WOOD WORK

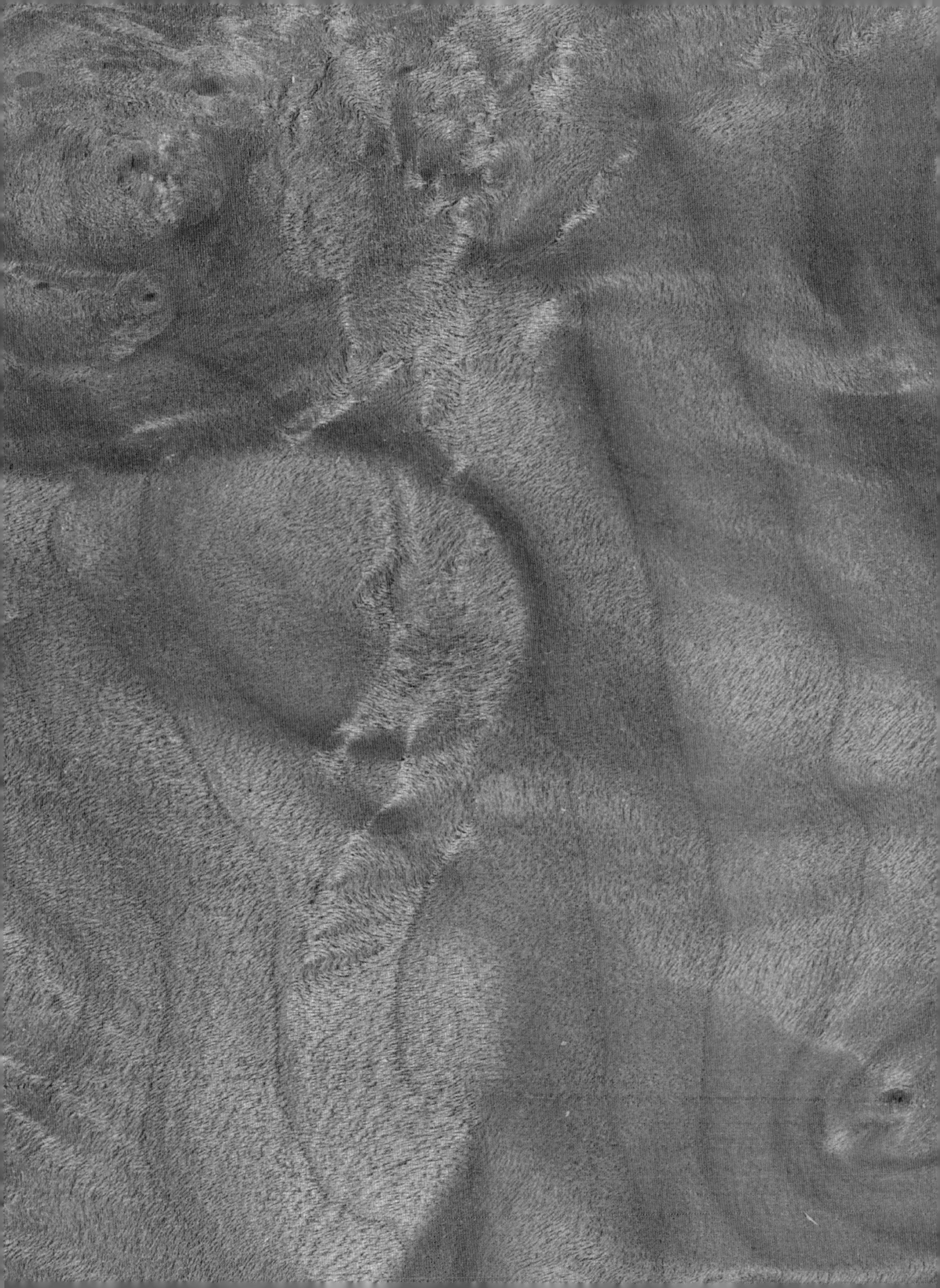

WOOD WORK

A STEP-BY-STEP PHOTOGRAPHIC GUIDE TO SUCCESSFUL WOODWORKING

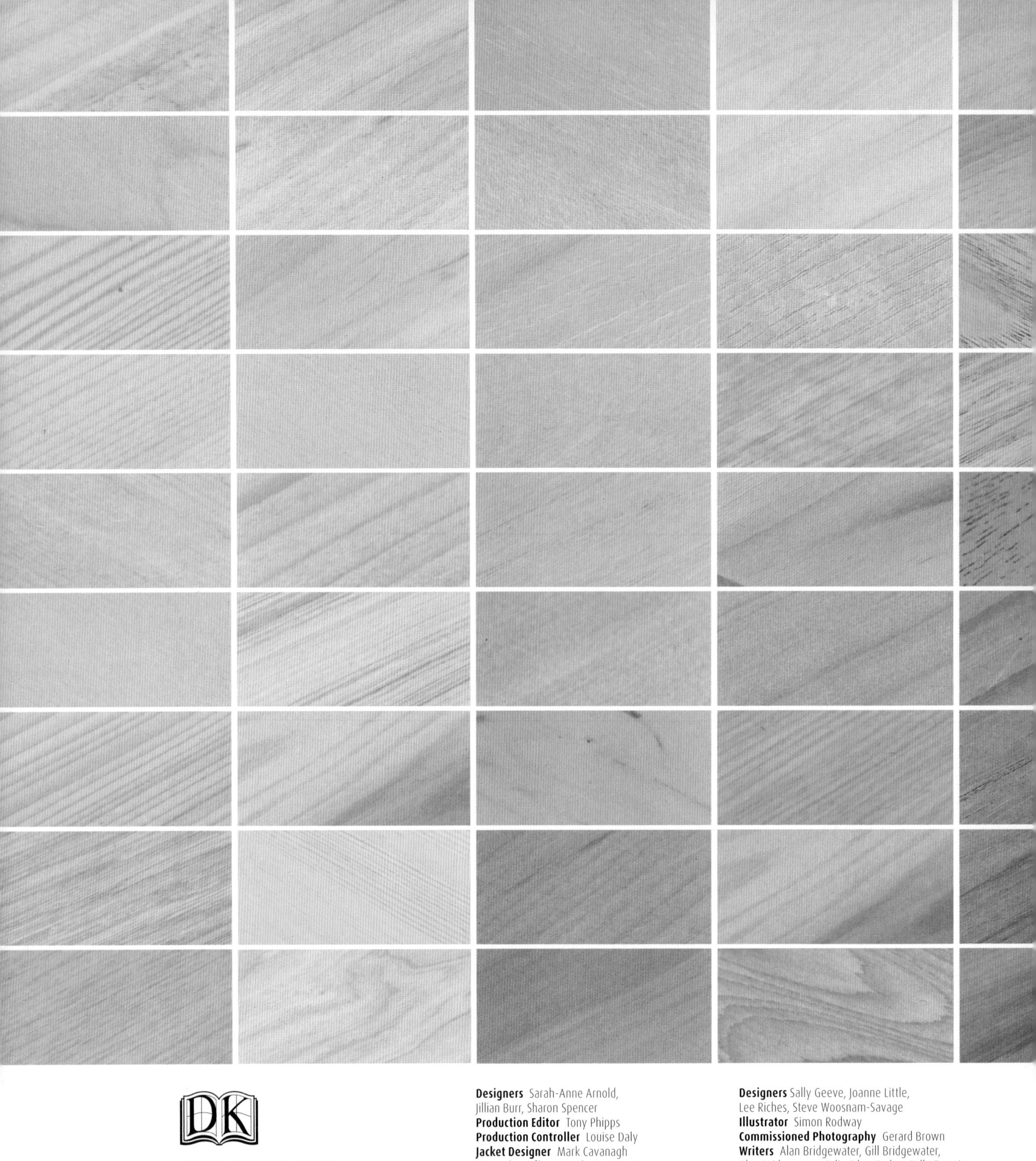

DK

LONDON, NEW YORK, MUNICH, MELBOURNE, DELHI

Senior Editor Gareth Jones
Senior Art Editor Gillian Andrews
Editors Bob Bridle, Joanna Edwards, Gill Pitts, Miezan Van Zyl, Clare Weber
US Editor Charles Willis
US Consultant Marc Schmidt

Designers Sarah-Anne Arnold, Jillian Burr, Sharon Spencer
Production Editor Tony Phipps
Production Controller Louise Daly
Jacket Designer Mark Cavanagh
Managing Editor Stephanie Farrow
Managing Art Editor Lee Griffiths
Publisher Jonathan Metcalf
Art Director Bryn Walls
Produced for Dorling Kindersley by
Schermuly Design Co.
Creative Director Hugh Schermuly
Project Manager Cathy Meeus
Editors Richard Gilbert, Mary Lindsay,

Designers Sally Geeve, Joanne Little, Lee Riches, Steve Woosnam-Savage
Illustrator Simon Rodway
Commissioned Photography Gerard Brown
Writers Alan Bridgewater, Gill Bridgewater, Glyn Bridgewater, Colin Eden-Eadon, Sally Francis, John Lloyd, Jonathan Tibbs, J.M. Wilkie

Published in the United States by
DK Publishing, 375 Hudson Street
New York, New York 10014

12 13 10 9 8 7 6 5 4
011— WD168— April 2010

Published in Great Britain by Dorling Kindersley Limited.

A catalog record for this book is available from the Library of Congress.

ISBN 978-0-7566-4306-5

DK books are available at special discounts when purchased in bulk for sales promotions, premiums, fund-raising, or educational use. For details, contact: DK Publishing Special Markets, 375 Hudson Street, New York, New York 10014 or SpecialSales@dk.com.

Printed and bound in China by Toppan.

Discover more at
www.dk.com

Neither the authors nor the publisher take any responsibility for any injury or damage resulting from the use of techniques shown or described in this book. The reader is advised to follow all safety instructions carefully, wear the correct protective clothing, and, where appropriate, follow all manufacturers' instructions. For more detailed information on Health and Safety, please see pages 17 and 78–79.

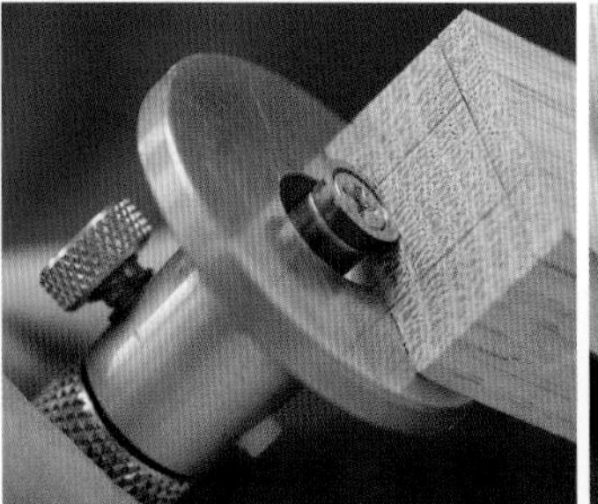

CONTENTS

TOOLS

HAND TOOLS

POWER TOOLS

STATIONARY AND MACHINE TOOLS

TECHNIQUES

JOINERY

WOODS

PROJECTS

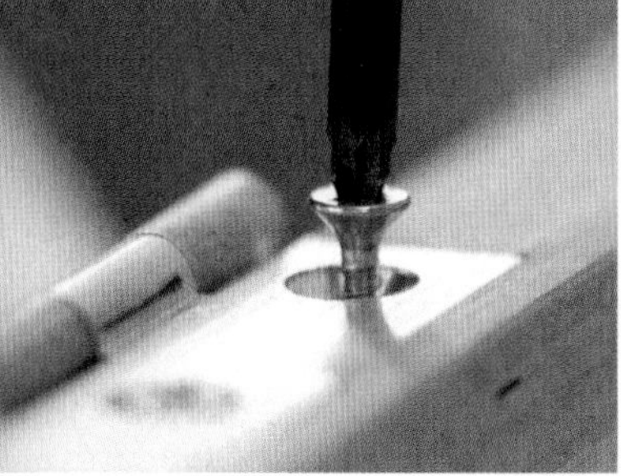
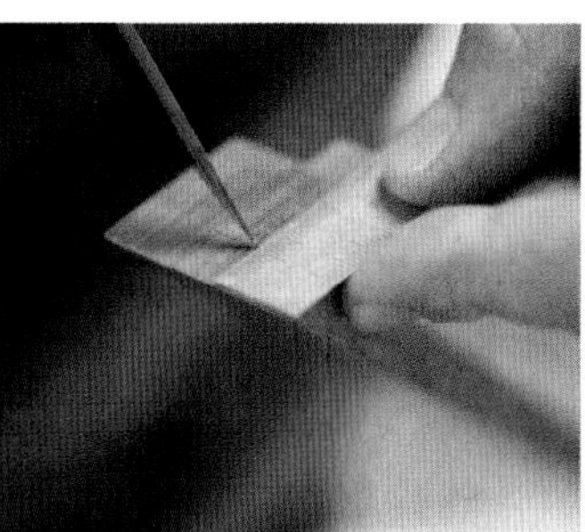

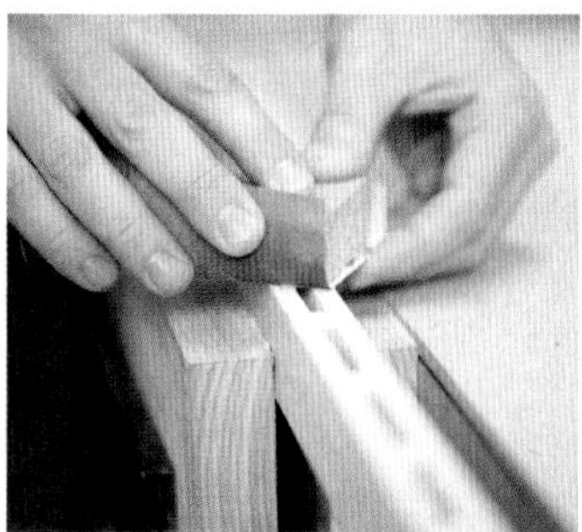

APPENDIX

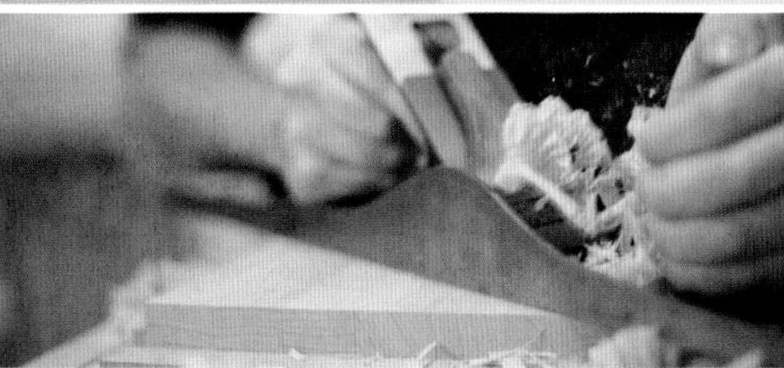

Introduction

Wood has been fundamental to the development and survival of mankind throughout history. Trees have provided us with the essentials for living—oxygen, food, warmth, medicine, and shelter—as well as offering the raw ingredients for key markers of cultural progress, such as paper, furniture, musical instruments, and works of art. Even nowadays, in a world of sophisticated technology and materials, we still use wood for much of our work on buildings and furniture, because of its versatility, beauty, and availability.

Because of this long tradition, wooden furniture has a rich and diverse heritage of styles, while examples that are centuries old can be found all around us, everywhere from museums and antiques shops to museums and galleries. This range of styles and sense of tradition and craftsmanship offers the modern woodworker an inspirational archive to draw upon, whether designing or constructing their own pieces.

Creating furniture by hand is a skill that has to an extent been supplanted by the development of power tools and machinery, yet the importance of using hand tools cannot be underestimated. Tools may have advanced in sophistication throughout history, but the fundamentals of woodworking have not changed significantly over the centuries, and this age-old craft is still the cornerstone of all furniture-making. Of course, it is possible to make furniture entirely by machine, but this requires a large workshop and a very large wallet. By contrast, hand skills allow you to create furniture within a limited space and with a limited budget, while experiencing the pleasure of working closely with wood to craft an object of your choice.

Woodwork celebrates the joys of creating furniture. It provides a core grounding in the fundamental woodworking skills and techniques, and the use of both hand and power tools; it shows you how to set up a workshop that is compatible with your budget and space; it showcases a catalog of the various types of timber available, and their individual working properties; and it presents you with achievable, yet challenging, projects.

Whether you are a novice or more experienced in the art of carpentry, *Woodwork* is an essential addition to your bookshelf.

About this book

Woodwork provides everything you need to know to get the best out of your carpentry. Not only it is an invaluable resource, providing you with detailed information on tools and timbers, but it is also a user-friendly and clearly illustrated guide that helps you progress from constructing individual joints to producing and adapting beautiful pieces of furniture.

TOOLS SPREADS—pp.14–79

The Tools section provides everything you need to know about woodworking tools, from the essential to the more specialized, with key advice for each on technique, safety, and maintenance.

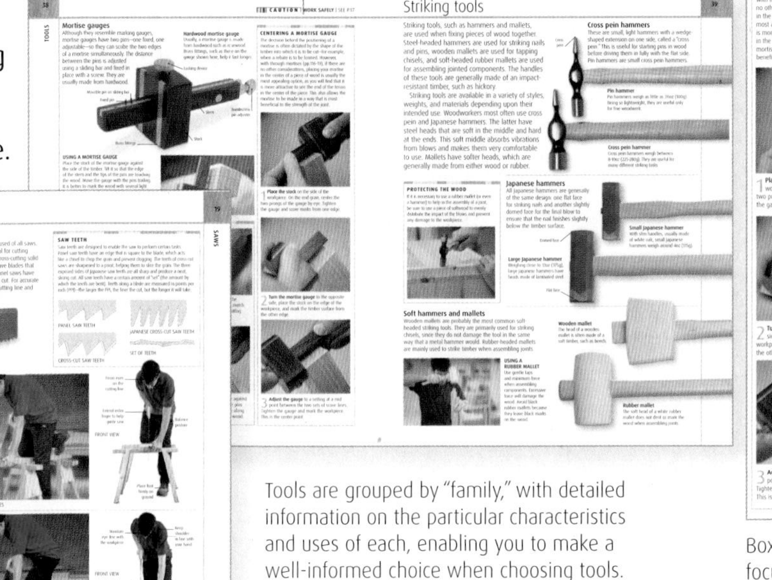

Tools are grouped by "family," with detailed information on the particular characteristics and uses of each, enabling you to make a well-informed choice when choosing tools.

Boxed features focus on specific subjects in detail, such as tool use and maintenance.

CAUTION | WORK SAFELY | SEE P.17

For ease of use, a cross-reference to the Safety information on page 17 is provided throughout the section.

TECHNIQUES SPREADS—pp.80–175

This section guides you step-by-step through all of the main traditional woodworking joints, including those that use modern commercial connectors, with advice on finishing and restoration.

PARTS OF THE JOINT

Parts of the Joint boxes provide a clearly illustrated explanation of how each joint fits together, along with information on its strengths and weaknesses.

Tools & Materials boxes list clearly all of the equipment you need to make each joint.

TOOLS AND MATERIALS

Pencil
Square
Mortise gauge
Marking knife
Drill and bits
Masking tape
Mortise chisel
Tenon saw
Bench hook
Sandpaper
Wood glue and brush
Clamps

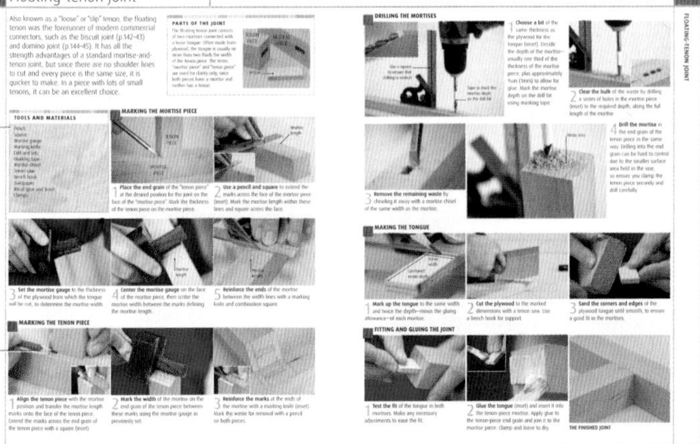

Each of the techniques (and the projects) are subdivided into individual sequences, to make them as managable as possible.

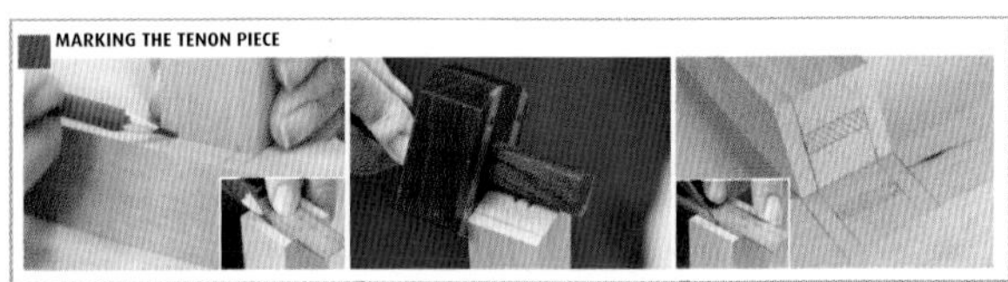

WOODS SPREADS—pp.176–99

Divided into hardwoods, softwoods, and veneers, the listed timbers are organized in order of color. The entries provide all the information you need to decide on the best wood to use for any project you have in mind.

Entries provide full details of the timber's other common names; the tree's characteristics; the colors and working and finishing properties of the timber; and its various uses.

Each of the timbers is fully illustrated to show the characteristics of its surface and grain at a glance.

Each wood is listed under its common name.

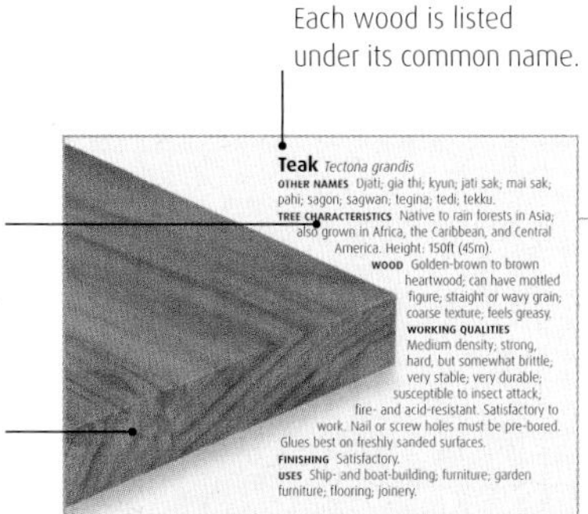

Teak *Tectona grandis*
OTHER NAMES Djati; gia thi; kyun; jati sak; mai sak; pahi; sagon; sagwan; tegina; tedi; tekku.
TREE CHARACTERISTICS Native to rain forests in Asia; also grown in Africa, the Caribbean, and Central America. Height: 150ft (45m).
WOOD Golden-brown to brown heartwood; can have mottled figure; straight or wavy grain; coarse texture; feels greasy.
WORKING QUALITIES Medium density; strong, hard, but somewhat brittle; very stable; very durable; susceptible to insect attack; fire- and acid-resistant. Satisfactory to work. Nail or screw holes must be pre-bored. Glues best on freshly sanded surfaces.
FINISHING Satisfactory.
USES Ship- and boat-building; furniture; garden furniture; flooring; joinery.

ENDANGERED SPECIES

Any timbers from endangered species are clearly labelled. You should always use timbers from a FSC-approved source (see p.178).

PROJECTS SPREADS—pp.200–379

The Projects section contains 25 projects arranged in order of complexity, which enable you to put your newly-acquired knowledge of tools, techniques and materials to practical use.

CUTTING LIST

Item	Material	No.	Length	Width	Thickness
Long box sides	Pine	6	28in* (700mm)	5 5/16in* (135mm)	13/16in* (20mm)
Short box sides	Pine	6	28in* (700mm)	5 5/16in* (135mm)	13/16in* (20mm)
Plinth	Pine	1	8ft 2½in* (2500mm)	2 9/16in (65mm)	9/16in (15mm)
Long lid surround	Pine	1	29½in* (750mm)	1¾in (45mm)	9/16in (15mm)
Short lid surround	Pine	2	21¾in* (550mm)	1¾in (45mm)	9/16in (15mm)
Lid panel	Pine	5	28in* (700mm)	4in* (100mm)	13/16in* (20mm)
Lid frame	Pine	1	8ft 2½in* (2500mm)	1⅜in (35mm)	9/16in (15mm)
Base	Birch ply	1	24 3/32in (612mm)	18¼in (462mm)	¼in (6mm)

*Includes excess to allow for cutting and/or planing to size

A detailed Cutting List helps you prepare all of the wood elements in advance.

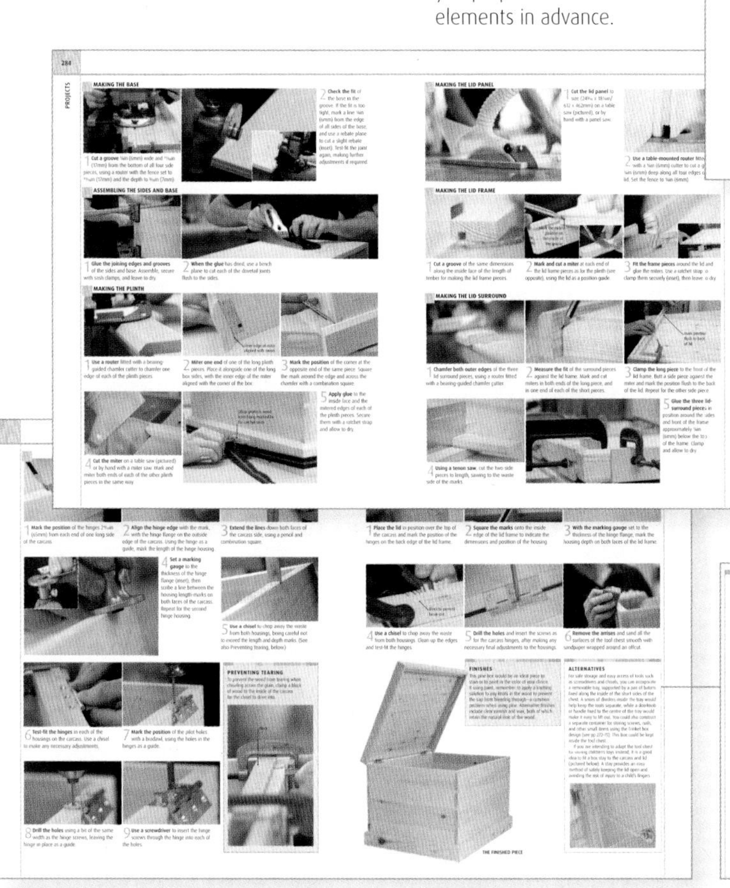

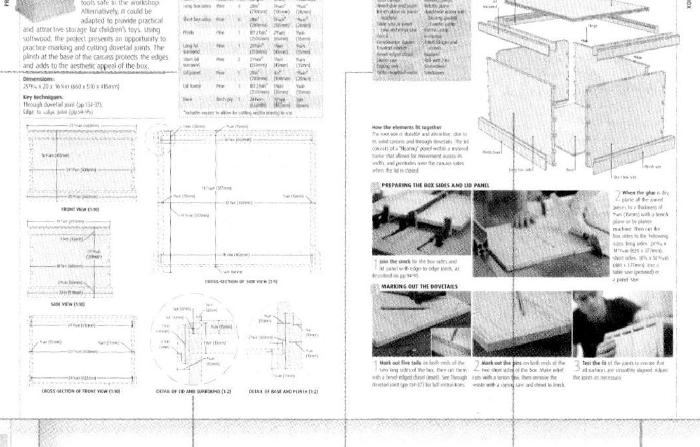

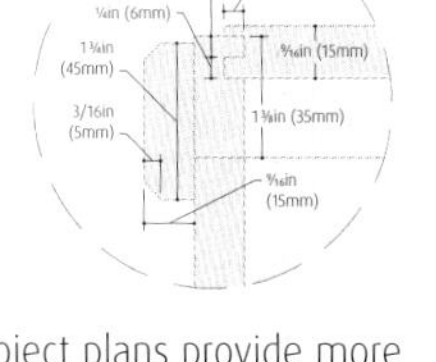

Project plans provide more detail for complex joints The dotted line around the detail corresponds to the main plan for easy navigation.

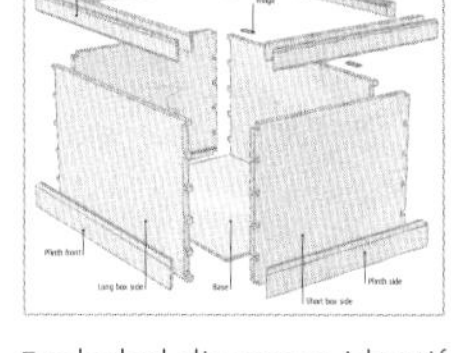

Exploded diagrams identify all of the elements listed in the Cuttting Lists and show you how they fit together.

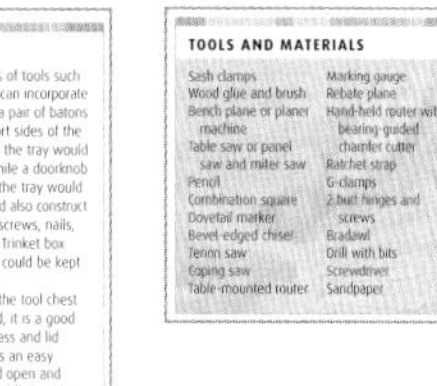

ALTERNATIVES

For safe storage and easy access of tools such as screwdrivers and chisels, you can incorporate a removable tray, supported by a pair of batons fixed along the inside of the short sides of the chest. A series of dividers inside the tray would help keep the tools separate, while a doorknob or handle fixed to the centre of the tray would make it easy to lift out. You could also construct a separate container for storing screws, nails, and other small items using the Trinket box design (see pp.272–75). This box could be kept inside the tool chest.

If you are intending to adapt the tool chest for storing children's toys instead, it is a good idea to fit a box stay to the carcass and lid (pictured below). A stay provides an easy method of safely keeping the lid open and avoiding the risk of injury to a child's fingers.

TOOLS AND MATERIALS

Sash clamps
Wood glue and brush
Bench plane or planer machine
Table saw or panel saw and miter saw
Pencil
Combination square
Dovetail marker
Bevel-edged chisel
Tenon saw
Coping saw
Table-mounted router
Marking gauge
Rebate plane
Hand-held router with bearing-guided chamfer cutter
Ratchet strap
G-clamps
2 butt hinges and screws
Bradawl
Drill with bits
Screwdriver
Sandpaper

Tools & Materials boxes clearly list all of the equipment you need to construct each piece.

Alternatives boxes at the end of each project offer you suggestions on how to vary the look of the piece, or adapt it for a different purpose.

TO

OLS

Much of the pleasure of woodworking comes from the appreciation of the many tools used. Handling and using a metal hand plane, for example, should be enjoyable—the way the crisp wood shavings curl up from a workpiece is a pure delight to the woodworking devotee. Equally, a carving gouge should be a joy to work with, and even a hammer or a power drill are beautiful objects in their own right. That said, tools are only enjoyable (and safe) to use if they are well balanced and are kept clean and sharp. It is also important to always use the correct tool for the task at hand.

Using the right tools for the job

You should avoid the temptation to simply browse a manufacturer's catalog and order a vast range of tools. When starting out in woodworking it is best to carefully consider your first project—its size and shape, the materials and techniques required—and then visit a quality tool supplier and select the minimum amount of tools necessary to complete the job. Once you start work, you may of course discover that you need more tools—a different plane or another clamp, for example—but at least these extra purchases will be guided by your actual needs.

Another important issue to address when buying tools is whether to opt for power tools or hand tools. This decision depends on whether you want the job done quickly and easily—but with the noise, dust, set-up requirements, and potential hazards associated with power tools—or whether you would prefer to work more slowly and enjoy the quieter, subtler pleasures of working with hand tools.

If you are an absolute beginner and have concerns about your own abilities, the best way to seek advise and gain confidence is either to work alongside an experienced woodworker or join a woodworking group. If you are slight of statue or not particularly strong, for example, you will be able to discuss what you can and can't feasibly achieve in the workshop. Equally, if you have limited funds, or your working space is restricted, you will be able to discuss your options. Above all, talking to and working with other woodworkers will inspire you to make the most of your newfound interest.

NEW OR SECOND-HAND TOOLS?

As a general rule, hand tools should last a lifetime and power tools and machines are only as good as their electrical parts. When deciding between buying new or second-hand tools, the best advise is to buy new power tools and machines and consider buying some hand tools that are second-hand. The main advantage of buying second-hand tools is that it may be possible to acquire a complete set of tools—in their own dedicated storage chest—that have been lovingly cared for by the previous owner.

BASIC TOOLS AND MATERIALS LIST

HAND TOOLS

MARKING AND MEASURING TOOLS
Pencil
2 metal rulers—12in (300mm) and 39in (1m)
Tape measure—16ft (5m)
Marking knife
Try square or combination square 9in (225mm)
Protractor (if no combination square)
Sliding-bevel gauge
Mortise gauge
Marking gauge
Dovetail marker

SAWS
Panel saw
Tenon saw
Dovetail saw
Coping saw

PLANES
Jack plane
Smoothing plane
Block plane
Combination oilstone and oil

CHISELS
Set of mortise chisels—¼–1in (6–25mm)
Set of bevel-edged chisels—¼–1in (6–25mm)

HAMMERS
Cross-pein hammer
Pin hammer

MISCELLANEOUS HAND TOOLS
Mallet
Flat spokeshave
Double-cut flat file
Pincers
Bradawl
Set of screwdrivers
PVA wood glue and paintbrush—½in (12mm)
Rubber mallet
4 C-clamps— 6in (150mm)
4 sash clamps— 60in (1.5m)

FINISHING TOOLS
Straight cabinet scraper
Scraper burnisher
Cork sanding block
Sandpapers—120-grit, 180-grit, 220-grit, and 320-grit
Paintbrush— 1½in (40mm)
Clean cotton cloths

HAND-HELD POWER TOOLS

Jigsaw and selection of blades
Drill/driver (cordless) with set of lip-and-spur wood drill bits, countersink bit, and selection of driver bit
Router with ¾in (10mm) straight cutter, and bearing-mounted cutter—buy further cutters as required
Orbital sander
(Circular saw is a useful addition)

MACHINE TOOLS

Band saw
Planer-thicknesser
Mobile dust extractor (attach to above machines; essential for planer-thicknesser)
Compound miter saw
Drill press with selection of Forstner bits
(Table saw is a useful addition if you have enough space)

STORING TOOLS

You should treat the phrase "a place for everything and everything in its place" as a golden rule in the workshop. It is important that you know the location of every tool at all times. Your tools should also be close at hand. This will allow you to access each tool as required, quickly and safely. Carefully storing your tools will help to prolong their life; make sure that they are clean, well oiled, and carefully stored in a dry box or chest, or in a designated storage rack. The working area needs to be dry, well-lit, dust-free, and clean—for the benefit of both you and your tools. While woodworking should be a rewarding, even therapeutic, activity, these benefits will only be realized if the workshop is a safe, comfortable, and orderly place to work. This is true for all sizes of workshop, from the largest production workshop to the smallest garden shed. See pp.68–69 for specific advice about how to set up your workshop.

Work safely

Tools can be very dangerous, so correct and safe use is crucial. The chart below outlines the hazards associated with common tools, and the precautions that you should take. However, you should also refer to the manufacturer's instructions and seek formal training whenever possible. For information about personal protective gear (PPE), see pp.78–79.

SAFETY IN THE WORKSHOP

- Keep the working area tidy
- Keep tools and equipment well maintained
- Seek training in the correct use of all equipment
- Use the appropriate personal protective equipment (PPE)
- Follow the correct procedures—never cut corners or rush a job
- Never work when tired or under the influence of alcohol or drugs
- Disconnect the power before adjusting machines or power tools, or touching blades, or cutters
- Do not wear loose clothing or jewelry, and keep hair away from rotating power tools or machines
- Properly support a workpiece

HAND TOOLS	TOOL	HAZARDS	SAFETY PRECAUTIONS
Look after your hand tools. Keep them clean and well maintained—a dirty chisel, for example, is hard to hold steady, and the badly fitting head of a hammer may fly off. Keep your blades sharp. While a blunt cutting tool may inflict less damage than a sharp one, it is more dangerous to use—you will need to use more force, which means it is more likely to slip.	**HAND SAW; MARKING KNIFE**	■ Cuts to hands	■ Cover blade when not in use ■ Support workpiece ■ Never force the saw while cutting ■ Take extra care when starting a cut
	PLANE	■ Cuts to hands when handling blades	■ Wear gloves when handling sharp blades
	CHISEL AND OTHER CUTTING TOOLS; SCREWDRIVER	■ Piercing wounds	■ Never place hand or body in front of blade
HAND-HELD POWER TOOLS	**POWER TOOL**	**HAZARDS**	**PRECAUTIONS**
Ensure your hand-held power tools are electrically safe and that all blades and cutters are securely and correctly mounted on the tool. While these tools may seem small and unlikely to cause serious injury, they work at very high speeds and are powerful enough to cause considerable injury.	**DRILL**	■ Lacerations to hands	■ Support the workpiece correctly (not with hands)
	ROUTER	■ Cutter breakage ■ Lacerations to hands ■ Flying debris ■ Tool "jumping"	■ Follow good practice; set router to correct speed ■ Support the workpiece correctly (not with hands) ■ Never start/stop tool while the cutter is in contact with a surface ■ Make cuts in the correct direction ■ Mount the cutter correctly
	CIRCULAR SAW	■ Cuts and lacerations	■ Always use the safety guards ■ Support the workpiece correctly (not with hands)
	SANDER	■ Respiratory damage	■ Wear PPE
	JIGSAW; JOINTER	■ Cuts and lacerations	■ Take general precautions
	NAILER	■ Piercing wounds	■ Never hold the tip of the nailer ■ Support the workpiece correctly (not with hands)
MACHINE TOOLS	**MACHINE**	**HAZARDS**	**PRECAUTIONS**
These powerful machines are potentially highly dangerous and should be treated with respect. This is not to say, however, that you should use them in a timid way; hold a workpiece firmly and feed it in in a controlled—and deliberate—manner. **General precautions for machine tools** ■ Use push sticks to feed in a workpiece ■ Always use the blade/cutter guards ■ Always set the machine up correctly, especially the cutter's speed and position ■ Never stand behind the workpiece in case of kick-back (the workpiece being "thrown") ■ Do not wear loose clothing or jewelry; tie back long hair	**TABLE SAW**	■ Kick-back (workpiece being "thrown")	■ Adjust side fence correctly ■ Seek assistance to help keep the kerf (width of cut) open when machining thick boards
	BAND SAW	■ Cuts and lacerations to hands	■ Follow general precautions for machine tools
	RADIAL-ARM SAW	■ Saw "climbing" the workpiece	■ Use a negative-rake blade
	PLANER	■ Kick-back	■ Ensure that the in-feed table is adjusted correctly
	PLANER-THICKNESSER	■ Trapped fingers	■ Ensure that the workpiece is fully on the roller
	LATHE; MORTISER; DRILL PRESS	■ Cuts and lacerations to hands	■ Follow general precautions for machine tools
	ROUTER TABLE	■ Cuts and lacerations to hands	■ Ensure cutter guards are correctly positioned ■ Make several small cuts rather than one large cut

Saws

Saws are an essential part of every woodworker's tool kit. Saw blades have serrated edges called "teeth," which are bent at an angle and set to alternate sides. When cutting through wood, the teeth create a slot, or "kerf," that is wider than the blade. This helps the blade to move freely through the wood without getting stuck.

There are many different types of saws—such as panel saws (opposite), back saws (p.20), and coping saws (p.21)—each designed for specific woodworking tasks. Coping saws, for example, are used for cutting curves. Western (or European) saws cut on the "push" stroke, while Japanese saws (p.21) cut on the "pull" stroke.

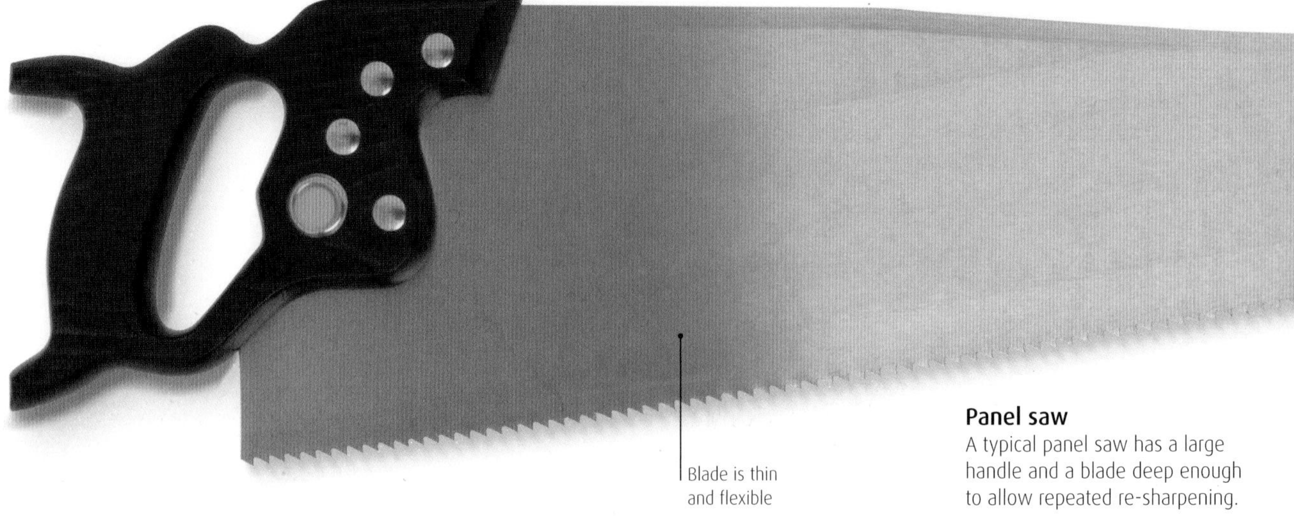

Blade is thin and flexible

Panel saw
A typical panel saw has a large handle and a blade deep enough to allow repeated re-sharpening.

SHARPENING A SAW

Each type of saw is sharpened differently, depending on its teeth. To sharpen a panel saw, you need two types of file (one to flatten the teeth and another to sharpen them), clamps, rulers, and a saw set. The saw set—used for adjusting the angle or "set" of each tooth—has a rotating anvil, which changes the angle of the surface, and a "punch" that bends the tooth in the right direction. Sharpening cross-cut saws (inset) requires a special file to sharpen the edges of two consecutive teeth. Sharpening any saw requires great skill, so it is worth bearing in mind that using and sharpening traditional saws may not suit all situations—sometimes it may be more time-efficient to use power tools and disposable hardpoint panel and back saws.

1 **Position the saw** securely in a specially made clamp, with the teeth facing upward. File to ensure the teeth are of equal height—some may have worn out and become uneven.

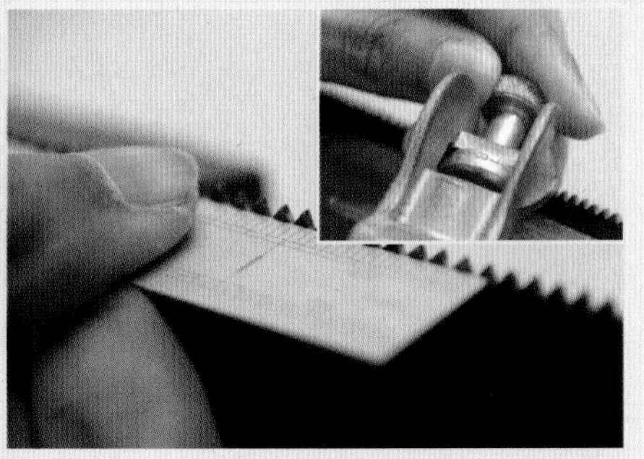

2 **Use a ruler** to measure the number of teeth per inch or centimeter and adjust the anvil of the saw set accordingly (inset). (The anvil is a flat surface against which each tooth is pushed.)

3 **Working from one side**, and starting with the teeth angled away from you, squeeze the saw set on alternate teeth to align them. Change sides and repeat the process.

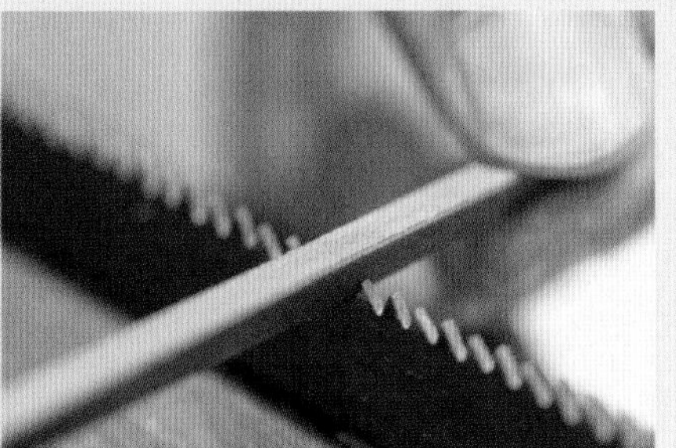

4 **Using a triangular file**, sharpen the teeth at right angles to the blade, starting with all the teeth angled away from you. Change sides and sharpen the remaining teeth. Use the same number of strokes for each tooth.

Cross-cut saw
Follow Steps 1, 2, and 3, but use a special file fixed on a jig to file the edges of adjacent teeth at the desired angles. Repeat on the other side.

Panel saws

Panel saws are among the most commonly used of all saws. They have long, flexible blades and are ideal for cutting boards and panels, as well as for ripping or cross-cutting solid timber (below). Good-quality panel saws have blades that are ground to a taper to ease sawing. All panel saws have relatively large teeth, which produce a rough cut. For accurate work, always cut to the waste side of the cutting line and plane the remainder.

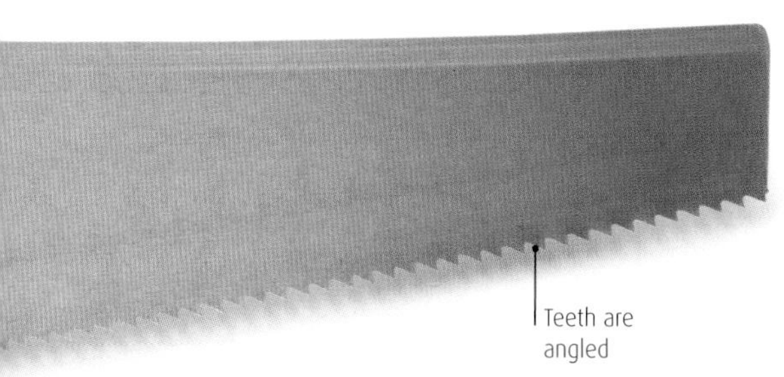

SAW TEETH

Saw teeth are designed to enable the saw to perform certain tasks. Panel saw teeth have an edge that is square to the blade, which acts like a chisel to chop the grain and prevent clogging. The teeth of cross-cut saws are sharpened to a point, helping them to slice the grain. The three exposed sides of Japanese saw teeth are all sharp and produce a neat, slicing cut. All saw teeth have a certain amount of "set" (the amount by which the teeth are bent). Teeth along a blade are measured in points per inch (PPI)—the larger the PPI, the finer the cut, but the longer it will take.

PANEL SAW TEETH

JAPANESE CROSS-CUT SAW TEETH

CROSS-CUT SAW TEETH

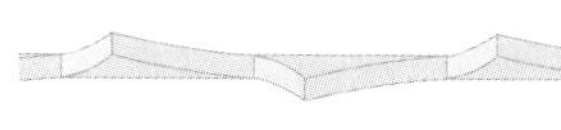

SET OF TEETH

RIPPING WITH A PANEL SAW

To rip (cut down the grain) with a panel saw, hold the wood securely on two trestles, and position yourself as comfortably as possible. As you saw closer to the trestle, move the wood forward carefully, ensuring that the other end does not drop down. When necessary, move the wood back and cut between the trestles. Finish the cut by working from the other end.

RIPPING ON TRESTLES

FRONT VIEW

CROSS-CUTTING WITH A PANEL SAW

To cross-cut (cut across the grain) with a panel saw, position yourself in the same way as you would for ripping, but with your saw parallel to the end grain. Place the saw to the waste side of the cutting line and carefully rest the thumb of your free hand on the side of the blade for added stability. Move your thumb after the first few carefully guided strokes.

CROSS-CUTTING ON TRESTLES

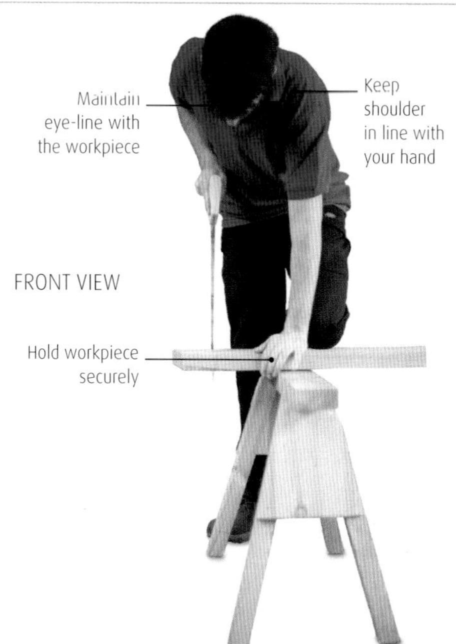

FRONT VIEW

Back saws

Used primarily for cutting tenons (pp.116–27), the back saw gets its name from the piece of folded, or cast, metal that runs along its back edge, supporting the blade. This heavy metal spine keeps the saw steady when cutting through wood, but limits the depth of your cut. Back saws have smaller teeth than panel saws, which results in a finer cut but at a slower pace. There are two types of back saw: the tenon saw and the dovetail saw. Back saws are multi-purpose tools that can be used for many sawing jobs.

LOOKING AFTER YOUR SAW

When not in use, always cover your saw's teeth to protect them and to avoid injuries. If you are planning to store your saw for a while, oil the blade lightly with tea seed oil or similar. If the handle feels rough, smooth it with sandpaper.

OILING THE BLADE

PROTECTING THE TEETH

Cast or folded metal spine

Large tenon saw

The large tenon saw has a long blade that cuts deep joints with ease. It has around 4 points, or teeth, per cm (approximately 11 per inch). Its larger size makes it slightly harder to handle than a small tenon saw.

Closed wooden handle

Small tenon saw

The small tenon saw has around 6 teeth per cm (approximately 14 teeth per inch). As well as cutting tenons, it can be used for numerous smaller cutting tasks.

Dovetail saw

Similar in appearance to a tenon saw, the dovetail saw is smaller with more teeth—approximately 7 per cm (around 18 per inch). These produce the fine cuts useful for cutting joints.

Handle held with screws

USING A BACK SAW

Place the saw on the timber, to the waste side of your cutting line. Carefully rest the thumb of your free hand against both the timber and the side of the blade to steady and guide the cut. To begin, push the saw forward smoothly. Continue pushing with a steady back-and-forth movement until the cut is complete. The tenon saw may start to judder when ripping (cutting down the grain) . This can be easily rectified by altering the angle of the cut slightly.

PUSH THE SAW FORWARD

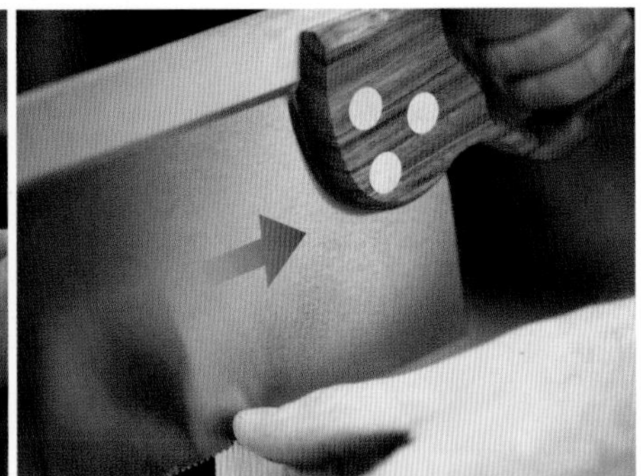

DRAW THE SAW BACK

Coping saws

When performing tricky tasks, such as cutting curves or removing waste from joints, such as dovetails (pp.134–39), a coping saw is indispensable. The blade is thin and narrow, which allows it to be turned easily. Use a fret saw, which is similar to a coping saw but has a finer blade, for intricate fretwork in thin board or veneer.

Fitting the blade in a coping saw
The blade of a coping saw must be fitted in the frame so that the teeth cut on the pull stroke. If fitted with the teeth pointing the wrong way, it might break.

Frame provides tension

Handle is turned clockwise to tension blade

Two pegs hold blade in position. These can be twisted in unison to rotate blade

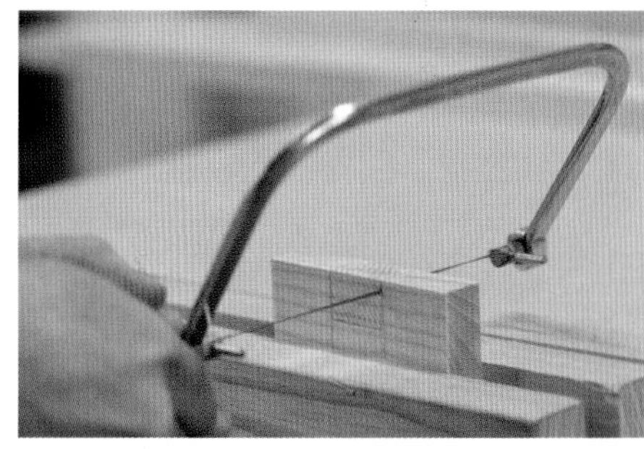

USING A COPING SAW
Place the central part of the coping saw blade on the workpiece and pull it toward you. Use short, steady strokes to produce the cut. Coping saws are not very accurate so always cut to the waste side of the line.

Japanese saws

As with Western saws, a variety of Japanese saws are available for a number of different purposes. The blades of Japanese saws are designed to cut on the pull stroke, and are much thinner than their Western counterparts. The blades are kept steady by the pulling action, unlike those of Western saws, which depend on their thickness to prevent bending. The teeth of Japanese saws are sharp on all sides, which results in a clean, slicing cut.

USING A JAPANESE SAW
Place the end of the Japanese saw on the cutting line and pull the tool backward, then push it forward. Take care not to apply too much pressure or the saw may go off course. Repeat to make the cut.

REMOVING THE BLADE

Turn the saw onto its back and, with a quick chopping action, strike the end of the blade on a piece of scrap wood. This will release the blade.

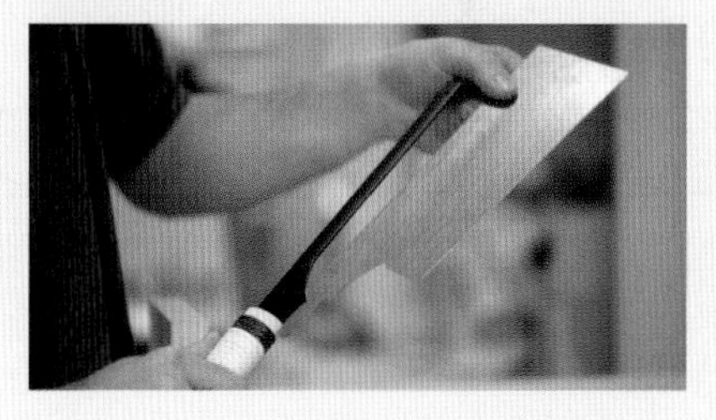

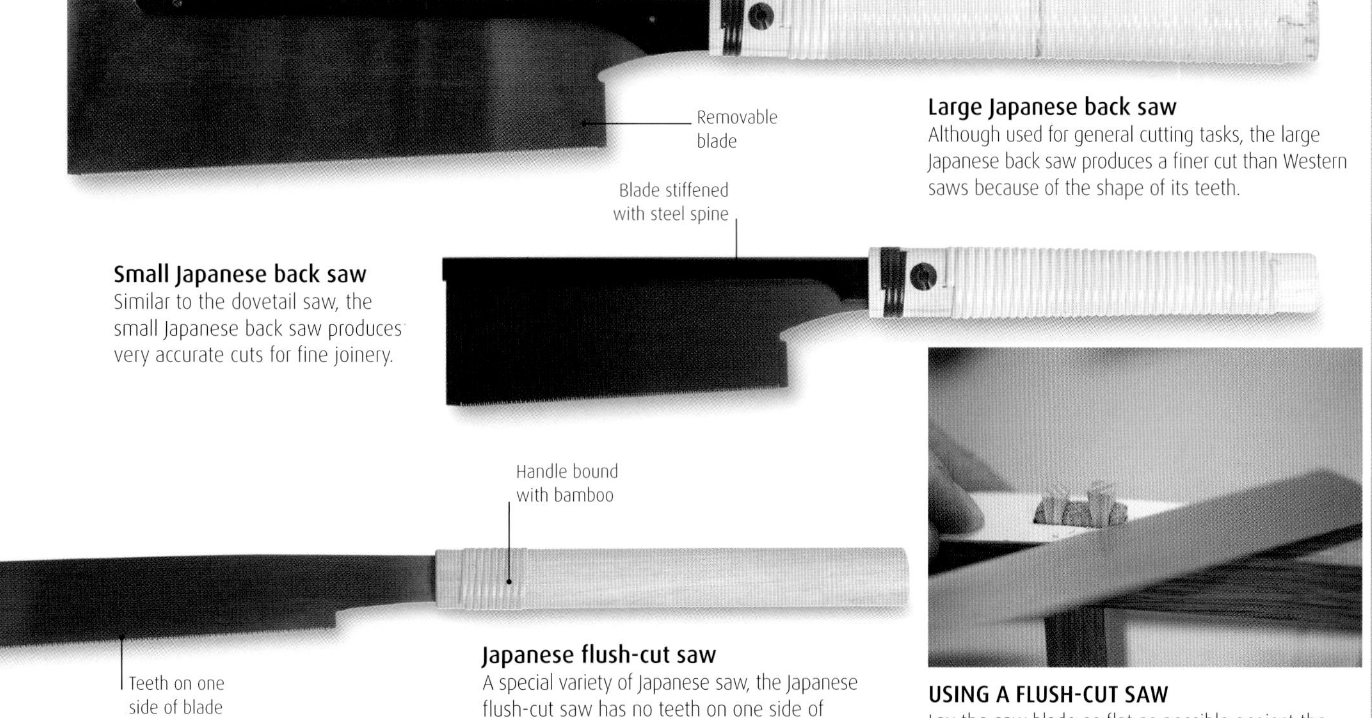

Large Japanese back saw
Although used for general cutting tasks, the large Japanese back saw produces a finer cut than Western saws because of the shape of its teeth.

Small Japanese back saw
Similar to the dovetail saw, the small Japanese back saw produces very accurate cuts for fine joinery.

Japanese flush-cut saw
A special variety of Japanese saw, the Japanese flush-cut saw has no teeth on one side of its blade. As a result, its teeth do not leave a mark when used to cut timber.

USING A FLUSH-CUT SAW
Lay the saw blade as flat as possible against the wood you wish to cut (you may need to angle the handle up slightly). Start the cut on a pull stroke.

Planes

Planes are used to smooth, flatten, shape, or reduce the thickness of timber. As the plane glides over the wood, the angled blade shaves the surface to create a uniform finish. The thickness of the shaving can be controlled by adjusting the position of the blade within the body. The most common type of plane is the bench plane (see below); however, there is a large variety of planes available for different woodworking purposes. Block planes (p.26)—an effective tool for trimming end grains—are smaller than bench planes and can be operated using just one hand. Other types include rebate and shoulder planes (p.27), and more specialized planes, such as router planes, plow planes, and spokeshaves (pp.28–29). These can be used to make grooves, trim joints, and smooth awkwardly shaped surfaces, such as curves.

Bench planes

Most bench planes have a blade fixed at an angle, or "pitch," of 45 degrees, with the bevel facing downward (if it were facing upward, the resultant pitch would be too great for general planing). Planes with a pitch greater than 45 degrees (sometimes called a "York pitch") are used for hard timbers, whereas low-angle planes—with pitches of approximately 42 degrees—are useful for cutting end grains. Bench planes come in different body lengths: short lengths clean rough edges and smooth surfaces effectively, while longer lengths create very straight edges. Planes are also known as either "Bailey" or "Bedrock" types—the main difference centers around the "frog" (the sliding iron wedge that holds the blade at the correct angle). With Bailey planes, the blade must be removed before adjustments to the frog are made; with Bedrock planes, you do not have to remove the blade to make adjustments.

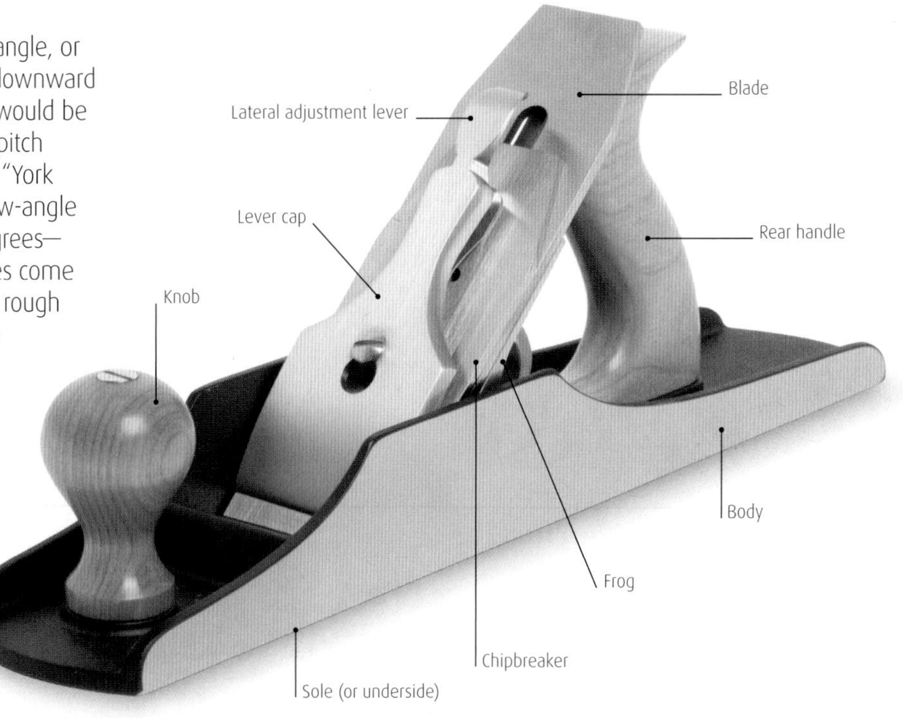

WOODEN PLANES

Although metal planes are more widely used than wooden planes, wooden models are still popular in some countries. The body of a modern wooden plane is made from beech or pear and the sole (the base of the plane) is made from lignum vitae, a durable "self-lubricating" hardwood. The two wooden parts are joined using mortise-and-tenon joints. The blades of wooden planes are easy to adjust and produce excellent results.

WOODEN BLOCK PLANE

WOODEN SMOOTHING PLANE

No. 4 plane

This size of plane is very easy to control and is an excellent choice for small, light work. The no. 4 bench plane is ideal for trimming surfaces and planing joints.

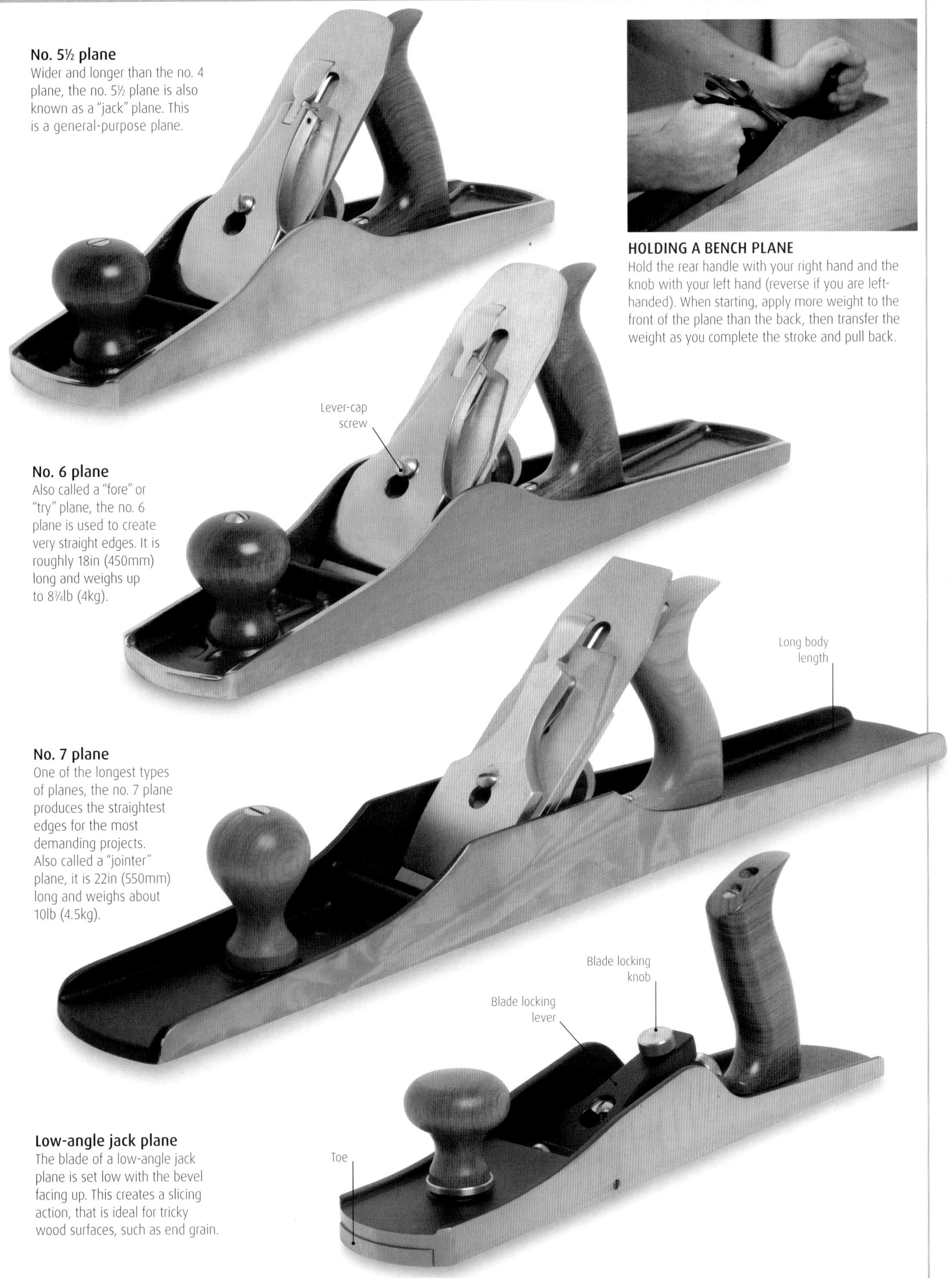

No. 5½ plane
Wider and longer than the no. 4 plane, the no. 5½ plane is also known as a "jack" plane. This is a general-purpose plane.

HOLDING A BENCH PLANE
Hold the rear handle with your right hand and the knob with your left hand (reverse if you are left-handed). When starting, apply more weight to the front of the plane than the back, then transfer the weight as you complete the stroke and pull back.

No. 6 plane
Also called a "fore" or "try" plane, the no. 6 plane is used to create very straight edges. It is roughly 18in (450mm) long and weighs up to 8¾lb (4kg).

No. 7 plane
One of the longest types of planes, the no. 7 plane produces the straightest edges for the most demanding projects. Also called a "jointer" plane, it is 22in (550mm) long and weighs about 10lb (4.5kg).

Low-angle jack plane
The blade of a low-angle jack plane is set low with the bevel facing up. This creates a slicing action, that is ideal for tricky wood surfaces, such as end grain.

Adjusting a bench plane

In order to achieve the best results, it is important that you know how to adjust a plane. Use the frog-adjusting screw to change the size of the "mouth" (the gap between the face of the blade and the edge of the opening in the sole). A large mouth is used for coarse grain while fine work requires a small mouth. To control the blade extension and set the depth of the cut, use the depth wheel at the back of the blade. Use the lateral adjustment lever behind the frog to make sure that the blade sits parallel with the sole.

CHECKING THE PLANE IS TRUE

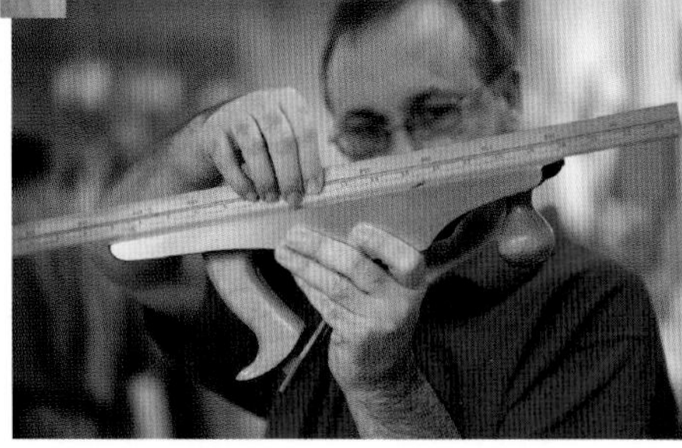

1 **Check the flatness** of the sole against the edge of a straight surface (such as a ruler). A very slightly concave sole is acceptable, but the sole must never be convex.

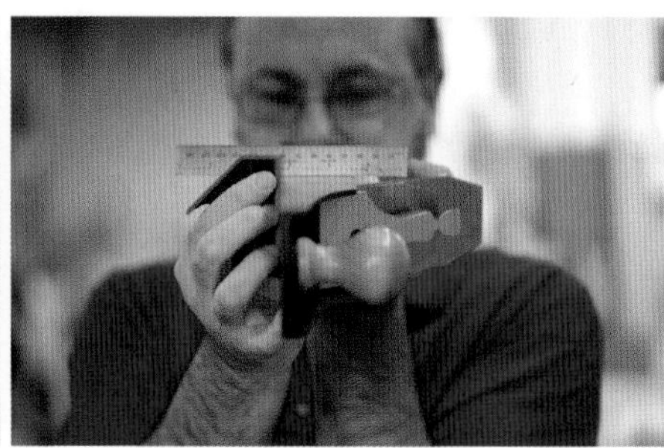

2 **Use a combination square** (p.36) to check that the plane is square. This is helpful if the plane is to be used on a shooting board (a flat board with grooves used for guiding a plane).

REMOVING THE BLADE

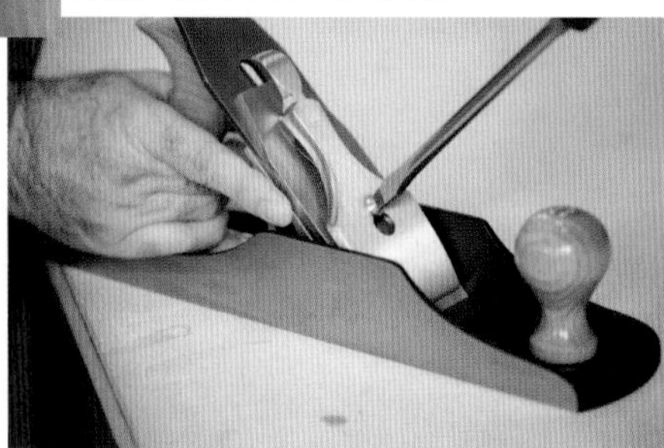

1 **Lift up the handle** of the lever cap. If the cap does not move easily, loosen it with a screwdriver. Make sure you use the correct screwdriver (p.43) for the job.

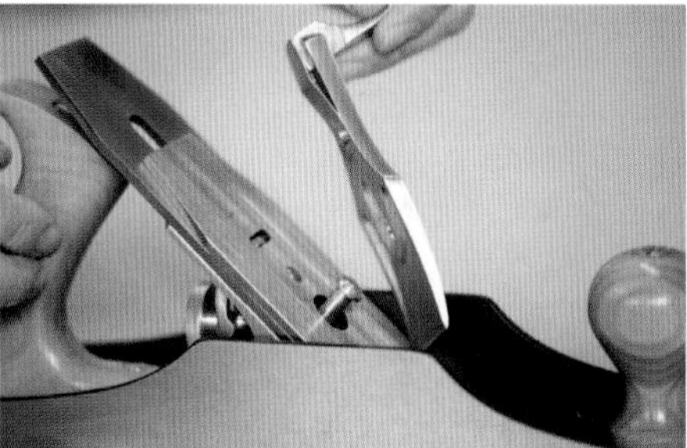

2 **Remove the lever cap** from the plane. The cap will lift off to expose the blade assembly. Unscrew the chipbreaker that sits on top of the blade.

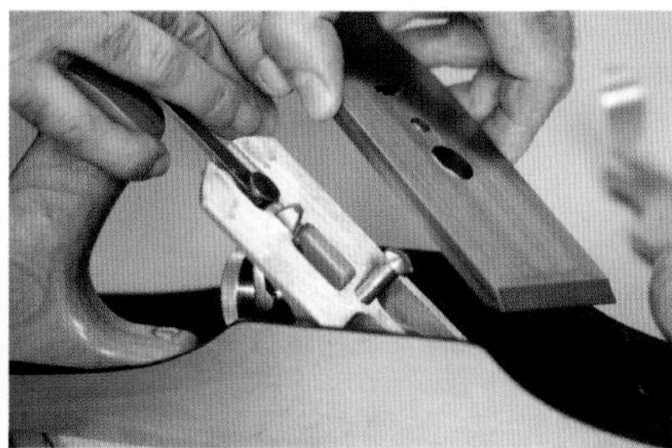

3 **Carefully lift the blade** off the frog. Hold it from behind and ensure you avoid bringing your hands too close to the sharp cutting edge of the blade.

ADJUSTING THE FROG

To adjust the frog on a Bailey plane, first remove the blade to bring the frog-locking screws into view. Loosen the screws, then move the frog in the required direction. Re-tighten the screws and fix the blade back onto the frog. Look along the sole of the plane and check the throat to ensure you have adjusted the opening to the desired measurement. Make adjustments, if necessary. On a Bedrock plane, the locking screws are located behind the frog, so you do not need to remove the blade to access them.

CHECKING THE CHIPBREAKER

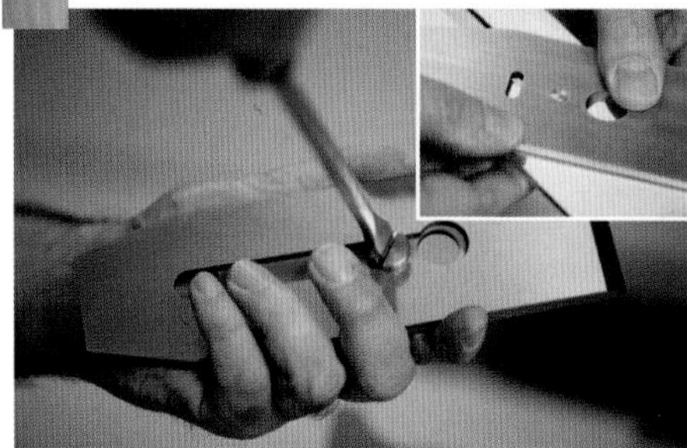

1 **Undo the screw** on the blade assembly to release the chipbreaker. Slide the elements apart (inset). To make this task easier, turn the chipbreaker away from the blade's edge.

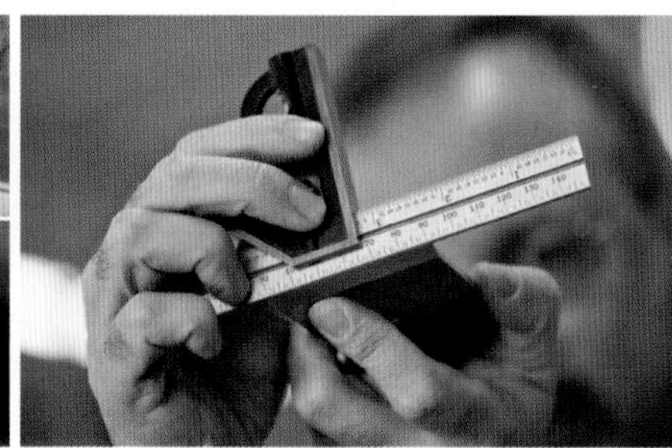

2 **Check the flatness** of the chipbreaker with a combination square placed first along its length, then its width. A gap between the blade and the chipbreaker will result in chips getting trapped.

GRINDING THE BLADE

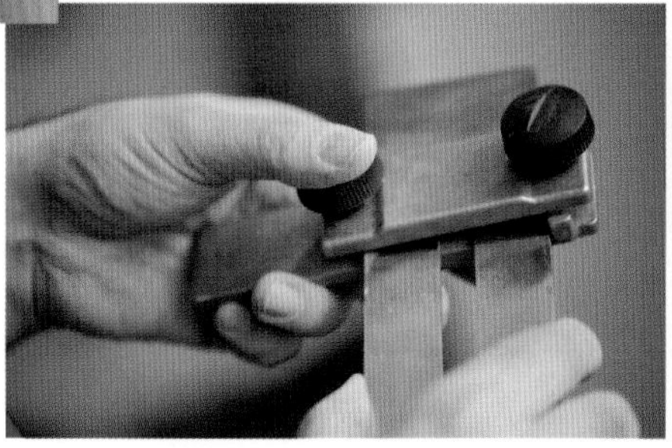

1 **Fit the blade** into the holder of a purpose-made jig. Slide it up firmly to the side stops and ensure that it is square.

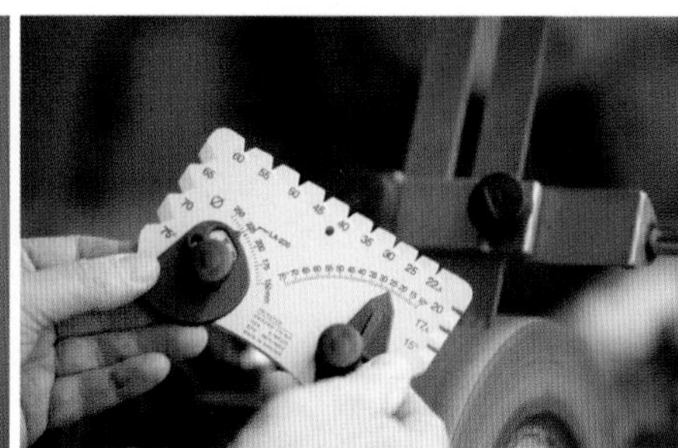

2 **Set the gauge** to the size of the grinding wheel and fix the angle at which the blade is to be sharpened (usually 25 degrees).

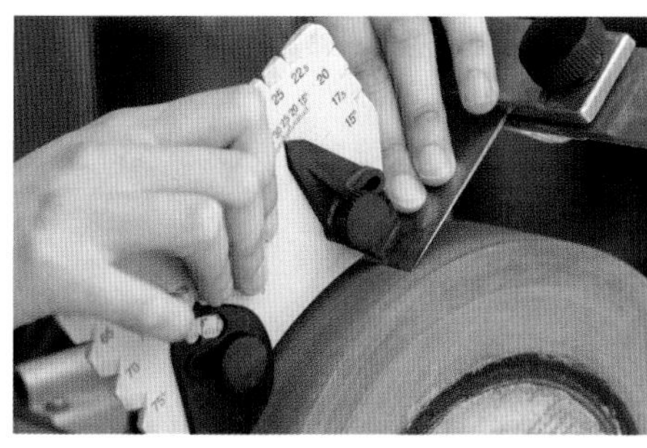

3 **Set the blade** on the grinding wheel (use a coarse benchstone if you want to grind by hand), place the gauge on top, and adjust the angle of the blade's cutting edge to match the gauge.

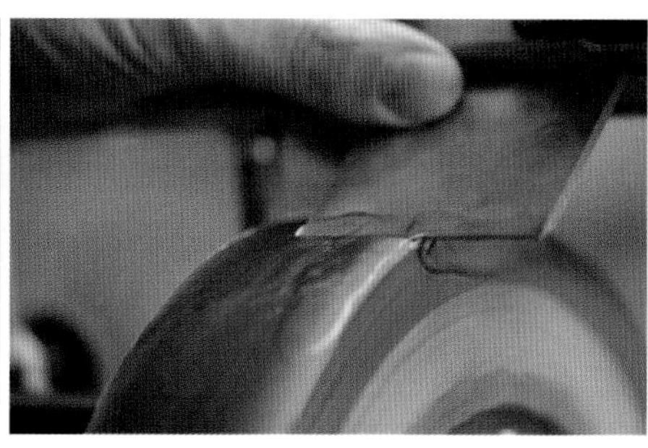

4 **Fill the trough** with water and start the grinder. During the grinding process, continuously move the blade back and forth over the grinding wheel.

5 **Check the blade** during grinding and ensure that the new edge is forming equally along the width of the blade. When the cutting edge is perfectly flat, the blade is ready to be honed.

HONING THE BLADE

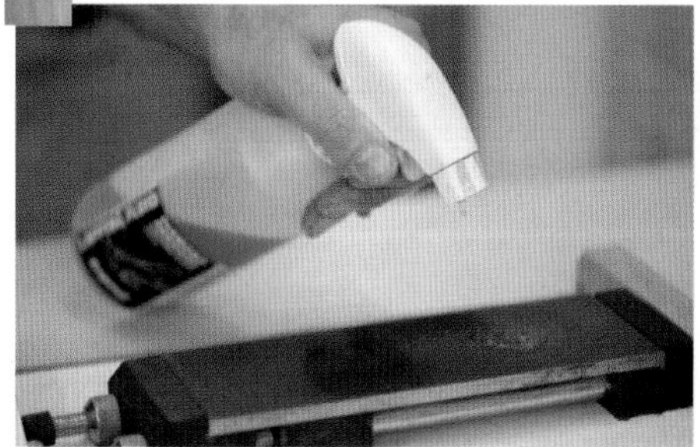

1 **Use a diamond whetstone** (1,000 grit) set in a stone holder to hone the blade. Secure this to the workbench and lubricate it with proprietary lapping fluid (petroleum-based).

2 **Flatten the back** of the blade to remove any burr that has formed during the grinding process. Rub the blade, flat side down, across the whetstone.

3 **Set the angle** of the honing guide, which is used to keep the angle and flatness of the bevel edge consistent while sharpening. The honing angle for planes is usually 30 degrees.

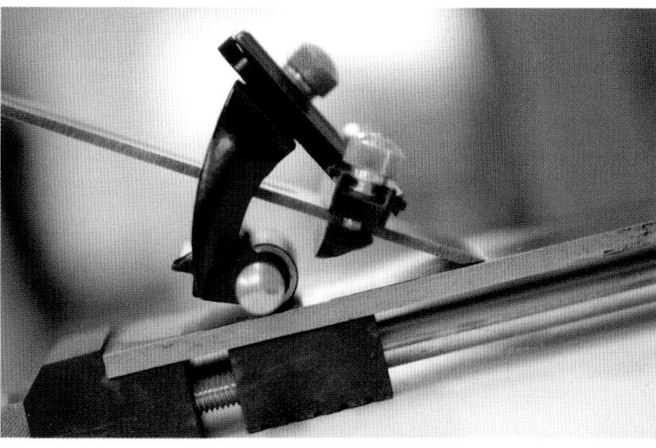

4 **Set the width** of the honing guide to the same width as the blade. Insert the blade and tighten the guide to secure it. Then place this assembly on the whetstone.

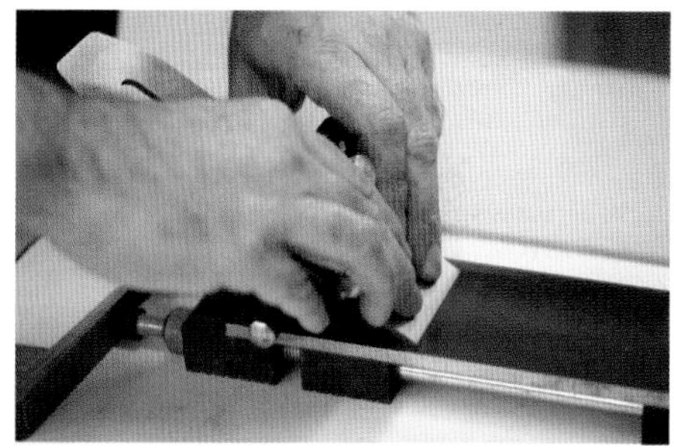

5 **Starting with a backward stroke,** hone the blade by working it back and forth with firm and even pressure. Use the entire surface of the whetstone to prevent any grooves forming.

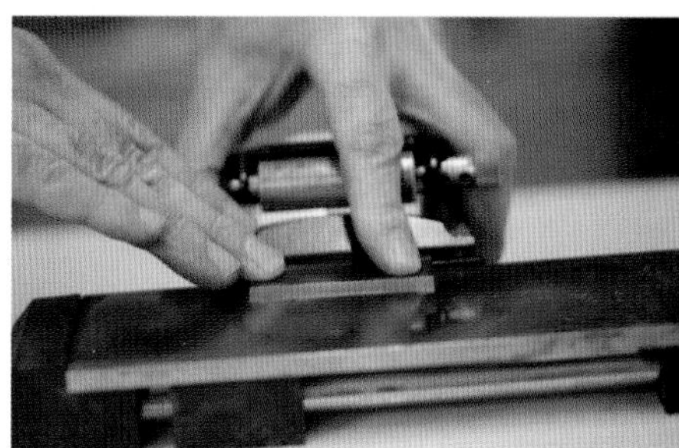

6 **Rub the flat side** of the blade to remove any burrs and continue rubbing until an even secondary bevel of about 1⁄32–1⁄16in (1–2mm) has formed along the width of the blade.

7 **Change to a stone** of a finer grit, such as a 4,000- to 6,000-grit waterstone. Lubricate with water and repeat steps 4–6. Keep turning the stone from time to time as you work.

8 **For the finest "mirror" finish**, repeat steps 4–6 with an 8,000-grit waterstone. To finish off, rub the flat side on the stone to remove any burrs.

REASSEMBLING THE PLANE

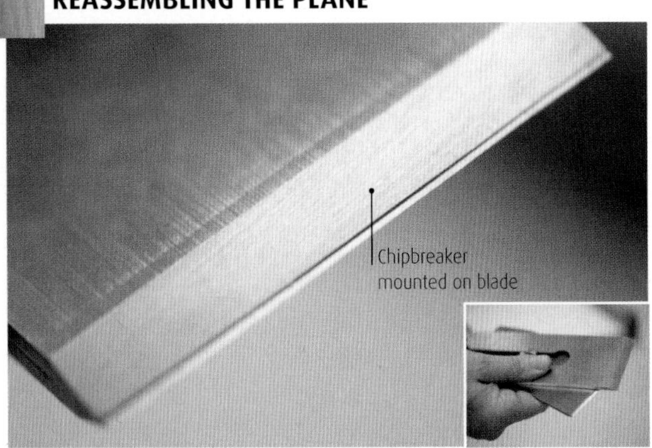

1 **Assemble the blade** and the chipbreaker, so that the end of the chipbreaker is aligned no more than ¹⁄₁₆in (1mm) from the edge of the blade. This not only prevents the blade from chattering (vibrating) when cutting difficult timbers, but also supports the cutting edge as the level of grinding becomes thinner.

2 **Slot the blade assembly** onto the frog and ensure that the lateral adjustment lever, an adjusting lever located on the back of the frog, is central.

ADJUSTING THE CUT

1 **Set the plane** vertically on a piece of paper and look through the mouth. Turn the blade depth lever, located on the back of the frog at its base, until you can see the blade sitting squarely.

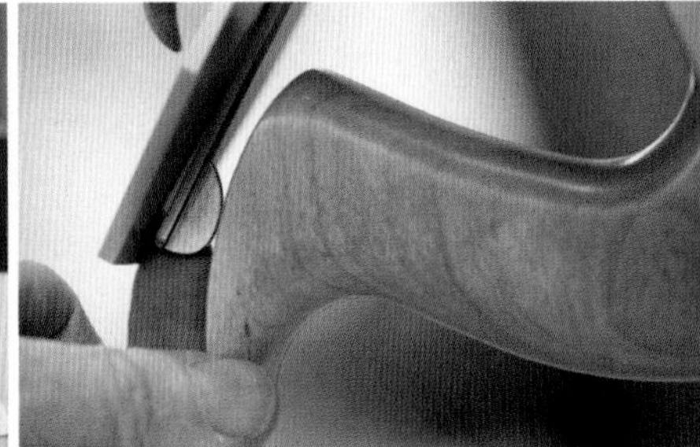

2 **Adjust the lateral adjustment lever** until the blade is parallel to the sole of the plane. When parallel, use the blade depth wheel to extend the blade back below the sole.

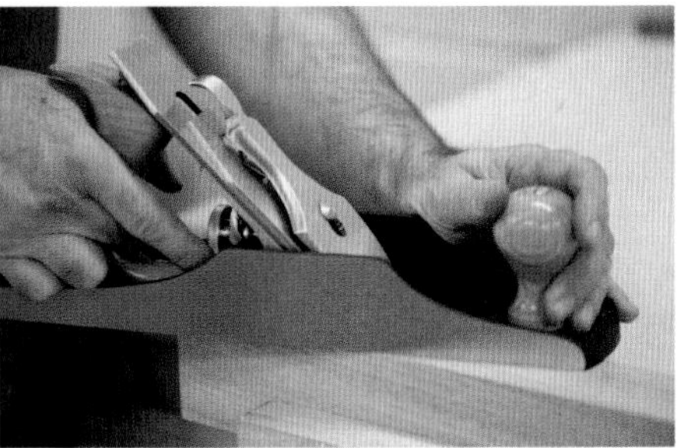

3 **Place the plane** on a piece of wood and continue extending the blade as you move it across the wood's surface. The blade is correctly set when it starts to remove a fine curl of wood.

LOOKING AFTER YOUR PLANE

To keep your plane in good working order, protect it from the damp and keep the blade sharp. Rub the sole of the plane with an abrasive block and apply tea seed oil. To avoid damaging the sole of the plane, always store the plane on its side or with one end raised.

CLEANING WITH AN ABRASIVE BLOCK

APPLYING TEA SEED OIL

Block planes

Smaller than bench planes, block planes can be used with one hand. Their blades are mounted with the bevel facing up and can be of low-angle, rebate, or skewed-blade type. Block planes are used for cutting end grain, trimming dovetails (pp.102–03, pp.134–37), fitting miters (pp.112–15), and forming small chamfers (small beveled edges).

USING A BLOCK PLANE
Use both hands for greater control when working small areas. However, when making simple cuts, hold the block plane in one hand.

Block plane
Many block planes have an adjustable mouth. Fine work will require you to use a small mouth, while coarse woods or resinous timbers may need a large mouth.

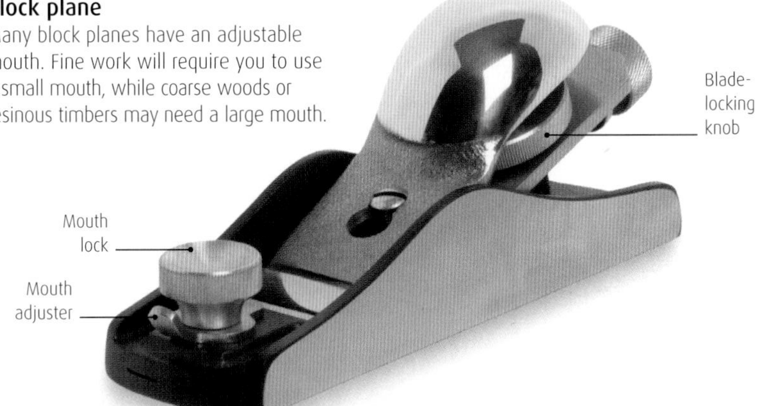

Rebate planes

Rebate and shoulder planes have blades that extend to the full width of the plane, which allows them to reach fully into the corners of rebate or shoulder joints (pp.108–09). Rebate planes are used to create, clean, and adjust rebates. Some have two fences—one controls the width of the rebate and the other sets the depth.

Rebate plane

A rebate plane, such as the one shown here, can be used to cut stopped rebates by mounting the blade at the front.

Side rebate planes

The blades of side rebate planes sit in a very flat body and are used to trim the sides of small grooves or housings. Left- or right-handed versions (or both combined) can be used when the rebate is restricted.

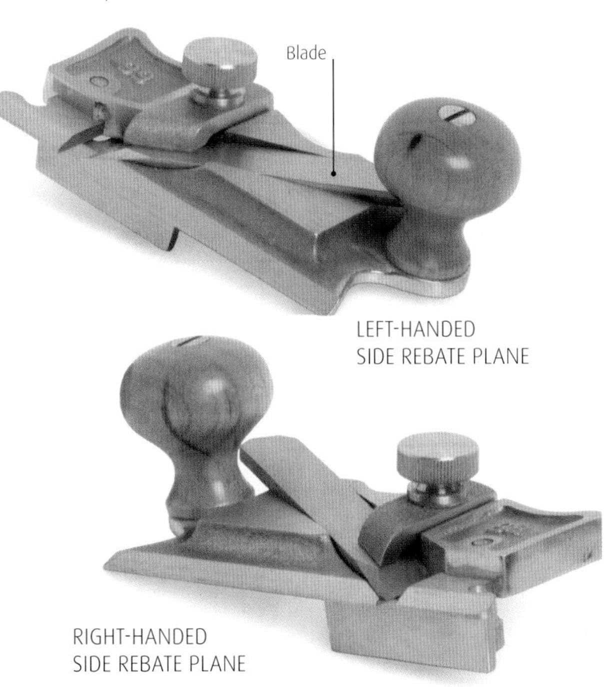

LEFT-HANDED SIDE REBATE PLANE

RIGHT-HANDED SIDE REBATE PLANE

Shoulder planes

Shoulder planes are tall with sides at right angles to their soles. This allows them to trim the shoulders of joints, such as tenons (pp.116–27), squarely. Also used for trimming the end grain of shoulder joints (pp.108–09), shoulder planes have a low-angle blade set with the bevel facing up. They come in a wide variety of sizes to suit different-sized shoulders.

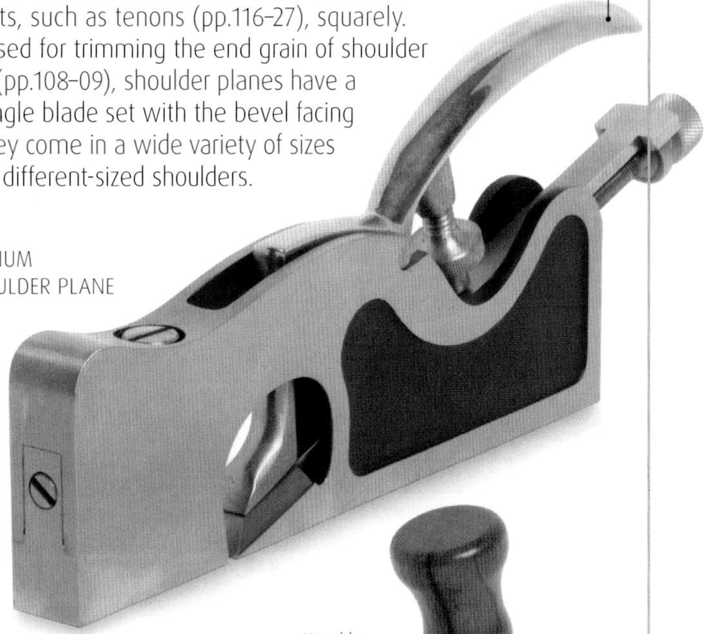

Blade locking lever and handle

MEDIUM SHOULDER PLANE

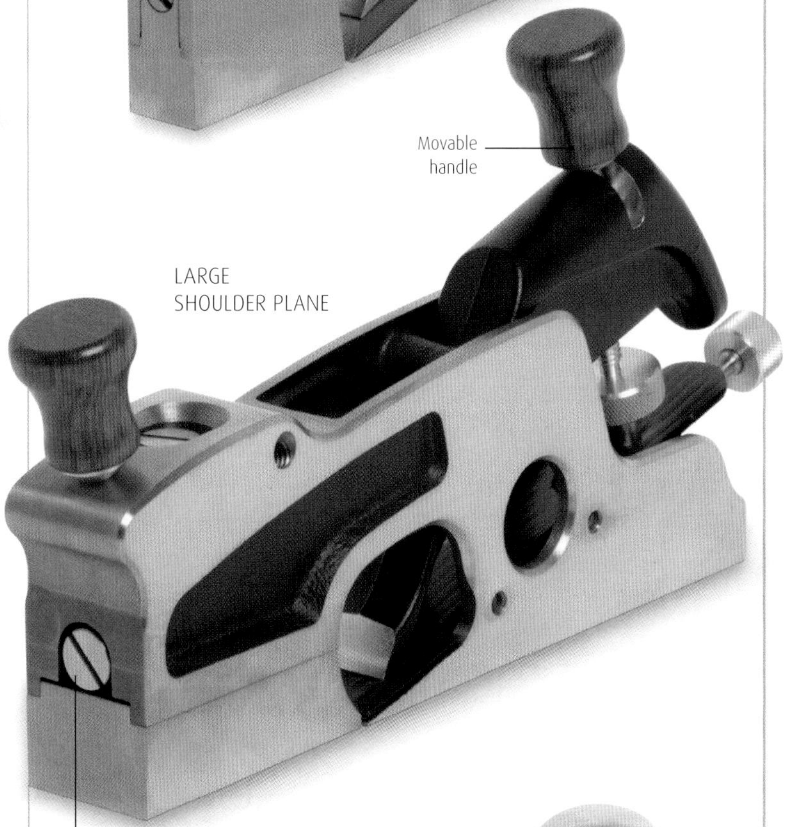

Movable handle

LARGE SHOULDER PLANE

Mouth adjuster and lock

Blade-locking lever and handle

Bullnose plane

A variation on shoulder planes, the bullnose plane has a very short length of sole in front of the blade. This allows the blade to access tight corners and other awkward areas.

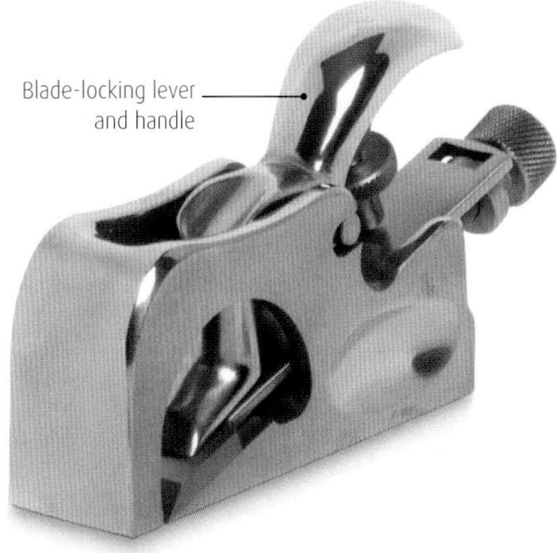

Specialized planes

Basic types of planes, such as bench planes and block planes, are used for simple tasks, such as smoothing surfaces and creating straight edges over large, unrestricted surfaces. However, when smoothing tight or corner edges, such as those in joinery work, it is useful to use specialized planes, such as iron miter planes, router planes, plow planes, and spokeshaves. Scraping planes have blades set to work on very hard timbers where simple planes are not as useful.

Iron miter planes

Miter planes are heavy, robust tools; their design allows them to be used on their sides with a shooting board. The blades of these planes are set at much lower angles than they are on other planes.

Side handle

Router planes

Specially designed to form and clean up housings, the blade of a router plane is suspended below the body. Blades for these planes are available in different shapes and sizes depending on the work being carried out.

ROUTER PLANE

SMALL ROUTER PLANE

USING A ROUTER PLANE

Router planes are used to remove waste from housings, halving joints, and other similar areas. Initially, adjust the blade to remove only a small amount of timber, before resetting it to shave off enough wood to achieve the required depth.

HONING A ROUTER PLANE

Follow the instructions for honing a bench plane (p.25), but place the whetstone near the edge of the workbench to provide clearance for the shaft.

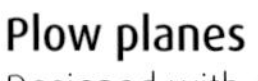

Plow planes

Designed with a narrow sole, plow planes are used to form grooves in the timber. Levers on plow planes can be adjusted to form grooves of desired depths, and the fence can be moved to create the groove at a specific distance from the edge.

USING A PLOW PLANE

Plow planes are one of the trickiest types of planes to use. The start point of the first cut should be near the end that is furthest away from you. As the cut deepens, begin to move the blade toward you.

Scraping planes

The blade of a scraping plane is set so that it leans forward in the direction of the cut. These planes are used to finish a surface and are useful for tackling very difficult timbers, or those with a coarse grain.

Blade

Handle

Blade-locking screw

LARGE SCRAPING PLANE

Blade

Handle

Blade-locking screw

Body

CABINET SCRAPING PLANE

PREVENTING RUST

Planes made from cast iron are prone to rust. To prevent this, periodically apply a light coating of oil to any exposed metal. If your tools are stored in a damp or humid place, wrap them up in a rag or sacking.

Spokeshaves

The body of a spokeshave plane has a very short sole held between two handles. It is used to form curves or chamfers as it is drawn along the timber. Other types of spokeshave plane include the travisher and pullshave, which have convex blades for planing concave surfaces.

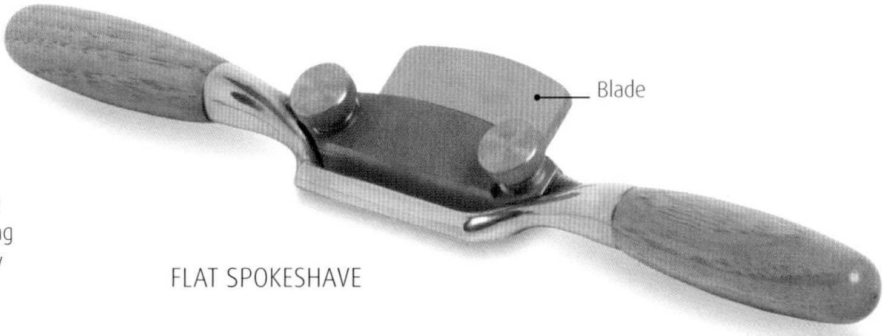

Blade

FLAT SPOKESHAVE

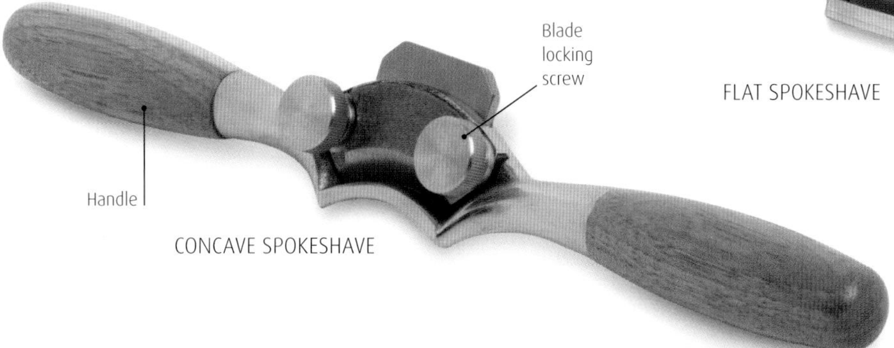

CONCAVE SPOKESHAVE

USING A SPOKESHAVE

Grasping both handles of the spokeshave, push it away from you. Since spokeshaves have such short soles, they may need to be rotated slightly to ensure the blade is correctly aligned and in contact with the surface being planed.

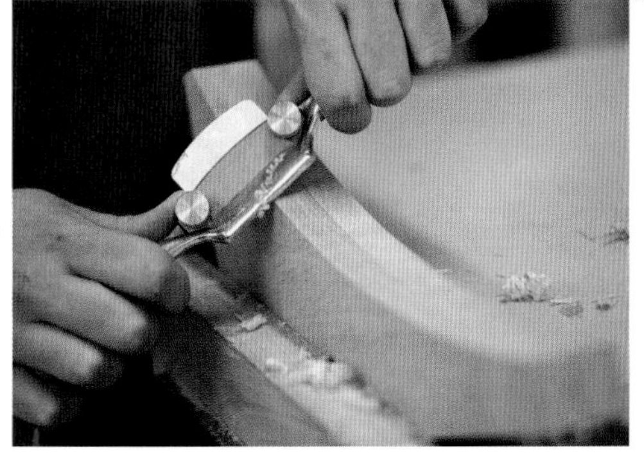

WAXING A PLANE

Sometimes, especially when working with resinous timbers, the friction between the plane and the timber makes planing very hard work. Applying a little candle wax to the sole of the plane will reduce the effort required.

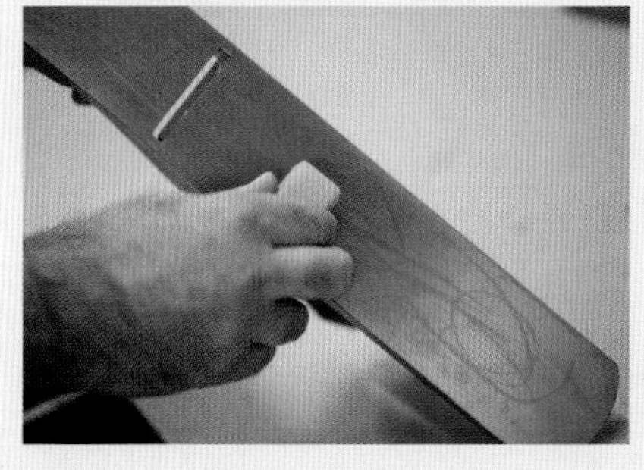

Chisels

Chisels are probably the most important cutting tools used by woodworkers. Comprised of a steel blade with one end sharpened and the other mounted in a handle, they can cut with, across, or along the grain, removing large amounts of wood or the thinnest of shavings. Chisel blades are sharpened on one side only. The slope that forms on the sharpened edge is normally at an angle of 30 degrees to the flat surface. If maintained well and sharpened regularly, chisels can help you execute complex cutting tasks fairly easily. The variety of chisels available is very large due to their many different uses. Bevel-edged chisels (below) are the most common, while Japanese chisels (p.32) are also popular with woodworkers. These often have a large iron cap or hoop on the handle—chisels in Japan are commonly used with hammers and the hoop prevents the handle from splitting. For heavy work, such as chopping mortises (pp.116–19), there are chisels available with large-section blades and impact-resistant handles that may be struck with a mallet.

LARGE BEVEL-EDGED CHISEL

MEDIUM BEVEL-EDGED CHISEL

SMALL BEVEL-EDGED CHISEL

SIDE VIEW

Bevel-edged chisels

The most common of all chisels, bevel-edged chisels get their name from the bevels running down on both sides of the blade. The blades of these chisels taper toward the cutting edge, and the sides have a small surface area. This allows them to reach easily into corners and joints, unlike chisels with rectangular blades. For cutting, bevel-edged chisels can be pushed by hand or used with a mallet (p.39). Some are even strong enough to be struck with a hammer. The handles vary between manufacturers, giving you plenty of choices.

CHOPPING VERTICALLY AND HORIZONTALLY

When chopping a workpiece vertically, it is important to keep the chisel aligned correctly. A combination square (p.36) can, sometimes, be used to check the angle of the cut. Place the workpiece directly over the leg of the bench to maximize the effectiveness of the mallet blows. When working horizontally, make sure that you keep the workpiece stationary—secure it by placing the other end against a solid object. If you are using cramps (pp.40–41), be sure to tighten them properly. If the cramp is loose, the workpiece may be damaged during chiseling.

CHOPPING VERTICALLY

CHOPPING HORIZONTALLY

Paring chisels

Although they look like bevel-edged chisels, paring chisels have longer, thinner blades. They are used, flat side down, for taking off small amounts of timber. These chisels are especially useful for smoothing out roughly chopped joints, for example, when you need to clean out the sides of a mortise joint. When working on large surfaces, the long blade of paring chisels allows them to reach further inside from the edge of the workpiece. The thinner blade also gives a degree of flexibility to assist in this process. However, this also makes them weak, so paring chisels should not be struck with mallets.

LARGE PARING CHISEL

MEDIUM PARING CHISEL

PARING WITH A GUIDE

To help keep the blade square to the cut, use a thick board as a guide. To keep the guide from moving, hold it in place with a vise. Its jaws (the part of the vise that holds the wood) are lined with hardwood, which does not harm the workpiece. When making either vertical or horizontal cuts, pinch the blade of the paring chisel between your thumb and forefinger, and rest the back of your fingers against the guide to steady the tool.

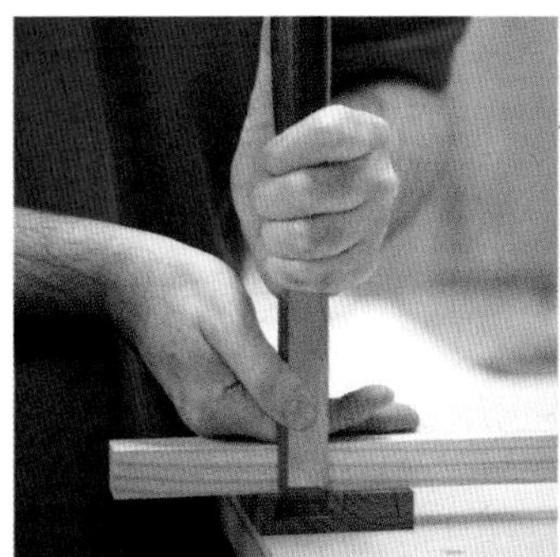
PARING VERTICALLY WITH A GUIDE

PARING HORIZONTALLY WITH A GUIDE

Mortise chisels

As their name suggests, the main function of mortise chisels is to chop mortises. They have large-section blades and very robust handles, which means they can be struck with a mallet repeatedly without any risk of damage. It helps to keep the blade sharpened, however, since fewer blows will be needed to drive the chisel in. The handle of a mortise chisel is made of hard timber such as ash or ironwood. A metal cap is also sometimes fitted at the top of the handle to prevent the wood from splitting.

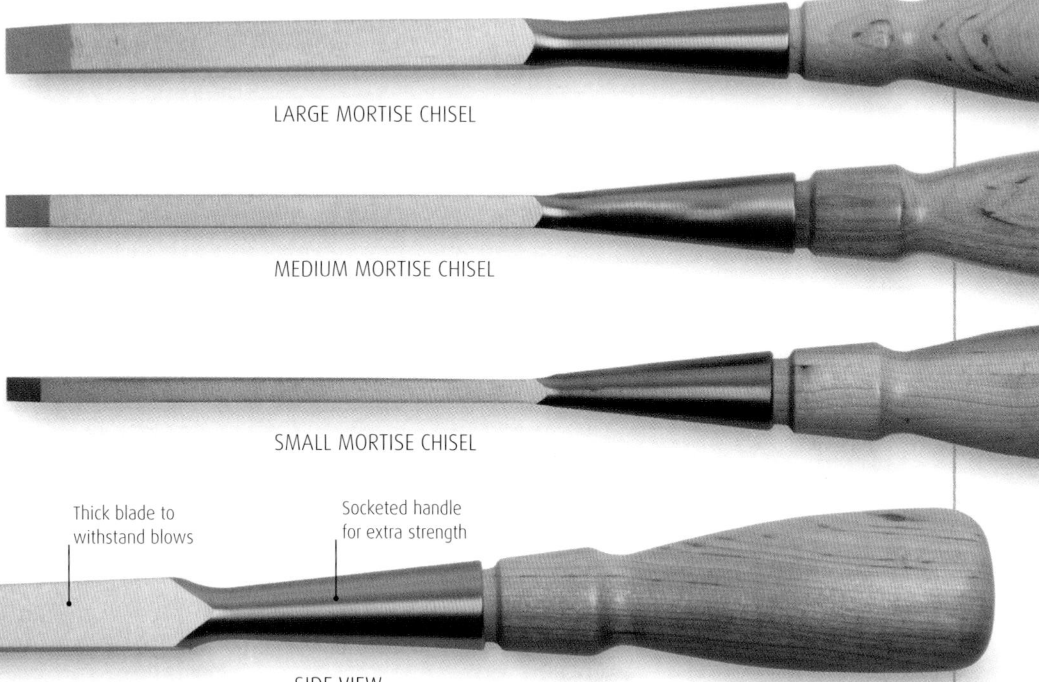

LARGE MORTISE CHISEL

MEDIUM MORTISE CHISEL

SMALL MORTISE CHISEL

SIDE VIEW

Skewed chisels

A variation of the bevel-edged chisel, skewed chisels have a cutting edge that is at an angle to the blade. They are used to clean out joints where the point of the cutting edge will easily trim into tight corners. Left- and right-handed versons of skewed chisels are available for ease of use, especially when performing tricky joinery work, such as the pin piece for a lapped dovetail joint (pp.138–39). The handles of skewed chisels are fitted with bands, which prevents the wood from splitting when struck with a mallet.

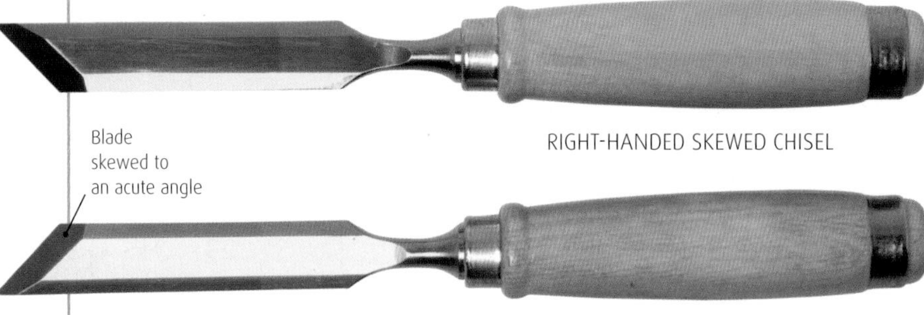

RIGHT-HANDED SKEWED CHISEL

LEFT-HANDED SKEWED CHISEL

Japanese chisels

The blades of Japanese chisels are sometimes made from the same type of steel used to make samurai swords, which allows them to be sharpened to a very fine edge. The backs of these chisels are also ground hollow, which reduces the friction when paring and also speeds up the process. When sharpening a Japanese chisel, there is a chance that the flat area directly behind the cutting edge will be removed during the process. Should this happen, you can easily restore it by using a whetstone.

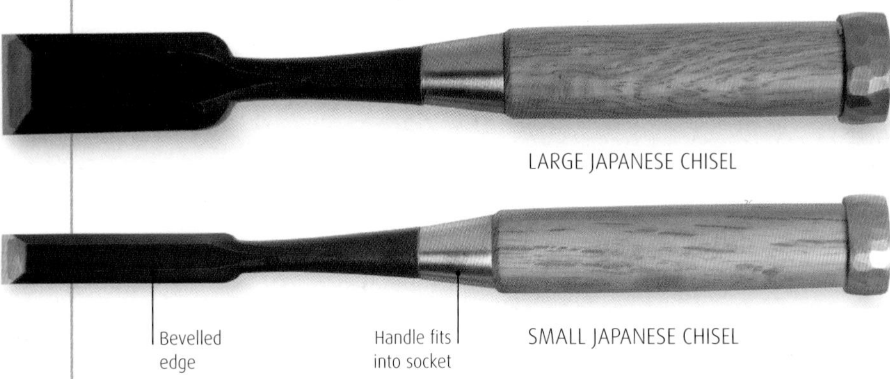

LARGE JAPANESE CHISEL

SMALL JAPANESE CHISEL

CARE AND STORAGE

Chisels should be treated with care if you want them to perform well. It is important to keep them sharp, mainly because it is safer to use a sharp chisel than a blunt one since less force is required to make a cut. After sharpening a chisel or before storing it away for any length of time, it is advisable to oil the metal surfaces with tea seed oil or similar. A good way to store chisels is in a leather roll, which will keep them separate, and therefore protect the cutting edges.

LEATHER ROLL, OPEN

LEATHER ROLL, FASTENED

Cranked paring chisels

Sometimes called swan-necked chisels, cranked paring chisels perform the same functions as ordinary paring chisels. However, the angled crank between the blade and the handle means they can be used flat, which is useful when paring in the center of large, flat surfaces. Cranked paring chisels are especially helpful for trimming the plugs used to hide screw heads.

Handle is raised above the plane of the blade

Cranked neck

Cranked paring chisel
The handle is set at an angle so that you can keep the blade flat without your fingers and knuckles coming into contact with the surface of the workpiece.

SHARPENING A CHISEL

Using a sharp chisel means that you will not have to exert as much force as you would with a blunt chisel. A sharp chisel will also improve the quality of your work. There are many ways to sharpen chisels, but using a water-cooled grindstone with purpose-made jigs is a popular method. This technique ensures that only a small amount of metal is removed to form the final bevel. It also allows you to fix common settings, which is helpful in saving time, especially when several chisels have to be sharpened together. You will need a jig to hold the chisel in place, a measuring devise to set the angle of the cutting edge, and a grindstone for sharpening. For honing, you will need a honing guide and whetstones ranging between 1,000–8,000 grit.

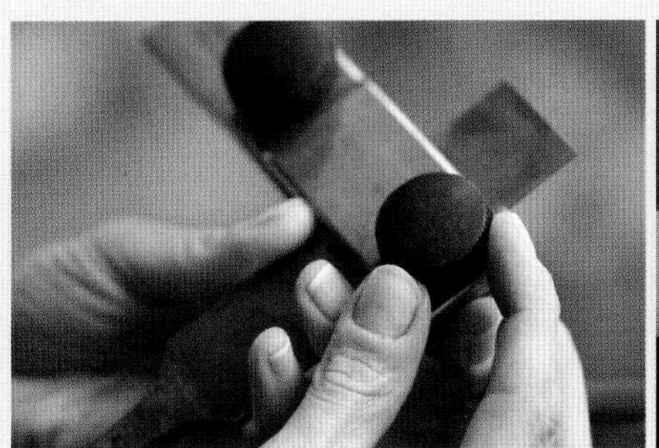

1 **Fit the chisel** into the jig with the blade extending beyond the jig by the desired amount, depending upon the width of the blade. Ensure the jig is tightened properly and the chisel is not loose.

2 **Place the chisel** on the stone and set the grinding angle to 25 degrees using an angle-measuring devise. Ensure you allow for the size of the grindstone.

3 **Start the machine** and, using gentle pressure, move the chisel from side to side across the grindstone. Ensure that the stone is well lubricated at all times.

4 **After grinding the chisel**, you will need to hone the blade. In preparation for this, fix the angle of the honing guide to 30 degrees so that the bevel will lie flat against the stone.

5 **Set the width** of the honing guide. This measurement must be the same as the width of the blade so that the blade will be held securely in place.

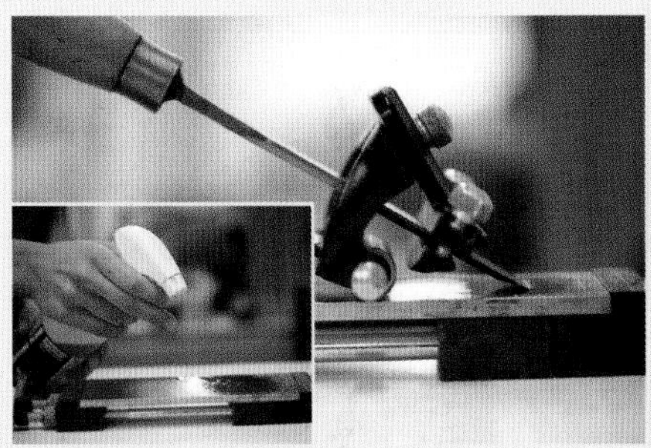

6 **Lubricate a 1,000 grit stone** (such as the diamond whetstone, inset). To start honing, work the underside of the blade from side to side to remove any burr formed during grinding.

7 **Starting with a backward stroke**, move the blade back and forth over the stone with firm, even pressure. Try to use the entire stone to avoid creating a groove in it.

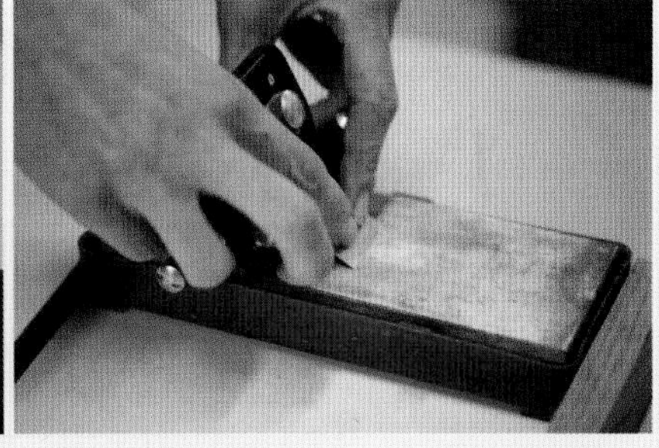

8 **Change to a stone** of a finer grit when an even, secondary bevel has formed on the blade. Continue grinding the chisel with a back and forth movement.

9 **Repeat steps 6–8** using a 4,000 grit whetstone. You will also need to flatten the back of the chisel on the whetstone (pictured) and remove any burr.

10 **Repeat steps 6–8** using an 8,000 grit whetstone. The fully sharpened chisel blade should have an even bevel with a mirror-like finish.

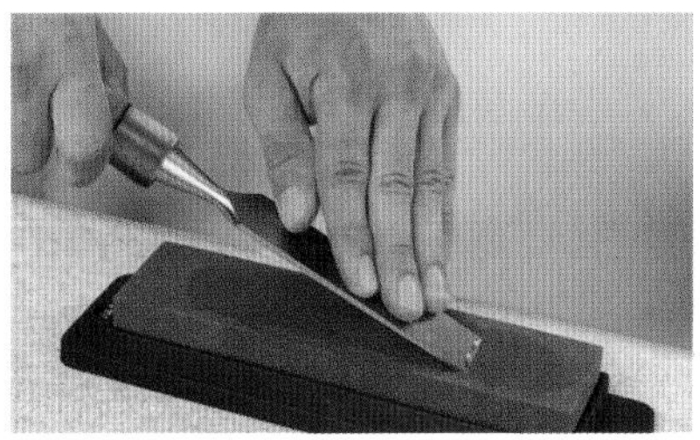

Sharpening a chisel by hand

Place your fingertips on top of the blade and rub the blade back and forth across the whole length of the whetstone.

Measuring and marking tools

Measuring and marking tools are essential for producing accurate work. They can be divided into three main groups: measuring tools, tools for marking the wood (such as a bradawl), and directional or guiding tools (such as a combination square). Generally, you will need a selection from each group when carrying out woodworking projects. Always choose the tools that will enable you to complete the task at hand most successfully. For example, a retractable tape measure is ideal for measuring along a board before cross-cutting, and a steel ruler or pair of dividers is best for measuring out cuts for a dovetail joint (pp.102–03, pp.134–39).

Basic measuring tools

Having access to a good selection of measuring tools is important for producing accurate work. A basic selection includes a retractable tape measure and steel rulers of various lengths. For more complex measurements, you will also need dividers and a vernier caliper. Dividers may also be used for marking out geometrical patterns onto the surface of wood for carving or fretting.

Rulers

Choose steel rulers with a matt surface—unlike rulers with polished surfaces, they do not reflect light and can be read accurately. Rulers reach up to 39⅜in (1000mm) in length.

SMALL RULER

LARGE RULER

Dividers

Dividers are spring-loaded and can be adjusted by means of a knurled knob running on a threaded rod—keep the points sharpened and cover them when not in use.

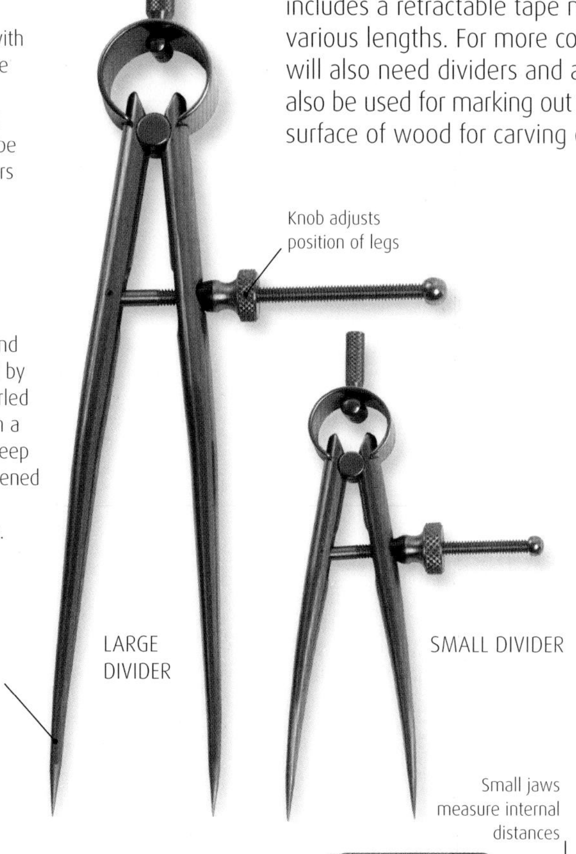

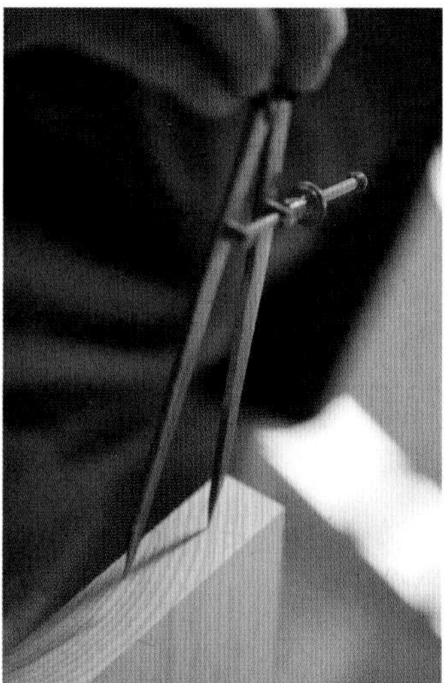

USING A DIVIDER
Use a divider when marking a series of regular intervals. Loosen the knob to set the prongs to the required length, then tighten it to lock them in place. Use the sharp ends to mark the timber.

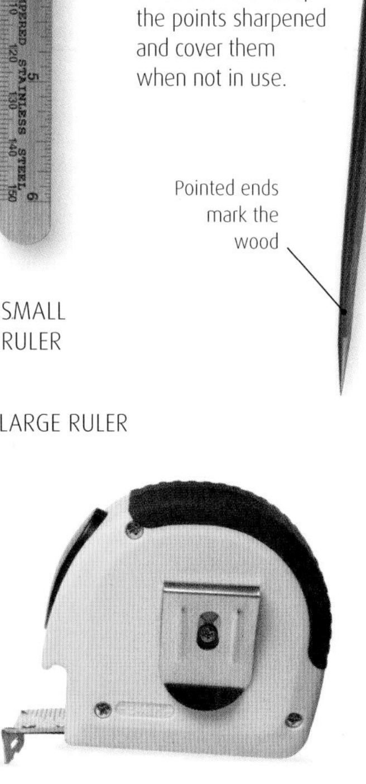

Retractable tape measure

The most common tape measures are 9¾ft (3m) or 16½ft (5m). Use the end hook only for rough measurements as it is often inaccurate. To get an exact measurement, measure from the 1in, 1ft, or 100mm mark and deduct this from the reading.

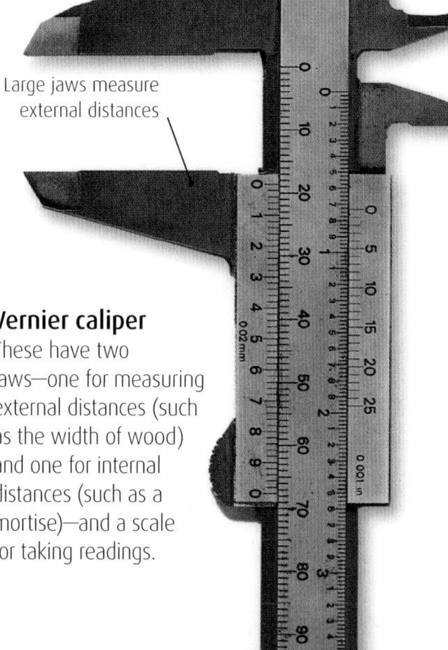

Vernier caliper

These have two jaws—one for measuring external distances (such as the width of wood) and one for internal distances (such as a mortise)—and a scale for taking readings.

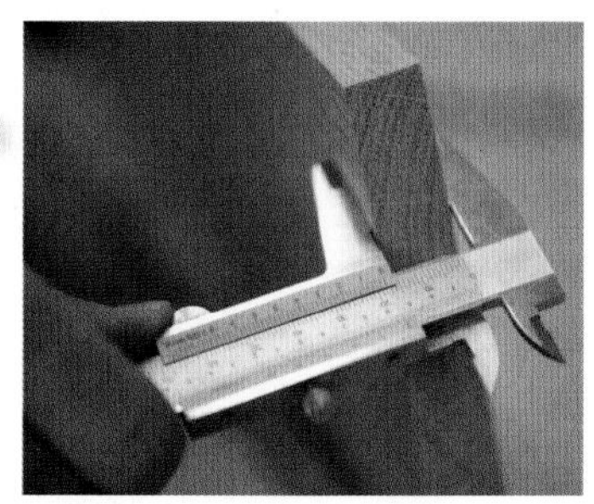

USING A VERNIER CALIPER
Use a caliper to measure between two parallel surfaces, such as the thickness of a piece of wood. Close the jaws on the object to ensure accuracy and take several readings—for external distances the correct one will be the smallest.

Basic marking tools

Pencils are indispensible for marking guiding lines on workpieces. For more accurate work, use V-point marking knives or Japanese marking knives. These leave a precise indent in the wood, which is very useful when sawing, chiseling, or marking joints. It is important to keep the blades of your marking knives sharp to ensure accurate lines—sharpen them to a chisel-like edge. Bradawls can be used to mark points for screw fittings.

LARGE MARKING KNIFE

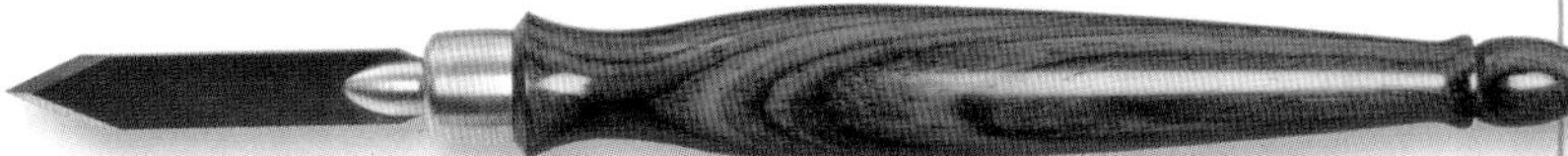

SMALL MARKING KNIFE

V-point marking knives
The two chisel-like blades of V-point marking knives differentiate them from Japanese marking knives (see below), which only have one.

Japanese marking knife
The blade of a Japanese marking knife is extremely hard and sharp, which means that it marks wood precisely and is ideal for fine woodworking.

Pencil
Choose a pencil with a hard lead, such as a 2H pencil. These are tough and work well on wood, leaving a dark, precise line to follow.

2H LEAD PENCIL

Bradawl
A pointed bradawl is useful for marking positions and making holes for screws. Bradawls also come with a chisel-like tip to cut across the grain.

MARKING THE CENTER

To find the center of a square piece of timber, draw two diagonal lines from the opposing corners. The point where the lines meet is the center. For round-section timber, use a center square.

Squares

Metal blades or "scales," fixed in wood or steel-based stocks, are called squares, and are used for measuring and marking right angles, as well as checking for squareness. Squares can knock out of alignment if dropped—check them for accuracy by marking a line from a straight-edged piece of board, reversing the square, repeating, and comparing the two lines.

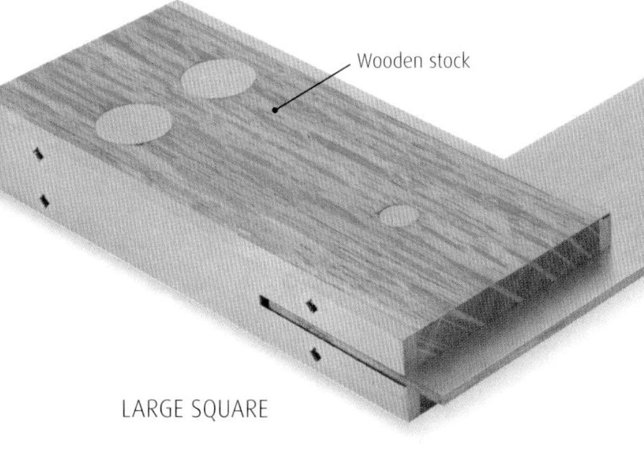

LARGE SQUARE

A range of sizes
Squares are available in various sizes. Long blades extend further across the wood, whereas short blades are good for working around end grains and edges.

SMALL SQUARE

Combination Squares

Made entirely of metal, combination squares are more robust than squares with wooden stocks. They are so called because the stock has a 90-degree face as well as one at 45 degrees, which is useful when marking and checking the two halves of miter joints (pp.112–15), for example. Some models come with a small built-in spirit level and a hardened steel scribing point.

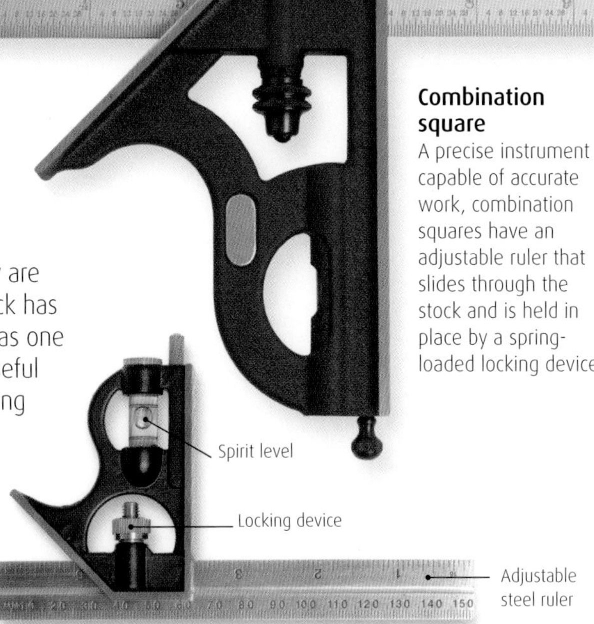

SMALL COMBINATION SQUARE

Combination square
A precise instrument capable of accurate work, combination squares have an adjustable ruler that slides through the stock and is held in place by a spring-loaded locking device.

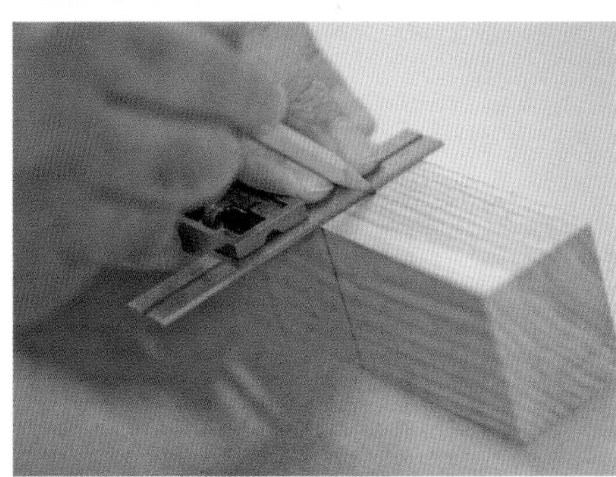

Squaring around
To square a line around a corner, place the combination square at the required distance from the end of the timber and mark the first line. Re-align the square on an adjacent face so that the point of your pencil is at the end of the first line, then draw the second line. Repeat for the two remaining faces. The end of the last line should meet the start of the first, if you have aligned the square accurately.

USING A COMBINATION SQUARE

A combination square is used in the same way as a square, but the adjustable ruler allows it to measure depths and also to mark set distances from an edge (see box, below). To use a combination square, simply loosen the knob, set the ruler to the required distance and angle (either 90 degrees or 45 degrees), and re-tighten the knob. Use a pencil or marking knife to mark the wood.

COMBINATION SQUARE—AT 45 DEGREES

COMBINATION SQUARE—AT 90 DEGREES

MARKING A LINE

When you need to make repeated markings the same distance from the edge of several pieces of wood, use a combination square to ensure that the lengths are consistent. Setting the ruler to the required distance and locking it into position means that you do not have to measure each length individually, thus saving time and increasing accuracy.

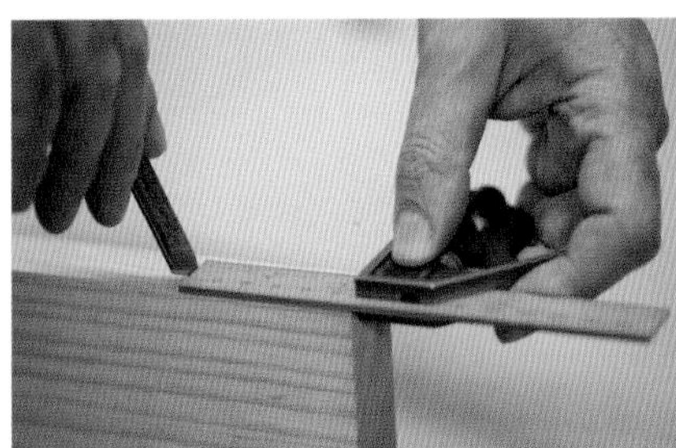

1 **Set the ruler** to the required distance. Place the stock at the end of the timber, then use a marking knife to mark the workpiece at the end of the ruler.

2 **Still holding the knife** at this mark, move the square and slide it along the edge of the timber until the ruler of the square rests against the blade of the marking knife.

3 **With the combination square** aligned next to the marking knife, and ensuring that the square does not move, mark a straight line across the surface of the workpiece.

Sliding bevels

The adjustable blades of sliding bevels, held in a timber stock, are used for measuring and marking angles. Locking mechanisms maintain their position, so it is easy to transfer consistent angles onto a number of pieces of wood. You can also adjust the length of the bevels from the stock.

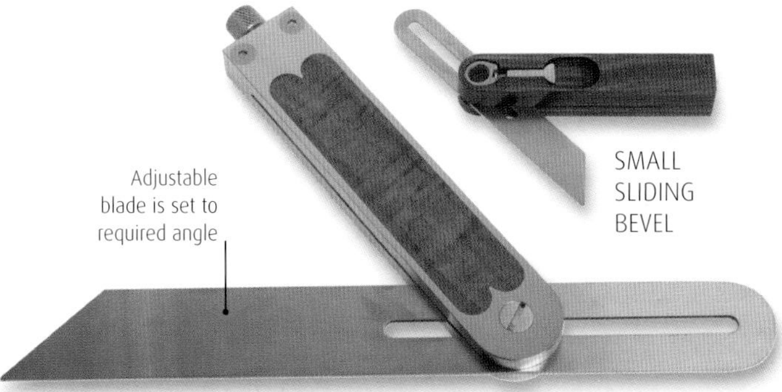

Sliding bevels
The bevel blade extends over the wood, and the stock rests against its edge. Use in conjunction with a protractor to measure and mark exact angles.

Dovetail markers

Simple yet useful, dovetail markers are tools that are set at the angles required to mark out dovetail joints. They are available in different measurements and can be used with both softwood and hardwood.

WOODEN DOVETAIL MARKER

METAL DOVETAIL MARKER

Dovetail markers
Using dovetail markers, like the two kinds shown here, makes marking dovetail joints on pieces of work simple, accurate, and fast.

USING A DOVETAIL MARKER
Hook the dovetail marker over the end of the timber. Align it with the marks that define the position of the tails. Mark the tail on the side of the timber using a pencil.

Marking gauges

These adjustable tools are used to transfer precise measurements onto wood, and are useful for tasks such as marking out hinge rebates and joint housings. Always retract the pin into the stock when not in use. Marking gauges are often inlaid with brass to resist wear.

Tite marking gauge
A built-in micrometer makes a tite marking gauge extremely accurate for detailed work.

USING A MARKING GAUGE
Once a marking gauge has been set to a required distance (see right), you can easily transfer that specific measurement to a piece of wood. Align the stock against the edge of the wood and run the pin or wheel across it to scribe a fine line.

SETTING A MARKING GAUGE
First loosen the locking device. Align the wheel or pin of your marking gauge with one end of the measurement you wish to mark. Move the stock along the stem to butt up against the other end of the measurement and then lock in place.

USING TIMBER TO SET A GAUGE

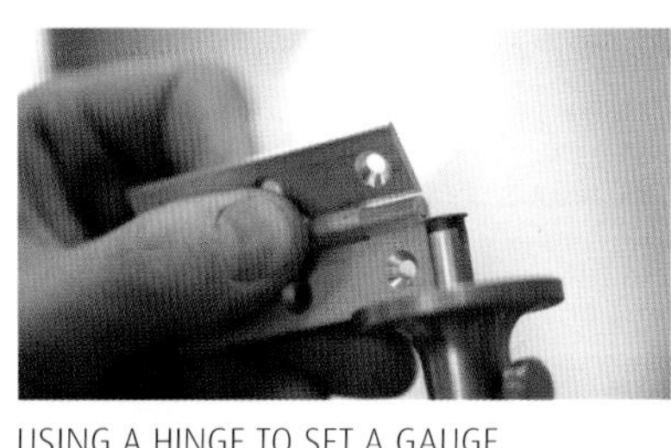
USING A HINGE TO SET A GAUGE

USING A TAPE MEASURE TO SET A GAUGE

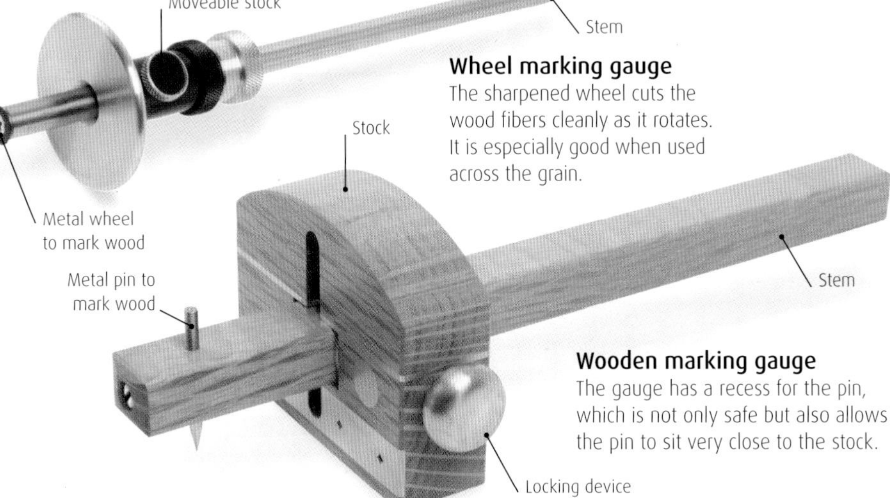

Wheel marking gauge
The sharpened wheel cuts the wood fibers cleanly as it rotates. It is especially good when used across the grain.

Wooden marking gauge
The gauge has a recess for the pin, which is not only safe but also allows the pin to sit very close to the stock.

CAUTION | WORK SAFELY | SEE P.17

Mortise gauges

Although they resemble marking gauges, mortise gauges have two pins—one fixed, one adjustable—so they can scribe the two edges of a mortise simultaneously. The distance between the pins is adjusted using a sliding bar and fixed in place with a screw. They are usually made from hardwood.

Hardwood mortise gauge

Usually, a mortise gauge is made from hardwood such as rosewood. Brass fittings, such as those on the gauge shown here, help it last longer.

USING A MORTISE GAUGE

Place the stock of the mortise gauge against the side of the timber. Tilt it so that the edge of the stem and the tips of the pins are touching the wood. Move the gauge with the pins trailing. It is better to mark the wood with several light passes rather than a single heavy one.

SETTING A MORTISE GAUGE

When setting a mortise gauge it is important to set the distance between the pins using the chisel with which the mortise is to be chopped. Do not rely on a standard measurement alone, as the chisel may vary slightly from its nominal size. This is more likely to happen with the chisels used in mortisers (pp.62–63), as they are tapered to reduce friction with the sides of the mortise. In addition, the size of a chisel will also reduce when it is sharpened.

1 **Loosen the thumbscrew** to adjust the sliding brass bar, and set the pins to match the width of the chisel to be used for cutting out the mortise.

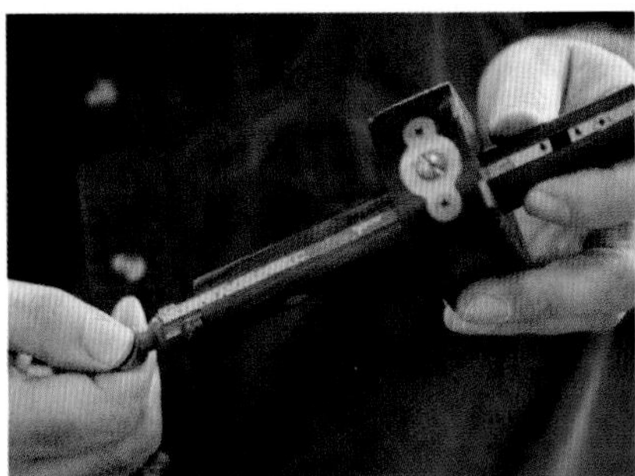

2 **Fix the pins** into the desired position by using the thumbscrew at the end of the mortise gauge to retighten and lock the sliding bar into place.

3 **Set the stock** of the mortise gauge against the edge of timber, making sure the pins are touching the surface. Run the gauge along the length of the mortise and mark the wood.

CENTERING A MORTISE GAUGE

The decision behind the positioning of a mortise is often dictated by the shape of the timber into which it is to be cut—for example, when a rebate is to be formed. However, with through mortises (pp.116–19), if there are no other considerations, placing your mortise in the center of a piece of wood is usually the most appealing option, as you will find that it is more attractive to see the end of the tenon in the center of the piece. This also allows the mortise to be made in a way that is most beneficial to the strength of the joint.

1 **Place the stock** on the side of the workpiece. On the end grain, center the two prongs of the gauge by eye. Tighten the gauge and score marks from one edge.

2 **Turn the mortise gauge** to the opposite side, place the stock on the edge of the workpiece, and mark the timber surface from the other edge.

3 **Adjust the gauge** to a setting at a mid point between the two sets of score lines. Tighten the gauge and mark the workpiece. This is the center point.

Striking tools

Striking tools, such as hammers and mallets, are used when fixing pieces of wood together. Steel-headed hammers are used for striking nails and pins, wooden mallets are used for tapping chisels, and soft-headed rubber mallets are used for assembling jointed components. The handles of these tools are generally made of an impact-resistant timber, such as hickory.

Striking tools are available in a variety of styles, weights, and materials depending upon their intended use. Woodworkers most often use cross pein and Japanese hammers. The latter have steel heads that are soft in the middle and hard at the ends. This soft middle absorbs vibrations from blows and makes them very comfortable to use. Mallets have softer heads, which are generally made from either wood or rubber.

Cross pein hammers

These are small, light hammers with a wedge-shaped extension on one side, called a "cross pein." This is useful for starting pins in wood before driving them in fully with the flat side. Pin hammers are small cross pein hammers.

Cross pein

Pin hammer
Pin hammers weigh as little as 3½oz (100g). Being so lightweight, they are useful only for fine woodwork.

Cross pein hammer
Cross pein hammers weigh between 8–10oz (225–280g). They are useful for many different striking tasks.

PROTECTING THE WOOD

If it is necessary to use a rubber mallet (or even a hammer) to help in the assembly of a joint, be sure to use a piece of softwood to evenly distribute the impact of the blows and prevent any damage to the workpiece.

Japanese hammers

All Japanese hammers are generally of the same design: one flat face for striking nails and another slightly domed face for the final blow to ensure that the nail finishes slightly below the timber surface.

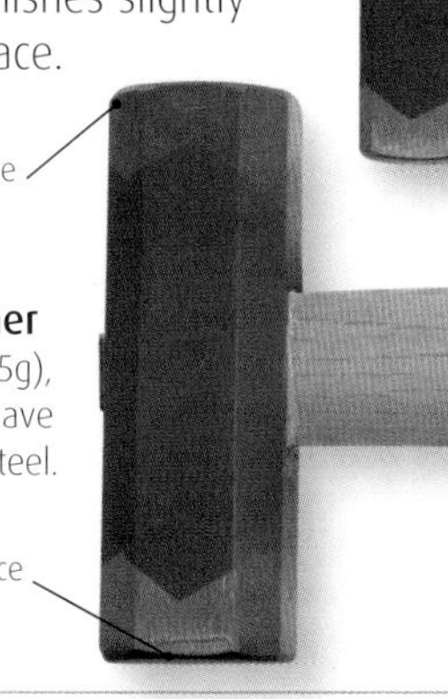

Domed face

Flat face

Small Japanese hammer
With slim handles, usually made of white oak, small Japanese hammers weigh around 4oz (115g).

Large Japanese hammer
Weighing close to 13oz (375g), large Japanese hammers have heads made of laminated steel.

Soft hammers and mallets

Wooden mallets are probably the most common soft-headed striking tools. They are primarily used for striking chisels, since they do not damage the tool in the same way that a metal hammer would. Rubber-headed mallets are mainly used to strike timber when assembling joints.

USING A RUBBER MALLET
Use gentle taps and minimum force when assembling components. Excessive force will damage the wood. Avoid black rubber mallets because they leave black marks on the wood.

Wooden mallet
The head of a wooden mallet is often made of a soft timber, such as beech.

Rubber mallet
The soft head of a white rubber mallet does not dent or mark the wood when assembling joints.

Clamps

Clamps (also known as cramps) are tools that hold pieces of wood in place. A woodworker will need a large number and variety of clamps to complete projects successfully. Clamps are used to hold pieces in position while work is being carried out, and to clasp joints while the adhesive dries. However, if used incorrectly they can spoil an otherwise good piece of work, so always have a dry-run to determine how the clamps should be arranged before applying adhesive.

Clamps are one of the most varied groups of woodworking tools. C-clamps (also known as G-clamps) are the most recognizable type—they are made of metal castings and sections, and can exert a considerable load. A sub-group known as speed clamps are often operated by a trigger, but the load they exert is much less than that of a standard C-clamp. There are also several types of specialized clamps that can be used, for example, to clamp very small joints, or frames.

C-clamps

Available in many sizes, C-clamps are probably the strongest clamps available. They are considered essential by many woodworkers, with a threaded bar that can be adjusted to the required jaw size. However, using too much force on the tommy bar can damage the clamp.

4in (100mm) C-clamp
This is an extremely useful size of clamp; most woodworkers have several 4in (100mm) C-clamps in their toolboxes. The fine pitch of the thread on this clamp makes it easy to increase the load.

10in (250mm) C-clamp
Although it is a fairly large clamp, a 10in (250mm) C-clamp should find a place in most toolboxes. This clamp can exert so much load that care is needed to prevent damage to the workpiece (see box, opposite).

Movable shoe

Threaded bar

10 INCH

Tommy bar is rotated to tighten clamp

Speed clamps

Capable of being operated with one hand, speed clamps are useful to quickly hold two items together. They cannot exert a large clamping load, so should only be used for small gluing operations.

USING SPEED CLAMPS
Speed clamps should be spaced at regular intervals to ensure an even pressure is applied at the glue line. Always have enough to hand before starting to glue a piece.

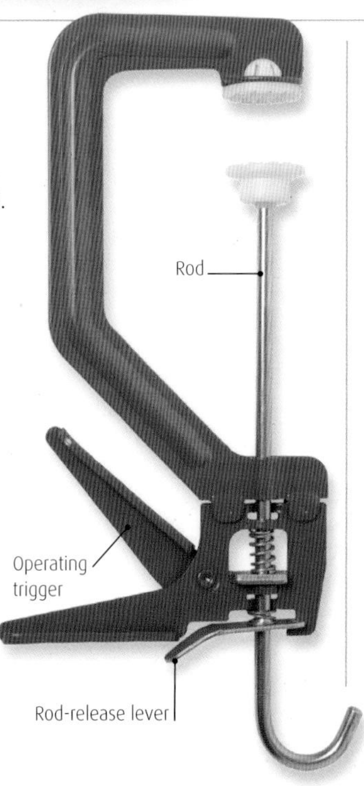

F-clamps

Much quicker to adjust to the required size than C-clamps, F-clamps also have a greater reach into the workpiece. However, they cannot exert as much load as a C-clamp.

Sash and long F-clamps

Available in a variety of lengths, sash and long F-clamps have a bar or rod, at one end of which is a screw-operated jaw and, at the other end, a jaw that is adjustable in fixed increments. The length of the bar can be increased through extensions. A longer length, however, means that the clamp may deflect when tightened, and the jaws may not be square. For best results, these clamps should be used in pairs—one on each side of the workpiece.

PROTECTING THE WOOD

If the piece being clamped is not protected, clamping may cause considerable damage. The easiest form of protection is to place a piece of softwood between the jaws and the workpiece; this spreads the load and cushions the hard metal edges of the clamp. It is also important to ensure that the steel of the clamp does not come into contact with wet glue and timber, as it can get stained due to the tannin in the wood. Clamps must be kept clean to ensure easy working.

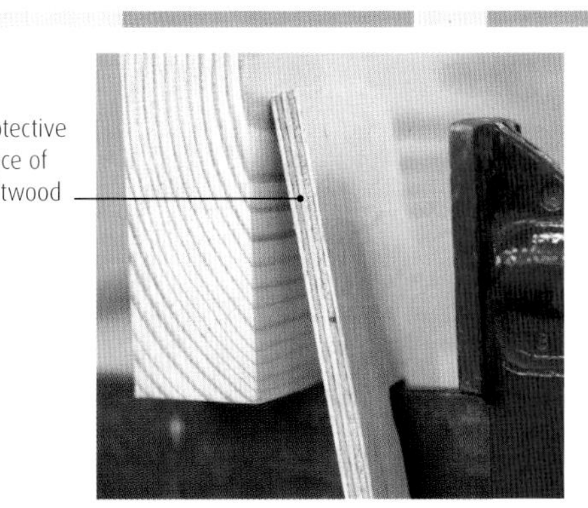

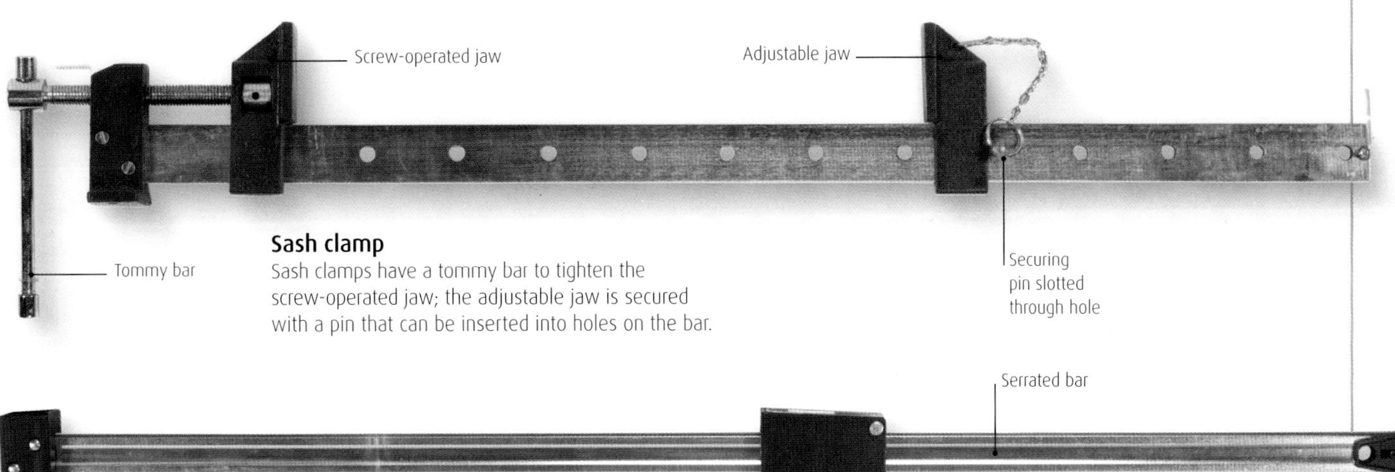

Sash clamp
Sash clamps have a tommy bar to tighten the screw-operated jaw; the adjustable jaw is secured with a pin that can be inserted into holes on the bar.

Long F-clamp
The jaws of an F-clamp are encased in plastic to protect the workpiece. They may also be reversible to allow spreading as well as clamping.

Hand clamps

A selection of small hand- or spring-operated clamps are available for clamping small joints and for holding items during construction and assembly. Their simple design ensures that they can be used with just one hand.

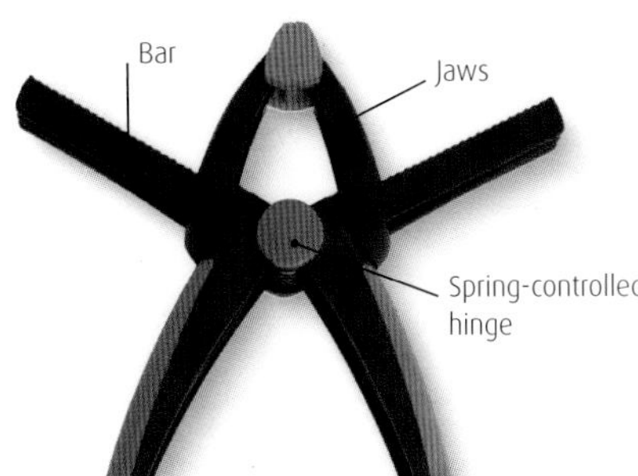

Star clamp
A small spring-operated clamp, the jaws of which can be slid along the bar to give a range of cramping widths.

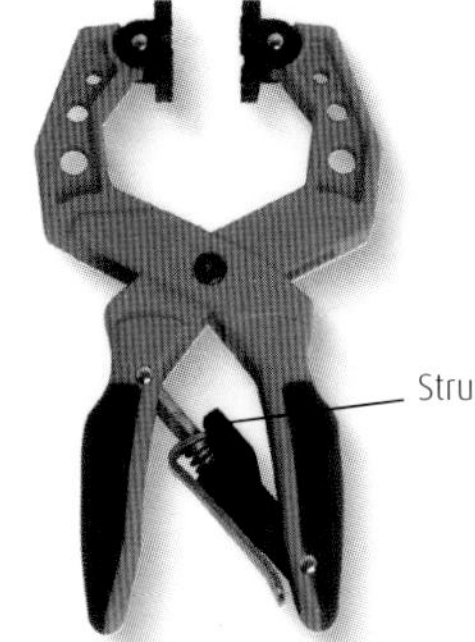

Pliers-type clamp
With this clamp, the load is applied by hand and the clamp is then locked in place by a strut.

Band and ratchet strap clamps

Useful for holding frames and coopered work, such as barrels or casks, band clamps are tensioned around the workpiece and exert their load inward. Ratchet strap clamps are similar to band clamps but intended for heavier work. Their straps are tightened by a ratchet mechanism, and can exert a greater load.

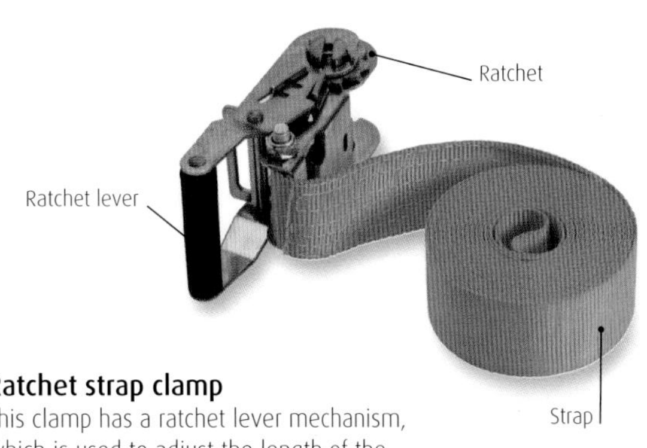

Ratchet strap clamp
This clamp has a ratchet lever mechanism, which is used to adjust the length of the strap and tighten it.

Drills and drivers

A drill is an essential tool for creating holes in wood to accommodate screws (p.67) and other fittings. Various drill bits are available, the most useful being lip-and-spur bits and forstner bits. Equally, the job of driving in screws once a hole has been drilled has also been made easy with the introduction of powered drivers, although a selection of hand-held screwdrivers is still a must in every toolbox.

There are two main types of drills: hand-operated drills and power drills. Power drills come in two forms: those that are connected to a power-supply cable, and cordless, battery-operated models. Drills adapted to hold a screwdriving bit are called drivers. The availability of many different kinds of accessories, such as drill bits and chucks, make drills and drivers especially versatile.

HAND DRILLS

Single- or double-pinion hand drills are useful for simple drilling operations. Being hand-operated, they can be used for delicate drilling tasks—for example, where the drilled hole must not exceed a certain depth. Hand drills can also be used in areas that are inaccessible to a power drill.

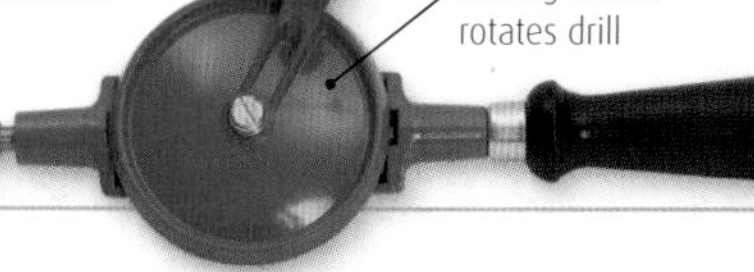

Power drills

Modern power drills typically have variable-speed controls and chucks that can take shank sizes of up to ⅜in (10mm) or more. With the improved efficiency of modern batteries, cordless drills are increasing in popularity due to their portability. The strength and type of battery determines the speed of the motor: the more powerful the battery, the faster the drill and the greater the torque. Most drill-drivers have a torque setting that limits the amount of force used when driving in screw fixings. It is important to buy a drill that is powerful enough for your needs.

Drill-drivers

Tools that perform the dual task of drilling and driving are known as drill-drivers. These can also be found in power-supply cable and cordless varieties (right). Cordless drill-drivers with batteries ranging between 9.6-volt and 18-volt are adequate for general-purpose use.

CORDLESS DRILL-DRIVER

USING A DRILL

To ensure that you drill a straight hole, place a small square near the drill bit and use it as a support and visual guide to keep the drill upright. To ensure that you drill to the correct depth, use masking tape wrapped around the drill bit as a guide.

DRILL BITS

Three of the most useful drill bits are high-speed steel (HSS) bits, lip-and-spur bits, and forstner bits. HSS bits are for use with a variety of materials, from steel to timber. Lip-and-spur bits are for accurate drilling in timber. Forstner bits are used for drilling large diameter, clean-sided, flat-bottomed holes. Other bits include the combination counterbore bit, which is used to cut all of the holes needed for counterboring (p.43) in one operation.

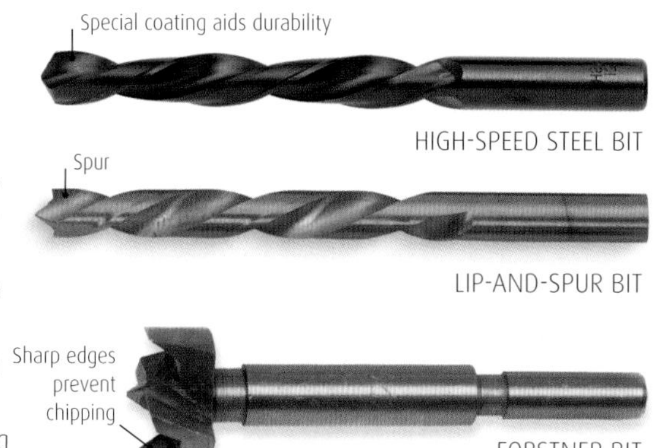

HIGH-SPEED STEEL BIT

LIP-AND-SPUR BIT

FORSTNER BIT

COUNTERSINK BIT

PLUG CUTTER BIT

COMBINATION COUNTERBORE BIT

COUNTERSINKING

The best way to achieve a neat finish on your workpiece is to ensure that the screw's head is flush with the surface. This is achieved by using a special drill bit called a countersink bit. It drills out a conical space from the top of the clearance hole. The screw's head then fits into this space.

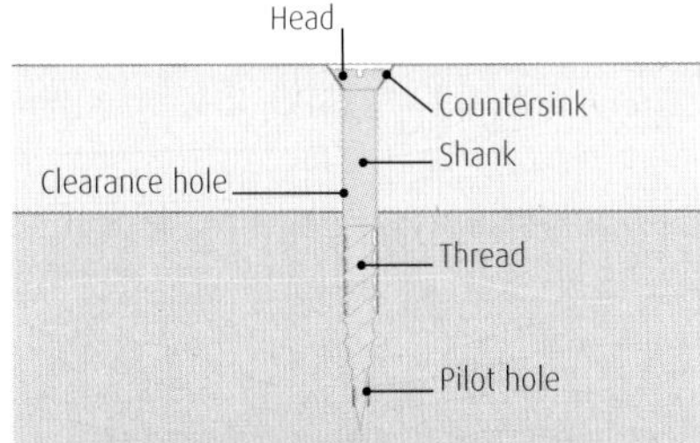

1 **Mark the position** where the screw needs to be inserted. Drill a pilot hole if necessary. Using a drill bit that matches the shank size of the screw, drill a clearance hole.

2 **Change to a countersink bit** and drill to the depth required. Be sure to place the drill directly over the clearance hole. The countersink bit will drill a conical space over the hole.

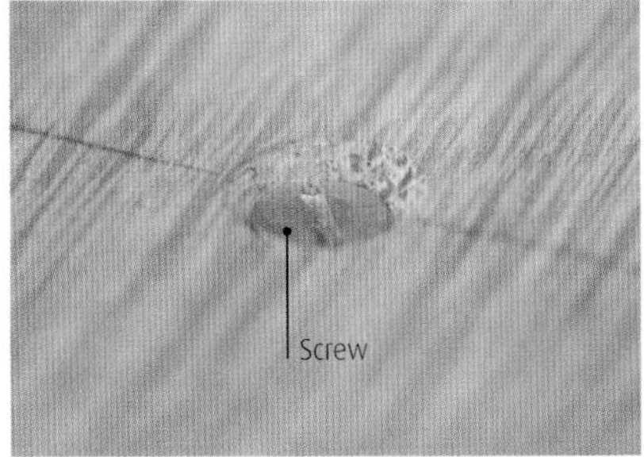

3 **Insert the screw** into the clearance hole using a driver. The head of the screw should sit in line with, or slightly below, the surface of the workpiece.

COUNTERBORING

Counterboring is a technique that recesses the head of a screw. The recess can be filled with a plug of wood to hide the screw. Use a drill bit with a diameter that is larger than the head of the screw being inserted to drill a hole on the same line as the pilot and clearance holes. This counterbore allows a shorter screw to be used and the hole can be plugged to completely hide the screw head if needed.

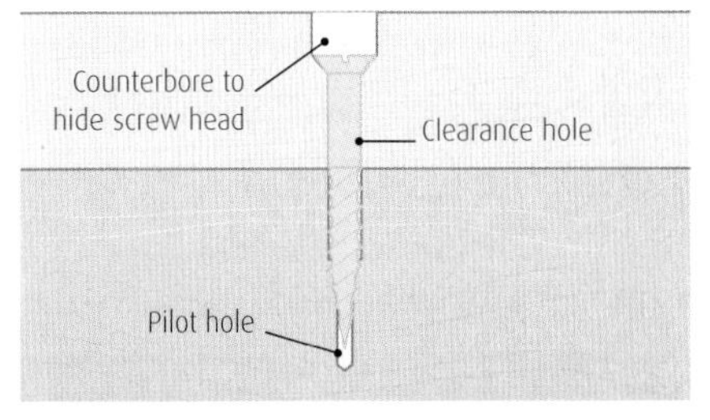

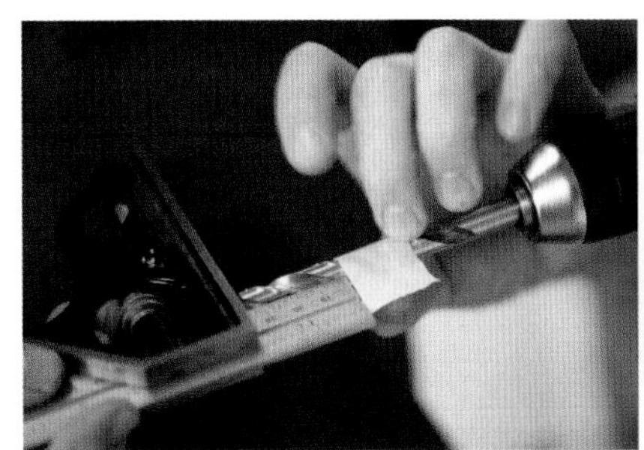

1 **Fit a drill bit** that is larger than the screw head. Set the required depth using masking tape (do not try to insert the screw too deep in case it breaks through the bottom of the timber).

2 **Drill the counterbore** into the top piece of timber to the depth indicated by the masking tape. Drill a straight hole, keeping the drill in an upright position.

3 **Use masking tape** to mark the required depth for the pilot hole (use a small diameter bit) and the clearance hole (use a bit big enough to prevent the screw from gripping the wood).

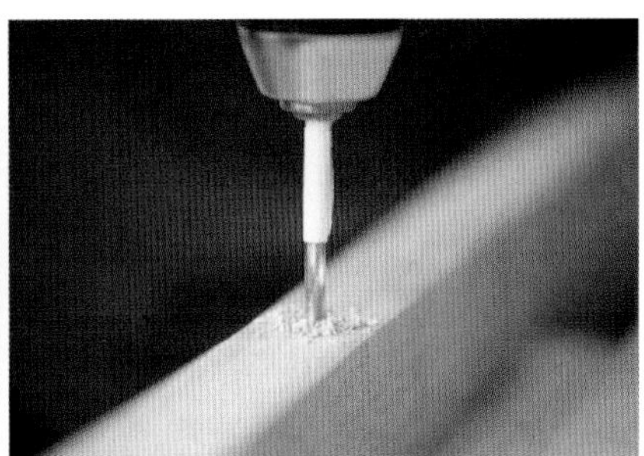

4 **Using the masking tape** as a guide, drill the pilot hole into both pieces of timber. Finally, drill the clearance hole through the top piece of wood only.

SCREWDRIVERS

Woodworkers typically use two types of screwdrivers: slot-headed drivers and cross-headed drivers, such as Phillips and Pozidriv. Cross-headed drivers fit into the screw head more securely and, therefore, are now used for most jobs. A stubby screwdriver is useful for driving screws when space is tight, and an electric screwdriver makes it easier to drive screws in awkward places. Always use a screwdriver that matches the size and shape of the screw: this will help prevent damage to the screw and driver.

STUBBY SCREWDRIVER

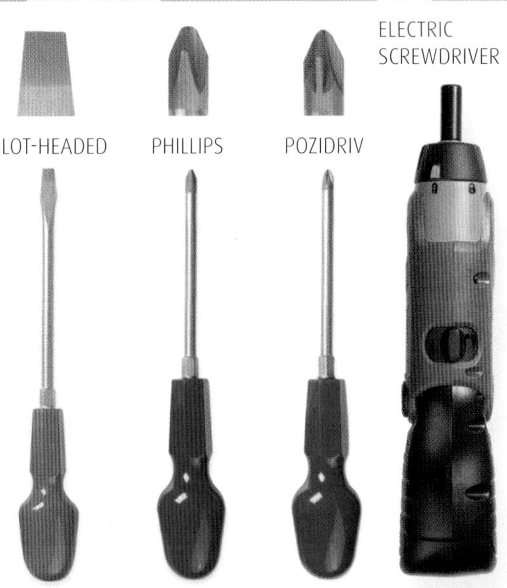

SLOT-HEADED

PHILLIPS

POZIDRIV

ELECTRIC SCREWDRIVER

Routers

A router is a power tool that routs (mills) channels, holes, and profiles in timber. The versatility and relative affordability of a router allows the woodworker to produce complex joints and carry out advanced techniques quickly and easily. The tool consists of a basic electric motor (with a speed of 20,000–25,000 rpm) connected to a tapered collet (chuck or metal collar), which holds a cutter. Router tables (p.49), in which the router is fixed beneath a benchtop, are also available.

Hand-held routers

There are two main types of hand-held router: the fixed-base router, which is popular in the US; and the plunge router, which is more widely used in Europe. On a fixed-base router, a screw mechanism fixes the cutter depth before use; on a plunge router, the cutter is lowered into position during use. Routers are available in a range of sizes (specified by the diameter of the collet), with the most common being ¼in (6mm) and ½in (12mm). An array of cutters is also available; it is this diversity of cutter types and sizes that makes a router so versatile.

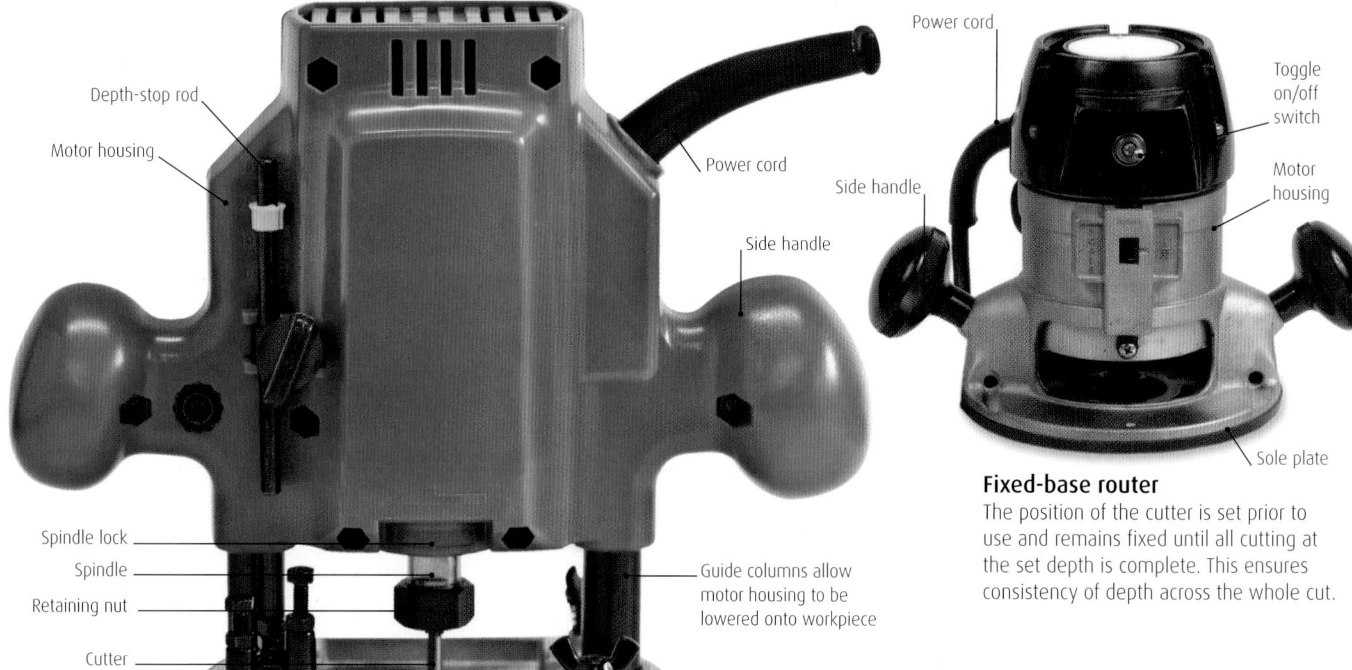

PLUNGE ROUTER—FRONT

Fixed-base router
The position of the cutter is set prior to use and remains fixed until all cutting at the set depth is complete. This ensures consistency of depth across the whole cut.

¼in (6mm) plunge router
Ideal for general-purpose use, this router has enough power (typically 1000–1400 watts) and weight to tackle most jobs, without being too heavy or cumbersome. A dust extractor (not shown) is usually fitted as standard.

PLUNGE ROUTER—BASE

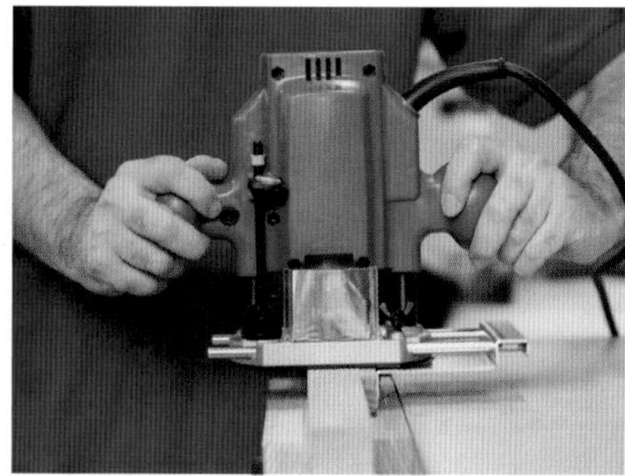

HOLDING A PLUNGE ROUTER
Grip the router with both hands, plunge it, and lock the motor housing in position using the plunge lock. Practice holding and plunging the router with the power off before making your first cut.

INSERTING A COLLET AND CUTTER

A router is sometimes supplied with more than one collet but, if the model-type permits, you may be able to insert a number of different collets to further increase the tool's versatility. You will need to remove a collet occasionally to clean it—and to clean the housing into which the collet fits (always clean the housing when changing a collet). Be aware that a collet can be damaged if it is not holding a cutter when the retaining nut is tightened. When fitting a cutter, however, ensure that the retaining nut is firmly tightened—this removes the risk of the cutter workiing itself loose during use.

1 **Ensure that the openings** in both the spindle and collet are clean and free of obstructions. Insert the collet into the opening until it locks into position (do not force it).

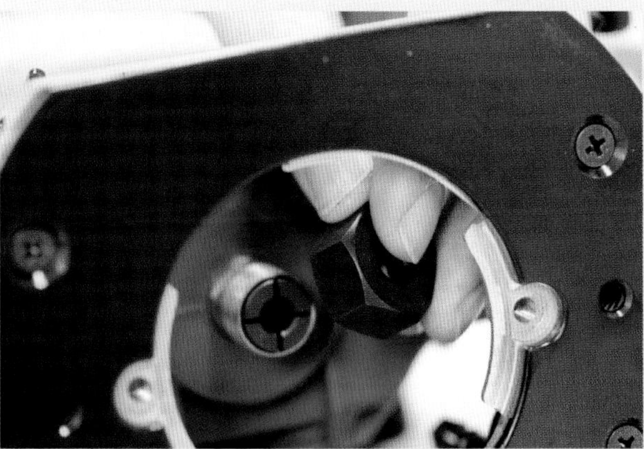

2 **Fit the retaining nut** onto the spindle and twist it several times to ensure that the thread is fully engaged. Do not tighten the nut onto the collet itself.

3 **Slot the cutter into the collet** so that three-quarters of the cutter's shank is inserted. Do not allow the shank to touch the far end of the spindle.

4 **Lock the spindle** (using its button- or lever-operated locking mechanism) to prevent it from freely rotating. Using a spanner, fully tighten the retaining nut.

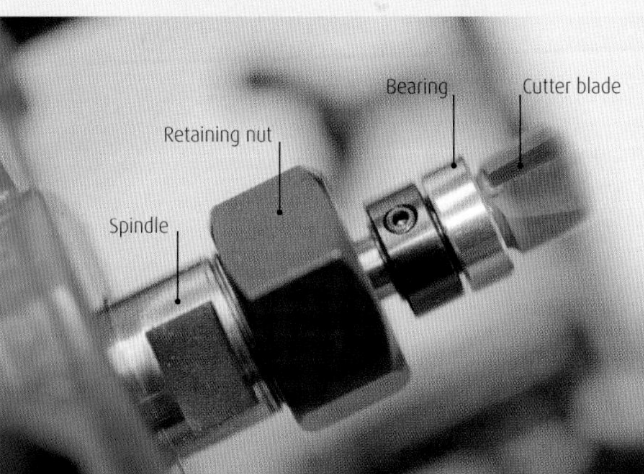

5 **Closely inspect** the cutter to ensure that it does not sit too close to the collet or retaining nut, as this may restrict its movement.

ROUTER CUTTERS

Most cutters have hard tungsten carbide cutting edges. Cutters are available in a range of shapes and sizes; the following cutters will enable you to carry out the majority of routing tasks.

GROOVE CUTTERS

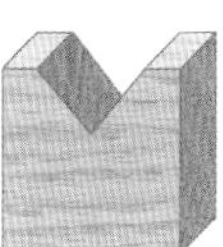

V-groove/Chamfer cutter
Cuts V-shaped grooves; if a fence is attached to the router, cuts chamfers (bevels) on the edges of a workpiece.

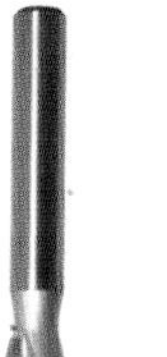
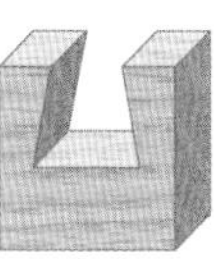

Dovetail groove cutter
Cuts dovetail housings (pp.110–11); note that the cutter will remove the sides of the dovetail as it is plunged in and out.

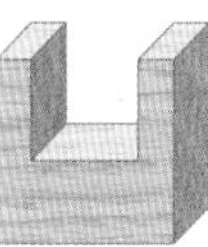

Straight groove cutter
Used to cut straight, square-section grooves and housings; can be used to cut out mortises (pp.116–19).

EDGE CUTTERS

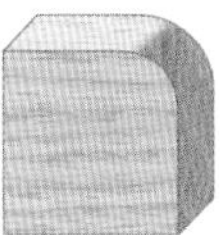

Round-over cutter
Used together with bearings of different sizes to cut ovolo and round-over (types of convex) moldings.

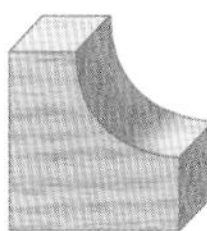

Cove cutter
Used for cutting concave moldings; the bearing acts as a guide along the edge of the wood.

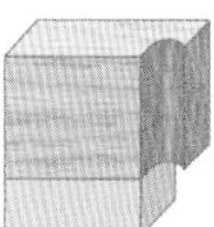

Flush-cut cutter
Used with a bearing to trim laminates flush with the edge of a board; also used to cut templates.

ADJUSTING THE DEPTH OF THE CUT

All plunge routers have a system for controlling the depth of cut. Typically this consists of an adjustable depth-stop rod fixed to the motor housing. This rod is aligned with one of the depth stops mounted on a revolving turret on the sole plate of the router. By setting the gap between the end of the rod and the stop on the turret, the downward travel of the motor housing is halted at a predetermined point.

1 **Ensuring that the power is off,** grip the router firmly by its side handles. Plunge down the router until the cutter touches the surface of the workpiece.

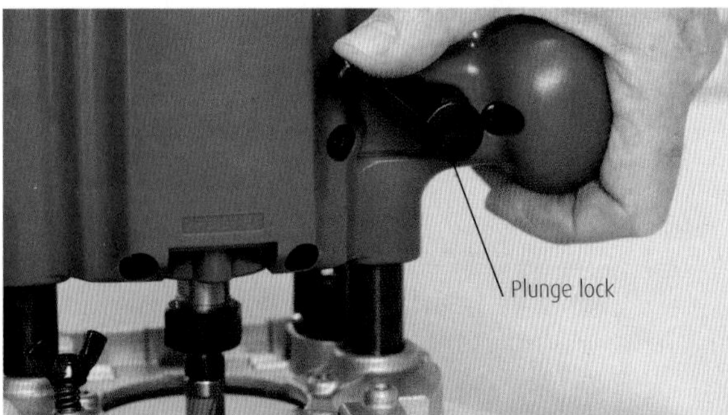

2 **Lock the motor** housing into this position by depressing the plunge lock—usually located on the back of one of the handles.

3 **Set the depth-stop rod** so that the gap between the rod and the stop matches the required depth of cut; make fine adjustments by screwing the stop either slightly up or down.

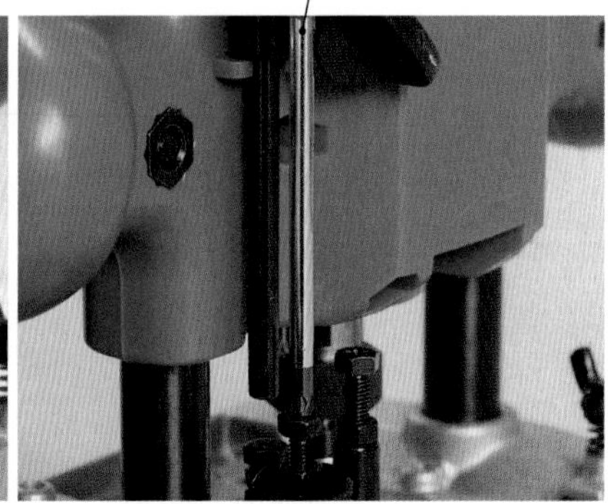

4 **If required, adjust the height** of the remaining stops using a screwdriver; this will allow you to make different depths of cut without having to re-set the depth-stop rod.

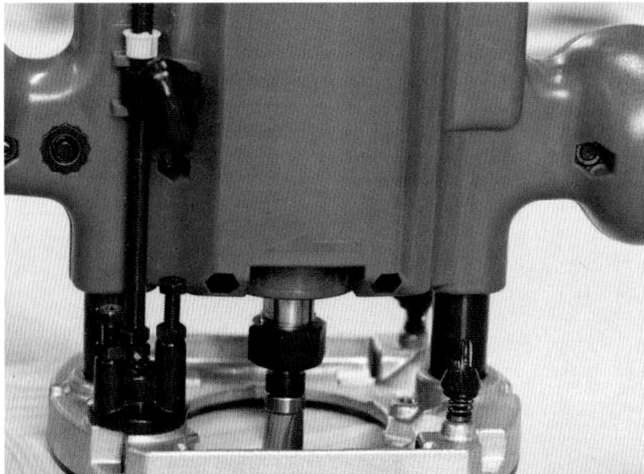

5 **Make trial cuts** for each depth of cut setting in offcuts of wood. Measure the results and make any further adjustments to the router as necessary.

SETTING THE FENCE

The side fence is a guide that determines how far in from the edge of a workpiece the cutter will sit. It also guides the router in a straight line along a workpiece. If the router's cutter rotates in a clockwise direction, the side fence should be attached to the left-hand side of the router. This will ensure that the fence is pulled in flush to the edge of the workpiece as the router is moved along the timber, keeping the router on its line and preventing it from from running away from you.

1 **Fix a short length** of smooth timber to the fence. This timber will butt up against the workpiece and, being smooth, will glide easily along its surface.

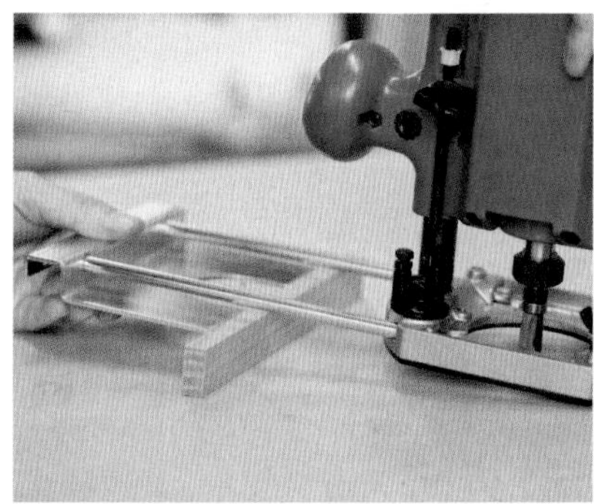

2 **Slide the fence** into the holes in the router's sole plate. Remember to attach it to the correct side of the router to allow for the direction in which the cutter rotates.

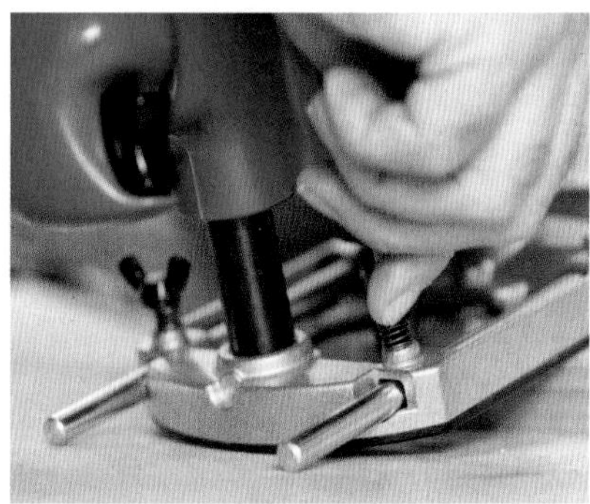

3 **Place the router** on the workpiece with the cutter in the correct position to make the cut. Slide the fence up to the edge of the workpiece and lock it into position.

FITTING A DUST-EXTRACTION SYSTEM

All routers are fitted with a dust-extraction system. Although these systems differ from model to model, most routers have a transparent plastic hood that fits over the sole plate and encloses the cutter. This hood contains the dust and waste produced while routing; it is attached to the hose of a vacuum extractor, which extracts and collects the waste. Many vacuum extractors are automatically activated when the router is switched on, and turn off approximately 10 seconds after the router is switched off.

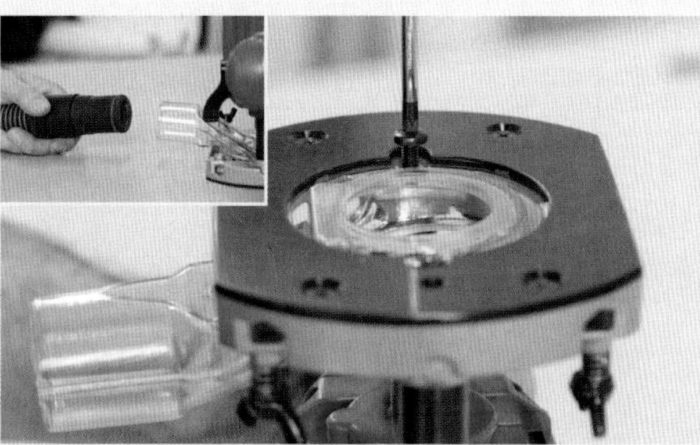

Fitting a dust-extraction hood
Screw the base of the dust-extraction hood into position on the sole plate. Some models allow for the hood to be clipped into place. For the system to work effectively, it is important to ensure that there is a tight seal between the hood and the vacuum extractor hose.

CUTTING A STRAIGHT LINE

To accurately cut a straight line you will need to either fit a side fence or, as shown, use a straight piece of timber as a guide. This is useful in situations in which you need to cut a groove or housing so far in from the edge of a workpiece that a fence will not reach. Position the timber guide so that it is on the left-hand side of the router cutter's clockwise rotation—this helps prevent the router from moving off the line. Place the flat part of the router's sole plate against the timber guide.

Forming a housing
Housings are normally cut using a straight-sided parallel cutter. If the correct size of cutter is not available, use a smaller one and make repeated cuts until the required size of housing is achieved.

SUPPORTING THE ROUTER

When routing a particularly narrow or short workpiece, it is easier to keep the router steady if you increase the surface area on which the sole plate sits. A piece of timber clamped alongside the workpiece, with its top edge flush with the top of the workpiece, will effectively widen the overall working surface.

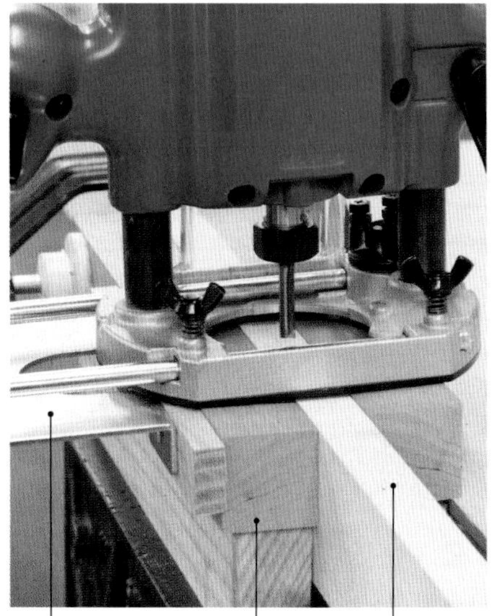

CUTTING A GROOVE

The best way to cut a straight groove is to use a side fence. Mark out the position of the groove and place the router on the workpiece, aligning the cutter with the groove markings. Slide the fence up to the edge of the workpiece and lock it in place. Use an offcut of timber to cut a trial groove to check that the fence is set correctly; adjust if necessary. Never start or stop the router when the cutter is in contact with the workpiece.

1 **Position the router** and fence on the workpiece. When steadied, switch on the power. Plunge the cutter to the required depth and make the first cut, moving the router along the workpiece.

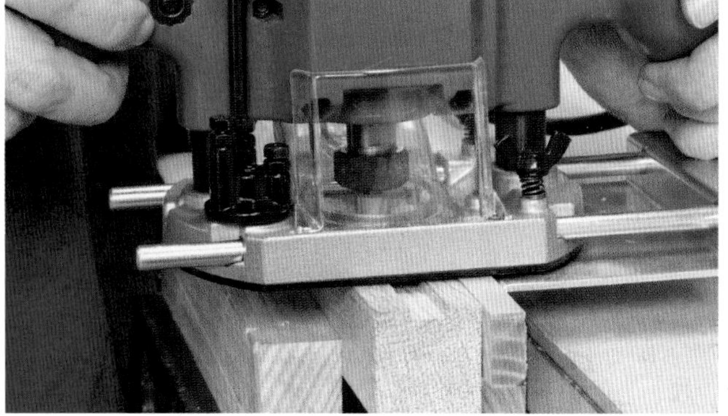

2 **Release the plunge lock** after making each cut. Allow the router to fully rise and the cutter to clear the workpiece before switching off the power. Repeat the process until the groove is finished.

CUTTING A CURVE

The easiest way to cut a radius is to attach a trammel to the router. This describes a circle in the same way as a pair of compasses. A trammel can be made very simply in the workshop, using a material such as thin MDF. When setting the depth of cut on the router, you must remember to take into account the thickness of the trammel and adjust the setting accordingly.

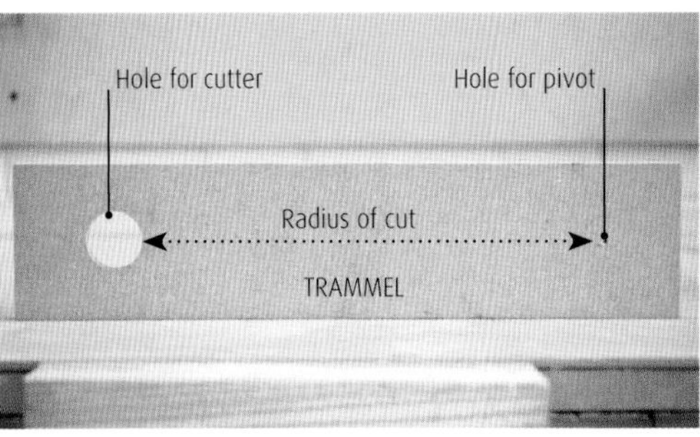

1 **Cut the MDF to size—**it should be the same width as the router's sole plate and slightly longer than the diameter of the curve. Drill a large hole at one end for the cutter, and a small hole at the other for the pivot.

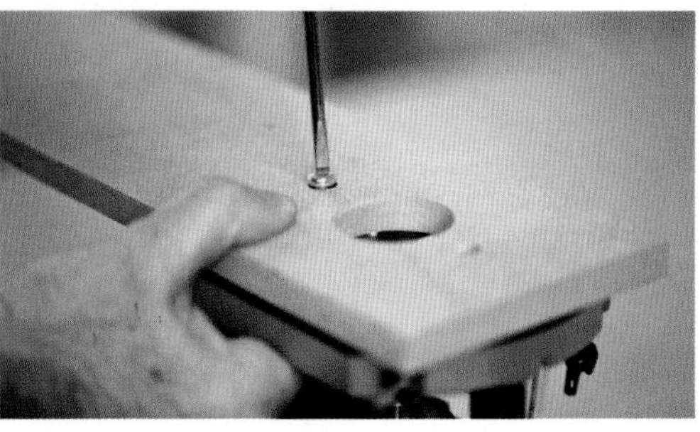

2 **Drill countersunk holes** for the screws that will fix the trammel to the sole plate. Ensure that the large hole aligns with the cutter. Insert the screws so that they are flush with the MDF.

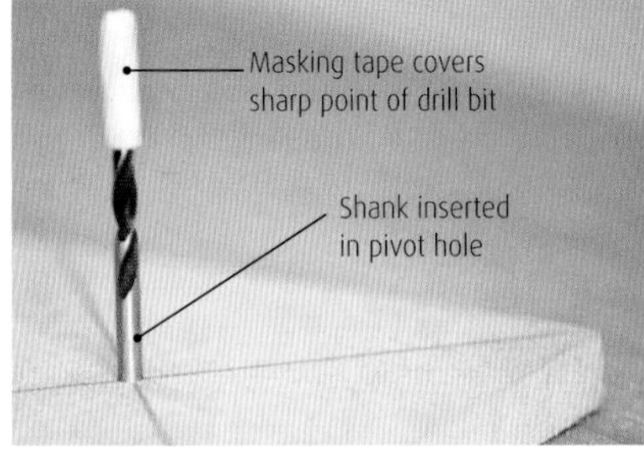

3 **Drill a ⅖in (10mm) hole** through the pivot hole and into the workpiece. Take the bit and slot it, shank first, through the pivot hole and into the hole in the workpiece.

4 **Plunge the router** and start the cut. It is simpler to do this in sections to prevent the cable and extraction hose from becoming entangled. Always cut in the same direction.

USING A TRAMMEL BAR

An alternative method to making and using a self-made trammel (above) is to use a proprietary trammel. Specially designed to help you cut curves with a router, it usually consists of a bar, which fits into a slot on the router, and a pin attached to an adjustable collar at the opposite end of the bar, which acts as a compass point. To prevent the pin from damaging the surface of the workpiece, an offcut of material, such as MDF, can be fixed at the point of rotation using double-sided tape.

CLEANING AND SHARPENING A CUTTER

Resin will accumulate on the router cutter, particularly if you are working with softwood. To prolong a cutter's life, you will need to clean it periodically. While denatured alcohol will do the job, there are more effective and environmentally friendly cleaning agents available. First spray on the cleaning agent, and then scrub the cutter with a tooth brush. If a cutter has been used a lot, you can further prolong its life by honing the back of the cutter on a "credit card" style diamond whetsone (p.72). Do not hone the beveled cutting edge or you will alter the diameter of the cut.

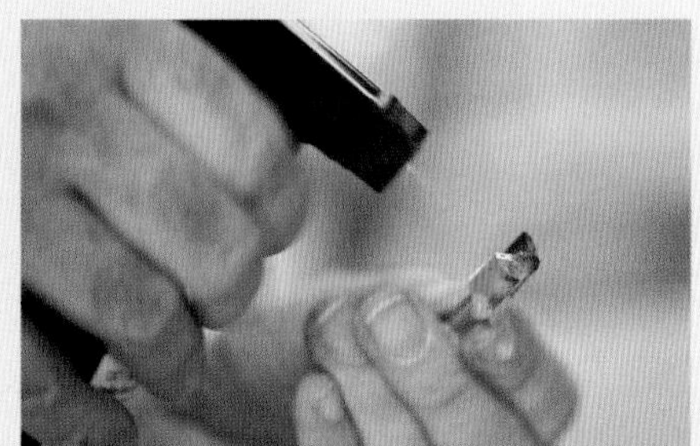

1 **After brushing off any loose dust,** apply the cleaning agent. If several cutters need to be cleaned, it may be easier to stand them in a small pot of the cleaning agent.

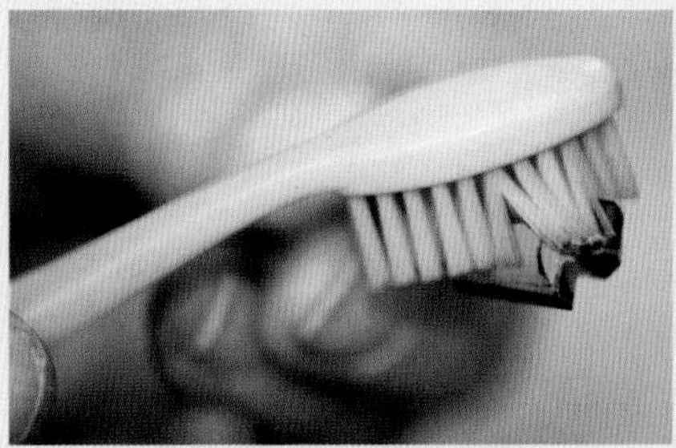

2 **Leave the cleaning agent** to work for a few minutes until the resin is soft enough to remove. An old toothbrush is ideal for removing the softened resin.

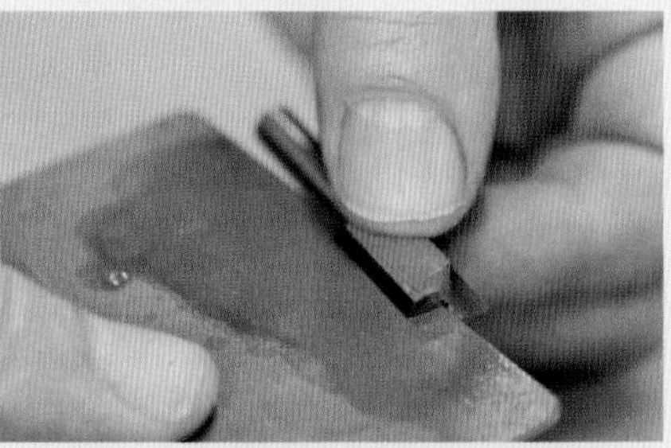

3 **Sharpen the inside edge** of the cutting blades using a diamond "credit card" sharpening stone. Do not work on the outside edges or you may alter the dimension of the cut.

CUTTING A PROFILE

When cutting a profile on the edge of a workpiece, make sure you have a support timber at both the front and back of the workpiece to act as a "lead on" and "take off" support. This will help you achieve a cleaner finish to the cut. Use a bearing-guided cutter to cut a profile—while it is possible to use an ordinary cutter and a side fence for straight lines, a bearing guarantees perfect alignment and can also be used on curved outlines.

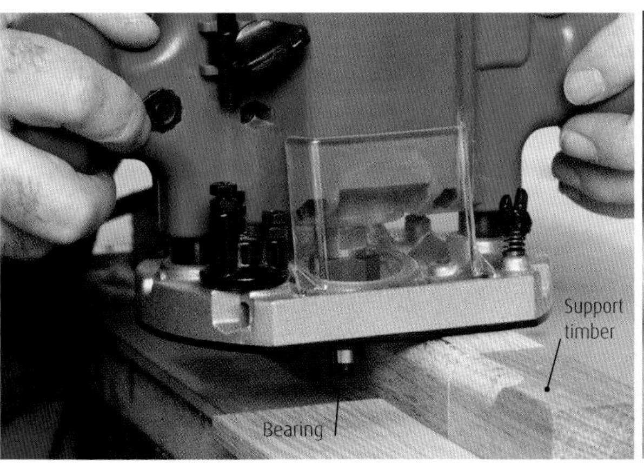

CUTTING A PROFILE WITH A BEARING-GUIDED CUTTER

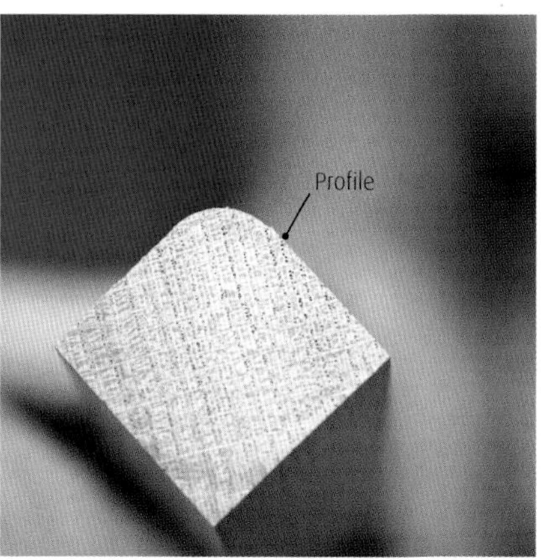

CROSS-SECTION OF WORKPIECE

CUTTING TO A TEMPLATE

By cutting a template of the finished shape and positioning it either on top of or underneath (pictured) an oversized workpiece, you can use a bearing-guided cutter to trim either straight or curved edges. You will need to create a template of the required shape from a board material such as MDF (as the bearing needs a smooth edge along which to run, MDF is particularly appropriate). The cutter length depends on the thickness of the edge you are cleaning up. You should not trim more than ⅛in (3mm) of material off the edge of the workpiece.

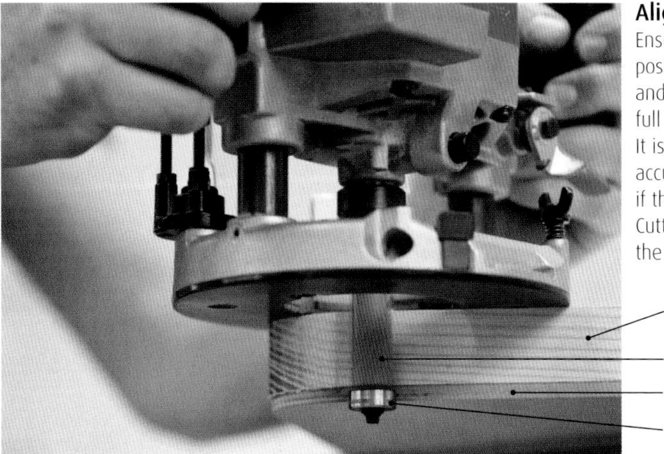

Align the bearing

Ensure that the bearing is positioned to run on the template, and that the cutter covers the full thickness of the workpiece. It is especially important to accurately position the bearing if the template is very thin. Cutters are also available with the bearing mounted at the top.

Router table

Proprietary router tables consist of a table side fence and sliding fence with provision for fixing a router upside down beneath the table with the cutter protruding through the surface. The workpiece is fed into the cutter (instead of the router being moved across the workpiece). Using a router table makes it easier to control the cut, as both hands are free to feed in a workpiece, and the cutter is clearly visable. A great benefit of a router table is the ability to rout small pieces of wood that would otherwise be very difficult to support and hold for routing in the conventional way.

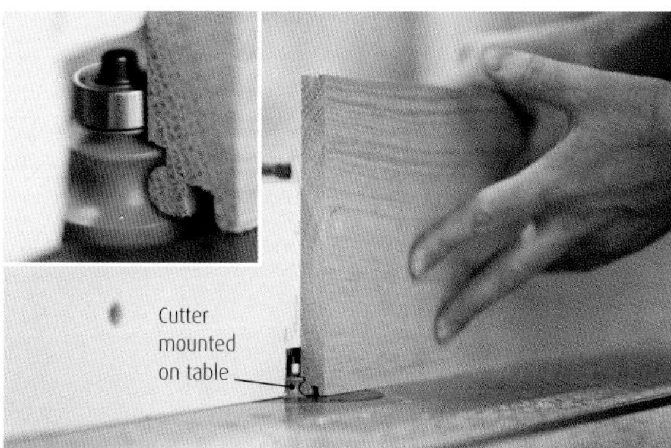

USING A ROUTER TABLE

The depth of cut is set using the router's plunge facility or a rise-and-fall mechanism usually located beneath the table top. The width is set by an adjustable fence mounted behind the cutter. Use push sticks to feed in a workpiece, and support it using featherboards.

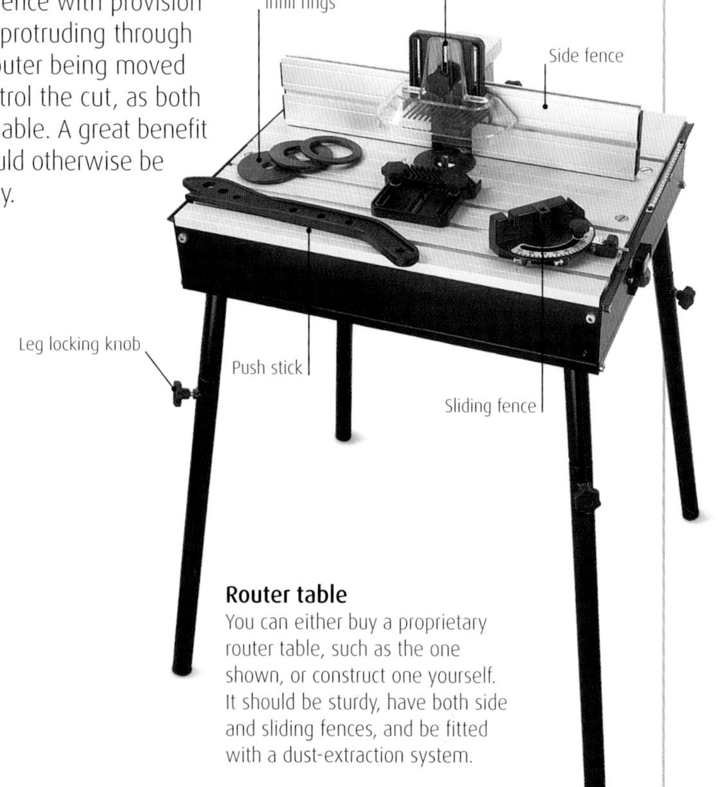

Router table

You can either buy a proprietary router table, such as the one shown, or construct one yourself. It should be sturdy, have both side and sliding fences, and be fitted with a dust-extraction system.

Hand-held power saws

Power saws are becoming increasingly popular among woodworkers. When used safely and correctly, they are a great labor-saving devise. Three types of saw are available: circular saws, jigsaws, and reciprocating saws, although the latter is more suited to DIY tasks than woodwork. Circular saws and jigsaws can perform most of the jobs that do not require more heavy-duty machine saws, such as table saws (pp.54–55) and band saws (pp.56–57). Both are ideal for carpentry work and cutting timber and manufactured boards to a rough size prior to machining or trimming with a plane (pp.22–29) or router (44–49). Power saws can be either AC- or battery-powered. AC-powered saws provide more power than cordless saws, but the cable can be restrictive. Battery-powered saws are more convenient to use, but may need recharging several times a day.

Circular saws

The blade of a circular saw is connected to the rotor of an electric motor. This assembly is carried inside a body that allows the blade to be both raised or lowered to give cuts at different depths, and also to be tilted to make angled cuts. There are two types of circular saw. The first type has a sole plate that is set to the desired depth and fixed before use; this type of saw is fed into the work from the edge. The second type has an adjustable sole plate. As the saw is lowered, the base plate stops moving once the blade reaches the preset depth. This type of saw is also used to perform plunging cuts.

Battery-powered circular saw
Circular saws tend to produce a coarse cut, especially when used freehand. If a fine finish is required, the cut face can be planed afterward. Always support the workpiece when using a circular saw.

CUTTING ALONG A LINE
Use a side fence or a guide when cutting along a line. You can also use the guide marks on the sole plate for freehand cutting.

RIPSAW BLADE

HOLDING THE SAW
The pistol grip should be held in the right hand. Always keep the left hand on the other hold, unless you are using it to raise the guard. Apply steady pressure on the circular saw as it cuts to avoid the machine from bouncing up.

CUTTING AT ANGLES

To set the blade of the circular saw to cut at an angle, release the angle-locking lever. Set the blade to the required angle and lock the lever back. The cut is made in the same manner as a vertical cut. However, the maximum depth of the cut is reduced because of the angle of the blade.

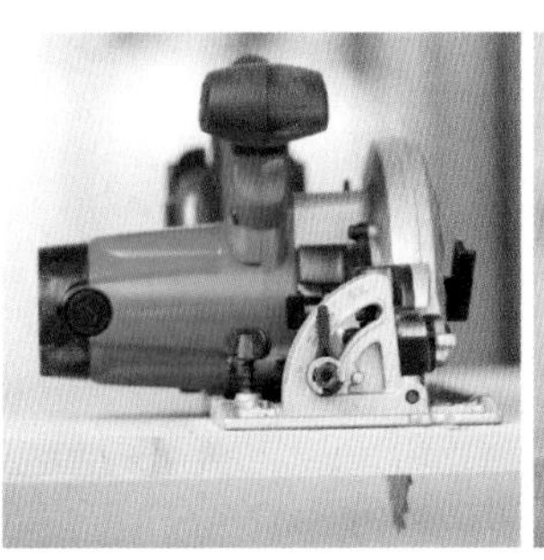

CUTTING VERTICALLY

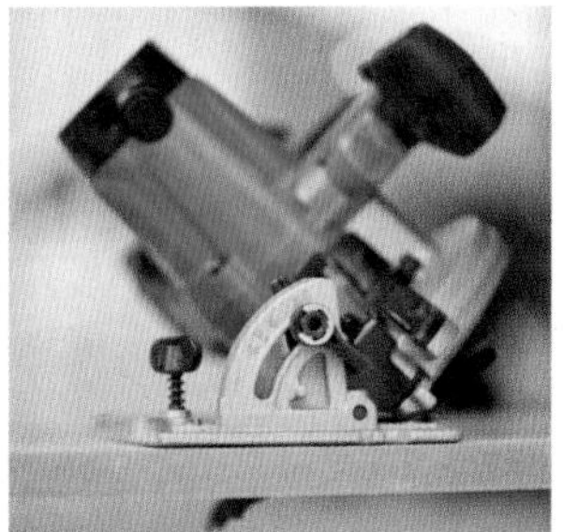

CUTTING AT AN ANGLE

CAUTION | WORK SAFELY | TAKE EXTRA CARE WHEN USING POWER TOOLS | SEE P.17

Jigsaws

Slower than other hand-held power saws, jigsaws are best suited for cutting boards and thin sections of timber. Due to the narrow sizes of the blades used, jigsaws can be used to cut curves as well as to make straight cuts. The blades of basic machines move straight up and down. However, jigsaws with an orbital or pendulum action cut into the work on the upstroke and away from it on the downstroke. This back-and-forth swinging action aids in chip removal. You can adjust the extent of the pendulum action to get the desired result.

Lock-on button
Blade guard
Pendulum action control lever
Rechargeable battery
Sole plate
Blade

Battery-powered jigsaw
Jigsaws work best when used for cutting thin materials and are capable of making fine cuts; however, when deeper cuts are attempted, there is a tendency for the blade to wander.

JIGSAW BLADES

There are a wide range of jigsaw blades available, with a blade to suit any given situation. Some blades are designed for fast cutting, while others are best suited for curved work. Jigsaw blades are disposable and need frequent replacement because the relatively short length of blade quickly becomes dull.

Small teeth give a fine, smooth cut

Downward-pointing teeth prevent damage to the top of a workpiece

Coarse teeth allow the blade to cut fast

Specialized blades
A narrow blade with small teeth (top) allows the saw to turn quickly, which enables you to cut curves with small radii. A blade with downward-pointing teeth (middle) is useful for cutting worktops, as it cuts wood on the down stroke and does not cause breakout on the top surface. A blade with coarse teeth (bottom) enables fast cutting. Set the pendulum action to maximum when using this blade.

USING A JIGSAW

A jigsaw can be used freehand to follow a line—whether straight or curved—starting from the edge of a workpiece. It can also be used with its own fence to make cuts of uniform width, or you can guide it with the help of a rail (a guiding tool) clamped to the workpiece. A jigsaw is particularly useful for making cuts that start from within the workpiece, such as those needed to fit a sink into a worktop.

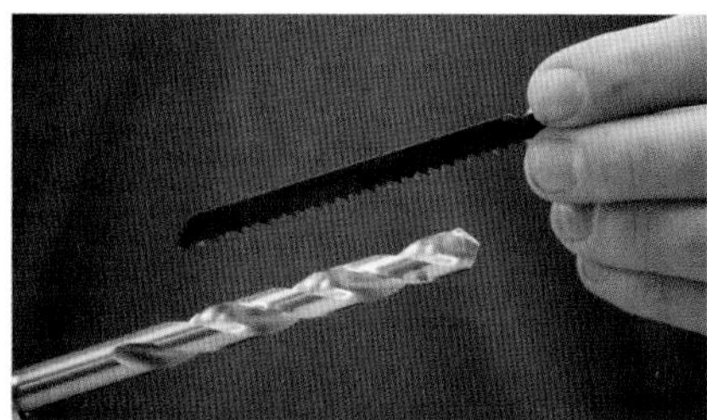

1 **To cut a shape** from within a workpiece, a hole must first be drilled for the jigsaw blade to pass through. Select a drill with a diameter just larger than the blade width.

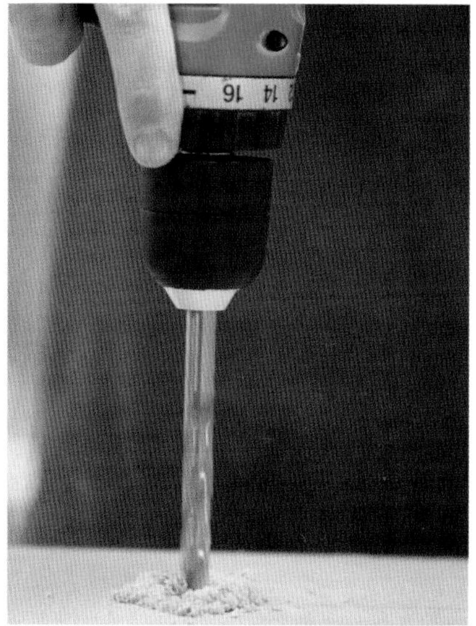

2 **Drill holes inside** the required cut-out shape at the start and finish of the cuts. Avoid any breakouts by using a scrap piece of timber under the workpiece.

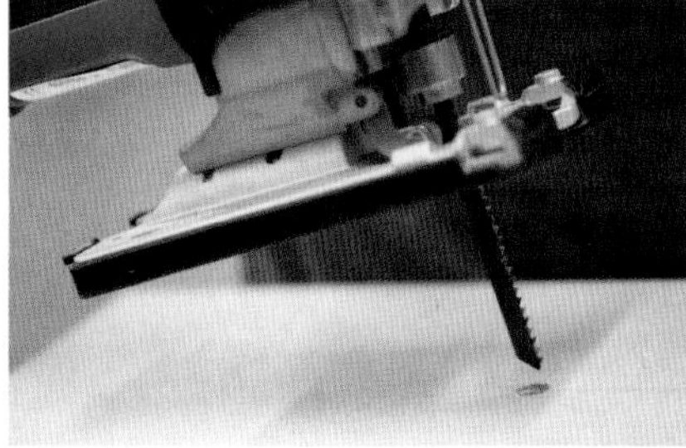

3 **With the saw turned off**, insert the blade into the hole and lower the sole plate onto the workpiece. Ensure the saw teeth are not touching the wood before starting the saw.

4 **Start the saw** and move it forward, cutting to the waste side of the line. Repeat until the waste can be removed. Always stop the saw before removing it from a cut.

Sanders and nailers

Power sanders make the often laborious task of sanding quick and easy. As well as hand-held power sanders, there are a number of bench-mounted sanding machines available that are suited to the home workshop. For large-scale commercial work consider using pad or drum sanders. Similarly, hammering in nails by hand can be taxing, so try using a nailer for jobs that include a large amount of nailing. There is a wide range of sanders and nailers available. Always wear a dust mask when sanding.

Orbital sanders

An orbital sander is used to sand large surfaces. It has a relatively large sanding pad that moves at high speed in an elliptical motion (tracing a circular path). This form of sanding means that an orbital sander can be used for a wood grain in any direction, but it does leave small circular marks on the finished work. While this may be acceptable on wood that is going to be painted, these marks can be unsightly. To minimize this problem, the random orbital sander (below) was developed. These machines have a circular pad that moves in random orbits. The irregular movements give a cleaner finish that needs less hand-sanding.

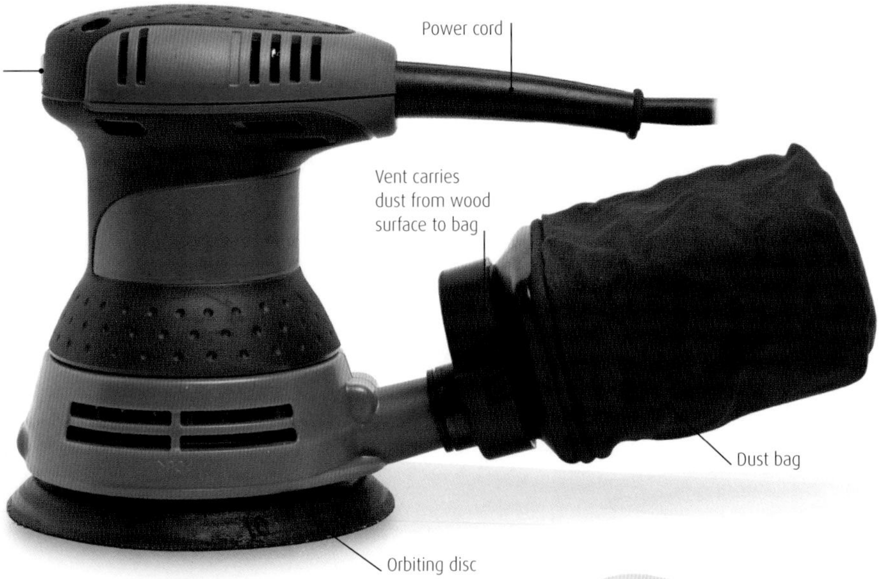

Random orbital sander
A random orbital sander is used for sanding large areas of wood. The paper is held in place with a Velcro system. A soft pad can also be attached to turn the sander into a polishing tool.

On/off switch
Power cord
Vent carries dust from wood surface to bag
Dust bag
Orbiting disc

Palm sander
A palm sander is a smaller version of the random orbital sander. It is used on small wood surfaces and finishing work. The paper is held in place with a lever clamp and is easy to change.

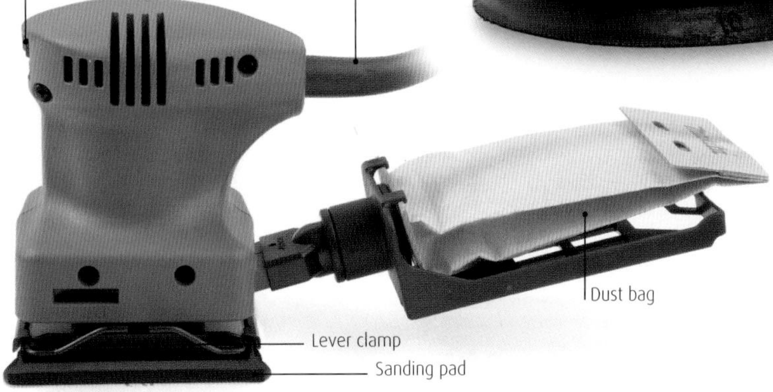

On/off switch
Power cord
Dust bag
Lever clamp
Sanding pad

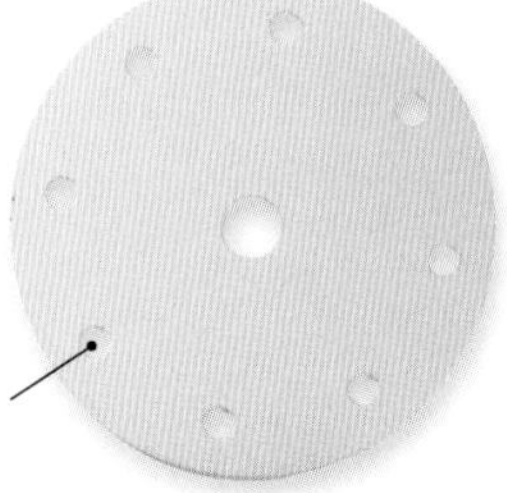

Holes aid dust extraction

ABRASIVE PAPER

REPLACING THE ABRASIVE PAPER

You will frequently need to replace the abrasive paper attached to the orbital sander's pad. To do this, first peel off the old paper from the surface of the pad. The replacement abrasive paper should be of an appropriate grit size. Fix the new paper onto the pad, making sure that you align the dust extraction holes in the abrasive paper with those that are on the pad.

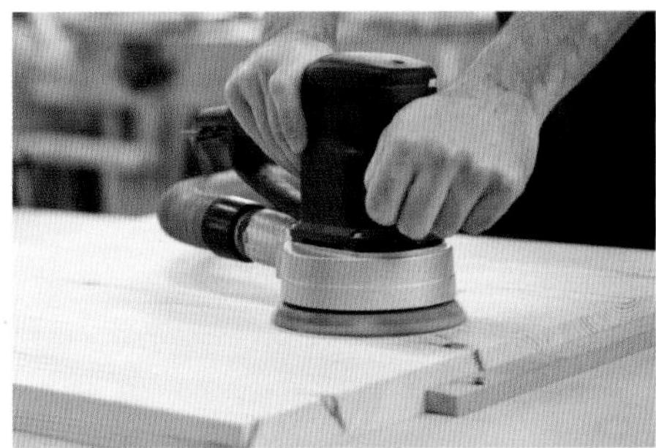

USING A SANDER
Switch the sander on before placing it on the surface. Grip the sander (use both hands for larger models) and move it slowly over the wood. Sand the whole area equally. Avoid applying too much pressure, as this can wear out the sander and result in uneven sanding.

Belt sanders

A belt sander is comprised of two rollers, around which runs a loop, or belt, of sandpaper. They are used to smooth large wooden surfaces, such as floors, decks, and porches. Belt sanders remove waste very agressively, so you should always take great care when using this tool. Available in a range of sizes, you can choose between hand-held and bench-mounted models. As with the circular abrasive papers used with orbital sanders (left), sandpaper belts are available in a variety of grit sizes. When replacing a belt, always check its alignment, as the machine and belt may be damaged if wrongly placed.

Abrasive paper belt

Hand-held belt sander
Attachments are available to help prevent hand-held belt sanders from digging into the wood. Due to the large amount of dust created, vacuum extraction is recommended.

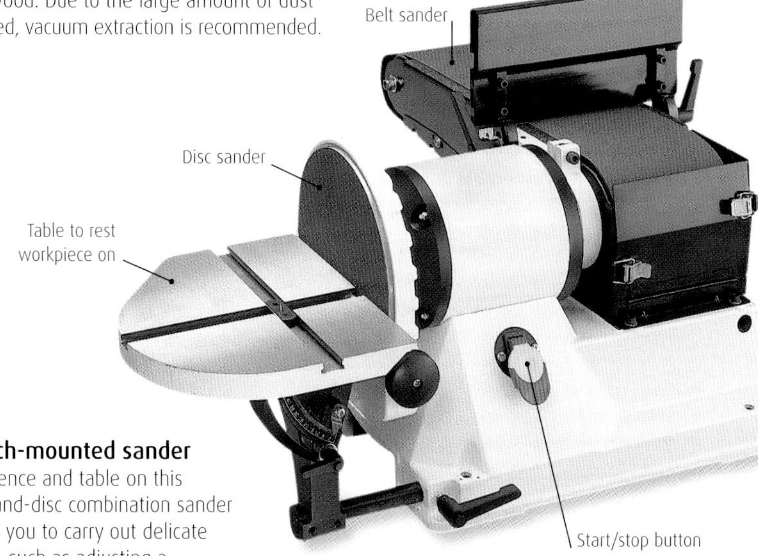

Bench-mounted sander
The fence and table on this belt-and-disc combination sander allow you to carry out delicate work, such as adjusting a miter (pp.112–15).

Spindle sanders

Using a spindle sander is the best way to sand curved edges and other shaped woodwork. These machines are ideal for smoothing complex surfaces, such as the inside edges of concave curves. Spindle sanders use replaceable spindles, or bobbins, for the sanding operation. Spindles are available in a range of sizes depending on the job. To increase the life of the abrasive paper, some machines have a spindle that oscillates vertically, spreading the wear over the length of the spindle. Keep moving the workpiece to avoid grooves from forming due to over-sanding.

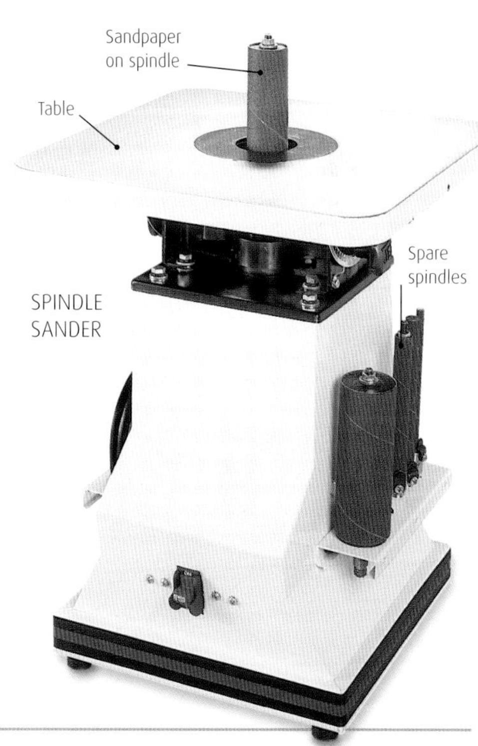

SPINDLE SANDER

Nail guns

Used for tasks that involve the insertion of a large number of nails or pins, nail guns can be gas-, compressed air-, AC-, battery-, or hand-powered. Always take extreme care when operating a nail gun, as it can be a dangerous tool. Be very careful when working with thin materials, as there is a danger that the nail will pass straight through the workpiece. While nail guns can be used with a range of nail sizes, they will not take every size of nail. It is important that you choose the correct machine for your needs.

Magazine

Nail gun
Some nail guns, such as the one pictured, have a magazine that holds the nails in a long strip. Other models feature a flexible string of nails wound up in a coil.

USING A NAIL GUN
Mark the workpiece with a pencil or a bradawl (p.35) to indicate where nails are to be inserted. Place the nail gun's nozzle over each mark and press the trigger. The nails will be pushed straight into the workpiece.

Table saws

Consisting of a flat table through which a rotary saw-blade protrudes, the table saw is the workhorse of the workshop. Mainly used for cutting solid timbers and flat boards , the size of the machine is defined by the size of the blade. A typical blade has a diameter of 10–18in (250–450mm); the larger the blade,the deeper the cut it can make. Although some table saws are available with heavy cast-iron tables and folded steel-plate bodies, modern table saws are also made of aluminum.

A basic modern table saw has a side fence for guiding the workpiece and a blade that can be raised, lowered, or tilted. Most models have a sliding table which, combined with a tiltable blade, enables the woodworker to cut compound angles. For cutting large boards, such as those used for making fitted furniture, a panel saw is needed. This is similar in design to the table saw, but has a sliding table used to perform very long cuts, and a side carriage that is large enough to carry sizeable boards through the saw.

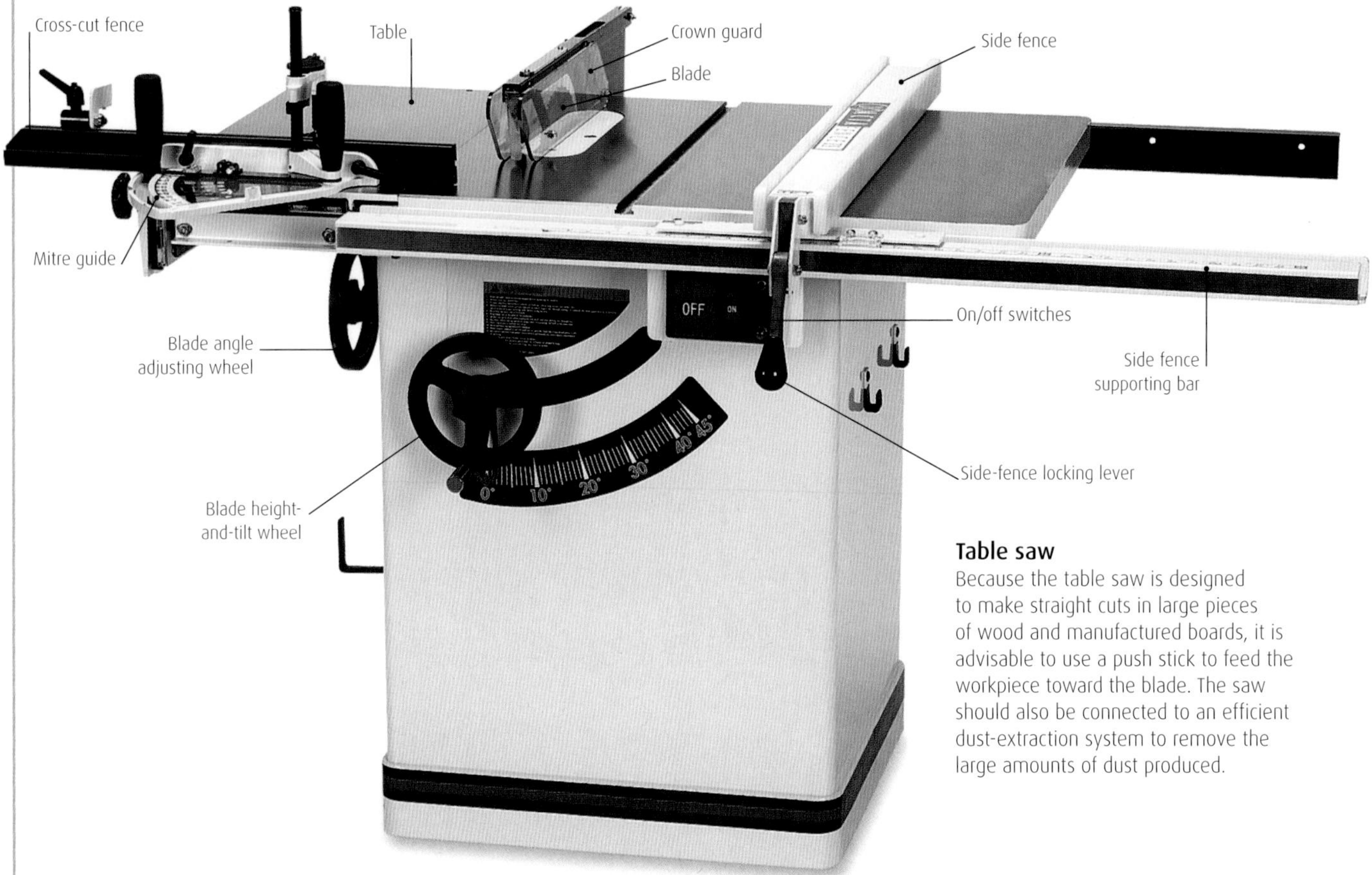

Table saw
Because the table saw is designed to make straight cuts in large pieces of wood and manufactured boards, it is advisable to use a push stick to feed the workpiece toward the blade. The saw should also be connected to an efficient dust-extraction system to remove the large amounts of dust produced.

TABLE-SAW BLADES

A range of blades is available for use with the table saw and you should always use the correct blade for each type of cut. For example, for general-purpose cutting work, a "universal" blade—which has a combination of rip and cross-cut teeth—should suffice. However, for fine work, use blades that are specially designed for either cross-cutting or ripping. These blades produce less heat and remove wood chips more efficiently.

CARING FOR SAW BLADES

Blades should be cleaned and sharpened regularly to maintain their cutting efficiency. Take care when using or handling a blade, as its teeth, which are usually made of tungsten carbide, are brittle.

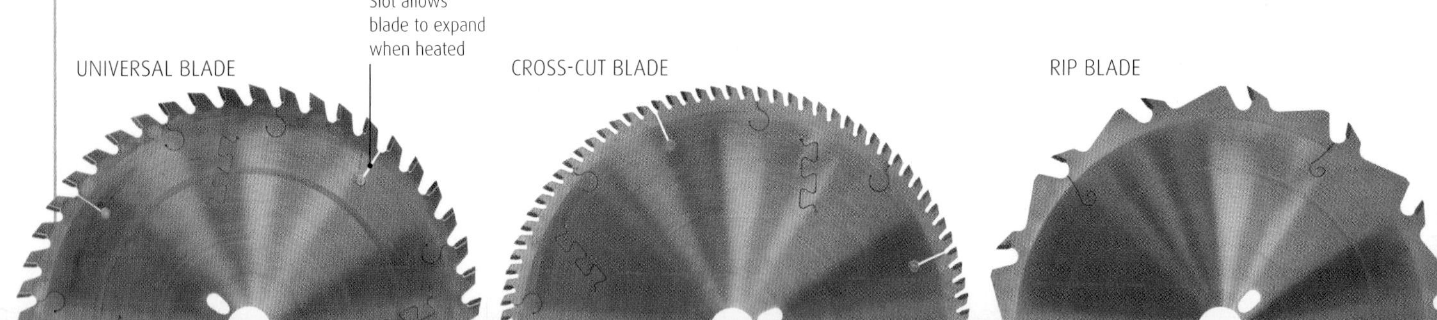

WORK SAFELY

If used incorrectly, woodworking machines have the potential to be extremely dangerous. It is important that you are aware of the risks, take proper safety precautions, and undergo appropriate training—especially when using powered cutting tools. Always read the manufacturers' safety instructions before starting work. Follow the correct procedures at all times, and never be tempted to rush a job or take short cuts.

Isolating switch
All table saws should have an isolating switch. This is used to disconnect, or isolate, the saw from its power source. Once the machine has been isolated, you are safe to make adjustments or carry out repairs.

Crown guard
A crown guard covers the top of the blade—you should never operate a table saw unless this guard is correctly in position. An extraction system sits on top of the crown guard to carry away excess dust.

RIPPING WITH A TABLE SAW

When ripping, it is important not to allow the timber to move out of position as you feed it toward the blade, as the workpiece may become trapped between the blade and the side fence. To avoid this, position the fence so that its end lies approximately 1in (25mm) behind the leading edge of the blade.

1 **Adjust the blade height** and position the fence to the required size. Remember to adjust the fence so that its end rests just behind the leading edge of the blade.

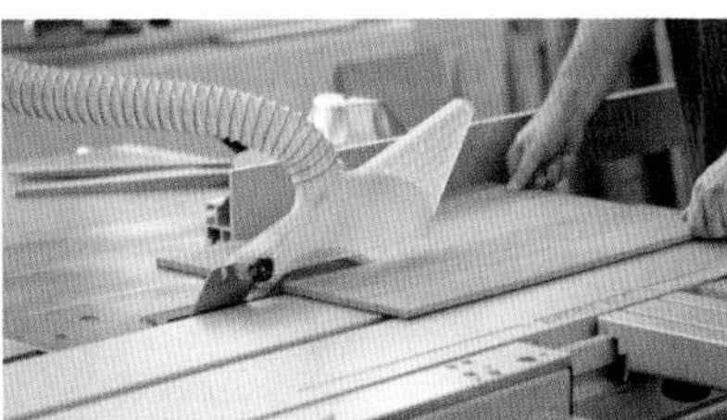

2 **Feed the workpiece** into the blade. Use one hand to hold the wood simultaneously against the fence and flat to the table, and use your other hand to move the wood forward.

3 **As your hands get closer** to the blade, use push sticks to move the workpiece forward. Never let go of the wood—one hand or a push stick should always be controlling the workpiece.

CROSS-CUTTING WITH A TABLE SAW

Set the saw blade as for ripping (left) but, if cross-cutting with a sliding table, do not use the side fence. This is to ensure that the offcut does not become trapped between the fence and blade. For the best results, use a cross-cutting blade. When changing blades, first turn off the isolating switch (see box, left).

1 **Fit the cross-cut fence** on the sliding table. Set the blade to the correct height with the help of the blade-height adjusting wheel. Move the side fence out of the way.

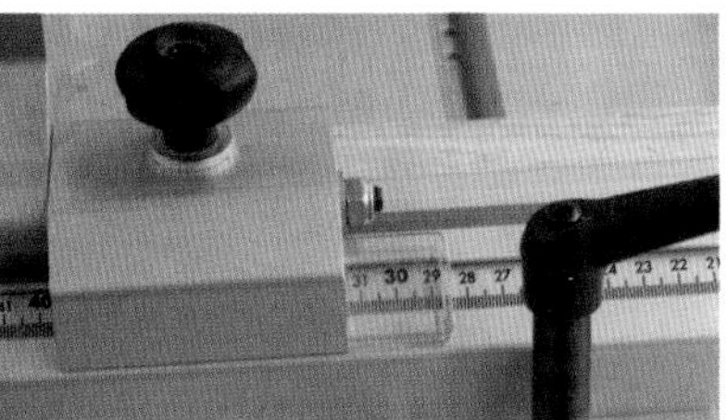

2 **Set the required length** on the cross-cut fence. If the dimension is critical, do a test cut first with a scrap piece of timber to verify that the reading is true and the fence square.

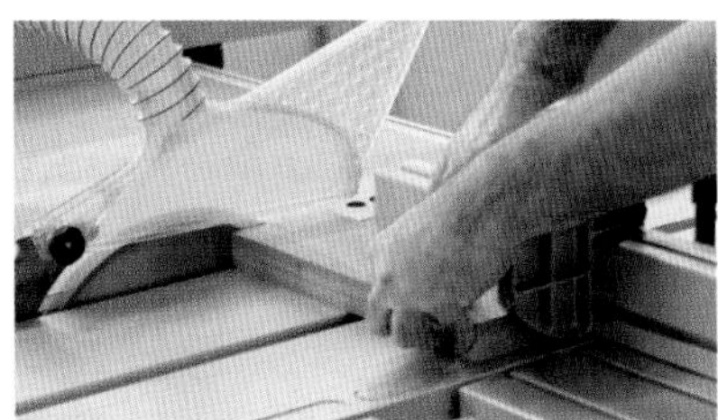

3 **Set the workpiece** against the fence and the end stop. Hold in place and push the fence forward to make the cut. Move the fence back and away before making any adjustments.

TILTING THE BLADE

The blade on a table saw can be tilted to any angle between 45 and 90 degrees. If a specific angle is desired, it is best to make test cuts first to ensure that the blade is angled correctly. On some table saws, you may have to adjust the sliding table to allow clearance for the tilted blade. You will also need to bear in mind that the maximum height of a cut is reduced when the blade is tilted. For narrow cuts, you may have to alter the fence as the blade will restrict its movement.

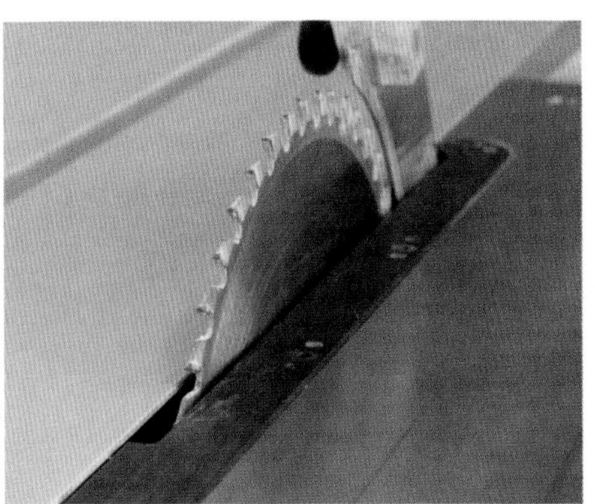

BLADE AT 90 DEGREES

BLADE AT 45 DEGREES

Band saws

Band saws are simple yet versatile cutting machines. They consist of a flexible steel blade that runs around two (or sometimes three) wheels in a continuous loop. The blade passes through a table that holds the workpiece. Available in a range of sizes, band saws can cut curves and perform deep ripping cuts—a task impossible on a table saw (pp.54–55).

Most woodworkers use narrow band saws. Wide band saws are also available, but are reserved for specialized projects. Band saw blades are available with a variety of different tooth counts—measured as teeth per inch (TPI)—and in a variety of widths. In general, the more teeth a blade has, the finer its cut will be, and the narrower the width of a blade, the smaller the radius of curve it will cut.

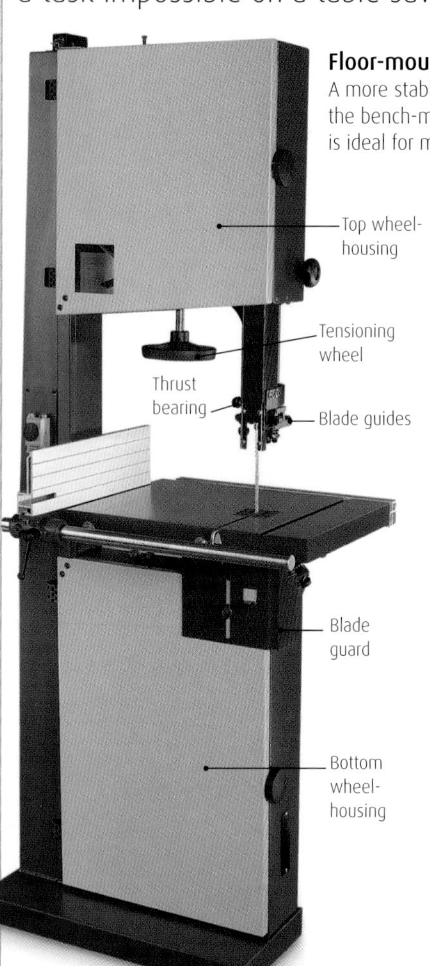

Floor-mounted band saw
A more stable and powerful machine than the bench-mounted band saw, this machine is ideal for making heavy ripping cuts.

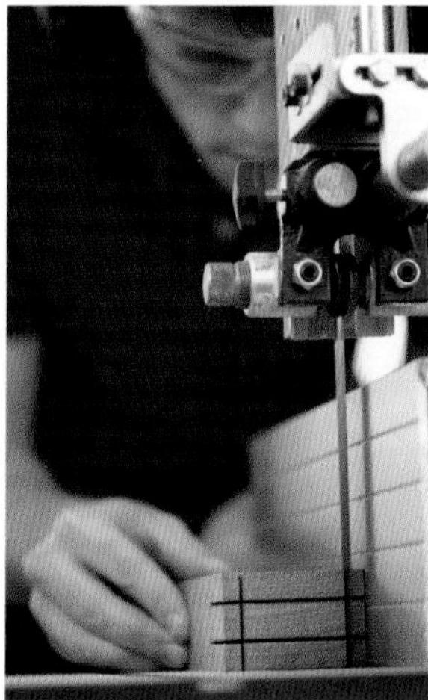

USING A BAND SAW
Lower the blade guard as far down the blade as the fence allows. Start the machine. When the blade has reached full speed, start feeding in the workpiece, using the fence as a guide. As you reach the end of the cut, use push sticks to feed the workpiece safely onto the blade.

RADIAL-ARM SAW

A radial-arm saw consists of a circular saw attached to a movable arm. Most commonly used for cross-cutting, it is a highly versatile tool (although not all radial-arm saws are designed to make rip cuts, which can be very dangerous). For example, its head can be raised to make partial cuts when kerfing (producing a curve) or tilted for angled cuts. You can also rotate the arm to cut the wood at a variety of angles.

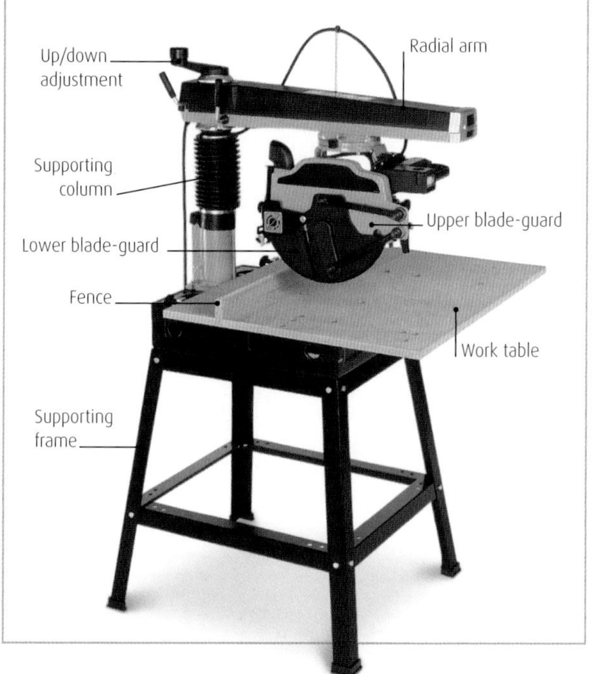

CUTTING CURVES WITH A BAND SAW

A band saw is useful for cutting curves in timber. Choose the widest possible blade for the tightest section of curve and use an offcut (waste piece of timber) to guide you. Make a series of straight relief cuts perpendicular to the proposed curve. These relief cuts will reduce the tension between the board and blade, and ease tension on the saw. This will avoid the need to withdraw the workpiece from the blade when cutting (which can pull the blade off its wheels). You will not be able to use a band saw to cut shapes (holes) in a sheet of timber—for that you will need a jigsaw (p.51).

1 **Draw the proposed curve** on the workpiece with a pencil or marking knife (p.35). Make a series of relief cuts at right angles to the curve, stopping very close to the line.

2 **Start cutting along the curve**. As you proceed, the waste will fall away as each relief cut is reached, making it easier for the band saw to move around the curved line.

CHANGING A BAND-SAW BLADE

To achieve the best results from a band saw, it is necessary to change the blade to suit the type of cut required. You will also need to replace a blade if it becomes blunt. With practice, you will find that this is a relatively straightforward task. Always use as wide a blade as possible to produce the cut—the wider the blade, the less likely it is to deflect under the load of the workpiece as the cut progresses. All the blade guides on the band saw should be reset whenever a new blade is fitted. Make sure that you check these guides regularly. Band-saw blades can be resharpened, but it is more usual to dispose of the blade. Take care when uncoiling a new blade.

1 **Make sure the machine** is isolated (see Work Safely, p.55). Open the top wheel-housing of the machine to expose the top wheel. Carefully release the blade guard.

2 **Release the tension** on the blade by turning the tensioning wheel in a counter--clockwise direction. Loosen the blade so that you can take it off the wheel with ease.

3 **Wearing protective gloves**, remove the blade from the wheel and slide it out. Hold the blade in one hand and steady it with your foot. Turn the blade over so that it folds into coils.

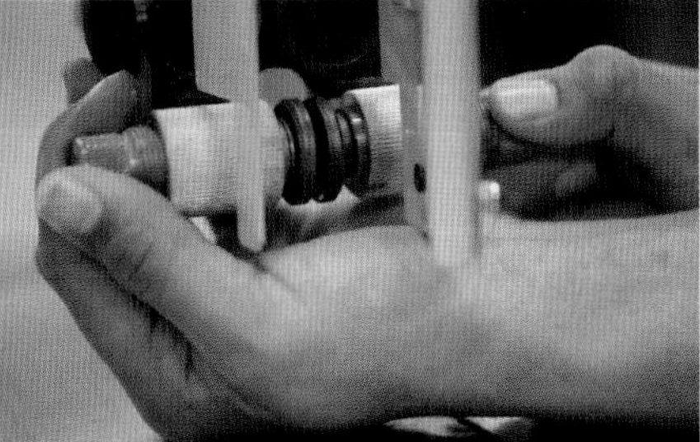

4 **Loosen all the blade guides** by unscrewing the knobs on the sides. The guides are used for keeping the blade in place and stopping it from moving sideways.

5 **Release the thrust bearing**. This provides support to the blade from the back. Before you fix the new blade, check to see that its teeth are pointing downward.

6 **Place the new blade** first over the crown of the top wheel and then around the bottom wheel, making sure it is centered on both wheels. Position the blade within the guides.

7 **Turn the tensioning wheel** to add a little tension to the blade. At this stage, do not over-tighten the tensioning wheel, as you may need to make a few adjustments.

8 **Turn the wheel by hand** and check for sideways movement in the blade as it runs through the guides. Make adjustments until the blade moves with no lateral movement.

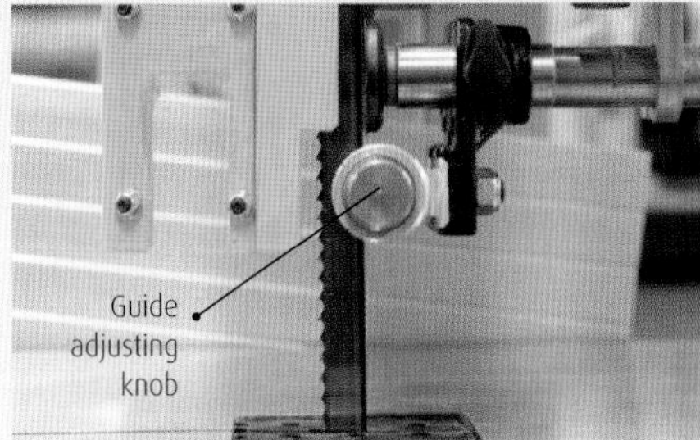

9 **Adjust the width** of the blade guides so that they sit within a piece of paper's width of the blade. Similarly, adjust the guides to the same width in the bottom wheel-housing.

10 **Set the blade** to full tension (as determined by the blade width) by adjusting the tensioning wheel. Re-check the guides and adjust them if necessary.

11 **Run the blade** under power to check that it runs smoothly. Listen carefully to the sound it makes. If you hear anything unusual, isolate the machine and make further adjustments.

Planers and thicknessers

Planers and thicknessers allow you to produce flat and square timber sections, which are a basic requirement for furniture-making and joinery. Planers are used to smooth faces and edges, while thicknessers shave off wood to produce sections of uniform thickness or width. The cutting action is achieved by a series of knives set in a circular block, with the number of knives ranging from two on small domestic models, to six on large industrial machines. Small capacity machines are available for the home workshop.

Planer-thicknessers

To save space, a combination machine called a planer-thicknesser has been developed. Planing takes place on the upper section of the machine, which consists of "in-feed" and "out-feed" tables. The in-feed table can be adjusted to control the depth of cut. A bridge-guard covers the cutter block and can be adjusted to the width and thickness of the wood being planed. The fence can also be moved back and forth to accommodate the workpiece. The fence is set square for most tasks, but can be angled at up to 45 degrees for planing bevels. The planing tables can be lifted to reveal a lower thicknessing table. Converting the machine between planing and thicknessing modes takes about two to three minutes.

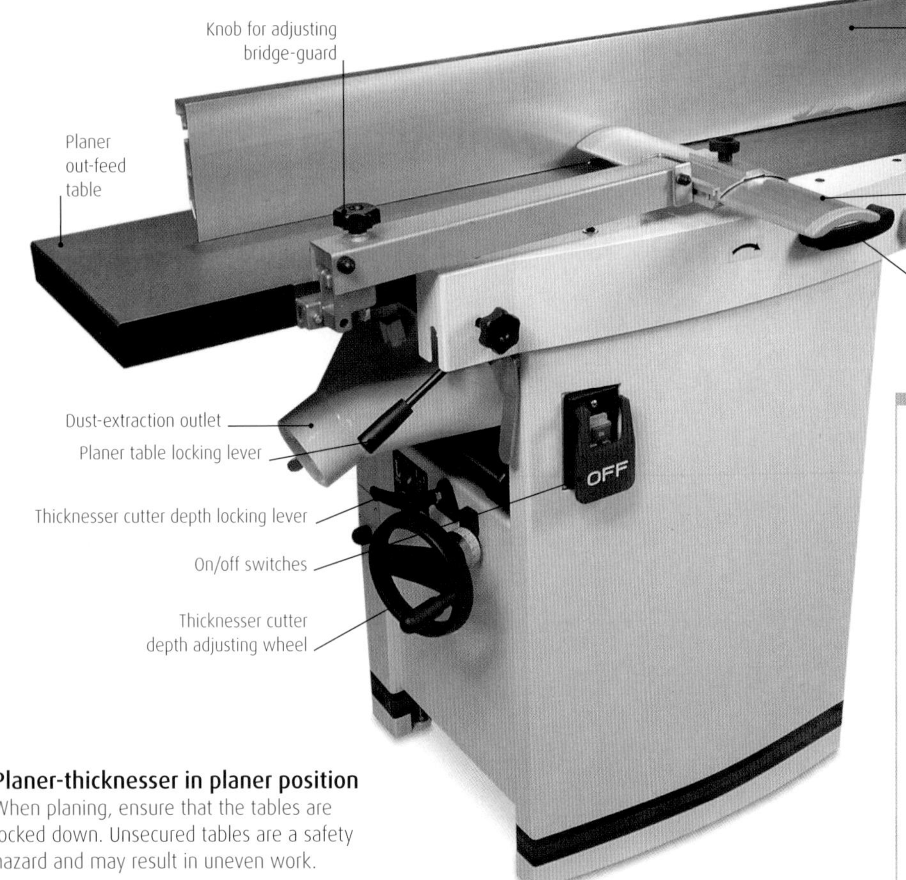

Planer-thicknesser in planer position
When planing, ensure that the tables are locked down. Unsecured tables are a safety hazard and may result in uneven work.

PLANING BOWED TIMBER

Before you start to plane, study the rough-sawn surface of the face side of the wood. If the surface is bowed concavely from side-to-side, it is likely that the machine will plane unevenly; adjust the pressure on the wood as you feed it through the planer to avoid this. If the surface is cupped convexly from side-to-side, the board will rock; you should either hand-plane it with a jack plane (p.23) to establish a partial level surface before using the machine, or choose the opposite surface as the face side. If the board is bowed along its length, you should also consider hand-planing first. Never attempt to force a bowed plank downward—it will not produce a flat board and your hand may slip onto the blade.

USING A PLANER

The main function of a planer is to produce smooth, flat faces and edges on wood stocks. These smoothed surfaces act as a reference for subsequent work, helping you to achieve parallel surfaces. Unlock the in-feed table, adjust the depth of cut (the amount of wood you want to remove), and then relock the table. You will have to pass the stock across the planer a number of times to achieve a smooth surface. Never plane stock smaller than 18in (450mm) in length; stock with lengths shorter than this is difficult and dangerous to work with.

PLANING A FACE
At the first pass, set the cutters to take off no more than 1⁄16in (5mm) of wood. Set the bridge-guard to approximately 1⁄32in (1mm) above your work.

PLANING AN EDGE
Adjust the bridge-guard to the thickness of your stock. Always ensure that the fence is square to the bed of the planer, or at the desired angle to create a bevel.

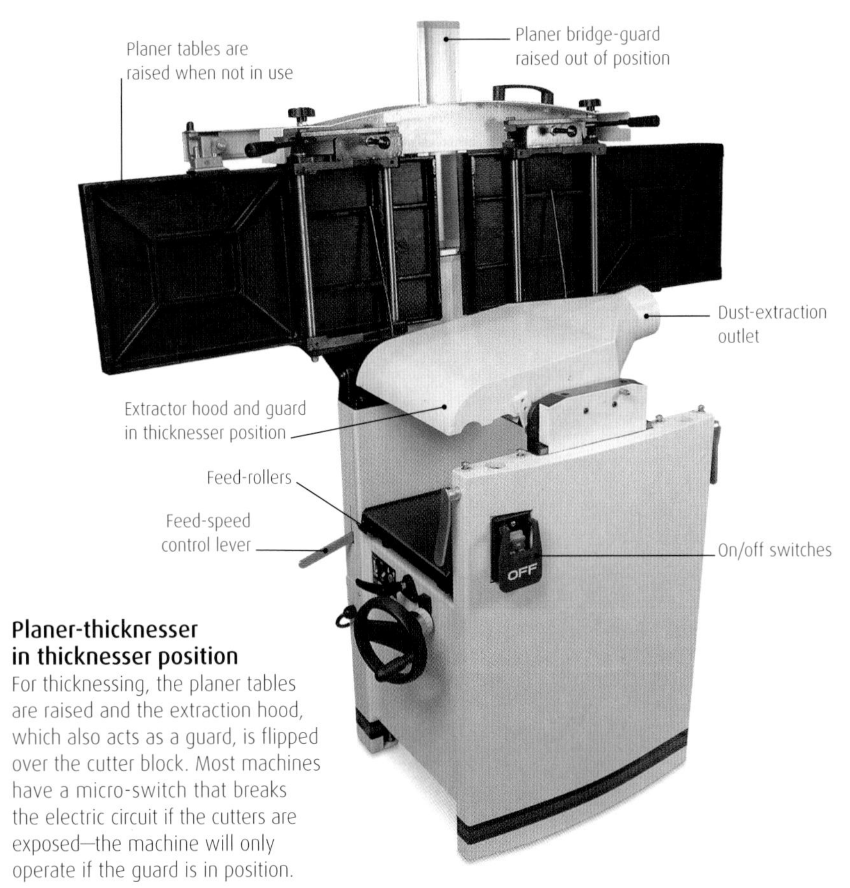

Planer-thicknesser in thicknesser position
For thicknessing, the planer tables are raised and the extraction hood, which also acts as a guard, is flipped over the cutter block. Most machines have a micro-switch that breaks the electric circuit if the cutters are exposed—the machine will only operate if the guard is in position.

USING A THICKNESSER

Set the height of the thicknessing table to the desired thickness. Check that the feed-rollers are in gear (most machines have a lever that engages the drive mechanism). Feed the piece in smoothly from the left-hand side of the machine, pressing its flat face down onto the table. Once the feed-rollers grip the workpiece, let it go and allow the rollers to take it through.

THICKNESSING A FACE
As for planing, do not use stock that is smaller than 18in (450mm) in length. After feeding in the stock, move to the other side of the machine to support the workpiece as it emerges, keeping it level.

THICKNESSING AN EDGE
Feed the stock smoothly with the flat edge on the bed of the table. Always stand to the side of the machine while working in case the stock bounces back or chips of wood fly out.

BENCH-TOP THICKNESSERS

A small version of the industrial machines found in large workshops, the bench-top thicknesser is an ideal machine for use in the home workshop as it can be easily mounted on a bench or trestles. However, keep in mind that the bench-top thicknesser is only designed for cutting workpieces to the required thickness. If you need to plane your workpieces first, you will also have to consider purchasing a dedicated planer machine (also available as a small bench-top machine).

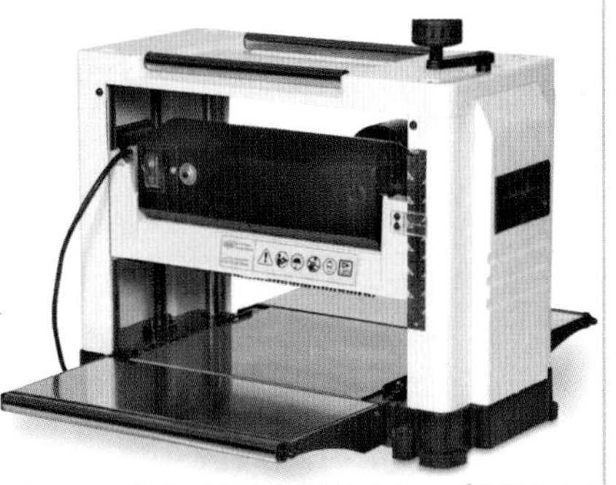

Planers

Woodworkers sometimes use a separate machine, called a planer, for smoothing the face and edge of a workpiece. These bulky machines are found only in large workshops, where a separate thicknesser will also be present. A planer has the same features as the planing element of a planer-thicknesser (left). However, its table is longer, allowing it to smooth long pieces. An advantage of using separate machines is that several operations can be performed simultaneously.

Planer
You will only ever need to work from one side of a dedicated planer machine. The dust extractor remains in a fixed position.

Lathes and cutting tools

Known as "turning," the most effective method of shaping round or cylindrical objects—such as knobs or table legs—is to use a powered machine called a lathe. The lathe spins the workpiece around a central axis of rotation at a constant speed. You can then shape or sand the workpiece symmetrically by holding a hand-held cutting tool or abrasive paper against it.

Woodturning lathes

Modern lathes—some of which can be controlled by computer—consist of a head- and tailstock mounted on a horizontal bed, together with a tool rest, locking lever, and adjusting wheel. Lathes can be used in two ways: long, thin workpieces can be suspended and shaped between two "centers" (one located on the headstock and the other on the tailstock); alternatively a faceplate can be attached to the headstock to turn shorter items, such as bowls.

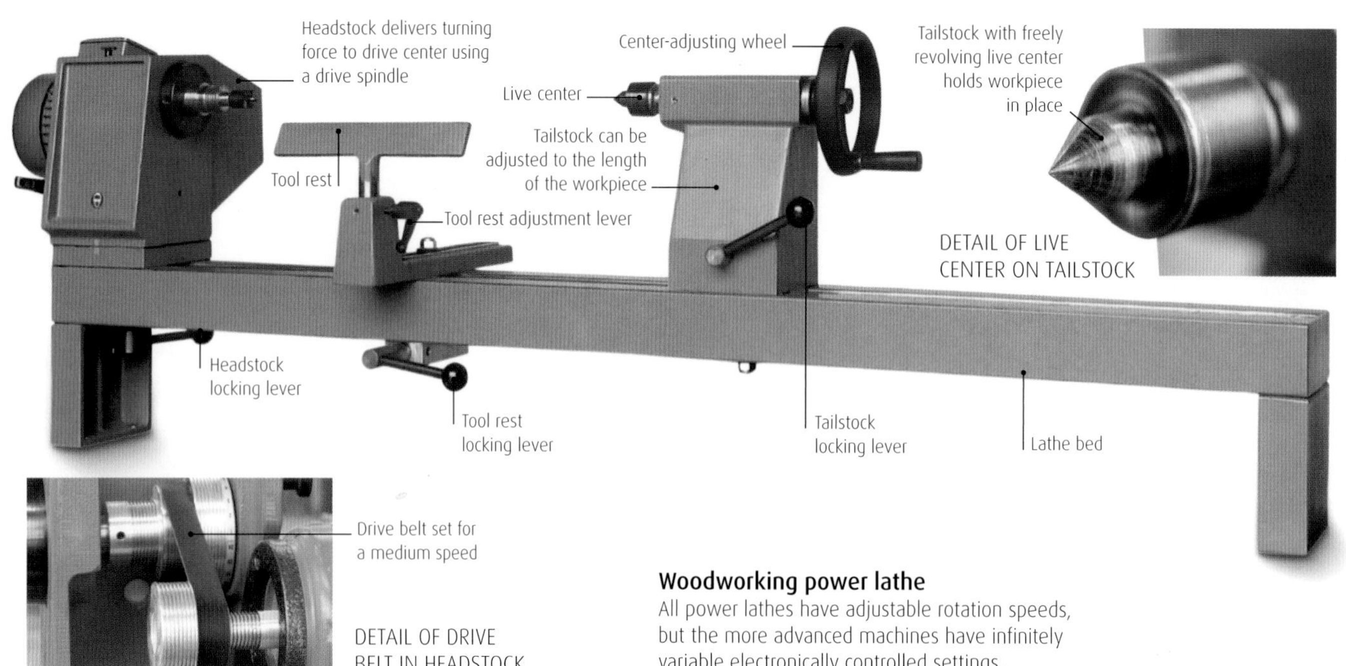

Woodworking power lathe
All power lathes have adjustable rotation speeds, but the more advanced machines have infinitely variable electronically controlled settings.

MOUNTING A WORKPIECE ON A LATHE

The height at which a lathe should be positioned is a matter of personal comfort, but a good rule of thumb is to fix it so that the centerline of the workpiece is at elbow height. When working between the drive and live centers, you can use the same basic technique to mount a workpiece, although there are several types of center to cope with different shapes and sizes of workpieces. The most basic arrangement involves a 2- or 4-prong drive center in the headstock, and a standard 60-degree live revolving centerin the tailstock.

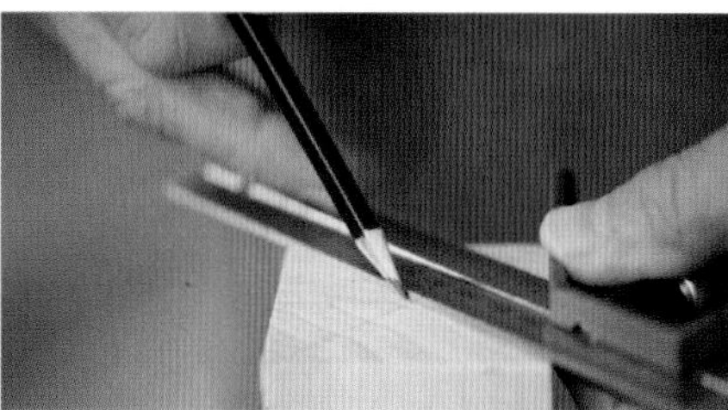

1 **Find the center** of one end grain by drawing diagonals between the corners. Use a center-finder for round-section material.

2 **Drill a hole** $\frac{3}{16}$in (4mm) in diameter and $\frac{3}{16}$in (4mm) deep into the marked point. Repeat Steps 1–2 on the other end grain of the workpiece.

3 **Insert the appropriate drive center** into the headstock. Fix the workpiece by placing one of the end-grain centerholes on the drive center.

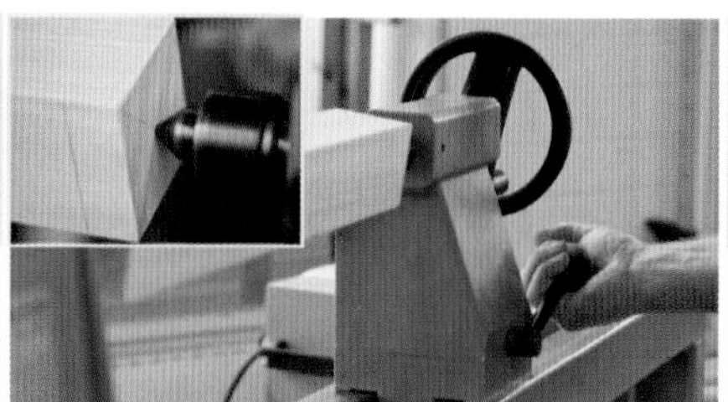

4 **Hold the workpiece** parallel to the lathe bed and slide the tailstock up until its live center engages with the other hole. Lock the tailstock.

5 **Advance the tailstock center** by rotating the wheel until the workpiece fixes onto the drive center. Lock the tailstock cente rin place (inset).

Cutting tools

Lathe cutting tools can be divided into three main categories: gouges, parting tools, and scrapers. Gouges have curved blades and are used for the initial shaping of the wood, as well as for forming beads (rounded, convex sections), coves (rounded, concave sections), and hollowing out bowls. Parting tools are used to form grooves and shoulders, and to plane surfaces. Scrapers are used as finishing tools prior to sanding. There are also specialized lathe tools for more advanced woodworking.

Gouges

Roughing gouges are used for the initial stages of turning square stock into a cylinder. Spindle gouges, often used next, are thinner with a rounded tip, and are useful for forming coves.

ROUGHING GOUGE

SPINDLE GOUGE

Parting tools

Used for cutting grooves and recesses, parting tools are also capable of forming shoulders, beads, and other convex curves.

LARGE PARTING TOOL

SMALL PARTING TOOL

Scraper tools

The main purpose of scraper tools is to remove marks left by other tools before sanding. Their shallow cutting angle leaves a smooth finish on the workpiece.

ROUND-NOSED SCRAPER

FLAT-NOSED SCRAPER

Skewed chisels

Also used as a general cutting tool (p.32), skewed chisels are used to form beads and to make V-cuts.

SKEWED CHISEL

Beading tools

Used to form grooves and beads, beading tools are specialized scrapers that have the shape of a bead formed on the blade's tip.

Beaded tip

BEADING TOOL

USING LATHE TOOLS

When using a gouge or parting tool, always position its handle lower than the tool rest. The handle of a scraper should be angled slightly above the tool rest or roughly horizontal. Your dominant hand should hold the handle and your other hand should hold the blade against the tool rest—either above the tool (for rough-cutting) or below it (for delicate work). Maintain this steady contact to ensure good control.

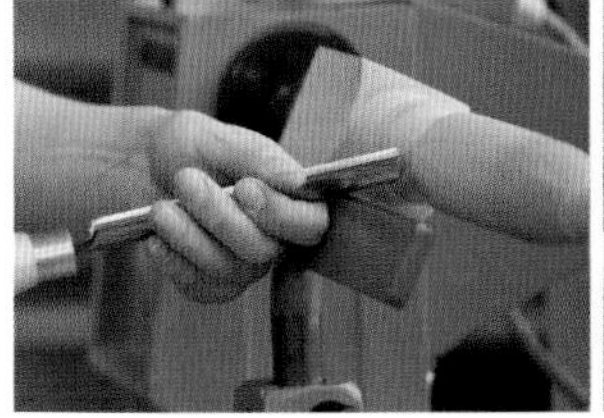

CUTTING TOOLS—UNDERHAND

CUTTING TOOLS—OVERHAND

SCRAPERS—ANGLED UP

CALIPERS

To measure the diameter of a piece of work, use calipers (p.34). When turning a workpiece, use outside calipers for measuring the diameter of spindles, and inside calipers for measuring the internal diameter of bowls and other hollows. Spring-loaded calipers are best as they cannot be altered easily by mistake.

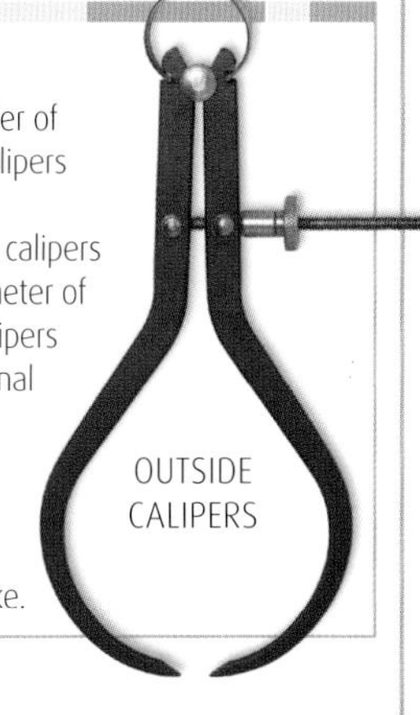

OUTSIDE CALIPERS

Mortisers

A mortiser is a machine used to cut out mortises (pp.116–19). While you can adapt alternative tools to do the same job—such as a drill press (p.66) or router (pp.44–49)—a mortiser is better suited as it produces clean, square-cornered mortises. Mortisers are available in either bench- or floor-mounted models. Machines called tenoners are also available for cutting the tenons that slot inside mortises, but these are larger machines suited to production workshops.

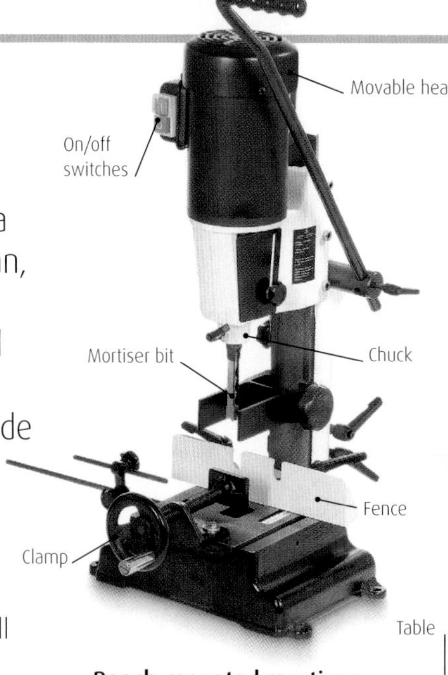

Bench-mounted mortiser
Ideal for the home workshop, the bench-mounted mortiser is used for more precise work than floor-mounted models.

Bench-mounted mortiser

A bench-mounted mortiser is used for relatively small jobs, such as mortises measuring approximately ⅝in (16mm) in size. Some bench-mounted mortisers have a maneuverable head that can be used on a variety of different-sized timbers at a variety of angles.

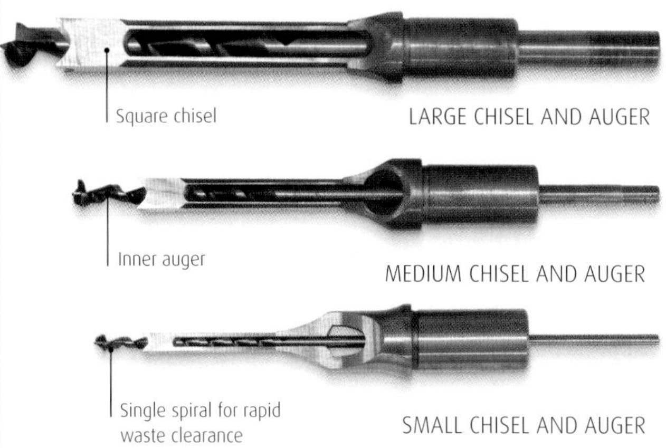

Mortiser bits
There is a wide range of mortiser bits available, with each one consisting of a square, outer chisel, which cuts the wood, and an inner auger, which removes the waste.

Floor-mounted mortiser

Due to their substantial size, free-standing floor-mounted mortisers are used to cut out large mortises that measure up to 1in (25mm) in width. The table of a floor-mounted mortiser is also capable of a large amount of longitudinal and lateral travel.

Floor-mounted mortiser
A floor-mounted mortiser is used to chop large mortises in large pieces of timber, and is almost essential in production workshops.

USING A MORTISER

A mortiser removes waste from the workpiece much faster than is possible by hand. However, you should avoid plunging the machine too quickly as this can lead to the chisel overheating and becoming damaged. Adjust the height of the chisel to give clearance for large timbers and to place the handle at a convenient height—you can even sit down for some types of work. To ensure your own safety, check that the chisel is secure and remember to wear protective eye goggles.

1 **To make the first cut**, align the chisel with the markings on the surface of the workpiece, which indicate the intended position of the mortise. Lower the chisel into the timber but do not cut too deeply.

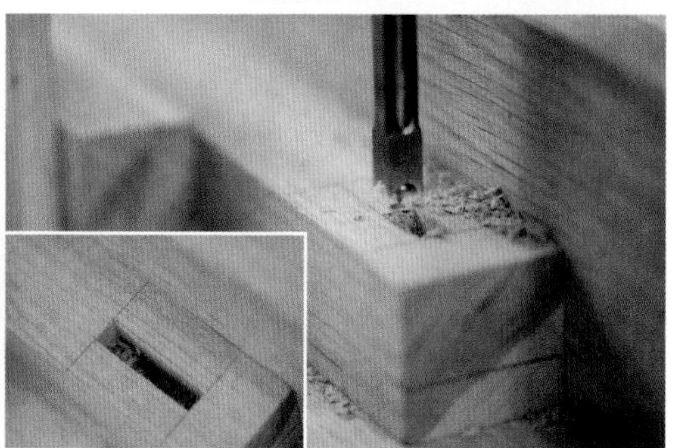

2 **After making the first cut**, take the chisel out of the mortise and move the timber sideways to make a new cut. Space the cuts so that the last one is made using the full width of the chisel (inset).

SETTING UP A MORTISER

Although setting up a mortiser is relatively easy, it is important that you do so correctly. If it is set up incorrectly, the chisel may not sit squarely with the workpiece. This could result in a mortise consisting of a series of diamond shapes, or one with jagged edges instead of clean, smooth edges. When fitting the mortiser bit into the machine, be sure to leave a gap of 1/16in (2mm) between the chisel and the auger. A smaller gap could lead to wood fragments becoming trapped, or the auger and chisel coming into contact with each other. Either scenario will generate excessive heat, which can severely damage the bit. Use a small coin to correctly measure the gap.

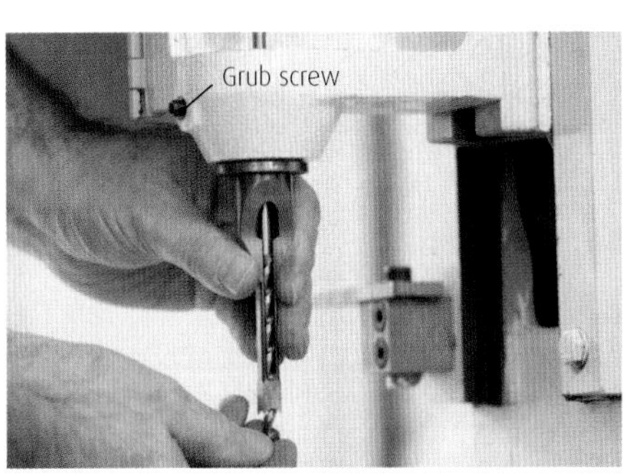

1 **Insert the auger and chisel** into the mortiser and lightly lock the grub screw. Use a small coin to check the spacing between the chisel's shoulder and the machine's collar.

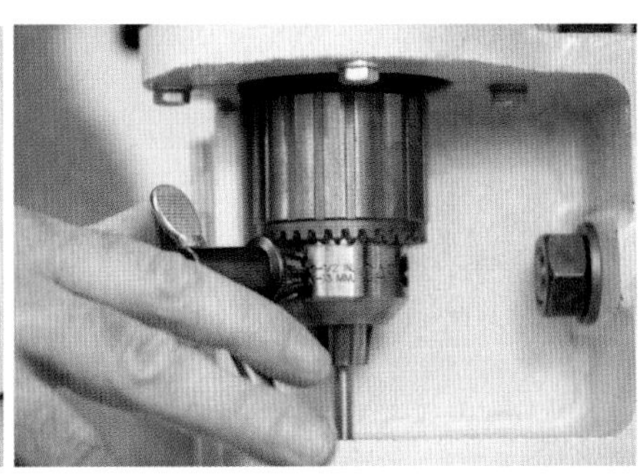

2 **Push the auger** fully up into the chisel and hold both pieces tightly against the coin. Tighten the chuck firmly onto the auger to prevent it from slipping when in use.

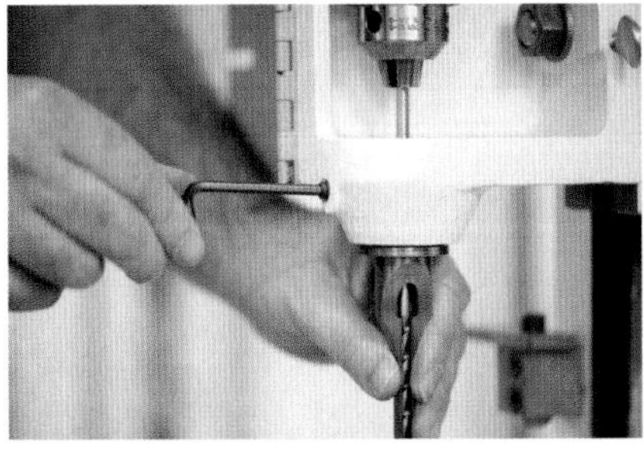

3 **Remove the coin** and slide the chisel up to the collar. Tighten the grub screw. The chisel and auger are now set with the correct amount of spacing between them.

4 **If the angle** of the chisel looks a little tilted, release the grub screw again and, using a square (p.35), adjust the chisel until it is correctly aligned. The chisel should be flush with the blade of the square and its edge should sit parallel to the fence. If the chisel is not aligned correctly, the finished mortise could be crooked.

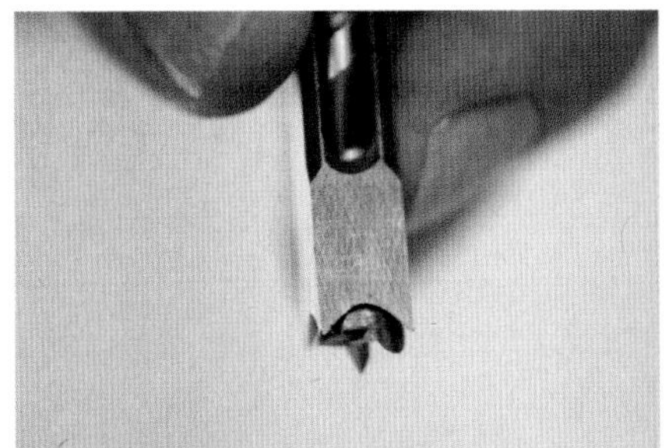

5 **When the chisel and auger** are in place, check the gap between them by pressing on the side of the auger. If there is no movement, there is no gap.

6 **To set the depth** of cut on the mortiser, first mark the desired depth of the mortise on the side of the workpiece. Lower the chisel and align it to the marking.

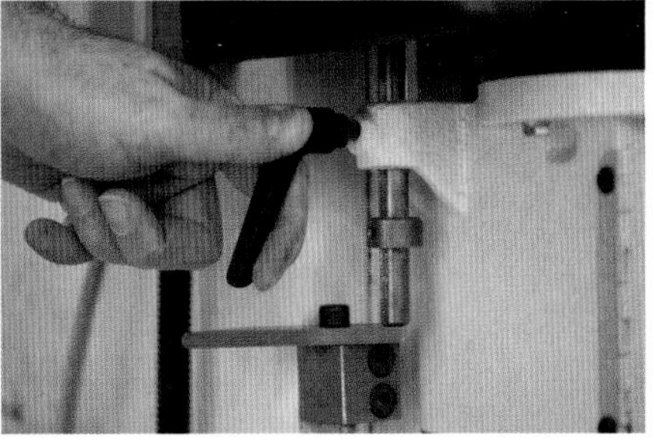

7 **When you are satisfied** that the chisel (and not the auger, which should protrude just below the marked line) is correctly aligned, lock the depth control-gauge into position.

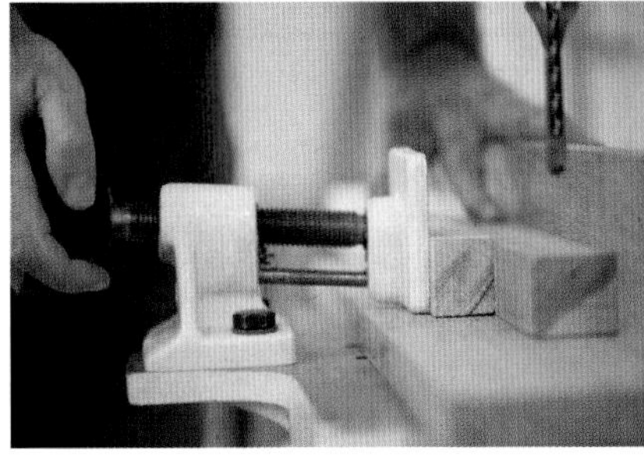

8 **Clamp the workpiece** onto the table (use a scrap of wood to protect the workpiece) and use the control wheel to adjust the position of the table to align the chisel with the mortise.

9 **Start the machine** and check that the auger is running freely in the chisel. When you are ready to cut, bring the handle down to lower the chisel onto the workpiece and then start the machine. Cut the mortise to a maximum depth of 3/8in (10mm) at a time. Raise the chisel up before moving the workpiece sideways as you proceed with the cut.

Commercial joining systems

Dowel, pocket-hole, biscuit, and domino joining systems are effective and discreet methods of connecting timbers. Similar to a mortise-and-tenon (pp.116–19), they are used when it is not possible or desirable to use conventional woodworking joints, or when basic connectors, such as nails and screws (p.67), are not up to the job. Jigs and jointers are available for aligning and cutting the holes and slots into which the relevant connectors are fitted.

Dowels and accessories
Use a drill bit of the same diameter as the dowel. A depth stop fits over the bit and marks the depth to which the hole should be drilled. A center point, temporarily slotted into the first hole, marks the position for an adjoining hole.

DEPTH STOP

CENTER POINT

WOOD DOWEL

DRILL BIT

Dowel-based systems

In a dowel-based system, the dowel acts as a loose tenon; dowel systems have many of the same attributes of the conventional mortise-and-tenon joint. The design of the dowel affects the performance of the joint, so it is important to choose the correct type. Dowels can be used individually or in multiples, and it is important to correctly align each side of the joint for an effective and attractive connection. Use a center point (above right) to align the holes for a single-dowel joint, or a dowel jig (below) to align the holes for a multiple-dowel joint.

USING A DOWEL CENTER POINT
Drill a hole in the first piece of timber and insert a center point. Align both parts of the joint and press together. The center point will mark the position for the second hole.

CREATING A DOWEL JOINT
To maximize the strength of the joint, insert the dowel to the same depth into each piece of wood. To do this, set the depth stop to just greater than half the dowel's length.

Dowel jig
Use a dowel jig to align the pieces of timber to be connected. Use a power drill (p.42) to drill through each bush to create a series of holes for the dowels.

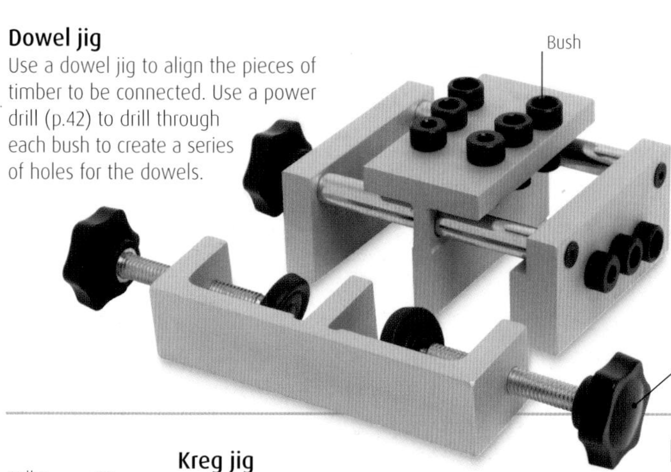

USING A DOWEL JIG
Clamp both parts of the joint into the jig. Drill through each hole in the jig, using the bush to help keep the drill upright. The jig will enable you to align each hole correctly, and to drill a series of holes in one continuous operation.

Kreg jig
The Kreg drill allows a series of pocketed screws to be drilled into a workpiece at the required angle. A clamp holds the workpiece in position.

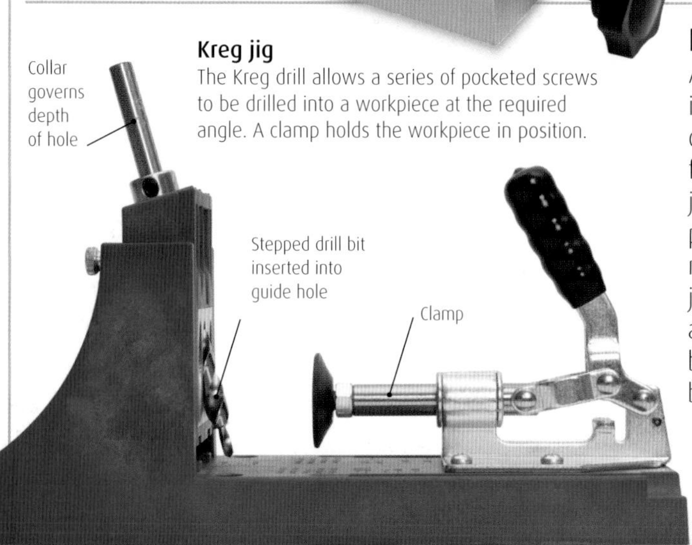

Pocket-hole systems

A pocket-hole system is used when it is necessary to hide a screw head, or when it is not possible to drill from the outside of a joint. A Kreg jig is used to make the acute-angled, pocketed (counterbored) holes necessary for this type of joint. The jig simplifies this process and ensures accuracy. The stepped drill bit allows both the pocket and the pilot hole to be drilled in one operation.

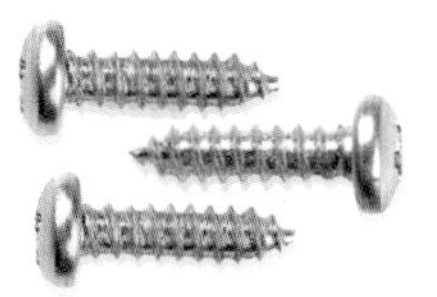

Self-tapping screws
Use steel self-tapping screws with the Kreg jig. These are stronger than wood dowels and exert a large amount of clamping pressure, which forms a solid joint.

Biscuit-based systems

A biscuit is a thin, oval-shaped piece of compressed wood that acts in the same way as a loose tenon in a conventional mortise-and-tenon joint. A biscuit jointer is used to cut the circular slot into which the biscuit is fitted. The jointer's depth stop ensures the slots are of the correct depth for the size of biscuit being used. The fence can be adjusted for different thicknesses of timber and to match the angle of the joint face.

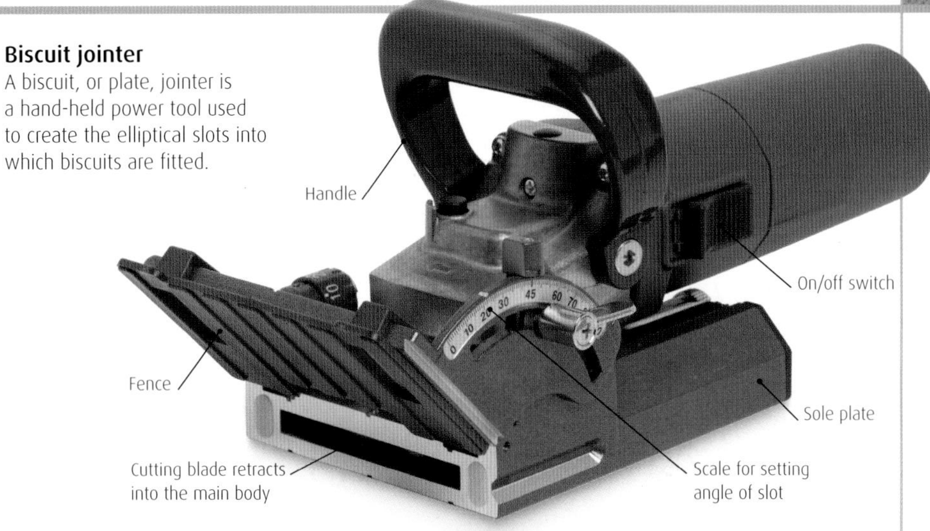

Biscuit jointer
A biscuit, or plate, jointer is a hand-held power tool used to create the elliptical slots into which biscuits are fitted.

Biscuits
Biscuits are usually made of compressed beech and are a standard thickness. They are available in three sizes: 0 (smallest), 10, and 20 (largest).

POSITIONING A BISCUIT JOINTER
Adjust the jointer to the width of the biscuit being used. Align the center line of the cutter with your pencil mark and machine the slot.

CREATING A BISCUIT JOINT
Use a biscuit jointer to cut slots that are slightly larger than the biscuits being used (to allow for any minor adjustments). Glue the biscuits into position.

Domino-based systems

Domino joints are similar to small mortise and tenon joints (pp.116–19). The slot, or mortise, is formed by a cutter that both rotates and oscillates laterally. The cutter can be set to the required depth and width, while the fence can be set square or angled. Attachments help with awkward shapes or for making a series of cuts.

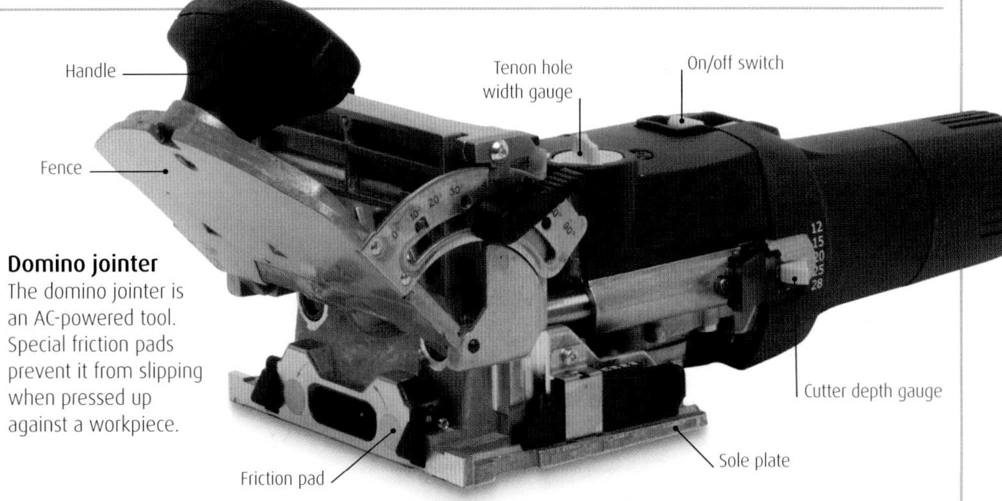

Domino jointer
The domino jointer is an AC-powered tool. Special friction pads prevent it from slipping when pressed up against a workpiece.

Cutter and domino sizes
Dominos and cutters are available in a variety of matching lengths and thicknesses. Changing the cutter in the jointer is a simple task.

HOLDING A DOMINO JOINTER
Hold the jointer with both hands. Use one hand to steady the tool against the workpiece, and the other to depress the jointer and form the cut.

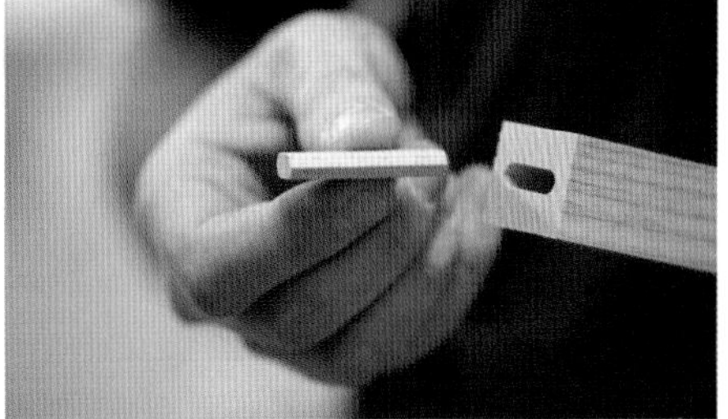

CREATING A DOMINO JOINT
Use a domino jointer, fitted with the correct cutter, to cut slots for the domino. Check that the domino fits correctly and then glue it into position.

Drill presses

CAUTION | WORK SAFELY | SEE P.17

A drill press is a heavy-duty machine that is used for drilling very precise holes. While there are many different ways to drill holes in timber, such as with hand or power drills (pp.42–43), it is sometimes necessary to produce work that is particularly accurate. This is especially important when drilling deep holes, large diameter holes, or those that must be drilled at a specific angle. To produce such precise work, a drill press is the most appropriate machine to use.

Drill presses have a movable drilling column that—in conjunction with drill bits of different sizes—can be used to make holes of varying depths. As well as being capable of vertical drilling, some pillar drills have an adjustable head that can be rotated for angled drilling, and most have an adjustable table that can be raised, lowered, or tilted. Pillar drills are available as smaller bench-mounted models or larger floor-mounted machines. Both types, however, must be bolted down, as they are top-heavy and can be unstable (especially when working at the end of long workpieces).

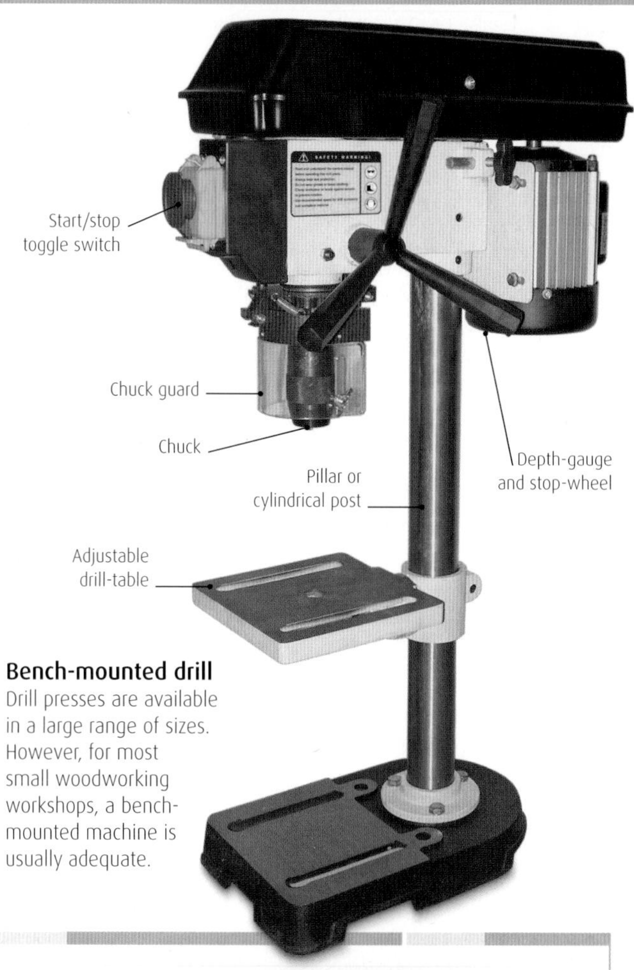

Bench-mounted drill
Drill presses are available in a large range of sizes. However, for most small woodworking workshops, a bench-mounted machine is usually adequate.

HOW TO USE A DRILL PRESS

Although relatively simple to use, a drill press takes practice to master and must be used with great care to achieve the best results. The required speed of rotation depends on the material being drilled and the size of the drill bit being used. This often involves changing the position of the drive belt on a series of pulleys. To ensure that the drill table is square to the drill bit, you can fit a rod into the chuck that is long enough to pass through the table, allowing the angle to be checked. However, always remember to turn off the power before making any adjustments to the drill press.

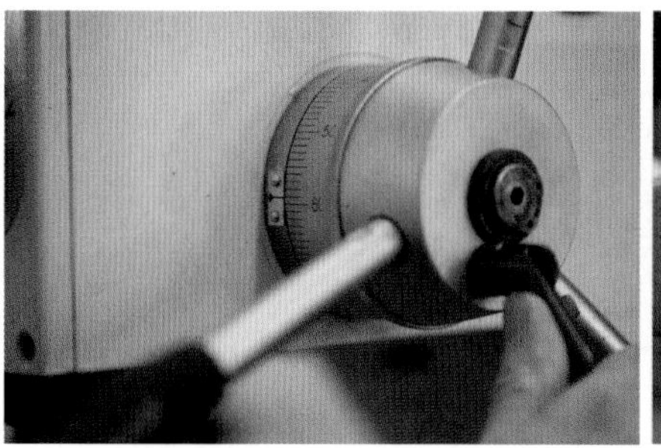

1 **To set the depth**, lower the drill to the required depth by rotating the depth-gauge and stop wheel on the side of the machine. Use the scale on top of the wheel to fix the depth.

2 **To change the bit**, use the chuck key to open the chuck to the required size. Insert the drill bit to be used and then retighten. Check that the drill bit is perfectly centred in the chuck.

3 **To hold the workpiece** securely, use drill vises, which can be fixed to the drill table and allow safe working. Alternatively, use C-cramps or jigs to hold and position the work.

4 **When you have aligned** the workpiece, start the machine and turn the wheel to lower the drill onto the timber. Drilling will stop automatically when the desired depth is reached.

5 **If the holes** will be visible on the face of the workpiece, place an offcut underneath as you drill. This will prevent any breakout on the surface of the timber as the drill emerges.

Fixings

Metal fixings are a quick and simple means of holding pieces of timber together when joints or connectors are not appropriate. Available in a wide variety of shapes and sizes, metal fixings vary in terms of purpose and quality. Some are purely functional, while others have an aesthetic quality that makes them attractive enough to be visible on the finished work.

KNOCK-DOWN FIXINGS

These are used when a joint may need to be taken apart some time after its assembly, such as in the case of "flat pack" furniture or large woodworking projects such as a bed (pp.318–25). However, they are also useful when working on difficult materials, such as chipboard.

CROSS-DOWEL AND BOLT

Screws

Forming a particularly large group of fixings, screws are an excellent choice when a mechanical fixing is needed to join timber. Screws come in various lengths and diameters, and have heads in different designs to suit the work at hand. When using traditional woodscrews, it is advisable to drill both a pilot and a clearance hole so that they are easier to drive in. This also prevents the timber from splitting. The choice of head depends on the desired look and the pieces being joined together.

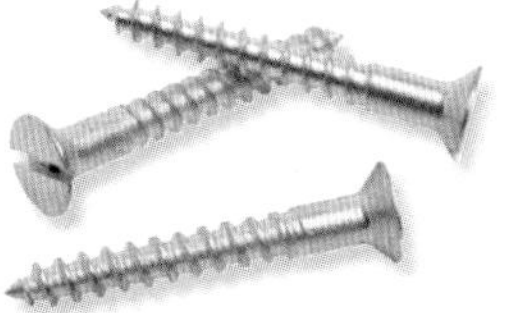

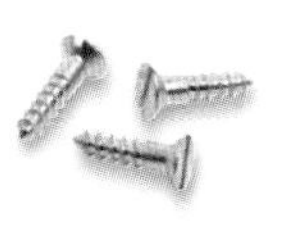

Brass slot-headed screws
Used predominantly when appearance is an important factor, these metal screws are relatively soft. They are therefore easily damaged if used with a screwdriver of the wrong type or size. Brass screws are also liable to break if the pilot hole is too small.

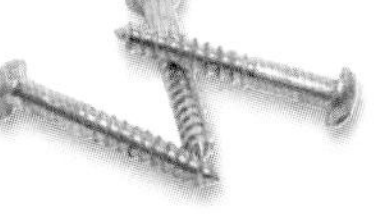

Brass round-headed screws
Brass round-headed screws are typically used to fix metal objects, such as name plates and escutcheons, onto a timber surface.

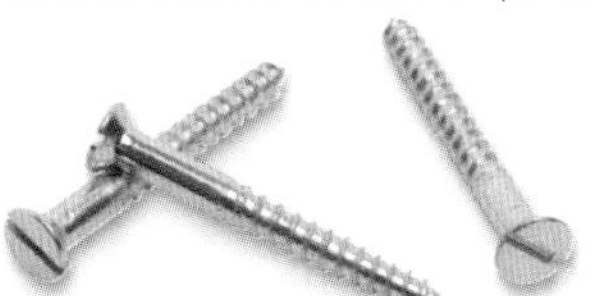

Steel slot-headed screws
These traditional screws can be difficult to use with a power driver but, used with both a clearance and pilot hole, will fit very tightly.

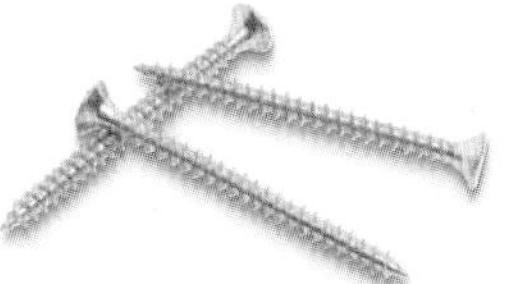

Chipboard screws
The thread extends over most of the shaft (useful for gripping the rough fibers of chipboard) and the heads are shaped for countersinking (p.43).

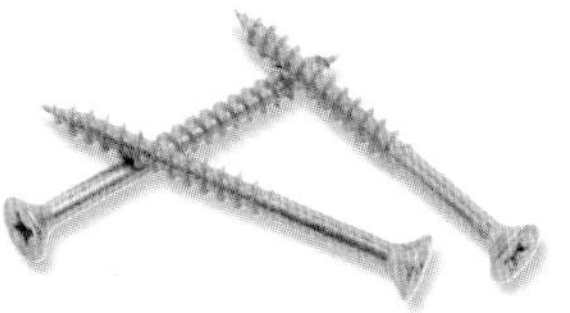

Pozidriv screws
Used with power drivers, these screws are cross-headed with extra divisions between the cross's slots. This makes the driver less likely to slip.

Nails and pins

Used for basic fixings in which the extra strength of a screw is unnecessary, nails are an easy way of holding pieces of timber together. Most, however, will become loose if there is any movement in the pieces being joined. Pins are thinner with smaller heads.

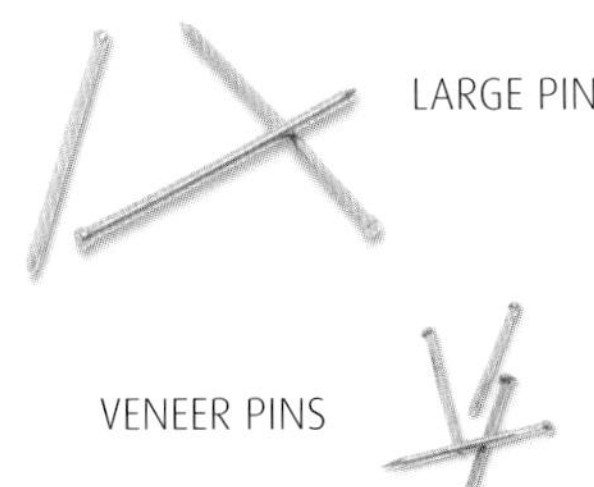

Pins
Popular when making temporary fixings, pins cause minimal damage to timber. The thinnest types are used to hold veneers.

Hinges

Used to attach two components together that still need to move relative to each other, hinges are available in a wide range of styles and sizes. Always use the correct hinge for the job, such as a table hinge for a drop-leaf table, and check for quality—for example, each one of a pair should be exactly alike and move smoothly on the pivot.

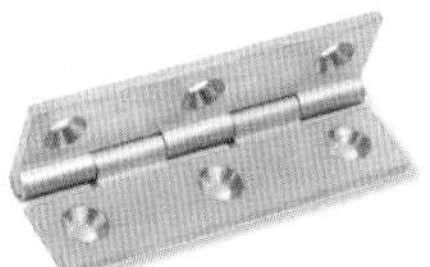

Brass butt hinge
A common fixing, brass butt hinges are an attractive and traditional option. The screws should fit flush with the surface of the hinge leaf.

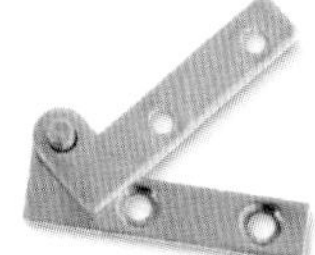

Scissor hinge
These hinges (so-called because of the design) fit onto the top and bottom edges of a door. They are less noticeable than brass butt hinges.

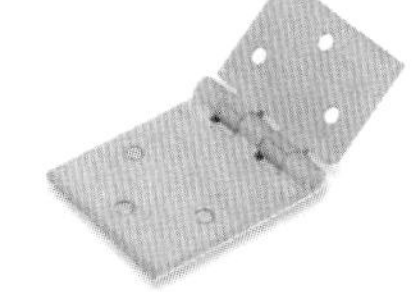

Table hinge
The leaves of table hinges are of different lengths, which allows the fixing screws sufficient depth of timber on drop-leaf tables.

Soss hinge
Hidden completely from view when the door is closed, soss hinges are designed to be fitted with the use of a router (pp.44–49).

Soss barrel-hinge
Similar in operation to standard soss hinges, soss barrel-hinges are held in place with a tensioning mechanism rather than screws.

Concealed hinge
Available in different styles, concealed hinges are invisible from the outside, and allow for a range of opening angles and thicknesses of material.

Workshop

Unfortunately, there is no such thing as the ideal home workshop because most people are limited by the space available and by their budget. However, the information and diagram here acts as a guide to help you formulate a sensible workshop layout and a machinery "wish list." Ample lighting is essential.

Planning a workshop layout

Obviously the more space you have available the better, as it will enable you to work on large-scale projects as well as accommodate specialized equipment that will help speed up your work. It is possible to work in a very small space, but you may have to limit the size of your chosen projects, and work with hand tools and power tools alone. This is easily achieved, especially if you are willing to spend a little bit extra on prepared timber sections—look for a local timber suppliers who are equipped to supply hardwood planed to your specification. Alternatively, commandeer a garage, or build yourself a substantial workshop if outdoor space and building codes allow—however, do consider the impact of machinery noise on your neighbors. The plan view of the workshop layout shown opposite employs a space 25 x 20ft (7.6 x 6.1m), and can be used as a basis for your own workshop. Each grid square represents 1 x 1ft 305 x (305mm).

YOUR SPACE

Your workshop is likely to be a different size and shape from the one shown here (doors and windows will also fall in different positions) so you will need to rearrange everything to suit your requirements. Find some graph paper and use the scale of one grid square to represent 1 x 1ft (305 x 305mm) to help you design the space. Use the machinery sizes shown in the main diagram as a guide. The workbench area needs good lighting and is best located near a window, and each machine needs space around it as indicated by the blue arrows.

KEY

SCALE: 1 SQUARE = 1 X 1FT (305 X 305MM)

- PLASTIC/METAL BINS
- FLOOR-STANDING EQUIPMENT
- SPACE REQUIRED AROUND MACHINERY. INDICATES DIRECTION WOOD PASSES THROUGH
- WORK AREAS AND STORAGE

PILLAR DRILL
Ideal for drilling accurate holes (in metal as well as wood), particularly large diameter holes, angled holes, and batch production using jigs.

MOBILE ROLLER STAND
Use this to support the end of a large workpiece as it runs off the table of a machine. Mobile on rollers or balls, it can be used with any of the machines used here.

OFF-CUT BIN
This is a handy place to store off-cuts for completing projects or making jigs.

LEANING BOARDS
Clear an area for leaning boards up against the wall (make sure they are stable).

TIMBER STORAGE RACK
Open racking for storing rough sawn planks, keeping them flat, dry, and accessible. Fix to the ceiling to keep it sturdy.

FLOOR-STANDING MORTISER
A sturdy machine with control wheels and positive depth stop is a great time-saving investment.

RECYCLE BIN
Recycle home workshop waste as you would household waste according to local regulations.

TRASH CAN
A metal trash can is ideal. Wood products can be burned, or small amounts disposed of with your household trash. For larger amounts, consult your local waste-management authorities.

TABLE SAW
If space allows, choose a panel saw that can cope with a 8 x 4ft (2440 x 1220mm) board. These have telescopic support legs. Alternatively, opt for smaller table saws, a radial arm saw, or a compound miter saw on a stand.

Bench Station, Workbench with storage and Engineer's vice images courtesy of Axminster Tool Centre, www.axminster.co.uk http://www.axminster.co.uk

BENCH STATION
Any heavy, sturdy table will do. This is a place for mounting a bench grinder and a bench vise.

ENGINEER'S VISE
Extremely useful for holding scrapers while re-sharpening, and for metalwork (cutting fixings, shaping metal).

BENCH GRINDER
Invest in a high-quality grinder, with large-diameter, wide grinding wheels.

STORAGE

The more shelving, cabinets, and drawers you have available the better. Over time you will accumulate many hand tools and power tool accessories that should be organized and stored in order to preserve them in good condition, while leaving maximum space for working. Often it is more time-efficient to display all your frequently-used hand tools on the wall near to your workbench. Power tools are normally kept in cabinets.

SHELF UNIT
Use this space for general equipment, for example jigs, fixings, glue, polish.

WALL-HUNG STORAGE
Arrange frequently used tools on the wall within easy reach. Keep planes or chisels on a shelf to avoid damaging the cutting edges. Use low cabinets to store power tools and accessories.

WORKBENCH WITH STORAGE
Choose a heavy solid construction, preferably with a surface of 6ft 6in x 2ft (2000 x 600mm) or larger. Built-in drawers, cabinets, and a tool storage well are a huge benefit. Site near to a window.

MOBILE DUST COLLECTOR
Essential for extracting shavings from a planer-thicknesser, this can also be moved near to other machines such as bandsaws or table saws, to collect dust. Shavings are collected in a reusable bag.

WINDOW
Natural light is essential for bench work, especially when judging the results of carving or finishing.

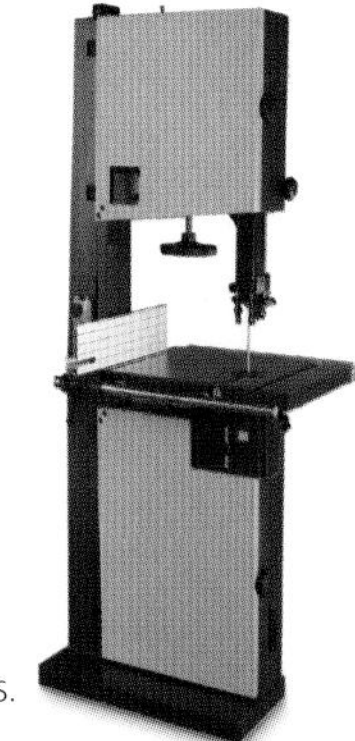

BANDSAW
An extremely useful, versatile machine used for rip sawing planks, shaping components, and joint-making. Always keep at least one spare blade, and preferably a range of blade widths for different radius curves.

WOODTURNING LATHE
A bench-mounted lathe is a useful addition to a workshop. Fix to the top of a sturdy bench with bolts. Position a shelf or cabinet nearby to hold wood-turning gouges, chisels, and scrapers.

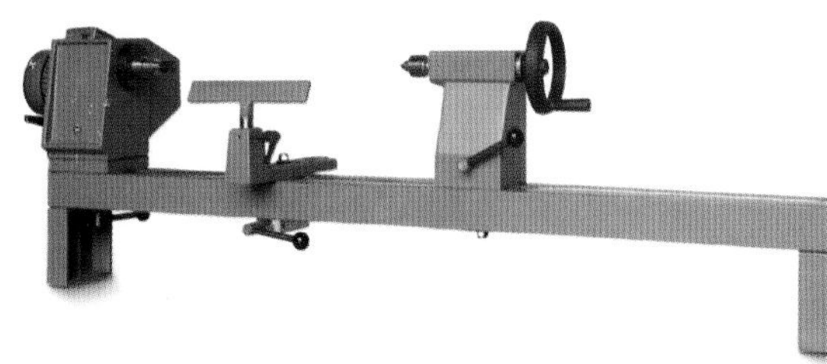

GARAGE DOOR
Open the door to increase the natural light. (Keep closed when applying finishes to avoid drafts.)

PLANER-THICKNESSER
Modern versions of this compact money-saving combination of a planer and thicknesser are good for a home workshop. Choose one with a powerful, quiet induction motor, cast-iron tables and a cast-iron fence.

Workbenches and work supports

No matter what type of task is being carried out, the woodworker will always need a suitable surface on which to work—this can range from a large, sophisticated workbench to a simple pair of trestle tables. The type of workbench you choose will depend on a number of factors, such as whether or not the bench needs to be portable, and the height at which a workpiece needs to be supported. If possible, choose a bench that has drawers and cabinets for storing tools.

Workbenches

Most woodworkers will need a workbench—either bought or self-built—that is tailored to his or her own needs. The bench should be as sturdy as possible, as this will prevent movement during use and will allow it to withstand heavy impacts, such as those caused by a mallet (p.39). The most important item on any workbench is the front vise, which is used to hold a workpiece securely in position. Other useful features include a second vise (end vise), which is usually located at one end of the bench. Together with "bench dogs" (securing pegs), this second vise allows long workpieces to be held in place.

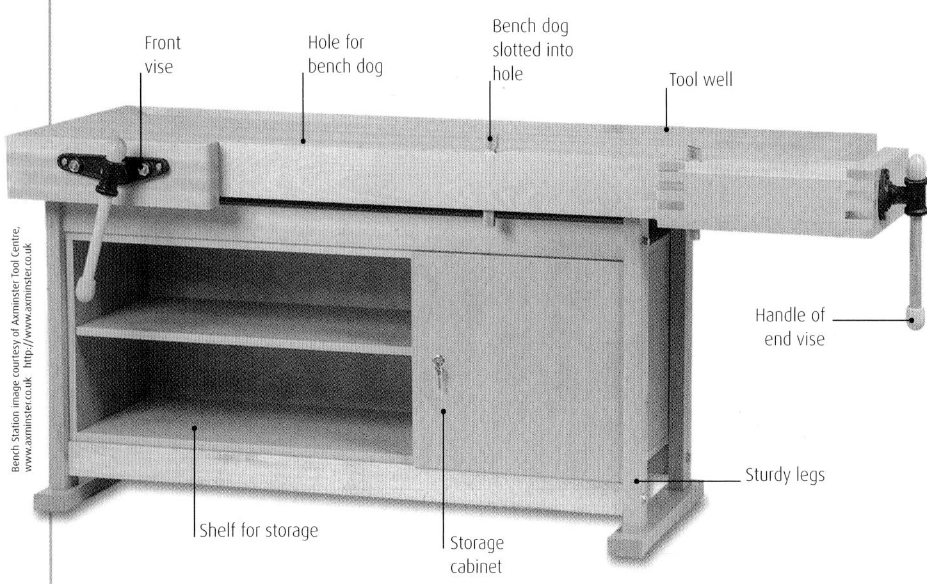

Workbench
This workbench is made of beech and features a tool well at the rear—used for storing tools while working—and bench dogs in both vises. Bench dogs are used for additional support when holding items in place.

PROPRIETARY WORKBENCHES

Small purpose-built workbenches are also available. These are portable and can be folded away. Despite their small size they will carry a considerable load when locked in the open position. The user can increase the bench's stability by placing a foot on the step. Controlled by handles, the rear half of the benchtop acts as a vise. Plastic pegs fit into holes to help support a workpiece.

Bench hooks

A bench hook is used to hold timber in place on a workbench. It is a useful addition to any bench and can be bought or easily constructed by the woodworker. It consists of either a solid board or piece of plywood, with a cross timber or square of wood fixed at each end on opposite sides. These cross timbers allow it to be hooked over the edge of the workbench. Sizes vary, but a typical bench hook measures 10 x 10in (250 x 250mm).

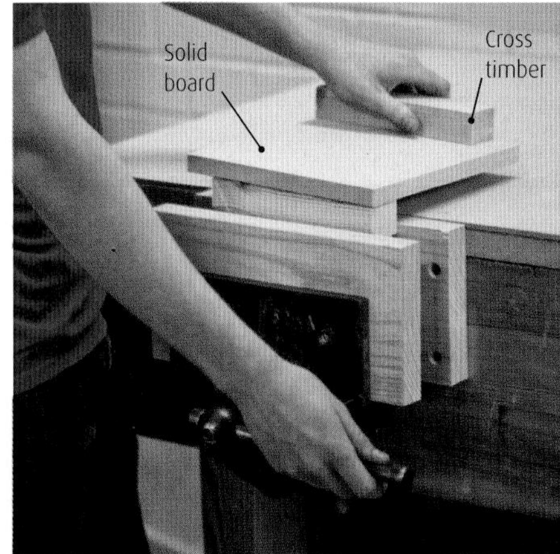

SETTING UP A BENCH HOOK
Hook the front cross timber over the edge of the bench or, as shown here, hold it in a vise. Using a vise is preferable as it eliminates movement and leaves one hand free to hold the workpiece.

USING A BENCH HOOK
Slide the workpiece forward until it rests against the back cross timber of the bench hook. Hold it in place with the heel of one hand, while using the thumb of the same hand to guide the edge of the saw.

Shooting boards

Shooting is the process of taking a few shavings from the edge or end of a board in order to correct an angle, straighten an edge, or clean up its surface. Similar in nature to a bench hook, a shooting board is designed to hold a workpiece in position, although a shooting board has an additional board fixed to its underside. This bottom board is wider than the top board and extends out to the side. It is along this board extension that a plane (pp.22–29)—which must be turned on its side— is run. The plane then trims the edge of the workpiece.

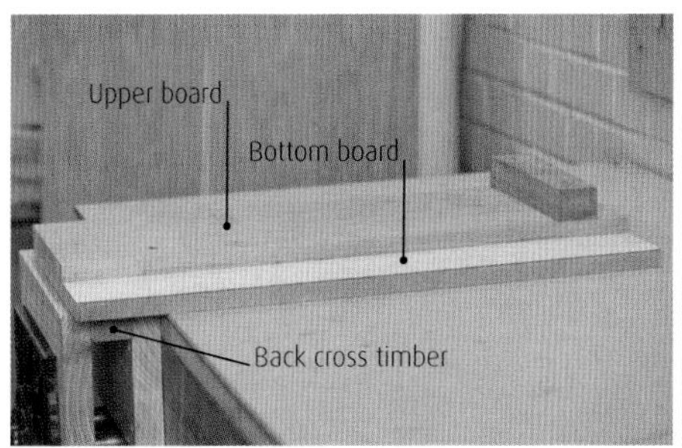

SETTING UP A SHOOTING BOARD
Hook the back cross timber over the edge of the bench, or grip it in a vise (shown above). Check that the front cross timber is square to the upper board.

USING A SHOOTING BOARD
Rest the side of the plane on the bottom board. Press its sole against the upper board. Push the workpiece up to the front cross timber and against the plane.

Front cross timber set at 45 degrees

Hook thumb behind the plane's frog

USING A SHOOTING BOARD AT 45 DEGREES
The front cross timber can be set at an angle of 45 degrees to allow for the trimming of a miter (pp.112–15). The best way of checking that the cross timber is set to the correct angle is to trim two offcuts. When these offcuts are placed together, they should form a right angle.

Bench vises

A vise is an important part of any workbench, making the task of firmly gripping a workpiece quick and easy. A large vise is generally more versatile than a smaller one because it can hold a workpiece in a variety of different positions. A large vise is also easier to tighten as the load is spread over a wider area. To speed up the process of adjusting a vise, quick-release mechanisms are available. Cast-iron vises should be used with wooden "cheeks," which prevent a workpiece from slipping or becoming damaged.

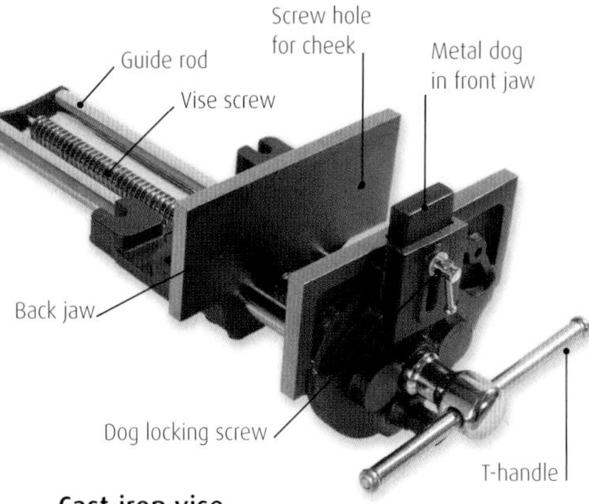

Cast-iron vise
Many woodworkers choose to work with a cast-iron vise. For supporting a workpiece, the model shown here has an adjustable metal dog (peg), which can be lowered out of the way.

CHANGING THE CHEEKS OF A VISE

After prolonged use, the wooden cheeks used with a cast-iron vise will need to be replaced. Beech and ash timbers make the best vise cheeks, as they are strong enough to resist the pressure of the vise's jaws but soft enough to protect the workpiece. The thickness of the vise cheeks also needs careful consideration, as the greater the thickness, the more the usable space between the vise's jaws will be taken up—a thickness of 13⁄16–13⁄16in (20–30mm) will be adequate. It is a good idea to fit the cheeks so that they sit slightly above the surface of the bench top. This means that any minor damage to the cheeks can be planed off, which will prolong their usability.

1 **Cut the cheeks** from offcuts of hardwood. Aim for a width of 8–12in (200–300mm); the top of the cheeks should sit just above the bench top. Mark positions for screw holes.

2 **Drill countersunk holes** in the cheek where marked. With the back cheek in position, drill pilot holes into the workbench and screw it into position.

3 **Place the front cheek** in the front of the vise and align both cheeks. Tighten the vise. Drill pilot holes through the screw holes in the vise and screw the front cheek into position.

Sharpening tools

Tool manufacturers are in the business of trying to sell as many tools as possible, but you should resist the temptation to buy every new piece of gear that comes onto the market. However, the serious woodworker may wish to consider adding some specialized tools and pieces of equipment to his or her workshop—especially those wanting to concentrate on a particular aspect of woodwork, such as antique restoration (pp.172–75). All woodworkers, however, will need to keep their tools sharp, and investing in a grinding wheel, for example, or a selction of sharpening stones, could be a wise investment. Tools for creating good finishes are also useful.

Grinders

Motorized grinders are used to grind the blades of tools such as planes (pp.22–29) and chisels (pp.30–33). To remove large amounts of metal, you will need a high-speed grinder. However, for general re-sharpening, a motorized whetstone is preferable. The slower speed of this machine makes it easy to control, and the grindstone is cooled by water, which prevents overheating and helps to preserve a blade's temper.

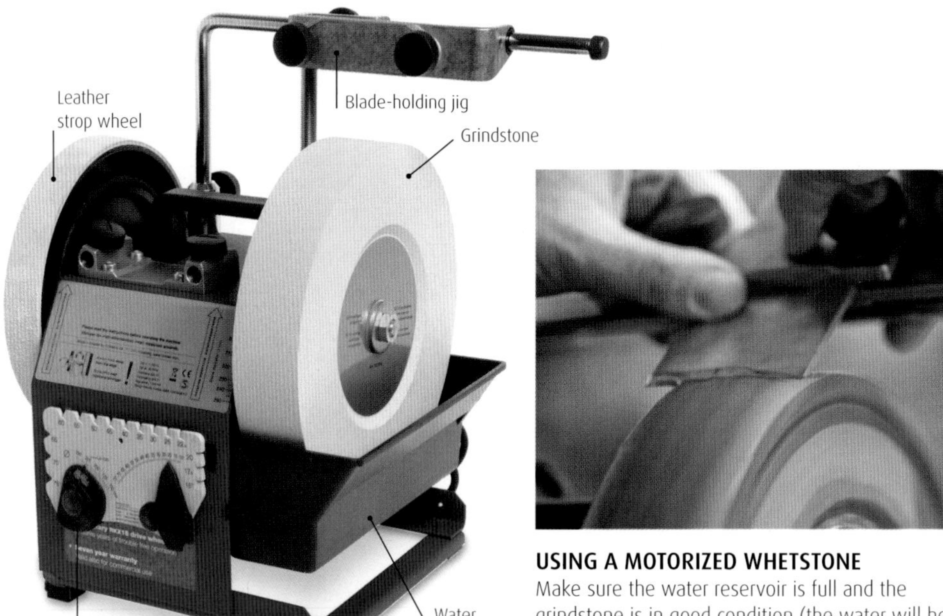

MOTORIZED WHETSTONE

USING A MOTORIZED WHETSTONE
Make sure the water reservoir is full and the grindstone is in good condition (the water will help to remove debris from the grindstone as well as keep it cool). Always wear protective goggles.

Sharpening stones

Bladed tools must be kept sharp, so you will need a variety of sharpening stones made from either natural stone or synthetic materials. Most stones should be lubricated before use: as the names suggest, oilstones are lubricated with oil, and waterstones (also called whetstones) with water. A honing guide will also help you to achieve an accurate finish.

Diamond whetsone

While very expensive, diamond whetsones are far more efficient to use than other stones, as they need no lubricant and stay flat (they can also be used to flatten man-made waterstones). The steel plate is coated with diamond grit and the holes in the plate capture the swarf. Available in various grits or as a combination stone.

DIAMOND WHETSTONE

SINGLE 1000-GRIT STONE

Single 1000-grit whetstone

Man-made oilstones and waterstones of various grits are available. A 1000 grit stone is coarse and used for initial honing or restoring an edge.

COMBINATION 1000/6000-GRIT JAPANESE WATERSTONE

Combination 1000/6000-grit Japanese waterstone

A rough (coarse grit) stone bonded to a medium-fine stone. Use the coarse side for initial honing and the finer one for finishing. Lubricate with water (oil will damage the stone). Japanese stones wear out more quickly than alternatives but are easier to flatten, meaning they last longer.

COMBINATION OIL STONE

Combination oilstone

Used by most woodworkers, oilstones come in different qualities, the best being Novaculite ("Arkansas") and cheaper versions made from silicon carbide. Again, a combination stone is a popular choice. Lubricate with oil.

Honing guides
Used for holding a blade at the correct angle while it is being sharpened, a honing guide will also help to preserve a blade's beveled edge. This means that it will require less re-grinding, increasing its lifespan.

LUBRICATING THE SHARPENING STONE
Most types of sharpening stone need to be used in conjunction with a lubricant (oil or water), which removes waste and aids ease of use. Make sure you use the correct lubricant with each stone.

USING A HONING GUIDE
Applying gentle downward pressure, roll the guide up and down the stone. Avoid making sideways movements, with the guide as this may damage it.

Scraper burnisher

The merit of a completed workpiece often depends on the quality of its finish (pp.164–71) so it is important that finishing tools are kept as sharp as possible. To sharpen a cabinet scraper (p.76)—one of the most common finishing tools—you will need to use a dedicated tool called a scraper burnisher. This sharpening tool has a cylindrical blade made of a particularly hard steel, which is not marked or damaged by the sharp edge of the cabinet scraper.

Scraper burnisher
Used during the process of sharpening a cabinet scraper, most scraper burnishers have an attractive hardwood handle and brass ferrule.

SHARPENING A CABINET SCRAPER

A cabinet scraper takes fine wood shavings off the surface of timber, and it is a burr running along the edge of the scraper that does the cutting work. This burr is created and angled by a scraper burnisher. To sharpen a cabinet scraper, you must first remove the old burr and prepare its edges. You will know when a scraper needs to be sharpened because it will form dust instead of shavings when drawn across timber. The edge of the cabinet scraper must be straight and the corners must be square before it is sharpened. This sharpening technique takes practice, so don't expect perfect results right away.

1 **Hold the cabinet scraper** vertically and carefully rub it along the surface of a sharpening stone to flatten the edges of the scraper.

2 **Place the scraper** flat to the stone, and rub it back and forth in order to remove the remains of the old burr from each side.

3 **Place the scraper** on the edge of the workbench and run the burnisher along the long edges of the scraper. Angle the burnisher downwards slightly to raise the burr.

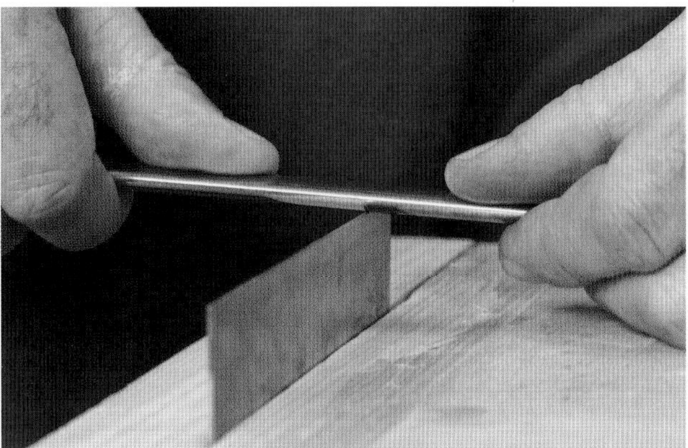

4 **Place the scraper in a vise** and run the burnisher along the edge in order to "turn" the burr. The burr should be angled at approximately 90 degrees to the flat sides.

Gluing and clamping

Gluing and clamping are important stages in any woodworking project. Glue has long been used to join wood (traditional animal glue is still used by some woodworkers and restorers), and is often the strongest part of a joint. You should keep more than one type of glue in your workshop, as different glues have different properties, and therefore different advantages for the woodworker. For example, slow-drying glues are useful for complex joints that will take time to assemble, while fast-setting glues may be more appropriate for smaller, quicker jobs. Once glue has been applied, clamping holds the joint firmly together while the glue cures (sets), and ensures that the joint is square.

Glues and gluing

As most glues are water-based, evaporation plays a key role in the curing process. The time taken for a glue to cure is therefore affected by its rate of evaporation, which in turn is affected by the ambient temperature—the warmer it is, the faster the process, and the less time you will have to make any adjustments. Be aware, however, that in cold conditions a glue may completely fail to cure. Three types of glue are of most use: PVA, polyurethane, and powdered-resin wood glue.

Smooth consistency

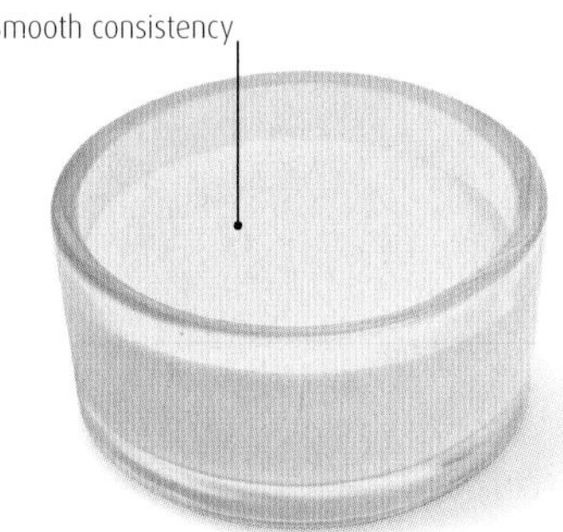

Polyvinyl acetate (PVA)

PVA is a versatile and inexpensive glue. It is easy to spread and forms a strong bond, although it leaves a gray glue-line and melts if sanded. The curing process relies on clamping pressure and water evaporation. Although clamps can be removed after just one or two hours, it may take up to 12 hours for the glue to cure completely.

Viscous solution

Polyurethane

This is a durable, water-resistant glue that is ideal for outdoor use. Since it relies on moisture to cure, it is useful for gluing timbers that already contain some moisture. Applied directly from the container, most types can be painted. It is stronger than other glues in end-grain-to-grain joints, but can be messy to use.

Fine powder

Powdered-resin wood glue

Ideal for fine cabinet making and laminating, this glue comes in powder form and must be mixed with water (right) before use. It has a longer "open time" than ready-mixed glues, so you will have more time to assemble your workpiece before the glue cures. It is waterproof and does not "creep," since it is not rubbery like PVA.

MIXING POWDERED-RESIN WOOD GLUE

Powdered-resin wood glue requires the addition of water to become active. Use equal amounts of powder and water. Start by adding half of the water. Mix well to form a smooth paste before stirring in the remaining water.

APPLYING GLUE

Before applying glue, make sure that the surfaces to be bonded are clean and free from any existing varnish or paint. To create a strong, even bond, it is important that you apply the glue in a controlled manner. The best way to do this is to use a brush or a roller. Aim for an even coating of glue on all surfaces (but not so much that there is an excessive amount to clean up). If you have mixed the glue yourself, pour it directly onto the largest surface. For gluing small components, decant a small amount of glue into a plastic tub, such as an old yogurt container.

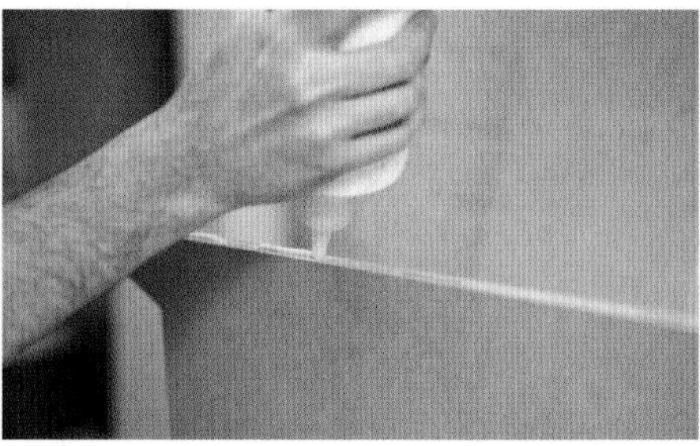

Applying glue straight from a bottle

For some jobs—such as running a line of glue along the edge of a board (above)—you can apply glue directly from the bottle. A special nozzle makes it simple for you to direct the flow.

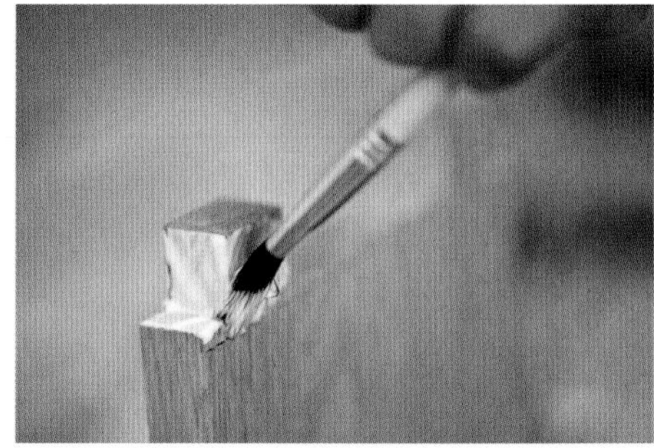

Applying glue with a brush

Use a brush to apply glue to joint areas, such as mortises and tenons, and for accessing hard to reach places, such as dovetail sockets and dowel holes. A brush will help you to apply an even coat.

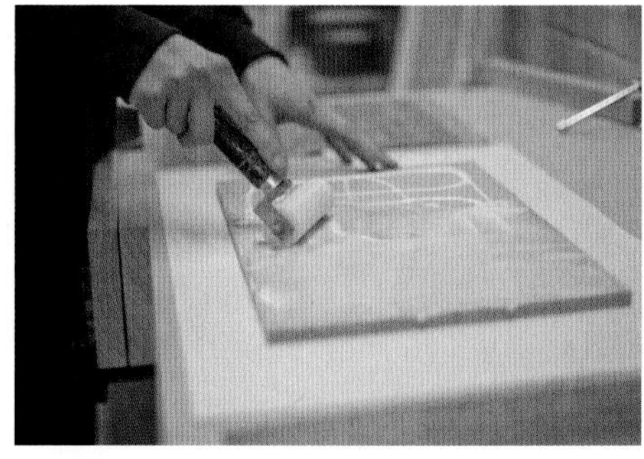

Applying glue with a roller

A roller is useful for applying glue to large surfaces, since it can help spread the glue evenly and quickly. Start from the center and work outward, making sure that the edges, in particular, are well covered.

Clamping

Clamping is an essential part of the "gluing up" process. Clamps (pp.40–41) are used to hold a carcass together until the glue has had time to fully cure. Clamps are also used to check for squareness. This is a vital consideration—if just one section of a piece is not square, it can affect the whole work. Different jobs require different types of clamps and you should always keep a good selection in your workshop. The key to successful clamping is careful preparation.

Before you start, always complete a "dry run." This will allow you to practice the assembly procedure, and check that you have the required tools and clamps, and that all of the pieces fit accurately together. It is also a good idea to plan your work so that gluing up is the last job of the day. You can then leave the glue to cure overnight (although you should never leave glue to cure in very cold conditions since it may fail).

Clamping miter joints

There are several ways to clamp miter joints. However, if they are being used to form a frame, one of the best methods is to use a band clamp. This fits around the frame and forces the joints together as the clamp is tightened. Always remember to check for squareness (see right).

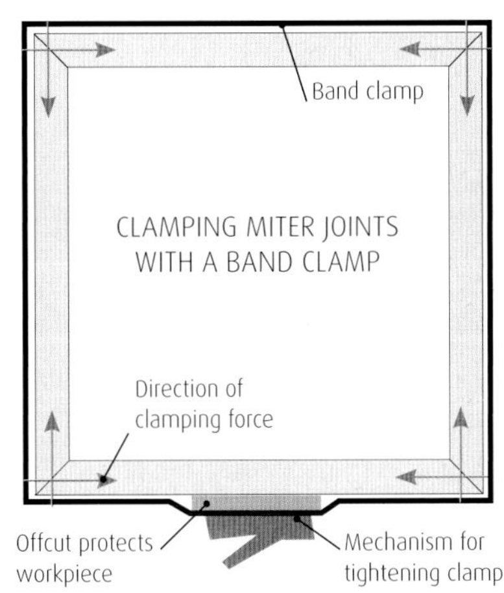

CLAMPING MITER JOINTS WITH A BAND CLAMP

Clamping mortise- and-tenon joints

Mortise-and-tenon joints must be properly clamped to ensure that the shoulders are closed up, and to prevent any air trapped in the mortise from opening up the joint before the glue has cured. It is usually best to use a sash clamp for this type of joint.

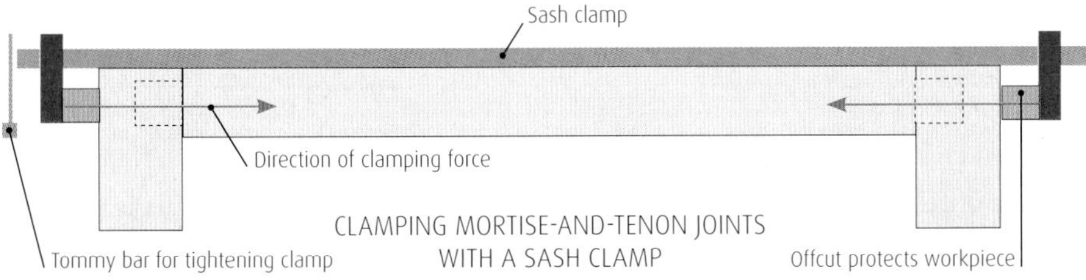

CLAMPING MORTISE-AND-TENON JOINTS WITH A SASH CLAMP

Clamping flat boards

To clamp a series of flat boards, you will need a number of sash clamps spaced at intervals of approximately 10in (25cm). The clamping force will fan out across the boards at approximately 45 degrees, and using several clamps will ensure even coverage. Lay the clamps alternately above and below the boards, tighten the clamps gently and uniformly, and check for flatness with the straight edge of a piece of timber.

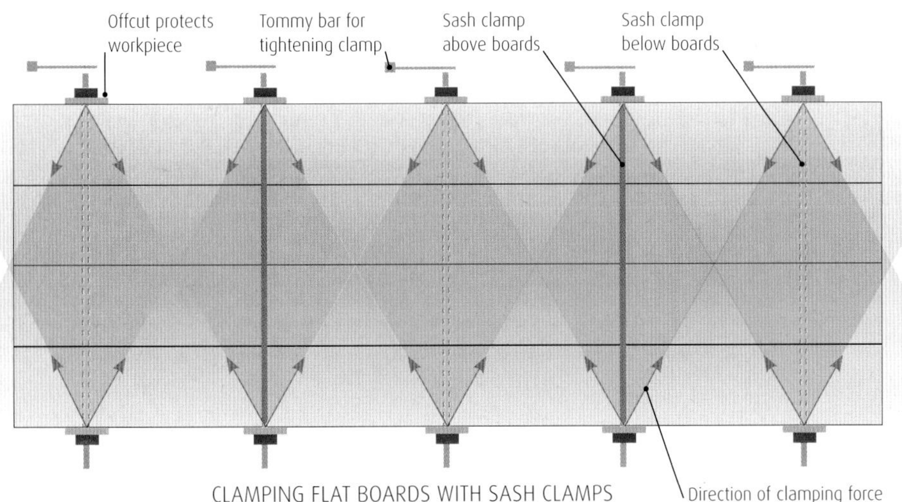

CLAMPING FLAT BOARDS WITH SASH CLAMPS

CHECKING FOR SQUARENESS

When gluing a square or rectangular frame or carcass, it is important to check that it is square as soon as the clamps are in place, as you will need to make any adjustments before the glue has cured. To do this, measure the length of each diagonal. If they are equal, the frame is square. A try-square can be used to check small pieces.

CHECKING FIRST DIAGONAL

CHECKING SECOND DIAGONAL

Clamping to make square

To use a clamp to correct the squareness of a frame, find the corners of the longest diagonal and move the clamp jaws at these corners slightly away from the frame. Retighten the clamps and check for squareness again. The frame is square when both diagonals are equal.

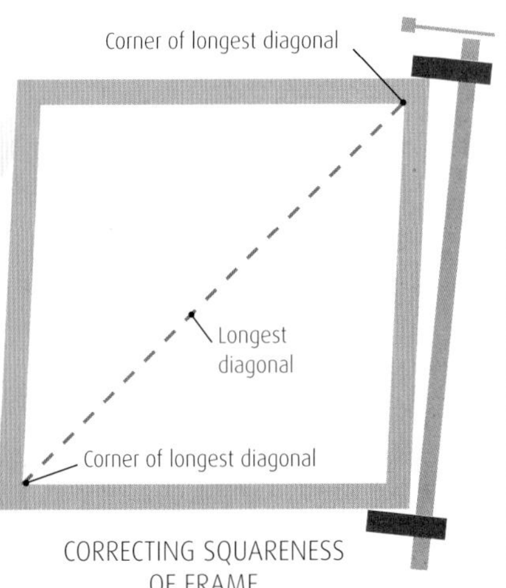

CORRECTING SQUARENESS OF FRAME

Scrapers and abrasives

Scrapers and adhesives are used to prepare the surface of a workpiece before a finish (pp.164–71) is applied. Preparing a surface involves the use of a scraper to remove surface blemishes, followed by a succession of abrasives of varying grit sizes to achieve the desired level of smoothness. The surface should be prepared only to the standard demanded of it by the intended finish. For example, it is a waste of time finishing a surface that is going to be painted to the same high quality as a surface that will ultimately be finished with French polish.

Cabinet scrapers

Used to remove fine shavings from the surface of timber, a cabinet scraper is a thin, sharp-edged sheet of tempered steel. Standard rectangular scrapers are used for flat surfaces, while goose-neck and concave/convex models are suited to moldings and shaped work. You should keep a variety of scrapers, especially as you will want to have a replacement to hand if one you are using becomes blunt (a scraper that produces dust instead of wood shavings needs to be sharpened—see p.73). Avoid over-working a particular area as a dip may form; this will become more pronounced when a finish is applied. As a cabinet scraper can be hard on the thumbs, you may prefer to use a scraping plane (p.29) instead.

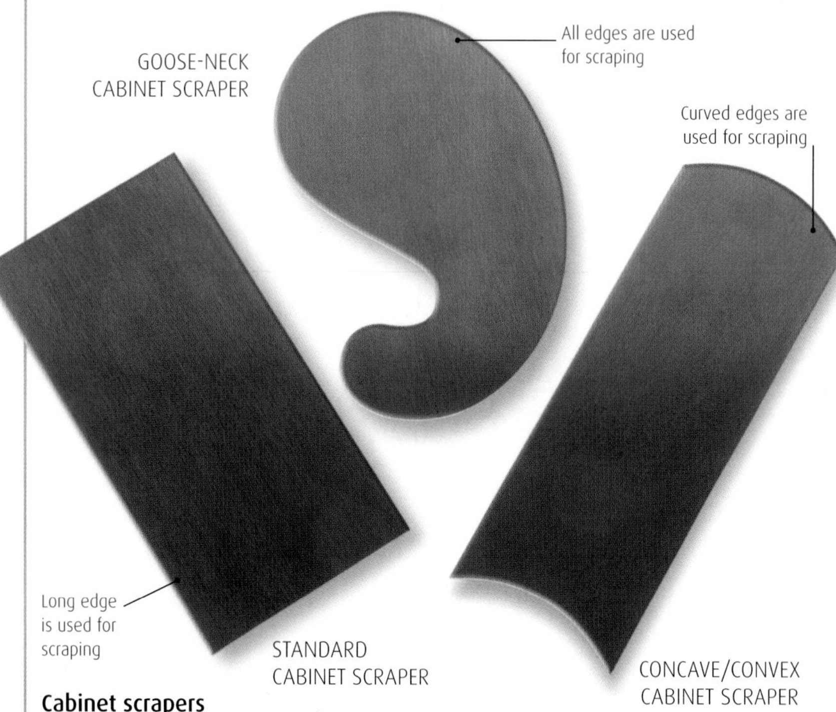

Cabinet scrapers
Cabinet scrapers are available in a range of standard shapes, which are capable of dealing with the demands of most projects. If necessary, however, it is possible to re-shape a scraper as required.

USING A CABINET SCRAPER
Hold the scraper in both hands, bend it slightly with your thumbs, and tilt it forward. Push it away from you, scraping it across the surface of the timber. You may need to adjust the angle or tilt to achieve the best cut. The scraper will become hot with use.

Abrasives

The term abrasive refers to any material that abrades (wears away) the surface of a workpiece. Sandpaper, which is also called abrasive paper (although sand is no longer used as an abrasive), is one of the most commonly used general-purpose abrasives. Papers are available in a range of grit sizes (below) for preparing wood to varying degrees of quality. Steel wool, another popular abrasive, is used for both applying and stripping finishes. Other abrasives include pumice and rottenstone, which are used to create a very fine finish.

GRIT SIZES

The coarseness of sandpaper is determined by the size of the abrasive particles bonded to the paper. A paper's coarseness is measured in grit sizes:

Grit size	Typical uses
100–120 (Coarse)	Initial sanding of timber that will be finished with oil or wax
	Final sanding of timber that will be finished with paint
150–180 (Medium)	Improving the surface of timber that will be finished with oil or wax
	Final sanding of timber that will be finished with varnish
240–320 (Fine)	Final sanding of timber that will be finished with oil or wax
360+ (Very fine)	Final sanding of timber that will be finished with the very finest finishes, such as French polish

SANDPAPER MEDIUMS

Sandpaper is available in a variety of mediums—such as in sheet form or as a disc—to suit its intended method of application:

Abrasive medium	Typical uses
Sheet	General sanding
Disc	For use with appropriate random orbital sander (p.52)
Sanding sponge	General sanding; profiles
Strip	General sanding; turning
Cord and tape	Sanding awkward areas; turning

Sandpaper backing
The abrasive grit on sandpaper is bonded onto backing paper, which can be folded or cut to size to suit the timber being finished. The type of bonding agent and the weight of paper used vary according to the intended use.

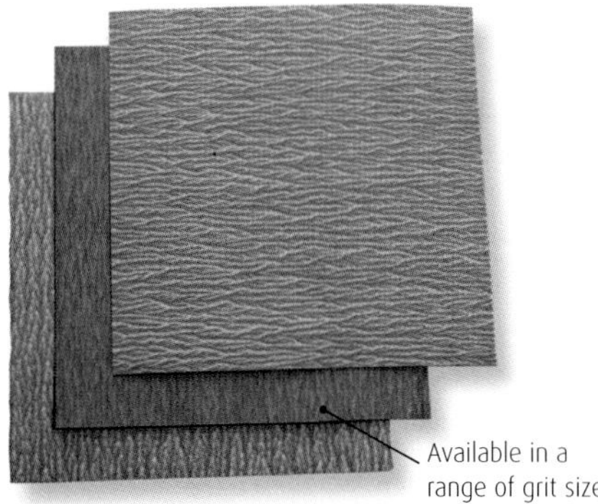

Abranet
As the name implies, this proprietary sand paper consists of a fine abrasive net or mesh. The mesh allows for easy dust extraction, which makes Abranet particularly resistant to clogging. It is available in various grit sizes.

Aluminium oxide paper
This type of abrasive paper is available in sheet form for sanding by hand, as well as in disc or belt form for use with sanders (p.52–53). Grit sizes range from a very coarse 40, to 240, which is suitable for creating a final finish.

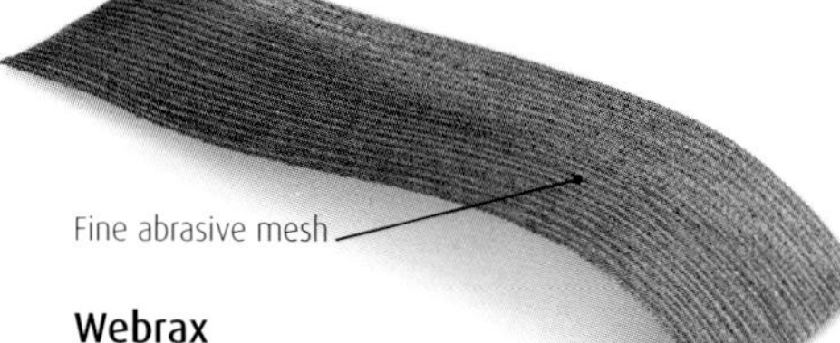

Webrax
A commercial web-like material, Webrax is highly flexible, which makes it ideal for use on contoured timber. It does not easily clog up with dust, and is also available in a non-abrasive form for applying finishes.

SANDING BLOCK

Sandpaper shoud be used in conjunction with a sanding block. This is simply a block of wood around which the woodworker wraps a piece of abrasive paper. The block will help support the paper and enable you to improve the quality of the finish. When sanding rough timber, using a block will also reduce the risk of sustaining injury from splinters. See p.165 for how to make a sanding block.

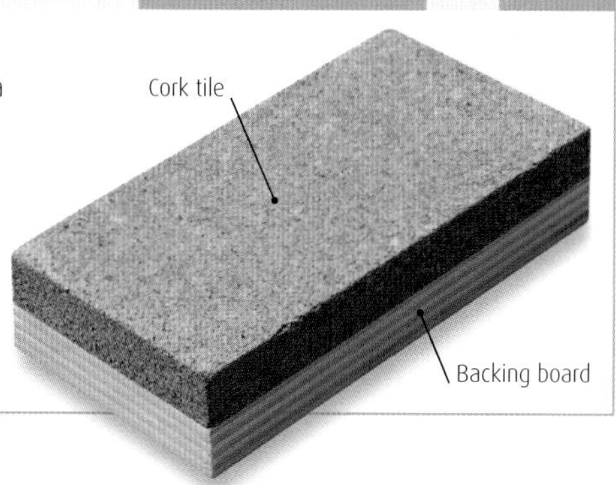

PREPARING A SANDING BLOCK

Ready-made sanding blocks are available to purchase, but you can easily make one in the workshop. Cork is the preferred material, as it is more comfortable to work with than hardwood and offers the right amount of resilience during use. Cork is available in tile form, which can be glued to a backing board (this increases the overall depth of the block) and cut to size.

1 **Cut a standard sheet** of sandpaper into smaller sections to produce a conveniently sized piece that will fit neatly around the sanding block.

2 **Fold the sheet of paper** around the sanding block and hold it in place with your thumb and three fingers. Press your forefinger on top of the block as a guide. The sanding block is now ready to use.

USING A SANDING BLOCK
Move the block smoothly over the required area, applying only gently pressure. If you have a large area to sand, you may wish to wear gloves or protect the tips of your fingers with tape.

TACK CLOTH

Before a finish such as oil is applied, it is vital that any dust is removed from the timber. While this can be achieved by brushing or vacuuming, for the best results you will need to use a tack cloth, which is specially designed for the task. The cloth is impregnated with a substance that is sticky enough to lift and retain dust, but not so sticky that it leaves a residue on the surface.

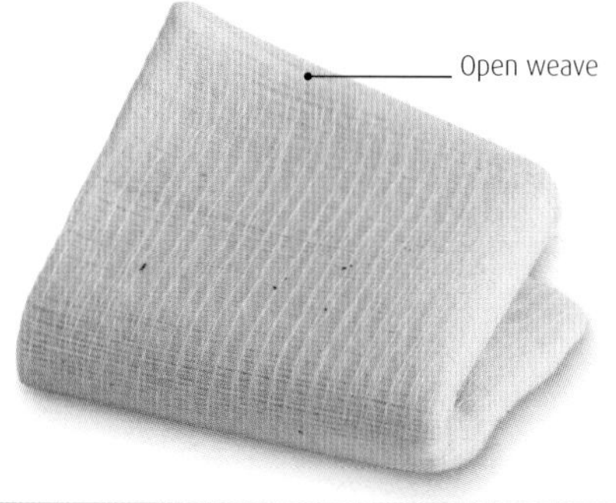

Safety clothing and first aid

Power tools and machines can be hazardous—many are noisy, create large amounts of dust, and have sharp, fast-moving blades. However, as long as you wear the correct safety clothing and take the necessary precautions (see p.17 for the safe use of tools), woodworking should be a safe and rewarding occupation. A well-stocked first-aid kit must be the first fixture in your workshop. Learn first-aid techniques, seek training in the correct use of all tools and equipment, and always follow the manufacturer's instructions. Remember also that timbers can be heavy, so research and use the correct lifting techniques and protect your hands and feet by wearing gloves and safety boots.

Personal Protective Equipment (PPE)

A term that encompasses all of the clothing and equipment used to protect an individual's body, PPE includes items as diverse as jumpsuits and body armor. While not every item of PPE will be needed by the woodworker, those shown below should be considered essential. It is important that PPE is worn or used correctly, looked after properly, and replaced before it becomes worns out. As you will often have to wear several items of PPE at the same time—such as a dust mask, safety goggles, and acoustic earmuffs (ear defenders)—choose items that complement each other and do not cause discomfort.While many hazards can be avoided by the wearing of protective clothing, inappropriate clothing in itself can be hazardous. For example, loose clothing should be avoided as it can become entangled in the rotating parts of a machine or power tool. For the same reason, don't wear loose jewelry, and if you have long hair, tie it back.

Protecting your eyes

It is essential that you protect your eyes from dust and from any flying objects or particles, such as a disintegrating router cutter. Safety goggles are rated by the level of impact resistance they offer; if in doubt, use a higher resistance than seems necessary. Goggles should also offer protection to the side of your face. If you wear glasses, look for safety goggles that have plenty of ventilation, as this will prevent fogging; goggles with prescription lenses are available.

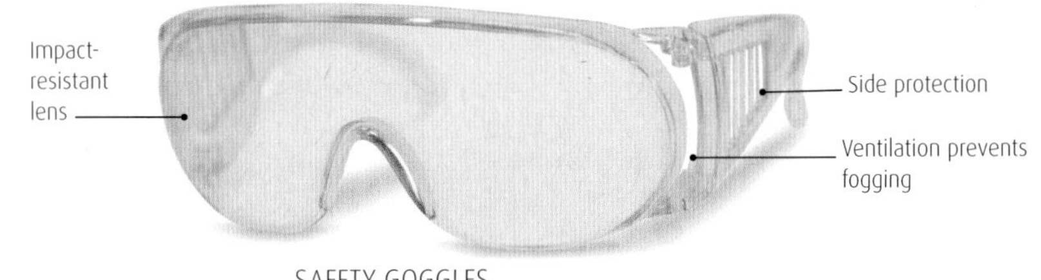

SAFETY GOGGLES

Protecting your ears

Many machines and power tools produce a significant amount of noise. As a general rule, if you cannot understand normal speech from a distance of 3ft (1m) with a machine switched on, you need to wear ear protection. You may decide to wear ear plugs, which are inserted into your ears, or headphone-style ear defenders, which sit over your head and cover the outside of your ears.

EAR DEFENDERS

Working with noisy machinery

You will need to wear ear protection when working with noisy machinery. Check that you can wear separate items of PPE in conjunction with each other. For example, you may find it uncomfortable to wear headphone-style ear defenders while wearing safety goggles (which should always be worn when operating machines and power tools), as the headphones can press against the arms of the goggles.

Protecting your lungs

Dust and noxious fumes are a major hazard when working with wood, glue, varnish, and other active agents. Dust, for example, will cause irritation to your respiratory tract (and some species of wood, such as blackbean, produce dust that can be carcinogenic)—so it is vital to protect your nose and mouth. A simple dust mask with a filter will provide adequate general-purpose protection, while full-face respirators with cartridges designed to filter specific particles are available for use with more harmful substances.

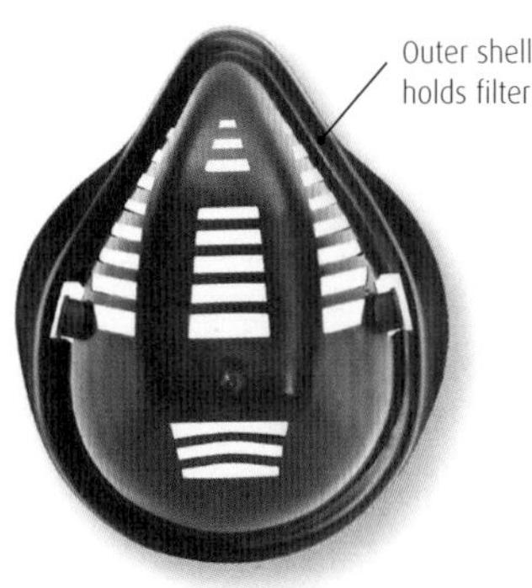

DUST MASK

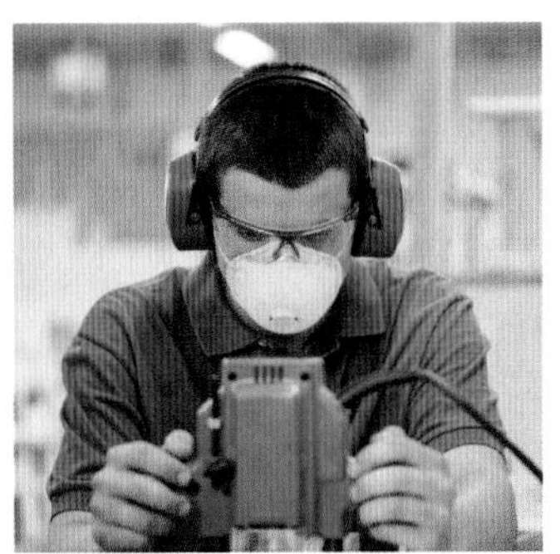

Working in a dusty environment

Ensure that your mask fits snugly to your face to prevent dust particles from passing through any gaps. You can change the fit of a mask by adjusting the elasticated straps. You may find that wearing a mask will cause safety goggles to mist up; choose a pair of goggles with ventilation slots behind the lens.

Protecting your hands

It is essential to wear tough protective gloves when changing or handling blades and cutters; these will prevent cuts and loss of grip. When handling timber, gloves will protect your hands from splinters and increase your grip when maneuvering large workpieces. However, be aware that gloves will reduce your level of control when operating machines and power tools, so should be avoided in these circumstances. Wear rubber gloves and apply barrier ointment when working with toxic finishes.

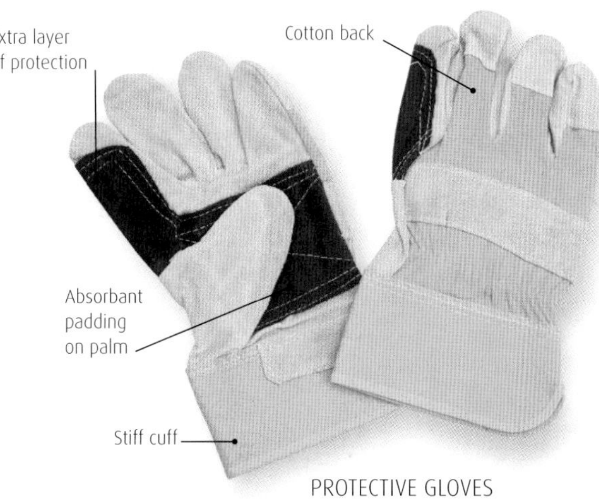

PROTECTIVE GLOVES

Protecting your feet

If a large workpiece were to slip from your grasp and fall on your feet, it could cause serious injury. Safety boots or shoes with steel toe caps will protect your toes; many boots also have steel in-soles to protect the soles of your feet should you step on a nail. Boots must be comfortable and have slip-resistant soles.

STEEL TOE-CAPPED SAFETY BOOTS

BASIC FIRST-AID KIT

Always keep a well-stocked first-aid kit in your workshop. Use an easily identifiable cabinet and place it in a conspicuous place (someone unfamiliar with the layout of your workshop may need to access it).

A basic first-aid kit should contain the following items:

- Bandages
- Butterfly bandages
- Scissors
- Tweezers
- Safety pins
- Antibiotic ointment
- Antiseptic ointment
- Iodine or similar prep pads
- Alcohol prep pads
- Gauze pads
- Medical adhesive tape
- Pain relievers
- Eye drops
- Burn medication

WORK SAFELY

Wearing the correct personal protective gear is a basic requirement—you must also follow safe working practices, seek appropriate training, and keep your tools well-maintained. Keep in mind the following safety advise as you work, and see p.17 for more information.

Work tidily and don't rush

Tripping is one of the most common causes of injury in the workshop. To reduce the risk, always work in a tidy manner, carefully stowing all tools, equipment, and workpieces; if your workshop is tidy and well-organized, you will be able to move around it more safely and freely. Plan your work schedule so that you are never tempted to rush a job or cut corners; following safety procedures correctly and thoroughly takes time.

Working with hazardous materials

You are likely to come into contact with a variety of hazardous materials while woodworking. For example, all wood dust poses a risk if inhaled or caught in the eyes, and some woods can be harmful to handle. Adhesives and finishes are also potentially harmful. You should research all potential dangers and take necessary precautions, such as wearing a dust mask, safety goggles, and protective gloves.

Working with machines and power tools

Machines and power tools can cause severe injury if used incorrectly. Always follow the manufacturer's instructions and never attempt operations beyond your experience or ability. Always disconnect the power supply before removing or handling blades or cutters. Regular maintenance will keep machines and tools safe and in good working order. For information about the safe use of specific tools, see the chart on p.17.

TRAINING CLASSES

As a woodworker, you will need to acquire a huge amount of information in order to work safely and to the best of your ability. As such, you should consider attending formal training classes—of which there are many to choose from. Your first priority should be to seek training in first aid, and the correct and safe use of machines and power tools. You may then wish to move on to training classes that focus on more specialized woodworking techniques. The advantages of attending dedicated training classes include keeping up-to-date with the latest practices and techniques, and receiving personalized advise from expert woodworkers.

TECHN

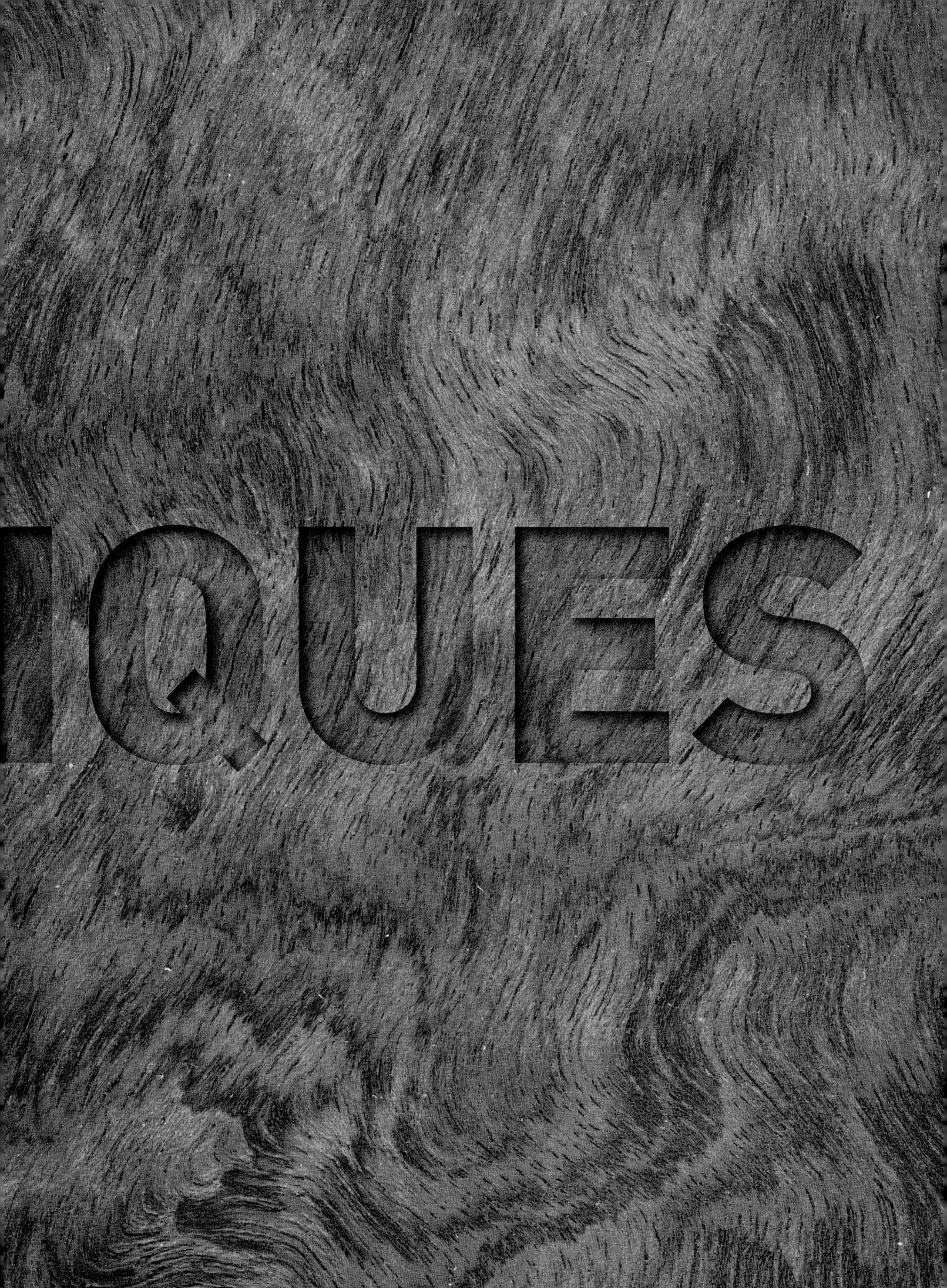
IQUES

Introduction

This section details the core woodworking techniques that, with practice, will enable you to complete all of the projects in the Projects chapter (see pp.200–379). In effect, any woodworking project is simply the sum of many different, well-executed techniques. For example, the ability to make careful measurements, establish well-placed cutting lines, make crisp cuts with a saw, assemble a joint, or create a smooth finish, is the result of practicing the techniques that you will find outlined on the following pages. So be assured that by working through these techniques you will gain all the knowledge you need to produce successful projects, even if mastering them all to produce beautifully finished pieces may seem a long way off.

BEFORE YOU BEGIN

When working on wood for the first time, you are likely to encounter various problems and difficulties. There are a few basic rules that you can bear in mind to help keep any setbacks to a minimum:

- **Read it through**—make sure you read through every step of the instructions in full before you start working on the wood. It is important to know what you are trying to achieve, otherwise you may not notice if you have done something wrong along the way.
- **Equipment**—assemble all the equipment you'll need in advance of starting a project (this is listed in the Tools and Materials panel on each project). You don't want to get halfway through and realize you haven't got a vital tool.
- **Patience**—learning to craft and shape wood can be time-consuming and at times tricky, but don't let this put you off. Patient practice is the only way to build up your skills and proficiency.
- **Off-cuts**—it is more than likely that your skills will take time to hone, so make sure that you practice on off-cuts until you feel fully confident. Mistakes on large pieces of wood can prove expensive.
- **Unfamiliar terminology**—the glossary (see pp.384–89) will explain any unfamiliar terms that you may encounter in the instructions.

Learning the techniques

Woodworking techniques are best developed by using a practical, methodical approach. This will encourage you to learn how the tools and wood come together. There is plenty of material available to help you with this. As well as using practical manuals (such as this one), there are instructional DVDs, and the internet. Ideally, you could back this up with some hands-on instruction by attending a training course or a workshop or, in a perfect world, work alongside an experienced woodworker who can show you first-hand how best to work.

Whatever combination of instructions you choose, you will only really improve by constant practice. Once you understand the anatomy of a technique, such as how a carefully maintained tool can be used to make a predictable mark or cut, then the only way to perfect that technique is to practice it repeatedly. For example, to successfully smooth a piece of wood with a hand plane, you must devote time to learning how to hold the plane in both hands, set it down on the firmly clamped piece of wood, align the sole of the plane with the workpiece, brace your shoulders and forearms, and make the cut. Repeating the process will make you fully proficient, and learning and exploring the potential of your tools and wood will improve your skills dramatically.

No matter how skilled or experienced you are with your hands, you will not achieve precise results if you do not keep your tools in good working order, so ensure that you keep them sharp and clean. For example, a blunt blade is likely to tear the wood rather than slice it. This means that you need to do extra work, such as laborious, heavy sanding, to produce a smooth cut. This can be avoided by taking the time to keep the blade sharp—it only takes a few minutes to improve the condition of a cutting edge and it really is worth doing to save time and effort later on. Even newly bought tools may still require sharpening before they are good enough to use.

As well as taking the time to learn techniques and keep your tools working properly, the last major consideration is making sure that you are properly organized and work patiently. At the start of any session, set out your tools and check that the cutting edges are keen and well honed. Work at an easy, controlled pace, frequently stopping to consult the drawings, feel the texture of the wood, check that each procedure has been carefully worked through, and re-hone the cutting edges. Eventually, performing a technique will become a pleasureable, skill-stretching adventure—your only problem will be how to stay away from your workshop.

WORKING ACCURATELY

Accurate woodworking relies on two main considerations: the position of the cutting lines you've marked and the position of your tool in relation to that line. While this may sound obvious, if your line is not exact, or your cut is a fraction over or under the line, you will end up with a sloppy joint, or a component part that is less than perfect.

To avoid this, mark out all cutting lines with the flat side of a beveled marking knife. Once you have made a crisp knife cut, and you have established which side of the cutting line will go to waste, then you can run the tool to the waste side of the cutting line in the confident knowledge that your cut cannot go wrong.

As well as this, the success of any woodworking technique is dependent on the quality of the tools that you are using. For good, accurate work, ensure that your tools are in good condition before you begin.

Alternative techniques

There is often more than one way of working to achieve the same result. For example, wood can be sawn and planed by hand, using a hand saw and plane, or by machine, using a table saw and planer-thicknesser. The same principle applies to cutting joints. This book explains both hand and machine techniques in detail so you can choose your preferred way of working.

Techniques checklist

The woodworking techniques on the following pages will provide you with the building blocks you need to make a whole range of different pieces of furniture. The table below lists each of the projects in the Projects chapter, together with the key techniques that are required to complete each one. Putting the techniques in their proper context helps make it clear how they relate to each project, and helps you choose which project to work on next.

PROJECTS AND THEIR TECHNIQUES

Project	Techniques	Project	Techniques
CHOPPING BOARD	■ Edge-to-edge joint (pp.94–95)	DEMI-LUNE TABLE	■ Wedged through mortise-and-tenon joint (pp.122-24) ■ Jigs and templates (pp.150–51)
COAT RACK	■ Basic mortise-and-tenon joint (pp.116–17)	TRINKET BOX	■ Through dovetail joint (pp.134-35)
MIRROR FRAME	■ Keyed miter joint (p.115)	COFFEE TABLE	■ Edge-to-edge joint (pp.94-95) ■ Domino joint (p.144)
WINE RACK	■ Dowel joint (pp.145–48)	TOOL BOX	■ Through dovetail joint (pp.134-35) ■ Edge-to-edge joint (pp.94-95)
HALL SHELF	■ Full housing joint (pp.106–07) ■ Jigs and templates (pp.150–51)	BEDSIDE TABLE	■ Dovetail half-lap joint (pp.102–03) ■ Basic mortise-and-tenon joint (pp.116–17) ■ Lapped dovetail joint (pp.138-39)
LAUNDRY BOX	■ Dowel joint (pp.145–48)	LINEN CHEST	■ Basic mortise-and-tenon joint (pp.116–17) ■ Edge-to-edge joint (pp.94-95)
PLATE RACK	■ Dowel joint (pp.145–48)	CHEST OF DRAWERS	■ Edge-to-edge joint (pp.94-95) ■ Domino joint (p.144) ■ Jigs and templates (pp.150–51)
SCREEN	■ T-bridle joint (pp. 128-30) ■ Basic mortise-and-tenon joint (pp.116–17)	BED	■ Basic mortise-and-tenon joint (pp.116–17)
BOOKCASE	■ Wedged through mortise-and-tenon joint (pp.122-24) ■ Jigs and templates (pp.150–51) ■ Edge-to-edge joint (pp.94–95)	GLASS-FRONTED CABINET	■ Dovetail housing joint (pp.110–11) ■ Domino joint (p.144)
BREAKFAST TABLE	■ Edge-to-edge joint (pp.94–95) ■ Haunched tenon joint (p.120)	GATELEG TABLE	■ Basic mortise-and-tenon joint (pp.116–17)
WALL CABINET	■ Shouldered and stopped housing joint (pp.108–09) ■ Comb joint (pp.132–33)	CHAIR	■ Basic mortise-and-tenon joint (pp.116–17) ■ Dowel joint (pp.145–48)
GARDEN TABLE	■ Basic mortise-and-tenon joint (pp.116–17) ■ Jigs and templates (pp.150–51)	BUFFET	■ Domino joint (p.144) ■ Cross-halving joint (pp.100–01) ■ Loose tongue-and-groove joint (pp.96–97) ■ Dovetail half-lap joint (102–03)
GARDEN BENCH	■ Basic mortise-and-tenon joint (pp.116–17) ■ Jigs and templates (pp.150–51)		

Preparing wood

Every piece of wood is unique, and when planning a project you need to be selective about which pieces you use and where. In mass-produced furniture you will often see mismatched colors, defective areas, and bland or clashing grain patterns, while handmade furniture should avoid these mistakes and instead display the strength and beauty of the wood. This section describes how to select timber and how to convert rough-sawn planks and manufactured boards into accurately sized components.

Rough-sawn planks
When planks are purchased they are often in a rough-sawn state and may be green (wet), air-dried, or kilned. Choose planks with an attractive figure and check for defects (see below).

Selecting timber

Timber varies not only in species (see pp.178–97) but also in quality. Grain or figure, color, and "defects" (see below) are the main aspects that define each piece both structurally and visually. The exception is manufactured boards, which are intentionally uniform in quality. In order to purchase suitable planks and use them efficiently, choose the species and arrangement of timber at the design and planning stage of a project (the exception to this rule is when a particular piece of wood is itself the inspiration for a design, as in some one-off creations like a table top made from a single plank or a bowl made from a burr). Check with suppliers to see what plank sizes are available. For most projects—especially table tops, solid chair seats, cabinet sides, and door panels, which are often made by gluing a number of narrow boards edge-to-edge—the planks should be straight, flat, and match up to each other (color and grain). Sapwood (p.178) should be avoided in handmade furniture, so ensure the planks are sufficiently wide that you can exclude it altogether. Choose quarter-sawn planks (p.178) for projects that require the stability (wide planks that stay flat) or decorative figure (ray flecks or ribbon effects, for example) offered by this method of conversion.

WOOD DEFECTS

Defective wood can be ugly and, worse still, it may fail structurally. Common imperfections in boards are knots, worm holes, and stains or rot caused by fungi. All knots weaken the timber, especially "dead" knots, where a branch has died and become encased; these often fall out when the plank is dried or planed, leaving a hole. Softwood that has no dead knots is called "clear." Different parts of the world use different grading terms for hardwoods, but always buy the best grade possible. Grain that runs diagonally across the face of the board is a defect due to poor conversion and will limit its use (grain that runs diagonally across the thickness may be unusable). An extremely warped plank may be due to poor seasoning or storage and will only be useful for very small components.

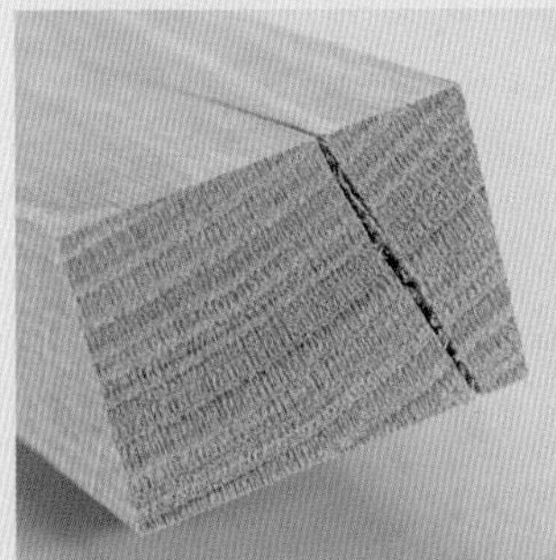

Splits
Splits are sometimes due to poor seasoning. Here, the end of a board has been allowed to dry too quickly.

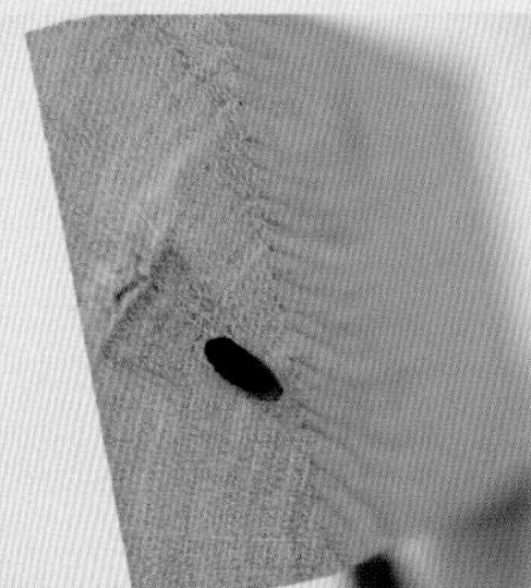

Worm holes
Insects such as ants, beetles, and termites leave obvious signs of where they have attacked the wood.

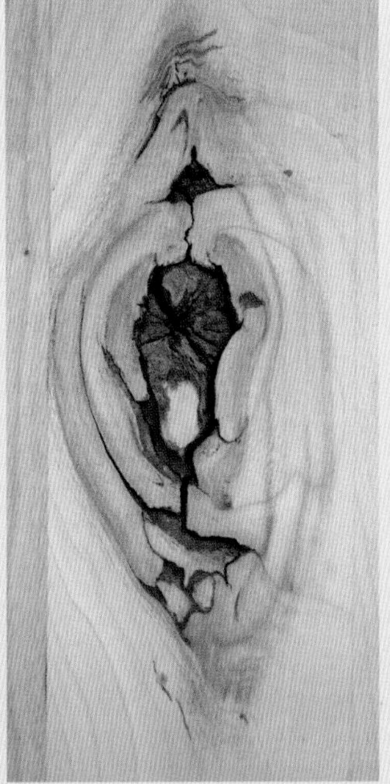

Knots
Knots have variable grain direction so are difficult to work. Dead knots (pictured) may result in cavities.

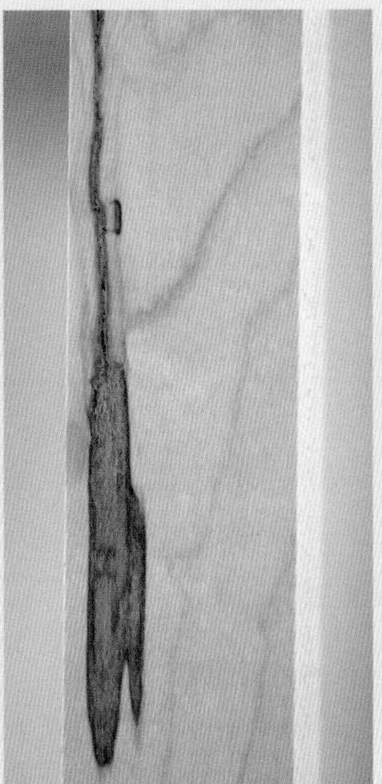

Scars
These marks, which are ingrown bark, may run deep and render the timber unusable.

Rough sizing

Work out the most efficient way to cut the components needed from the rough-sawn boards that are available. The board must be flat and about ¼in (6mm) thicker than the finished thickness. So, for example, choose 1in (25mm) board for a ¾in (19mm) component. The extra ¼in (6mm) will be removed during planing and thicknessing. Allow additional length for each component (2in/50mm is sufficient) and additional width (for long components, allow 1½in/ 40mm extra, while for smaller components, ½in/12mm is enough). Large components that take up a whole board are easy to mark out as there are no choices to make regarding placement. Mark out the length of these with a tape measure, straight edge, and carpenter's pencil, avoiding defects and sapwood. Mid-size components (over 16in/ 400mm long) need careful placement and, where possible, should be cut from the same plank as shorter components to make use of the whole length. Small components (under 16in/ 400mm long) should not be rough sized at this stage but rather marked out as groups of components that are planed first and only cut later. Keep in mind that some components should have matching grain. As a general rule when cutting short pieces, cross-cut first and rip second.

ROUGH SIZING BY HAND

1 **Use a tape measure** and carpenter's pencil to mark the rough sizes of a component or group of components onto the rough-sawn board. Allow 2in (50mm) extra length and ½in–1½in (12–40mm) extra width (see above).

2 **Support the board** on trestles and saw along the marked lines with a panel saw. If the plank is to be cut across, dividing it into two or more pieces, then make these cuts first; the smaller pieces are more manageable. A jigsaw or hand-held circular saw may also be used.

ROUGH SIZING BY MACHINE

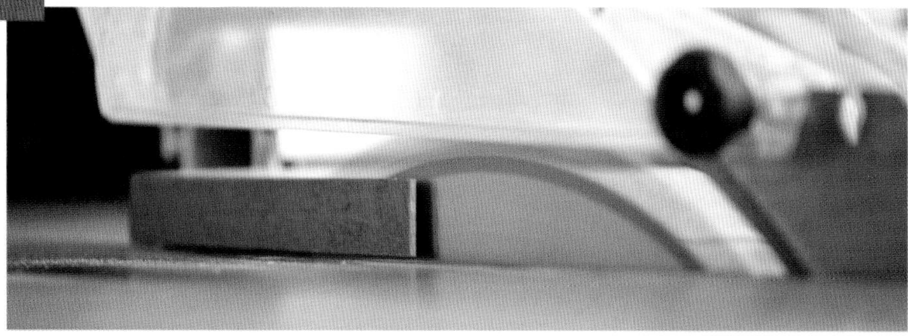

1 **Use the table saw** to cut off the rough ends of boards, especially those that are painted or may have grit embedded in the end grain. If the board is log-sawn and therefore has two waney (naturally wavy) edges, at least one edge will need to be sawn off straight so that the straight edge can be used against the fences of the table saw. The quickest way is to use a hand-guided bandsaw (see p.56) or jigsaw.

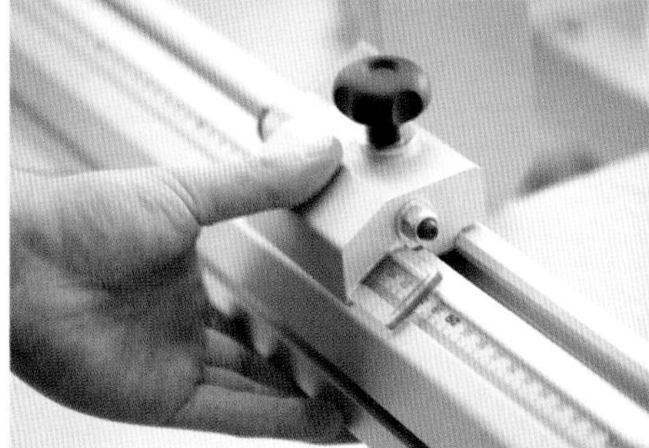

2 **To cut the boards** to rough length using the table saw, first mark where to cut on the piece, allowing 2in (50mm) extra, then set the cross-cut fence end-stop to the desired length.

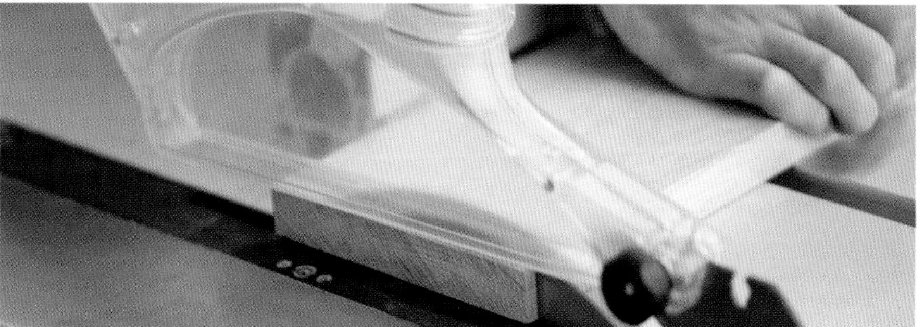

3 **Hold the piece** against the fence and end-stop and carefully make the cut. To make cuts along the grain, set the rip-fence scale to the desired width (or set with a tape measure) and make the cut.

For further information on cross-cutting and ripping with a table saw and on how to use a table saw safely, see pp.54–55.

Planing a face and edge

The techniques on the following pages describe the method by which roughly sized components are planed to make a rectangular-section component with flat and smooth sides. The piece is first planed flat on one face (across the width) and then planed flat on an adjacent surface (the edge), ensuring it is 90 degrees to the face. The remaining rough face and edge are then planed smooth and parallel with the first face and edge. Planing by hand may not be necessary if you have machines to do the work for you (see p.89 for the machine method), but nevertheless it is a good planing excercise.

SQUARING-UP

When planing, the "face side" is the first and widest surface to be planed flat. It is often also selected as the most attractive surface that will be most visible. After planing, it is marked with a loop. The second, adjacent surface is called the "face edge" and is planed at 90 degrees ("squared up") to the face side and marked with a V-shaped arrowhead.

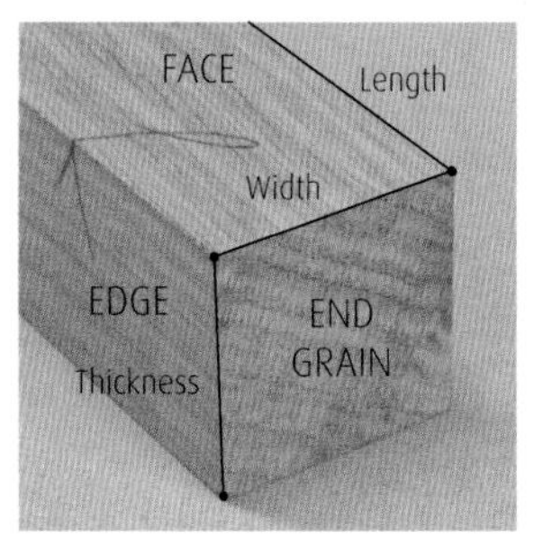

Creating a face and edge by hand

Planing the first and widest surface by hand is usually performed with a no. 5½ plane (also called a "jack" plane, see p.23), which has a sole about 15in (380mm) long. For boards wider than 6in (150mm), consider using a no. 7 plane (also called a "jointer" or "try" plane) with a sole about 24in (600mm) long, as this will produce a flatter surface. The plane should be set to a coarse cut and used at a slight angle to the direction in which it is pushed (a shearing angle). If the board is greater than 6in (150mm) wide, work the plane at an angle to the grain and then follow up with an opposing angle. This levels the board across the width, after which you can proceed to planing the edge. In all cases, ensure that you are working the plane in the direction that lays the grain to produce a smooth surface. If the grain tears, try working from the opposite end. Keep the pressure on the front of the plane as you begin a stroke, then transfer the pressure to the back of the plane as you complete the stroke. This avoids rounding over at the ends.

CREATING A FACE SIDE

1 **Choose the face side**, then assess where the high points are and which direction to plane in order to lay the grain.

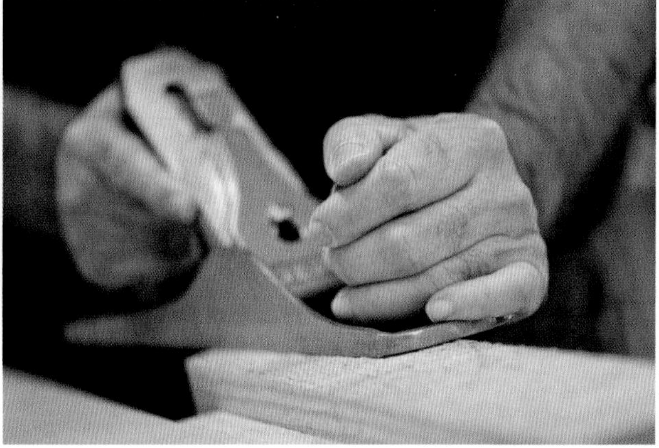

2 **Place the wood** in the vise and start planing with a bench plane. Concentrate on the obvious high points first and work at a slight angle to the grain. Continue planing until the rough sawn surface and the "shadows" of the saw have been removed and the surface is clean, flat, and smooth.

WINDING STICKS

A winding stick consists of two pieces of light and dark wood glued together to form a straight stick about 24in (600mm) long. Used in pairs and placed at each end of a piece of wood, they give a visual indication of flatness or of winding ("wind"), which is a twist along the length. All points on a flat surface are in the same plane but a twisted surface will have points in different planes. Because the sticks are longer than the width of the board they extend and exaggerate any twist, making it easier to spot.

Far winding stick is placed the other way up to the near stick, with the dark wood on top

STICKS PLACED AT EITHER END

Brown wood of far stick is visible above the pale wood of the near stick, meaning the surface is not flat

WINDING STICKS NOT PARALLEL

3 **Use winding sticks** to check if the surface is flat and that you are planing square. Place a stick at each end of the face side of the piece of wood. Sight across the sticks with your eyes at the level of the closest stick and compare their position. If they are exactly parallel, then the surface is flat.

4 **A long, straight edge** such as a metal ruler turned on its side is used to assess the flatness of the face side from end to end in various positions, both straight and diagonally. Sighting along the ruler with your eyes at its level will help you to spot any defects.

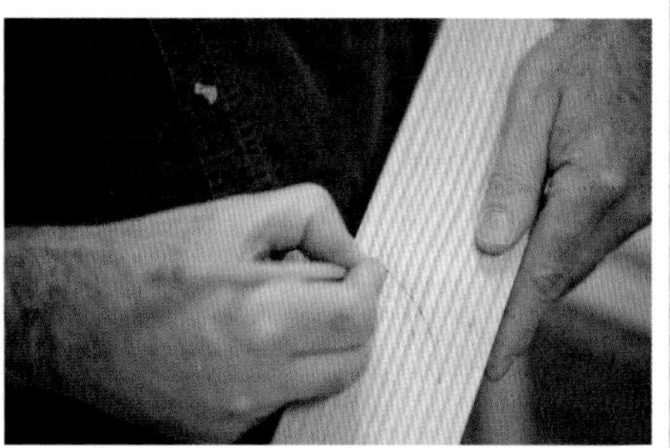

5 **Complete the face side**, planing with the no. 5½ plane set for a fine cut, until the surface is perfectly flat and smooth. Annotate it with a standard face-side mark that points to what will be the face edge.

CREATING THE FACE EDGE

1 **Plane the face edge** flat and square (at 90 degrees) to the face side.

2 **Check the squareness** with a carpenter's or combination square.

3 **Mark any locations** that are out of square and require further planing.

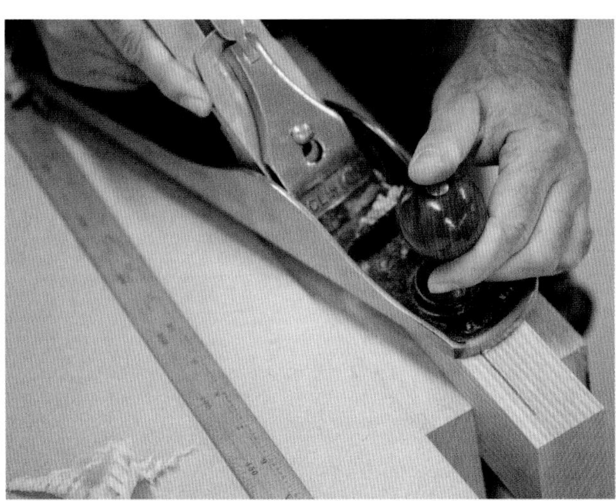

4 **Plane the face edge** again, concentrating on the marked locations. Continue planing until all of the pencil marks have been removed.

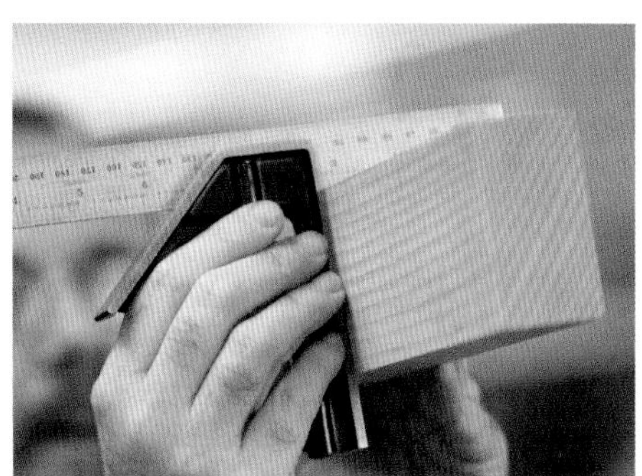

5 **Check the squareness again**. Holding the piece of wood at eye level against the light helps to reveal any discrepancies.

6 **Use a metal ruler to check** the end-to-end flatness in the same way as for the face side (see Step 4). If the face edge is a similar width to the face side, check for twisting using the winding sticks (see opposite).

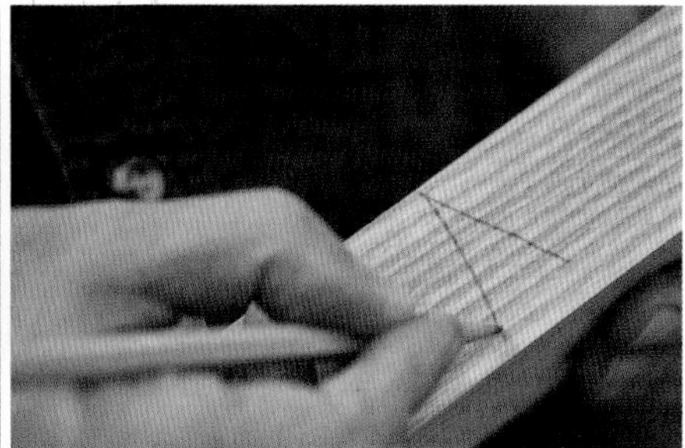

7 **When the face edge is flat** and smooth, use a pencil to annotate it with the standard face-edge mark, pointing to the face-side mark.

MARKING THE THICKNESS

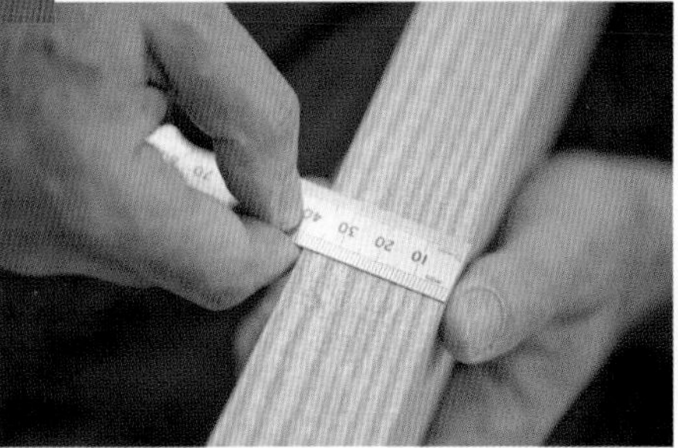

1 **Having prepared the face side** and the face edge, all subsequent measurements should be taken from these surfaces.

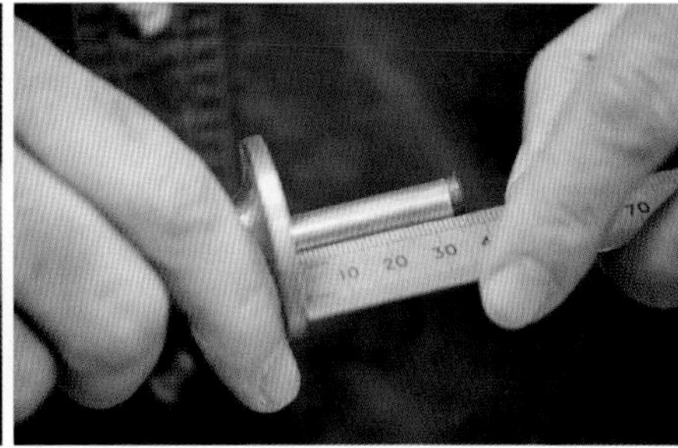

2 **Set the marking gauge** to the desired thickness of the face edge measured with a ruler in Step 1.

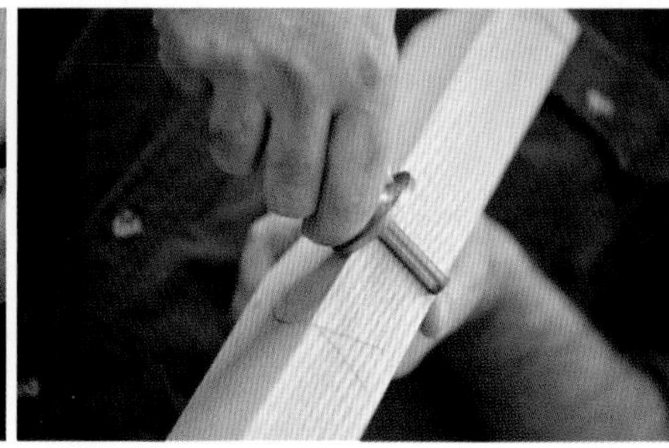

3 **Place the marking gauge** against the face side and score the thickness along the face edge.

4 **Use the marking gauge** to score the thickness along the other edge and both ends of the piece. A standard wooden marking gauge with a pin (see p.37) can be used but this often fails to mark a clean line on the end grain.

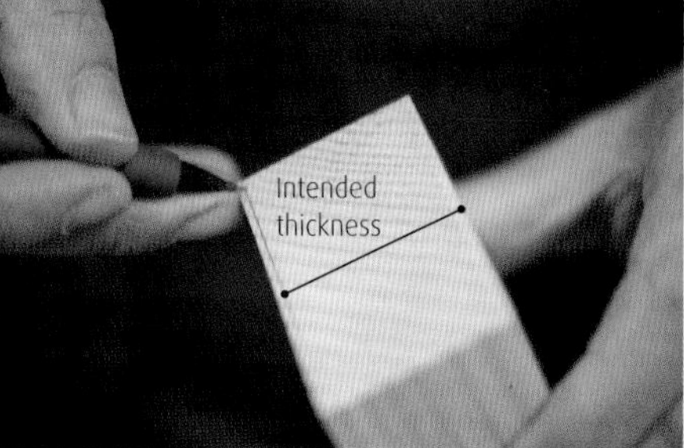

5 **If necessary**, make the line easier to see by drawing into the scored line with a fine pencil.

CUTTING THE THICKNESS

1 **Ascertain how much material** needs to be removed to get down to the desired thickness. If ¼in (6mm) or more, consider sawing off the bulk of the waste. If less than ¼in (6mm), remove the excess material from the non-face side with a plane.

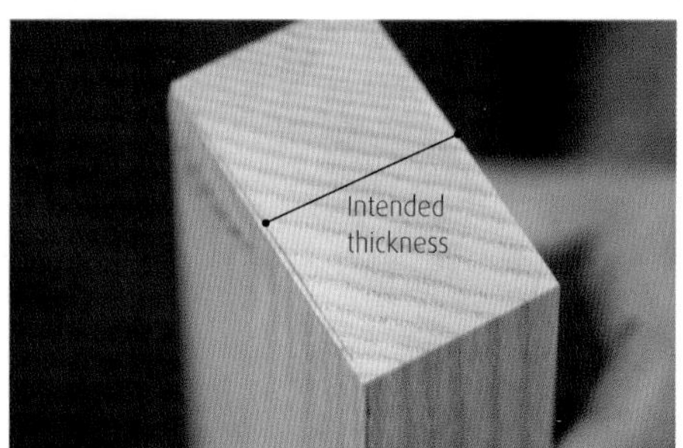

2 **During planing**, routinely check the relative position of the scored line all around the piece.

3 **Continue planing** until you have reached the scored line denoting the thickness and the surface is smooth. This non-face surface is now square to the face edge.

MARKING AND CUTTING THE WIDTH

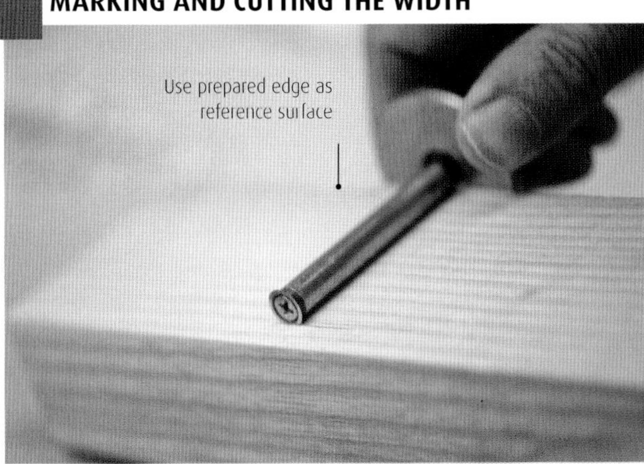

1 **Mark the desired width** on the face side with the marking gauge. Mark both sides of the wood. Small amounts (less than ¼in/6mm) can be planed. Larger reductions need to be sawn—either by hand (using a rip saw) or, more commonly, with a band saw.

2 **Cut the width** with a band saw using a fence, making a test cut before continuing. Always "undercut" to allow for hand-finishing by plane to the exact width.

3 **Use the no. 5½ plane** to remove the excess material on the remaining rough edge. As you work, check the relative position of the scored line all around. Continue until you have reached the line and achieved a smooth, flat surface.

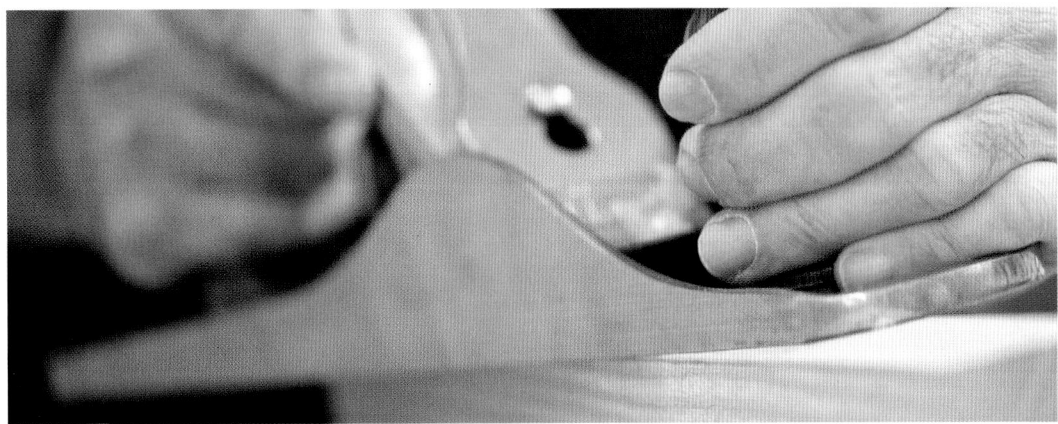

Facing and edging by machine

This procedure describes planing the face side (the widest and often best side) and the face edge (an edge at 90 degrees and adjacent to the face side) flat and smooth. The purpose of this is to establish two good flat surfaces that are perfectly square to each other, which can be used to work from when "thicknessing" (thicknessing creates the two remaining surfaces that establish the thickness and width of the component). Never machine-plane stock that is less than 18in (450mm) in length as the rollers will not grip it properly. The planer is an extremely dangerous machine if used incorrectly. See p.17 and pp.58–59 for information on how to use the planer safely, and always ensure follow the manufacturer's guidelines.

USING A PLANER

1 **Plane off** only the minimum amount of the rough-sawn face side to achieve a flat, smooth, and clean surface. Set the cutters to take off no more than 1⁄24in (1.5mm) of wood at a time.

2 **Check the fence** is set to 90 degrees using a square. Press the face side of the piece against the fence and plane the face edge.

3 **Use a square to check** the finished planed edge is 90 degrees to the face. If it is not, the fence may be out of square or you may not be holding the wood firmly against the fence.

USING A THICKNESSER

1 **Use a caliper** to find and measure the thickest part of the piece. Bear in mind a warped plank may be substantially thicker in the central area. Adjust the thicknesser to the caliper measurement minus 1⁄32in (1mm).

2 **Pass the wood** through the thicknesser, face-side down in the direction that lays the grain. If the machine motor sound indicates that it is struggling quickly (but safely), release the bed lock (if it has one) and wind down the bed. Avoid allowing the motor to grind to a halt. Reset the machine to a greater thickness and try again. Continue, reducing the thickness by 1⁄32in (1mm) increments or less for hardwoods and 1⁄16in (2mm) or less for softwoods until the desired thickness is achieved.

3 **Measure the width** with a caliper. If the piece needs reducing by more than 3⁄8in (10mm) to achieve the desired width, saw off the bulk of the waste first.

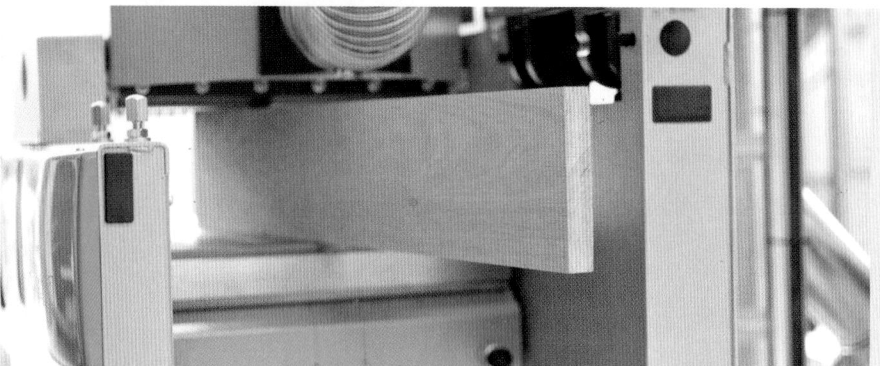

4 **Set the thicknesser** to the desired reduction and pass the wood through the machine face-edge down in the direction that lays the grain. Continue reducing the width by small increments (as in Step 2) until the desired width is reached.

Cutting to final size

When components have been planed square to the correct thickness and width, they can be cut to the precise finished length on a table saw (or radial arm saw, see p.56). Check on an offcut that the machine is producing precise 90-degree cross-cuts then make the necessary adjustments before proceeding. On a table saw, adjust the height of the blade to give the best results (see below). If the component first requires cutting along the grain to reduce its width, this procedure can be carried out on the table saw using a short-rip fence (see p.55).

CROSS-CUTTING TO FINAL SIZE USING A TABLE SAW

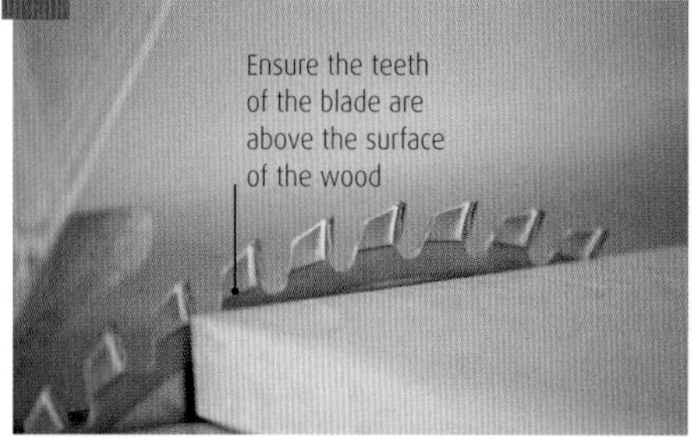

1 **For the best results**, adjust the blade height so that the teeth are about 3⁄8in (10mm) above the surface of the board or the base of the uppermost tooth is just above the surface of the wood. This will result in a cleaner cut.

2 **Cut off the rough end** of the piece. Hold the wood against the cross-cut fence and cut off the minimum amount to leave a clean, square end.

3 **Set the cross-cut end-stop scale** for cutting the piece to the desired length, then make the cut. Use the same setting for cutting identical length components.

Cutting sheet materials

It is often necessary to cut a 96in x 48in (2440mm x 1220mm) sheet of plywood or MDF into smaller pieces. Many hobby-rated table saws cannot accommodate this size of sheet, in which case one of the methods illustrated below can be used. If a large table saw can be used, ask for help to maneuver the board. To cut the piece accurately, you must ensure that there is adequate support for the board as you saw by using trestles, extending supports, or roller stands, and the person helping you, if possible. Manufactured boards are "inert" and therefore will not trap the table saw blade—this means that it is safe to use the full extent of the rip fence when "rip" sawing. Vertical panel saws are the ultimate solution for cutting up sheets, but they are not usually found in small workshops.

Breakout (splintering) is often a problem with plywood or veneered boards, especially when cutting across the grain. An effective technique to obtain the best results is to cut 1⁄32–1⁄8in (1–3mm) short of the finished line with the saw (the amount depends on the extent of the breakout) and then cut back to the finished size using a router and guide (see p.47).

CUTTING SHEETS BY HAND USING A PANEL SAW

1 **Support the board on trestles**. Measure and mark the cut-line with a square or straight edge and pencil. Double check the measurements.

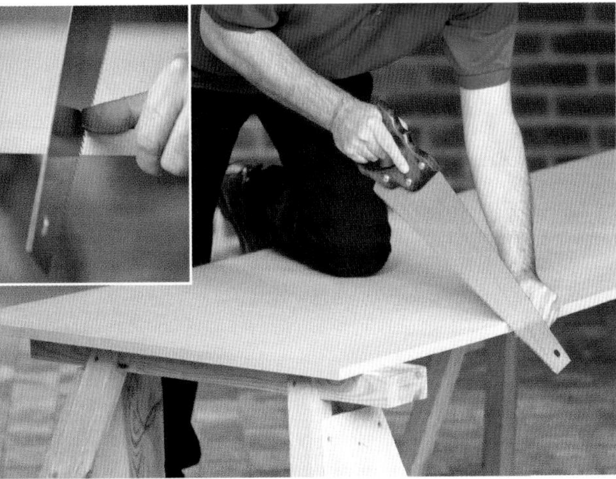

2 **Position yourself over** the line of cut, using your body weight to hold the board still. Use your thumb to guide the first few carefully aligned strokes to the waste side of the line (inset), and once the start of the cut is established, move your thumb away and continue sawing.

CUTTING SHEETS BY CIRCULAR SAW

1 **Mark the position** of the cut in pencil as described in Step 1 above. Ensure the board is fully supported either side of the cut-line (otherwise, when you complete the cut, the waste will fall down or swing up, or you could lose your balance, resulting in an accident).

2 **Mark the position** of a fence on the stock (non-waste) side of the cutting line to align the saw blade with the marked cutting line.

3 **Clamp a fence** in position, then use a square to ensure that the fence is square to the cutting line.

4 **Saw through the wood** with the circular saw, placing the edge of the saw up against the fence and using your weight to steady the board on the supporting trestles as you cut.

Choosing a joint

Joints are an integral part of woodwork—they literally hold a piece together—so the joint you choose and where it fits in the piece are both critical to the strength and longevity of the overall construction. Various factors should be taken into account when selecting a joint, not least of which is the fact that wood is a natural material and not an inert, man-made substance. The joint should be selected according to the type of wood, the function and aesthetics of the item, and the role that the joint will play within it.

JOINT TERMS

Woodworkers describe the shapes created when cutting joints using the terminology shown here. Other terms are "groove" (a narrow housing), "tongue" (created by two rebates), and "dovetails" and "pins" (parts of an interlocking "dovetail" joint employing tapered shapes).

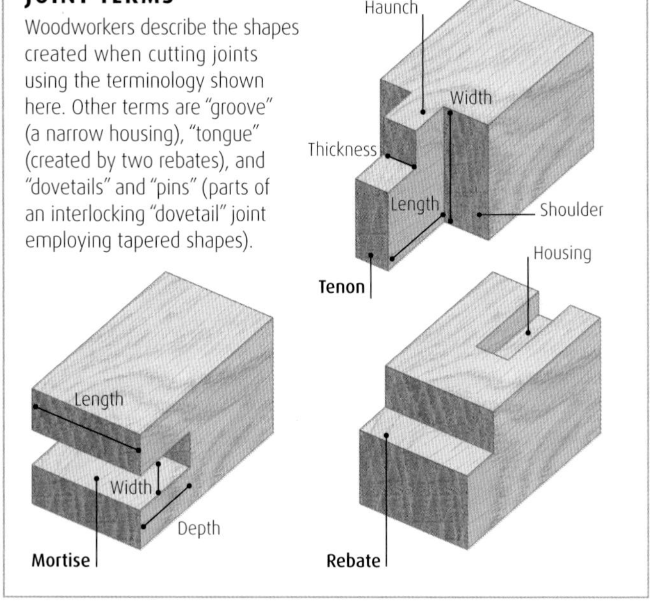

Joint stresses

When selecting a joint, bear in mind that various stresses and strains will affect it throughout the life of the piece. There are four main types of joint stress—tension, shear, racking (also known as bending), and compression—each of which affect the joint in a different way.

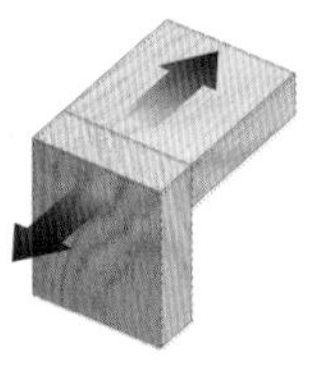

Result

Tension

Occurring when the forces on a joint combine to pull it apart, tension is commonly found on a drawer front when pulling the drawer open. The physical force applied to the joint is increased by the weight of the drawer contents, increasing the tension. Dovetails, which have an inherent mechanical strength, are used in drawer fronts to counteract the tension.

Result

Racking

Common in chairs, tables, frames, or carcasses that are unsupported, racking (or bending) can be resisted in a number of ways. A wedged through-tenon or twin tenon can be used, or another shoulder can be added to a stub tenon. Gluing in a carcass back reduces racking potential, while a deeper rail or additional stretcher rail can reinforce a table or chair.

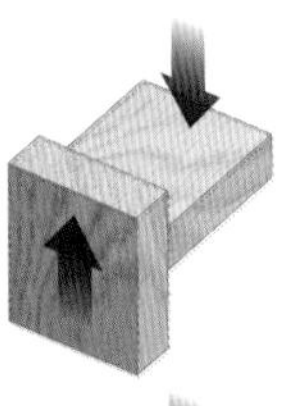

Result

Shear

Occurring when pressure is applied to a joint line, shear can cause the joint to fail. For example, a scarf joint or butt miter, which rely on glue to hold them together, could shear due to the lack of mechanical lock. Modern glues are very strong but it is always good practice to reinforce a joint by pegging or using a loose tongue, or even screwing.

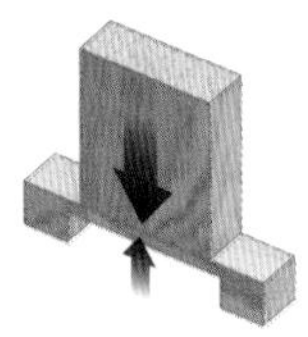

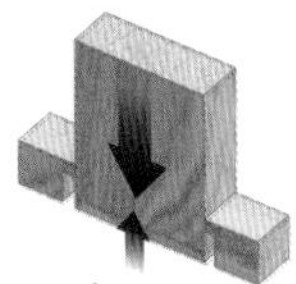

Result

Compression

Occurring when a joint is subject to down-force, compression is counteracted by choosing a joint that will resist load. The weight of a sideboard carcass on a mortise-and-tenoned plinth is a good example of this kind of stress, so in addition to ensuring that the joints and rails are deep enough, inserting glue blocks into the corners can also help.

JOINTS AND THEIR USES

Joint name	Strengths	Weaknesses	Uses
Edge-to-edge joint	Modern glue makes the joint stronger than the wood itself.	On thick sections, it may need reinforcing with a tongue.	All flat carcass sections, panels, and table tops.
Loose tongue-and-groove joint or spline	Makes locating boards easier and increases gluing area.	The joints can be weak if the tongue and grooves are too wide.	Constructing a carcass and panels.
Fixed tongue-and-groove joint	Increased gluing area increases strength; very versatile.	Time-consuming to make and can be weak if joints are too big.	Decorative paneling for the back of pieces such as bookcases; floorboards.
Cross-halving joint	Stronger than corner halving, and with a good resistance to racking.	No real weakness, but joints need careful cutting to look good.	Often used in stretcher rails and lattice frames.

Joint name	Strengths	Weaknesses	Uses and examples
Dovetail half-lap joint	Capable of resisting pull-out and sideways racking.	No great weakness, this is the strongest of the lapped joints.	Any type of framing, carcass pieces, and rails for drawers.
Corner halving joint	A simple and quick joint to make.	Relies on glue only and can be subject to racking.	Basic frames.
Scarf joint	Used in carpentry for lengthening mostly decorative pieces.	Not useful for making furniture; cannot take much strain.	Used to extend dado rails, architraves, and skirting boards; also used in some guitars.
Full housing joint	A simple joint that has no strength in tension, but good load capability.	Needs careful cutting or the joints can look shoddy.	Used in bookcases and chests of drawers.
Shouldered housing joint	Very strong and If used with a shoulder looks very neat.	No mechanical resistance against tension and little against racking.	Drawer divisions or dividers in boxes, desks, and carcasses.
Dovetail housing joint	Strong, resists racking, and does not suffer from pull-out.	No weaknesses. Requires careful work to achieve a tight fit.	Bookshelves, carver chairs, bed frames, or for joining a stiffening rail to any frame.
Butt-miter joint	Quick to make and looks attractive.	No very strong, even when glued up.	Picture frames and coffee table tops, used a lot in veneered work.
Mitered half-lap joint	An attractive joint, with a good gluing area.	No strength until glued.	Frames and panels, most useful for tops.
Loose-tongue miter joint	Easy to adapt for various situations and very strong.	Has none of the weaknesses of the butt joint.	Attractive and can be used in any frame construction.
Keyed miter joint	This is a strong and attractive joint.	No mechanical resistance against tension unless keys at opposing angles.	Picture frames and boxes.
Mortise-and-tenon joint	Good against racking if used with top and bottom shoulders.	Only weak if the tenon is not made thick enough.	The staple joint of furniture making, used almost any construction.
Haunched tenon joint	The haunch increases the gluing area, making the joint stronger.	The haunch remains visible and is not always attractive.	Good for frame and panel work where the groove runs all the way through
Secret haunched tenon joint	Extra gluing area, but haunch remains hidden.	The joint can be fragile if not cut correctly.	Classy joint often used for front chair legs.
Wedged through mortise-and-tenon	Extremely strong, this joint cannot be withdrawn.	No weaknesses. Requires careful work to achieve an attractive result.	Chairs, chests of drawers, or any carcass piece that needs extra support.
Knock-down tenon joint	Joint easy to disassemble or knock-down.	The end of the tenon can split if the piece is subjected to racking.	Large pieces of furniture, such as bookcases and beds.
Draw-bore tenon	A strong joint that does not require any glue.	The quality of modern glues means this joint is no longer used as often.	Decorative features; lends a traditional feel to furniture.
T-bridle joint	Very strong joint that is resistant to racking.	Requires great accuracy, especially when used in curved tables.	Used in the middle of rails.
Corner bridle joint	Increased gluing areas, particularly if used in multiples.	Like an open topped mortise, not very strong until glued up.	Sometimes used double or even triple on chairs very strong joint used in this way.
Comb joint	Its large gluing surface means that, once glued, it is very strong.	Little mechanical strength.	Boxes and carcass pieces.
Through dovetail joint	One the strongest woodwork joints there is, it resists load well.	No weaknesses.Requires careful work to achieve an attractive result.	Used decoratively in boxes and carcass pieces.
Lapped dovetail joint	Resists tension.	No weaknesses. Requires careful work to avoid breaking the laps.	Drawer fronts.
Floating tenon joint	A strong joint that is useful in many situations and quick to make.	It is made of two mortises and can only be used in certain areas.	A good choice for a piece that uses small tenons.
Biscuits	Very quick to make for a huge variety of joints; can be used in most situations.	No real mechanical strength until the joint is glued.	Used for attaching frames to carcasses, making carcasses, and mitered frames.
Dominos	A version of the loose tenon a piece which is quick and easy to make.	Can only be used where there is room for a mortise in both sections.	Can be used just about anywhere there is a tenon even for chair making.
Dowels	A quick method of construction—very easy to use in the home workshop.	Many areas used with this joint are end grain, and harder to glue.	Can be used in most carcass work in multiples and as a mortise and tenon.
Joint with pocket-screw jig	Very useful if space for joints is limited.	Tension and racking will eventually pull the screws loose.	Kitchen-cabinet carcass work.

Edge-to-edge joint

The edge-to-edge joint—also known as the butt joint—is the most basic joint in woodworking, and it is also one of the most important. Without it, almost nothing could be made, since it allows individual boards to be joined together to create pieces wider than the width of wood available straight from a tree. Wide boards are commonly used for furniture elements such as table tops, or the carcass sides of large pieces of furniture, such as sideboards or chests of drawers. In addition, the frequency of wood defects, such as shakes and knots (see p.84), mean that it is rare to find a single board that is totally clean. It is therefore often necessary to join pieces in order to achieve a defect-free finish. The edge-to-edge joint can also be used decoratively—for example, for joining figured panels in frame-and-panel carcass work, doors, and the sides of furniture pieces. Due to the strength of modern glues, panels joined in this way are strong enough for most of these applications, especially since they are usually connected to the rest of a carcass with other joints, which add to the overall strength of the piece.

PARTS OF THE JOINT

The individual boards that make up the edge-to-edge joint must be perfectly square and true. To minimize warping, lay the boards so that the grain lies in alternate directions. Longer joints should have a slight hollow of approximately 1/16in (0.5mm) in the middle, which creates a sprung tension at the ends that prevents any shrinkage from pulling the joint apart.

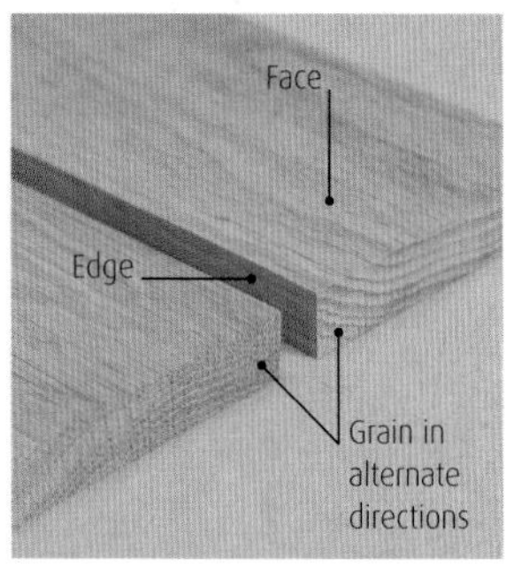

Variations of the edge-to-edge joint

There are several joints that are related to the edge-to-edge joint, such as the loose tongue-and-groove joint (pp.96–97) and the fixed tongue-and groove joint (pp.98–99), as well as joints formed by biscuit jointers (pp.142–43) and domino jointers (pp.144–45). These methods incorporate additional features to improve the accuracy with which the pieces are joined, and also add to the strength of the joint.

TOOLS AND MATERIALS

- Bench plane
- Pencil
- Sash clamps
- Masking tape
- Wood glue and brush
- Rubber mallet

PREPARING THE JOINT

1 **Place the first piece of wood** in a vise with the edge to be joined uppermost, then tighten the vise.

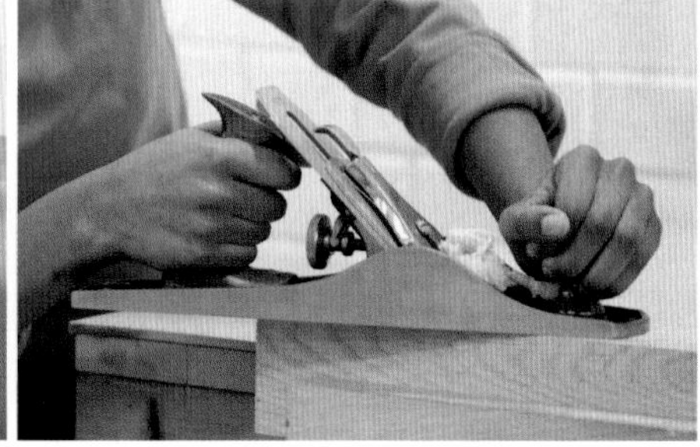

2 **Plane along the edge** with a bench plane to create a flat surface for the joint. Repeat Steps 1–2 for the second piece of wood.

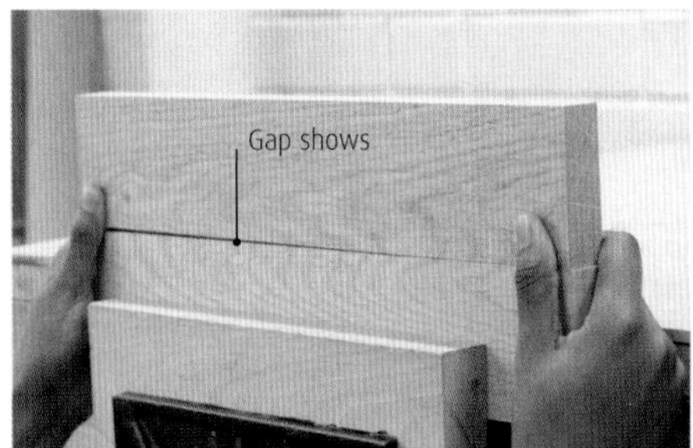

3 **Lay the joining edges** on top of each other to check for gaps, which reveal an area that needs to be planed again.

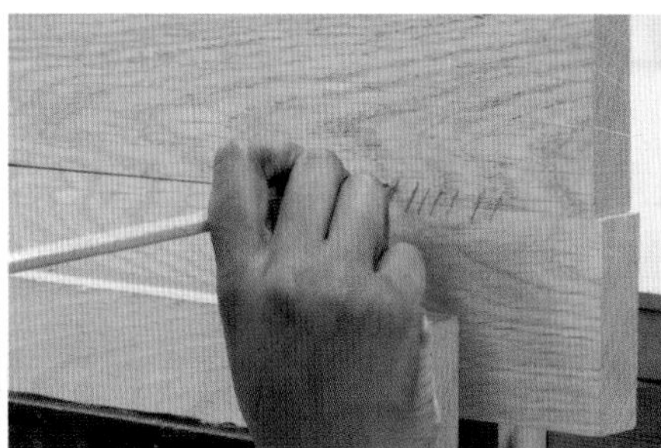

4 **Use a pencil** to mark any excess that needs to be planed further to level off the joining edges.

5 **Plane the marked area** with a bench plane, removing a little at a time. Ensure you check the edge against the other piece to avoid removing too much material.

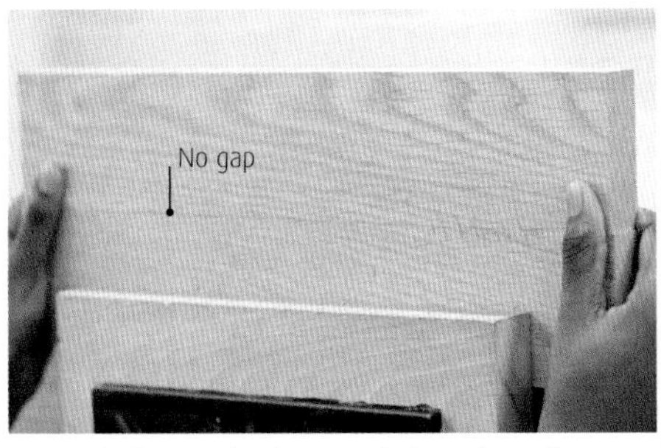

6 **Continue planing** until the edges fit together closely with no gaps between the two pieces of wood.

7 **Mark the exact position** of the pieces in relation to each other when joined, by drawing a V-mark in pencil.

ASSEMBLING THE JOINT

1 **Set up the clamps** before gluing the joint. Insert the two pieces of wood and adjust the sash clamps to the correct width.

2 **Protect the wood** from staining by sticking masking tape to the bars of the clamps that will be in contact with the wood.

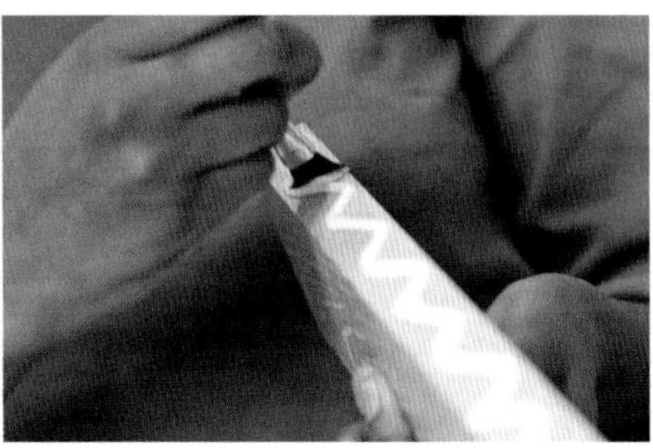

3 **Apply wood glue** to one surface of the joint, spreading it evenly along the full length of the edge with a brush.

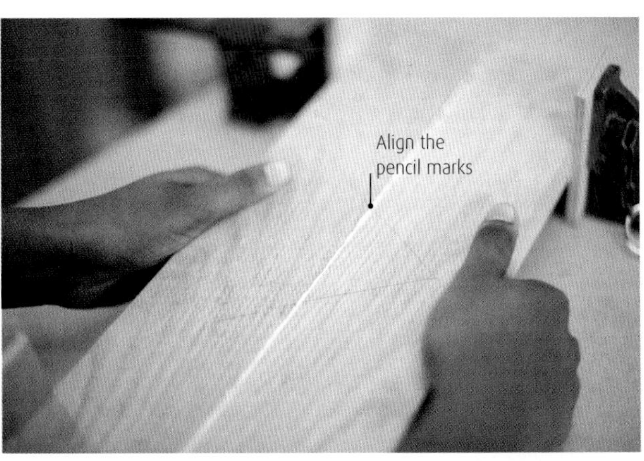

4 **Place the pieces** together with the V-mark aligned. Clamp the two pieces in position.

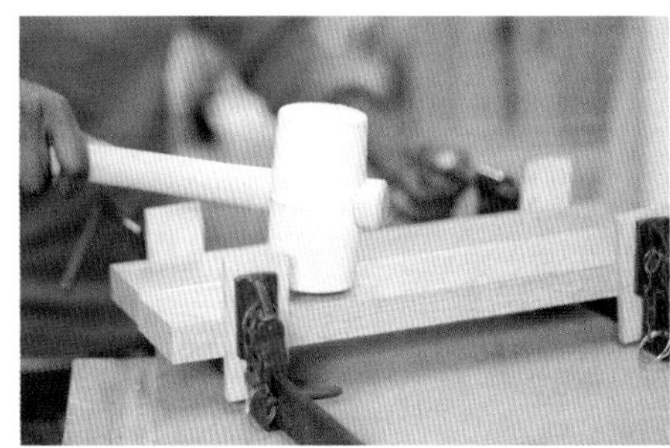

5 **Gently tap along the join** with a rubber mallet to ensure that the edges are flush with each other.

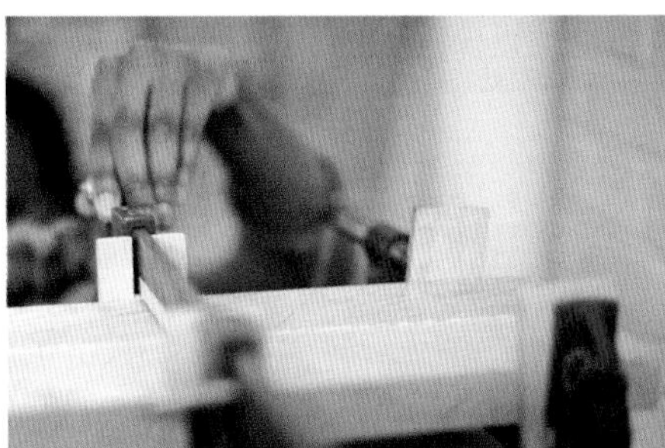

6 **Tighten the sash clamps**, being careful to check that the two pieces remain perfectly aligned with each other.

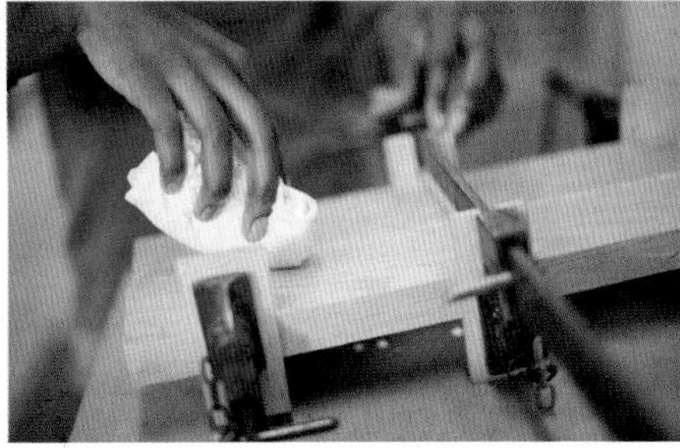

7 **Wipe away any excess glue** with a rag and leave to dry for several hours or, ideally, overnight.

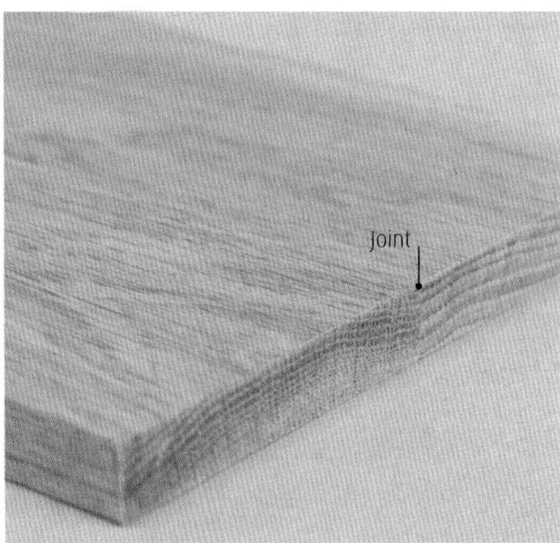

THE FINISHED JOINT

Loose tongue-and-groove joint

The loose tongue-and-groove joint has many uses in furniture-making. Although termed "loose," the tongue is actually glued into place in the grooves of the two connecting boards. It can be used in either a single-tongue form (described here) to join standard-width boards, or in a double-tongue assembly to join thicker boards—two grooves are cut in the edge of each piece, which allows two tongues to be used. When a contrasting wood is used for the tongue, it can form a decorative detail in the edge of the two boards. A similar effect can be achieved by cutting the tongue shorter than the full length of the boards, and inserting a contrasting piece of wood into the end of the grooves. The loose tongue-and-groove is a modern variant of the fixed tongue-and-groove (p.98).

PARTS OF THE JOINT

The joint is formed by cutting a groove in the each of the joining edges of the two pieces. A separate tongue of wood is inserted in the grooves and glued in place to hold the pieces together. Plywood is the usual material for the tongue, and since it is supplied in a standard thickness, the width of the grooves will always be the same, simplifying the cutting process.

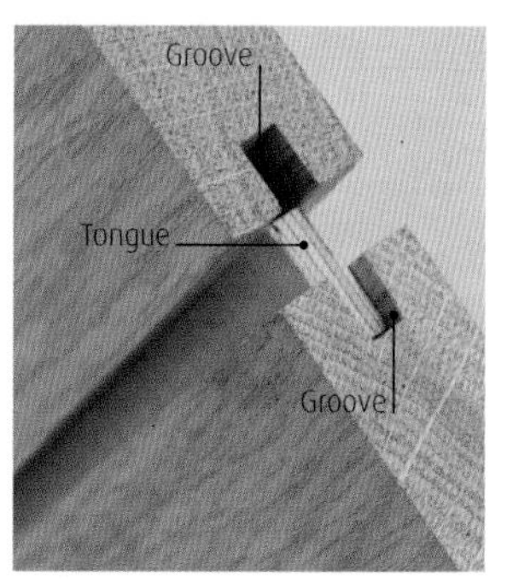

Getting it right

When marking up a loose tongue-and-groove joint, it is essential to achieve the right ratio between the thickness of the tongue and the thickness of the board. If the tongue is too thick, the grooves will take up too much of the width of the board, which will weaken the joint. There is no firm rule, but a general guideline is that the tongue needs to be less than a third of the thickness of the board.

The most important consideration when using this joint is the alignment of the boards, rather than the overall strength, which is provided by strong, modern glues. A common problem when gluing a large side panel or table top is the number of boards that must be correctly aligned and kept flat. The big advantage of using loose tongues in this situation is that they can all be positioned in the same place on the edge of the boards, thereby ensuring that the boards will line up with ease and greater accuracy.

TOOLS AND MATERIALS

Bench plane
Mortise gauge
Plow plane
Ruler
Band saw or circular saw
Pencil
Wood glue and brush
Sash clamps

PREPARING AND MARKING OUT THE GROOVE

1 **Flatten the edges** of both boards by planing them with a bench plane, as if preparing for making an edge-to-edge joint (see pp.94–95).

2 **Set a mortise gauge** to the width of the blade of the plow plane. The choice of blade is determined by the thickness of the tongue.

3 **Use the mortise gauge** to scribe the width of the groove centrally on one edge of each of the two pieces (see Centering a Mortise Gauge, p.38).

SETTING THE PLANE AND CUTTING THE GROOVE

1 **Adjust the fence** of the plow plane to align the blade within the scribed groove marks.

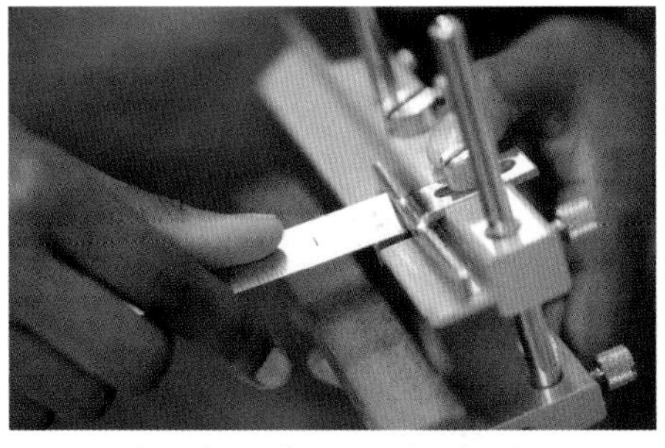

2 **Set the plow plane** to the depth of the groove required. Usually, this is a little more than the width of the groove.

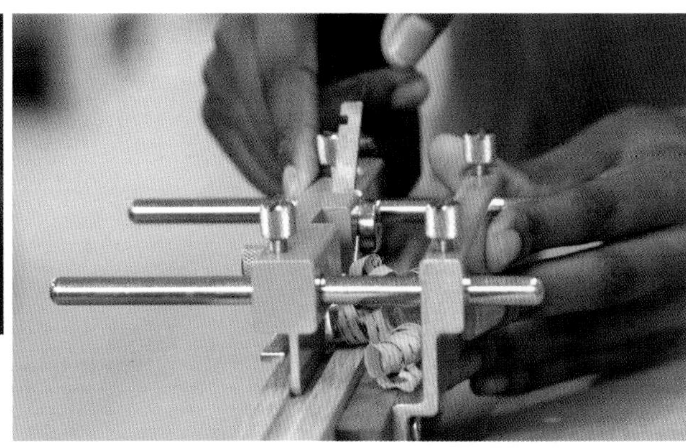

3 **Use the plow plane** to cut the grooves on the edges of both of the pieces being joined.

MAKING THE TONGUE

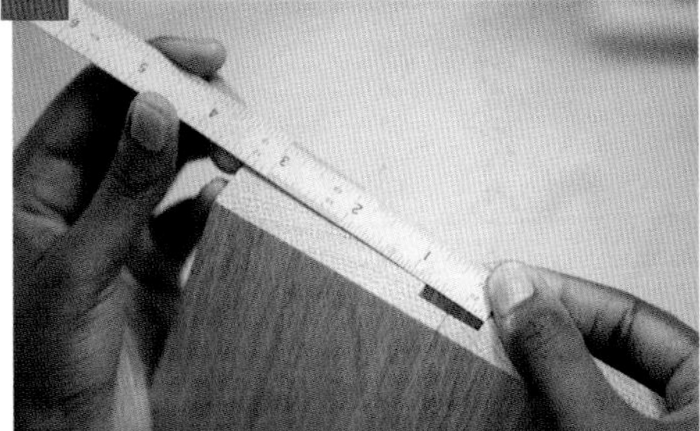

1 **Place the pieces together** and measure the combined width of the grooves in order to calculate the width of the tongue.

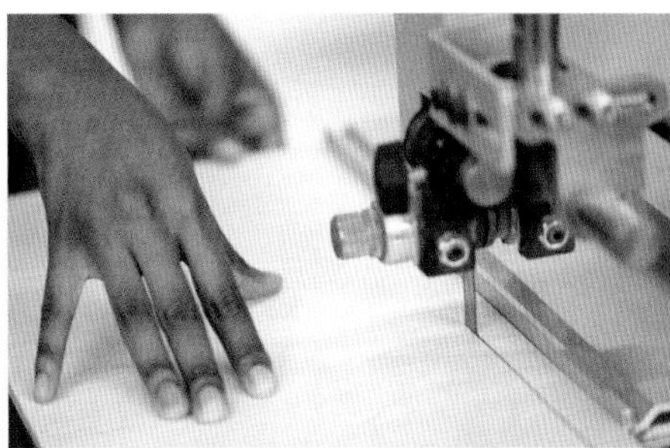

2 **Cut the tongue** to the length and width required using a band saw (pictured) or a circular saw. The width should be about 1⁄16 in (2mm) less than the combined measurement of both grooves.

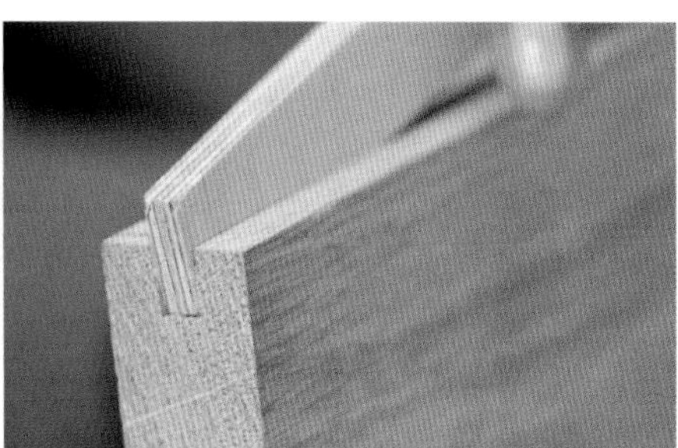

3 **Test-fit the tongue** in the grooves. Mark the joining position on the faces of the pieces to be joined (see Marking the Joint, below left).

MARKING THE JOINT

Before you glue the joint, it is a good idea to mark the exact position of the two pieces of the joint. You can then dismantle the joint for gluing with the assurance that it can easily be reassembled in the desired position.

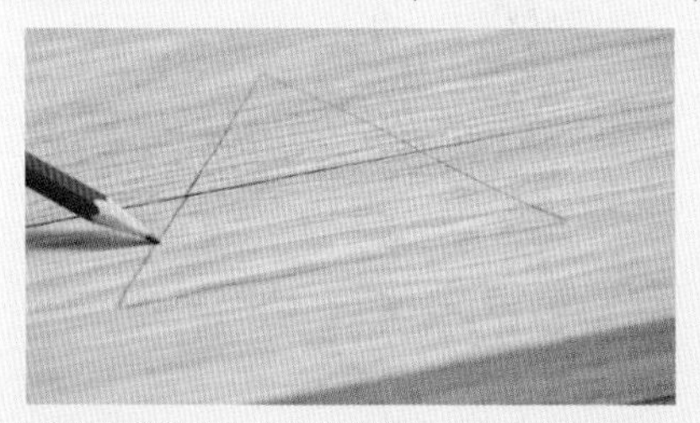

GLUING THE JOINT

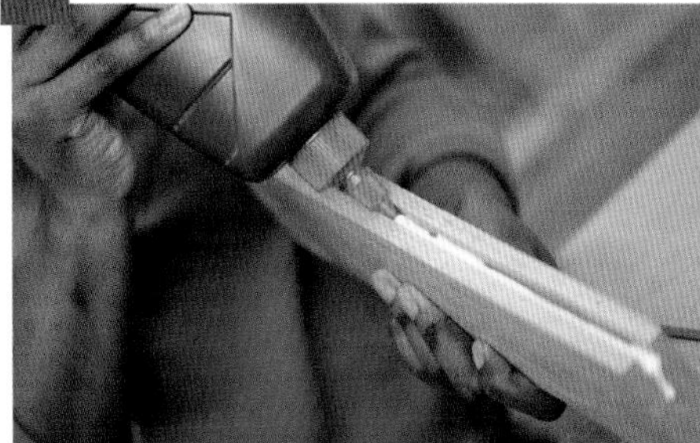

1 **Apply a generous amount** of wood glue into the grooves of both of the pieces that are to be joined.

2 **Insert the tongue** into the groove of the first piece, then clean any excess glue from the end grain.

3 **Brush glue onto the joining edge** of each piece, then assemble the joint by placing the second piece over the tongue.

4 **Clamp and leave to dry**. When the glue is dry, plane the surface of the assembled pieces flush.

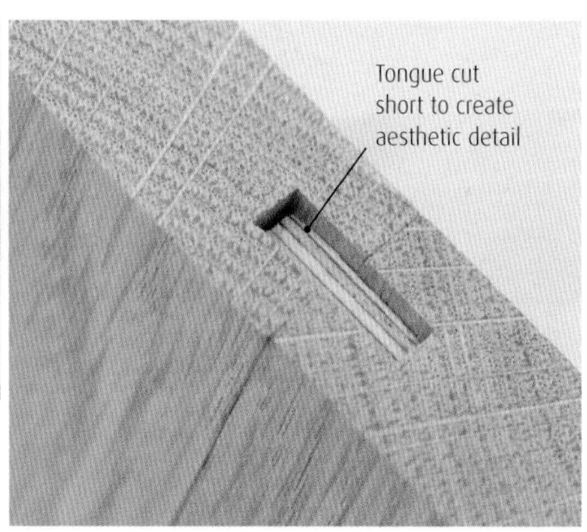

THE FINAL JOINT

Fixed tongue-and-groove joint

This is a versatile edge-to-edge joint that has many applications. It is most commonly used as a decorative feature for the back of pieces such as bookcases or dressers; for floorboards or paneling; or simply to join boards together, although the strength of modern glues means that this usage has become less common. The joint can also be used to make a panel within a frame for carcass work, as in cupboard doors.

PARTS OF THE JOINT

A fixed tongue-and-groove has an integral tongue created by a double rebate on one piece that marries with the groove on the joining piece. The timber must be very flat for this joint to work, as it is easy to misalign the groove. The groove must be cut slightly deeper than the tongue in order to allow space for the glue.

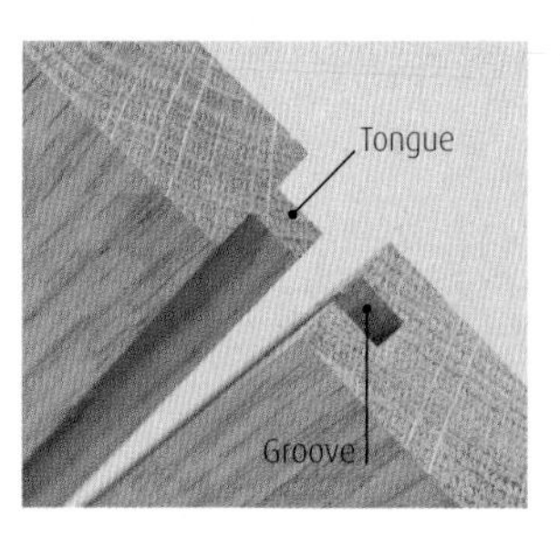

TOOLS AND MATERIALS

- Plow plane
- Ruler
- Rebate plane
- Double-sided tape
- Hammer and nails
- Spare strips of wood
- Wood glue and brush
- Sash clamps

CUTTING THE GROOVE AND SETTING THE PLANE

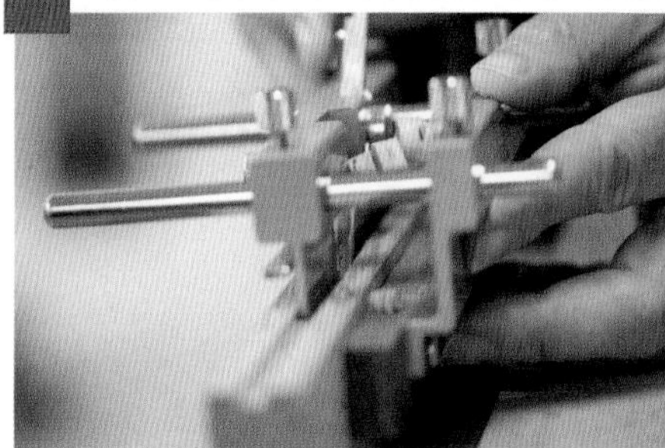

1 **Prepare the edge** and use a plow plane to cut a groove of the required dimensions, as for the loose tongue-and-groove joint (pp.96–97).

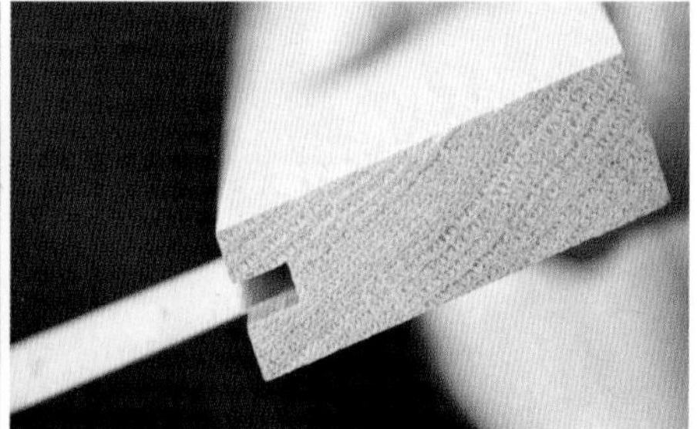

2 **Measure the depth** of the groove to determine the length of the tongue, which will be cut with a rebate plane.

3 **Set the fence** of the rebate plane to 1/32in (1mm) less than the depth of the groove, to allow space for the glue. (The fence governs the width of the rebate.)

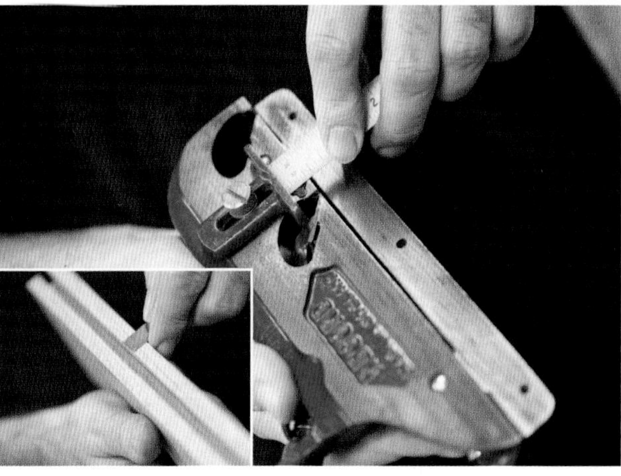

4 **Set the foot** of the plane to the same measurement as that of each side of the groove (inset). (The foot governs the depth of the rebate.)

CUTTING THE TONGUE

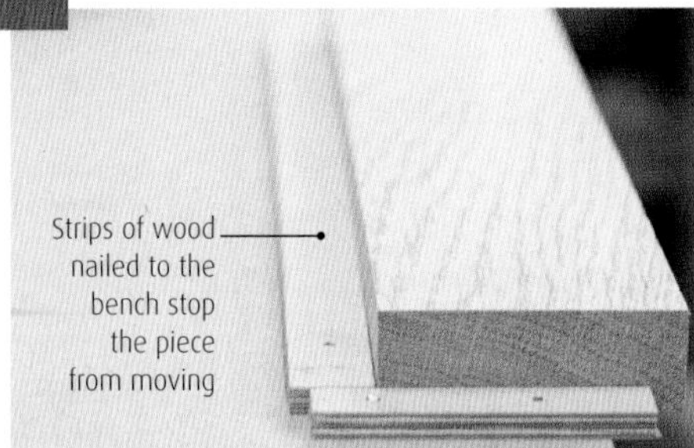

1 **Secure the tongue piece** to the bench face uppermost, using double-sided tape and strips of wood to hold it firmly in place as you plane the rebate.

2 **Use the rebate plane** to cut along one side of the tongue piece until you have achieved the desired depth of rebate.

3 **Turn the piece over** and secure it to the bench, then plane the second rebate to create the tongue.

ASSEMBLING THE JOINT

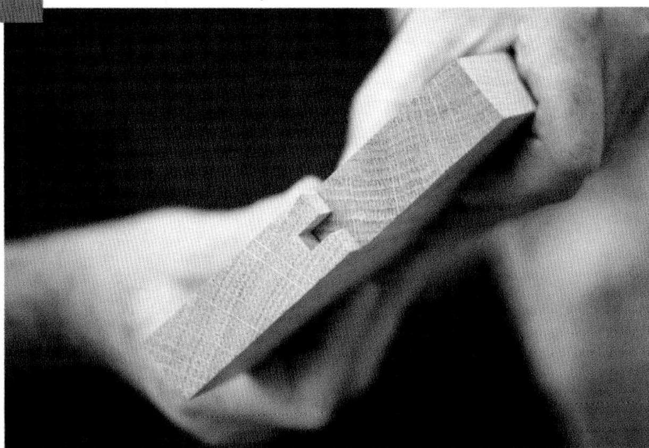

1 **Check the fit of the tongue** in the groove. Make any necessary adjustments to the pieces by further planing.

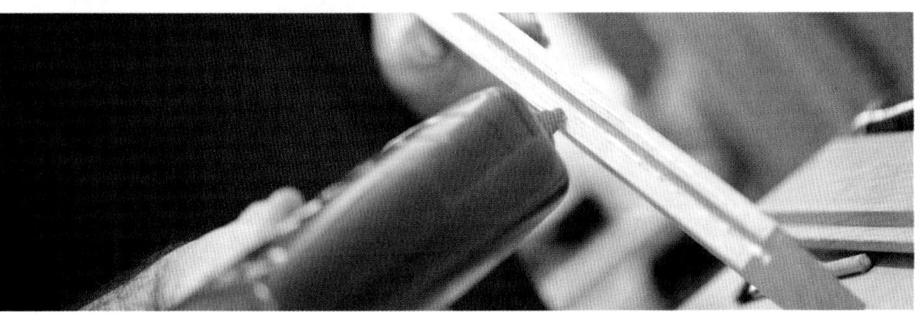

2 **When you are sure** that the fit of the tongue into the groove is satisfactory, squeeze a generous amount of wood glue into the groove and along the joining edges of both elements of the joint.

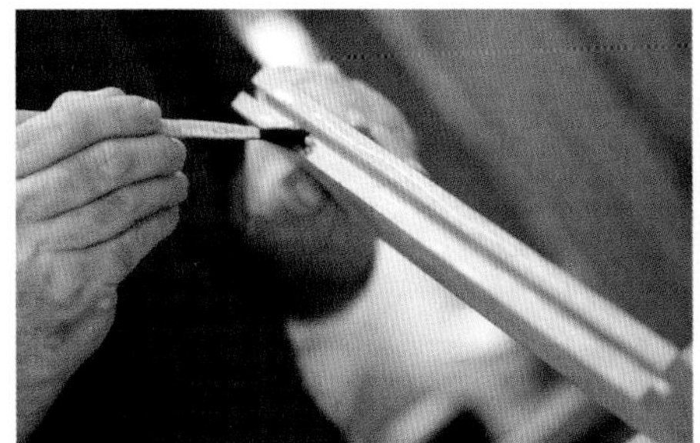

3 **Spread the glue** with a brush to distribute the adhesive evenly on all of the surfaces to be joined.

4 **Assemble the glued elements** and clamp together using sash clamps placed at regular intervals along the length of the joined pieces.

5 **Wipe away any excess glue** with a damp cloth and leave the joint to dry, ideally for several hours.

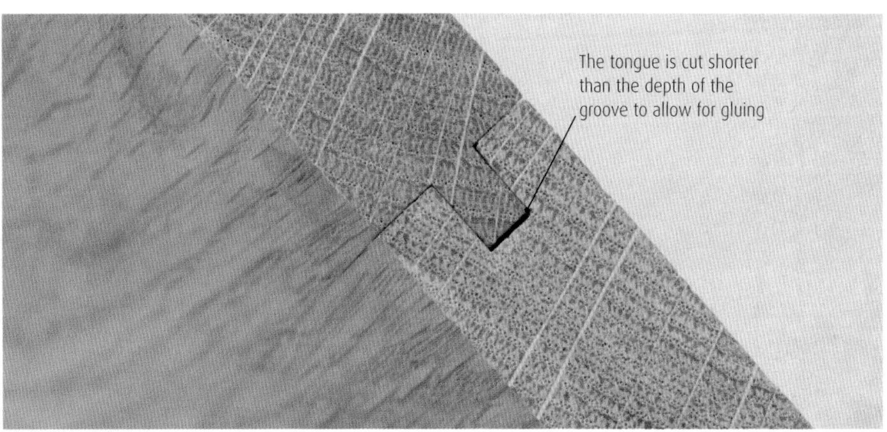

THE FINAL JOINT

USING A ROUTER TABLE

Cutting the groove
You can cut the groove using a table-mounted router (see p.45). Fit a cutter to suit the groove width. Set the fence to the distance of the groove from the face (the width of the shoulder) and the depth to that of the groove.

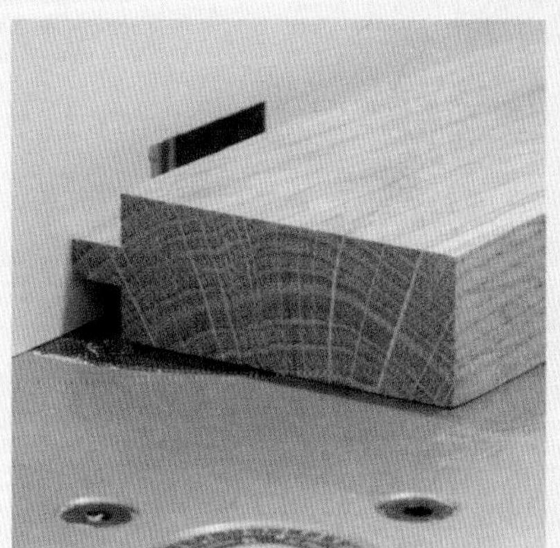

Cutting the tongue
You can also cut the rebates for the tongue on a table-mounted router. Working with the piece on its side, set the fence to the length required for the tongue (that is, the depth of the groove, less an allowance for glue), and set the depth of the cut to the width measurement of the shoulder.

Cross-halving joint

The cross-halving joint (sometimes called a cross-halved lap joint or center lap) is one of a family of joints, known as lap joints, that are useful whenever it is necessary to join two pieces of wood that cross each other. When subjected to lateral force, each long-grain piece is locked against an end-grain shoulder and cannot move, making this a very strong joint. The cross-halving joint is commonly used in various types of building joinery and furniture construction, for example on a range of basic carpentry frames and on stretcher rails for tables and chairs. It can also be used on frames in carcass work, and when constructing "shoji"—Japanese lattice screens.

Related joints

The most basic form of lap joint—the simple lap joint—is used on carcass work, where there is no mechanical strength needed. This joint consists simply of a rebate with the second component butted and glued into it. The simple lap joint relies solely on end grain gluing for its strength, and can be strengthened by using additional veneer pins. It is often used to make simple trays or boxes.

PARTS OF THE JOINT

The cross-halving joint consists of two pieces with exactly half of their material removed to create four shoulders that cross each other. The fit of the components must be perfect, otherwise the joint will be sloppy and unsightly. Although the amount of material removed incurs a risk of weakness, once the two parts are glued together it is a very strong joint.

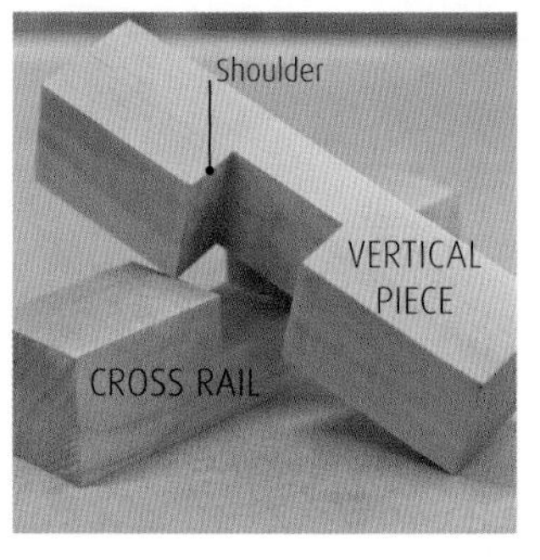

There are many types of halving joint, including the corner halving joint (p.104), in which the lap joint is created in the ends of both pieces. Another joint in this family, similar to the corner halving joint, is the "T" halving joint, which, as its name suggests, forms a T-shape. This is a very useful joint for bracing and is often used in large plinths—for example, as a form of stretcher rail on a sideboard. In the dovetail half-lap joint (pp.102–103), both elements are cut into the shape of a dovetail, providing additional mechanical strength. In some work, an angled or oblique halving is a useful variation of the cross-halving joint. The basic construction is the same as for a cross-halving joint, but a combination square or an adjustable bevel is required to mark out the angles.

TOOLS AND MATERIALS

- Pencil
- Combination square
- Marking gauge
- Marking knife
- Small tenon saw
- Bevel-edged chisel
- Hand router (optional)
- Wood glue and brush

MARKING UP THE JOINT

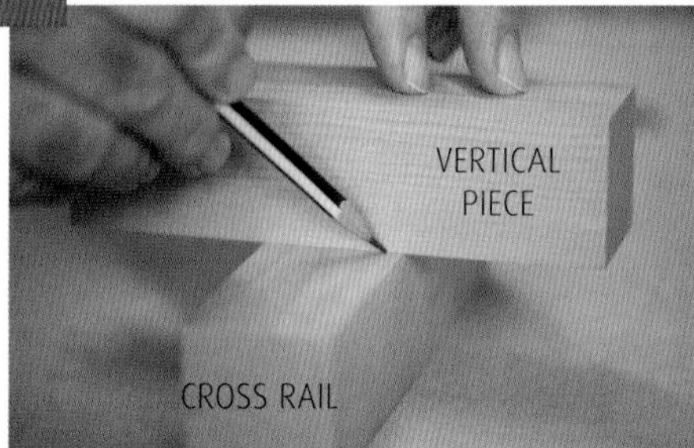

1 **Mark the position** of the joint on the cross rail by marking the width of the lap with a line either side of the vertical piece.

2 **Extend the marks** around three sides of the cross rail using a combination square and pencil or a marking knife.

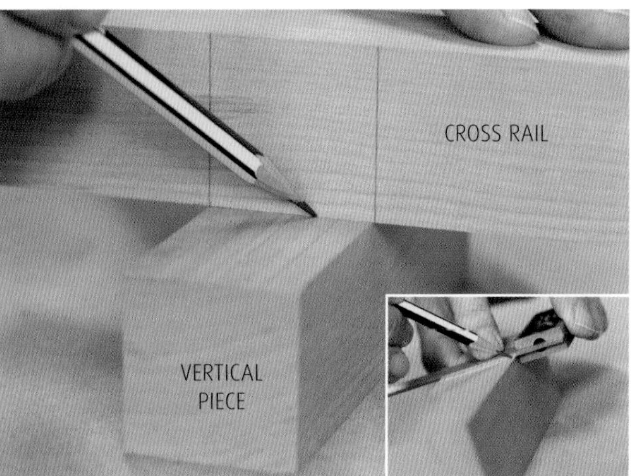

3 **Reverse the pieces** and mark the shoulders on the vertical piece, using the cross rail as a guide. Square the marks onto three sides of the vertical piece (inset).

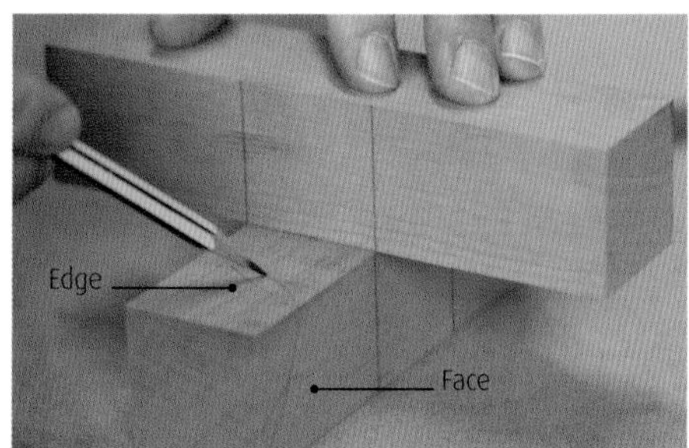

4 **Position the pieces** in the desired position and mark the faces (see Preparing the wood, pp.84–91).

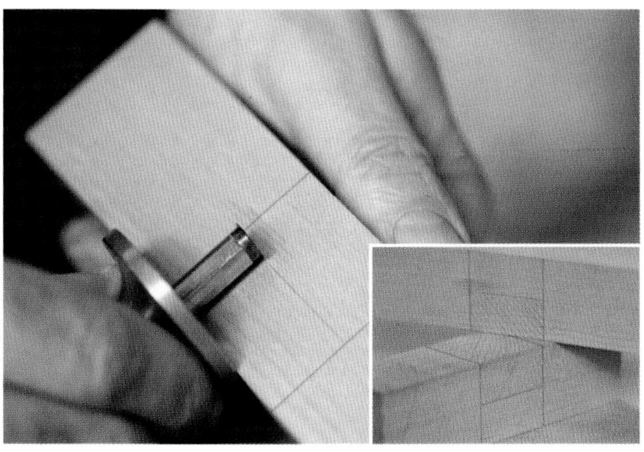

5 **Set the marking gauge** to half the thickness of the stock and mark the depth of the lap between the shoulder lines on the edges of both pieces. With the pieces aligned so that the faces that will be cut to create the laps are touching, mark the waste for removal (inset).

6 **Scribe the edges** of the waste on both pieces with a marking knife, to ensure a clean cut across the grain.

CUTTING AND FITTING THE JOINT

1 **Using a small tenon saw**, cut on the waste side of the vertical marks until you reach the depth mark.

2 **Make a series** of relief cuts vertically through the waste, being careful not to cut through the depth mark.

3 **Remove the waste** with a bevel-edged chisel, chopping horizontally from one edge of the piece.

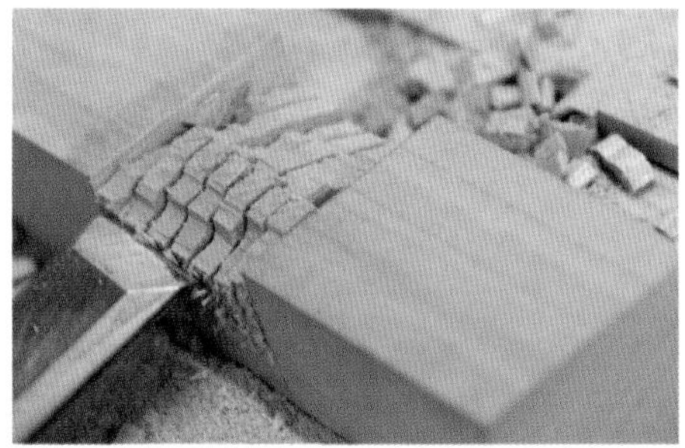

4 **Reverse the piece** in the vise and chop away the remaining waste, working horizontally from the other edge.

5 **Use the chisel** to pare the edges and base of the lap to the marks, and to create a smooth finish. Alternatively, use a hand router (see right) if available.

USING A HAND ROUTER

The hand router has a sheer cut across the grain that makes it ideal for leveling off surfaces. With the cutter set to the depth of the housing, work the tool across the bottom surface at a slight angle to give a clean, sheer cut.

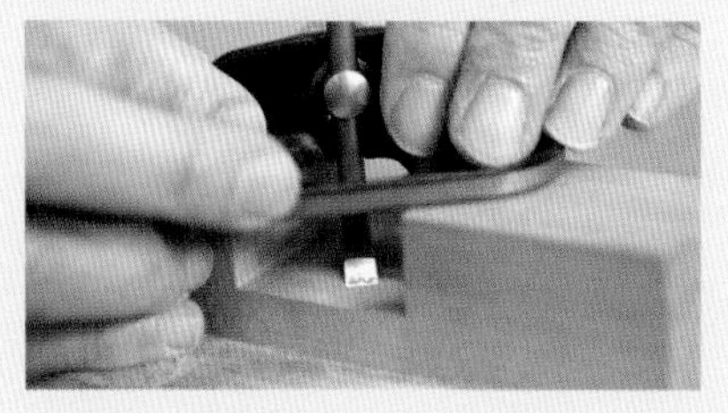

6 **Remove the waste** from the second piece in the same way, using a tenon saw, chisel, and hand router if available.

7 **Check the fit** of the two pieces and adjust by paring further if necessary. When the fit is good, glue the joint, clamp, and leave to dry.

THE FINISHED JOINT

Dovetail half-lap joint

A member of the family of lap joints, the dovetail half-lap is capable of resisting pull-out and sideways racking, so is mechanically the strongest of all lap joints. It can be used on any type of framing and is often utilized on carcass pieces, particularly for top drawer-rails and back-rails, since it can be easily inserted into an existing frame. It is occasionally used doubled up as a twin dovetail on a wide top-rail.

PARTS OF THE JOINT

As with all half-lap joints, the tail piece of the dovetail half-lap measures half the thickness of the wood, and in most cases the socket piece into which it is to be fitted is of the same width and thickness. But in some instances, the socket piece can be of a different thickness.

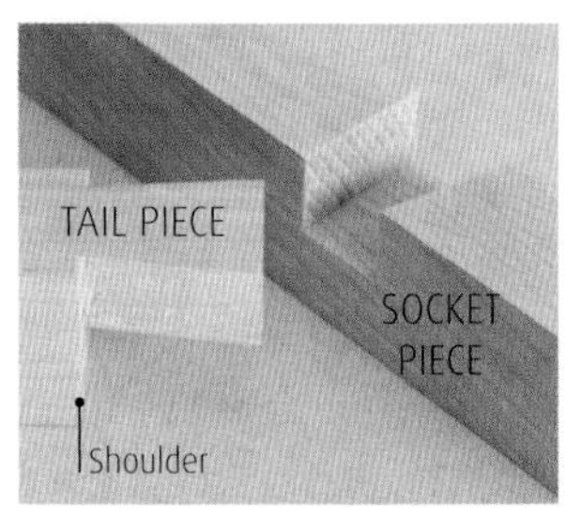

TOOLS AND MATERIALS

- Pencil
- Square
- Marking gauge
- Marking knife
- Dovetail marker
- Tenon saw
- Bevel-edged chisel
- Wood glue and brush
- Clamp
- Bench plane

MARKING OUT THE TAIL

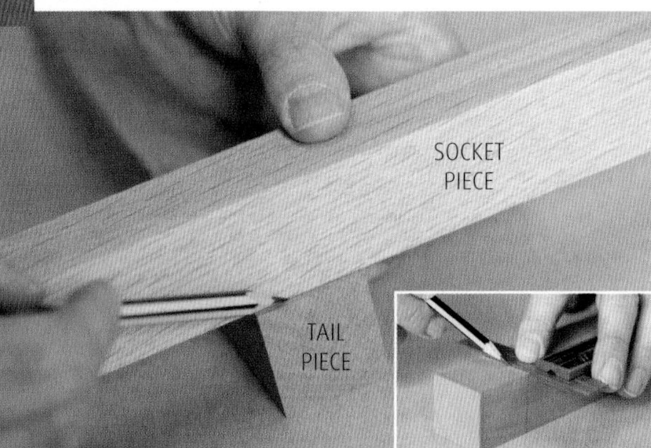

1 **Set the socket piece** on top of the tail piece, with the end grain of the tail piece protruding by up to 1/16in (2mm). Mark a line either side of the socket piece, and extend the lines onto all four sides of the tail piece with a square (inset).

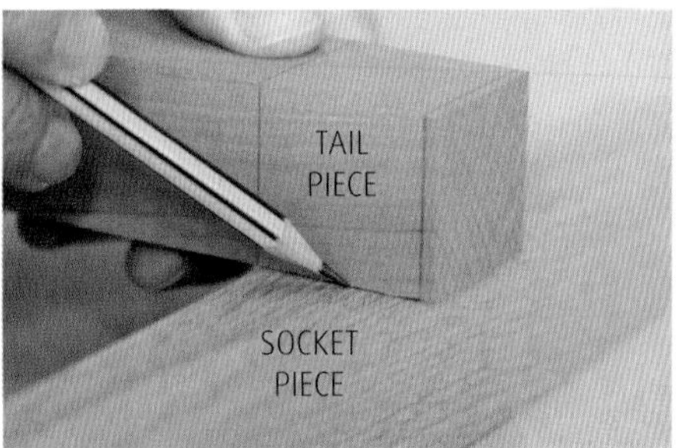

2 **Mark the position** of the lap on the socket piece, using the tail piece as a guide. Square the measurements around all four sides.

3 **Decide on the depth** of the lap (see Parts of the joint, above) and scribe this measurement around the edges and end grain of the tail piece.

4 **Scribe with a marking knife** to reinforce the shoulder lines on both edges and on the underside (the waste side) of the tail piece.

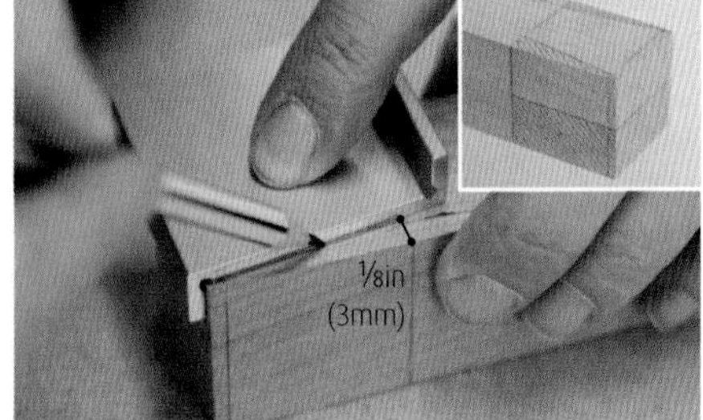

5 **Using a dovetail marker** as a guide, mark the tail from the end grain to the shoulders on the face side of the tail piece. Set the marker at least 1/8in (3mm) from the edge at the shoulder. Mark the waste (inset).

CUTTING THE TAIL

1 **Secure the tail piece** in a vise at an angle and cut the waste from the back of the tail using a tenon saw. Saw diagonally through the end grain to the shoulder.

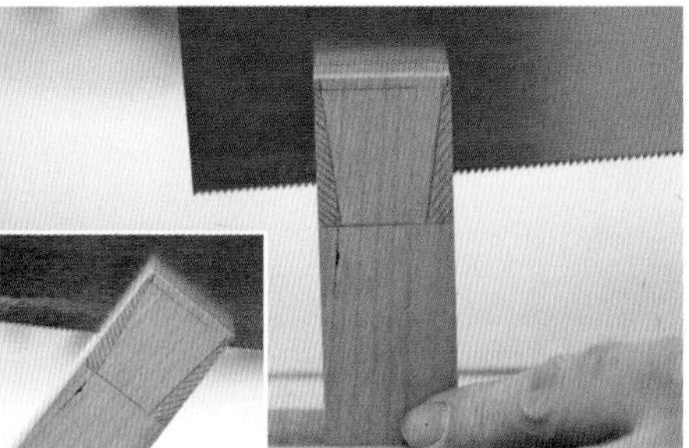

2 **Turn the piece** in the vise and saw diagonally from the other direction (inset). Finally, saw vertically to the shoulder.

3 **Using a bevel-edged chisel**, cut a V-groove along the shoulder line at the back of the tail.

4 **Release the waste** by cross-cutting along the shoulder line with a tenon saw (inset). Clean up the shoulder and edges with a chisel.

5 **Scribe across the end grain** from the marks made in Step 5 (opposite) with a marking knife and square.

6 **Set the tail piece** in the vise so that the line marking one side of the tail is vertical. Cut down the end grain to the shoulder with a tenon saw. Repeat to cut the other side of the tail.

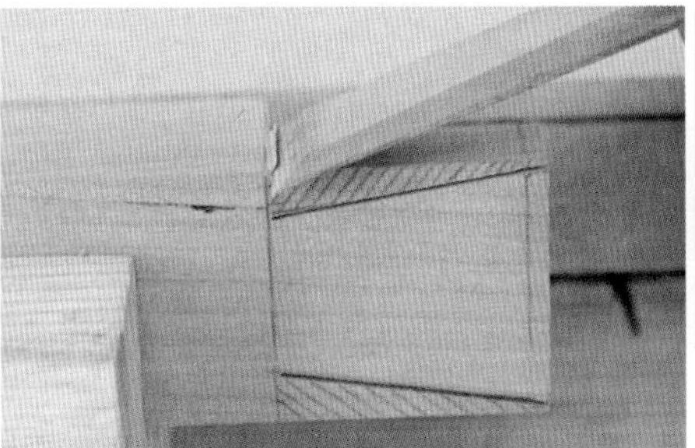

7 **With the tail piece secured** in a vise, chisel a V-groove along the shoulder line on the edges of the tail.

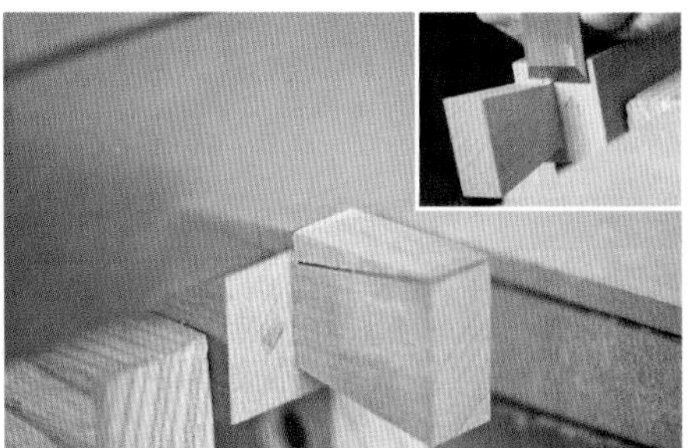

8 **Release the waste** by sawing down the shoulder line on each edge and the back face. Clean up the shoulders with a chisel (inset).

MARKING OUT THE SOCKET

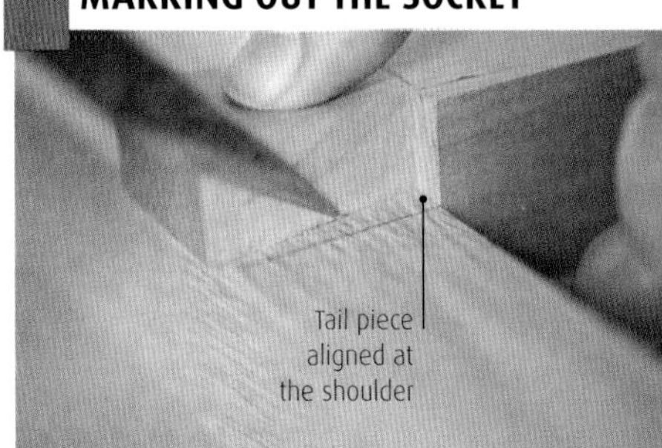

1 **Set the tail** in position over the socket piece, aligned at the shoulder. Scribe around the tail with a marking knife. Square the marks onto the edges.

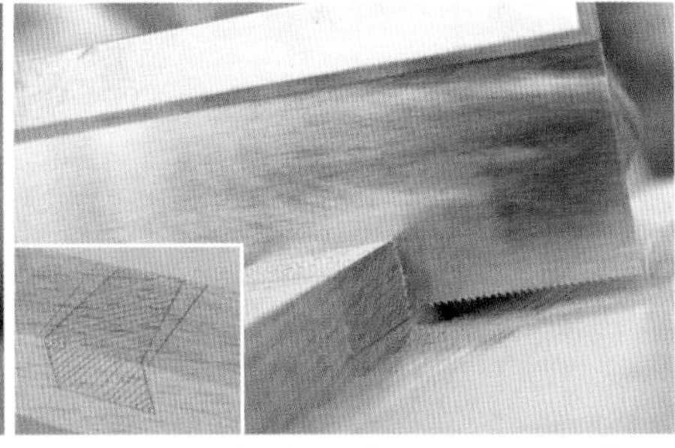

2 **Mark the depth** of the socket on both edges using the marking gauge as previously set (inset). Use a tenon saw to cut the edges of the socket to this depth.

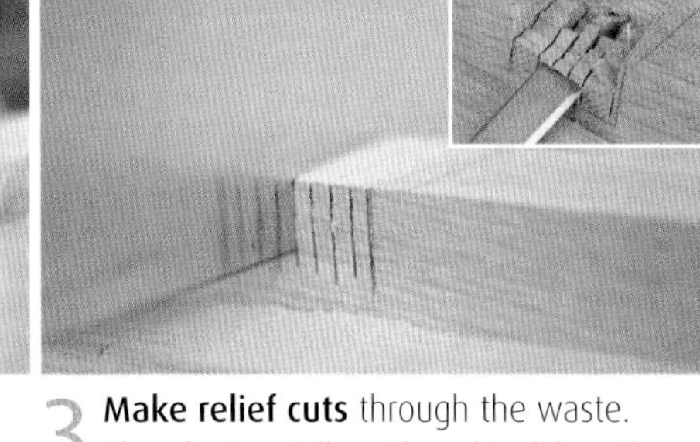

3 **Make relief cuts** through the waste. Chop horizontally with a chisel (inset) to release the waste. Clean up the base and edges with a chisel.

4 **Test the fit** of the joint and adjust as necessary. Saw off the excess length of the tail and plane flush to the edge of the socket piece using a bench plane (inset).

THE FINISHED JOINT

Corner-halving joint

One of the simplest types of joint, the corner-halving joint has no mechanical lock or resistance to racking or twist, so should not be subjected to lateral strain. It has large gluing surfaces and relies on glue for its strength, but can be reinforced with screws or dowels. Its main advantage is that it is quick to make, and it can be used for frames on the backs of carcasses, internal frames holding dividers, or dust frames in chests of drawers.

PARTS OF THE JOINT

This joint utilizes components of equal thickness, and each piece is a mirror image of the other. Each long-grain piece is half the width of the stock, and mates against the end-grain shoulder of the opposite piece.

TOOLS AND MATERIALS

- Pencil
- Square
- Marking gauge
- Marking knife
- Tenon saw
- Bevel-edged chisel
- Wood glue and brush
- C-clamp
- Bench plane

MARKING OUT AND CUTTING THE JOINT

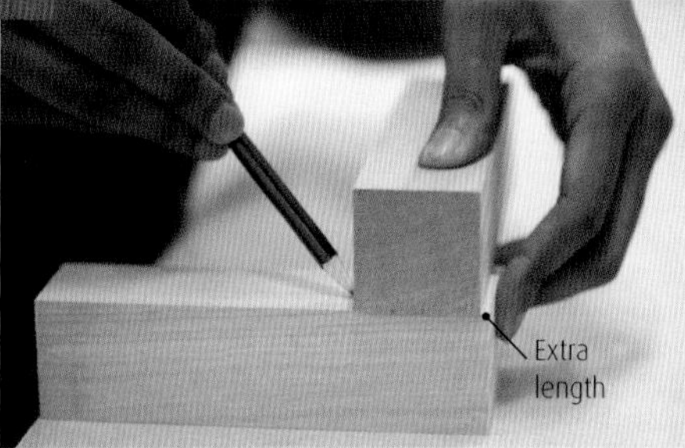

1 **Mark the position** of the joint on the first piece using the thickness of the other piece, aligned approximately 1⁄16in (2mm) from the end grain, as a guide.

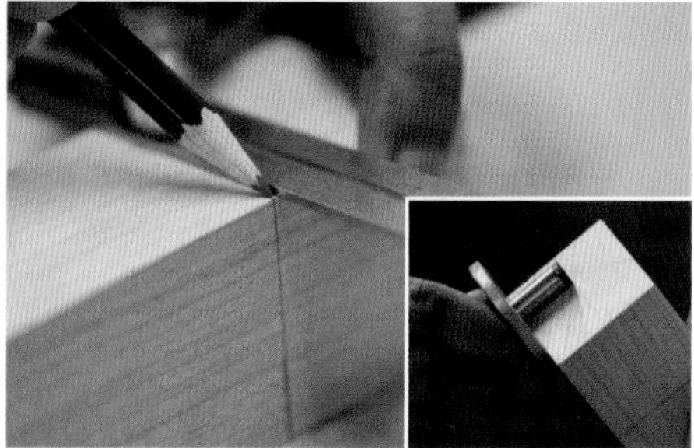

2 **Extend the mark** around three sides with a square. With the marking gauge set to half the width of the wood, scribe around the three marked sides (inset).

3 **Score the lines** with a marking knife, then cut the waste with a tenon saw (inset). Make sure you cut to the waste side of the scored line.

4 **Clean up the joint** with a bevel-edged chisel, then follow Steps 1–4 to cut a joint in the second piece of wood.

FINISHING THE JOINT

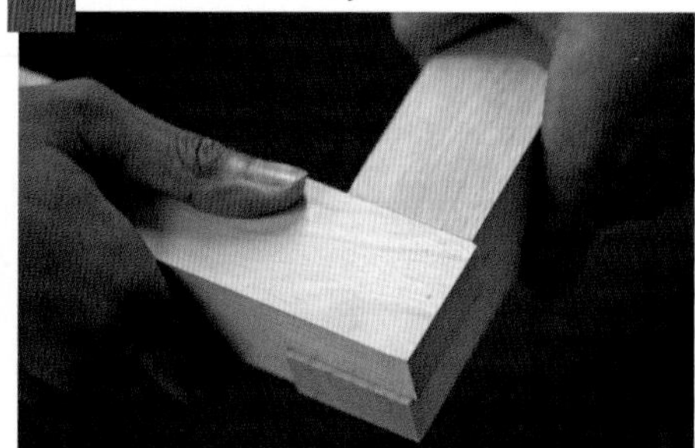

1 **Test-fit the joint** to ensure that all the faces are flush (although the ends of the joint should protrude beyond the edges). Adjust the fit by paring further if necessary.

2 **Once a good fit** has been achieved, use a brush to apply glue to the joint, clamp the joint with a G-clamp (inset), and leave it to dry.

3 **Once the glue has dried**, use a bench plane to remove the excess length from the ends of the joint to achieve a flush finish on both edges.

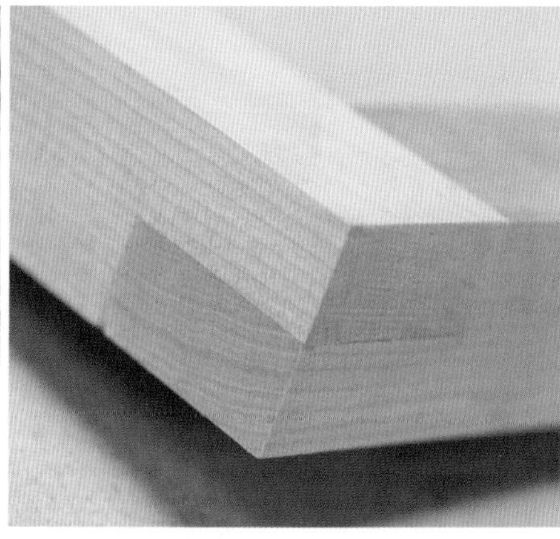

THE FINISHED JOINT

Scarf joint

Primarily used to lengthen material, scarf joints are not usually found in the construction of furniture, but are used in carpentry to extend dado rails, architraves, and skirting boards. Guitar makers use a scarf joint on steel-strung and classic guitars to join the head to the neck. It can be reinforced by using a loose tongue (pp.96–97), and should be strengthened with screws, nails, or a fixing plate if it is to take any strain.

PARTS OF THE JOINT

The joining pieces form a bevel that slides together, and are simply butt-jointed. Identical in shape and size, they are cut at a shallow angle to give a larger gluing area and greater shear strength. The faces of the joint are end grains and will absorb more glue than a face or edge, so apply primer before gluing.

TOOLS AND MATERIALS

Pencil
Square
Ruler
Band saw or tenon saw
Bench plane
Wood glue and brush
C-clamp

MARKING OUT THE FIRST PIECE

1 **Use a pencil** and square to mark the start of the taper across the face of the first piece of wood that is going to be joined.

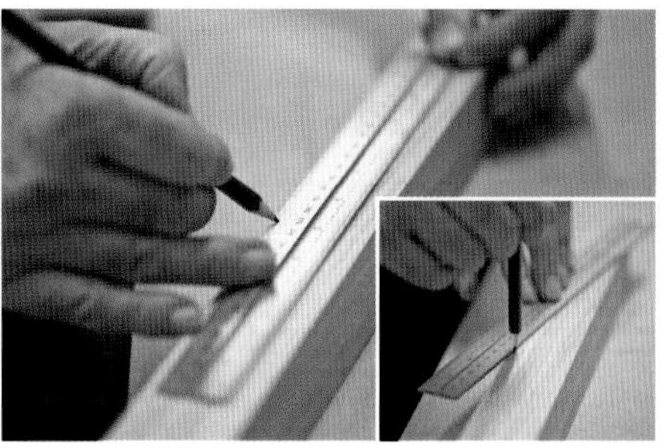

2 **Mark the other end** of the taper approximately four times the width of the wood from the first mark. Draw a diagonal line from one edge to the other (inset).

3 **Extend both marks** around the adjacent sides as a guide for cutting, using a pencil and square.

CUTTING AND FINISHING THE JOINT

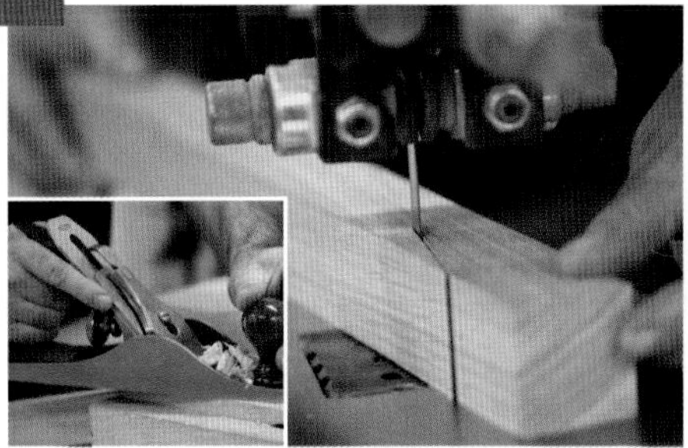

1 **Use a band saw** to cut along the line. (A tenon saw can be used instead, but requires great skill.) Plane the sawn edge smooth with a bench plane (inset).

2 **Use the first piece** as a template for marking out the second piece, which should be cut and planed in the same way as the first.

3 **Check that the pieces** fit together precisely, then mark them to indicate the exact position of the joint.

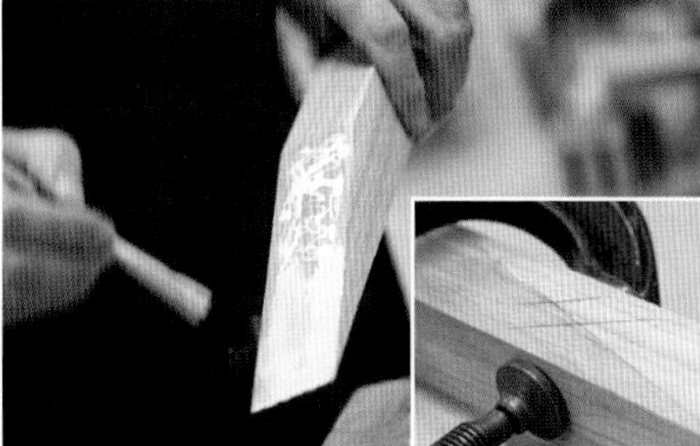

4 **Apply glue** to one surface of the joint with a brush, then clamp the two pieces together so that the marks are aligned (inset).

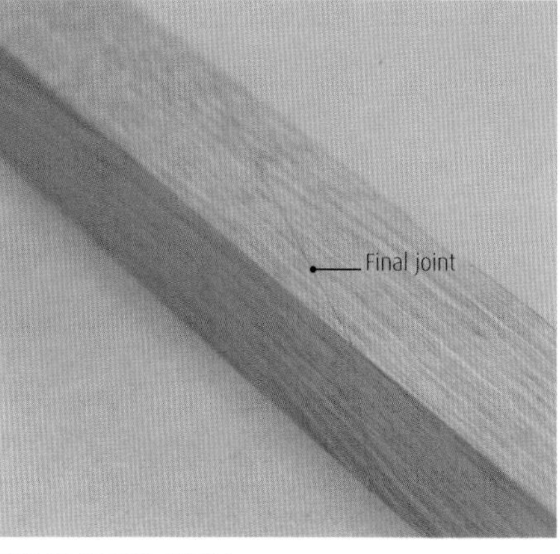

THE FINISHED JOINT

Full housing joint

Among the most basic types of joint, the housing joint consists of a groove—the "housing"—into which the end grain of the joining piece of wood—the "tenon"—is inserted. Ideal for making shelves for bookcases and plinths for pieces such as sideboards, it may also be used to make carcass furniture, such as desks and chests of drawers. While the housing joint is strong in terms of the downward force it can withstand, it has no resistance to sideways tension because the gluing area is limited to the end grain, although it can be strengthened by cutting a shoulder into the tenon. The full (or "through") housing joint described here is the simplest form; variations include the shouldered and stopped housing joint, in which the housing is cut shorter than the full width of the housing piece and a shoulder is incorporated into the end grain of the tenon piece (p.108), and a dovetail housing (p.110), in which the tenon and housing are cut into matching dovetail shapes.

PARTS OF THE JOINT

The housing is made to the exact thickness of the tenon piece and extends across the full width of the housing piece and into both edges. The depth of the housing is usually one third of the thickness of the housing piece, and certainly no more than half—any more than this will weaken the overall structure sof the piece.

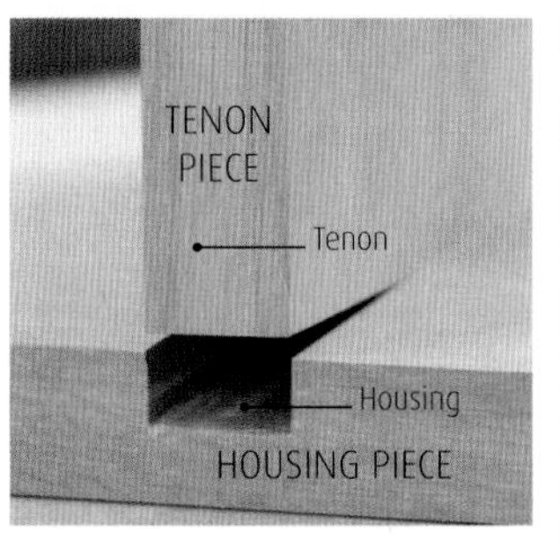

Making the full housing joint

With careful construction of each component, the full housing joint is useful for a range of applications. Be aware, however, that any slight discrepancy in the build will be revealed in the finished joint. For example, in your zeal to achieve a good finish, it can be all too easy to sand the shelves a little thinner than intended, resulting in a loose fit in the housing. Pay close attention to your markings at all times.

The main disadvantage of the full housing joint is that, because the housing runs the full width of the housing piece, the tenon is visible on the face edges, which can mar the finish. This may not matter if the joint is used internally in a carcass piece, or if it is concealed, for example, by a door.

TOOLS AND MATERIALS

- Marking knife
- Square
- Ruler
- Marking gauge
- Pencil
- Appropriately sized chisel (slightly smaller than the thickness of the housing)
- Tenon saw
- Wooden mallet
- Rubber mallet
- Wood glue and brush
- Clamps

MARKING OUT THE HOUSING

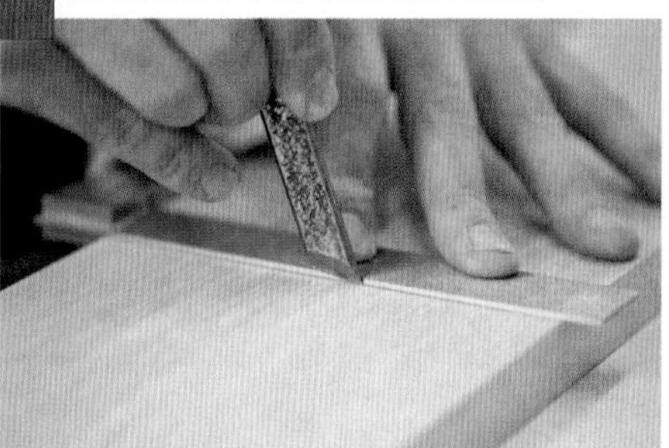

1 **Score a single line** on the face of the housing piece with a marking knife and square to mark the position of the housing.

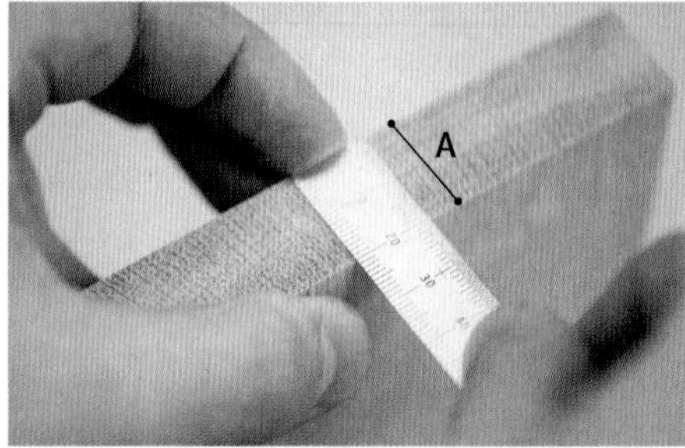

2 **Measure the width** of the end grain of the tenon piece (A) to determine how wide you will need to cut the housing.

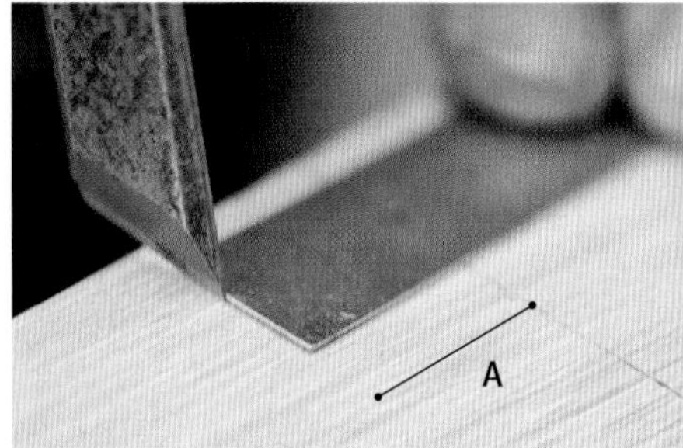

3 **Mark the width** of the tenon (A) on the housing piece. This defines the width of the housing.

4 **Square this line** across the face of the housing piece, using the marking knife and square.

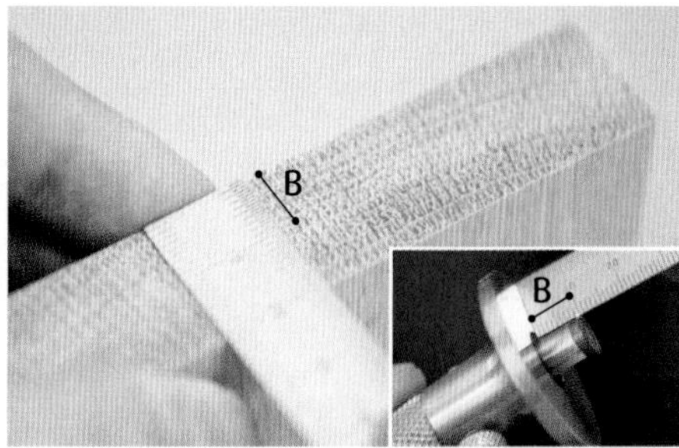

5 **The thickness of the housing piece** determines the housing depth. Set the marking gauge to between one third and one half of this measurement (B).

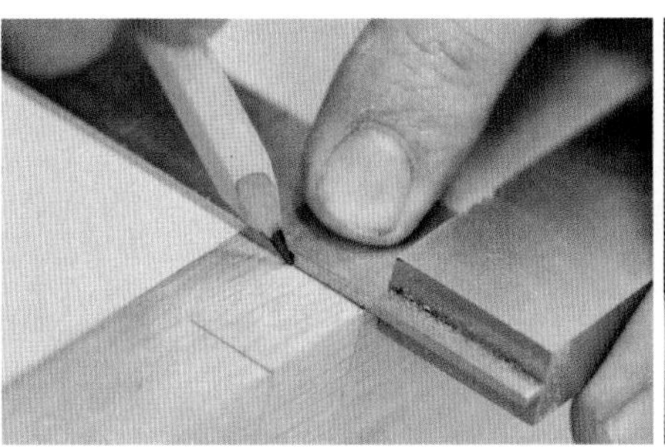

6 **Extend the width marks** around the edge of the housing piece on both edges, using a pencil and square.

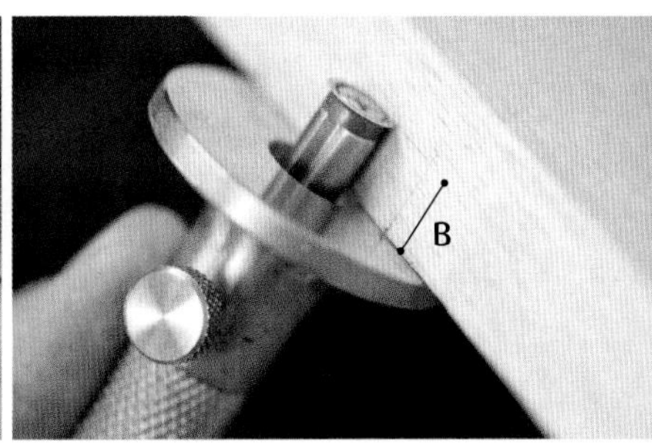

7 **Use the marking gauge** to scribe the depth of the housing between the width marks on both edges.

8 **Score along the width marks** that you have made in pencil, using the marking knife and square.

CUTTING THE HOUSING

1 **Use a chisel** to make a V-groove along each of the housing lines on the face of the housing piece. Cut along the grooves with a tenon saw to the depth indicated by the edge markings (inset).

2 **Loosen the waste** with a chisel by making vertical cuts along the width of the housing.

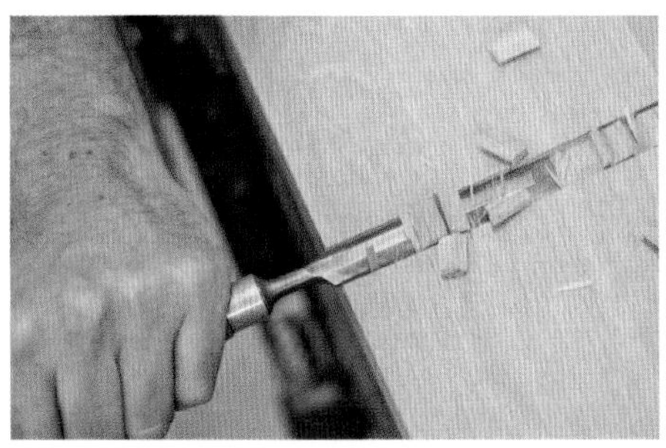

3 **Use a chisel and wooden mallet** to remove the bulk of the waste from the housing by chopping horizontally.

4 **Trim the base and edges** with the chisel, smoothing off any loose cuts, splinters, and rough edges.

ASSEMBLING THE JOINT

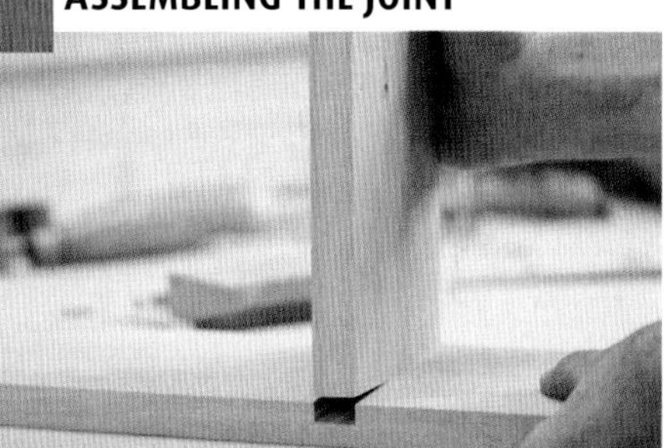

1 **Insert the tenon piece** into the housing, taking care not to damage the edges as you bring the two pieces together.

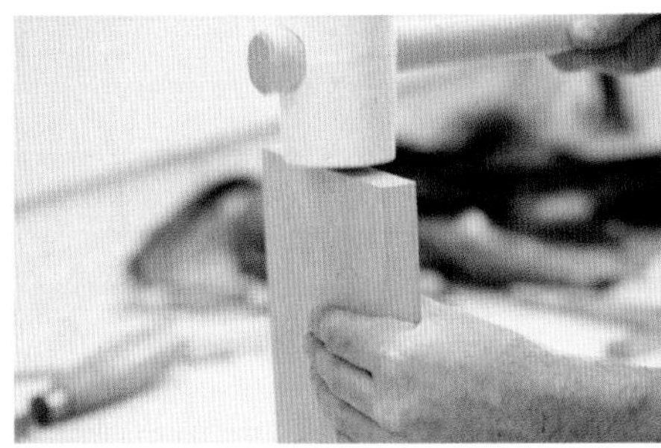

2 **Use a rubber mallet** to lodge the tenon in place—the fit should be snug. If the fit is too tight, adjust the width of the housing by paring with a chisel.

3 **Check that the fit is square** by holding a square against the joint. When you are satisfied with the accuracy of the join, glue and clamp the joint.

THE FINISHED JOINT

Shouldered and stopped housing joint

A variation on the full housing joint (p.106), the shouldered and stopped version is neat and clever. The stopped housing hides the joint from view, and a small shoulder on the two mating faces prevents any undercutting from being visible. Because of this, it is particularly useful for drawer divisions or dividers in boxes, desks, and other carcass applications for which aesthetics are important. It is in some ways easier to make than a full housing; although the shoulder must be cut precisely, the fit of the joint itself is less critical.

PARTS OF THE JOINT

The end grain of the tenon piece is cut to form a shoulder along one side, and the housing is stopped short of the front edge of the housing piece. The housing width is narrower than the full thickness of the tenon piece, and the depth of the housing can be up to half the thickness of the housing piece. The stopped shoulder allows the front edge of the housing piece to be shaped—for example, by rounding.

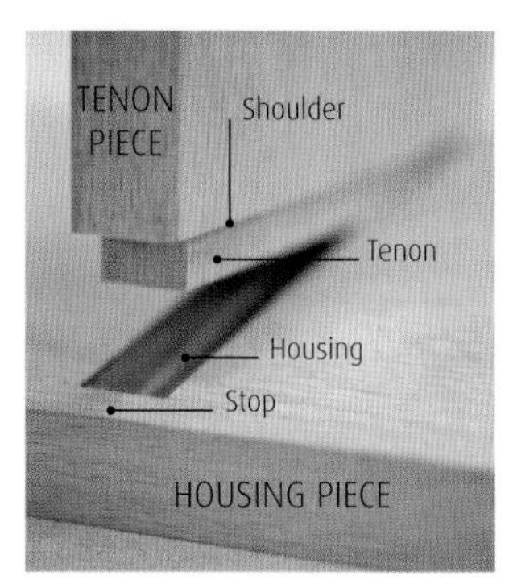

TOOLS AND MATERIALS

- Pencil
- Square
- Ruler
- Marking gauge
- Marking knife
- Appropriately sized bevel-edged chisel (to match housing width)
- Tenon saw
- Rebate plane
- Wood glue and brush
- Clamps

MARKING OUT THE HOUSING

1 **Using a pencil and square**, draw a single line to mark the required position of the housing on the housing piece.

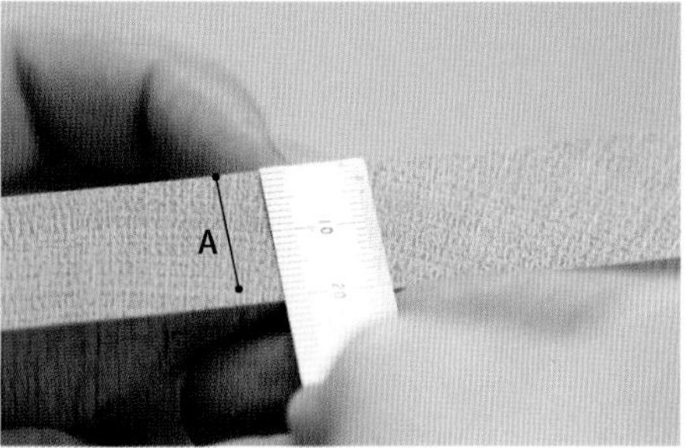

2 **Decide the width** of the tenon (A). Be sure not to make it too narrow or it will not be strong enough.

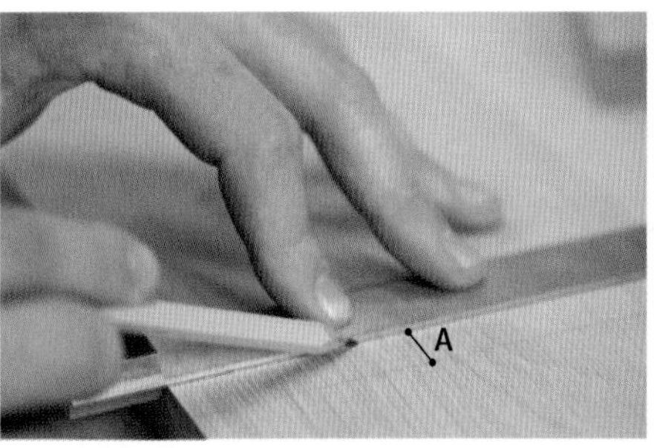

3 **Mark the tenon width** (A) on the housing piece and square the mark across the face using the pencil and square.

4 **Extend the width marks** around the back edge of the housing piece using the pencil and square.

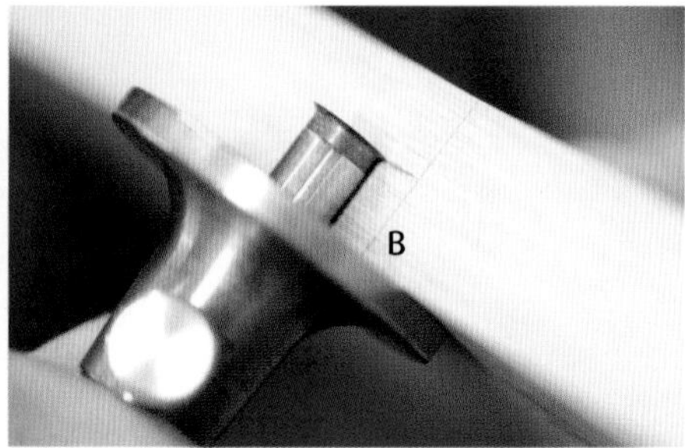

5 **Decide the depth** of the housing (B), and use a marking gauge to scribe that measurement onto the marked edge.

6 **Set the marking gauge** to the width required for the stop of the housing (C), and mark that distance from the front edge between the housing lines.

CUTTING THE HOUSING

1 **Use a marking knife and square** to score the grain along the lines marking the edges of the housing, avoiding the area at the front edge marked for the stop.

2 **With the housing piece** secured in a vise, use a bevel-edged chisel to cut a narrow, vertical-sided groove along each side of the housing.

3 **Saw down the sides of the housing** to the marked depth with a tenon saw. Always saw on the waste side of the lines.

4 **Clamp the housing piece** to the bench. Using a bevel-edged chisel of the same width as the housing, first make vertical cuts (inset), then chisel horizontally to the required depth. Clean up any rough edges.

MARKING OUT THE TENON

1 **Set the marking gauge** to the tenon width (A) and scribe this measurement along the end grain of the tenon. This defines the width of the single shoulder of the tenon.

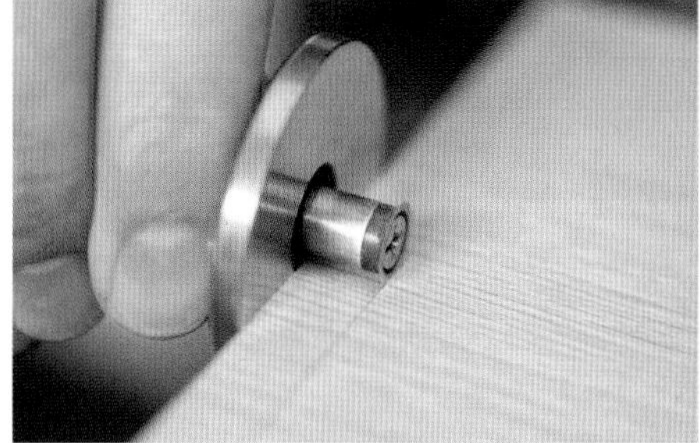

2 **Mark the length of the tenon,** which is the housing depth (B) less about 1/32in (1mm) for glue, on the face and edge of the tenon piece.

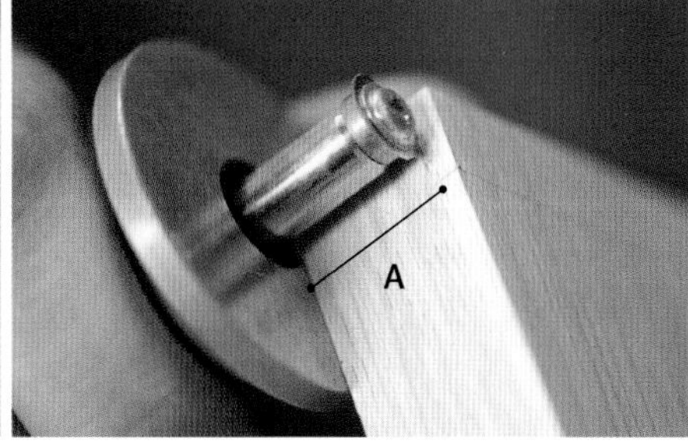

3 **Set the marking gauge** to the housing width (A), and continue the mark to the edge to meet the depth measurement.

4 **Set the marking gauge** to the length of the stop (C). Scribe this measurement onto the front edge of the tenon piece.

CUTTING THE TENON

1 **Use the rebate plane** to cut the tenon to the required width (A), as marked on the tenon edge. Check the thickness of the tenon with the marking gauge (inset).

2 **Use a bevel-edged chisel** to cut a V-groove along the marked line of the stop on the front edge of the tenon piece.

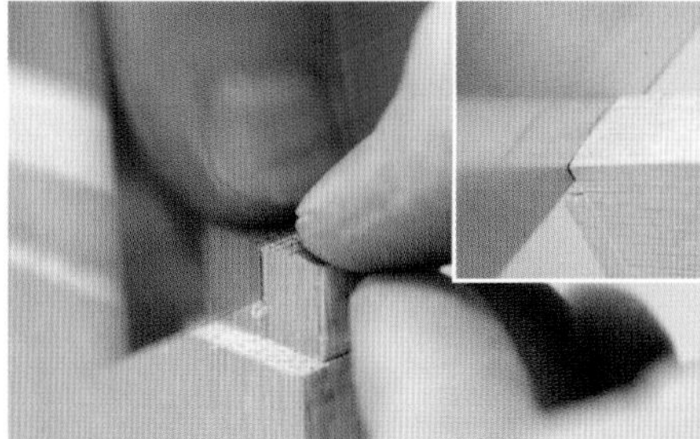

3 **Use a tenon saw** to cut the stop from the tenon piece. Saw along the groove, first ripping through the end grain. Then cross cut down the shoulder (inset).

4 **Check that the tenon** fits the housing. If necessary, adjust the tenon piece by paring with the chisel (inset). Glue, clamp, and allow the joint to dry.

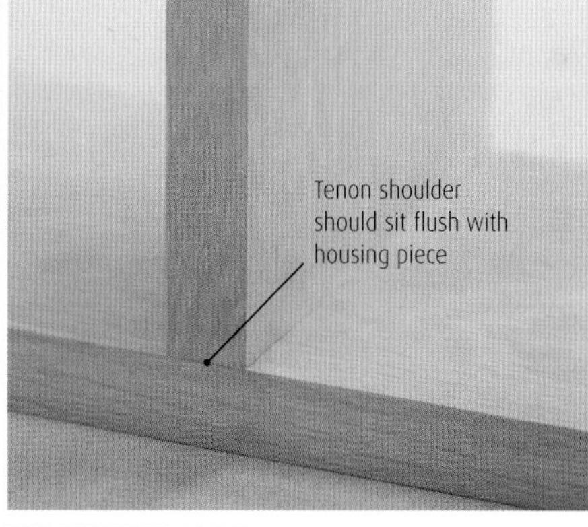

THE FINISHED JOINT

Dovetail housing joint

The dovetail housing is the strongest type of housing joint—it resists racking and does not suffer from pull-out, thanks to its shape. It is useful for carcass constructions where strength is important—such as open bookshelves, arm-to-side-rail joints on carver chairs, bed frames, or for joining a stiffening rail to any frame. It can also be used as a knock-down element of a piece, making it a very adaptable and versatile joint.

PARTS OF THE JOINT

The housing depth can be from a third to half the thickness of the stock, and the tail angle should be at the standard 1:8 ratio for hardwood (1:6 ratio for softwood). The shoulders of the tail produce a very neat joint. The tail piece is usually cut and driven in from the back of the carcass, so the housing is often stopped at the front.

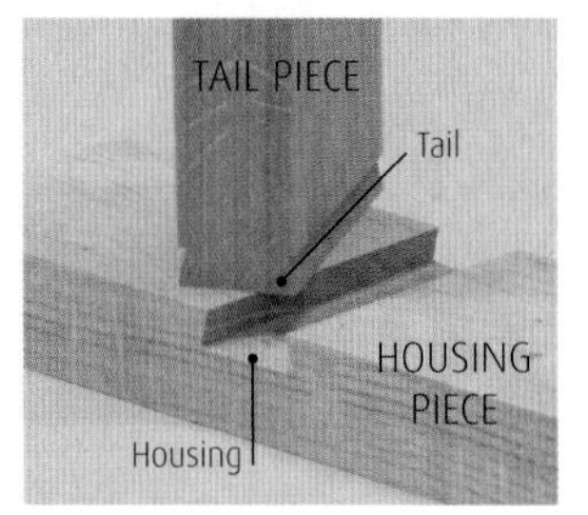

TOOLS AND MATERIALS

Squares
Pencil
Marking gauge
Hand-held router with straight and dovetail cutters
Chisel
Table-mounted router
Wood glue and brush

MARKING OUT THE HOUSING

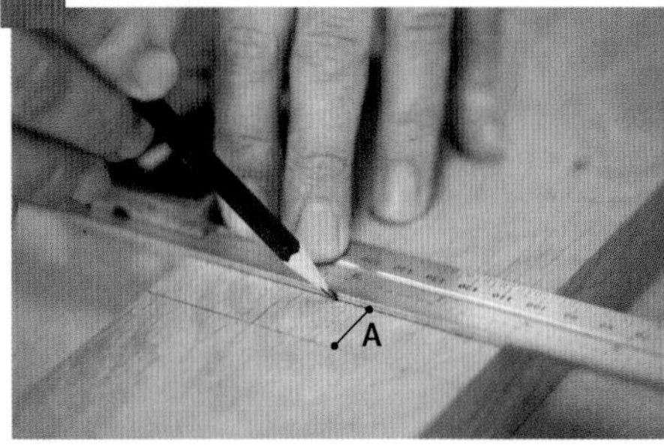

1 **Draw a pencil line** square across the housing piece to define the position of the housing. Mark the housing width (A) approximately ¼in (6mm) less than the thickness of the tail piece.

2 **Square the marks** onto both edges of the housing.

CUTTING THE HOUSING

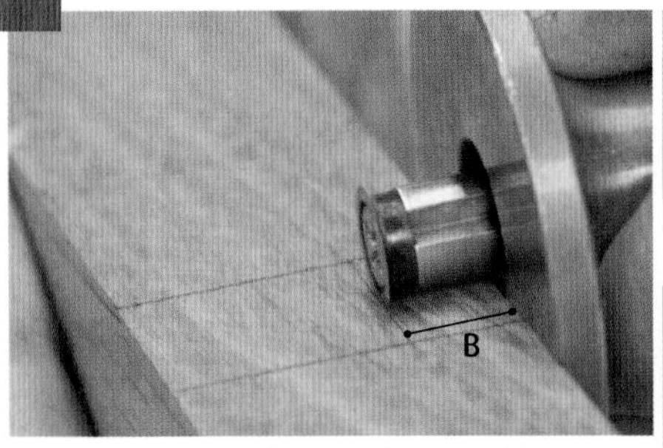

1 **Mark the depth** of the housing (B) on both edges with a marking gauge. The depth should be about one third of the thickness of the housing.

2 **Use a hand-held router** and straight cutter to cut the housing. Secure a fence to guide the router (see pp.46–47) square to the housing, in order to align the cutter to one of the marks that define the edge of the housing (inset).

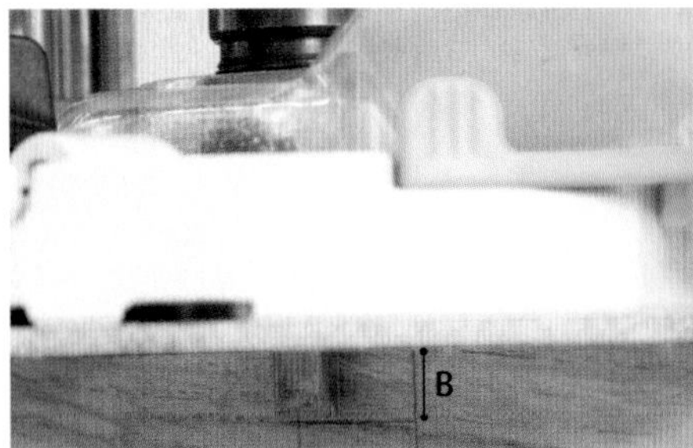

3 **Set the router** to the same depth as the housing (B).

4 **Cut along the length** of the housing to the mark defining the edge (see Step 2). Do not attempt to cut the full depth of the housing in one pass—instead, make several passes of the router until you reach the desired depth. Note that the waste material either side of the workpiece helps support the router and contains breakout.

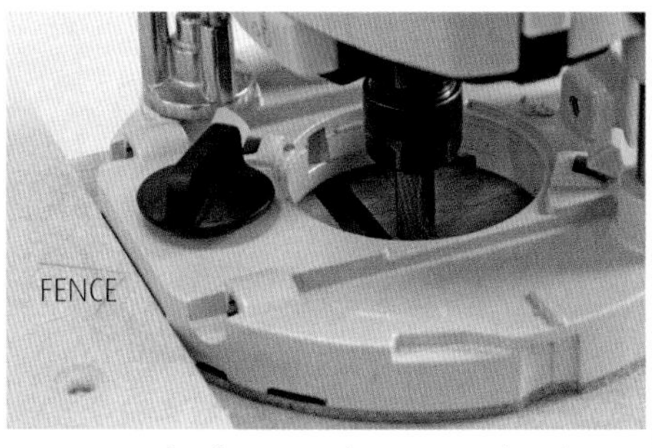

5 **Move the fence** and router so that the cutter is aligned to the other marked edge of the housing, then make a further pass of the router.

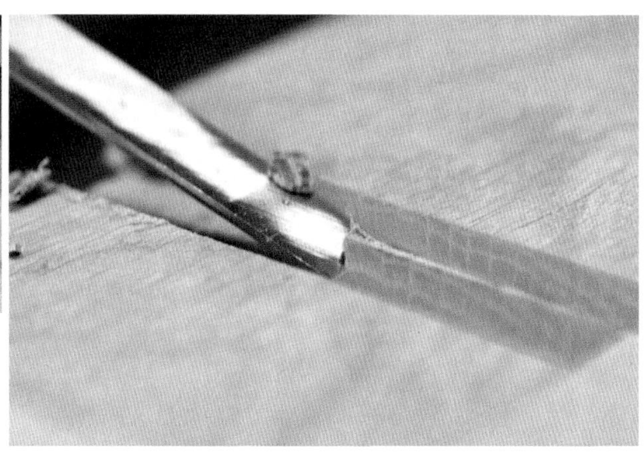

6 **Remove the remaining waste** by chiseling. Alternatively, make additional passes of the router until all the waste is removed.

7 **Insert a dovetail cutter** in the router. Adjust the fence to align the upper part of the cutter with one edge of the housing, so that a dovetail profile is cut without increasing the width at the top of the housing. Cut along the edge to the full depth (B).

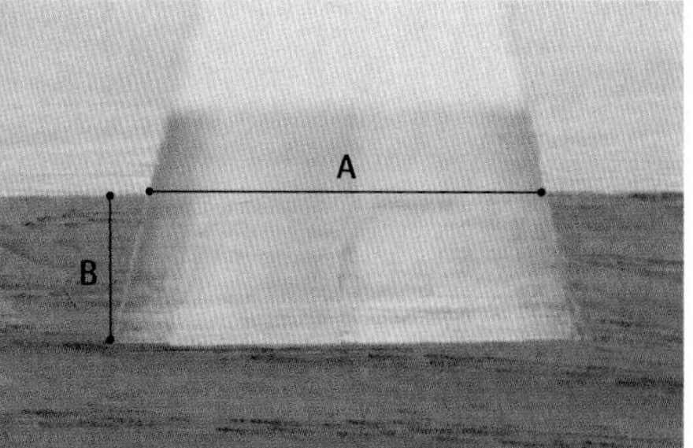

8 **Adjust the fence** to set the dovetail cutter against the other edge. Cut along this edge, then clean up the base and both edges with a chisel.

MARKING OUT AND CUTTING THE TAIL

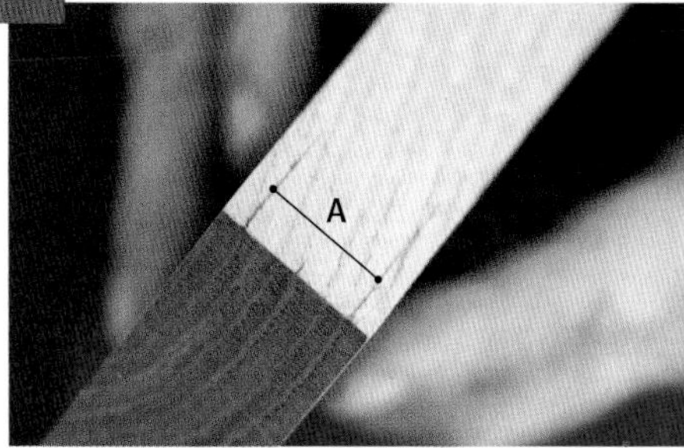

1 **Mark the width** of the top of the housing (A) onto the edge of the tail piece. Ensure you center this measurement within the thickness of the piece.

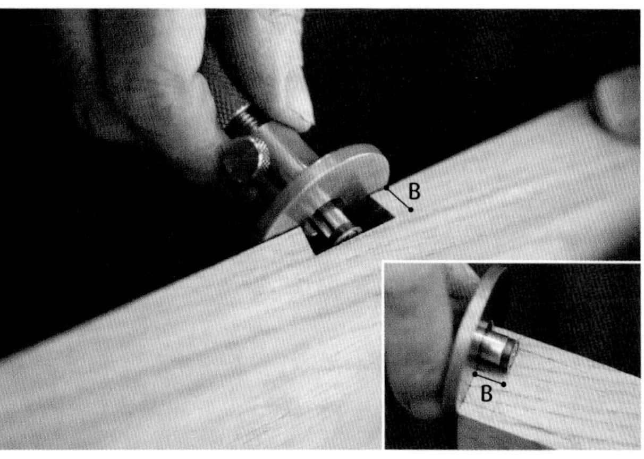

2 **Set a marking gauge** to the depth of the housing (B), then scribe this measurement onto the edge of the tail piece (inset). Scribe the line around all four sides of the tail piece to mark the length of the tail.

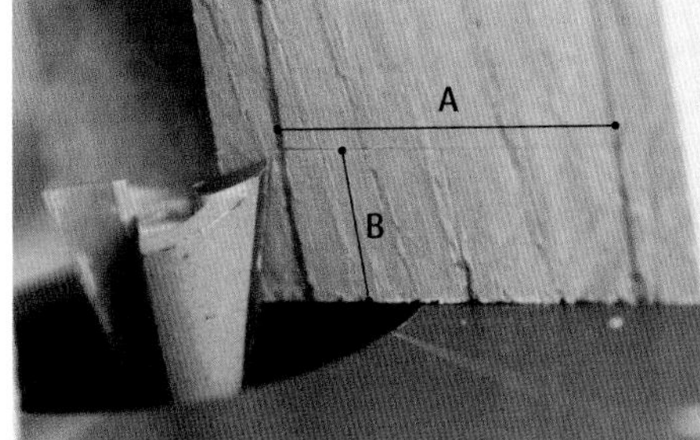

3 **Use a table-mounted router** to cut the tail. Set the depth of the cutter to the tail-length mark, then set the fence so that the outer tips of the cutter are aligned to the housing-width lines.

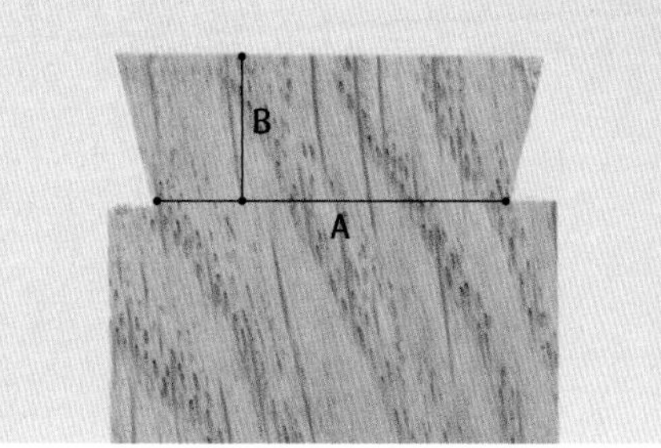

4 **Cut both sides** of the tail on the router. Check the fit within the housing, make any necessary adjustments, and re-fit. Glue the joint, check it is at a 90-degree angle, and then wipe off any excess glue.

THE FINISHED JOINT

Butt-miter joint

Possibly the most common joint, the butt-miter is instantly recognizable as the joint frequently used to make wooden picture frames, and is an attractive way of adding a frame to a table top or a panel. It is simply a 45-degree butt-jointed end grain. Sharp blades are particularly important for this joint, as any bluntness will knock it out of alignment. Reliable and accurate methods of cutting this joint include using a miter block, a compound miter saw, or a miter trimmer. Gluing up the joint can be difficult, since the joining surfaces may slide when wet glue is applied, and the miter can open up over a period of time because the wood shrinks across the grain. There are various ways of fitting the pieces together to make gluing easier, as well as reinforcing and improving the joint to increase its longevity.

PARTS OF THE JOINT

This simple joint consists of two pieces of wood of the same width and thickness, joined at the end grain. These joining end grains are cut to an angle of 45 degrees. There is no mechanical reinforcement, and this joint instead relies on glue for its strength. Accurate cutting of the miter is essential for a successful joint.

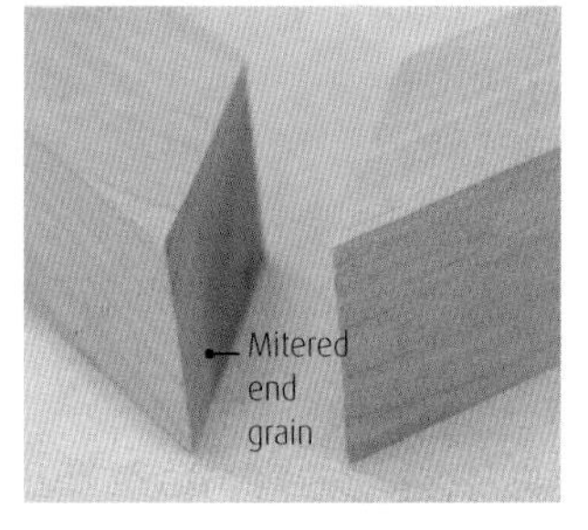

Strengthening the joint

Gluing the end grain is the weakest of jointing techniques, despite the strength of modern glues. If you do decide to use a butt-miter joint, making the miter as small as possible is the best way to maximize its strength. Alternatively, butt-mitered picture frames are often reinforced with a plate or picture framers' corrugated pins on the back of the joint.

An easy method of reinforcing a butt-miter is to insert a loose tongue in a slot in the face of each joining surface, which provides a hidden—and very neat—solution. A keyed miter (p.115) with veneer or solid keys is a decorative variation that is particularly effective on boxes, and can be an attractive feature if contrasting woods are used.

Commercial connectors—in particular, biscuits or dominoes (pp.142–44)—can also be used to strengthen a butt-miter joint. Simple dowel connectors (pp.145–48) are another method of reinforcement.

TOOLS AND MATERIALS

Combination square
Marking knife
Suitable clamp
Bench hook
Tenon saw
Bench plane
Shooting board
Wood glue and brush

MARKING AND CUTTING THE JOINT

1 **Use a combination square** and marking knife to score a line at a 45-degree angle across one face of the first piece of wood.

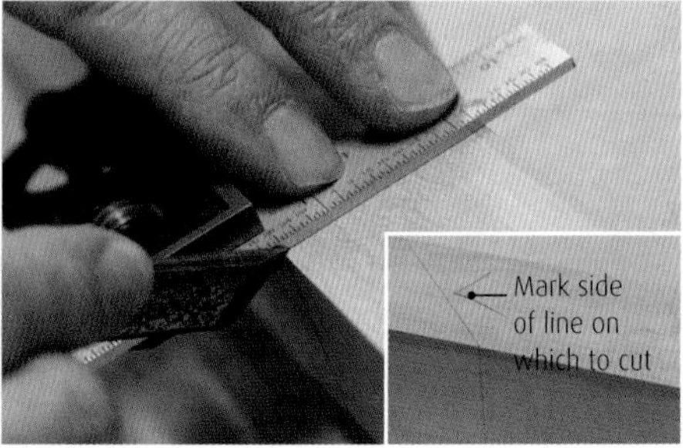

2 **Square the mark** across the two adjacent edges, then mark a line at 45 degrees across the remaining face. Make a V-mark on the side of the line on which you will make the cut (inset).

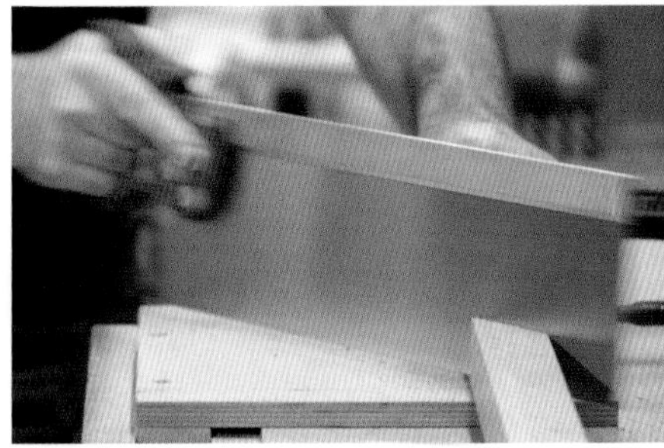

3 **Clamp the piece** to a bench hook to secure it for cutting. Cut along the angle drawn with a tenon saw.

4 **Plane the cut surface smooth**, using a 45-degree shooting board for accuracy. Cut the second piece in the same way. Check the fit of the pieces, apply glue, and clamp.

THE FINISHED JOINT

Mitered half-lap joint

The principal advantage of the mitered half-lap over a conventional corner lap is the attractive appearance of the finished joint—it leaves a neatly mitered face with only one of the end-grain areas exposed. It could be argued that it is weaker than a conventional corner lap or straight butt-miter, due to the smaller gluing and end-grain contact area; however, the glued area and lap part of the joint lend it greater strength.

PARTS OF THE JOINT

As with other lap joints, the components of each joining piece must be of exactly the same dimensions. The lap is exactly half the thickness of each piece, and a simple miter is cut on the top face of each piece. The two pieces are cut in slightly different ways, and are referred to as piece A and piece B for clarity.

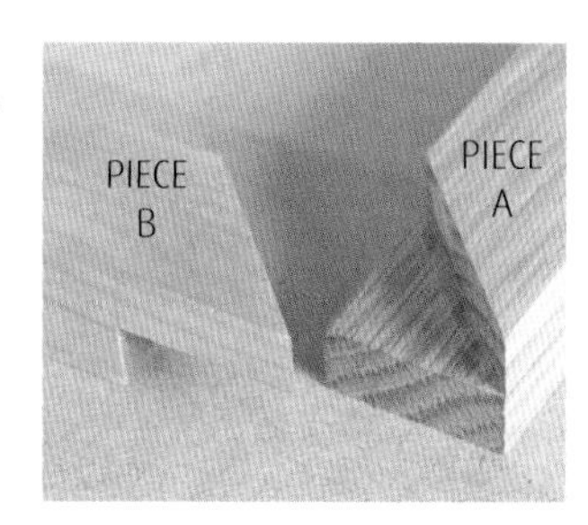

TOOLS AND MATERIALS

- Pencil
- Combination square
- Marking gauge
- Marking knife
- Tenon saw
- Bevel-edged chisel
- Wood glue and brush
- Suitable clamp
- Block plane

MARKING THE PIECES

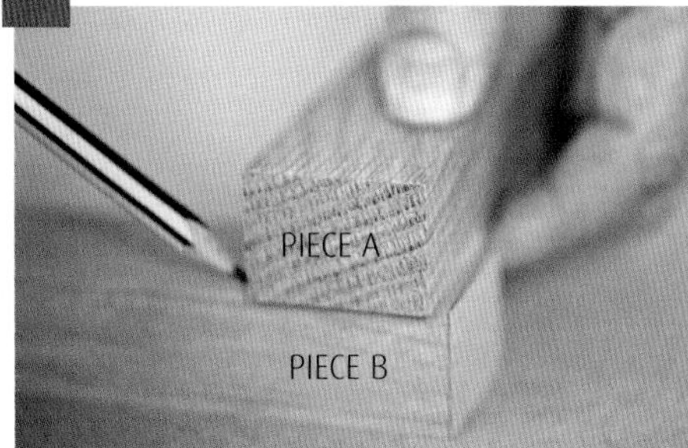

1 **Position piece A** over piece B close to the end grain, and mark the width on piece B, allowing an extra 1/16in (2mm) at the end grain. Reverse the pieces to mark piece A.

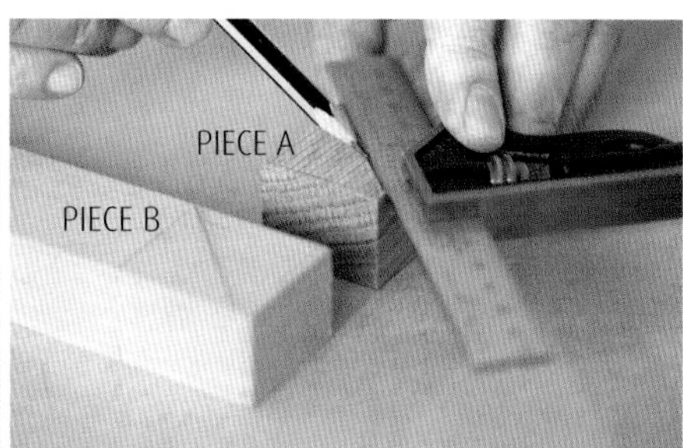

2 **Square the marks** onto all sides of both pieces. Then use a combination square set to 45 degrees to mark the angle of the miter between the marks on both pieces.

3 **Mark the lap** on the end grain and edges of both pieces with a marking gauge. Use a marking knife to extend the line of the miter onto the edge, then mark the waste (insets).

CUTTING THE PIECES

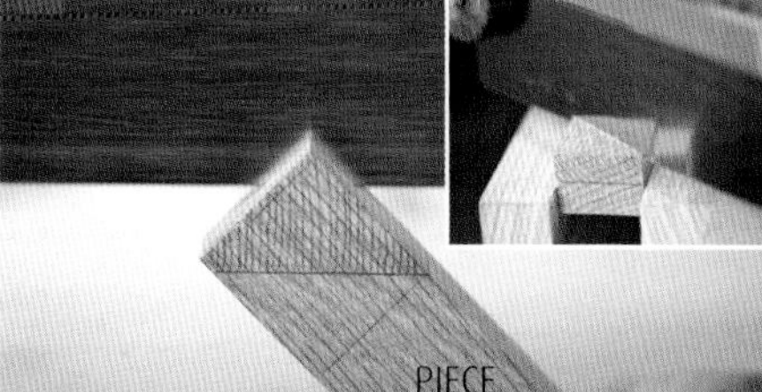

1 **Cut the lap** of piece A with a tenon saw until you reach the shoulder and the line marking the end of the miter. Saw along the line of the miter to release the waste (inset).

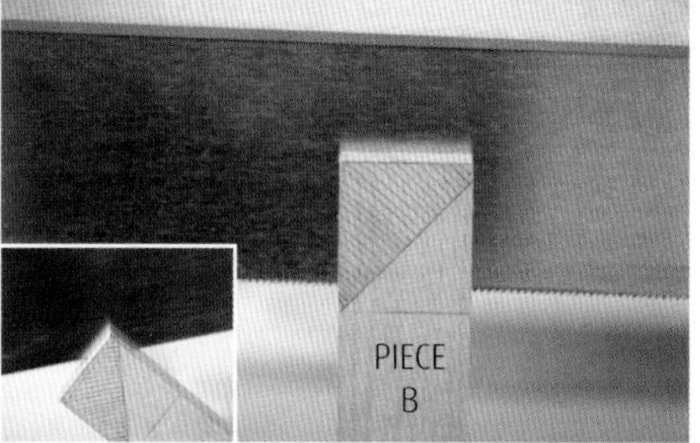

2 **Cut the lap** of piece B to the shoulder mark (inset). Make a cut through the other corner and then cut vertically to the shoulder.

3 **Set piece B** in the vice with the unmiterd section of waste uppermost. Chisel a V-groove along the shoulder, then saw to the marked depth. Saw along the line of the miter to release the remaining waste (inset).

4 **Check the fit** of the joint and, if necessary, pare with a bevel-edged chisel. Glue and clamp the joint, then once the glue has dried, use a block plane to cut the joint flush to the edge (inset).

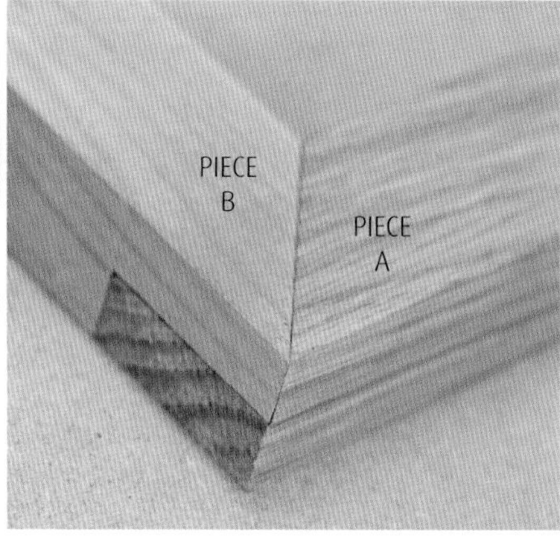

THE FINISHED JOINT

Loose-tongue miter joint

A mechanically strong joint, the loose-tongue miter is more versatile than the simple butt-miter joint (p.112): useful for framing, it resists racking and twist, and provides a larger surface gluing area. The tongue acts in the same way as a floating tenon (pp.140-41), and needs to be a good fit to prevent the miters from sliding. This joint is quick to build and the basic construction process is the same as for a butt-miter joint.

PARTS OF THE JOINT

Mortises in the joining end grains hold the loose tongue. The best material to use for the tongue is ¼in (6mm) birch plywood, since it is strong and uniform in thickness. It should be square to provide the maximum gluing area.

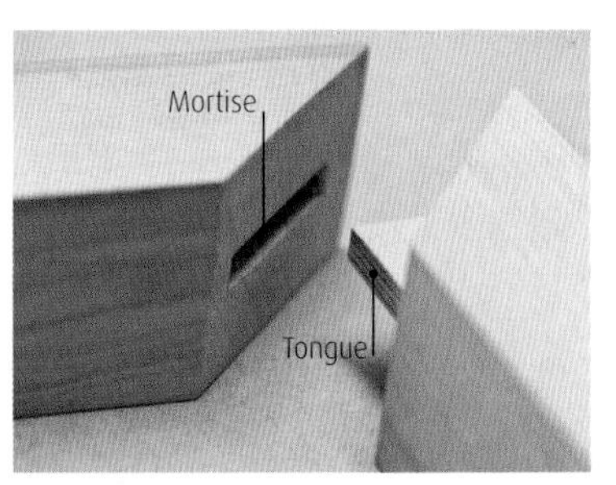

TOOLS AND MATERIALS

- Square
- Ruler
- Mortise gauge
- Mortise chisel
- Band saw or tenon saw
- Wood glue and brush
- Clamp

MARKING OUT AND CUTTING THE JOINT

1 **Miter two pieces** as described for the butt-miter joint (p.112). Set the mortise gauge to the width of the chisel, which should be selected to match the thickness of the plywood used to make the tongue (inset).

2 **Mark the length of the mortise** across the end grain with two horizontal lines (inset). Using the mortise gauge, mark the width of the mortise centrally between these lines. Repeat on the second piece.

3 **Cut the mortise** with the chisel. The slot should be triangular in section, with a vertical edge running from the upper end of the mortise and a horizontal edge from the lower end. Repeat on the second piece.

4 **Measure the depth** of the mortise, which will determine the dimensions of the tongue (see Step 5, below left).

5 **Cut a square plywood tongue**, using a band saw (pictured) or a tenon saw. The sides of the tongue should be the same length as the depth of the mortise.

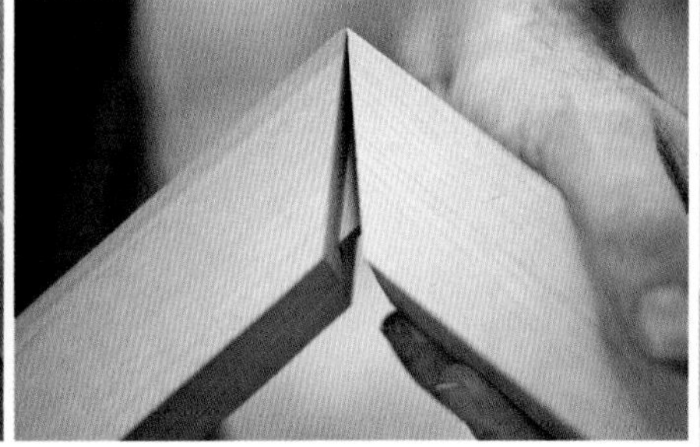

6 **Insert the tongue** into one of the mortises and test fit all three elements of the joint. Adjust as necessary to achieve a tight fit, then glue and clamp.

THE FINISHED JOINT

Keyed miter joint

This is a strong and attractive joint that can be used on any miter with a small section—such as a picture frame—but is most commonly used for boxes. Its strength comes from the veneer keys, which are inserted into slots cut in the glued miter. You can make a decorative feature of the keys by using sections of veneerin a contrasting color to the miter. You could even choose different colors for different keys.

PARTS OF THE JOINT

The basic construction is that of a simple butt-miter joint (p.112). Cuts are made through the corner of the joint, into which the veneer keys are inserted. The placing of the keys is purely aesthetic, but they are usually equally spaced on the stock.

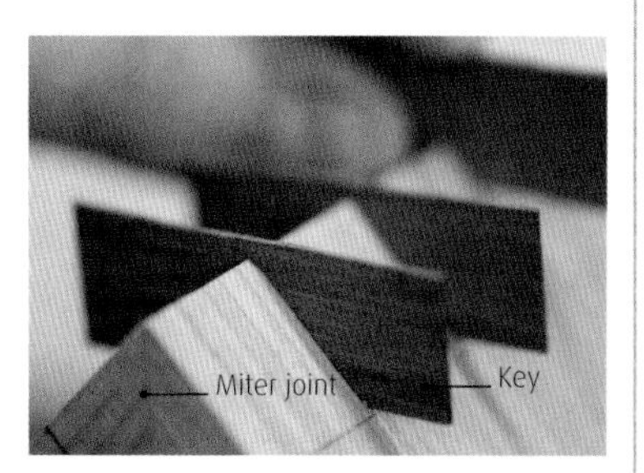

TOOLS AND MATERIALS

- Veneer
- Tenon saw
- Square
- Pencil
- Scalpel
- Wood glue and brush
- Marking knife
- Chisel or flush-cut saw
- Sandpaper

MARKING OUT AND CUTTING THE JOINT

1 **Join two pieces** in a butt miter joint (inset); see p.112. Use a tenon saw that has a kerf of the same width as the veneer, or cut the veneer to suit your saw. Make a test cut on spare wood with your saw to check the fit of the veneer within the kerf.

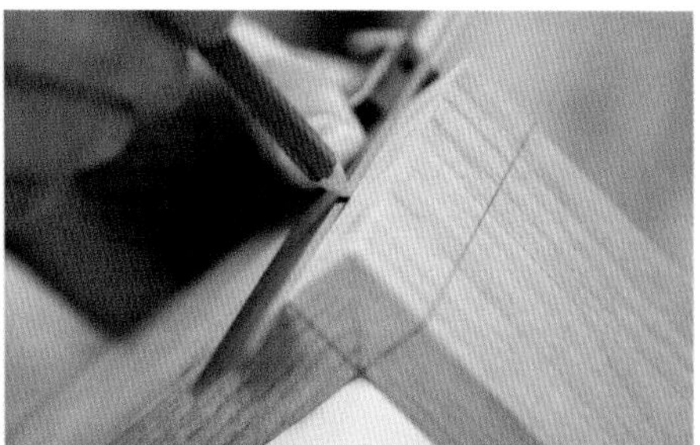

2 **Mark the thickness** of each piece square across both edges of the miter, and square the marks across the outside faces of both pieces to provide a guide for the depth of cut required.

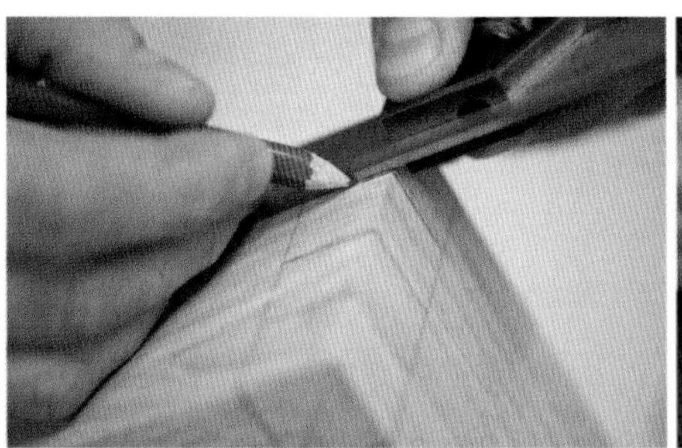

3 **Mark the positions of the keys** on the corner of the joint, and extend the lines to the depth of the cut guides on the faces.

4 **Secure the joint** in a vise with the corner uppermost, and use your chosen saw to cut the slots to the depth of the cut guides marked in Step 2 above.

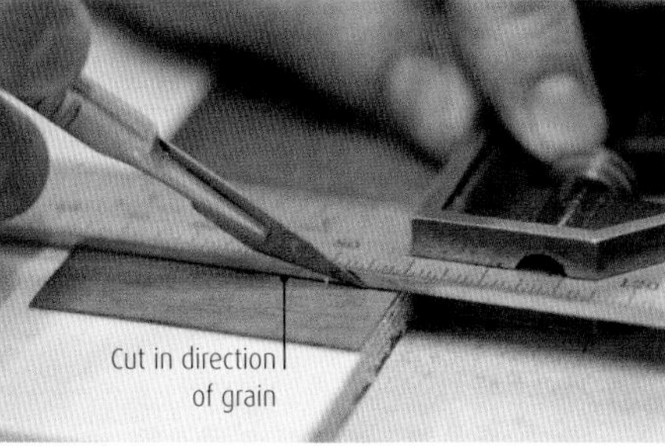

5 **Cut the required number of keys** from the veneer with a scalpel. Cut the pieces oversize, and with one straight edge along the direction of the grain.

6 **Test-fit the keys** in the slots. Adjust if necessary and glue in place. Clean off any excess glue and leave to dry.

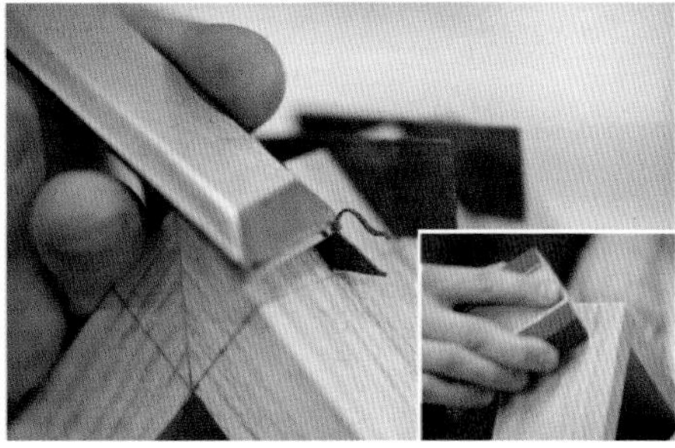

7 **Score the keys flush** with the surface using a marking knife. Then use a chisel (pictured) or flush-cut saw to pare away the excess. Sand smooth to finish (inset).

THE FINISHED JOINT

Basic mortise-and-tenon joint

The mortise-and-tenon is one of the most commonly used joints. It has been used for many centuries in a wide range of woodwork, such as the frame-and-panel furniture (linen chests, cabinets, and dressers) of the Middle Ages and the Tudor period, as well as in the construction of buildings. Today, it is still used for many of these pieces, as well as for doors, windows, and chairs. It is important to remember that tenons are weak in tension and are therefore easy to pull out, but draw-boring (pinning with a dowel), for example, is one of a number of methods of preventing this (see Draw-bore tenon, pp.126–27). The basic joint described here is a stopped mortise-and-tenon joint (see Parts of the joint, right) that has a shoulder around all four sides of the tenon.

PARTS OF THE JOINT

The mortise is a slot—either stopped (as here) or extending through the thickness of the wood—into which a matching tenon fits. The tenon sides are called cheeks and the end grain faces are called shoulders. The tenon thickness should be between a third and half that of the mortise piece—too thick and the joint will be weak, too thin and the tenon is weakened.

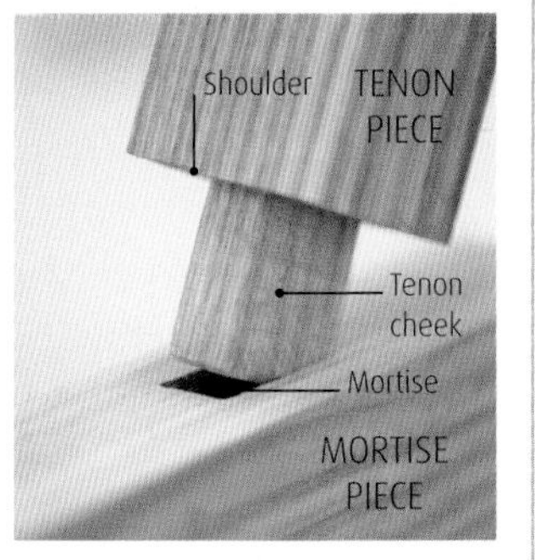

Types of mortise-and-tenon joints

There are many variations on the basic mortise-and-tenon joint. The double tenon (also known as the twin tenon), in which two tenons are cut in the end grain and fit into a matching pair of mortises, has the advantage of a larger gluing area than a standard mortise-and-tenon, and is very resistant to racking and twist, particularly if it has a shoulder. This joint is used in the Bedside table (pp.288–99). Other joints in this family include a knock-down version that has a peg to lock it in place (see p.125).

Through tenons are often wedged as a simple way of adding decorative detail to a piece. These wedged through mortise-and-tenon joints (pp.122–24) can also be used to increase the strength of both carcasses and chairs, most notably at the back-leg joint, which receives a lot of stress compared with the other leg joints. Carcass tenons are often added to housings in furniture to increase strength, while stub tenons (a smaller type of tenon that is generally square) are often used for fitting drawer rails to carcasses.

TOOLS AND MATERIALS

- Ruler
- Pencil
- Square
- Mortise gauge
- Mortise chisel or mortiser
- Marking knife
- Masking tape
- Wooden mallet
- Marking gauge
- Tenon saw or band saw
- Bevel-edged chisel
- Dovetail saw (optional)
- Bench hook
- Wood glue and brush

MARKING OUT THE MORTISE

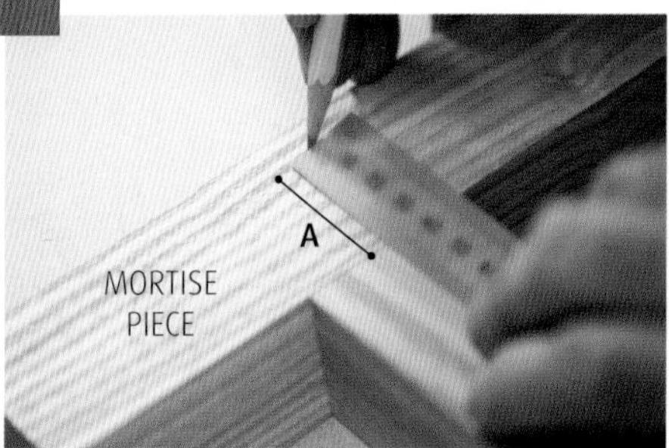

1 **Decide on the depth** of the mortise (A) and mark this measurement on the edge of the mortise piece.

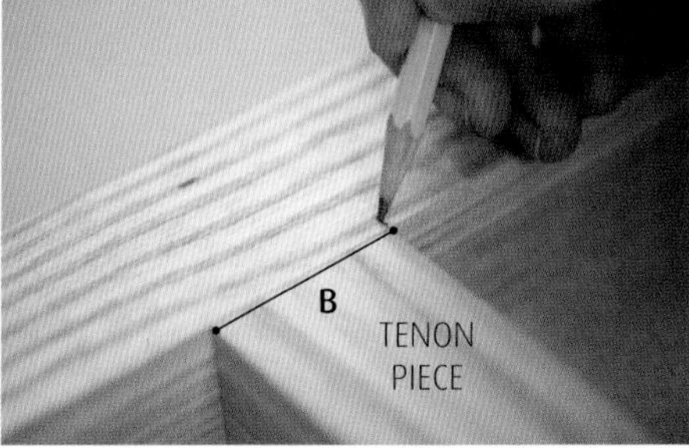

2 **Mark the width** of the tenon piece (B) on the mortise piece to provide a guide for the position of the mortise.

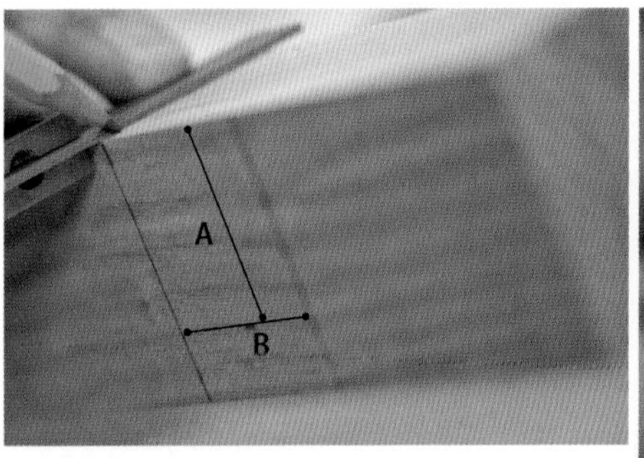

3 **Use a square** and pencil to extend the lines marking the width of the tenon piece (B) across the face and onto both edges.

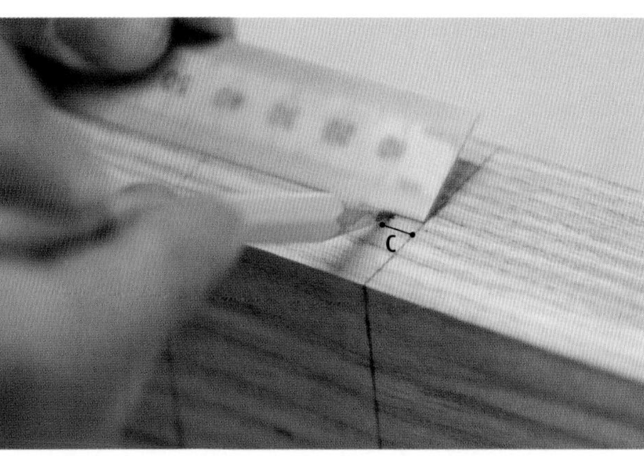

4 **Mark the shoulder** (C) on the face of the mortise piece inside both of the tenon width marks.

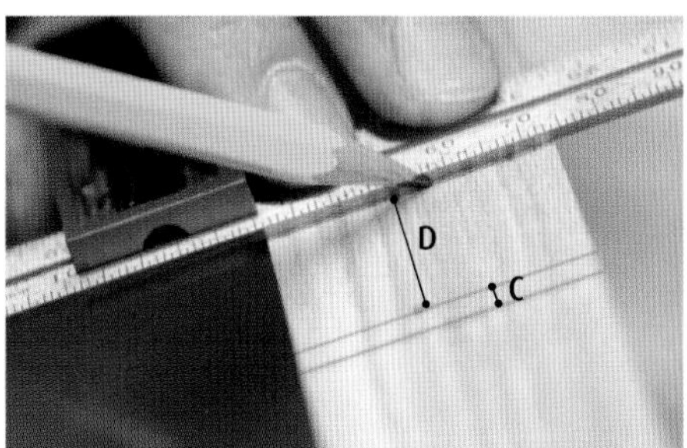

5 **Extend these marks** across the face. The distance between the shoulder marks is the length of the mortise (D).

6 **Set the pins** of the mortise gauge to the width of the mortise chisel, which should be chosen to match the planned mortise width (E).

7 **Set the fence** of the mortise gauge to the mortise width (E) in the desired position between the shoulder marks within the mortise length, then scribe.

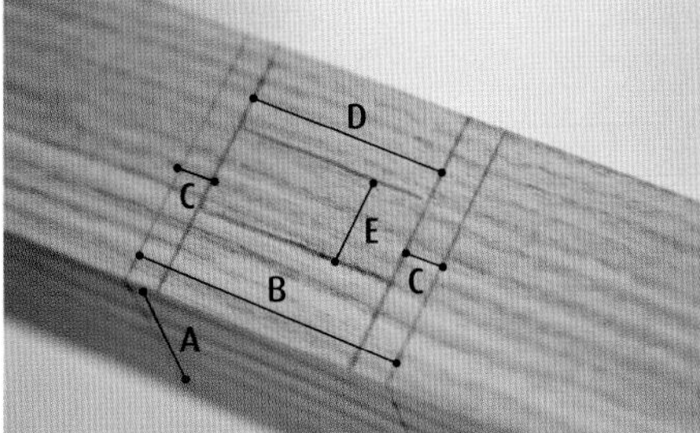

8 **Reinforce all scribed lines** in pencil (pictured). Then mark the waste within the mortise for removal.

CUTTING OUT THE MORTISE

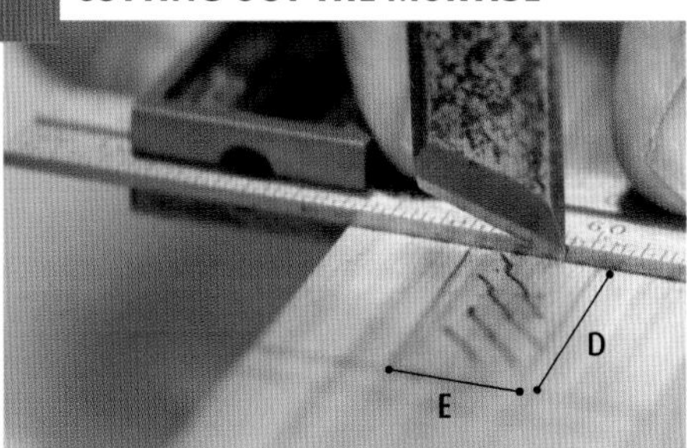

1 **Use a marking knife** and a square to reinforce the scribed marks defining the length of the mortise across the grain.

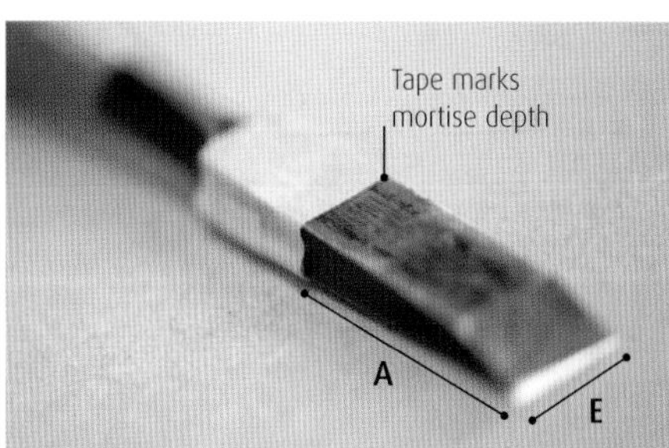

2 **Using the mortise chisel** selected to match the width of the mortise (E) (see Step 6, above), mark the desired mortise depth (A) on the chisel with tape.

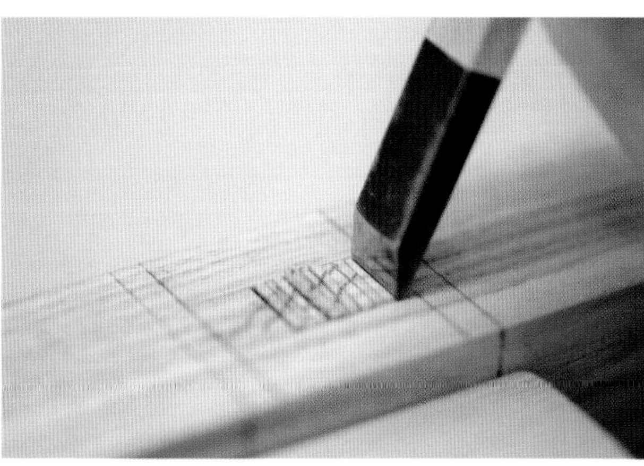

3 **Secure the mortise piece** to the bench, then make V-shaped cuts along the length of the mortise with the chisel and wooden mallet to release the waste.

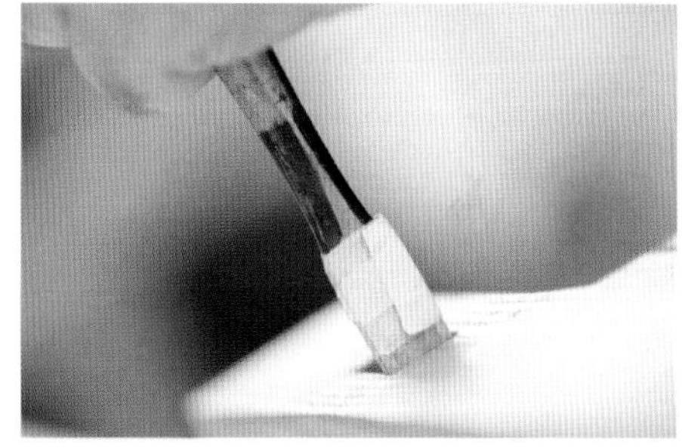

4 **Continue to remove the waste** until you reach the mortise depth marked on the chisel.

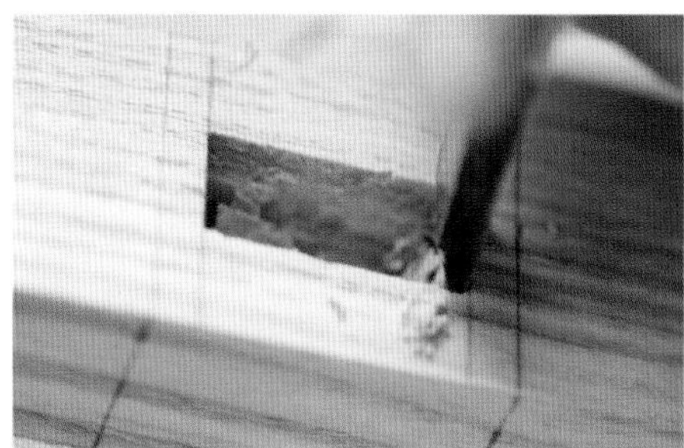

5 **When you have reached** the required depth, use the chisel to pare the sides and ends of the mortise precisely to the marked dimensions.

USING A MORTISER

Cutting a mortise by machine is usually done using a hollow chisel (of a gauge selected according to the width of mortise required) with an auger bit running through the center (see Mortisers, p.62). The auger drills as the chisel cuts with a downward plunging action. The machine is set to a repeatable position and depth. Once one mortise has been marked out, the others can all be cut using the same setting, so there is no need to mark out the other mortises fully. This considerably speeds up the process of making identical mortises on several pieces.

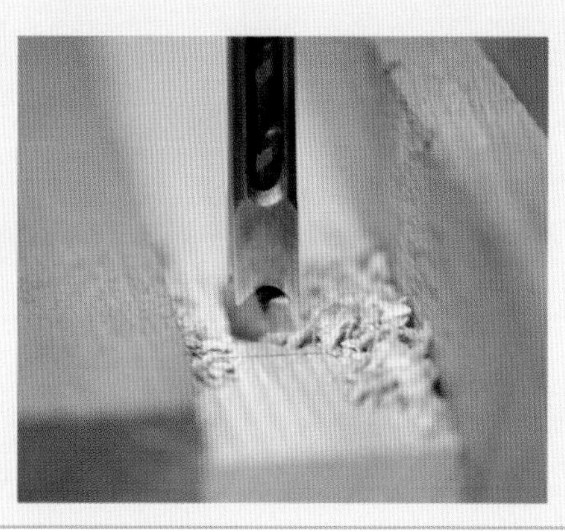

MARKING UP THE TENON

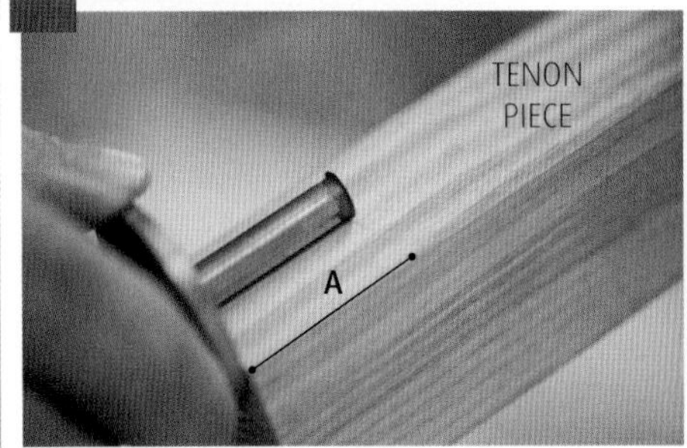

1 **Set the marking gauge** to the depth of the mortise (A). Mark the shoulder of the tenon on the face of the tenon piece.

2 **Extend and deepen** the scored lines around all four sides of the tenon piece using the square and marking knife.

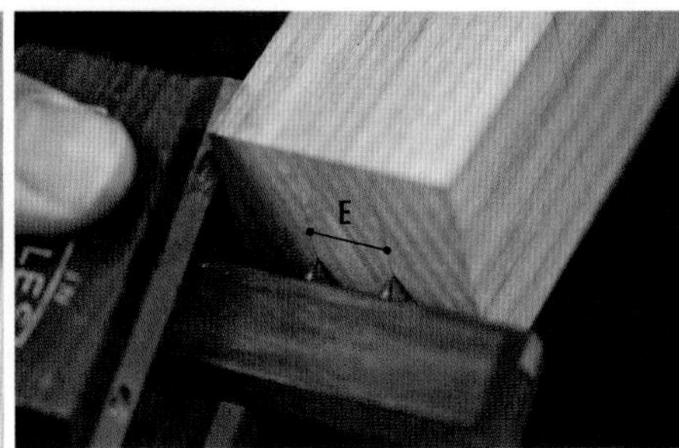

3 **Use the mortise gauge** as previously set to mark the thickness of the tenon (E) on the face. Extend the marks around the end grain and non-face side.

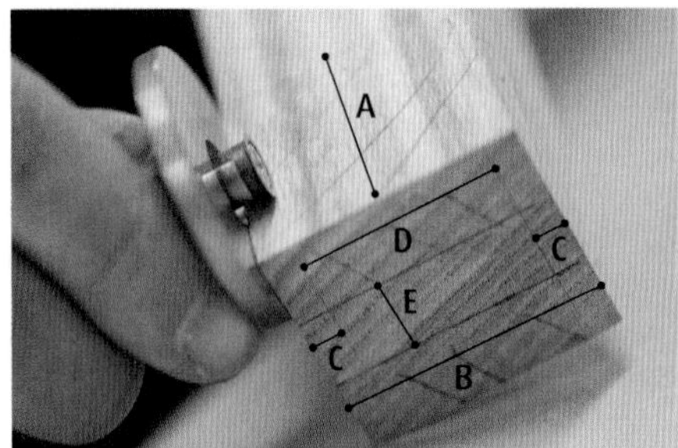

4 **Set the marking gauge** to the width of the shoulder (C) and scribe this measurement adjacent to both edges of the face, and across the end grain of the tenon.

CUTTING THE TENON CHEEKS

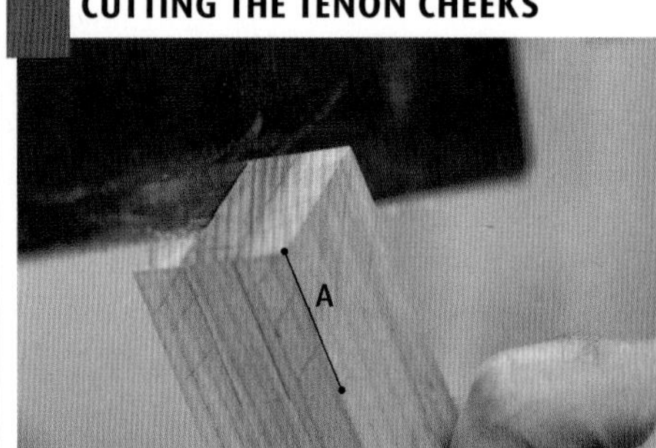

1 **Secure the tenon piece** in a vise at an angle, then saw along the tenon cheek with a tenon saw. Cut until you reach the depth mark on the edge nearest to you.

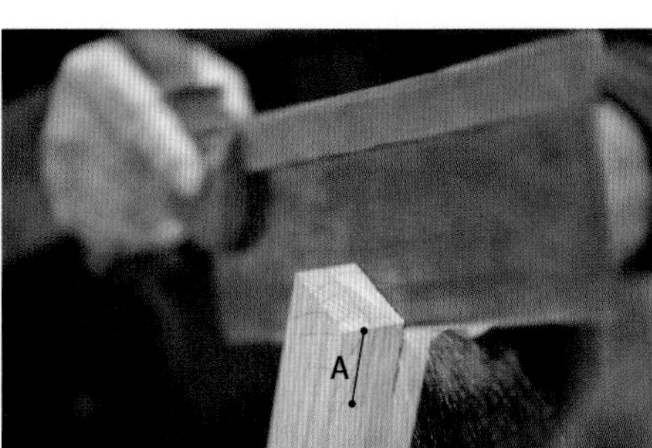

2 **Turn the wood** so that you can saw in the same cut from the other side, until you reach the depth mark on that edge.

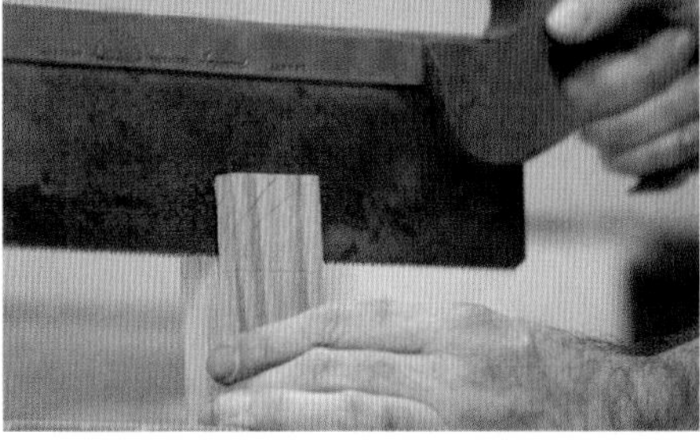

3 **With the wood secured vertically** in the vise, saw horizontally through the same cut. Repeat Steps 1–3 on the other tenon cheek.

4 **Secure the tenon piece** in the vise with the face uppermost. Use a bevel-edged chisel to cut a groove along the shoulder line to create a clean sawing line.

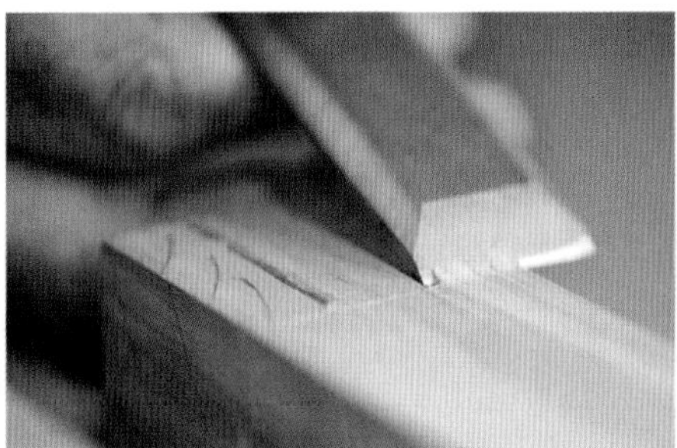

5 **Cut a groove** along the lines marking the edges of the cheeks, then chisel grooves on the other face and edge in the same way.

6 **Use a small tenon saw** or dovetail saw to cut along the groove in the first face to release the waste. Turn the tenon piece and saw off the other cheek.

USING A BAND SAW

To cut the tenon on a band saw, set up the fence to the marked lines on the end grain of the tenon piece. When satisfied that the settings are correct, cut the width of the tenon, then cut the small shoulders to trim the length of the tenon. Remove the cheeks by carefully setting the fence to the waste side of the marked lines. Cut to the lines, stopping well before the shoulder line. Once the first cheek is cut, the same setting should work for the other cheek. Finally, cross-cut to the waste side of the marked lines of the shoulders, taking care not to cut into the tenon itself.

CLEANING UP THE SHOULDERS

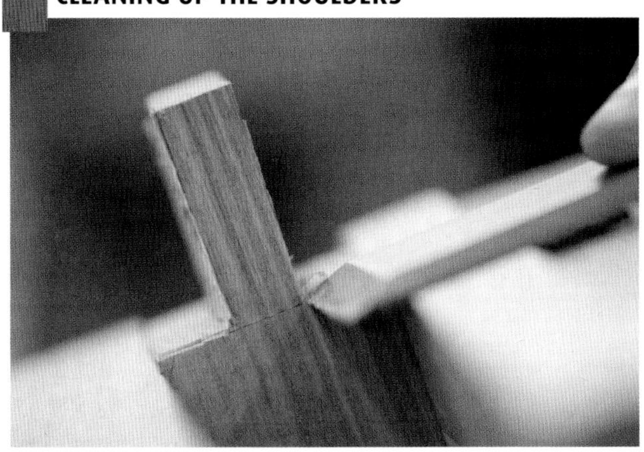

1 **Insert the tenon piece** in the vise with the tenon uppermost and a block alongside, level with the shoulder mark. Carefully chisel away the shoulder, using the block as a guide.

2 **Check the squareness** of the shoulders with a square, then adjust it by careful chiseling if necessary.

3 **Square the line** marking the width of the shoulder (C) from the end grain down the newly cut face of the tenon, using a marking knife.

4 **Cut down the shoulder line** with a tenon saw to remove the waste, then saw along the shoulder to release the waste. Repeat on the other side.

5 **Use a bevel-edged chisel** to pare accurately back to the scored line and neaten any rough edges left by sawing.

FINISHING AND FITTING THE MORTISE AND TENON

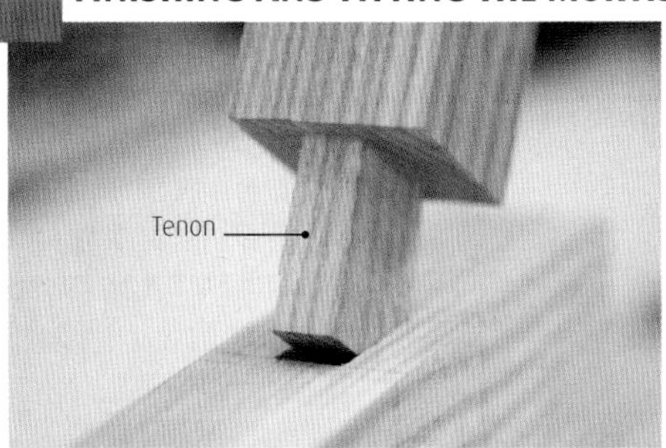

1 **Test the fit** of the tenon in the mortise. It should be snug—pare with a chisel to ease the fit if necessary.

2 **Check the depth** of the mortise and the length of the tenon to calculate how much material to trim from the tenon to create space for the glue in the joint.

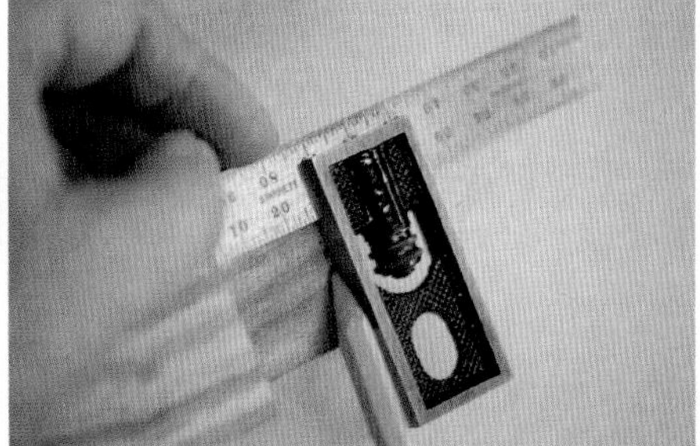

3 **Mark a line** on the face of the tenon to allow 1/16in (2mm) between the end of the tenon and the base of the mortise, then extend the line around all four sides.

4 **Holding the tenon piece** on a bench hook, cut along the line marked in Step 3 with a tenon saw to remove the excess length from the end grain of the tenon.

5 **To ease the fit**, chamfer the edges of the tenon with a chisel. When you are happy with the fit, glue, assemble, check the joint is square, and clamp it.

THE FINISHED JOINT

Haunched-tenon joint

The haunched tenon is a variation of the basic mortise-and-tenon joint (see pp.116–19). It evolved from frame-and-panel carcassing, in which the groove holding the panel runs the whole length of the stile. The haunch fills and therefore strengthens the end of the groove. This joint allows extra tenon width near the shoulder without adding extra depth to the entire mortise, thus providing additional strength.

PARTS OF THE JOINT

The joint consists of a mortise that is cut to a reduced depth at one end. The haunch in the tenon is cut to fit this shape. In the example on this page the full depth of the mortise extends through the thickness of the wood.

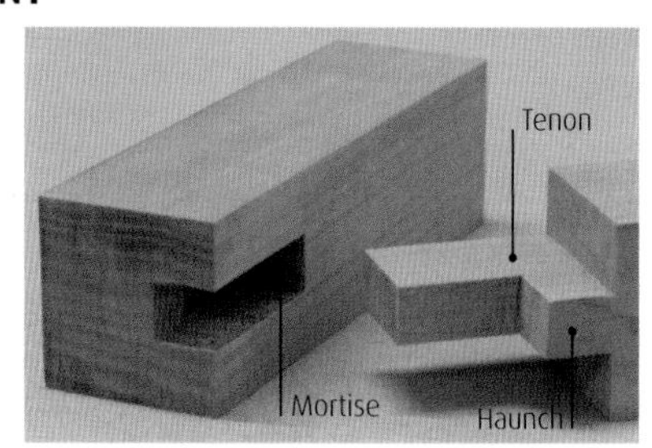

TOOLS AND MATERIALS

- Mortise gauge
- Mortise chisel
- Tenon saw
- Wood glue and brush
- Clamp
- Block plane

MAKING THE MORTISE AND THE HAUNCH

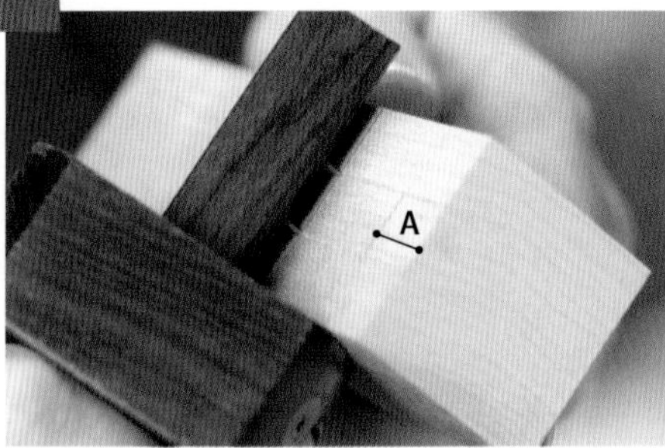

1 **Mark out the length** and width of the mortise in the position required (see pp.116 17). Mark the length of the haunch (A) across the mortise width. The haunch should be around one third of the mortise length.

2 **Extend the marks** around the end grain and mark the depth of the mortise and the haunch (B). Cut the full-depth part of the mortise using a mortise chisel.

3 **Cut the haunch**, using a tenon saw to cut through the end grain to the marked depth. Remove the waste with the chisel (inset).

MAKING THE TENON

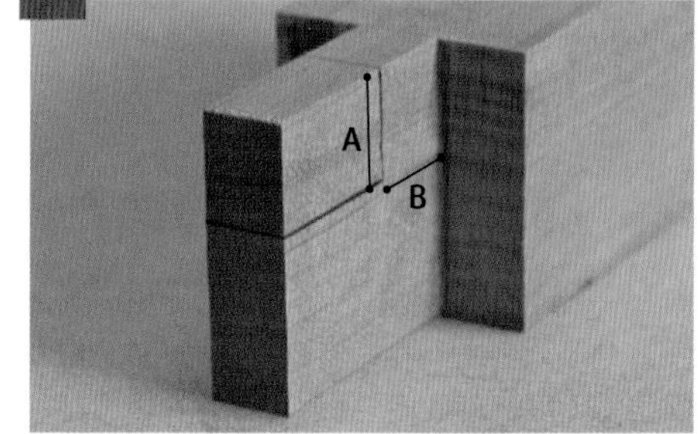

1 **Cut the tenon** to the full mortise width and depth (see p.118). Mark the length (A) and depth (B) of the haunch on the tenon.

2 **Cut the haunch** from the tenon with a small tenon saw, taking care not to exceed the marked lines.

3 **Test-fit the joint** and pare with the chisel to adjust, if necessary. Glue and clamp. When the glue is dry, plane both edges flush with the block plane.

THE FINISHED JOINT

Secret haunched-tenon joint

Although the strength of modern glues has diminished its necessity, the secret haunched-tenon joint is nevertheless useful when an extra-strong haunch is required, but aesthetics are also important. Particularly useful in furniture making, because the joint is hidden, it is often chosen in place of a standard haunched tenon (opposite) for joints such as the front rail-to-leg joints of a chair, or the door tops of a low cabinet.

PARTS OF THE JOINT

This joint differs from the standard haunched tenon (opposite) in that the haunch is sloped (or "tapered"), which strengthens the joint. The mortise is usually blind.

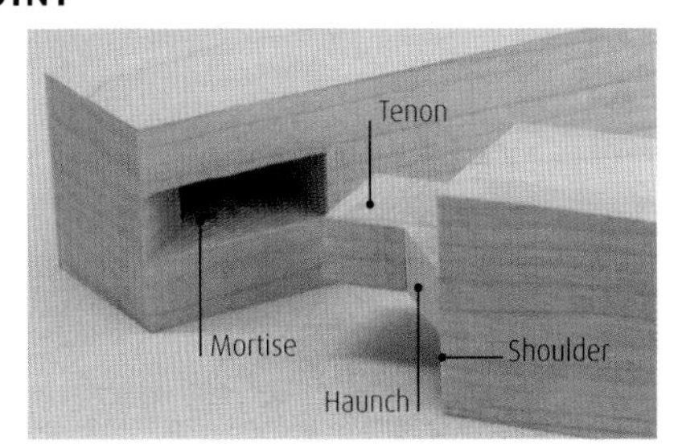

TOOLS AND MATERIALS

- Mortise gauge
- Mortise chisel or hand drill
- Bevel-edged chisel
- Masking tape
- Tenon saw or band saw
- Wood glue and brush
- Clamps
- Block plane

MAKING THE MORTISE

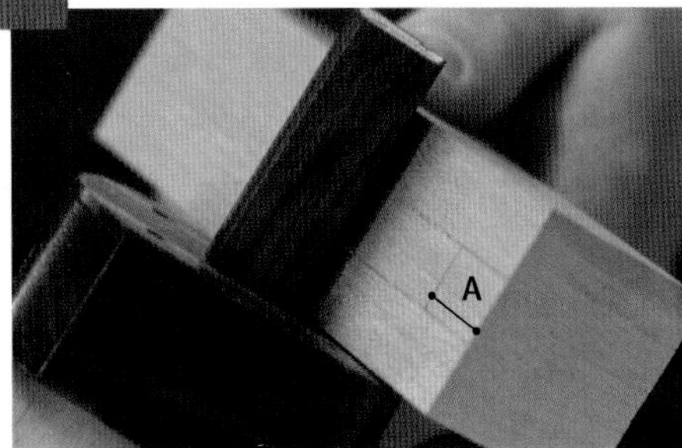

1 **Mark out a mortise** of the desired width and length onto the mortise piece with a mortise gauge (see pp.116–17), and then mark the length of the haunch (A) across the width.

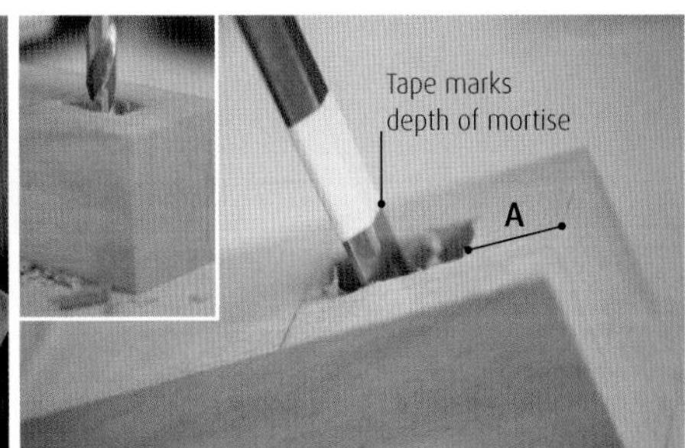

2 **Chop out the full-depth** section of the mortise with a mortise chisel or a hand drill (inset), finishing off the edges with a bevel-edged chisel.

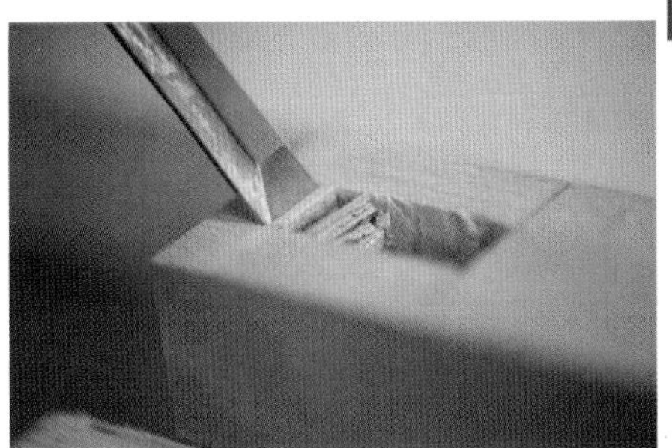

3 **Starting at the inside edge**, chisel the haunch at an angle of about 45 degrees from the outer edge of the mortise.

MAKING THE TENON

1 **Cut the tenon** to the full length and depth of the mortise (see p.118), using a tenon saw or band saw. Mark the length of the haunch (A) with a pencil line on the end grain of the tenon, extending the line around both faces of the tenon with a square. Measure the depth of the haunch (B)—the full depth of the mortise less the depth from the base to the lowest point of the haunch—and mark this position on the line indicating the haunch length. Draw a diagonal line from this point to the shoulder.

2 **Cut the bulk** of the haunch in a square section with a tenon saw (inset). Remove the remaining waste with a bevel-edged chisel, taking care to chisel down to the marks.

3 **Test-fit the joint** by interlocking the mortise and tenon, and adjust by paring with a bevel-edged chisel if necessary. Glue, clamp, and leave to dry. Plane the edges of the joint flush to finish.

THE FINISHED JOINT

Wedged through mortise-and-tenon joint

The wedged through mortise-and-tenon joint is a very strong joint that cannot be withdrawn, making it excellent for use in chairs (particularly the back legs), chests of drawers, or any carcass piece that needs extra support. It can form a decorative feature if contrasting wedges are used, as in the bookcase project (pp.238–43). Its strength comes from the snug fit of the tenon within the mortise when the wedges are inserted.

PARTS OF THE JOINT

In this strong and often decorative joint, the tenon extends through the mortise piece. The ends of the mortise are shaped to allow the tenon to spread to fit securely when tapered wedges are inserted into slots that have been cut in the end grain of the tenon.

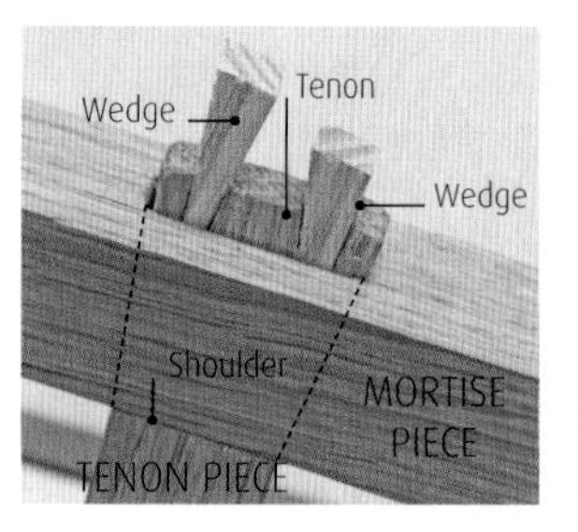

TOOLS AND MATERIALS

- Pencil
- Square
- Mortise gauge
- Marking knife
- Drill and bits
- Masking tape
- Mortise chisel
- Dovetail saw
- Bevel-edged chisel
- Hammer
- Band saw (optional)
- Flush-cut saw

MARKING OUT THE MORTISE

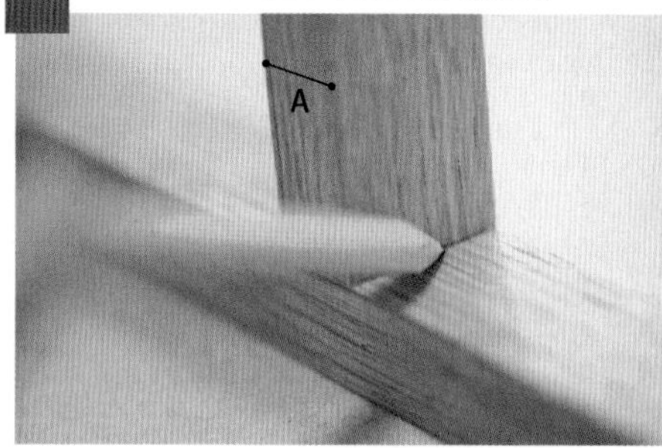

1 **Using the thickness** of the tenon piece (A) as a guide, use a pencil to mark the length of the mortise on the face of the mortise piece.

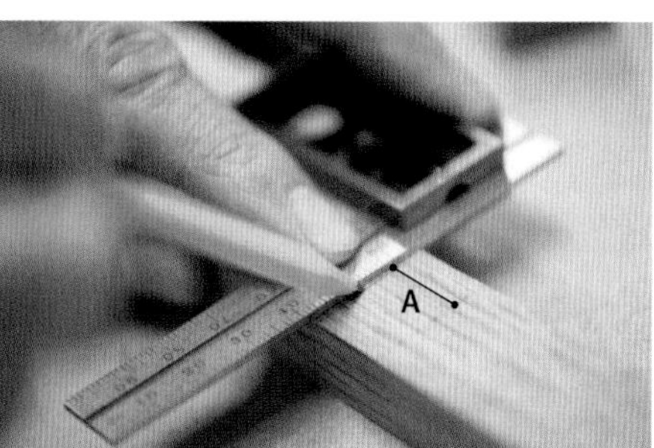

2 **Square the length marks** around all four sides of the mortise piece, using a square and pencil.

3 **Set a mortise gauge** to the thickness of the tenon required (B) and set the fence of the gauge to the desired position of the mortise. Scribe between the lines marking the length of the mortise on both faces of the mortise piece.

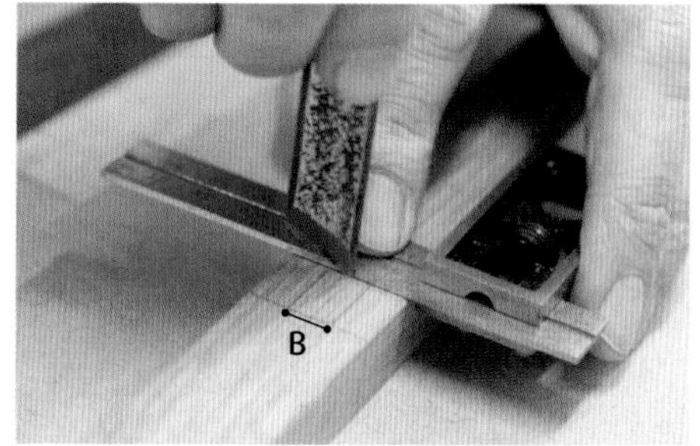

4 **Score across the grain** at the shoulders with a marking knife to link the tenon thickness marks (B) at both ends of the mortise.

MARKING OUT THE TENON

1 **Mark the position** of the tenon shoulder on the tenon piece, using the thickness of the mortise piece as a guide. Allow an extra ⅛in (3mm) in addition to the thickness of the mortise piece.

2 **Scribe the tenon shoulder line** around all four sides of the tenon piece, using a marking knife and square.

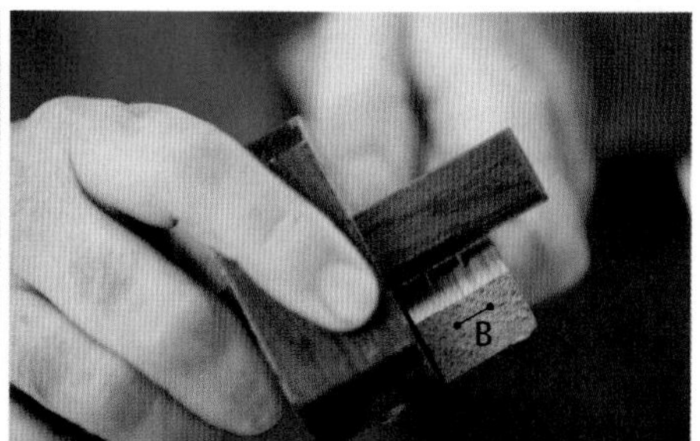

3 **Use the mortise gauge** as previously set to scribe the tenon thickness (B) onto the tenon piece. Scribe across the end grain and down both faces of the tenon to the shoulder line.

CUTTING THE MORTISE

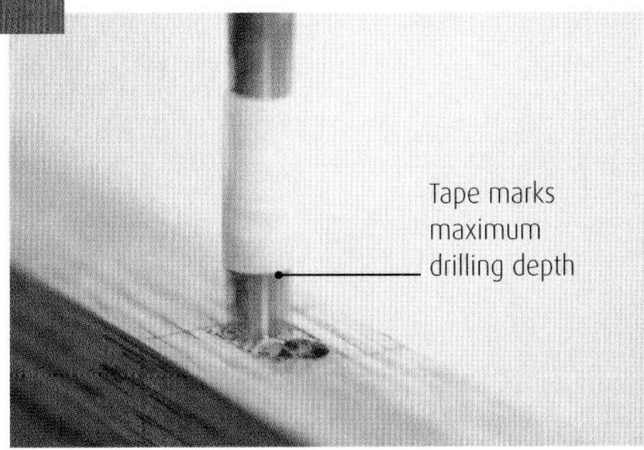

1 **Use a drill** fitted with a bit a little smaller than the width of the mortise to drill halfway through the mortise piece. Make more than one drill hole, if required.

2 **When drilling,** be careful to keep clear of the marked edges of the mortise. Drill from the other side to cut through the thickness of the mortise piece.

3 **Use a mortise chisel** of the same width as the mortise to remove the remainder of the waste and to clean up the edges on both sides of the mortise.

FLARING THE MORTISE

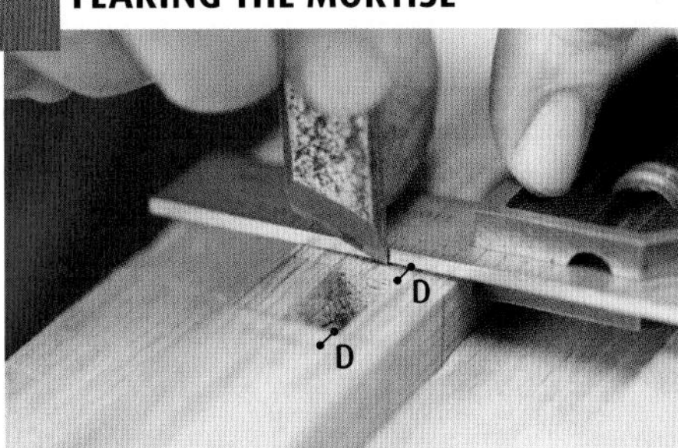

1 **Working on the outside face** of the mortise, mark the maximum desired thickness of the wedges (D) at both ends of the mortise with a marking knife.

2 **Chisel into the mortise** at an angle to almost the full depth of the mortise to create sloping sides (inset). Leave the lower inside edges of the mortise square.

CUTTING THE TENON

1 **Using a dovetail saw,** cut the cheeks of the tenon diagonally from each side and then vertically to the shoulder (see p.118). Turn the piece in the vise and cross cut along each shoulder to release the waste (inset).

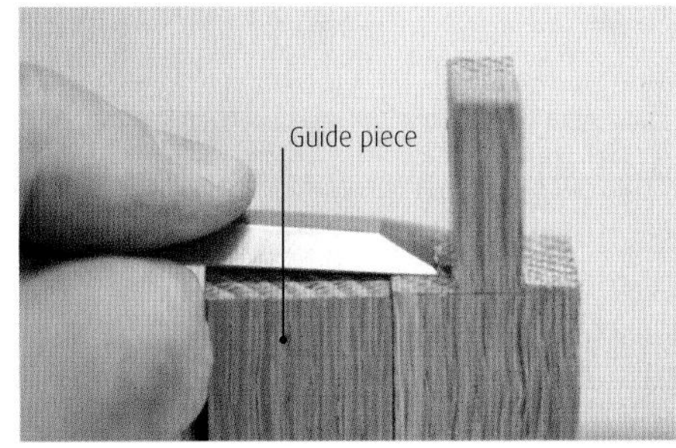

2 **Clean up the shoulders** with a bevel-edged chisel, using a guide piece clamped alongside the tenon piece.

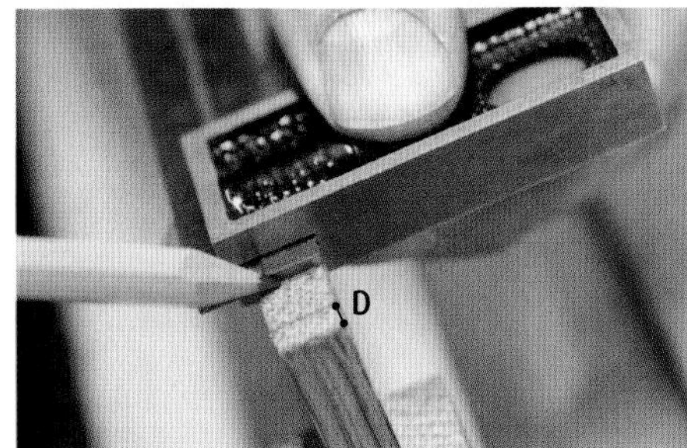

3 **On the end grain of the tenon,** mark the position of the slots for the wedges the same distance from the edge of the tenon as the width of the wedges (D).

4 **Mark the line of each slot** at a slight angle from the marks on the end grain of the tenon made in Step 3 to a point (X) about ⅛in (3mm) from the shoulder.

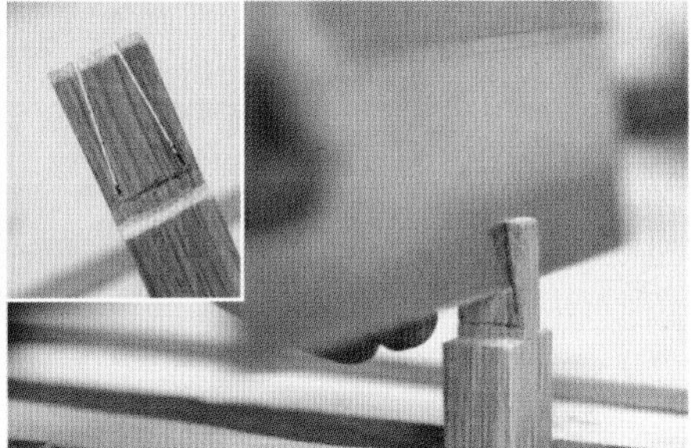

5 **Saw from each mark** on the end grain at an angle to the marked position near the bottom of the tenon to create two diagonal slots (inset).

MAKING THE WEDGES

1 **Cut the wedges from wood** of the same thickness as the mortise width (B). Check the fit of the chosen wood by inserting it in the mortise.

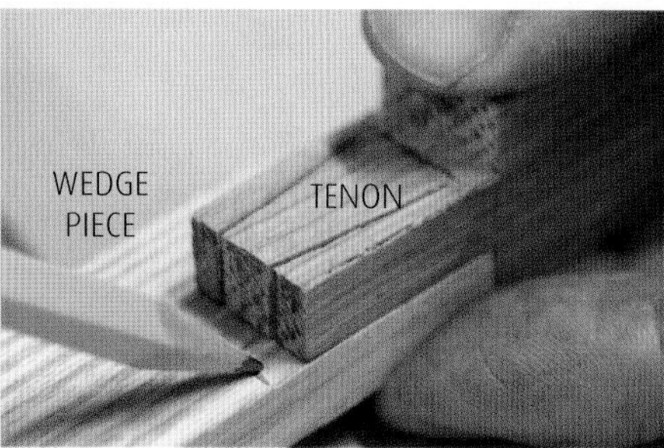

2 **Using the tenon as a guide**, mark the length of the wedges. (This should be a little longer than the length of the tenon.)

3 **Extend the mark** that indicates the length of the wedges across the face of the wedge piece using a square.

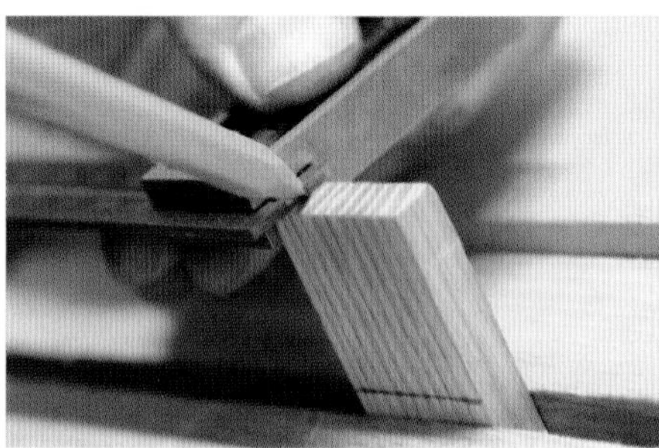

4 **From the edge** of the wedge piece, mark the width of the wedges (D) on the end grain.

5 **Saw from this point** toward the length mark, at an angle. Stop just before you reach the mark.

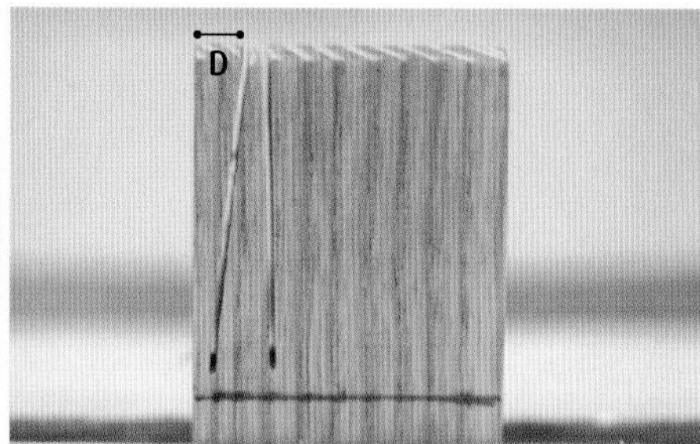

6 **To cut the second wedge**, saw vertically down from the same point in the end grain to a point level with the previous cut. Repeat Steps 4–6 to cut as many wedges as you require.

7 **Using a dovetail saw** (pictured) or a band saw, cut along the base of the wedges to separate them.

ASSEMBLING THE JOINT

1 **Insert the tenon into the mortise** so that the tenon end protrudes from the flared end of the mortise. Then use a hammer to tap the wedges into the slots.

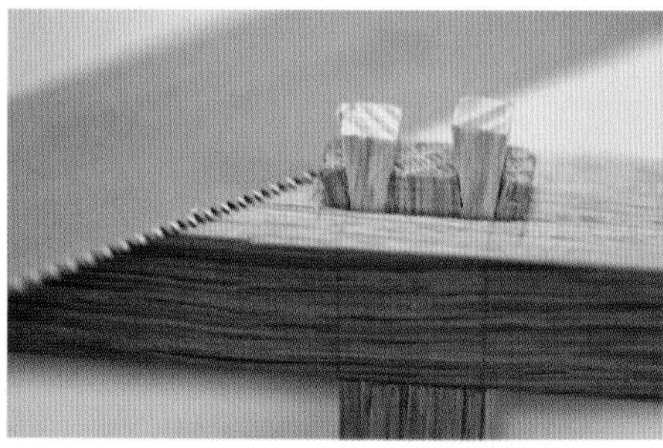

2 **Use a flush-cut saw** to trim the tenon and wedges as closely as possible to the face of the mortise piece.

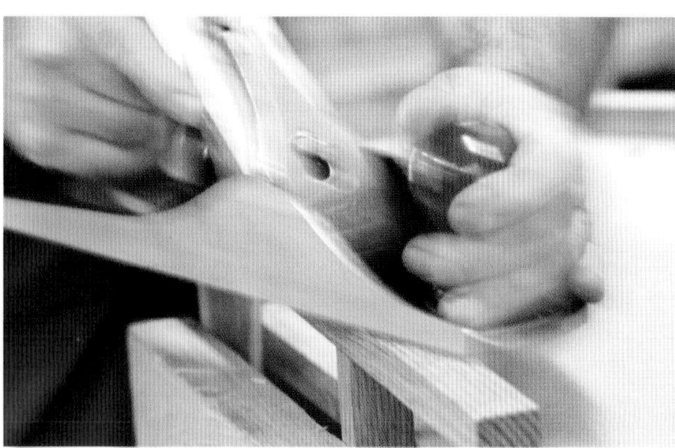

3 **Use a bench plane** to finish, smoothing the exposed end of the joint flush with the face of the mortise piece. This joint does not need to be glued, although glue may contribute to its long-term strength.

THE FINISHED JOINT

Knock-down tenon joint

A member of the mortise-and-tenon family, the knock-down tenon is commonly used in Asian furniture, as well as in the furniture of the Arts and Crafts movement. The peg that is inserted through the tenon is removable, which allows the joint to be disassembled easily. This means that pieces can be completely "knocked down" for transport, making the joint particularly useful for large items, such as bookcases and beds.

PARTS OF THE JOINT

This joint is formed by a tenon that protrudes from the mortise sufficiently to accommodate a mortise for a peg. When inserted, the peg acts as a stop against tension. The peg/mortise width should be no more than one third of the tenon width.

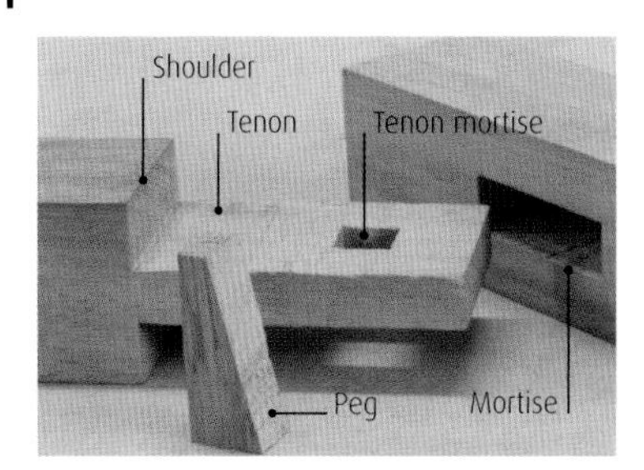

TOOLS AND MATERIALS

- Pencil
- Square
- Mortise gauge
- Drill and bits
- Mortise chisel
- Tenon saw
- Block plane
- Flush-cut saw (optional)

MAKING THE MORTISE AND TENON

1 **Mark up and cut** a mortise through the thickness of the wood, as described for a basic mortise-and-tenon joint (pp.116-19).

2 **Cut the tenon** to the required length (see Parts of the Joint, above, and p.118). Mark the thickness of the mortise piece on the face of the tenon.

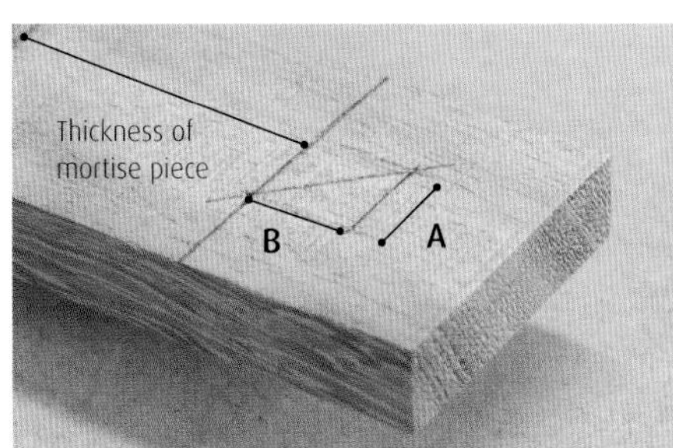

3 **Mark the size and position** of the tenon mortise on the tenon face. Scribe the mortise width (A) with a mortise gauge, then square the required length of the tenon mortise (B) between these marks.

4 **Drill out the waste** from the tenon mortise with a bit a little smaller than the size of the mortise (inset), then square off the sides of the hole with a chisel.

MAKING AND FITTING THE PEG

1 **Cut the peg** longer than required, using stock slightly larger than the tenon mortise. Plane the peg to fit the mortise (inset). Cut a taper along one edge so that the narrow end fits loosely in the mortise.

2 **With the joint assembled**, place the non-tapered edge flush to the face of the mortise piece, and push the peg into the tenon mortise until it fits tightly.

3 **Cut the ends of the peg** flush to the edges of the mortise piece, using a flush-cut saw or a tenon saw. No glue is required for this joint.

THE FINISHED JOINT

Draw-bore tenon joint

One of the oldest forms of mortise-and-tenon joint, the draw-bore tenon was commonly used in buildings and furniture from the 16th century onward. Devised before the introduction of reliable glues, the joint is assembled dry and then secured by a doweling peg that draws the shoulders tight against the bore. The draw-bore tenon can form a decorative feature, lending a traditional feel to furniture in which it is used.

PARTS OF THE JOINT

The peg hole ("bore") is drilled through both sides of the mortise, and the hole in the tenon is slightly offset so that the joint is pulled tight when the peg is knocked into the hole. The size of the peg is determined by the joint size. The bore should be located at least ½in (12mm) from the end of the tenon.

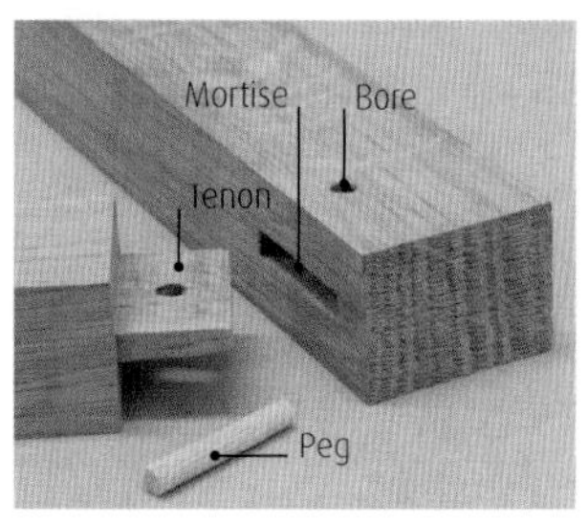

TOOLS AND MATERIALS

- Combination square
- Pencil
- Bradawl
- Marking gauge
- Drill and lip-and-spur bit
- Dividers
- Bevel-edged chisel
- Hammer
- Flush-cut saw

MARKING OUT THE BORE

1 **Mark out and cut** a basic mortise and tenon joint (pp.116–19). Using a combination square and pencil, mark the ends of the mortise and the tenon shoulder, and extend the marks across the adjacent face of the mortise piece.

2 **Mark a line** on the face of the mortise piece centered between the lines indicating the mortise length.

3 **Using a combination square** set flush to the edge, measure the depth of the mortise.

4 **Using a pencil**, transfer the measurement to the mortise face on each of the lines indicating the mortise length. Square the mark across the face.

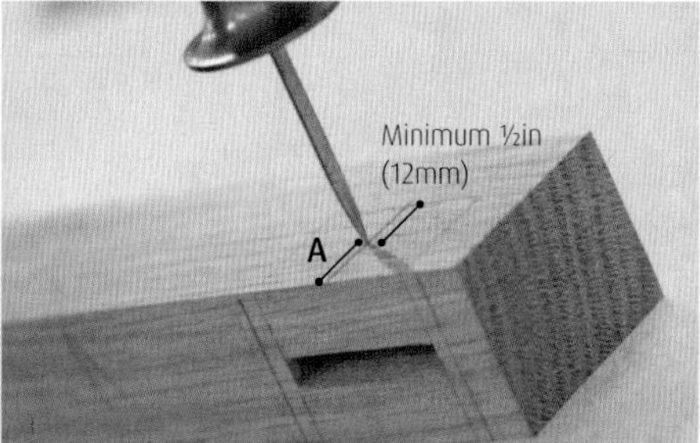

5 **Use a bradawl** to mark the position of the bore on the center line, at least ½in (12mm) from the line marked in Step 4. (Measurement A is the distance of the bore from the edge.)

6 **Repeat Steps 1 and 2** on the opposite face of the mortise. Use a marking gauge set to measurement A to scribe the position of the bore onto the other face.

DRILLING THE BORE

1 **Choose a lip-and-spur drill bit** to match the width of doweling you have selected for the peg (see Parts of the Joint, opposite).

2 **Drill vertically into the positions** marked for the bores through the mortise piece. (Be sure to drill from both sides to avoid break out.)

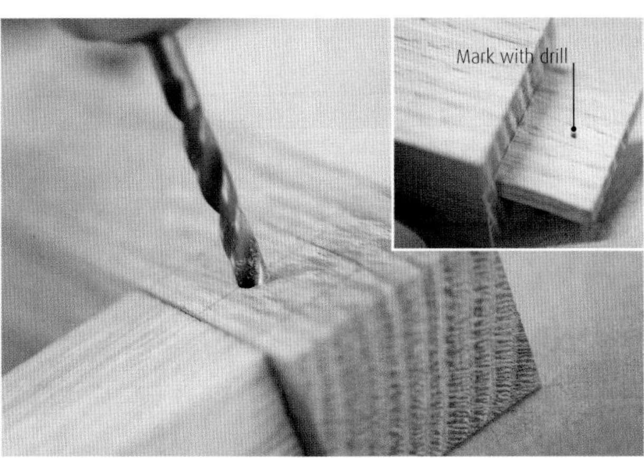

3 **Assemble the mortise and tenon** and use a short burst of the drill to mark the position of the bore on the tenon (inset). Be careful not to drill all the way through.

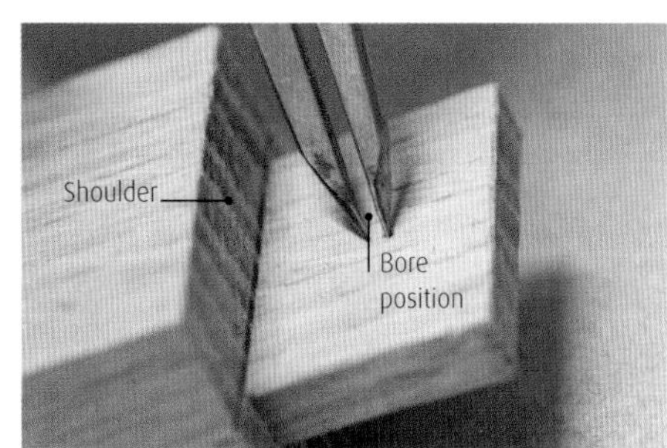

4 **Remove the tenon** and use dividers to mark the position of the bore 1⁄16in (2mm) closer to the shoulder than the point marked by the drill.

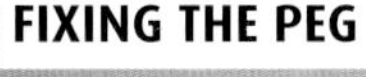

5 **Using the same drill bit,** drill a hole in the newly marked position, all the way through the tenon. Use an offcut to support the tenon during drilling.

FIXING THE PEG

1 **Cut the doweling** for the peg a little longer than the full thickness of the stock, and chamfer one end with a bevel-edged chisel.

2 **With the mortise and tenon assembled**, tap the peg through the hole in the top of the mortise piece and through the tenon.

3 **Cut the peg** flush with the joint, using a flush-cut saw. Pare any excess length with a chisel (inset). As an alternative to the fluted dowel, a non-fluted dowel made from matching wood can be used.

THE FINISHED JOINT

T-bridle joint

Bridle joints are part of the large family of joints related to the mortise-and-tenon joint (pp.116–19): they are essentially open mortises with a tenon. Although most types of bridle joint have no mechanical hold at all, the larger-than-normal gluing surface area means that, when joined with modern glues, they can be as strong as joints with a closed mortise. The exception to the rule is the T-bridle (also known as an open-slot mortise), which, even without glue, has great inherent strength—as well as resistance to racking—due to its construction, in which the mortise completely straddles the tenon. The T-bridle can be used for joints in the middle of rails, such as in carcass panel frames. It can also be used to connect a leg to a top rail in a table.

Types of bridle joint

Although the T-bridle is the strongest type of bridle joint in purely mechanical terms, other joints within this family can be very strong too. The simplest variant is the corner bridle (p.131), which is essentially the same as a T-bridle but has a mortise that crosses the tenon at the end of the tenon piece to create a corner. While it might appear to be a weak joint, since there is nothing—apart from a tight fit—to prevent it from being pulled apart, its main advantage is its large gluing surface area. Stronger variants of the corner-bridle joint include one in which a square peg is used and one in which two pegs are inserted diagonally through the joint.

Another useful bridle joint is the mitered bridle, which is used for the construction of frames. It is a neater method of joining a frame than the corner bridle, and can be used in a frame-and-panel construction. The use of woods of contrasting colors in bridle joints can be an effective way of creating added visual interest.

PARTS OF THE JOINT

In a T-bridle joint the mortise part is simply an open mortise, which forms a U-shape in the end of the mortise piece. The "bridle," which is enclosed within the mortise, is formed by the tenon. It is similar to a double-sided half lap, and has a housing in both sides. The shoulders on the housings enable it to resist sideways racking very well.

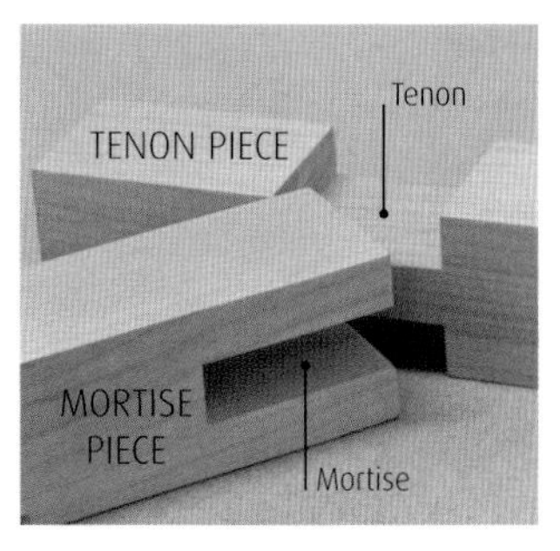

TOOLS AND MATERIALS

- Pencil
- Square
- Mortise gauge
- Marking knife
- Tenon saw
- Coping saw
- Mortise chisel
- Bevel-edged chisel
- Wood glue and brush
- Clamps
- Bench plane

MARKING OUT THE MORTISE AND TENON

1 **Set the mortise piece** at a right-angle to the tenon piece so that it protrudes slightly, and mark the position of the shoulder in pencil on the mortise piece.

2 **Use a square and pencil** to extend the shoulder line onto all four sides of the mortise piece.

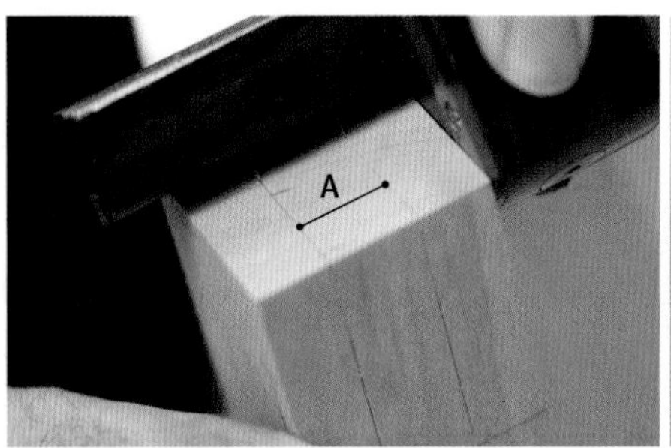

3 **Set the mortise gauge** to just over one third of the thickness of the mortise piece (A). Scribe the mortise width centrally along the end grain, and down both faces to the shoulder mark.

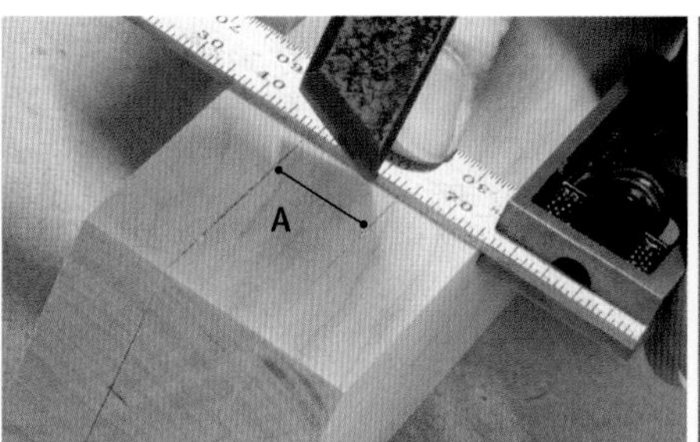

4 **Scribe the shoulder marks** between the scored width on both edges with a marking knife. Then mark the waste of the mortise for removal.

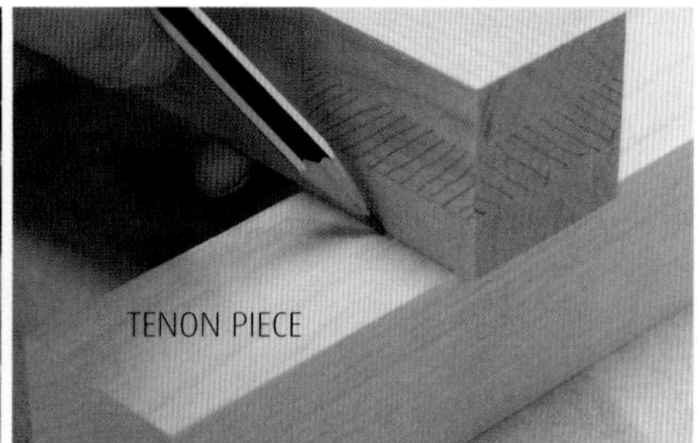

5 **Place the mortise piece** in position over the tenon piece, and mark the position and dimensions of the joint.

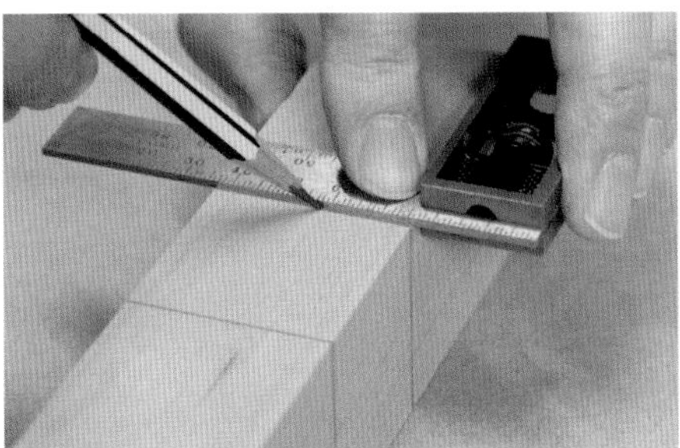

6 **Extend the marks** around all four sides of the tenon piece, using a square and pencil.

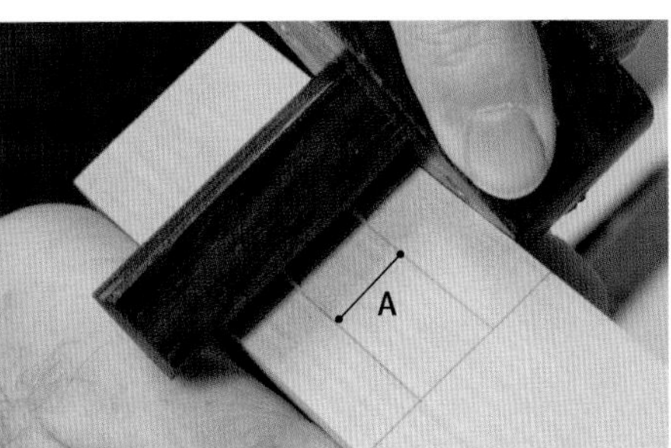

7 **With the mortise gauge** still set at the width of the mortise (A), scribe the thickness of the tenon centrally between the marks on both edges of the tenon piece.

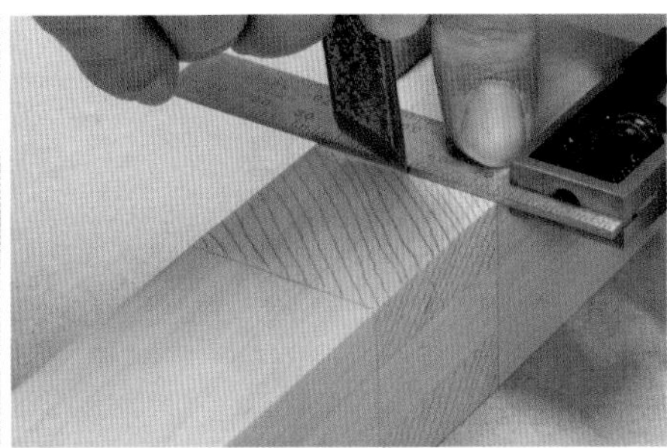

8 **Mark the waste** for removal. Then score the shoulder marks on both faces of the tenon piece, using a square and marking knife.

CUTTING THE MORTISE

1 **Secure the piece** in a vise and use a tenon saw to cut the mortise diagonally from the end grain to the shoulder mark.

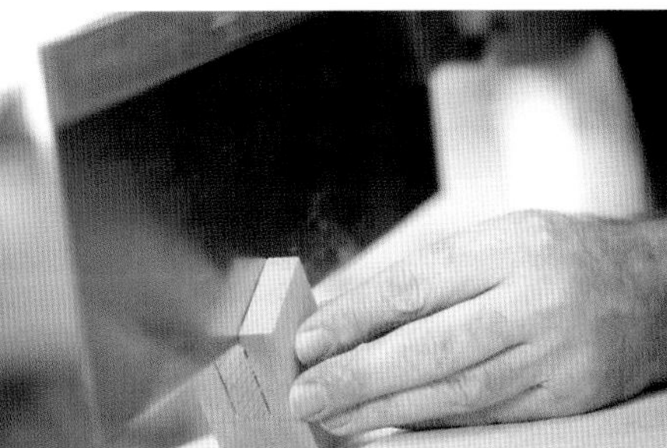

2 **Turn the piece** in the vise and cut from the other side, being careful to stay within the marks.

3 **Turn the piece** in the vise for a final time and cut vertically through the cuts to the shoulder mark.

4 **Make a relief cut** through the center of the mortise to enable you to remove the waste.

5 **Release the waste** by cutting from the relief cut to both edges of the mortise with a coping saw.

6 **Using a mortise chisel**, clean up the base of the mortise to the shoulder, removing any rough edges.

CUTTING THE TENON

1 **Place the tenon piece** in a vise and cut the tenon shoulders with a tenon saw. Be sure to cut to the waste side of the lines.

2 **Make relief cuts** through the waste. Turn the tenon piece upside down and repeat, cutting the shoulders and relief cuts.

3 **Chop away the waste** with a bevel-edged chisel, then repeat on the reverse face of the tenon piece.

4 **Clean up the tenon** on both sides by paring the base and edges of both sides with a mortise chisel.

5 **Test-fit the joint** and, if necessary, use a chisel to adjust the mortise and tenon in order to achieve a good fit.

FINISHING THE JOINT

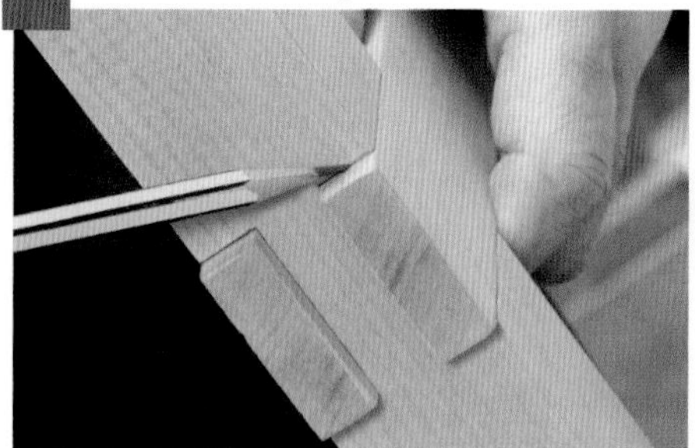

1 **Assemble the joint** and, using a pencil, mark the excess on the ends of the mortise piece.

2 **Disassemble the joint** and square the pencil lines on the end grains of the mortise onto both faces with a marking knife.

3 **Glue the joint** (inset) and assemble. Clamp and leave it to dry.

4 **Once the glue has dried**, cut along the scored lines with a tenon saw to remove most of the excess from the mortise ends.

5 **Prepare the remaining mortise ends** for planing by chiseling the edges. This will prevent the grain from breaking out when the ends are planed.

6 **Use a bench plane** to remove the remainder of the ends, planing them flush to the tenon piece.

THE FINISHED JOINT

Corner-bridle joint

The corner-bridle joint is essentially an open mortise and tenon. The exposed end grain makes it a very attractive joint but it has no resistance to racking and relies on glue for its strength. A good example of the use of a corner bridle joint is in chair making, where a leg can be securely attached to a solid seat with a triple corner bridle. The secret is that the gluing area is three times the size of the normal joint.

PARTS OF THE JOINT

This joint is used for two pieces of wood of the same dimensions. The tenon piece fits into a U-shaped open mortise. The end grains of both the mortise and the tenon are exposed, giving the joint its distinctive appearance.

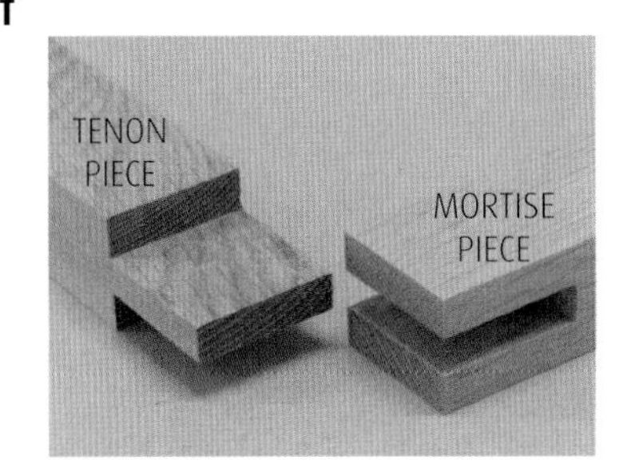

TOOLS AND MATERIALS

- Pencil
- Square
- Mortise gauge
- Marking knife
- Tenon saw
- Coping saw
- Bevel-edged chisel
- Wood glue and brush
- Block plane

MARKING THE JOINT

1 **Place the first piece of wood** on top of the second at right-angles so that the edge of the first is just short of the end grain of the second. Mark around both edges.

2 **Square the marks** around all four sides. Reverse the pieces and mark up the second piece in the same way.

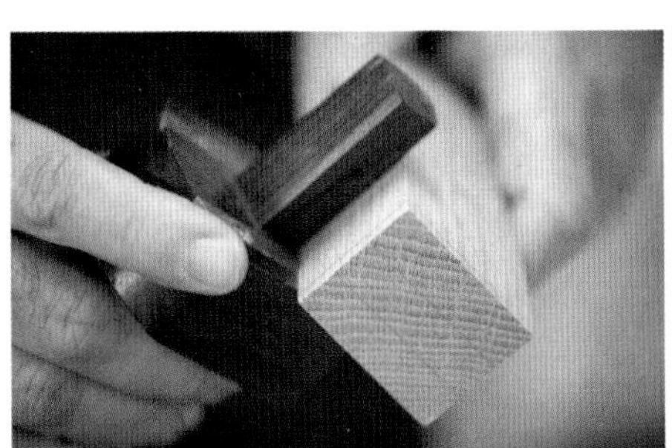

3 **Set a mortise gauge** to one third of the thickness of the wood. Scribe centrally around the end grain and down the edges to the marks on both pieces.

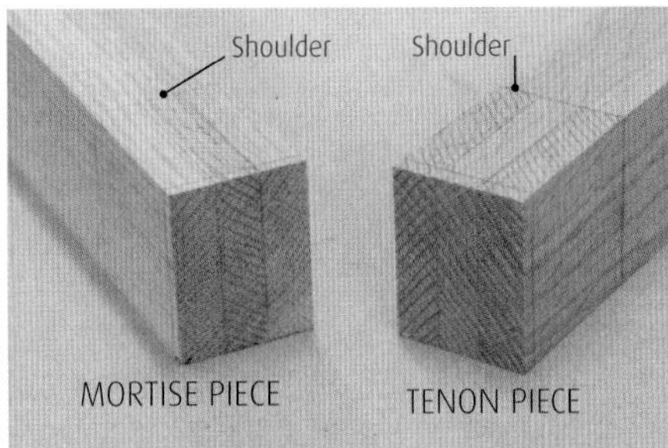

4 **Mark the waste** on both pieces—the central area of the mortise piece, and the sides (cheeks) of the tenon. Score the cutting line at both shoulders with a marking knife.

CUTTING AND FINISHING THE JOINT

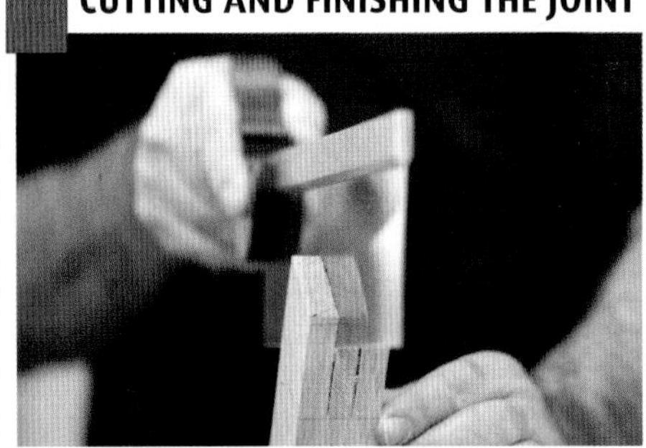

1 **Set the mortise piece** in a vise and remove the waste with a tenon saw and a coping saw, as described for a T-bridle Joint, Steps 1–6, (p.129).

2 **Set the tenon piece** in a vise and cut as described for a basic mortise-and-tenon joint (pp.116–19). Clean up the sides, base, and shoulders of both parts with a chisel.

3 **Test-fit the joint** and make any necessary adjustments. Glue the joint, assemble it, and when the glue is dry, plane the ends flush with a block plane.

THE FINISHED JOINT

Comb joint

The comb joint (also called a finger joint) is a simplified form of the through-dovetail joint (pp.134–37). Unlike the dovetail, it has little mechanical strength, but its large gluing surface area means that, once glued, it is very strong. The comb joint requires careful marking out but is quicker to make than a set of dovetails. It is useful for boxes and carcass pieces, and contrasting woods can be used for a decorative effect.

PARTS OF THE JOINT

This joint consists of two matched sets of interlocking "fingers" (or pins). The pins of one part lodge in the sockets of the other. The joint is strongest when the two sets of pins are of equal size.

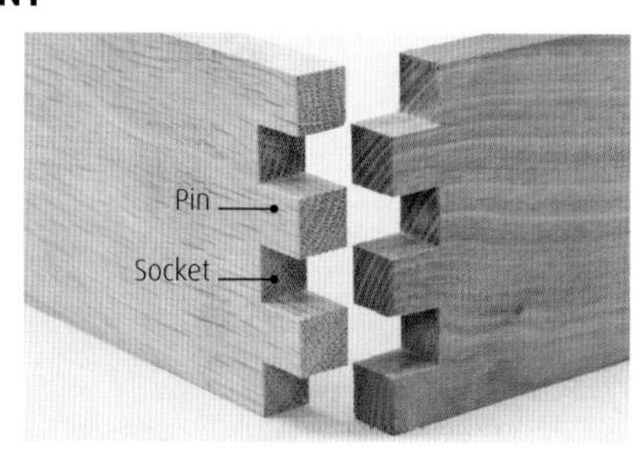

TOOLS AND MATERIALS

Square
Block plane
Marking gauge
Pencil
Dovetail saw
Coping saw
Bevel-edged chisel
Wood glue and brush
Clamps
Marking knife

MARKING AND CUTTING THE FIRST PIECE

1 **Check that both pieces of wood** are square, which is essential to achieve an accurate joint. Make any necessary adjustments by planing.

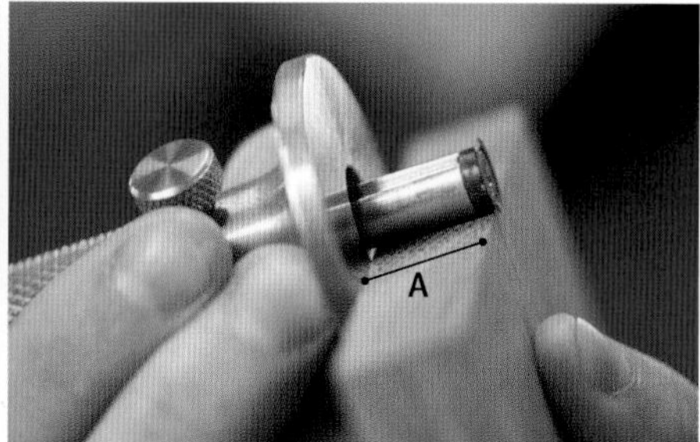

2 **Set a marking gauge** to slightly more than the thickness of the wood (A). This will create slightly oversized pins that can be trimmed flush when the joint is complete.

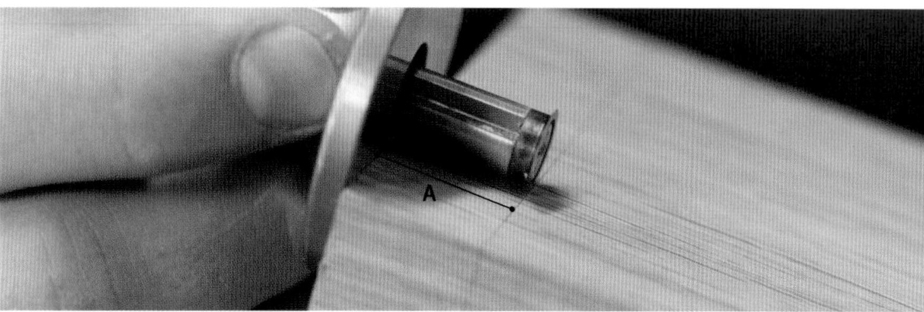

3 **Use the marking gauge** to scribe measurement (A) on both faces and one edge of each of the two pieces being joined, to indicate the position of the shoulders.

4 **Decide on the number and size** of pins required, and mark the pins square across the end grain of the first piece.

5 **Extend the pin marks** with a square and pencil from the end grain down each face as far as the shoulder.

6 **Secure the piece** in a vise and use a dovetail saw to cut the pins vertically to the shoulder.

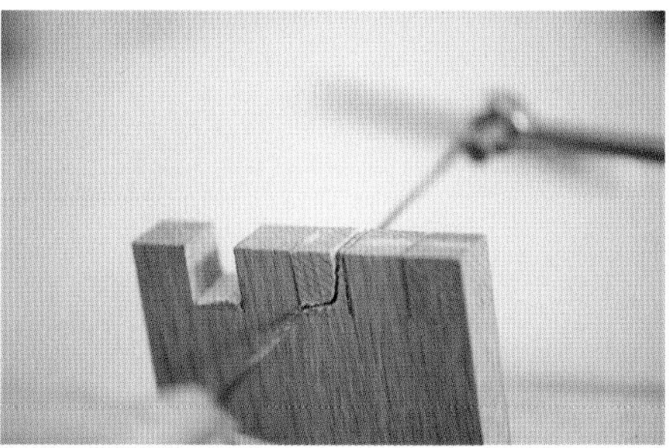

7 **Remove the bulk of the waste** with a coping saw, making a J-shaped cut into the adjacent vertical cut.

8 **Turn the piece in the vise** and cut the waste from the half pin with the dovetail saw.

9 **Remove the remaining waste** with a bevel-edged chisel, paring any excess material clean to the shoulder.

MARKING THE SECOND PIECE

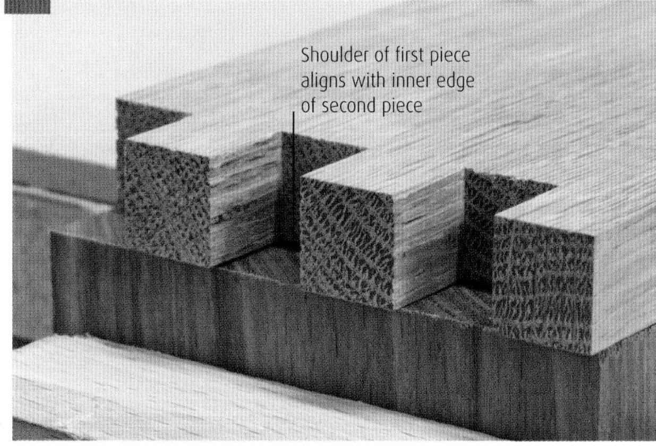

1 **Set the second piece** in a vise with the end grain uppermost. Place the pins of the first piece over the end grain of the second piece, aligned at the shoulder. The ends of the pins will slightly overhang the outer edge.

2 **Use a marking knife** to scribe the position of the pins on the end grain of the second piece.

3 **Using a square and marking knife**, reinforce the marks indicating the positions of the pins on the end grain of the second piece, then extend them down to the shoulder on both faces (inset).

ASSEMBLING THE JOINT

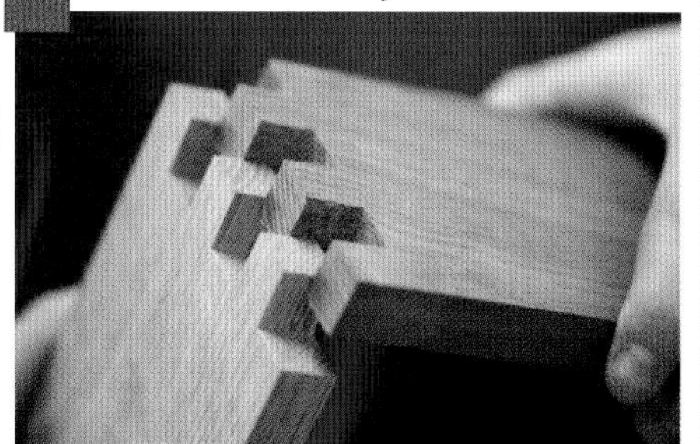

1 **Cut the pins as for the first piece**. Test-fit the joint and adjust by paring with a chisel, if necessary.

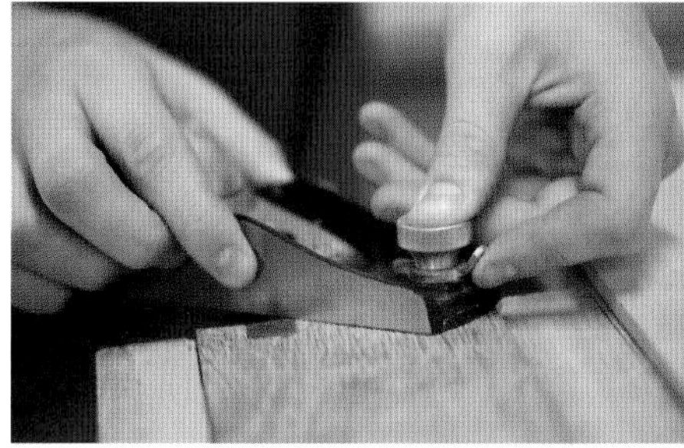

2 **Glue and assemble the joint**. Clamp the pieces. When the glue is dry, use a block plane to remove the excess from the ends of the pins.

THE FINISHED JOINT

Through-dovetail joint

In use since the time of the ancient Egyptians, the through dovetail is the most well known of all dovetail joints. It is commonly used on boxes and carcasses of all sizes, due to its strength and decorative look. Not only is it one of the most attractive joints in woodworking, it is also one of the best mechanically due to its strength in tension, and so is very sound in terms of its construction. It makes an excellent corner joint and is virtually indestructable when bonded with glue. Its full potential came to be recognized during the Arts and Crafts period of the late 19th and early 20th centuries, when it was used to great effect.

PARTS OF THE JOINT

The interlocking pattern of tails and pins is one of the strongest of all the woodworking joints. The through dovetail is particularly strong when used in the construction of all four corners of a piece, such as a box, since it has great strength in tension. The spacing of the pins and tails is largely a matter of taste, although using small pins will avoid a machine-made look.

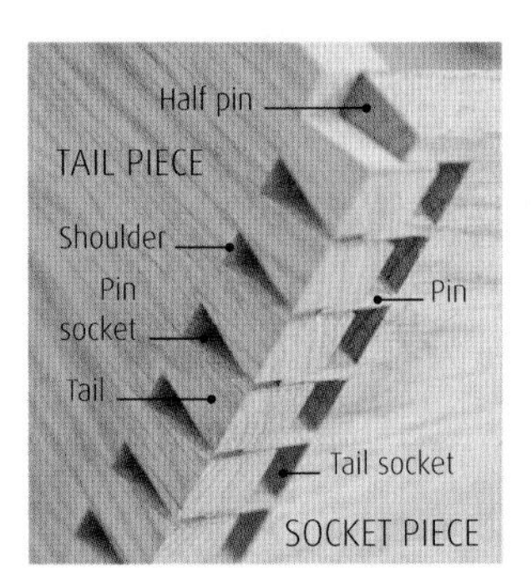

Types of dovetail joint

Lapped dovetails (pp.138–39) are a variation on the through dovetail used for drawer fronts, usually with a lighter wood for the sides and a darker wood for the front. A double-lapped version, which leaves a line of end grain, can be used on carcass work to hide the tails. If you want to hide the dovetails completely and achieve a very clean look, the secret-mitered dovetail is the best version to use, but it is a difficult joint to make and requires careful preparation—practice is essential. Single- and half-lap dovetails are often used for rails on the tops of drawer openings and connecting carcass sides. Dovetail keys and splines (thin inserts) use contrasting woods to highlight the dovetail shape, and are a very attractive way of joining box sides or even butt joints on table tops. Dovetail housing joints (pp.110–11) are commonly used for housings that need to be very strong, and where frames need an extra stretcher or strengthening rail.

TOOLS AND MATERIALS

- Dividers
- Pencil
- Square
- Marking gauge
- Marking knife
- Dovetail marker
- Dovetail saw
- Coping saw
- Mortise chisel
- Clamp
- Bevel-edged chisel
- Wood glue and brush
- Hammer

MARKING OUT THE TAILS AND PIN SOCKETS

1 **Mark the chosen half-pin** length on one end of the end grain of the tail-piece. Set a pair of dividers to this length and transfer the measurement to the opposite end of the end grain.

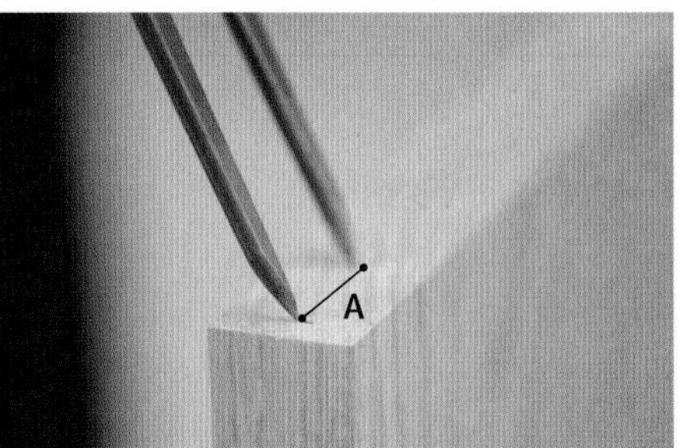

2 **Choose the number of pins** and tail sockets required. Set the dividers to the estimated combined length of one tail and pin socket (A).

3 **Walk the dividers** from one half-pin mark to the other, adjusting the (A) length until the chosen number of (A) lengths exactly matches the distance between the two half-pin marks. An alternative option would be to calculate length (A) using a ruler and calculator.

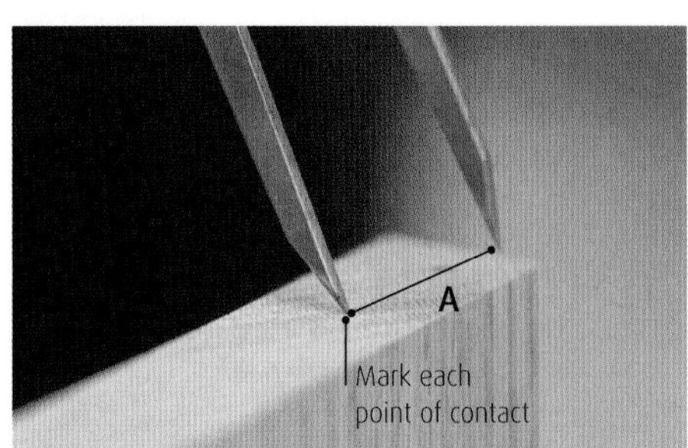

4 **With the dividers still set** to length (A), walk them from one end of the end grain toward the other, marking every point of contact. Repeat from the other end grain.

5 **Using a pencil** and square, extend these marks across the end grain. The longer lengths (B) are those of the tails, the shorter lengths (C) those of the pin sockets.

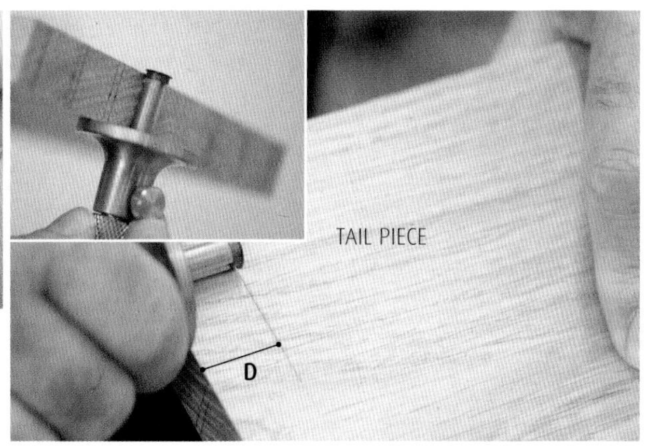

6 **Mark the shoulder** (D) on the tail piece by setting a marking gauge to a fraction more than the thickness of the tail piece (inset), then scribing from the end grain across both faces.

7 **Extend the shoulder line** onto both edges by scribing with a marking knife, guided by a square.

8 **Use a dovetail marker** as a guide for marking the desired angle for the tails. Draw the angles of the tails and pins to the shoulder on both faces in pencil.

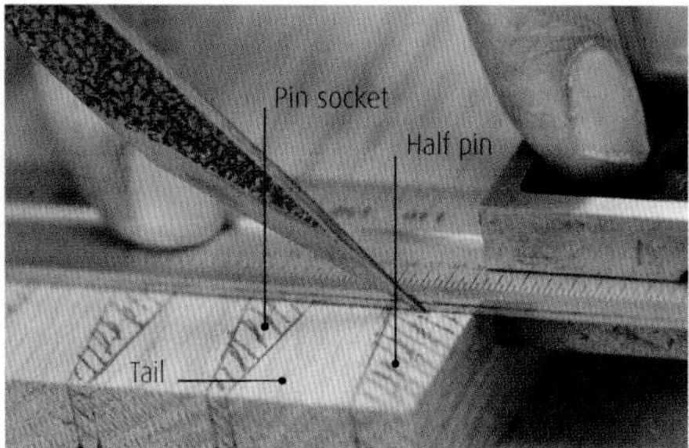

9 **Score the shoulders** along the base of the half pins and pin sockets on both faces with a marking knife, avoiding the base of the tails.

CUTTING THE TAILS

1 **Using a dovetail saw**, cut down through the end grain along the marks. Set the wood at an angle in the vise so you can cut vertically down each mark.

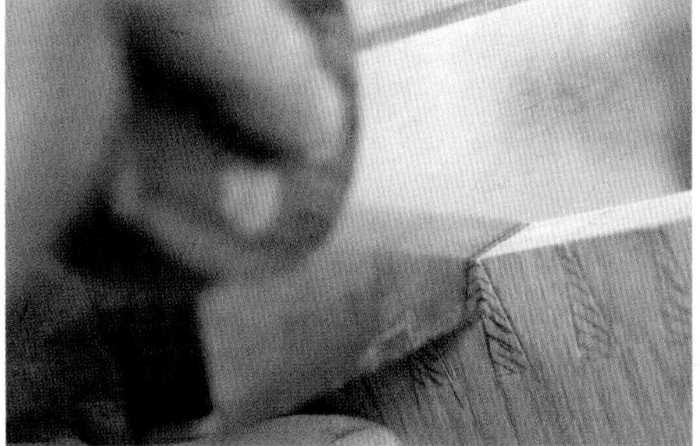

2 **Complete all the saw cuts** down the parallel socket edges. Then adjust the position of the wood in the vise and saw through the other side of the tails.

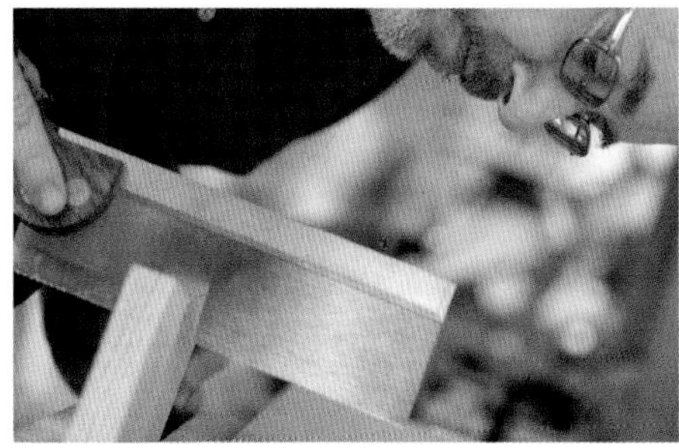

3 **Keep checking** that you do not cut past the shoulder line on the side of the wood facing away from you.

4 **Using a coping saw**, make a vertical cut through the center of each pin socket, then angle the cut to remove the waste.

5 **Use a dovetail saw** to remove the half pins at both ends of the joint, cutting to the waste side of the shoulder mark.

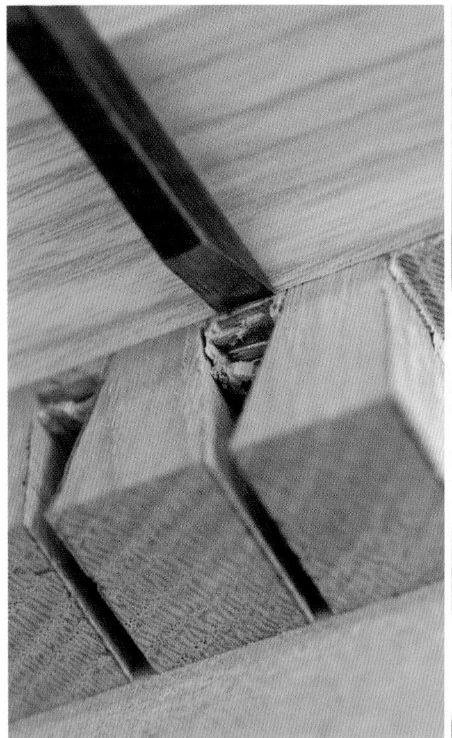

6 **Secure the wood** in a vise and use a mortise chisel to cut and square off the socket bases and edges.

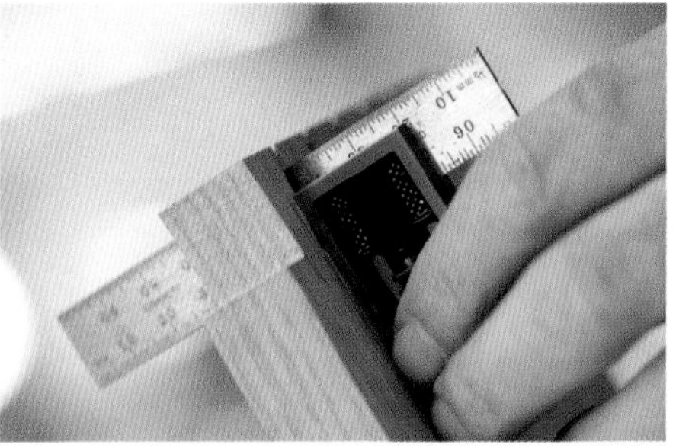

7 **Clamp the tail piece** against a squared guide piece. Use a bevel-edged chisel to pare the shoulders of the end-pin sockets so that they are clean and square to the marks.

8 **Check that the socket bases** are square at the shoulders by placing a square through each socket, against the face.

CUTTING TAILS ON A BAND SAW

If your piece requires lots of dovetails, using a band saw is a good way to cut them quickly and accurately. You can even cut more than one set at a time—when making drawers, for example, tape pairs of drawer sides together to cut both in one go. As well as cutting the tails themselves, you can also use the band saw to remove the waste in between them.

1 **Make a cut** with the band saw straight through the pin socket to the shoulder, and then make angled cuts along the tail marks.

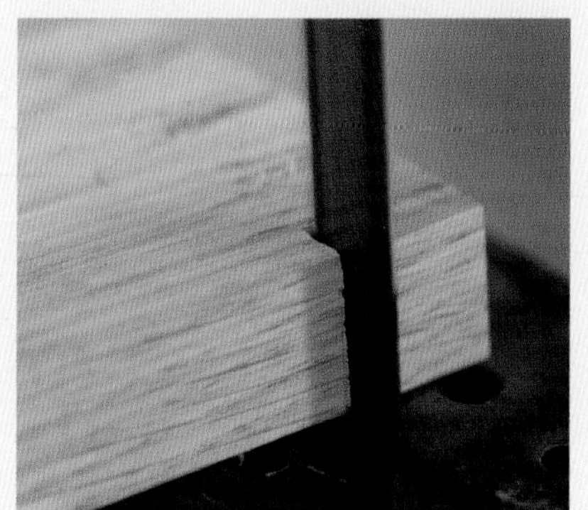

2 **Use the band saw** to cut the shoulder of each of the half pin sockets. Then remove the waste from each socket with a chisel, as described in Step 6 (above left).

MARKING OUT THE PINS

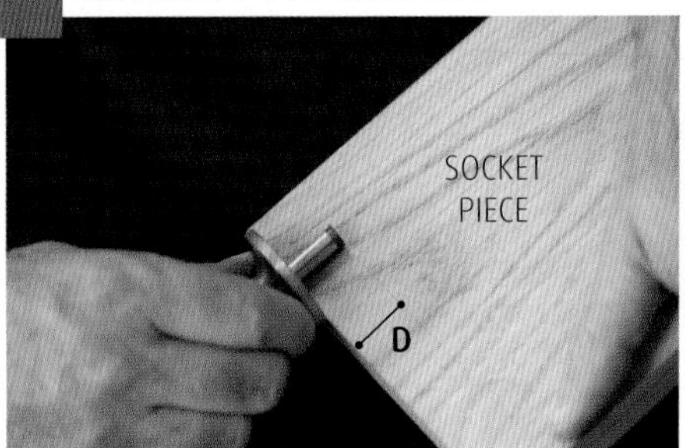

1 **Use the marking gauge**, set to measurement (D), to scribe the shoulder (the length of the pins) from the end grain across both faces of the socket piece.

2 **Secure the socket piece** in a vise, and set the tail piece at right-angles over the end grain, making sure the tail piece is precisely aligned at the edges and at the shoulder. Support and weight it to prevent any movement during marking up.

3 **Use a marking knife** to transfer the position of the tails and pins from the tail piece to the end grain of the socket piece.

4 **Square the lines** down to the shoulder mark on both faces of the wood, using a marking knife and square.

CUTTING THE PINS

1 **Using a dovetail saw**, cut down to the shoulder mark on each side of the pins, taking care not to exceed the lines.

2 **Use a coping saw** to remove the waste from the tail sockets, ensuring that you follow the lines carefully.

3 **Use a marking knife** to scribe along the shoulder of the sockets, avoiding the base of the pins. Repeat on the other side.

4 **Align a guide piece** to the socket piece shoulder and use a chisel to clean up the sides and bases. Check that the bases are square (see Step 8, opposite).

CUTTING PINS ON A BAND SAW

Although too delicate to be fully cut with a band saw, the pins can be roughly machined and the waste from the tail sockets removed.

1 **Cut into the tail sockets** at right angles with the band saw. Be sure to cut well clear of the marks.

2 **Remove the waste** by hand, using a coping saw to cut to the shoulder in each of the sockets.

ASSEMBLING THE JOINT

1 **Assemble the joint**. The fit should be snug. Make any necessary adjustments and then apply glue to the joint.

2 **Tap the glued pieces** into place using a hammer, protecting the wood with a block. Clamp if necessary.

3 **When the glue is dry,** place the joint in a vise and block-plane the ends of the pins and tails flush to both faces.

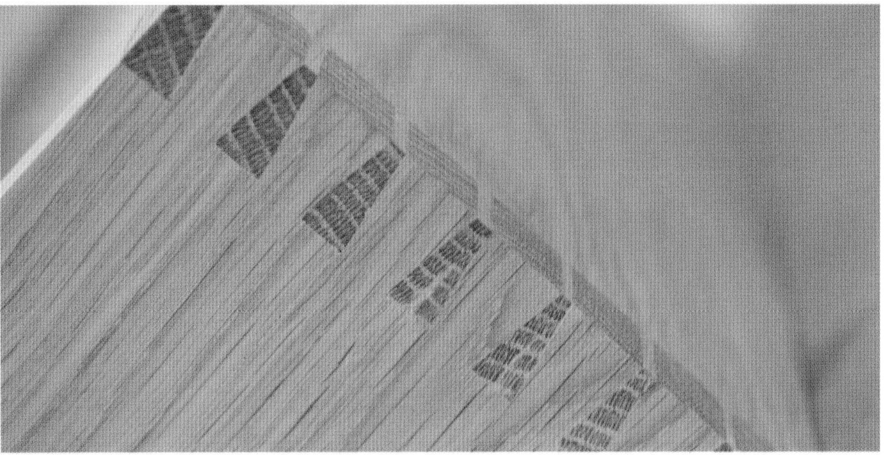

THE FINISHED JOINT

Lapped-dovetail joint

One of the most widely used joints in the dovetail family, the lapped dovetail has great strength so is ideal for drawers, which are often subject to heavy loads. It is particularly useful for securing the front of the drawer to the sides. The lapped dovetail can also be used as a carcass joint if you don't want the joint to show—the sides of a chest of drawers, for example. If the dovetails are going to be visible, you can use contrasting types of wood to accentuate them and utilize them as a decorative feature.

PARTS OF THE JOINT

The lapped dovetail is the same as a through dovetail, except that the sockets do not extend to the front of the socket piece, leaving an area called the "lap." The ratio of lap to dovetail is usually 1:3. It can be thinner—up to 1:4—but do not make it any thinner than this or you will run the risk of cutting through it when cleaning the sockets. The half pin needs to be reasonably strong, so will often be made thicker than the full pin.

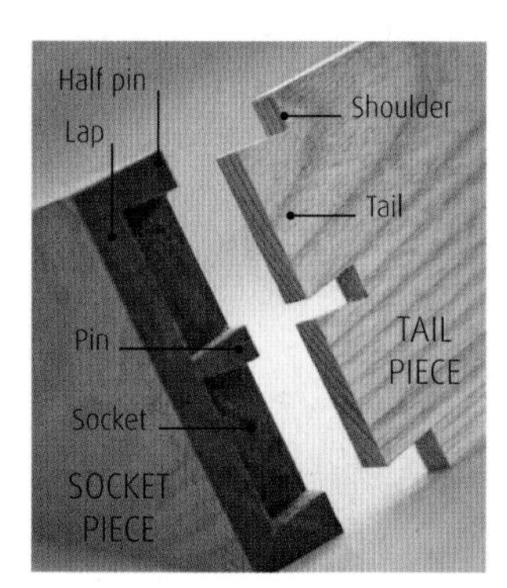

TOOLS AND MATERIALS

- Marking gauge
- Dividers
- Dovetail marker
- Pencil
- Coping saw
- Dental pick or scalpel
- Marking knife
- Square
- Dovetail saw
- Mortise chisel
- Mallet
- Bevel-edged chisel
- Hammer
- Wood glue and brush
- Clamps
- Hammer

MARKING OUT AND CUTTING THE TAILS

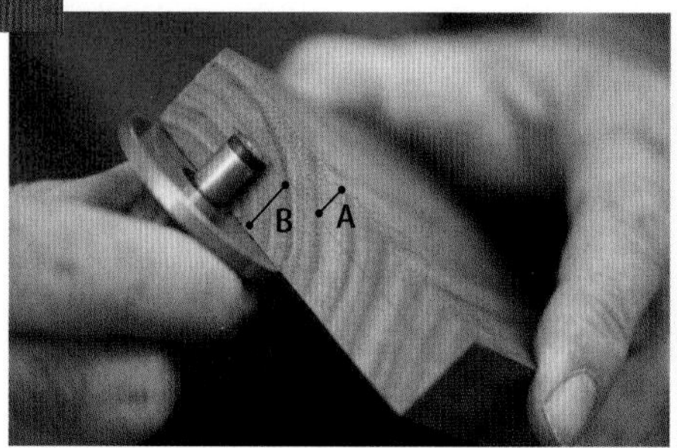

1 **Decide the depth of the lap (A)** on the socket piece. Set a marking gauge to the thickness of the wood minus (A), and scribe this measurement (B) along the end grain.

2 **Use the marking gauge** set to measurement (B), to scribe across the face of the tail piece to mark the shoulder around all sides of the tail piece.

3 **Mark out the half pins** on the end grain of the tail piece. Use dividers to mark the first half pin, then mark the second at the same distance from the other edge.

4 **Decide how many tails** are needed. Set the dividers to the required length and mark them out as described for a through-dovetail joint (pp.134–35).

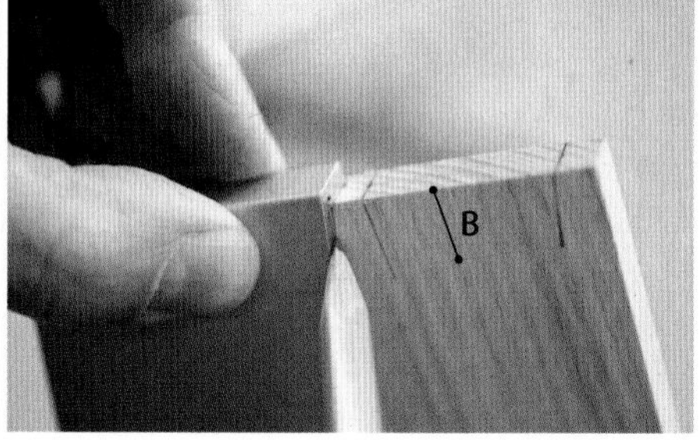

5 **Using a pencil**, draw around a dovetail marker to draw the angles of the tails to the line of the shoulder. Be careful to mark the tails squarely across the end grain.

6 **Secure the tail piece** in a vise, and cut out and tidy up the tails as described for a through-dovetail joint on pp.135–36.

MARKING OUT THE SOCKETS

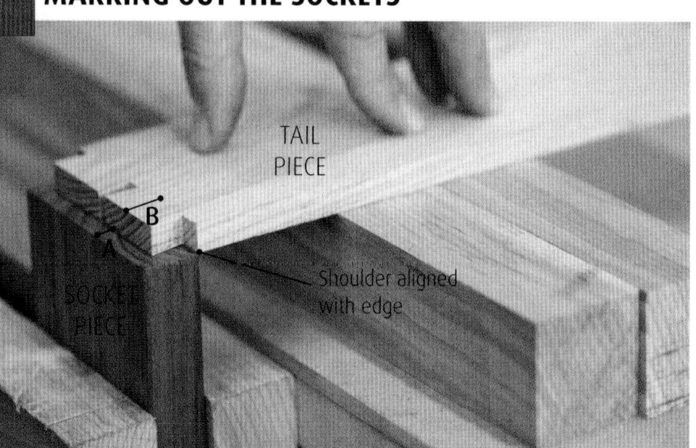

1 **Set the socket piece** in a vise. Position the tail piece at right angles over the end grain so that the shoulder is perfectly aligned with the edge of the socket piece, and the ends of the tails align with the line of the lap scribed on the end grain. Use a block of wood to support the tail piece.

2 **Scribe the position of the tails** onto the end grain of the socket piece by scribing around the tails. Use a dental pick, which is ideal for tight corners, or a scalpel.

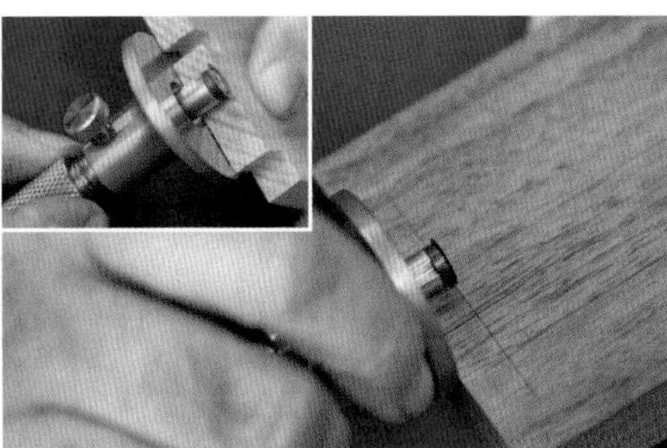

3 **Use a marking gauge** to scribe a line to mark the thickness of the tail piece (inset) onto the face of the socket piece.

4 **Use a marking knife** to reinforce the socket lines on the end grain of the socket piece.

5 **Score the vertical lines** of the tail sockets onto the face of the socket piece, using a square and marking knife.

CUTTING OUT THE SOCKETS

1 **Cut the sockets** with a dovetail saw following the angles of the marked lines, and angling the sawcut toward the corners.

2 **Secure the socket piece** to the bench and use a mortise chisel and mallet to remove the waste from the sockets. Carefully remove a little at a time.

3 **When most of the waste** has been removed, pare the sockets to the lines and neaten the edges with a bevel-edged chisel.

ASSEMBLING THE JOINT

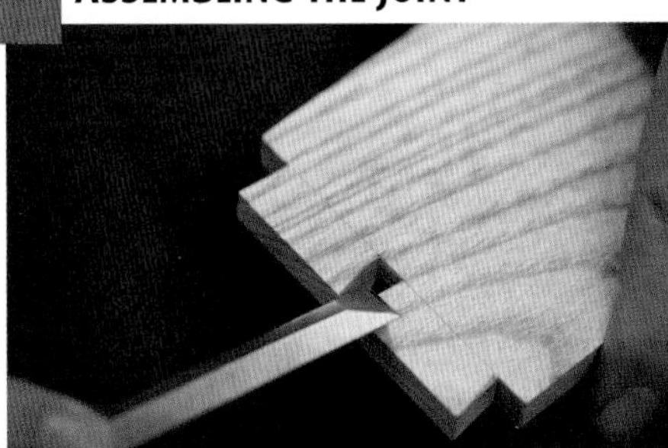

1 **Use a bevel-edged chisel** to cut a slight chamfer along the edges of the sides of the tails to ease the fit of the joint.

2 **Test the fit of the tails and sockets** by tapping the pieces together with a hammer. Adjust, if necessary, by paring. When the fit is satisfactory, glue and clamp.

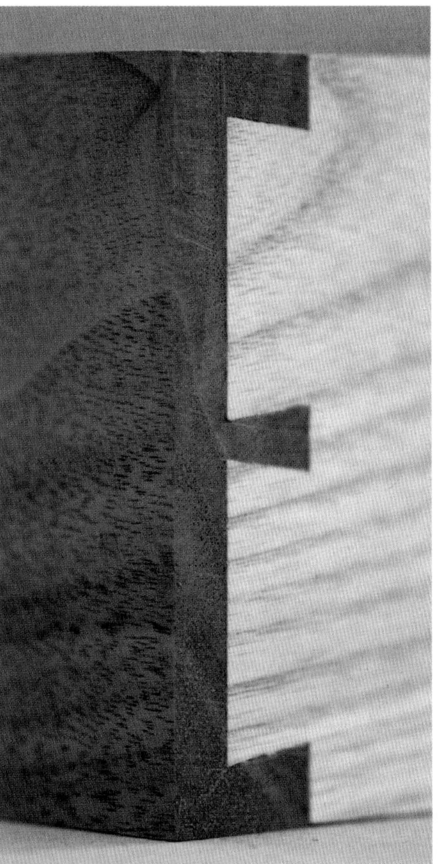

THE FINISHED JOINT

Floating-tenon joint

Also known as a "loose" or "slip" tenon, the floating tenon was the forerunner of modern commercial connectors, such as the biscuit joint (p.142–43) and domino joint (p.144–45). It has all the strength advantages of a standard mortise-and-tenon joint, but since there are no shoulder lines to cut and every piece is the same size, it is quicker to make. In a piece with lots of small tenons, it can be an excellent choice.

PARTS OF THE JOINT

The floating-tenon joint consists of two mortises connected with a loose tongue. Often made from plywood, the tongue is usually no more than two thirds the width of the tenon piece. The terms "mortise piece" and "tenon piece" are used for clarity only, since both pieces have a mortise and neither has a tenon.

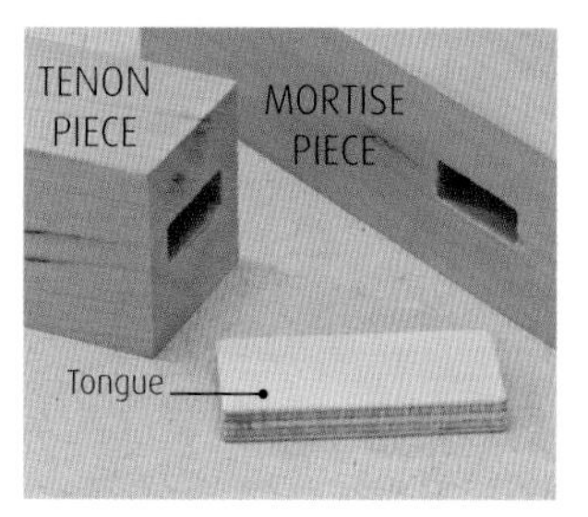

TOOLS AND MATERIALS

- Pencil
- Square
- Mortise gauge
- Marking knife
- Drill and bits
- Masking tape
- Mortise chisel
- Tenon saw
- Bench hook
- Sandpaper
- Wood glue and brush
- Clamps

MARKING THE MORTISE PIECE

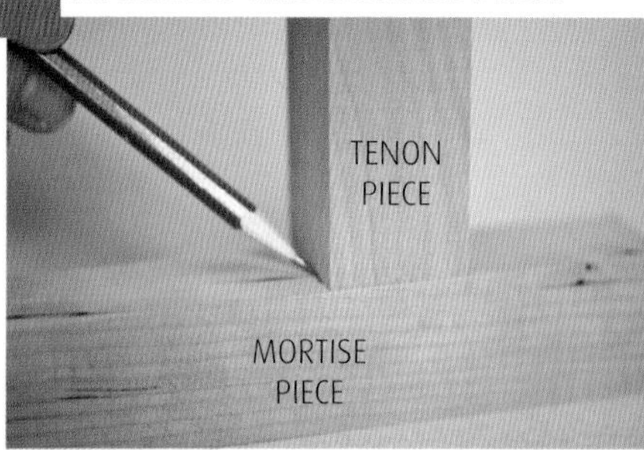

1 **Place the end grain** of the "tenon piece" at the desired position for the joint on the face of the "mortise piece". Mark the thickness of the tenon piece on the mortise piece.

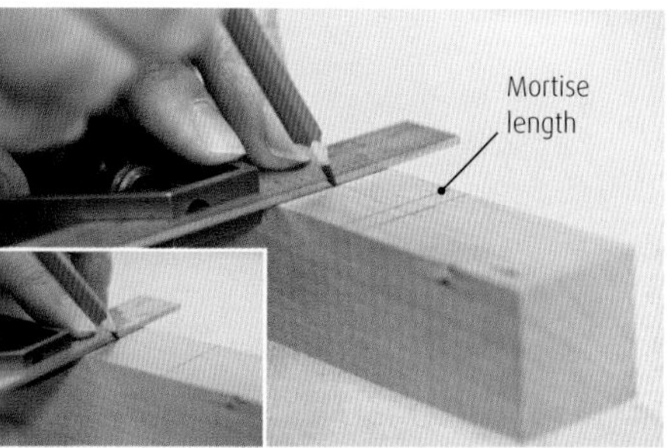

2 **Use a pencil and square** to extend the marks across the face of the mortise piece (inset). Mark the mortise length within these lines and square across the face.

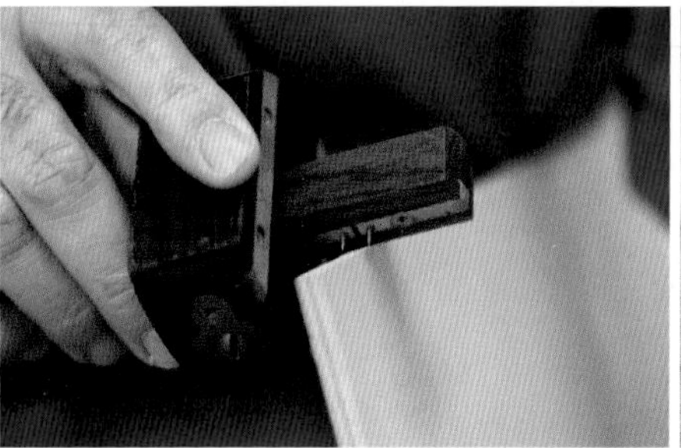

3 **Set the mortise gauge** to the thickness of the plywood from which the tongue will be cut, to determine the mortise width.

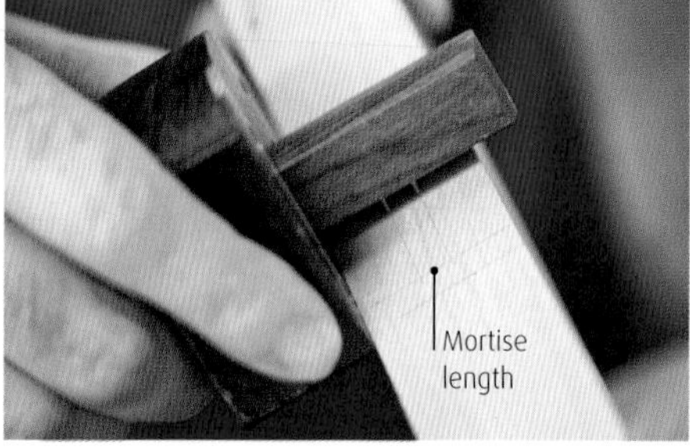

4 **Center the mortise gauge** on the face of the mortise piece, then scribe the mortise width between the marks defining the mortise length.

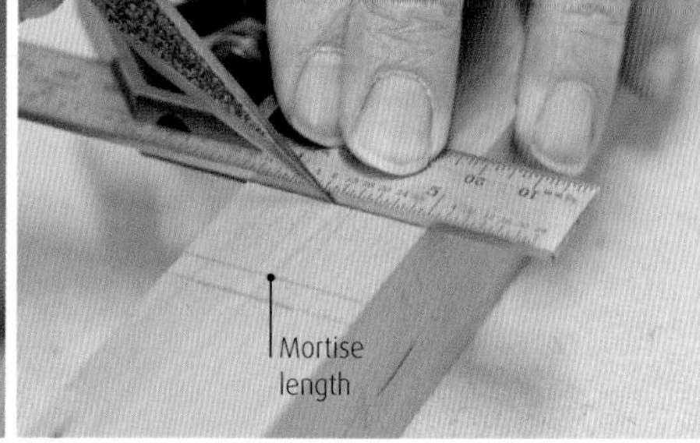

5 **Reinforce the ends** of the mortise between the width lines with a marking knife and combination square.

MARKING THE TENON PIECE

1 **Align the tenon piece** with the mortise position and transfer the mortise length marks onto the face of the tenon piece. Extend the marks across the end grain of the tenon piece with a square (inset).

2 **Mark the width** of the mortise on the end grain of the tenon piece between these marks using the mortise gauge as previously set.

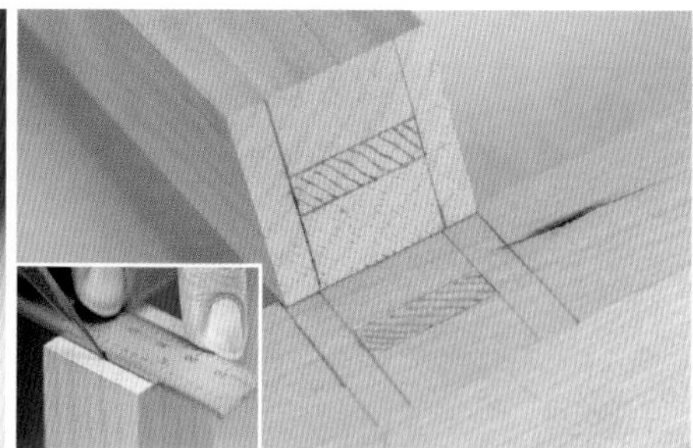

3 **Reinforce the marks** at the ends of the mortise with a marking knife (inset). Mark the waste for removal with a pencil on both pieces.

DRILLING THE MORTISES

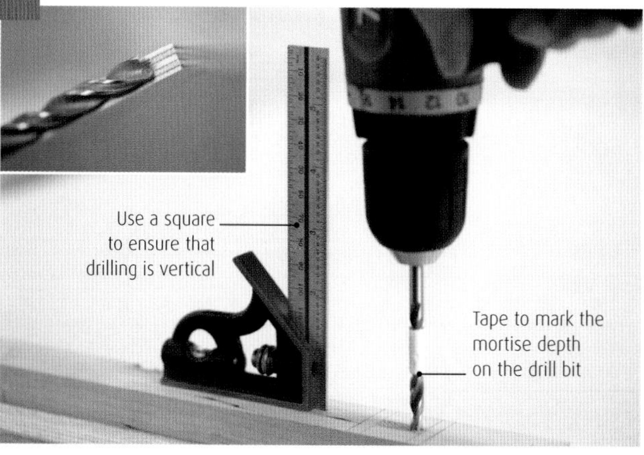

1 **Choose a bit** of the same thickness as the plywood for the tongue (inset). Decide the depth of the mortise—usually one third of the thickness of the mortise piece, plus approximately 1⁄32in (1mm) to allow for glue. Mark the mortise depth on the drill bit using masking tape.

2 **Clear the bulk** of the waste by drilling a series of holes in the mortise piece (inset) to the required depth, along the full length of the mortise.

3 **Remove the remaining waste** by chiseling it away with a mortise chisel of the same width as the mortise.

4 **Drill the mortise** in the end grain of the tenon piece in the same way. Drilling into the end grain can be hard to control due to the smaller surface area held in the vise, so ensure you clamp the tenon piece securely and drill carefully.

MAKING THE TONGUE

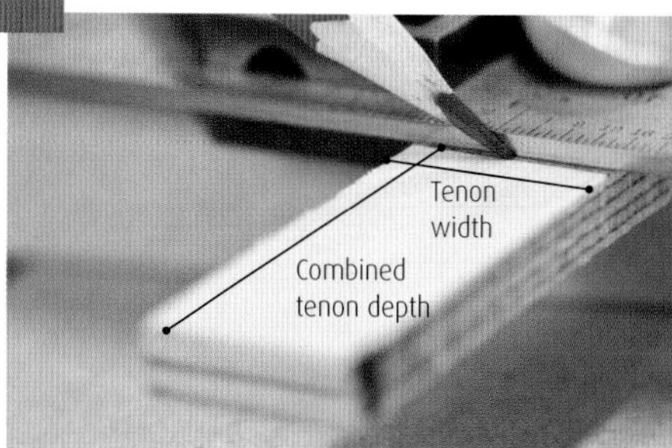

1 **Mark up the tongue** to the same width and twice the depth—minus the gluing allowance—of each mortise.

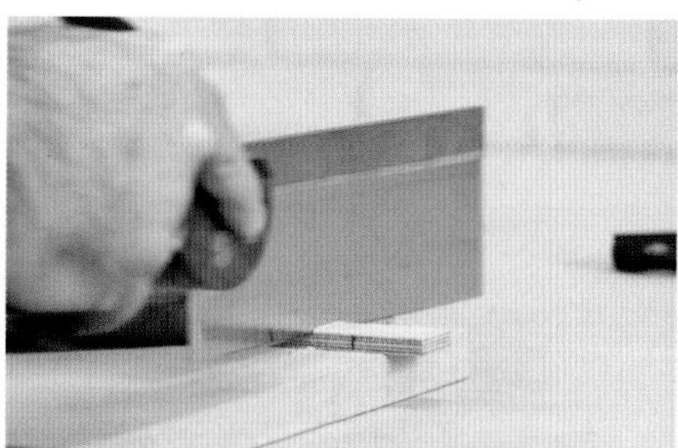

2 **Cut the plywood** to the marked dimensions with a tenon saw. Use a bench hook for support.

3 **Sand the corners and edges** of the plywood tongue until smooth, to ensure a good fit in the mortises.

FITTING AND GLUING THE JOINT

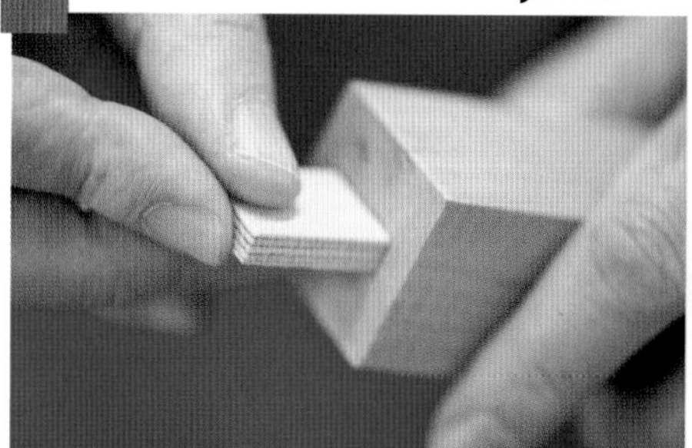

1 **Test the fit** of the tongue in both mortises. Make any necessary adjustments to ease the fit.

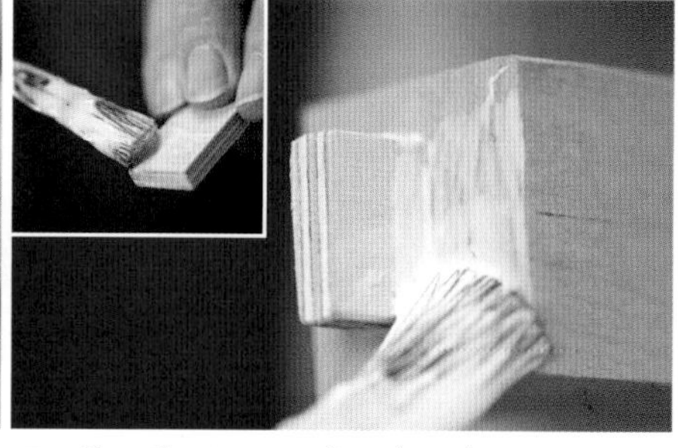

2 **Glue the tongue** (inset) and insert it into the tenon-piece mortise. Apply glue to the tenon-piece end grain and join it to the mortise piece. Clamp and leave to dry.

THE FINISHED JOINT

Joints using commercial connectors

A range of commercially produced connectors, most of which act like a loose tongue, can be used to add strength to joints. Dowels—a short length of doweling glued into a drilled hole—were the first type to be developed, and have been used in the furniture industry for many years (see pp.145–48). Biscuits (shown here) and dominos—pieces of compressed beech glued into a slot (pp.144–45)—improve on the dowel by being stronger and because the specialist tools used to cut the slots are easy to use. The pocket-screw jig (p.149) is another device that has simplified the method of making the centuries-old pocket-hole joint.

Biscuit joints

A relatively new method of joining wood, biscuits are made of compressed beech and perform the same function as a dowel, loose tenon, or tongue. They are oval in shape, a standard thickness, and come in three sizes (see p.65). The slots are made with a biscuit jointer, which has a small, circular saw-blade and various fences to allow straight and angled slots to be cut. The biscuit is a very easy and effective means of quickly assembling a joint. The jointer is easy to set up and use, and the biscuit itself has a major advantage over the dowel—it is long grain and so forms a much stronger joint. One disadvantage is the biscuit's shallowness, which makes it less effective in a frame situation, such as a tenon. The biscuit joint can be used in almost any configuration; it is especially good on carcass work with man-made board material, and it can also be used in both corner joints and "T" joints, as well as in divisions and miters.

PARTS OF THE JOINT

The biscuit fits into matching elliptical slots in the two joining faces, each of which houses exactly half of the biscuit. The biscuit acts in the same way as a tenon in a conventional mortise-and-tenon joint. Biscuits can be used either singly or as a double joint if there is sufficient thickness in the material. Using more biscuits, and arranging them in a double set-up, increases the gluing surface area and makes the joint stronger.

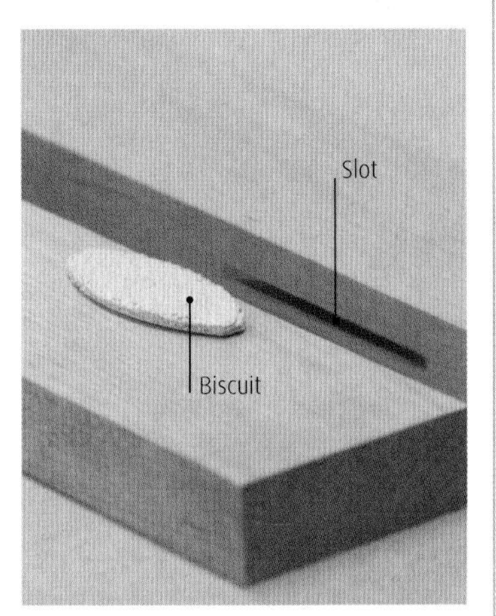

TOOLS AND MATERIALS

Square
Pencil
Biscuit jointer
Biscuits
Wood glue and brush

MAKING AN EDGE-TO-EDGE BISCUIT JOINT

1 **Place the two pieces** of wood to be joined side-by-side and square a pencil mark across both pieces to indicate where the center of each slot will be. When marking out slots at the ends of each piece, make sure that you leave sufficient space for the length of the biscuit on either side of the center-line.

2 **Set the height** of the biscuit jointer's cutting blade so that the slot will be cut in the middle of each piece of wood. You may need to raise either the base of the biscuit jointer or the piece of wood.

3 **Adjust the controls** of the blade to the correct setting for the size of biscuit that you plan to use. It should be marked with the different depths for standard biscuits.

4 **Align the machine mark** on the blade with the first pencil line on the first piece of wood, then machine the slot. Repeat at the other marked lines, then cut the slots in the other piece of wood.

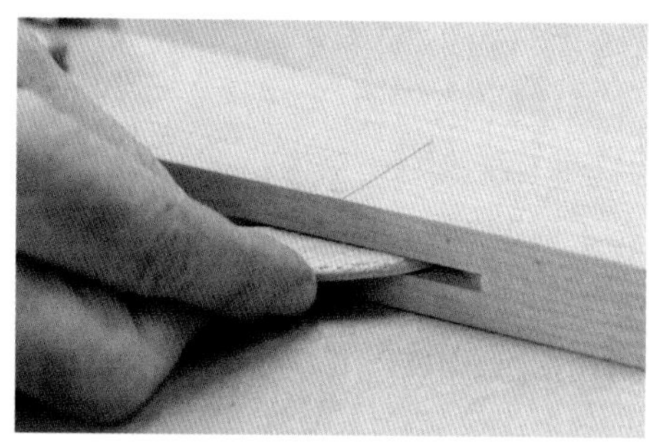

5 **Insert a biscuit** into each of the slots along the edge of one of the pieces of wood.

6 **Push the protruding biscuits** into the slots in the other piece of wood to test the fit of the joints.

7 **Once you are happy** with the fit of the biscuits in the slots, apply glue inside and around the slots, then fit the joint together.

THE FINISHED JOINT

MAKING A FACE-TO-EDGE BISCUIT JOINT

1 **Mark the positions of the slots** on the edge piece, then cut the slots as for an edge-to-edge biscuit joint (see Steps 1–3 opposite and Step 4 above).

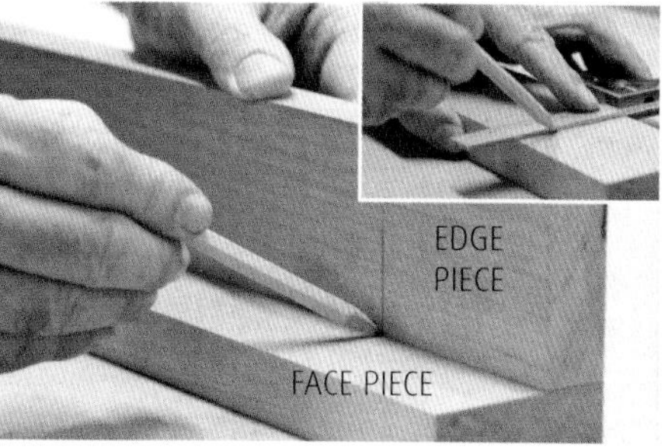

2 **Set the edge piece** in position on the face piece, then mark the position of the slots on the face. Extend a line square across the face (inset).

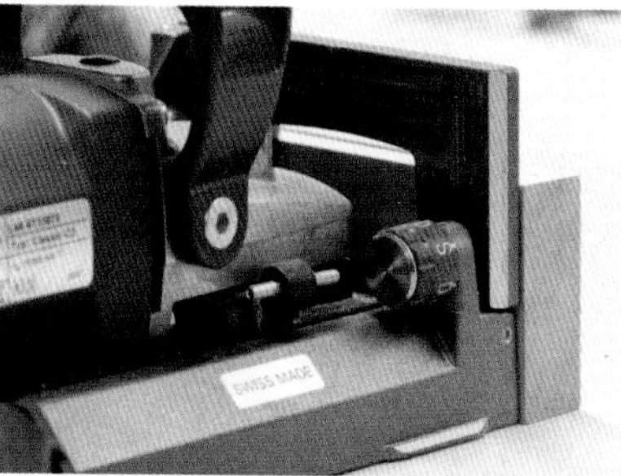

3 **Position the face piece** vertically against the cutter with the machine mark aligned with the line on the face, then cut the slots.

4 **Place the biscuits** in the slots of the face piece, then test the fit with the edge piece.

5 **Once you are happy** with the fit of the biscuits in the slots, apply glue inside and around the slots, then fit the joint together.

THE FINISHED JOINT

Domino joints

Similar in concept to the biscuit (see p.65 and p.142), the domino is even more effective and versatile, although it does not replace it. Essentially a floating tenon made of beech, the domino connector comes in different sizes and lengths for use in joints of different orientations and in components of different thicknesses (p.65). It is strong, partly due to its long-grain construction, and can be used in any setting in place of a conventional mortise-and-tenon joint, including chairs, doors, and butt-jointed edges to frame-and-panel constructions. The only situation in which it cannot be employed is when a thin carcass material is used, such as man-made board. The domino mortise is cut with a domino jointer fitted with a cutter selected to match the size of domino to be used. The required depth of cut is determined by setting the depth control of the jointer.

PARTS OF THE JOINT

Each component of the domino joint contains a mortise, and the "tenon" is the domino itself—a rectangular-shaped lozenge with rounded, fluted sides that fits into the mortises and connects the pieces. When inserted in its mortise, the domino naturally creates "shoulders," just like a standard mortise and tenon (see p.116). Extra strength can be given to the joint by using two dominos alongside each other, in a twin "tenon" set-up.

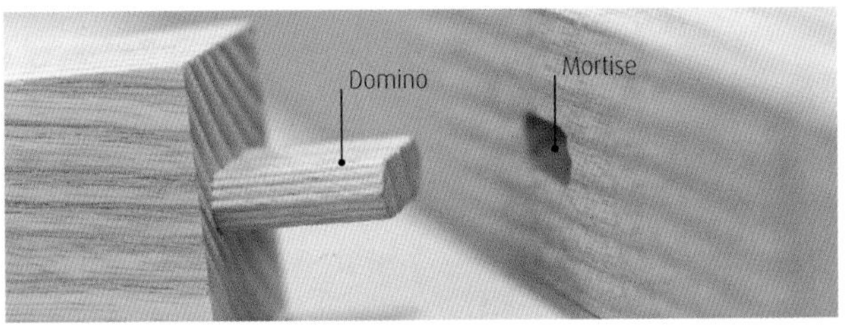

TOOLS AND MATERIALS

Square
Pencil
Domino jointer and cutters
Dominos
Wood glue and brush

MAKING A DOMINO JOINT

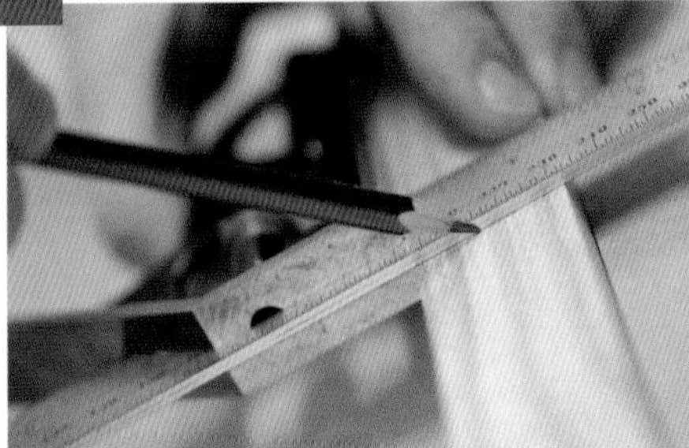

1 **Mark the position** of the domino mortise in one edge of the first piece by drawing a line on the adjacent face.

2 **Mark the position** of the domino mortise in the second piece by drawing a line on the adjacent face.

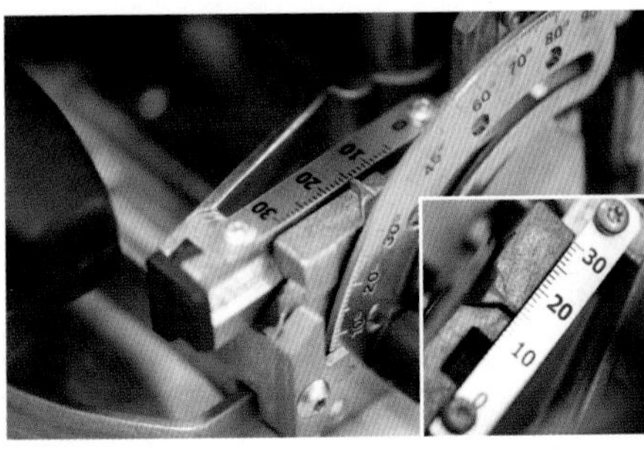

3 **Adjust the domino jointer** to set the position of the mortise on the first piece, then adjust it to set the height (inset).

4 **Adjust the fence** to set the position of the cut, then align the jointer with the edge of the first piece of wood.

5 **Set the depth** of the mortise to be cut and fit a cutter to match the size of domino that you intend to use.

6 **Position the domino jointer** by aligning the guide mark on the machine with the line on the wood.

7 **Cut the mortise** in the edge of the first piece. Re-set the jointer for the second piece and cut the mortise in the marked position (inset).

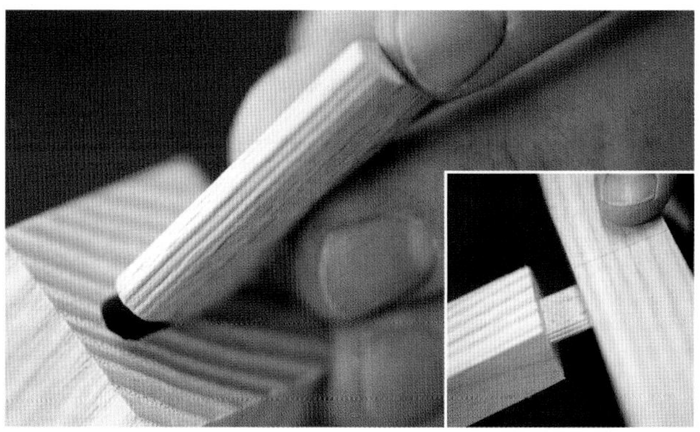

8 **Insert the domino** into one of the mortises, then join the pieces together to check the fit (inset). Once you are satisfied with the fit, apply glue to the mortises and fit the joint together.

THE FINAL JOINT

Dowel joint using center points

The main advantage of dowels is that they are quick to produce (see p.148) and can reinforce a simple butt-joint very easily. They can be used on just about any section of wood and in any configuration, and can offer a solution that wouldn't be possible with a conventional joint. They can be used to align butt-jointed edge joints, as in a corner joint, edge-to-face as in a T-joint, or as a mortise-and-tenon in a frame. They must be marked out accurately, using center points or a jig. The disadvantage of dowels is the lack of long-grain contact, since they are normally inserted into the end grain. More than one dowel—arranged in a row if possible—can be used, which increases gluing area and strength.

PARTS OF THE JOINT

Dowels consist of round pieces of wood that act, in constructional terms, like a series of mini-tenons inserted into holes—the equivalent of mortises—in each component. Commercially made dowels (see p.64) feature a series of flutes on them to relieve air pressure as they are inserted. Without this release of pressure, you may not be able to close the joint, especially once wet glue has been applied to the holes.

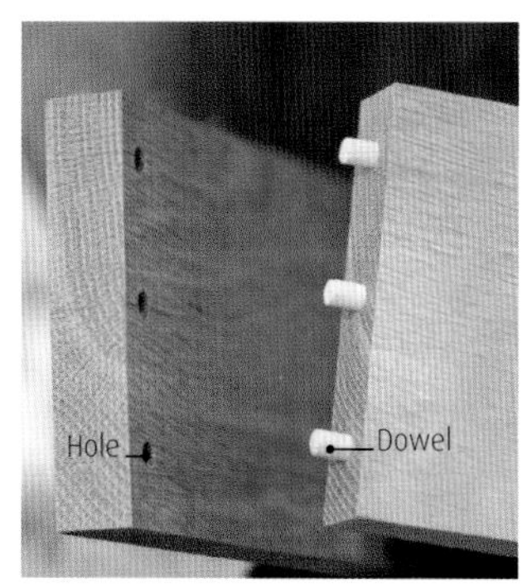

TOOLS AND MATERIALS

- Marking gauge
- Pencil
- Square
- Drill and bits
- Doweling
- Center points
- Mallet
- Wood glue and brush

MAKING A DOWEL JOINT

1 **Use a marking gauge** to scribe along the center of the end grain of the first piece, then place the piece in a vise.

2 **Mark the position** of each of the holes you require by squaring a pencil mark across the end grain.

3 **Select a drill bit** to match the diameter of the dowel.

4 **Decide on the depth** of the holes—usually up to half the thickness of the piece to be joined. Mark the drill bit to this depth and drill a hole at each marked position. Use a square to ensure that you drill vertically.

5 **Insert a center point** (selected to match the diameter of the dowel) into each of the holes in the end grain.

6 **Position the piece** to be joined over the end grain of the first piece, using a square to ensure it is centered. Use a mallet to tap the second piece so that the drilling positions are imprinted in it by the center points. Lift the second piece off and remove the center points from the first piece.

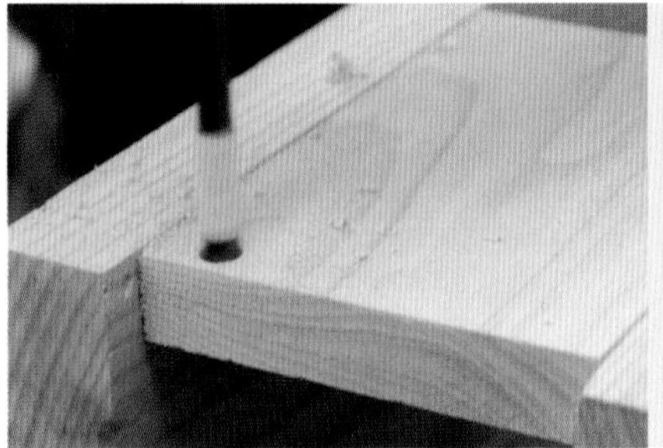

7 **Support the piece** in a vise and drill a hole in each of the marked positions to the same depth as in the first piece.

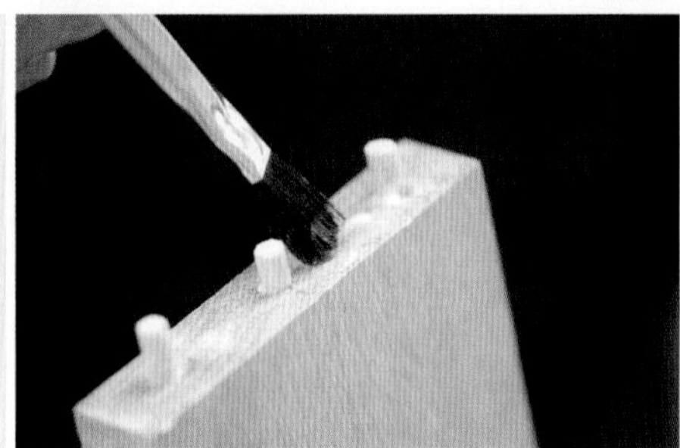

8 **Glue the end-grain holes** and insert the dowels. Apply glue to the surface of the end grain and fit the joint together.

THE FINAL JOINT

USING HANDMADE DOWEL PINS

This is a fairly accurate and simple method of marking both sets of dowel centers, and does not require any specialist equipment - just some panel pins and a pair of snippers. One set of centers are marked, pins are inserted, and then cut off to leave sharp points. These are used for marking the other piece of wood, and are later removed before drilling. When transferring the marks your accuracy can be improved by sliding the pieces up against a right angle jig. The holes that are made by the pins are then used for locating the drill bit.

1 **Mark the positions** of the holes on the end grain of the first piece (see Steps 1–2, p.145). Hammer a panel pin into each of the marked positions, inserting them deep enough to hold securely, but not so deep as to be difficult to remove.

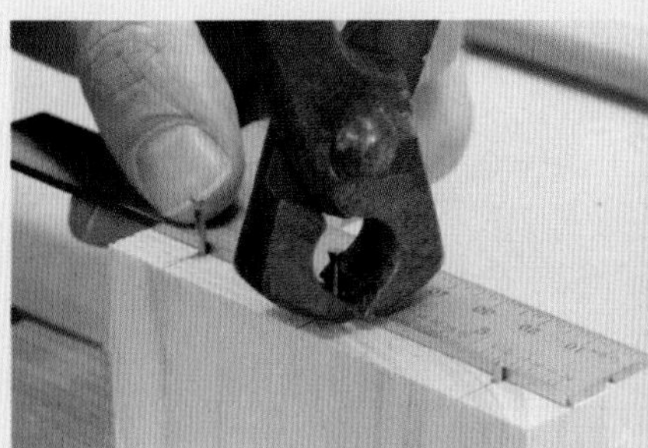

2 **Use a pair of snippers** to cut each of the panel pins to the same height—approximately ⅛in (3mm).

3 **Place the piece to be joined** in position over the pins and tap the top of the piece gently with a mallet to mark the positions of the holes. Remove the second piece.

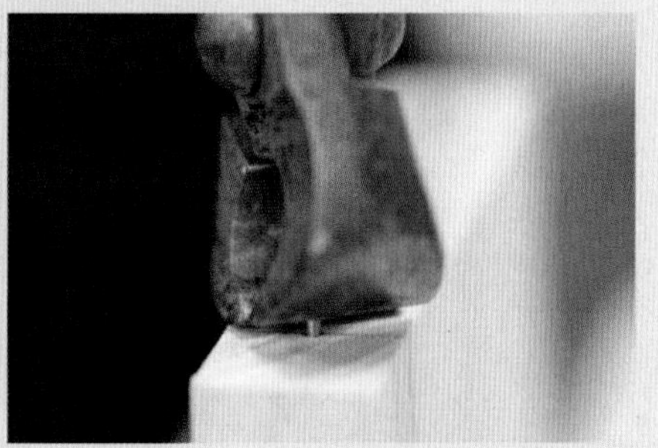

4 **Use the snippers** to remove the pins. Drill each of the marked positions, insert the dowels, then glue and assemble the joint (see Steps 3–8, p.145 and above).

Dowel joint using a commercial jig

Doweling jigs save the time spent marking out precise locations for the dowels, and ensure a greater level of accuracy than can be achieved by other methods. However, jigs are only capable of jointing a range of thicknesses—this should be considered when designing a project (the jigs assist in positioning the dowel in the center of a specified thickness). Cheap versions do not provide the same degree of accuracy as high quality jigs with metal guide bushes. Adjoining pieces (the sides of a drawer, for example) are clamped in alignment together, face-to-face, and worked on simultaneously.

TOOLS AND MATERIALS	
Vise	Power drill
Pencil	Chisel
Square	Sandpaper
Drill and bits	Wood glue and brush
Doweling	Hammer
Dowel jig and bushes	Clamp
Masking tape	

SETTING UP THE JIG

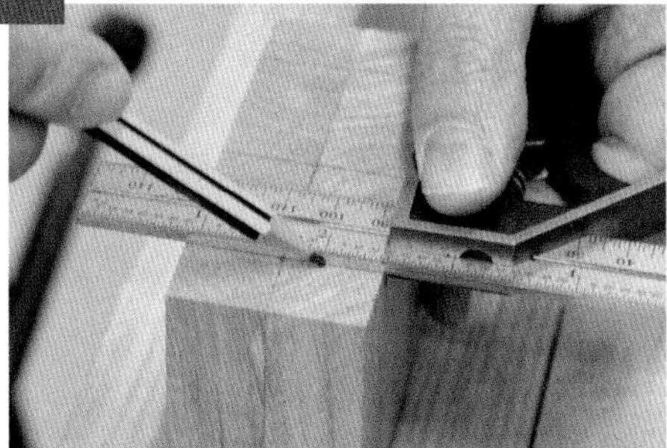

1 **Place both pieces** side-by-side in a vise and use a pencil and square to mark the position of each hole in their end grains.

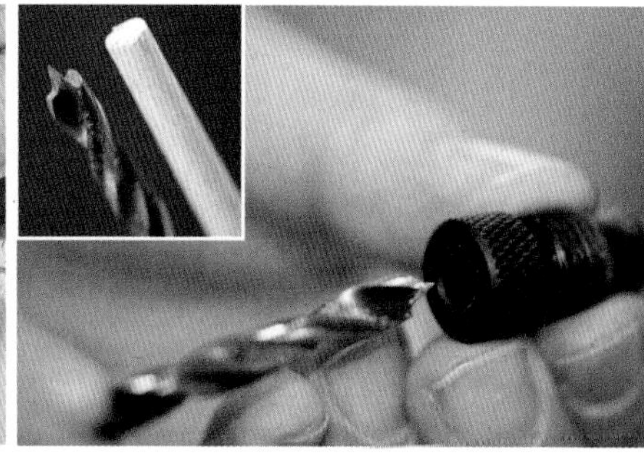

2 **Select a drill bit** and bush of the same diameter as that of your chosen piece of doweling (inset).

3 **Place the pieces** in the jig, then insert the first bush into the vertical hole that is centered over the thickness of the end grain.

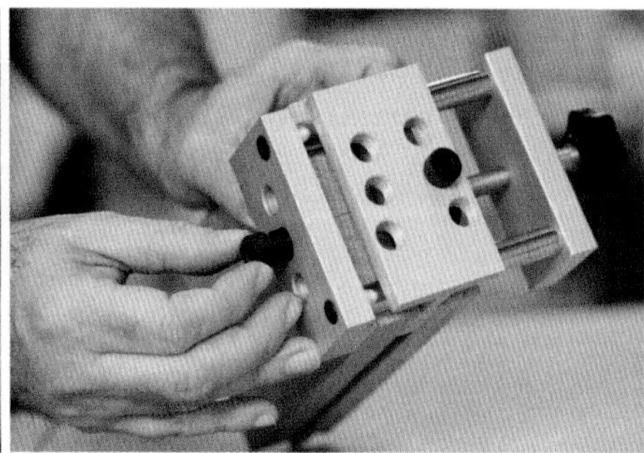

4 **Choose a horizontal hole** for the second bush so that it lines up with the first bush.

5 **Place the E-clamp** in position to keep the pieces equally spaced. When working with long lengths of wood, use an additional spacer piece of the same width as the E-clamp. Secure the whole set up in position in the vise.

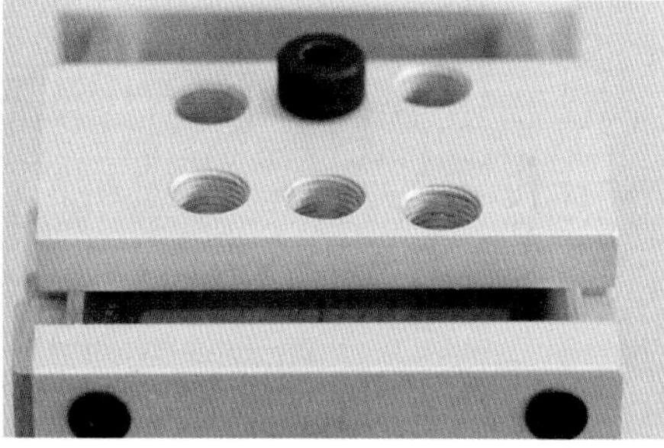

6 **Loosen the main part** of the jig and position it so that the bush is centered over the mark for the first hole. Tighten the jig in position.

SETTING UP THE DRILL BITS

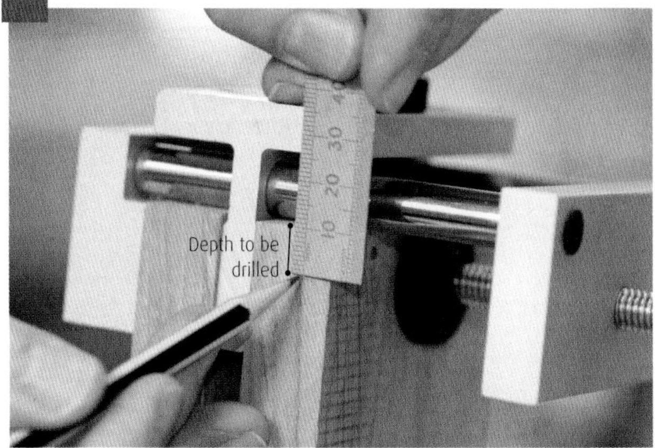

1 **Determine the depth** to be drilled—a maximum of half the thickness of the stock. Mark the edge of the piece that will be drilled through the end grain to the required depth.

2 **Measure the distance** from the end grain to the top of the bush and add this distance to the depth to be drilled.

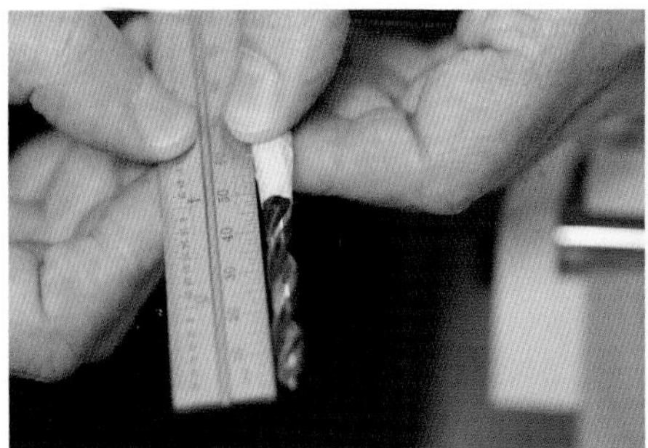

3 **Use masking tape** to mark the drill bit to the combined length of the drilling depth and the distance from the end grain to the top of the bush.

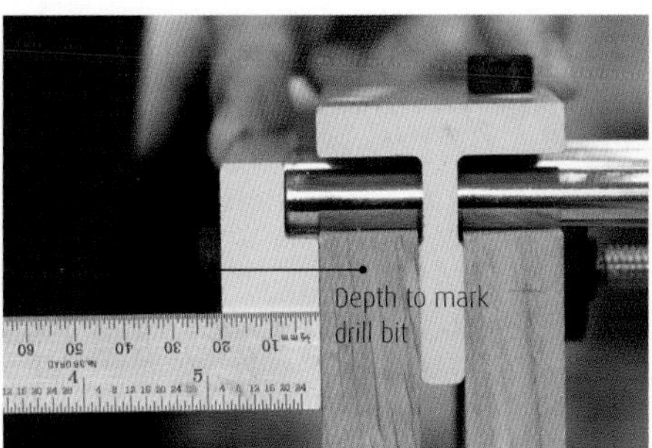

4 **For the horizontal drilling position**, measure the distance from the face of the wood to the top of the bush, and add it to the depth to be drilled.

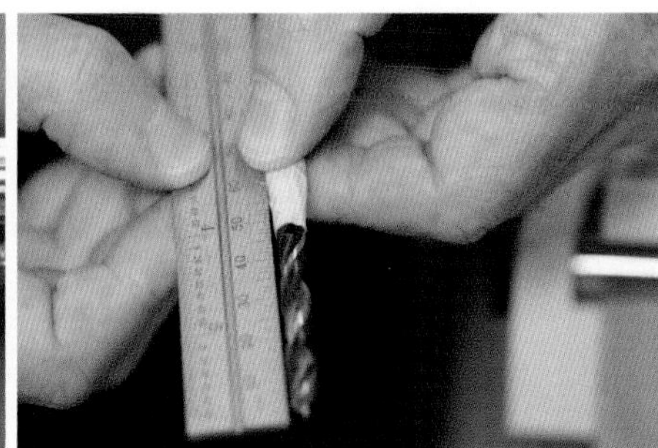

5 **Mark a second drill bit** to the combined measurement. Mark the tape on the bits to indicate which jig position—vertical or horizontal—each bit should be used for.

6 **Insert the correct bit** and drill into the vertical position in the first piece, being careful not to drill past the marked depth.

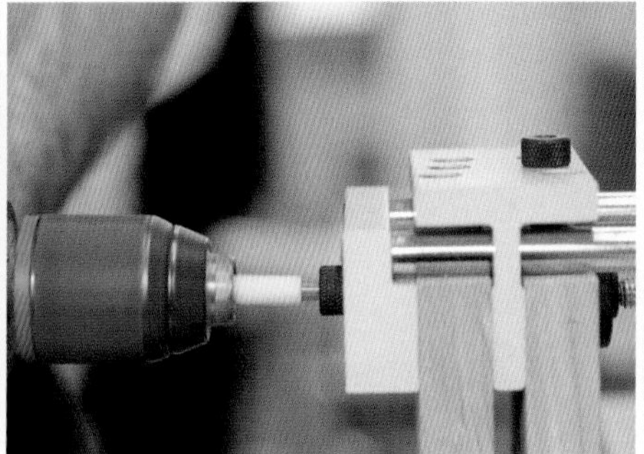

7 **Use the second bit** (marked for the horizontal position) to drill into the face of the second piece.

8 **Move the jig** to align with the next marked dowel position, then drill vertically and horizontally as before. Drill the remaining marked positions in the same way.

PREPARING THE DOWELS AND GLUING THE JOINT

1 **Use a chisel** to cut a V-groove along the length of the doweling to hold the glue. Then calculate the length of each dowel—the combined depth of each pair of holes, minus 1⁄16in (2mm) for glue (inset). Cut the doweling into the number of lengths required to join each pair of holes.

2 **Smooth the ends** of each dowel with sandpaper to remove any rough edges and ease the fit in the holes.

3 **Check the fit** of the dowels in the end-grain holes, then connect to the second piece to test the fit of the joint.

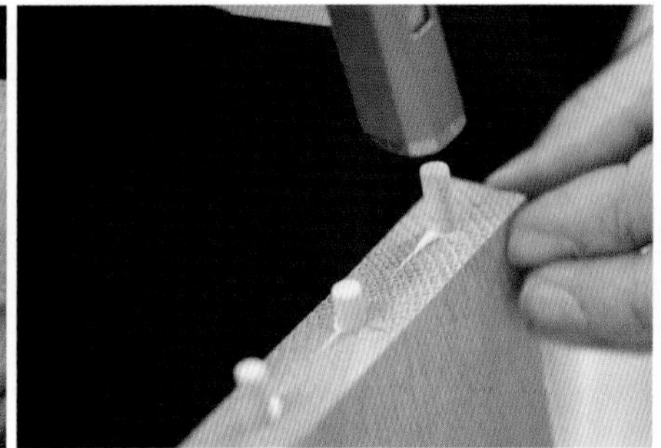

4 **Disassemble the joint** and apply glue to the holes and the end grain. Tap the dowels into the holes and assemble the joint.

THE FINAL JOINT

Joint with pocket-screw jig

The Kreg system is a commercial method of pocket-hole joinery, a type of joint that has been in use since at least the 18th century. It was originally used in applications such as attaching rails to table tops, but now performs the same function as other connectors. It can be extremely useful if space for joints is limited, such as kitchen-cabinet carcass work. A specialist jig (such as a Kreg jig), which can be adjusted for stock of different sizes, ensures that alignment is consistent and accurate, while a specialist bit (such as the Kreg bit) cuts the clearance and pilot holes, producing a precise hole every time. Its applications are extensive, from T-joints and edge-to-edge joints to corner joints and for connecting rails to legs.

PARTS OF THE JOINT

The pocket-hole joint is formed by a hole drilled at an acute angle that houses a self-tapping screw, which is used to connect the two pieces together. Each of the components are butted up against each other and the hole is then drilled to accept the screw—the type of screw varies according to the wood or woods that are being used.

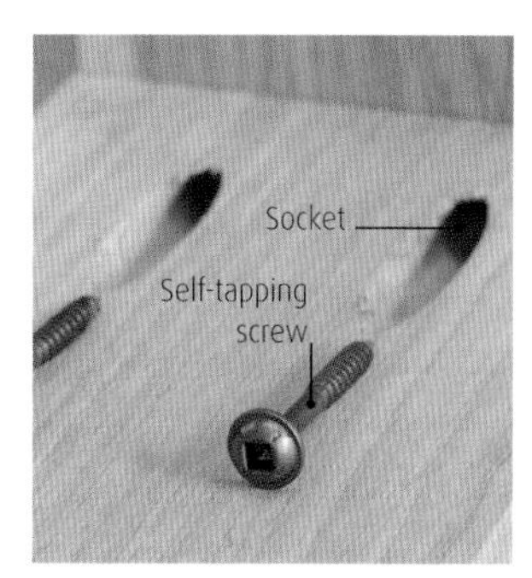

TOOLS AND MATERIALS

- Square
- Pocket-screw jig (Kreg jig)
- Clamp
- Specialized bit (Kreg bit)
- Power drill
- Bench hook
- Square-drive screws

USING A POCKET-SCREW JIG

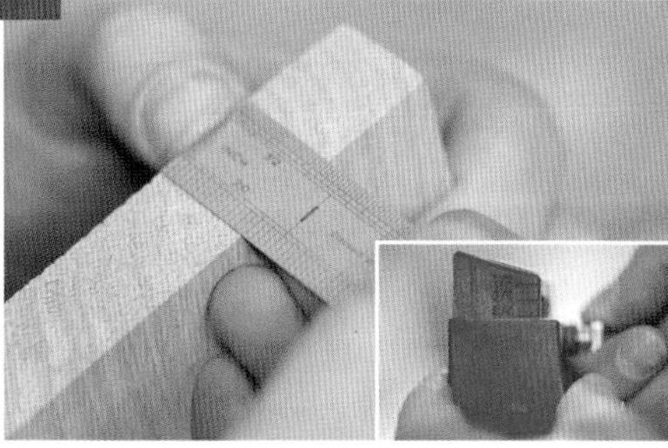

1 **Measure the thickness** of the stock to be drilled, then set the jig to match this measurement (inset).

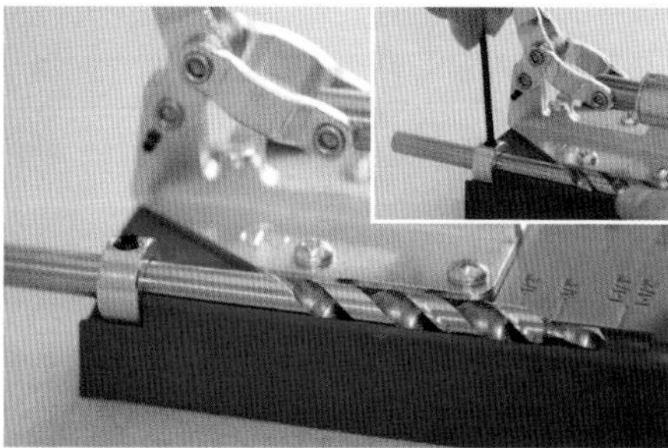

2 **Adjust the Kreg-bit collar** (inset) so that the tip aligns with the jig measurement that matches the thickness of the stock.

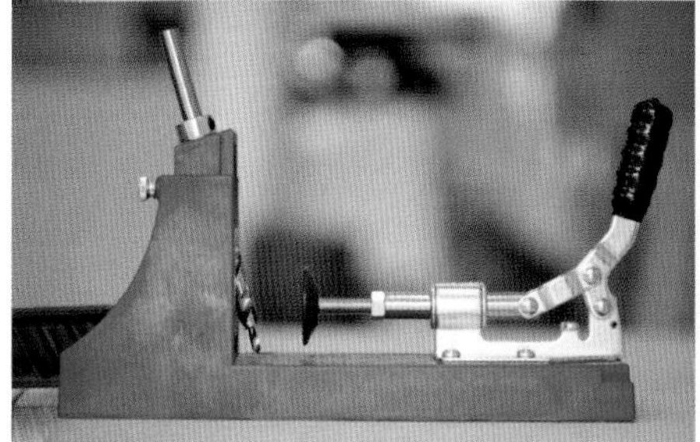

3 **Clamp the jig** to the bench, then insert the Kreg bit into the guide hole to check the alignment. Attach the bit to your drill.

4 **Place the piece** to be drilled within the jig, then close the clamp to secure it firmly in position.

5 **Insert the Kreg bit** into the guide hole and drill as far as you can. Reposition the piece and repeat as necessary.

6 **Place the undrilled piece** vertically against a bench hook with the drilled end of the other piece butted against it. Insert a square-drive screw through each hole, into the second piece. Set the drilling speed for the material—hardwoods require a much slower speed than softwoods or manufactured boards.

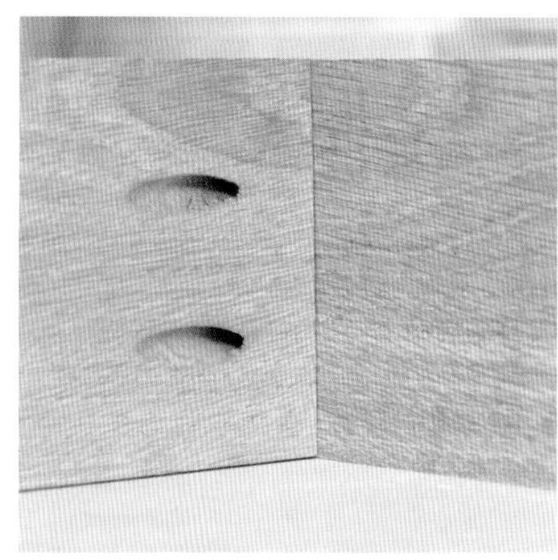

THE FINAL JOINT

Jigs and templates

A jig is a devise designed to hold a workpiece or guide a tool in a specific way. They are frequently used in combination with machines, improving both accuracy and safety and having the added benefit of speeding up a process. Templates share many of the attributes of a jig, but they are generally flat design-patterns of the outline of a component. Examples of useful jigs and templates are shown here.

MDF is an excellent choice of material for jigs and templates because it does not expand or shrink as solid wood does, thereby maintaining accuracy. In general, it is better to use screws rather than glue on a jig, as screws will enable it to be adjusted or dismantled. Screws should be countersunk below the surface of the MDF (raised heads may damage the workpiece or bed or fence of a machine).

Jig for drilling holes

Drilling a number of accurately placed holes can be very time-consuming without a jig. The jig shown here is one for drilling a repeat pattern of holes in the sides of a cabinet with adjustable shelves (see Glass-fronted cabinet, pp.326–333). The holes will receive metal shelf pegs. The sheet of MDF should be of the same size as the component or designed to line up with an edge or corner. Use an offcut underneath the MDF for drilling into. Similar jigs can be made with an additional fence for drilling into edges.

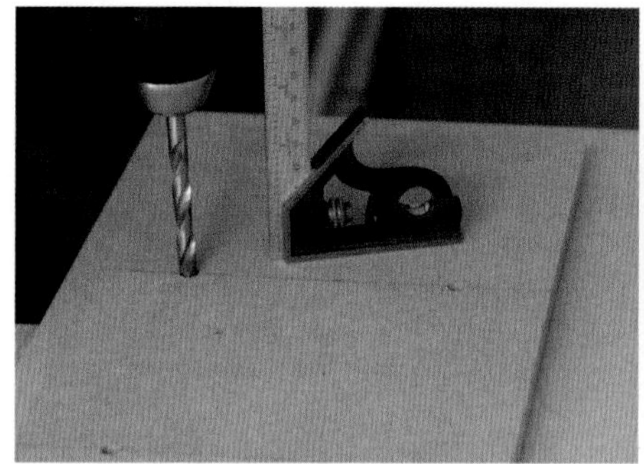

1 **Mark out the positions** of the holes onto a piece of MDF, then drill the holes through it. Use a square as a guide when drilling to ensure the hole is perpendicular.

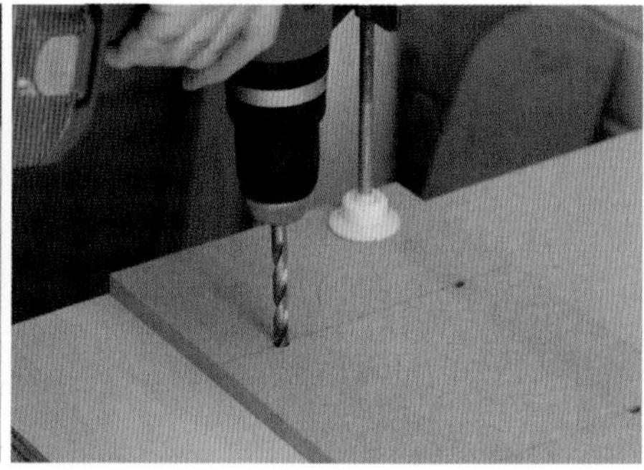

2 **Locate the jig** over the workpiece and secure it with a cramp. Drill through the holes in the jig to the required depth.

Jig for tapering thickness

The jig described here allows a component to be shaped by holding it at an angle as it is passed through a thicknesser (see pp.58–59). Please note that this method should only be used when the workpiece is more than 18in (500mm) long—any shorter and it may twist around in the machine. As is always the case when using a thicknesser, take extra care and always follow the manufacturer's guidelines for safe operation.

1 **Cut out a base board** that is about 4in (100mm) longer and 4in (100mm) wider than the workpiece. Mark out two identical shapes, 1in (25mm) high at the lowest point and with a sloping top edge representing the angle of taper. Fix them with countersunk screws (work from the underside) near to the ends of the baseboard.

2 **Screw side pieces** to the base, using the width of the workpiece to set their positions. The side pieces cradle the workpiece, preventing side-to-side movement.

3 **Fit a cleat** on one tapered end to prevent backward movement as the piece moves through the thicknesser.

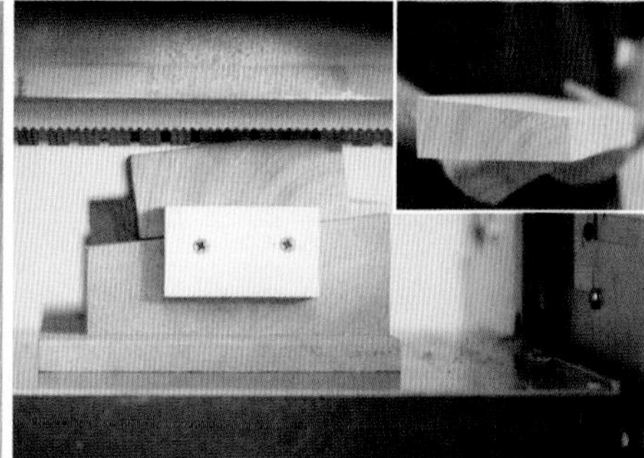

4 **With the workpiece set** in the jig, feed it repeatedly through the thicknesser, each time reducing the thickness by $\frac{1}{32}$–$\frac{1}{16}$in (1–2mm) until the desired profile is achieved.

Jig for tapering width

This simple jig, which is for use on a table saw, is quick to make and effective. It can be used to cut the same taper on a variety of widths (by adjusting the side fence), but it is normally used for cutting identically shaped workpieces. After sawing, the edge will need planing. Alternatively, use a rectangular base, an angled or adjustable fence, end stop, and toggle clamps to hold the workpiece in position. This kind of jig acts as a sled that is passed through the saw. For further information on how to use a table saw safely, see pp.54–55.

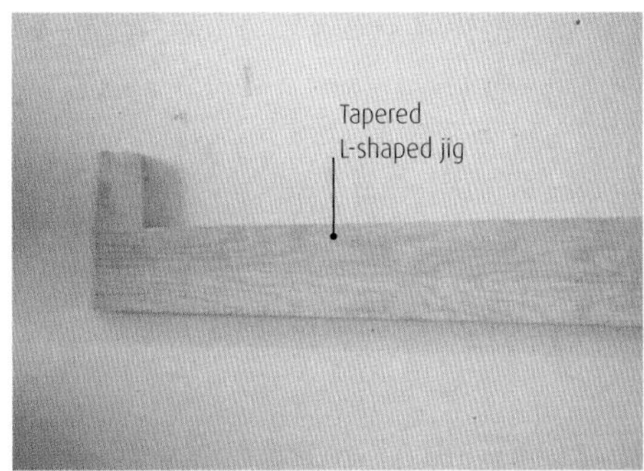

1 **Mark out and cut** the desired angle from a piece of wood, leaving an L-shape at the end to act as a stop during sawing.

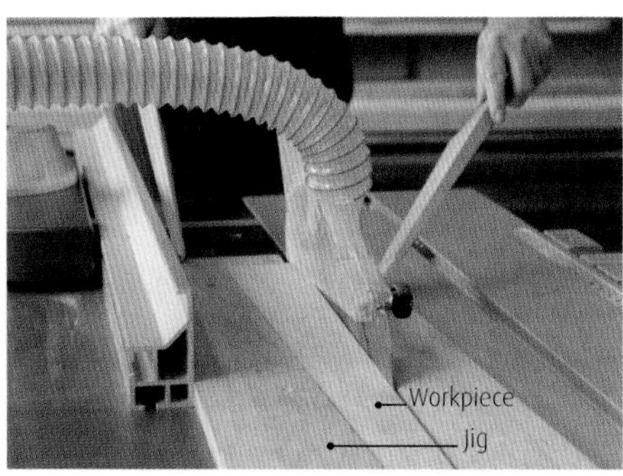

2 **Position the workpiece** on the table saw, located in the jig with the end butted up to the L-shape. Adjust the side fence to the required dimension. Feed the work through the saw using push sticks as shown.

Template for cutting a curve

This method produces smooth outlines that need only light sanding. It also provides a means of reproducing identical workpieces. The bulk of the waste is removed with a jigsaw and the finishing cut is made with a bearing-guided cutter. The bearing of the cutter traces the shape of the template. The same method can be used for routing intricate shapes.

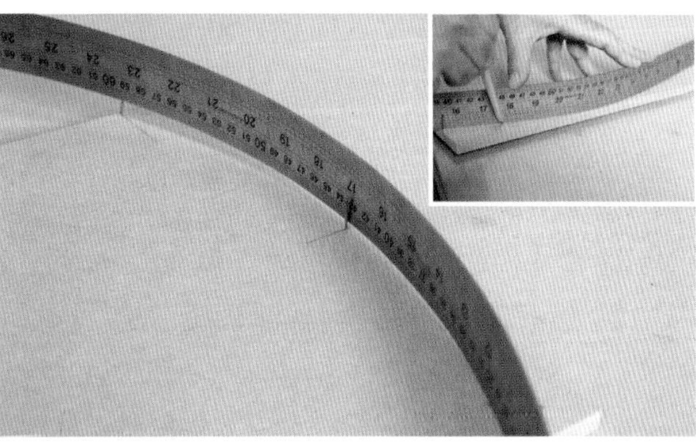

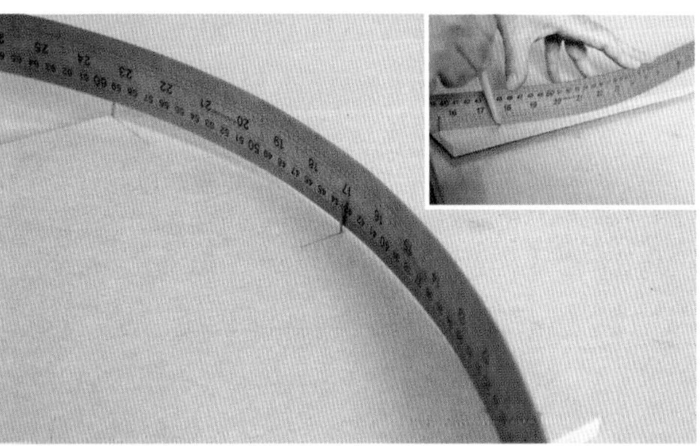

1 **Mark both ends** and the center of the curve on the top edge of the template. Hammer pins into the marked positions. Place the ruler behind the center pin and in front of the side pins to create a curve. Draw along the back of the ruler to transcribe the curve onto the template (inset).

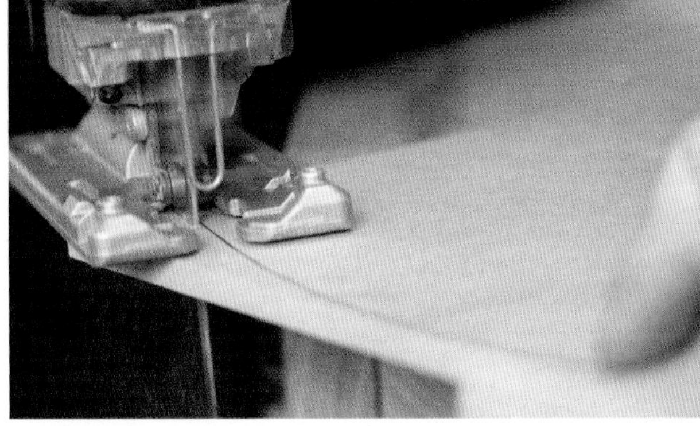

2 **Remove the ruler and the pins** and cut to the waste side of the line with a jigsaw (pictured) or band saw.

3 **Use a flat spokeshave** to smooth out the curve to the line. Finish with sandpaper.

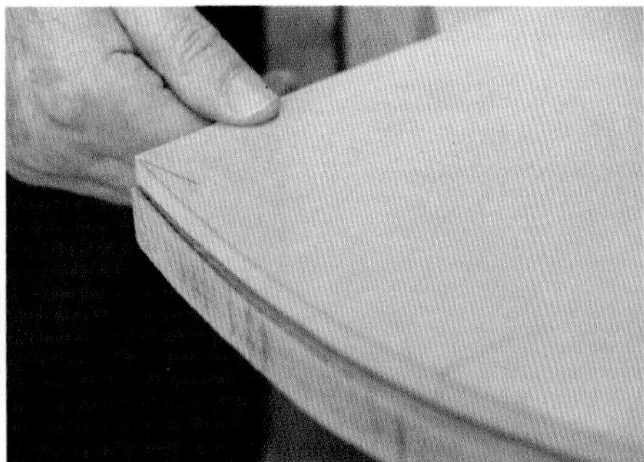

4 **Draw around the template** onto the workpiece. Remove the template and cut along the line drawn with a jigsaw. Stay $\frac{1}{16}$in (2mm) to the waste side of the line (inset).

5 **Position the template** over the workpiece with the curved edge of the template aligned precisely with the pencil line, and cramp in position for routing.

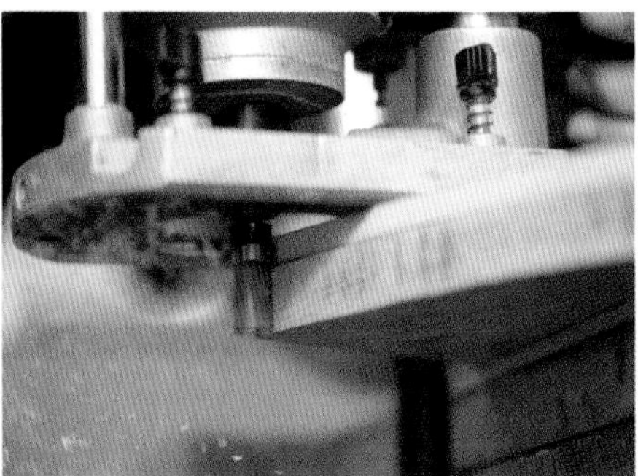

6 **Fit a bearing-guided cutter** in the router, adjust the router so that the bearing of the cutter aligns with the edge of the template, and trim off the waste.

Turning techniques

A wood lathe and cutting tools (woodturning chisels, scrapers, and gouges) are used for creating round-section components, such as legs for a chair (turning between centers), as well as complete items such as bowls (faceplate turning). Turning is a popular hobby, probably because it is a creative and enjoyable process, but mastering the techniques is definitely a challenge for the beginner. A lathe is basically a machine that spins a piece of wood while the turner skilfully maneuvers a hand-held cutting tool across the surface of the workpiece, removing shavings until the desired shape is achieved and then sanded smooth (polishing can also be performed on the lathe). As with most woodworking, seasoned wood is generally used, but green (wet) wood can also be used for artistic bowls and traditional Windsor chair legs, where the subsequent drying and shrinking process distorts the shape, resulting in irregular-shaped bowls and oval-section chair legs. Green wood is a joy to turn as the wood is soft and cuts without creating dust; tools must be extremely sharp to avoid tearing the wood, and sanding is not usually required. Most timbers can be turned; species such as beech or oak are often used in furniture making, and a burr or a piece of zebrano may be used for decorative objects.

TURNING BETWEEN CENTERS

Traditional chairs and tables often have turned legs that are made by mounting the blank, or stock, in the lathe between the headstock and the tailstock ("between centers"). Often these legs are left square at an end so that they can be mortised (pictured) and feature decorative hollows, beads, vases, and balls. Legs without square sections can be planed octagonally before turning.

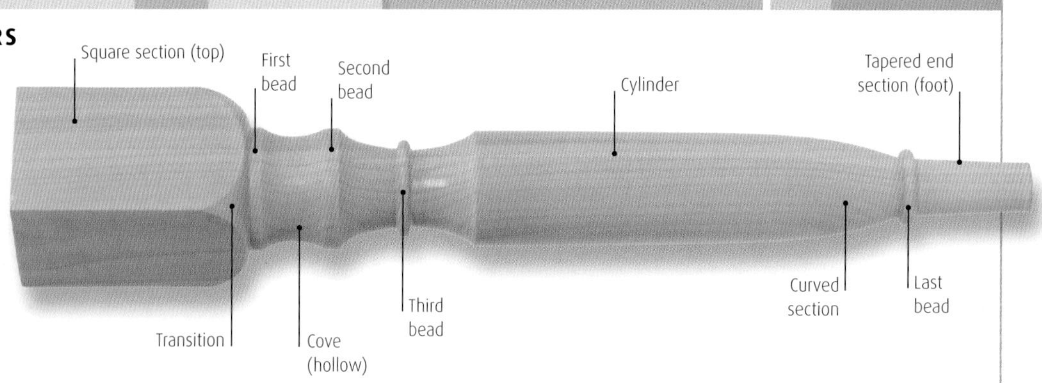

TOOLS AND MATERIALS

- Pencil
- Square
- Lathe
- Full-face visor
- Roughing-out gouge
- MDF for template (size to suit)
- Outside caliper
- Parting tool
- Spindle gouge
- Skew chisel
- Beading tool (optional)
- Flat scraper
- Round scraper
- Sandpaper
- Dust mask
- Cloth
- Friction wax-polish

CUTTING A CYLINDER

1 **Set the lathe** to the lowest speed. Draw diagonal lines on the ends of the stock to find the center points, and mount in the lathe between the head- and tailstock. Ensure the wood is centered, advance the tailstock, then lock its position. Mark the top end of the turning using a square (allow about 1in/25mm of waste) and the first bead position.

2 **Set the rest** about ⅜in (10mm) from the stock and at a height that is roughly in line with the center line.

3 **Spin the wood** manually to check that it is clear of the rest. Check that the stock is held firmly; if you can move (wobble) either end then tighten the tailstock.

4 **Place the gouge on the rest** and hand-spin the lathe to check the position and angle of the tool in relation to the wood. **Note**: The handle of the cutting tool should be slightly lower than the rest.

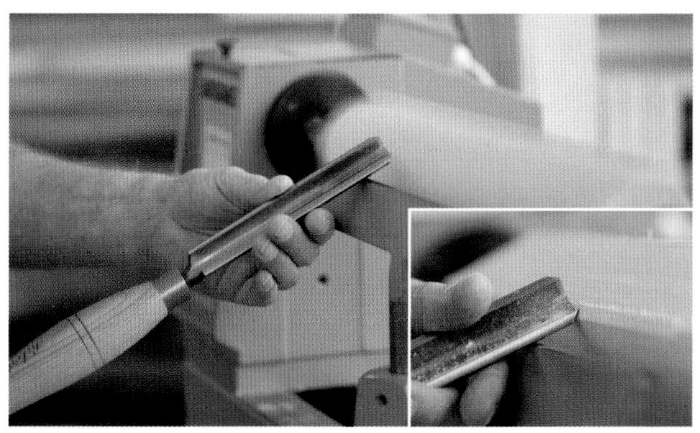

5 **Put a face visor on.** Turn the lathe on and then immediately off to check that the piece is balanced (strong vibration means it is off-center and needs remounting). Now turn the lathe on, increase the speed, and begin cutting. Advance the roughing-out gouge as shown (inset).

6 **Make light cuts at first.** Aim to convert the square stock to a rough cylinder, but avoid cutting the square-section top part.

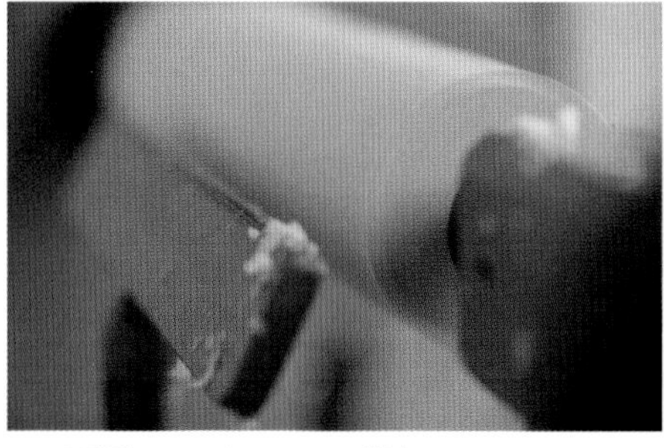

7 **While turning** you will have to reposition the rest; each time you do, check that it is clear of the wood.

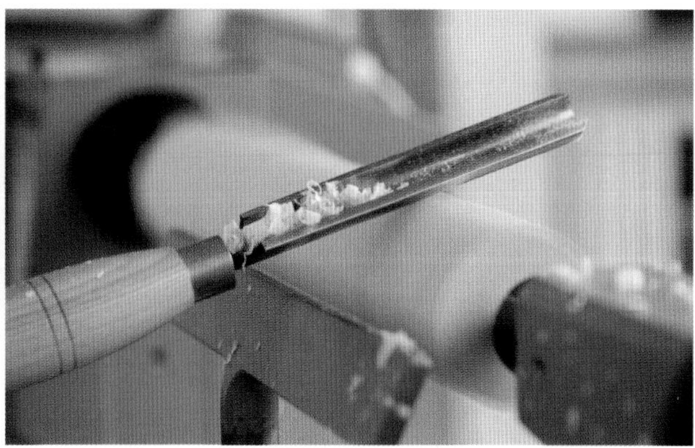

8 **Check the progress** of the cylinder by holding the tool lightly on the edge of the moving stock. When it sits without bouncing, the cylinder is finished.

PLANNING A TURNING PROFILE

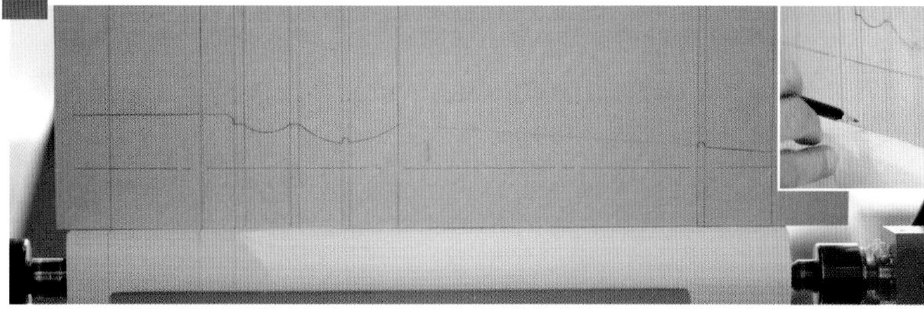

1 **Create a profile template** from rigid cardboard. Draw on it the shape and each transition point between sections. With the lathe turned off, sit the template on the stock (aligned with the top mark) and mark the transition points onto the stock (inset).

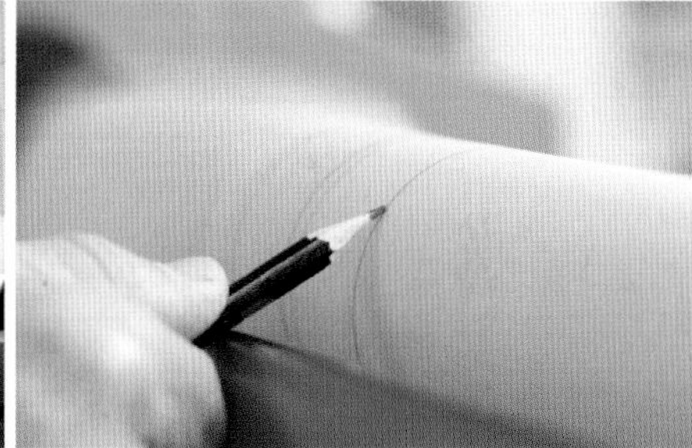

2 **Lift off the template**, turn on the lathe, and hold a pencil to the rotating surface to extend each mark around the workpiece.

CUTTING THE SQUARE SECTION

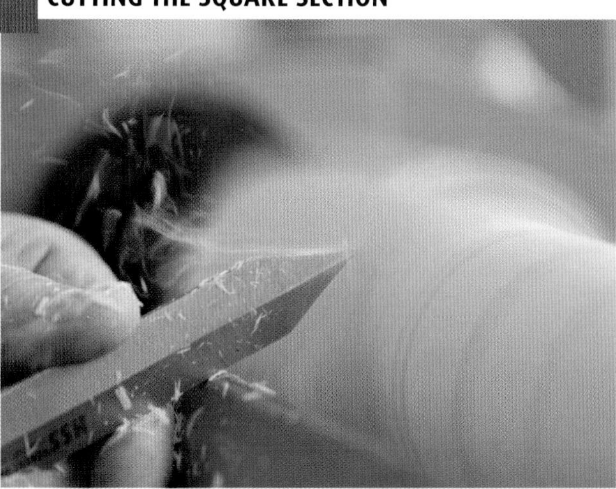

1 **Set the caliper** to the diameter of the first bead nearest the top (see Turning Between Centers, opposite). Increase the speed of the lathe to the halfway point. Use the parting tool to cut into the stock at the location of the first bead. Hold it square to the lathe and gently plunge into the wood. Repeat the plunges on either side to widen the cut.

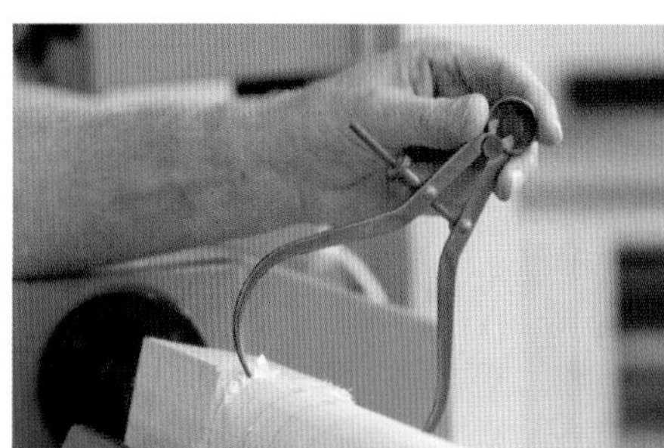

2 **Frequently stop the machine** and check the diameter of the cut section with the caliper so that you do not over-cut.

ALLOWING FOR BEADING

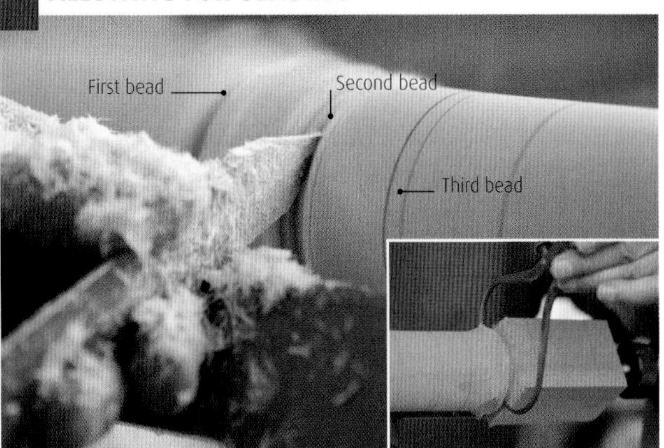

1 **Remove most of the waste** from the section to be beaded. Use the parting tool to cut to about 3⁄16in (5mm) over the intended diameter of the bead. Check the diameter with a caliper as you work (inset). Cut down to the second and third beads in the same way.

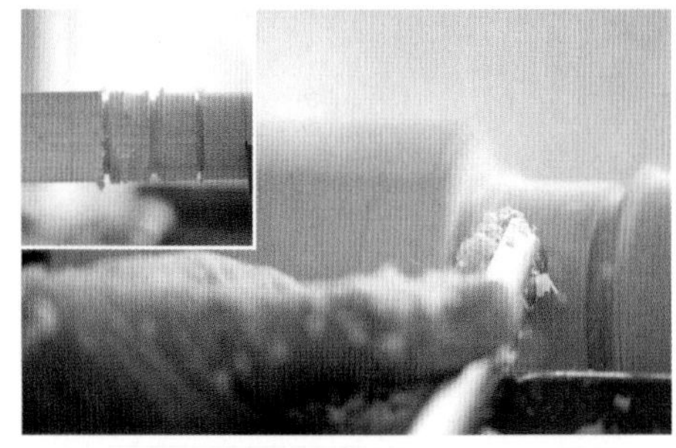

2 **Use the roughing-out gouge**, passed lightly over the surface, to smooth the section between the beads (inset).

CUTTING THE TRANSITION

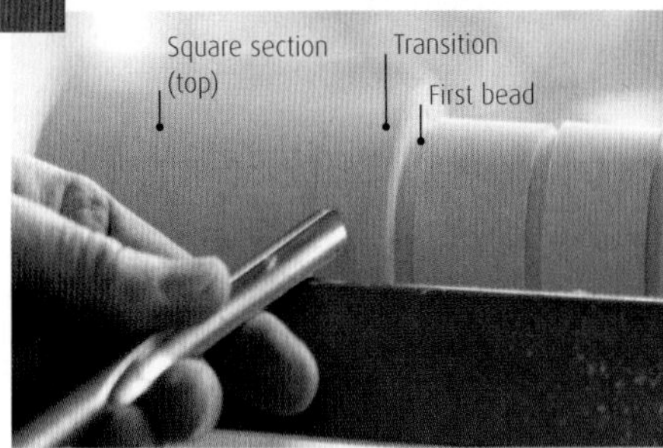

1 **Cut the transition** from the square section to the cylinder using the spindle gouge. This cuts the corners into a curve.

2 **Keep the bevel** of the gouge supported on the stock as you increase the depth of cut toward the cylindrical section. Resharpening the tool and increasing the speed of the lathe to three-quarter speed will help to achieve a cleanly cut result (inset).

CUTTING THE FIRST COVE

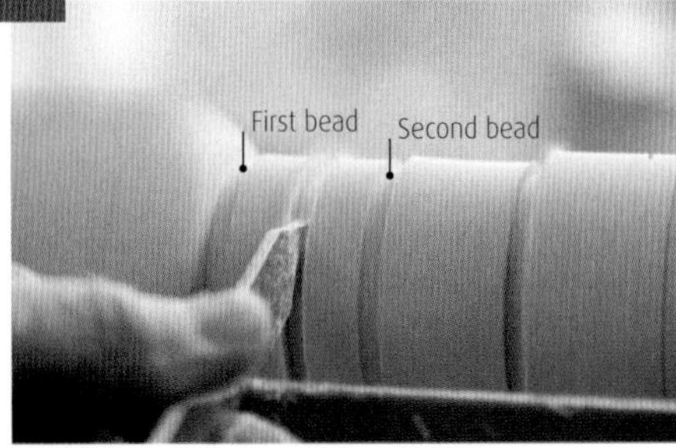

1 **Use the parting tool** to cut to about 1⁄16in (2mm) over the intended final diameter at the center of the cove.

2 **Use the spindle gouge** to cut toward the center of the cove alternately from the left and right.

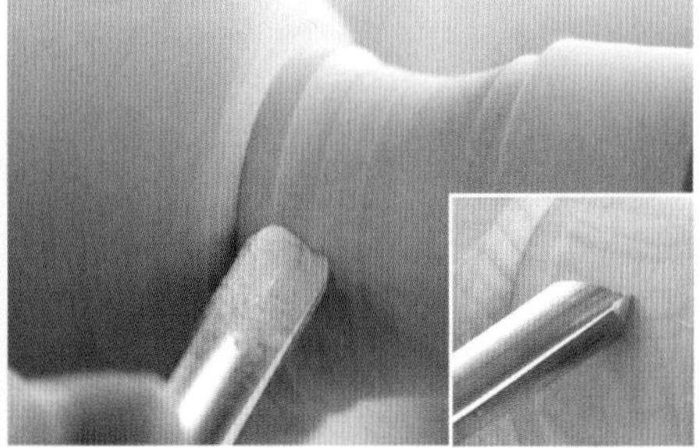

3 **As you work**, gradually turn the gouge from side-on to angle the open side of the gouge into an upward position (inset).

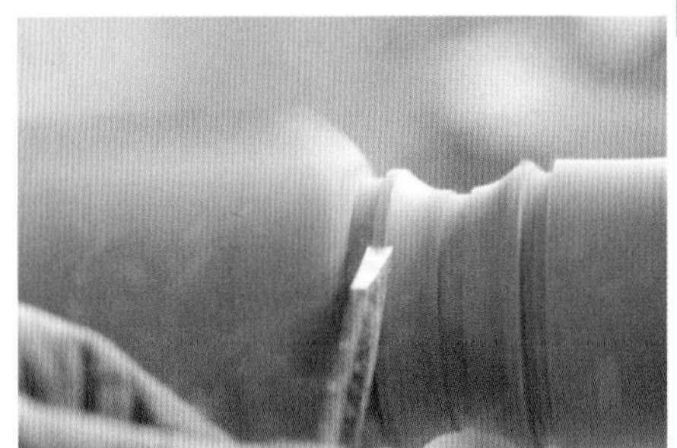

4 **Alternate cutting** with the spindle gouge with using the parting tool to cut back rough edges from the sides of the cove.

CUTTING A COVE WITH A BEAD

1 **Use a roughing-out gouge** to reduce the excess wood at the edge to the level of the shoulder.

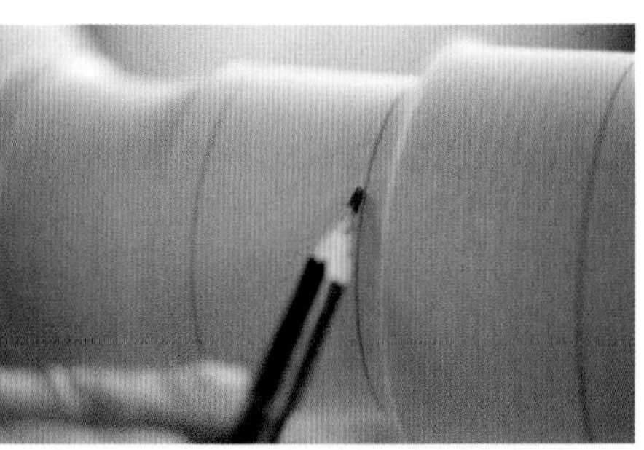

2 **With the lathe still turning**, carefully re-mark the bead position and that of the shoulder.

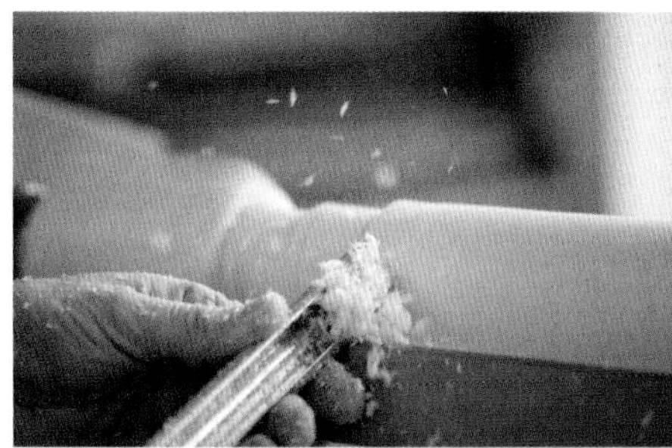

3 **Use the roughing-out gouge** to remove the excess from the stock, from the beaded cove to the tail stock.

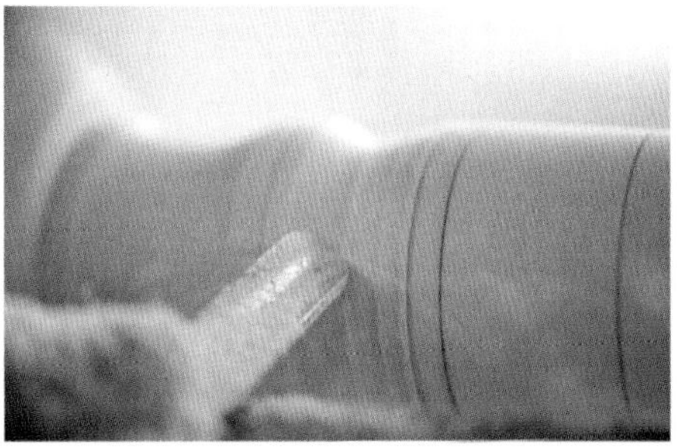

4 **Cut the cove** toward the center using the spindle gouge, stopping before you reach the beaded section.

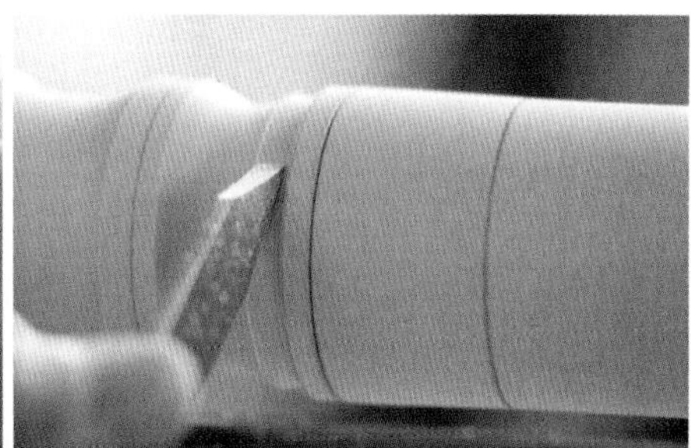

5 **Periodically use the parting tool** to cut back the rough edges close to the bead. Then use a skew chisel to create a straight edge close to the beading.

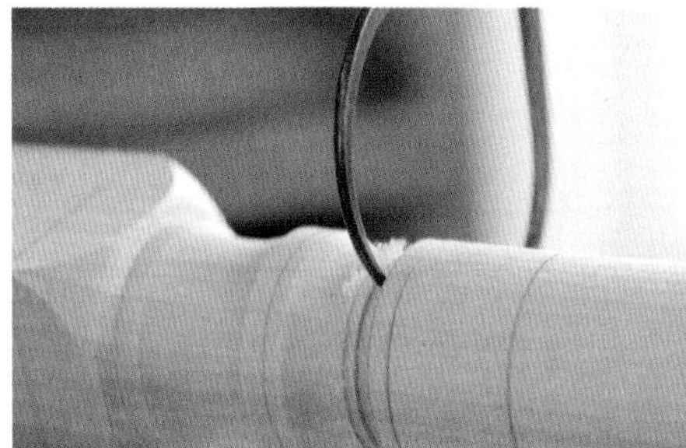

6 **As you work**, keep checking the diameter of the cove with the caliper (always turn the lathe off first).

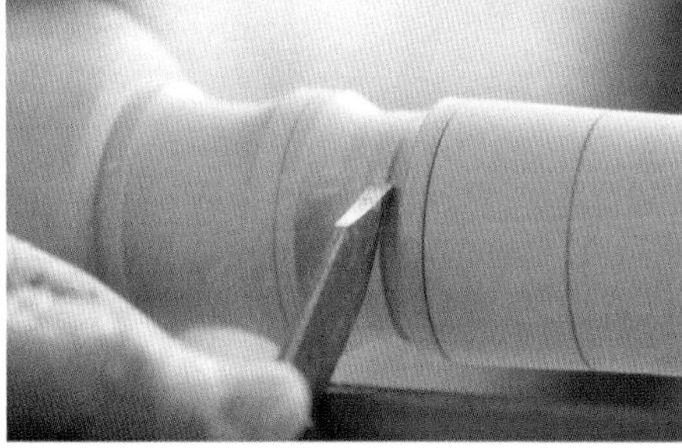

7 **Use the parting tool** (at a 90-degree angle to the lathe) to cut the edge of the bead to nearly the full depth of the cove.

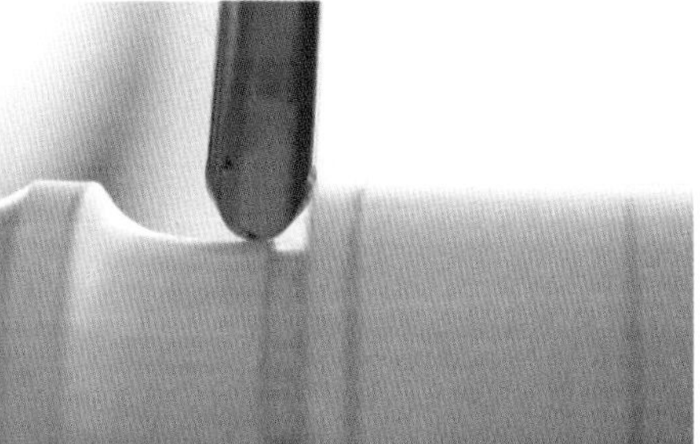

8 **Use the spindle gouge** to finish cutting the cove to the marks from shoulder to bead. Repeat Steps 1–7 to cut the other side of the cove from edge to center.

CREATING THE CURVED SECTION

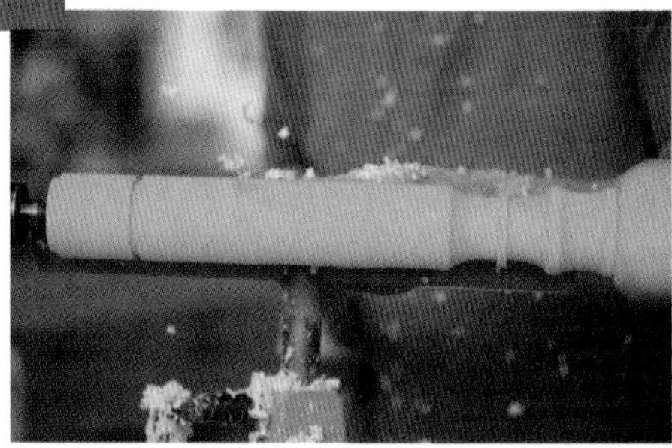

1 **Use the roughing-out gouge** to remove waste from the remaining section of the workpiece to produce a cylinder.

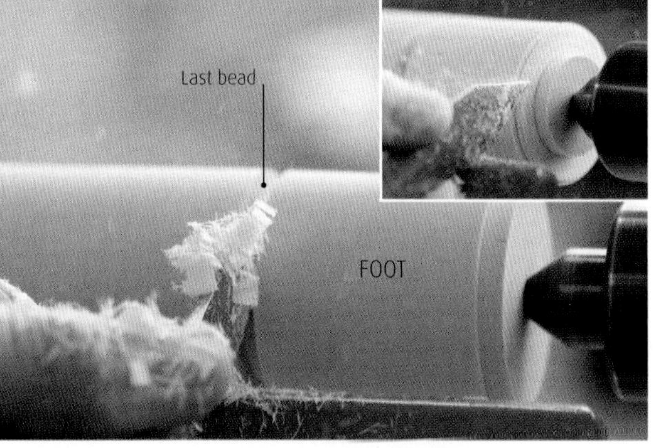

2 **Use the parting tool** to reduce further the shoulders on either side of the end section—the narrowest section. As before, use the template, a pencil, and the parting tool to mark the position of the bottom bead and the foot. Work carefully at the end (inset), avoiding contact with the tailstock.

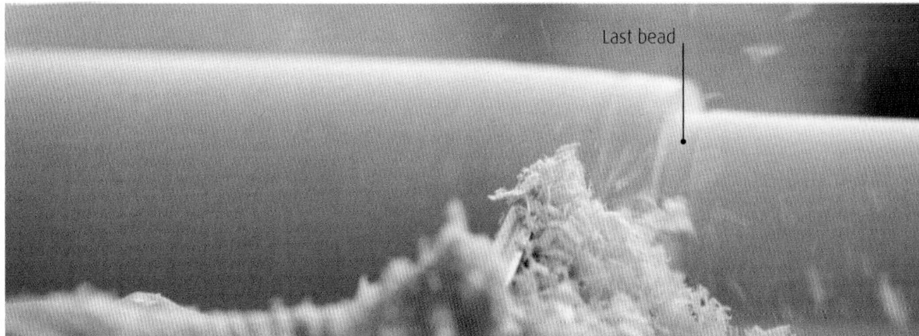

3 **Begin to cut** the curved section near the end of the workpiece. Use the roughing-out gouge to take smooth shearing cuts from the surface. Always work in a "downhill" direction (in this case from left to right) in order to "lay" the grain. Point the tool to the right and rotate in a clockwise direction.

4 **As you near the end** of the curved section, be careful not to cut into the bead.

5 **Once you have cut** some of the curve, return to the bead. Cut most of the excess from either side with the parting tool until you are at nearly the desired depth.

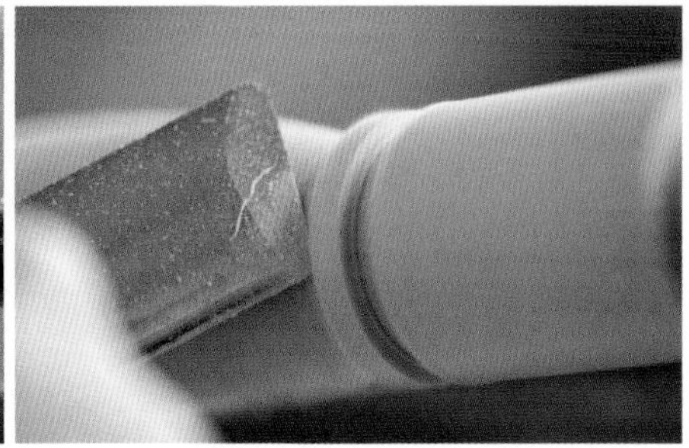

6 **Use a skew chisel** to cut into the bead at the end of the curve, a space too small for the roughing-out gouge.

USING A BEADING TOOL

A beading tool is a useful aid—it cuts the beading to a predetermined profile. When using this tool, raise the tool rest so that the tool is placed over the beaded section at the correct angle to the wood.

FINISHING THE TAPER AND BEAD

1 **Complete the taper** on the end (foot) of the workpiece. Use the roughing-out gouge to remove the waste between the shoulder cuts. As before, cut this tapered section with a "downhill" left-to-right motion.

2 **Finish the beading**. This can be done with a parting tool. Start at one edge of the beading and shave only a small amount at a time. Work the tool around the profile of the beading to achieve the desired shape.

SMOOTHING AND FINISHING

1 **Smooth off** the flat and convex sections with a flat scraper. Hold the tool square to the lathe and fairly horizontal.

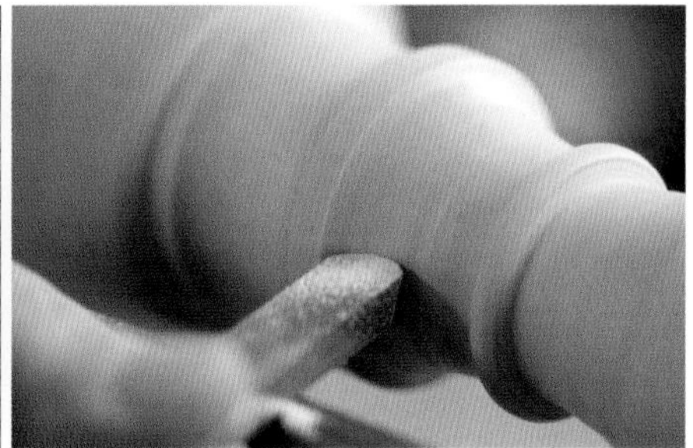

2 **Use a round scraper** to smooth the concave curves. Sweep the tip from side to side, aiming for a smooth, balanced curve.

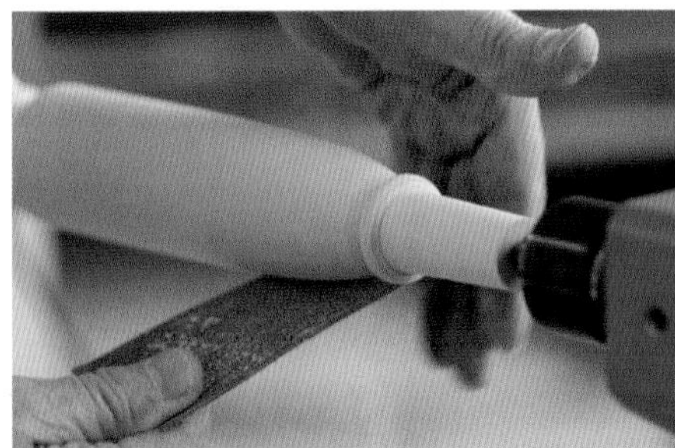

3 **Sand smooth** using conventional abrasive paper. Be sure to wear a dust mask.

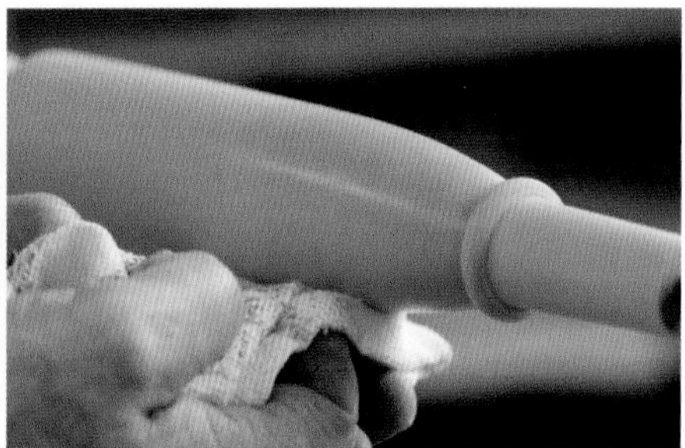

4 **If no further work is required**, such as mortising, a friction wax-polish can be applied while the piece is still spinning.

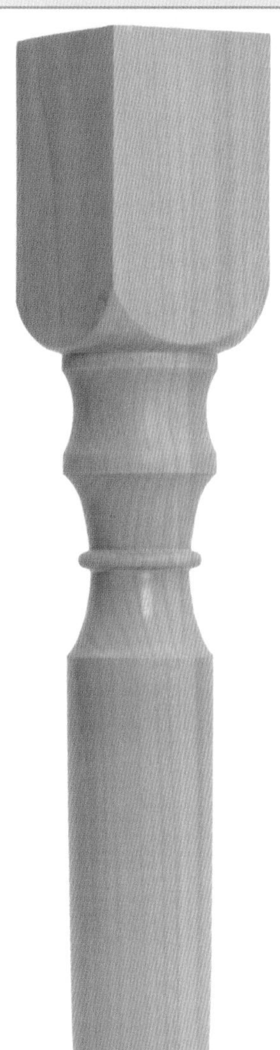

THE FINISHED PIECE

Veneering

Veneering was invented in Ancient Egypt and probably had its heyday in the 17th century. More recently, it has made a comeback for ecological reasons: because of the way veneers are cut (see p.198), their thinness makes much better use of the tree and, therefore, the world's wood resources in general. Veneering offers huge decorative potential and opportunities to create sculptural forms that would not be possible using solid wood. As well as providing an attractive surface, strips of veneer can be used to cover the edges of boards. An alternative method is to lip (see p.161) the edges with solid wood.

Arranging and checking veneer
To veneer large areas, you will have to join sheets of veneer side-by-side, using sheets from the same stack of veneer and maintaining the order in which it was cut. Check that the veneer does not require flattening before you start cutting or gluing (see below).

Choosing veneer

When designing a piece of furniture, it is worth considering the potential of veneers, since there are several areas in which they have an advantage over solid wood. For instance, veneering onto a moisture-resistant MDF core means that there are none of the movement problems associated with solid wood construction (cross-grain expansion and shrinkage). There are also many beautiful and distinctive grain patterns to choose from, such as bird's-eye, fiddleback, mottled, pommele, and quilted (see pp.198–99). Some of these veneers are cut from butts or burrs, which would otherwise not be used except for turning or sculptures. Another sensible reason to choose veneer is cost. An oak-veneered MDF board is a fraction of the cost of a solid oak board. Pre-veneered boards in popular woods such as ash, birch, and cherry are available and can save all the trouble of veneering, but present the challenge of how to cover exposed edges (see pp.161–62).

Veneers are limited in size so check what is available when planning a project. To cover large areas, for example, sheets of veneer 8in (200mm) wide can be joined side-by-side. Veneer is cut, stored, and sold in stacks that retain the same order in which the sheets were cut. When joining side-by-side, this order is maintained by a method known as slip-matching (each subsequent strip comes from beneath the preceding strip). Highly figured veneers can also be book-matched or quarter-matched: two or four identical leaves are turned and arranged so that they present a mirror image of each other.

Flattening veneer

Most veneers are flat enough to glue straight down, but those that are severely rippled or bubbled are best flattened before use, otherwise they may split while dry and under the pressure of clamps. Also, you will not be able to achieve a good result when assembling matched veneers or a pattern unless the veneers are flattened. Spraying water over the face surface just before gluing is good enough for moderately rippled veneer—it immediately becomes flexible enough to clamp. For pronounced rippling, use the technique described below.

BUCKLED VENEER

Burr veneers are especially prone to buckling. Before using them, you must flatten the sheets as described below but, instead of using just water, you must also use a traditional softening recipe or a proprietary veneer softener and place paper between the veneer and the boards.

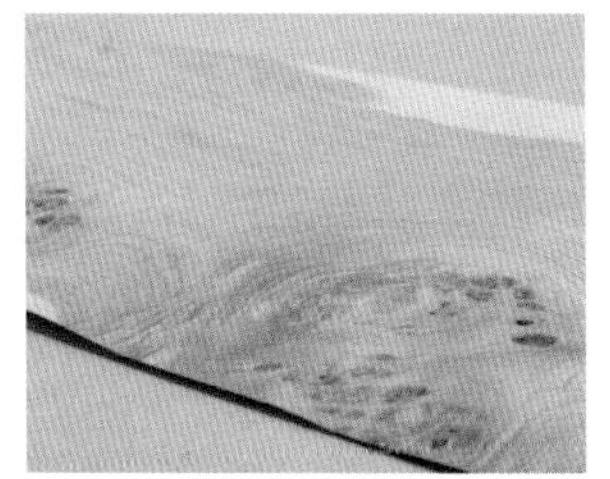

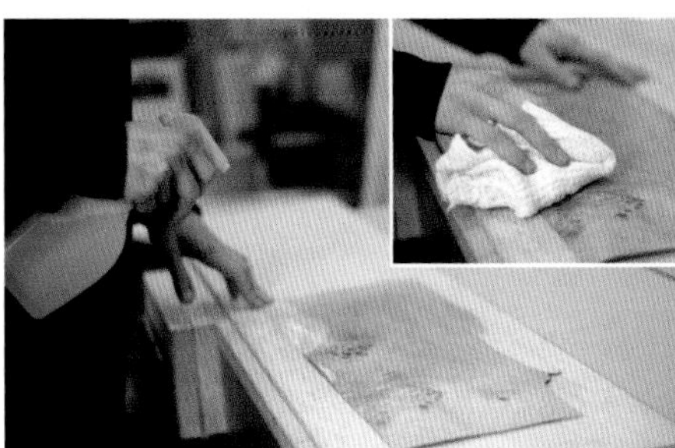

1 **Flatten veneer** that has warped by dampening it with a light misting of water. Wipe away any excess water with a cloth (inset).

2 **Place the dampened veneer** between two boards. You can flatten several sheets at a time, but you must put a sheet of absorbent paper between each sheet.

3 **Either clamp the boards** together or weigh them down. Check after a few days. If the veneer is still not flat, repeat the process and leave for a few more days.

Veneering a surface

Traditionally, veneers were stuck to a solid wood core using hot animal glue (see p.173). Hot glue is applied to the wood core, the veneer is laid in the direction of the grain, then rubbed down with a veneer hammer until the veneer is flat and the glue has cooled. The veneer can be laid on a flat or curved surface without clamping, but solid wood is inherently unstable so the glue bond weakens over time. Contact adhesive (see p.163) can be used in place of hot animal glue. In the veneering technique described below, PVA glue can be substituted by powder resin or specialized glues.

ELEMENTS OF A VENEERED PIECE

The core (also called "groundwork" or "substrate") is the structural component (made from MDF or solid wood) beneath the veneer. MDF is the ideal core because it is dimensionally stable and so the glue bond remains intact. As well as a face veneer, a balancing or "backing" veneer must be glued to the reverse side. If a balancing veneer is not used, the board will always warp, no matter how thick.

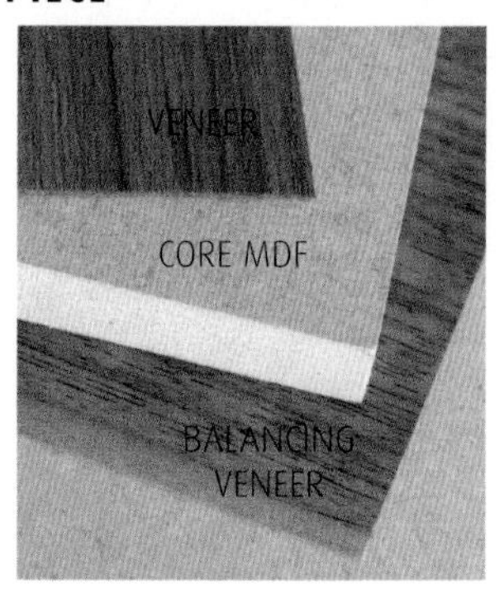

TOOLS AND MATERIALS

- Chinagraph pencil and lead pencil
- Metal ruler
- Scalpel
- Shooting board
- Bench plane
- Veneer tape
- Square (optional)
- Paper
- Offcut blocks (for cauls)
- PVA glue and roller
- Offcut boards (for clamping)
- C-clamps
- Cabinet scraper
- Fine-grade sandpaper

CUTTING THE VENEER

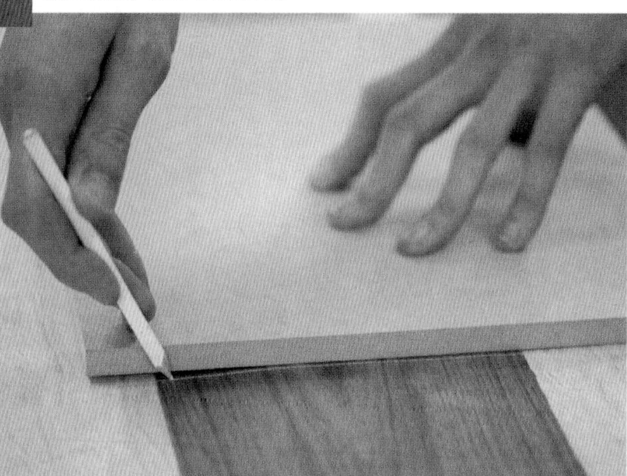

1 **Lay the core MDF** over the face veneer (when veneering MDF, the grain direction usually runs along the length of the core). Mark the length with 1/16in (2mm) extra either end. For large areas, it is likely you will have to join two or more sheets together, side-by-side (see p.157). Mark extra sheets as required.

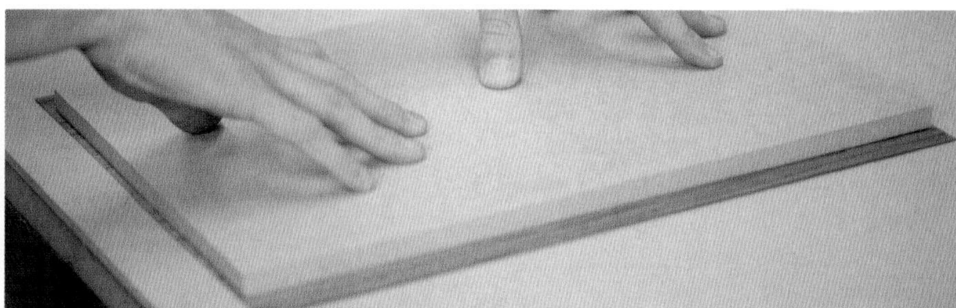

2 **Cut the veneer** along the marks using a scalpel. Mark the order of the pieces of veneer.

3 **If you are using** more than one piece of veneer, butt the pieces together loosely and check that they are larger than your core material on all sides. Where there is excess veneer, mark and trim, leaving at least 3/16in (5mm) extra width.

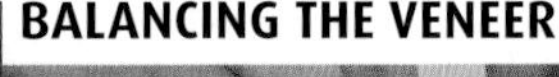

BALANCING THE VENEER

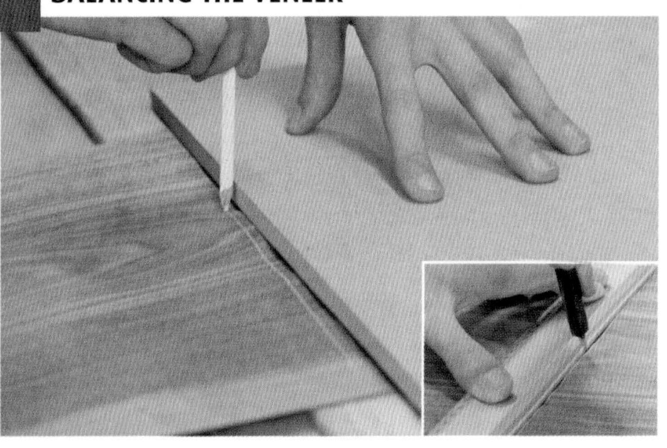

1 **Mark the balancing veneer** for the reverse side of the core in the same way as the face veneer and cut it to length (inset). A less expensive or less attractive veneer may be used, but the grain must run in the same direction as the face veneer.

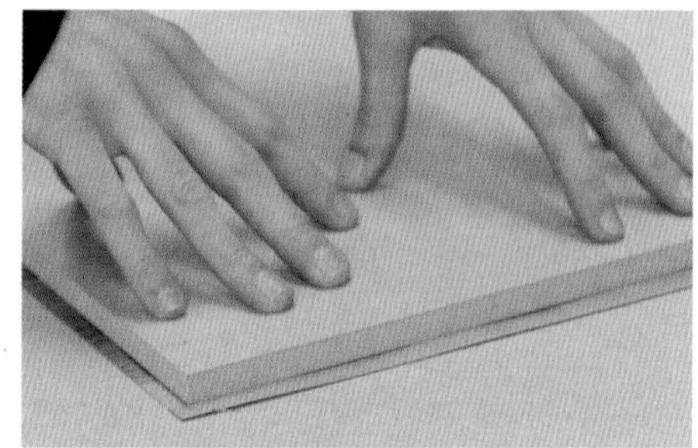

2 **Check the fit** of the core material over the balancing veneer, ensuring there is at least 3/16in (5mm) extra on all sides.

SHOOTING THE VENEER

1 **For veneers** that are to be joined side-by-side, use a shooting board (see p.71) to trim the inside edge of each of the pieces, clamping them firmly in place.

2 **Use a no.7 bench plane** to shoot the edge, being sure to cut in the direction of the grain to avoid tearing.

3 **Check that the inside edge** of the veneer is square along a straight edge, such as the side of a plane.

JOINING AND TRIMMING THE PIECES

1 **Where veneers** require joining, arrange them side-by-side on a flat surface in the order already marked. Push the pieces together tightly so that there is no gap, then place 2in (50mm) long strips of veneer tape at 6in (150mm) intervals along the join.

2 **If the join** in the face veneers must be centered on the core, mark center lines on the edge of the core as required.

3 **Mark center lines** on the tape on the face veneer to correspond with the marks on the core.

4 **Align the center marks**, then mark the excess veneer around the edge of the core, allowing for a 1/16in (2mm) overhang.

5 **Trim the excess** with a scalpel, using a metal ruler as a guide.

PREPARING TO GLUE THE VENEER

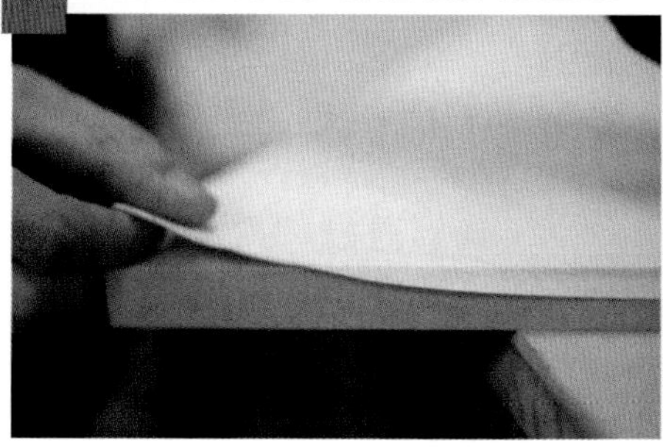

1 **Prepare for gluing** by taping paper to one surface of a board that is 4in (100mm) longer and wider than the core. Prepare two boards in this way.

2 **Make sufficient** specially shaped blocks, known as cauls, to clamp at 6in (150mm) intervals around the piece. Use a plane to taper the cauls slightly—about 1/16in (2mm)—on one side at each end. This ensures that when clamped at either end, pressure is also exerted in the middle of the piece. Untapered cauls will also be needed.

GLUING THE VENEER

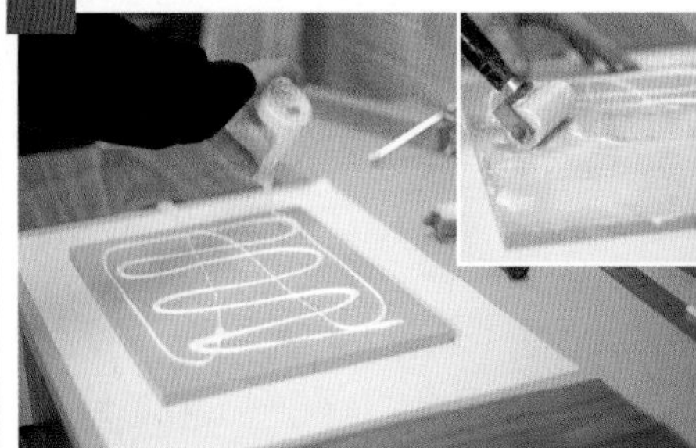

1 **Spread PVA adhesive** onto the face of the core material. Use a roller to spread the glue evenly (inset).

2 **Place the face veneer** face down on a surface and place the glued core over it, aligning the center seam of the veneer to the center marks on the edge of the core (inset).

3 **Apply PVA adhesive** to the other face of the core and spread it in the same way as in Step 1.

4 **Place the balancing veneer** face down. Turn the core over and place the second glued surface on top of the balancing veneer. Tape all three elements together at the edges.

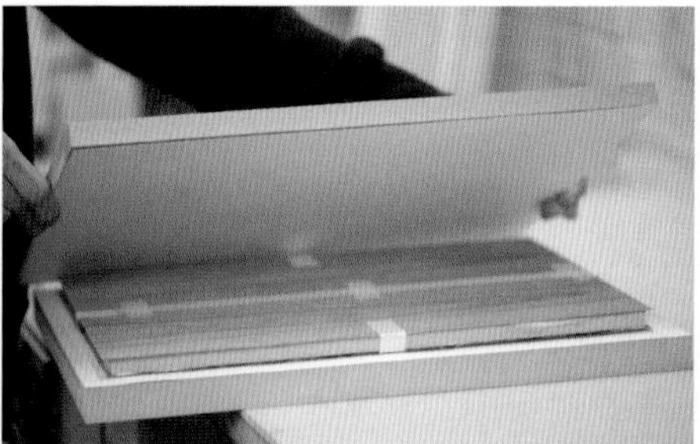

5 **Place the veneered piece** between the two paper-covered clamping boards prepared earlier (see p.159). Keep the face veneer uppermost when clamping.

6 **Clamp with the cauls on top** and the untapered blocks beneath (inset). Tighten the clamps until no gap is visible between the boards and the tapered ends of the cauls.

FINISHING THE VENEER

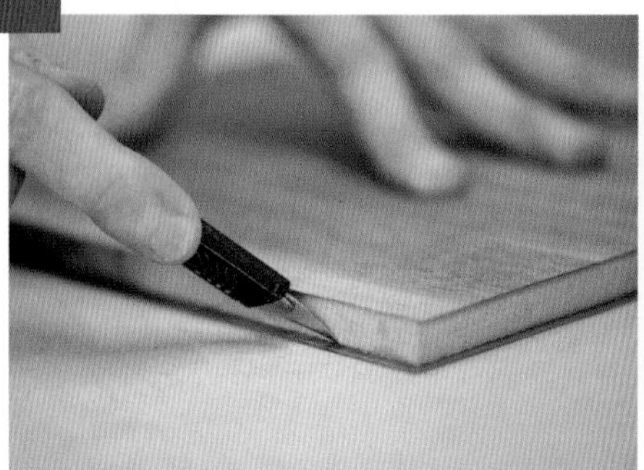

1 **Trim the edges** of both the face and balancing veneers. Use a knife or scalpel to score the excess.

2 **Remove the excess** by planing on a shooting board. Do not exert too much force; let the weight of the plane

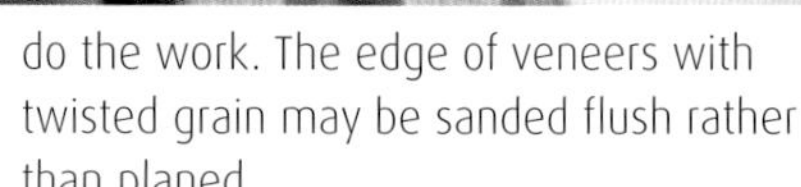

do the work. The edge of veneers with twisted grain may be sanded flush rather than planed.

3 **Remove the tape** from the face of the veneer using a cabinet scraper. After removing the tape, continue scraping to remove marks on the veneer. A pad sander may be used instead of a scraper for large areas, but take care not to oversand.

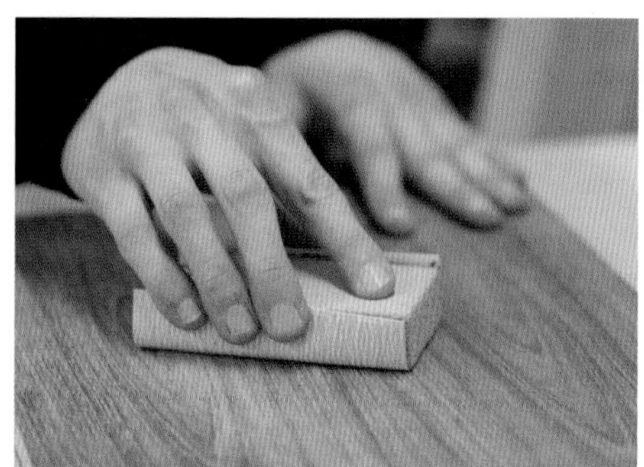

4 **Lightly sand** the face of the veneer with fine-grade sandpaper to finish.

Lipping

If the edges of a board are visible, as in a table top for example, the most effective way to cover the edges is by using a lipping—a solid wood strip stuck to the edge of the board. The technique below shows how to apply lipping to MDF prior to applying the face and balancing veneers. The solid wood lip provides an attractive edge that is resistant to knocks. The lipping is usually made from the same tree species as the veneer, and the veneer overlaps the thin edge of the lipping. In the case of pre-veneered boards, a much thinner lipping is used but applied in the same way. See also strip-edging veneer (p.162).

TOOLS AND MATERIALS

- Miter block, compound miter saw, or miter trimmer
- Lipping stock (width should be 1/32in/1mm greater than the thickness of the core)
- Pencil
- Masking tape
- Wood glue and brush
- Block plane

LIPPING THE EDGES

1 **With the lipping stock** cut overlength, cut a miter in one end grain of each piece using a miter trimmer.

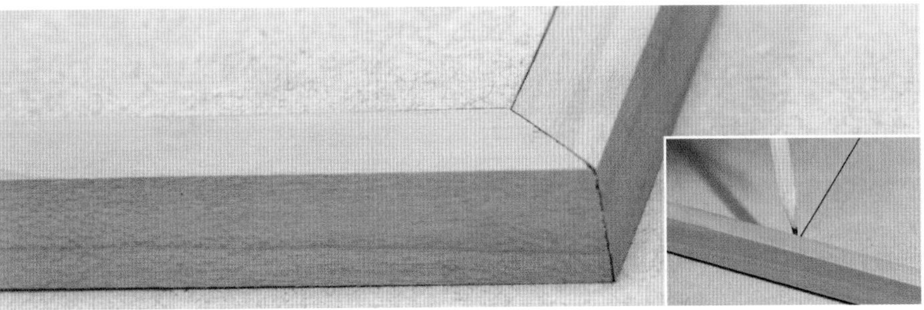

2 **Set the lipping** alongside the core, with the inner edge of the mitered end aligned to one corner. Match with the mitered end of another piece of lipping. Mark the corner position at the other end of each piece of lipping (inset).

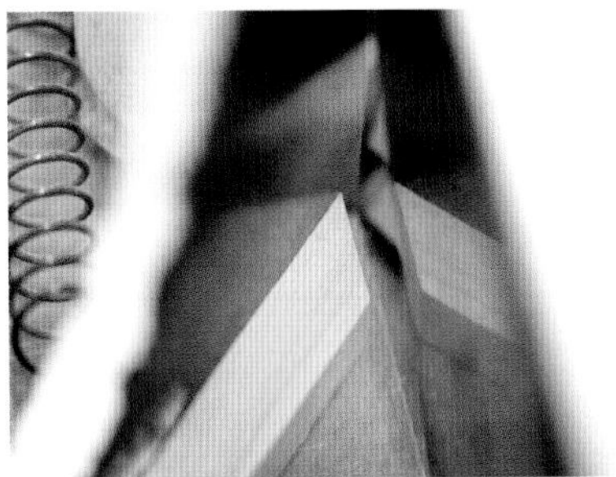

3 **Cut miters** in the marked position of each lipping piece. Continue in the same way until you have cut all four lipping pieces.

4 **Put the core in a vise**. Tape the first piece of lipping precisely in position on the edge of the core. Glue the adjacent edge of the core (inset).

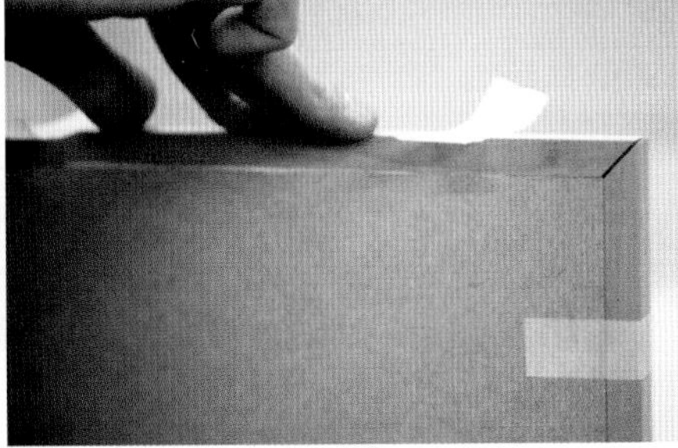

5 **Apply glue** to the second piece of lipping (to which you have already attached strips of tape) and set it in position on the glued edge, aligned to the first piece. Tape the lipping in place.

6 **Remove the unglued piece** and glue it and the remaining two lipping pieces around the core, following instructions in Step 6. Apply glue to the miters for the subsequent pieces of lipping (inset).

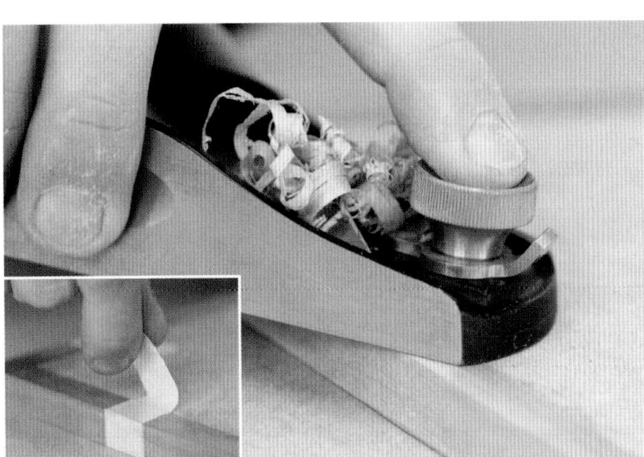

7 **When the glue** is dry, carefully remove the tape (inset). Then, on both surfaces, plane the edges of the lipping flush with the core using a block plane. If you wish to veneer the surface, see Veneering a surface, pp.158–60.

Strip-edging veneer

Covering the edge of a veneered board with a strip of the same face veneer has the advantage of a perfect color match. The technique described below, using PVA, is ideal for pieces that are small and decorative but is not recommended for situations where the edge may be frequently knocked (in those cases use lipping instead—see p.161). The veneer is applied in much the same way as for the face and must overlap the stock all around. Veneer edging-strip is also available as a coil, pre-glued with hot-melt glue that is easy to apply with machinery or with a household iron. A third option is to use contact adhesive (see Using contact adhesive, p.163). After gluing, the excess veneer is trimmed with a knife or block plane and sanded flush.

TOOLS AND MATERIALS

Metal ruler
Scalpel
Chinagraph pencil
Blocks (size to suit)
Parcel tape and veneer tape
Brush
PVA glue
Roller
Offcuts
Sash clamps
Knife or block plane (optional)
Sandpaper

CUTTING THE VENEER

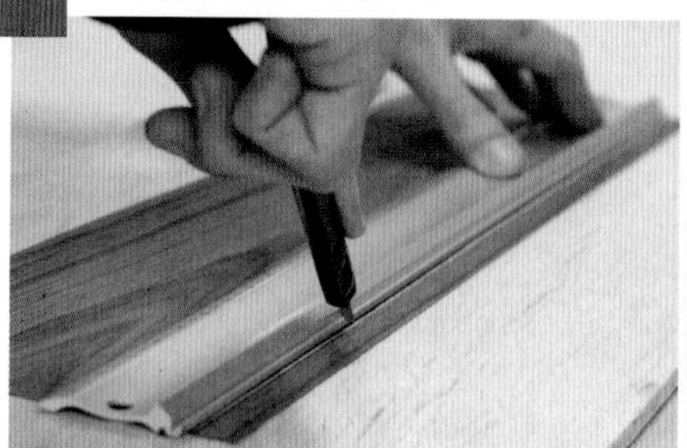

1 **Cut the veneer** for the edges. First cut one straight edge with a scalpel, using a metal ruler as a guide.

2 **Using the edge** to be veneered as a guide, mark the width of the edging piece of veneer, making it just a little bit wider than the stock.

3 **Cut the veneer** with a scalpel, using a metal ruler as a guide. Then, cut the edging pieces to length across the grain.

PREVENTING SPLITTING

When trimming veneer edge pieces across the grain, be careful to avoid splitting (or "break out") by pressing down firmly with the scalpel at the end of the cut.

GLUING AND CLAMPING THE VENEER

1 **Prepare the blocks** for the clamps by sticking parcel tape along the side that will be in contact with the veneer. This prevents any glue that seeps out from sticking the block to the veneer.

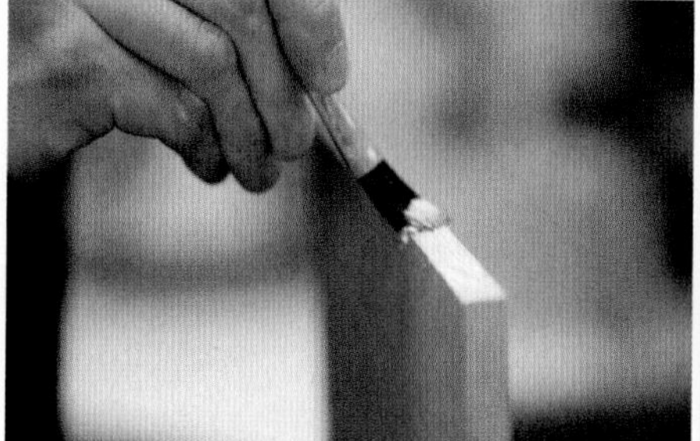

2 **Put the core piece in a vise**, then apply PVA adhesive to the edge of the core piece with a brush.

3 **Place the veneer** in position along the glued edge, being careful to avoid spreading glue on the face of the veneer.

4 **Press the veneer** firmly onto the edge. It is a good idea to use a clean roller to do this, if possible.

5 **Secure the veneer** in place using veneer tape.

6 **Remove the core** from the vise and use offcuts to raise it above the surface of the workbench.

7 **Set the taped block** prepared in Step 1 alongside the glued edge. If you wish to, you can apply veneer to two opposing edges and clamp them simultaneously.

8 **Clamp using sash clamps** above and below the piece. Wipe away excess glue with a clean, damp cloth (turn the core over to clean the other side). When the glue has dried, remove the clamps and trim the excess veneer with a knife or block plane and sand flush. Take great care not to sand more than is necessary in case you damage the veneers.

USING CONTACT ADHESIVE

The advantage of contact adhesive is that no clamping is necessary and the glue dries rapidly. It is also a quick way of veneering curved edges; follow the same instructions as here, but use a veneer hammer to smooth down the veneer (other glues would necessitate shaped blocks—that match the curves—for clamping). This technique is somewhat similar to using hot animal glue, but here the instant results are offset by the high odor of contact adhesive, which is a serious problem if large areas are to be glued. The "trick" to contact adhesive is applying a thin, clean, even thickness to both the core and the veneer and then waiting until the adhesive has become tacky ("gone off") before putting the veneer in position.

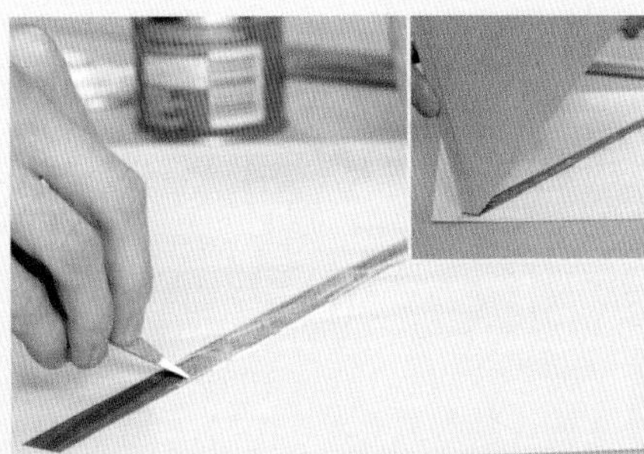
1 **Spread contact adhesive** thinly on the back of the veneer and on the edge of the core. When the glue has "gone off," place the glued edge of the core onto the veneer (inset).

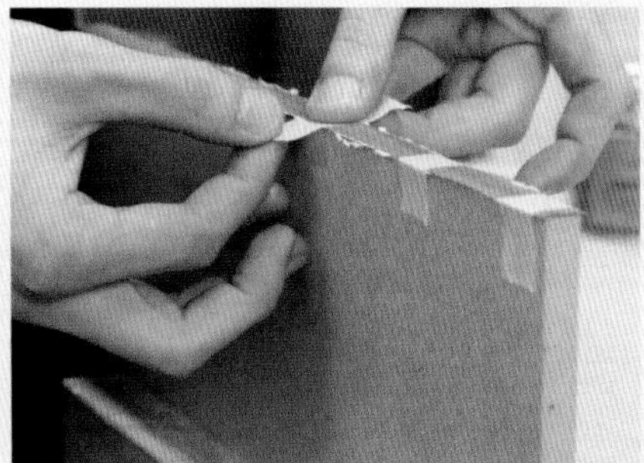
2 **Press the core** down firmly on the veneer, put the core in a vise, then lightly secure the veneer in place with strips of veneer tape. Do not place too much pressure on the edges.

3 **When the glue is dry**, clamp the piece to the workbench and carefully remove the veneer tape.

4 **Use a block plane** to clean up the excess veneer from the edges.

5 **Sand the edges** smooth with fine-grade sandpaper. Trim the veneer at the end grains with a scalpel (inset).

Finishing techniques

Finishing describes the process of creating a final finish that is both protective and decorative. Depending on the nature of the workpiece and various functional and aesthetic requirements, the timber may need to be sanded, the grain and knots filled, the surface re-sanded, the wood primed, and the surface either painted, varnished, oiled, waxed, or distressed. The exact procedure followed by a woodworker will depend on the character of the project, the type of timber, any functional requirements, and personal likes and dislikes. For example, while one woodworker's high-shine hardwood table top will require sanding, the grain to be raised, re-sanding, filling, more sanding, and then varnishing, another woodworker's distressed table top might only need to be worked over with steel wool and wax.

ORDER OF WORKING

Preparation is key when finishing, and this stage includes the initial planning of the job, followed by sanding, scraping, filling, staining, and either sealing and/or priming. The next stage is to apply the final finish; this may involve waxing, oiling, lacquering, varnishing or painting, perhaps followed by more polishing and waxing.

As the finishing process progresses from the dusty stages of preparation to the more delicate aspects of varnishing, for example, the workpiece will need to be moved to a dust-free environment (or the existing environment will need to be made dust-free). Most woodworkers carry out preparation in one area, clean up the dust and debris, and then move the workpiece to a clean, dry, dust-free area designated for final finishing.

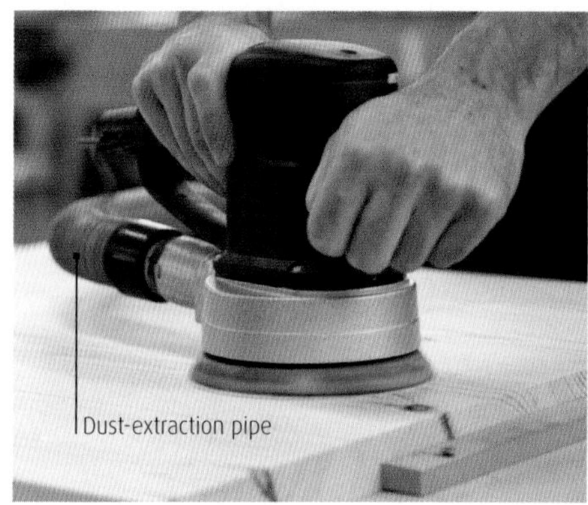

Sanding
When sanding, wear a suitable dust mask and fit a dust-extraction device to any power sanders. Be aware that some wood dusts are toxic.

Oiling
Apply oil in a swift motion, adding only small amounts at a time. Use a pad to spread the oil evenly across the surface of the timber.

Preparing surfaces

The level of preparation required will depend on the nature of the timber, but the surface may need to be sanded, planed, scraped, filled, bleached, stained, or otherwise modified. This work must be carried before a final finish is applied. A wood such as English oak, for example, might require no more preparation than a swift sanding prior to waxing. On the other hand, pine might need to be sealed, primed, or stained before a final finish is applied. These preparation procedures need to be thought through and carefully planned at the start of the project. If you have any doubts about how to prepare a workpiece or what finish to use, it is always advisable to carry out a number of "trial runs" on offcuts of wood. This will allow you to experiment and practice your technique—without jeopardizing the job.

REPAIRING HOLES

If you have clearly visible holes in your workpiece you may wish to fill them before applying a final finish. To do this, use wood filler or plug the hole with a peg of similar-looking wood. After you have applied a finish, you can fill small holes using coloured wax filler. If the hole is in a workpiece that is ultimately going to be painted, a good option is simply to fill the hole with two-mix wood filler, smooth it over with a putty knife—so that the filler is slightly proud—let it dry, and then rub it down so that the filler is flush with the surface. If, for example, you are presented with a hole in an oak workpiece that is going to be varnished or oiled, the hole must first be drilled out then plugged with a plug cut from the same cut of wood and from the same face, edge, or end grain within the wood. This procedure is best carried out with a drill and plug set. If the hole is no more than a small dent or dink in a polished surface, a quick solution is to take a wax filler of the same color, smear it into the damaged area, and then buff it to a finish. As with any other woodworking or finishing procedure, if you have doubts about how to proceed, carry out a trial run on an offcut or, if the hole is in an existing workpiece, carry out a trial run on a base or back that is hidden from view.

Spreading filler
Using a flexible filling knife, press the filler firmly into the hole. For small holes (inset), smear wax filler into the area with your thumb.

USING SCRAPERS

A scraper is a thin, flexible sheet of super-hard steel with a sharp, burred edge. It is used for smoothing flat or curved surfaces prior to sanding. Although scrapers are less popular now than they once were (orbital sanders are more efficient) many woodworkers still prefer them for smoothing small areas of torn grain (grain that has been ripped up by planing), smoothing small areas that have not been sanded properly, smoothing areas that are awkward to sand, and for smoothing surfaces after veneering (pp.157–63). Scrapers with convex and concave profiles are also available.

Using a scraper plane
Secure the workpiece to the bench and work in the same direction as the grain. Be sure to remove shavings and not dust—removing dust is a sign that the blade needs sharpening.

Using a cabinet scraper
Hold the scraper at either end to create a curve, lean it forward at 45 degrees, and work in the direction of the grain. When all tears in the grain have been removed, the wood is ready for sanding.

USING A RANDOM ORBITAL SANDER

Orbital sanders (p.52) with large rectangular bases are ideal for material removal and coarse sanding, but can also be used for fine sanding. Sanders with sanding disks 6in (150mm) in diameter are superb for final finishing, leaving only difficult-to-access areas to be sanded by hand. They can also be used for general-purpose sanding if fitted with coarse abrasive. Palm sanders (p.52) are small, lightweight orbital sanders held in one hand. They are convenient for sanding small components as the other hand is free to hold the workpiece.

Random sanding
Work up and down the surface of the workpiece. Do not exert pressure as the weight of the sander is sufficient to do the work. The random action of the machine helps to prevent ring marks.

MACHINE SANDING

In many workshops, the initial smoothing of a workpiece is carried out by a machine fitted with a coarse- to medium-grit abrasive. Fine sanding is then carried out by hand. Table tops, jointed doors, and wide boards are smoothed on a dimension or drum sander, or on a pad sander. A pad sander has a long sanding belt with a movable, hand-operated bed and pad, making it a versatile machine a medium-sized workshop. Belt-and-disc sanders (p.53) are useful for quickly smoothing either straight or curved components, as long as they are relatively narrow. Always wear a dust mask.

SANDING BY HAND

Hand sanding is sometimes favored over power sanding because it is quieter and tends to produce less dust. For very fine work, it is also far better to sand by hand to avoid ring marks; for some shaped and fretted workpieces, hand-sanding is the only option (see Sanding an awkward shape, p.166). Sanding veneer is also best done by hand unless dealing with large expanses (p.166). For flat surfaces always use a sanding block, either one that is homemade or store-bought, and sized to fit a quarter, or a sixth, of a sheet of sandpaper. The block distributes the pressure uniformly and helps maintain the flat surface. Always sand exactly parallel to the direction of the grain, otherwise scratches on the surface will be apparent (these are time-consuming to remove). Use several grades as described below. With each grade, continue sanding until the surface is free from blemishes and all the marks made by the previous grade of abrasive have been removed.

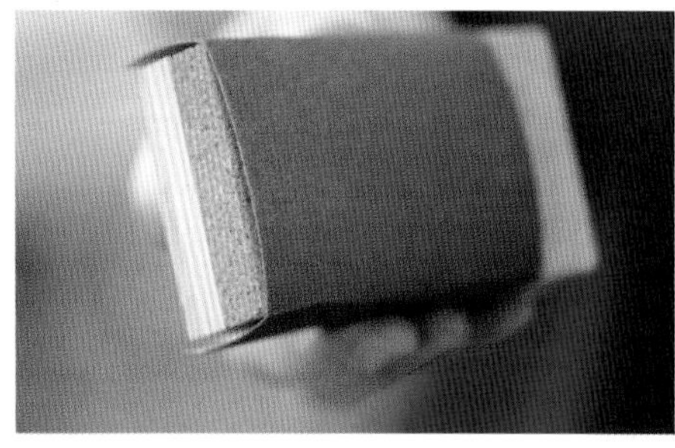

Making a sanding block
Glue cork to an offcut to make a block approximately 4¼ x 2⅜ x 1¼in (110 x 60 x 30mm).

Sanding a flat surface
Sand back and forth in the direction of the grain until you have covered the whole surface. Change to a finer grit of paper and repeat the process, using progressively finer paper from 120–240 grit.

Removing arrises
Use a cork sanding block and work in the direction of the grain. The flexiblilty of the cork produces a rounded edge. For a sharper, beveled effect, use a wooden sanding block.

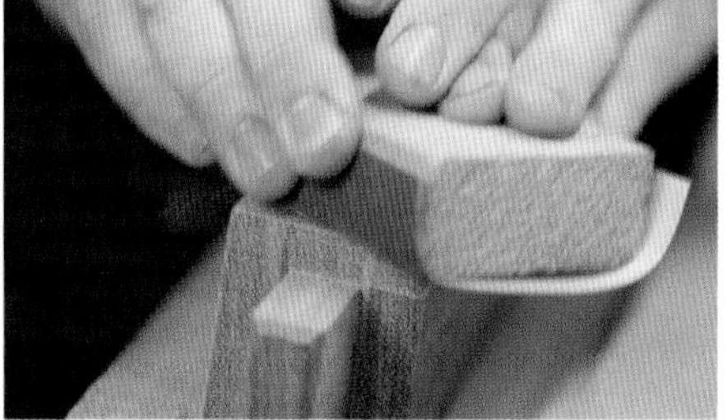

Supporting the workpiece
Small components can be held in a vice leaving both hands free to work the sanding block. This is highly efficient and allows greater control.

SANDING AN AWKWARD SHAPE

Whenever you need to sand a small, awkwardly shaped workpiece, you will need to find a "former" (improvised sanding block) that fits the shape of the workpiece and around which the sandpaper can be wrapped. The former could be anything from a dowel, or the back of a spoon, to the palm of your hand. It should fit the item being worked—for example, the convex back of a spoon might fit perfectly inside the concave hollow of a dish. Experienced woodworkers tend to accumulate a collection of formers that they know are going to suit a particular task in hand. Alternatively, a former can be hand-made for a specific job.

Sanding without a block
Wrap, hold, and support the sandpaper in your hands and work the surface with a gentle yet firm stroking action. Constantly reshape your hands and modify the pressure, allowing your hands to be guided by your sense of touch.

CHECKING SMOOTHNESS

Look carefully along the surface of the workpiece and use your sense of touch to check the level of smoothness. Run your hands along the workpiece in all directions, feeling and stroking the surface until you have a clear understanding of how the timber's planes and contours relate to each other.

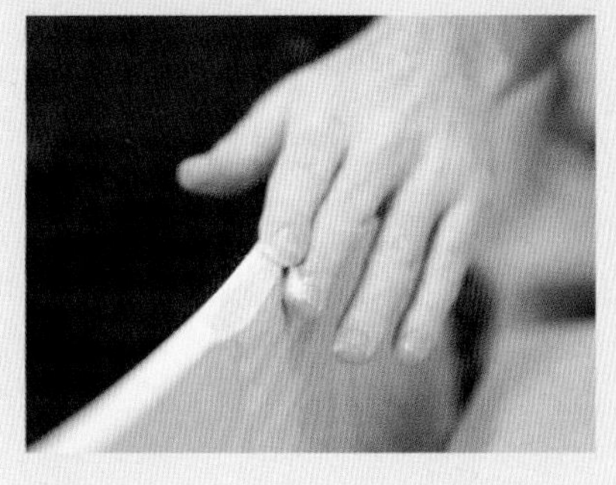

RAISING THE GRAIN

When trying to achieve a very fine finish, you may need to raise the grain of the wood. Raising the grain describes the process of raising the surface fibers of the timber (the nibs or tiny raised bumps of the grain) just prior to finishing. To do this, first dampen the workpiece slightly so that the nibs stand proud. Then leave the timber to dry naturally until the nibs feel stiff and brittle to the touch. Finally, rub down the surface of the wood with a fine-grade sand paper. The more time and effort you spend at this stage of the process, the smoother the final finish will be. However, you will only need to raise the grain when you want to achieve a polished high-shine finish.

SANDING ON THE FLAT

Small objects, such as a tray from a jewellery box, or a dowel or peg, are difficult to hold in a vice and sand smooth. Often it is more convenient and effective to fix a sheet of sandpaper to a flat surface—using contact adhesive or double-sided tape—and to sand by rubbing the workpiece back and forth over the sandpaper.

Sanding flat edges
Sanding on a flat surface ensures that all edges of a small tray are made perfectly flat (in the same plane) and smooth.

Sanding a small item
Sometimes the only way you will be able to sand a fiddly piece is to rub it across sandpaper stuck down to a flat surface.

SANDING VENEER

Sanding veneer is no different to sanding solid wood, except that it is important for you to avoid excessive sanding and earing right through to the core. You must take special care at the edges of the veneer, which will wear through more quickly. When the veneer pattern has grain running in various directions, you only sand it with fine grades. For general work begin with 120-grit and repeat the process with 180, then 240. For fine work finish with flour paper or 500-grit. A scraper plane can be used as directed.

SANDING VENEER

1 **Use a scraper plane** (or a cabinet scraper) on a veneered surface to remove any deposits of glue or remnants of tape adhesive.

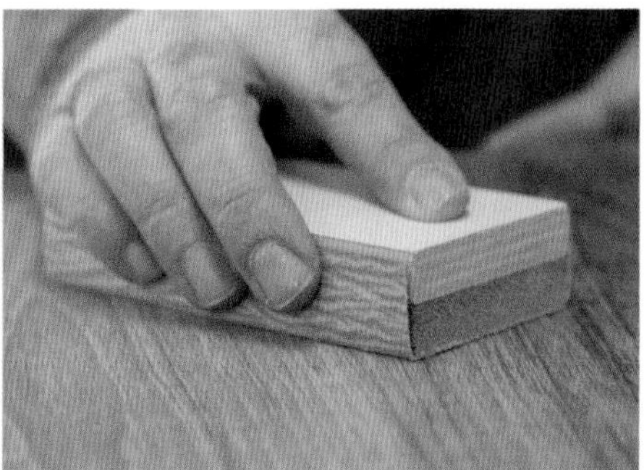

2 **Lightly sand the surface** by hand with fine-grade sandpaper. Work your way through the grit sizes as for solid timber, but taking extra care not to over-sand the veneer.

Sealing, staining, and finishing

Once the workpiece has been sanded to the required finish (this is a judgement that will vary hugely from workpiece to workpiece and woodworker to woodworker) the timber may need to be stained to add texture and colour, sealed to stabilize the surface of the wood, and finished with wax, paint, or varnish to give it texture and aesthetic appeal. Final finishes are a matter of personal taste—one person's ideal finish might be another person's worst nightmare!

FINISHING OPTIONS

Finish	Advantages	Disadvantages	Application methods
DANISH OIL (Low sheen; interior/exterior use)	■ Easy to apply and restore ■ Suitable for all types of timber ■ Does not chip, crack, or peel ■ Oils with stain added are available	■ Substantially darkens wood ■ Time-consuming to apply ■ Less protective than lacquer/varnish	Apply with a brush or cloth and wipe excess from surface. Allow 6 hours to dry. De-nib after first coat. Apply two more coats. Use wax to improve the luster (interior wood).
TUNG OIL (Low sheen; interior/exterior use)	■ Easy to apply and restore ■ Suitable for all types of timber ■ Does not chip, crack, or peel	■ Has a long drying time ■ Time-consuming to apply ■ Less protective than lacquer/varnish	Apply with a brush or cloth and wipe excess from surface. Allow 24 hours to dry. De-nib after first coat. Apply two more coats. Use wax to improve the luster (interior wood).
WAX POLISH (Medium sheen; interior use)	■ Easy to restore ■ Suitable for all types of timber ■ Does not chip, crack, or peel ■ Dark stain polishes are available	■ Requires re-applying/re-buffing ■ Time-consuming to apply ■ Less protective than lacquer/varnish	Apply with a cloth or 000-grade steel wool and allow to dry for 15 minutes before buffing to a sheen using a cloth or burnishing brush.
HARD WAX OIL (Low sheen; interior use)	■ Easy to apply and renovate ■ Suitable for all types of timber ■ Wear-resistant; does not peel or flake ■ Does not darken wood significantly	■ Less protective than lacquer/varnish	Apply undiluted using a synthetic brush; follow direction of grain. Wipe off excess; allow 4–6 hours to dry. Apply second coat. Buff with a soft cloth to increase the shine.
FRENCH POLISH (High sheen; interior use)	■ Quick to repair ■ Color can be fine-tuned/matched ■ White polish available for white woods ■ Highly resistant to cracking	■ Less protective than lacquer/varnish	Apply several coats using cotton wool inside cotton cloth. Leave 30 minutes between coats; allow to dry overnight. Apply 6+ additional coats. Remove streaking with denatured alcohol.
POLYURETHANE VARNISH (Matt-high sheen; interior/exterior use)	■ Easy to apply ■ Suitable for all types of timber ■ Durable ■ More protective than polish or lacquer	■ Shows brush marks and dust ■ High-build can detract from the wood ■ Darkens wood substantially ■ Can de-laminate or yellow	Apply with a synthetic brush. Brush in direction of grain. First application can be diluted. Allow to dry before de-nibbing. Reapply a second no-diluted coat. Can also be sprayed (*see* lacquer).
ACRYLIC VARNISH (Matt-high sheen; interior/exterior use)	■ Easy to apply ■ Suitable for all types of timber ■ Low odor, water based, and fast drying ■ Does not darken wood significantly	■ High-build can detract from wood ■ Prolonged exposure to skin oils/sweat can soften finish ■ Can de-laminate or yellow	Apply with a synthetic brush in the same way as polyurethane varnish.
WAX FINISH VARNISH (Low sheen; interior/exterior)	■ Easy to apply ■ Has appearance and feeling of wax but gives greater protection ■ Low odor, water based, and fast drying ■ Almost no darkening of wood	■ Prolonged exposure to skin oils/sweat can soften finish ■ Can de-laminate and yellow	Apply with a synthetic brush in the same way as polyurethane varnish.
CELLULOSE LACQUER (Matt-high sheen; interior)	■ Quick to apply; high build; self-leveling ■ Suitable for all types of timber ■ High level of protection ■ Almost no darkening of wood	■ Spray room setup required; high odor; hazardous and wasteful ■ Can crack, de-laminate, or yellow ■ Not possible to restore ■ Disallows patina	Requires ventilated spraying area and equipment. Thin first coat and allow to dry for 30 minutes. After de-nibbing, apply a second undiluted coat. Apply further coats for greater protection.
ACID CATALYST (COLD CURE) LACQUER (Matt-high sheen; interior)	■ Fast application, high build and self leveling ■ Suitable for all types of timber ■ Very high level of protection ■ Almost no darkening	■ Spray room setup required, high odor, hazardous and wasteful ■ Chipping, cold-checking (cracking), and de-laminating ■ Disallows patina and may yellow	Apply in the same way as cellulose lacquer, but mix in an acid catalyst hardener before spraying. Pre-catalyst lacquer has the hardener already mixed in.

STAINING

Wood can be stained to add interest and color to a workpiece, and to hide or remodel what may be an unattractive grain. If you are concerned about the impact some modern stains may have on the environment, there is no reason why you shouldn't produce your own eco-friendly stains using tried-and-tested traditional recipes. For exampe, iron filings soaked in vinegar will stain timber a dark gray or ebony color; tobacco-soaked ammonia or urine will stain timber brown; potassium permanganate crystals will stain timber reddish brown; and coffee and water will stain timber a ginger-brown color. Given that many stains are little more than thinned-down paint, you can simply thin any colored paint of your choice to create stain.

SOLVENTS

A wood stain consists of a combination of dyes and pigments suspended in a solvent; a stain is usually described and defined by its solvent. Stains containing solvents such as denatured alcohol and Stoddard solvent are usually used when a finish is required that will not raise the grain. Regardless of the choice of solvent, stains are characterized by the fact that they only soak into the surface of the wood. It is possible to achieve an especially delicate and subtle finish by rubbing down a stained surface. Make color swatches (see below) before proceeding.

DENATURED ALCOHOL

STODDARD SOLVENT

HOW TO STAIN WOOD

1 **Having tested the stain** on an offcut, wipe the workpiece with a damp cloth. When the timber has dried, rub it briskly with a fine-grade sandpaper.

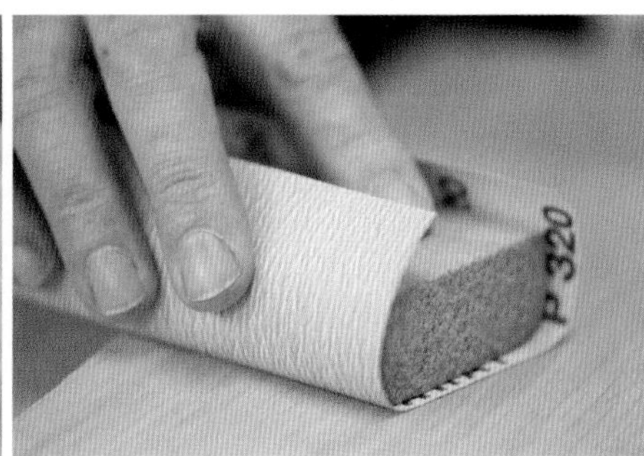

2 **Repeat step 1** several times. Switch to the finest grade of sandpaper and rub the surface of the workpiece until you have achieved an extremely fine finish.

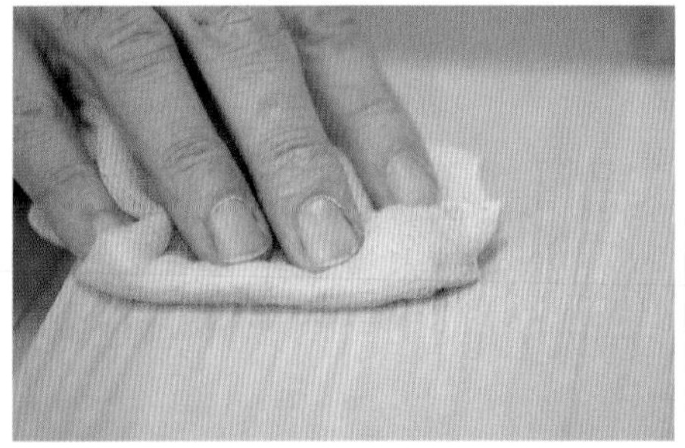

3 **When you have achieved** a very fine finish, use a clean, lint-free cloth to remove every trace of dust and debris from the surface of the workpiece.

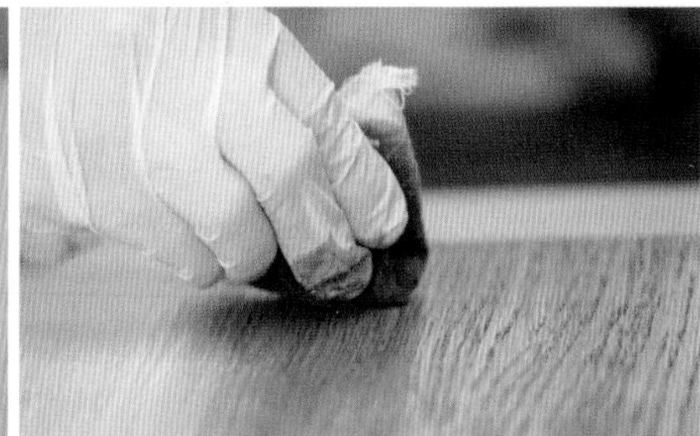

4 **Put on protective gloves** to prevent your skin from becoming stained. Soak a wad of lint-free cloth with the stain and apply it evenly over the whole surface.

COLOR SWATCHES

Before taking a workpiece to its final stained finish, it is always a good idea to work through the various finishing options on offcuts of timber. In order to identify and keep a record of how different finishes will appear, first number or label a selection of offcuts; these will act as color swatches. Treat each offcut with a different stain or finish, allow the offcuts to dry, and then write the date and type of finish on the back of each piece. Over time you will be able to build up a collection of different finishes so that you will know exactly how a "live" workpiece will appear before you apply a finish.

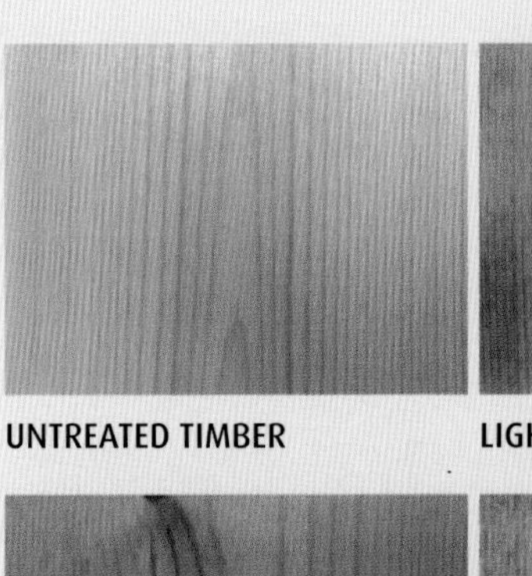

UNTREATED TIMBER

LIGHT OAK

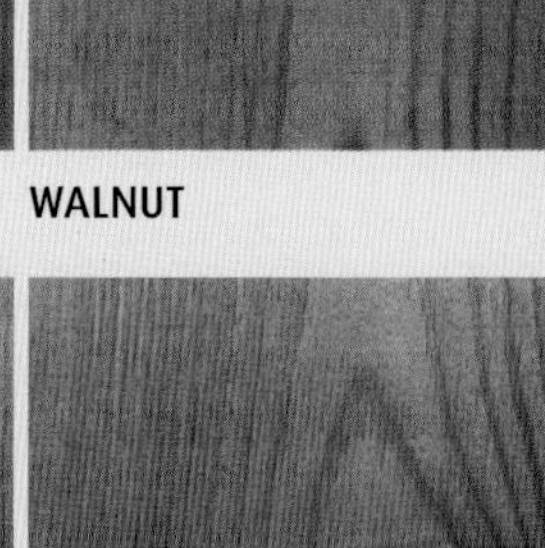

WALNUT

MEDIUM OAK

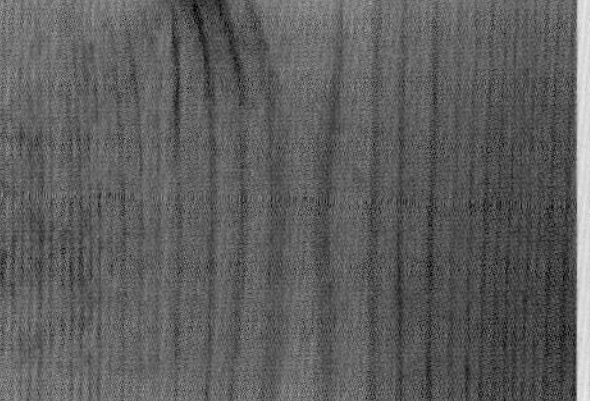

JACOBEAN DARK OAK

RED MAHOGANY

LIMING

Although liming is a procedure that traditionally involves working caustic-limewash mixes into the grain of the wood in order to create a weathered, driftwood like appearance, a similar finish can now be achieved by working liming wax or even a white acrylic wash into the wood. Prior to liming the wood—whether with a traditional limewash, liming wax, or white acrylic wash—you will need to work the surface of the wood with various grades of steel wool and/or wire brushes until the grain is clean and open. Once you have worked the wood to an open finish (the amount of work needed will depend on the nature of the workpiece and the required texture), tidy up any mess and move the workpiece to a clean area that you have set aside for liming.

LIMING THE WOOD

1 **Load fine-grade** steel wool or a soft cloth with liming wax (inset). Thoroughly rub the wax into the surface of the workpiece.

2 **Leave for three minutes**, then wipe away the excess wax with the wire wool or soft cloth. Once assembled, finish the workpiece by applying oil or wax (see below or p.170).

OILING

Oiling is a finishing technique that involves rubbing various mixes of oil into the surface of the wood to create a dull-to-medium sheen finish. The choice of oil and the working time (time spent oiling), will depend on your required depth of finish. For example, while a salad bowl might only need to be swiftly wiped over with olive oil, a table top might need three or more coats of tung oil and linseed oil. As a general rule, to achieve a tough, water resistant, light-reflecting surface, the more coats the better.

TEAK OIL

FINISHING OIL

DANISH OIL

LINSEED OIL

APPLYING OIL

1 **Using a clean, lint-free cloth,** work the oil into the grain of the workpiece. Repeat the process until the surface of the timber is saturated or "puddled."

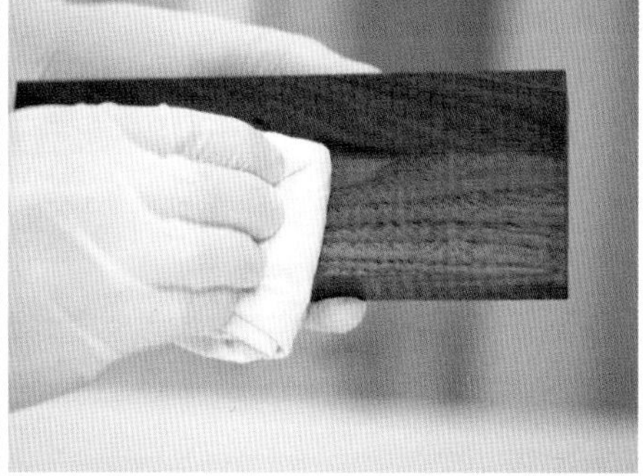

2 **Continue rubbing the surface** until you have worked it dry. After approximately 20 minutes, change to a dry cloth and wipe away any remaining "puddles."

3 **Depending on the workpiece,** the chosen oil, and the intended finish, you may wish to repeat steps 1–2 three times or more.

4 **Wipe off any excess oil** that has bled from open joints and intersections. Re-work the timber with a dry cloth until you have produced the required finish.

WAXING

In the context of wood finishes, wax is a generic term for a finish that contains either a natural or synthetic wax. This includes animal waxes such as beeswax and lanolin, vegetable waxes such as carnauba and candelilla, mineral waxes such as montan and paraffin, and synthetic waxes such as fatty acid amine and polyamide. Depending on the type of workpiece being waxed—and its intended use—apply the wax with either a lint-free cotton cloth or a fine, soft brush, before buffing it with either a stiff brush or a hard cotton cloth until the wax softens and compacts to create a transparent or opaque finish. Always research individual waxes before use as some can be toxic and may cause irritation of the skin.

Clear wax
So called "clear waxes" vary from white, waxy, candle-like varieties to soft, honey-colored varieties such as beeswax.

WAXING A SMOOTH SURFACE

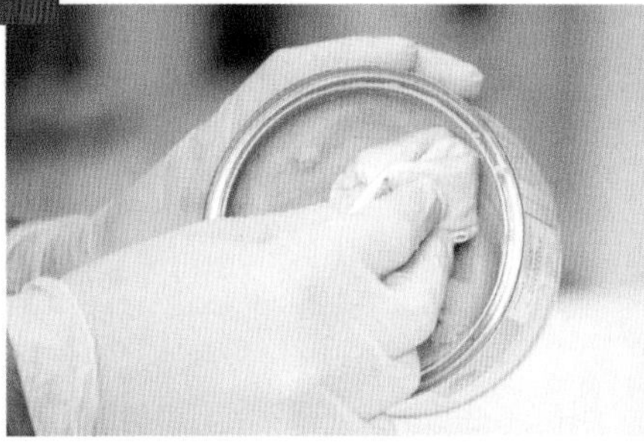

1 **Roll a clean, lint-free cloth** into a pad that suits the size of the workpiece. Wipe the cloth onto the wax to pick up just enough wax for the task in hand.

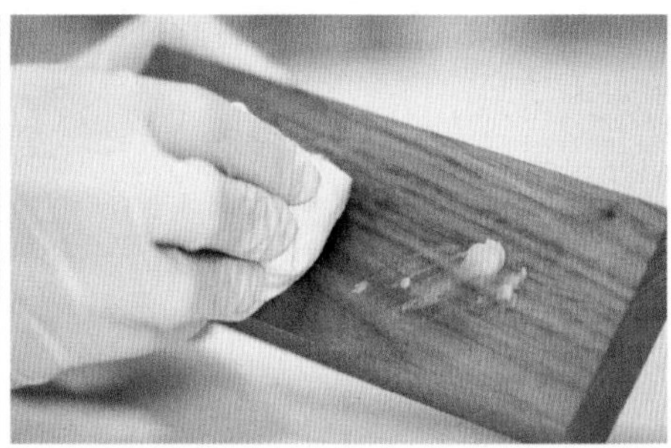

2 **Rub the wax across the workpiece** in all directions until you can see that it has filled the pores of the grain.

3 **Having loaded the grain with wax,** allow the wax to dry. Then, use a clean lint-free cloth to buff and work the wax to a high shine finish. Repeat steps 1–3 as required to achieve the desired finish.

VARNISHING

Varnish is a hard transparent finish primarily used on woods that have a decorative quality in their own right. Varnish can be applied directly onto timber or onto a surface that has previously been stained or patterned. Once applied, the varnish will gradually dry, cure, and harden. This process occurs either as the solvent carrier dries and evaporates (as is the case with resin or water-based acrylic varnish) or as part of a chemical reaction (as is the case with epoxy, polyurethane, and oil varnish). All types of varnish will harden best in an atmosphere that is dry, clean, and free from dust.

Clear varnish
Although diffent types of varnish may appear variously cloudy, watery, clear, or oily, they will all dry to a clear finish.

VARNISHING WOOD

1 **Using a clean, soft brush,** apply a thin coat of varnish to the workpiece. Always work in the direction of the grain.

2 **When the varnish is dry** to the touch, move the workpiece to a clean, dust-free area and rub it with fine-grade paper.

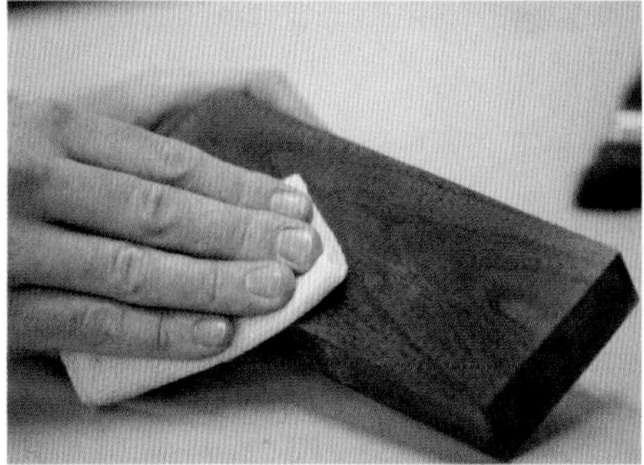

3 **Wipe the surface** of the timber with a clean, lint-free cloth; return it to the varnishing area and apply a second coat.

4 **Repeat steps 1–3,** varnishing and sanding the workpiece until you achieve a finish that meets your requirements.

COMPARISON OF FINISHES

Your choice of finish will be determined by both the functional and aesthetic requirements of the workpiece. Safety should always be a high priority for pieces intended for use with food and drink; untreated wood is often the best option for bowls and chopping boards, etc. Finishes such as waxes, oils, and varnishes—which may be toxic and not resistant to water—are usually better suited to decorative furniture.

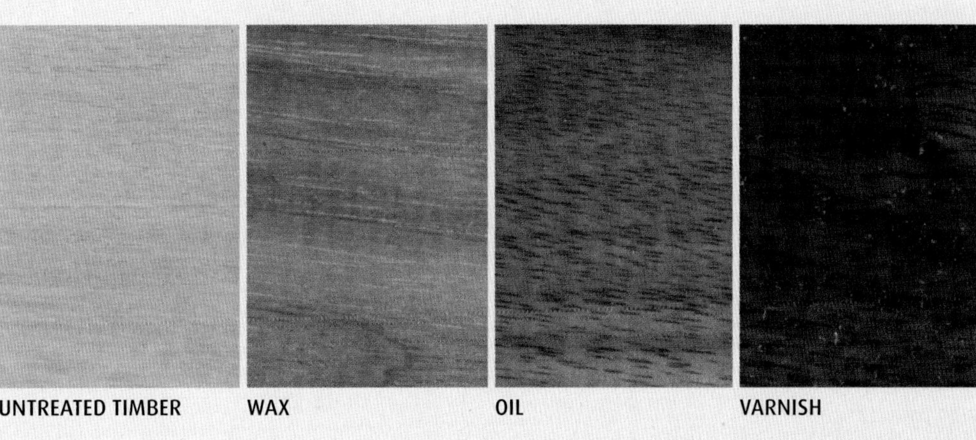

UNTREATED TIMBER WAX OIL VARNISH

CELLULOSE LACQUER

A sprayed on, solvent-based lacquer most commonly used in production workshops, cellulose lacquer is also used by fine furniture makers. Its advantages include a flawless sheen, which causes almost no darkening of the timber, and a high level of protection. While cellulose lacquer is not as protective as polyurethane varnish (left), it is far more attractive.

The main disadvantage of this finish is that it contains a volatile, flammable, and highly toxic solvent that poses a health risk. Always take extreme care when handling it and wear the correct protective clothing (pp.78–79); pregnant women should always avoid exposure to solvents. Non-toxic, water-based lacquers will ultimately replace solvent-based lacquers in the furniture industry, but these safer alternatives are currently not as durable.

Although the lacquer itself is cheap, the spray equipment required is not; therefore it is only a viable option if you intend producing batches of furniture. This method also requires space for a spraying room or "booth," which means it may not be suited to the home workshop. The spraying area must be fitted with an explosion-protected, safety-filtered extractor fan, and lighting and switches to the same specification.

PAINTING

New or bare timber will need to be sanded and primed before it can be painted. Primer is a thin paint that is used to minimize the porosity of the base wood. If a primer is not applied to new or bare timber, the top coat of any paint subsequently applied will be swiftly "sucked dry" as the wood absorbs the moisture from the paint. This will result in the paint eventually peeling. Once the wood has been primed and any knots have been sealed (see below) the next job is to swiftly rub down the surface with a fine-grade sandpaper, before wiping the surface with a lint-free cloth. When the workpiece is clean and dust-free, you can apply an undercoat. Once this has dried, apply a top coat. If you are at all unsure about your choice of paint color, or want to check that the primer, undercoat, and top coat are all compatible with each other, carry out a trial run on an offcut of wood.

Sealing knots

Wood knots are the dark and resinous circles in planed timber that indicate where small branches once grew from the trunk. As they are liable to bleed and stain the end finish, they should be sealed with several coats of knotting solution. It is usually best to apply knotting solution with a fine brush, but this can vary depending on the type of knot and your choice of finish.

CHOICE AND CARE OF BRUSHES

Brushes come in a huge range of sizes, materials, and prices. The best way to choose a brush is to find one of the correct size for your intended application and of a bristle type that suits your paint. Natural bristles such as ox and hog hair, for example, are good for use with oil-based paints as these bristles are long-lasting and hold their shape. A high-quality brush such as this will last for many years if it is correctly looked after—meaning that it is soaked in Stoddard solvent after use and then repeatedly washed with a soapy liquid. A top quality brush, however, is not always the best brush for the job. Sometimes a cheaper, disposable brush with synthetic bristles is better for quick jobs such as painting the back or underside of a workpiece. Ultimately, your choice of brush will depend on your attitude to the initial cost, the time spent cleaning, and the cost and toxicity of the required cleaning materials.

Restoring furniture

Your main aim when restoring a piece of antique furniture should always be to return it to its original condition—both in terms of functionality and appearance—in a sympathetic and inconspicuous way. It should be possible, for example, to use and admire a restored Queen Anne chair without either fearing that it might collapse or noticing any obvious signs of repair. In fact, careful, expert furniture restoration can add value to an antique and help preserve it for the enjoyment of future generations.

One of the most challenging aspects of furniture restoration—whether working with an antique or a more modern piece—is the removal of marks and stains, inconsistencies in color, such as bleaching caused by the sun, and damage to polish; the high level of skill required for this sort of work can take years to master. Although furniture restoration techniques are predominantly intended for use on antiques, many techniques are equally appropriate for use on contemporary pieces.

Principles of restoration

The first principle of furniture restoration says that every repair that is made should be reversible. This prevents the piece from being permanently altered and means that any repairs can themselves be revisited at a future date without the integrity of the original piece being compromised. While this principle applies to all restoration techniques, it is most relevant to the choice of glue (see Using animal glue, opposite).

The second principle states that original surfaces should be preserved wherever possible (this applies to contemporary as well as antique furniture). All wooden surfaces change color over time, so any careless work with a plane or chisel will remove the oxidized surface to reveal the original color of the wood, causing difficulties when re-polishing. If you are unsure as to how to proceed with a project—especially if the furniture is valuable—consult a trained restorer before you start.

To restore a piece of furniture, it is sometimes necessary to dismantle its parts. If a joint is loose, for example, there is a temptation to reinforce it with a screw or nail. While this might improve the joint in the short term, any added metalwork will ultimately weaken the joint and make future repairs more difficult and time-consuming. The only reliable solution is to dismantle and clean the joint, then re-glue and reassemble it. Before dismantling a joint, however, you should identify it and assess how it was assembled. This will allow you to ascertain in which direction to apply force in order to pry it apart. It is also important to establish whether other components attached to the loose part, which may be sound, must also be dismantled in order to loosen the joint without causing damage to the furniture. If the joint is firm, the glue must be "softened" before dismantling (see below).

DISMANTLING AN OLD JOINT

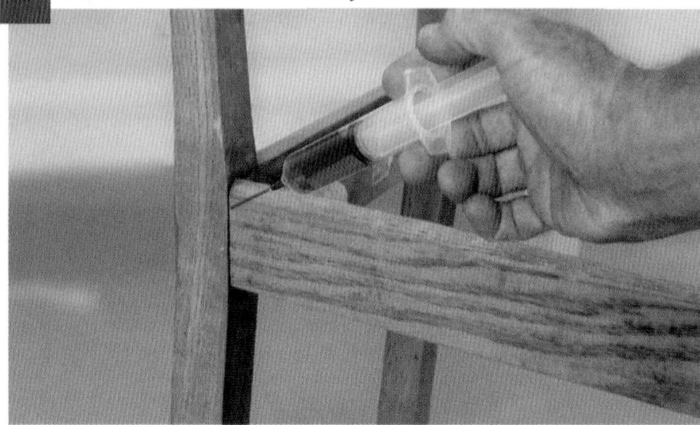

1 **Inject methanol** directly into the joint to break down or "soften" the old holding glue. Take care not to get any drops of methanol on the surrounding wood as it may damage any polish. Alternatively, apply steam or heat to the joint to soften the glue.

2 **Once the glue** has been softened, carefully apply pressure to the joint to dismantle it. Insert a softwood wedge into the joint, and tap it with a hammer until the joint comes apart.

DISMANTLING MODERN JOINTS

When dismantling a contemporary piece of furniture held together with a strong modern adhesive such as resin glue, you may not be able to take the joint apart as described, left. This is because the glue is not reversible and can not be softened. Instead, you will have no choice but to take apart the joint by cutting through it with a saw.

Using a Japanese saw
A Japanese saw is a good choice for cutting through joints, such as mortise-and-tenons, as the thin blade has a narrow kerf (width of cut) and will cause minimal damage to the piece.

USING ANIMAL GLUE

Animal glue, which is usually made from the hooves and hides of animals such as cows and horses, was commonly used in the construction of antique furniture. Although it has an unpleasant smell, animal glue is as strong as most modern glues and, because it is water-soluble and melts when heated, it has the advantage of being reversible. For these reasons—compatibility with the original glue, strength, and reversibility—animal glue should be the adhesive of choice when repairing and restoring antique furniture.

Most animal glues are available in pearl form or as a gel, and must be heated before use. One of the properties of hot animal glue is that it has a short "open time", meaning that it will start to set quickly. For more complex gluing jobs, it may be better to use "cold-set" animal glues, such as fish glue or liquid-hide glue, which don't require heating and have a much longer open time.

1 **Take a handful** of pearls of animal glue and place them in the top section of a double-boiler glue pot. Add water to the bottom section of the pot and apply heat.

2 **Stir the glue** while it heats. When there are no lumps and the glue has a smooth consistency, it is ready. Don't let the glue boil or the water run dry.

Repairing joints

If you have been unable to soften the glue in an old mortise-and-tenon joint, for example, and have had to cut through the tenon, you will now need to fit a replacement, or "false," tenon in order to successfully reassemble the joint. The replacement tenon must be positioned accurately, using the remnants of the original tenon as a guide. Accurate marking and cutting of this new joint is therefore critical, as a tenon will usually be of structural importance to the piece of furniture and a snug joint will ensure a strong repair.

MAKING A FALSE TENON

1 **Using a mortise gauge**, mark out the position of the false tenon on the new rail. Place the rail in a vise and make two angled saw cuts following the gauge lines.

2 **Remove the waste** with a chisel to create a mortise into which the false tenon will be fixed before being glued into the existing mortise on the piece of furniture.

3 **Use a sliding bevel** (p.35) to transfer the angle of the mortise to the new false tenon. Aim for between 30–40 degrees.

4 **Plane a matching tenon piece** that fits snugly in the mortise. Cut the angle to match but leave the piece oversized.

5 **Glue and clamp the false tenon** into the mortise. When the glue has set, trim the new tenon to fit the original mortise.

Repairing veneers

Veneers (pp.157–63 and pp.198–99) are thin decorative sheets of wood fixed onto a solid core. Any veneer covering of an antique will have been attached using animal glue (p.173), so a loose veneer can often be re-secured by re-activating the old glue using heat. A technique called "hot blocking" can be successful. This involves heating a block of MDF or plywood and placing it on top of a sheet of brown paper over the loose veneer. Pressure is then applied to the block with a clamp or weights. The heat from the hot block should soften the glue and the clamp or weights on the block will hold the veneer in contact with the glue while it cools and sets again. If this is not successful, warm animal glue will need to be introduced under the veneer, using a syringe. Animal glue should also be used when replacing pieces of damaged veneer with new veneer.

Hot blocking
The hot-blocking technique is often used to repair the veneer of antique furniture. In some cases, this method can be used to repair loose veneer on modern furniture—as long as thermoplastic PVA glue has been used.

French polishing

French polish is the finish most associated with antique furniture, although it only came into common usage in the 19th century. Prior to this, various varnishes and waxes were used instead. French polish is made from a natural product called shellac—a secretion from the lac insect that is dissolved in alcohol. Shellac has many other uses beyond French polish; for example, it can be used to stiffen ballet shoes and as a shiny coating for sweets and pills.

The technique of French polishing involves applying numerous coats of shellac with a brush or a pad. Each successive coat slightly softens the previous one, resulting in a homogenous build-up of polish. These layers are again slightly softened and evenly distributed around the piece of furniture using a pad, alcohol, and applied pressure. This technique burnishes the polish, ultimately achieving the high, blemish-free, shine most commonly associated with a grand piano. Although the process is simple in principle, it takes time and practice to perfect, and to develop a "feel" for the polish. Old shellac surfaces can be softened and "pulled-over" to rejuvenate them, but this requires exceptional skill and should not be attempted by the novice.

A newly French-polished surface is usually dulled with very fine steel wool and wax. The wax will not only soften the bright shine of the burnish, but will also protect the shellac.

COLORING REPLACEMENT PIECES

Blending new pieces of veneer (or wood) to their new surroundings might first require the application of a bleach or an acid to lighten the new piece (remember to always take great care when using chemicals). Having achieved a base color, ideally a shade lighter than the surrounding veneer, the color can be adjusted using a combination of water stains and/or artist's acrylic paints. Remember that the final color of the repair will be its "wet" color; to reveal this color and to seal the stain, apply shellac (a natural resin) to the repair.

Painting the figure
Having achieved a good background color, you can add grain, figure (natural pattern), and even fake scratches so that the repair blends in with the original piece. Apply water stains and/or acrylic paints with a fine artist's brush then seal with a coat or two of shellac.

Matching new and old wood

When a component, such as a chair leg, is broken, a repair or replacement part might be required. When working on antique furniture, this should be achieved by replacing as little as possible of the original piece. With contemporary furniture, however, it might be more practical to replace the whole part. In either situation, the challenge for the woodworker is to then finish the new part so that it blends in seamlessly with the existing piece of furniture. One way of doing this is to artificially accelerate the process of oxidation (newly cut wood gradually changes color as it reacts with the oxygen in the air). This can be achieved by bleaching the wood with an acid.

Removing water marks and stains

Marks and stains on an antique surface can usually be categorized as either "white" or "black." If the mark is white or light-colored, it is usually located on the surface film of the polish. If the mark is black or dark-colored, it is usually located on the wood itself, underneath the polish. The white, ring-shaped, marks that are often found on a French-polished surface are caused by either water or heat (typically from a glass or hot cup), which has discolored the surface of the shellac. These marks can be dealt with using a very fine abrasive to "cut" the marks out of the polish. A traditional way of doing this is to use a paste made of cigar ash mixed with a small amount of vegetable oil. Alternatively, use burnishing cream or fine steel wool (0000 grade) with a little paste wax.

Reducing black marks in the wood is relatively straightforward. However, as it involves first removing polish (to "access" the stain) and then re-applying polish, it can be a long process. Dark marks are generally caused by either iron staining (due to a reaction between the wood and a metal fixing) or ink, both of which can be reduced by applying oxalic acid. This process may be repeated as many times as is necessary to achieve the desired reduction in staining, with any final residue being washed off with water before polish is re-applied. Always take care when using oxalic acid and wear the appropriate safety equipment (see Work safely, right).

WORK SAFELY

Although oxalic acid is found naturally in many edible plants—such as parsley, spinach, and Swiss chard—in its purified form it is extremely toxic and corrosive. As such, you should always take great care when using oxalic acid. Wear the correct personal protective gear (pp.78–79), including gloves and goggles to protect your hands and eyes from splashes, and a dust mask to protect your respiratory tract from noxious fumes (always work in a well-ventilated area). Keep a supply of water to hand so that you can wash yourself if splashed. If swallowed, drink plenty of milk or water. Store oxalic acid safely and out of the reach of children.

REMOVING MARKS AND STAINS

1 **To remove marks** and stains from a damaged surface, first use fine steel wool (0000 grade) and paste wax to remove the surface polish. This will remove any "white" marks, and allow you to access any "black" stains ingrained in the wood itself.

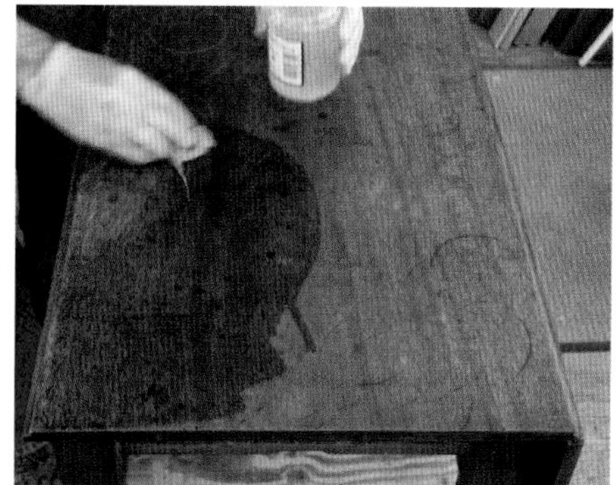

2 **Apply a coating of oxalic acid** to the wood. This will reduce the staining. Take great care when using oxalic acid.

3 **Wash off any oxalic acid residue** with water. Using a pad, apply layers of shellac. Carefully distribute it to produce an even finish.

4 **Apply more layers of shellac** as required, and continue to work the polish around the surface until you achieve a high finish.

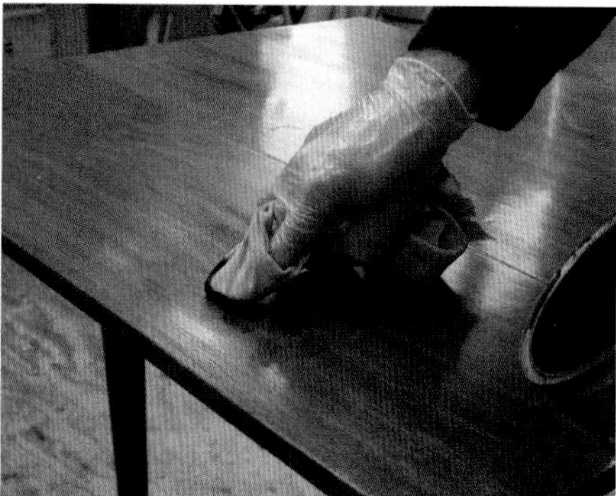

5 **You may wish to soften the shine** of the shellac by applying a layer of wax. This will also help protect the polished surface from water.

CARE OF ANTIQUES

Everyday care of antique furniture is relatively quick and easy:

- Sparingly apply a good quality furniture wax—one that contains beeswax and carnauba wax (derived from the leaves of the carnauba palm)—once or twice a year. Waxing more frequently than this can cause the surfaces to become too sticky, which attracts dirt and dust.
- Periodically wipe surfaces with a damp cloth and buff them with a dry cloth. This should be enough to keep antique furniture looking at its best between waxing. Take care when cleaning and dusting, as you may damage loose veneers or bandings.
- Regularly check for any loose joints, feet, veneers, or moldings; glue them back as soon as possible to prevent further damage.
- Check for evidence of woodworm; the first signs of an infestation are tiny holes in the wood, sometimes accompanied by fine dust. These holes are known as "flight" holes, indicating that beetle larvae have bored through the wood before metamorphosing into their adult form and exiting the wood as flying beetles. Where there is evidence of a previous infestation in a piece of furniture (flight holes and fine dust), it is best to assume that there is still woodworm active in the wood. This should be treated by applying a worm-killing solution; paint this onto any unpolished surface and inject it into flight holes. Worm-killing solution will not only kill existing woodworm but will prevent re-infestation.

WO

ODS

Woods

Wood is a sustainable commodity if managed responsibly. Each species of tree produces timber with different qualities, meaning that there is a vast array of woods available for a wide range of functions.

Types of wood

Timbers are classed as softwoods or hardwoods. This is based not on the actual hardness of the wood, but on the botanical classification of the species. The cell structure is more complex in hardwoods. The trunk of a tree consists of several distinct layers (see opposite and p.184). Trees growing in seasonal environments commence growth each spring, producing the earlywood. Later in the season, the latewood is produced, which is denser, has smaller cells, and is usually darker. This results in well-defined annual rings, while tropical trees growing in areas without distinct seasons do not have clear rings. The outer, youngest parts of the trunk form the sapwood and the inner, older parts comprise the heartwood.

Appearance and physical properties dictate a timber's end uses. The appearance is a combination of the wood's grain, texture, and figure (see panel, right). The way in which wood is converted (sawn) can accentuate special kinds of figuring and will also determine its stability (see below). A timber's physical and working qualities are described in many ways (see right) and vary from species to species.

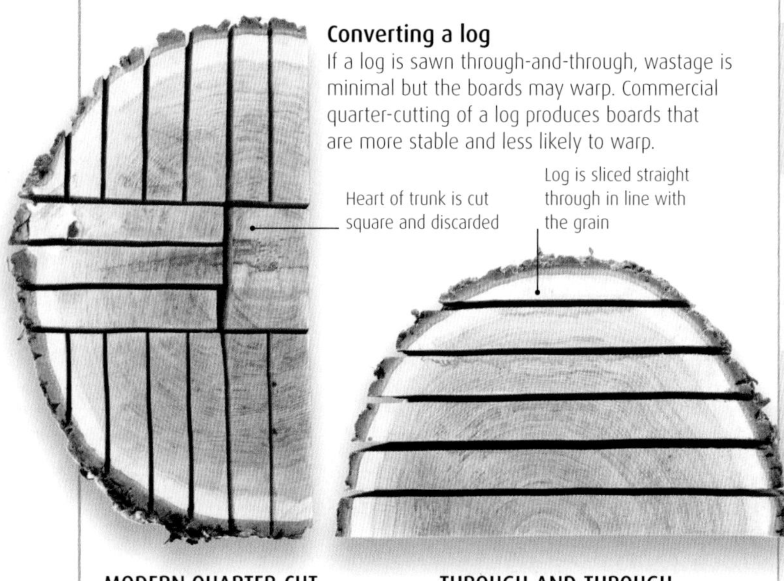

Converting a log
If a log is sawn through-and-through, wastage is minimal but the boards may warp. Commercial quarter-cutting of a log produces boards that are more stable and less likely to warp.

MODERN QUARTER-CUT

THROUGH-AND-THROUGH

WOOD TERMS

DENSITY	Density is a measure of the weight of a given volume of wood dried to a standard moisture content. Density is often linked with hardness, strength, and ease of working.
DURABILITY	A timber's durability—its resistance to fungal decay—is important in deciding whether it is suitable for outdoor use. Some woods are also notably susceptible (while others are resistant) to insect attack.
FIGURE	Figure is the wood's surface pattern and can be the result of contrasting streaks of color, conspicuous growth rings, grain pattern, knots, defects, or other natural features.
GRAIN	Grain describes the orientation of the wood's fibers within the tree. Straight grain is where the fibers lie parallel along the trunk. Interlocked grain occurs when the fibers alternate every few years between growing in a left-handed spiral and a right-handed spiral. Spiral grain is where the direction of the spiral is constant. Wavy-grained wood has fibers in regular short waves. Wood can also have irregular grain.
HEARTWOOD	Non-functioning xylem tissue at the center of the trunk is called heartwood. It is darker than sapwood, more durable, and more resistant to insect attack.
MEDULLARY RAYS	These are bands of cells that grow at 90 degrees to the growth rings. They are distinctive in some woods, such as oak (see Hardwood trunk p.184), while barely visible in others (see Softwood trunk, opposite).
SAPWOOD	The comparatively soft and perishable wood from the outer part of the trunk is called sapwood. While the tree is still alive, this xylem tissue transports water and minerals and stores food. Sapwood thickness varies between species.
SPECIES NAME	Timber can have many common and commercial names, which can vary from place to place. For example, the wood known as American sycamore in the US is called American plane in the UK. So, for positive identification, the species' scientific name must be used, in this case, *Platanus occidentalis*.
STABILITY	Even after seasoning (drying), wood reacts to seasonal changes in atmospheric humidity by expanding and contracting. The degree to which this occurs is described as the wood's stability.
TEXTURE	Texture describes the size of the pores and rays in wood. Wood with a coarse texture has large pores, which may need to be filled before a finish is applied.

ENDANGERED SPECIES

Illegal logging and over-exploitation have led to a shortage of some timbers—those species on the following pages that are vulnerable are flagged with a red leaf. When buying timber, therefore, it is important to ensure that it has come from a sustainable source—look for the stamp of a recognized body, such as that of the Forest Stewardship Council (FSC; see Resources, pp.380–82). Recycled timber should also be considered (see p.187).

FSC ©

WORK SAFELY

Wood dust can be a hazard in the workshop once it can irritate the eyes, skin, and respiratory tract. Depending on the species, inhaled dust may lead to shortness of breath or cause allergic bronchial asthma, rhinitis, nosebleeds, headaches, or nausea. In the worst cases, the dust of a particular species, such as the blackbean, can be carcinogenic. It is therefore important to wear protective equipment, such as a face mask, goggles, and gloves (see pp.78–79), when the woodwork technique produces a large amount of dust, and use a dust extractor if possible.

Softwoods

Softwoods are the timbers of a group of trees that are classified as gymnosperms, which means that their seeds are "naked". Many of the softwood species are conifers (they bear their seeds in cones). The trees have needle- or scale-like leaves and are mostly all evergreens. Softwood trees make up the vast boreal forests of the far nothern hemisphere. They also occur in mixed temperate forests and some southern hemisphere rain forests.

Distinguishing features

Timber from softwoods is characterized by the contrasting shades of the earlywood and latewood tissues, giving many softwoods a strong growth-ring figure. Colors range from pale yellow to reddish-brown in different species, but there is not the variety of textures and figures found in hardwoods. Although many softwoods are softer than many hardwoods, there is a large amount of overlap between the two groups. An important exception to the general rule is yew, which botanically is a softwood, but is harder and stronger than several commercial hardwoods.

Softwood timber often contains resin ducts, but it has none of the vessels found in hardwoods (see p.184), only the much smaller tracheids (elongated cells that transport water). In reaction to mechanical stress, softwood trees produce compression wood (on the underside of a branch, for example), which is unstable and rarely used. Softwoods are often aromatic and some are extremely durable. Most are less expensive than hardwoods, meaning they are widely used in the construction industry.

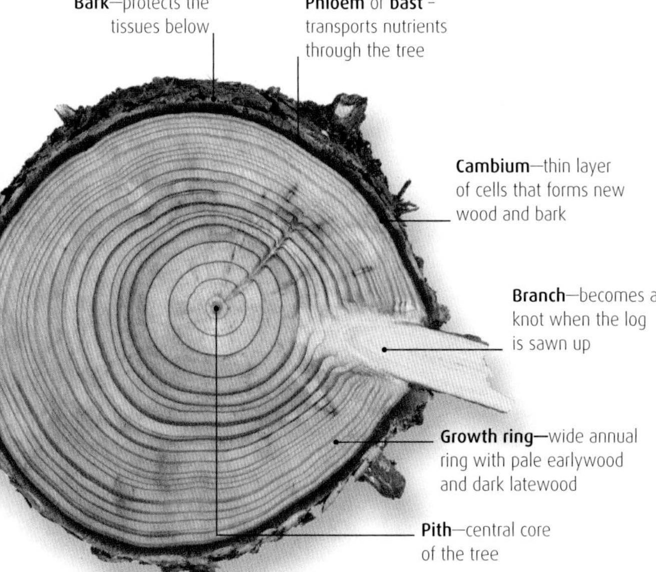

Softwood trunk
In light-colored woods, such as this pine tree, the difference between the outer sapwood and inner heartwood is hard to see. The distinct, wide annual rings reveal that this pine is a fast-growing species.

Yellow cedar *Xanthocyparis nootkatensis*
(synonyms *Callitropsis nootkatensis, Chamaecyparis nootkatensis, Cupressus nootkatensis*)

OTHER NAMES Alaska or Pacific Coast yellow cedar; Alaska, Nootka, Sitka, or yellow cypress; Nootka false cypress.
TREE CHARACTERISTICS Native to North American Pacific coastal forest belt, from Alaska to California. Height: 120ft (37m).
WOOD Pale yellow heartwood, whitish sapwood; straight grain; fine texture.
WORKING QUALITIES Medium density; medium strength, but low stiffness; stable; durable; acid-resistant. Easy to work.
FINISHING Good.
USES High-class joinery; boat-building; external joinery; battery separators.

Baltic whitewood *Picea abies*

OTHER NAMES European whitewood; Norway or European spruce; spruce; white deal.
TREE CHARACTERISTICS Native to Northern and Central Europe; also grown in UK. Height: 120ft (37m). Note: Whitewood shipments may also contain silver fir (see p.181).
WOOD Creamy-white to pale brown with distinct growth rings; straight grain; fine texture; good natural luster.
WORKING QUALITIES Medium density; weak; medium stability; non-durable; susceptible to insect attack. Easy to work. Hard knots can quickly blunt tools.
FINISHING Good.
USES Interior joinery; flooring; plywood. Swiss pine (selected quarter-cut material): soundboards for stringed instruments; violin bellies (front plates).

Northern white cedar *Thuja occidentalis*

OTHER NAMES Eastern white, white, or swamp cedar; American arborvitae.
TREE CHARACTERISTICS Native to southeastern Canada and northeastern USA, especially favoring swampy sites (also grows on cliff faces). Height: 50ft (15m).
WOOD Light brown heartwood, white sapwood; straight grain; fine texture; strongly aromatic.
WORKING QUALITIES Light; weak and soft; stable; very durable. Easy to work.
FINISHING Good.
USES Fencing and fence posts; cabins; roof shingles; telephone poles; boat-building, including canoes.

 **ENDANGERED SPECIES**

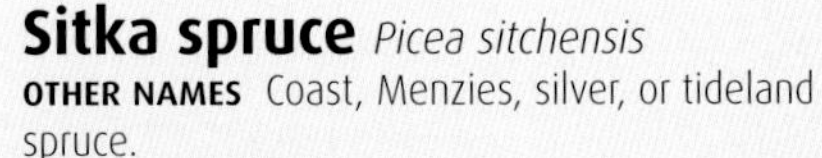

Sitka spruce *Picea sitchensis*

OTHER NAMES Coast, Menzies, silver, or tideland spruce.
TREE CHARACTERISTICS Native to North American Pacific coastal forest belt, from Alaska to California; also grown in Europe. Height: 175ft (53m).
WOOD Pinkish-yellow to pale brown heartwood, creamy-white sapwood; straight (sometimes spiral) grain; medium texture; non-resinous; good natural luster.
WORKING QUALITIES Light; medium strength; medium stability; non-durable; susceptible to insect attack. Easy to work. Good steam-bending timber.
FINISHING Very good.
USES Plywood; joinery; boat-building; musical-instrument soundboards.

Cedar of Lebanon *Cedrus libani*

OTHER NAMES True cedar.
TREE CHARACTERISTICS Native to mountains of Asia Minor, chiefly Lebanon; also grown in Europe (including UK, where it is planted as a parkland specimen tree) and USA. Height: 80ft (25m).
WOOD Yellowish-brown to pale brown heartwood with contrasting growth rings, yellowish-white sapwood; straight grain; medium-fine texture; strongly aromatic. Can have ingrown pockets of bark.
WORKING QUALITIES Medium density; soft and brittle; medium stability; durable; susceptible to insect attack. Easy to work, but large knots may cause problems. Unsuitable for steam-bending.
FINISHING Good.
USES Drawer linings; linen chests; fences and gates; decorative veneers.

Douglas fir *Pseudotsuga menziesii*

OTHER NAMES Douglas spruce; British Columbian or Oregon pine.
TREE CHARACTERISTICS Native to western North America; also grown in Europe and New Zealand. Height: 200ft (60m). Not a true fir.
WOOD Light red- or orange-brown heartwood with wide, darker growth rings, pale yellow sapwood; straight (but can be spiral or wavy) grain; medium texture.
WORKING QUALITIES Medium density; strong and stiff; stable; moderate durability. Blunts tools quickly. Nail or screw holes must be pre-bored.
FINISHING Good, but material with high resin content is best varnished or painted.
USES Plywood; heavy and light construction work; joinery; shipbuilding; mining timber.

Common larch *Larix decidua*

OTHER NAMES European larch.
TREE CHARACTERISTICS Native to mountains of Central Europe; also grown in UK, western Russia, and New Zealand. Height: 70ft (20m).
WOOD Pale reddish-brown to brick-red heartwood with distinct growth rings; may be knotty; straight or spiral grain; fine texture.
WORKING QUALITIES Medium density; medium strength (50 percent harder than Baltic redwood); stable; moderate durability; susceptible to insect attack. Satisfactory to work. Knotty material quickly blunts tools. Nail or screw holes must be pre-bored. Dead or loose knots may cause problems during machining.
FINISHING Good.
USES Boat-building; joinery; fencing; shingles; telephone poles.

Ponderosa pine *Pinus ponderosa*

OTHER NAMES Big, bird's-eye, blackjack, bull, British Columbia soft, California white, or western yellow pine.
TREE CHARACTERISTICS Native to southwestern Canada, western USA, and northern Mexico; also grown in Australia, New Zealand, and South Africa. Height: 130ft (40m).
WOOD Reddish-brown heartwood, pale yellow sapwood; resin ducts apparent, but sapwood non-resinous; can be very knotty (knotty pine); straight grain; medium texture.
WORKING QUALITIES Medium density; soft; stable; non-durable. Easy to work.
FINISHING Satisfactory, but resin seeping from numerous knots can cause problems.
USES Sapwood: pattern-making. Heartwood: joinery; furniture; railroad ties. Knotty pine: paneling.

Western hemlock *Tsuga heterophylla*

OTHER NAMES British Columbia or Pacific hemlock; Alaskan pine; hemlock spruce.
TREE CHARACTERISTICS Native to Pacific coastal rain forest and the northern Rocky Mountains in North America; also grown in UK, China, and Japan. Height: 150ft (45m).
WOOD Pale yellowish-brown heartwood with distinct growth rings that have a purplish tinge; straight grain; fine texture; non-resinous; good natural luster.
WORKING QUALITIES Medium density; medium–low strength; stable; non-durable; susceptible to insect attack. Easy to work. Hard, brittle knots. Nail or screw holes near edges must be pre-bored.
FINISHING Good.
USES Construction; joinery; railroad ties; pallets; turnery; plywood; veneers.

ENDANGERED SPECIES

Silver fir *Abies alba*

OTHER NAMES Whitewood; white fir.
TREE CHARACTERISTICS Native to mountains of Europe, including Pyrenees, Carpathians, and Alps; also grown in UK. Height 145ft (45m). Note: shipments of whitewood may also contain Baltic whitewood (see p.179).
WOOD White to pale yellowish-brown; straight grain; fine texture; good natural luster.
WORKING QUALITIES Medium density; relatively weak; medium stability; non-durable; susceptible to insect attack. Easy to work.
FINISHING Good
USES Construction; joinery; flooring; plywood. Central and Eastern European-grown timber: musical instrument soundboards and violin bellies (front plates).

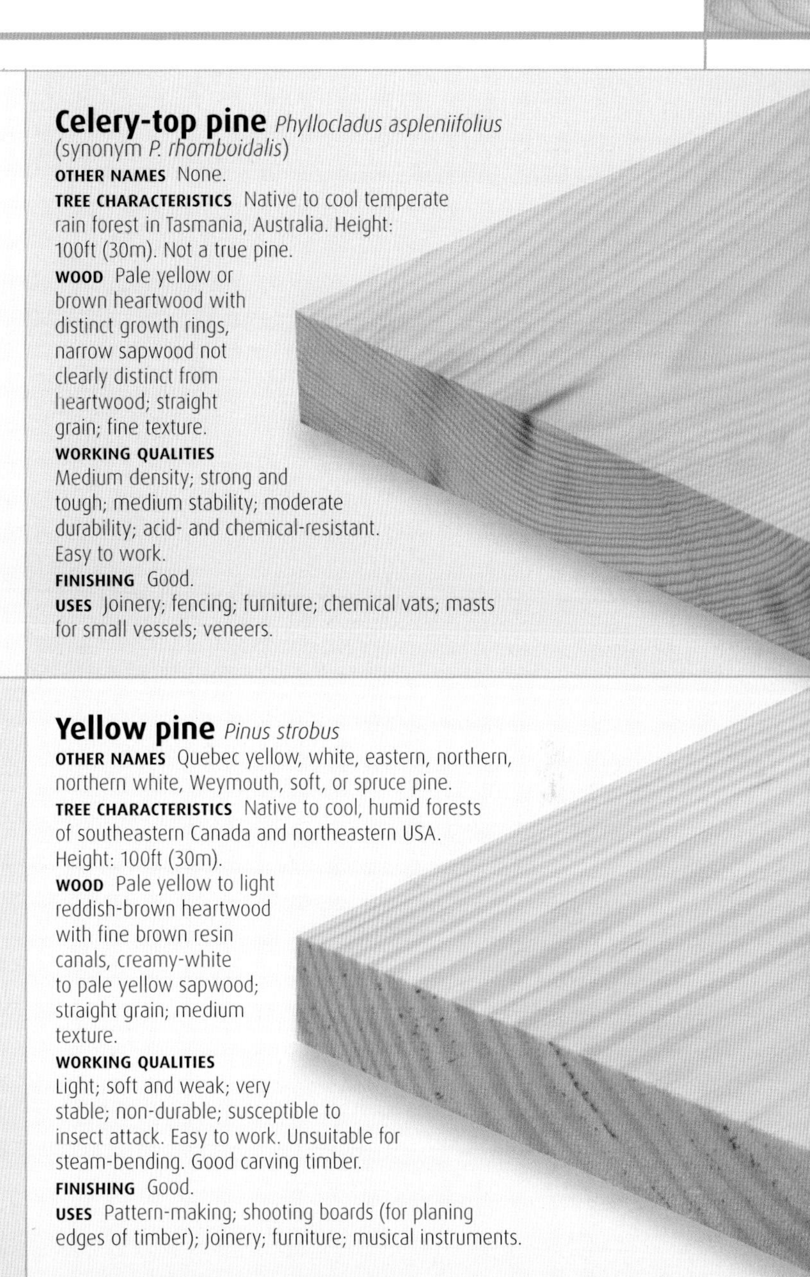

Celery-top pine *Phyllocladus aspleniifolius* (synonym *P. rhomboidalis*)

OTHER NAMES None.
TREE CHARACTERISTICS Native to cool temperate rain forest in Tasmania, Australia. Height: 100ft (30m). Not a true pine.
WOOD Pale yellow or brown heartwood with distinct growth rings, narrow sapwood not clearly distinct from heartwood; straight grain; fine texture.
WORKING QUALITIES Medium density; strong and tough; medium stability; moderate durability; acid- and chemical-resistant. Easy to work.
FINISHING Good.
USES Joinery; fencing; furniture; chemical vats; masts for small vessels; veneers.

Baltic redwood *Pinus sylvestris*

OTHER NAMES Scots pine (UK-grown timber only); red or yellow deal; Archangel, European, Scandinavian, or Russian redwood; Norway or Scots fir.
TREE CHARACTERISTICS Native to Europe and northwestern Asia; also grown in North America. Height: 70ft (20m).
WOOD Pale reddish-brown heartwood with distinct growth rings, creamy-white to pale yellow sapwood; usually straight grain; often knotty; variable texture, depending on origin.
WORKING QUALITIES Medium density; variable strength; medium stability; non-durable. Easy to work. Gluing is hard if high in resin. Unsuitable for steam-bending.
FINISHING Satisfactory.
USES Furniture; joinery, including turnery; construction; railroad ties; telephone poles; plywood.

Yellow pine *Pinus strobus*

OTHER NAMES Quebec yellow, white, eastern, northern, northern white, Weymouth, soft, or spruce pine.
TREE CHARACTERISTICS Native to cool, humid forests of southeastern Canada and northeastern USA. Height: 100ft (30m).
WOOD Pale yellow to light reddish-brown heartwood with fine brown resin canals, creamy-white to pale yellow sapwood; straight grain; medium texture.
WORKING QUALITIES Light; soft and weak; very stable; non-durable; susceptible to insect attack. Easy to work. Unsuitable for steam-bending. Good carving timber.
FINISHING Good.
USES Pattern-making; shooting boards (for planing edges of timber); joinery; furniture; musical instruments.

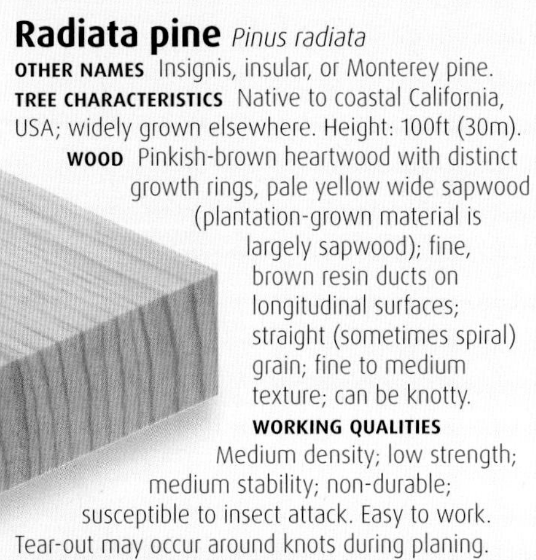

Radiata pine *Pinus radiata*

OTHER NAMES Insignis, insular, or Monterey pine.
TREE CHARACTERISTICS Native to coastal California, USA; widely grown elsewhere. Height: 100ft (30m).
WOOD Pinkish-brown heartwood with distinct growth rings, pale yellow wide sapwood (plantation-grown material is largely sapwood); fine, brown resin ducts on longitudinal surfaces; straight (sometimes spiral) grain; fine to medium texture; can be knotty.
WORKING QUALITIES Medium density; low strength; medium stability; non-durable; susceptible to insect attack. Easy to work. Tear-out may occur around knots during planing. Unsuitable for steam-bending.
FINISHING Satisfactory.
USES Construction; joinery; plywood.

Huon pine *Lagarostrobos franklinii* (synonym *Dacrydium franklinii*)

OTHER NAMES Macquarie or white pine.
TREE CHARACTERISTICS Native to southwestern Tasmania, Australia. Height: 100ft (30m). Not a true pine.
WOODS Creamy-white to pale brown with distinct growth rings; can have attractive bird's-eye figure; straight grain; very fine texture; strongly aromatic.
WORKING QUALITIES Medium density; weak; medium stability; very durable. Easy to work. Nail or screw holes must be pre-bored. Unsuitable for steam-bending.
FINISHING Very good.
USES Furniture; joinery; boat-building; decorative veneers.

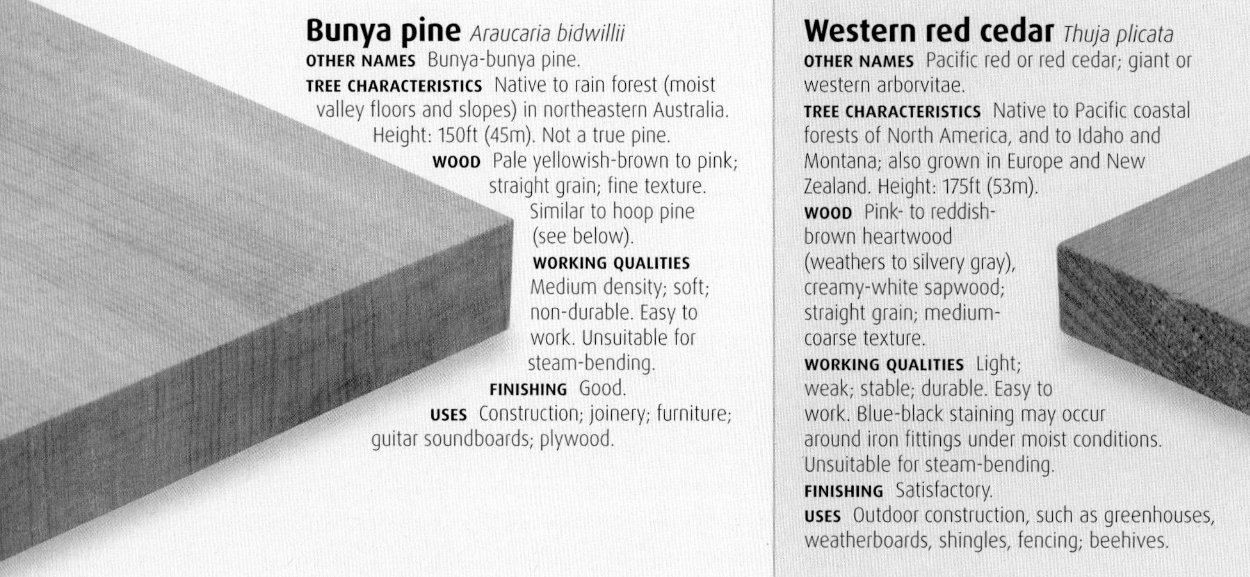

Bunya pine *Araucaria bidwillii*

OTHER NAMES Bunya-bunya pine.
TREE CHARACTERISTICS Native to rain forest (moist valley floors and slopes) in northeastern Australia. Height: 150ft (45m). Not a true pine.
WOOD Pale yellowish-brown to pink; straight grain; fine texture. Similar to hoop pine (see below).
WORKING QUALITIES Medium density; soft; non-durable. Easy to work. Unsuitable for steam-bending.
FINISHING Good.
USES Construction; joinery; furniture; guitar soundboards; plywood.

Western red cedar *Thuja plicata*

OTHER NAMES Pacific red or red cedar; giant or western arborvitae.
TREE CHARACTERISTICS Native to Pacific coastal forests of North America, and to Idaho and Montana; also grown in Europe and New Zealand. Height: 175ft (53m).
WOOD Pink- to reddish-brown heartwood (weathers to silvery gray), creamy-white sapwood; straight grain; medium-coarse texture.
WORKING QUALITIES Light; weak; stable; durable. Easy to work. Blue-black staining may occur around iron fittings under moist conditions. Unsuitable for steam-bending.
FINISHING Satisfactory.
USES Outdoor construction, such as greenhouses, weatherboards, shingles, fencing; beehives.

Hoop pine *Araucaria cunninghamii*

OTHER NAMES Colonial, Dorrigo, Moreton Bay, Norfolk Island, Queensland, or Richmond River pine; Australian Araucaria; Arakaria.
TREE CHARACTERISTICS Native to drier rain forests of coastal eastern Australia and mountains of Papua New Guinea. Height: 165ft (50m). Not a true pine.
WOOD Pale brown heartwood, whitish sapwood; straight (sometimes spiral) grain; fine texture.
WORKING QUALITIES Medium density; soft; stable; non-durable; susceptible to insect attack. Easy to work. Tear-out may occur around knots during planing. Unsuitable for steam-bending.
FINISHING Good.
USES Furniture; joinery; turnery; boat-building.

King William pine *Athrotaxis selaginoides*

OTHER NAMES King Billy pine; Tasmanian cedar.
TREE CHARACTERISTICS Native to mountains of Tasmania, Australia. Height: 100ft (30m). Not a true pine or cedar.
WOOD Pinkish- to reddish-brown heartwood, pale yellow sapwood; straight grain; fine texture.
WORKING QUALITIES Light; soft and fissile (readily split); very durable. Easy to work. Good steam-bending timber. End grain can tear out during turning.
FINISHING Excellent.
USES Boat-building; joinery; musical-instrument soundboards; Venetian blind slats.

Kauri *Agathis* spp.

OTHER NAMES New Zealand, Queensland, or Malaysian kauri; kauri pine.
TREE CHARACTERISTICS Native to North Island, New Zealand; Queensland, Australia; Papua New Guinea; and Southeast Asia. Height: 165ft (50m). Not true pines.
WOOD Creamy white to dark reddish-brown heartwood; can have a flecked or mottled figure; straight grain; fine texture; good natural luster.
WORKING QUALITIES Medium density; stiff, with medium strength; stable; moderate to good durability; susceptible to insect attack. Easy to work. Unsuitable for steam-bending.
FINISHING Excellent.
USES Joinery; furniture; boat-building; pattern-making; flooring; plywood; decorative veneers.

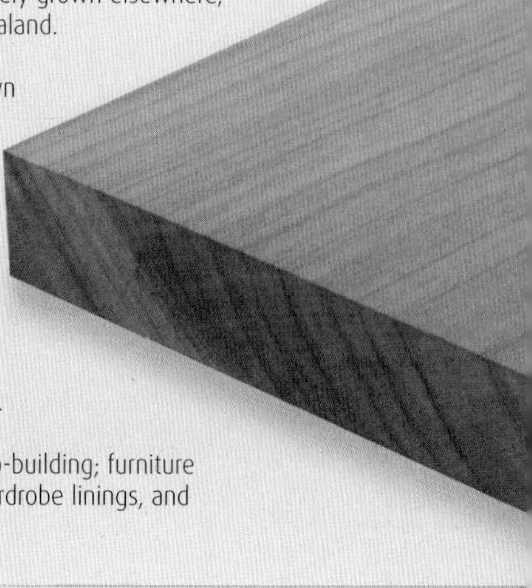

Macrocarpa *Cupressus macrocarpa*

OTHER NAMES Monterey cypress; cypress.
TREE CHARACTERISTICS Native to coastal rocky outcrops in California, USA; widely grown elsewhere, including Australia and New Zealand. Height: 80ft (25m).
WOOD Orange- to pinkish-brown heartwood; straight grain; fine texture; may have tiny knots; strongly aromatic.
WORKING QUALITIES Light–medium density; strong; stable; very durable. Satisfactory to work. Unsuitable for steam-bending. Reduced cutting angle may be required for planing or molding.
FINISHING Satisfactory.
USES Construction; joinery; ship-building; furniture (especially for bookshelves, wardrobe linings, and linen chests).

ENDANGERED SPECIES

Yew *Taxus baccata*

OTHER NAMES Common or European yew.
TREE CHARACTERISTICS Native to Europe, Asia Minor, Algeria; also grown in Burma (Myanmar) and the Himalayas. Height: 50ft (15m).
WOOD Orangey-brown heartwood with black or purple streaks, creamy-yellow sapwood; tiny knots and ingrown bark often present; straight, curly or irregular grain; medium texture.
WORKING QUALITIES Dense; medium strength; stable; durable; susceptible to insect attack. Hard to work. Curly or irregular-grained samples may tear-out during planing. Nail or screw holes must be pre-bored. Hard to glue. Excellent steam-bending and turning timber.
FINISHING Excellent.
USES Turnery; veneers; bent chair parts; longbows.

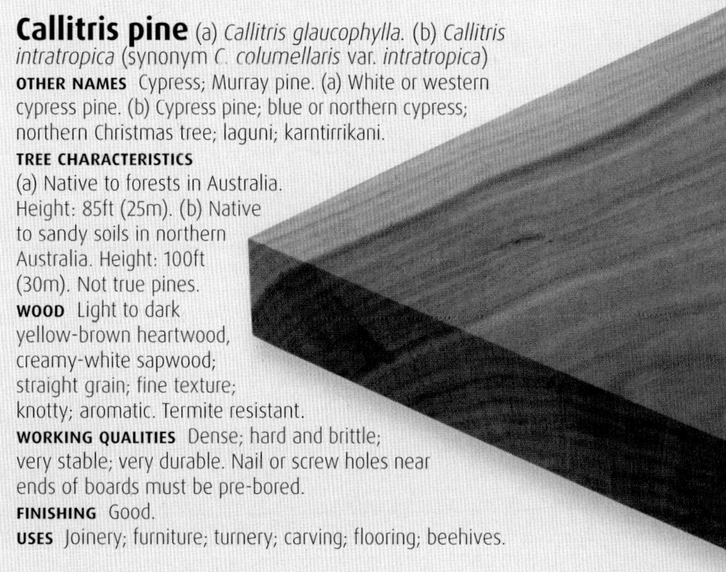

Callitris pine (a) *Callitris glaucophylla.* (b) *Callitris intratropica* (synonym *C. columellaris* var. *intratropica*)

OTHER NAMES Cypress; Murray pine. (a) White or western cypress pine. (b) Cypress pine; blue or northern cypress; northern Christmas tree; laguni; karntirrikani.
TREE CHARACTERISTICS (a) Native to forests in Australia. Height: 85ft (25m). (b) Native to sandy soils in northern Australia. Height: 100ft (30m). Not true pines.
WOOD Light to dark yellow-brown heartwood, creamy-white sapwood; straight grain; fine texture; knotty; aromatic. Termite resistant.
WORKING QUALITIES Dense; hard and brittle; very stable; very durable. Nail or screw holes near ends of boards must be pre-bored.
FINISHING Good.
USES Joinery; furniture; turnery; carving; flooring; beehives.

Virginian pencil cedar
Juniperus virginiana

OTHER NAMES Pencil, eastern red, or red cedar; juniper; eastern or red juniper.
TREE CHARACTERISTICS Native to a wide range of habitats (rocky outcrops to moist swampy soils) in southeastern Canada and eastern USA. Height: 60ft (18m). Not a true cedar.
WOOD Reddish-brown heartwood with darker growth rings, creamy-white sapwood; straight grain; fine texture; strongly aromatic.
WORKING QUALITIES Medium density; soft; stable; durable. Easy to work. May tear around knots during planing. Nail or screw holes must be pre-bored. Unsuitable for steam-bending.
FINISHING Very good.
USES Pencils; cigar boxes; coffins; decorative veneers.

Rimu *Dacrydium cupressinum*

OTHER NAMES Red pine.
TREE CHARACTERISTICS Native to temperate rain forest of New Zealand. Height: 100ft (30m). Not a true pine.
WOOD Yellowish- to reddish-brown heartwood, pale brown sapwood; good figure in some logs due to dark streaks; straight grain; fine texture.
WORKING QUALITIES Medium density; medium strength; medium stability; moderate durability; sapwood susceptible to insect attack. Easy to work. Nail or screw holes must be pre-bored. Unsuitable for steam-bending.
FINISHING Good.
USES Furniture; joinery; flooring; weatherboards; plywood; architectural veneers.

Sequoia *Sequoia sempervirens*

OTHER NAMES California or coast redwood.
TREE CHARACTERISTICS Native to coastal strip of California and extreme southeast of Oregon, USA; also grown in Europe, Australia, and New Zealand. Height: 300ft (90m).
WOOD Reddish-brown heartwood with distinct growth rings, dull white sapwood; straight grain; mostly fine texture (some is coarse); non-resinous.
WORKING QUALITIES Light; somewhat brittle; stable; medium-durability; susceptible to insect attack. Easy to work. Can splinter when being machined. Nails do not hold well.
FINISHING Very good.
USES Joinery; weatherboards and shingles; organ pipes; plywood; telephone poles.

OTHER SOFTWOODS TO CONSIDER

American pitch pine (a) *Pinus palustris.* (b) *P. elliottii*
OTHER NAMES (a and b) Southern pine; Gulf Coast pitch pine. (a) Longleaf, yellow, pitch, or turpentine pine. (b) Slash or longleaf pitch pine.
USES Heavy construction work; shipbuilding; joinery; flooring; plywood; pallets.

Sugar pine *Pinus lambertiana*
OTHER NAMES Big, California sugar, gigantic, great sugar, or shade pine.
USES Joinery; pattern-making; organ pipes and piano keys; food containers; flooring; plywood.

Western white pine *Pinus monticola*
OTHER NAMES Idaho white, mountain, silver, or white pine.
USES Joinery; furniture; packing cases; boatbuilding; plywood.

Thuya burr *Tetraclinis articulata*
OTHER NAMES Arar; alerce; citron burl; thyine wood.
USES Mostly used for decorative veneers as size availability is limited.

Hardwoods

Hardwoods are the timbers from a wide range of broadleaved trees that belong to the flowering plant group, the angiosperms, which produces "covered" seeds. Hardwood species grow in a variety of habitats, ranging from tropical rain forests to savannah to temperate woodlands, but they do not extend as far north as softwood species.

Distinguishing features

A significant feature of hardwoods is that the many different species contain a larger range of colors, textures, and kinds of figure than softwoods. Hardwoods are often slower-growing and more durable than softwoods, and are usually more expensive. As their name suggests, hardwoods are harder than most softwoods, but exceptions include balsa (see opposite), which is actually the softest of all commercial timbers.

Hardwood timber contains several kinds of cells, including small tracheids and large tubes, called vessels, which transport water. In some species, for example, oaks, the vessels are large enough to be seen with the naked eye. Pores on the surface of a piece of timber are actually the severed ends of these vessels. The relative sizes and arrangements of the vessels dictate the timber's texture, with larger vessels giving a coarser texture.

When their wood is subjected to mechanical stress, for example, in a horizontally growing branch, hardwood species produce tension wood on the branch's upper surface to help support it. Branches are therefore rarely used by woodworkers because the tension wood cannot be seasoned to make stable, large-dimension timber.

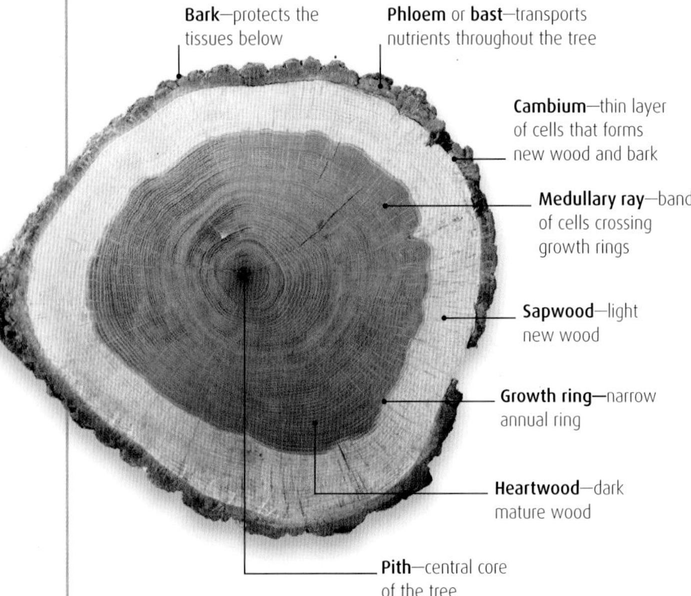

Hardwood trunk
This cross-section of an oak trunk shows the heartwood and the sapwood, numerous thin annual rings (which, when counted, give the age of the tree), and the distinctive medullary rays radiating from the center.

Holly (a) *Ilex aquifolium.* (b) *I. opaca*

OTHER NAMES (a) European holly. (b) American or white holly.
TREE CHARACTERISTICS (a) Native to Europe and western Asia. Height: 65ft (20m). (b) Native to southeastern USA. Height: 65ft (20m).
WOOD Pale creamy white, sometimes with greenish tinge; little or no figure; irregular grain; fine texture.
WORKING QUALITIES Very dense; hard and tough; not stable; perishable; susceptible to insect attack. Hard to work. Reduced cutting angle required for planing or molding. Excellent turning timber. Only available in comparatively small sizes.
FINISHING Excellent. Sometimes dyed black to imitate ebony.
USES Decorative inlay lines and marquetry motifs (substitute for boxwood); musical-instrument parts; turnery.

American ash (a) *Fraxinus americana.* (b) *F. pennsylvanica.* (c) *F. nigra*

OTHER NAMES (a) Canadian or white ash. (b) Green or red ash. (c) Black or brown ash.
TREE CHARACTERISTICS Native to North America. Height: 130ft (40m).
WOOD Grayish brown heartwood sometimes with pink tinge; straight grain; coarse texture.
WORKING QUALITIES Medium density; strong and elastic, with excellent shock resistance; stable; non-durable; susceptible to insect attack. Easy to work. Nail or screw holes must be pre-bored in harder grades of the timber. Very good steam-bending timber provided knots are absent.
FINISHING Very good.
USES Sporting goods; tool handles; boat-building; furniture.

Soft maple (a) *Acer rubrum.* (b) *A. saccharinum.* (c) *A. macrophyllum*

OTHER NAMES (a) Red maple. (b) Silver maple. (c) Big-leaf or Oregon maple.
TREE CHARACTERISTICS (a) and (b) Native to eastern North America. (c) Native to Pacific coastal forest of North America. Height: 100ft (30m).
WOOD Creamy white or pale reddish-brown heartwood, grayish-white sapwood; usually little figure; straight grain; fine texture.
WORKING QUALITIES Medium density; medium strength; stable; non-durable; susceptible to insect attack. Satisfactory to work. Can be hard to glue. Nail or screw holes must be pre-bored.
FINISHING Excellent.
USES Furniture; joinery; flooring; turnery; musical instruments.

 **ENDANGERED SPECIES**

Jelutong *Dyera costulata*

OTHER NAMES Jelutong pukit; jelutong paya.
TREE CHARACTERISTICS Grows in Brunei, Indonesia, and Malaysia. Height: 200ft (60m).
WOOD Creamy white to straw colored, sometimes with darker discoloration if tree had been tapped for latex; little figure; straight grain; fine texture.
WORKING QUALITIES Medium density; weak and soft; stable; non-durable; sapwood susceptible to insect attack. Easy to work.
FINISHING Very good.
USES Pattern-making; carving; light joinery; picture frames; plywood corestock.

Balsa *Ochroma pyrimidale* (synonym *O. lagopus*)

OTHER NAMES Catillo; guano; lanero; polak; tami; topa.
TREE CHARACTERISTICS Native to West Indies and Central and South America; also grown in India and Indonesia. Height: 80ft (25m).
WOOD Commercial timber is chiefly the white to pinkish-oatmeal sapwood; straight grain; fine texture; good natural luster.
WORKING QUALITIES Extremely light; very soft, but strong in relation to its weight; stable; perishable; susceptible to insect attack. Easy to work. Nails and screws do not hold, but the timber glues well. Unsuitable for steam-bending.
FINISHING Satisfactory. Highly absorbent so needs large quantities of finishing material.
USES Model-making; insulating and buoyancy material; corestock for metal-faced sheets in aircraft and wind turbines.

Obeche *Triplochiton scleroxylon*

OTHER NAMES Abachi; arere; ayous; samba; wawa; whitewood.
TREE CHARACTERISTICS Grows in tropical West and Central Africa. Height: 180ft (55m).
WOOD Creamy-white to pale yellow; little figure; interlocked grain; fine texture.
WORKING QUALITIES Light; soft; stable; non-durable; sapwood susceptible to insect attack. Easy to work. Nails do not hold well. Blue or black staining may occur around iron fittings under moist conditions.
FINISHING Good, provided grain is filled.
USES Light furniture parts such as drawer sides; interior joinery; model-making; plywood and corestock; food containers.

Yellow birch *Betula alleghaniensis*

OTHER NAMES American, Canadian yellow, gray, hard, Quebec, or swamp birch; betula wood.
TREE CHARACTERISTICS Native to southeastern Canada and northeastern USA, especially in uplands and mountain ravines. Height: 70ft (20m).
WOOD Reddish-brown heartwood, white or pale brown sapwood; straight grain; fine texture; good natural luster.
WORKING QUALITIES Dense; strong; not stable; perishable; susceptible to insect attack. Easy to work. Reduced cutting angle required for planing areas with curly grain. Nail or screw holes must be pre-bored. Very good steam-bending timber.
FINISHING Excellent.
USES High-quality furniture; flooring; turnery; upholstery frames; high-quality plywood.

Hickory *Carya* spp.

OTHER NAMES Pignut, mockernut, red, shagbark, shellbark, and white hickory.
TREE CHARACTERISTICS Native to deciduous forests of eastern North America. Height: 100ft (30m).
WOOD Brown to reddish-brown heartwood, pale brown sapwood; straight (sometimes wavy or irregular) grain; coarse texture.
WORKING QUALITIES Very dense; strong and flexible; stable; non-durable; sapwood susceptible to insect attack. Hard to work. Reduced cutting angle required for planing or molding. Nail or screw holes must be pre-bored. Can be hard to glue. Excellent steam-bending timber.
FINISHING Good.
USES Ax handles; sporting goods; furniture.

Hard maple (a) *Acer saccharum.* (b) *A. nigrum*

OTHER NAMES Rock maple. (a) Sugar maple. (b) Black maple.
TREE CHARACTERISTICS Native to Canada and eastern USA; (b) grows further west than (a). Height: (a) 120ft (40m), (b) 80ft (25m).
WOOD Pale brown heartwood with reddish tinge and sometimes dark brown heart, white sapwood with reddish tinge; straight, curly or wavy grain; fine texture; good natural luster.
WORKING QUALITIES Dense; strong; medium stability; non-durable; sapwood susceptible to insect attack; abrasion-resistant. Hard to work. Reduced cutting angle required for planing or molding. Nail or screw holes must be pre-bored.
FINISHING Excellent.
USES Heavy-duty flooring; butcher blocks; turnery; furniture; decorative veneers (see bird's-eye maple, p.198).

Basswood *Tilia americana*

OTHER NAMES American lime; American linden; American linn; whitewood.
TREE CHARACTERISTICS Native to moist forests of southern Canada and northeastern USA. Height: 100ft (30m).
WOOD Creamy white to pale brown; little or no figure; straight grain; fine texture.
WORKING QUALITIES Light; weak and soft; stable; non-durable; susceptible to insect attack. Easy to work. Glues well. Unsuitable for steam-bending.
FINISHING Good.
USES Carving; pattern-making; picture frames; Venetian blind slats; food containers.

Mountain ash *Eucalyptus regnans*

OTHER NAMES Australian or Tasmanian mountain oak; Victoria or white ash; stringy or swamp gum.
TREE CHARACTERISTICS Native to southeastern Australia and Victoria. Height: 120ft (37m).
WOOD Pale to light brown with a pinkish tinge and distinct gum veins; can have fiddleback figure; straight, interlocked or wavy grain; coarse texture.
WORKING QUALITIES Medium density, strength, and stability; moderate durability; susceptible to insect attack. Satisfactory to work. Nail or screw holes must be pre-bored. Unsuitable for steam-bending.
FINISHING Good.
USES Furniture; flooring; weatherboards; plywood; decorative veneers from selected logs.

American plane *Platanus occidentalis*

OTHER NAMES Aliso; buttonwood; American sycamore.
TREE CHARACTERISTICS Native to deciduous forests in southeastern USA; also grown in mountains of northeastern Mexico. Height: 120ft (37m).
WOOD Pale to dark brown heartwood, pale brown sapwood; distinctive fleck figure on quarter-cut material (called lacewood in the United States); irregular grain; fine texture.
WORKING QUALITIES Medium density; medium strength; stable; non-durable; susceptible to insect attack; resistant to splitting. Satisfactory to work. Flat-sawn material can warp.
FINISHING Good.
USES Furniture; joinery; flooring; butcher blocks; veneers.

European ash *Fraxinus excelsior*

OTHER NAMES Common ash.
TREE CHARACTERISTICS Native to Europe and southwestern Asia. Height: 120ft (37m).
WOOD Cream to pale brown heartwood; can have fiddleback figure; straight grain; coarse texture; good natural luster. Olive ash has dark brown heartwood, sometimes with black streaks, resembling olivewood.
WORKING QUALITIES Dense; tough and strong; medium stability; non-durable; susceptible to insect attack. Easy to work. Nail or screw holes must be pre-bored. Excellent steam-bending timber.
FINISHING Excellent.
USES Tool handles; sporting goods; boat-building; furniture; turnery; decorative veneers (see p.198).

Linden *Tilia × europea* (synonym *T. × vulgaris*)

OTHER NAMES Common or European lime.
TREE CHARACTERISTICS Native to Northern, Central, and Southern Europe. Height: 100ft (30m).
WOOD Creamy yellow to pale brown; no figure; straight grain; fine texture.
WORKING QUALITIES Medium density; medium strength; medium stability; perishable; susceptible to insect attack; resistant to splitting. Easy to work. Can be woolly. Reduced cutting angle required for planing.
FINISHING Good.
USES Toys; musical-instrument parts; architectural models; the preferred timber choice for carving.

Hornbeam *Carpinus betulus*

OTHER NAMES Hardbeam.
TREE CHARACTERISTICS Native to Europe, eastward to Iran. Height: 80ft (25m).
WOOD Grayish-white heartwood with greenish streaks; has fleck figure on quarter-cut material, can also have mottle figure; irregular grain; fine texture.
WORKING QUALITIES Dense; strong; not stable; perishable; susceptible to insect attack; split-resistant; abrasion-resistant. Satisfactory to work. Nail or screw holes must be pre-bored. Good turning and steam-bending timber.
FINISHING Very good.
USES Musical-instrument parts; flooring; drumsticks; decorative veneers.

ENDANGERED SPECIES

Sweet chestnut *Castanea sativa*

OTHER NAMES European or Spanish chestnut.
TREE CHARACTERISTICS Native to southeastern Europe. Height: 115ft (35m).
WOOD Pale brown heartwood similar to European oak, but without oak's flake figure (see p.189), creamy white sapwood; straight or spiral grain; coarse texture.
WORKING QUALITIES Medium density; medium strength; stable; durable; sapwood susceptible to insect attack. Easy to work. Blue or black staining may occur around iron fittings under moist conditions, and fittings may corrode. Good steam-bending timber.
FINISHING Excellent.
USES Furniture; coffins; fencing and posts.

European birch
(a) *Betula pendula*. (b) *B. pubescens*

OTHER NAMES (a and b) Common birch. (a) Silver birch. (b) Downy, hairy, or brown birch.
TREE CHARACTERISTICS Native to Europe as far north as Lapland. Height: 70ft (20m).
WOOD Creamy white to pale brown; straight grain; fine texture; good natural luster; many decorative figures.
WORKING QUALITIES Medium density and strength; stable; perishable. Easy to work. Reduced cutting angle required for planing areas with curly grain. Can be woolly. Good steam-bending timber if knots are absent.
FINISHING Very good.
USES High-quality joinery and plywood; turnery, such as bobbins and domestic ware; decorative veneers.

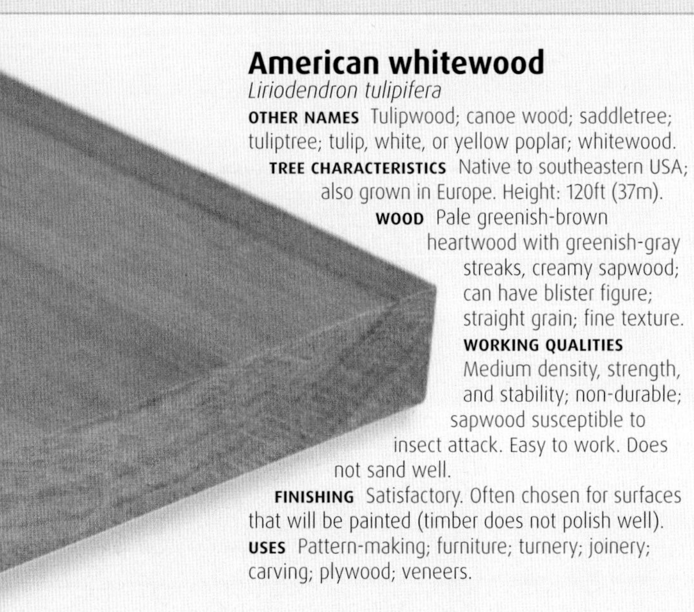

American whitewood
Liriodendron tulipifera

OTHER NAMES Tulipwood; canoe wood; saddletree; tuliptree; tulip, white, or yellow poplar; whitewood.
TREE CHARACTERISTICS Native to southeastern USA; also grown in Europe. Height: 120ft (37m).
WOOD Pale greenish-brown heartwood with greenish-gray streaks, creamy sapwood; can have blister figure; straight grain; fine texture.
WORKING QUALITIES Medium density, strength, and stability; non-durable; sapwood susceptible to insect attack. Easy to work. Does not sand well.
FINISHING Satisfactory. Often chosen for surfaces that will be painted (timber does not polish well).
USES Pattern-making; furniture; turnery; joinery; carving; plywood; veneers.

Continued on p.188 ▸

RECYCLING WOOD

When planning a project, consider whether you can use old wood for part or all of it. Timber, and particularly structural timber (such as beams or joists, for example), is usually suitable for reuse so long as it is sound. Check for damage when buying old wood from a reclamation yard or other sources of recycled timber (see Resources, pp.380–82). As well as having the advantage of being thoroughly seasoned, reclaimed wood may look better than new timber. And, where a species is endangered and therefore protected, reclaimed wood may be the only option.

Recycled floorboards
Old floorboards made from good-quality wood, such as oak (above), can be refurbished and reused for new flooring or other projects, once trimmed, stripped, and stained or varnished.

PREPARING RECYCLED WOOD

Old timbers often have areas of woodworm or rot, but, once the worst areas are removed, the remaining wood is usually structurally sound. Old nails and other fixings should also be removed.

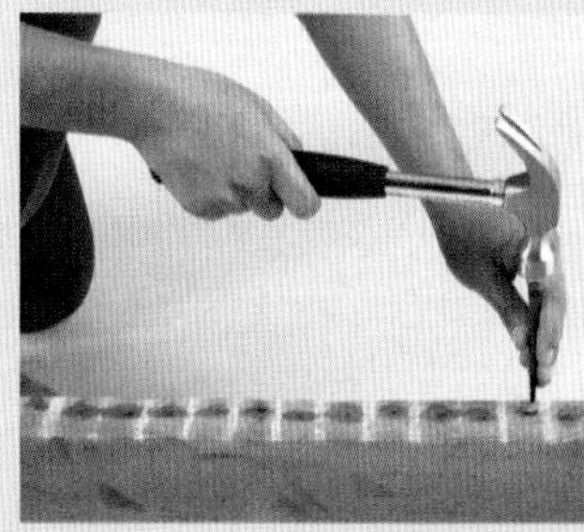

1 **Rusted nails** may snap off if you try to pry them out of a piece of timber with a claw hammer or pry bar. If this happens, use a hammer and punch to knock the broken shaft of the nail below the wood's surface.

2 **With large timbers** that are affected with woodworm or rot, use an ax or hatchet to cut away the affected wood.

3 **Once the worst bits** have been cut away, brush the wood down and treat it to kill any woodworm and protect it from further attack by insects or rot.

American white oak *Quercus alba*

OTHER NAMES Arizona, Appalachian, Quebec, stave, or white oak.
TREE CHARACTERISTICS Native to eastern USA and southeastern Canada. Height: 100ft (30m)
WOOD Pale yellowish- to pinkish-brown heartwood, creamy white to pale brown sapwood; has flake figure on quarter-cut material; straight grain; medium-coarse texture.
WORKING QUALITIES Dense; strong; medium stability; durable; susceptible to insect attack; abrasion-resistant. Northern-grown wood is easier to work than southern-grown. Excellent steam-bending timber. Can be hard to glue. Nail or screw holes must be pre-bored.
FINISHING Good. Does not fume well.
USES Furniture; boat-building; flooring; barrels.

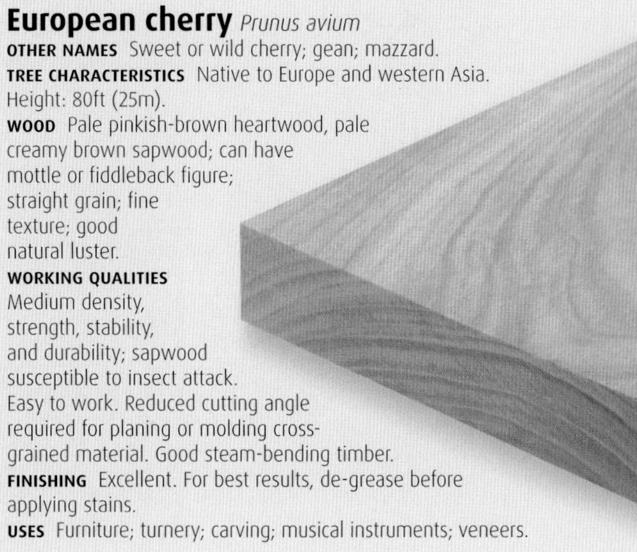

European cherry *Prunus avium*

OTHER NAMES Sweet or wild cherry; gean; mazzard.
TREE CHARACTERISTICS Native to Europe and western Asia. Height: 80ft (25m).
WOOD Pale pinkish-brown heartwood, pale creamy brown sapwood; can have mottle or fiddleback figure; straight grain; fine texture; good natural luster.
WORKING QUALITIES Medium density, strength, stability, and durability; sapwood susceptible to insect attack. Easy to work. Reduced cutting angle required for planing or molding cross-grained material. Good steam-bending timber.
FINISHING Excellent. For best results, de-grease before applying stains.
USES Furniture; turnery; carving; musical instruments; veneers.

European beech *Fagus sylvatica*

OTHER NAMES Common Beech.
TREE CHARACTERISTICS Native to Europe, as far east as the Caucasus. Height: 100ft (30m).
WOOD Pale pinkish-brown sometimes with dark veining or heart (steamed beech is reddish brown); has fleck figure on quarter-cut material; straight grain; fine texture.
WORKING QUALITIES Dense; medium strength; medium stability; perishable; susceptible to insect attack. Easy to work. Nail or screw holes must be pre-bored. Good turning and steam-bending timber.
FINISHING Excellent.
USES Furniture; high-class joinery; turnery; domestic ware; tools and tool handles; plywood; decorative veneers. Warning: Do not use spalted beech (formed when logs are attacked by fungus) for food utensils.

Red oak *Quercus rubra*

OTHER NAMES American, Northern, or Southern red oak.
TREE CHARACTERISTICS Native to eastern USA and southeastern Canada; also grown in Europe. Height: 90ft (27m).
WOOD Pale brown heartwood with reddish tinge; less figure than other oaks; straight grain; coarse texture.
WORKING QUALITIES Dense (less so than European oak); hard; medium stability; non-durable; sapwood susceptible to insect attack. Northern-grown wood is easier to work than southern-grown. Excellent steam-bending timber. Can be hard to glue. Nail or screw holes must be pre-bored.
FINISHING Good.
USES Furniture; joinery; boat-building; flooring; plywood.

London plane *Platanus × hispanica* "Acerifolia" (synonym *P. acerifolia*)

OTHER NAMES Common or European plane.
TREE CHARACTERISTICS A man-made hybrid, unknown in the wild, planted in Europe and the Americas. Height: 100ft (30m).
WOOD Light reddish-brown heartwood; highly decorative figure on quarter-cut material (see lacewood, p.198); straight grain; fine-medium texture.
WORKING QUALITIES Medium density; medium strength; stable; perishable; sapwood susceptible to insect attack. Satisfactory to work. Can bind during sawing. Medullary rays can tear-out during planing. Good steam-bending timber.
FINISHING Excellent.
USES Furniture; joinery; decorative veneers; turnery.

American cherry *Prunus serotina*

OTHER NAMES Black, cabinet, choke, Edwards Plateau, rum, wild, or whiskey cherry; capulin; New England mahogany.
TREE CHARACTERISTICS Native to eastern North America; also grown in Central and Eastern Europe. Height: 80ft (25m).
WOOD Reddish-brown heartwood, creamy- to pinkish-white sapwood; straight grain; fine texture; good luster.
WORKING QUALITIES Medium density; medium strength; medium stability; medium durability; sapwood susceptible to insect attack. Easy to work. Good steam-bending timber.
FINISHING Excellent. Can be stained to imitate mahogany.
USES Furniture; high-quality joinery; turnery; carving; musical-instrument parts; decorative veneers.

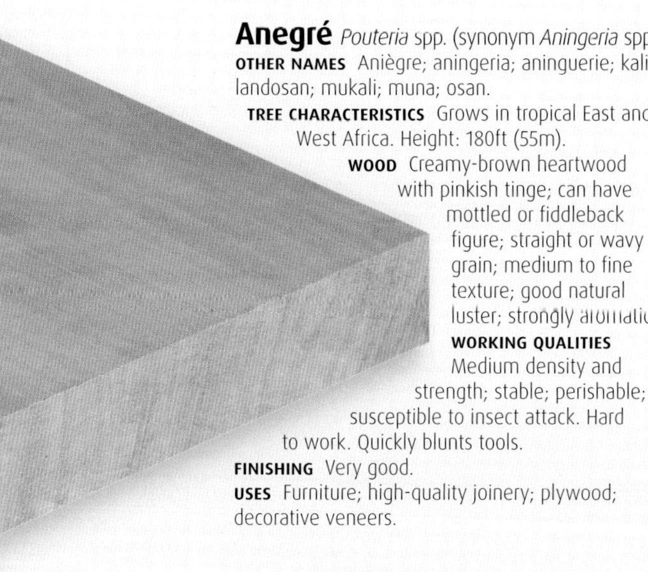

Anegré *Pouteria* spp. (synonym *Aningeria* spp.)

OTHER NAMES Aniègre; aningeria; aninguerie; kali; landosan; mukali; muna; osan.

TREE CHARACTERISTICS Grows in tropical East and West Africa. Height: 180ft (55m).

WOOD Creamy-brown heartwood with pinkish tinge; can have mottled or fiddleback figure; straight or wavy grain; medium to fine texture; good natural luster; strongly aromatic.

WORKING QUALITIES Medium density and strength; stable; perishable; susceptible to insect attack. Hard to work. Quickly blunts tools.

FINISHING Very good.

USES Furniture; high-quality joinery; plywood; decorative veneers.

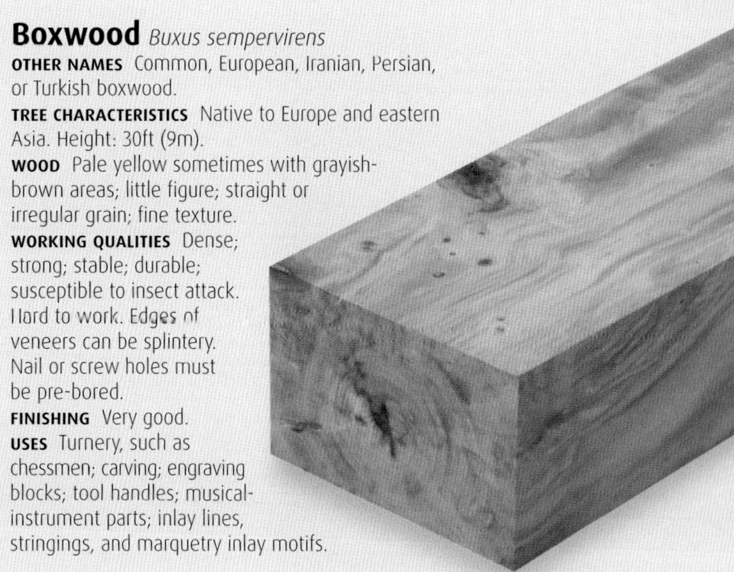

Boxwood *Buxus sempervirens*

OTHER NAMES Common, European, Iranian, Persian, or Turkish boxwood.

TREE CHARACTERISTICS Native to Europe and eastern Asia. Height: 30ft (9m).

WOOD Pale yellow sometimes with grayish-brown areas; little figure; straight or irregular grain; fine texture.

WORKING QUALITIES Dense; strong; stable; durable; susceptible to insect attack. Hard to work. Edges of veneers can be splintery. Nail or screw holes must be pre-bored.

FINISHING Very good.

USES Turnery, such as chessmen; carving; engraving blocks; tool handles; musical-instrument parts; inlay lines, stringings, and marquetry inlay motifs.

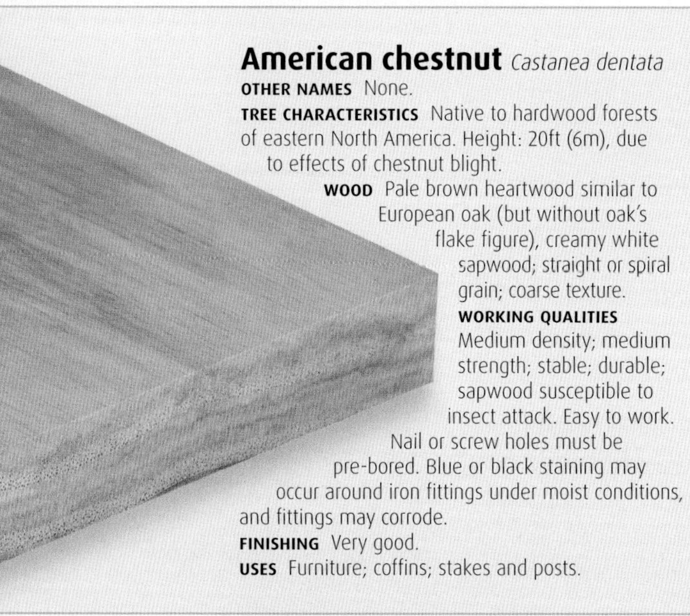

American chestnut *Castanea dentata*

OTHER NAMES None.

TREE CHARACTERISTICS Native to hardwood forests of eastern North America. Height: 20ft (6m), due to effects of chestnut blight.

WOOD Pale brown heartwood similar to European oak (but without oak's flake figure), creamy white sapwood; straight or spiral grain; coarse texture.

WORKING QUALITIES Medium density; medium strength; stable; durable; sapwood susceptible to insect attack. Easy to work. Nail or screw holes must be pre-bored. Blue or black staining may occur around iron fittings under moist conditions, and fittings may corrode.

FINISHING Very good.

USES Furniture; coffins; stakes and posts.

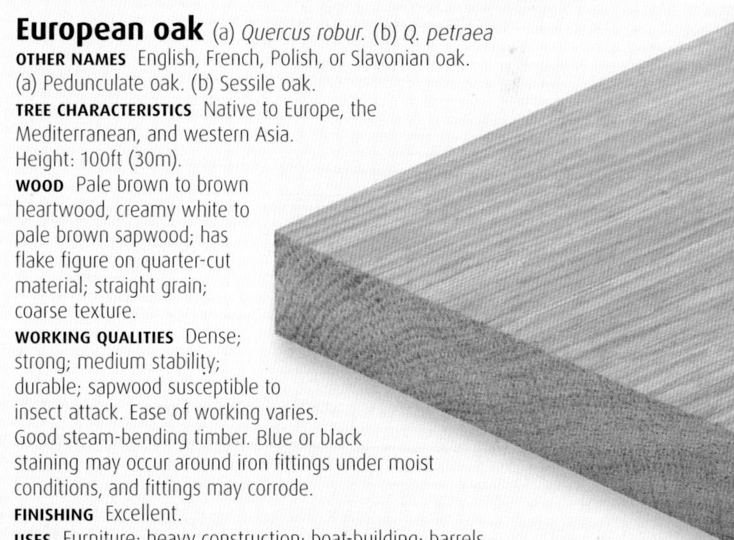

European oak (a) *Quercus robur.* (b) *Q. petraea*

OTHER NAMES English, French, Polish, or Slavonian oak. (a) Pedunculate oak. (b) Sessile oak.

TREE CHARACTERISTICS Native to Europe, the Mediterranean, and western Asia. Height: 100ft (30m).

WOOD Pale brown to brown heartwood, creamy white to pale brown sapwood; has flake figure on quarter-cut material; straight grain; coarse texture.

WORKING QUALITIES Dense; strong; medium stability; durable; sapwood susceptible to insect attack. Ease of working varies. Good steam-bending timber. Blue or black staining may occur around iron fittings under moist conditions, and fittings may corrode.

FINISHING Excellent.

USES Furniture; heavy construction; boat-building; barrels.

American mahogany *Swietenia macrophylla*

OTHER NAMES Large-leaved mahogany; acajou; acahou; aguano; baywood; caoba; zopilote gateado.

TREE CHARACTERISTICS Grows in tropical Central and South America. Height: 150ft (45m).

WOOD Light to dark reddish-brown heartwood; can have curly, pommelle, fiddleback or other figuring; straight or interlocked grain; medium–coarse texture; good natural luster.

WORKING QUALITIES Medium density; low-medium strength; stable; durable; sapwood susceptible to insect attack. Easy to work.

FINISHING Excellent.

USES (Reproduction) furniture; joinery; boat-building; musical instruments; turnery; decorative veneers.

American beech *Fagus grandifolia*

OTHER NAMES Beech.

TREE CHARACTERISTICS Native to hardwood forests of eastern North America. Height: 150ft (45m).

WOOD Reddish-brown heartwood, creamy white sapwood; has fleck figure on quarter-cut material; straight grain; fine texture (but slightly coarser than European beech).

WORKING QUALITIES Dense (slightly more so than European Beech); medium strength; medium stability; perishable; susceptible to insect attack. Easy to work. Can burn when cross-cutting or drilling. Good turning and steam-bending timber.

FINISHING Good.

USES Furniture; high-class joinery; turnery; tools and tool handles; plywood; decorative veneers; food containers.

Ramin *Gonystylus bancanus* and *G. macrophyllum*

OTHER NAMES Lanutan-bagyo; melawis; ramin telur.
TREE CHARACTERISTICS Native to freshwater swamps in Southeast Asia, including Sarawak and western Malaysia. Height: 80ft (25m).
WOOD Straw-yellow to yellowish-brown; little figure; straight or interlocked grain; fine texture.
WORKING QUALITIES Dense; hard but not stiff; not stable; perishable; sapwood susceptible to insect attack. Satisfactory to work. Unsuitable for steam-bending. Nail or screw holes must be pre-bored.
FINISHING Satisfactory, provided grain is filled.
USES Furniture; joinery; carving; turnery; veneers; plywood; doweling; picture frames.

Sassafras *Sassafras albidum* (synonym *S. officinale*)

OTHER NAMES Aguetree; black ash; cinnamon wood; golden elm; red sassafras; saxifrax tree.
TREE CHARACTERISTICS Native to eastern USA and southern Ontario, Canada. Height: 90ft (27m).
WOOD Pale to dark brown heartwood; straight grain; coarse texture; strong scent.
WORKING QUALITIES Light-medium density; soft and flexible; stable; moderate durability; sapwood susceptible to insect attack. Easy to work. Nail or screw holes near edges of boards must be pre-bored. Not available in very large sizes.
FINISHING Good.
USES Furniture; boat-building; fencing; decorative veneers.

European elm (a) *Ulmus glabra.* (b) *Ulmus × hollandica.* (c) *U. procera* and other species

OTHER NAMES (a) Mountain, Scots, Scottish, white, or wych elm; Irish leamhan. (b) Cork bark or Dutch elm. (c) English or nave elm.
TREE CHARACTERISTICS Native to (a) and (b) Northern Europe; (c) England and Wales. Height: 150ft (45m).
WOOD Pinkish-brown or dull brown heartwood sometimes with olive-green streaks; has fleck figure on quarter-cut material; straight or irregular grain; coarse texture.
WORKING QUALITIES Medium density, strength, and stability; non-durable in air but very durable under water; susceptible to insect attack; split-resistant. Satisfactory to work. Can be woolly. (c) is unsuitable for steam-bending.
FINISHING Very good; (b) is best.
USES Boat-building; furniture; flooring; veneers.

American red gum *Liquidambar styraciflua*

OTHER NAMES Heartwood sold as: American sweet gum; bilsted; redgum; satin walnut. Sapwood sold as: sapgum; hazel pine.
TREE CHARACTERISTICS Native to southeastern USA, Mexico, and Central America. Height: 150ft (45m).
WOOD Pinkish- to reddish-brown heartwood with dark streaks, creamy white sapwood; mottled or marbled figure; irregular grain; fine texture; good luster.
WORKING QUALITIES Medium density and strength; low stability; non-durable; susceptible to insect attack. Easy to work. Unsuitable for steam-bending.
FINISHING Excellent. Can be stained to imitate walnut.
USES Furniture; joinery; plywood; turnery.

Japanese oak *Quercus mongolica*

OTHER NAMES Manchurian Oak; Ohnara.
TREE CHARACTERISTICS Grows in northeastern Asia, including Japan. Height: 100ft (30m).
WOOD Pale brown heartwood with pinkish tinge; has flake figure on quarter-cut material; straight grain; coarse texture. In Japan, slow-grown timber from Hokkaido is traditionally preferred to that from Honshu.
WORKING QUALITIES Dense; medium strength; medium stability; durable; sapwood susceptible to insect attack. Easy to work. Good steam-bending timber.
FINISHING Very good. The timber has particularly good staining qualities.
USES Furniture; joinery; flooring; boat-building; plywood; decorative veneers.

Butternut *Juglans cinerea*

OTHER NAMES White walnut; oilnut; nogal; nogal blanco; nuez meca.
TREE CHARACTERISTICS Native to mixed hardwood forests in northeastern USA and Canada, favouring stream-side banks. Height: 70ft (20m).
WOOD Brown heartwood with darker streaks, creamy- or grayish-white sapwood; straight grain; coarse texture; good natural luster.
WORKING QUALITIES Medium density; soft; medium stability; non-durable; susceptible to insect attack. Easy to work. Cutting edges must be kept sharp because of timber's softness.
FINISHING Excellent.
USES Joinery; boat-building; furniture; carving. A black walnut substitute.

 ENDANGERED SPECIES

African mahogany *Khaya antotheca, K. ivorensis,* and related species

OTHER NAMES Khaya.
TREE CHARACTERISTICS Grows in tropical Africa. Height: 140ft (43m).
WOOD Light pinkish- to deep reddish-brown heartwood; straight or interlocked grain; can have striped or roey figure on quarter-cut material; medium-coarse texture; good natural luster.
WORKING QUALITIES Medium density; low–medium strength; stable; moderate durability; susceptible to insect attack. Easy to work. Can be woolly. Reduced cutting angle required for planing or molding.
FINISHING Excellent.
USES Furniture; boat-building; plywood.

Silky oak (a) *Cardwellia sublimis.* (b) *Grevillea robusta.* (c) *Roupala brasiliensis* and *R. montana*

OTHER NAMES (a) Australian, northern, or Queensland silky oak; bull oak; golden spanglewood; lacewood; oongaary. (b) Australian or southern silky oak; grevillea. (c) Brazilian or ropala lacewood; carne de vaca; louro faia.
TREE CHARACTERISTICS Native to: (a) Queensland, (b) eastern Australia, (c) tropical South America. Height: (a) 120ft (37m), (b) 150ft (45m), (c) 60ft (18m).
WOOD Pinkish- to reddish-brown heartwood; large rays give strong figure on quarter-cut material; mostly straight grain; coarse texture.
WOOD CHARACTERISTICS Medium density, strength, and stability; moderate durability; abrasion-resistant. Easy to work.
FINISHING Good.
USES Decorative veneers; (a) furniture; (c) musical instruments.

Red alder *Alnus rubra*

OTHER NAMES Oregon, Pacific Coast, or Western alder.
TREE CHARACTERISTICS Native to lowland areas of the Pacific coastal forests of North America. Height: 120ft (37m).
WOODS Pale yellow to reddish-brown; usually little figure; straight grain; fine texture.
WORKING QUALITIES Medium density; soft and weak; stable; perishable (but durable under water); susceptible to insect attack. Easy to work. Reduced cutting angle required for planing. Good steam-bending timber.
FINISHING Good.
USES Turnery; carving; kitchen cabinets; plywood; veneers.

South American cedar *Cedrela fissilis*

OTHER NAMES Brazilian or Peruvian cedar; cigar-box cedar; cedro batata, rosa, or vermelho.
TREE CHARACTERISTICS Grows in South and Central America, but not Chile. Height: 95ft (30m). Not a softwood, despite its common name.
WOOD Pinkish-brown to dark reddish-brown; straight or interlocked grain; medium-coarse texture; resinous; strongly aromatic.
WORKING QUALITIES Medium density; medium strength; very stable; durable; susceptible to insect attack. Easy to work. Can be woolly.
FINISHING Good, but presence of resin can affect staining and polishing.
USES Furniture, including blanket boxes; high-quality joinery; cigar boxes; flooring; construction; boat-building; plywood; decorative veneers.

Pear (a) *Pyrus communis.* (b) *Sorbus torminalis*

OTHER NAMES (a) Common pear; pearwood. (b) Swiss pear; wild servise tree.
TREE CHARACTERISTICS Native to Europe and western Asia. Height: (a) 40ft (12m); (b) 85ft (25m).
WOOD Pinkish-brown heartwood (steamed pear is slightly darker); usually little figure, but can have mottling on quarter-cut material; straight grain; fine texture.
WORKING QUALITIES Dense; hard but brittle; stable; perishable; susceptible to insect attack. Satisfactory to work. Excellent for turning. Unsuitable for steam-bending.
FINISHING Excellent. Can be stained black as an ebony substitute.
USES Decorative turnery; musical instruments.

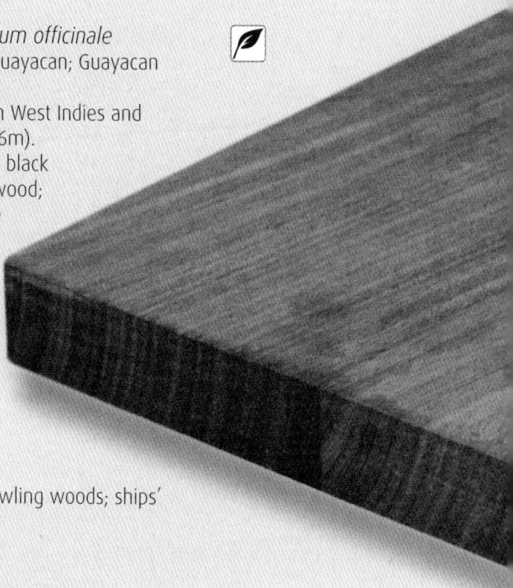

Lignum vitae *Guaiacum officinale*

OTHER NAMES Bois de Gaiac; Guayacan; Guayacan negro; ironwood; palo santo.
TREE CHARACTERISTICS Grows in West Indies and tropical America. Height: 20ft (6m).
WOOD Dark greenish-brown to black heartwood, creamy white sapwood; irregular, interlocked grain; fine texture; feels greasy.
WORKING QUALITIES Extremely dense; hard and strong, but can be splintery; medium stability; very durable; self-lubricating. Hard to work. Hard to glue. Unsuitable for steam-bending. Excellent turning timber.
FINISHING Excellent.
USES Carving mallet heads; bowling woods; ships' propeller bearings; turnery.

Gonçalo alves *(a) Astronium fraxinifolium. (b) A. graveolens*

OTHER NAMES Bossona; kingwood; locustwood; tigerwood; zebrawood; zorrowood. (a) Mura; urunday-para. (b) Aderno; chitibao; guarita; urunday.
TREE CHARACTERISTICS Grows in (a) Brazil, (b) Mexico. Height: 120ft (37m).
WOOD Reddish-brown heartwood with dark brown streaks giving highly decorative figure, pale grayish-brown sapwood; interlocked grain; medium texture; feels greasy.
WORKING QUALITIES Very dense; strong; stable; very durable. Hard to work. Reduced cutting angle required for planing or molding. Nail or screw holes must be pre-bored. Unsuitable for steam-bending.
FINISHING Excellent.
USES High-quality furniture; turnery; veneers.

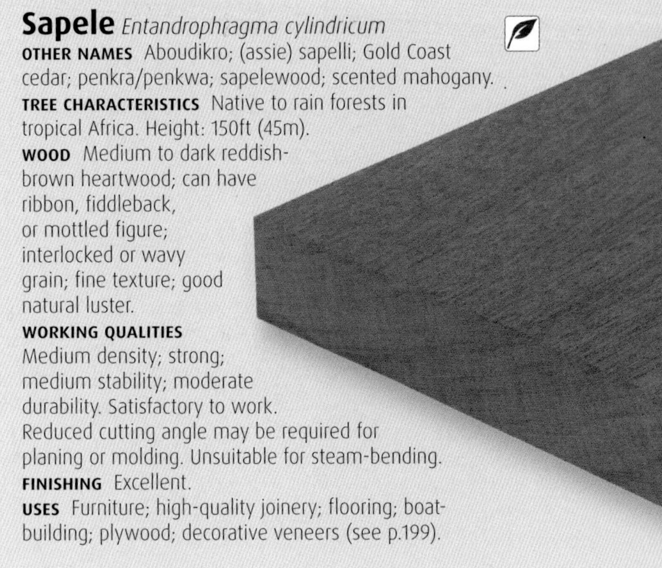

Sapele *Entandrophragma cylindricum*

OTHER NAMES Aboudikro; (assie) sapelli; Gold Coast cedar; penkra/penkwa; sapelewood; scented mahogany.
TREE CHARACTERISTICS Native to rain forests in tropical Africa. Height: 150ft (45m).
WOOD Medium to dark reddish-brown heartwood; can have ribbon, fiddleback, or mottled figure; interlocked or wavy grain; fine texture; good natural luster.
WORKING QUALITIES Medium density; strong; medium stability; moderate durability. Satisfactory to work. Reduced cutting angle may be required for planing or molding. Unsuitable for steam-bending.
FINISHING Excellent.
USES Furniture; high-quality joinery; flooring; boat-building; plywood; decorative veneers (see p.199).

Osage orange *Maclura pomifera*

OTHER NAMES Bow wood; bodare; bodark; bois d'arc; hedge-apple; horse-apple; naranjo chino; mock-orange; osage.
TREE CHARACTERISTICS Native to Oklahoma, Texas, and Arkansas (planted elsewhere in USA), growing on valley floors and prairies. Height: 50ft (15m).
WOOD Orangey-brown heartwood, pale yellow sapwood; straight grain; coarse texture; good natural luster.
WORKING QUALITIES Dense; strong; very stable; extremely durable. Hard to work. Quickly blunts tools. Nail or screw holes must be pre-bored.
FINISHING Good.
USES Posts and stakes; railroad ties; tobacco pipes; turnery.

Bubinga *Guibourtia demeusei*

OTHER NAMES African rosewood; buvenga; essingang; kevazingo.
TREE CHARACTERISTICS Grows in Cameroon, Gabon, and DRC. Height: 70ft (20m).
WOOD Reddish-brown heartwood with purplish-brown veining, creamy white sapwood; straight or irregular grain; coarse texture; good natural luster.
WORKING QUALITIES Very dense; medium strength; stable; medium durability; susceptible to insect attack. Satisfactory to work. Reduced cutting angle required for planing or molding. Nail or screw holes must be pre-bored. Unsuitable for steam-bending. Can be hard to glue.
FINISHING Excellent.
USES Turnery; boat-building; flooring; decorative veneers (see kevasingo, p.199).

Teak *Tectona grandis*

OTHER NAMES Djati; gia thi; kyun; jati sak; mai sak; pahi; sagon; sagwan; tegina; tedi; tekku.
TREE CHARACTERISTICS Native to rain forests in Asia; also grown in Africa, the Caribbean, and Central America. Height: 150ft (45m).
WOOD Golden-brown to brown heartwood; can have mottled figure; straight or wavy grain; coarse texture; feels greasy.
WORKING QUALITIES Medium density; strong, hard, but somewhat brittle; very stable; very durable; susceptible to insect attack; fire- and acid-resistant. Satisfactory to work. Nail or screw holes must be pre-bored. Glues best on freshly sanded surfaces.
FINISHING Satisfactory.
USES Ship- and boat-building; furniture; garden furniture; flooring; joinery.

Red meranti *Shorea spp.*

OTHER NAMES Dark red meranti; Philippine mahogany; red lauan; red seraya.
TREE CHARACTERISTICS Grows in Sabah, Brunei, Philippines, Sarawak, and western Malaysia. Height: 200ft (60m). Not a true mahogany.
WOOD Medium to dark brownish-red heartwood with white resin streaks; interlocked grain; coarse texture.
WORKING QUALITIES Dense; medium strength; stable; moderate durability; sapwood susceptible to insect attack. Easy to work. Unsuitable for steam-bending.
FINISHING Good.
USES Boat-building; flooring; mahogany substitute for furniture and joinery.

ENDANGERED SPECIES

Zebrano *Microberlinia brazzavillensis* and *M. bisulcata*

OTHER NAMES (African) zebrawood; allen ele; amouk; ele; okwen; zingana.

TREE CHARACTERISTICS Native to West Africa. Height: 150ft (45m).

WOOD Brownish-yellow heartwood with dark brown or black streaks giving bold striped figure on quarter-cut material, creamy white sapwood; interlocked or wavy grain; coarse texture; good natural luster.

WORKING QUALITIES Dense; strong and hard; stable; non-durable. Hard to work. Sanding gives a better finish than planing. Nail or screw holes must be pre-bored. Unsuitable for steam-bending.

FINISHING Very good, provided grain is filled.

USES Decorative veneers; turnery; furniture.

Karri *Eucalyptus diversicolor*

OTHER NAMES None.

TREE CHARACTERISTICS Native to high-rainfall forests of southwestern Australia; also grown in South Africa. Height: 200ft (60m).

WOOD Reddish-brown heartwood; stripe figure on quarter-cut material; interlocked or wavy grain; moderately coarse texture. Similar to jarrah (see p.194).

WORKING QUALITIES Very dense; strong and hard; not stable; durable; fire-resistant. Hard to work. Quickly blunts tools. Reduced cutting angle required for planing or molding. Nail or screw holes must be pre-bored. Good steam-bending timber provided knots are absent.

FINISHING Satisfactory.

USES Heavy construction; ship-building; furniture.

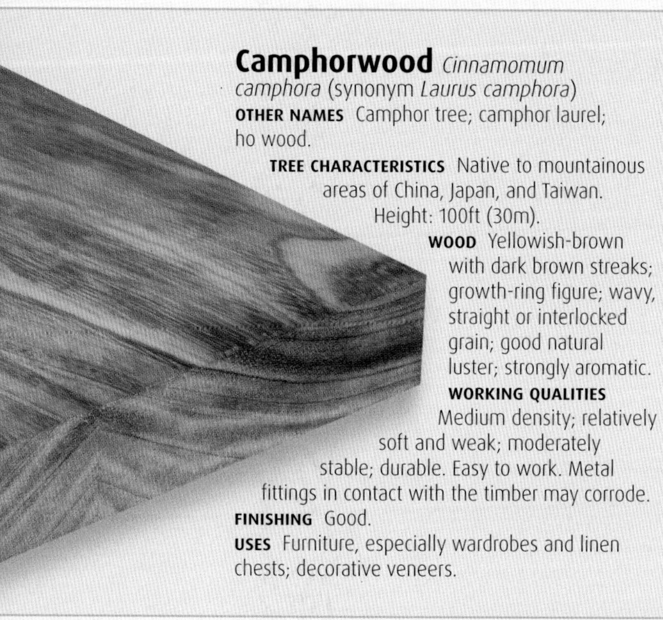

Camphorwood *Cinnamomum camphora* (synonym *Laurus camphora*)

OTHER NAMES Camphor tree; camphor laurel; ho wood.

TREE CHARACTERISTICS Native to mountainous areas of China, Japan, and Taiwan. Height: 100ft (30m).

WOOD Yellowish-brown with dark brown streaks; growth-ring figure; wavy, straight or interlocked grain; good natural luster; strongly aromatic.

WORKING QUALITIES Medium density; relatively soft and weak; moderately stable; durable. Easy to work. Metal fittings in contact with the timber may corrode.

FINISHING Good.

USES Furniture, especially wardrobes and linen chests; decorative veneers.

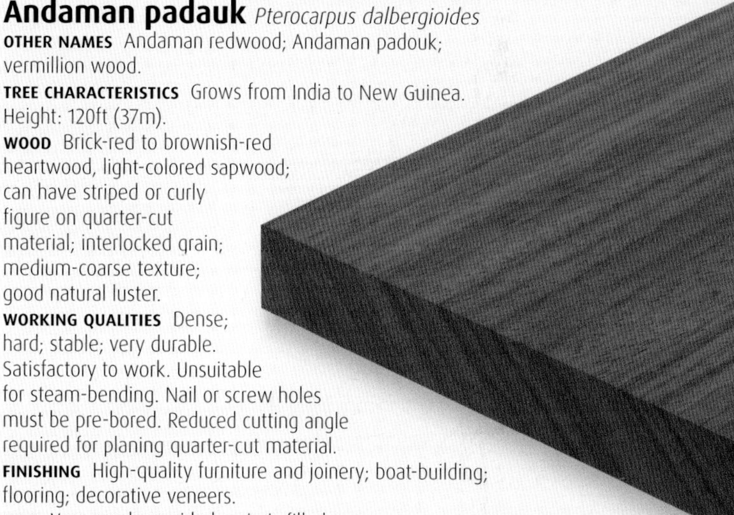

Andaman padauk *Pterocarpus dalbergioides*

OTHER NAMES Andaman redwood; Andaman padouk; vermillion wood.

TREE CHARACTERISTICS Grows from India to New Guinea. Height: 120ft (37m).

WOOD Brick-red to brownish-red heartwood, light-colored sapwood; can have striped or curly figure on quarter-cut material; interlocked grain; medium-coarse texture; good natural luster.

WORKING QUALITIES Dense; hard; stable; very durable. Satisfactory to work. Unsuitable for steam-bending. Nail or screw holes must be pre-bored. Reduced cutting angle required for planing quarter-cut material.

FINISHING High-quality furniture and joinery; boat-building; flooring; decorative veneers.

USES Very good, provided grain is filled.

Tasmanian blue gum *Eucalyptus globulus*

OTHER NAMES Blue or southern blue gum; bluegum eucalyptus; fever tree.

TREE CHARACTERISTICS Native to southern Australia and Tasmania; also grown in USA, Chile, and the Mediterranean region. Height: 150ft (45m).

WOOD Pale brown heartwood with pinkish tinge; interlocked grain; medium texture.

WORKING QUALITIES Very dense; very hard and strong; not stable; moderately durable; susceptible to insect attack. Easy to work.

FINISHING Good.

USES Construction; joinery; flooring; furniture.

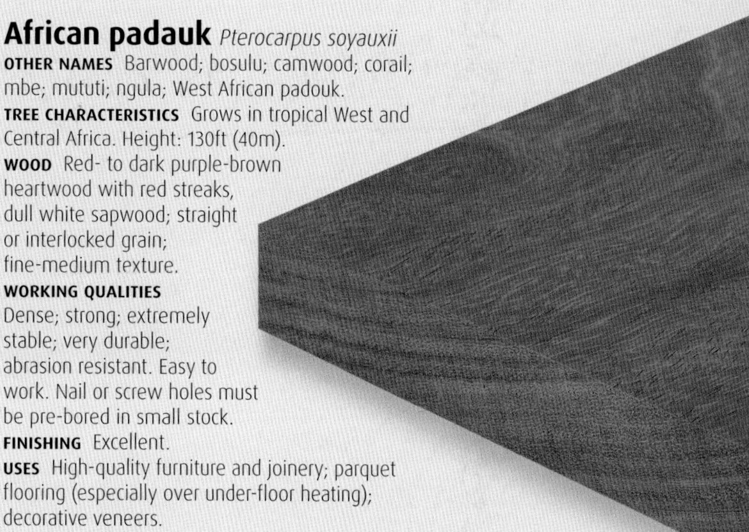

African padauk *Pterocarpus soyauxii*

OTHER NAMES Barwood; bosulu; camwood; corail; mbe; mututi; ngula; West African padouk.

TREE CHARACTERISTICS Grows in tropical West and Central Africa. Height: 130ft (40m).

WOOD Red- to dark purple-brown heartwood with red streaks, dull white sapwood; straight or interlocked grain; fine-medium texture.

WORKING QUALITIES Dense; strong; extremely stable; very durable; abrasion resistant. Easy to work. Nail or screw holes must be pre-bored in small stock.

FINISHING Excellent.

USES High-quality furniture and joinery; parquet flooring (especially over under-floor heating); decorative veneers.

River red gum *Eucalyptus camaldulensis* (synonym *E. rostrata*)

OTHER NAMES Murray red gum; red gum.
TREE CHARACTERISTICS Native to riverbanks in southern Australia; also grown in South Africa and the Iberian peninsula. Height: 165ft (50m).
WOOD Pink to brownish-red heartwood, distinct from paler sapwood; can have fiddleback figure; interlocked grain; fine texture; resinous.
WORKING QUALITIES Very dense; strong; very durable. Hard to work. Reduced cutting angle required for planing or molding. Nail or screw holes must be pre-bored. Unsuitable for steam-bending. Hard to glue.
FINISHING Very good.
USES Shipbuilding; heavy construction; joinery; weatherboards; flooring; decorative veneers.

Makoré (a) *Tieghemella heckelii* (synonym *Mimusops heckelii*). (b) *T. africana*

OTHER NAMES (a) Abacu; agamokwe; African cherry; bacu; baku; cherry mahogany. (b) Douka; dumori.
TREE CHARACTERISTICS Native to rain forest in tropical West Africa. Height: 150ft (45m). Not a true cherry or mahogany.
WOOD Pink to reddish-brown heartwood; can have attractive moiré figure; grain usually straight; fine texture; good natural luster.
WORKING QUALITIES Medium density; medium strength; stable; very durable. Hard to work. Quickly blunts tools. Nail or screw holes must be pre-bored.
FINISHING Excellent, provided grain is filled.
USES Furniture; joinery; laboratory benches; marine plywood; decorative veneers. A mahogany substitute.

Jarrah *Eucalyptus marginata*

OTHER NAMES Swan or Western Australian mahogany.
TREE CHARACTERISTICS Native to coastal belt of southwestern Western Australia. Height: 150ft (45m).
WOOD Dark brownish-red heartwood, pale yellow sapwood; boat-shaped marks caused by beefsteak fungus give attractive figure on flat-sawn material; straight, interlocked, or wavy grain; coarse texture.
WORKING QUALITIES Very dense; hard and strong; medium stability; very durable. Hard to work. Reduced cutting angle required for planing or molding. Nail or screw holes must be pre-bored.
FINISHING Very good.
USES Marine construction; shipbuilding; railroad ties; weatherboards; furniture; decorative veneers.

Blackbean *Castanospermum australe*

OTHER NAMES Bean tree; Moreton Bay bean; Australian or Moreton Bay chestnut.
TREE CHARACTERISTICS Native to rain forest in northeastern Australia; also grows in New Caledonia, Canada, and Vanuatu. Height: 120ft (37m).
WOOD Chocolate-brown heartwood with grayish streaks, white-yellow sapwood; straight or interlocked grain; coarse texture; feels greasy.
WORKING QUALITIES Dense; hard and brittle; medium stability; durable. Hard to work. Lighter colored areas can crumble when planed. Can be hard to glue. Unsuitable for steam-bending.
FINISHING Excellent.
USES High-quality furniture and joinery; turnery.

Spotted gum (a) *Corymbia maculata* (synonym *Eucalyptus maculata*). (b) *E. citriodora*

OTHER NAMES (a) Spotted iron gum. (b) Lemon eucalyptus, lemon-scented gum.
TREE CHARACTERISTICS Native to eastern Australia. Height: 130ft (40m).
WOOD Light brown to dark reddish-brown heartwood, white sapwood; can have fiddleback figure; straight or wavy grain; coarse texture; feels greasy.
WORKING QUALITIES Very dense; hard and strong; moderate stability; durable; sapwood susceptible to insect attack. Satisfactory to work. Reduced cutting angle required for planing or molding. Nail or screw holes must be pre-bored. (a) Good steam-bending timber.
FINISHING Very good.
USES Tool handles; boat-building; flooring; joinery.

Iroko *Milicia excelsa* (synonym *Chlorophora excelsa*)

OTHER NAMES African teak; band; counter wood; intule; kambala; lusanga; mokongo; moreira; mvule; mvulu; odum; rokko; tule; yellowwood.
TREE CHARACTERISTICS Grows in tropical Africa. Height: 160ft (50m).
WOOD Golden-orange to brown heartwood, creamy- to yellowish-white sapwood; can have mottle figure; interlocked grain; coarse texture.
WORKING QUALITIES Medium density; medium strength; stable; very durable; susceptible to insect attack. Satisfactory to work. Quickly blunts tools. Reduced cutting angle required for planing or molding quarter-cut material.
FINISHING Excellent, provided grain is filled.
USES Ship-building; joinery; furniture. A teak substitute.

ENDANGERED SPECIES

Courbaril *Hymenaea courbaril*

OTHER NAMES Algarrobo; Brazilian cherry; copal; Courbaril plum; guapinal; locust gum; Jatai vermelho; jutaby; marbre; West Indian locust; Surinam teak.
TREE CHARACTERISTICS Grows in Central and South America, and the West Indies. Height: 100ft (30m).
WOODS Reddish to orange-brown heartwood with dark streaks giving highly decorative figure, creamy white sapwood; interlocked grain; medium-coarse texture.
WORKING QUALITIES Very dense; very strong and hard; stable; moderate durability. Satisfactory to work. Reduced cutting angle required for planing or molding.
FINISHING Good.
USES Furniture; joinery; turnery; flooring.

Afrormosia *Pericopsis elata*

OTHER NAMES Assamela; ayin; egbi; ejen; eyen; kokrodua; mohole; ole; olel pardo; tento.
TREE CHARACTERISTICS Grows in West Africa. Height: 150ft (45m).
WOOD Orangey-brown heartwood, pale brown sapwood; can have "ropey" or mottled figure; straight or interlocked grain; medium-fine texture; good natural luster.
WORKING QUALITIES Dense; strong; stable; very durable. Easy to work. Reduced cutting angle required for planing. Nail or screw holes must be pre-bored. Blue-black staining may occur around iron fittings under moist conditions, and fittings may corrode.
FINISHING Excellent.
USES Boat-building; joinery; furniture; flooring; veneers.

Brush box *Lophostemon confertus* (synonym *Tristania conferta*)

OTHER NAMES Brisbane or red box.
TREE CHARACTERISTICS Native to wet sclerophyll and moist open forests in eastern Australia; also grown in Hawaii and Madagascar. Height: 100ft (30m).
WOOD Pinkish-gray to reddish-brown heartwood; interlocked grain; fine texture.
WORKING QUALITIES Very dense; hard; durable; abrasion-resistant. Hard to work. Quickly blunts tools. Unsuitable for steam-bending. Can be hard to glue.
FINISHING Good.
USES Flooring, including bridge decking; mallets; pulley blocks; weatherboards.

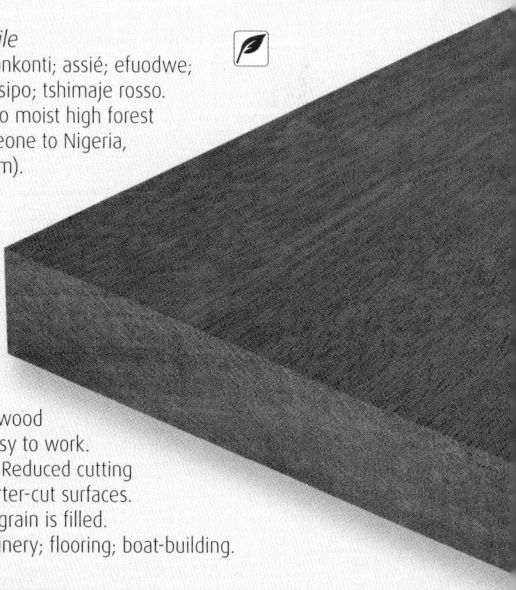

Utile *Entandrophragma utile*

OTHER NAMES Abebay; afau-konkonti; assié; efuodwe; liboyo; kisi-kosi; mebrou zuiri; sipo; tshimaje rosso.
TREE CHARACTERISTICS Native to moist high forest in tropical Africa, from Sierra Leone to Nigeria, and Uganda. Height: 200ft (60m).
WOOD Dark reddish-brown heartwood, pale brown sapwood; can have striped figure on quarter-cut material; interlocked grain; medium texture; good natural luster.
WORKING QUALITIES Medium density; hard; medium stability; durable; sapwood susceptible to insect attack. Easy to work. Unsuitable for steam-bending. Reduced cutting angle required for planing quarter-cut surfaces.
FINISHING Excellent, provided grain is filled.
USES Furniture; high-quality joinery; flooring; boat-building.

Black walnut *Juglans nigra*

OTHER NAMES (Black) American, Canadian, or Virginia walnut; walnut; canaletto.
TREE CHARACTERISTICS Native to mixed hardwood forests of eastern USA and Canada; also grown in Europe. Height: 70ft (20m).
WOOD Dark brown to purplish-black heartwood, pale brown sapwood; highly figured, often burry, timber comes from stumpwood; straight or wavy grain; medium-coarse texture.
WORKING QUALITIES Medium density; tough and hard; stable; very durable; sapwood susceptible to insect attack. Easy to work. Good steam-bending timber.
FINISHING Excellent.
USES High-quality furniture; gunstocks; veneers.

Australian blackwood *Acacia melanoxylon*

OTHER NAMES Tasmanian blackwood; black wattle.
TREE CHARACTERISTICS Native to mountains of southeast Australia; also grown in South Africa, India, Sri Lanka, Chile, and Argentina. Height: 80ft (25m).
WOOD Yellow-brown to dark reddish-brown heartwood with darker brown growth rings, creamy- to grayish-white sapwood; can have fiddleback figuring; straight, interlocked, or wavy grain; medium texture; good natural luster.
WORKING QUALITIES Medium density; hard; stable; very durable; susceptible to insect attack. Satisfactory to work. Reduced cutting angle required for planing or molding. Can be hard to glue. Good steam-bending timber.
FINISHING Excellent.
USES High-quality furniture; turnery; boat-building; veneers.

Purpleheart *Peltogyne* spp.

OTHER NAMES Amaranth; aramante; guarabu; koroboreli; morado; nazareno; pau roxo; purplewood; saka; sakavalli; tananeo; violetwood.
TREE CHARACTERISTICS Grows in tropical Central and South America. Height: 150ft (45m).
WOOD Vivid purple heartwood matures to dark brown, dull white sapwood; striped or roey figure on quarter-cut timber; straight or interlocked grain; fine to moderate texture; good natural luster.
WORKING QUALITIES Very dense; stiff and strong; stable; very durable. Hard to work. Quickly blunts tools. Nail or screw holes must be pre-bored. Good turning timber.
FINISHING Excellent.
USES Heavy construction work such as bridges or docks; flooring; furniture; turnery; veneers.

Cocobolo *Dalbergia retusa*

OTHER NAMES Granadillo; grenadillo.
TREE CHARACTERISTICS Grows in western Central America. Height: 60ft (18m).
WOOD Red-brown heartwood, with yellow, black, or purple streaks giving highly decorative figure, yellowish-white sapwood; irregular grain; fine texture; good natural luster.
WORKING QUALITIES Extremely dense; hard and very strong; stable; very durable. Satisfactory to work. Reduced cutting angle required for planing or molding. Hard to glue. Good turning timber.
FINISHING Excellent.
USES Turnery; small decorative items; clubs; cutlery handles; decorative veneers.

Queensland walnut
Endiandra palmerstonii

OTHER NAMES Australian (black) walnut; Australian laurel; oriental wood; walnut bean.
TREE CHARACTERISTICS Native to coastal tableland rain forest in northeast Australia. Height: 140ft (43m). Not a true walnut.
WOOD Dark brown heartwood with pink, green, or black streaks, pale brown sapwood; can have attractive checkered figure; irregular grain; medium texture; good natural luster.
WORKING QUALITIES Dense; hard but brittle; non-durable; susceptible to insect attack. Hard to work. Quickly blunts tools. Tungsten-carbide tipped (TCT) blades advised for sawing and planing.
FINISHING Very good.
USES High-quality furniture; flooring; veneers.

Indian rosewood *Dalbergia latifolia*

OTHER NAMES Black, Bombay, East Indian, Indonesian, or Sonokeling rosewood; Indian or Bombay blackwood; biti; eravidi; Indian or Java palisander; kalaruk; malabar; shisham; sissoo.
TREE CHARACTERISTICS Grows in southern India and Indonesia; Height: 100ft (30m).
WOOD Dark purplish-brown heartwood with darker streaks, creamy white sapwood; can have ribbon figure; interlocked grain; moderately coarse texture; strongly aromatic.
WORKING QUALITIES Very dense; strong but not stiff; extremely stable; very durable. Hard to work. Unsuitable for nailing.
FINISHING Excellent, provided grain is filled.
USES High-quality furniture; musical instruments; veneers.

Pau ferro *Swartzia madagascariensis*

OTHER NAMES Boto; cimbe; kampanga; kisasamba; msekeseke; mussacuasso; nacuata; oken.
TREE CHARACTERISTICS Grows in Sudan, Mozambique, and Zimbabwe. Height: 130ft (40m).
WOOD Dark reddish-brown heartwood, with yellow or dark brown bands; wavy or interlocked grain; medium texture.
WORKING QUALITIES Extremely dense; strong, hard, and stiff; medium stability; durable; susceptible to insect attack. Hard to work. Nail or screw holes must be pre-bored.
FINISHING Excellent.
USES Construction; furniture; flooring; musical-instrument parts; turnery. Note: The pau ferro of Brazil and Bolivia (*Machaerium scleroxylon*) is used as a Brazilian rosewood substitute; also for musical-instrument parts especially guitars; turnery.

Ipê *Handroanthus* spp. (synonym *Tabebuia* spp.)

OTHER NAMES Amapa prieta; bastard lignum vitae; bethabara; green ebony; hakia; ironwood; lapacho; pau d'arco; surinam greenheart; wassiba; yellow poui.
TREE CHARACTERISTICS Grows in Central and South America and Caribbean. Height: 85ft (25m).
WOOD Olive-brown heartwood with lighter or darker streaks, creamy white sapwood; straight or irregular grain; fine texture.
WORKING QUALITIES Extremely dense; very strong; stable; very durable. Hard to work. Reduced cutting angle required for planing or molding. Nail or screw holes must be pre-bored. Unsuitable for steam-bending.
FINISHING Very good.
USES Heavy construction; flooring; furniture; turnery; bows.

ENDANGERED SPECIES

Wengé *Millettia laurentii*

OTHER NAMES Awong; bokonge; dikela; mibotu; nson-so; palissandre du Congo; tshikalakala
TREE CHARACTERISTICS Grows from Cameroon to Mozambique and Tanzania. Height: 60ft (18m).
WOOD Dark brown heartwood with closely-spaced black veins, creamy white or pale yellow sapwood; straight grain; coarse texture.
WORKING QUALITIES Very dense; strong; stable; durable; abrasion-resistant. Satisfactory to work. Hard to glue. Nail or screw holes must be pre-bored.
FINISHING Good, provided grain is filled.
USES Flooring; turnery; joinery; boat-building; decorative veneers.

Kingwood *Dalbergia cearensis*

OTHER NAMES Bois violet; violet wood; violetta.
TREE CHARACTERISTICS Grows in South America (chiefly Brazil). Height: 30ft (10m).
WOOD Purplish-brown heartwood with black or yellow streaks giving highly decorative growth-ring figure, whitish-brown sapwood; straight grain; fine texture; good natural luster; feels waxy.
WORKING QUALITIES Extremely dense; very strong; stable; durable. Satisfactory to work. Only available in small sizes or as veneers.
FINISHING Very good, especially with wax finishes.
USES Decorative veneers and bandings; antique restoration; turnery.

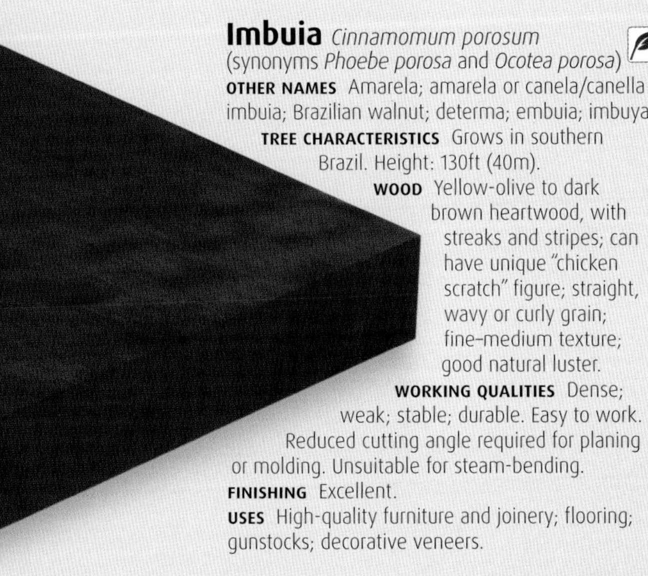

Imbuia *Cinnamomum porosum*

(synonyms *Phoebe porosa* and *Ocotea porosa*)
OTHER NAMES Amarela; amarela or canela/canella imbuia; Brazilian walnut; determa; embuia; imbuya.
TREE CHARACTERISTICS Grows in southern Brazil. Height: 130ft (40m).
WOOD Yellow-olive to dark brown heartwood, with streaks and stripes; can have unique "chicken scratch" figure; straight, wavy or curly grain; fine–medium texture; good natural luster.
WORKING QUALITIES Dense; weak; stable; durable. Easy to work. Reduced cutting angle required for planing or molding. Unsuitable for steam-bending.
FINISHING Excellent.
USES High-quality furniture and joinery; flooring; gunstocks; decorative veneers.

African blackwood *Dalbergia melanoxylon*

OTHER NAMES African grenadillo; Mozambique ebony; mpingo; pau preto.
TREE CHARACTERISTICS Grows in East Africa. Height: 20ft (6m). Not a true ebony.
WOOD Dark brown heartwood with black streaks giving black appearance, creamy-yellow sapwood; little figuring; straight grain; very fine texture; feels greasy.
WORKING QUALITIES Extremely dense; extremely hard and strong; stable; very durable; sapwood susceptible to insect attack. Hard to work. Quickly blunts tools. Nail or screw holes must be pre-bored. Unsuitable for steam-bending.
FINISHING Excellent.
USES Woodwind instruments; turnery; carving.

Ziricote *Cordia dodecandra*

OTHER NAMES Bocote; canalete; laurel; peterebi; sericote; siricote; ziracote. (Note: Other *Cordia* species may be be sold as ziricote.)
TREE CHARACTERISTICS Grows in Belize, Guatemala, Honduras, and Mexico. Height: 90ft (27m).
WOOD Reddish brown heartwood with irregular dark streaks, yellowish-brown sapwood; straight or interlocked grain; medium texture; good natural luster.
WORKING QUALITIES Dense to very dense; hard; stable; moderately durable. Satisfactory to work.
FINISHING Very good.
USES High-class furniture; turnery; gunstocks; flooring; boat-building; decorative veneers.

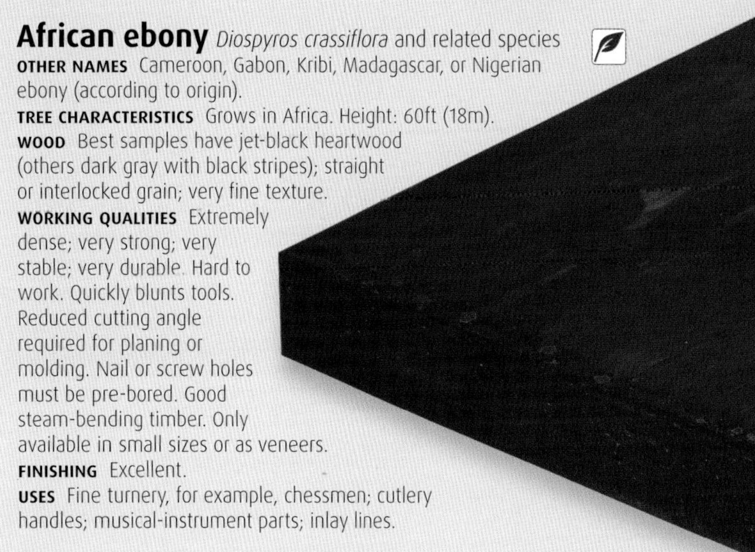

African ebony *Diospyros crassiflora* and related species

OTHER NAMES Cameroon, Gabon, Kribi, Madagascar, or Nigerian ebony (according to origin).
TREE CHARACTERISTICS Grows in Africa. Height: 60ft (18m).
WOOD Best samples have jet-black heartwood (others dark gray with black stripes); straight or interlocked grain; very fine texture.
WORKING QUALITIES Extremely dense; very strong; very stable; very durable. Hard to work. Quickly blunts tools. Reduced cutting angle required for planing or molding. Nail or screw holes must be pre-bored. Good steam-bending timber. Only available in small sizes or as veneers.
FINISHING Excellent.
USES Fine turnery, for example, chessmen; cutlery handles; musical-instrument parts; inlay lines.

Veneers

Veneers are thin sheets of wood that are sliced from a log and used for decoration or construction (as plywood). Today, special cutting equipment can produce large decorative "leaves" less than 1⁄64in (0.5mm) thick. Traditionally, however, veneers were produced by carefully sawing logs into thin layers about 1⁄8in (3mm) thick. Such saw-cut veneers are still made today, and are largely used for antique restoration.

Types of veneers

Veneers are available in a range of natural colors and a variety of figures. The type of figure is determined by the species of wood, and where and how it is cut from the tree. This means that each sheet of veneer is unique. Cutting methods include flat-slicing to display flat grain; quarter-slicing to display side grain and medullary rays, if present; and rotary cutting, which peels off a continuous sheet of veneer from the log's circumference.

Veneers allow the use of timbers that are fragile due to their irregular grain, such as burrs (see below), and therefore have insufficient strength for most projects, such 0as furniture or even jewelry boxes, because the grain might crumble under the weight of the finished item. Cutting such timbers into veneers solves this problem as the solid "ground" onto which the veneer is fixed (see p.158) carries the physical load of the item. Fragile veneers can therefore be used for the same projects as veneers cut from straight-grained timbers, but they must be handled with great care.

Burrs (or burls) are abnormal growths on trunks. Veneers cut from them are extremely beautiful, with their masses of dark knots, but they are weak, due to their irregular grain, and the leaves come in odd shapes and sizes. Wavy-grained woods give a 3D effect figure known as "fiddleback," with bands of light and dark grain "rippling" across the veneer leaf. Other veneers with unusual patterns caused by irregular or wavy grains include bird's-eye maple and masur birch.

Bird's-eye maple *Acer saccharum* and *A. nigrum*

OTHER NAMES None.
TREE CHARACTERISTICS Native to Canada and eastern USA. Height: 120ft (37m).
WOOD Special form of hard maple (see p.185) with pale brown background with reddish tinge, containing tiny knot-like features that are widely spaced apart (unlike in burr timbers); irregular or wavy grain; fine texture; good natural luster.
SIZE AVAILABILITY Veneer sheets are wide, but not long (less than 10ft/ 3m).
FINISHING Excellent.
USES Decorative veneering of high-quality furniture, paneling, doors, and jewelry boxes.

Masur birch *Betula pendula* and *B. pubescens.*

OTHER NAMES Karelian birch or birch burr (but not a true burr).
TREE CHARACTERISTICS Native to Europe, as far north as Lapland. Height: 70ft (20m).
WOOD Special form of birch (see p.187) that has a creamy white to pale brown background with irregular dark brown markings and streaks, which are often curved; irregular grain; fine texture; good natural luster.
SIZE AVAILABILITY Sourced from the base of selected trees. Veneer sheets are wide, but not long (less than 6½ft/ 2m).
FINISHING Very good.
USES Decorative veneering of high-quality furniture, boxes, and paneling.

Fiddleback ash *Fraxinus excelsior*

OTHER NAMES Figured ash.
TREE CHARACTERISTICS Native to Europe (where it favours moist, rich soils) and southwestern Asia. Height: 120ft (37m).
WOOD Special form of ash (see p.186) with cream to pale brown heartwood; rippled grain, giving an undulating 3D-effect figure; coarse texture; good natural luster.
SIZE AVAILABILITY Medium-size widths and lengths.
FINISHING Excellent.
USES Decorative veneering of high-quality furniture.

Fiddleback sycamore *Acer pseudoplatanus*

OTHER NAMES Figured sycamore.
TREE CHARACTERISTICS Native to Europe and western Asia. Height: 100ft (30m).
WOOD Special form of sycamore with creamy white to pale brown heartwood; rippled grain, giving an undulating 3D-effect figure; good natural luster.
SIZE AVAILABILITY Large.
FINISHING Excellent.
USES Decorative veneering of high-quality furniture, paneling, and musical instruments.

Lacewood *Platanus × hispanica* "Acerifolia" (synonym *P. acerifolia*)

OTHER NAMES Quartered planetree.
TREE CHARACTERISTICS A man-made hybrid, unknown in the wild, planted in Europe and the Americas. Height: 100ft (30m).
WOOD Quarter-cut form of London plane (see p.188) with light reddish-brown heartwood; highly decorative "snakeskin" figure comprising flecks of ray tissue; straight grain; fine-medium texture.
SIZE AVAILABILITY Long, medium-width sheets.
FINISHING Excellent.
USES Decorative veneering of high-quality furniture and paneling.

 **ENDANGERED SPECIES**

Cedar of Lebanon *Cedrus libani*

OTHER NAMES True cedar.
TREE CHARACTERISTICS Native to mountains in Asia Minor, chiefly Lebanon; also grown in Europe and USA. Height: 80ft (25m).
WOOD Yellowish-brown to pale brown heartwood with contrasting growth rings, yellowish-white sapwood; straight grain; medium–fine texture; strongly aromatic. Can have ingrown pockets of bark (see p.180).
SIZE AVAILABILITY Good.
FINISHING Good.
USES Decorative veneering, especially for the insides of boxes and wardrobes; also paneling.

European burr walnut *Juglans regia*

OTHER NAMES Common, Black Sea, English, or Persian walnut.
TREE CHARACTERISTICS Native to southeastern Europe, Central Asia, and western China. Height: 100ft (30m).
WOOD Special form of walnut that has grayish-brown background with dark brown streaks, crammed with numerous darker brown knots with circular "eyes"; irregular grain; medium–coarse texture.
SIZE AVAILABILITY Small sheets, sometimes in irregular shapes matching the original outline of the burr.
FINISHING Excellent.
USES Decorative veneering, especially car dashboards and antique–replica furniture.

Steamed pear (a) *Pyrus communis.* (b) *Sorbus torminalis*

OTHER NAMES (a) Common pear; pearwood. (b) Wild servise tree; Swiss pear.
TREE CHARACTERISTICS Native to Europe and western Asia. Height: (a) 40ft (12m); (b) 85ft (25m).
WOOD Medium pinkish-brown heartwood (see p.191); color enhanced by steaming; usually little figure (in the most highly prized veneers), but can have mottling on quarter-cut material; straight grain; fine texture.
SIZE AVAILABILITY Limited by size of tree.
FINISHING Excellent.
USES Decorative veneering of high-quality furniture.

Burr elm *Ulmus glabra, Ulmus × hollandica, U. procera* and other species.

OTHER NAMES Elm burr.
TREE CHARACTERISTICS Native to Europe. Height 150ft (45m).
WOOD Special form of elm (see p.190) with dull brown, orangey-brown or pinkish background, crammed with numerous darker brown knots with circular "eyes"; sometimes has olive-green streaks; irregular grain; coarse texture. Cluster elm has small areas of burrs surrounded by normal straight grain.
SIZE AVAILABILITY Small sheets, sometimes in irregular shapes.
FINISHING Very good.
USES Decorative veneering of small items.

Brown oak *Quercus robur* and *Q. petraea*

OTHER NAMES None.
TREE CHARACTERISTICS Native to Europe and western Asia. Height: 100ft (30m).
WOOD Special form of oak (see p.189) with rich chocolate-brown color; flake figure on quarter-cut material; straight grain; coarse texture. Tiger oak has irregular dark brown streaks. Brown oak and tiger oak burrs are sometimes offered for sale.
SIZE AVAILABILITY Good.
FINISHING Excellent.
USES Decorative veneering of high-quality furniture and paneling.

Pommele sapele *Entandrophragma cylindricum*

OTHER NAMES Pommele.
TREE CHARACTERISTICS Native to rain forests in tropical Africa (Ivory Coast, Cameroon, Uganda, and Tanzania). Height: 150ft (45m).
WOOD Special form of sapele (see p.192) with medium to dark reddish-brown heartwood; mottled figure, giving a "bubbly" 3D appearance with a pattern running perpendicular to the log's axis; interlocked or wavy grain; fine texture; good natural luster.
SIZE AVAILABILITY Very large.
FINISHING Excellent.
USES Decorative veneering, especially doors and paneling.

Kevasingo *Guibourtia demeusei*

OTHER NAMES Pommele bubinga.
TREE CHARACTERISTICS Grows in Cameroon, Gabon, and DRC. Height: 70ft (20m).
WOOD Special form of bubinga (see p.192) with purplish-brown veining on a reddish-brown background; marbled figure of concentric circles, ovals, or irregular shapes defined by the dark-colored veins; irregular grain; coarse texture; good natural luster.
SIZE AVAILABILITY Very large.
FINISHING Excellent.
USES Decorative veneering of high-quality furniture and paneling; humidors.

Vavona burr *Sequoia sempervirens*

OTHER NAMES Redwood burr or sequioa burr.
TREE CHARACTERISTICS Native to coastal strip of California and southeastern Oregon, USA. Height: 300ft (90m).
WOOD Special form of sequioa (see p.183) that has a reddish-brown background with distinct growth rings, crammed with numerous small knots with elliptical "eyes"; irregular grain; mostly fine texture (some is coarse); non-resinous.
SIZE AVAILABILITY Larger sheets than burrs from other species.
FINISHING Decorative veneering of high-quality furniture, jewelry boxes, and paneling.
USES Very good.

PROJ

ECTS

Introduction

The projects are all about taking the skills you have learned in the Techniques chapter (see pp.80–175) and using them creatively to make some wonderful pieces of furniture for your home. Each of the projects on the following pages is broken down into detailed steps, from thinking about initial designs to the last dust-down and polish. Before you start, make sure that you are comfortable with the project you have chosen to make and that you have the right tools and materials at hand.

Choosing a project

Deciding what to make is an exciting prospect and of course you are free to choose any of the projects on the following pages. But before you jump in, consider that the projects progress in difficulty, from the simple chopping board to the more complex chair. Although a novice can make the chair right away using the techniques learned on pages 80–175, you may want to consider practicing your skills on an easier project. However, if the buffet inspires you and you think that it would be perfect for your home, there is no reason why you shouldn't start on it—just be aware that the more difficult projects require more time and patience than the easier ones. Whichever project you choose, don't be afraid of making mistakes—this is a normal part of the learning process. Just don't forget to enjoy yourself along the way.

Getting started

Once you have decided on a project, you will need to choose your wood and finalize your design. When choosing your wood, make a list of the various sections and lengths you need and then make a trip to your local supplier. That way you will get to see and feel what you are buying. Spend as long as you need to with the supplier, to make sure that every piece is fit for purpose. If you see a piece of wood that is less than perfect—it may have too many knots, not have enough character in the grain, or even has a split—don't be afraid to ask for another instead.

Lastly, don't be afraid to change the design as you see fit, but make sure you apply any changes throughout the project to achieve a consistent result.

USING YOUR OWN IDEAS

As you build up your experience as a woodworker, you may want to try out detailed variations on the ideas given in the projects. The list of what is possible is almost limitless, but, for example, could include using different joints or finishes, applying a variety of different veneers, or adding decorative elements such as beading to your work. Here are some points to consider:

- Be aware at every step that the designs suggested here are only ideas. The projects have been conceived by experienced woodworkers but if you have strong views about color, form, materials, or design then always be alert to the possibility of making changes.
- Don't be afraid of trying out alternative techniques as well as materials and finishes—being creative is the key to flourishing as a woodworker.
- Be careful to make sure that your changes don't threaten the structural integrity of the piece you are working on.

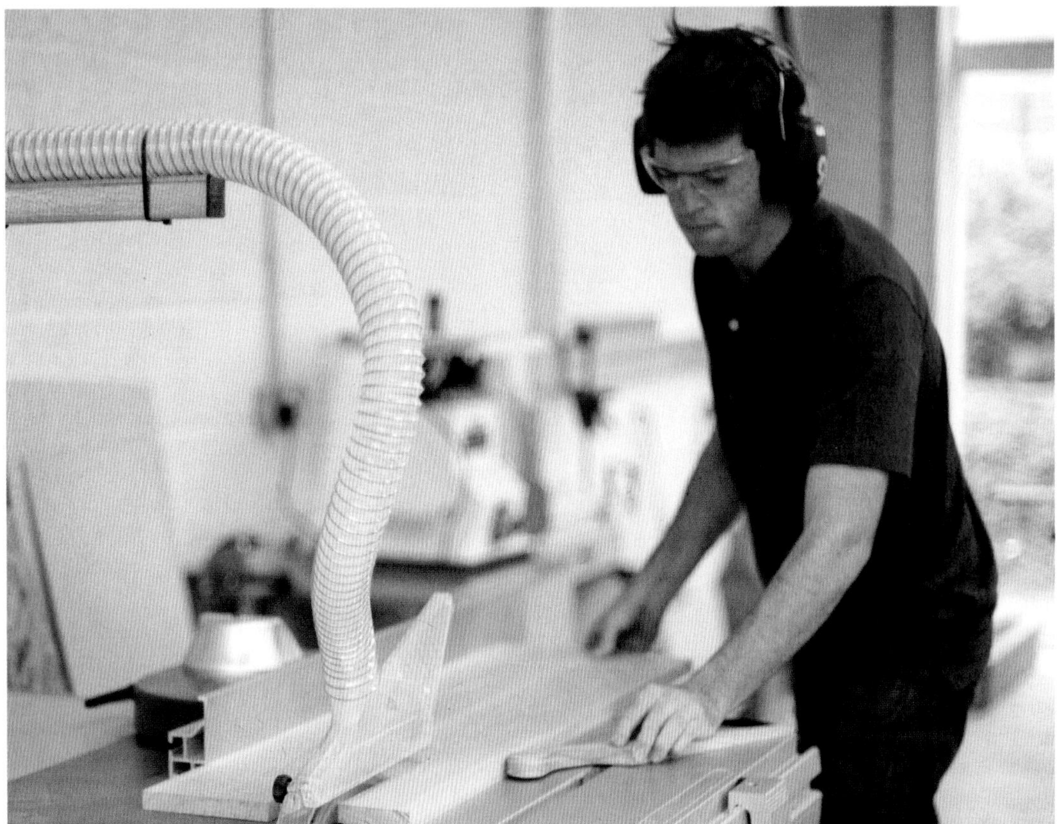

Putting your skills into practice
As you work through the projects in this chapter, putting your new-found skills into practice, always remember to follow the correct safety procedures. Wear the necessary protective gear (pp.78–79), such as safety goggles and ear defenders, and make sure that any power tool or machine is fitted with a dust extractor. When "feeding in" a workpiece (left), for example, it is particularly important to use a push stick.

Working through your project

To make sure that you've covered all the bases and haven't left anything out, refer to the checklist below. This provides a detailed roadmap of all the points you should consider so you work safely and produce successful results that you will be happy with for years to come. But don't feel that you have to follow the checklist slavishly– depending on your project and existing level of skill some tasks will be more familiar and relevant than others.

PROJECT CHECKLIST

Task	Action
CHOOSE YOUR PROJECT 1	■ Consider how difficult a project is relative to your current experience—you may be better off practicing your skills on an easier project to start with. ■ See which projects inspire you—woodworking should be fun and creative. ■ Assess what you actually need for your home.
SAFETY FIRST 2	■ Throughout the project, ensure that you are following the safety guidance given both in this book and on the tool manufacturer's instructions. ■ Make sure that friends and family know where you are and that there is a phone and first-aid kit close at hand in case you have an accident
READ THROUGH THE PROJECT 3	■ Before you start work, read through the whole project and make sure you are clear about every process. Try to visualize each action required so that you always know what is coming next. ■ If you have doubts about the correctness of a cut or mark or procedure, think it through first.
IDENTIFY THE TECHNIQUES 4	■ Assess the different techniques you will need to complete the project. Perhaps highlight each one as you read through the project so you are completely clear about the skills you will need to demonstrate. Refer back to the Techniques chapter (see pp.80–175) if you are in any doubt.
WHAT DO YOU NEED? 5	■ Refer to the Tools and Materials list at the start of every project to check that you have everything you need. It is much better to do this before you start work than to stop and start, which destroys your rhythm.
ASSEMBLE YOUR TOOLS 6	■ Assemble all your tools and materials in your workspace, putting everything within easy reach. ■ Don't worry too much about the arrangement of the tools other than to make sure that they are close at hand and safely arranged.
TEST YOUR TOOLS 7	■ Try out your tools at the start and before you use them at each stage. You don't want to be caught out by an unexpectedly blunt blade. ■ There is no such thing as an unexpectedly sharp blade—sharp means with swift, accurate, safe cuts; blunt means slow, rough, unsafe cuts.
SELECT YOUR WOOD 8	■ The timber proposed for each project is intended as a guide only. If you don't want to use the wood suggested, check through the Wood chapter (see pp.176–99) to find a suitable alternative. ■ If choosing your own wood, make sure it is user-friendly, non-toxic, and comes from a sustainable source.
MAKE SPACE 9	■ Read through the project to ensure you are aware of its physical scale—you need to give yourself enough room to maneuver. ■ Adjust your workspace accordingly. Perhaps you could erect an awning or other covered area, or find an alternative space to make larger sections of a project.
PRACTICE 10	■ If you have any doubt as to your proficiency at any of the techniques then make sure you practice on some off-cuts first. As you move through the steps, if there is anything that you are unsure of, return to the relevant technique page for information. It is better to be slow and patient than to make expensive mistakes.
MEASURE AND CUT 11	■ When measuring and cutting your materials, make sure you follow EITHER the imperial OR the metric measurements—do not follow a mixture of both as the pieces will not fit together. ■ Be aware that tools such as levels and squares can sometimes give false readings, so check them.
DOUBLE CHECK 12	■ The accuracy of your cutting and measuring is going to dictate whether or not your project will be successful, so it is worth double-checking your measurements, just to be absolutely sure that you have not made an error. ■ Follow the old adage: "Measure twice and cut once."
WORK PATIENTLY 13	■ Work your way steadily through the steps, taking your time and ensuring you are clear about every action. ■ Don't rush a step if you are tired. It is much better to leave it until the next day.
APPLY A FINISH 14	■ Before adding any finishes to the wood, make sure that you rub off any pencil marks, as they will show through and spoil the effect.
UNDERSTAND THE TERMINOLOGY 15	■ Refer to the glossary (see pp.384–87) if you do not understand any of the terms or jargon used in the projects.
TROUBLESHOOT 16	■ If in doubt about a dimension or cut, put together the component parts in a dry run. ■ If you make an irreversible mistake, ask yourself if you can modify the design to accommodate the mistake, before rushing off to buy more wood.

Chopping board

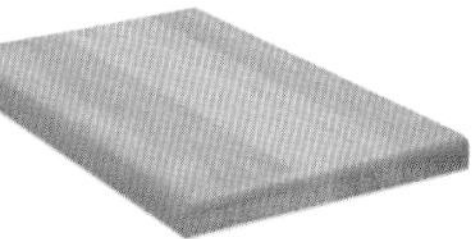

Making a chopping board is a great way to familiarize yourself with the technique of joining sections of timber to create a single piece with a larger surface area. The simple design featured here uses edge-to-edge joints, which can be very strong when modern glue is used. Beech is the traditional wood for chopping boards, but you could try tight-grained timbers, such as maple or pear, for an alternative finish.

Dimensions:
17 11⁄16 x 11 x 1¾in (450 x 280 x 45mm)

Key technique:
Edge-to-edge joint (pp.94–95)

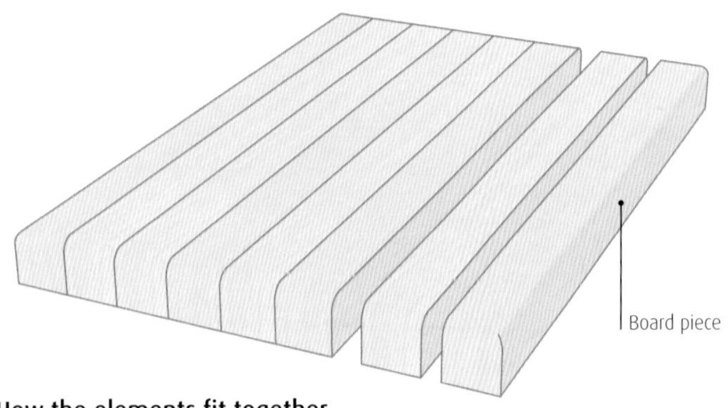

How the elements fit together
Each of the sections are glued together to make an oversized board, which is then cut to size. All four top edges of the board are smoothed to a rounded profile using a bench plane.

CUTTING LIST

Item	Material	No.	Length	Width	Thickness
Board pieces	Beech	8	23⅝in* (600mm)	1⅜in (35mm)	1¾in (45mm)

*Includes excess to allow for cutting to size

TOOLS AND MATERIALS

Pencil
Ruler
Wood glue and brush
Sash clamps
Square
Panel saw or band saw
Bench plane
Shooting board
Cabinet scraper (optional)
Sandpaper
Food-safe oil

TOP VIEW (1:5)

END VIEW (1:5)

GLUING AND SIZING THE BOARD

1 **Arrange the pieces** according to appearance and grain direction (see pp.94–95). Check they fit together accurately.

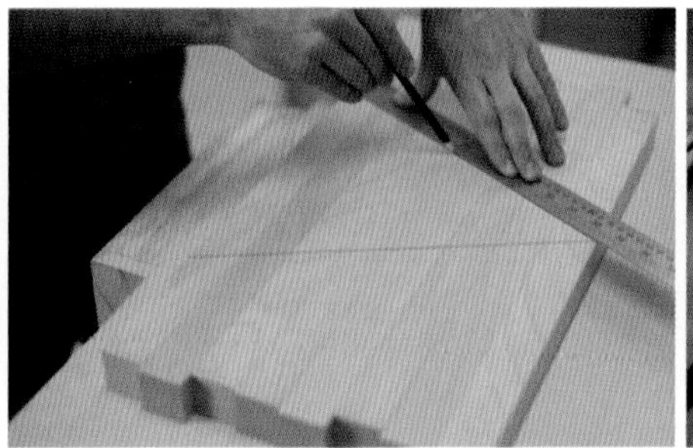

2 **Draw a V-mark** across the assembly with a pencil and metal ruler to mark the position of the pieces.

3 **Apply glue to the joining edges** and assemble the pieces in the sash clamps, lining up the V-mark.

4 **Clamp the assembly** tightly in the sash clamps and wipe away any excess glue. Leave to dry overnight.

5 **Mark the finished length**— 17 11/16in (450mm)—and square the lines across the assembled pieces using a square.

6 **Cut the end grains** to the length lines either by hand, using a panel saw (pictured), or on a band saw.

7 **Shoot the end grains** smooth and square using a bench plane guided by a shooting board.

FINISHING THE BOARD

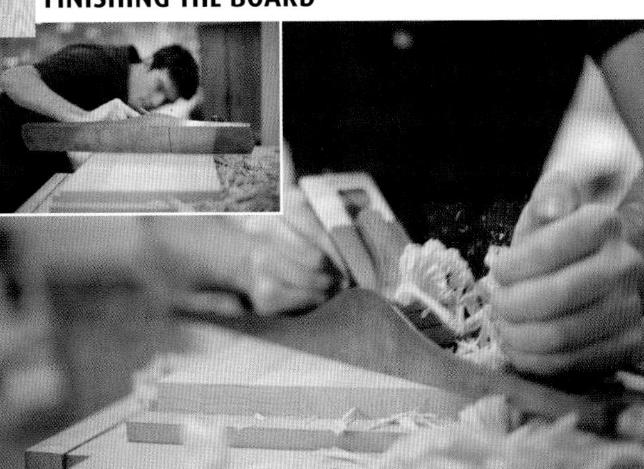

1 **Secure the board** against an end-stop and plane both surfaces flat, working across the grain first. As you work, use the edge of the plane to check the board for flatness (inset).

2 **Smooth both surfaces** flat with either a cabinet scraper (pictured) or a piece of sandpaper.

3 **Use a bench plane** to chamfer the edges of the upper face of the board. Work across the grain (along the short sides)—first, then with the grain (along the long sides).

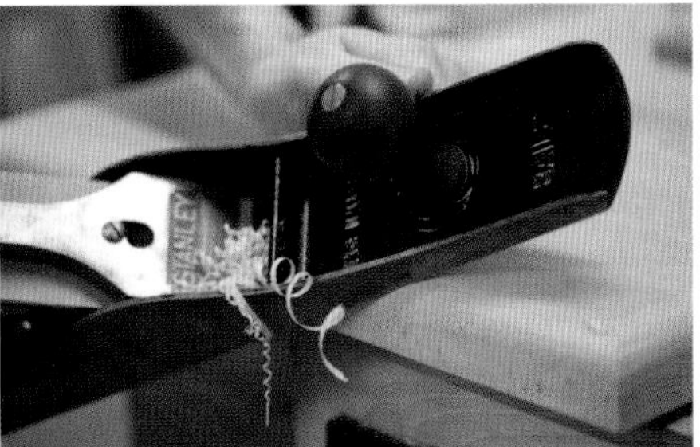

4 **Work around all four edges** in the same order several more times, progressively taking more off each edge until you have achieved a finished, rounded shape.

5 **Sand all four edges** smooth. Apply olive oil or a similar food-safe oil for a non-toxic finish.

THE FINISHED PIECE

Coat rack

A row of sturdy pegs is an indispensible storage aid in most homes. This simple coat rack requires minimal materials and a basic range of tools, and is a great way to use up offcuts from the workshop. The traditional look is reminiscent of Shaker designs, and is perhaps more attractive than modern versions that use metal hooks. The length of the backboard and number of pegs can easily be modified to fit the space available and the amount of hanging capacity required. The "look" of the piece could also be altered by choosing a different wood or peg shape to fit the décor of the room for which it is intended (see p.208, Alternatives). You will need to attach fixings to the backboard, appropriate to the wall surface, to secure the coat rack safely in the chosen position.

Dimensions:
47 1/4 x 3 9/16 x 1 3/4in (1200 x 90 x 45mm)

Key techniques:
Basic mortise-and-tenon joint (pp.116–17)

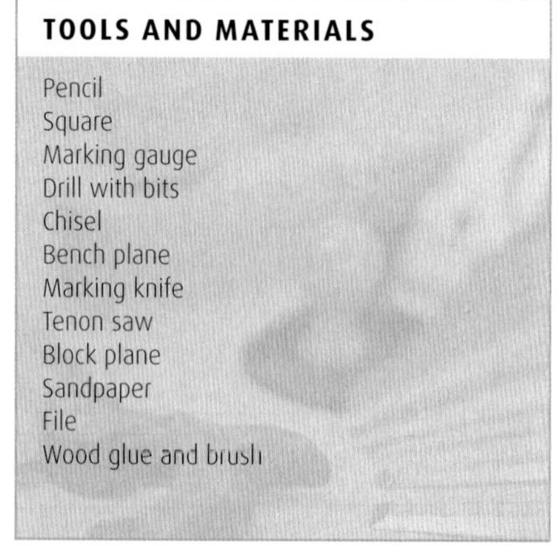
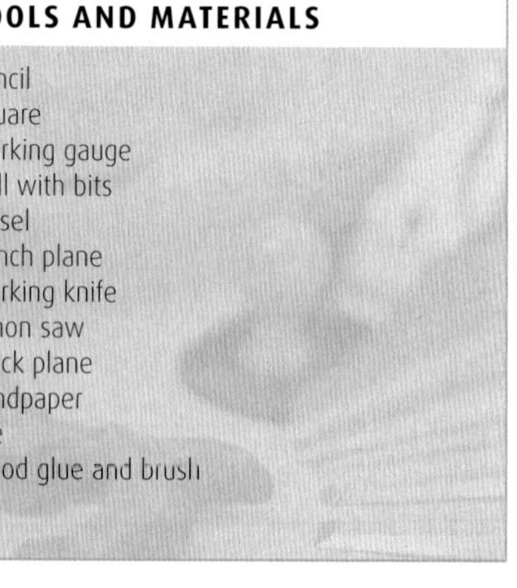

TOOLS AND MATERIALS

- Pencil
- Square
- Marking gauge
- Drill with bits
- Chisel
- Bench plane
- Marking knife
- Tenon saw
- Block plane
- Sandpaper
- File
- Wood glue and brush

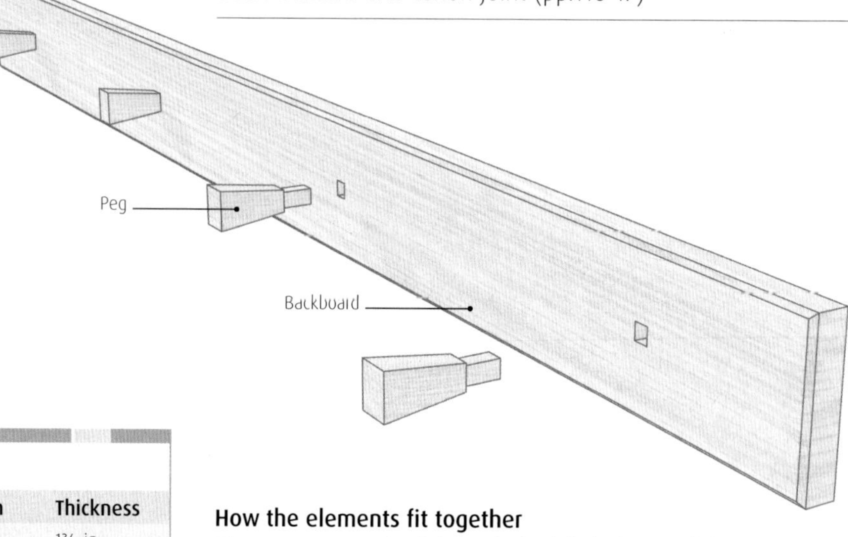

CUTTING LIST

Item	Material	No.	Length	Width	Thickness
Backboard	Oak	1	47 1/4in (1200mm)	3 9/16in (90mm)	13/16in (20mm)
Pegs	Oak	4	2 9/16inin (65mm)	1in (25mm)	13/16in (20mm)

How the elements fit together

The pegs are mortised through the full thickness of the backboard for maximum strength and durability. The peg tenons have a shoulder all around, which lends them extra strength for taking the weight of heavy coats or other items.

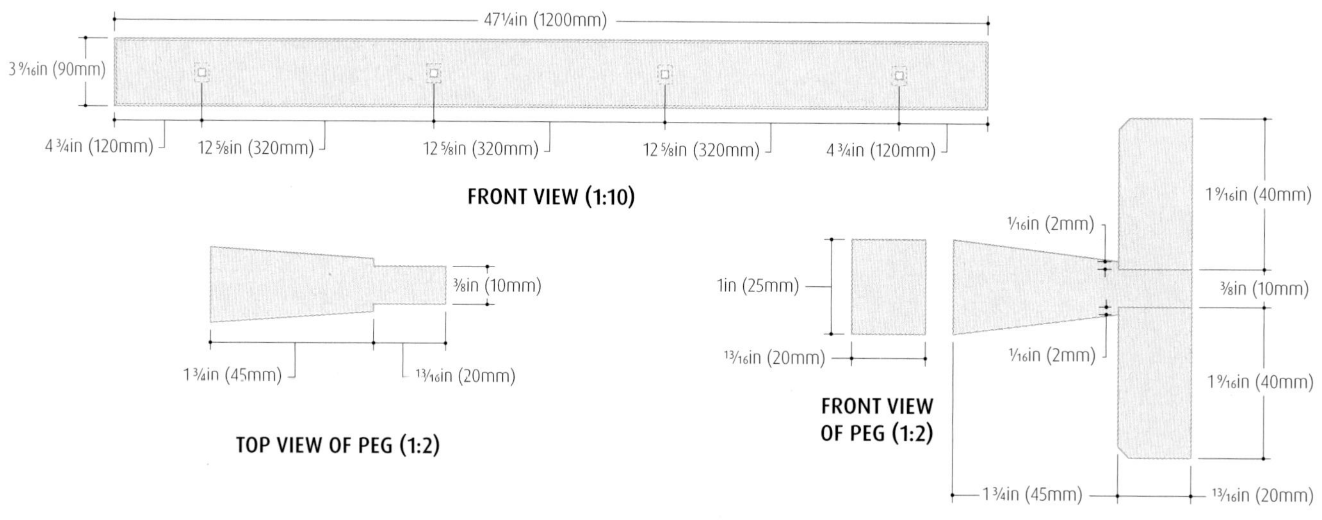

MARKING THE MORTISES ON THE BACKBOARD

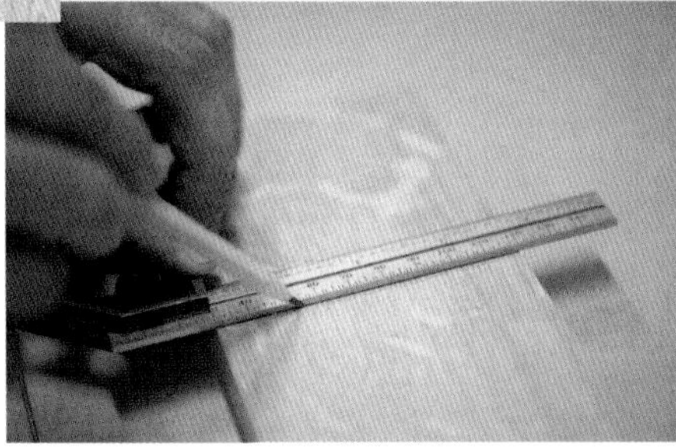

1 **With the backboard** cut to size, square a line across the width of the board to mark the center-point of each peg mortise (see diagram, opposite, for positions).

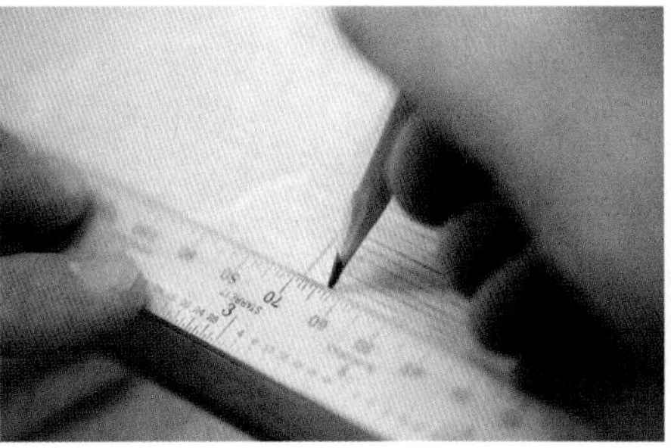

2 **Mark the mortise width** with a pencil ¼in (6mm) to either side of the centre-point line.

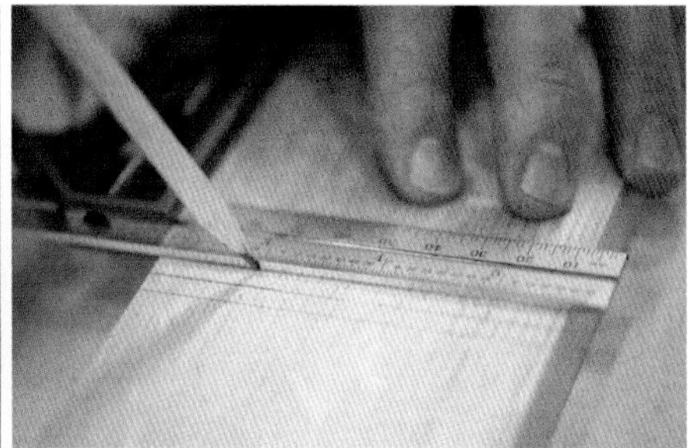

3 **Extend the marks** across the full width of the backboard with a pencil and square.

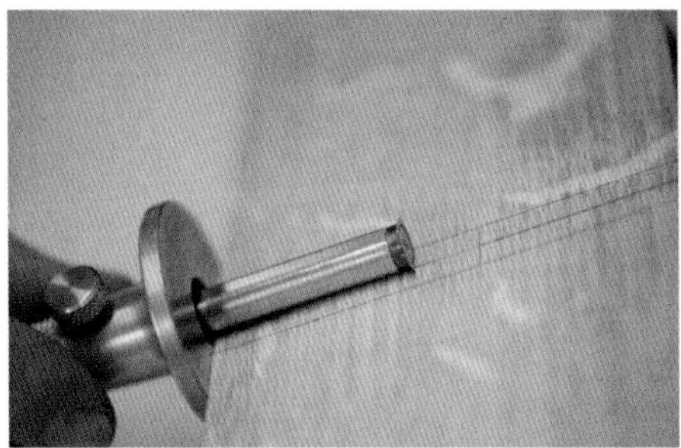

4 **Use a marking gauge** set to 1⁹⁄₁₆in (40mm) to scribe a line between the mortise width marks from each edge of the backboard to mark the mortise length.

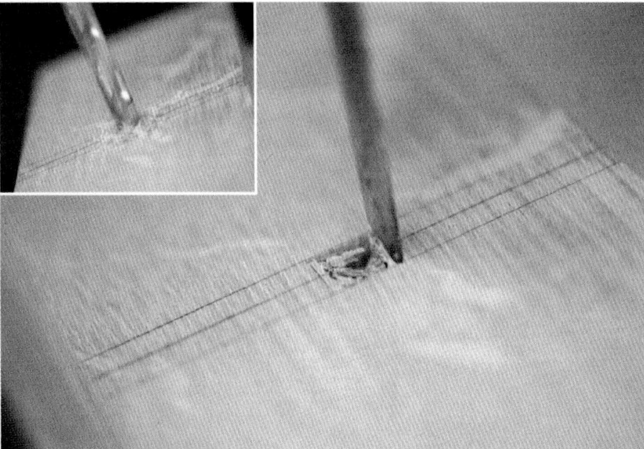

5 **Use a drill** to remove the bulk of the mortise waste (inset), then clean up the edges with a chisel. Repeat Steps 1–5 for all mortises.

6 **Secure the backboard** in a vise, then chamfer the front edges of the backboard with a bench plane.

MARKING OUT THE PEGS

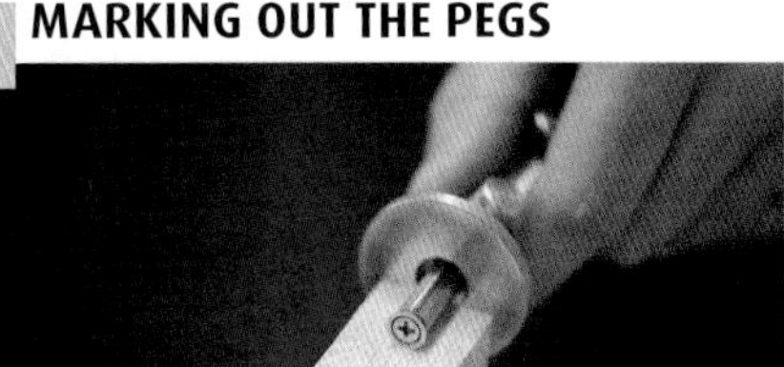

1 **Mark the tenon shoulder** on each peg piece ¹³⁄₁₆in (20mm) from one end grain, then square the mark around all four sides.

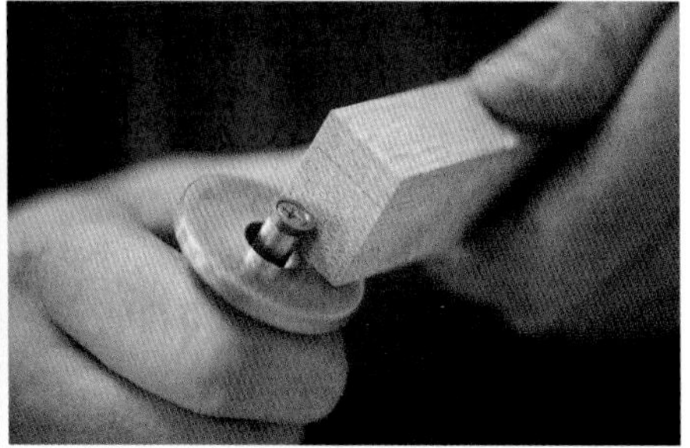

2 **Use a marking gauge** set to ⁵⁄₁₆in (7.5mm) to scribe across the same end grain from the short edges. Extend the marks down both faces to the shoulder.

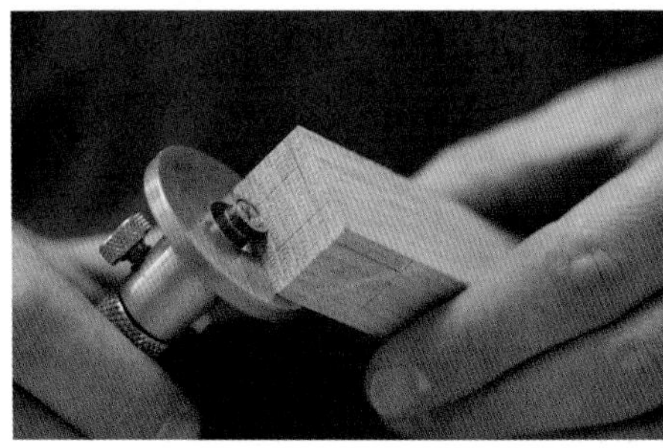

3 **Reset the marking gauge** to ³⁄₁₆in (5mm) and scribe along the end grain from each face and down the edges to the shoulder.

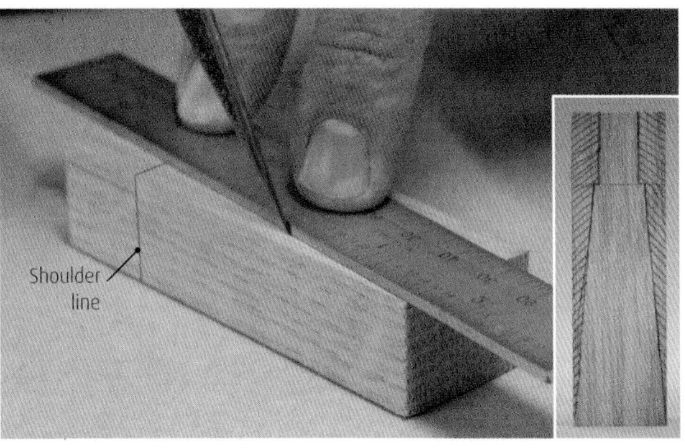

4 **Use a marking knife** to make two marks on the shoulder line on each face, ¼in (6mm) from each edge. Score a diagonal line from each mark to the untenoned corners. Mark both faces of all four peg pieces in the same way, and use a pencil to mark the waste for removal (inset).

CUTTING THE TENONS AND TAPERS

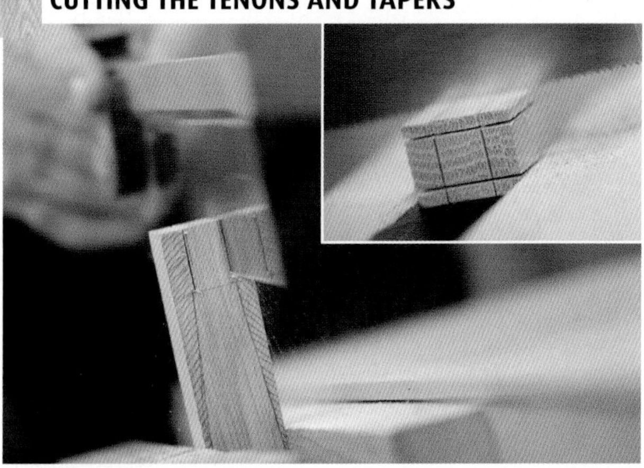

1 **Use a tenon saw** to cut the tenons down the scribed lines to the shoulder, then cross-cut along the shoulders (inset). Repeat on the remaining three pegs.

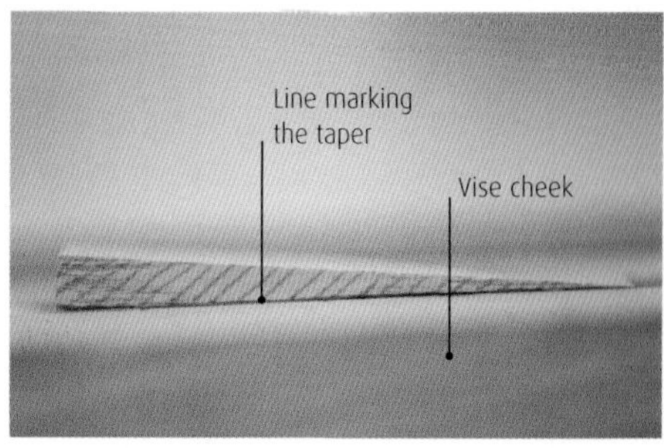

2 **Set a peg** in the vise with the line that marks the taper in alignment with the top of the vise cheeks.

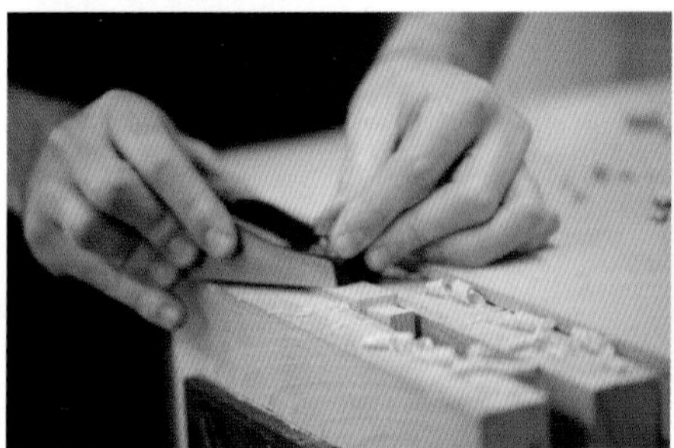

3 **Plane to the line** with a block plane, then repeat on the opposite edge. Taper all of the pegs in the same way.

4 **Smooth all of the surfaces** and remove any arrises with sandpaper. File the edges at the untenoned ends of the pegs (inset).

FIXING THE PEGS

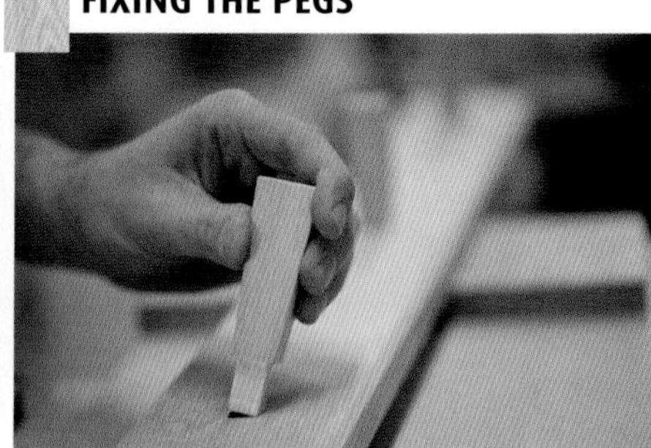

1 **After testing the fit**, apply glue to all of the peg tenons and insert each firmly into its mortise. Clean up any excess glue.

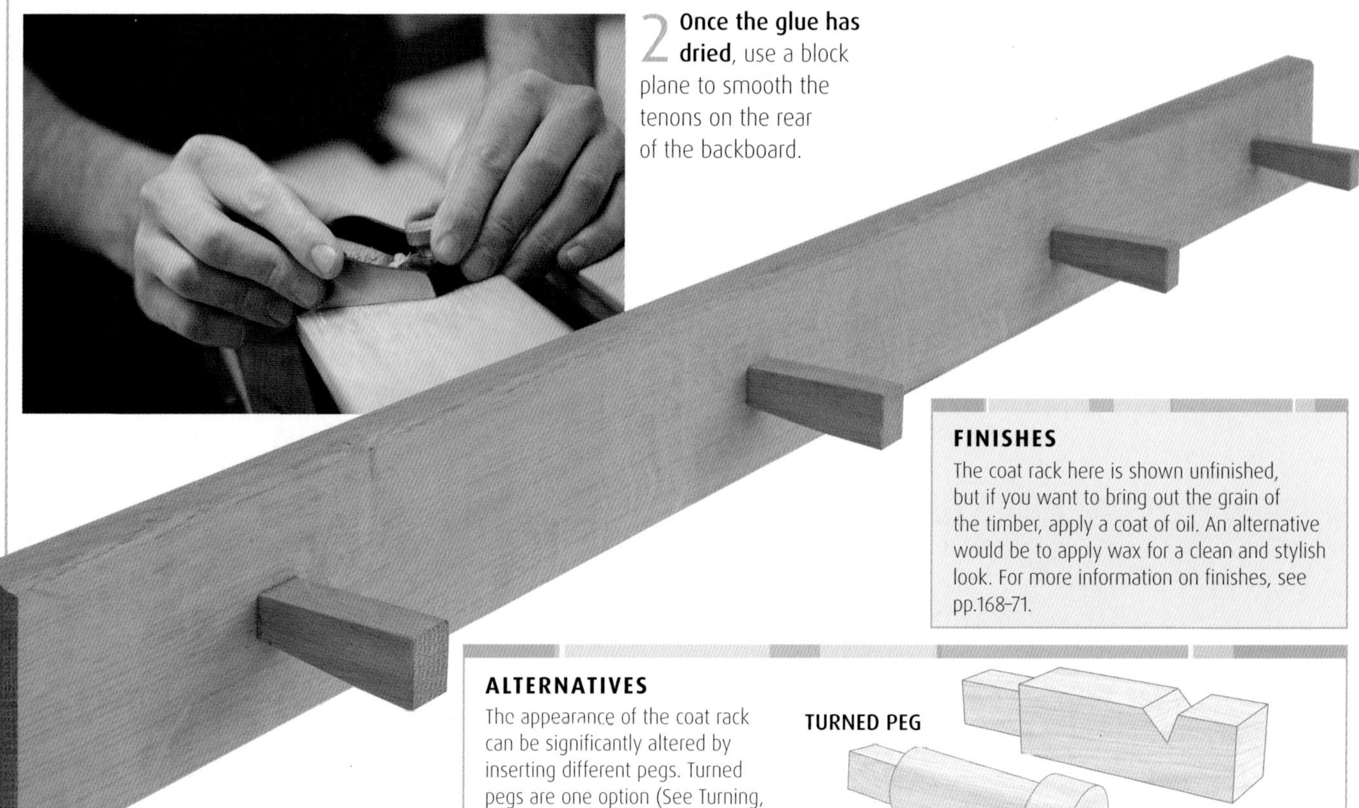

2 **Once the glue has dried**, use a block plane to smooth the tenons on the rear of the backboard.

THE FINISHED PIECE

FINISHES

The coat rack here is shown unfinished, but if you want to bring out the grain of the timber, apply a coat of oil. An alternative would be to apply wax for a clean and stylish look. For more information on finishes, see pp.168–71.

ALTERNATIVES

The appearance of the coat rack can be significantly altered by inserting different pegs. Turned pegs are one option (See Turning, pp.152–56), as are notched pegs, which help to hold items securely.

TURNED PEG

NOTCHED PEG

Mirror frame

The basic principles utilized in this project are simple, yet extremely important to master. Being able to produce a good miter joint is an invaluable woodworking skill, since it can be employed in a range of projects, including picture frames, boxes, plinths, skirting boards, and architraves. This particular frame uses a slightly more advanced keyed miter joint (p.115), which increases the surface area onto which glue can be applied.

Dimensions:
17 15/16 x 17 15/16in x 1 3/8in (455 x 455mm x 35mm)

Key technique:
Keyed miter joint (p.115)

TOOLS AND MATERIALS

- Sash clamp
- Marking gauge
- Shoulder plane or router
- Marking knife
- Ruler
- Bench plane
- Combination square
- Miter saw or miter block
- 45-degree shooting board
- Bevel-edged chisel
- Wood glue and brush
- Ratchet strap cramp
- Finishing oil
- Sandpaper and block
- Mirror (16 x 16in/406 x 406mm)
- Small hammer
- Panel pins

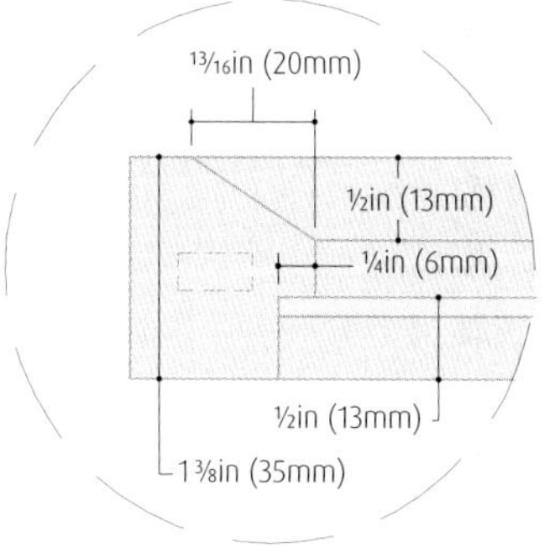

DETAIL OF MITER SECTION (1:2)

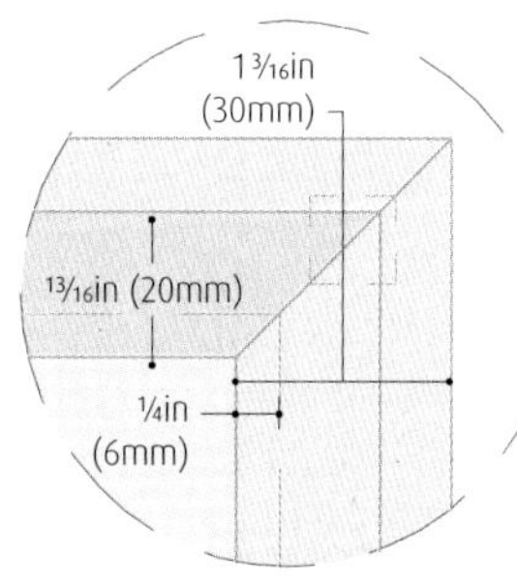

DETAIL OF FRONT OF MITER (1:2)

CUTTING LIST

Item	Material	No.	Length	Width	Thickness
Frame pieces	Walnut	4	19 11/16in* (500mm)	1 3/8in (35mm)	1 3/16in (30mm)
Keys	Ply	4	3/8in (10mm)	3/8in (10mm)	1/4in (6mm)
Backing board	Hardboard	1	16in (406mm)	16in (406mm)	1/8in (3mm)

*Includes excess to allow for cutting to size

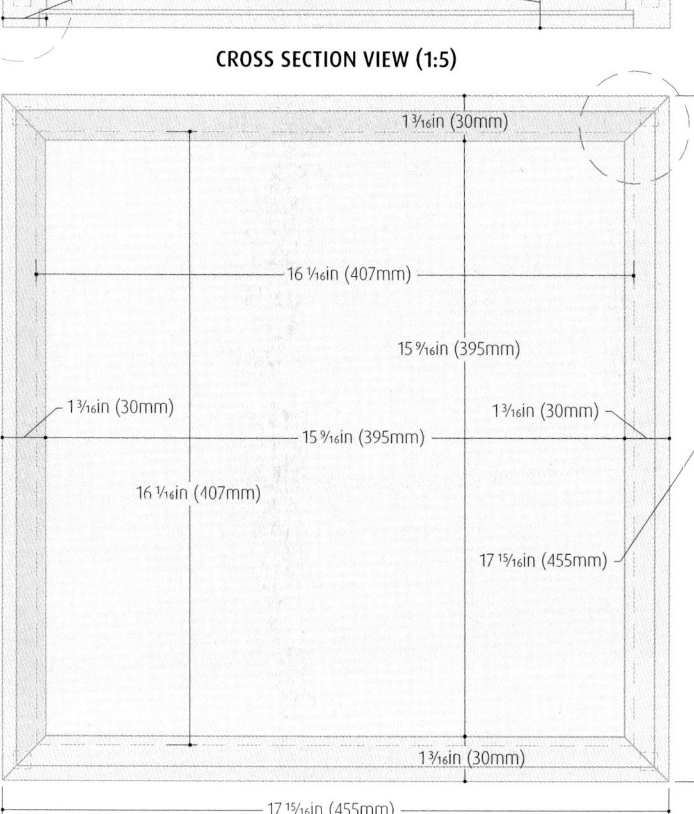

FRONT VIEW (1:5)

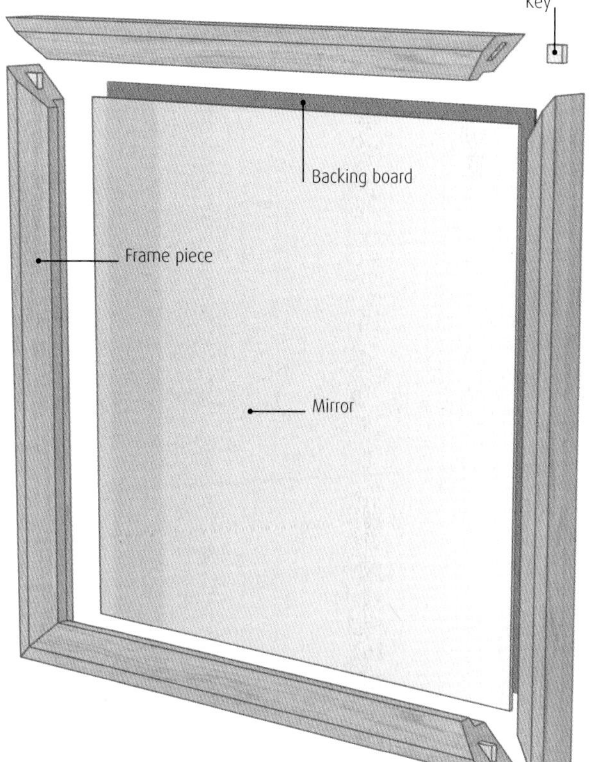

How the elements fit together
The mitered corners are strengthened by the use of plywood "keys," which also help to keep the miters flush with one another when being glued. A rebate in the back of the frame accommodates the mirror, which is held in place with pins.

MARKING OUT AND CUTTING THE FRAME PIECES

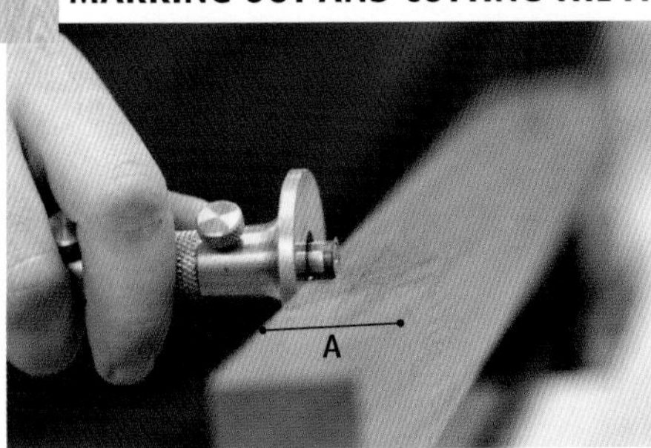

1 **Secure each frame piece** edge-up and score a line along the edge (A) with a marking gauge set to ¼in (6mm). Then score another line along face B (see Step 2) with the gauge set to ½in (13mm).

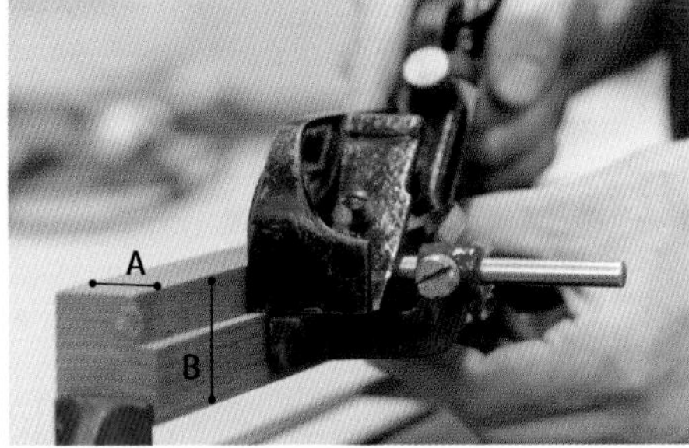

2 **Cut a rebate** to the marked lines with a shoulder plane (pictured) or a router (see panel, right). Repeat Steps 1 and 2 for the remaining three frame pieces.

MACHINE-CUTTING THE REBATE

You can use a router with a straight cutter to cut a rebate ¼in (6mm) wide by ½in (13mm) deep between the scored lines along the length of each frame piece.

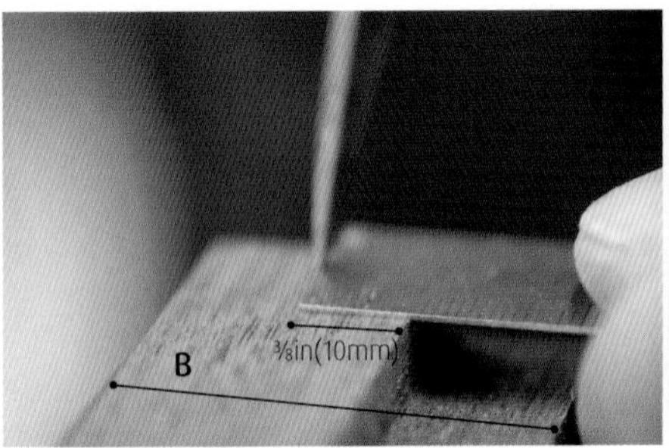

3 **At the end** of the first piece, measure ⅜in (10mm) from the edge of the rebate on the face (B), and extend the line along the length of the face with a marking gauge.

4 **On the adjacent side (C)**, mark ⅜in (10mm) from the outside edge of the frame. Scribe the line along the length of the piece.

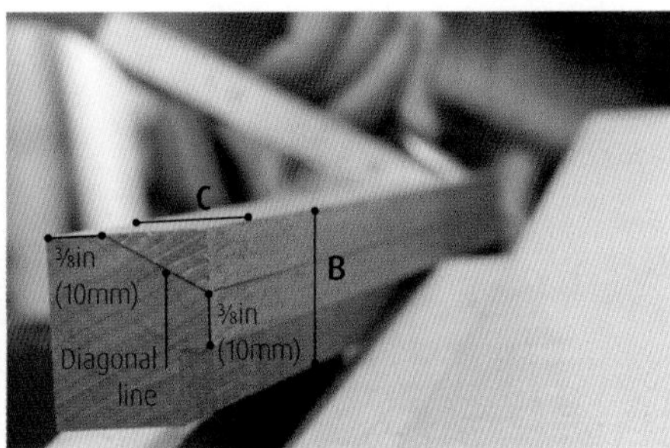

5 **Join the marks** by scribing a diagonal line across the corner on both end grains. Mark all three remaining frame pieces in the same way.

6 **Secure the piece** in a vise with the corner just marked uppermost. Plane the waste to create the splay. Repeat Steps 3–6 for the remaining pieces.

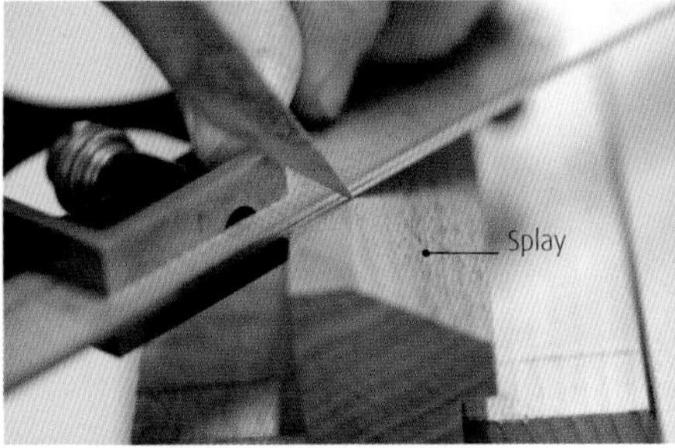

7 **Use a combination square** and marking knife to scribe a 45-degree angle (see diagram on p.209 for measurements) on both ends of each piece, the splay uppermost.

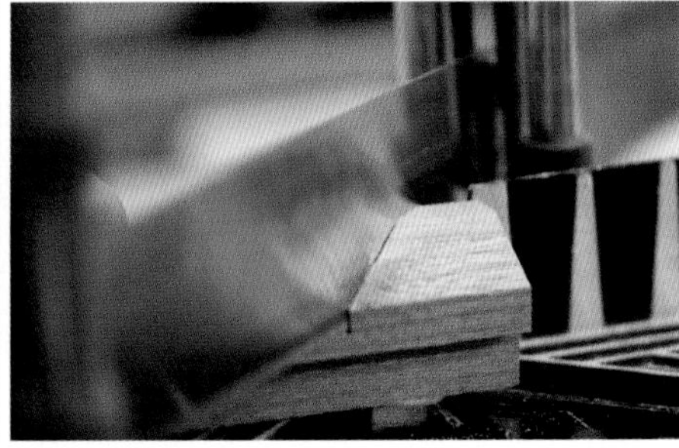

8 **Cut the miters** to the waste side of the marks to allow for finishing with a plane. Use a miter saw (pictured) or a miter block.

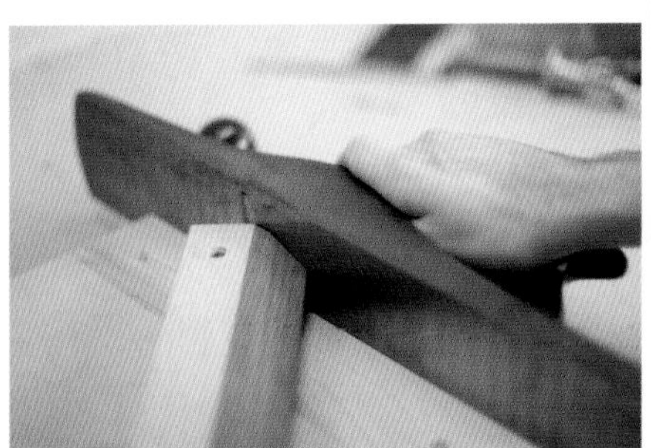

9 **Place each piece** on a 45-degree shooting board (see pp.72–73) and plane each end exactly to size.

MARKING OUT THE MORTISE

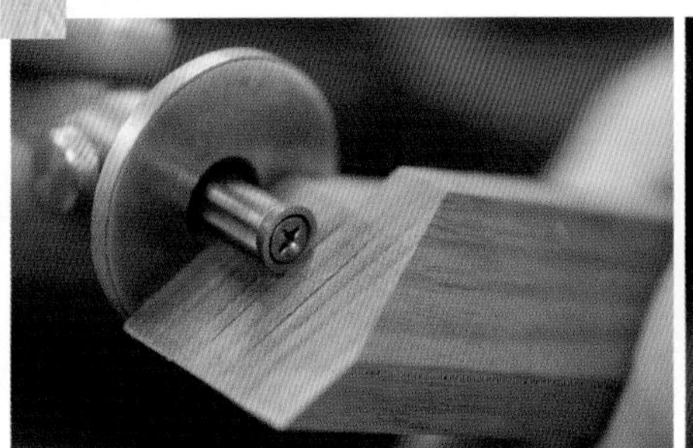

1 **Mark the mortise position** on the mitered surface. Set the gauge to 9⁄16in (14.5mm). Score a line from edge to edge.

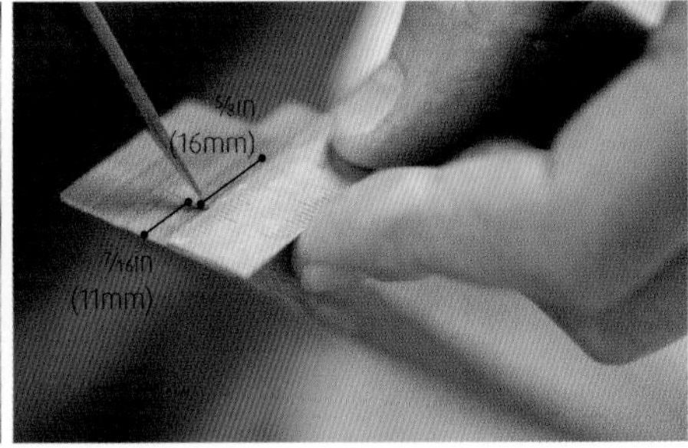

2 **Mark the mortise length** of ⅝in (16mm), with the base of the mortise 7⁄16in (11mm) from the bottom of the miter.

CUTTING AND FITTING THE MORTISES AND KEYS

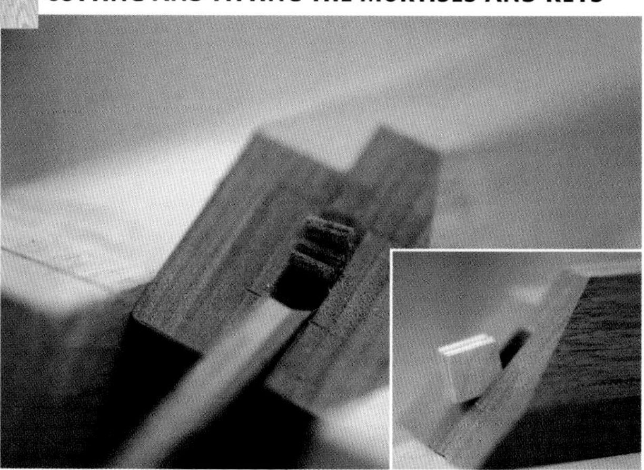

1 **Cut the mortise** by hand with a bevel-edged chisel to a depth of 3/8in (10mm) from the maximum extent of the miter. Cut four "keys" 3/8in (10mm) square from 1/4in (6mm) plywood, and insert a key into one mortise of each piece (inset).

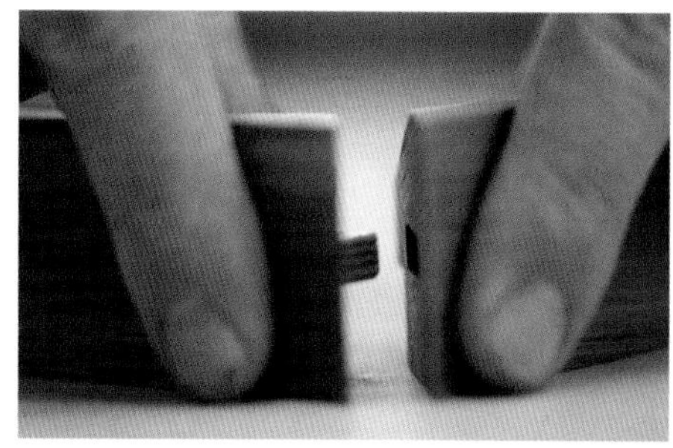

2 **After checking the fit**, glue all the mortises and keys and assemble the frame, carefully inserting each key into its matching mortise.

3 **Clamp the assembled frame** firmly with a ratchet strap, and leave the glue to dry overnight.

FINISHING THE FRAME

1 **Sand all the surfaces** of the frame assembly smooth once the glue is dry. Securing the frame in a vise makes this job easier.

2 **Carefully apply one or two coats** of finishing oil to all parts of the frame and leave it to dry.

SECURING THE MIRROR

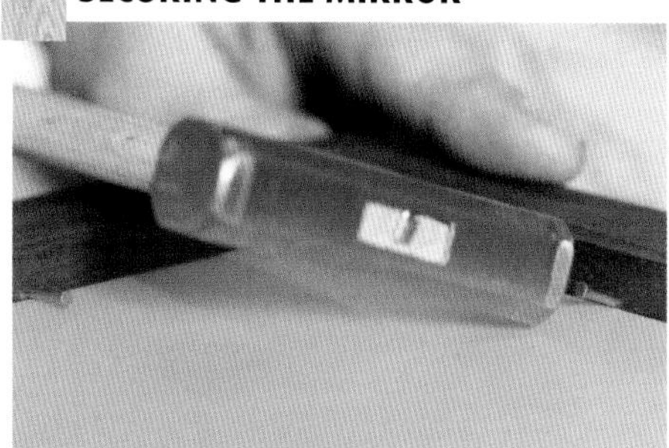

1 **Place the mirror** in the frame. Use a small hammer to insert panel pins at an angle at regular intervals into the inside edge of the back of the frame.

2 **Use your thumb** to push the pins horizontal to hold the mirror securely within the rebate.

THE FINISHED PIECE

Wine rack

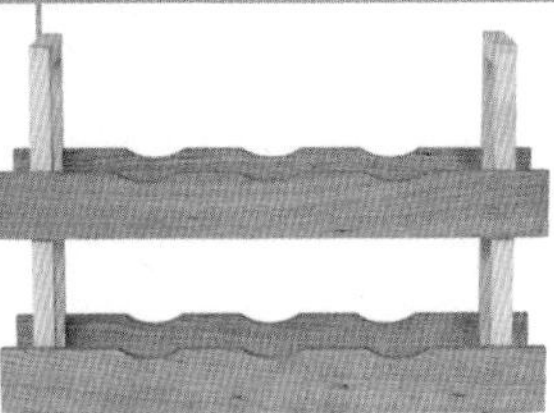

This straightforward and accessible project is an excellent way for the novice woodworker to gain confidence in the technique of using dowels as a method of jointing. The project requires only a minimum amount of basic equipment and materials and is therefore a good choice if you want to try out your woodworking skills without making a huge investment in tools.

The instructions here are suitable for a six-bottle unit, but you can increase its capacity by either incorporating longer façades or by making the stiles longer and adding an extra row of façades (see Alternatives, p.215).

Dimensions:
19 15/16 x 13 3/4 x 5 3/16in (505 x 350 x 130mm)

Key technique:
Dowel joints using center points (pp.147–48)

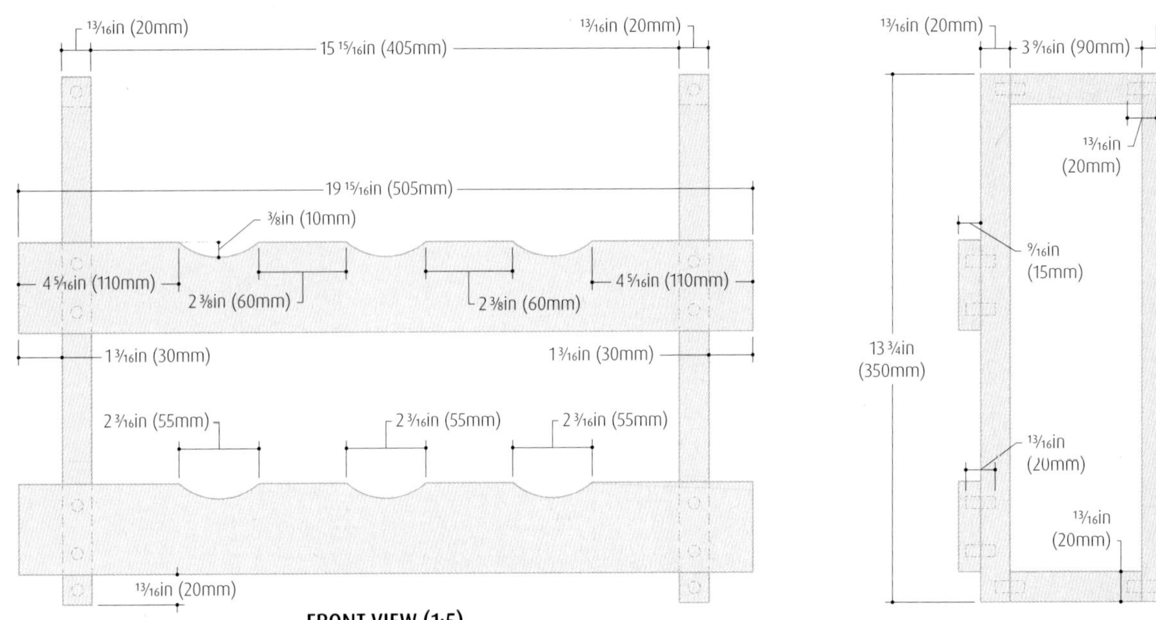

FRONT VIEW (1:5)

SIDE VIEW (1:5)

Stile

Dowel connector

Façade

Rail

How the elements fit together

The stiles and rails of the upright frames are joined by dowel connectors, which also attach the façades to the front and back. Three scoops on each rail provide support for six bottles.

TOOLS AND MATERIALS

- Pencil
- Ruler
- Drill with 3/8in (10mm) bit
- Masking tape
- Wood glue and brush
- F-clamps
- Tape measure
- C-clamps
- Combination square
- Protractor
- Coping saw
- Sandpaper

CUTTING LIST

Item	Material	No.	Length	Width	Thickness
Stiles	Maple	4	13 3/4in (350mm)	13/16in (20mm)	13/16in (20mm)
Rails	Maple	4	3 9/16in (90mm)	13/16in (20mm)	13/16in (20mm)
Façades	Cherry	4	19 15/16in (505mm)	2 3/8in (60mm)	9/16in (15mm)
Dowel connectors	Beech	24	13/16in (20mm)	3/8in (10mm)	3/8in (10mm)

MAKING THE END FRAMES

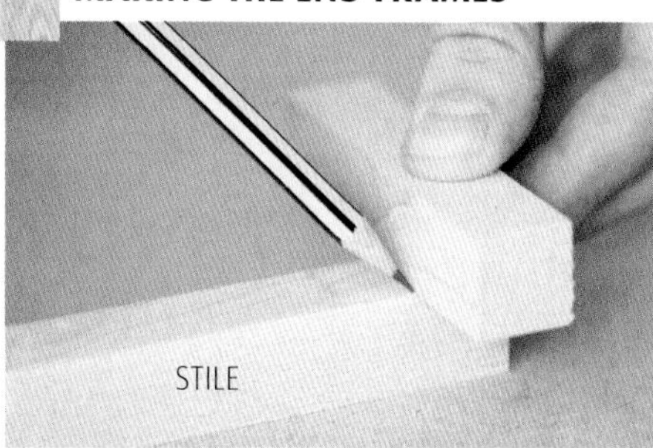

1 **Mark the width** of a rail at one end of a stile with a pencil line, aligning the rail against the end grain of the stile.

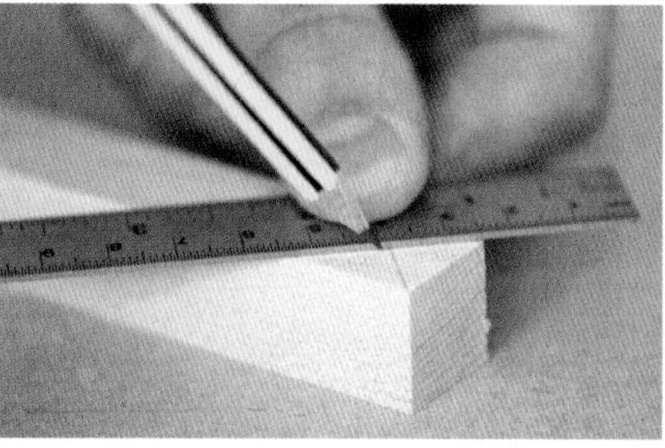

2 **Mark the centerpoint** between this mark and the end grain by drawing diagonals from corner to corner. Mark both ends of all four stiles in the same way.

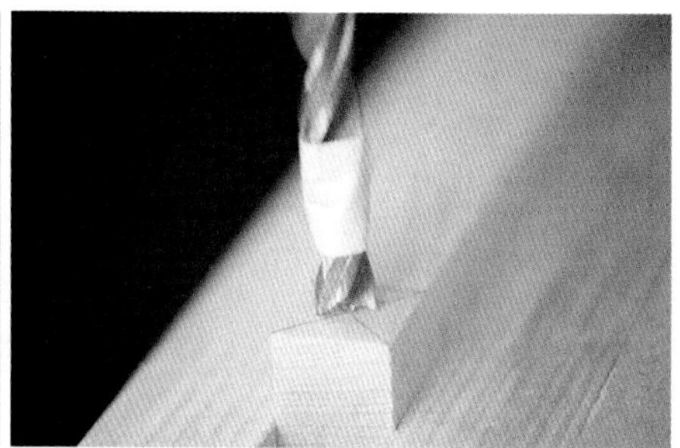

3 **Use masking tape** to mark a drilling depth of ⅜in (10mm) on a ⅜in (10mm) drill bit. Drill a hole to this depth in each of the marked positions.

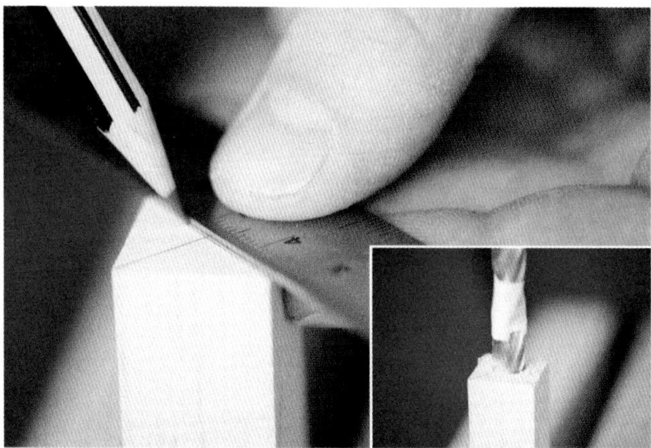

4 **Mark the center** of the end grain at both ends of all four rails (horizontal pieces), then drill through each mark to a depth of ⅜in (10mm) and a width of ⅜in (10mm) (inset).

5 **Test the fit** of the dowels in the holes in the stiles and rails. Adjust if necessary to ease the fit.

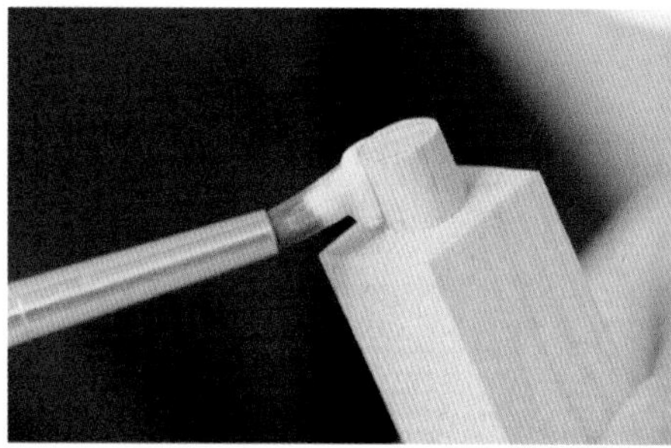

6 **Use a brush** to apply glue to the holes and dowels of the stiles and rails, then assemble the frames.

7 **Clamp the frames** and use a tape measure to check for squareness (see p.75). Wipe off any excess glue and leave to dry.

MARKING UP THE BOTTLE SUPPORTS IN THE FAÇADES

1 **Clamp all four façades** together with the top edge and end grains aligned. Mark a line square across the edges of all the pieces at the mid-point of the length.

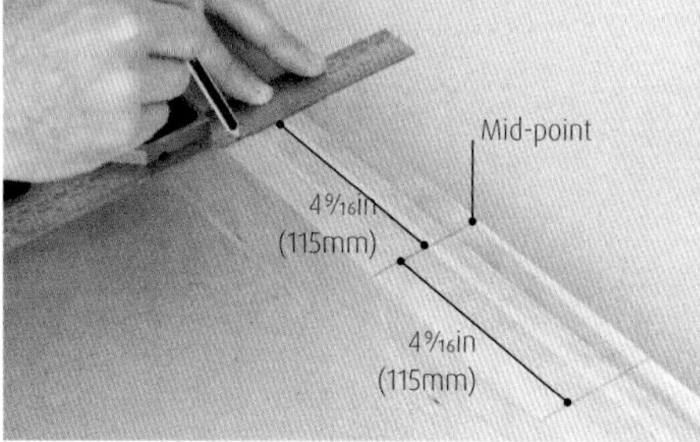

2 **Draw a line** 4⁹⁄₁₆in (115mm) from either side of the mid-point and square the marks across the edges.

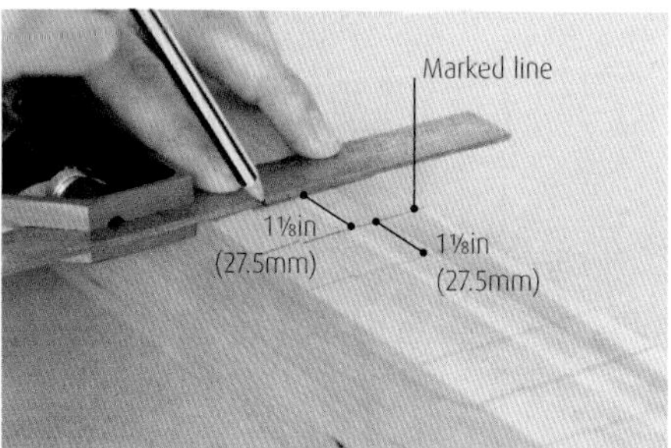

3 **Mark 1⅛in (27.5mm)** on each side of both of these marked lines, then square the marks across the edges.

4 **Unclamp the pieces**, then extend the marks made in Step 3 across one face of each piece.

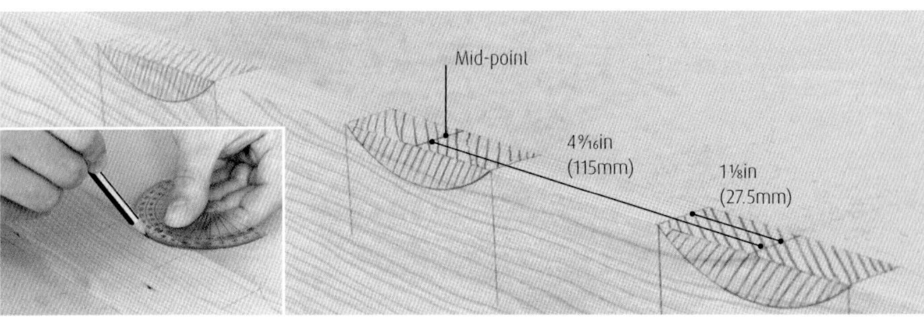

5 **Place a protractor** between each pair of lines so that the edges intersect at the top edge of the façade (inset). Draw around the protractor to mark a uniform curve for the bottle holders in each position. Mark the waste for removal.

CUTTING THE BOTTLE SUPPORTS

1 **Secure one façade** in the vise, then cut the bottle supports on the waste side of the marks with a coping saw.

2 **Use coarse sandpaper** to remove the waste to the marks. Repeat Steps 1–2 for the remaining façades.

ASSEMBLING THE RACK

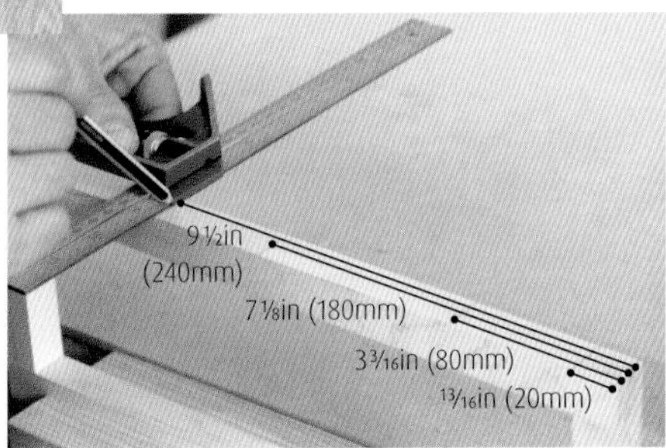

1 **Set one end frame** in a vise with the edge of the stile positioned horizontally. Square four lines across the outer edge at the distances shown from the end grain.

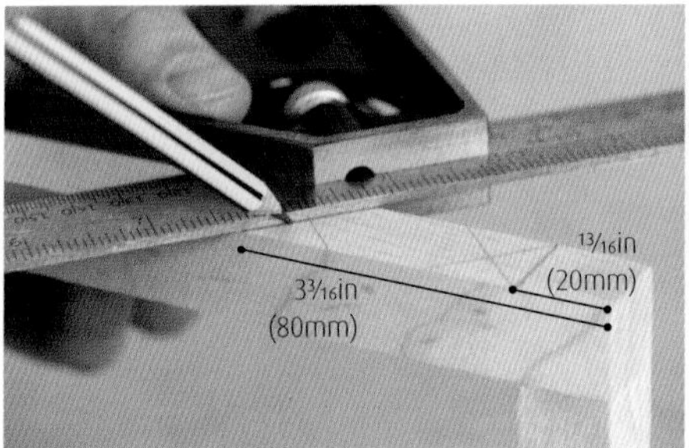

2 **Use a combination square** at 45 degrees to project diagonals as shown. The point at which the diagonal lines intersect is the centerpoint for the dowel holes.

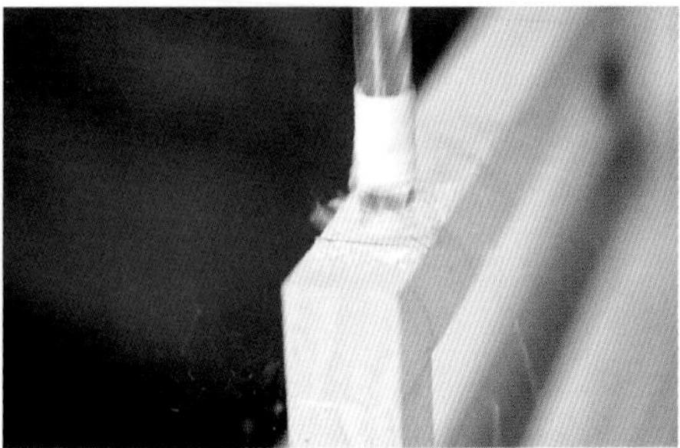

3 **Drill into the point** of each intersection to a depth of ⅜in (10mm), using a ⅜in (10mm) drill bit.

4 **Repeat Steps 1–3** for the outer edges of the remaining three stiles. Check that all marks for hole placement are aligned with the marks on the first stile before drilling any holes.

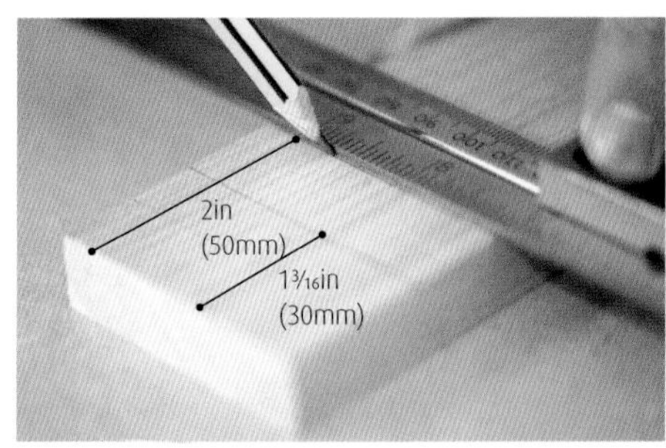

5 **Mark the position** of the dowels on the rear face of each façade. Square two lines across the face 1³⁄₁₆in (30mm) and 2in (50mm) from the end grain at both ends of the façade.

6 **Set the combination square** to 45 degrees and mark four intersecting diagonals from each edge, within the lines.

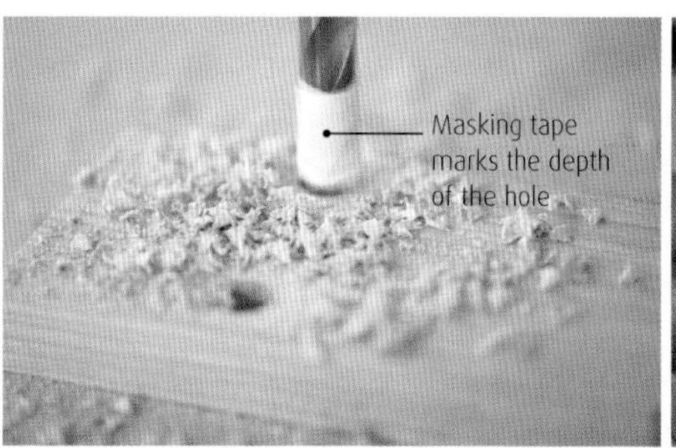

7 **Drill a hole** into each of the positions marked by the intersecting diagonals to a depth of ⅜in (10mm). Repeat Steps 5–7 for the other three façades.

8 **Insert a dowel connector** into every hole in each façade, then insert them into the holes in the end frames to check the fit.

FINISHING AND GLUING

1 **Remove the façades** from the end frames, then sand all elements to remove any rough edges.

2 **Brush glue** into the dowel holes in the façades and end-frame stiles, then assemble the wine rack.

3 **Securely clamp each façade** and end-frame joint, then leave the assembly to dry.

THE FINISHED PIECE

ALTERNATIVES

If you are a more confident woodworker, try adapting the wine rack to your specific needs, or to the décor of the room for which it is intended. You could, for example, increase (or decrease) the height of the stiles and add additional façades if applicable. Alternatively, increase the length of the façades themselves to fit the space available (you may need to incorporate an additional central stile for support).

Aesthetic alternatives could involve experimenting with different shapes (perhaps you could shape the bottom edge of the façade to complement the curves in the top edge). Or try using different woods—walnut would be a suitable dark wood.

FINISHES

The wine rack featured here has been finished with Danish oil, which brings out the grain of the wood and emphasizes the contrast between the colors of the maple and cherry woods used. A clear acrylic varnish would be a good alternative if you want to preserve the natural colors of the wood. This project would also look good made in oak and finished with lime wax.

Hall shelf

This practical piece of wall furniture, designed for hanging coats and storing items such as hats, is an ideal way of using space in a narrow hallway. Its simple design, using minimal materials and basic techniques, can easily be altered to suit different requirements. Curved brackets with diminishing chamfers give structural stability and a graceful appearance to the piece. A chamfer is also run along the shelf edges. The wooden pegs have only minimal shaping and are mortised securely into the peg board.

Dimensions:
30¹¹⁄₁₆ x 8¼ x 14¼in (780 x 210 x 362mm)

Key techniques:
Full housing joint (pp.106–107);
Jigs and templates (pp.150–51)

TOOLS AND MATERIALS

- Metal ruler
- Pencil
- MDF (7 1⁄16 x 13 ¾ x ¼in/ 180 x 350mm x 6mm)
- Band saw or coping saw
- Flat spokeshave or router and chamfer cutter
- Marking knife
- Square
- Marking gauge
- Tenon saw
- Bevel-edged chisel
- Shoulder plane
- Mortise chisel
- Drill and bits
- Mortiser (optional)
- Sander
- Wood glue and brush
- Screwdriver and 8 screws
- Block plane

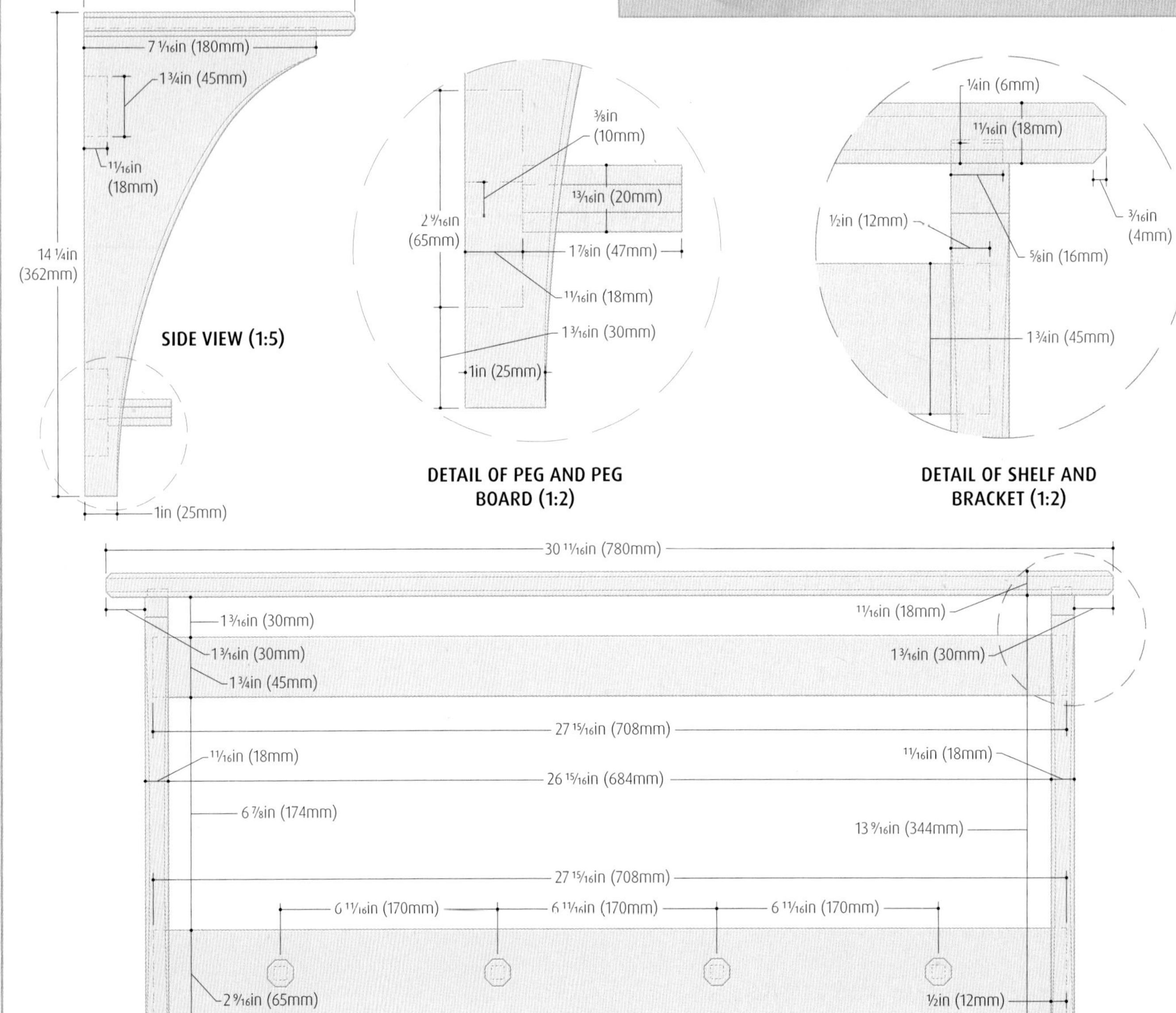

How the elements fit together
The curved brackets fit in a housing cut in the underside of the shelf. The top brace and peg board are attached to the brackets by means of halving joints and screws. The chamfered pegs are tenoned through the rail for maximum strength.

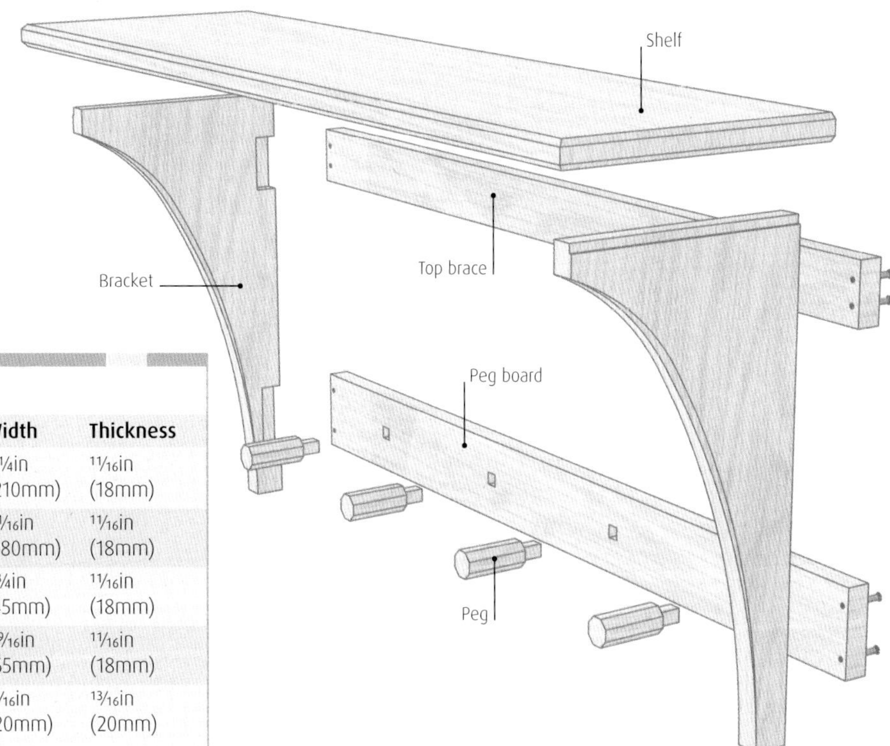

CUTTING LIST

Item	Material	No.	Length	Width	Thickness
Shelf	Oak	1	30 11/16in (780mm)	8 1/4in (210mm)	11/16in (18mm)
Brackets	Oak	2	13 3/4in (350mm)	7 1/16in (180mm)	11/16in (18mm)
Top brace	Oak	1	27 15/16in (708mm)	1 3/4in (45mm)	11/16in (18mm)
Peg board	Oak	1	27 15/16in (708mm)	2 9/16in (65mm)	11/16in (18mm)
Pegs	Oak	4	2 9/16in (65mm)	13/16in (20mm)	13/16in (20mm)

MAKING THE CURVED BRACKETS

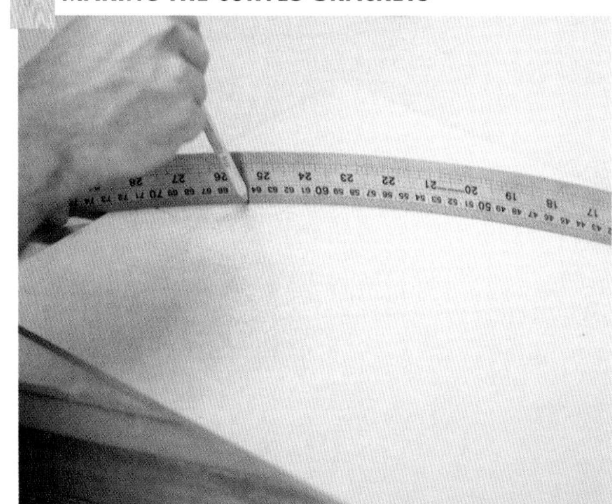

1 **Make a template** for the brackets from MDF (see Tools and materials, opposite, for the size). Mark 1in (25mm) from one corner along one short side and 1in (25mm) from the opposite corner along the adjacent long side. Form the curve with a metal ruler held between the two points—it is easier if a helper holds one end of the ruler. Cut out the template with a coping saw or band saw.

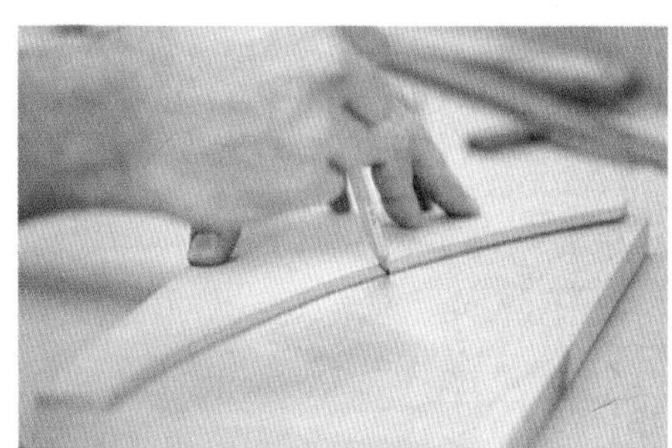

2 **Mark the shape** of the brackets on each bracket piece by aligning the jig to one corner and drawing around it with a pencil.

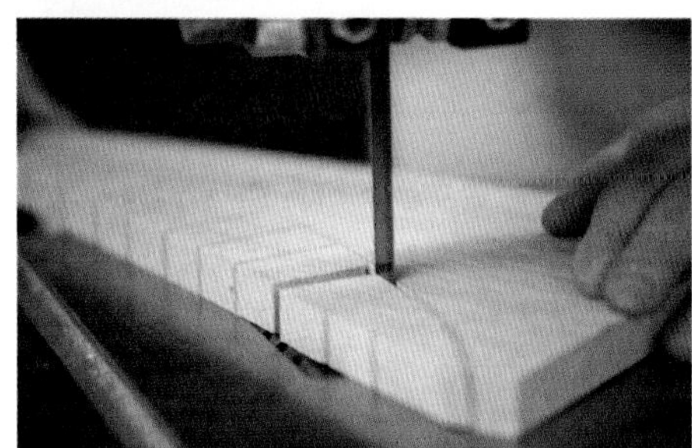

3 **Roughly cut the curved shape** of each bracket piece, using a band saw (pictured) or a coping saw.

4 **Smooth the curves** either by hand, using a spokeshave (pictured), or by machine, using a router. Place the two brackets side by side and smooth them at the same time for a good match.

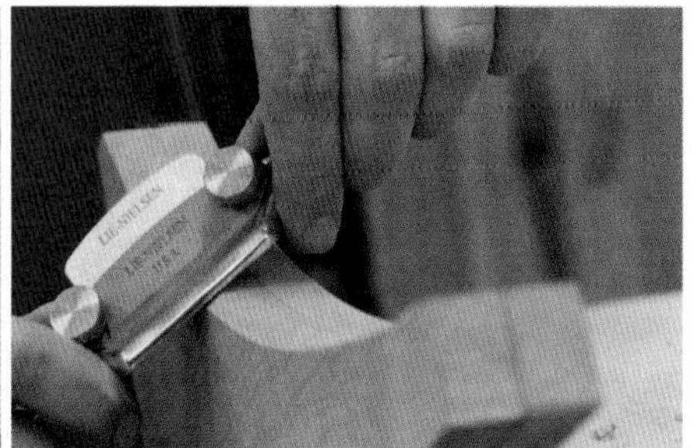

5 **Chamfer the center** of the curves on the outside edges of the brackets to create a diminishing stopped chamfer, either by hand with a spokeshave (pictured), or with a router fitted with a chamfer bit.

MARKING OUT AND CUTTING THE BRACKET HOUSINGS

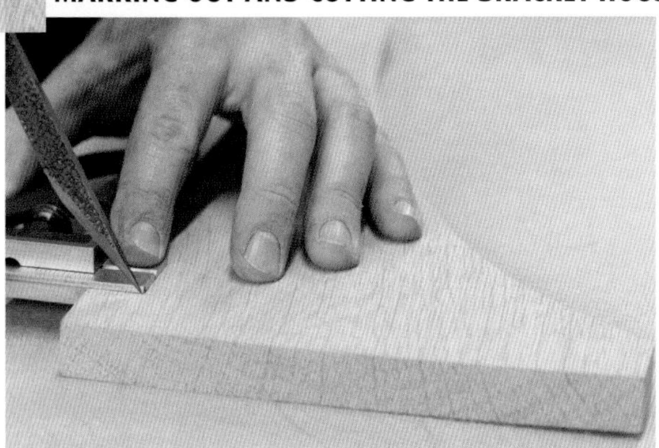

1 **Mark the housings** on the inside face of the long side of the first bracket piece. The upper housing is 1⅝in (42mm) long by 11⁄16in (18mm) wide, and starts 13⁄16in (30mm) from the top. The lower housing is 29⁄16in (65mm) long and 11⁄16in (18mm) wide, and starts 13⁄16in (30mm) from the other end of the bracket.

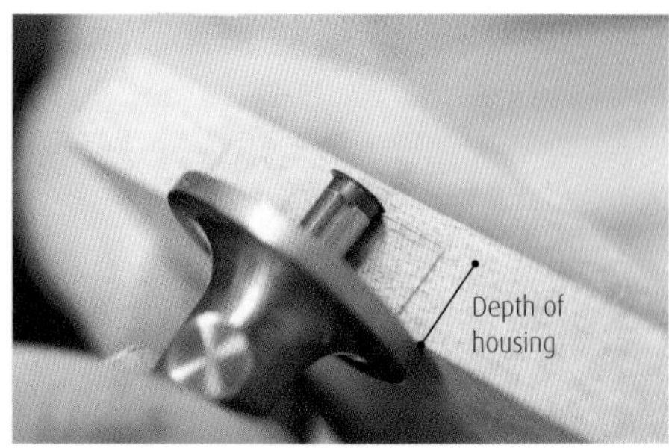

2 **Extend the marks** around onto the edge, and continue the line to mark the depth of the housings to ½in (12mm).

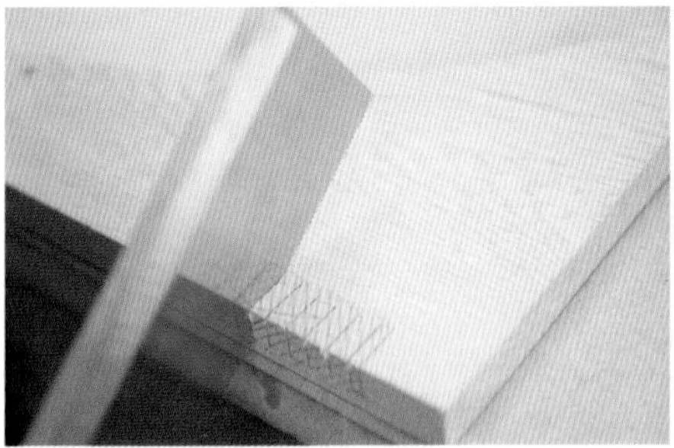

3 **Remove the waste** using a tenon saw. Make several cuts diagonally from corner to corner inside the marked area.

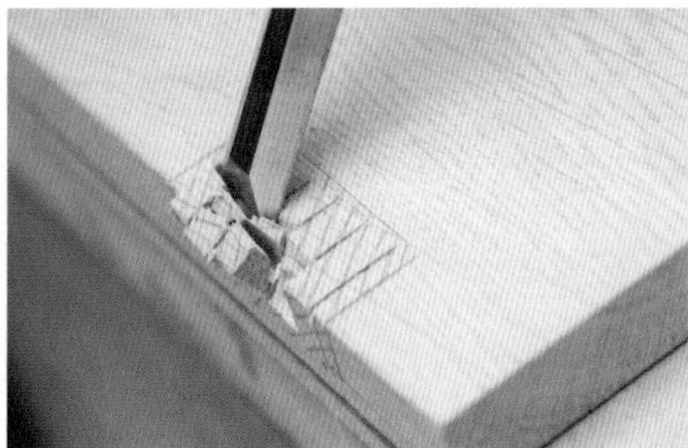

4 **Chop away the waste** from both housings and clean up the edges using a bevel-edge chisel.

5 **Mark and cut the housings** on the inside face of the second bracket in the same way.

MARKING OUT AND CUTTING THE SHOULDER

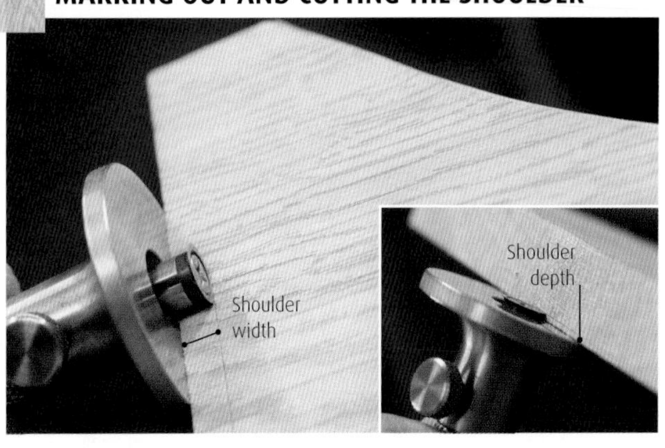

1 **Mark the width** of the shoulder along the face of the short side of the bracket with a marking gauge set to ¼in (6mm). Then mark the shoulder depth of 1⁄16in (2mm) on the bracket edge (inset).

2 **Set the bracket** in a vise and use a shoulder plane to cut the shoulder, taking care not to exceed the marked depth.

MARKING OUT THE HOUSINGS AND CHAMFERING THE SHELF

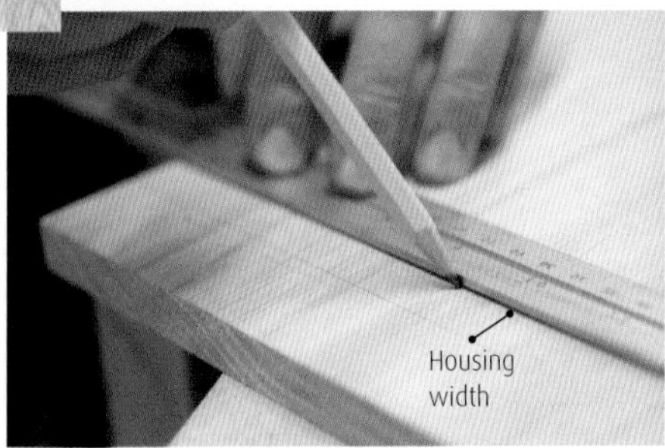

1 **Mark the positions** of the housings on the underside of the shelf 13⁄16in (30mm) from each end grain. Then mark the housing width of ⅝in (16mm).

2 **Mark the housing stop** 13⁄16in (30mm) from the front edge of the shelf. Mark the housing depth of 5⁄16in (7mm) on the back edge.

3 **Remove the waste** from the housing, using a mortise chisel. First chop vertically, then pare horizonally to the marked depth.

4 **Finish the shelf** by chamfering the front edges with a spokeshave to create a pleasing, smoothly angled effect.

MAKING THE PEG BOARD

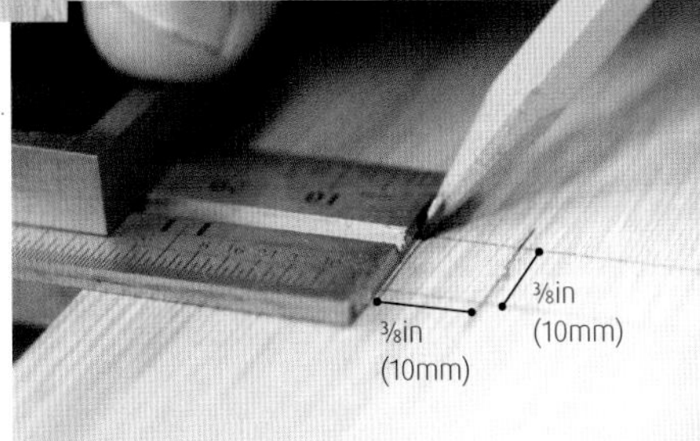

1 **Mark the four mortises** on the peg rail with a pencil and square. Each mortise is 3/8in (10mm) square.

2 **Drill away the bulk** of the waste with a drill (pictured) or a mortiser, extending the mortise all the way through the wood. Square off the holes with a chisel (inset). Assemble the shelf and brackets to check the fit.

FIXING THE TOP BRACE

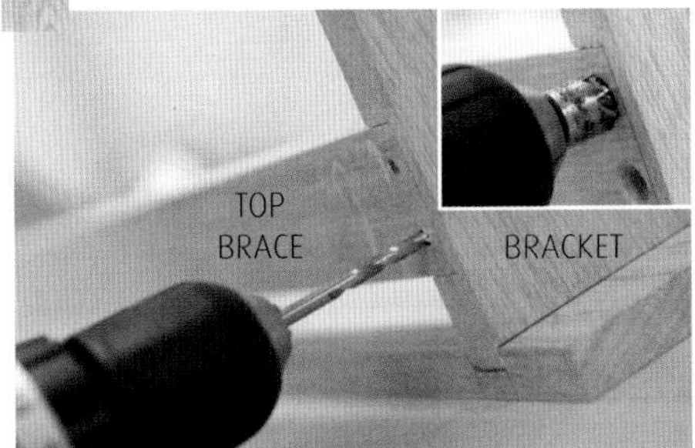

1 **Drill two screw holes** through each end of the top brace and peg board into the back edge of the brackets, centered on the thickness. Countersink the holes (inset).

2 **Disassemble the hall shelf** and sand each component, smoothing off any splinters and rough edges.

3 **Glue the housings** for the shelf and brackets, and assemble them. Screw the top brace and peg board into position in the housings on the brackets (inset).

MAKING AND FIXING THE PEGS

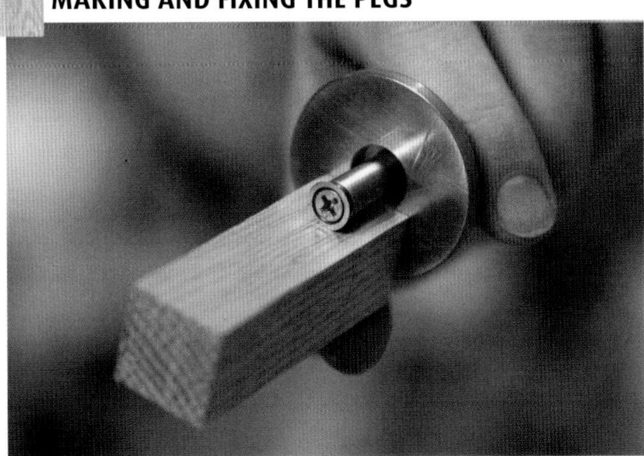

1 **Make a tenon** in the end of each peg. Set the marking gauge to 11/16in (18mm) and score the shoulder around all four sides.

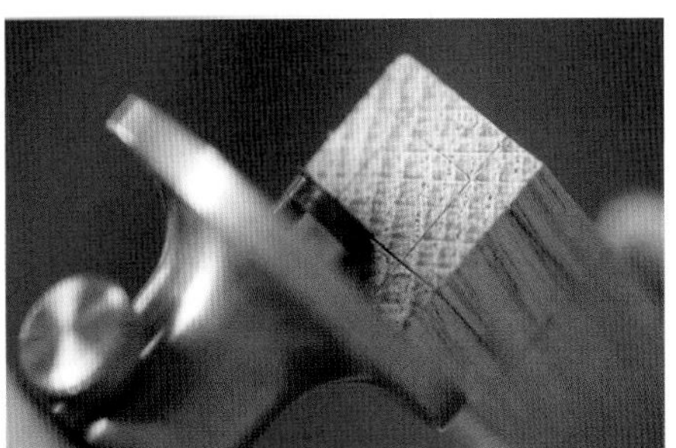

2 **Set the marking gauge** to 3/16in (5mm) and scribe the width of the shoulder on the end grain from each side. Extend the lines down all four sides to the shoulder.

3 Cut the tenon using a tenon saw, carefully sawing along each mark with the peg held securely in a vise.

4 Clean up the shoulders with a chisel, then check the fit of each peg in the mortises. Adjust if necessary.

5 Secure each peg in turn horizontally in the vise and chamfer all four edges with a block plane.

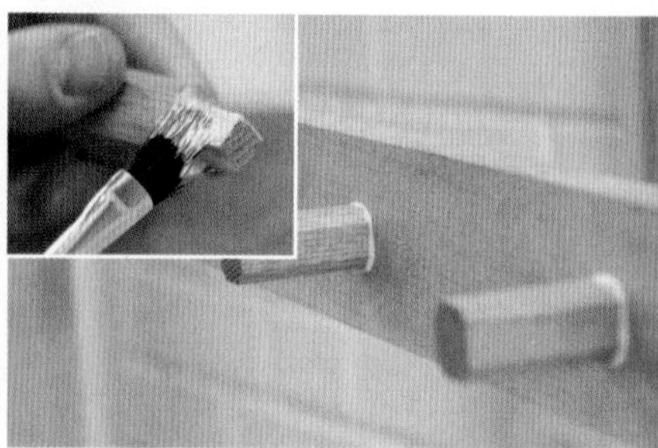

6 Glue the peg tenons (inset) and insert each one into its mortise, taking care to clean up any excess glue.

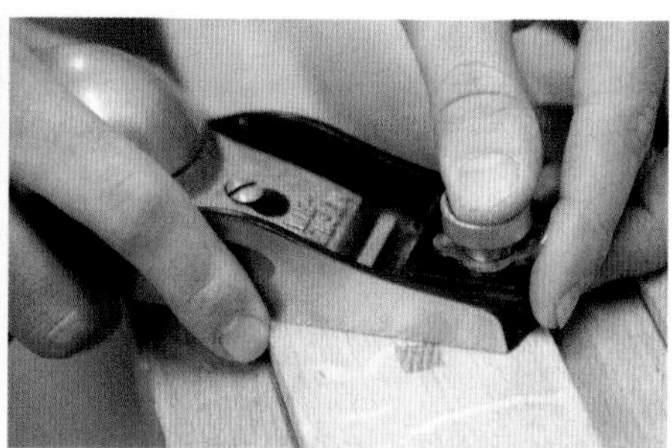

7 Unscrew the bottom rail and use a block plane to shave the ends of the pegs flush with the back of the rail. Screw in place again.

THE FINISHED PIECE

FINISHES

Either oil or wax would provide a suitable finish for this piece. If you are aiming to achieve an "antique" look—perhaps to match existing pieces of furniture in your home—you could apply a dark wood stain first. Be sure to choose an appropriate finish for the type of wood stain used (see Staining, p.166).

ALTERNATIVE PEGS

To adapt the design to suit a longer wallspace, you can increase the length of the shelf, top brace, and peg board, and use additional pegs, as required. Do bear in mind, however, that if you would like the hall shelf to be more than a third longer, you should use an extra bracket halfway across to provide additional support. Similarly, you can increase the width of the shelf to provide extra storage space or fit a larger hallway. You can also change the appearance of the piece by using notched or turned pegs, as for the coat rack (see pp. 208), or painting or staining it (see left) to suit the surrounding decor.

Laundry box

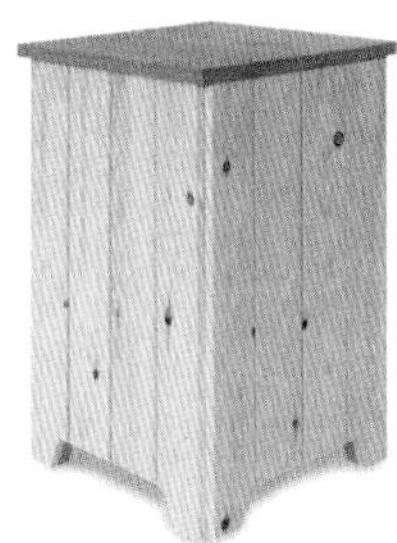

A simple project for the woodworker, this laundry box is a practical item to have in the home. It is also versatile, being robust and tall enough to be used as a seat as well as for storage. The design utilizes a biscuit-jointed MDF box for its internal structure—a useful technique that can be employed in a range of woodworking projects since it provides a quick, strong corner joint. The tongue-and-groove cladding is pinned and glued to the MDF core—another adaptable technique that can be used for covering surfaces around the home, such as boxes built around pipe work or cladding on the sides of a bathtub. The tongue-and-groove sections can be handmade, but it is worth checking to see what is available at your local timber merchants—it is often cheaper to buy cladding of a standard width and thickness.

Dimensions:
24 7/16 x 14 7/16 x 14 7/16in (620 x 366 x 366mm)

Key techniques:
Biscuit joints (pp.142–43);
Fixed tongue-and-groove joint (pp.98–99);
Edge-to-edge joint (pp.94–95)

14 7/16in (366mm)
1 15/16in (50mm)
13 1/4in (336mm)
14in (356mm)

SIDE VIEW (1:8)

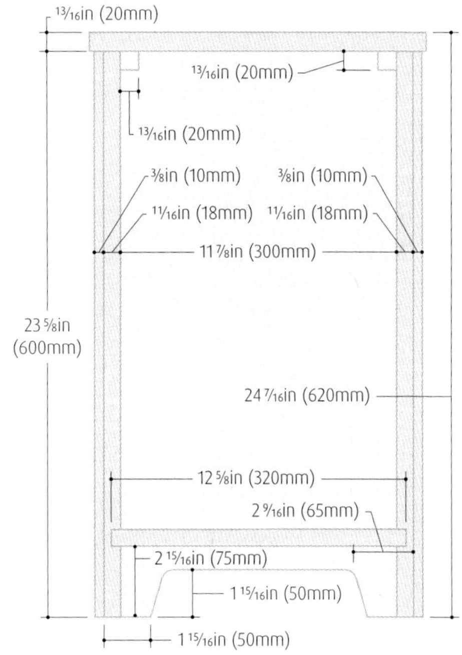

13/16in (20mm)
13/16in (20mm)
13/16in (20mm)
3/8in (10mm)
3/8in (10mm)
11/16in (18mm)
11/16in (18mm)
11 7/8in (300mm)
23 5/8in (600mm)
24 7/16in (620mm)
12 5/8in (320mm)
2 9/16in (65mm)
2 15/16in (75mm)
1 15/16in (50mm)
1 15/16in (50mm)

CROSS SECTION (1:8)

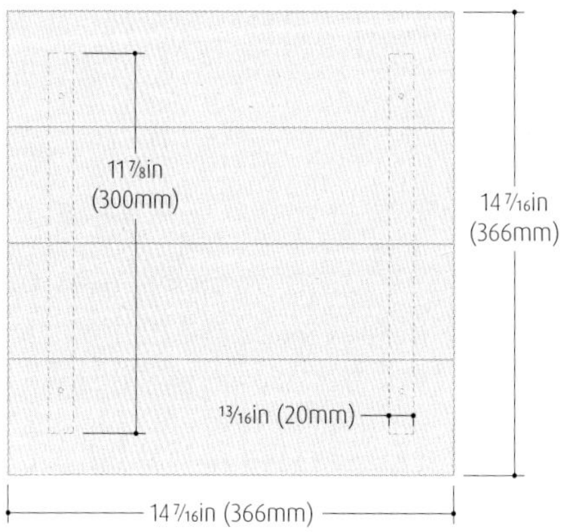

11 7/8in (300mm)
14 7/16in (366mm)
13/16in (20mm)
14 7/16in (366mm)

UNDERSIDE OF LID (1:8)

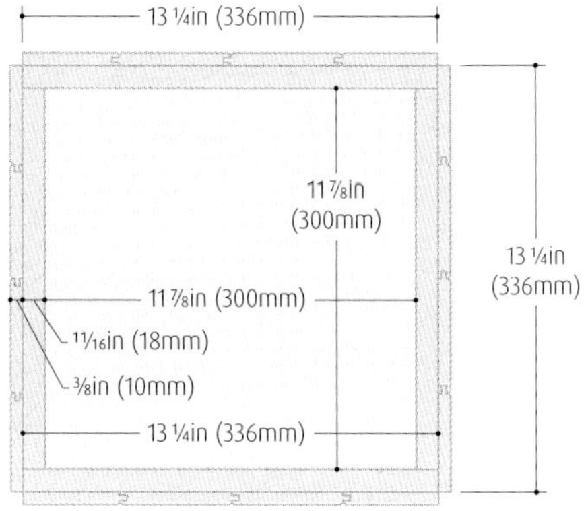

13 1/4in (336mm)
11 7/8in (300mm)
13 1/4in (336mm)
11 7/8in (300mm)
11/16in (18mm)
3/8in (10mm)
13 1/4in (336mm)

TOP VIEW (1:8)

How the elements fit together
The MDF core is biscuit-jointed and concealed within tongue-and-groove jointed pine cladding. The lid is a panel made from oak boards. It is secured over the box by two battens screwed to its underside.

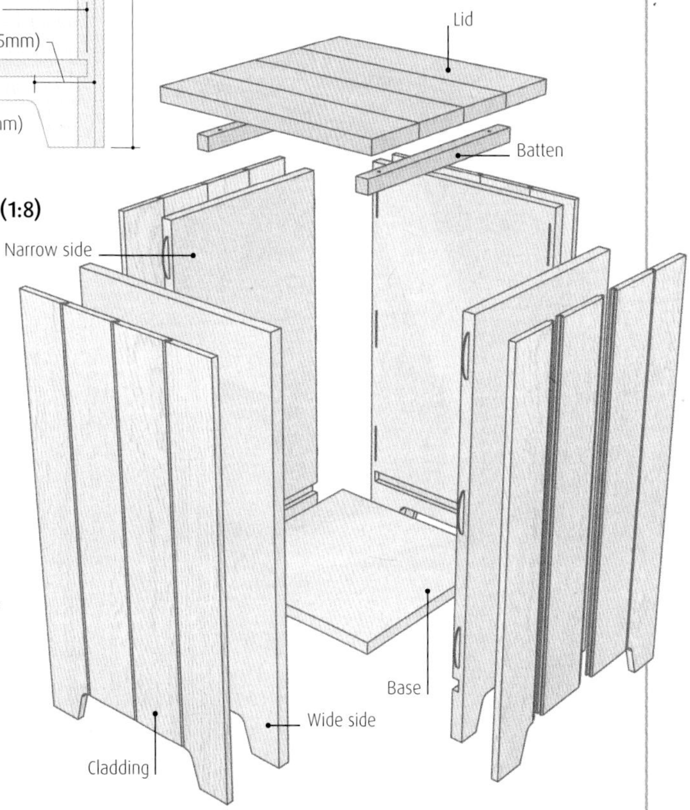

Lid
Batten
Narrow side
Base
Wide side
Cladding

TOOLS AND MATERIALS

- Pencil
- Square
- Router and cutters
- Chisel
- Band saw or jig saw
- Metal ruler
- Biscuit jointer
- 12 size 10 biscuits
- Wood glue and brush
- Sash clamps
- Tape measure
- Sandpaper
- Drill with bits
- 4 screws (8 x 1¼in/ 4 x 30mm)
- Block plane
- Bench plane
- Nail gun or hammer
- Coping saw

CUTTING LIST

Item	Material	No.	Length	Width	Thickness
Wide sides	MDF	2	23⅝in (600mm)	13¼in (336mm)	11/16in (18mm)
Narrow sides	MDF	2	23⅝in (600mm)	11⅞in (300mm)	11/16in (18mm)
Tongue-and-groove cladding	Pine	16	23⅝in (600mm)	3 9/16in (90mm)	⅜in (10mm)
Lid	Oak	4	15¾in* (400mm)	3in* (100mm)	13/16in (20mm)
Battens	Oak	2	11⅞in (300mm)	13/16in (20mm)	13/16in (20mm)
Base	MDF	1	12⅝in (320mm)	12⅝in (320mm)	11/16in (18mm)

*Includes excess to allow for cutting to size

CUTTING THE HOUSING FOR THE BASE

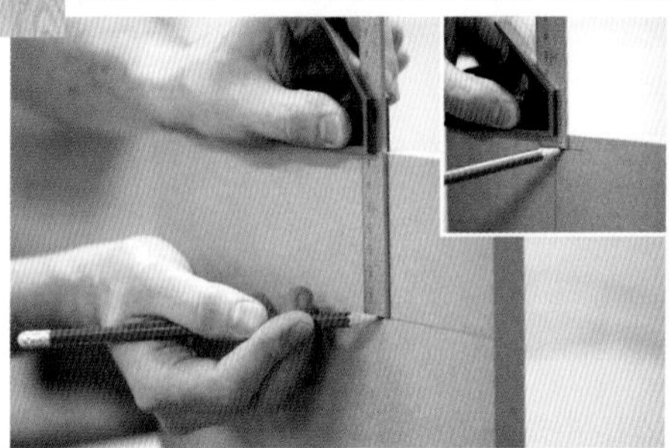

1 **Mark the lower edge** of the housing 2 15/16in (75mm) from the bottom of the four side pieces. Mark a stop ¼in (7mm) from both edges of the two wide sides (inset).

2 **Use a router** to cut the housing on the two narrow sides above the marked lines to a width of 11/16in (18mm) and a depth of ⅜in (10mm). Extend the housing through the full width of each piece.

3 **Cut the housing** on the wide sides to the marked stop (inset), then square off the ends with a chisel.

MARKING OUT THE FEET

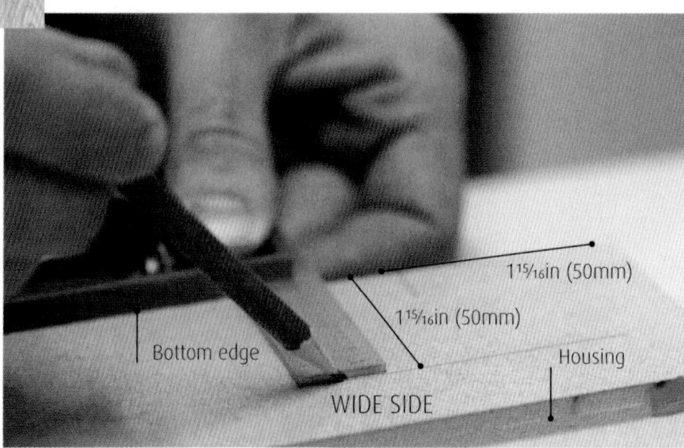

1 **Mark a point** on the bottom edge of a wide side, on the same face as the housing, 1 15/16in (50mm) from one side. Repeat from the other side, on the same face. Then draw a line across the width of the side 1 15/16in (50mm) from the bottom edge. Repeat on the other wide side.

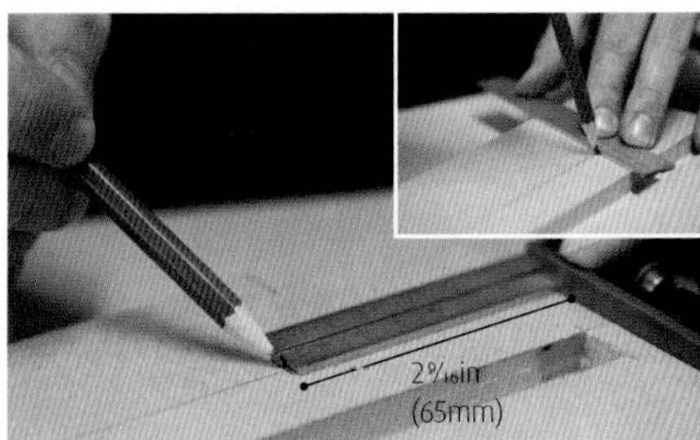

2 **Mark a point** 2 9/16in (65mm) from each edge on the lines just drawn. Draw lines to join those points to the marks made on the bottom edges in Step 1 (inset).

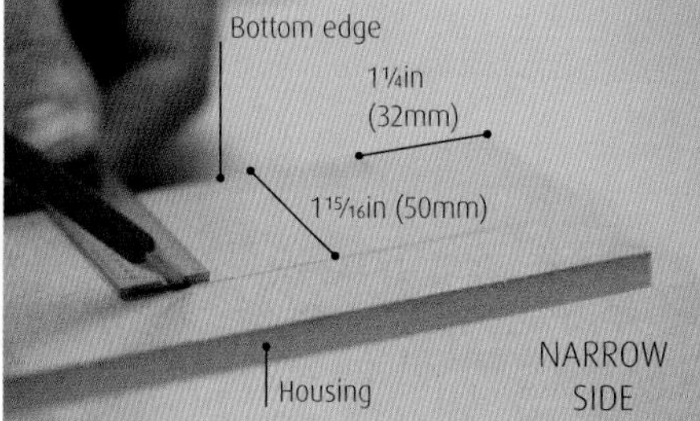

3 **Mark 1¼in (32mm)** from both edges of one narrow side, on the same face as the housing. Then draw a line across the side 1 15/16in (50mm) from the bottom edge.

4 **Mark a point** 1⅞in (47mm) from both edges along the lines just drawn, then join the points to the marks made in Step 3. Repeat Steps 3–4 on the other narrow side.

CUTTING OUT THE FEET

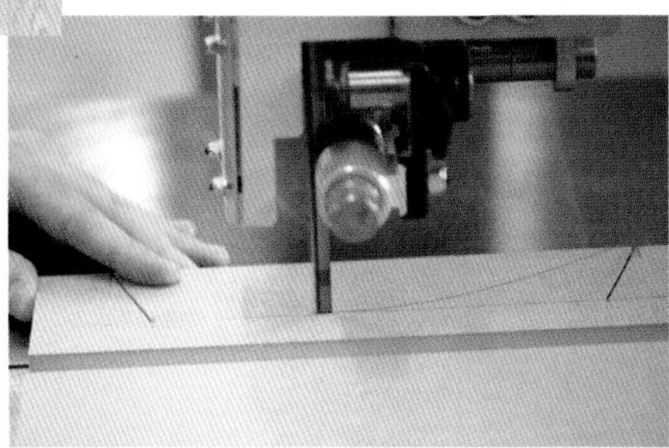

1 **Cut out the feet** of all four sides using a band saw (pictured) or jig saw. Cut on the waste side of the marked lines.

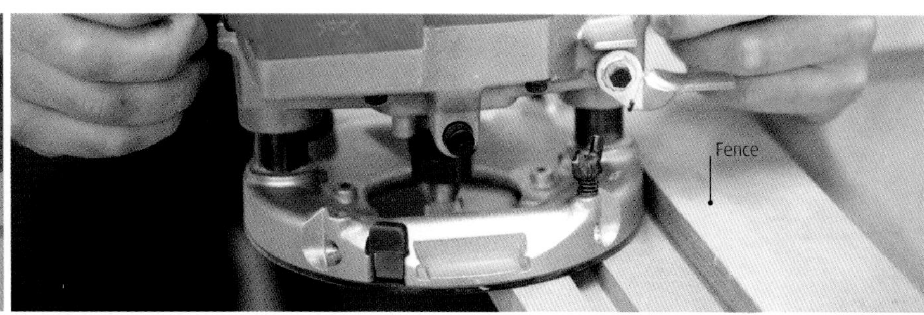

2 **Trim back to the marked lines** with a router. Cramp a straight edge of spare wood to the piece to act as a fence (guide) for the router.

JOINTING THE SIDES

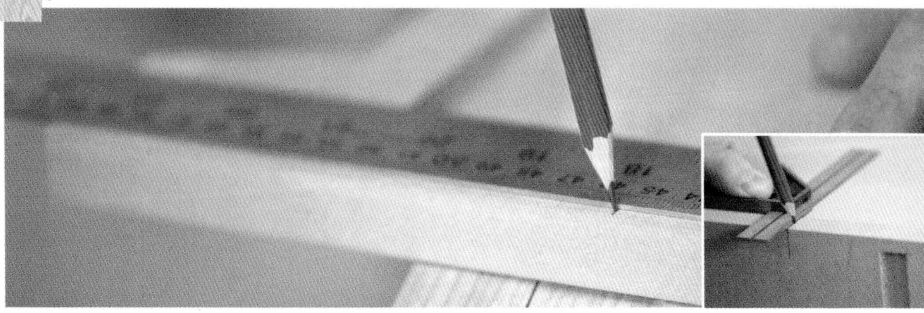

1 **Mark the positions** for three biscuit joints along both vertical (long) edges of each wide side, spaced approximately equidistantly above the base housing. Extend the marks across the full width of the edges (inset).

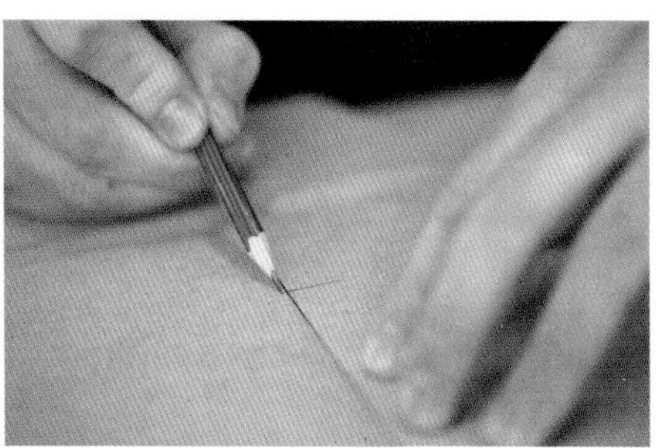

2 **Set a narrow side** alongside a wide side and transfer the marks onto the inner face of the narrow side.

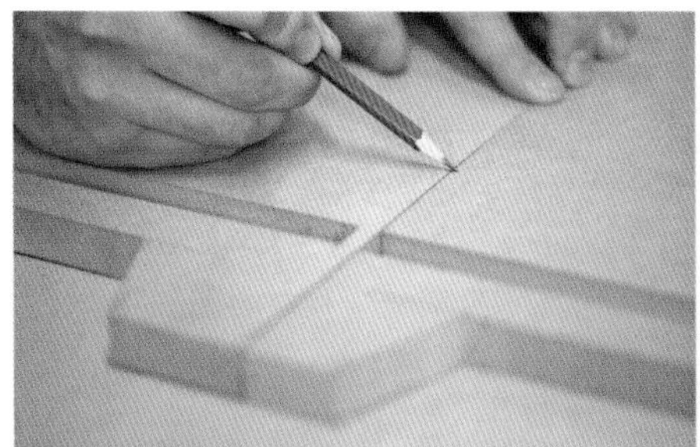

3 **Repeat this process** to mark the guide positions for the biscuit jointer on the opposite side of the inner face. Repeat Steps 2 and 3 for the remaining narrow side.

4 **Use a biscuit jointer** to cut size 10 slots in both vertical (long) edges of the narrow sides. Center the biscuit jointer on each of the marks on the inner face.

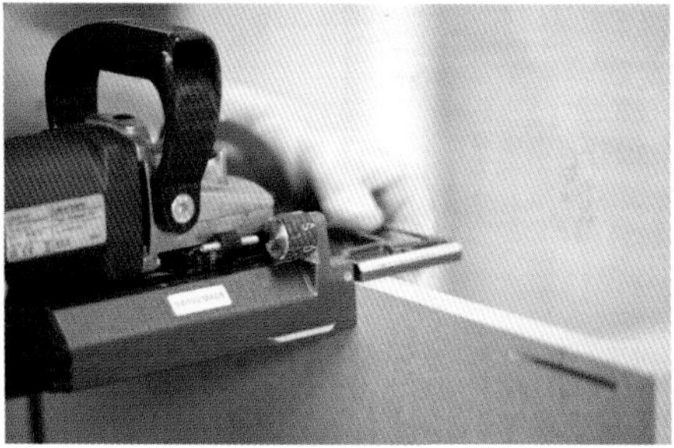

5 **Cut the slots** in the wide sides in the same way, but in the inner face. This time, center the biscuit jointer on each of the marks on the edges.

ASSEMBLING THE SIDES AND BASE

1 **Insert a size 10 biscuit** into each of the slots in the edges of the narrow sides, then test-assemble the structure. Insert the base in the housing to check the fit.

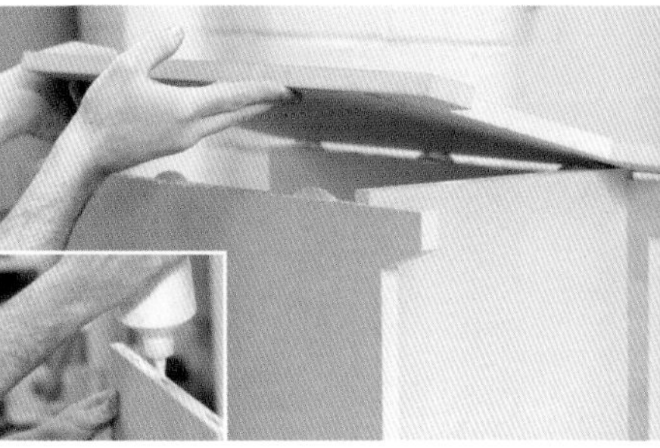

2 **Apply glue liberally** to the biscuits and the edges of the sides (inset). Assemble three sides, insert the base, and then place the fourth side in position.

3 **Clamp the assembly** with sash clamps and check for squareness with a tape measure. Clean up any excess glue.

MAKING THE LID

1 **Join the lid pieces** (see Edge-to-edge joint, pp.94–95) and cut to the final size (see the diagram on p.221). Sand smooth.

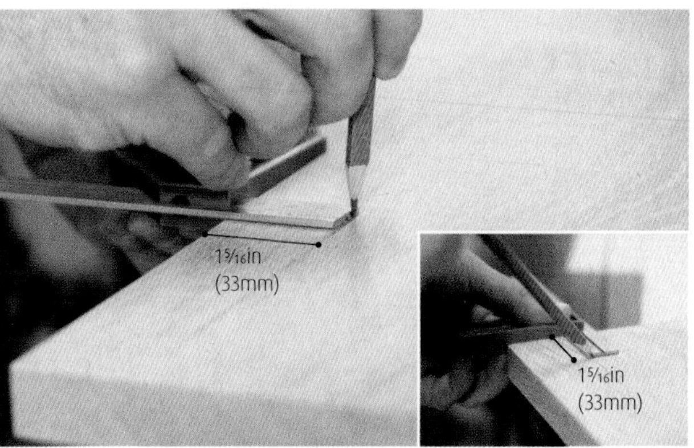

2 **Mark a line** 1⁵⁄₁₆in (33mm) from each edge on the underside of the lid. Then mark a point 1⁵⁄₁₆in (33mm) from the end grain at each end of both lines (inset). These marks define the positions of the battens.

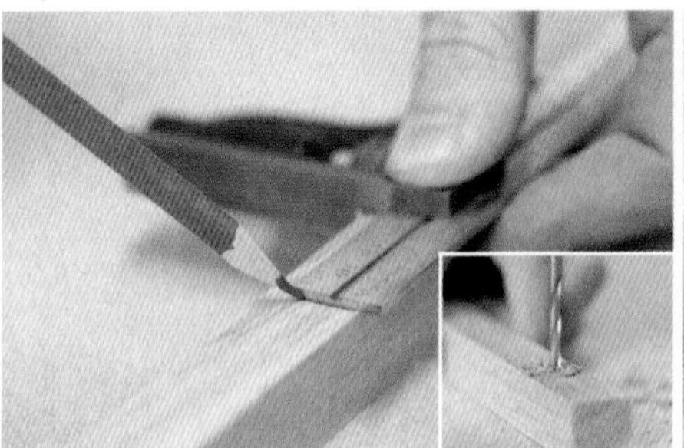

3 **Mark a screw hole** ¹³⁄₁₆in (20mm) from each end of both battens. Drill clearance holes to match the screws, centered within the batten width (inset).

4 **Countersink the holes** (inset). Place the battens on the underside of the lid in the marked positions, then drill pilot holes part way into the lid through the clearance holes.

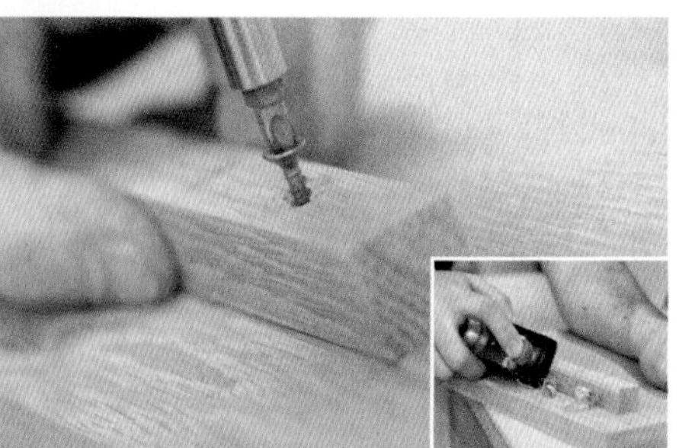

5 **Screw the battens** into position. Use a block plane to chamfer the outside edges of the battens (inset).

FIXING THE TONGUE-AND-GROOVE CLADDING

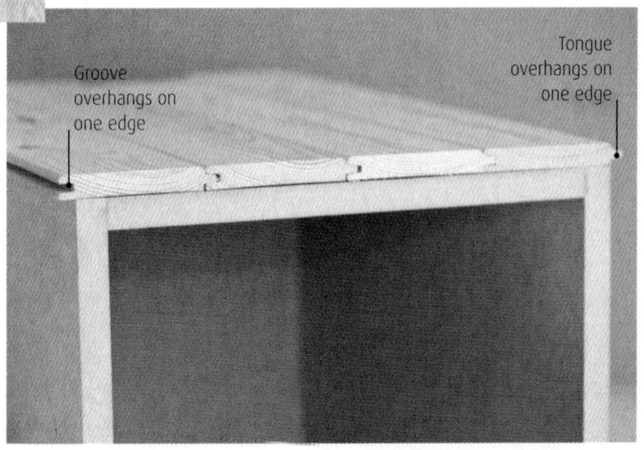

1 **Assemble four pieces** of tongue-and-groove cladding and position them against one side of the box. Align them flush to the top edge so that the tongue and the groove of the outside pieces overhang the sides.

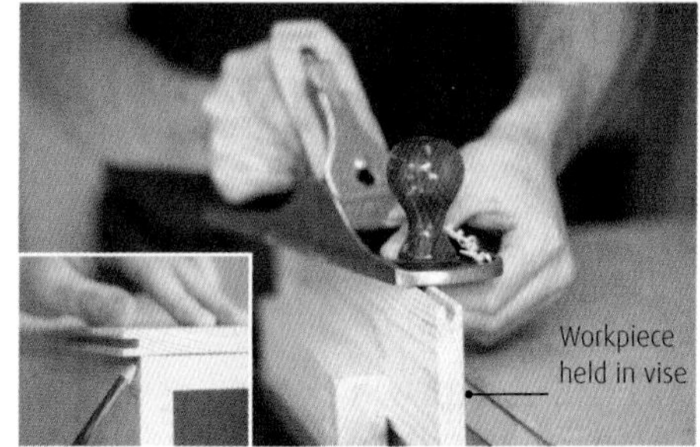

2 **Draw a pencil line** to mark the position of the overhang on the underside of each of the outer slats (inset). Use a bench plane to trim the outer edges to the line.

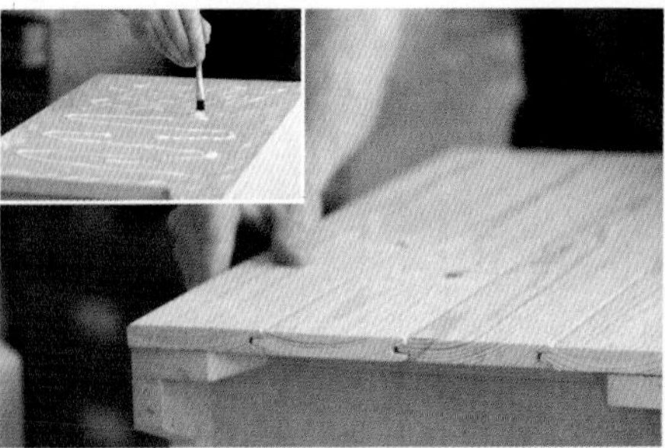

3 **Apply wood glue** to the side of the box, spreading it evenly over the entire surface with a brush (inset). Then set the assembled slats in position on the glued side. Adjust them to align as in Step 1 (above).

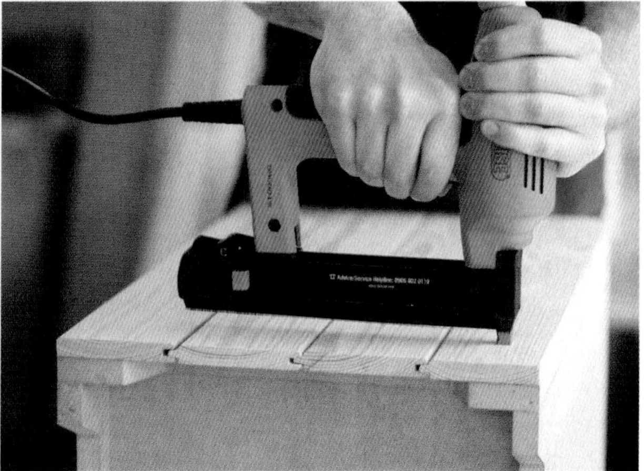

4 **Nail the cladding** to the box side with panel pins using a nail gun (pictured), or by hand with a hammer. Insert a pin at the top and bottom of each slat approximately 1in (25mm) from the end. Allow the glue to dry.

CUTTING OUT THE LEGS AND FINISHING THE BOX

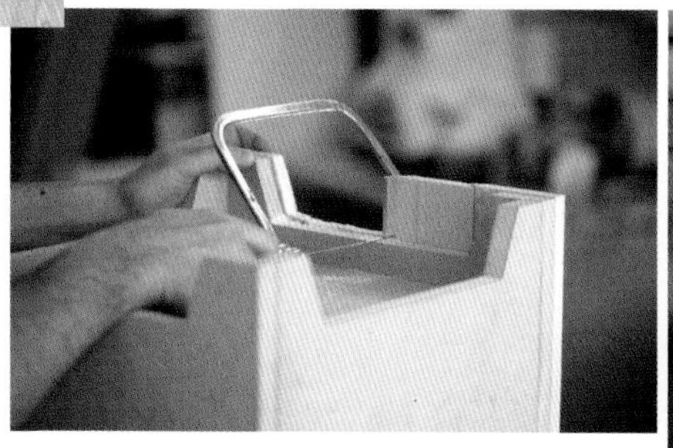

1 **Roughly cut the shape** of the legs from the cladding using a coping saw, following the shape of the MDF carcass.

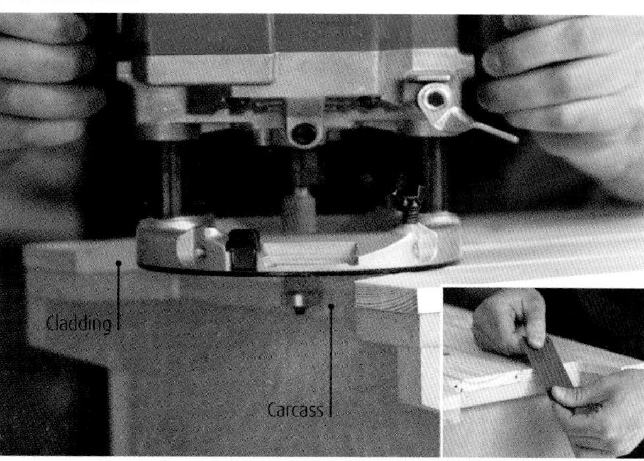

2 **Use a router** fitted with a bearing-guided straight cutter to trim the cladding flush to the carcass base. Sand the edges smooth (inset).

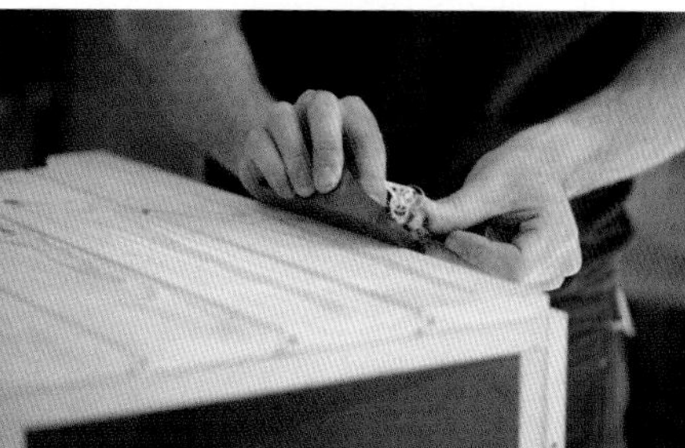

3 **Repeat steps 1–4**, fixing the tongue-and-groove cladding (opposite), for the remaining three sides. Then repeat Steps 1–2 (above) to cut out the remaining legs.

4 **Once all the cladding** is in place, use a block plane to chamfer the outer edges of the cladding along each corner of the box.

UNDERSIDE OF THE LID

FINISHES

You can paint the box in a color to fit the color scheme of the room for which it is intended. Be sure to apply knotting solution (see Painting, p.69) first to any knots in the pine. Alternatively, you can achieve a natural finish on the pine cladding by applying clear varnish (see p.171). The oak of the lid needs only a few coats of finishing oil to achieve a rich color and provide a good protective layer.

THE FINISHED PIECE

Plate rack

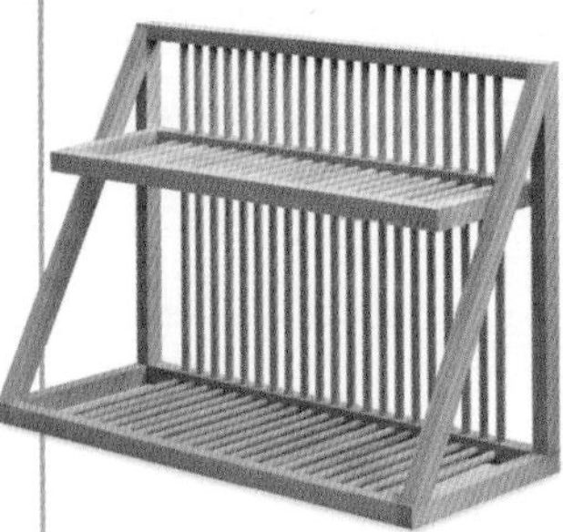

A wall-mounted plate rack is a functional solution for the kitchen, providing a space where dishes can be left to dry and stored afterward. This accessible project involves only a few basic woodworking techniques. Its design features dowel joints made using dowel centerpoints and shop-bought beech doweling—the most common type of doweling—as the primary method of jointing. The close grain of beech, a traditional timber choice for kitchen furniture and accessories, makes it a suitable material for this project. The dimensions of the plate rack can be enlarged to a maximum of approximately 31½in (800mm), or reduced to fit the space available, by changing the length of the rails and the number of shelf dowels. You will need to fix wall-mountings suitable for your wall surface to the back of the rack.

Dimensions:
25⁹⁄₁₆ x 10¼ x 18⅛in (650 x 260 x 460mm)

Key technique:
Dowel joints using centerpoints (pp.147–48)

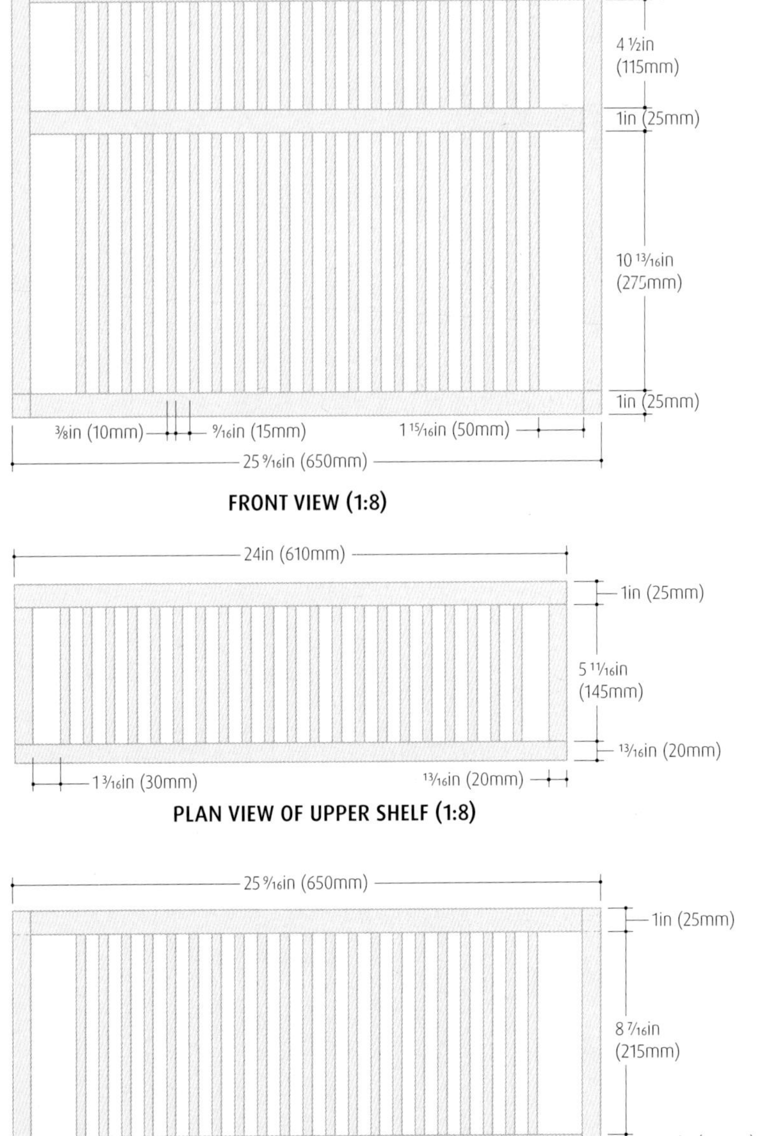

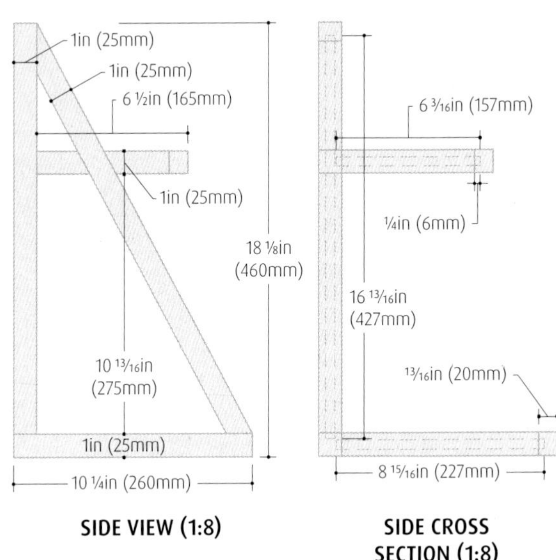

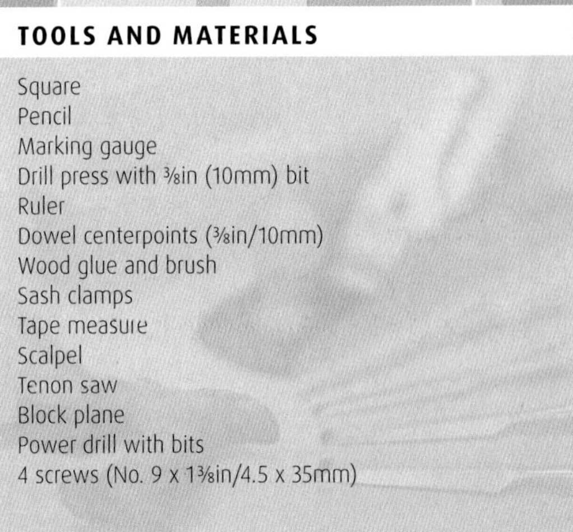

TOOLS AND MATERIALS

Square
Pencil
Marking gauge
Drill press with ⅜in (10mm) bit
Ruler
Dowel centerpoints (⅜in/10mm)
Wood glue and brush
Sash clamps
Tape measure
Scalpel
Tenon saw
Block plane
Power drill with bits
4 screws (No. 9 x 1⅜in/4.5 x 35mm)

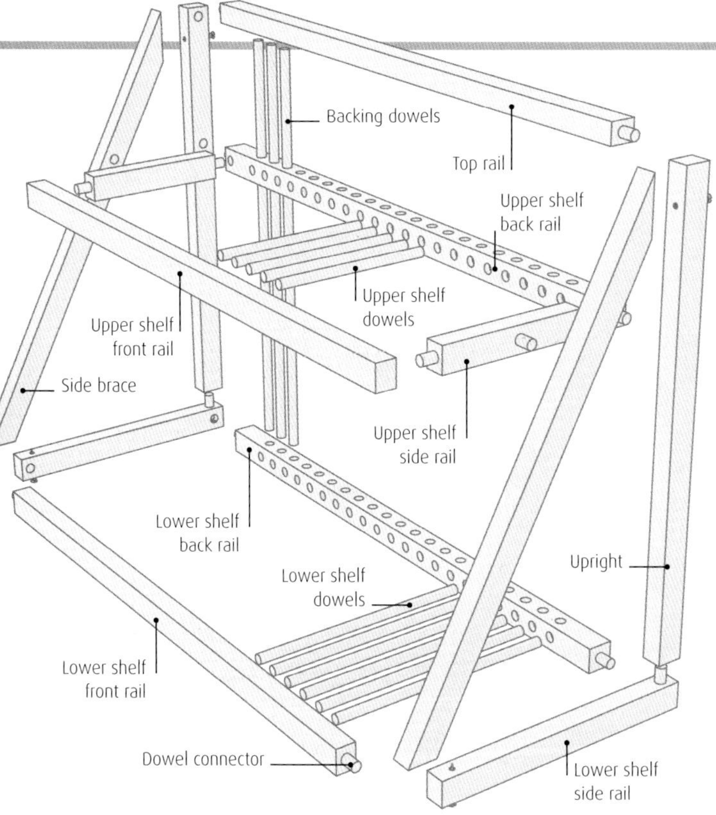

How the elements fit together
The shelves, uprights, and top rail are joined with 10mm (⅜in) beech dowels, while the diagonal side braces are secured to the uprights and lower shelf with screws, and to the upper shelf with dowels.

CUTTING LIST

Item	Material	No.	Length	Width	Thickness
Uprights	Beech	2	17⅛in (435mm)	1in (25mm)	13/16in (20mm)
Side braces	Beech	2	23⅝in* (600mm)	1in (25mm)	13/16in (20mm)
Lower shelf back rail	Beech	1	24in (610mm)	1in (25mm)	1in (25mm)
Lower shelf front rail	Beech	1	24in (610mm)	1in (25mm)	13/16in (20mm)
Lower shelf side rails	Beech	2	10¼in (260mm)	1in (25mm)	13/16in (20mm)
Upper shelf back rail	Beech	1	24in (610mm)	1in (25mm)	1in (25mm)
Upper shelf front rail	Beech	1	24in (610mm)	1in (25mm)	13/16in (20mm)
Upper shelf side rails	Beech	2	5 11/16in (145mm)	1in (25mm)	13/16in (20mm)
Top rail	Beech	1	24in (610mm)	1in (25mm)	13/16in (20mm)
Backing dowels	Beech	21	16 13/16in (427mm)	⅜in (10mm)	⅜in (10mm)
Lower shelf dowels	Beech	21	8 5/16in (227mm)	⅜in (10mm)	⅜in (10mm)
Upper shelf dowels	Beech	21	6 3/16in (157mm)	⅜in (10mm)	⅜in (10mm)
Dowel connectors	Beech	16	1⅛in (28mm)	⅜in (10mm)	⅜in (10mm)

*Includes excess to allow for cutting to size

MAKING THE LOWER SHELF BACK RAIL

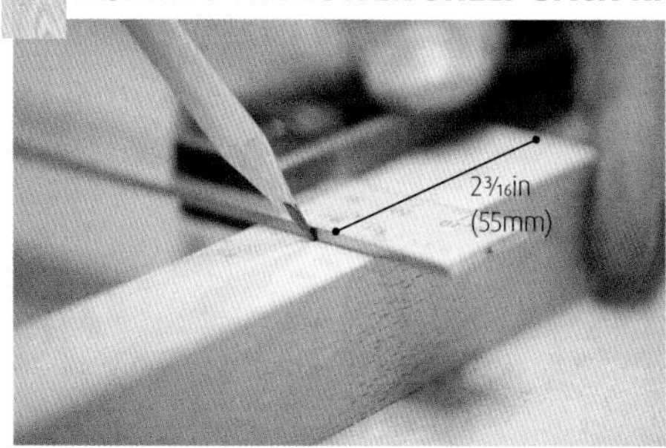

1 **Mark the positions** of the holes for the horizontal dowels on the face of the lower shelf back rail, starting with the two end holes, which are 2 3/16in (55mm) from each end grain.

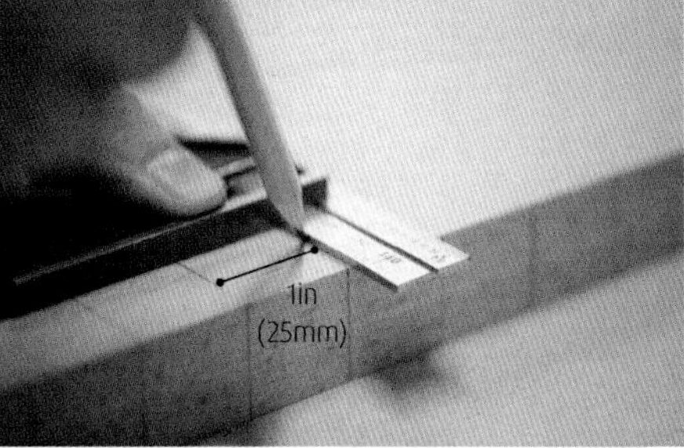

2 **Mark the positions** of the remaining 20 holes at 1in (25mm) intervals. Extend each of the marks onto one adjacent edge.

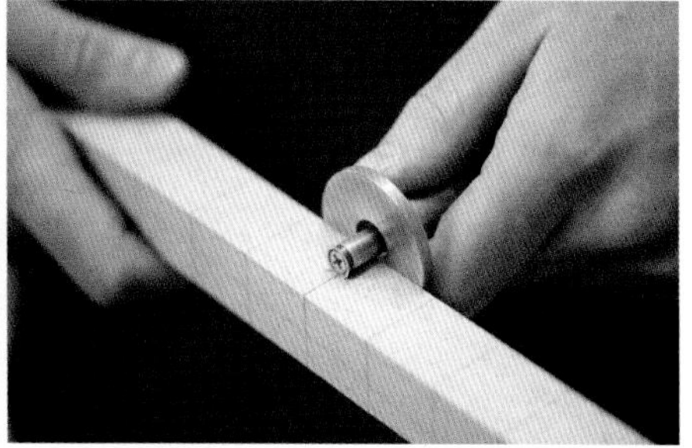

3 **Use a marking gauge** to scribe along the center of the width of both marked sides to mark the exact position of the hole on each line.

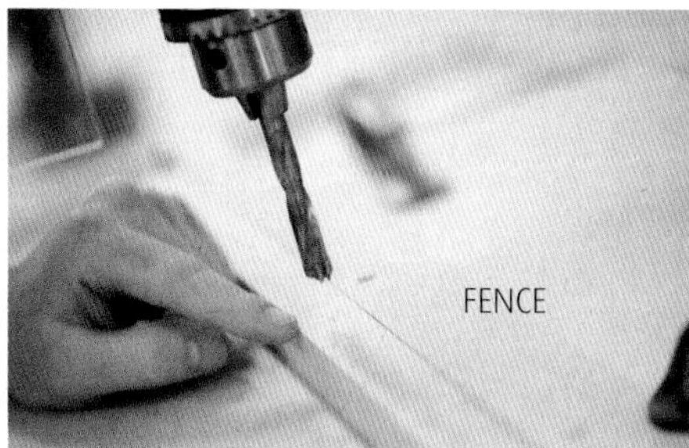

4 **Secure a fence** to the base of a drill press to fix the drilling position over the center the rail, ½in (12.5mm) from the edge. Attach a ⅜in (10mm) bit.

5 **Drill the holes** in the face of the rail, 5/16in (7mm) in depth. Turn the rail and drill the holes in the marked edge to a depth of 5/16in (7mm) (inset).

MAKING THE LOWER SHELF FRONT RAIL

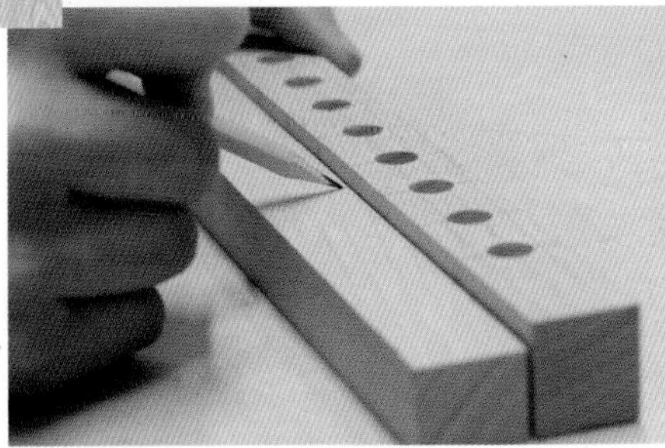

1 **Align the lower shelf front rail** against the lower shelf back rail and transfer the positions of the 21 holes onto one face.

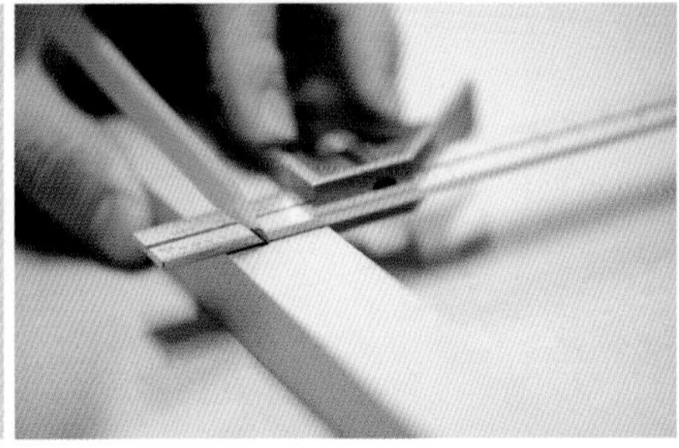

2 **Use a square** and pencil to extend the marks across the face of the lower shelf front rail.

3 **With the drill press** set up as before, drill holes in the marked positions to a depth of 5⁄16in (7mm).

MAKING THE DOWEL JOINT HOLES IN THE LOWER SHELF

1 **Mark the center** of both end grains on the lower shelf back rail by drawing diagonals from corner to corner. Mark the front rail in the same way.

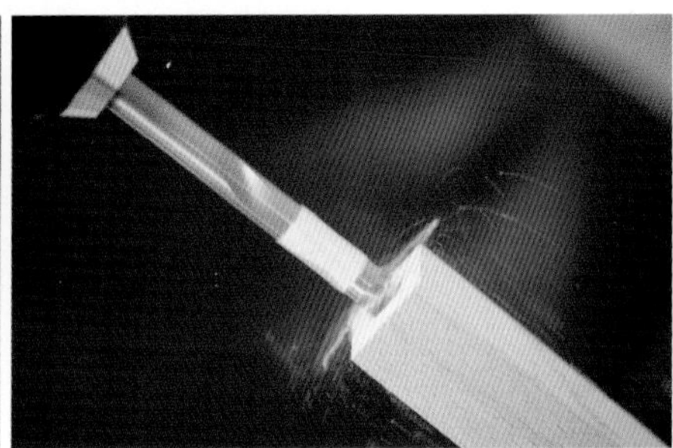

2 **Use a drill** fitted with a 3⁄8in (10mm) bit to drill into the marked center of each end grain to a depth of 9⁄16in (15mm).

3 **Insert a dowel centerpoint** into each of the holes in the end grains of the lower shelf front and back rails.

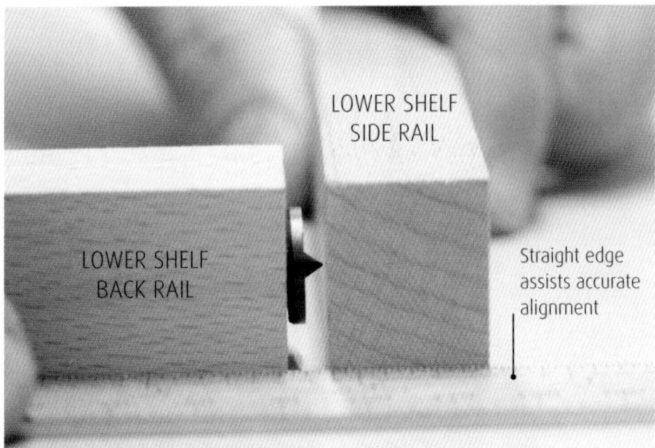

4 **Set the end** of the lower shelf back rail at right angles to the face of a lower shelf side rail, then press the two pieces together to mark the position of the dowel. Repeat Steps 1–4 to match all dowel centerpoints on the back and front rails of the lower shelf to their positions in relation to both side rails.

5 **Drill a hole** 3⁄8in (10mm) in diameter into each marked position in the lower shelf side rails, to a depth of 5⁄8in (15mm).

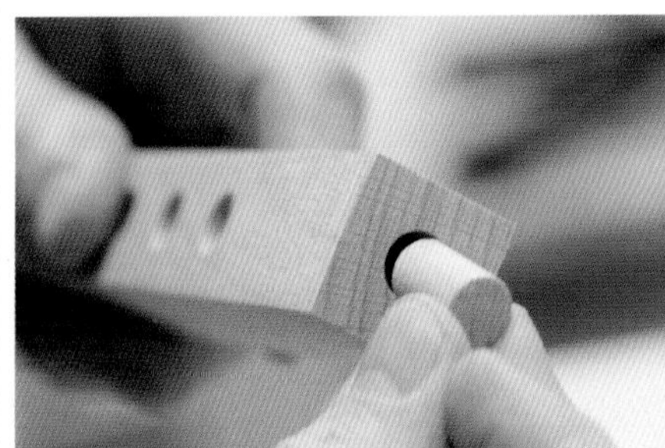

6 **Cut four 1 1⁄8in (28mm) pieces** of dowel and insert a piece into each end of the lower shelf front and back rails. Check the lower shelf assembles correctly.

ASSEMBLING THE LOWER SHELF

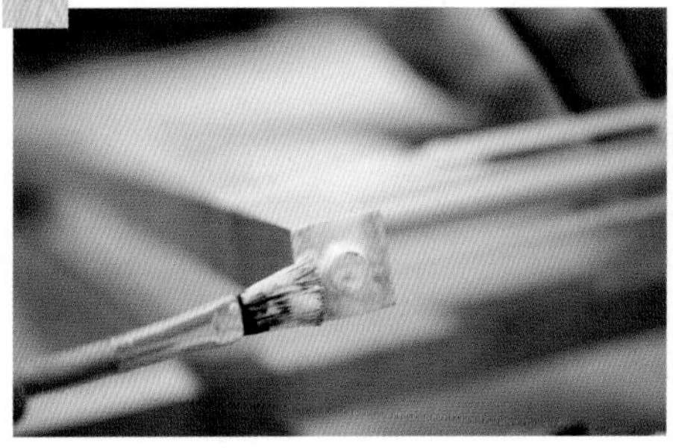

1 **Insert the dowels** unglued into the holes on the inside faces of the front and back rails. Remove, brush glue into the joint holes and over the end grains, and reassemble.

2 **Clamp the assembly** with sash clamps and use a tape measure to check for squareness (see p.75). Leave the shelf to dry.

MAKING THE UPPER SHELF

1 **Set the upper shelf back rail** alongside the lower shelf back rail, then transfer the marks for the position of the 21 dowels.

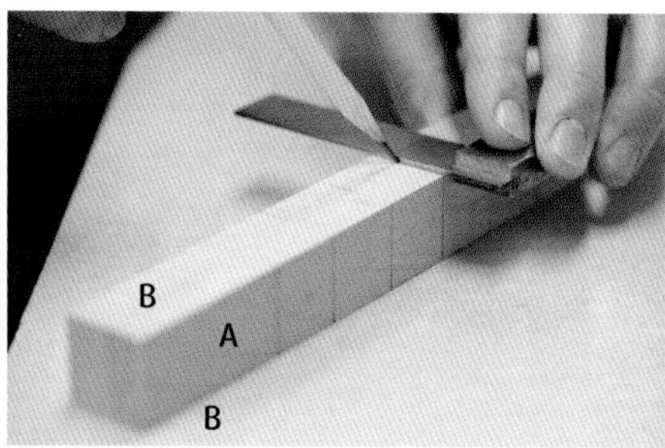

2 **Square the marks** across the face of the upper shelf back rail (A) and onto both adjacent edges (B).

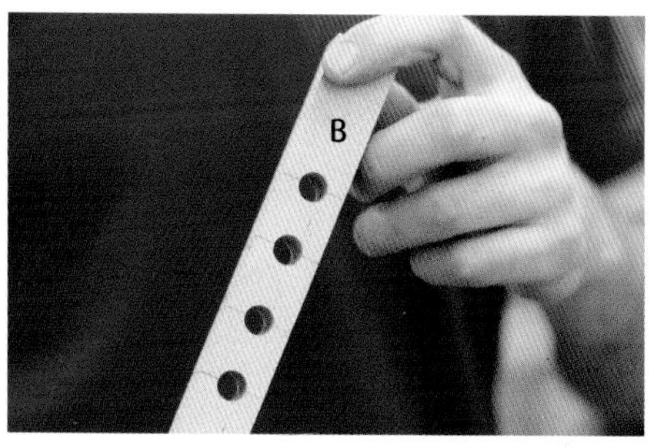

3 **Using the drill press** as previously set (with a ⅜in/10mm bit), drill holes in each of the marked positions. Drill through the wood from both edges (B).

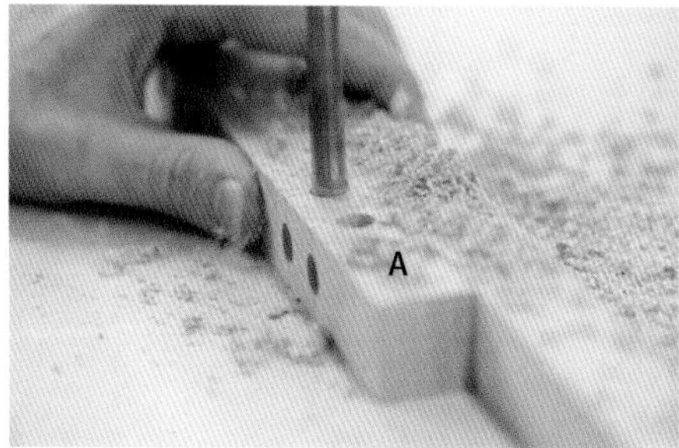

4 **Drill to a depth** of 5⁄16in (7mm) in the positions marked on the face (A), using the drill press as previously set.

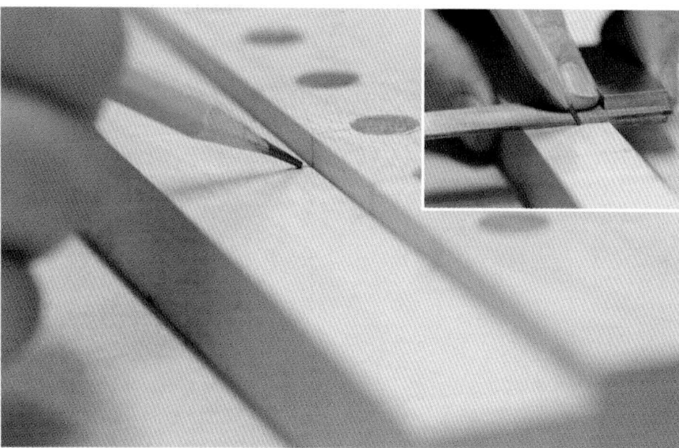

5 **Set the upper shelf front rail** against the upper shelf back rail and transfer the positions of the holes onto the face. Square off the marks with a pencil and square (inset).

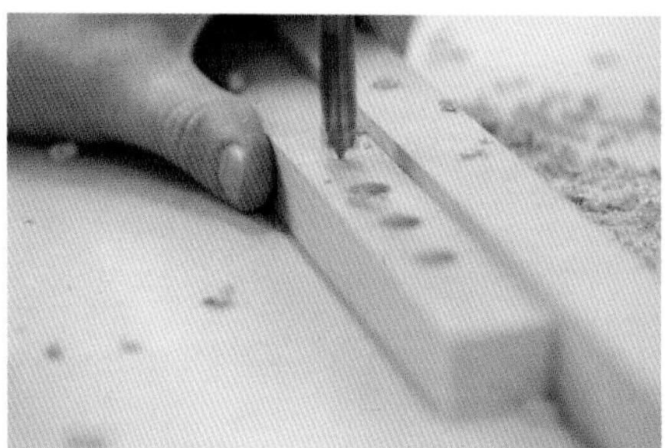

6 **Drill holes** in each of the marked positions to a depth of 5⁄16in (7mm), using the drill press as previously set.

MAKING THE DOWEL JOINT HOLES IN THE UPPER SHELF

1 **Mark the centerpoint** of both end grains of both upper shelf side rails by drawing diagonals from corner to corner.

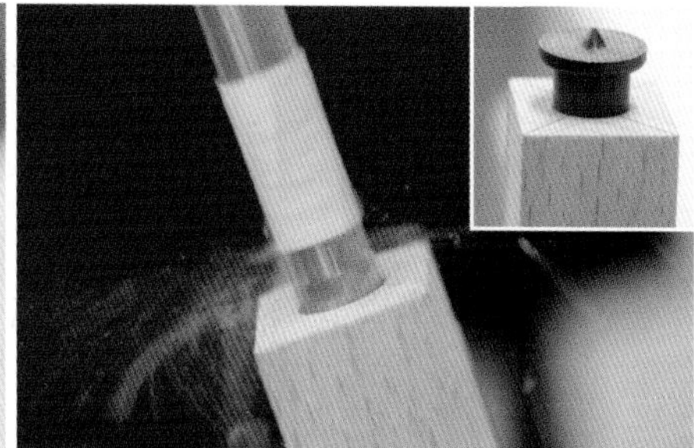

2 **Drill into each position** with a ⅜in (10mm) bit to a depth of 9⁄16in (15mm). Insert a dowel centerpoint into each hole (inset).

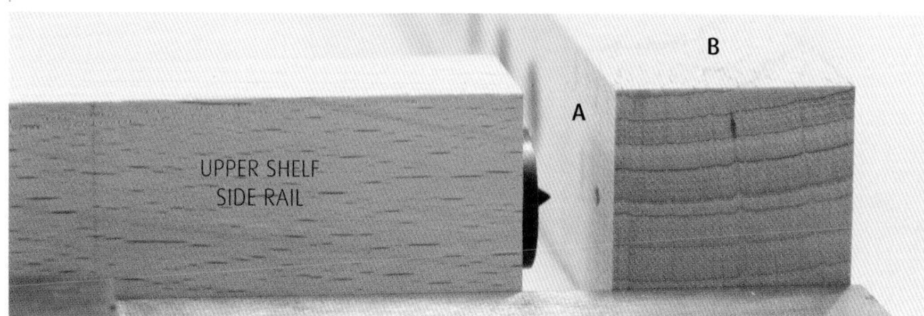

3 **Press the points** into the upper shelf front and back rails against face A on the back rail and the drilled face of the front rail. Ensure that the outer faces of the side rails are aligned to the end grains of the front and back rails.

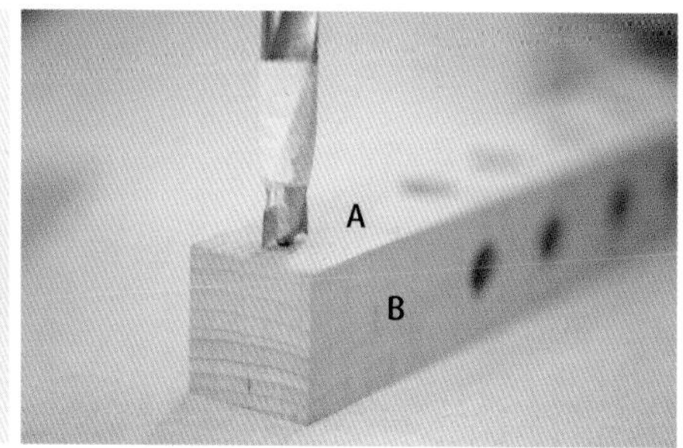

4 **Drill holes** to a depth of 9⁄16in (15mm) in the marked positions in the upper shelf front and back rails.

ASSEMBLING THE UPPER SHELF

1 **Insert a dowel** 1⅛in (28mm) in length into the hole in each of the end grains of the upper shelf side rails to test the joints.

2 **Disassemble then apply glue** to the end grains and dowel joint holes using a brush (inset). Then assemble the shelf frame with the unglued shelving dowels in place. Clamp, check for squareness (see p.75), and allow to dry.

ASSEMBLING THE TOP RAIL

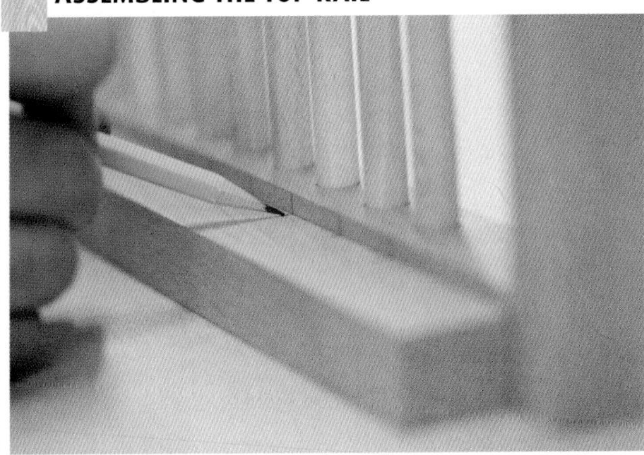

1 **Transfer the dowel** positions from the lower shelf back rail onto the face of the top rail.

2 **Square the marks** across the face and use the drill press as previously set (with a ⅜in/10mm bit) to drill the dowel holes to a depth of 5⁄16in (7mm).

3 **Mark the center** both end grains with diagonal lines drawn from opposing corners, then use a ⅜in (10mm) bit to drill a 9⁄16in (15mm) deep hole.

MAKING THE UPRIGHTS

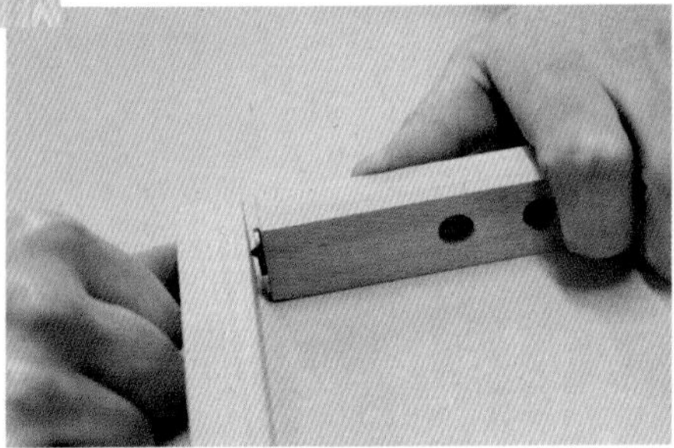

1 **Insert a dowel centerpoint** into each end grain of the top rail, then align each end against the face of each upright to mark the dowel positions.

2 **Use a 10mm (⅜in) bit** to drill the dowel position into both uprights to a depth of 15mm (9⁄16in).

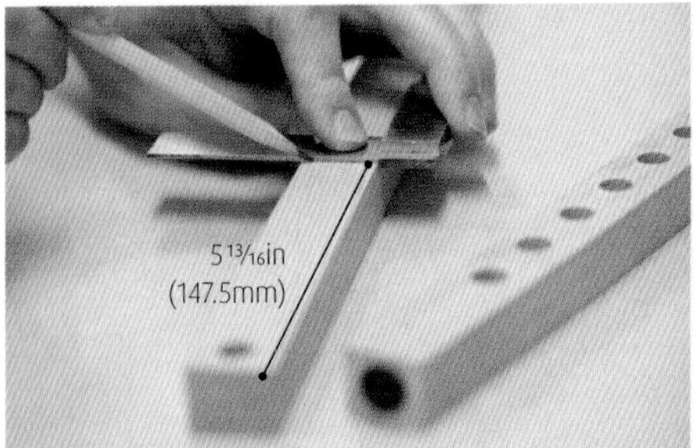

3 **Mark a line** across the width of the face of each upright, 5 13⁄16in (147.5mm) from the end grain.

4 **Mark the centerpoint** of the line with a marking gauge (inset), then drill a ⅜in (10mm) hole to a depth of 9⁄16in (15mm).

5 **Mark the centerpoint** of the bottom end grain of each upright (see Step 3, Assembling the Top Rail, opposite), then drill a hole for a dowel centerpoint (inset).

6 **Insert a dowel centerpoint** into each hole, then align the end grain with the corner of the lower shelf side rail. Press down to mark the position.

7 **Drill a hole** in each marked position on the lower shelf to a depth of 9/16in (15mm).

ASSEMBLING THE UPPER SHELF

1 **Once the glue has dried**, drill a 3/8in (10mm) hole in the center of each end grain of the upper shelf back rail, to a depth of 9/16in (15mm).

2 **Arrange the top rail**, upper shelf, and uprights in position. Glue dowel connectors into the ends of the rails (inset) and insert them into their matching position in the uprights.

3 **Clamp the upper shelf assembly** with sash clamps. Check that the shelf is at a right angle to the uprights using a square. Leave to dry.

INSERTING THE BACKING DOWELS

1 **Insert the backing dowels** through the holes in the upper shelf back rail and locate them in the holes in the underside of the top rail.

2 **Test the fit** of the dowels in the holes of the lower shelf back rail.

3 **Remove the lower shelf**, then insert glued dowel connectors into the ends of the uprights. Re-attach the lower shelf.

4 **Clamp the assembly** with sash clamps, then check the back for squareness with a tape measure (see p.75).

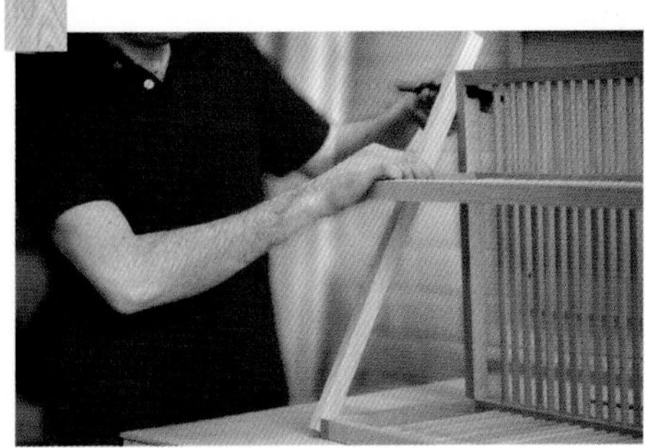

1 **Set the first side brace**, cut overlength, against the assembled rack with the bottom end grain aligned to the lower shelf.

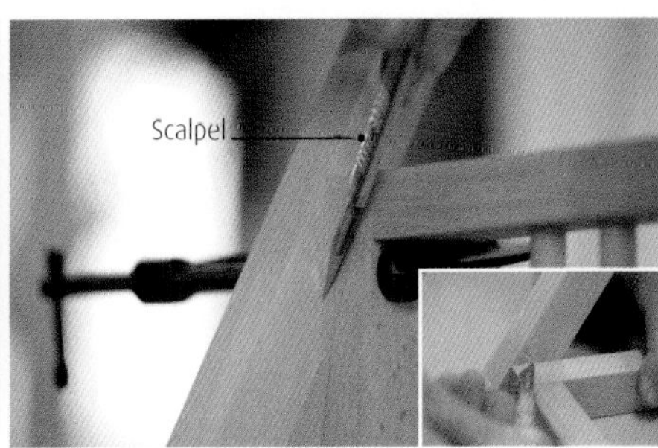

2 **Scribe the position** of the front edge of the upright and the top edge of the lower shelf (inset) on the inside edge of the brace.

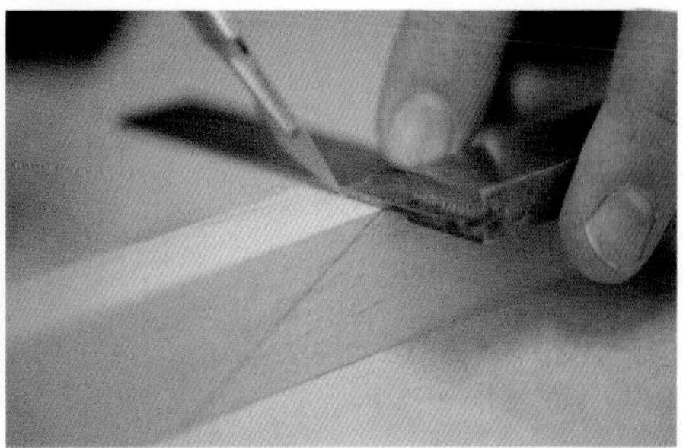

3 **Extend the marks** around all four sides of the brace. Repeat Steps 1–3 for the second side brace.

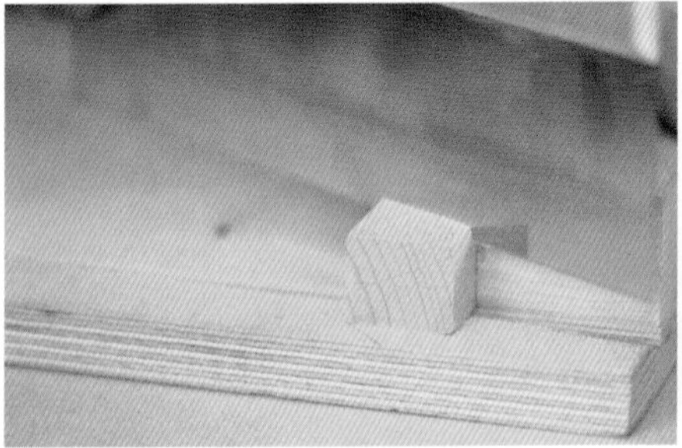

4 **Use a tenon saw** to cut along the marked lines at the top and bottom of each brace. Ensure that you cut to the waste side of the marks.

5 **Plane the excess** from both end grains of each brace to the marked lines with a block plane.

6 **Check the fit** of both braces against the rack, and adjust the end grain with the block plane as necessary.

MAKING THE DOWEL JOINTS

1 **With the brace** held in position, mark either side of the brace on the outside edge of the upper shelf. Mark the center of this position using diagonal lines (inset). Repeat for the second side brace.

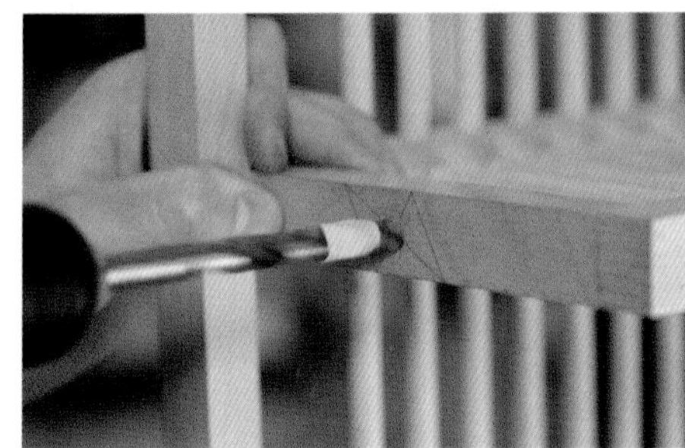

2 **Drill a hole** with a 3/8in (10mm) drill bit into each of the marked positions, to a depth of 9/16in (15mm).

3 **Insert a dowel centerpoint** into each of the holes drilled in the side of the upper shelf in the previous step.

4 **Press each side brace** into position against the centerpoint to mark the position for the dowel joint.

5 **Drill a hole** with a 3/8in (10mm) drill bit to a depth of 9/16in (15mm) in each side brace. Insert a dowel connector to join the pieces.

INSERTING THE SCREWS

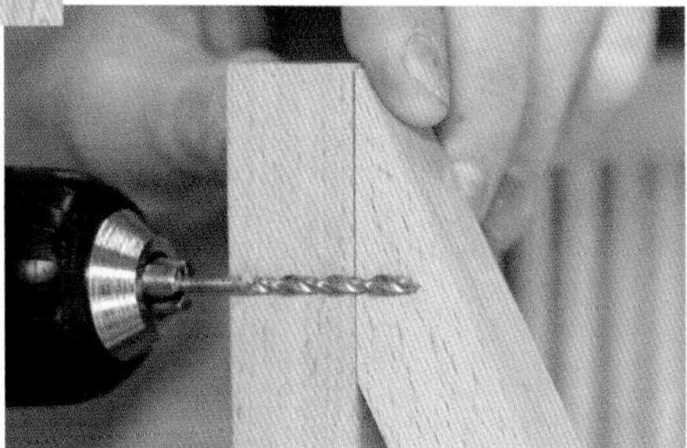

1 **Drill a pilot hole** all the way through the upright and into, but not completely through, the brace.

2 **Drill a clearance hole** to match the screw size all the way through the upright, but not into the brace.

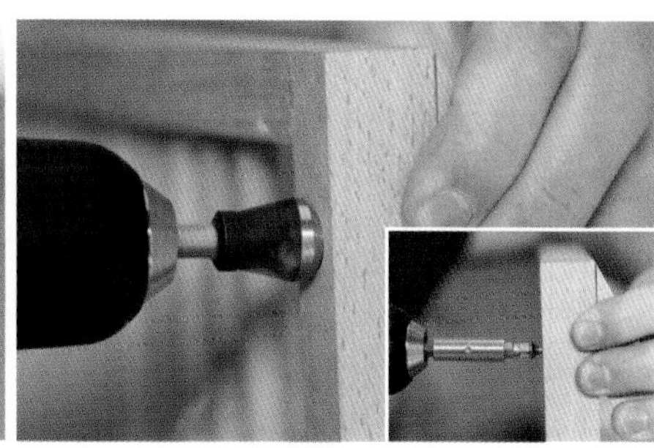

3 **Fit a countersink bit** into the drill, countersink the hole, and insert a screw (inset).

4 **To fix the brace** to the lower shelf, insert a screw in the underside of the shelf (inset), drilling the holes as in Steps 1–3. Repeat Steps 1–4 for the second side brace.

FINISHES

The plate rack is likely to be exposed to a lot of water and will therefore need protection. After assembly, you can apply several coats of finishing oil, which will give the wood a subtle sheen. Alternatively, you could use a matt or gloss waterproof varnish to help preserve the wood.

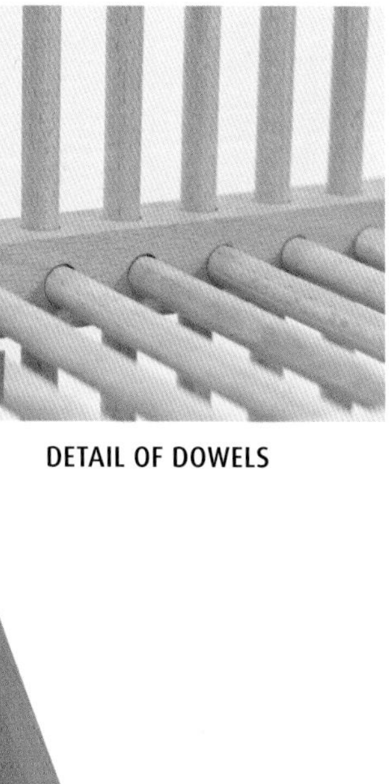

DETAIL OF DOWELS

THE FINISHED PIECE

Screen

This screen provides an attractive way of temporarily dividing up room areas or disguising cluttered corners. The design utilizes straightforward methods of construction, involving the repetition of a few simple processes. A mortiser is almost essential for cutting the numerous mortises for the screen joints in order to achieve the consistent accuracy required for a uniform overall appearance.

CUTTING LIST

Item	Material	No.	Length	Width	Thickness
Uprights	Ash	6	63in (1600mm)	1⅜in (35mm)	13⁄16in (20mm)
Rails	Ash	9	21⅝in (550mm)	1⅜in (35mm)	13⁄16in (20mm)
Slats	Ash	60	19 11⁄16in (500mm)	1¾in (45mm)	¼in (6mm)

Dimensions:
63 x 21⅝ x 13⁄16in (1600 x 550 x 20mm)

Key techniques:
T-bridle joints (pp.128–31); Basic mortise-and-tenon joint (pp116–19)

TOOLS AND MATERIALS

- Pencil
- Combination square
- Mortise gauge
- Tenon saw or band saw
- Bevel-edged chisel
- Tape measure
- Marking knife
- Mortiser or mortise chisel
- Sandpaper
- Wood glue and brush
- Sash clamps
- G-clamps
- 4 "Soss hinges" and screws
- Router
- Straight router cutter
- Drill with bits

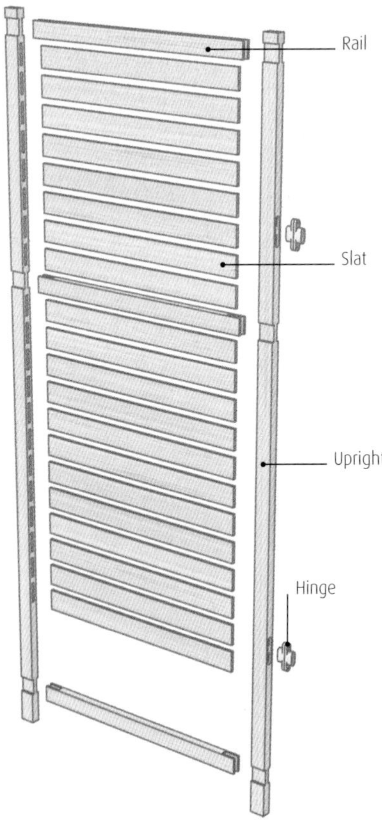

Rail
Slat
Upright
Hinge

How the elements fit together
Bridle joints connect the uprights to the three main horizontal rails. The slats are then straight-mortised into the uprights without shoulders, and left unglued for ease of assembly.

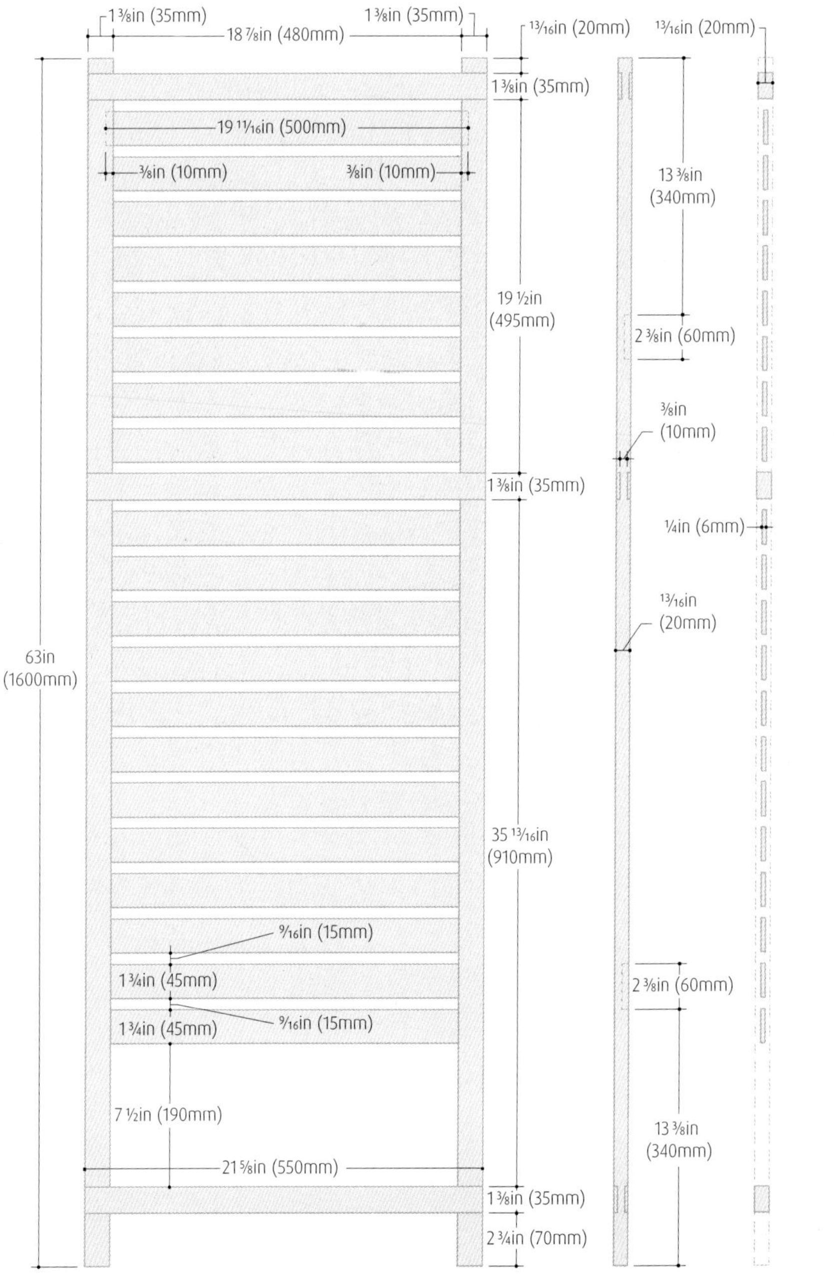

1⅜in (35mm)
18 ⅞in (480mm)
1⅜in (35mm)
19 11⁄16in (500mm)
⅜in (10mm)
⅜in (10mm)
63in (1600mm)
1⅜in (35mm)
19 ½in (495mm)
1⅜in (35mm)
35 13⁄16in (910mm)
9⁄16in (15mm)
1¾in (45mm)
1¾in (45mm)
9⁄16in (15mm)
7 ½in (190mm)
21⅝in (550mm)
1⅜in (35mm)
2 ¾in (70mm)

FRONT VIEW (1:10)

13⁄16in (20mm)
13⁄16in (20mm)
13 ⅜in (340mm)
2 ⅜in (60mm)
⅜in (10mm)
¼in (6mm)
13⁄16in (20mm)
2 ⅜in (60mm)
13 ⅜in (340mm)

SIDE VIEW (1:10)

SIDE SECTION VIEW (1:10)

MAKING THE BRIDLE JOINTS IN THE RAILS

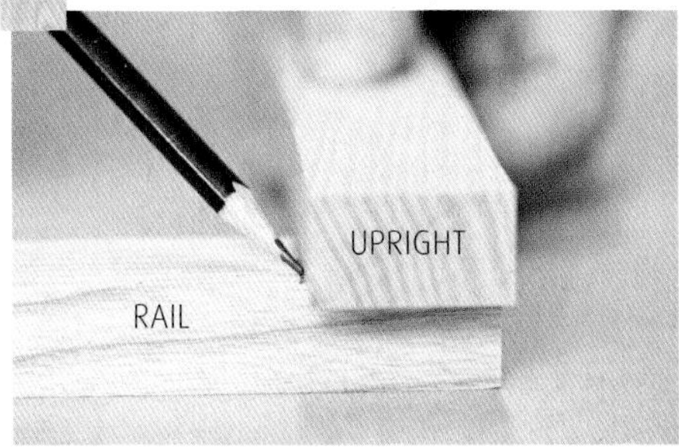

1 **Mark the shoulder** of the T-bridle joint mortise on the end of a rail by marking the width of the upright, positioned flush to the end grain.

2 **Square the shoulder mark** across all four sides of the rail, using a pencil and combination square.

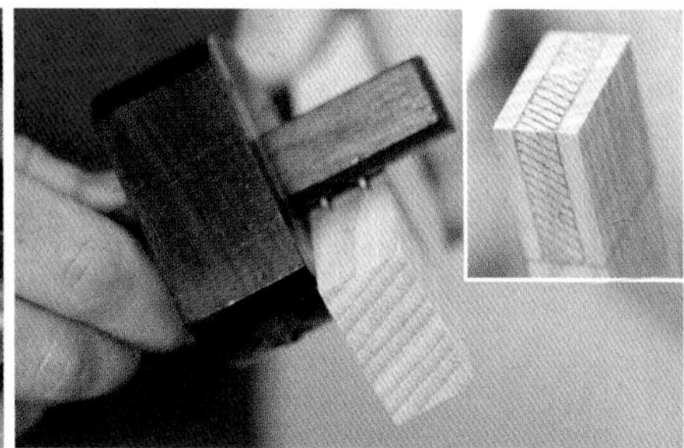

3 **Use a mortise gauge** to scribe the width of the mortise— ⅜in (10mm)— across the end grain and onto both edges to the shoulder marks. Mark the waste (inset).

4 **Cut the mortise** with either a tenon saw or band saw (see p.128). If cutting by hand, use a combination square to set the wood at a 45-degree angle in the vise.

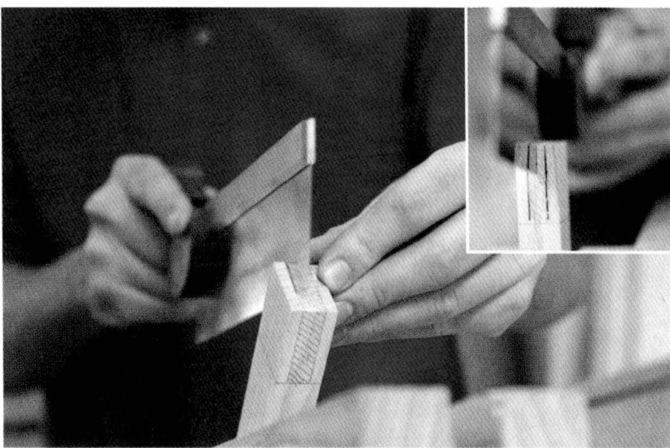

5 **Cut diagonally down each edge** of the mortise in one direction, then change the position of the wood in the vise to cut diagonally in the other direction. Finally, cut vertically to the shoulder down each edge and make a vertical relief cut in the center of the waste (inset).

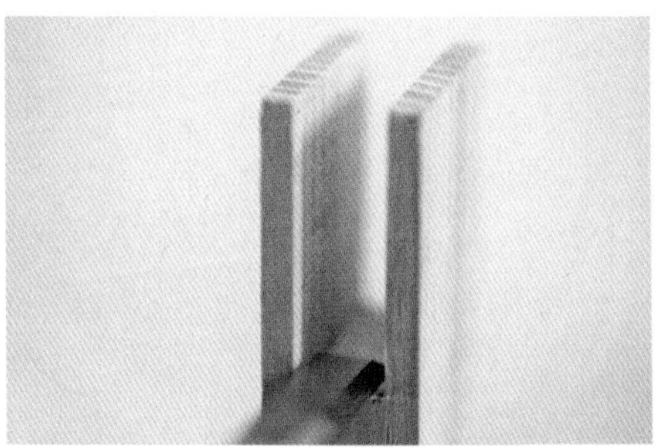

6 **Chop out the waste** with a bevel-edged chisel. Repeat Steps 4–6 on the other end of the rail and on both ends of the remaining eight rails.

MARKING THE TENON POSITIONS IN THE UPRIGHTS

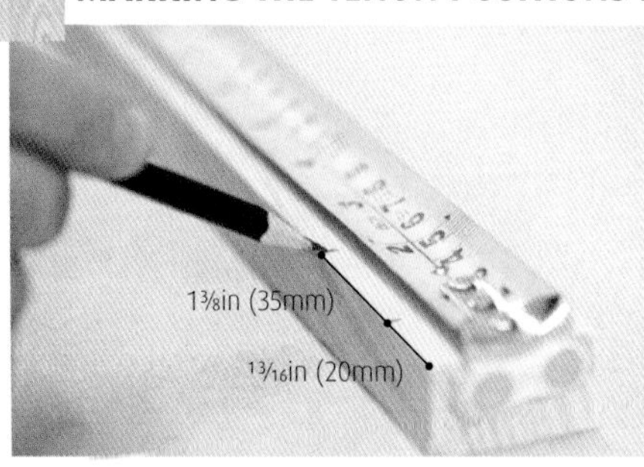

1 **Mark the position** of the three tenons, each to a width of 1⅜in (35mm), on one of the six uprights. Mark the first tenon 13⁄16in (20mm) from the top end grain.

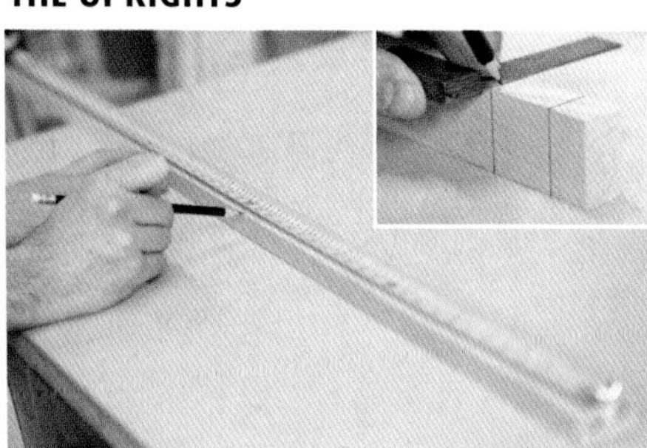

2 **Mark the start** of the second and third tenons 21⅝in (550mm) and 58⅞in (1495mm) respectively from the end grain. Square all the marks around all sides (inset).

3 **Use the mortise gauge** as previously set— ⅜in (10mm)—to scribe the thickness of the tenons between the marks on both edges. Mark the waste (inset).

4 **Reinforce the shoulder marks** with a marking knife, then cut a V-groove with a chisel to achieve a clean edge.

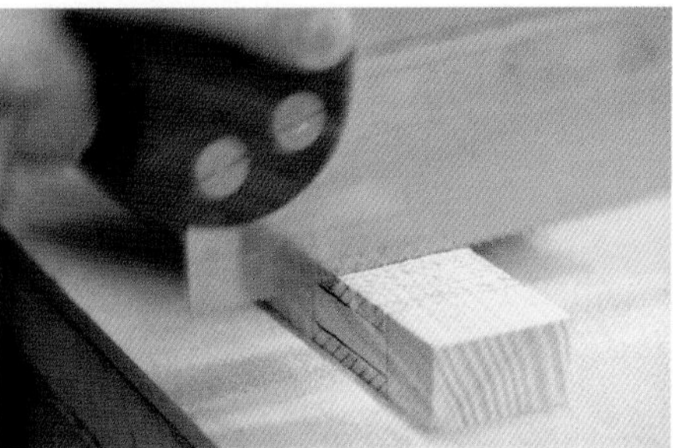

5 Cut the tenons by hand with a tenon saw (pictured) or with a band saw, then make vertical relief cuts into the waste.

6 Chop out the waste with the chisel, then pare the surfaces clean. Repeat Steps 1–6 for the remaining uprights.

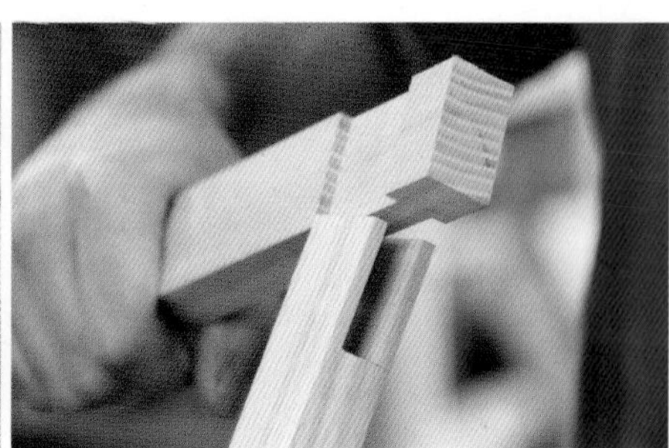

7 Test the fit of the tenons within their matching mortises in the rails and adjust if necessary.

MAKING THE SLAT MORTISES ON THE UPRIGHTS

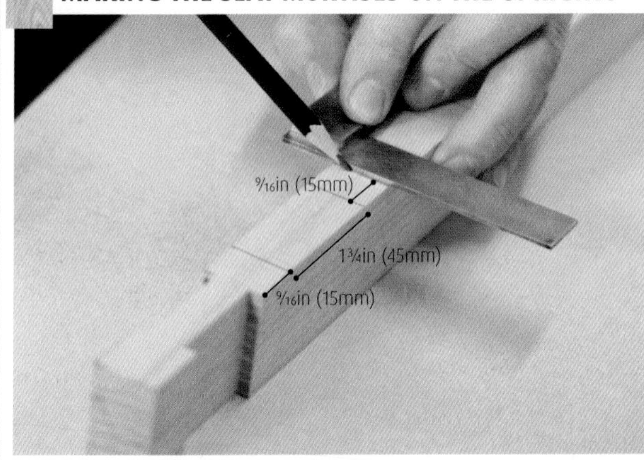

1 Mark the positions of the slat mortises on the inside edges of the upright. Mark a line across one upright 9⁄16in (15mm) from the upper tenon to indicate the top of the first mortise. The mortise length is 1¾in (45mm). Mark a further eight mortises at 9⁄16in (15mm) intervals until the middle tenon is reached.

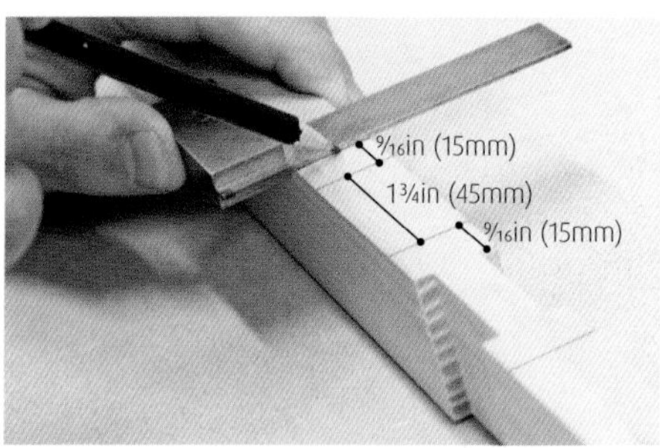

2 From the middle tenon, mark a further 12 mortises of the same length at 9⁄16in (15mm) intervals.

3 Set the mortise gauge to ¼in (6mm) and mark the width of the first mortise (centered on the inside edge) by scribing between the two length marks.

4 Set the mortiser fence to the marked mortise position and the depth to ⅜in (10mm). Cut all the mortises and sand (inset). Repeat Steps 1–4 for the remaining uprights.

5 Test the fit of all the elements in each panel: first fit the rails into one of the uprights, then insert the slats into the mortises, and then attach the other upright.

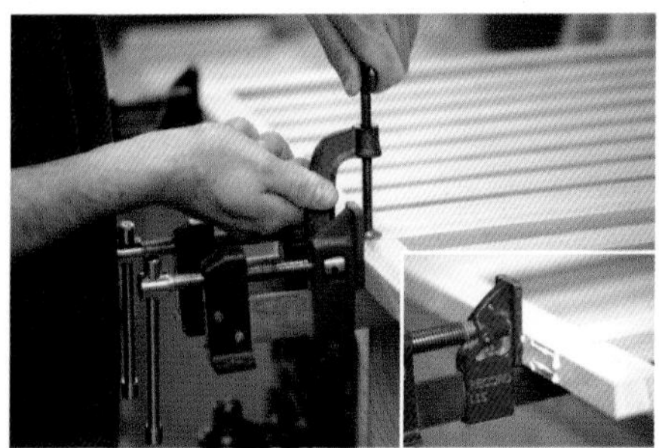

6 Once satisfied with the fit, glue the bridle joints on all three panels and clamp with sash clamps and G-clamps. Check for squareness (see p.75).

FITTING THE HINGES

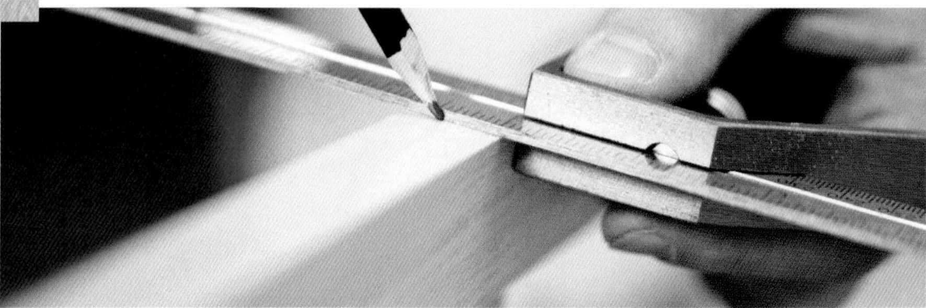

1 Mark the position of two Soss hinges 13⅜in (340mm) from each end grain of the panel uprights, then square the mark across the outside edge. The hinges are positioned on both uprights of the central panel and the adjacent upright of each of the side panels.

2 **Measure and then mark** the length of the hinges square across the edges of each of the uprights.

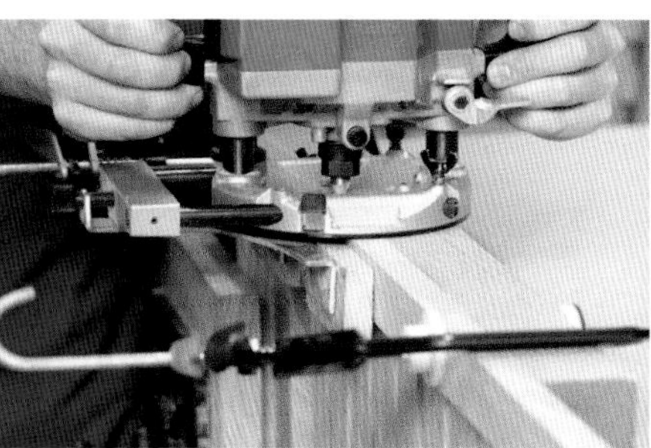

3 **Use a router** fitted with an appropriately sized cutter to cut a housing to match the hinge dimensions in each marked position. Clamp a block alongside the upright to support the router.

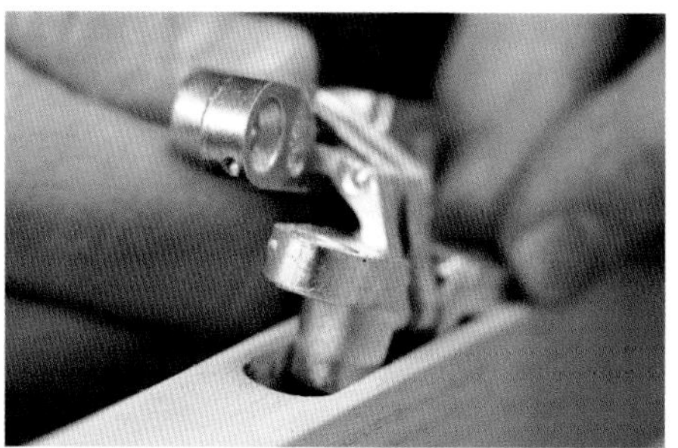

4 **Test the fit** of the hinges in the housings, and make any necessary adjustments with a chisel.

5 **With the hinges** placed in each housing on the central panel, drill pilot holes into each of the hinge screw positions, then screw in place (inset). Be sure to orient the hinges in opposing directions on each side of the panel to enable the screen to fold in a zig-zag.

6 **Set the first side panel** to be joined with its hinge housings over the hinges on the central panel, then slot in the hinge. Screw in position as before. Repeat for the remaining side panel.

FINISHES

The screen can be left unfinished, but if you do want to apply a finish, be sure to do it before assembly. It would be very hard to apply finishing oil or wax into all the corners once glued up. A couple of coats of clear acrylic varnish would be a good choice of finish here as it would not discolor the timber, therefore avoiding adding unwanted weight to the overall look.

THE FINISHED PIECE

Bookcase

This bookcase uses wedged through mortise-and-tenon joints (pp.122–24) for both aesthetic effect and structural strength. Wedged tenons are capable of holding a piece of furniture tight with no glue at all, although glue is used in this project. The wedges, made from a contrasting color of timber, fulfil a visual as well as structural role, forming a key decorative feature of the piece. The shelves are progressively deeper from top to bottom and are spaced at different heights to accommodate a range of book sizes.

Dimensions:
37⅜ x 21½ x 8 7/16in (951 x 545 x 215mm)

Key techniques:
Edge-to-edge joints (pp.94–95)
Wedged through mortise-and-tenon joint (pp.122–24);
Jigs and templates (pp.150–51);

TOOLS AND MATERIALS

- Wood glue and brush
- Sash clamps and C-clamps
- Planer-thicknesser or bench plane
- Table saw or panel saw
- MDF 39 x 10 x ¼in/ (1000 x 250 x 6mm)
- Ruler
- Pencil
- Pair of compasses
- Band saw or coping saw
- Block plane
- Sandpaper
- Router and cutters
- Square
- Bevel-edged chisel
- Marking gauge
- Drill with bits
- Small tenon saw
- Router table (optional)
- Screwdriver
- 4 screws (No.8 x 1¼in/4 x 30mm)
- Hammer
- Flush-cut saw
- Finishing oil

CUTTING LIST

Item	Material	No.	Length	Width	Thickness
Sides	Oak	4	39⅜in* (1000mm)	4¾in (120mm)	13/16in (20mm)
Shelf 1	Oak	1	21⅝in* (550mm)	7⅞in (200mm)	13/16in (20mm)
Shelf 2	Oak	1	21⅝in* (550mm)	6 11/16in (170mm)	13/16in (20mm)
Shelf 3	Oak	1	21⅝in* (550mm)	5 11/16in (145mm)	13/16in (20mm)
Shelf 4	Oak	1	21⅝in* (550mm)	5⅛in (130mm)	13/16in (20mm)
Brace	Oak	1	20⅝in (525mm)	2 9/16in (65mm)	13/16in (20mm)
Wedge	Walnut	1	19 11/16in (500mm)	1 1/16in (27mm)	1/16in (2mm)

*Includes excess to allow for cutting to size

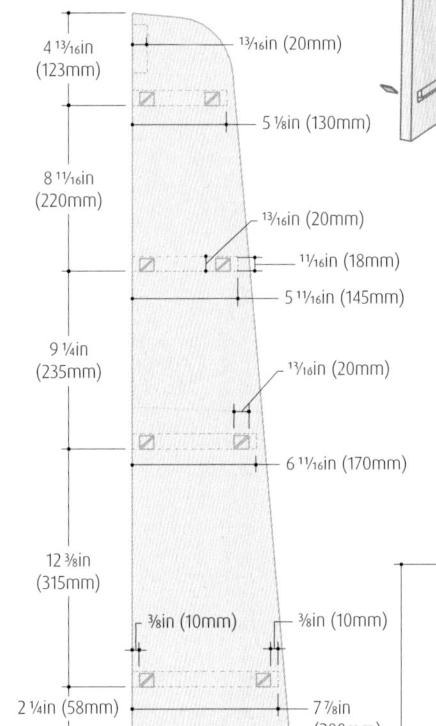

SIDE VIEW (1:10)

Brace
Shelf 4
Shelf 3
Shelf 2
Wedge
Side
Shelf 1

How the elements fit together
The shelves have two through tenons on each end and a stub tenon (short-tenoned section) between the two which locates into a housing. The insertion of wedges into the tenons firmly locks the joint in the mortise. A brace is also screwed across the top to provide extra stability.

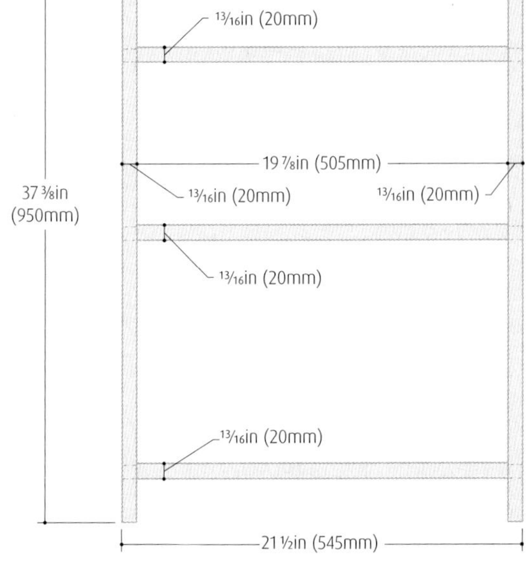

FRONT VIEW (1:10)

PREPARING THE SIDE PIECES

1 **Join the side pieces** with glue (see Edge- to-edge joint, pp.94–95) and clamp. Wipe off any excess glue and leave to dry.

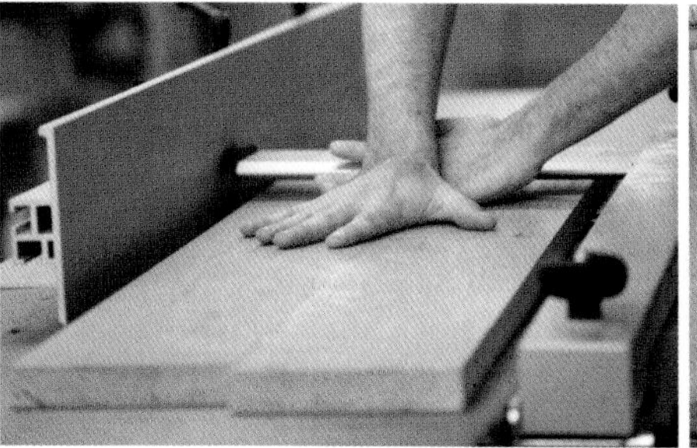

2 **Plane the joined side pieces** on a planer (pictured) or by hand using a bench plane.

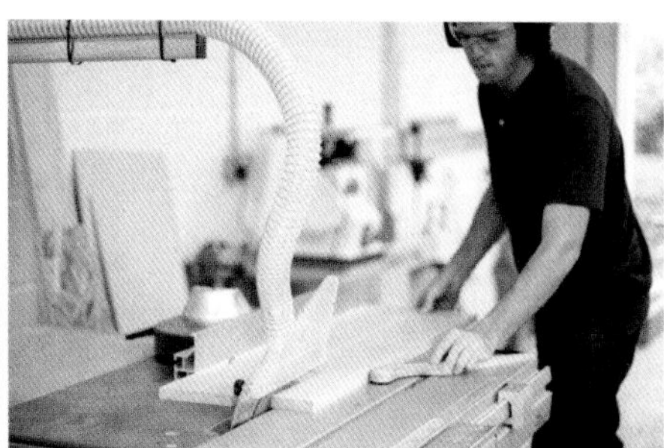

3 **Cut the pieces** to a width of 8⁷⁄₁₆in (215mm) and length of 37⅜in (950mm) with a table saw or by hand with a panel saw.

MAKING THE TEMPLATE FOR THE SIDES

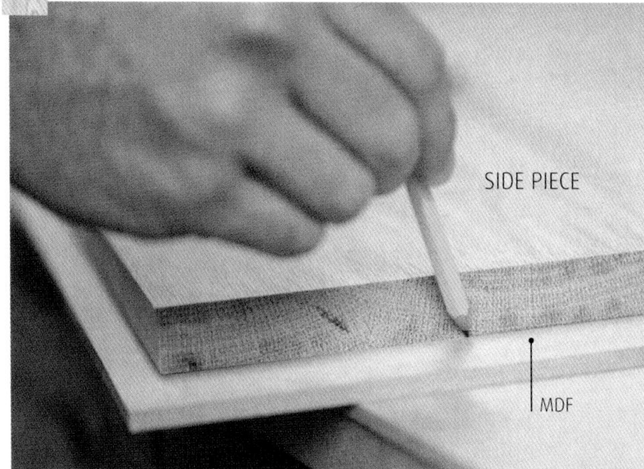

1 **Set a side piece** over the MDF, aligned to one corner, and draw around it. On the MDF, working from the same corner, mark 3⁹⁄₁₆in (90mm) along the long edge and 5½in (140mm) along the short edge. Use a square to extend the marks across the MDF to the point at which they intersect.

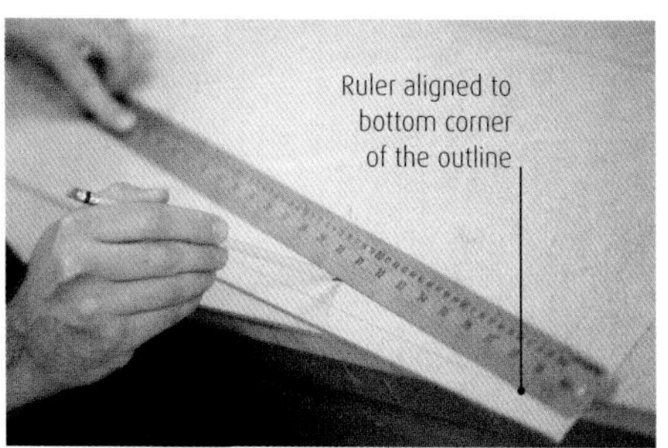

2 **On the MDF**, mark a diagonal line from the bottom corner of the outline of the side piece to the intersection point marked in the previous step. This will form the start of the curve of the shelf side.

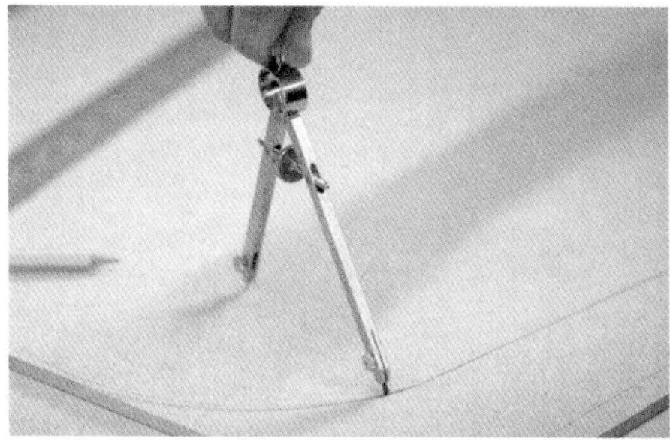

3 **Use a pair of compasses** to draw the curve between the top of the diagonal line and the top corner of the MDF.

4 **Cut out the template** from the MDF on a band saw (pictured), or by hand with a coping saw. Cut away the waste in sections.

5 **Clean up the template edges**. Use a block plane to smooth the straight edges, and sandpaper for the curved edge.

CUTTING THE SIDE PIECES

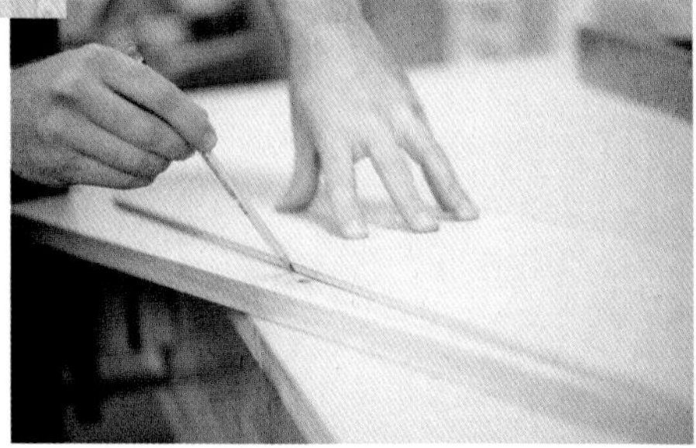

1 **Place the template** onto each of the side pieces in turn, and draw around it to mark the shape.

2 **Cut each side piece** roughly to shape with a band saw, removing the waste in stages using relief cuts (see p.56) and giving the blade room to maneuver. Be sure to cut to the waste side of the marks to allow for finishing (see next step).

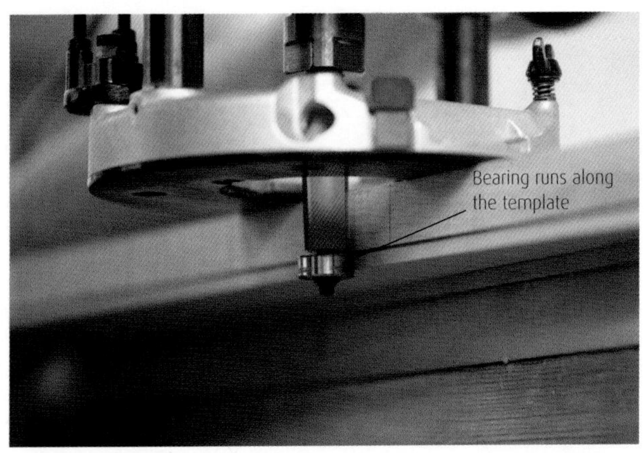

3 **Clamp the template** under a side piece, then adjust a router and bearing-mounted cutter so that the bearing runs along the template.

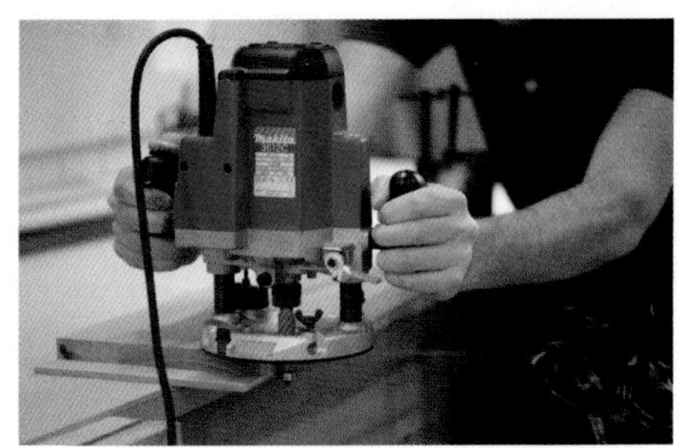

4 **Cut the side to shape**, working in the direction of the grain to avoid tearing the wood. Repeat on the second side piece.

MARKING OUT AND CUTTING THE SHELF HOUSINGS

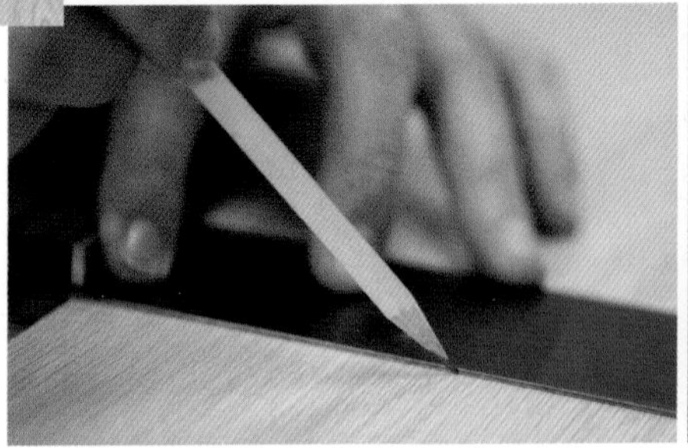

1 **Mark the position** of the first shelf housing on one side piece (see the diagram on p.238), using a pencil and square.

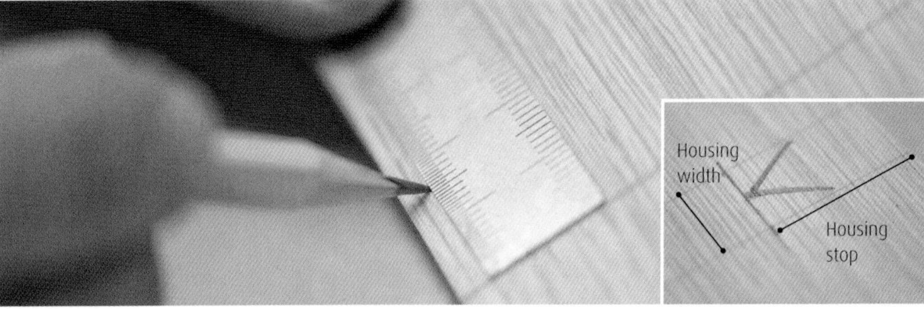

2 **Mark the width** of the housing at 11⁄16in (18mm)— 1⁄16in (2mm) less than the thickness of the shelf piece. Mark the length of the housing, which is calculated as the length of the shelf less a 3⁄8in (10mm) stop from the front edge (inset).

3 **Set the router** to a depth of 1⁄8in (3mm), then insert a router cutter no larger than the width of the housing. Using a straight edge as a guide, cut the housing.

4 **Use a bevel-edged chisel** to square off the housing stop. Repeat Steps 1–4 for the remaining housings on both side pieces.

5 **Use a pencil** and square to mark the width of each housing on the back edge and outside face of the side pieces.

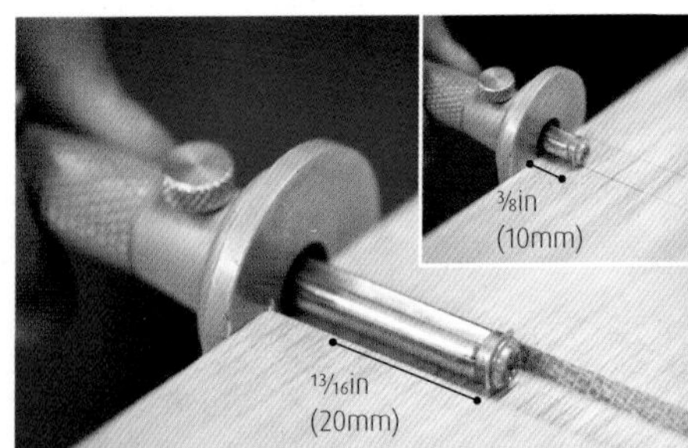

6 **Using a marking gauge**, mark two mortises 13⁄16in (20mm) in length within each housing, 3⁄8in (10mm) from each edge. Mark the mortise positions on the outside face of the side piece (inset).

7 **Clamp the side piece** over a piece of spare wood and remove most of the waste from each mortise using a drill fitted with a bit no wider than the housing. Drill completely through the side piece.

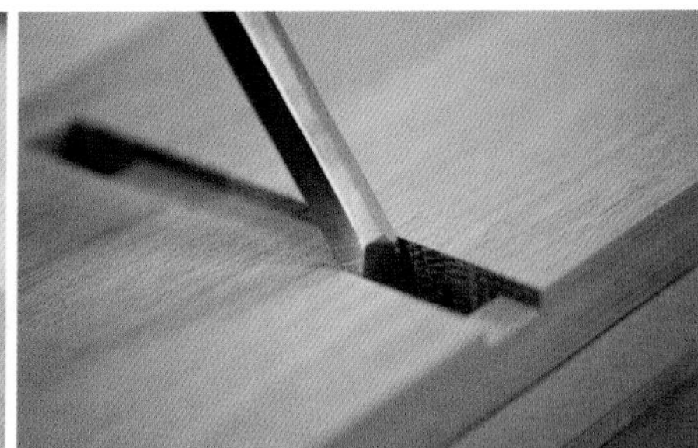

8 **Square off** the sides of the mortises with the chisel. Turn the piece over and complete the edges on the other side. Cut all of the mortises in all of the housings in the same way.

CUTTING THE TENONS

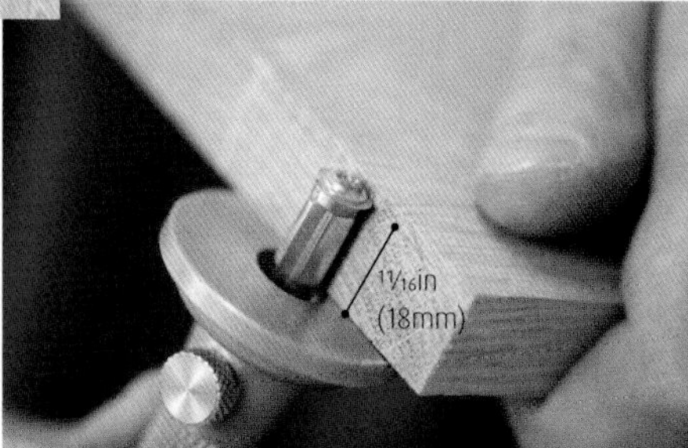

1 **Use a marking gauge** to scribe the tenon thickness—11⁄16in (18mm)—on the end grain at both ends of Shelf 1.

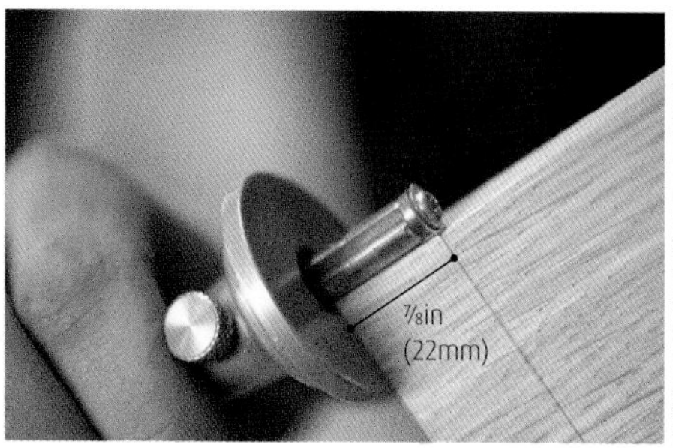

2 **Scribe the length** of the tenons on the face of the shelf piece at both ends using the marking gauge set to 7⁄8in (22mm).

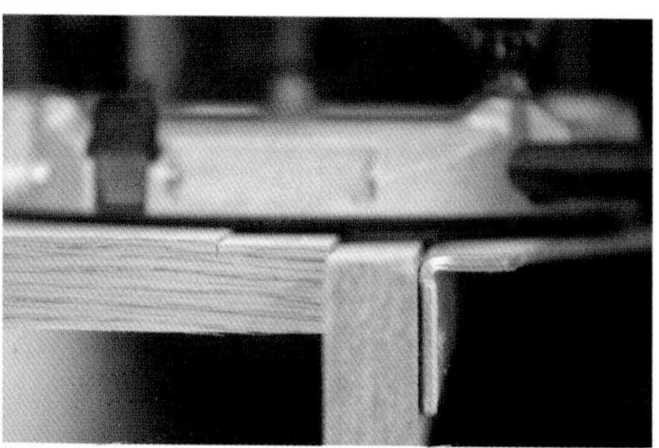

3 **Cut a 1⁄16in (2mm) shoulder** for the tenons at both ends using a router. Set the fence on the router against the end grain to position the cutter accurately, and set the depth to 1⁄16in (2mm).

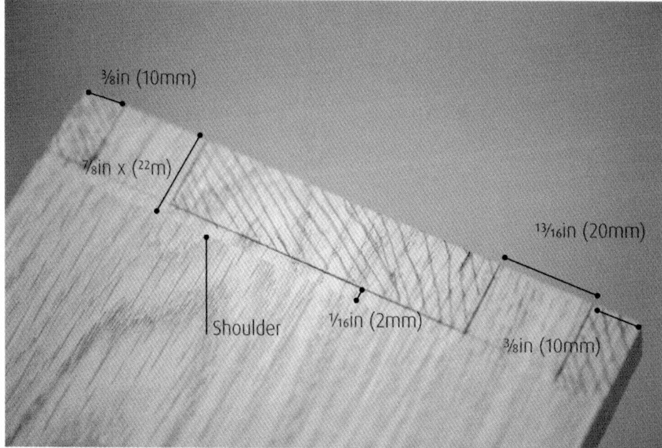

4 **Mark the position** and width of the tenons on both ends of Shelf 1. Repeat Steps 1–4 for Shelves 2–4.

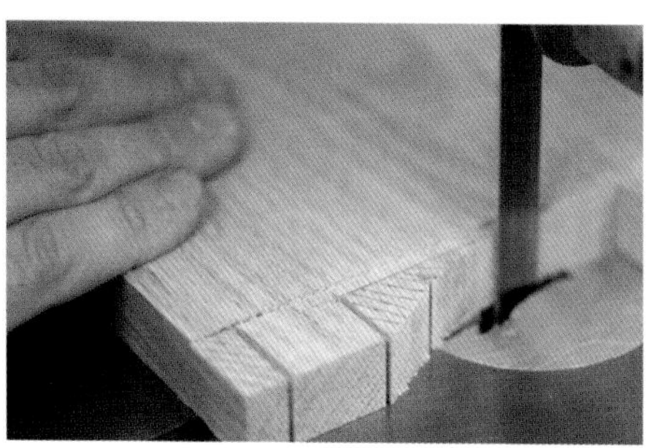

5 **Cut out the tenons** with a band saw (pictured) or by hand with a coping saw. Repeat the tenons on Shelves 2-4.

MAKING THE SLOTS AND WEDGES

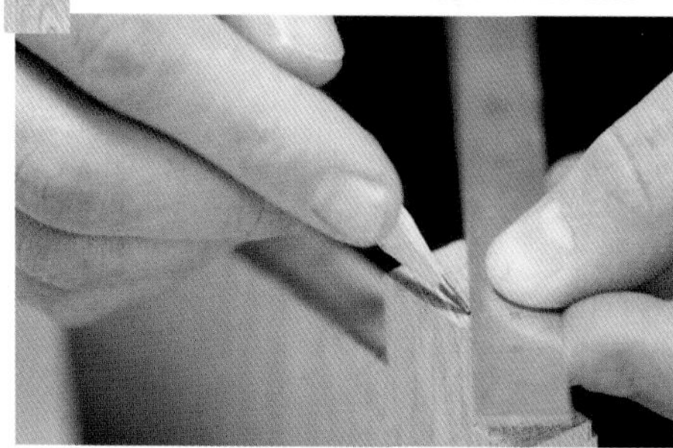

1 **Draw a diagonal line** from corner to corner on the end grain of each tenon, ensuring that all the diagonals are parallel.

2 **Using a small tenon saw**, cut a diagonal slot along the marks to the full length of each tenon.

3 **Cut the veneer pieces** for the wedges to the required length of 11⁄16in/27mm with a small tenon saw.

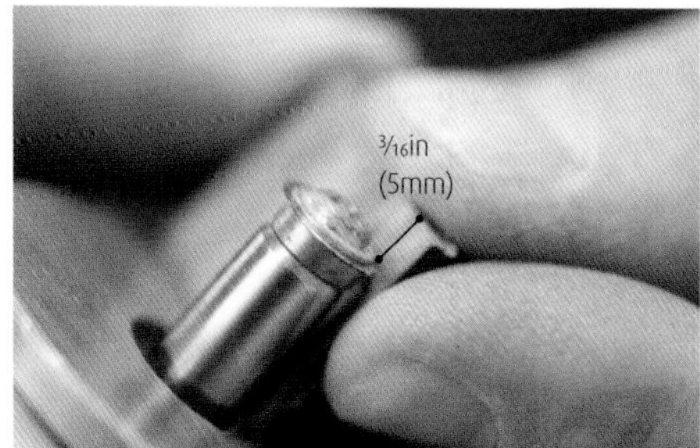

4 **Mark the start** of the taper 3⁄16in (5mm) from the edge of each wedge. Repeat on the other side.

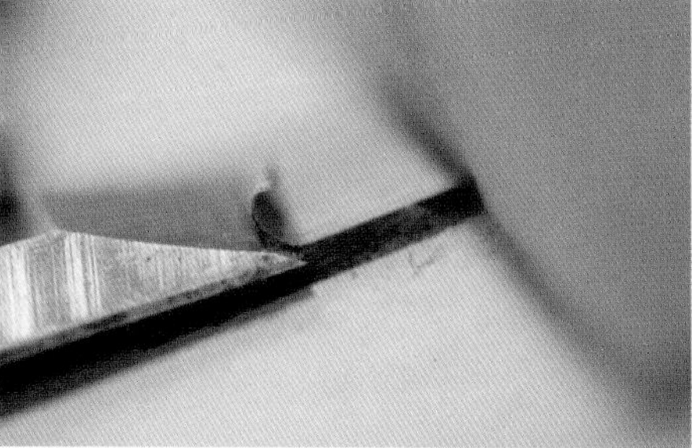

5 **With a chisel angled** downward, pare the wedges, starting at the mark, to achieve a taper. Repeat on the other side.

6 **The thin end** of the wedges should be narrow enough to fit into the diagonal slot in the end grain of the tenon.

CUTTING AND FITTING THE TOP BRACE

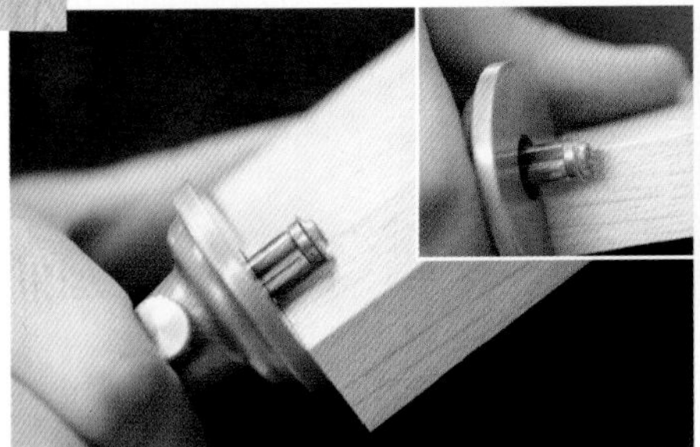

1 **Measure and mark the shoulder** at ⅜in (10mm) from the end grain on the face of the brace. Extend the marks halfway down each of the edges (inset).

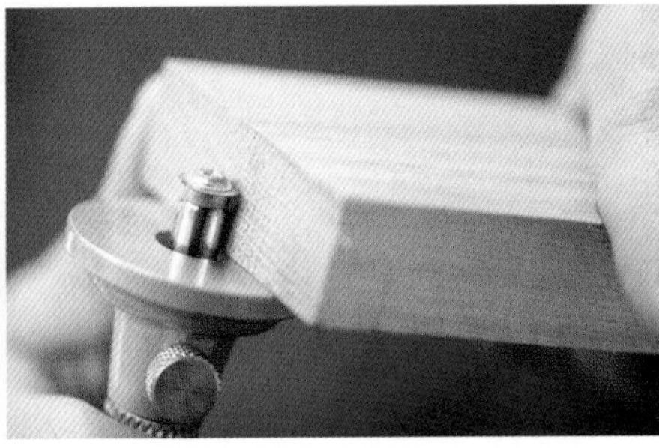

2 **Reset the marking gauge** to half the thickness of the brace, then mark this measurement on the end grain and around the edges of the brace.

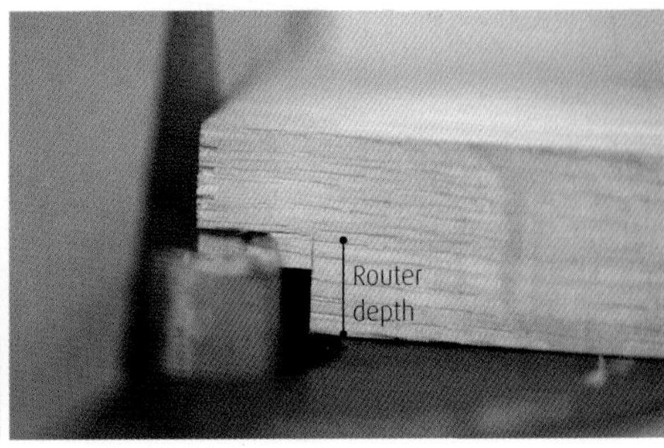

3 **Cut the shoulder on the brace** with a table-mounted router (pictured), or chisel the shoulder by hand. Set the router depth to half the thickness of the brace.

4 **Place the brace** in the desired position on the side piece, and mark it with a pencil.

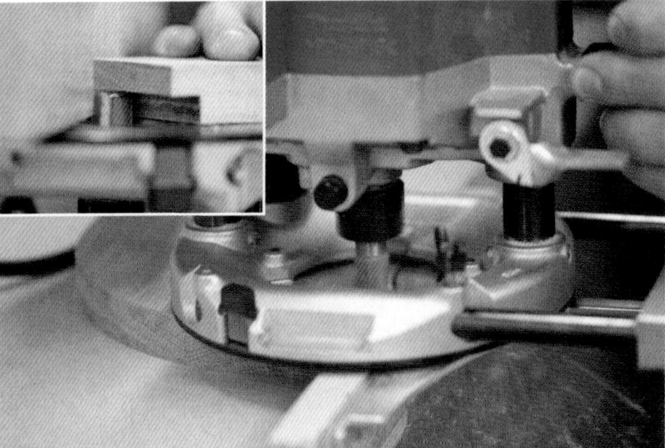

5 **Set the router** to the depth of the rebate of the brace (inset). Cut the rebate in the side piece with the router.

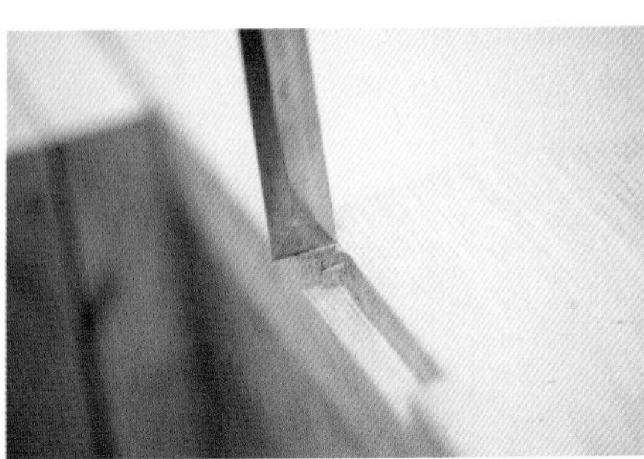

6 **Square up the edges** of the rebate with the chisel. Repeat Steps 1–6 to cut the rebate on the second side piece.

ASSEMBLING THE BOOKCASE

1 **Assemble and test-fit** all the parts except for the wedges of the bookcase. Make any necessary adjustments.

2 **With the brace in position**, mark two screw holes at each end of the back of the brace, centered within the rebate width.

3 **Drill pilot holes** through the brace and into the rebate, and finish with a countersink bit. Insert the screws (inset).

4 **When you are happy with the fit**, dismantle the bookcase and sand all the surfaces, except the outward facing surfaces of each side, prior to gluing.

GLUING AND CLAMPING

1 **Apply wood glue** to all of the tenons and housings using a brush, then assemble the main elements of the bookcase.

2 **Clamp one shelf at a time** to prepare it to receive the wedges. Apply glue to the tip of each wedge and hammer each one into its slot. Place a block between the hammer and wedge to prevent splitting.

3 **Complete the clamping**, using blocks to distribute the pressure on either side of each shelf.

4 **Wipe away any excess glue** and leave to dry. Pare off any glue that remains when partly dry with a chisel or pointed stick.

CUTTING THE TENONS FLUSH

1 **Use a flush-cut saw** to cut each of the wedged tenon ends flush to the sides of the bookcase.

2 **Use a block plane** to plane the wedged tenon ends smooth to the face of the bookcase sides. Sand and finish with oil.

THE FINISHED PIECE

WEDGED TENON DETAIL

ALTERNATIVES

You can adapt this design by increasing the height of the sides and adding more shelves. You can also increase the length of the shelves, although if you require them to be more than a third longer, you should create an extra vertical support in the center to carry the additional weight of the loaded shelves. In the alternative version pictured here, the wedged tenons have been left proud of the bookcase sides.

Breakfast table

This simple table uses haunched and mitered mortise-and-tenon joints to strengthen the frame, and buttons engaged in slots for fixing the table top, which allow for shrinkage or expansion. The table can be enlarged by extending the size of the top and the length of the rails.

Dimensions:
28⅜ x 31⅛ x 31⅛in (720 x 790 x 790mm)

Key techniques:
Edge-to-edge joint (pp.94–95);
Haunched tenon joint (p.120)

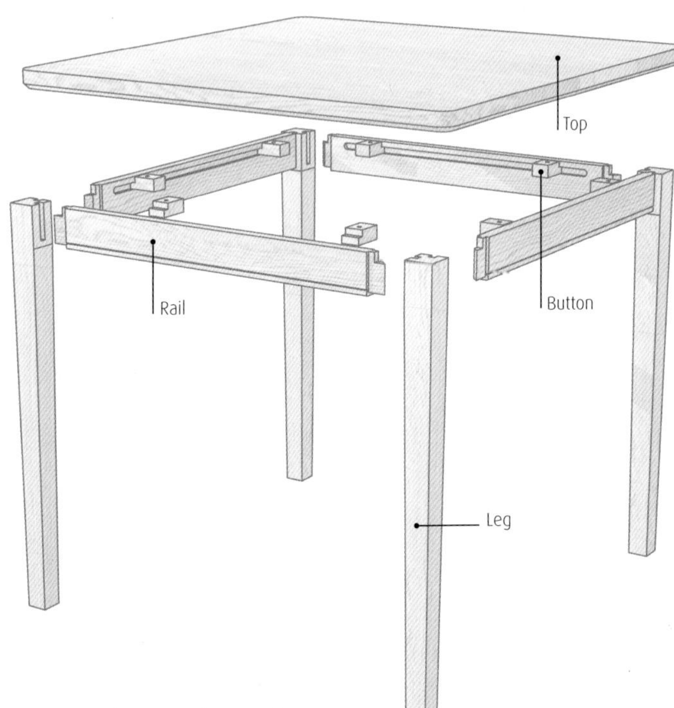

How the elements fit together
The legs are fixed to four rails, forming a frame to support the table top. The table top is secured to the frame by buttons located in a groove on the inside of the rails.

TOOLS AND MATERIALS

- Pencil
- Mortise gauge
- Combination square
- Mortiser and ⅜in (10mm) bit or ⅜in (10mm) mortise chisel
- Ruler
- Bench plane
- Marking gauge
- Band saw or tenon saw
- Marking knife
- Chisel
- Router and cutters
- Drill and bits
- Shooting board
- Wood glue and brush
- Sash clamps
- Table saw or panel saw
- Orbital sander and sandpaper
- MDF offcut
- Screwdriver
- 8 screws (No.9 x 1¼in/4.5 x 30mm)

CUTTING LIST

Item	Material	No.	Length	Width	Thickness
Legs	Pine	4	27³⁄₁₆in (690mm)	1¾in (45mm)	1¾in (45mm)
Rails	Pine	4	24¹³⁄₁₆in* (630mm)	2⁹⁄₁₆in (65mm)	¹³⁄₁₆in (20mm)
Tops	Pine	6	35⁷⁄₁₆in* (900mm)	5⅞in (150mm)	1³⁄₁₆in (30mm)

*Includes excess to allow for cutting to size

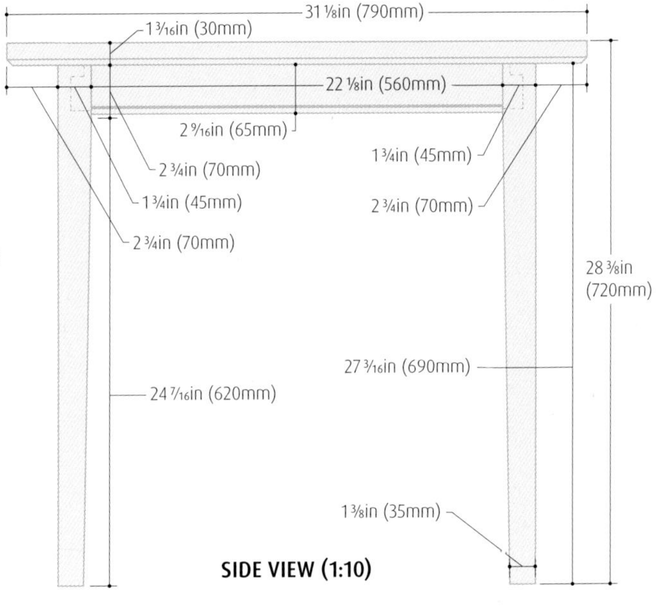

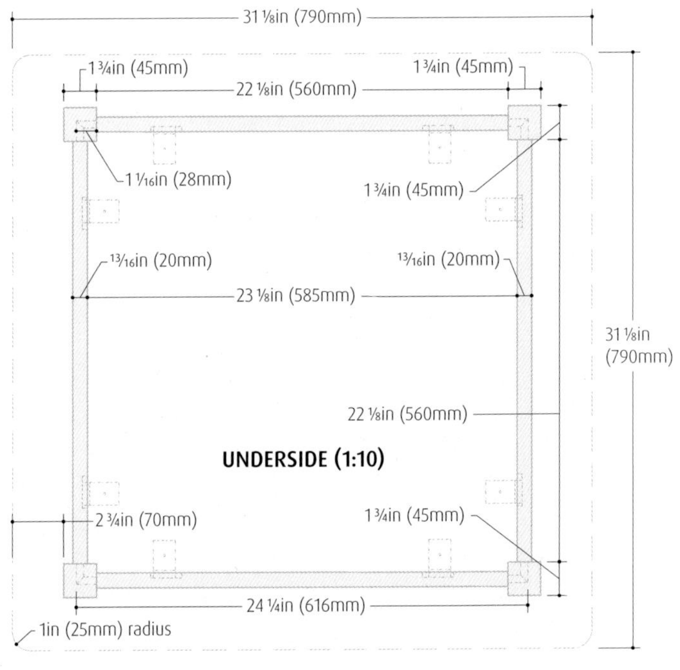

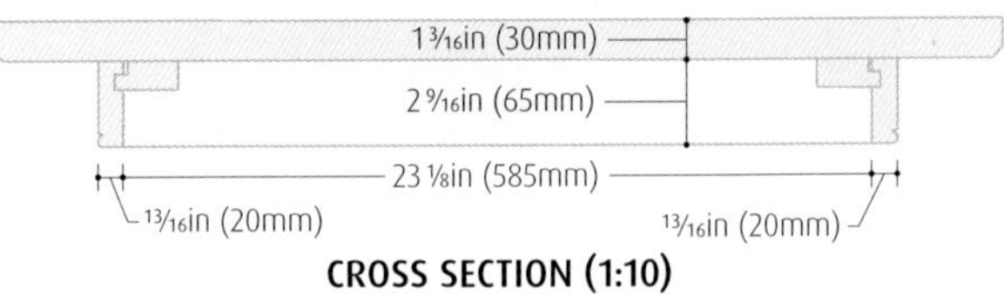

MARKING OUT AND CUTTING THE LEG MORTISES

1 **Mark the full length** of the mortise on the top of the leg, using the width of the rail piece aligned to the end grain as a guide.

2 **Set the mortise gauge** to ⅜in (10mm)— the width of the mortise and of the mortise chisel to be used.

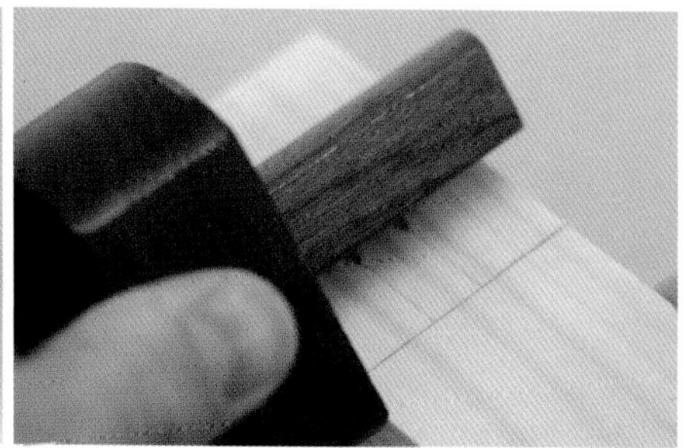

3 **Set the mortise gauge** to the center of the thickness of the leg and scribe the mortise width between the lines marking the mortise length.

4 **Mark the position** of the mortise haunch 9⁄16in (15mm) from the top of the leg and square the mark across the width of the mortise.

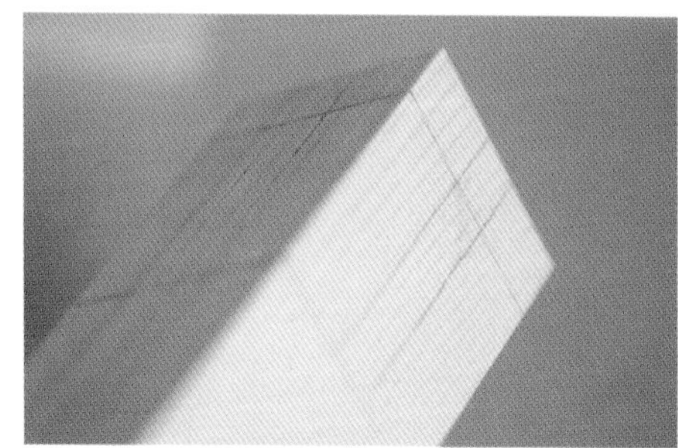

5 **Repeat the marks** on one of the adjacent sides. Mark out the remaining three legs in the same way.

6 **Using a mortiser** fitted with a ⅜in (10mm) bit (pictured) or by hand with a ⅜in (10mm) mortise chisel, cut the waste from the full-depth section of the mortise to a depth of 1 1⁄16in (27mm).

7 **Cut the mortise haunch** within the marks to a depth of ⅜in (10mm) using a mortiser or mortise chisel.

8 **Cut the mortise** on the adjacent side of the leg in the same way. The base of the second mortise joins the side of the first. Repeat Steps 6–8 for the other legs.

TAPERING THE LEGS

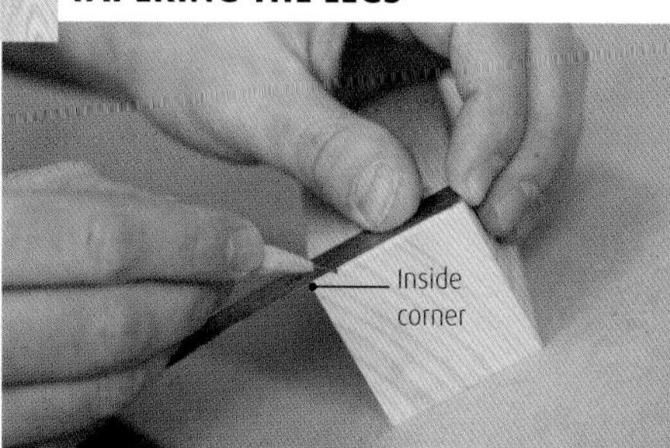

1 **Taper the legs** on the two inside edges, which also hold the mortises. On the end of the leg, mark a point ¼in (7mm) from the inside corner.

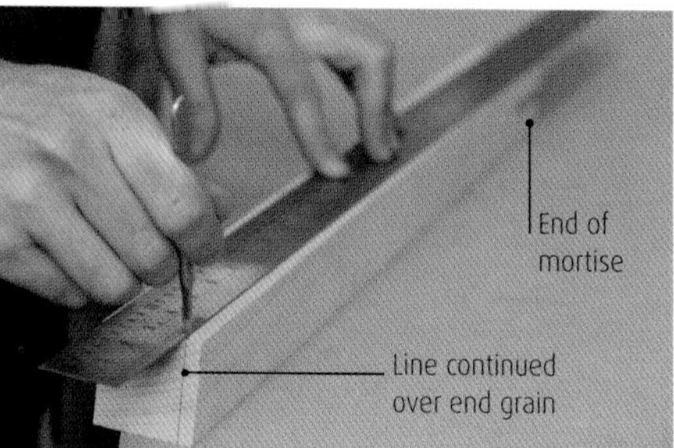

2 **Score a diagonal** from that mark to the edge of the leg at the marked position of the end of the mortise. Draw the same diagonal on the opposite face.

3 **Plane the taper** with the leg held in a vise. Work toward the end of the leg that is to be the narrowest.

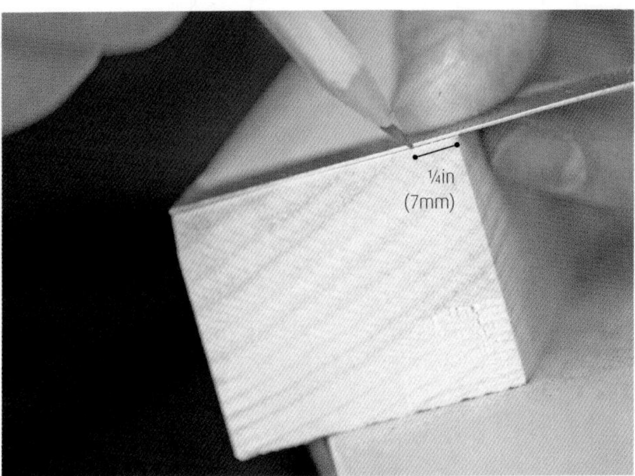

4 **When you have planed down** to the marks, mark the taper for the adjacent inside edge ¼in (7mm) from the corner of the edge you have just planed. Plane the second side and then repeat for the remaining three legs.

MARKING OUT AND CUTTING THE RAIL TENONS

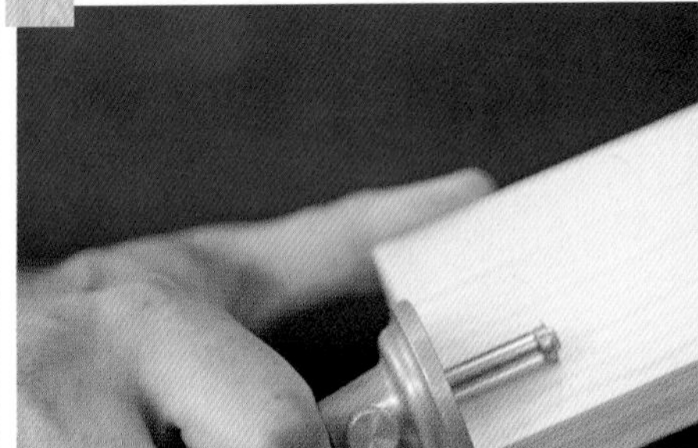

1 **Measure and scribe the length** of the tenon— 1in (25mm)—on all sides of both ends of each rail with a marking gauge.

2 **Set the mortise gauge** to the thickness of the tenon— ⅜in (10mm)—and scribe centrally around the edges and end grain. Repeat on both ends of all four rail pieces.

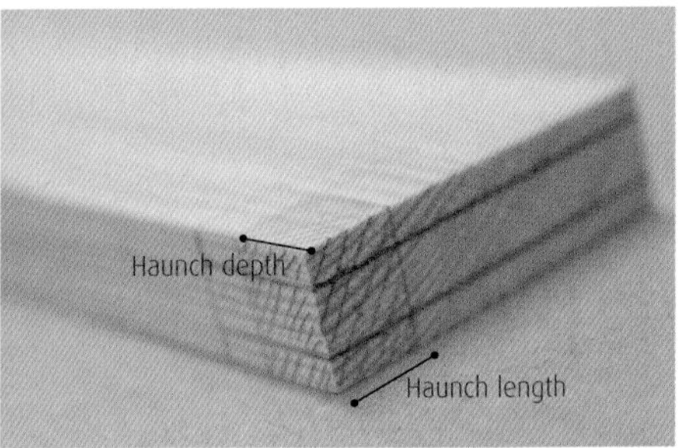

3 **Mark the length** of the haunch ⅜in (10mm) from the shoulder of the tenon and a depth of 9⁄16in (15mm) on the face and end grain. Repeat for all the other tenons.

4 **Cut the tenons** either on a band saw (pictured) or by hand with a tenon saw. Start with the cheeks, then cut the haunch.

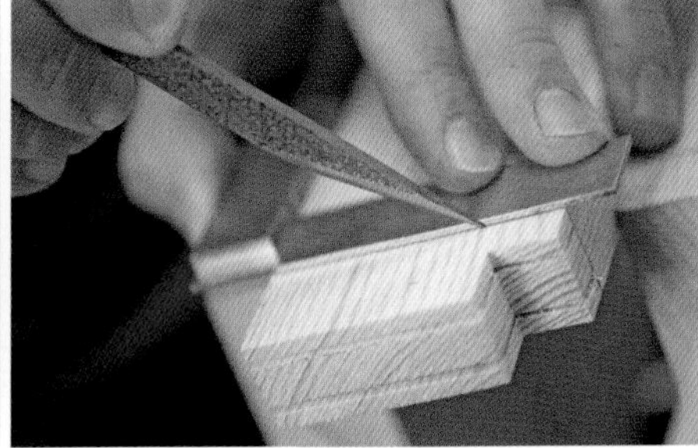

5 **Reinforce the shoulder marks** of each tenon by scribing with a marking knife, guided by a square.

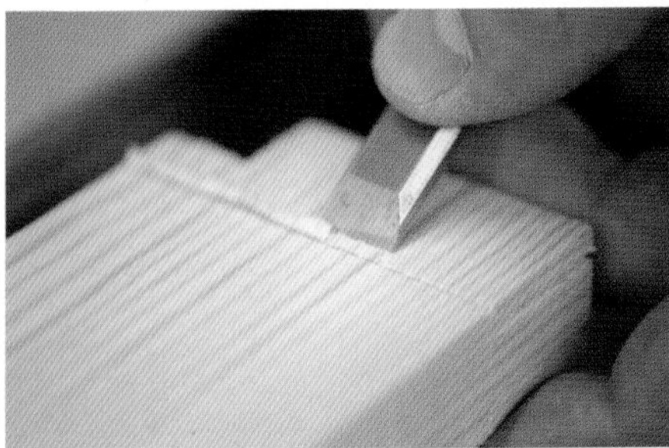

6 **Chisel a V-groove** along the shoulder, making shallow diagonal cuts to ensure a clean edge.

7 **Cut the shoulder** with a tenon saw, cutting along the chiseled groove. Repeat for all eight tenons.

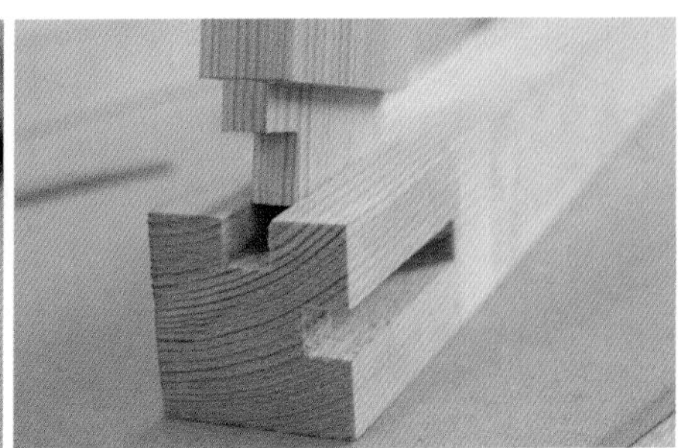

8 **Check the fit** of each tenon in its mortise on the leg. See the diagram on p.244 for the assembly of the rails and legs.

MITERING THE TENONS

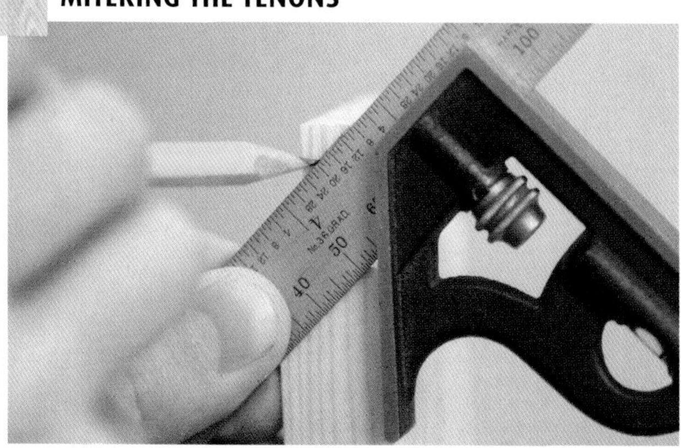

1 **Use a pencil** and combination square to mark a 45-degree angle on the edge of one the tenons.

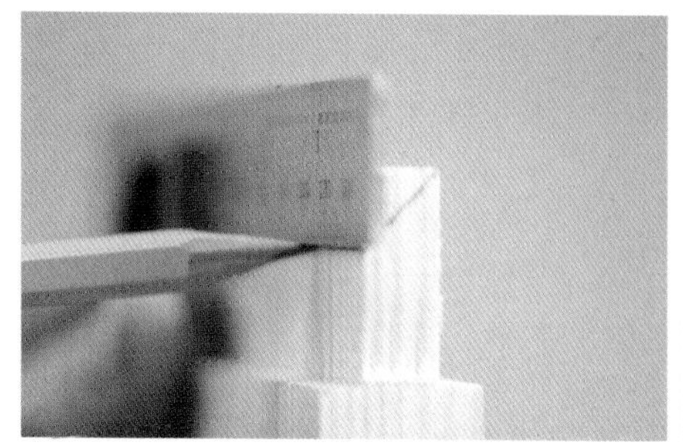

2 **Extend the line** square across the face of the tenon, using a pencil and combination square.

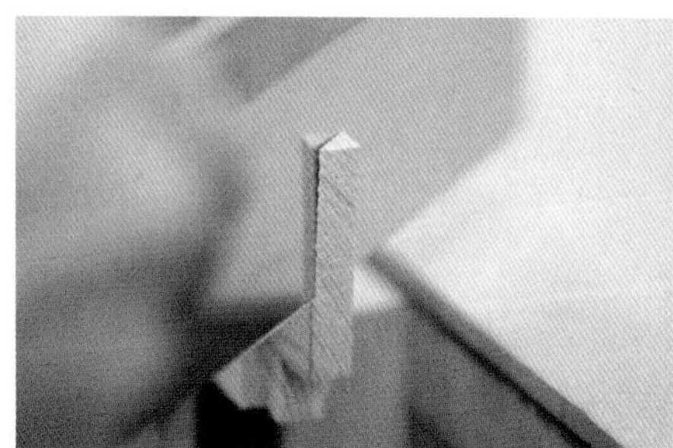

3 **Cut the miter** with a tenon saw. Repeat for all of the tenons, making sure that the miters on each tenon are angled toward the inside of the rail (see diagram on p.244).

FINISHING THE RAILS

1 **Use a router** fitted with a bearing-guided beading cutter to cut the bead detail on the outside face of each rail. It is easiest and quickest to clamp two pieces "back to back" in the vise, and work along one side in one direction and back along the other in the opposite direction. Cut the beading on all four pieces.

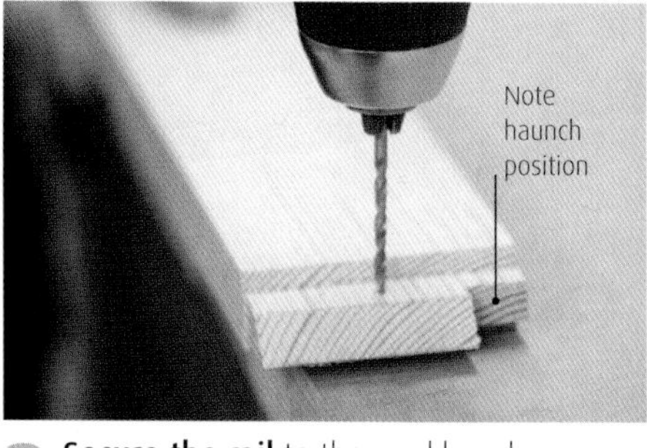

2 **Secure the rail** to the workbench, with the inside face uppermost and the haunch on the inside, by screwing through the tenon (pictured) or by clamping.

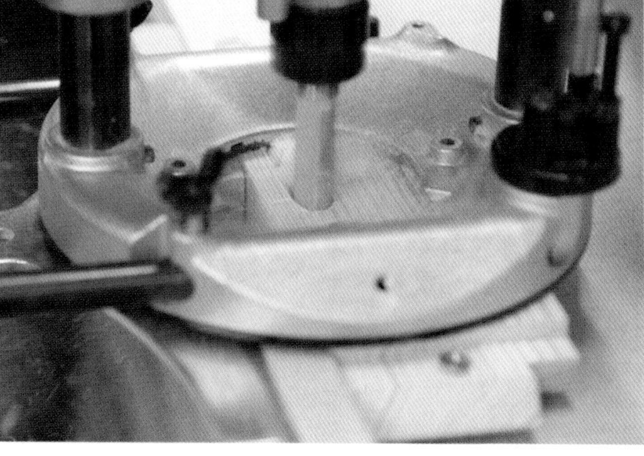

3 **Set the router** to a depth of 5⁄16in (8mm) and fit a ½in (12.5mm) straight bit. Cut a groove to create a slot for the "buttons" (see below), stopping 1in (25mm) from the tenon shoulder at each end.

MAKING THE "BUTTONS"

1 **Cut eight "buttons"** (fixings for the table top) from spare wood. Place each piece on a shooting board and use a bench plane to smooth and square the end grain.

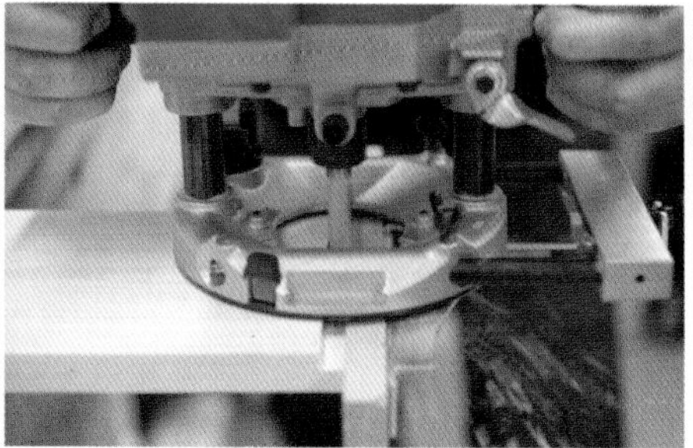

2 **Fit the router** with a ½in (12.5mm) bit. Set the fence to ⅜in (10mm) and the depth to ¼in (7mm). Use the router to cut a rebate across the end grain of the wood.

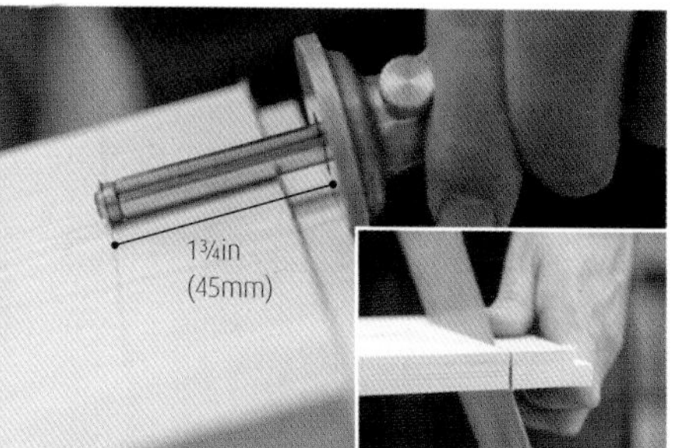

3 **Using a marking gauge**, mark 1¾in (45mm) from the end grain and cut along the line with a panel saw (inset).

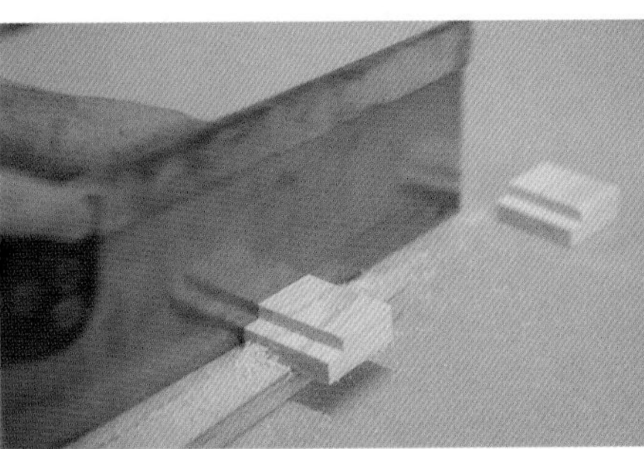

4 **Repeat Steps 2 and 3** twice more to make two further sections. Mark off each section into three equal widths of 2in (50mm) and cut to make eight buttons.

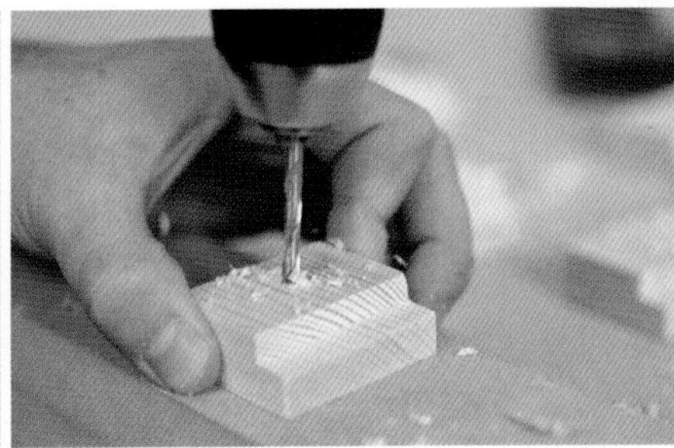

5 **Holding the button** securely, use a bit to match the screw size and drill a hole in the center of each button.

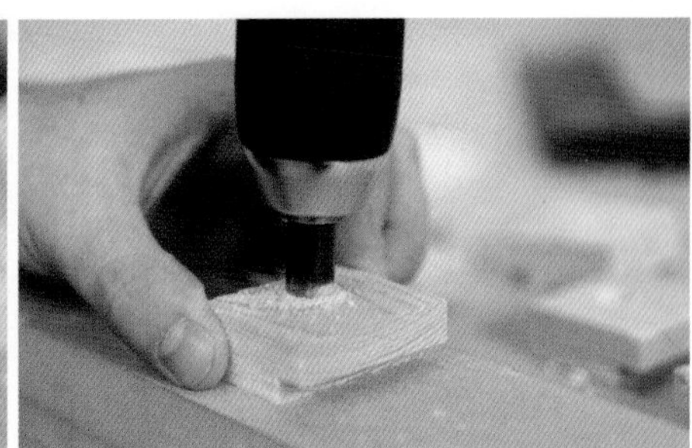

6 **Fit a countersink** into the drill. Turn the button upside-down and countersink the hole on the underside.

ASSEMBLING THE TABLE TOP

1 **Join the pieces** for the table top. Take into account the visual effect of the wood and the need to alternate the grain direction (see p.94). Glue and clamp securely. Leave to dry overnight.

2 **When the glue is dry,** unclamp the table top and cut it to size using a table saw (pictured) or by hand with a panel saw.

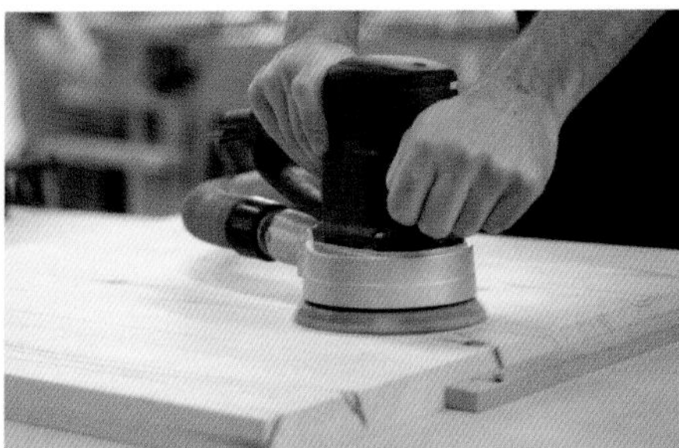

3 **Sand the table top** flat and smooth with an orbital sander, using progressively finer grades of sandpaper.

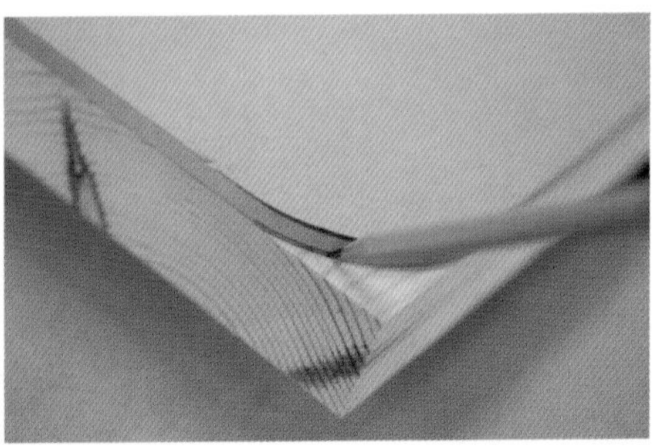

4 **Using a simple curved template** (see Jigs and templates, pp.150–51), mark rounded corners on the table top.

5 **Remove the bulk** of the waste from the corners of the table top with a band saw, cutting to the waste side of the marks.

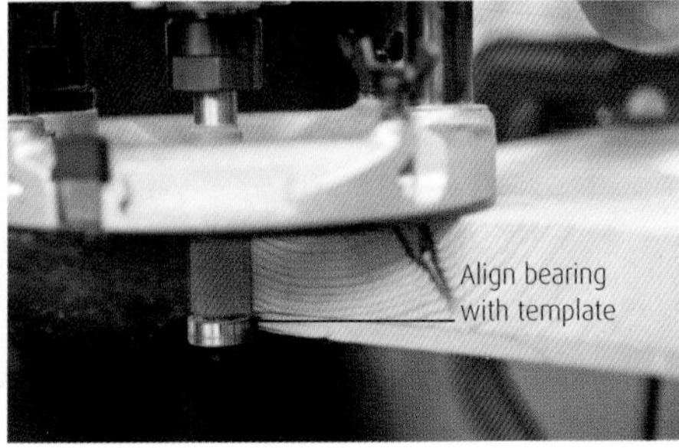

6 **To finish the corners**, use a router fitted with a bearing-guided cutter aligned to the template and clamped underneath the table top. Work in the direction of the grain.

7 **Chamfer the edges** on the underside of the table top using the router and a bearing-guided chamfer cutter.

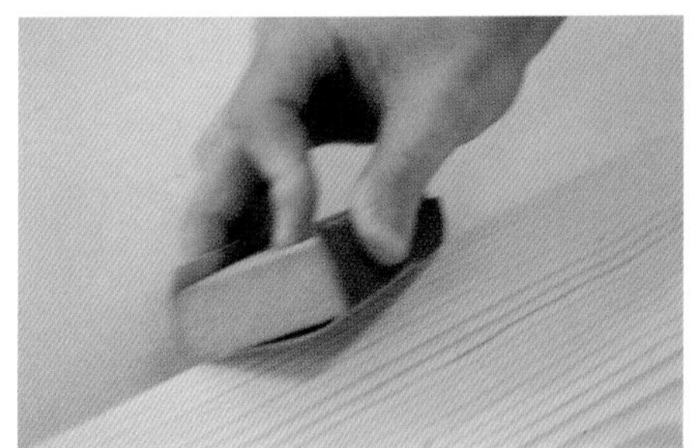

8 **Sand the edges** of the upper side of the table top by hand to remove any sharp corners and create a smooth finish.

GLUING THE FRAME

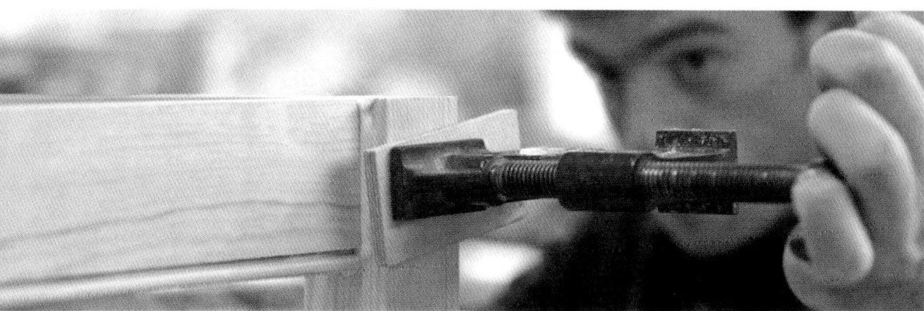

1 **Assemble the joints** of the legs and rails to check for fit. Adjust if necessary, then glue.

2 **Clamp the frame assembly** using sash clamps. Protect the wood from damage by placing spare offcuts between the clamp and the frame. Clean up any excess glue and allow the assembly to dry overnight.

ATTACHING THE TOP

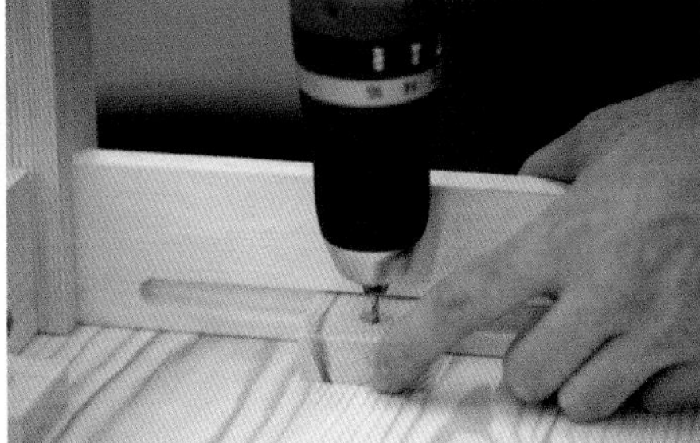

1 **Place the table top** upside down and center the leg assembly on it. Position two buttons in the slot of each rail, at regular intervals around the frame.

2 **Drill a pilot hole** to match the screw size through each button and into the table top. Mark the drill bit so that you do not drill right though the table top.

3 **Insert screws** to secure each of the buttons in position on the underside of the table top.

THE FINISHED PIECE

ALTERNATIVE LEG DESIGN

If you want a more traditional look, you could turn the table legs on a lathe (see Turning, pp.152–56).

FINISHES

A breakfast table gets a lot of wear and therefore needs a tough, protective finish. Use either a clear varnish or multiple coats of oil. Alternatively, you could paint or stain the table to match your decor. Be sure to check that any stain you use is compatible with the finish to be applied afterward.

Wall cabinet

This small wall-mounted cabinet is a practical storage unit for the bathroom or kitchen. Consisting of a jointed carcass, internal shelf, door, and back, it is a good piece for the novise woodworker to make to get to grips with the basic principles of cabinet design. There are many kinds of wall fixings available: choose one that is suitable for the wall on which you intend to place the cabinet.

Dimensions:
17 11/16 x 14 3/16 x 6 9/16in (450 x 360 x 168mm)

Key techniques:
Shouldered and stopped housing joint (pp.108–109);
Comb joint (pp.132–33)

CUTTING LIST

Item	Material	No.	Length	Width	Thickness
Sides	Oak	2	17 13/16in* (452mm)	5 7/8in (150mm)	11/16in (18mm)
Ends	Oak	2	13 7/8in* (352mm)	5 7/8in (150mm)	11/16in (18mm)
Shelf	Oak	1	13 1/8in (334mm)	5 1/8in (130mm)	11/16in (18mm)
Back	Oak-faced MDF	1	17 1/16in (434mm)	13 1/8in (334mm)	3/16in (4mm)
Door	Oak	1	17 11/16in (450mm)	14 3/16in (360mm)	11/16in (18mm)

*Includes excess to allow for cutting to size

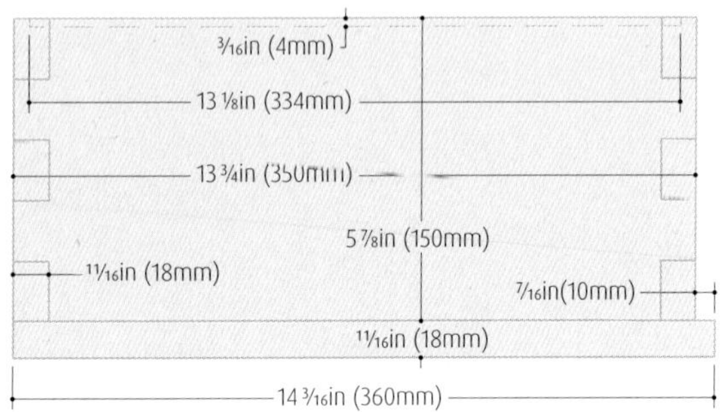

TOP VIEW (1:5)

How the elements fit together
The carcass is comb jointed. The interior shelf is fitted into stopped housings on the inside of each side piece. Pinned into a rebate, the back panel helps to keep the carcass square.

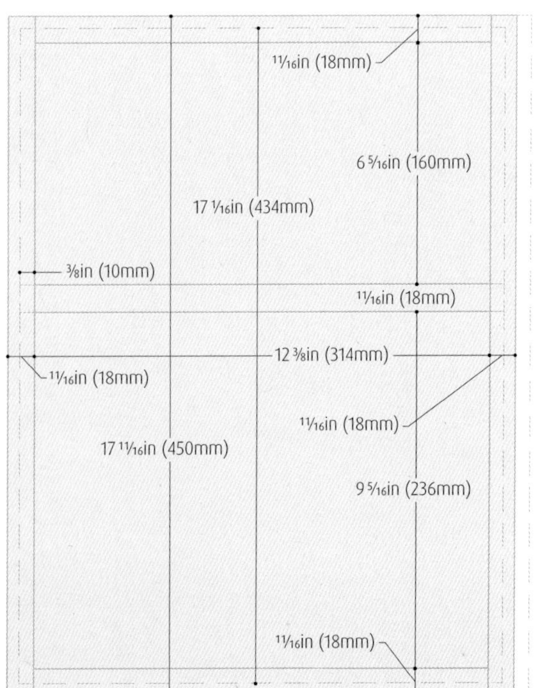

FRONT VIEW (1:5)

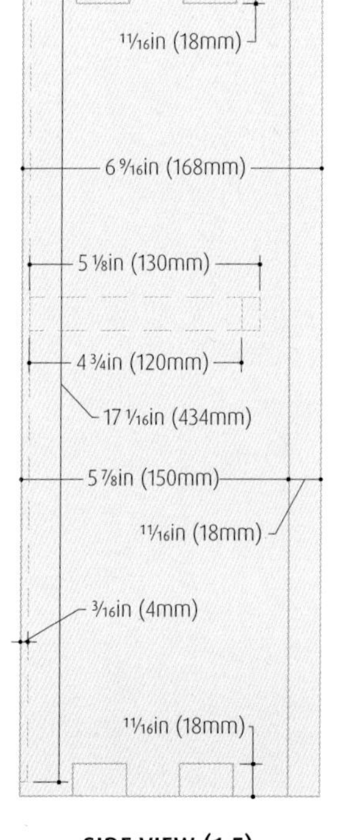

SIDE VIEW (1:5)

TOOLS AND MATERIALS

- Marking gauge
- Dividers
- Marking knife
- Square
- Pencil
- Tenon saw or band saw
- Coping saw
- Bevel-edged chisel
- Ruler
- Rubber mallet
- Wood glue and brush
- Masking tape
- Sash clamps
- Bench plane
- Router and bearing-guided rebate cutter
- Hammer
- 8 panel pins
- 2 brass butt-hinges and screws
- Bradawl
- Drill with bits
- Screwdriver
- Sandpaper
- Wax
- Door catch

MARKING OUT THE COMB JOINTS ON THE SIDES AND ENDS

1 **Set the marking gauge** to 13/16in (20mm)—the thickness of the timber of the carcass pieces plus 1/16in (2mm).

2 **Scribe this measurement** around all sides of both ends of the four carcass pieces to indicate the shoulder of the joint.

3 **Set a pair of dividers** to 1 3/16in (30mm) and mark holes to divide the end grains of each piece into five equal segments.

4 **Mark the divisions** with a marking knife and square, scoring across the width of the end grains of each piece.

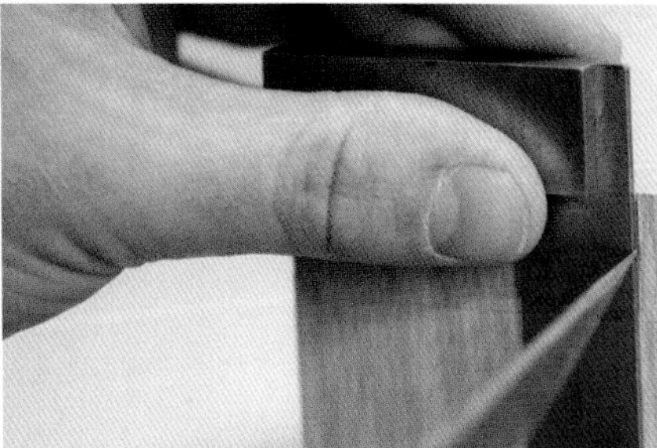

5 **Extend the marks** to the shoulder on both faces of all four pieces, using the square and marking knife.

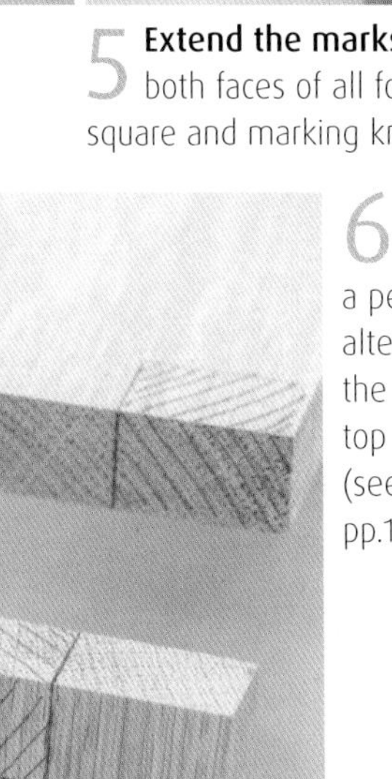

6 **Mark the waste** to be removed with a pencil. Be sure to mark alternating segments on the side pieces, and the top and bottom pieces (see Comb joint, pp.132–33).

CUTTING COMBS WITH A BAND SAW

You can use a band saw to cut the comb joints. To remove the central sections, you will need to use a chisel as well.

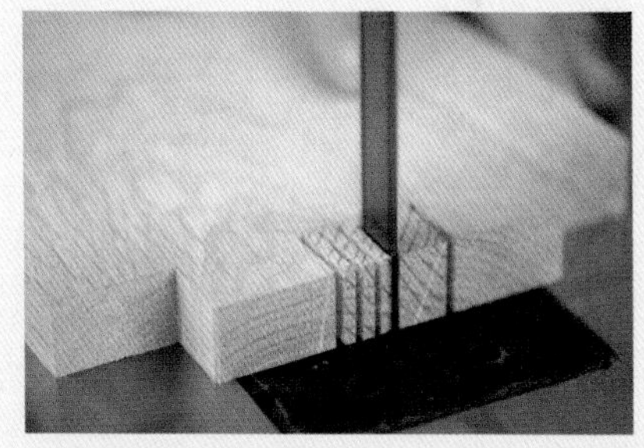

1 **Make a series** of relief cuts through the waste with the band saw to ease its removal with a chisel (below).

2 **Use a bevel-edged chisel** to chop away the waste, being careful not to exceed the marking lines.

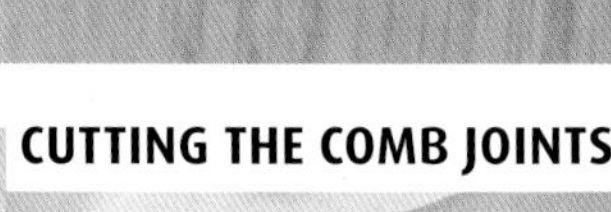

CUTTING THE COMB JOINTS

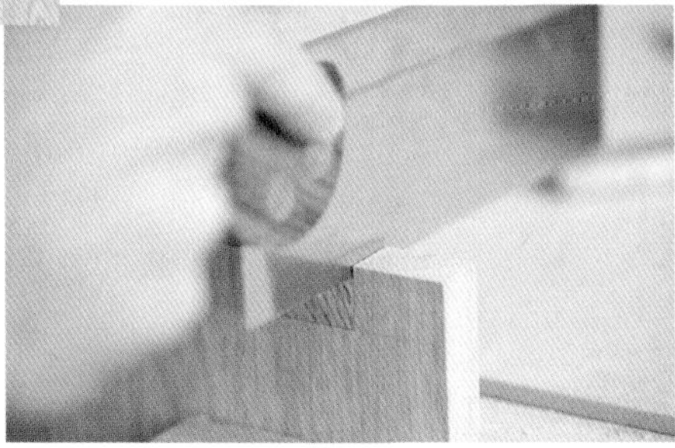

1 **With the piece secured in a vise**, cut through the end grain with a small tenon saw, keeping to the waste side of the marks.

2 **Release the waste** with a coping saw. Cut slightly clear of the marks to allow for finishing.

3 **Trim the bases** and edges of the sockets with a bevel-edged chisel. If necessary, clamp a guide to allow you to chisel accurately.

4 **Test the fit** of the comb joints and, if necessary, chisel away excess material to allow a tight fit.

MARKING AND CUTTING THE STOPPED HOUSING

1 **Mark the housing** for the shelf on the inside face of each side piece, 6⁵⁄₁₆in (160mm) from the shoulder at the top.

2 **Mark the thickness** of the wood—¹¹⁄₁₆in (18mm)—at a point 7in (178mm) from the shoulder at the base of the comb.

3 **Square the marks** from both of these positions 4¾in (120mm) across the face to define the length of the housing.

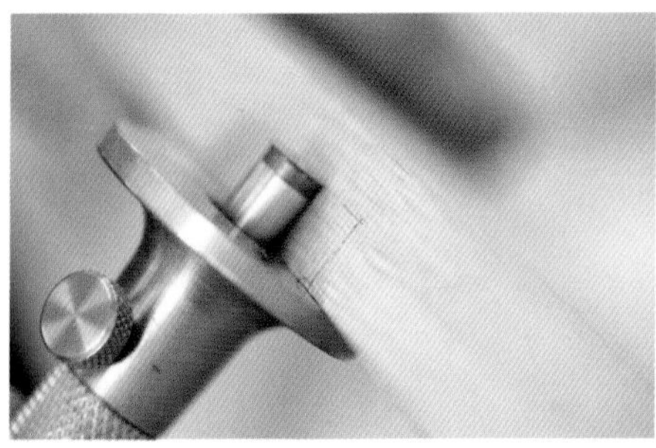

4 **Extend the marks** down the back edge of the piece, and use the marking gauge to scribe the housing depth of ⅜in (10mm).

5 **Scribe the housing stop** ⅞in (23mm) from the front edge. Repeat Steps 1–5 to mark the housing on the other side piece in the same way.

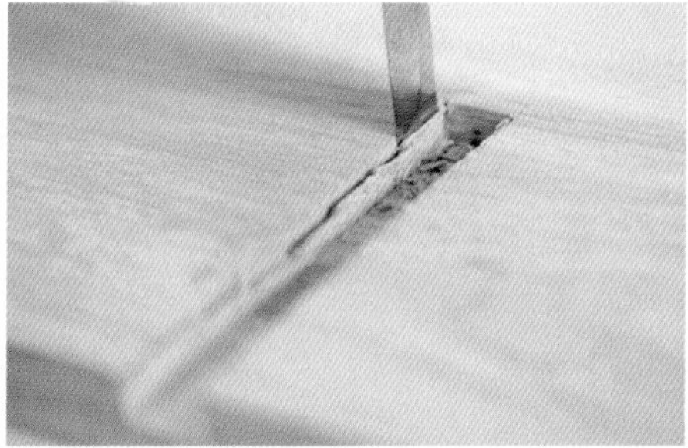

6 **Remove the waste** from each housing by hand or machine, as described for full housing joints (pp.106–07). Finish the edges by hand with a bevel-edge chisel.

MAKING THE SHELF

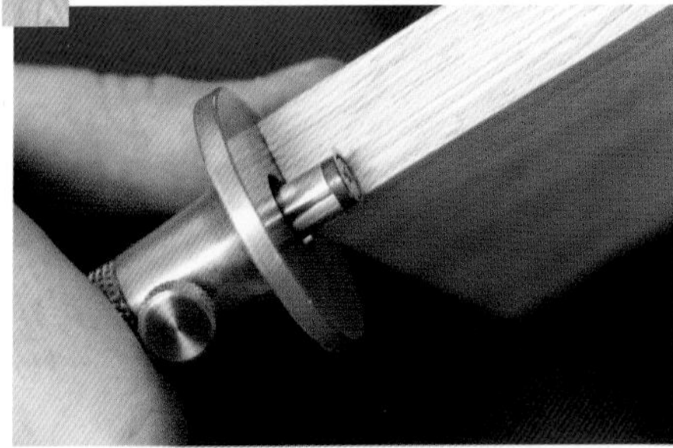

1 **Mark the stop** on the front edge of both ends of each shelf piece, ⅜in (10mm) deep (to match the housing depth) and ³⁄₁₆in (5mm) along the face. Extend the marks onto the end grain and the other face.

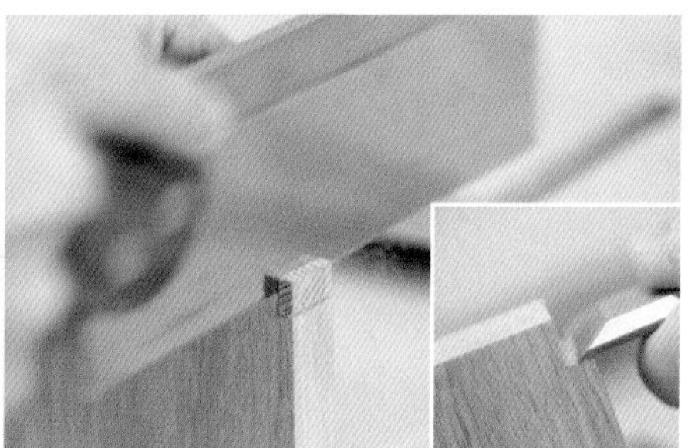

2 **Remove the waste** by cutting to the waste side of the marks with a small tenon saw. Finish cutting with a bevel-edged chisel (inset).

3 **Check the fit** of the shelf in the housings. Note that the back of the shelf should not be flush with the side piece, to allow space for the back piece.

ASSEMBLING THE CARCASS

1 **Do a test-assembly** of the carcass elements and shelf. Check the joints for squareness and adjust if necessary.

2 **Dismantle and apply glue**. Protect the wood from the glue with masking tape (to be removed before assembly).

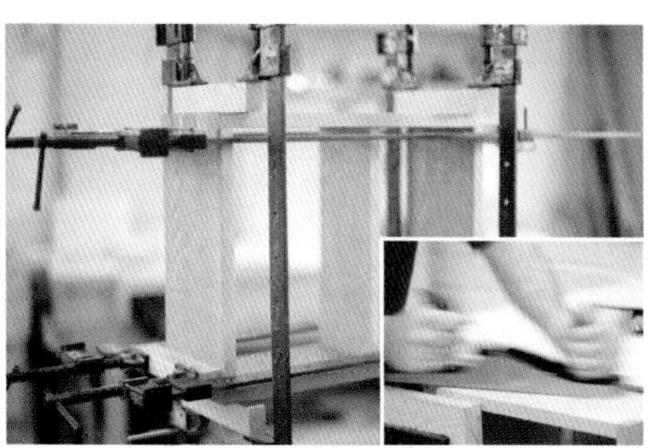

3 **Assemble the pieces** and then clamp together to ensure that the carcass dries squarely. Once the glue is dry, remove the clamps and plane the joints flush (inset).

FITTING THE CUPBOARD BACK

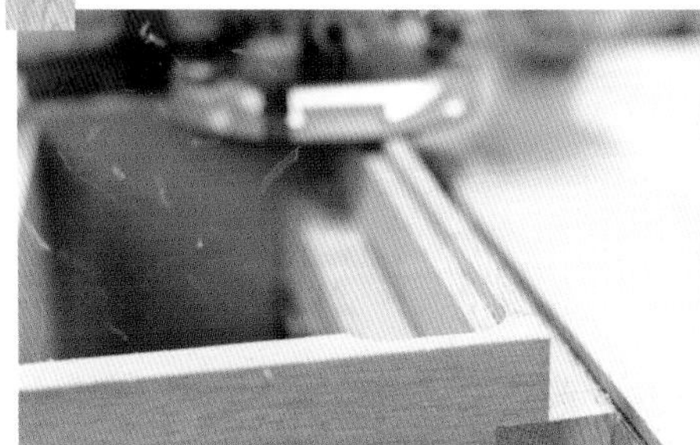

1 **Use a router** fitted with a bearing-guided rebate cutter set to a depth of 3⁄16in (4mm) and width of 3⁄8in (10mm) to cut a rebate along the inner edge of the frame.

2 **Square off the corners** and clean up the edges around the shelf housing, using a bevel-edged chisel.

3 **Test-fit the cupboard back** and adjust it if necessary. Make a mark 3⁄16in (5mm) from the edge of the back piece on all sides, and tap in two panel pins on each side.

FIXING THE HINGES TO THE CARCASS

1 **Mark the position** of the rebates for the two brass butt-hinges on the front edge of one side of the carcass frame. The first is 2in (50mm) from the bottom and the second 2in (50mm) from the top.

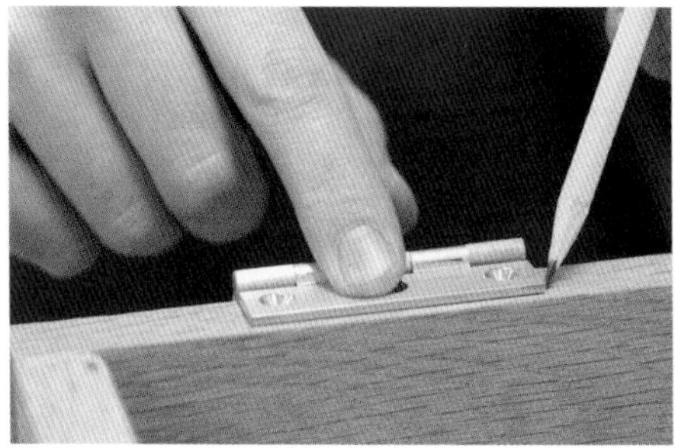

2 **Place the hinge** in the first position and mark its length. Repeat for the second hinge position.

3 **Extend the marks** onto the outside face of the carcass side. Repeat for the second rebate.

4 **Set a marking gauge** to the thickness of the hinge (inset), and scribe between the length marks for each hinge on the outside face of the carcass.

5 **Chisel away the waste** to the marks for both hinge rebates and clean up, being careful not to exceed the marks.

6 **Insert the hinge** into the rebate, checking that it is flush with the wood. Mark the screw holes with a bradawl.

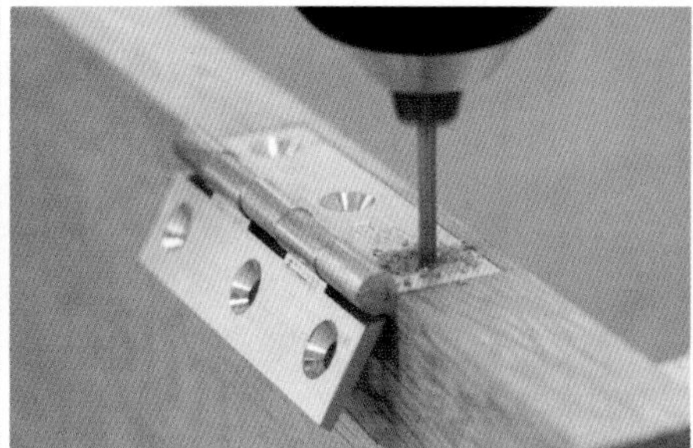

7 **Drill pilot holes** (and clearance holes if using traditional screws). Choose the drill bit and gauge the depth to suit the screws.

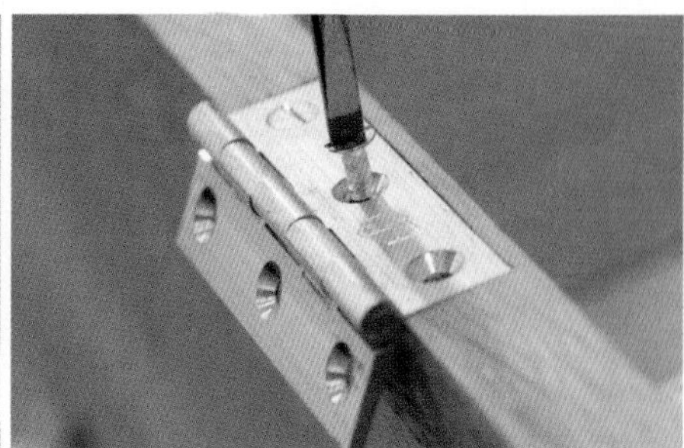

8 **Insert the screws** by hand with a screwdriver. Fit the second hinge, drill the screw holes, and insert the screws.

FIXING THE HINGES TO THE DOOR

1 **Mark the hinge positions** on the inside face of the door, using the same measurements as on the carcass.

2 **Cut the rebates** with a chisel and check the fit, then screw in the other flap of the hinges to fit the door.

FINISHING THE CABINET

1 **Sand the surfaces and edges** of every part of the cabinet to achieve a perfectly smooth finish.

2 **Finish the outside** of the wall cabinet. Remove the door and apply wax (pictured), following the instructions on p.167, or use a different finish of your choice.

3 **Screw a ball catch** or other catch of your choice into position in the top corner of the cabinet on the opposite side to the door hinges (inset). Hold the door against the carcass and mark the position of the catch on the inside face. Fit the other part of the catch in that position. Refit the door.

THE FINISHED PIECE

Garden table

Designed for outdoor use, the garden table is a perfect piece to accompany the garden bench (pp.260–63). Although it is an uncomplicated design, the deep, long mortises of each joining component are time-consuming and strenuous to cut by hand, so a machine mortiser, while not essential, is recommended for this project. Iroko is the timber of choice, since its water-resistant qualities make it good for exterior use, but any hardwood is suitable. This table can be enlarged easily by increasing the length of the cross rails and table-top rails, and adding more table-top slats.

Dimensions:
27 3/16 x 33 13/16 x 33 13/16in (690 x 860 x 860mm)

Key techniques:
Basic mortise-and-tenon joint (pp.116–19);
Jigs and templates (pp.150–51)

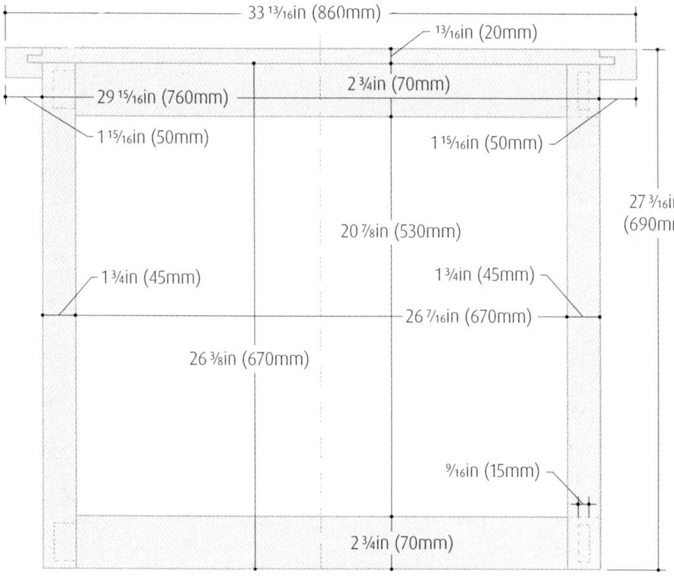

33 13/16in (860mm)
13/16in (20mm)
2 3/4in (70mm)
29 15/16in (760mm)
1 15/16in (50mm)
1 15/16in (50mm)
27 3/16in (690mm)
20 7/8in (530mm)
1 3/4in (45mm)
1 3/4in (45mm)
26 7/16in (670mm)
26 3/8in (670mm)
9/16in (15mm)
2 3/4in (70mm)

FRONT CROSS SECTION VIEW (1:10)

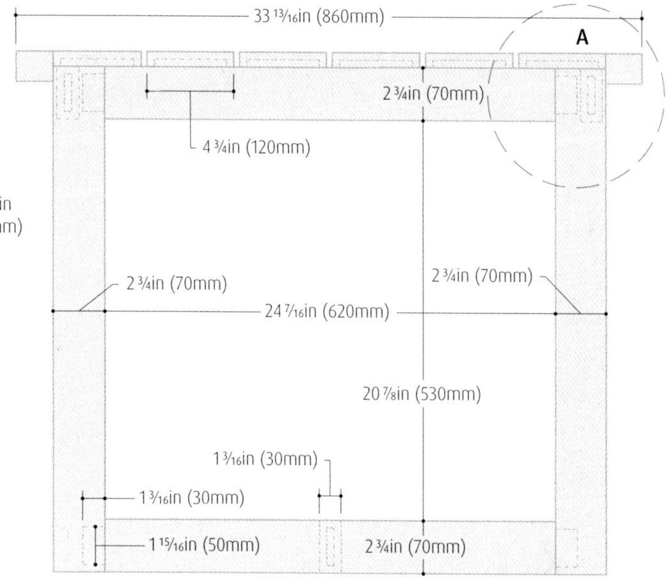

33 13/16in (860mm)
A
2 3/4in (70mm)
4 3/4in (120mm)
2 3/4in (70mm)
2 3/4in (70mm)
24 7/16in (620mm)
20 7/8in (530mm)
1 3/16in (30mm)
1 3/16in (30mm)
1 15/16in (50mm)
2 3/4in (70mm)

SIDE VIEW (1:10)

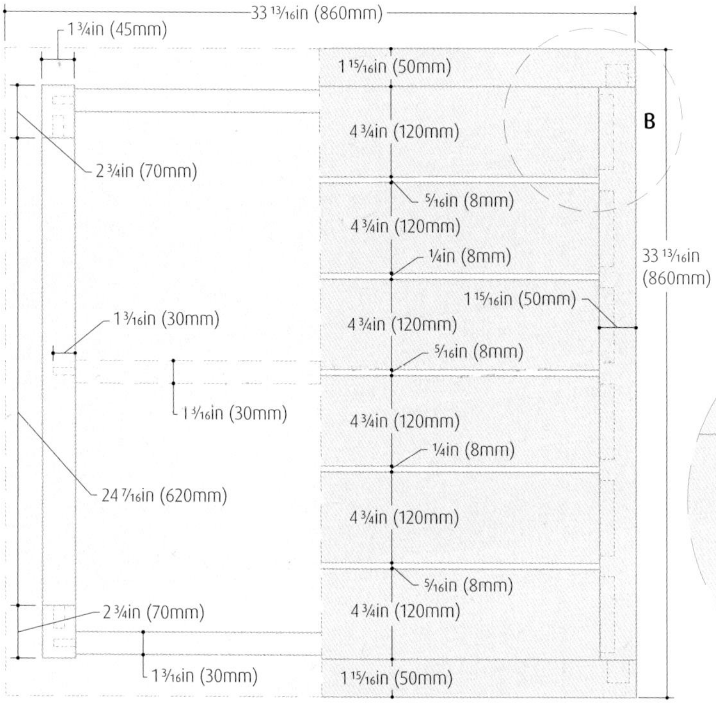

33 13/16in (860mm)
1 3/4in (45mm)
1 15/16in (50mm)
4 3/4in (120mm)
B
2 3/4in (70mm)
5/16in (8mm)
4 3/4in (120mm)
1/4in (8mm)
33 13/16in (860mm)
1 15/16in (50mm)
1 3/16in (30mm)
4 3/4in (120mm)
5/16in (8mm)
1 3/16in (30mm)
4 3/4in (120mm)
1/4in (8mm)
24 7/16in (620mm)
4 3/4in (120mm)
5/16in (8mm)
2 3/4in (70mm)
4 3/4in (120mm)
1 3/16in (30mm)
1 15/16in (50mm)

PLAN VIEW (1:10)

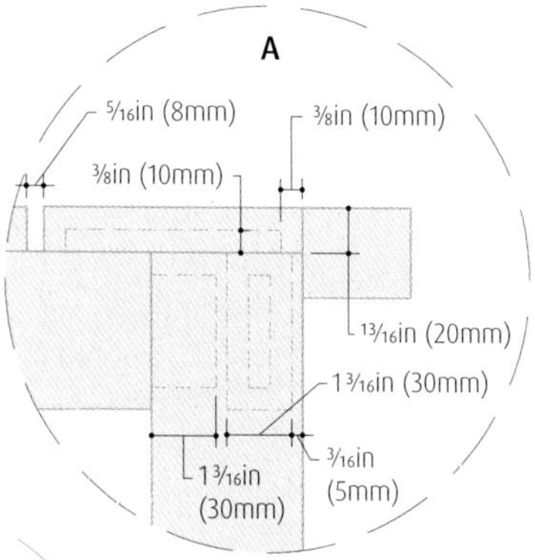

A
5/16in (8mm)
3/8in (10mm)
3/8in (10mm)
13/16in (20mm)
1 3/16in (30mm)
1 3/16in (30mm)
3/16in (5mm)

TOP CORNER DETAIL (1:5)

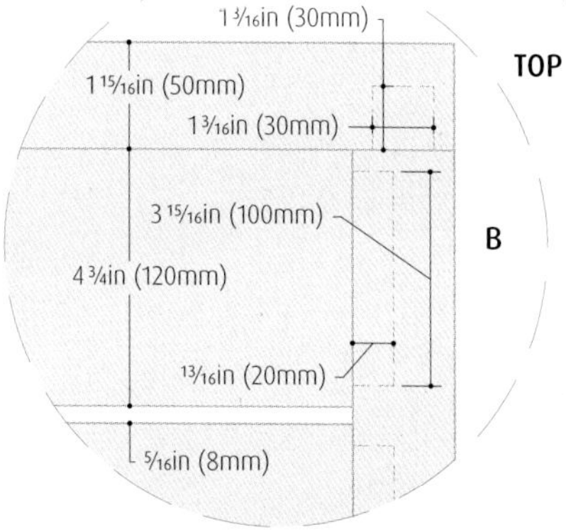

1 3/16in (30mm)
1 15/16in (50mm)
1 3/16in (30mm)
3 15/16in (100mm)
B
4 3/4in (120mm)
13/16in (20mm)
5/16in (8mm)

TABLE-TOP CORNER DETAIL (1:5)

How the elements fit together
The garden bench utilizes large mortise-and-tenon joints to provide ample strength, and should be bonded with good-quality waterproof glue. The table top fits over the frame without additional fixings for ease of transport and storage.

TOOLS AND MATERIALS

Pencil
Square
Mortise gauge
Mortiser or ⅜in (10mm) and 9⁄16in (16mm) mortise chisels
Marking gauge
Band saw or tenon saw
Block plane
Waterproof wood glue and brush
Sash clamps
Tape measure
Bevel-edged chisel

CUTTING LIST

Item	Material	No.	Length	Width	Thickness
End-frame stiles	Iroko	4	26⅜in (670mm)	2¾in (70mm)	1¾in (45mm)
End-frame rails	Iroko	4	27³⁄₁₆in (690mm)	2¾in (70mm)	1¾in (45mm)
Cross rails	Iroko	3	29⅛in (740mm)	2¾in (70mm)	1³⁄₁₆in (30mm)
Long table-top rails	Iroko	2	33⅞in (860mm)	1¹⁵⁄₁₆in (50mm)	1⁹⁄₁₆in (40mm)
Short table-top rails	Iroko	2	32⁵⁄₁₆in (820mm)	1¹⁵⁄₁₆in (50mm)	1⁹⁄₁₆in (40mm)
Table-top slats	Iroko	6	31½in (800mm)	4¾in (120mm)	¹³⁄₁₆in (20mm)

MAKING THE MORTISES IN THE END-FRAME STILES

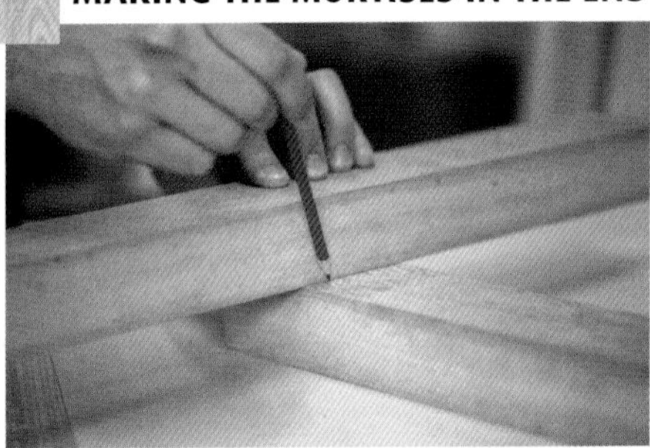

1 **Using the width** of an end-frame rail aligned to the end grain of an end-frame stile as a guide, mark a mortise shoulder at each end of the same edge of both end-frame stiles.

2 **Mark the mortise length** ⅜in (10mm) from the end grain and ⅜in (10mm) from the shoulder line. Set the gauge to ⅝in (16mm)—the width of the mortise—and scribe centrally between the width marks.

3 **Cut the mortise** to a depth of 1⅜in (35mm). Use a mortiser fitted with a ⅝in (16mm) bit (pictured), or cut the mortise by hand with a mortise chisel (pp.30–33).

4 **Mark a second mortise** on the inside face at one end of each stile (see diagram, above). Square the dimensions of the existing mortise onto the face and use the mortise gauge set to ⅝in (16mm) to scribe the mortise width ½in (12mm) from the non-mortised edge of the stile (inset).

5 **Cut the second mortise** to a depth of 1⅜in (35mm) using a mortiser (pictured), or by hand with a mortise chisel.

MAKING THE TENONS AND MORTISES IN THE END-FRAME RAILS

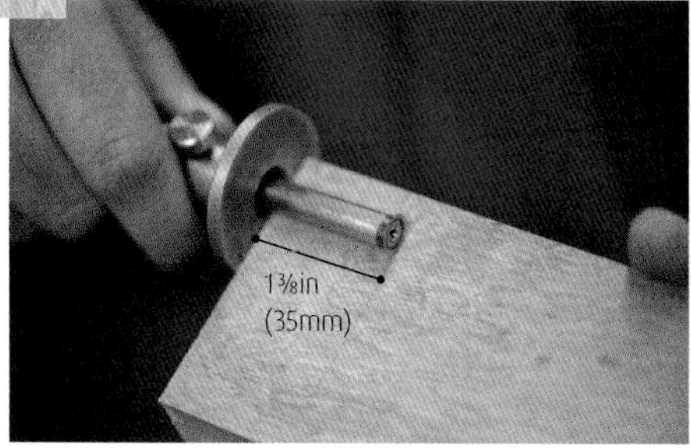

1 **Make a tenon** at each end of all of the end-frame rails. Set the marking gauge to 1⅜in (35mm) and scribe the shoulder line on the face of the rails.

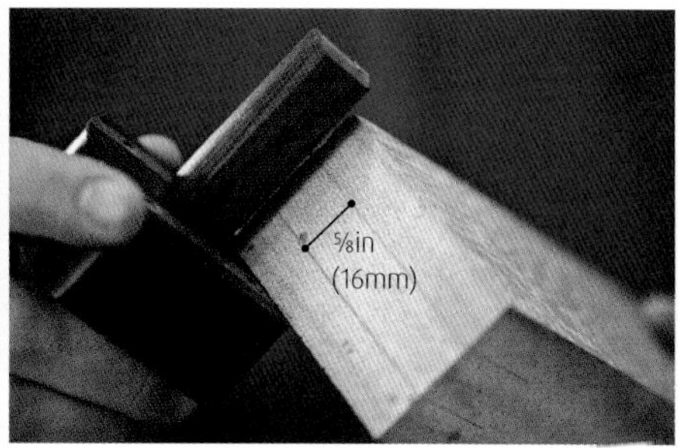

2 **Use the mortise gauge** as previously set to mark the thickness of each tenon. Scribe around the end grain and onto both adjacent edges, to the shoulder mark.

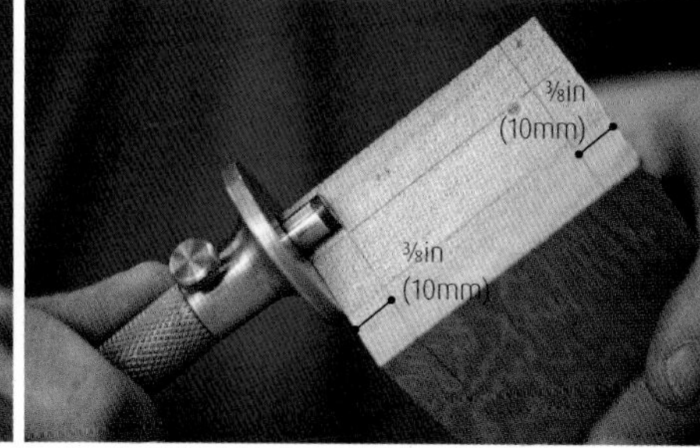

3 **Set the marking gauge** to ⅜in (10mm) and scribe two lines from each edge of the end grain to define the tenon width. Extend the lines to the shoulder on both faces.

4 **Cut the tenon** on a band saw (pictured) or by hand with a tenon saw. Repeat on all the end-frame rails. Chamfer the edges of the tenons with a block plane (inset).

5 **Find the halfway point** on the inside face of the two lower end-frame rails and square two lines 5⁄16in (8mm) to either side of it, across the width of the face.

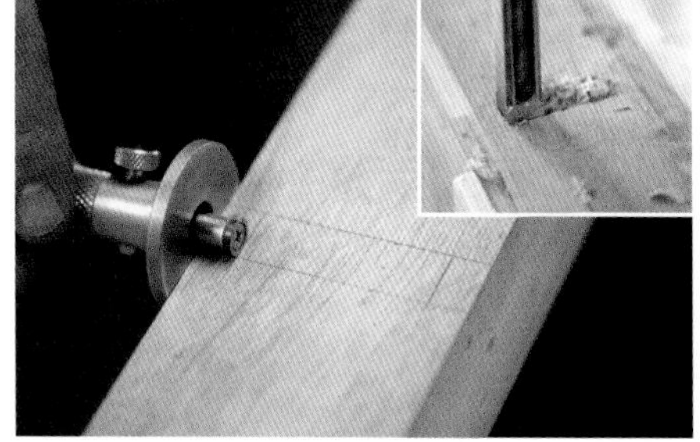

6 **Use the marking gauge** set to ⅜in (10mm) to mark the length of the mortise from each edge. Cut the mortises to 1⅜in (35mm) using a mortiser or by hand.

ASSEMBLING THE END FRAMES

1 **Test the fit** of the joints of the end frames, and make any adjustments necessary to achieve a tight fit.

2 **Glue the elements** using waterproof glue (inset). Assemble both end frames and cramp with sash clamps. Use a tape measure to check for squareness, then leave to dry.

MAKING THE TENONS IN THE CROSS RAILS

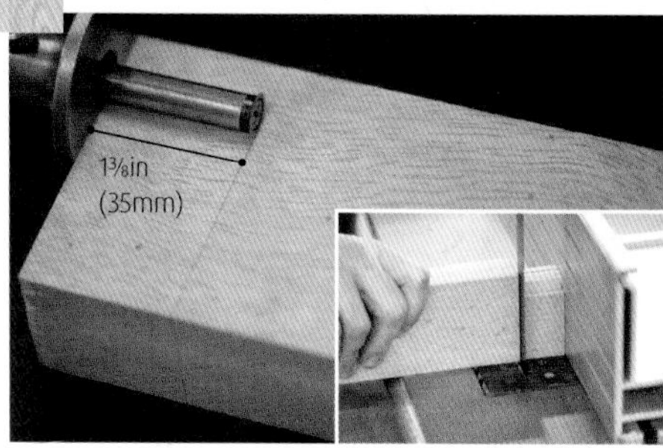

1 **Mark and cut a tenon** (inset) in each end of the cross rails in the same way as those on the end-frame rails (see above, Steps 1–4).

2 **Once the two end frames** have dried, apply waterproof glue to the cross-rail tenons (inset) and insert them into the mortises in the center of the lower end-frame rails. Clamp with sash clamps and leave to dry.

MAKING THE TABLE-TOP FRAME

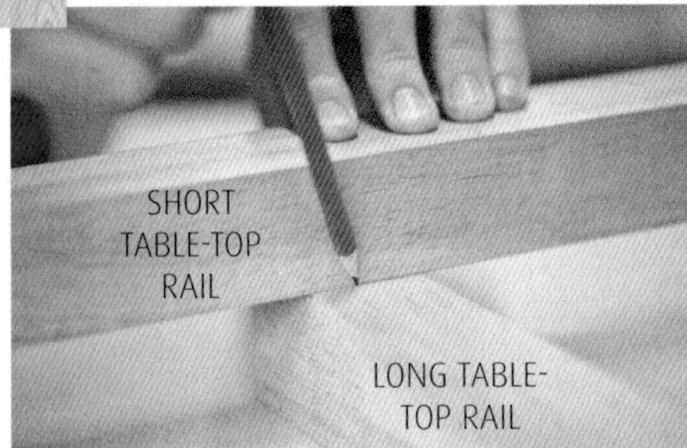

1 **Use the thickness** 1 9⁄16in (40mm) of a short table-top rail as a guide to mark a mortise shoulder on the same 1 9⁄16in (40mm) edge at each end of the long rails.

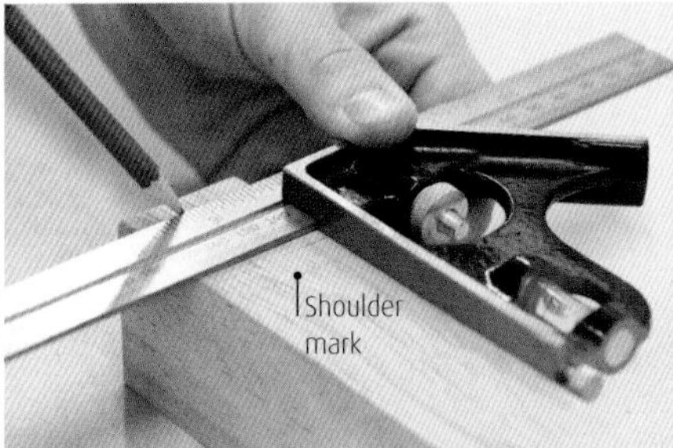

2 **Mark the mortise length** with two lines 3⁄8in (10mm) from the end grain and shoulder line, then square the marks across the face.

3 **With the mortise gauge** set to 5⁄8in (16mm), scribe the mortise width centrally between the marks. Cut the mortise to 1 3⁄16in (30mm) on a mortiser (inset) or by hand.

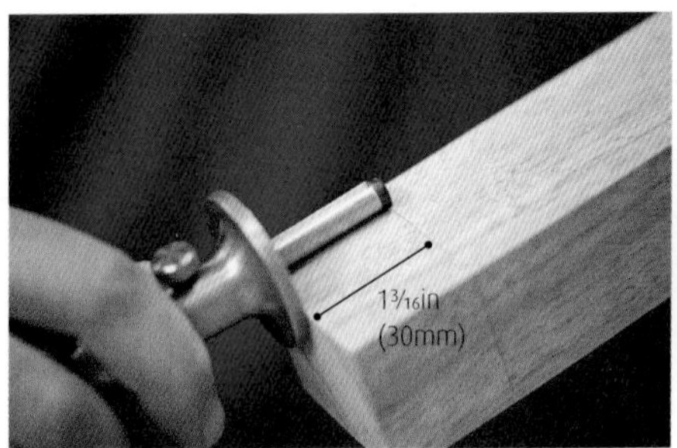

4 **Mark a tenon** on each end of both short table-top rails. Use the marking gauge to scribe a 1 3⁄16in (30mm) shoulder around all four sides.

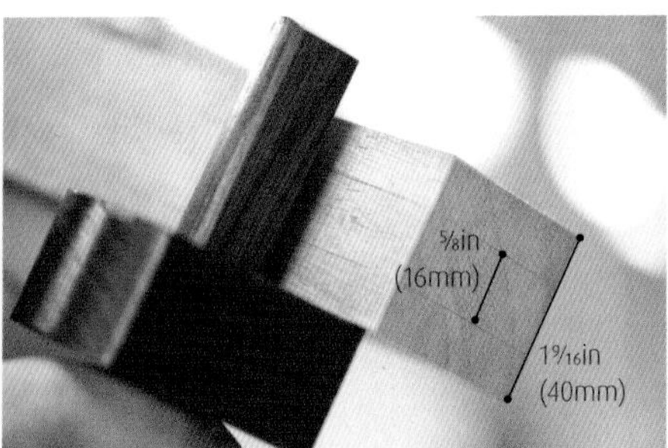

5 **Use the mortise gauge** as previously set 5⁄8in (16mm) to scribe the tenon thickness on both edges and across the end grain.

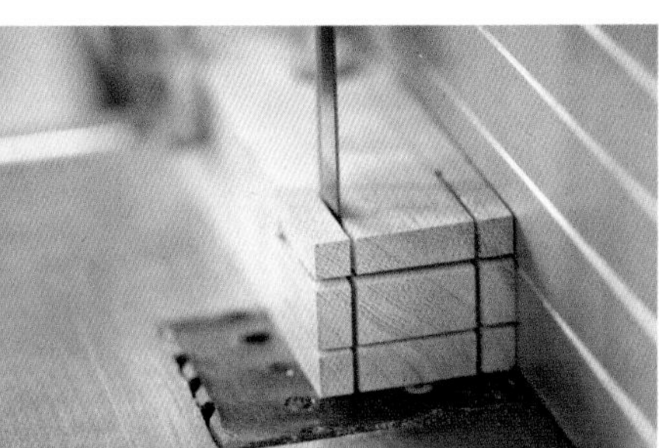

6 **Mark the tenon width** on the end grain and both faces with the marking gauge set to 10mm (3⁄8in). Cut the tenons on a band saw (pictured) or by hand with a tenon saw.

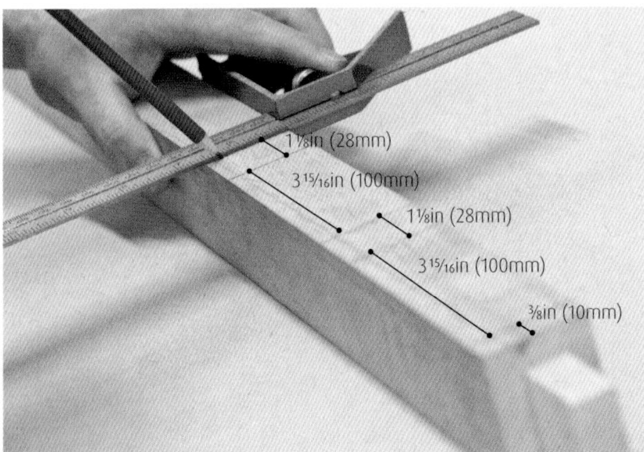

7 **Mark the mortises** for the table-top slats on the inside edge of each short table-top rail. Mark the first mortise 3⁄8in (10mm) from the tenon shoulder with a length of 3 15⁄16in (100mm). Mark the next mortise 1 1⁄8in (28mm) from this mark, with the same length. Continue to mark the mortises for all six slats along both rails.

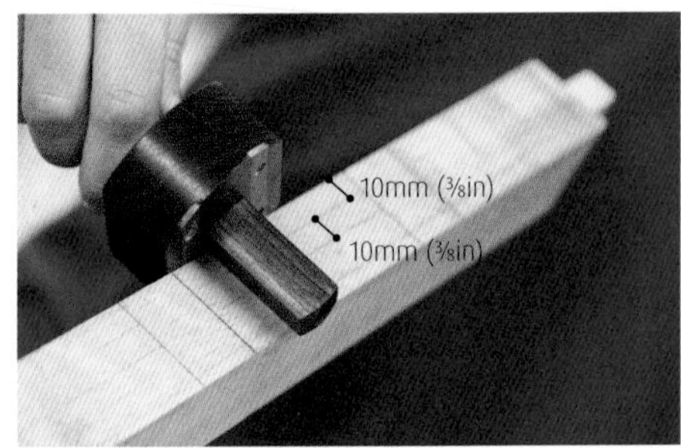

8 **Mark the width** of each mortise on the short table-top rail, using the mortise gauge set to 3⁄8in (10mm). Set the fence to 3⁄8in (10mm) and scribe from the top edge.

9 **Cut the mortises** in the short table-top rails to a depth of 13⁄16in (20mm) using a mortiser fitted with a 3⁄8in (10mm) bit.

MAKING THE TABLE-TOP SLATS

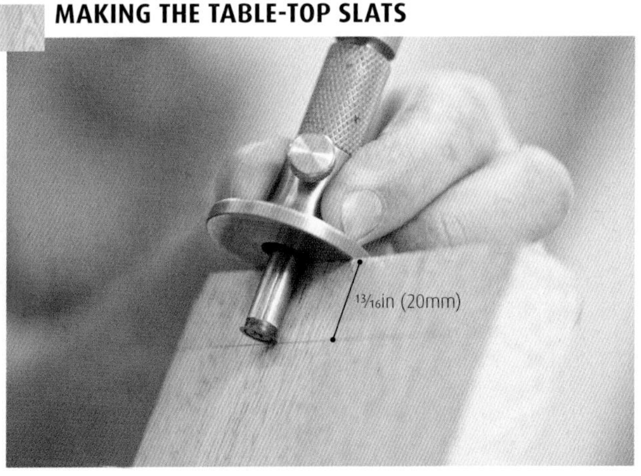

1 **Mark a "barefaced tenon"**—a tenon with only one shoulder—in both ends of all of the table-top slats. Set the marking gauge to 13⁄16in (20mm) and mark the shoulders on all four sides of each of the slats.

2 **Set the marking gauge** to 3/8in (10mm) and scribe a line along the end grain and to the shoulder on both edges of the slats.

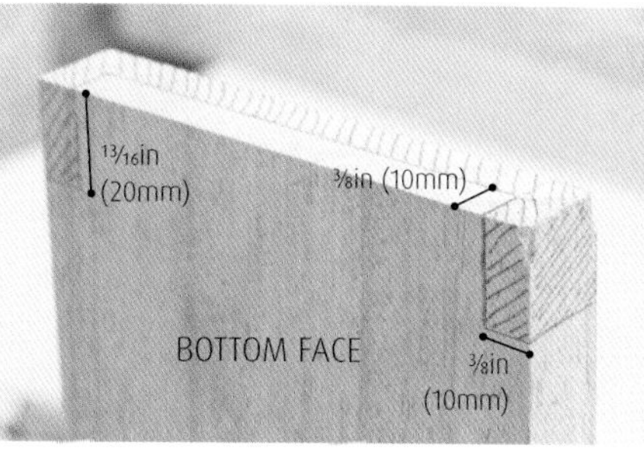

3 **Use the marking gauge** to scribe the same measurement across the end grain from each edge, and down both faces to the shoulder. Mark the waste for removal.

4 **Cut the tenons** on a band saw (pictured) or with a tenon saw, then clean up with a bevel-edged chisel. Chamfer the upper edges of the slats with a block plane (inset).

ASSEMBLING THE TABLE

1 **Test-fit all of the elements** of the table top, and make any necessary adjustments to achieve a good fit.

2 **Glue and assemble** the table-top rails and slats. Clamp with sash clamps and leave to dry.

3 **Assemble the frame** and table top. (The table top fits over the frame without fixings for ease of removal and storage.)

DETAIL OF TABLE TOP

FINISHES

A coating of Danish oil can be applied to the finished piece (pictured), to bring out the richness of the cherry wood and provide a good protective layer. For added protection against rain, use teak oil instead. As an alternative you could source some specialized Outdoor Furniture Oil, and then follow the manufacturer's instructions when applying.

THE FINISHED PIECE

Garden bench

This sturdy outdoor bench is a simple design with relatively few elements. It features a gently concaved seat, shaped by planing the boards with the aid of a jig. Although other woods could be chosen, the dense grain and high oil-content of iroko make it the ideal timber for outdoor furniture.

Dimensions:
40 9/16 x 18 7/16 x 17 1/8in (1030 x 470 x 435mm)

Key techniques:
Basic mortise-and-tenon joint (pp.116–19);
Jigs and templates (pp.150–51)

TOOLS AND MATERIALS

- Square
- Pencil
- Mortise gauge
- Mortiser or 3/8in (10mm) mortise chisel
- Marking gauge
- Band saw or tenon saw
- Bevel-edged chisel
- Ply or MDF and offcuts (47 x 22 x 3/4in/1200 x 550 x 18mm)
- Thicknesser or bench plane
- Masking tape
- Drill with bits
- Sandpaper
- Wood glue and brush
- Sash clamps
- Screwdriver
- 8 screws (No.10 x 1 1/2in/ 5 x 40mm)

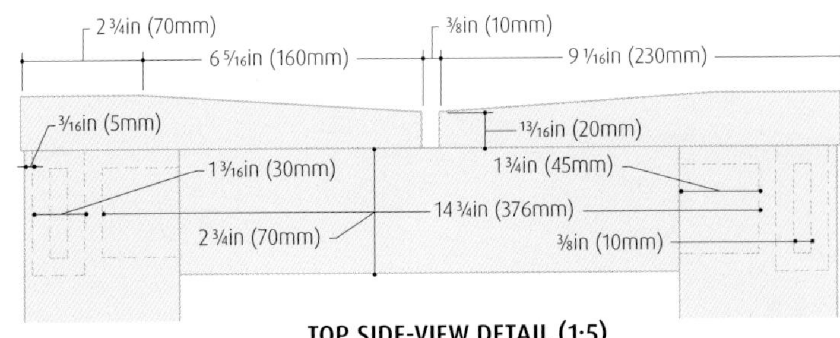

TOP SIDE-VIEW DETAIL (1:5)

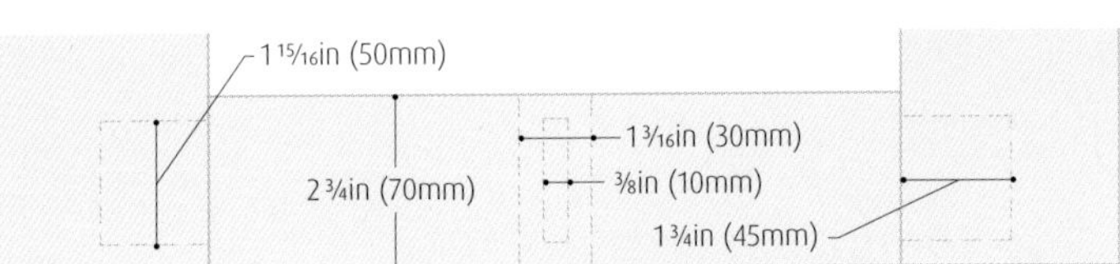

BOTTOM SIDE-VIEW DETAIL (1:5)

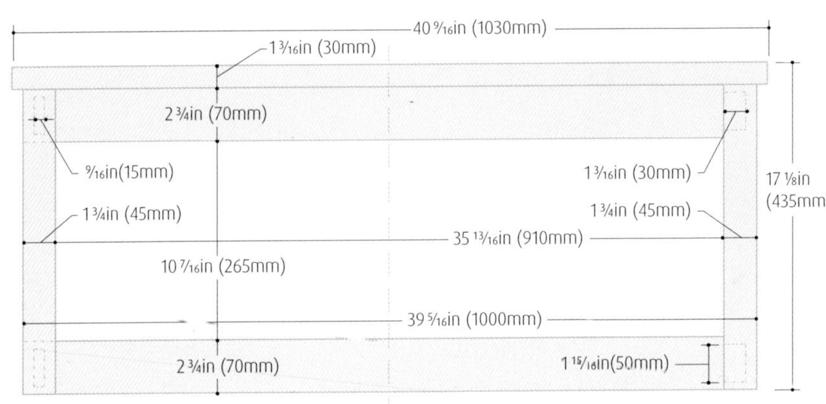

FRONT VIEW (1:10)

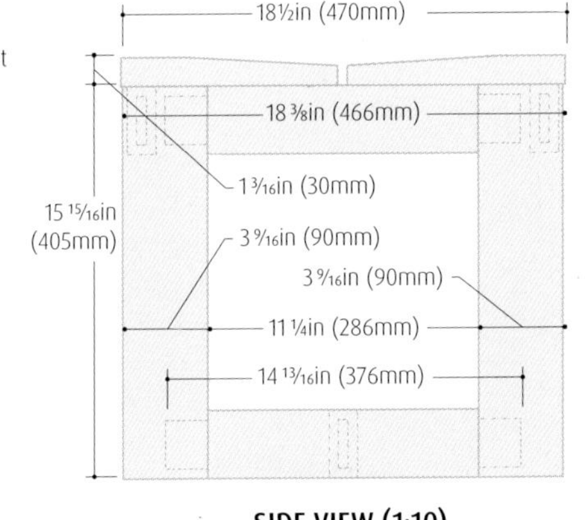

SIDE VIEW (1:10)

Seat slat
Upper long-rail
Upper short-rail
Stile
Lower short-rail
Lower long-rail

How the elements fit together
The end frames are assembled using mortise-and-tenon joints. These are connected by the three long rails—also joined in the same way. The seat is screwed in place through the rails.

CUTTING LIST

Item	Material	No.	Length	Width	Thickness
Seat slats	Iroko	2	40 9/16in (1030mm)	9 1/16in (230mm)	1 3/16in (30mm)
Long rails	Iroko	3	38 3/16in (970mm)	2 3/4in (70mm)	1 3/16in (30mm)
Short rails	Iroko	4	14 13/16in (376mm)	2 3/4in (70mm)	1 3/4in (45mm)
Stiles	Iroko	4	15 15/16in (405mm)	3 9/16in (90mm)	1 3/4in (45mm)

MAKING THE END-FRAME MORTISES AND TENONS

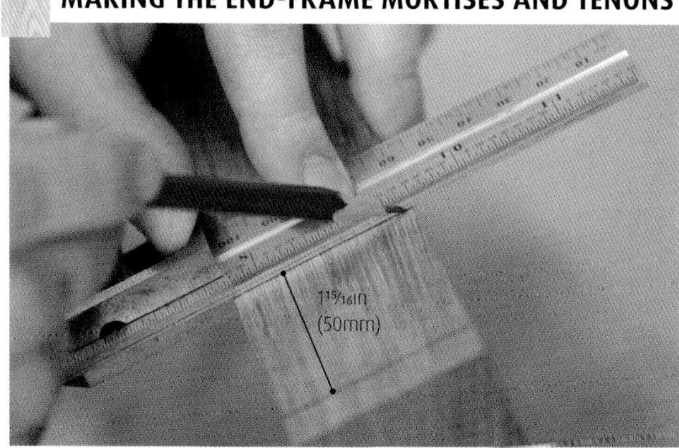

1 **Mark out the length** and position of two mortises 1¹⁵⁄₁₆in (50mm) in length on each end of the inside edge of each stile. Square two lines across the edge: the first ⅜in (10mm) and the second 2⅜in (60mm) from the end grain of each end.

2 **Use a mortise gauge** set to ⅜in (10mm) to mark the mortise width and scribe centrally between the marked lines.

3 **Cut out the mortises** to a depth of 1¾in (45mm), using either a mortiser fitted with a bit of the correct size (pictured), or by hand with a mortise chisel.

4 **Mark the length** of the tenons—1¾in (45mm)—on all four sides of each short rail, using a marking gauge.

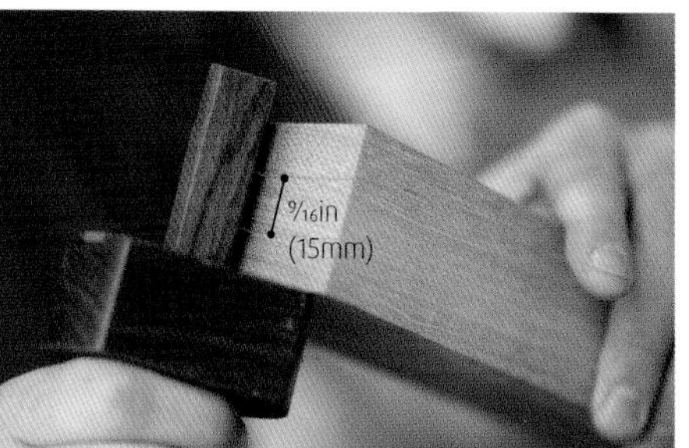

5 **Mark the thickness** of each tenon on the end grains of each short rail with the mortise gauge, as previously set.

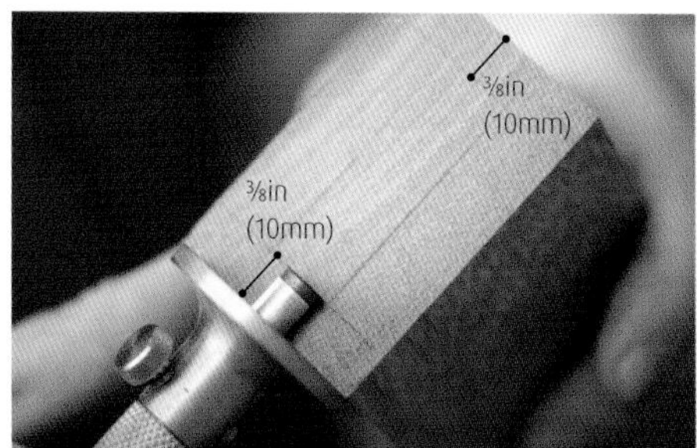

6 **Mark the width** of the tenon shoulders by scribing across the end grain of each tenon piece ⅜in (10mm) from the edge, creating a tenon width of 2in (50mm).

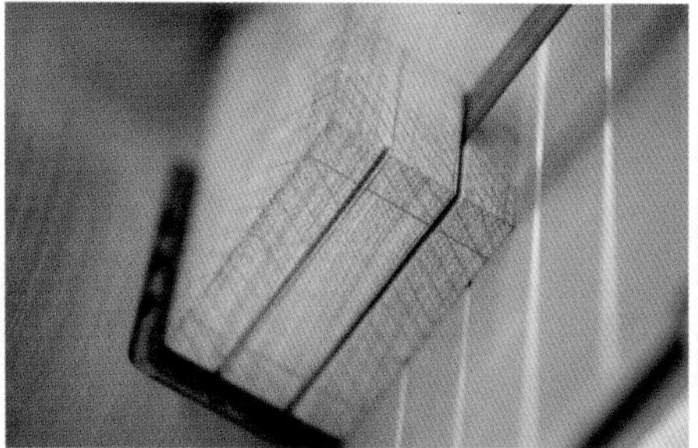

7 **After extending the marks** down each face of the tenon pieces, cut the tenons with a band saw (pictured) or by hand with a tenon saw.

8 **Clean up the tenons** with a chisel, then check the fit of the mortise-and-tenon joints of the two end frames.

MAKING THE MORTISES AND TENONS FOR THE LONG RAILS

1 **From the outside edge**, mark out a second mortise ⅜in (10mm) wide on the inside face of each of the stiles (inset), using the mortise gauge as previously set. Cut the mortises to a depth of 1¾in (45mm) using a mortiser or mortise chisel (see Step 3, above).

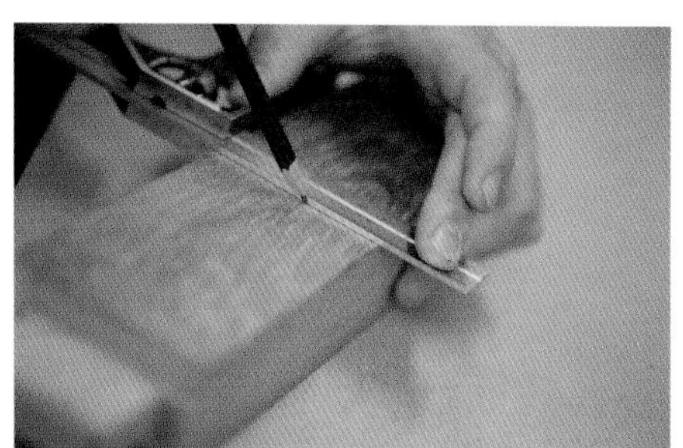

2 **Mark the position** of a mortise ⅜in/10mm in width in the center of each of the two lower short rails.

3 **To center the mortise** on both of the lower short rails, mark half the mortise width—3⁄16in (5mm)—to one side of the centre line and half to the other side.

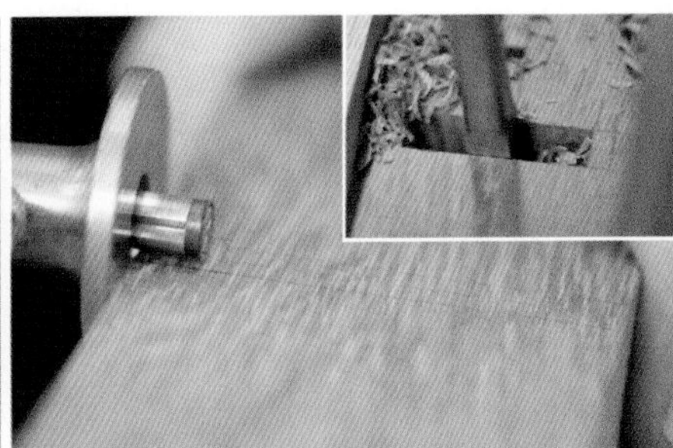

4 **Mark the length** of the mortises—2in (50mm)—with a marking gauge and then cut the mortises (inset).

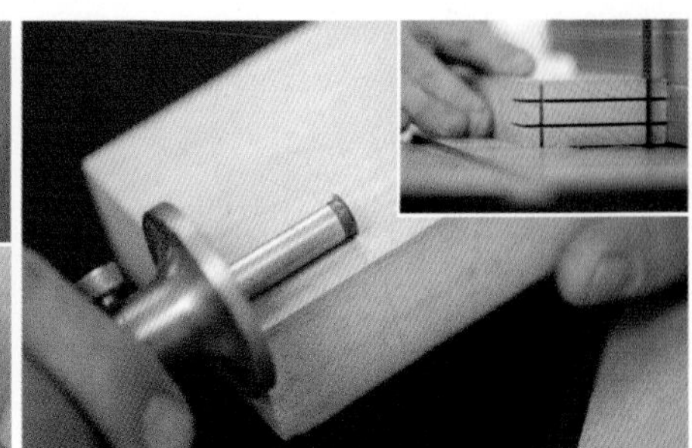

5 **Mark the length** and width—1 3⁄16in (30mm) and 2in (50mm)—of the tenon on both ends of all three long rails. Cut the tenons in both ends of the rails (inset).

TAPERING THE SEAT PIECES

1 **Make a jig** with a baseboard of ply or MDF to cradle each seat slat. Screw tapered blocks (made from offcuts) to support the seat slat at the desired angle for planing by machine or hand. Fix end- and side-stops to prevent the seat moving within the jig during planing.

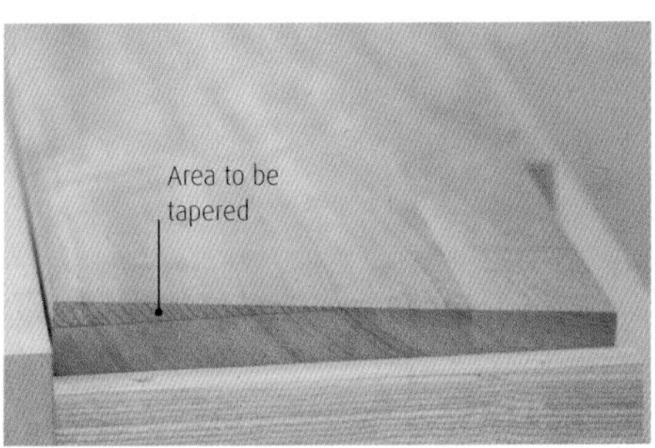

2 **Mark the end grain** of both seat pieces to indicate the amount to be tapered, then set the first piece in the jig.

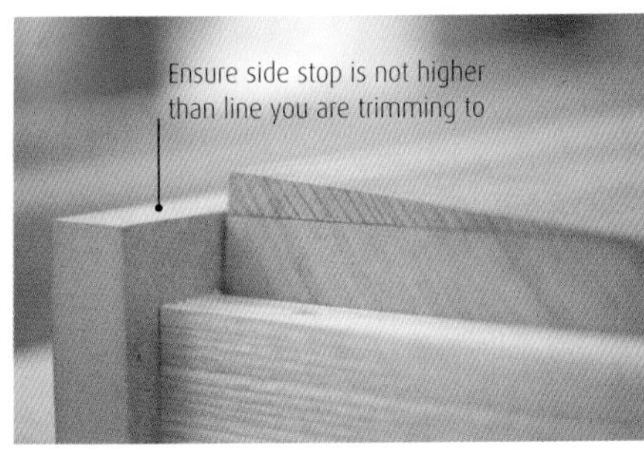

3 **Pass the seat piece** supported by the jig through a thicknesser, taking off about 1⁄32in (1mm) at each pass, or plane the pieces by hand. Taper the second seat piece in the same way.

MAKING THE SCREW HOLES

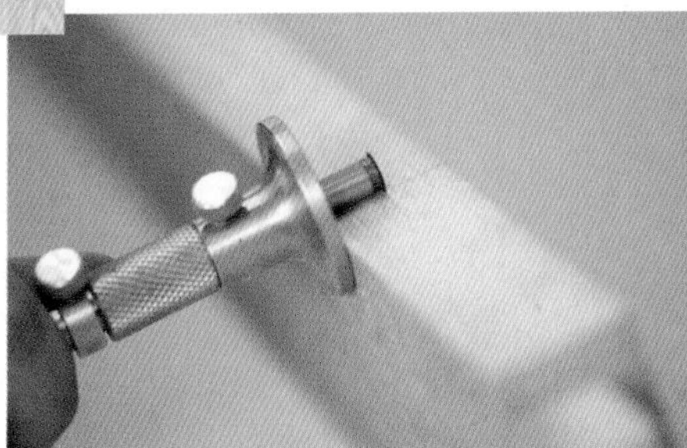

1 **Mark the screw holes**, centered on the thickness, on both edges of the two upper long-rails and the upper short-rails. Mark four holes equidistantly along the upper long-rails and two along the upper short-rails.

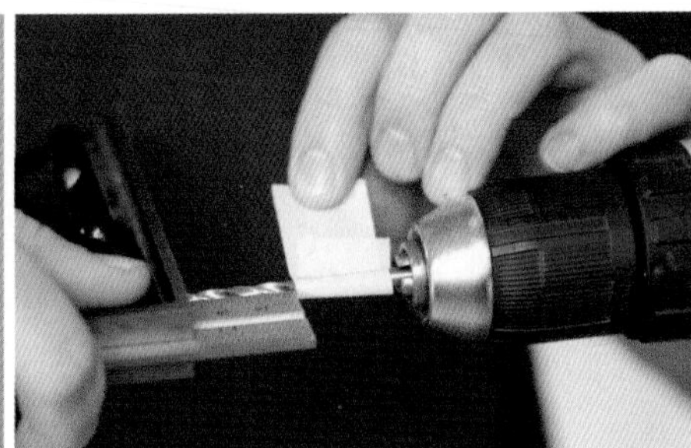

2 **Use masking tape** to mark a drilling depth of 1 9⁄16in (40mm) on a 3⁄16in (5mm) drill bit.

3 **Drill clearance holes** to the depth indicated by the masking tape in all the marked positions on the upper rails.

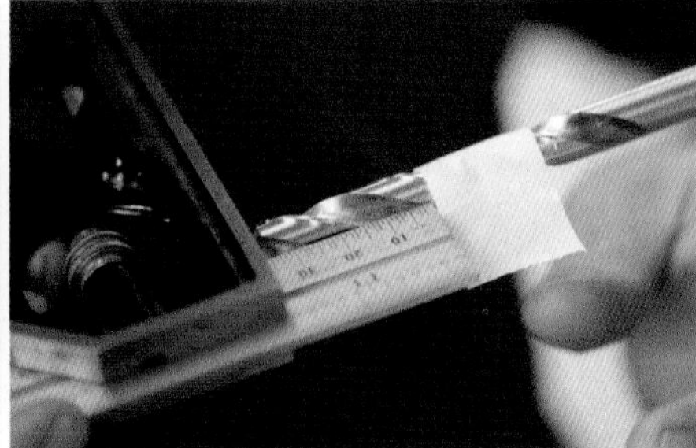

4 **Mark a depth** of ½in (13mm) on a 3⁄8in (10mm) drill bit. Drill to this depth into all the clearance holes on the top edges.

5 **Drill counterbore holes** to a depth of 1 9⁄16in (40mm)in the underside edge, still using the 3⁄8in (10mm) drill bit.

ASSEMBLING THE BENCH

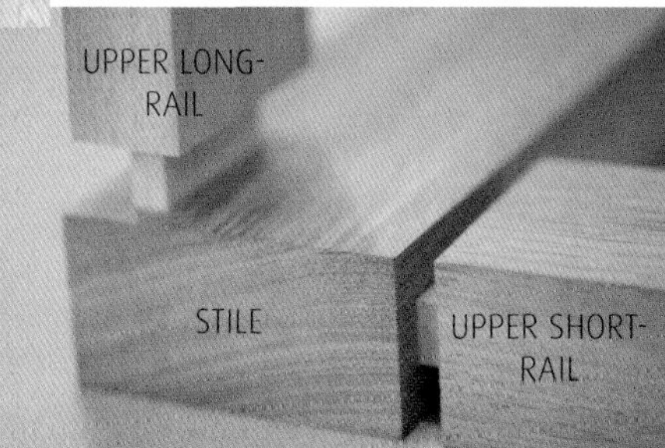

1 **Test-assemble all the elements** of the upper part of the end frames and adjust if necessary.

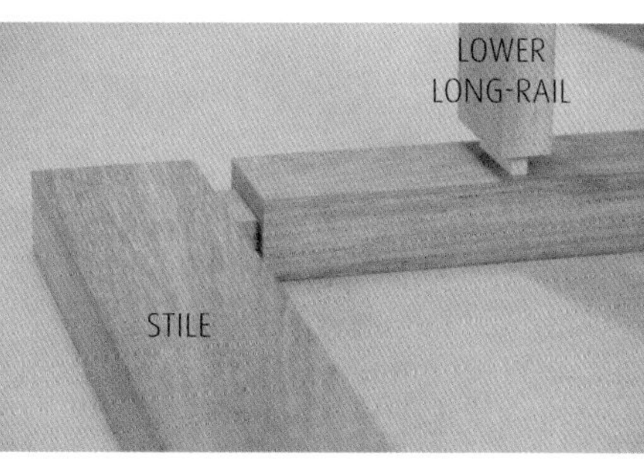

2 **Assemble all the elements** of the lower part of the end frames, including the lower long-rail, and adjust if necessary.

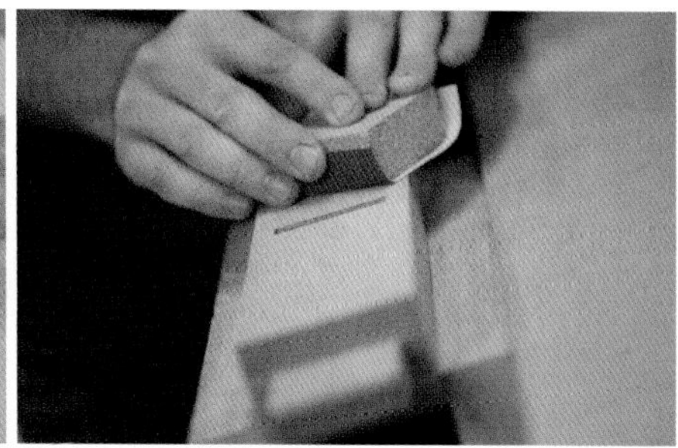

3 **Smooth each of the elements** of the bench with sandpaper before you glue the joints.

4 **Glue and assemble** the end frames. Then clamp, check for squareness, and leave overnight to dry.

5 **Once the end frames** have dried, glue the long rails into the end frames and clamp with sash clamps. Leave to dry.

FITTING THE SEAT

1 **Clamp the seat pieces** to the frame with a ⅜in (10mm) gap between the two seat slats.

2 **Drive screws** about $\frac{1}{32}$in (1mm) into the seat – just enough to mark their positions. Disassemble, and drill pilot holes into the seat. Reassemble.

FINISHES

The high oil-content of some timbers, such as teak or iroko, can mean that no special finish is required. However, depending on the desired look, one or more coats of teak oil can be applied to achieve a richer finish.

THE FINISHED PIECE

Demi-lune table

This clean, simple console table would look good in a hallway or small room. The project demonstrates how a simple jig can solve a variety of problems, including drawing an ellipse or cutting a circle. The method for ellipse drawing featured here is a simple process that will produce accurate results.

Dimensions:
32 11/16 x 35 7/16 x 14in (830 x 900 x 355mm)

Key techniques:
Wedged through mortise-and-tenon joint (pp.116–19);
Making templates and jigs (see pp.150–51)
Edge-to-edge joint (pp.94–95)

TOOLS AND MATERIALS

- Wood glue and brush
- Sash clamps
- MDF (39½ x 15¾ x ¼in/1000 x 400 x 6mm)
- Pencil
- Long metal ruler
- Hammer
- Panel pins
- String
- Pincers
- Band saw
- Sandpaper (coarse, medium, and fine grades)
- Table saw or panel saw
- C-clamp
- Router with bearing-guided straight cutter
- MDF (31⅞ x 1⅜ x ¼in/810 x 35 x 6mm)
- Square
- Coping saw (optional)
- Mortise gauge
- Mortiser or mortise chisel
- Marking gauge
- Small tenon saw
- Bevel-edged chisel
- Tenon saw with wide kerf
- Rubber mallet
- Flush-cut saw and card
- Block plane
- Drill with bits
- Tape measure
- 10 screws (No. 8 x 1⅜in/4 x 35mm)

CUTTING LIST

Item	Material	No.	Length	Width	Thickness
Table top	Maple	2	39⅜in* (1000mm)	7⅞in* (200mm)	13/16in (20mm)
Shelves	Maple	2	39⅜in* (1000mm)	5⅞in* (150mm)	13/16in (20mm)
Legs	Maple	4	31⅞in (810mm)	1⅜in (35mm)	1⅜in (35mm)
Upper short rails	Maple	2	9 13/16in (250mm)	1 3/16in (30mm)	13/16in (20mm)
Upper long rail	Maple	1	29 15/16in (760mm)	1 3/16in (30mm)	13/16in (20mm)
Lower short rails	Maple	2	10¼in (260mm)	1 3/16in (30mm)	13/16in (20mm)
Lower long rail	Maple	1	30 11/16in (780mm)	1 3/16in (30mm)	13/16in (20mm)
Wedge	Walnut	1	19¾in* (500mm)	⅜in (10mm)	⅛in (3mm)

*Includes excess to allow for cutting to size

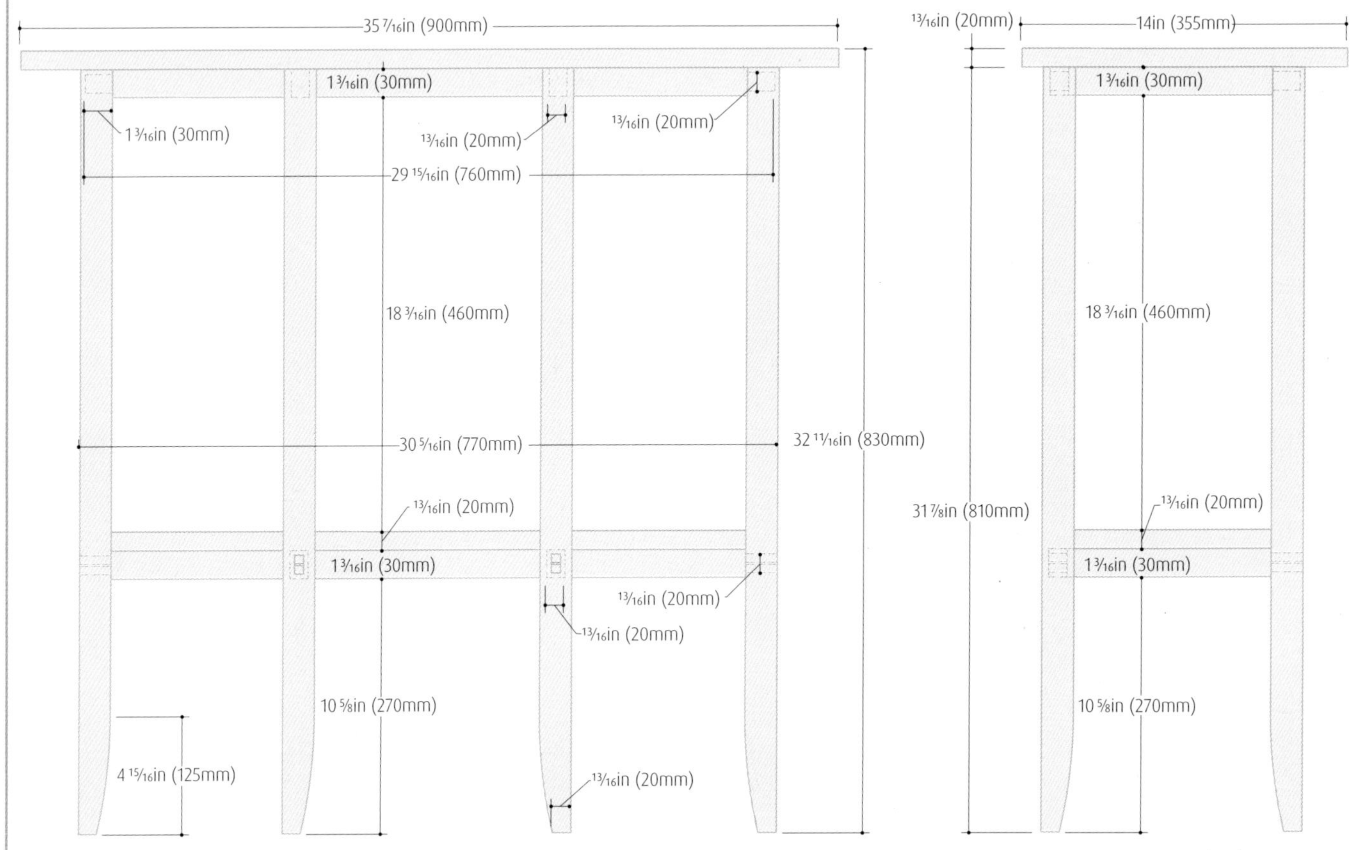

FRONT VIEW (1:8)

SIDE VIEW (1:8)

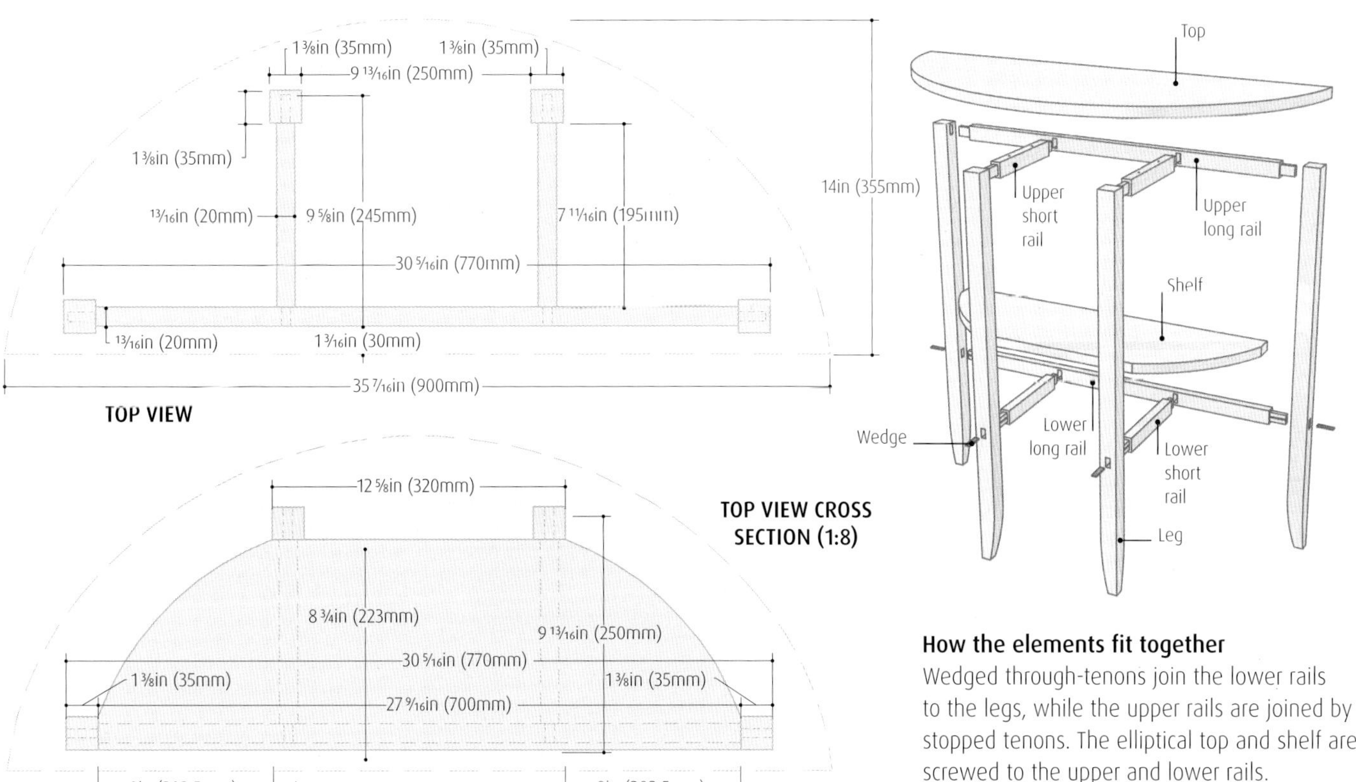

How the elements fit together
Wedged through-tenons join the lower rails to the legs, while the upper rails are joined by stopped tenons. The elliptical top and shelf are screwed to the upper and lower rails.

JOINING THE TABLE TOP AND SHELF

1 **Join the pieces** for the table top using an edge-to-edge joint (see pp.94–95). Secure with sash clamps and leave to dry.

2 **Use the same method** to join the pieces for the shelf, then clamp and set aside to dry.

MAKING THE ELLIPTICAL TEMPLATE FOR THE TABLE TOP

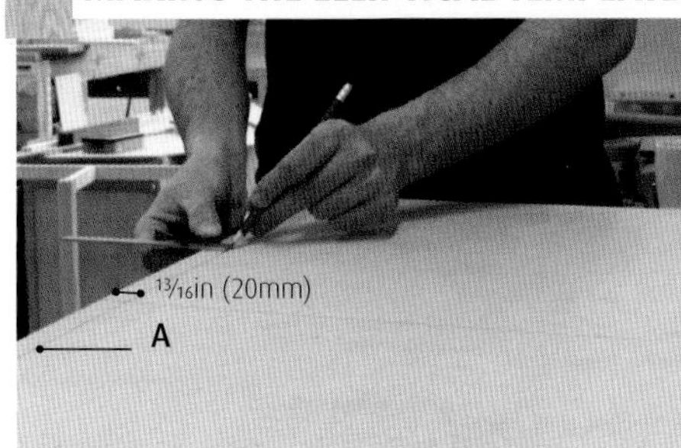

1 **Mark the halfway point** of a long side of the larger piece of MDF, then square the measurement across. Mark a line (A) 13/16in (20mm) from one edge of the long sides.

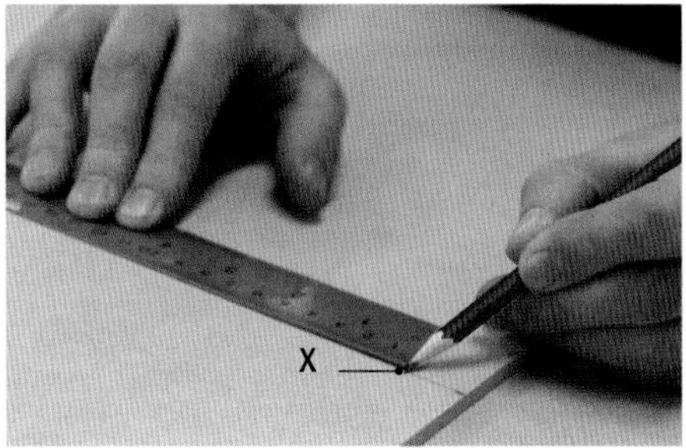

2 **Mark a point (X)** 14in (355mm) along the halfway line from the intersection with line A.

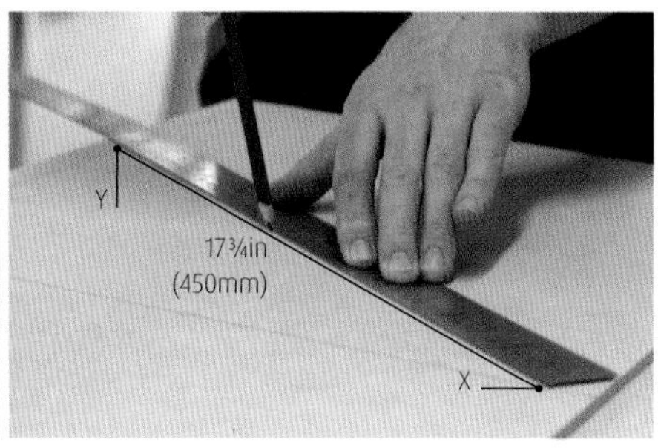

3 **Set the ruler** with the zero marker at point X. Align the other end of the ruler to measure 17 3/4in (450mm) at line A, and mark the point at which they cross (Y). Mark a second point Y on the other side of the centerline in the same way.

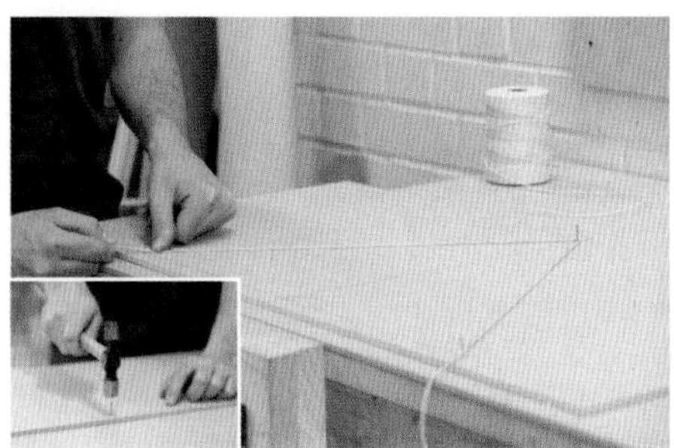

4 Mark each marked point (X and both Ys) by hammering in a panel pin (inset). Tie a taut length of string between both points Y, taking it around point X.

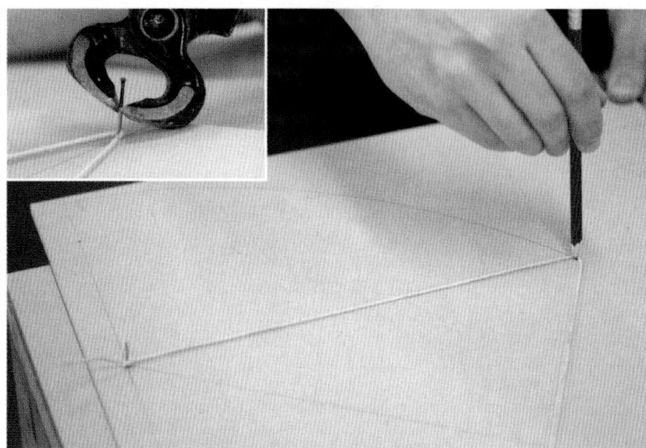

5 Remove the pin from point X with a pair of pincers (inset). Place the pencil within the loop of string on line A and pull it taut. Keeping the string tight, draw an ellipse starting at one point Y, passing through point X, and finishing at the other point Y.

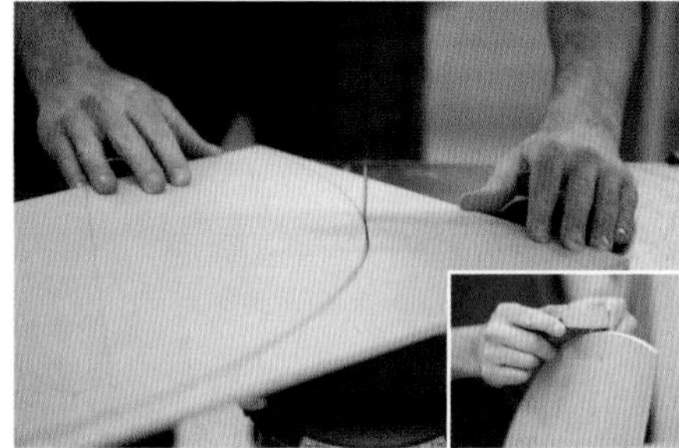

6 Cut out the template on a band saw, cutting to the waste side of the curve just drawn. Smooth the edges with sandpaper (inset).

CUTTING THE TABLE TOP

1 Cut the table top to the required width— 35 7⁄16in (900mm)—on a table saw (pictured) or panel saw.

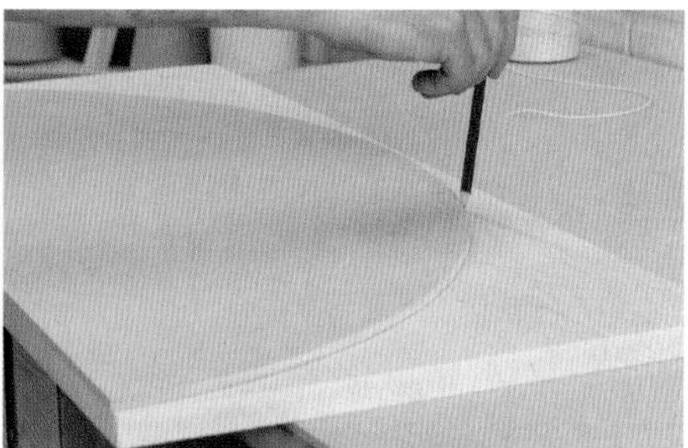

2 Place the template over the table top with the straight edge aligned with a long side, then draw the curved outline onto the prepared board.

3 Use a band saw to cut out the curved table top, cutting to the waste side of the marked line.

4 Clamp the template beneath the table top using a C-clamp. Use a router fitted with a bearing-guided straight cutter to trim the table top to the exact dimensions of the template. Sand with a block and medium-grade paper to remove the arrises (inset).

SHAPING THE LEGS

1 Make a template for the legs from a piece of MDF of the same width. Mark a point 13⁄16in (20mm) along the bottom edge, then square a line across the face 10 7⁄8in (275mm) up the side.

2 Draw a curved line between the points, either freehand (pictured) or by drawing along a steel ruler bent between the points (see Hall shelf, pp.216–20).

3 Set the piece in a vise and cut along the marked line with a coping saw (pictured), or using a band saw.

4 **Use a block** and sandpaper to remove any rough edges and create a smooth finish on the curve.

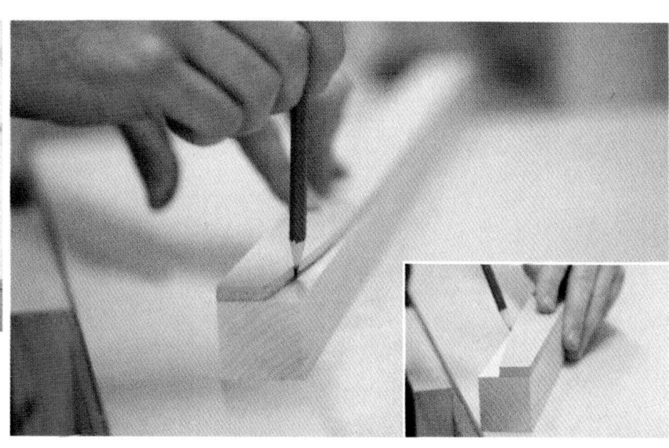

5 **Place the template** over a leg and transfer the shape onto a face. Then turn the template over, position it on the side adjacent to the straight edge, and draw a curve in the opposite direction (inset).

6 **Use a square** to extend the marks across the end grain, then mark the waste for removal.

7 **Cut to the waste side** of both marked lines on a band saw. Repeat Steps 5–7 for the other three legs.

8 **Sand back to the marked lines** of each leg with very coarse, then progressively finer, sandpaper.

CUTTING THE MORTISES IN THE LEGS

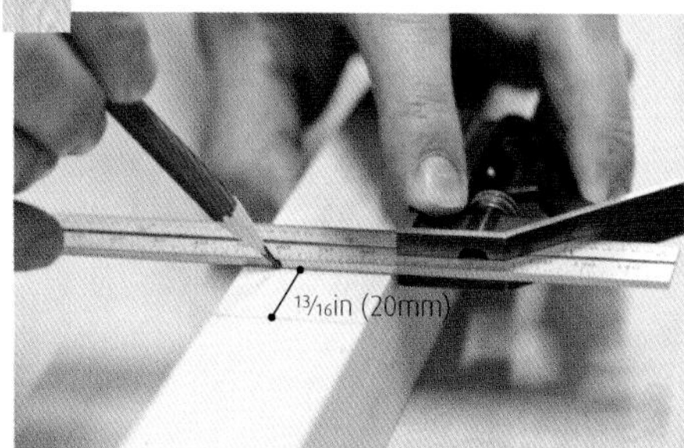

1 **Square a line** across an unshaped edge 20 1/4in (515mm) from the top end grain, and a second line 13/16in (20mm) away. Repeat on another leg, but for the last two legs, mark the mortise on the other unshaped edge.

2 **Use the mortise gauge** to mark a mortise width of 3/8in (10mm), centered between the marks. Square the marks around all sides (inset), then mark the mortise width on the opposite side. Repeat on the other legs.

3 **Cut the lower mortises** on each leg with a mortiser (pictured), or a mortise chisel. Cut halfway through from one side, then cut the rest of the way through from the other side.

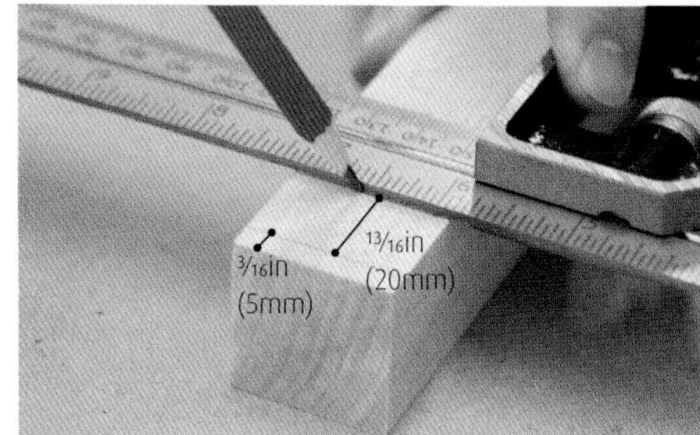

4 **Mark the position** of the top mortise 3/16in (5mm) from the end grain at the top of the leg. Mark the mortise length of 13/16in (20mm).

5 **With the mortise gauge** set to 3/8in (10mm) and the fence to 3/16in (5mm), scribe the mortise width from the outside (unshaped) face of each leg.

6 **Cut the mortise** on each leg to a depth of 1in (25mm). You now have two pairs of legs, with one of each pair shaped on the opposite edge to the other (inset).

MAKING THE UPPER LONG RAIL

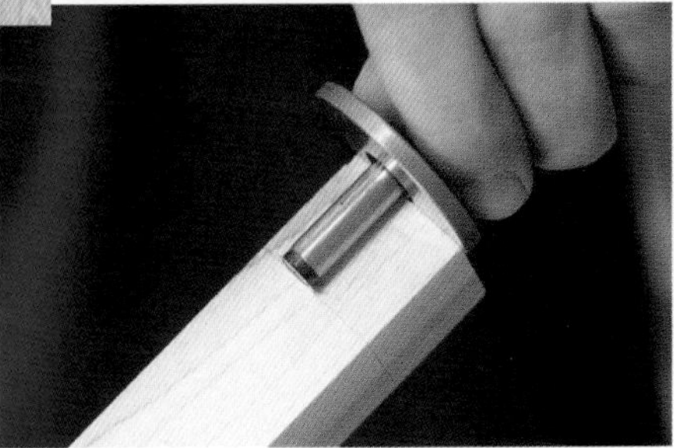

1 **Mark out a tenon** in both end grains of the upper long rail to fit the top leg mortises. Scribe the shoulder with a marking gauge 1³⁄₁₆in (30mm) from the end grain.

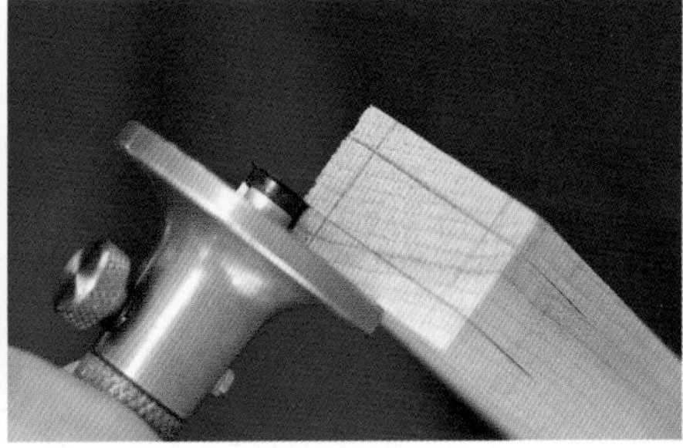

2 **Use the marking gauge** set to ³⁄₁₆in (5mm) to scribe the width and thickness of the tenon across the end grain and down each face and edge to the shoulder.

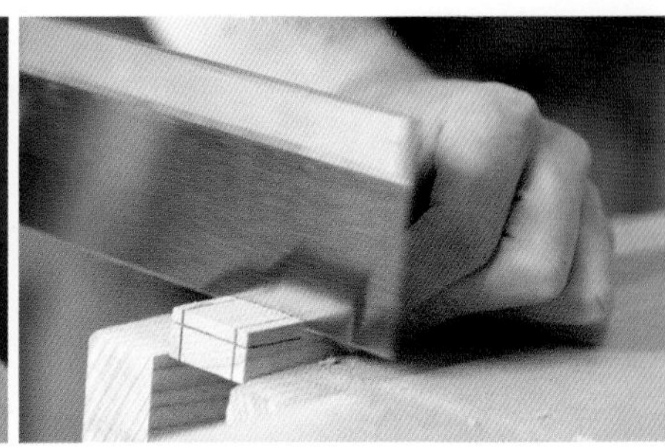

3 **Saw along the marked lines** to cut both tenons, either by hand with a small tenon saw (pictured), or on a band saw.

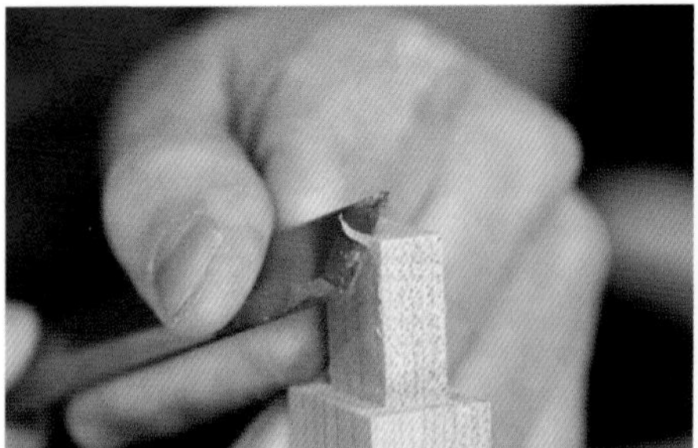

4 **Clean up the shoulders** and chamfer the ends of each tenon with a bevel-edged chisel.

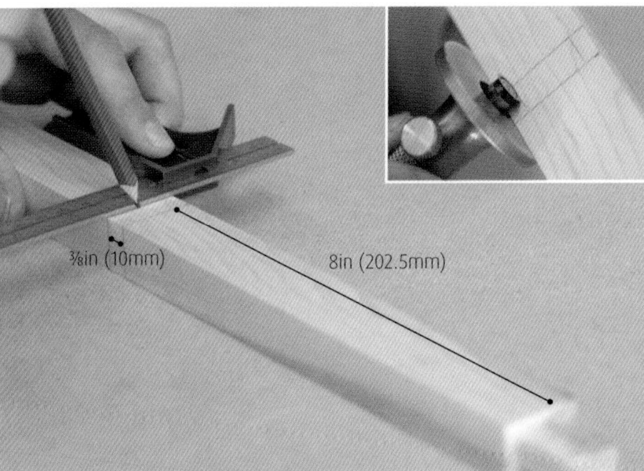

5 **Mark two through mortises** on the inside face of the rail. Measure 8in (202.5mm), then a further ⅜in (10mm), from each tenon shoulder, then square the marks across all four sides. Use the marking gauge as previously set to scribe the width of both mortises from each edge on both faces (inset).

6 **Cut the mortises** with a mortiser (pictured) or by hand using a mortise chisel. Cut part-way through from one side, then complete from the other side.

MAKING THE LOWER LONG RAIL

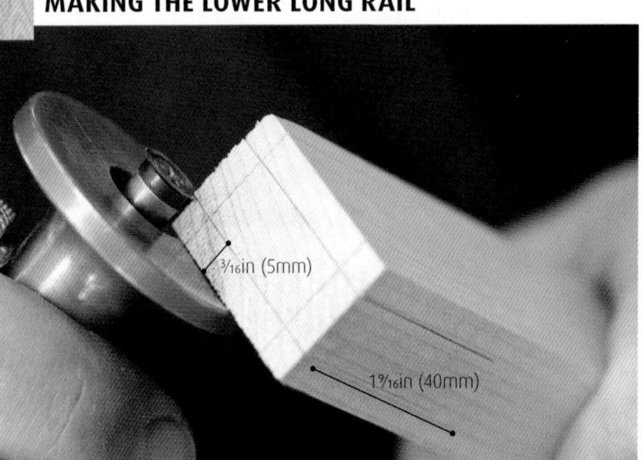

1 **Mark a tenon** in both end grains of the lower long rail. Mark a shoulder of 1⁹⁄₁₆in (40mm) to allow a ³⁄₁₆in (5mm) protrusion to be trimmed off after the wedges (see opposite) have been inserted. As with the upper long rail (see Step 2, above), set the marking gauge to ³⁄₁₆in (5mm) to scribe the tenon width and thickness.

2 **Set the rail in a vise** and cut along the marked lines by hand with a small tenon saw (pictured), or using a band saw.

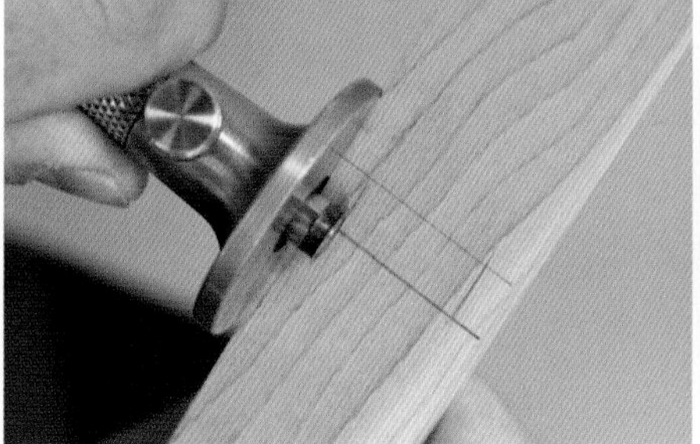

3 **Mark and cut two mortises** of the same size and in the same position as those in the upper long rail (see Steps 5–6, above).

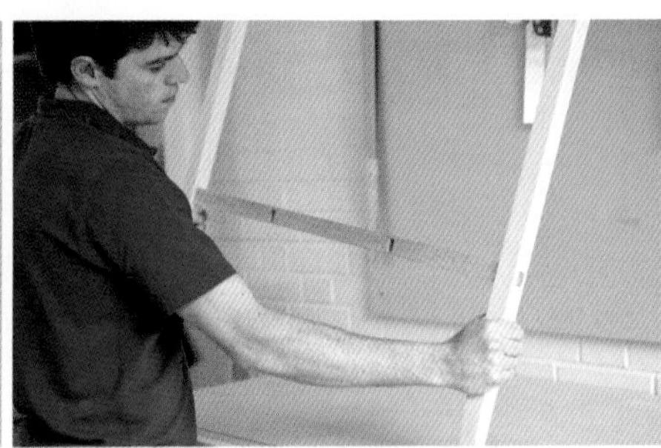

4 **Test the fit** of the upper and lower long rails and the back legs, and make any adjustments that are necessary.

MAKING THE SHORT RAILS

1 **Set a marking gauge** to 1in (25mm) and scribe the shoulder around both ends of the two upper short rails. Reset the gauge to 3/16in (5mm) and scribe across the end grain and down both faces and edges.

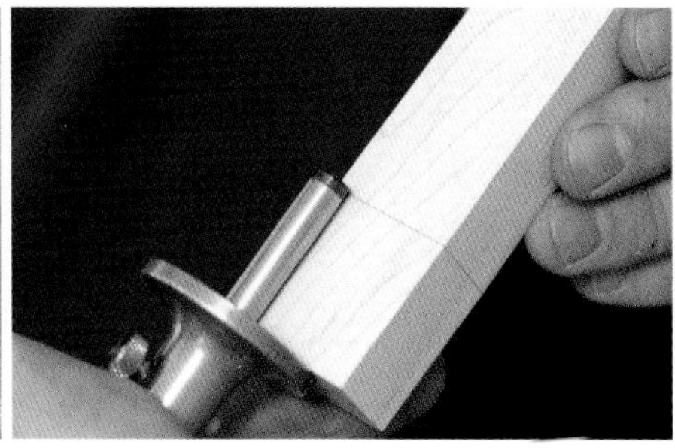

2 **Mark out a tenon** in both ends of the two lower short rails. Mark one tenon in each rail as described in Step 1. Mark out the second tenon in each rail in the same way but with a shoulder of 1⅜in (35mm).

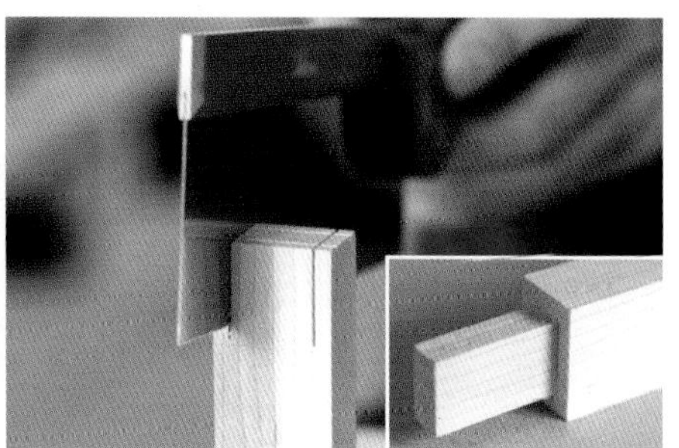

3 **Cut the tenons** by hand with a small tenon saw or using a band saw, then use a bevel-edged chisel to create a clean tenon and shoulder (inset).

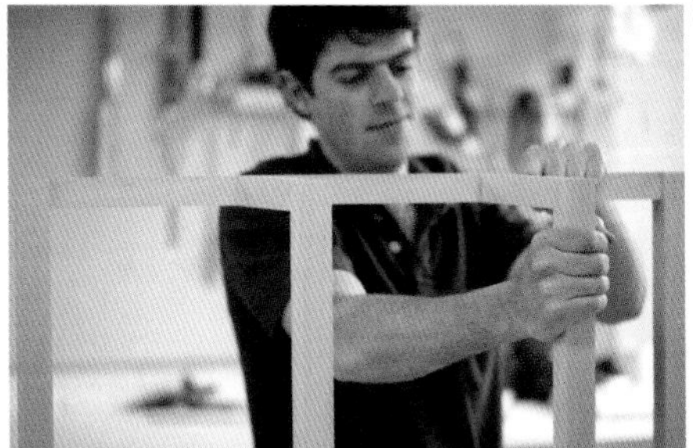

4 **Insert the short rails** and front legs to the back-leg and long-rail frame, as previously assembled.

CUTTING THE WEDGE SLOTS AND WEDGES

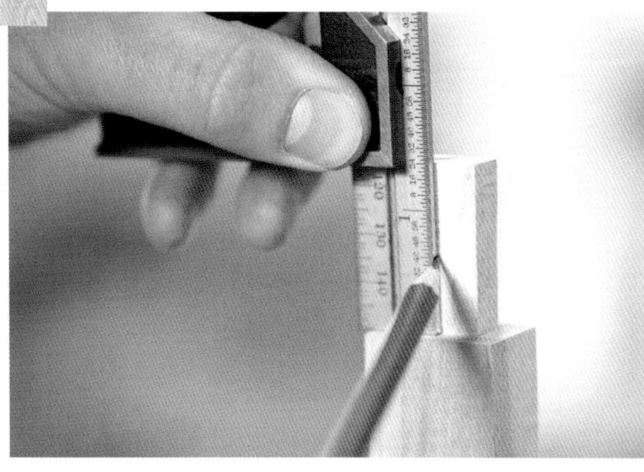

1 **Cut a slot** for a decorative wedge in the end of each long tenon in the lower short rails, and in both tenons of the lower long rail. Mark the center of the tenon width on the end grain, then square the mark down one face to the shoulder of each tenon.

2 **Use a tenon saw** with a wide kerf to saw a slot in each of the marked tenons, cutting all the way to the shoulder.

3 **Cut four wedges** to a length of 1³/16in (30mm) from a contrasting wood to that used for the rest of the piece, such as walnut.

4 **Taper each wedge** using a chisel, then check the fit in the slot of the tenon into which it is to be placed.

GLUING THE FRAME

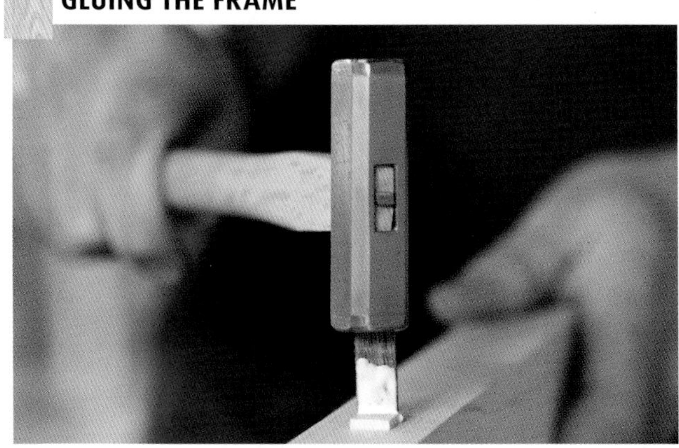

1 **Apply glue to the tenons** of all frame elements, then assemble. Insert a glued wedge into each tenon slot and tap in with a hammer.

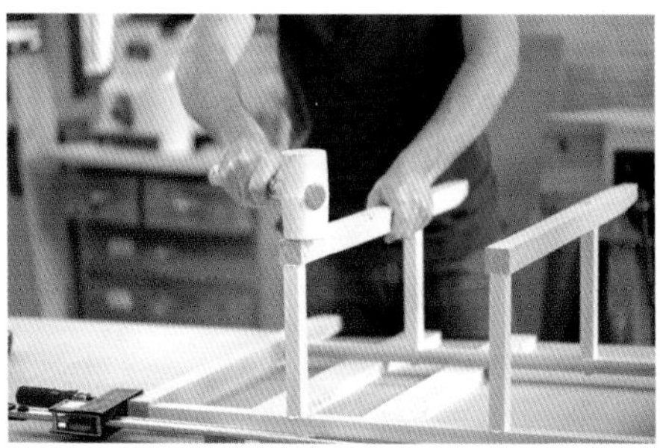

2 **Clamp the assembly** with sash clamps, then seat the upper front-leg joints by tapping with a rubber mallet. Set aside to dry.

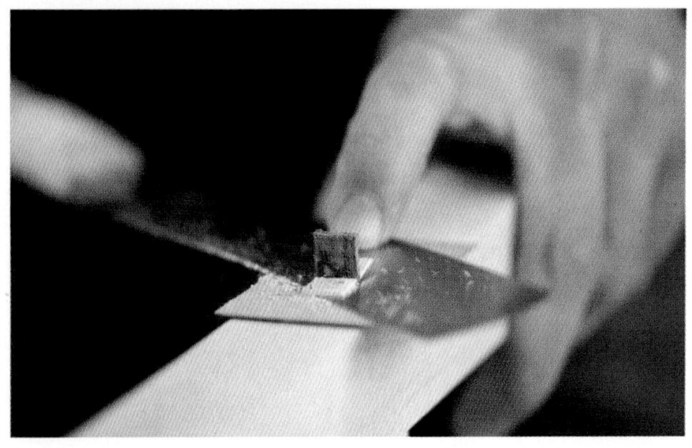

3 **Once the glue has dried**, cut the protruding tenons with a flush-cut saw. Protect the surrounding surface with a mask cut from cardboard.

4 **Use a block plane** to smooth the ends of the wedged tenons until fully flush with the surface of the leg.

CUTTING THE SHELF

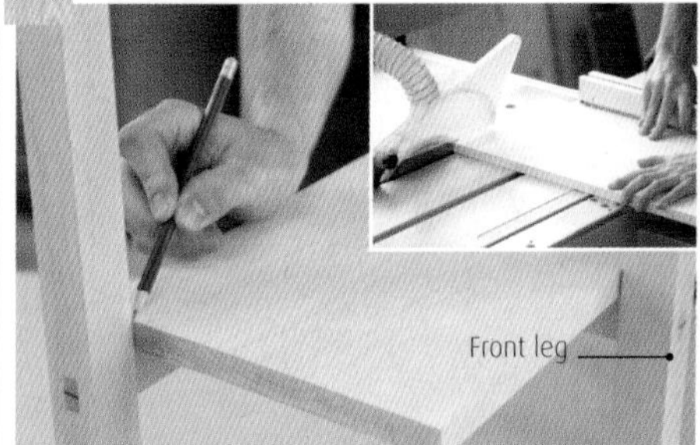

1 **Cut the shelf** to size on a table saw (inset), then place it on the lower frame, butted up to the front legs. Mark on the shelf the position of the front of the back legs, and the outside edge of the front legs.

2 **Place the table-top template** on top of the shelf. Align the back edge of the template with the marked position of the back leg, and the curved edge over the marked position of the front leg. Draw the curve of the template on the shelf, then repeat at the other end of the shelf. Cut along the marked lines on a band saw (inset).

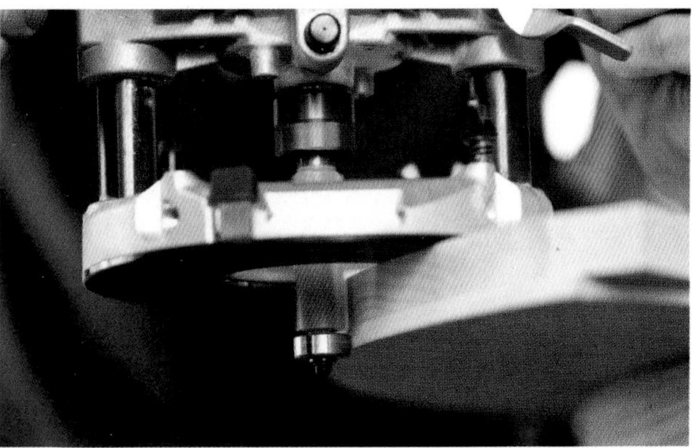

3 **Clamp the template** beneath the shelf aligned with the curve. Use a router fitted with a bearing-guided straight cutter set to run off the template to smooth the curved edges. Remove the arrises from the edges by sanding.

4 **Test the fit** of the shelf in the frame, sanding the curved edge to ease the fit if necessary.

FITTING THE TABLE TOP AND SHELF

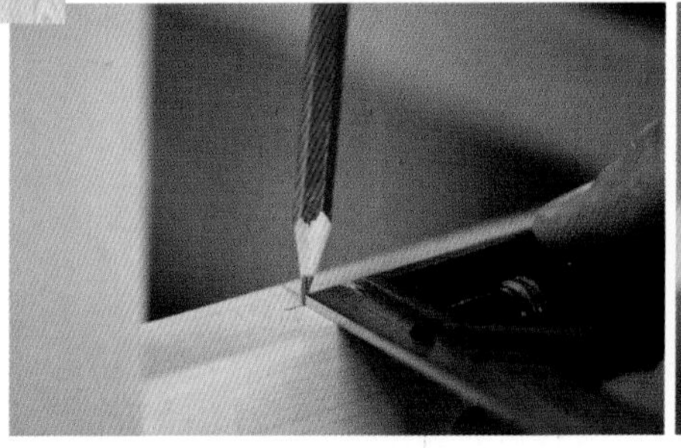

1 **With the frame upside down**, mark a clearance hole centered on the width of each short rail 2in (50mm) from the front legs. Mark further holes on both long rails 2in (50mm) from the back legs.

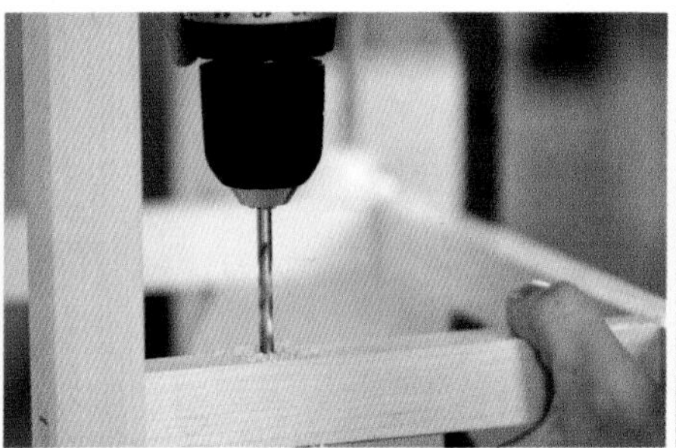

2 **Drill a clearance hole** for a No. 8 x 1⅜in (4 x 35mm) screw in each of the marked positions, securing an offcut of wood under each position to prevent "break out."

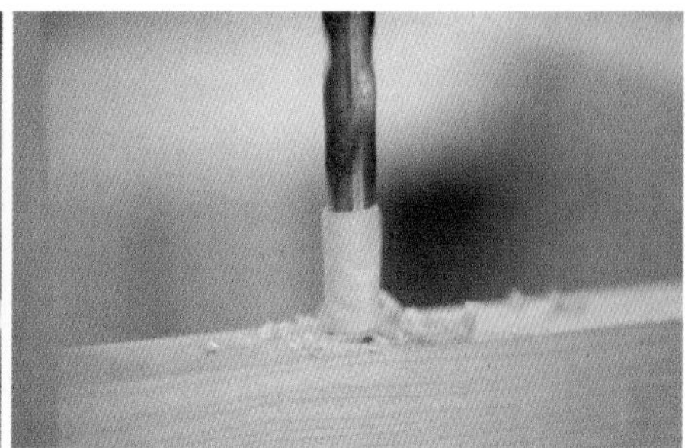

3 **Fit a slightly larger bit** to the drill, then counterbore the holes (see p.67) in the short rails to a depth of ⅜in (10mm) from each side.

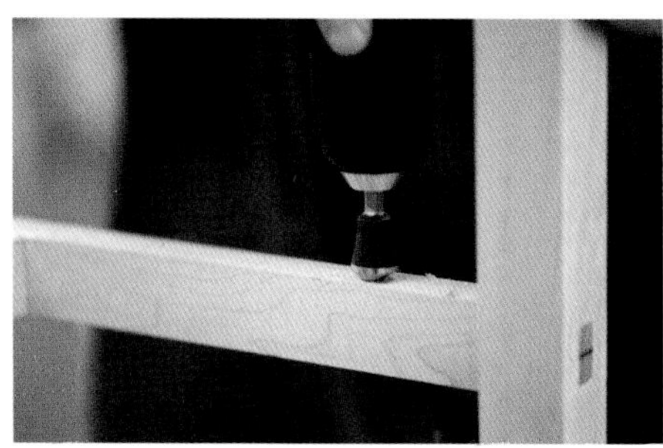

4 **Countersink each of the holes** in the underneath edge of the upper and lower long rails.

5 **Mark the mid-point** of the upper long rail, then do the same on the underside of the straight edge of the table top.

6 **Draw a line** on the underside of the table top 1³⁄₁₆in (30mm) from, and parallel to, the straight edge.

7 **Place the frame** over the underside of the table top with the back of the frame aligned with the line just drawn, and with the centermarks of both pieces aligned. Drill pilot holes into the table top through the holes in all of the top rails to a depth of ³⁄₁₆in (5mm). Insert a screw into each position (inset).

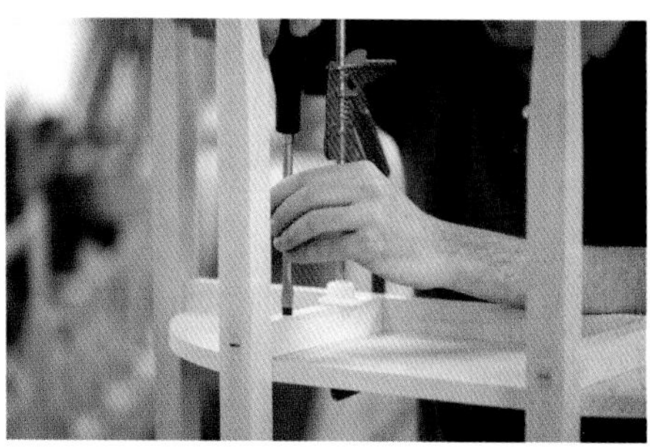

8 **Use a C-clamp** to secure the shelf on the upper side of the lower rails. Drill a pilot hole through each hole in the rails and into the underside of the shelf to a depth of ³⁄₁₆in (5mm). Insert a screw into each hole.

THE FINISHED PIECE

FINISHES

This piece has been finished with a protective clear, acrylic varnish, which prevents discoloration of the timber more effectively than an oil-based finish. It is a good idea to apply at least three coats of varnish to the table top, as a piece of furniture of this kind will get a lot of use and risks being scratched—for example, by heavy items such as vases being placed on it.

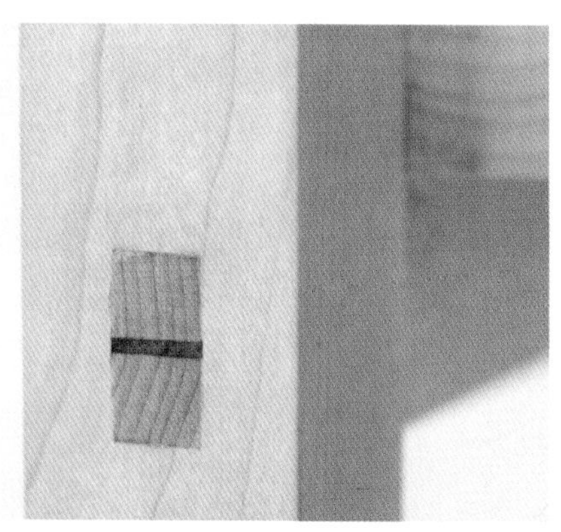

DETAIL OF THE WEDGED THROUGH TENON

Trinket box

Box-making is a complete genre of fine woodworking in its own right, and the design of this trinket box uses several classic approaches and techniques. When working on such a small scale, it is especially important to work accurately—any mistakes or gaps will be obvious, especially when working with lighter timbers, such as maple or sycamore. The outer box is constructed as an enclosed cube before being cut in two to make the box and lid.

Dimensions:
5 7/8in x 5 7/8in x 1 9/16in 1 (50 x 150 x 41mm)

Key techniques:
Through dovetail joint (pp.134–37)

TOOLS AND MATERIALS

Bench plane	Shoulder or rebate plane
Shooting board	Several grades of sandpaper
Marking gauge	Double-sided tape
1-in-8 dovetail marker	Masking tape (optional)
Marking knife	Finishing oil (optional)
Pencil	Wood glue and brush
Combination square	Clamps
Dovetail saw	Tape measure or ruler
Coping saw	Block plane
Narrow-bladed chisel	Band saw
Table-mounted router	45-degree shooting board

CUTTING LIST

Item	Material	No.	Length	Width	Thickness
Tail side-pieces	Maple	2	5 15/16in* (152mm)	1 11/16in* (43mm)	5/16in (8mm)
Socket side-pieces	Maple	2	5 15/16in* (152mm)	1 11/16in* (43mm)	5/16in (8mm)
Lid piece	Maple	1	5 9/16in (142mm)	5 9/16in (142mm)	5/16in (7mm)
Base piece	Walnut	1	5 9/16in (142mm)	5 9/16in (142mm)	5/16in (7mm)
Lining pieces	Walnut	4	5 7/16in* (139mm)	7/8in (22mm)	1/8in (3mm)

*Includes excess to allow for cutting to size

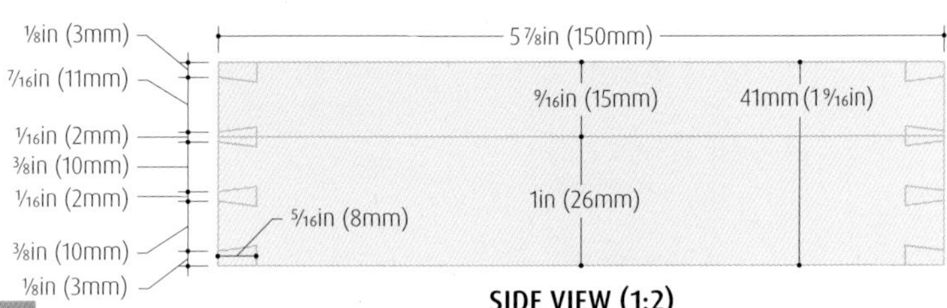

SIDE VIEW (1:2)

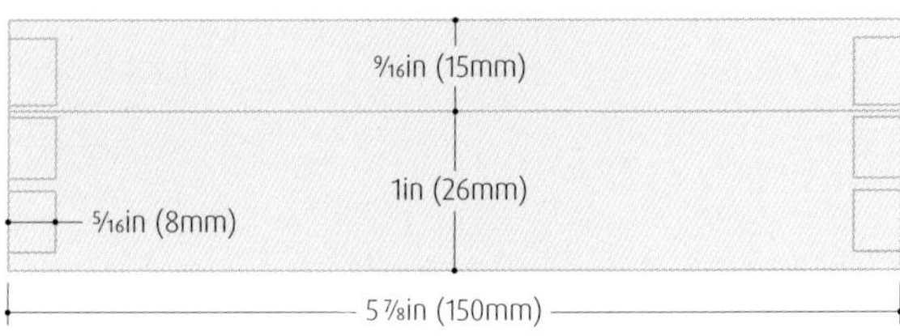

FRONT VIEW (1:2)

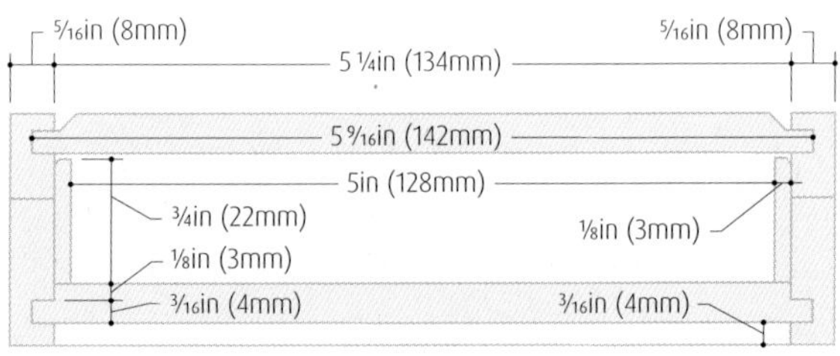

CROSS SECTION (1:2)

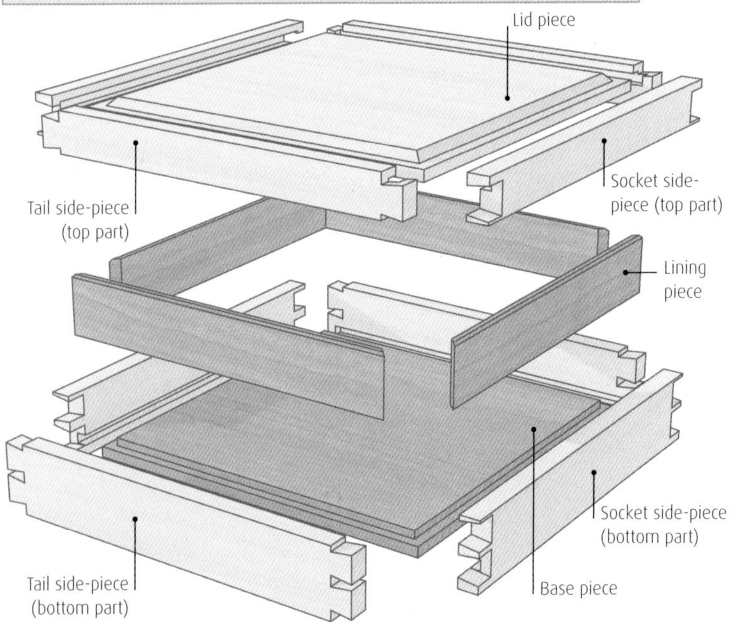

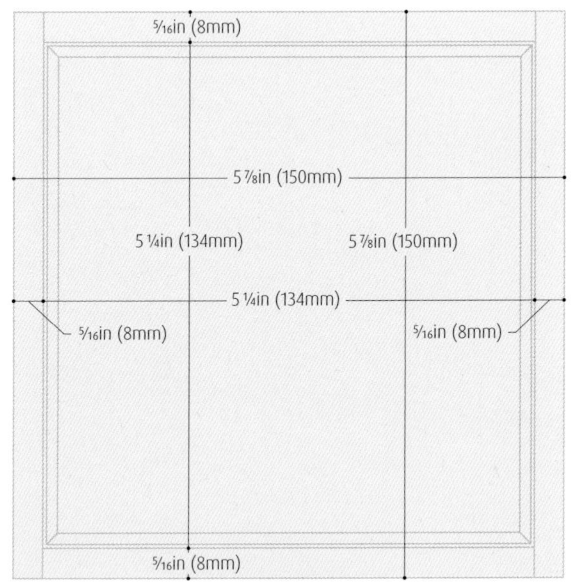

TOP VIEW (1:2)

How the elements fit together
Two grooves that run along the inside edges of the sides provide a housing for the base and lid panels. The box lining has mitered corners and provides a lipping over which the lid fits.

MAKING THE TAILS

1 **Using a bench plane** and shooting board, square off the end grains of all four side pieces to approximately 1⁄16in (2mm) oversize.

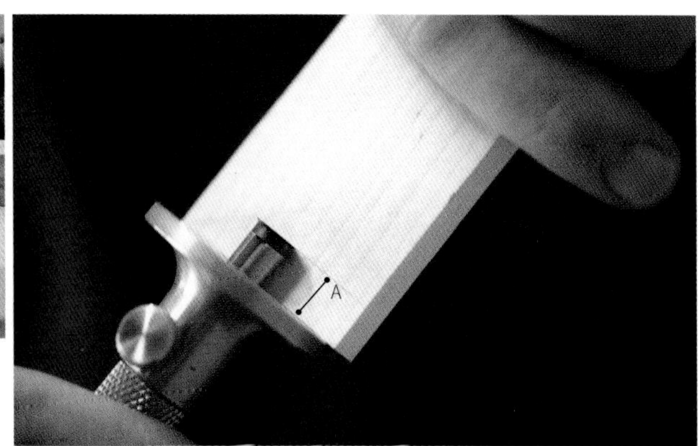

2 **Mark the shoulder** of the tails and pins (A) on both sides of each end of the four side pieces, using a marking gauge set to 1⁄32in (1mm) more than the thickness of the side pieces. (See also Through dovetail joint, pp.134–37, for detailed instructions on making dovetail joints.)

3 **Use a 1-in-8 dovetail marker** to mark tail angles on both faces and ends of the two tail side-pieces. Leave a gap between two tails to create a wide pin socket, which should be twice as wide as the other sockets.

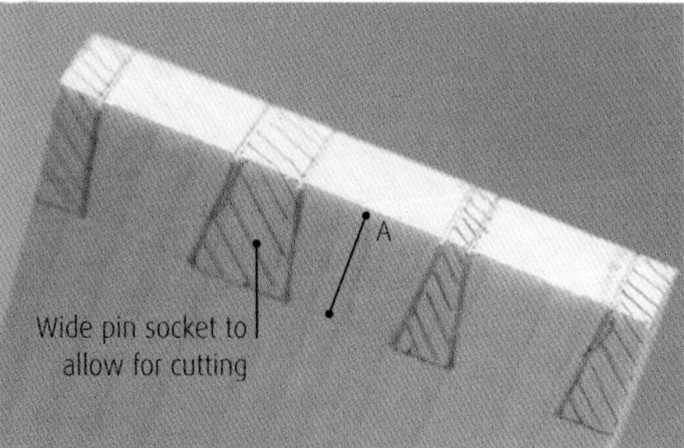

4 **Mark the waste** with a pencil. The wide pin socket mentioned in Step 3 allows the box to be split (see Step 2, Separating the lid from the box, p.275).

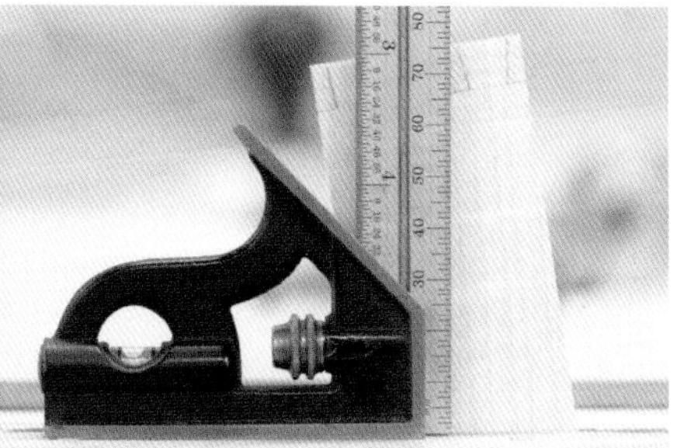

5 **Secure one of the tail side-pieces** in a vise, using a combination square to align it so that one set of tail marks is perpendicular to the bench.

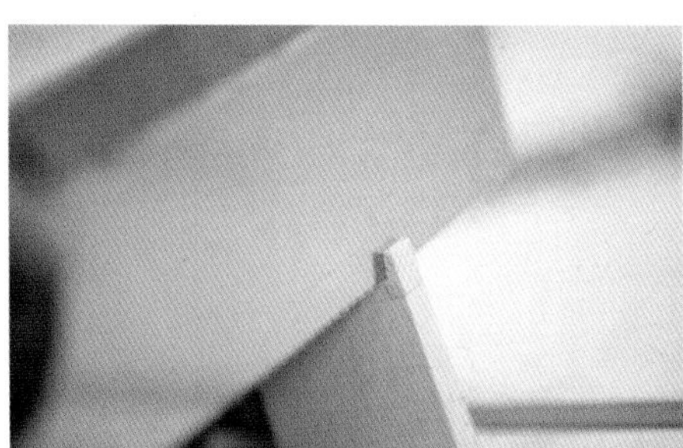

6 **Use a dovetail saw** to cut along the vertical marks to the shoulder. Then adjust the wood so that the remaining tail marks are vertical. Cut and repeat on the other end.

7 **Remove the waste** from between the tails by cutting with a coping saw and narrow-bladed chisel. Repeat Steps 5–7 for the other tail side piece.

MAKING THE PINS

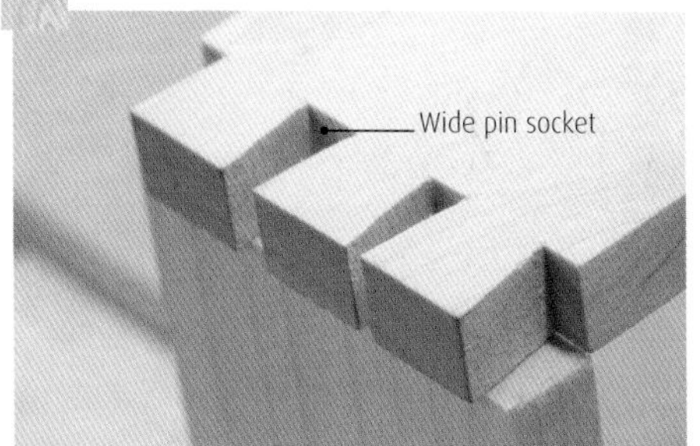

1 **Secure one of the remaining** two side pieces (the socket side-pieces) in a vise. Rest a tail side-piece on its end grain, touching its shoulder at right angles.

2 **Scribe the tail positions** onto the end grain of the socket side piece with a marking knife, ensuring that the tail side-piece is supported securely.

3 **Use a square to extend** the marks vertically down both faces to the shoulder. Repeat for both ends of both socket side-pieces.

4 **Cut the pins** to the shoulder with a dovetail saw (as per Steps 5–7, Making the tails), then remove the waste cleanly with a narrow-bladed chisel.

CUTTING THE GROOVES AND REBATES

1 Using a table-mounted router fitted with a 3/16in (4mm) bit, with the fence and depth set to 3/16in (4mm), cut a groove along both edges of the inner side of all four pieces. Test the fit of the pins and sockets of all four side pieces.

2 Cut a rebate along all four upper edges of the base piece, either with a shoulder plane, or with the router. Set the fence to 1/8in (3mm) and the depth to 3/16in (4mm).

3 Using a shoulder plane, or the router with the same settings, cut a rebate along all four upper edges of the lid piece.

4 Mark a chamfer around all sides of the top of the lid piece with a marking gauge, 1/4in (6mm) from the edge.

5 Place the lid piece in a vise and cut the chamfer, using a shoulder or rebate plane. Work across the grain first.

ASSEMBLING THE BOX

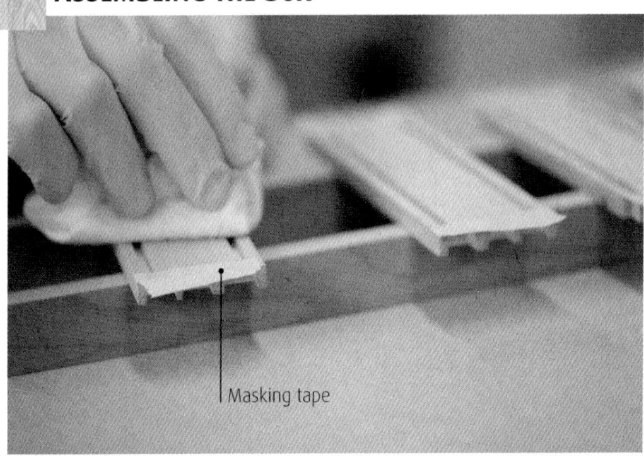

1 Sand the inside surfaces. If an oiled finish is desired, cover the inside faces of the tails and pins with masking tape to prevent them from being oiled, as oil reduces the effectiveness of the glue.

2 Use a clean rag to apply oil to the inside surfaces of the side, base, and lid pieces. For best results, apply three coats, allowing five hours' drying time between each coat.

3 When the oil has dried, use a fine brush to apply glue to the tails and pins, then assemble three of the side pieces.

4 Insert the lid piece and base piece into the grooves on the inside faces of the three side pieces, without applying glue. Glue the fourth side piece in place.

5 Clamp the assembly and check for squareness with a tape measure or ruler (see p.75). Make any necessary adjustments, then set aside to allow the glue to dry.

SEPARATING THE LID FROM THE BOX

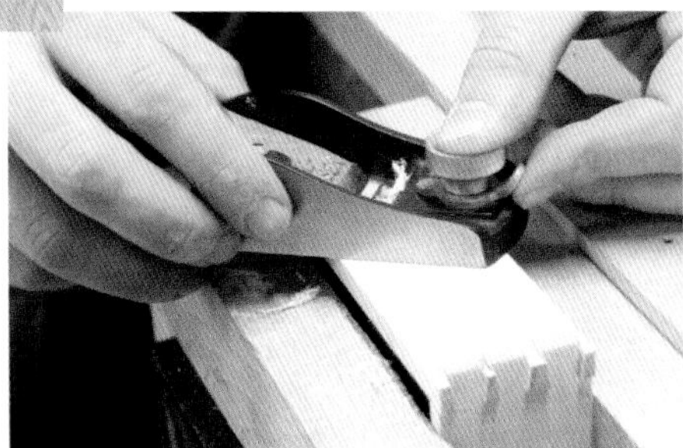

1 **Once the glue has dried**, use a block plane to remove the excess length of the tails and pins on all four sides of the box.

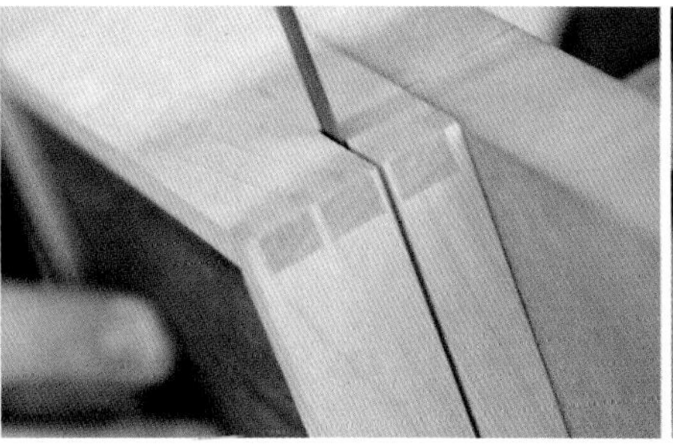

2 **Separate the box** into two parts by cutting it in two with a band saw. Line up the blade with the center of the largest pin (see Step 3, Making the tails, p.273).

3 **Clean any excess glue** from the internal corners with a chisel, then sand flat the newly sawn edges of both parts of the box, using progressively finer grades of sandpaper.

MAKING THE BOX LININGS

1 **Cut the lining pieces** to precise lengths by marking off exact dimensions from the inside of the box. Miter the ends with a bench plane guided by a 45-degree shooting board.

2 **Chamfer the outer face** of the upper edge of each of the lining pieces with a block plane. Fit the lining pieces inside the box (inset) without gluing.

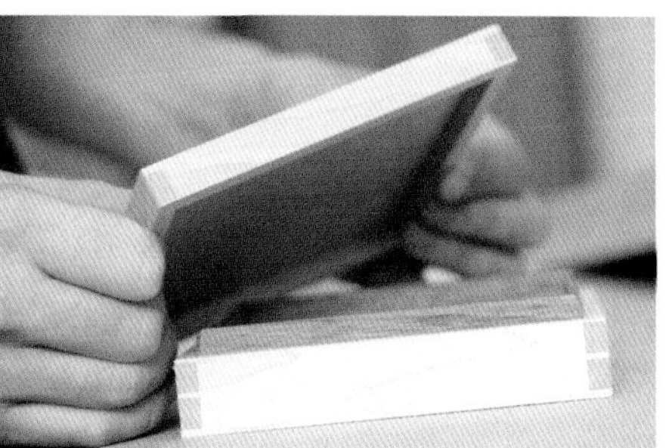

3 **Test the fit** of the lid. When you are happy with the fit, oil the lining pieces, and insert in position unglued.

FINISHES

Oil or wax are both good choices of finish for this piece. Both will create a strong and rich sheen, which is appropriate for a box intended for the storage of treasured items. It is important to apply the finish to the inside faces prior to assembly because, due to the box's small size, it would be difficult to get into the tight corners effectively after assembly.

ALTERNATIVES

A good way to add refinements to this piece would be to divide up the internal space to make compartments for different trinkets. Simply cut additional lengths of box lining and house them in the base or sides. You could also line the box with felt (as pictured).

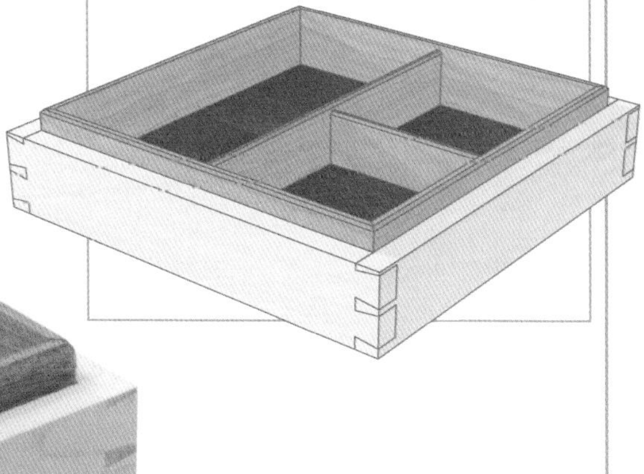

THE FINISHED PIECE

Coffee table

Clean lines, pale timber, and delicate sections make this ash coffee table an attractive addition to a modern home. The use of angled joints lends it a relaxed appearance and increases the feeling of solidity, without adding weight or bulk to the structure. This project is an example of how the domino jointing system (see pp.144–45) can be used as the principal construction technique within a piece of furniture, giving great results and saving time. The timber sections here are small, but, by ensuring a tight fit with the appropriate connector, this system can create a joint that rivals the traditional mortise-and-tenon joint for strength and stability.

Dimensions:
840 x 510 x 392mm (33 1/16 x 20 1/16 x 15 7/16in)

Key techniques:
Edge-to-edge joint (pp.94–95);
Domino joint (pp.144–45)

TOOLS AND MATERIALS

Pencil	Wood glue and brush
Square	Sash clamps
Protractor	Drill with bits
Sliding bevel	Chisel
Ruler	Rubber mallet
Bench plane	MDF (33 1/16 x 20 1/16 x 1/4in/840 x 510 x 6mm)
Band saw	Router with bearing-guided straight and chamfer cutters
Domino jointer	Screwdriver
20 size 5x30 domino connectors	6 screws (No. 9 x 1 3/8in/4.5 x 35mm)
Bench hook	Clear acrylic varnish
Tenon saw	
Marking gauge	
Sandpaper	

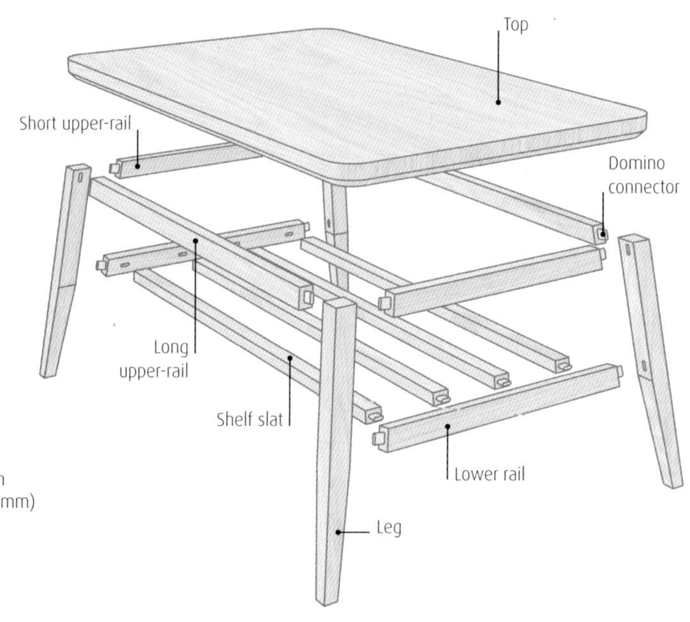

How the elements fit together

The legs are angled to 82 degrees, and taper downward from near the mid-point. All the rails employ the same angle across their end grain. The top is screwed in position through the rails.

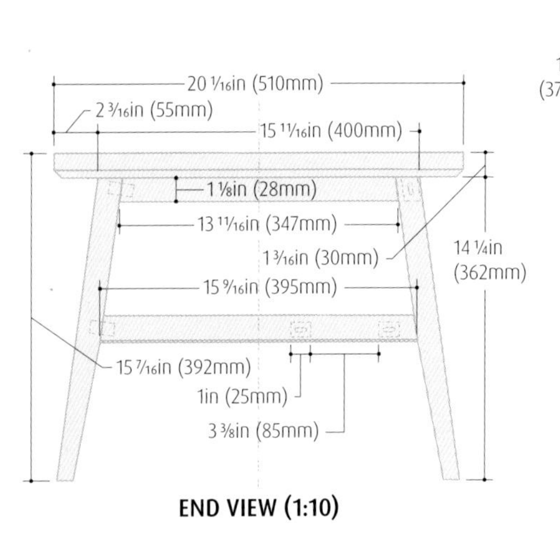

END VIEW (1:10)

14 9/16in (370mm)
7 7/8in (200mm)
1 3/16in (30mm)

LEG DETAIL (1:5)

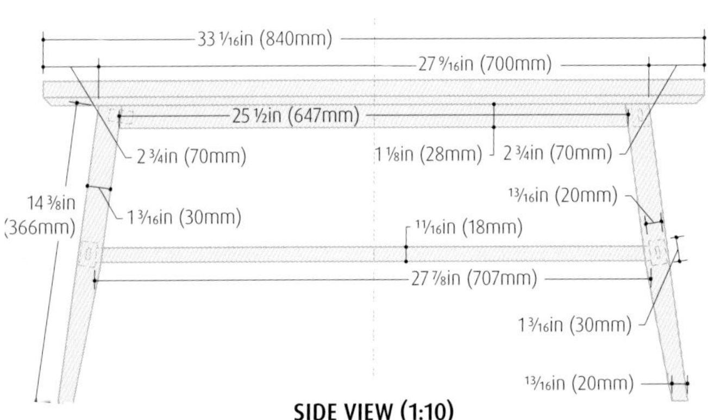

SIDE VIEW (1:10)

CUTTING LIST

Item	Material	No.	Length	Width	Thickness
Top	Ash	3	35 1/2in* (900mm)	7 1/8in* (180mm)	1 3/16in (30mm)
Legs	Ash	4	15 3/4in* (400mm)	1 3/16in (30mm)	1 3/16in (30mm)
Long upper rails	Ash	2	27 1/2in* (700mm)	1 3/16in (30mm)	13/16in (20mm)
Short upper rails	Ash	2	17 3/4in* (450mm)	1 3/16in (30mm)	13/16in (20mm)
Lower rails	Ash	2	17 3/4in* (450mm)	1 3/16in (30mm)	13/16in (20mm)
Shelf slats	Ash	4	29 1/2in* (750mm)	1in (25mm)	11/16in (18mm)

*Includes excess to allow for cutting to size

ESTABLISHING THE ANGLE

1 **On a smooth surface**, such as a spare piece of offcut, use a square to draw a line at 90 degrees from the edge.

2 **Use a protractor** to mark an angle of 82 degrees. This is the angle at which the table legs are set.

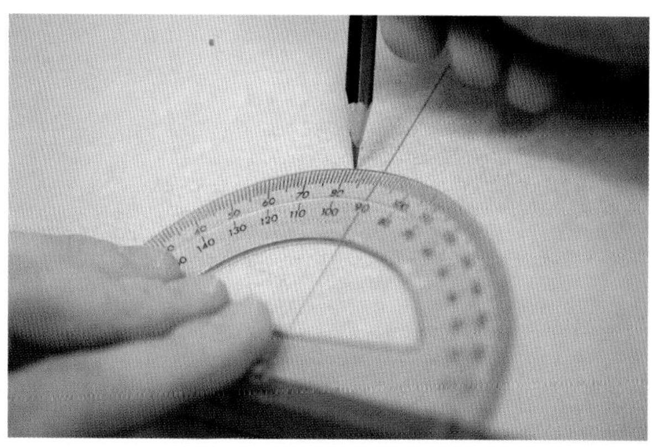

3 **Use the mark** as a reference for setting the sliding bevel. Keep the sliding bevel set to this 82-degree angle throughout.

MARKING OUT THE ANGLES AND SIZING THE LEGS

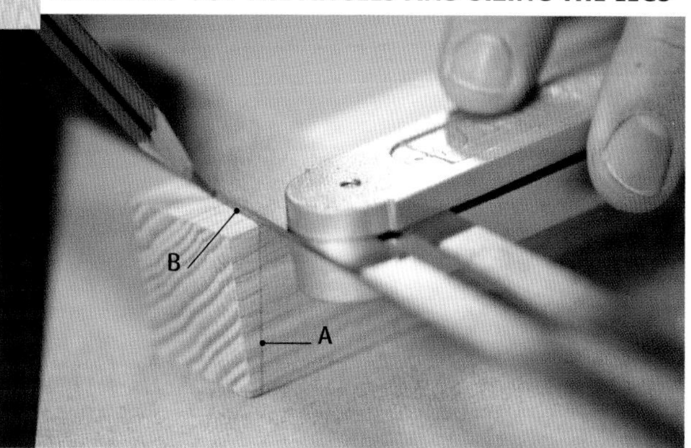

1 **Using the sliding bevel**, mark a line (A) at an 82-degree angle at a point 1/16in (2mm) from the end grain on one face of a leg piece. Draw a line (B) onto the next face, from the end of (A) that is furthest from the end grain, at the same angle. This end will be the top of the leg.

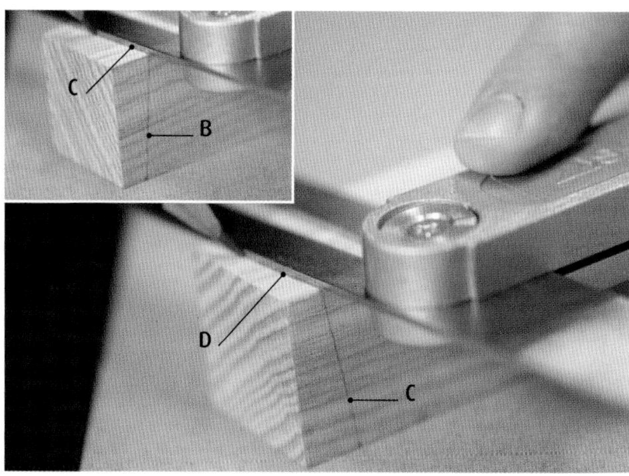

2 **Turn the wood** and draw a line (C) with the bevel at the same angle, but oriented to slope in the opposite direction to (B) (inset). Then turn the wood to the final face and join the marks with the end of line (A) to form line (D). Mark the waste for removal.

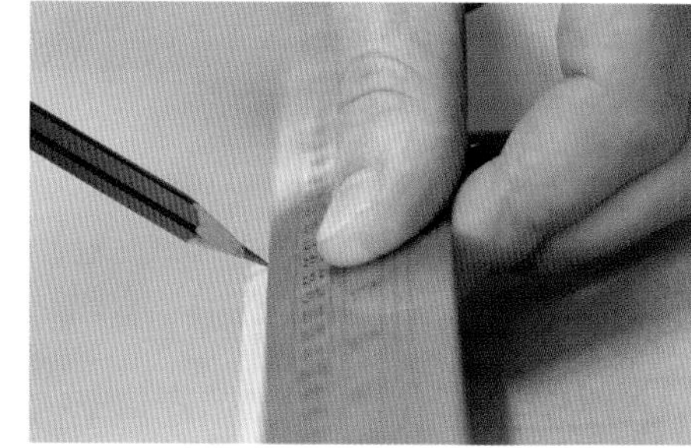

3 **Mark a point** 370mm (14 9/16in) from the corner where the lines (A) and (D) meet. From this point, draw lines parallel to those drawn in Steps 1–2. This will be the bottom of the leg. Repeat Steps 1–3 for all leg pieces.

MARKING OUT THE TAPERS ON THE LEGS

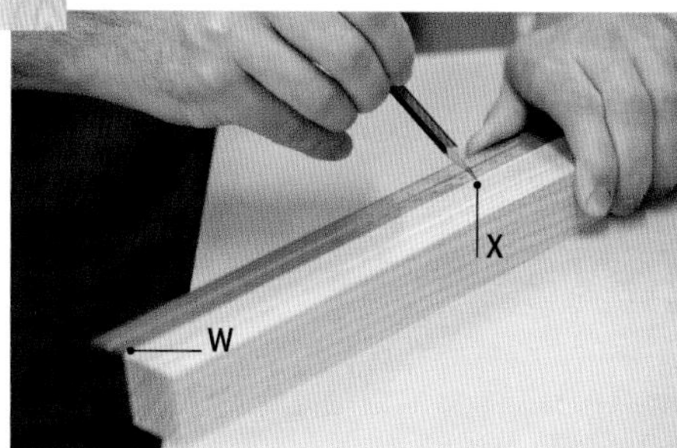

1 **Mark the start** of the taper (X) 200mm (7 7/8in) from the bottom of a leg, along the edge from the inside corner (W) nearest the end grain on the bottom of each leg.

2 **Use the sliding bevel**, still set at 82 degrees, to draw the lines across the faces of the wood, parallel to the lines (A, B, C, and D) drawn at the top of the leg.

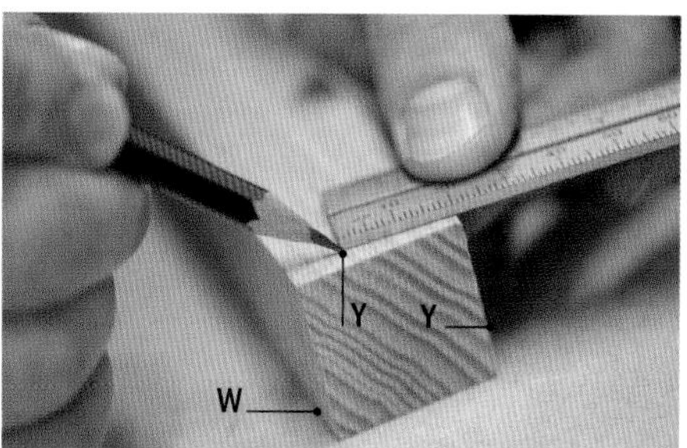

3 **Mark two points (Y)** on both outside edges of the bottom of the leg, 20mm (13/16in) along the angled lines parallel with (A) and (D).

4 **Using a pencil** and ruler, draw a line to join the points (Y) on both edges to the mark indicating the start of the taper (X).

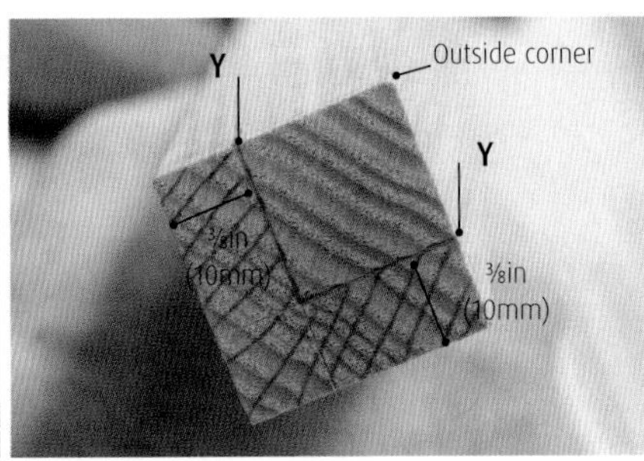

5 **With a marking gauge** set to ⅜in (10mm), scribe along the end grain from the base of both tapers and mark the waste for removal.

6 **Cut the taper** either by hand with a bench plane (pictured), or using a band saw and finish by hand-planing. Repeat Steps 1–6 for the remaining three legs.

MAKING THE MORTISES AND TRIMMING THE LEGS

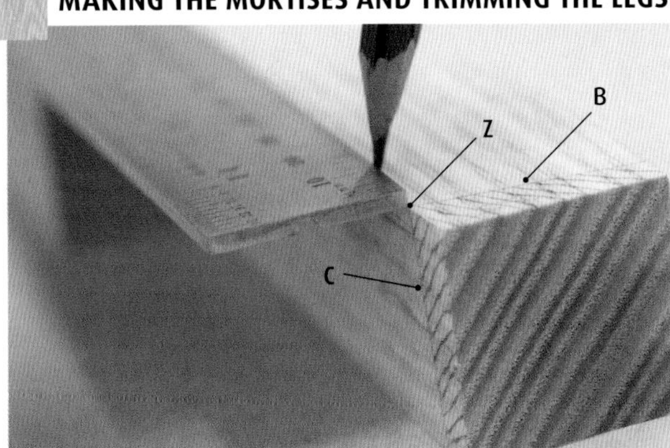

1 **Mark the centers** of the two domino mortises on each of the four leg pieces. The center of the upper mortises are ½in (12.5mm) from point (Z), which is the point furthest from the end grain at the top of the leg. The lower mortise on each leg is 6¾in (170mm) from the same position.

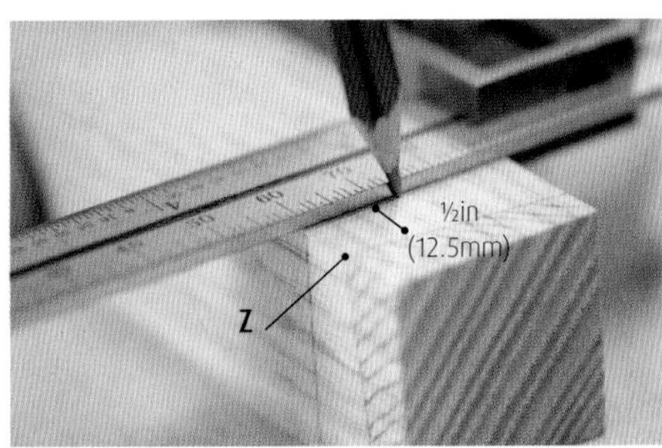

2 **Square a line** from each of these marks across the adjacent—outer—faces of each piece.

3 **Align the domino jointer**—with the height and depth set to ⅝in (15mm)—with the mark for the upper mortise. Using a $^3/_{16}$in (5mm) cutter, cut a mortise on both inside (unmarked) faces of all four legs.

4 **Using the same settings**, cut one lower mortise on each of the four legs, ensuring that you cut the mortises in the correct position in relation to the leg tapers (see the diagram on p.276).

5 **Secure one leg piece** against a bench hook, then cut along the angled lines using a tenon saw to remove the waste from the tops and bottoms of the leg. Repeat Step 5 on the remaining three legs.

MAKING THE LOWER AND UPPER RAILS

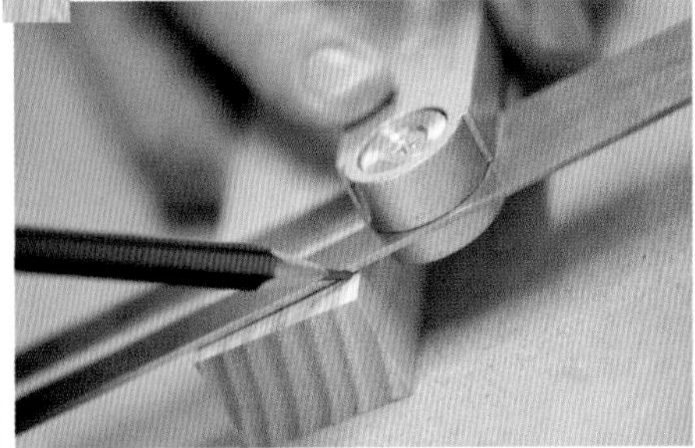

1 **Mark a line** on the face near one end grain of all upper and lower rails with the sliding bevel set at the standard angle of 82 degrees.

2 **Extend the line** onto both adjacent edges with a square. Then use the sliding bevel to join these lines on the remaining face. Mark out all lower and upper rails in the same way.

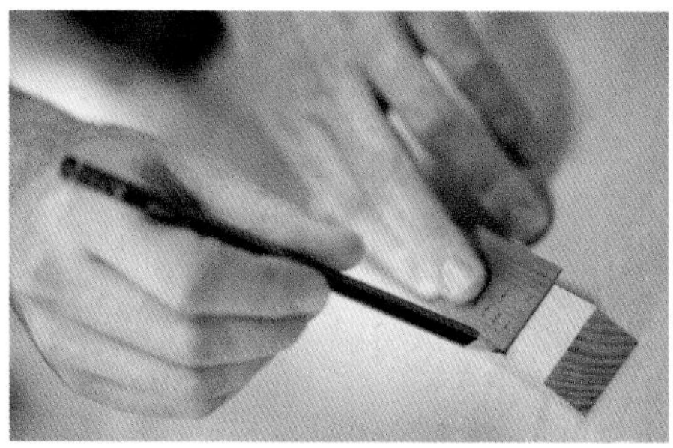

3 **Mark the exact length** of each rail (see diagram on p.276 for the measurements) from the end grain just marked onto the lower edge of the rail.

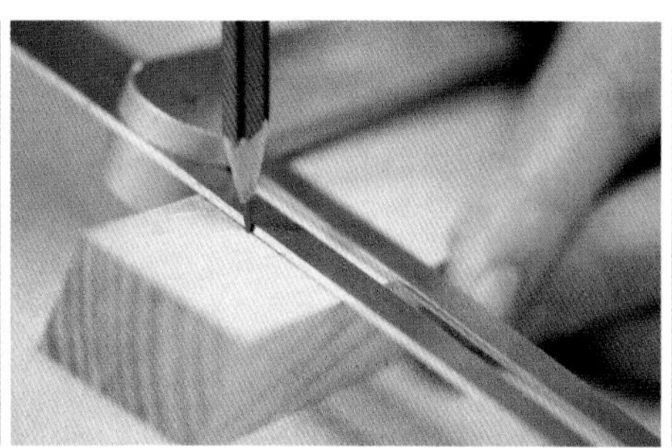

4 **Set the sliding bevel** against the upper edge of the rail and extend the mark made in Step 3 across both faces of the rail.

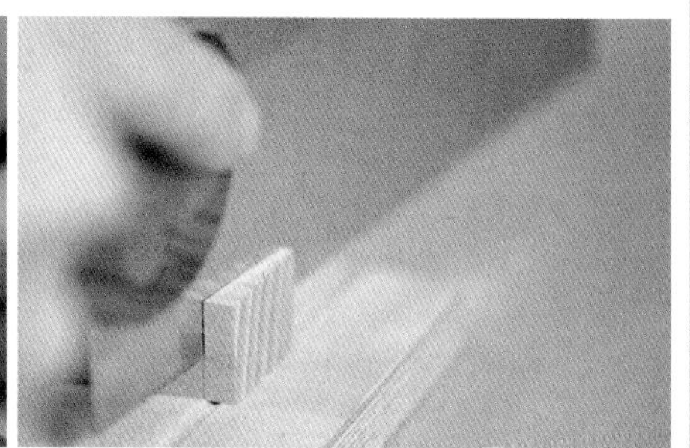

5 **Cut both lower rails** and all four upper rails to length along the angled marks at each end.

ANGLING THE UPPER RAILS

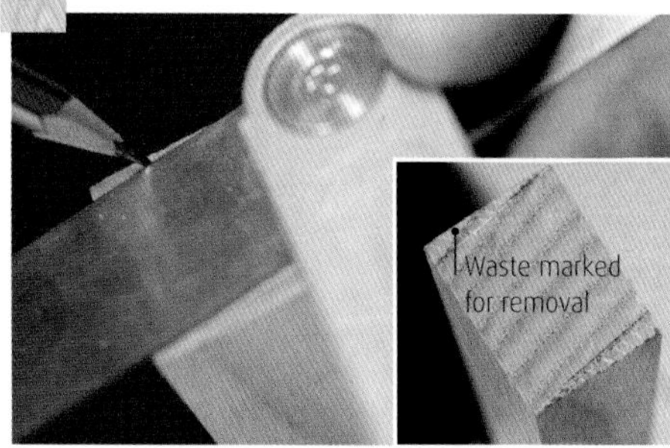

1 **Use the sliding bevel** to draw angled lines across the top and bottom of the end grains of each upper rail (inset).

2 **Use a marking gauge** to score a line on the face of the rail that joins the lower ends of the angled marks on the end grains.

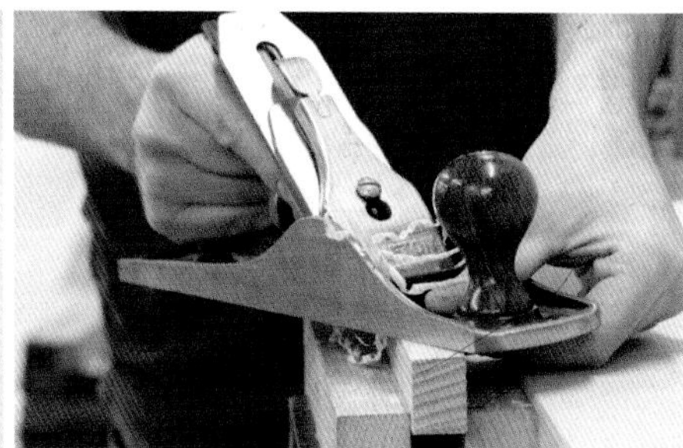

3 **Plane to the marks** to remove the waste along both edges of the rail. Angle all four upper rails in the same way.

MARKING AND CUTTING THE MORTISES ON THE RAILS

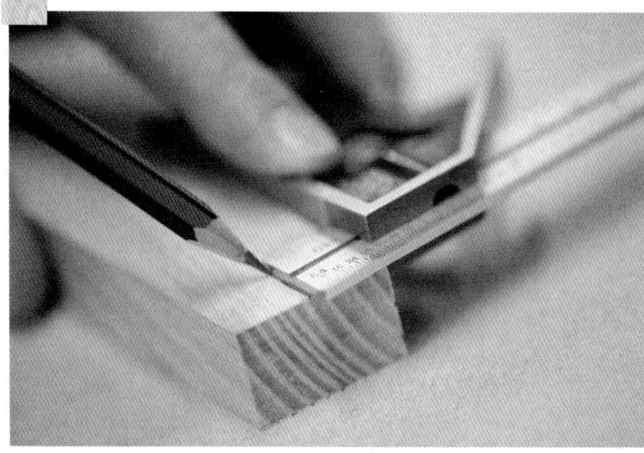

1 **Mark the center** of the width of the lower rail on the angled end to provide a guide for the domino jointer to cut a mortise into the end grain. Extend the guide line for the cutter onto the face, then square the line onto the end grain.

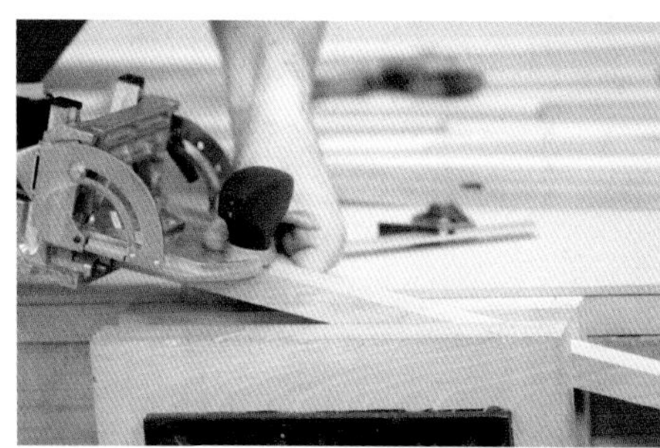

2 **Set the height** of the domino jointer to ⅜in (10mm) and cut the mortise. Repeat Steps 1–2 to cut a mortise in each end of all the upper and lower rails.

CUTTING THE SHELF-SLAT DOMINO MORTISES IN THE LOWER RAILS

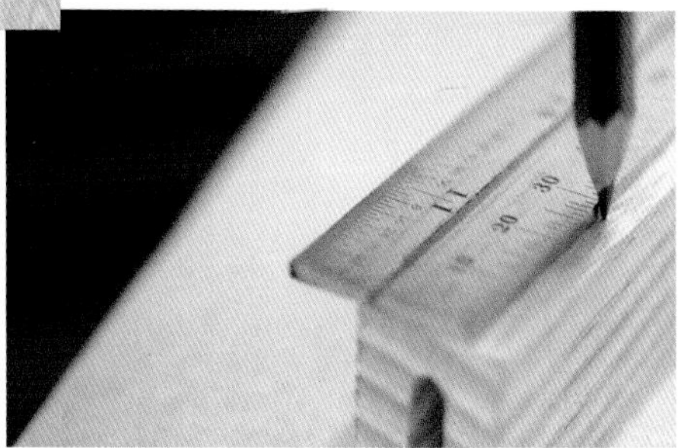

1 **On the top edge** of each of the lower rails, mark the position of the mortises for four of the slats at 1³⁄₁₆in (30mm) and 5½in (140mm) from each end.

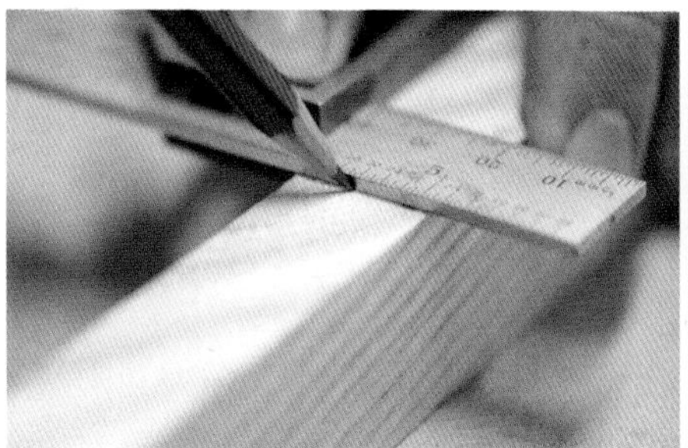

2 **Extend the marks** across the top edge of the rails with a square, to act as a guide for the domino jointer.

3 **Set the jointer** to a height and depth of ⅝in (15mm) and cut the mortises into the inside face of each rail using a ³⁄₁₆in (5mm) cutter.

MAKING THE SLATS

1 **Measure and mark** the top face of each slat to a length of 27⅞in (707mm) from a point about ⅜in (10mm) from one end. Square off the lines on the top face.

2 **Use the sliding bevel** to mark a line at an 82-degree angle toward the end grain from this mark across the edge of the slat. Repeat on both ends of each slat.

3 **Use a tenon saw** to cut both ends of all four slats precisely to length along the angled marks. Use a bench hook to support the wood as you saw.

4 **Use the marking gauge** to lightly score a center line on the top face near the ends of every slat. Use these marks as a guide when jointing.

5 **Set the fence** of the domino jointer to an 82-degree angle. Set the height to ⅜in (9mm) and cut a mortise ⅝in (15mm) deep in both end grains of all four slats (inset).

ASSEMBLING THE FRAME

1 **Sand all the components** and assemble the end frames using domino connectors. Be careful to orientate the mortises correctly. Glue only when you are confident of the fit.

2 **Clamp the frames** using blocks cut to an 82-degree angle to prevent distortion. Leave to dry.

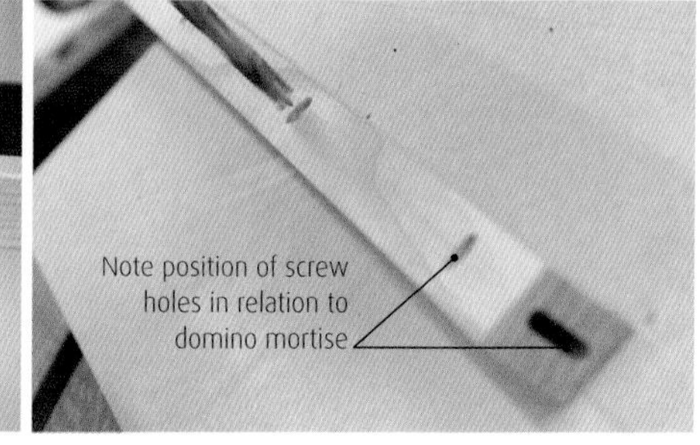

3 **Make cross-grain slotted holes** in each of the long upper rails; for each slot drill and counterbore closely spaced screw holes and chisel out the waste from in between.

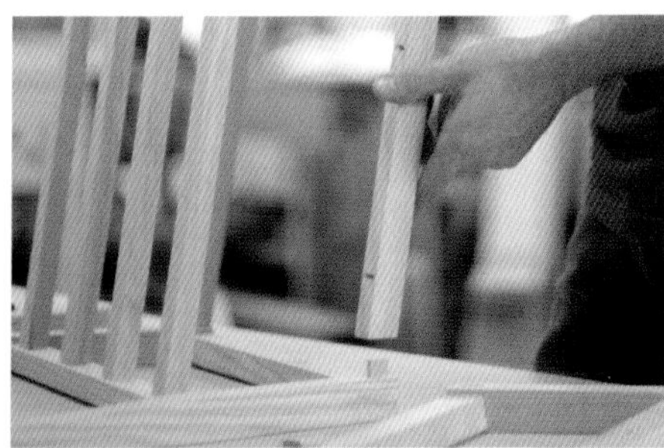

4 **When the glued end frames are dry**, use domino connectors to join the two end frames with the long rails and the slats.

5 **Be careful to orientate the rails** and slats at the correct angle, then assemble using a rubber mallet to knock the joints into place. Glue and clamp once you are confident of the fit.

MAKING AND FITTING THE TABLE TOP

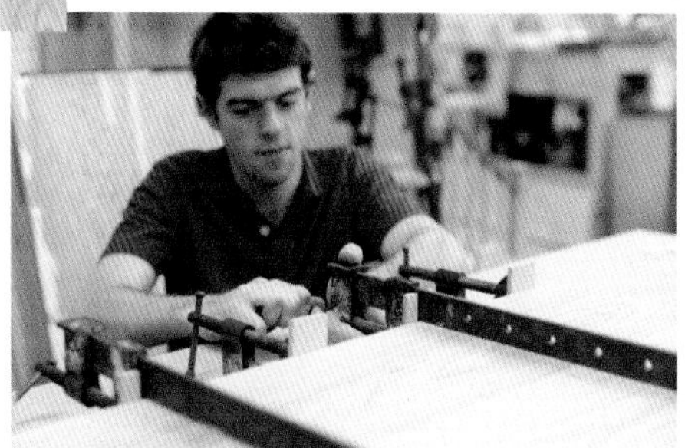

1 **Assemble the pieces** for the table top. Glue and clamp them together (see Edge-to-edge joint, pp.94–95). When the glue is dry, cut the table top to size.

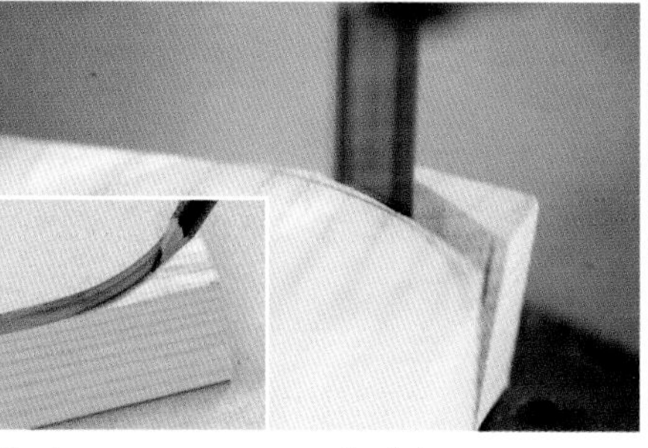

2 **Draw a curve** on each of the corners (inset) using an MDF template (see Jigs and templates, pp.150–51). Cut the curves to the waste side of the line with a band saw.

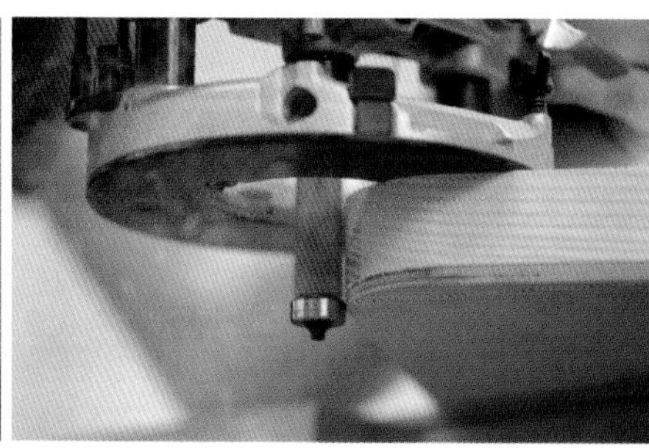

3 **Secure the table top** over the template. Complete the cutting of the curve and create a smooth finish using a router fitted with a bearing-guided router cutter.

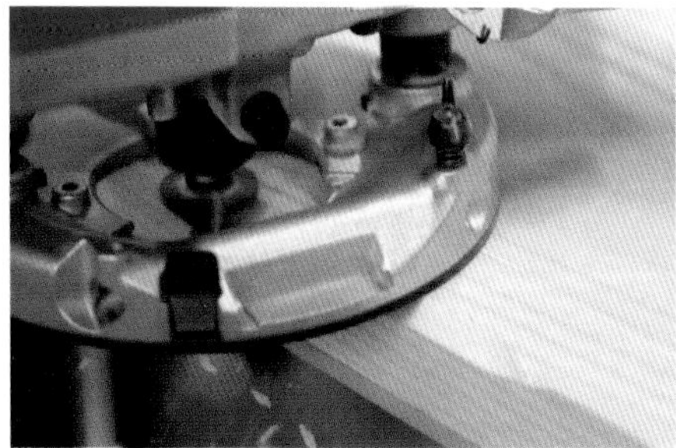

4 **Using a chamfer cutter** in the router, chamfer the underside edges of the table top.

5 **Use sandpaper** to achieve a smooth finish on all the surfaces and edges of the table top.

6 **Position the frame** centrally and upside down on the underside of the table top, and drill pilot holes into the table top using those in the upper rail of the frame as a guide. Insert screws to complete the assembly. Apply clear acrylic varnish or a finish of your choice.

THE FINISHED PIECE

DETAIL OF THE SLATS AND RAILS

ALTERNATIVES

A good way of adapting the design of this piece would be to use contrasting timbers for different parts of the table. The pictured design has a narrow panel of wood of a different color inserted through the middle of the table top.

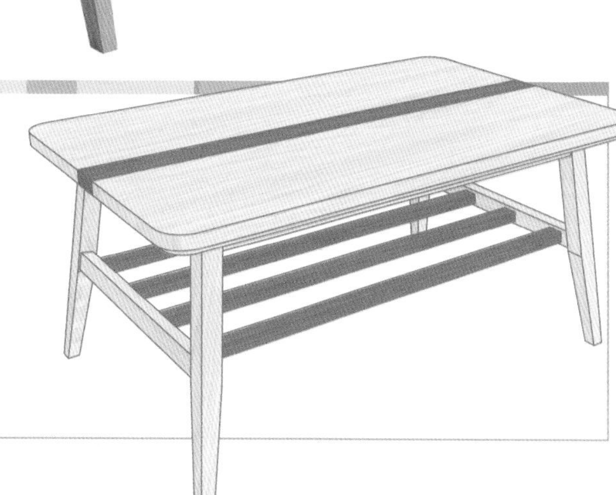

Tool box

A dovetailed chest can be an effective way of keeping your tools safe in the workshop. Alternatively, it could be adapted to provide practical and attractive storage for children's toys. Using softwood, the project presents an opportunity to practice marking and cutting dovetail joints. The plinth at the base of the carcass protects the edges and adds to the aesthetic appeal of the box.

Dimensions:
25 15/16 x 20 x 16 1/4in (660 x 510 x 415mm)

Key techniques:
Through dovetail joint (pp.134–37);
Edge-to-edge joint (pp.94–95)

CUTTING LIST

Item	Material	No.	Length	Width	Thickness
Long box sides	Pine	6	28in* (700mm)	5 5/16in* (135mm)	13/16in* (20mm)
Short box sides	Pine	6	28in* (700mm)	5 5/16in* (135mm)	13/16in* (20mm)
Plinth	Pine	1	8ft 2 1/2in* (2500mm)	2 9/16in (65mm)	9/16in (15mm)
Long lid surround	Pine	1	29 1/2in* (750mm)	1 3/4in (45mm)	9/16in (15mm)
Short lid surround	Pine	2	21 3/4in* (550mm)	1 3/4in (45mm)	9/16in (15mm)
Lid panel	Pine	5	28in* (700mm)	4in* (100mm)	13/16in* (20mm)
Lid frame	Pine	1	8ft 2 1/2in* (2500mm)	1 3/8in (35mm)	9/16in (15mm)
Base	Birch ply	1	24 3/16in (612mm)	18 1/4in (462mm)	1/4in (6mm)

*Includes excess to allow for cutting and/or planing to size

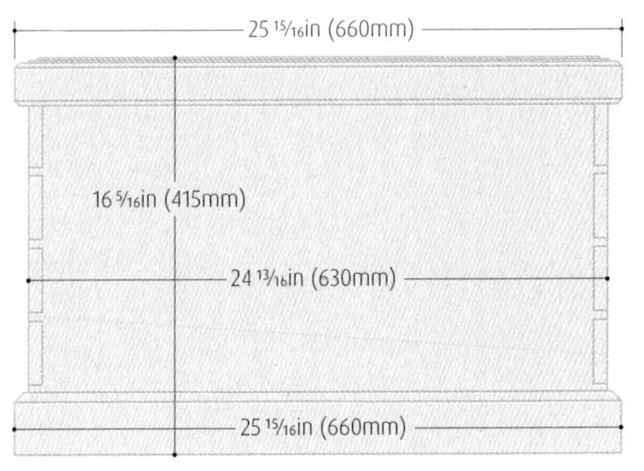

FRONT VIEW (1:10)

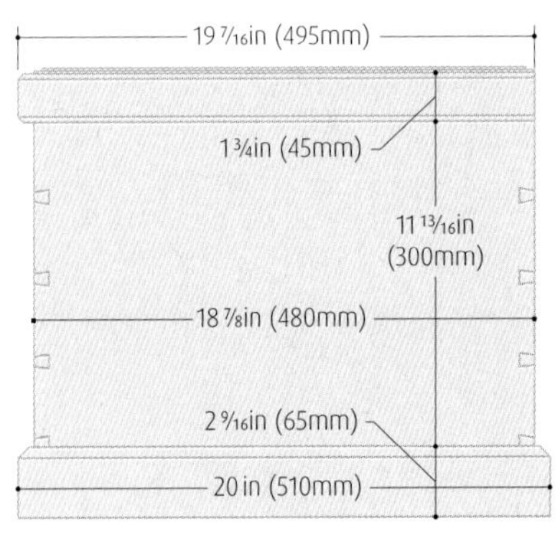

SIDE VIEW (1:10)

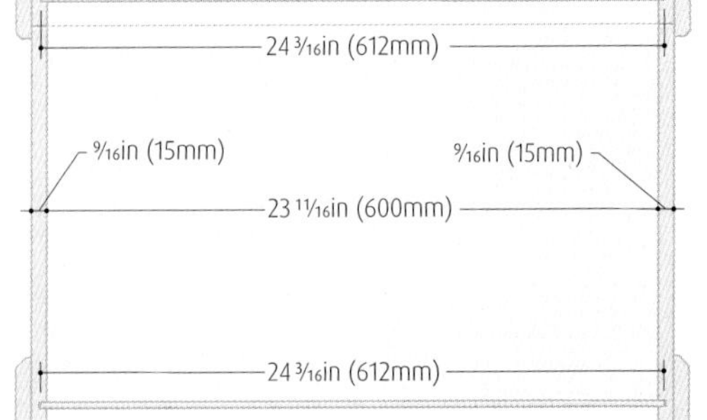

CROSS-SECTION OF FRONT VIEW (1:10)

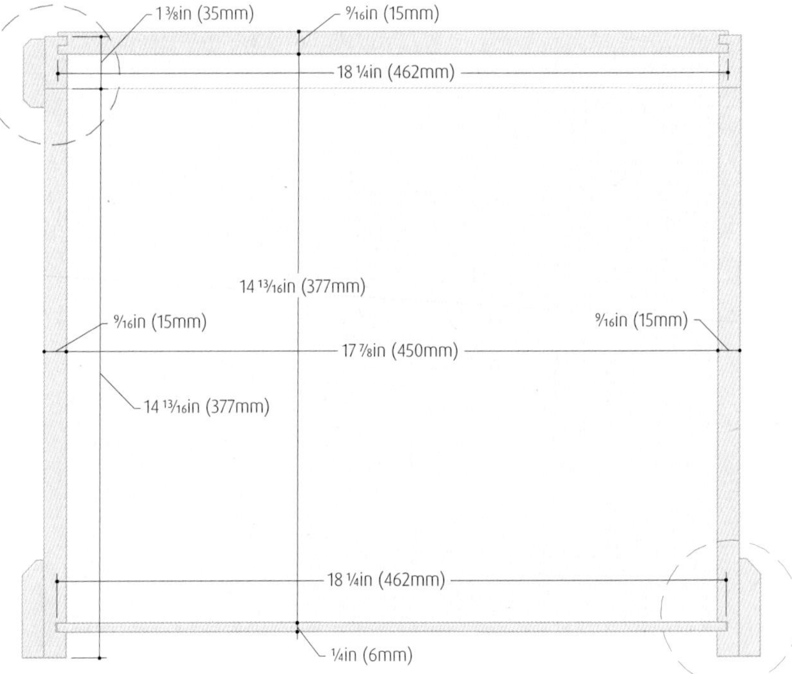

CROSS-SECTION OF SIDE VIEW (1:5)

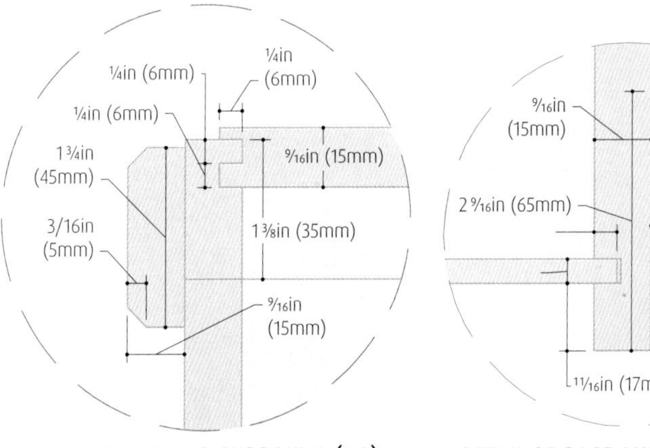

DETAIL OF LID AND SURROUND (1:2)

DETAIL OF BASE AND PLINTH (1:2)

TOOLS AND MATERIALS

Sash clamps	Marking gauge
Wood glue and brush	Rebate plane
Bench plane or planer machine	Hand-held router with bearing-guided chamfer cutter
Table saw or panel saw and miter saw	Ratchet strap
Pencil	G-clamps
Combination square	2 butt hinges and screws
Dovetail marker	Bradawl
Bevel-edged chisel	Drill with bits
Tenon saw	Screwdriver
Coping saw	Sandpaper
Table-mounted router	

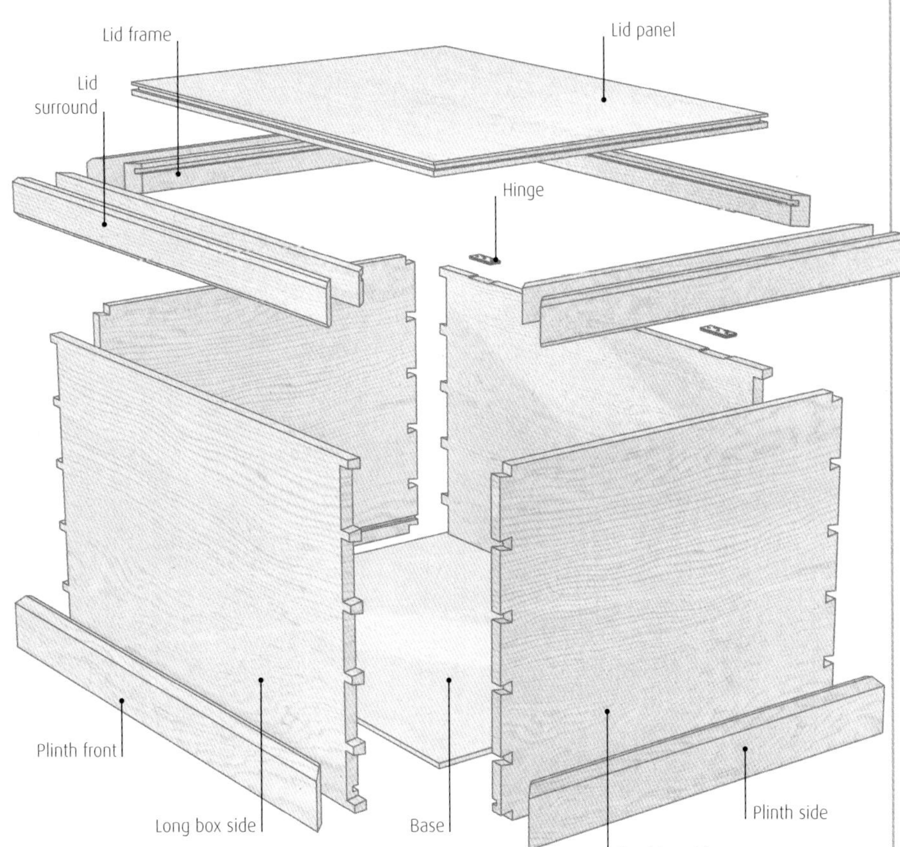

How the elements fit together
The tool box is durable and attractive, due to its solid carcass and through dovetails. The lid consists of a "floating" panel within a mitered frame that allows for movement across its width, and protrudes over the carcass sides when the lid is closed.

PREPARING THE BOX SIDES AND LID PANEL

1 **Join the stock** for the box sides and lid panel with edge-to-edge joints, as described on pp.94–95.

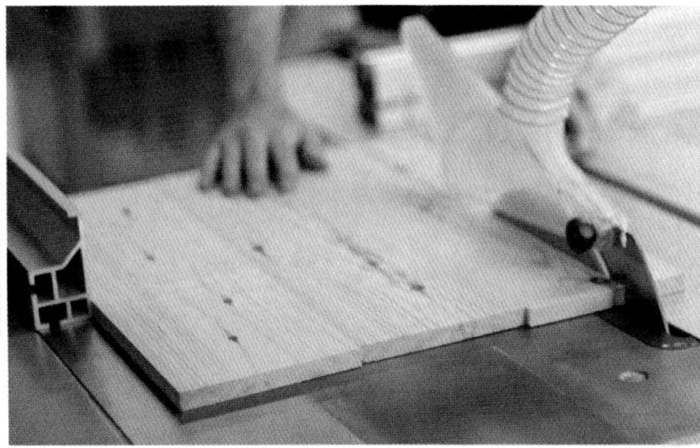

2 **When the glue** is dry, plane all the joined pieces to a thickness of 9⁄16in (15mm) with a bench plane or by planer machine. Then cut the box sides to the following sizes: long sides: 24 13⁄16 x 14 13⁄16in (630 x 377mm); short sides: 18 7⁄8 x 14 13⁄16in (480 x 377mm). Use a table saw (pictured) or a panel saw.

MARKING OUT THE DOVETAILS

1 **Mark out five tails** on both ends of the two long sides of the box, then cut them with a bevel-edged chisel (inset). See Through dovetail joint (pp.134–37) for full instructions.

2 **Mark out the pins** on both ends of the two short sides of the box. Make relief cuts with a tenon saw, then remove the waste with a coping saw and chisel to finish.

3 **Test the fit** of the joints to ensure that all surfaces are smoothly aligned. Adjust the joints as necessary.

MAKING THE BASE

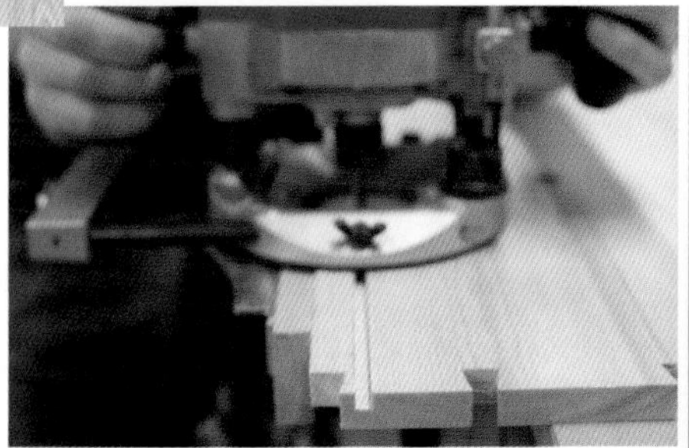

1 **Cut a groove** ¼in (6mm) wide and 11⁄16in (17mm) from the bottom of all four side pieces, using a router with the fence set to 11⁄16in (17mm) and the depth to 5⁄16in (7mm).

2 **Check the fit** of the base in the groove. If the fit is too tight, mark a line ¼in (6mm) from the edge of all sides of the base, and use a rebate plane to cut a slight rebate (inset). Test-fit the joint again, making further adjustments if required.

ASSEMBLING THE SIDES AND BASE

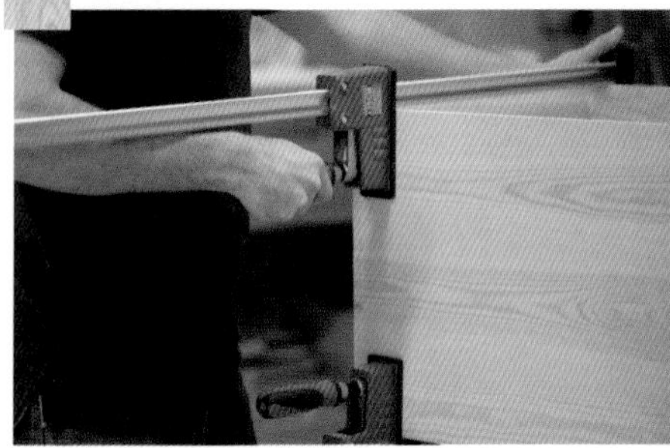

1 **Glue the joining edges and grooves** of the sides and base. Assemble, secure with sash clamps, and leave to dry.

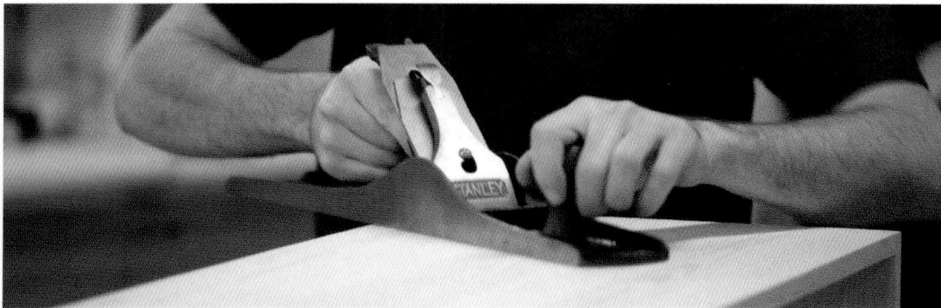

2 **When the glue** has dried, use a bench plane to cut each of the dovetail joints flush to the sides.

MAKING THE PLINTH

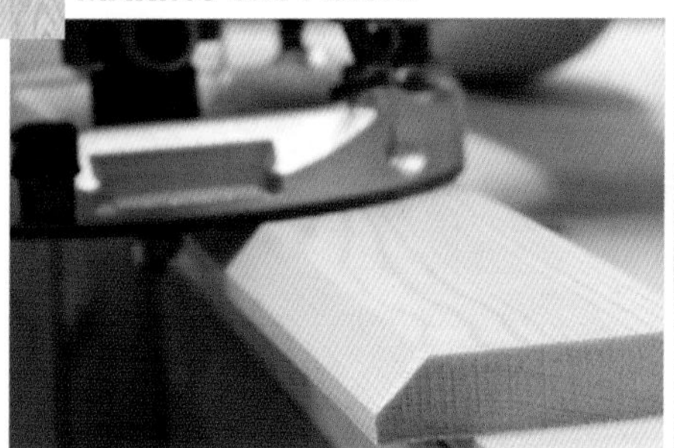

1 **Use a router** fitted with a bearing-guided chamfer cutter to chamfer one edge of each of the plinth pieces.

2 **Miter one end** of one of the long plinth pieces. Place it alongside one of the long box sides, with the inner edge of the miter aligned with the corner of the box.

3 **Mark the position** of the corner at the opposite end of the same piece. Square the mark around the edge and across the chamfer with a combination square.

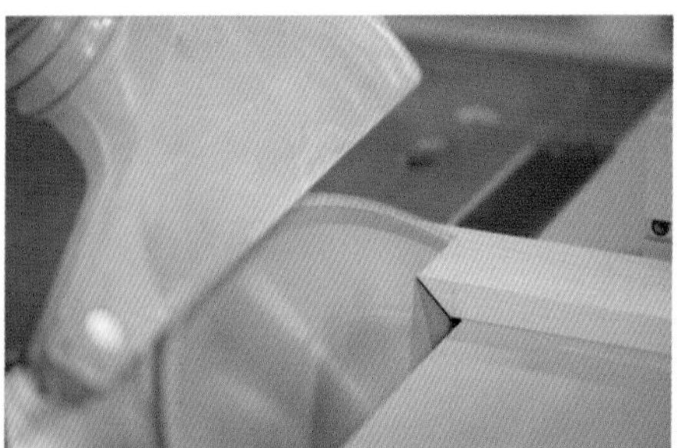

4 **Cut the miter** on a table saw (pictured) or by hand with a miter saw. Mark and miter both ends of each of the other plinth pieces in the same way.

5 **Apply glue** to the inside face and the mitered edges of each of the plinth pieces. Secure them with a ratchet strap and allow to dry.

MAKING THE LID PANEL

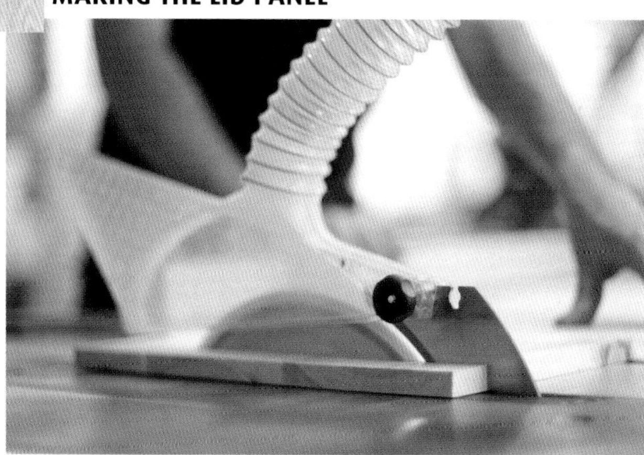

1 **Cut the lid panel** to size (24³⁄₁₆ x 18¼in/ 612 x 462mm) on a table saw (pictured), or by hand with a panel saw.

2 **Use a table-mounted router** fitted with a ¼in (6mm) cutter to cut a groove ¼in (6mm) deep along all four edges of the lid. Set the fence to ¼in (6mm).

MAKING THE LID FRAME

1 **Cut a groove** of the same dimensions along the inside face of the length of timber for making the lid frame pieces.

2 **Mark and cut a miter** at each end of the lid frame pieces as for the plinth (see opposite), using the lid as a position guide.

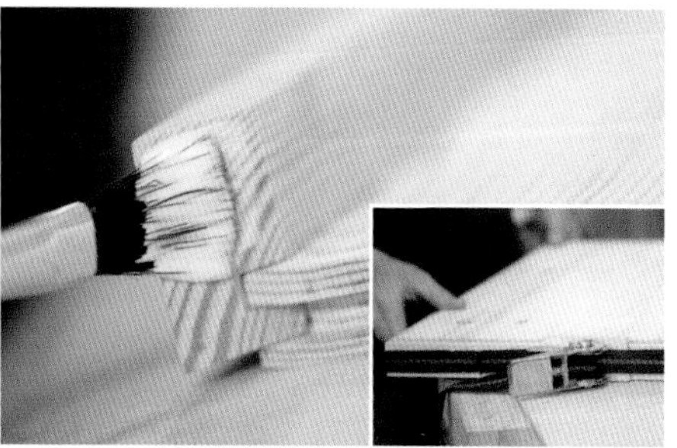

3 **Fit the frame pieces** around the lid and glue the miters. Use a ratchet strap to clamp them securely (inset), then leave to dry.

MAKING THE LID SURROUND

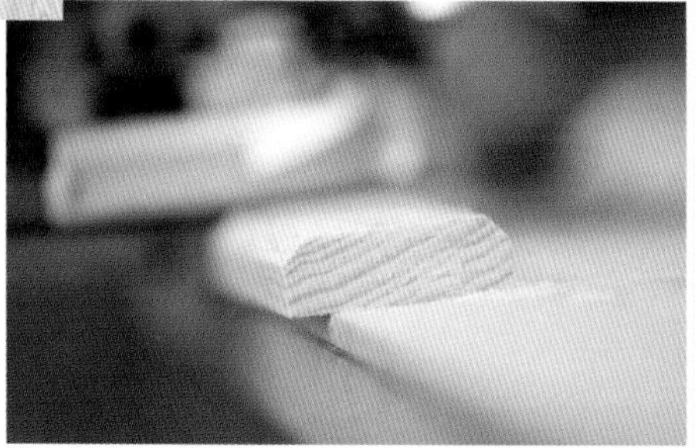

1 **Chamfer both outer edges** of the three lid surround pieces, using a router fitted with a bearing-guided chamfer cutter.

2 **Measure the fit** of the surround pieces against the lid frame. Mark and cut miters in both ends of the long piece, and in one end of each of the short pieces.

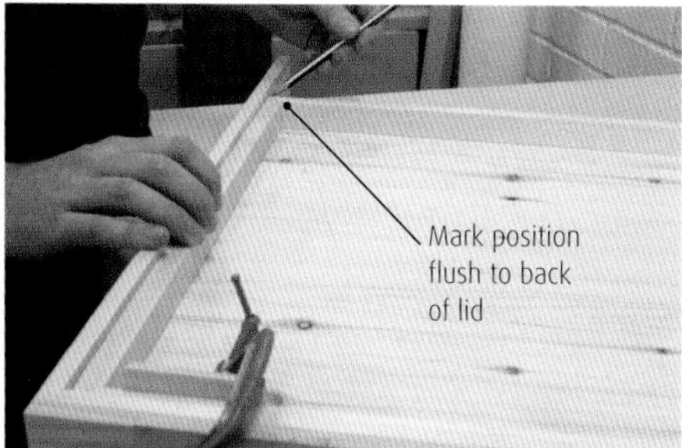

3 **Clamp the long piece** to the front of the lid frame. Butt a side piece against the miter and mark the position flush to the back of the lid. Repeat for the other side piece.

4 **Using a tenon saw**, cut the two side pieces to length, sawing to the waste side of the marks.

5 **Glue the three lid-surround pieces** in position around the sides and front of the frame approximately ¼in (6mm) below the top of the frame. Clamp and allow to dry.

FITTING THE HINGES TO THE CARCASS

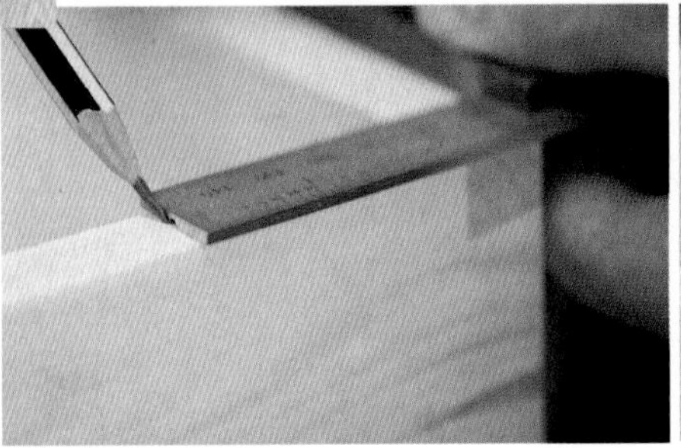

1 **Mark the position** of the hinges 2⁹⁄₁₆in (65mm) from each end of one long side of the carcass.

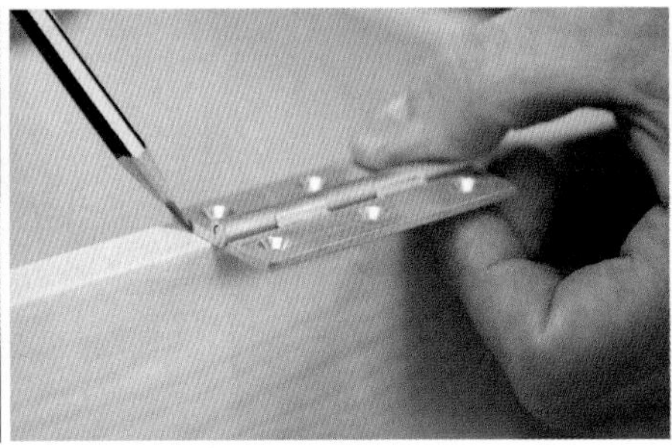

2 **Align the hinge edge** with the mark, with the hinge flange on the outside edge of the carcass. Using the hinge as a guide, mark the length of the hinge housing.

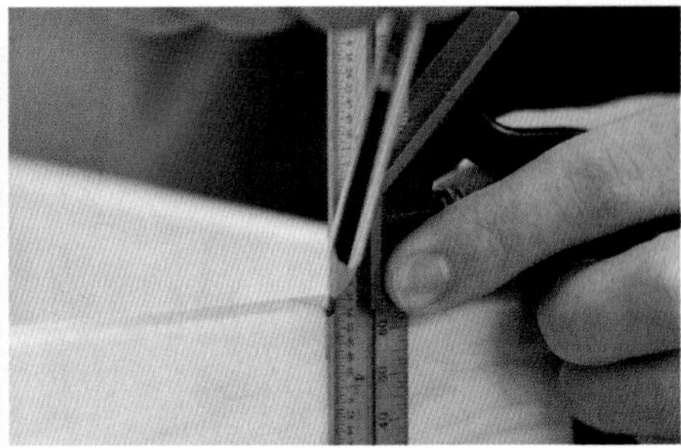

3 **Extend the lines** down both faces of the carcass side, using a pencil and combination square.

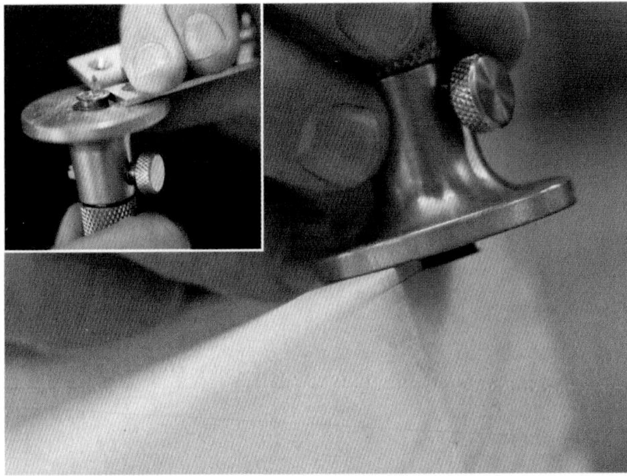

4 **Set a marking gauge** to the thickness of the hinge flange (inset), then scribe a line between the housing length-marks on both faces of the carcass. Repeat for the second hinge housing.

5 **Use a chisel** to chop away the waste from both housings, being careful not to exceed the length and depth marks. (See also Preventing tearing, below.)

6 **Test-fit the hinges** in each of the housings on the carcass. Use a chisel to make any necessary adjustments.

7 **Mark the position** of the pilot holes with a bradawl, using the holes in the hinges as a guide.

8 **Drill the holes** using a bit of the same width as the hinge screws, leaving the hinge in place as a guide.

9 **Use a screwdriver** to insert the hinge screws through the hinge into each of the holes.

PREVENTING TEARING

To prevent the wood from tearing when chiseling across the grain, clamp a block of wood to the inside of the carcass for the chisel to drive into.

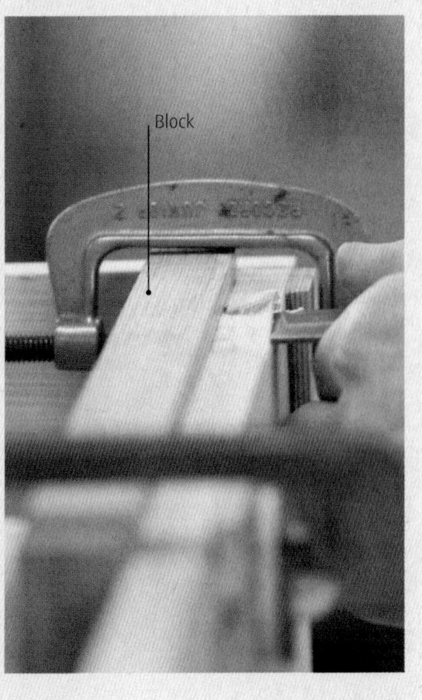

FITTING THE HINGES TO THE LID

1 **Place the lid** in position over the top of the carcass and mark the position of the hinges on the back edge of the lid frame.

2 **Square the marks** onto the inside edge of the lid frame to indicate the dimensions and position of the housing.

3 **With the marking gauge** set to the thickness of the hinge flange, mark the housing depth on both faces of the lid frame.

4 **Use a chisel** to chop away the waste from both housings. Clean up the edges and test-fit the hinges.

5 **Drill the holes** and insert the screws as for the carcass hinges, after making any necessary final adjustments to the housings.

6 **Remove the arrises** and sand all the surfaces of the tool chest smooth with sandpaper wrapped around an offcut.

THE FINISHED PIECE

FINISHES

This pine box would be an ideal piece to stain or to paint in the color of your choice. If using paint, remember to apply a knotting solution to any knots in the wood to prevent the sap from bleeding through—a common problem when using pine. Alternative finishes include clear varnish and wax, both of which retain the natural look of the wood.

ALTERNATIVES

For safe storage and easy access of tools such as screwdrivers and chisels, you can incorporate a removable tray, supported by a pair of batons fixed along the inside of the short sides of the chest. A series of dividers inside the tray would help keep the tools separate, while a doorknob or handle fixed to the centre of the tray would make it easy to lift out. You could also construct a separate container for storing screws, nails, and other small items using the Trinket box design (see pp.272–75). This box could be kept inside the tool chest.

If you are intending to adapt the tool chest for storing children's toys instead, it is a good idea to fit a box stay to the carcass and lid (pictured below). A stay provides an easy method of safely keeping the lid open and avoiding the risk of injury to a child's fingers.

Bedside table

This simple but elegant Shaker-style cherry-wood bedside table utilizes a traditional type of carcass construction and a dovetailed drawer. The construction method is similar to that of a simple mortise-and-tenoned table—except that the rails are designed to be wide enough to accommodate a drawer within the table's internal space. The top is solid with a rounded upper edge to give a soft profile. The legs are tapered to provide a small footprint at the base, which adds to the overall appearance of lightness.

TOOLS AND MATERIALS

- Ruler and pencil
- Combination square
- Mortise gauge
- Mortiser or mortise chisel
- Marking gauge
- Tenon saw or band saw
- Coping saw
- Bevel-edged chisel
- Bench plane
- Dovetail marker
- Marking knife
- Dovetail saw
- Drill with bits
- Screwdriver
- 8 screws (No. 9 x 1¼in/4.5 x 30mm); 12 screws (No. 9 x 1⅜in/4.5 x 35mm)
- Wood glue and brush
- Sash clamps
- Cabinet scraper
- Hand-held router and bearing-guided round-over cutter
- Tape measure
- Table-mounted router
- Block plane
- Drawer knob
- Wood stain and wax
- Bradawl
- Hammer
- File

CUTTING LIST

Item	Material	No.	Length	Width	Thickness
Legs	Cherry	4	25³⁄₁₆in (640mm)	1⅜in (35mm)	1⅜in (35mm)
Side rails	Cherry	2	14in (355mm)	7⁵⁄₁₆in (185mm)	¹³⁄₁₆in (20mm)
Back rail	Cherry	1	19½in (495mm)	7⁵⁄₁₆in (185mm)	¹³⁄₁₆in (20mm)
Upper front rail	Cherry	1	18⁵⁄₁₆in (465mm)	1³⁄₁₆in (30mm)	¹³⁄₁₆in (20mm)
Lower front rail	Cherry	1	18⁵⁄₁₆in (465mm)	1³⁄₁₆in (30mm)	¹³⁄₁₆in (20mm)
Runners	Cherry	2	12in (305mm)	1in (25mm)	¹³⁄₁₆in (20mm)
Kickers	Cherry	2	12in (305mm)	1in (25mm)	¹³⁄₁₆in (20mm)
Rear kicker	Cherry	1	15³⁄₁₆in (385mm)	1in (25mm)	¹³⁄₁₆in (20mm)
Table top	Cherry	1	23¹³⁄₁₆in* (605mm)	18⁵⁄₁₆in* (465mm)	¹³⁄₁₆in (20mm)
Drawer front	Cherry	1	17½in* (445mm)	5¹¹⁄₁₆in* (145mm)	¹³⁄₁₆in (20mm)
Drawer sides	Ash	2	13⅛in (333mm)	5¹¹⁄₁₆in* (145mm)	⅜in (10mm)
Drawer back	Ash	1	17⅛in* (435mm)	4¹⁵⁄₁₆in (125mm)	⅜in (10mm)
Drawer base	Birch ply	1	17⅛in (435mm)	13in (330mm)	¼in (6mm)
Guides	Pine	2	12in (305mm)	⁹⁄₁₆in (15mm)	⅜in* (10mm)

*Includes excess to allow for cutting to size.

Dimensions:
660 x 605 x 465mm (26 x 23¹³⁄₁₆ x 18⁵⁄₁₆in)

Key techniques:
Dovetail half-lap joint (pp.102–103);
Basic mortise-and-tenon joint (pp.116–19);
Lapped dovetail joint (pp.138–39)

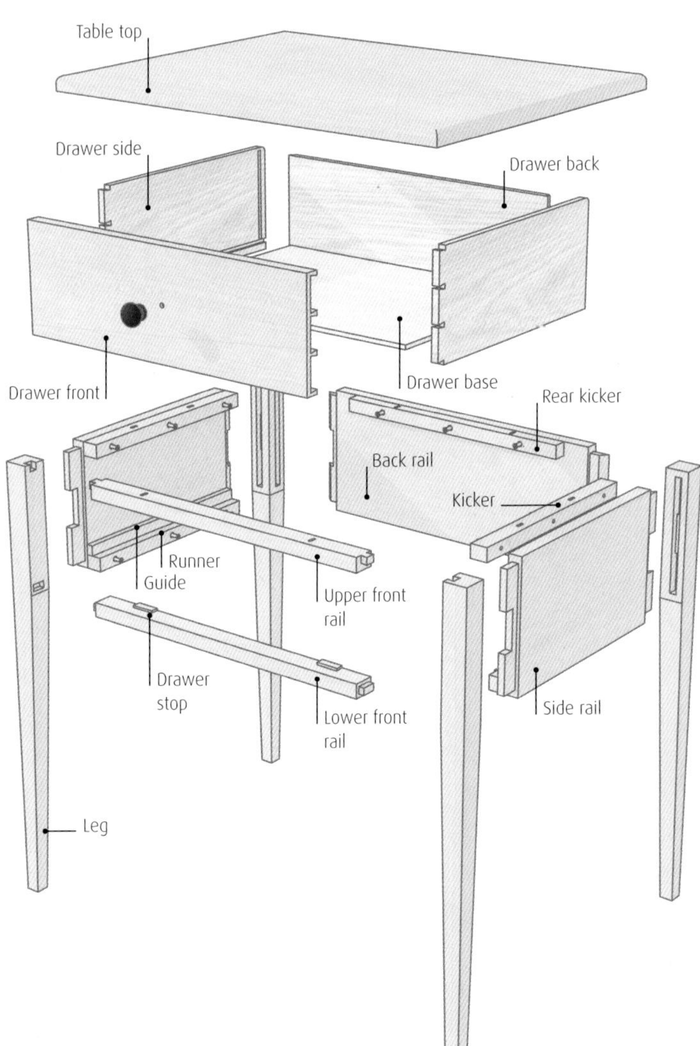

How the elements fit together
The side and back rails are fitted to the legs by double tenons. A dovetail half-lap joint joins the upper front rail to the legs. Drawer runners and kickers are screwed to the rails and the drawer itself has lapped dovetails at the front and a housing at the back.

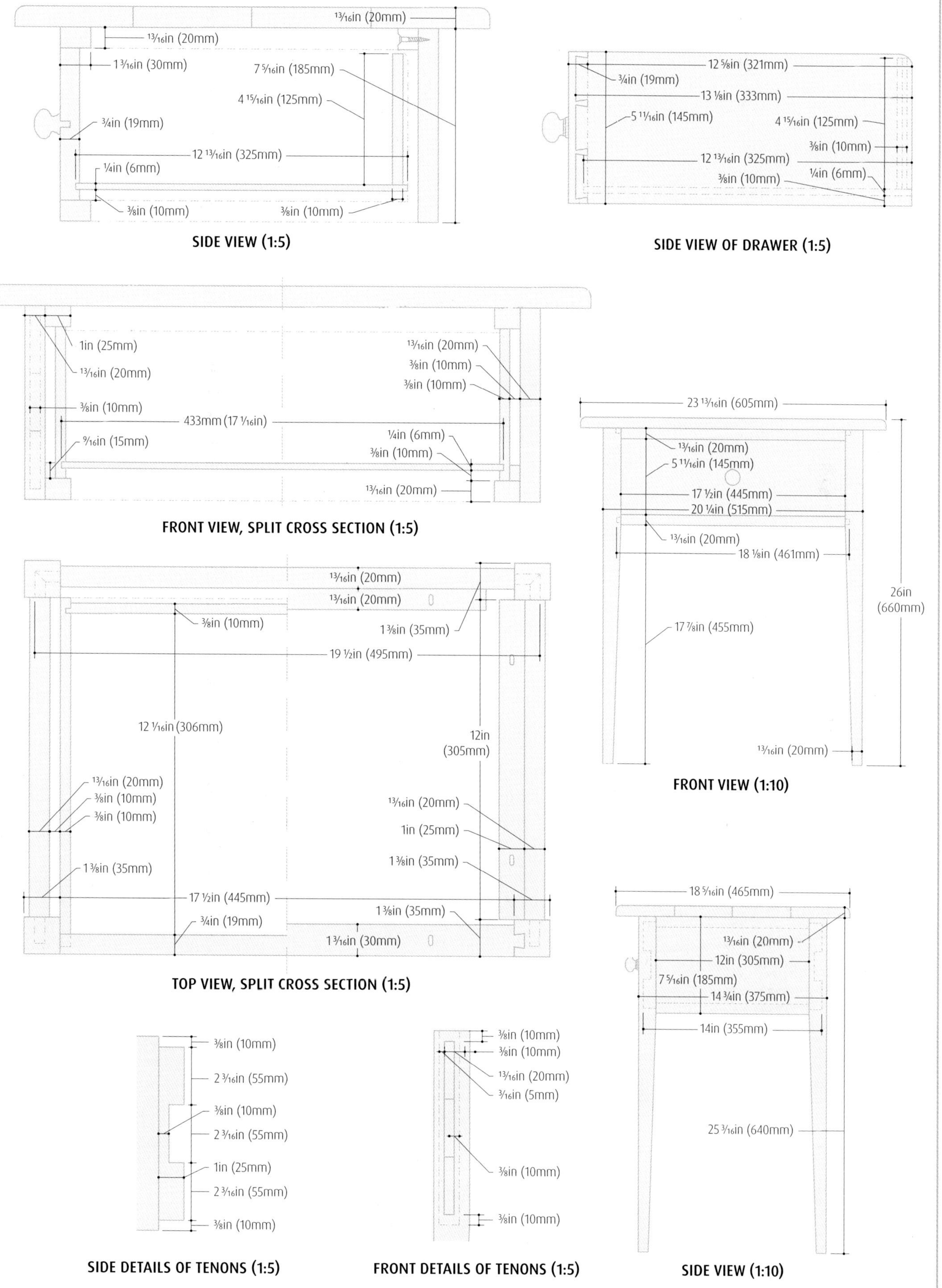

SIDE VIEW (1:5)

SIDE VIEW OF DRAWER (1:5)

FRONT VIEW, SPLIT CROSS SECTION (1:5)

FRONT VIEW (1:10)

TOP VIEW, SPLIT CROSS SECTION (1:5)

SIDE DETAILS OF TENONS (1:5)

FRONT DETAILS OF TENONS (1:5)

SIDE VIEW (1:10)

MAKING THE LONG MORTISES IN THE LEGS

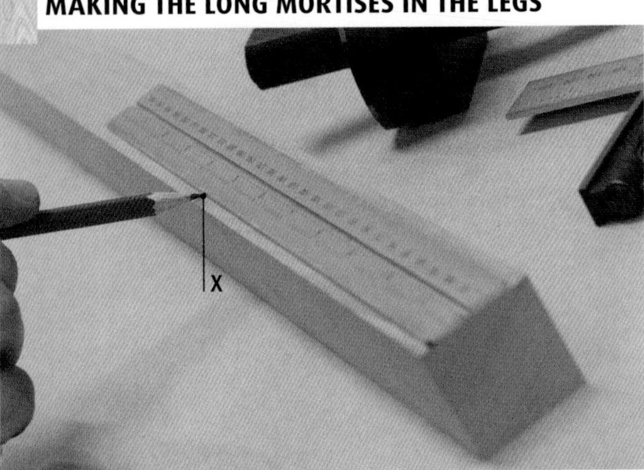

1 **Make a long mortise** with a haunch in each of the leg pieces. On one corner, mark the position of the bottom of the rail (X) 7⁵⁄₁₆in (185mm) from the top end grain.

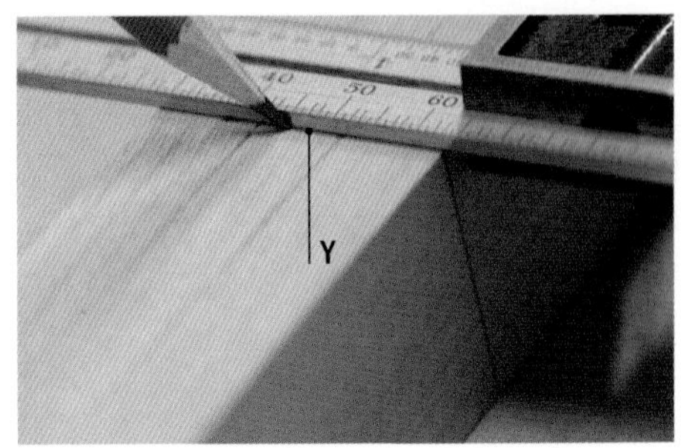

2 **Extend the marks** square across both adjacent sides to form line Y, using a square and pencil. These sides will become the inside faces of the leg.

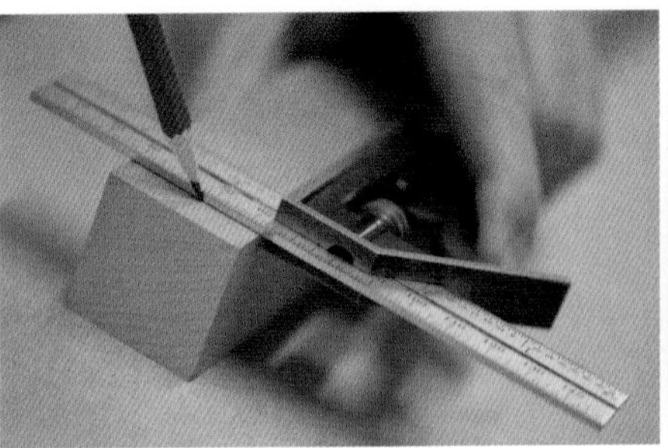

3 **Mark one end** of the mortise ⅜in (10mm) and the other 6¹⁵⁄₁₆in (175mm) from the top end grain. Square the marks onto both inside faces of the legs.

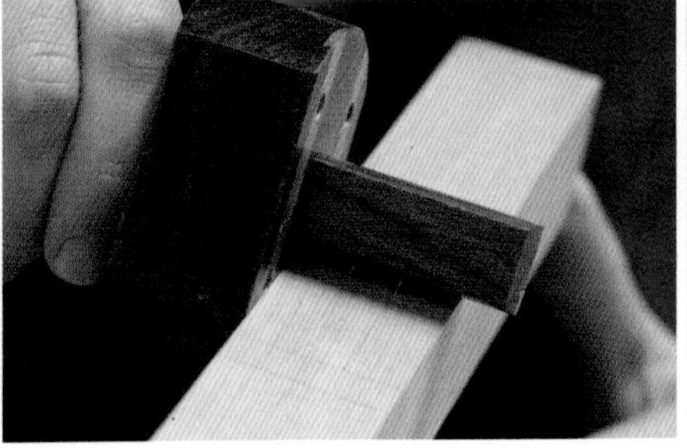

4 **Set a mortise gauge** to a width of ⅜in (10mm) and scribe the mortise width centrally between the ends of the mortise marked in the previous step.

5 **Divide the mortise length** into thirds. You will be cutting the middle third more shallowly to accommodate the haunch of the double tenon (see opposite).

6 **Use a mortiser** to cut the mortise to a depth of ⅜in (10mm) in the middle third, and 1in (25mm) on either side.

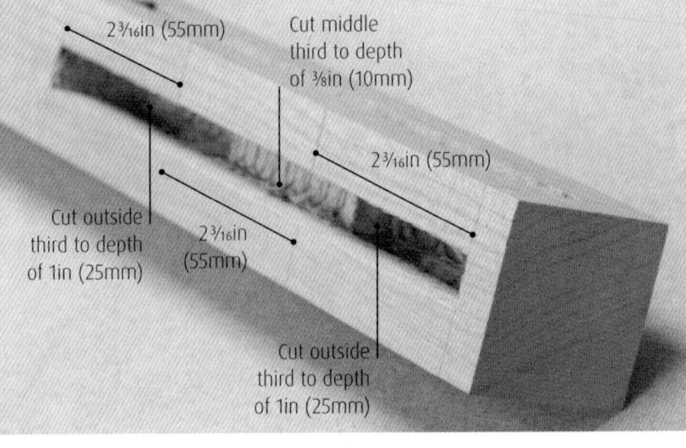

7 **Repeat Steps 1–6** for each of the remaining three leg pieces. For the two back legs, cut a second mortise of the same dimensions in the other inside face.

MAKING THE BACK- AND SIDE-RAIL TENONS

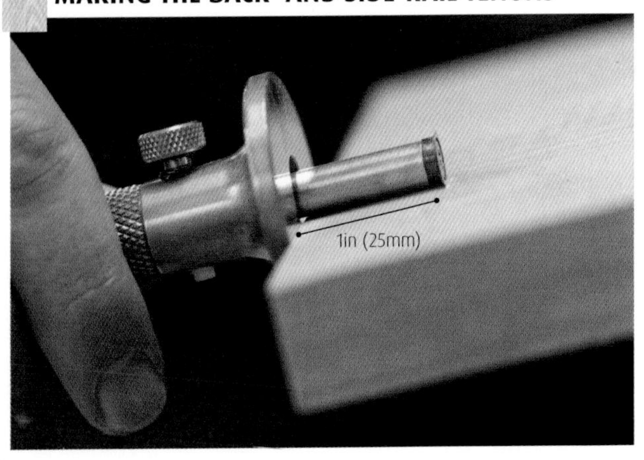

1 **With a marking gauge** set to 1in (25mm), scribe the tenon shoulder around the ends of the back rail.

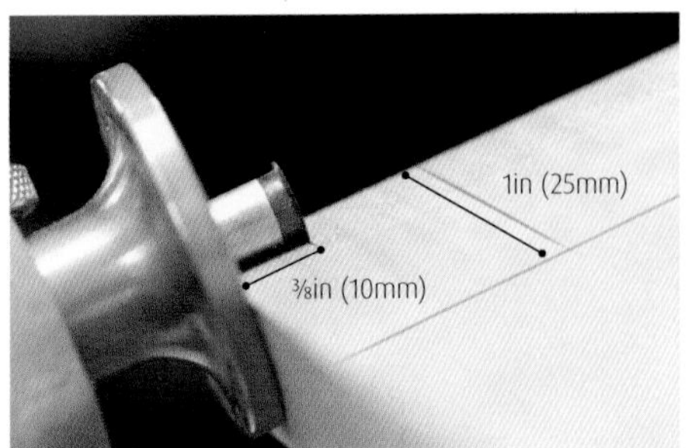

2 **Set the marking gauge** to ⅜in (10mm) and scribe the shoulder of the tenon around the end grain and both faces of the back rail.

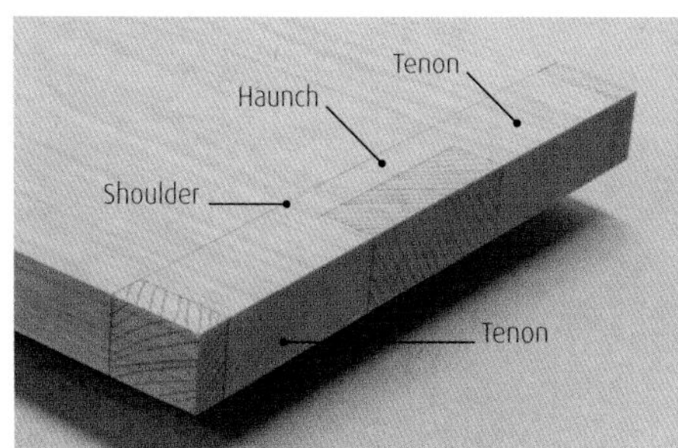

3 **Mark the width** of each tenon— 2³⁄₁₆in (55mm)—and the haunch in the middle. Mark the depth of the haunch ⅜in (10mm) from the shoulder and mark up the waste.

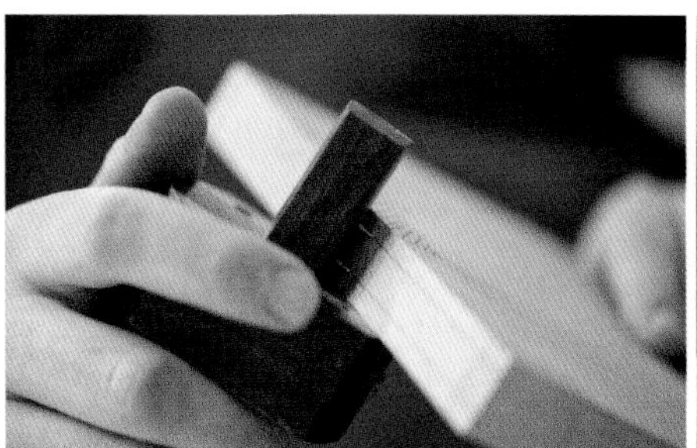

4 **Scribe the thickness** of the tenon along the center of the end grain with the mortise gauge set to ⅜in (10mm), as before.

5 **Cut the tenon** by hand with a tenon saw (pictured) or with a band saw. Use a coping saw to remove the waste from the haunch (inset).

6 **Clean up all of the edges** with a bevel-edged chisel. Repeat Steps 1–6 for the other end of the back rail and each end of both side rails.

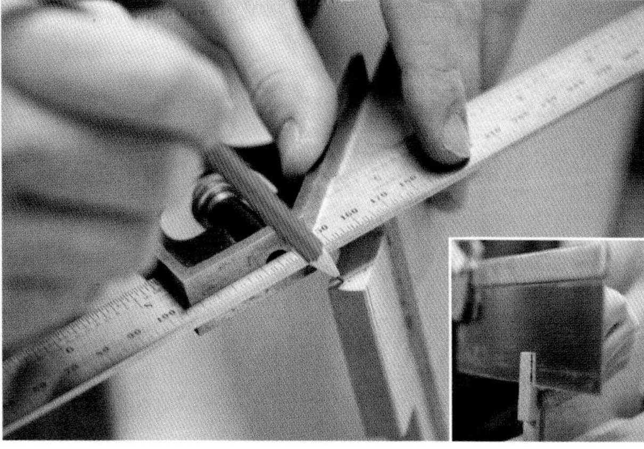

7 **Mark a miter** angled inward in the ends of the back rail tenons, along the side of the tenon. Use the combination square as a guide. Extend the mark square along the width of the tenon and cut the miter with the tenon saw (inset). Cut a miter of the same dimensions in one end of each of the side rails.

8 **Test the fit** of the side and back rail tenons in the matching leg mortises. Make any necessary adjustments.

MAKING THE SMALL MORTISES IN THE LEGS

1 **Each front leg** has a small mortise on the inner face. Mark 6¾in (170mm) from the end grain at the top of the leg, and scribe across to indicate the position of the top of the mortise. Make a second mark ⅜in (10mm) further down the leg to indicate the width of the mortise.

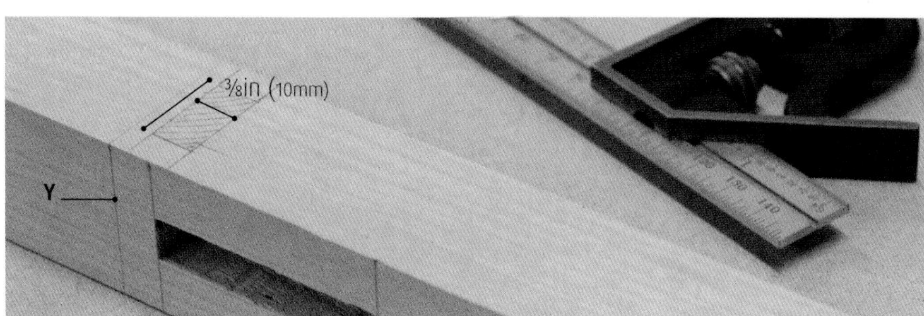

2 **Mark the length** of the mortise—¹³⁄₁₆in (20mm)—centrally within the width marks made in the previous step.

Note that the position of the mortise overlaps that of the large mortise in the adjacent face.

3 **Cut the mortise** on a mortiser to a depth of ⅜in (10mm), or by hand with a mortise chisel of a suitable size.

TAPERING THE LEGS

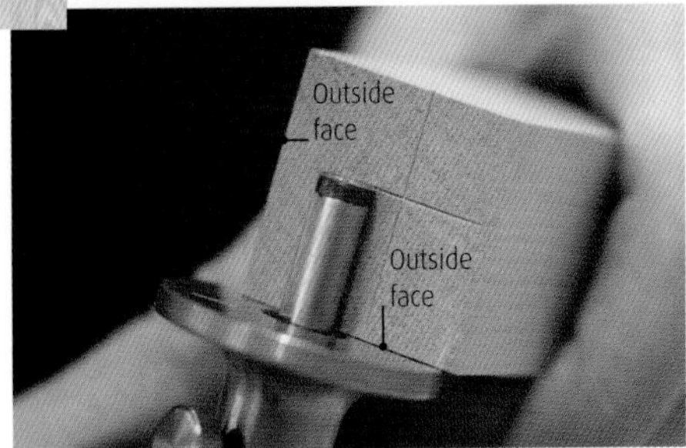

1 **To taper the legs** on the two inside faces, first set the marking gauge to 13⁄16in (20mm) and scribe the measurement on the end grain at the bottom of the leg from the two outside faces.

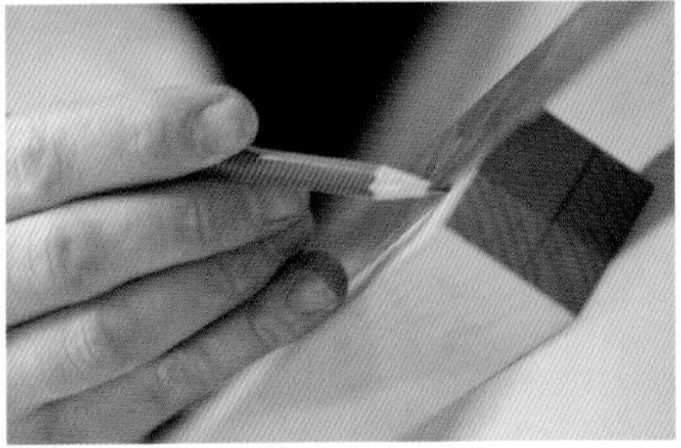

2 **Extend the marks** at each edge diagonally along the adjacent face to the edge at point X as previously marked (p.290), which will be the start of the taper.

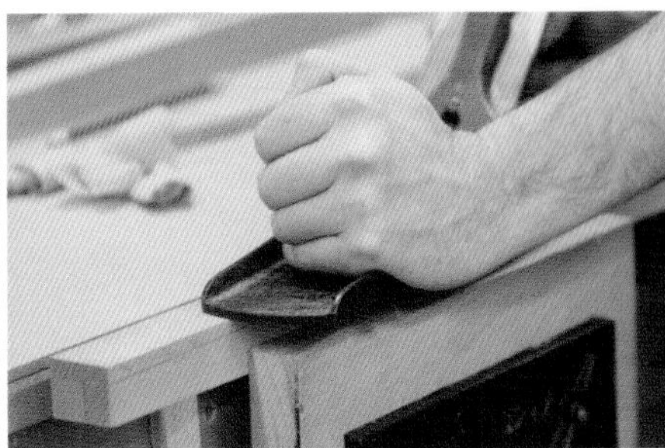

3 **With the wood secured** in a vise, use a bench plane to cut the taper along both inside faces of each leg to the marks.

MAKING THE TENONS IN THE LOWER FRONT RAIL

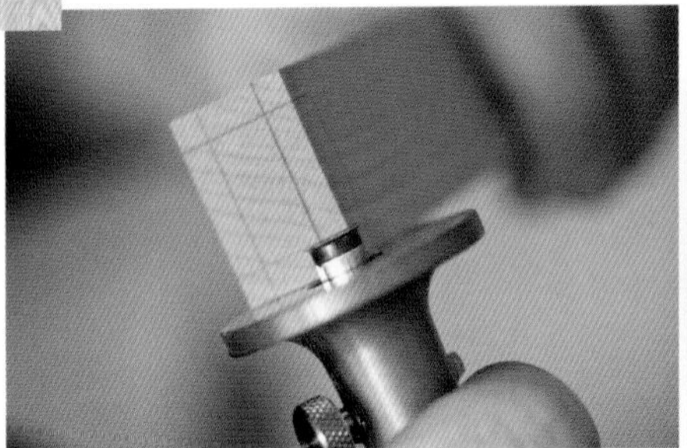

1 **Mark a tenon** 13⁄16in (20mm) wide, 3⁄8in (10mm) thick, and 3⁄8in (10mm) long in both end grains of the lower front rail.

2 **Cut the tenons** with a tenon saw, then clean up the shoulders with a bevel-edged chisel (inset).

3 **Test the fit** of the tenons in the small mortises in the front legs. Make any necessary adjustments to ease the fit.

MARKING THE UPPER FRONT-RAIL TAILS

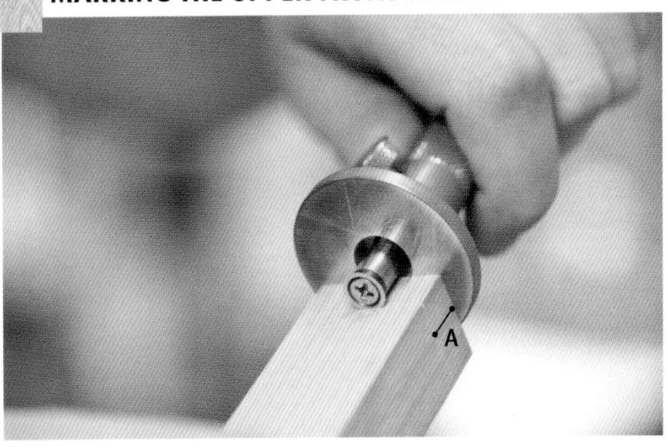

1 **The upper front rail** is joined to the front legs by half-lapped dovetail joints (pp.102–103). Mark up the tails in both end grains of the upper front rail. Use the marking gauge to scribe 3⁄8in (10mm) (A) around all four sides from one end grain of the rail.

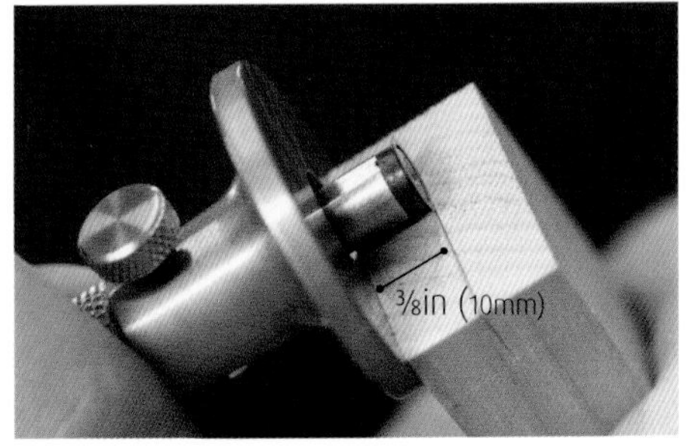

2 **Scribe the same measurement** from edge to edge across the end grain. Extend the mark around both edges.

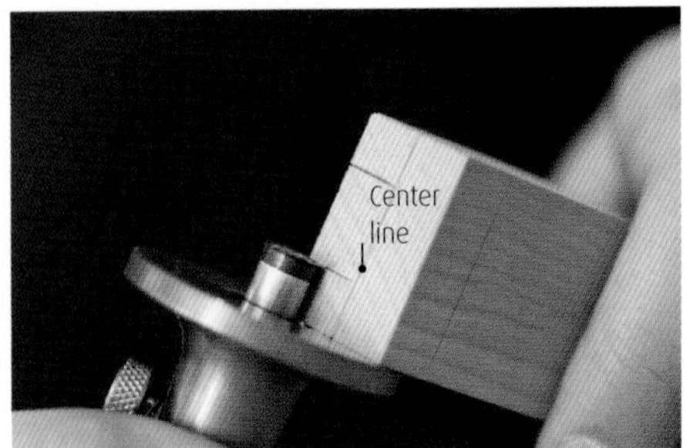

3 **Set the marking gauge** to 5⁄16in (8mm) and mark the end grain from each edge on one side of the center line.

4 **Using the hardwood angle** of a dovetail marker as a guide (see Dovetail markers, p.37), scribe the angle of the tails on the upper face of the upper front rail with a marking knife. Mark the waste with a pencil (inset). Repeat Steps 1–4 for the other end of the rail.

CUTTING THE TAILS IN THE UPPER FRONT RAIL

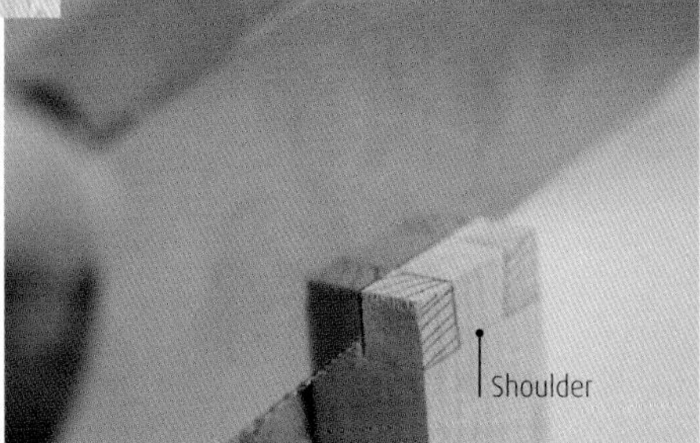

1 **Use a dovetail saw** to make a vertical cut to the shoulder along the center line of one end grain.

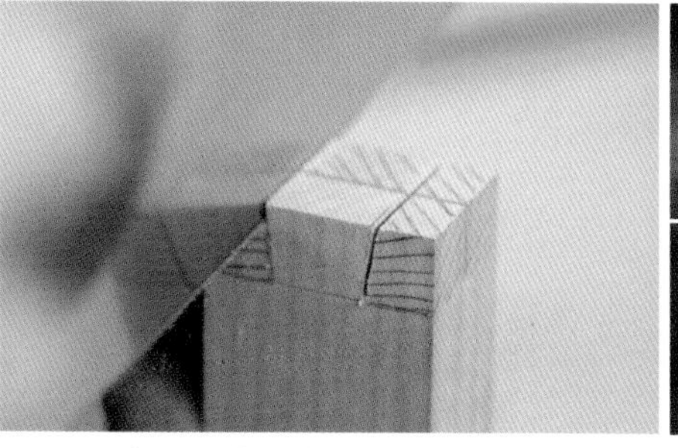

2 **Cut the angles** of the tail through the end grain to the shoulder. Be careful to cut to the waste side of the marks.

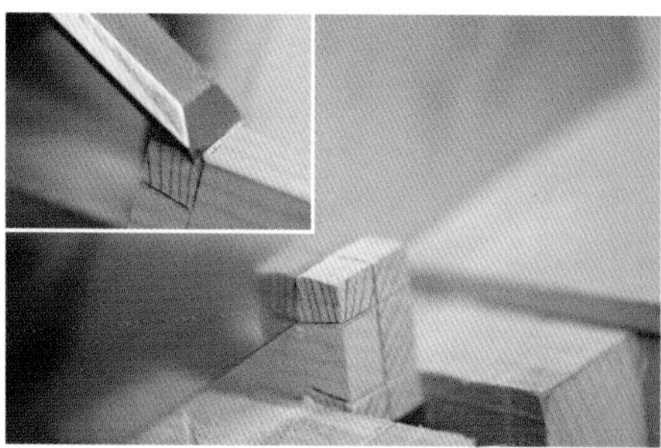

3 **Chisel a V-groove** along the shoulder mark (inset) to ensure a clean cut. Cross-cut from each edge to the shoulder mark.

4 **Make a final cross-cut** to remove the waste from the underside of the tail, then clean up the tail with a chisel (inset). Repeat Steps 1–4 for the other end grain.

MAKING THE FRONT LEG DOVETAIL SOCKETS

1 **Mark up and cut a socket** for the tails in each of the front legs. Set the tail at right angles over the top end grain of one leg with the upper front rail aligned to the front of the leg. Scribe around the tail on the end grain with a marking knife. Repeat on the other leg.

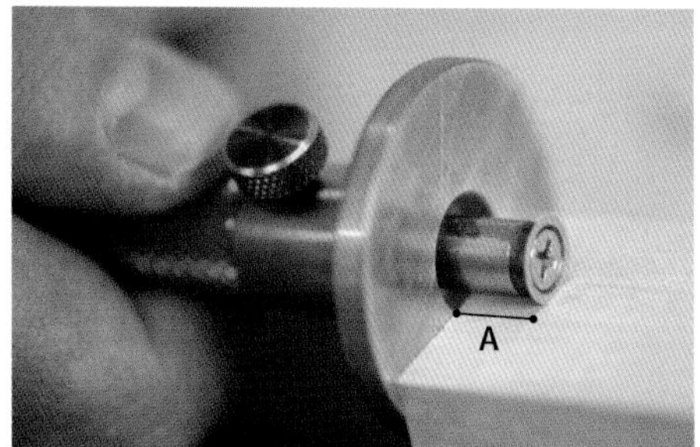

2 **Scribe the depth** of the socket (A)— ⅜in (10mm)—on the inside face of the leg.

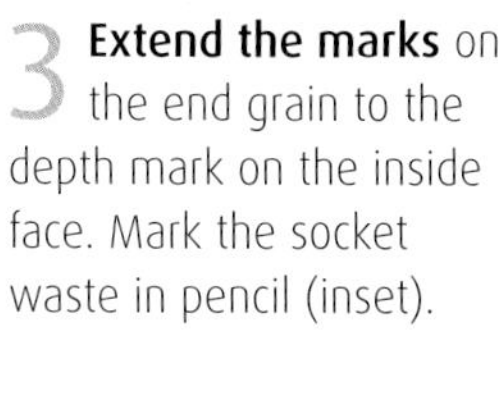

3 **Extend the marks** on the end grain to the depth mark on the inside face. Mark the socket waste in pencil (inset).

4 **Cut the sockets** with a dovetail saw. Start by making relief cuts into the socket waste.

5 **Remove the waste** all the way to the marks with a bevel-edged chisel of a suitable size.

6 **Check the fit** of each tail in its matching socket on the front legs. Adjust if necessary to achieve a tight fit.

MAKING THE SCREW SLOTS IN THE UPPER FRONT RAIL

1 **Draw two lines** on the top face of the upper front rail 5⁵⁄₁₆in (135mm) from each shoulder to mark the position of the two screw slots. Extend the marks across the full width of the face with a pencil and square.

2 **Using a drill** with a ³⁄₁₆in (4mm) bit, drill two holes through the rail approximately ³⁄₈in (10mm) apart.

3 **Countersink both holes** in each position on the rail.

4 **Using a chisel**, remove the waste between each of the pairs of drill holes to create two slots.

MAKING THE DRAWER RUNNERS AND KICKERS

1 **Using the same method**, cut two slots in each of the kickers the same distance from each end grain, with the slots running lengthways along the grain.

2 **Align a runner** along the bottom of the inside face of one of the side rail pieces and clamp in position. Drill three pilot holes approximately equidistant from each other into the rail. Countersink the holes and then screw in place. Repeat Steps 1–2 for the other runner and side rail.

3 **Join the kickers** to the top of the inner face of each of the side rails in the same way as the runners. Make sure that the countersunk slots are underneath.

4 **Drill two screw slots** as for the upper front rail in the rear kicker. Align the piece on the top inner face of the back rail. Drill and countersink three pilot holes through the kicker into the rail and insert screws.

5 **Test-fit the frame elements**. Make any necessary adjustments to the fit of the joints.

MAKING THE TABLE TOP

1 **Glue and clamp the pieces** for the table top (see Edge-to-edge joint, pp.94–95). Leave overnight to dry.

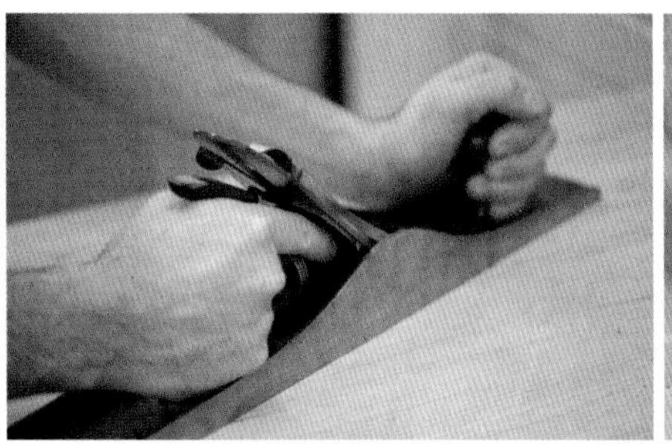

2 **Cut the table-top assembly** to size—23 13⁄16in (605mm) x 18 5⁄16in (465mm)—and plane flat with a bench plane.

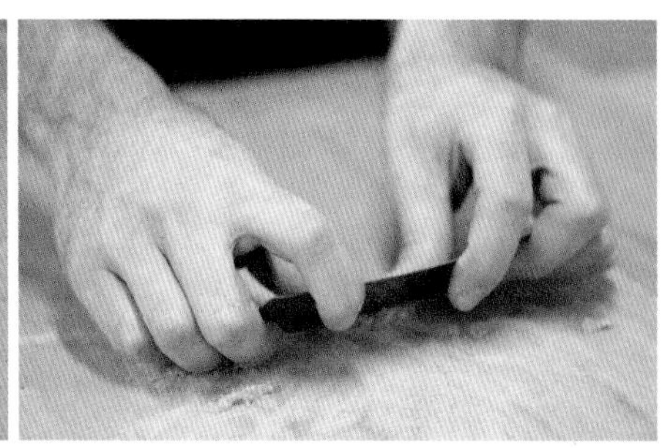

3 **Use a cabinet scraper** to achieve a perfectly smooth finish on the upper surface of the table top.

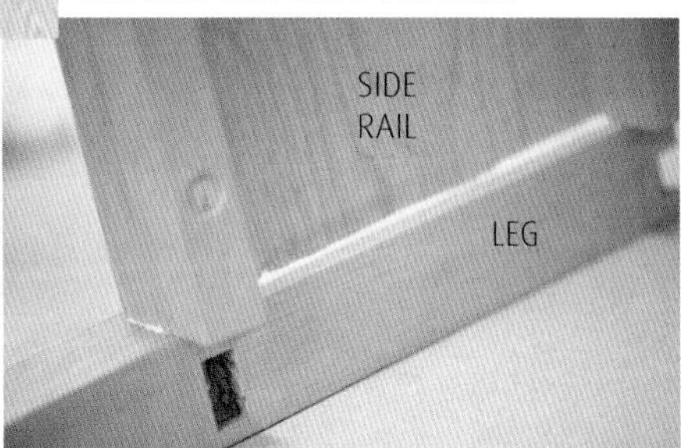

4 **Round off the top edge** of the table top with a router fitted with a bearing-guided round-over cutter. Sand it smooth.

GLUING THE SIDE FRAMES

1 **Glue and assemble the side rails** and legs to construct the two side frames of the piece.

2 **Clamp each side frame** with sash clamps, clean off any excess glue, then leave to dry. Once the glue has dried fully, fit the front and back rails to the side frames.

MAKING THE DRAWER FRONT

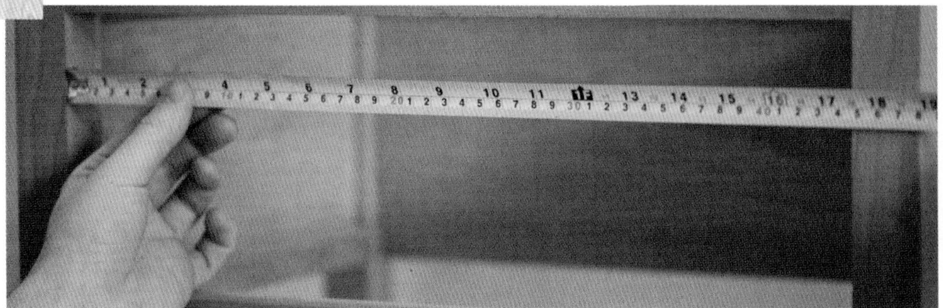

1 **Measure the aperture** in the frame for the drawer, then fine-tune the dimensions of the drawer front to fit.

2 **Check the fit** of the drawer front against the aperture. Ensure that the fit is snug (not loose) to allow for further adjustment.

MAKING THE DRAWER SIDE DOVETAILS

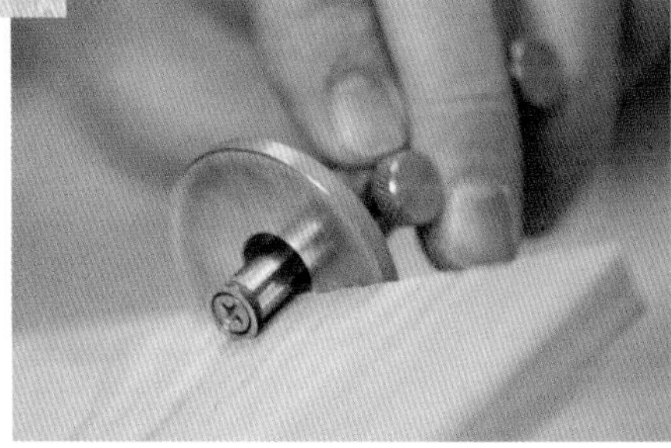

1 **The drawer front** and sides are joined with lapped dovetail joints (pp.138–39). Scribe a shoulder of ½in (12mm) at one end of each drawer side with a marking gauge.

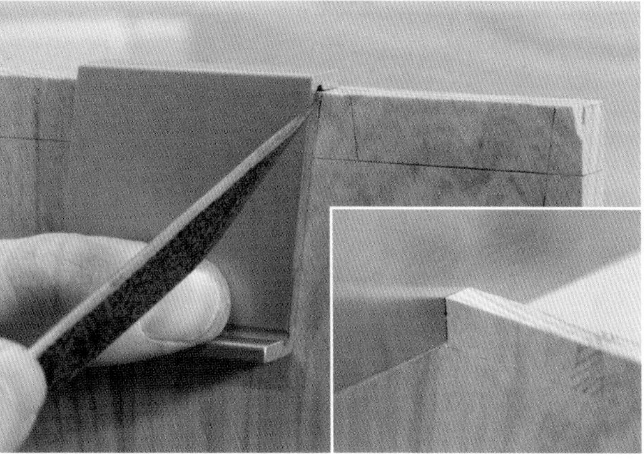

2 **Mark out three tails** on the end grain of the marked end of each drawer side. The end pins are ¼in (6mm) wide at the shoulder. Using a dovetail marker, extend the marks down the face to the shoulder, and cut the tails with a dovetail saw (inset).

MAKING THE DOVETAIL SOCKETS IN THE THE DRAWER FRONT

1 **Mark the depth** of the sockets in the drawer front by scribing the tail length—½in (12mm)—on the end grain.

2 **Mark the thickness** of the drawer side—⅜in (10mm)—on the inside face of the drawer front.

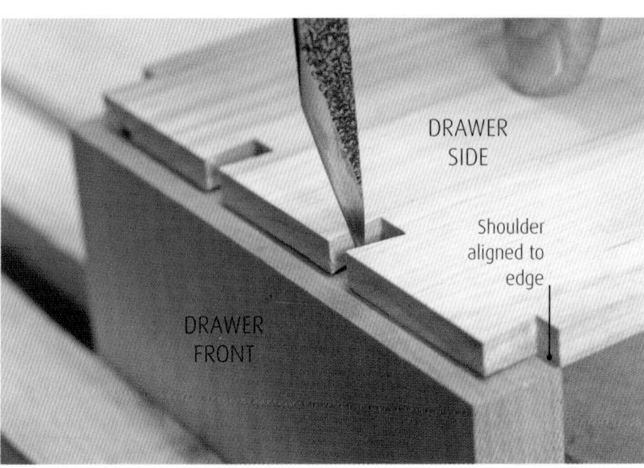

3 **Set the tails** of a drawer side at right angles to one end grain of the drawer front. Align the shoulder to the back edge of the end grain of the drawer front. Mark the position of the sockets by scribing around the tails with a marking knife.

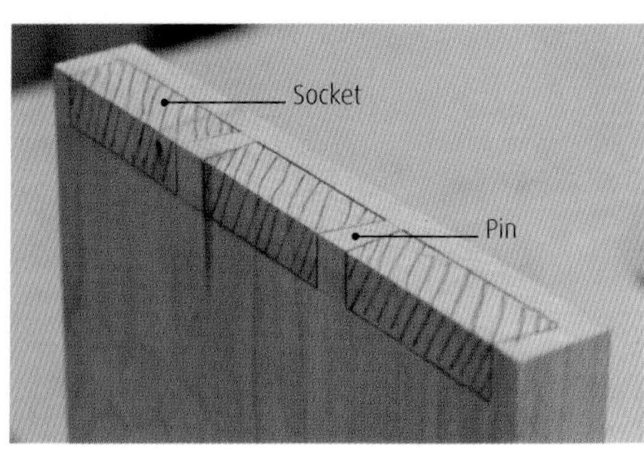

4 **Mark the sockets** on the other end grain of the drawer front in the same way, using the other drawer side as a guide.

5 **Cut the waste** from the sockets by making relief cuts with a tenon saw, then chopping and cleaning up with a chisel.

6 **Using a chisel**, chamfer the inner edges of the tails on each of the drawer sides to ease the fit in the sockets.

7 **Test the fit** of both of the lapped dovetails joining the drawer front and sides, and adjust if necessary.

MAKING THE GROOVES FOR THE DRAWER BASE

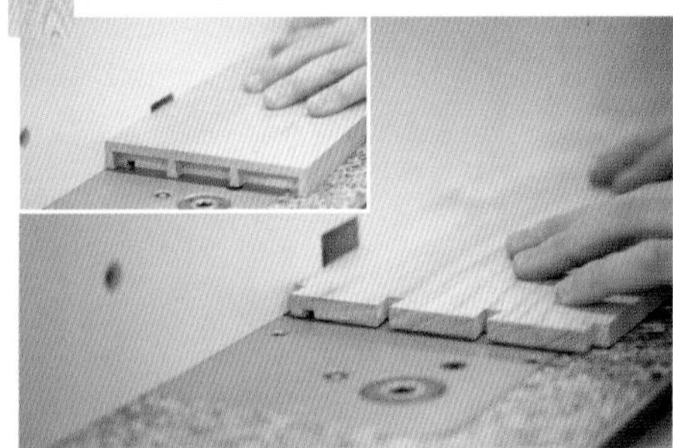

1 **Using a table-mounted router**, cut a groove ¼in (6mm) wide and $^{3}/_{16}$in (4mm) deep, 10mm (⅜in) from the bottom edge along the length of the inside of the drawer front (inset) and sides.

2 **Cut a groove** ¼in (6mm) wide and $^{3}/_{16}$in (5mm) deep 10mm (⅜in) from the back end grain of both drawer sides to, but not beyond, the groove along the bottom edge.

3 **Cut a rebate** along both end grains on the inside of the drawer back. Set the fence to $^{3}/_{16}$in (5mm) and cut to a depth of $^{3}/_{16}$in (4mm).

ASSEMBLING THE DRAWER

1 **Ease the fit** of the drawer base into the grooves by planing the edges with a block plane.

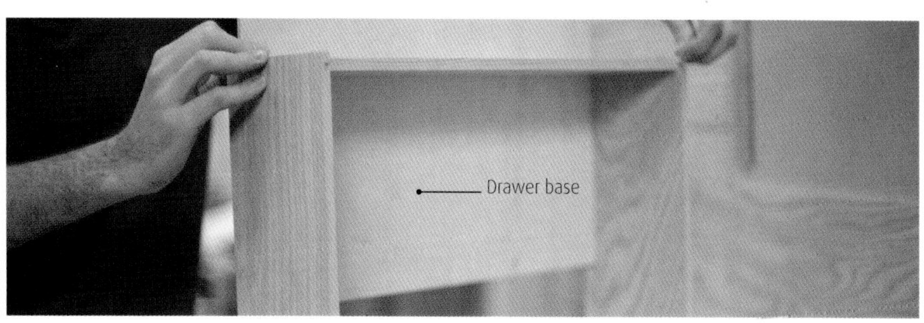

2 **Dry-fit the drawer assembly**, piecing together the sides and back first and then sliding in the base. Adjust if necessary.

3 **Glue the dovetails** and rebates of the drawer front, sides, and back, then assemble. Insert the base unglued and clamp. Leave to dry before progressing to Step 4.

4 **Fix the base** to the drawer back using one screw that passes through the center line of the base and into the edge of the drawer back (approximately ⅜in/10mm from the back edge of the base). Drill and countersink a hole, then use a screwdriver to insert the screw (inset).

FITTING THE DRAWER

1 **With the drawer clamped** in a vise, use a bench plane to cut the pins on each drawer side flush. Work on each side in turn.

2 **Use a block plane** to round off the back edges of the drawer to ease its fit within the carcass frame.

3 **Insert the assembled drawer** into the carcass frame to check the fit of each of the elements.

4 **Mark any areas** that require further planing with a pencil, then plane to fit (inset). Make two guides (see p.288) from pine, loosely position them on the runners, and test the fit of the drawer. Adjust the guides by planing thinner if necessary, then glue and clamp them into position. Leave to dry.

FITTING THE DRAWER KNOB

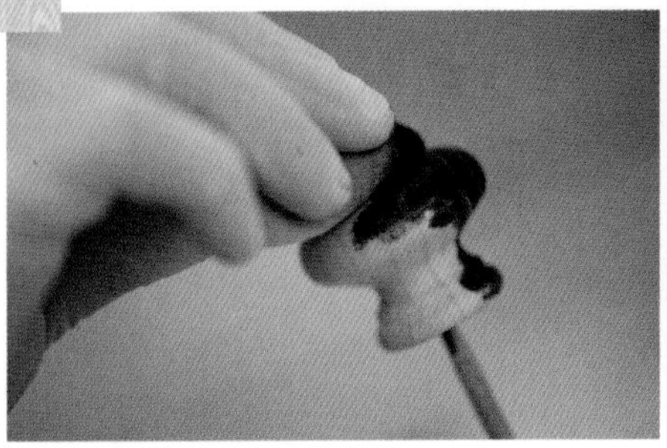

1 **Apply a dark stain** of your choice to the store-bought drawer knob. (See Staining, pp.166–67.)

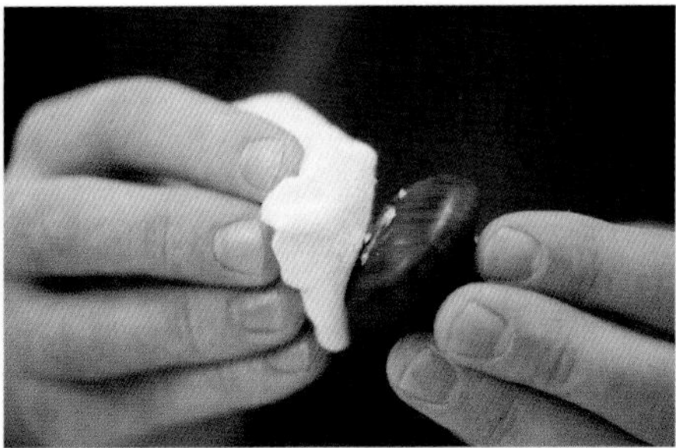

2 **Once the stain** has dried, apply wood wax with a clean cloth (see Applying wax, p.171) and leave to dry.

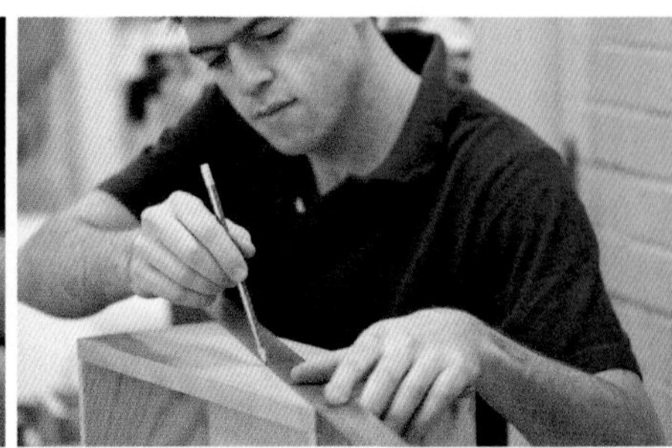

3 **Draw diagonal lines** across the drawer front from corner to corner. The point of intersection is the center: this is where the drawer knob will be positioned.

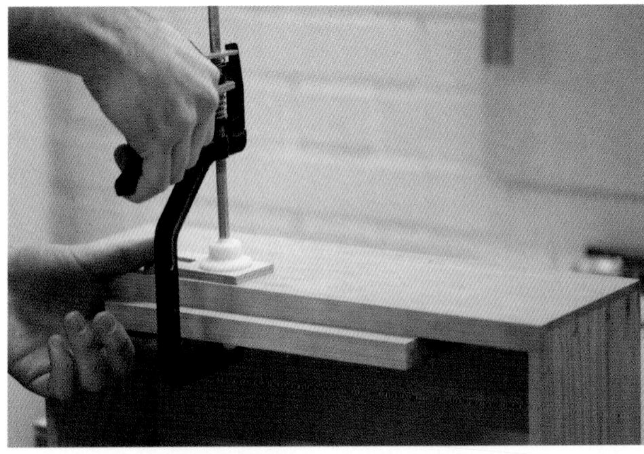

4 **Before you drill** the hole for the drawer knob, clamp a block of wood under the drawer front to prevent "break out" during drilling.

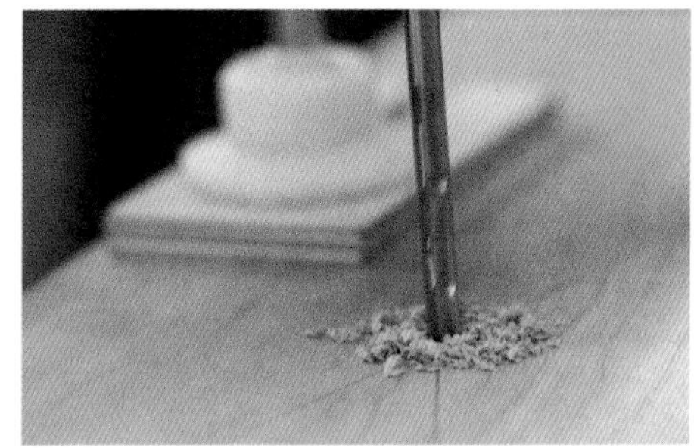

5 **Use a drill bit** slightly bigger than the gauge of the screw to drill the screw hole from the outside of the drawer front at the marked position.

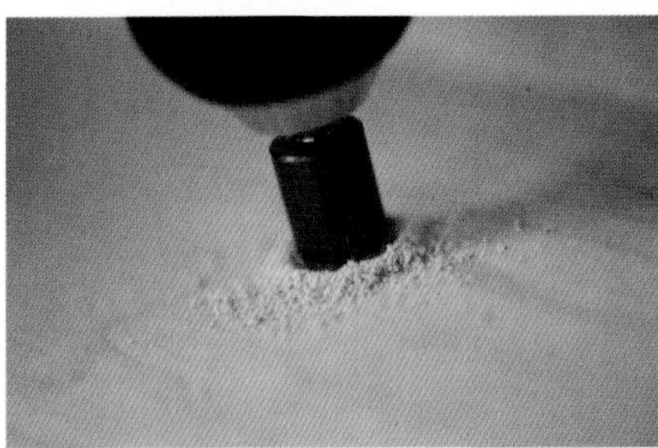

6 **On the inside face** of the drawer front, countersink the hole for the screw to secure the drawer knob.

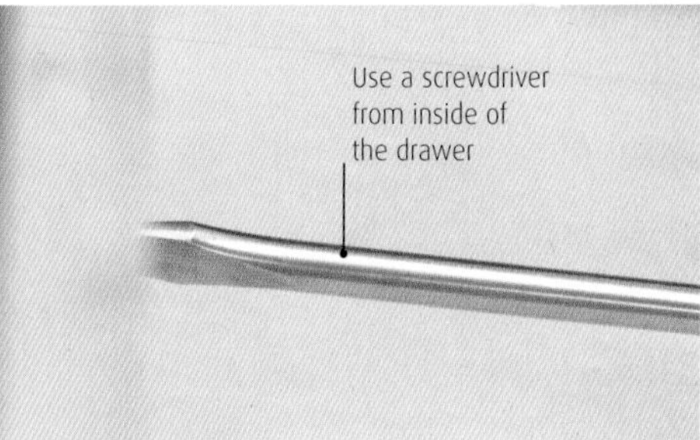

7 **Clean up the drawer front** by sanding it smooth, then screw the knob firmly into position.

FITTING THE TABLE TOP

1 **Position the carcass** upside down and centered on the underside of the table top. Use a bradawl to mark the position of the screw holes through each of the slots in the frame. Remove the frame and drill pilot holes into the underside of the table top at the marked positions, no deeper than half the thickness of the table top.

2 **Reposition the frame** over the table top and insert screws into each of the marked positions.

MAKING THE DRAWER STOPS AND FINISHING THE LEGS

1 **Measure the thickness** of the drawer front with a marking gauge, then scribe that measurement along the top edge of the lower front rail from the outer face.

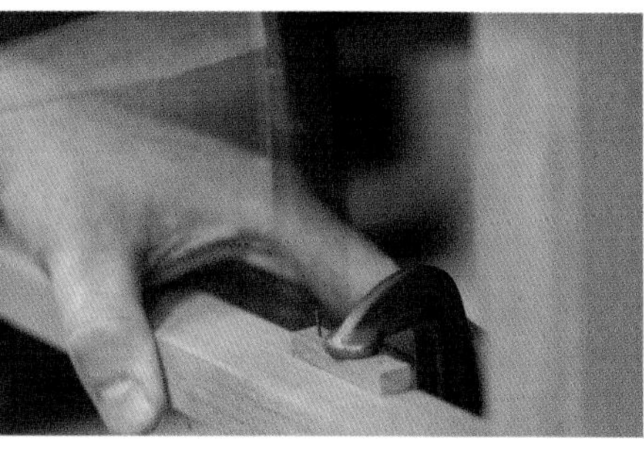

2 **Using a hammer**, pin two small blocks (offcuts) to the back edge of the lower front rail aligned to the scribed line. These will serve as drawer stops.

3 **Finish the piece** by filing the bottom edges of the legs smooth—this will prevent splitting of the wood.

DETAIL OF THE LAPPED DOVETAIL

DETAIL OF THE DRAWER KNOB

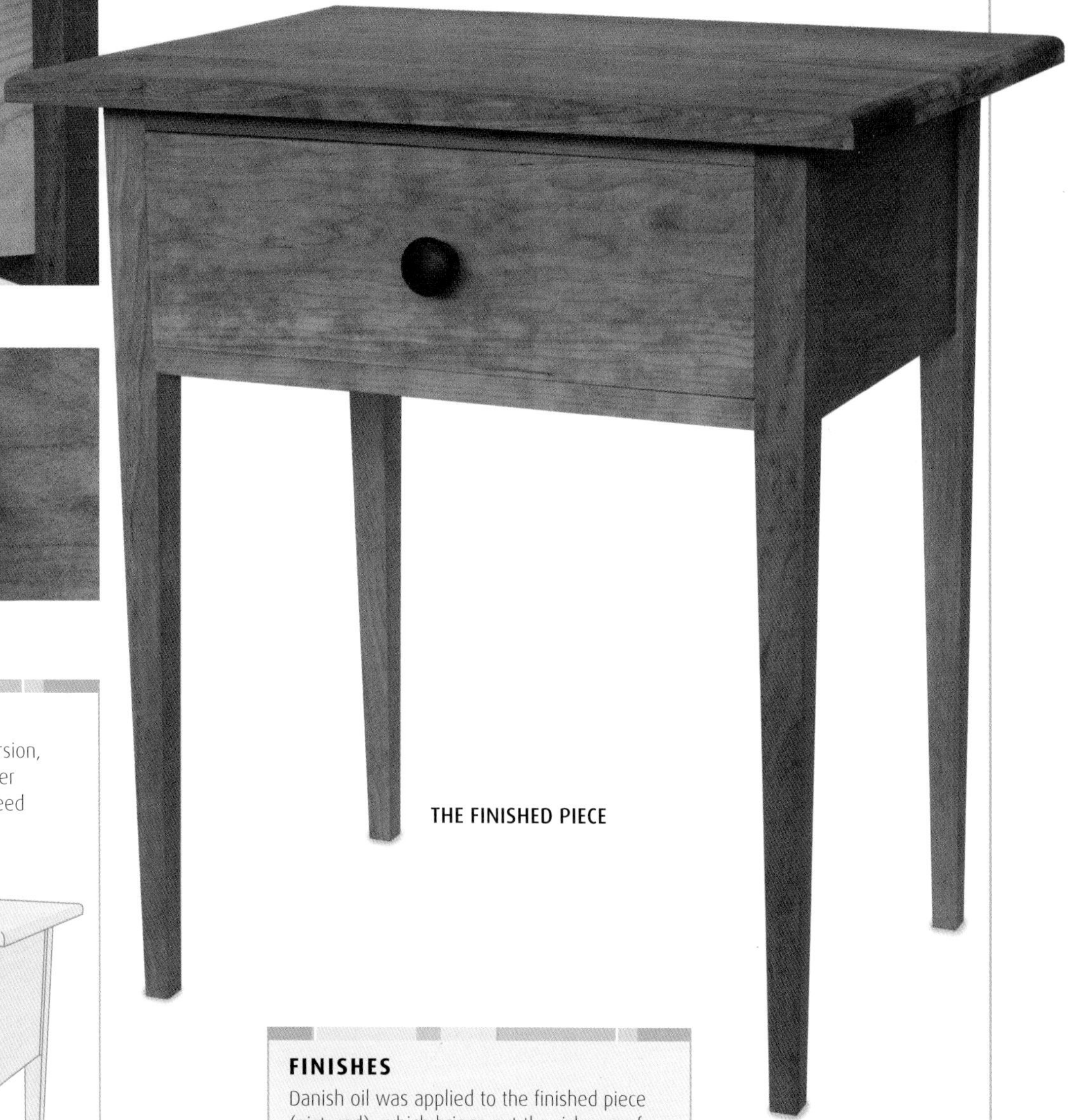

TWO-DRAWER DESIGN

If you want to make a two-drawer version, simply insert a dividing rail and another set of drawer runners. You will also need to increase the size of the side rail to accommodate the additional drawer.

THE FINISHED PIECE

FINISHES

Danish oil was applied to the finished piece (pictured), which brings out the richness of the cherry and provides a good protective layer. If you want to give the piece a deeper shine, apply a few coats of clear wax and buff to a high finish.

Linen chest

A linen chest is a versatile piece of furniture that provides useful storage space and can also double up as a low table. The frame-and-panel design has a traditional look. Floating (rather than glued) panels allow the timber to expand and contract, and the sides protrude from the frame, adding visual bulk. A wax or oil finish will retain the natural appearance of the wood.

Dimensions:
33 7/8 x 18 1/8 x 17 11/16in (860 x 460 x 450mm)

Key techniques:
Basic mortise-and-tenon joint (pp.116–19)
Edge-to-edge joint (pp.94–95)

TOOLS AND MATERIALS

- Pencil
- Ruler
- Combination square
- Mortise gauge
- Mortiser and 3/8in (10mm) bit or 3/8in (10mm) mortise chisel
- Router and 1/4in (6mm) straight router cutter, 45-degree router cutter, and bearing-guided chamfer cutter
- Marking gauge
- Band saw
- Tenon saw
- Bevel-edged chisel (optional)
- Measuring tape
- Router table (optional)
- Rubber mallet
- Sash clamps
- Wood glue and brush
- 2 "Soss 204" concealed hinges and screws
- Drill with bits
- Bench plane
- Spokeshave
- File
- Screwdriver

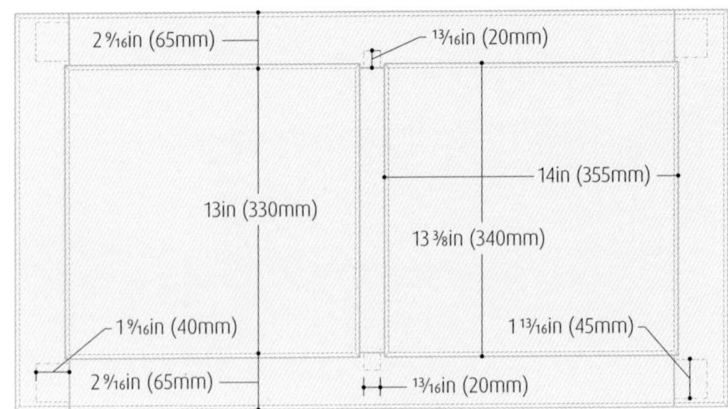

TOP VIEW (1:10)

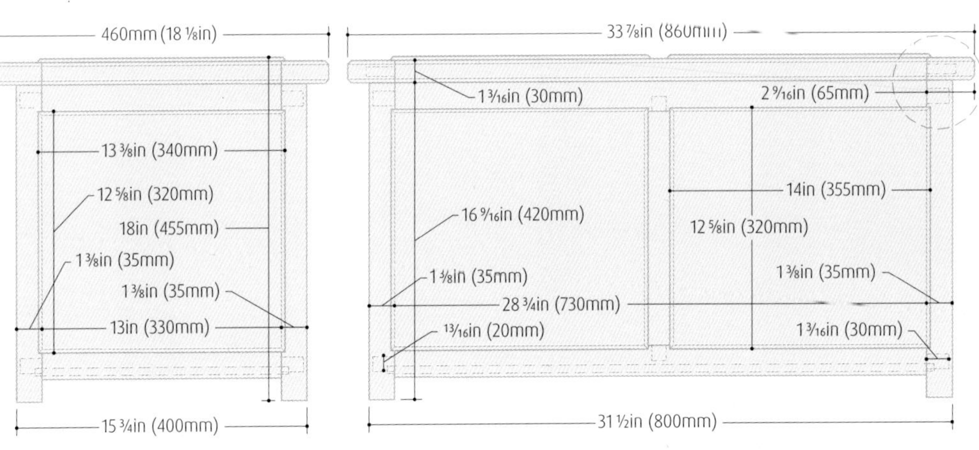

SIDE VIEW (1:10)

FRONT VIEW (1:10)

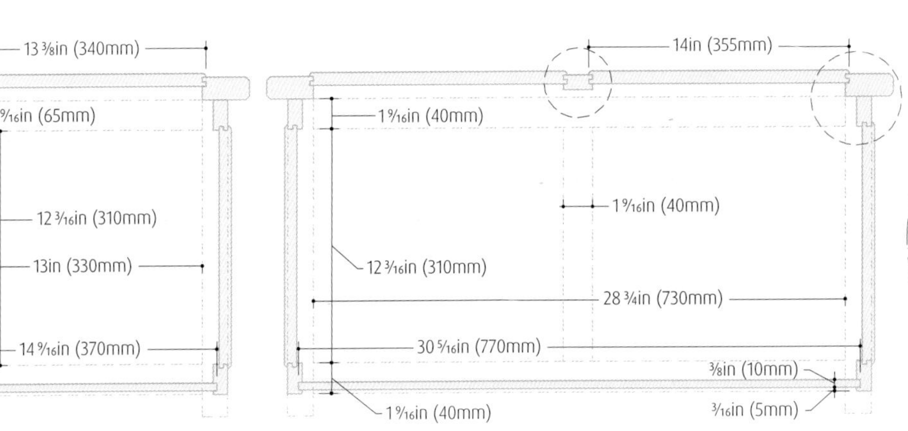

SIDE CROSS SECTION (1:10)

FRONT CROSS SECTION (1:10)

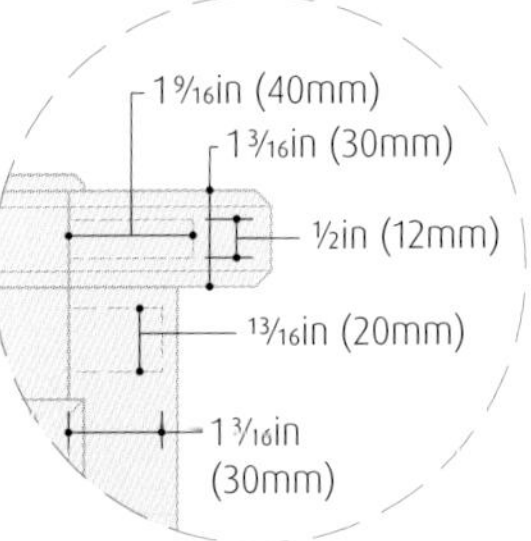

CROSS SECTION OF TOP CORNER DETAIL (1:5)

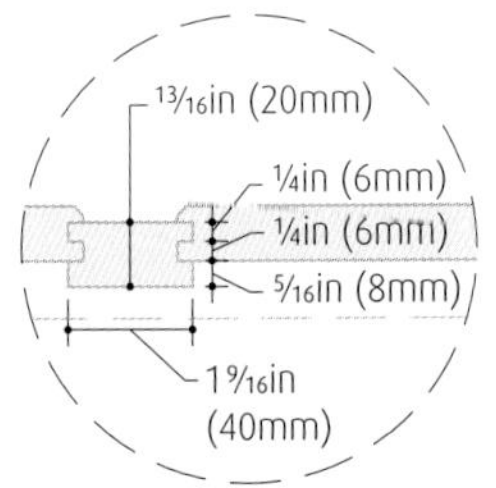

CROSS SECTION OF LID MUNTIN DETAIL (1:5)

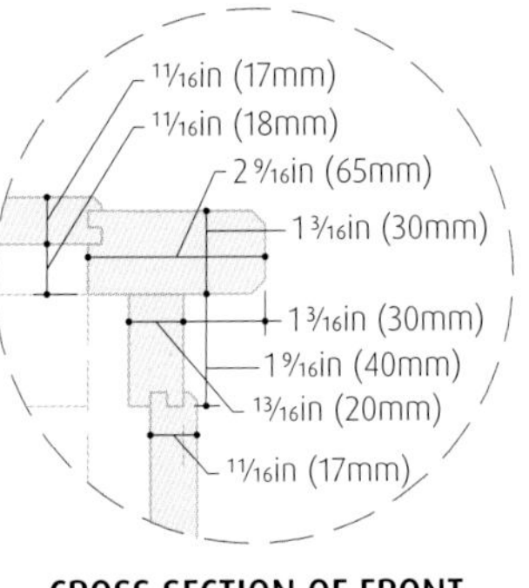

CROSS SECTION OF FRONT CORNER DETAIL (1:5)

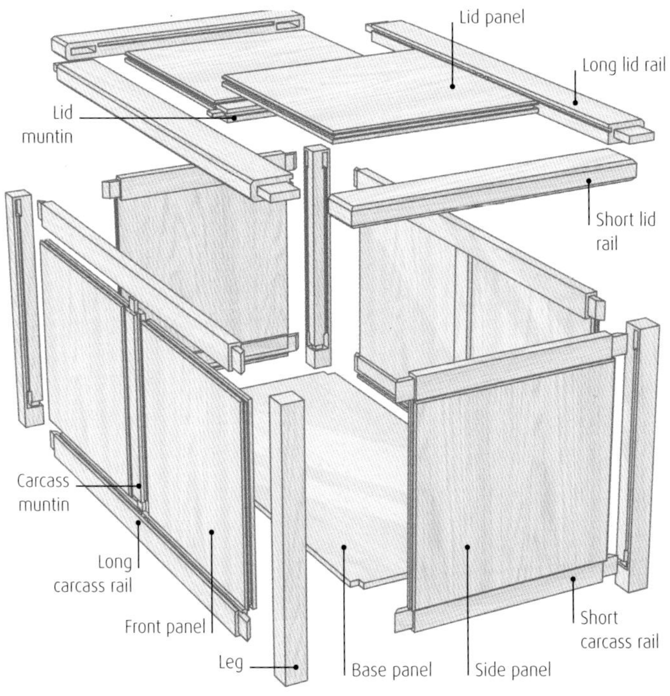

How the elements fit together
The dual panels on the lid and both of the long sides are separated by a central rail known as a "muntin." The lid, fitted with concealed hinges, overhangs the carcass.

CUTTING LIST

Item	Material	No.	Length	Width	Thickness
Carcass					
Legs	Oak	4	16 9⁄16in (420mm)	1 3⁄8in (35mm)	1 3⁄8in (35mm)
Long rails	Oak	4	31 1⁄8in (790mm)	1 9⁄16in (40mm)	13⁄16in (20mm)
Short rails	Oak	4	15 3⁄8in (390mm)	1 9⁄16in (40mm)	13⁄16in (20mm)
Muntins	Oak	2	13 3⁄4in (350mm)	1 9⁄16in (40mm)	13⁄16in (20mm)
Front and back panels	Oak	12	15 3⁄8in* (390mm)	5 1⁄8in* (130mm)	11⁄16in (17mm)
Side panels	Oak	6	15 3⁄8in* (390mm)	5 1⁄8in* (130mm)	11⁄16in (17mm)
Base panel	Oak-faced ply	1	30 5⁄16in (770mm)	14 9⁄16in (370mm)	1⁄4in (6mm)
Lid					
Long rails	Oak	2	32 7⁄8in (810mm)	2 9⁄16in (65mm)	1 3⁄16in (30mm)
Short rails	Oak	2	16 1⁄8in (410mm)	2 9⁄16in (65mm)	1 3⁄16in (30mm)
Muntin	Oak	1	14 9⁄16in (370mm)	1 9⁄16in (40mm)	13⁄16in (20mm)
Panels	Oak	6	15 3⁄8in* (390mm)	5 1⁄8in* (130mm)	11⁄16in (17mm)

*Includes excess to allow for cutting to size

MAKING THE MORTISES AND GROOVES IN THE LEGS

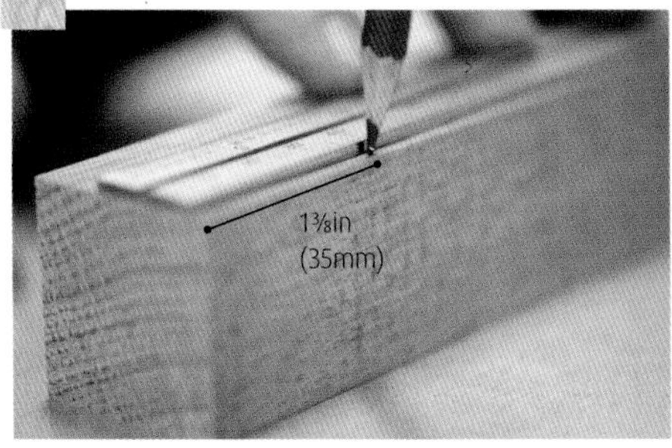

1 **Mark the position** of the lower mortise on the inside edge 1 3⁄8in (35mm) from the end grain of the first leg. Repeat on the other three legs.

2 **For each leg**, mark the mortise length (13⁄16in/20mm). Square the marks across two sides. Mark the mortises 3⁄8in (10mm) from the other end of the leg in the same way.

3 **Set the mortise gauge** to a width of 3⁄8in (10mm) to match the size of the mortise bit (pictured) or the width of the chisel to be used.

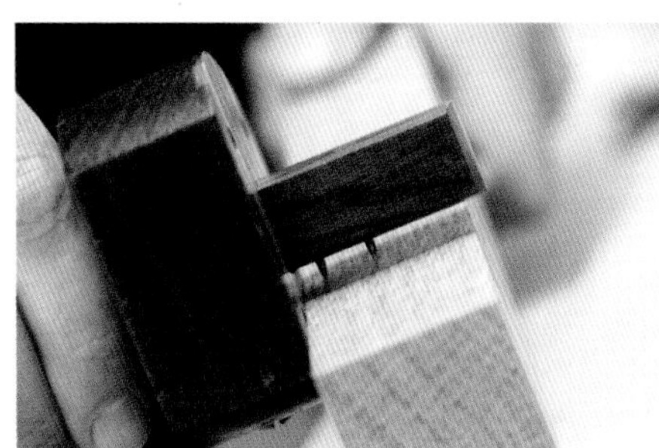

4 **Scribe the width** of all four mortises 3⁄16in (5mm) from the outer edge onto the inside edge of each leg piece.

5 **Cut the mortises** to a depth of 1 3⁄16in (30mm). Use a mortiser (pictured) or cut the mortise by hand with a mortise chisel (see p.117).

6 **Use a router** fitted with a 1⁄4in (6mm) cutter to cut a groove for the panels in each leg between the upper and lower mortises. Set the depth of cut to 5⁄16in (8mm) and the router fence to 1⁄4in (6mm).

CUTTING THE TENONS AND GROOVES IN THE CARCASS RAILS

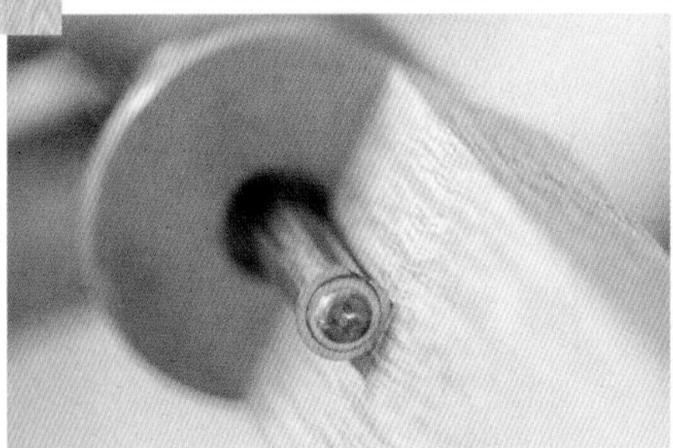

1 **Scribe two lines** 1³⁄₁₆in (30mm) from both ends of each carcass rail to mark the length of the tenons. (There are eight carcass rails—two for each of the chest's four sides.)

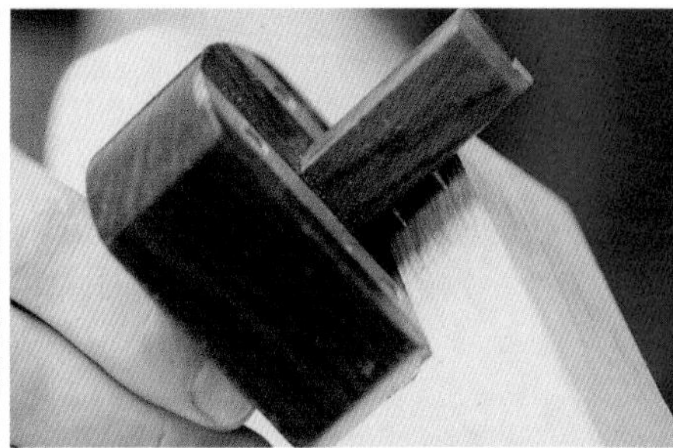

2 **Using the mortise gauge** as previously set at ³⁄₈in (10mm), mark the thickness of each tenon on both edges and the end grain of the eight carcass rail pieces.

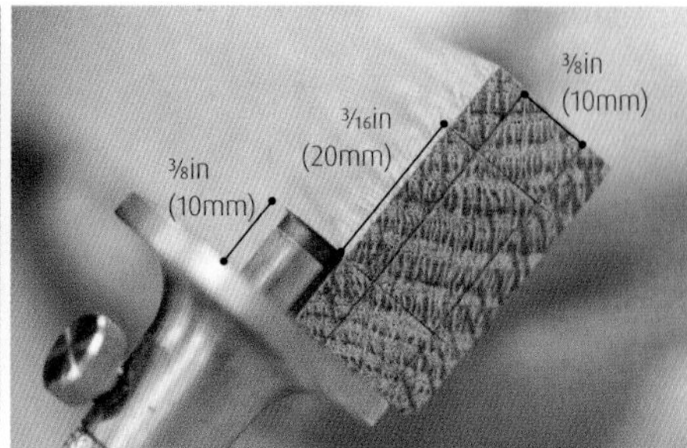

3 **Mark the tenon width**— ¹³⁄₁₆in (20mm)—with the marking gauge set to ³⁄₈in (10mm) across both faces to the shoulder and across each end grain.

4 **Cut the tenons** using a band saw (pictured) or with a tenon saw. Cut the cheeks first, then the shoulders.

5 **Use a combination square** to mark a 45-degree angle on the end of each tenon. The marked angle on the pair of tenons on each carcass rail should face the same way (inward). Continue the lines around the tenons and then cut with a tenon saw (inset).

6 **Check the fit** of the tenons of the carcass rail in the leg mortises. Square up the shoulders of the tenons with a bevel-edged chisel if necessary.

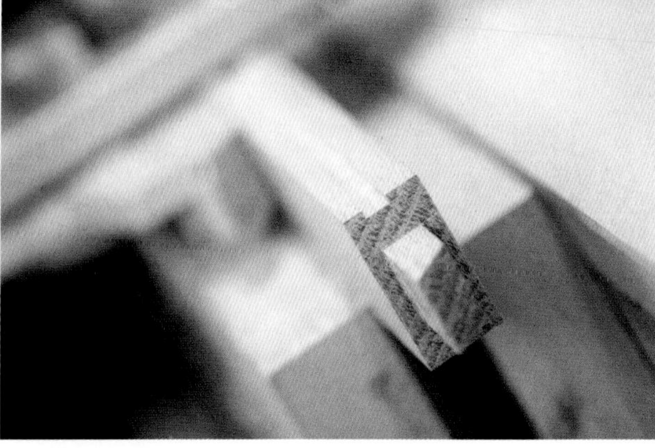

7 **Cut a groove** along one edge of each carcass rail with the router. For the four top carcass-rails, cut the groove in the lower edge, and for the four lower carcass-rails, in the upper edge. Set the router as it was for cutting the groove in the legs (see Step 6, p.301).

MAKING THE MORTISES IN THE LONG CARCASS RAILS

1 **Mark a mortise** ¹³⁄₁₆in (20mm) long half-way along the grooved edge of each of the four long carcass-rails. Measure 14in (355mm) from each tenon shoulder and extend the marks across the edge.

2 **Using the mortise gauge** as previously set at ³⁄₈in (10mm), scribe the mortise width within the two length marks, with the fence set to the side closest to the groove.

3 **Cut the mortises** in each carcass rail to a depth of ¹³⁄₁₆in (20mm), using a mortiser (pictured) or a mortise chisel.

MAKING THE CARCASS MUNTINS

1 **Use a marking gauge** set to 13⁄16in (20mm) to scribe the length of the tenons. Extend the marks around each face of both ends of the two carcass muntins.

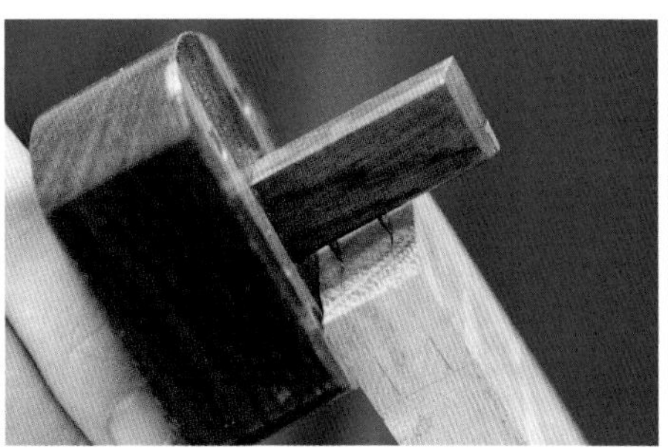

2 **Mark the thickness** of the tenons around the edges and the end grains of both carcass muntins, using the mortise gauge as previously set.

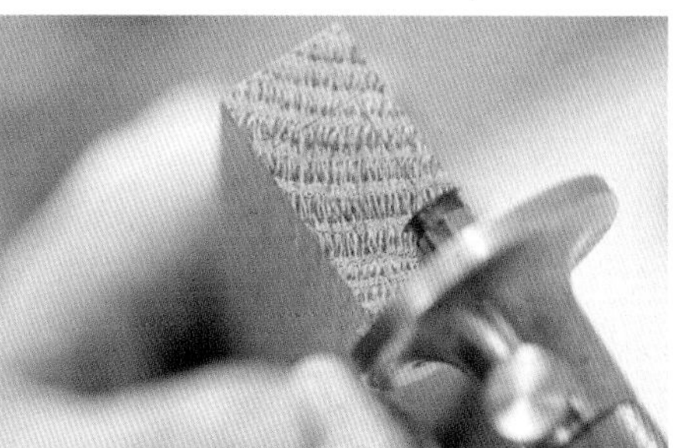

3 **Mark the width** of the tenons on the end grains. Set the marking gauge to 3⁄8in (10mm) and scribe across the width from each edge of both end grains.

4 **Cut all four tenons** on the two carcass muntins, using a band saw (pictured) or with a tenon saw.

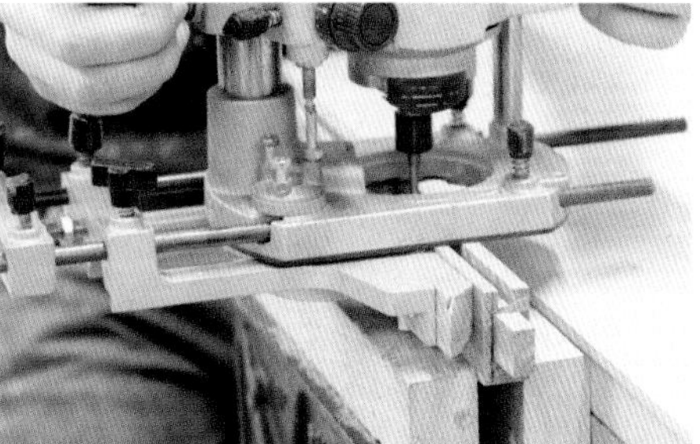

5 **Cut a groove** along both edges of both carcass muntins, using the router as previously set (see Step 6, p.301). Be careful to run the router off the same face on both edges.

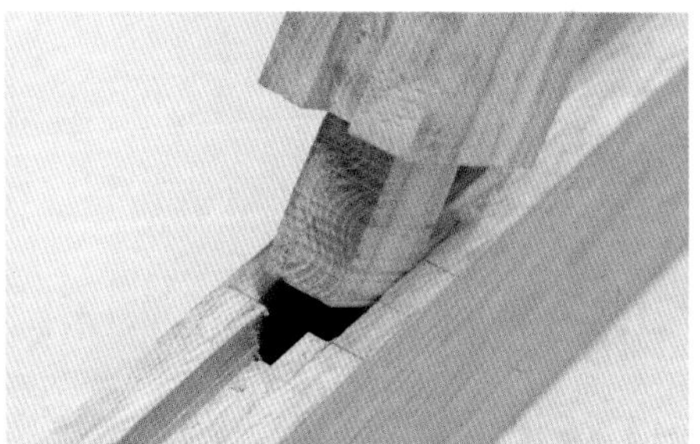

6 **Test the fit** of the carcass-muntin tenons in the mortises of the long carcass rails. Make any necessary adjustments.

MAKING THE GROOVES AND NOTCHES FOR THE BASE

1 **Fit a 3⁄8in (10mm) cutter** in the router and set the fence and depth to 3⁄16in (5mm). Cut a groove along the bottom edge of all the lower carcass rails.

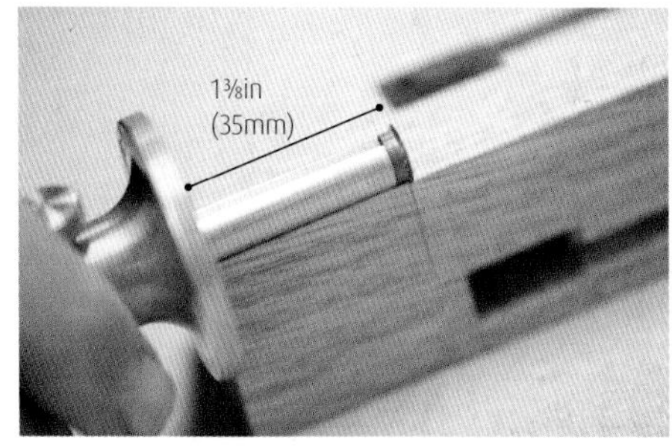

2 **Mark the position** of a notch in the inner corner of each leg 1⅜in (35mm) from the bottom of the leg on the two faces between the two mortises.

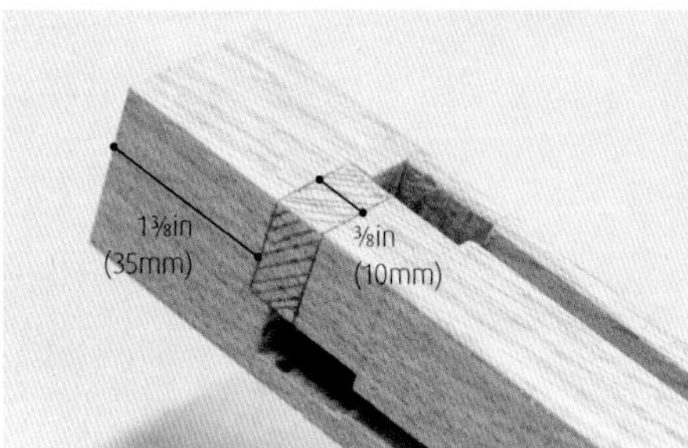

3 **Scribe a second line** 3⁄8in (10mm) from the first, then use a pencil to mark the waste for removal.

4 **Cut the notch** to a depth of 3⁄16in (5mm) with a mortiser (or a mortise chisel). Repeat on all leg pieces.

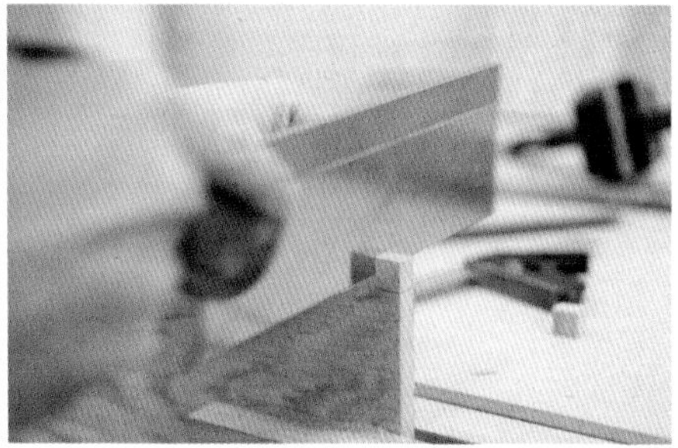

5 **Cut a ½in (13mm) square** from each corner of the base piece to fit around the corners of the legs.

MAKING THE MORTISES IN THE SHORT LID RAILS

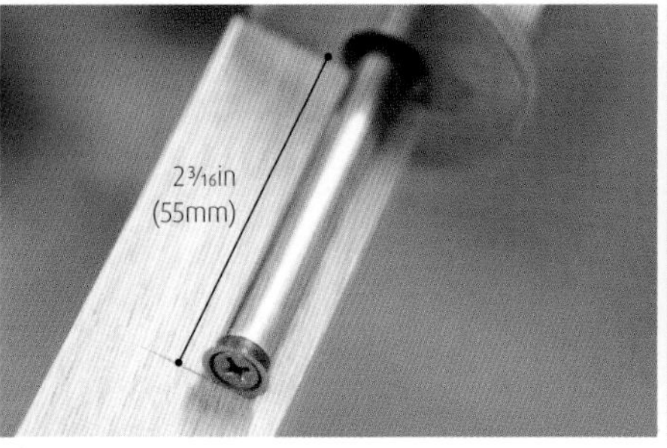

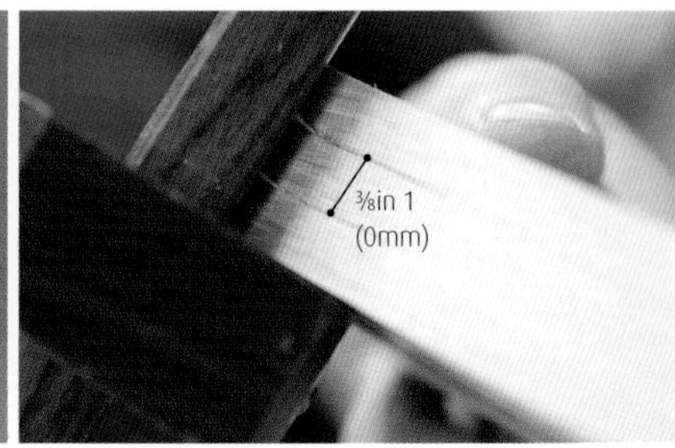

1 **With the lid rails cut to length**, make mortises in the two short lid-rails. Mark the start of the mortises on the edge ⅜in (10mm) from each end grain of both short lid-rail pieces.

2 **Make a second mark** 2³⁄₁₆in (55mm) from each end grain to define a mortise length of 1¾in (45mm).

3 **Using the mortise gauge** set to ⅜in (10mm), scribe the mortise width centrally between the marks.

4 **Cut the mortises** to a depth of 1⁹⁄₁₆in (40mm) using a mortiser fitted with a ⅜in (10mm) bit (shown), or a mortise chisel.

MAKING THE TENONS IN THE LONG LID-RAILS

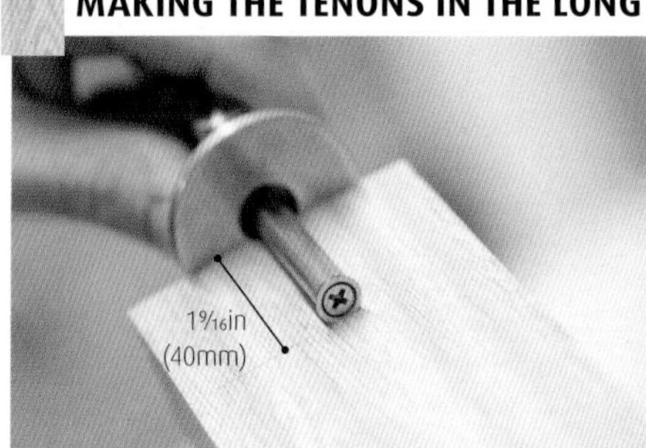

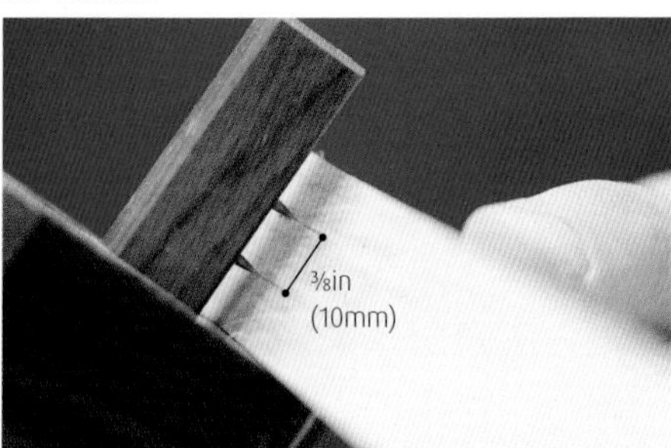

1 **Mark the tenon shoulder** 1⁹⁄₁₆in (40mm) from each end of both long lid-rails. Extend the line around all four faces and edges.

2 **Using the mortise gauge** as previously set, scribe the tenon thickness around the edges and end grain.

3 **Mark the tenon width** on the end grain using a marking gauge set to ⅜in (10mm).

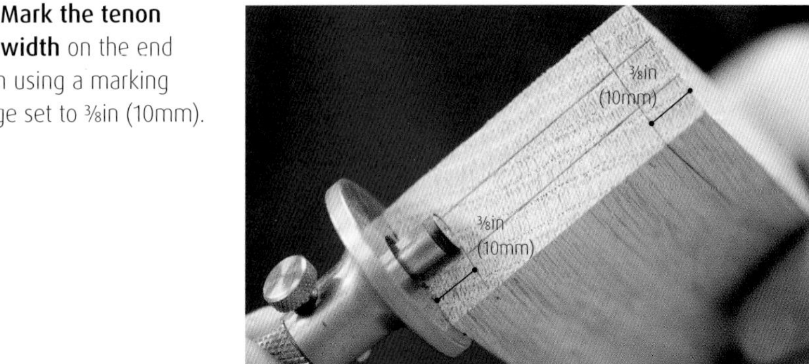

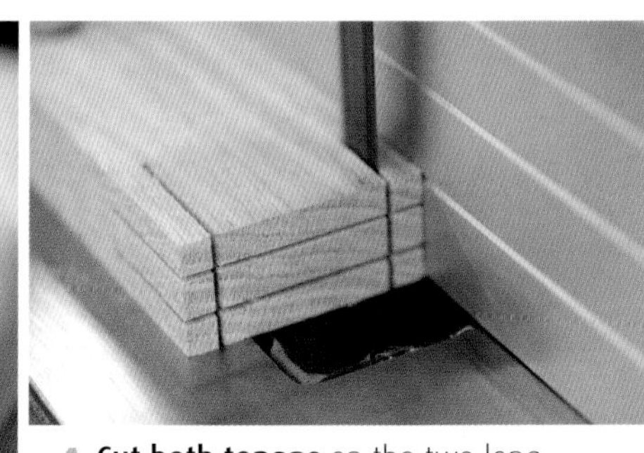

4 **Cut both tenons** on the two long lid-rails using a band saw (pictured), or by hand with a tenon saw.

CUTTING THE GROOVES IN THE LID RAILS

1 **Cut a groove** to accommodate the panels in all four lid rails. Use the router with the fence and cutter set to ¼in (6mm), and the depth set to ⁵⁄₁₆in (8mm). Cut the groove in the short lid-rails in the same edge as the mortises and, for ease of assembly, continue the groove ⅜in (10mm) into each mortise.

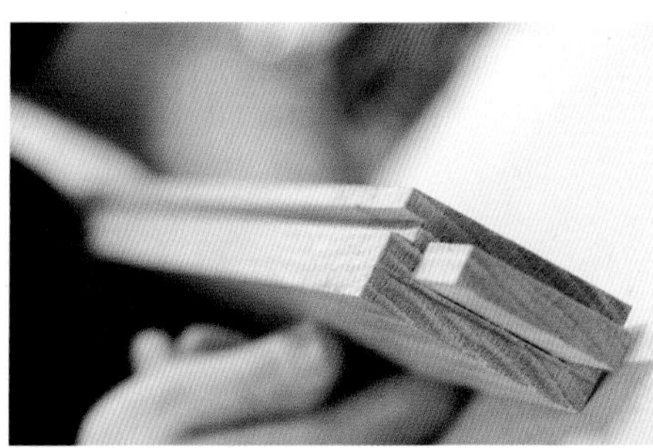

2 **In each of the long lid-rails**, cut the groove along the full length of one edge, extending into the shoulder of the tenon. Use the router as previously set.

CUTTING THE CENTRAL MORTISE IN THE LONG LID-RAILS

1 **Using the mortise gauge** as previously set (width: 3/8in/10mm; fence: 3/8in/10mm), mark the mortise in the center of each of the long rails. Mark the length of the mortise at 13/16in (20mm).

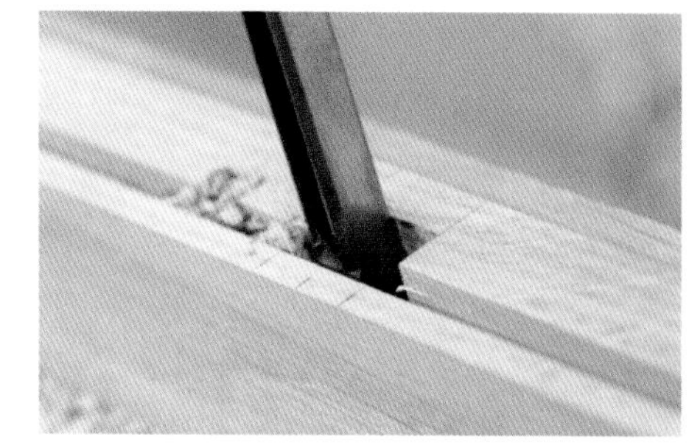

2 **Cut the mortise** in the marked position to a depth of 13/16in (20mm). Use a mortiser (pictured) or cut it by hand with a mortise chisel.

MAKING THE LID MUNTIN

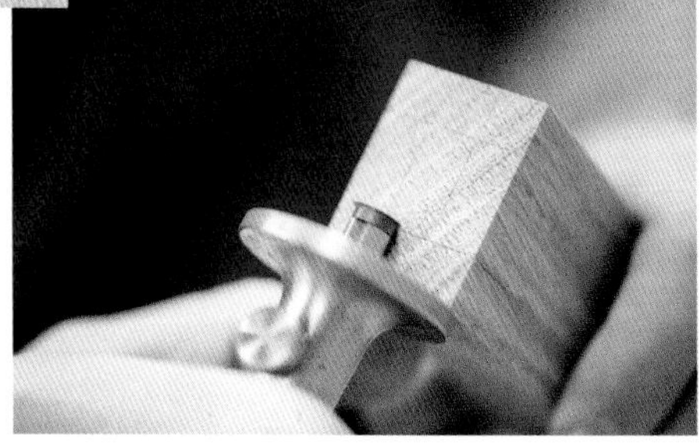

1 **Mark up a tenon** at each end of the lid muntin to a length and width of 13/16in (20mm) and a thickness of 3/8in (10mm).

2 **Cut the tenons** in each end of the lid muntin, either by hand with a tenon saw, or on a band saw (pictured).

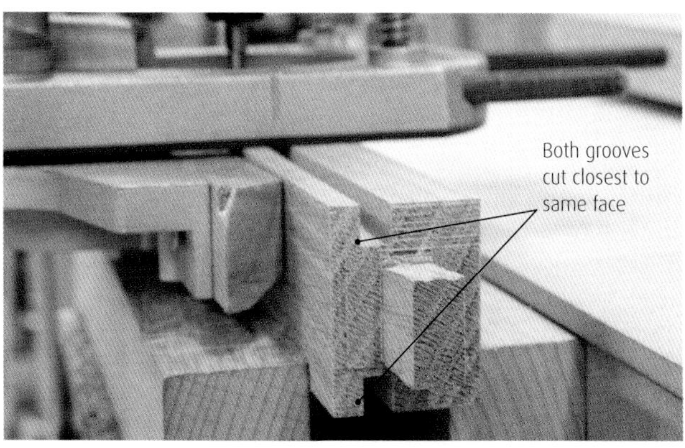

3 **Using the router** as previously set, cut a groove along the full length of both edges of the lid muntin. Run the router off the same face on both sides.

4 **Test-assemble the lid frame** to check the fit of the joints, particularly that of the lid and the long lid-rail mortises (inset).

MAKING THE PANELS

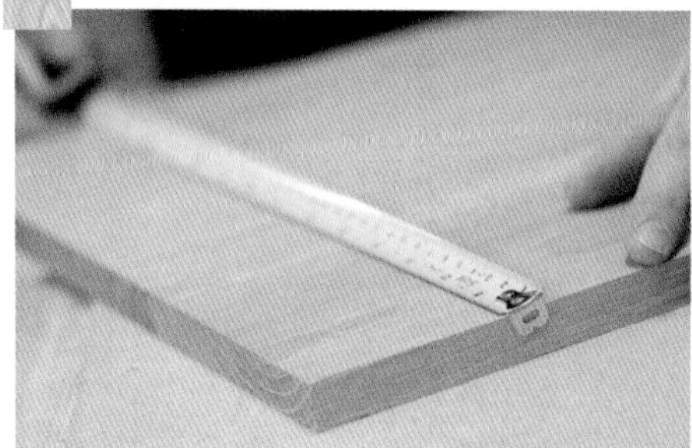

1 **Join three boards** for each side panel and the front, back, and lid panels (see Edge-to-edge joint, pp.94–95). Use a band saw to cut the panels: sides—13 3/8 x 12 5/8in (340 x 320mm); front and back—14 x 12 5/8in (355 x 320mm); lid—13 3/8 x 14in (340 x 355mm).

2 **Cut a 1/4in (6mm) groove** in all four edges of each panel. A table-mounted router is the best tool for the job, but a hand-held router can also be used (see pp.46–49). Set the fence 1/4in (6mm) from the inside face of each panel.

3 **Chamfer all four outside edges** of each panel using a bearing-guided chamfer cutter fitted to a table-mounted router.

ASSEMBLING THE CARCASS

1 **Before gluing the pieces**, test-assemble the carcass of the chest to check the fit. Make any adjustments that may be necessary. Dismantle the frame in order to insert the panels (see Step 2).

2 **Use a rubber mallet** to tap the panels into the grooves on the rails and muntins of the carcass and lid, with the chamfered edges on the outside.

3 **Slide the base** into the grooves on the lower carcass-rails, and adjust the grooves with a chisel if necessary.

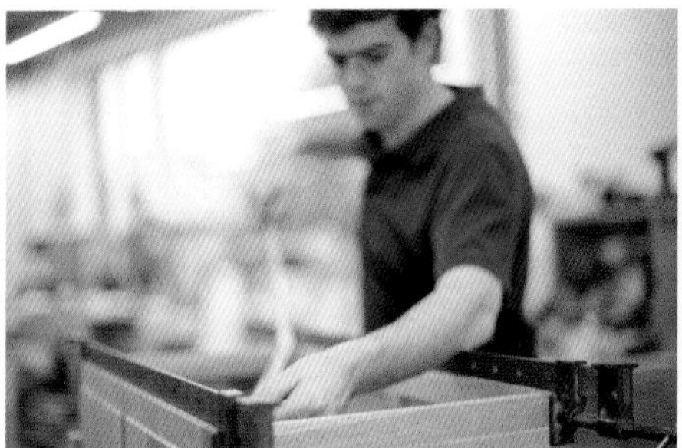

4 **When all elements** of the lid and carcass are correctly fitted, check for squareness (see p.75), then dismantle.

5 **Glue all mortises** and tenons of the lid frames and carcass. Do not glue the base or panels. Assemble, clamp, and allow to dry.

FITTING THE HINGES

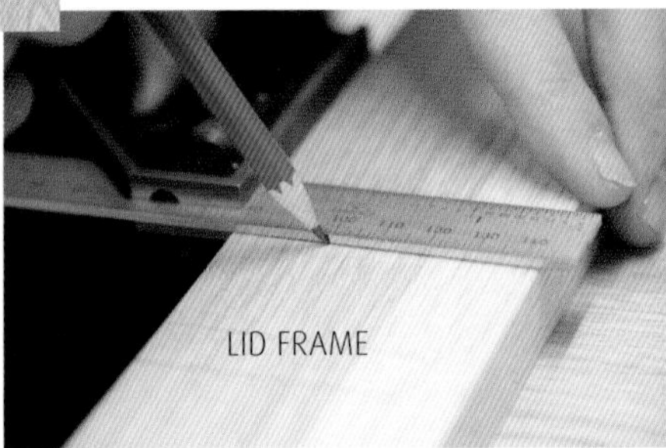

1 **Mark up two mortises** to fit the hinges 4¾in (120mm) from each end of the underside of the back long-lid-rail. Make sure the lid overhangs the frame by 1³⁄₁₆in (30mm) on all sides. Mark matching mortises on the back edge of the carcass frame.

2 **Cut the mortises** in the marked positions in the lid with a router fitted with a bit of the appropriate size (inset) or with a mortise chisel. Clamp an offcut at each end of the desired cut to restrict the router path and prevent it from overcutting.

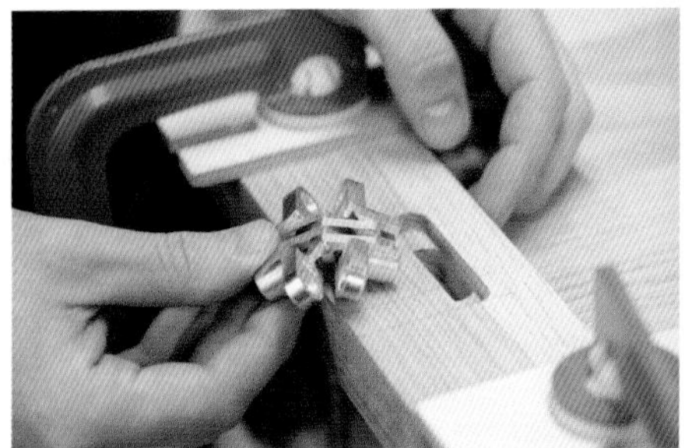

3 **Check the fit** of the hinges in the mortises and adjust with a mortise chisel if necessary.

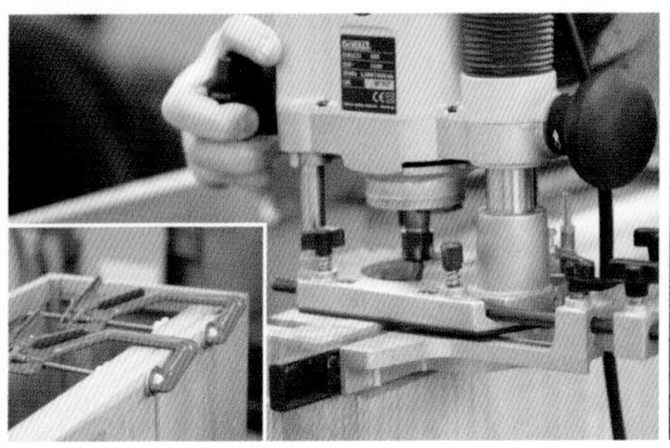

4 **Clamp an additional piece** of wood to the carcass to support the router (inset). Cut the mortises in the carcass with the router.

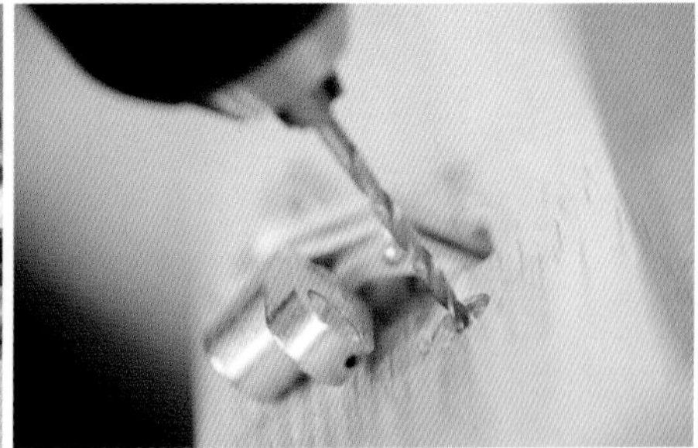

5 **Insert the hinges** into the lid mortises and drill pilot holes for the screws using a drill.

FINISHING THE EDGES

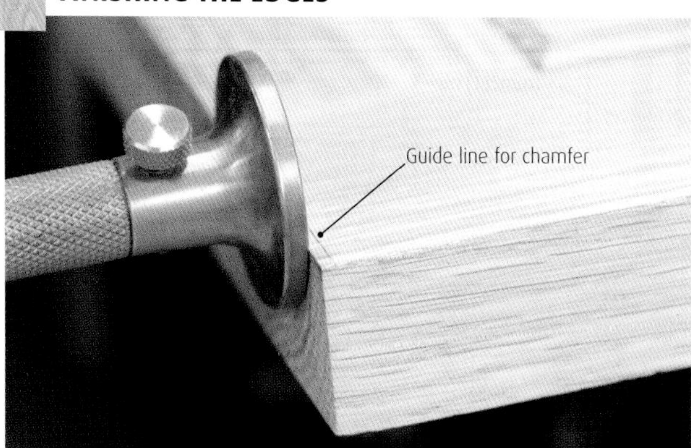

1 **Use a marking gauge** to scribe a guide line for a 1/16in (2mm) chamfer along the upper and lower lid edges.

2 **Chamfer the upper** and lower edges of the lid using a bench plane, ensuring that you do not exceed the guide line.

3 **Use a flat spokeshave** to remove the arrises from all the outside edges of the carcass.

4 **File the edges** of the base of each leg to prevent the grain from splitting when the chest is fully loaded.

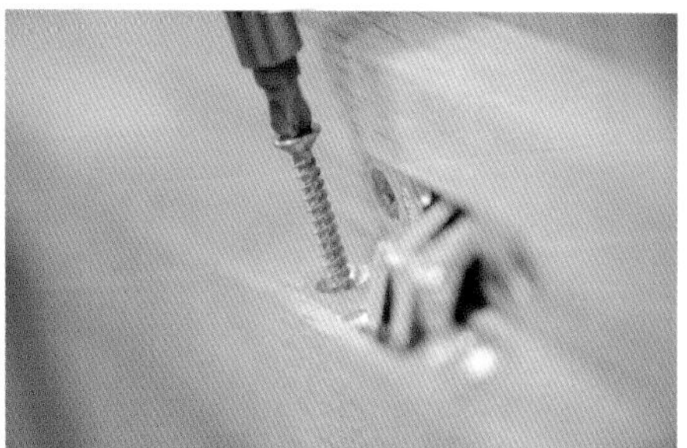

5 **Insert the hinges** into the carcass and screw in place, then screw into the lid to finish.

THE FINISHED PIECE

ALTERNATIVES

The design can be easily enlarged to suit your needs by inserting extra panels divided by additional muntins in the carcass and lid.

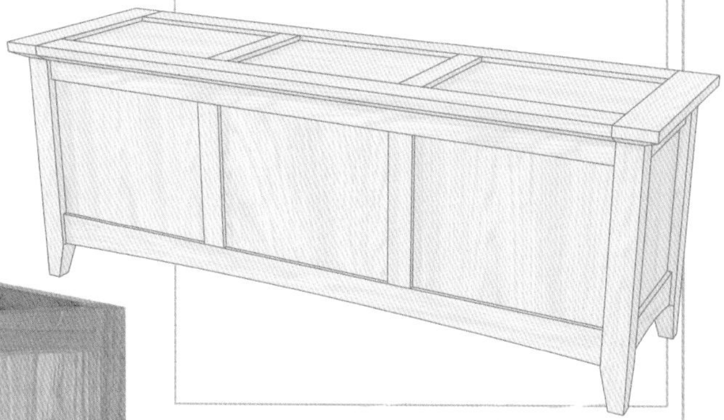

HINGE DETAIL

Chest of drawers

The curved lines of the drawer-fronts on this chest of drawers not only provide visual interest, but also act as functional, secret handles. Careful timber selection for the drawer fronts can also create real impact in the finished piece. The chest comprises three main sections—the plinth, the carcass, and the top. Separating each section is a thin space, known as a "shadow gap." The drawer handles are cut by spokeshaving a scoop out from the underside of each false drawer-front. The project features the use of the domino jointing system (see p.65 and pp.144–45), but could be adapted to use mortise-and-tenon joints.

CUTTING LIST

Item	Material	No.	Length	Width	Thickness
Carcass					
Top	Ash	2	39 1/2in* (1000mm)	8 1/4in* (210mm)	1 3/16in (30mm)
Sides	Ash	4	25 1/2in* (650mm)	8 1/4in* (210mm)	1in (25mm)
Rails	Ash	6	31in (790mm)	1 3/16in (30mm)	1 3/16in (30mm)
Runners	Ash	6	12 3/8in (314mm)	1 3/16in (30mm)	1 3/16in (30mm)
Top rails	Ash	2	31in (790mm)	1 3/16in (30mm)	9/16in (15mm)
Top kickers	Ash	2	12 5/8in (320mm)	1 3/16in (30mm)	9/16in (15mm)
Back	Birch ply	1	31in (790mm)	22 3/4in (579mm)	3/16in (4mm)
Shadow gaps (side)	Ash	4	15 3/4in* (400mm)	13/16in (20mm)	3/16in (5mm)
Shadow gaps (front and back)	Ash	4	33 1/2in* (850mm)	13/16in (20mm)	3/16in (5mm)
Plinth					
Legs	Ash	4	3 15/16in (100mm)	1 3/4in (45mm)	1 3/4in (45mm)
Long rails	Ash	2	29 1/2in (750mm)	1 3/16in (30mm)	1in (25mm)
Short rails	Ash	2	11 7/16in (290mm)	1 3/16in (30mm)	1in (25mm)
Top Drawer					
Front	Ash	1	30 5/16in (770mm)	6in (152mm)	9/16in (15mm)
Sides	Ash	2	14 3/8in (365mm)	6in (152mm)	9/16in (15mm)
Back	Ash	1	30 5/16in (770mm)	5 3/8in (136mm)	3/8in (10mm)
Middle and Bottom Drawers					
Front	Ash	2	30 5/16in (770mm)	6 9/16in (167mm)	9/16in (15mm)
Sides	Ash	4	14 3/8in (365mm)	6 9/16in (167mm)	9/16in (15mm)
Back	Ash	2	30 5/16in (770mm)	6in (151mm)	3/8in (10mm)
All Drawers					
False fronts	Ash	3	33in (840mm)	7 11/16in (195mm)	9/16in (15mm)
Bases	Birch ply	3	30 1/8in (768mm)	13 7/8in (353mm)	1/4in (6mm)

*Includes excess to allow for cutting to size

Dimensions:
33 1/16 x 28 7/8 x 16 9/16in (840 x 734 x 395mm)

Key techniques:
Edge-to-edge joint (pp.94-95);
Domino joints (pp.144–45);
Jigs and templates (pp.150–51)

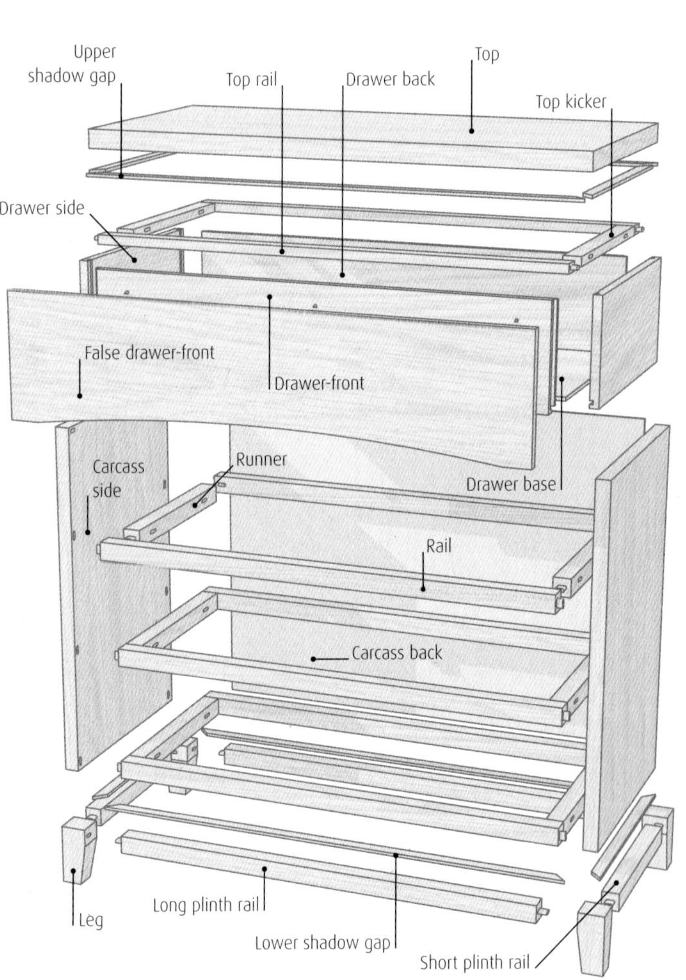

How the elements fit together

The design of the chest features a straightforward construction method that utilizes the domino jointing system, which permits a quick and accurate build. The drawer sides are joined by rebate joints and have false fronts screwed on from the inside. The back of the carcass is simply pinned in place.

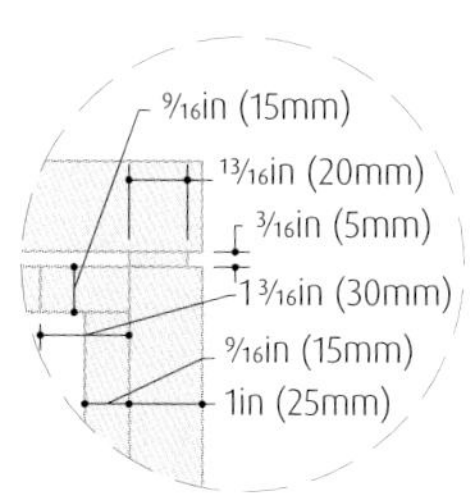

TOP CORNER DETAIL (1:5)

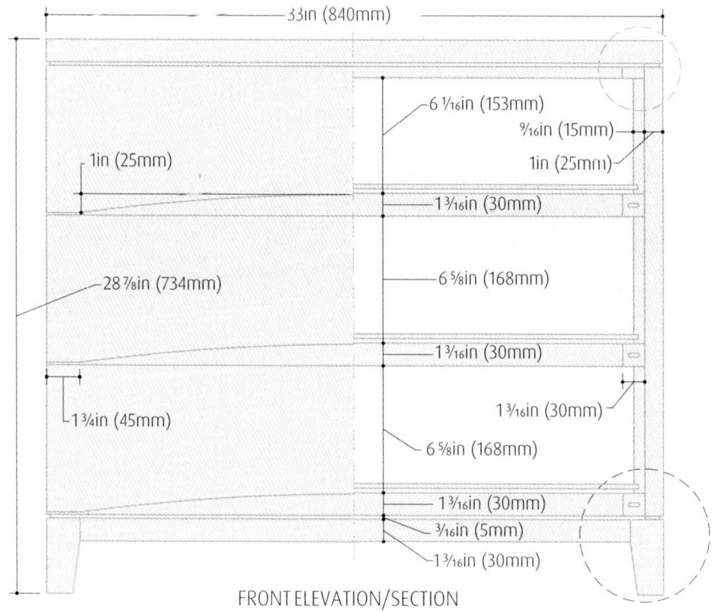

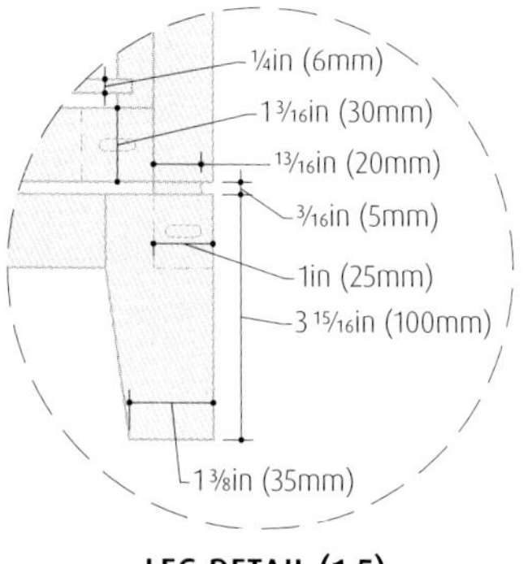

LEG DETAIL (1:5)

3/16in (4mm)
1/4in (6mm)
1/4in (6mm)
9/16in (15mm)

BACK CORNER DETAIL (1:5)

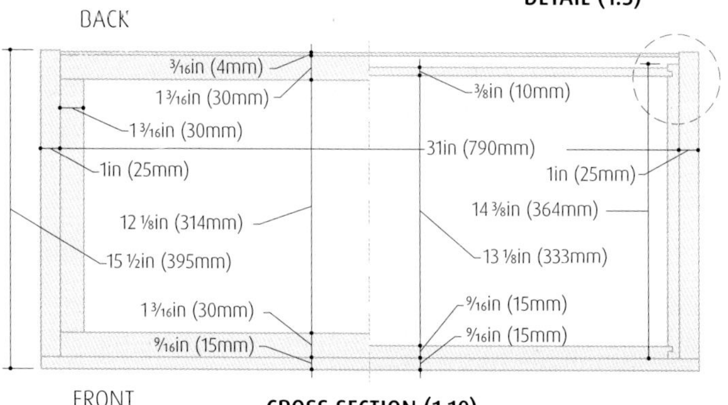

CROSS SECTION (1:10)

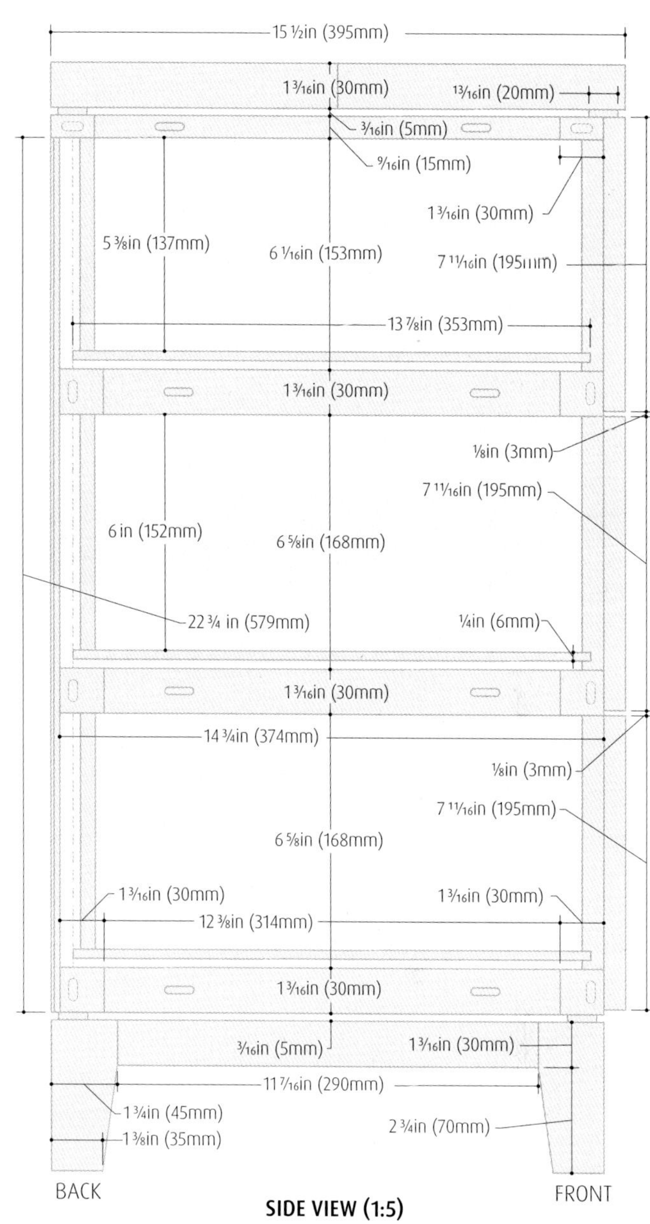

SIDE VIEW (1:5)

TOOLS AND MATERIALS

- Marking gauge
- Domino jointer
- Pencil
- Square
- 20 size 5x30 domino connectors
- Hand-held router and slot cutter or drill and chisel
- 20 size 8x40 domino connectors
- Table saw or panel saw
- Long metal ruler
- Wood glue and brush
- Sash clamps
- 20 size 6x40 domino connectors
- Block plane
- File
- Miter block or miter saw
- Tenon saw
- Masking tape
- Hammer and pins
- Drill with bits
- 22 screws (No.8 x 1¼in/4 x 30mm)
- Screwdriver
- Sandpaper
- Table-mounted router, straight cutter (¼in/6mm), and bearing-guided straight router cutter
- Bench plane
- 2 screws (No.4 x ½in/3 x 12mm)
- MDF (33 x 7⅞in/840 x 200mm)
- Band saw
- Spokeshave
- C-clamps
- 18 screws (No.8 x ¾in/4 x 20mm)

MAKING THE DRAWER-RUNNER FRAMES

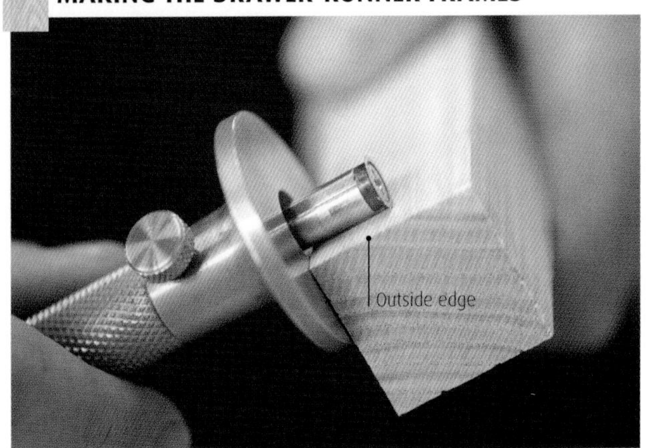

1 **With the runners and rails** cut to length, (see Cutting list, p.308), scribe the center of the outside edge of all the rails with a marking gauge, as a position guide for the domino jointer.

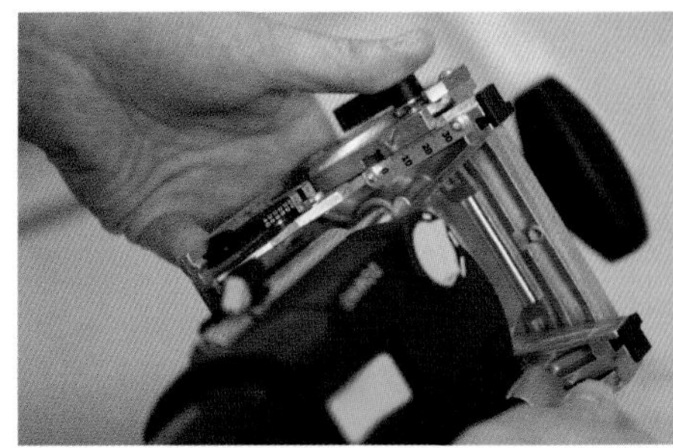

2 **Set the fence height** of the domino jointer to 5⁄16in (7mm) and the depth to 13⁄16in (20mm). Fit a cutter for an 8x40 domino (see also Domino jointers, p.65).

3 **With the domino jointer aligned** to the mark on the edge, cut a domino mortise in both end grains of all the rails.

4 **Draw a line** 5⁄8in (15mm) from each end grain and square around each face of all the rails with a pencil and square.

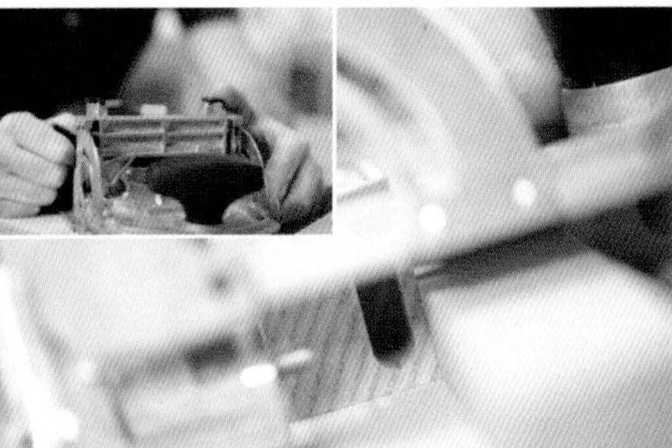

5 **Fit a cutter** for a 5x30 domino and set the fence to 5⁄8in (15mm) and the depth to 3⁄8in (10mm) (inset). With the jointer aligned to the mark drawn in Step 4, cut a mortise on the inner face of each rail

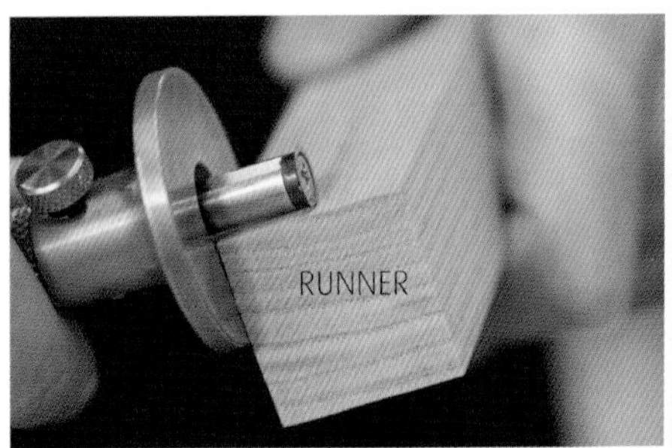

6 **Use a marking gauge** to scribe the center-point of each end grain on the top edge of the runners.

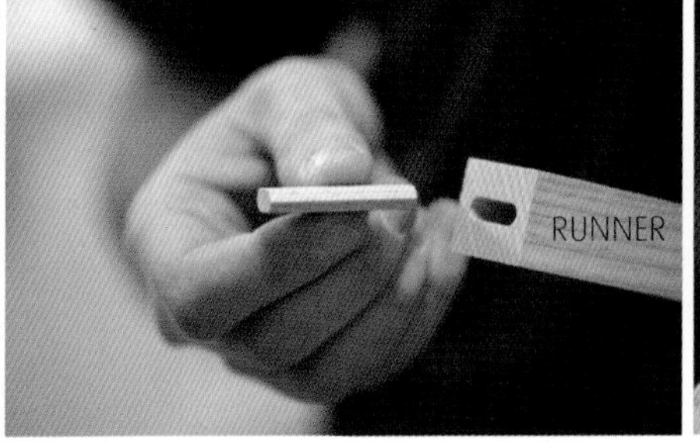

7 **With the fence set to 5⁄8in (15mm)**, cut a domino mortise to a depth of 13⁄16in (20mm) in the center of each end grain of all the runners, and insert a 5x30 domino.

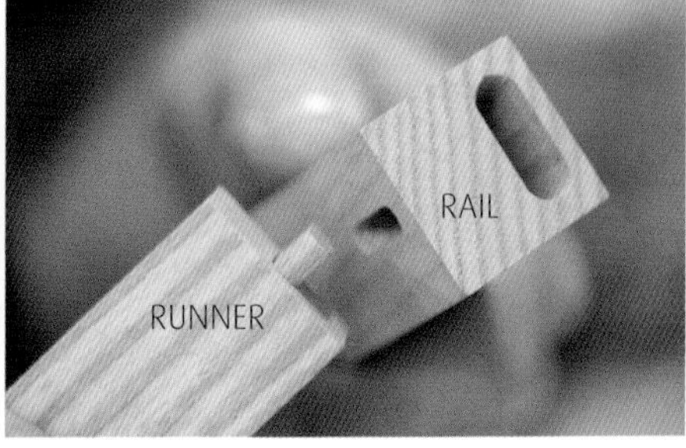

8 **Test the fit** of the 5x30 domino connectors in each of the mortises marked and cut in Steps 1–7.

MAKING THE SCREW SLOTS IN THE RUNNERS

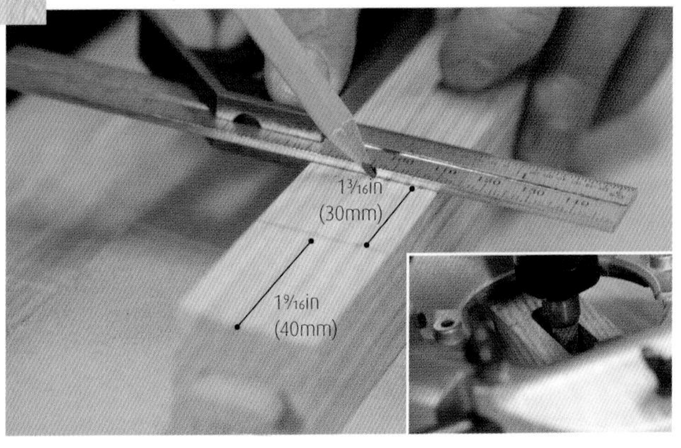

1 **Mark the position** of two screw slots 13⁄16in (30mm) in width, centered on the inside edge of each of the runners, 19⁄16in (40mm) from the end grain. Cut the slots with a router fitted with a slot cutter (inset) or with a drill and chisel, as described for the Bedside table (p.288).

2 **Dry-assemble** all three drawer-runner frames of the chest. Make any necessary adjustments.

MAKING THE TOP RAILS

1 **Mark the position of a domino mortise** aligned to the face in the center of each of the end grains of the two top rails.

2 **Set the fence** of the domino jointer to 5⁄16in (7mm) and the depth to 13⁄16in (20mm). Fit a cutter to match a 5x30 domino and cut mortises in each of the positions marked in Step 1.

MAKING THE CARCASS SIDES AND TOP

1 **Join the panels** for the carcass sides and top with edge-to-edge joints (pp.94–95). Cut them to size: top 33 x 15½in (840 x 395mm); sides 23⅜ x 14 15⁄16in (594 x 380mm).

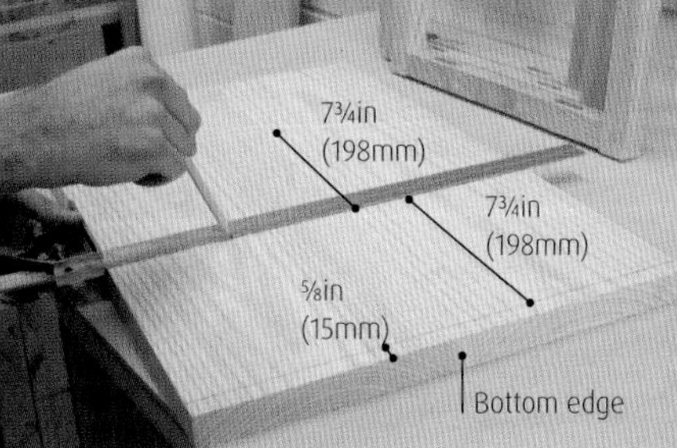

2 **Mark the positions** of the mortises for each of the runner frames on the inside face of the carcass sides—three along the front edge and three along the back.

3 **Extend the marks** from the face onto the edges of both carcass sides using a pencil and square.

4 **Cut mortises** for 8x40 dominoes in each marked position aligned to the front and back edges. Set the fence to 5⁄16in (7mm) (front edge) and ½in (13mm) (back edge).

5 **Mark two mortise positions** on the top edge of each carcass side: ⅝in (15mm) from the front edge; ⅝in (15mm) from the back edge.

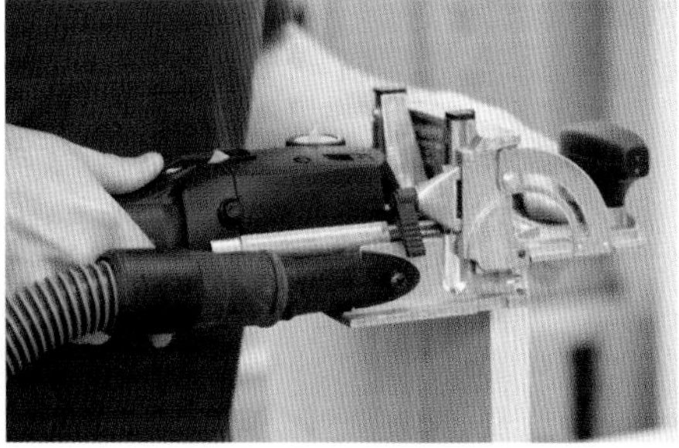

6 **Using a 3⁄16in (5mm) domino cutter**, with the fence set to ⅜in (10mm), cut both mortises to a depth of 13⁄16in (20mm).

7 **Assemble the runners**, kickers, and rails to make four dry-jointed frames. Glue the dominoes into the mortises in the sides. Assemble the frames and sides. Drill pilot holes through the slots and fix with screws.

MAKING THE PLINTH

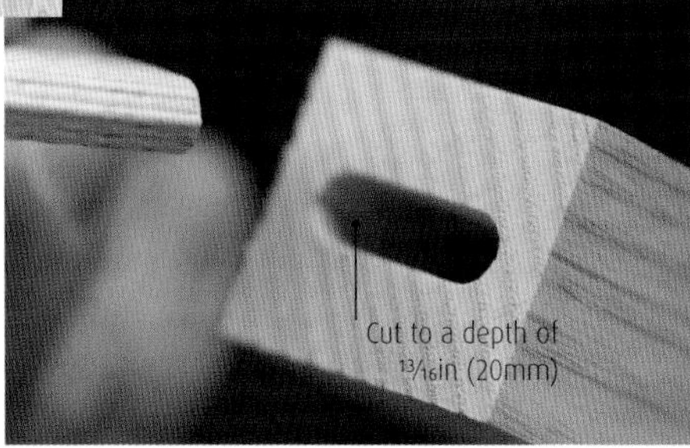

1 **Mark a mortise** parallel with the long edge of each end grain of all plinth rails. Set the jointer fence to ⅝in (15mm). Cut mortises for 6x40 dominoes in each position.

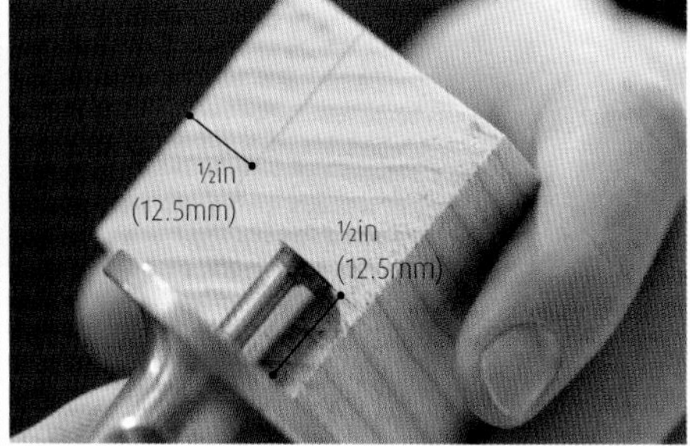

2 **Use a marking gauge** to scribe a line ½in (12.5mm) from the edge of the end grain on two adjacent sides of each leg piece.

3 **With the jointer set** for a 6x40 domino and the fence to ⅝in (15mm), cut mortises to a depth of 13⁄16in (20mm) in the two sides of the legs marked in Step 2, centered on the marks on the end grain.

4 **Measure 1³⁄₁₆in (30mm)** from the mortised end and square the line around all sides to mark the start of the tapers on all four leg pieces.

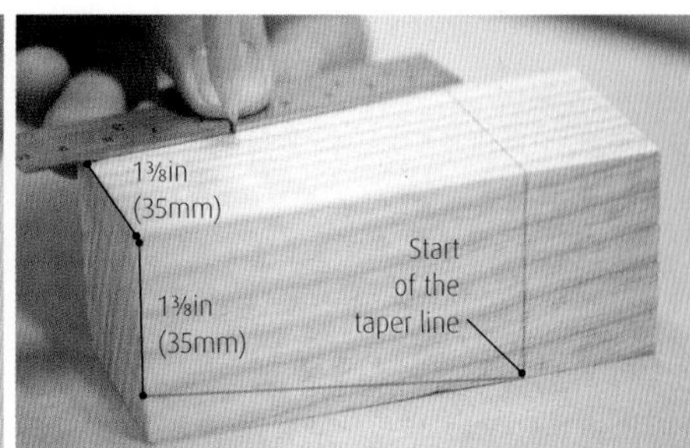

5 **Mark 1⅜in (35mm)** from the outside corner of the end grain on the two non-mortised sides. Join each mark to the corner at the start of the taper. Square the marks across the end grain and mark the waste.

6 **With the waste marks** protruding above the jaws of a vise (inset), plane each leg piece to remove the waste with a block plane.

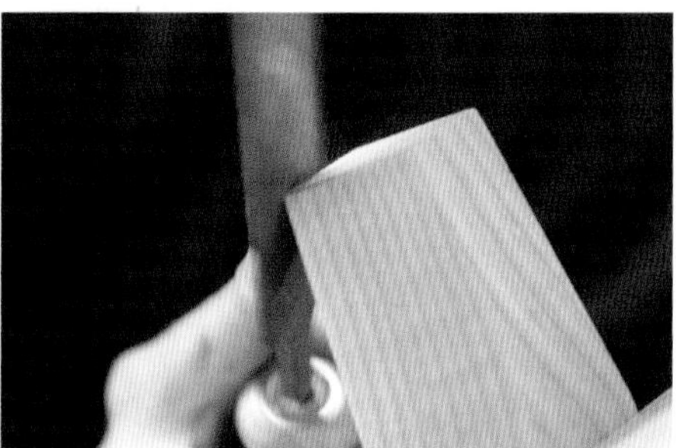

7 **File the bottom edges** of the end grains of all four leg pieces to prevent splitting in use.

MAKING THE UPPER AND LOWER SHADOW GAPS

8 **Test-fit then glue the mortises** and dominoes to join the legs to the short plinth-rails. Clamp and allow to dry. Then glue the long plinth-rails in position.

1 **Miter the ends** of the shadow gap pieces to 32⅝ x 15⅛in (830 x 385mm) for the upper shadow gap, and 32⅝ x 14⅝in (830 x 370mm) for the lower shadow gap.

2 **Mark a line** ³⁄₁₆in (5mm) from the outer face around the top edge of the plinth, using a pencil and square.

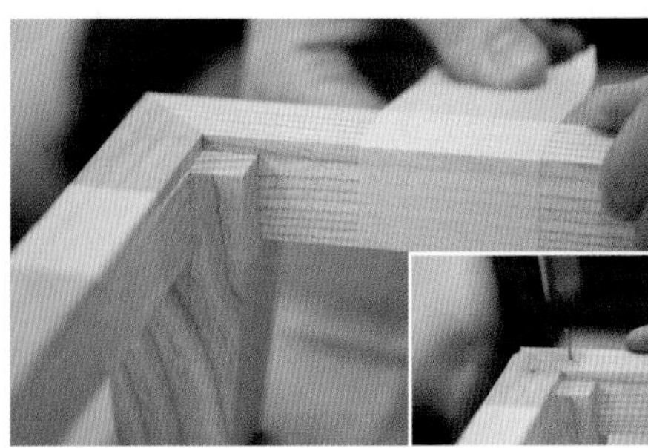

3 **Place the lower shadow-gap pieces** on the upper edge of the plinth and align them with the marks, flush to the inner face. Tape them to the plinth and pin in place (inset).

4 **Remove the masking tape** and secure the plinth in place upside down over the carcass. Drill three countersunk holes for 2in (50mm) screws into the underside of each of the long plinth-rails. You will use the upper shadow-gap pieces in Step 1, Fitting the top (opposite).

FITTING THE TOP KICKER-RAIL AND DRAWER-RUNNER FRAMES TO THE CARCASS

1 **Make two screw slots** in the inner edge of each top kicker-rail (see Steps 1 and 2, Making the screw slots in the runners, p.310). Make shorter screw slots in the center of the underside of each rail and two cross-grain slots spaced equidistantly in the center of the underside of the top rail at the back. Screw the rails along the top edge of each side.

2 **Secure the glued drawer runner-frames** to the carcass by inserting screws through the screw slots into the carcass sides.

FITTING THE TOP

1 **Fix the mitered pieces** for the upper shadow gap 3⁄16in (5mm) from the outer edge of the top of the carcass. Secure with masking tape as for the lower shadow gap (see Steps 2–3, Making the upper and lower shadow gaps, opposite) and pin to the carcass sides.

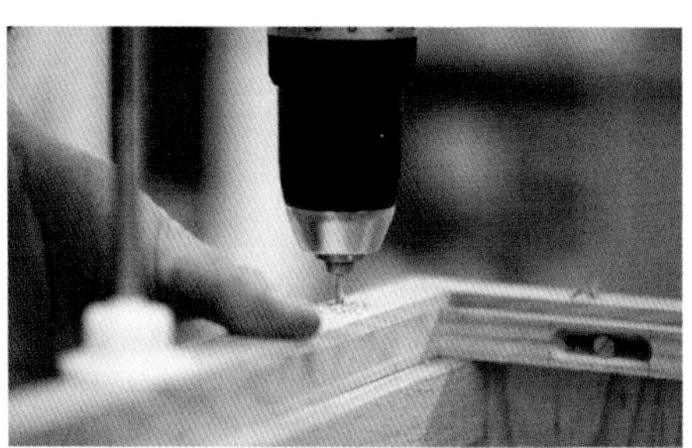

2 **Drill three screw holes** through the shadow gap and through the top rail at the front of the carcass.

3 **Make three cross-grain slotted screw holes** in the top rail at the back. Countersink the holes on the rails' undersides.

4 **Sand the edges** of the top and place it in position on the top of the carcass, flush to the back of the frame and overhanging at the front. Drill pilot holes into the underside of the top through the holes and slots in the rails and kickers, then insert the screws to secure the top.

MAKING THE DRAWERS

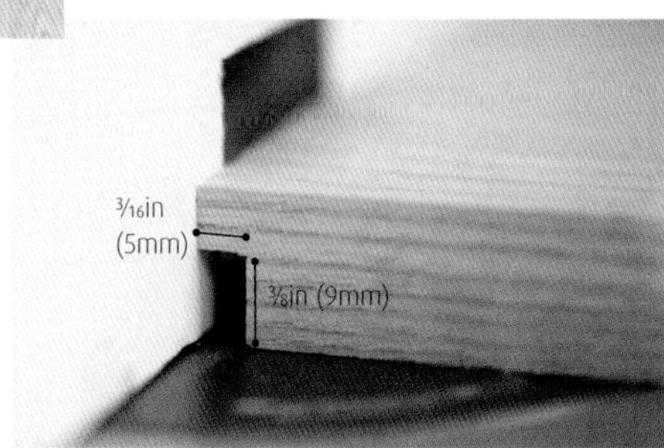

1 **Use a table-mounted router** to cut all the grooves and rebates on the inside faces of the drawer pieces. Cut a rebate along both end grains of each drawer front to the dimensions shown.

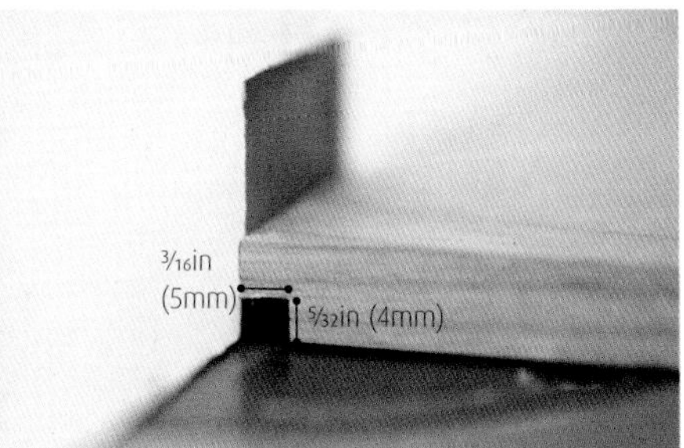

2 **Cut a rebate** along the inside face and both end grains of each drawer back. Set the fence to 3⁄16in (5mm) and cut to a height of 5⁄32in (4mm).

3 **Cut a groove** along the inside face of each drawer front. Use a 1⁄4in (6mm) bit with the fence set to 3⁄8in (10mm) and the height to 3⁄16in (5mm).

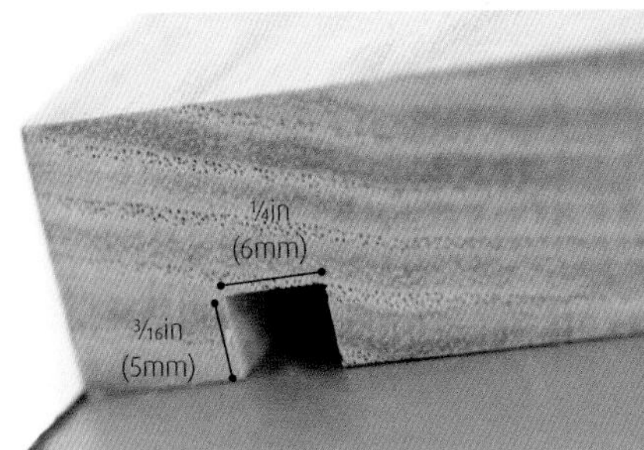

4 **Cut a groove** ¼in (6mm) wide and to a depth of ³⁄₁₆in (5mm) parallel to the bottom edge of the inside face of each of the drawer sides.

5 **Cut two more grooves** of the same dimensions along the short sides on the inside face of each drawer side.

6 **Use a block plane** to chamfer the edges of each drawer bottom on both short sides and one of the long sides, to ease the fit in the grooves.

7 **Test-fit the drawer pieces** and make any adjustments that are necessary. Glue the pieces, assemble, and clamp.

8 **When the drawer** has dried, plane the edges flush. Drill a countersunk hole for a 4 x ½in (3 x 12mm) screw though the drawer base into the center of the edge of the drawer back. Insert the screws (inset). Repeat for all drawers.

MAKING THE FALSE DRAWER-FRONT TEMPLATE

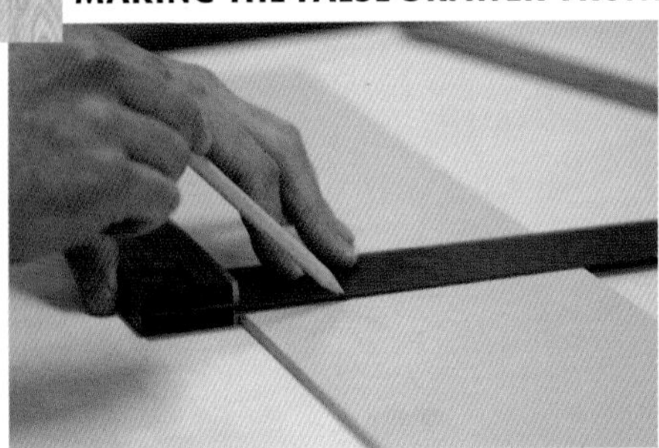

1 **Cut a piece of MDF** to the same length as the false drawer-front, but ³⁄₁₆in (5mm) wider. Mark the center-point of the long side and extend a pencil line across the face.

2 **Measure 1¾in (45mm)** from each end of the template and square the mark off across the face (inset).

3 **Mark a line** along one long side of the template ³⁄₁₆in (5mm) from the bottom edge. Extend the line across the face.

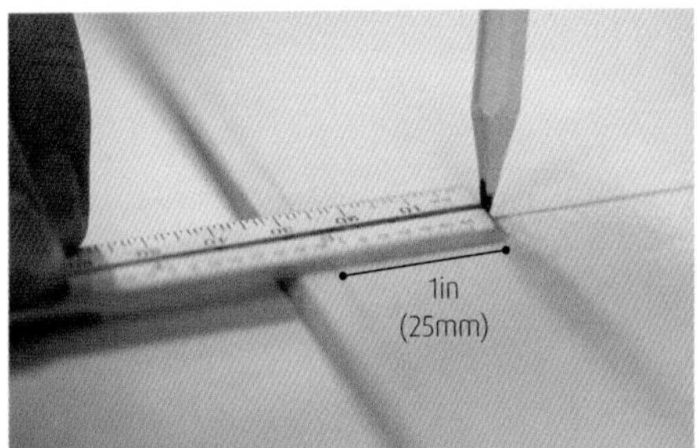

4 **Mark a point on the center line** 1in (25mm) from the width line, using a pencil and square.

5 **Hammer three panel pins** into the template: one at the mark drawn on the center line in Step 4 and the other two the thickness of a metal ruler above each intersection of the width and side lines.

6 **Place the metal ruler** above the center pin and below the side pins to create a curve, and mark it on to the face of the template with a pencil.

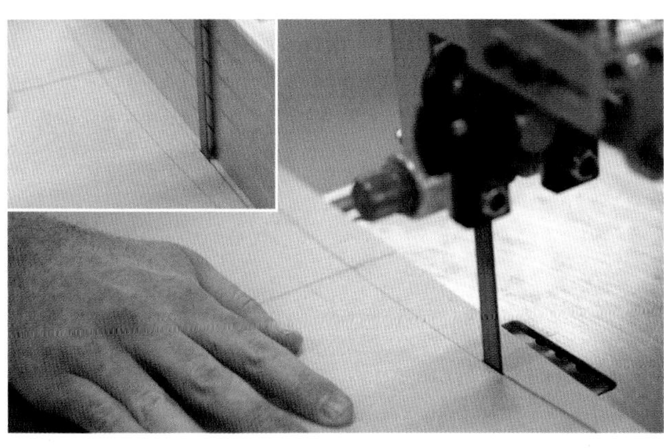

7 **Cut to the waste side** of the width line (inset) and then cut along the curved line with a band saw.

8 **Use sandpaper** to remove any remaining waste and sand the edges smooth.

MAKING THE FALSE DRAWER-FRONTS

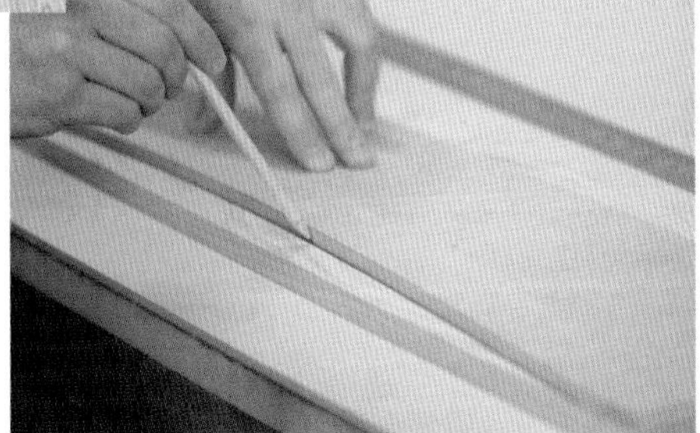

1 **Align the template precisely** over the false drawer-front. Use the template as a guide to draw the curve along the bottom edge of the false drawer-front.

2 **Cut the curve** in the false drawer-front on a band saw. Be careful to cut to the waste side of the line to prevent over-cutting and to allow for finishing.

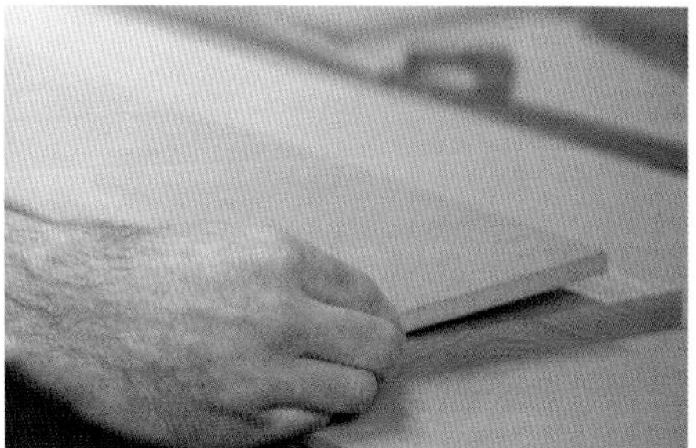

3 **Secure the template** over the false drawer-front with clamps or using double-sided tape (pictured).

4 **With the template** positioned beneath the false drawer-front, align a bearing-guided straight router cutter to the template and cut back to the marked line. Repeat Steps 1–4 for the remaining drawer fronts.

MAKING THE FINGER GRIPS

1 **On the back of a false drawer-front** mark a line down the center to act as a guide for the middle of the molded—or "scalloped"—finger grip on the inside lower edge.

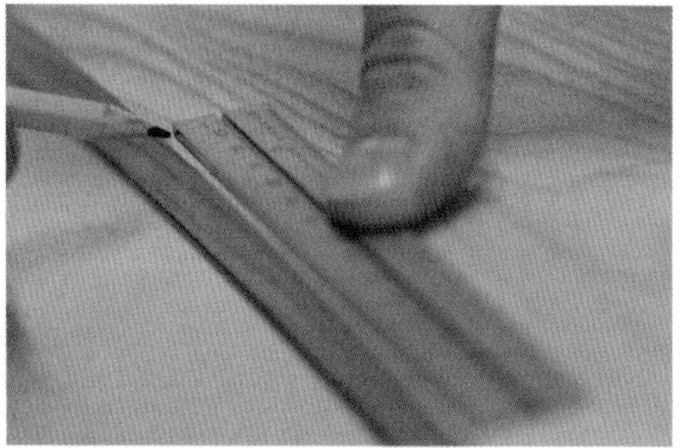

2 **Mark the width** of the finger grip on the curved edge 2⁹⁄₁₆in (65mm) to either side of the center line.

3 **Extend the width line** across the edge of the false drawer-front using a pencil and square.

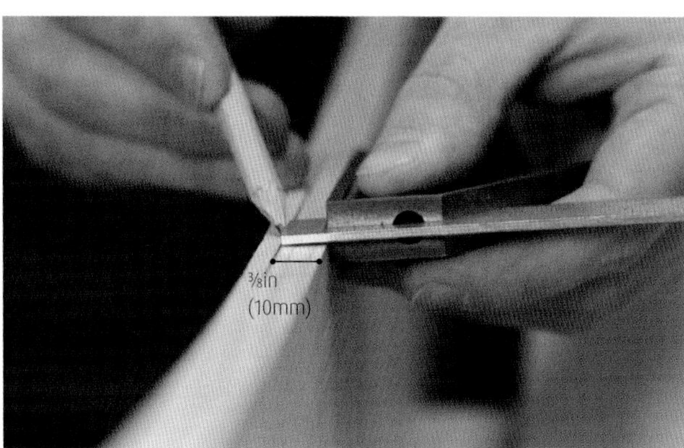

4 **Mark the start** of the finger grip 3⁄8in (10mm) from the back edge of the false drawer-front.

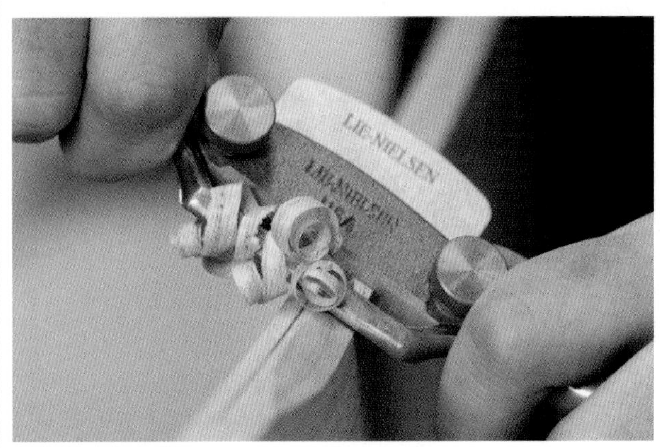

5 **Use a spokeshave** at an angle of approximately 45 degrees to create the finger grip, removing the waste to the marked lines. Repeat Steps 1–5 for the remaining two false drawer-fronts.

6 **When you have cut** all three false drawer-fronts, sand smooth and remove any sharp edges.

FITTING THE FALSE DRAWER-FRONTS

1 **Mark the center** of the lower edge of the back of the false fronts, and the center of the lower edge of all the drawer fronts. Extend the marks onto the edges.

2 **Place the front** of the bottom drawer on the back of one false front with the center marks aligned. Position the lower edge of the false front 1$\frac{1}{16}$in (27mm) below the lower edge of the drawer front.

3 **Clamp the components** of the drawer together with G-clamps to secure them accurately in position for drilling.

4 **Working from the inside** of the drawer, drill and countersink two pilot holes for the screws along the center line of the drawer front, with the drill marked to a depth of 1in (25mm). Drill four more holes, two on each side approximately 1in (25mm) from the sides of the drawer.

5 **Insert the screws** with a screwdriver. Fit the false drawer-fronts to the remaining two drawers in the same way.

INSERTING THE CARCASS BACK

1 **With the back panel cut to size**, place it in position against the back of the carcass. Mark the position of the center of the drawer rails onto the back.

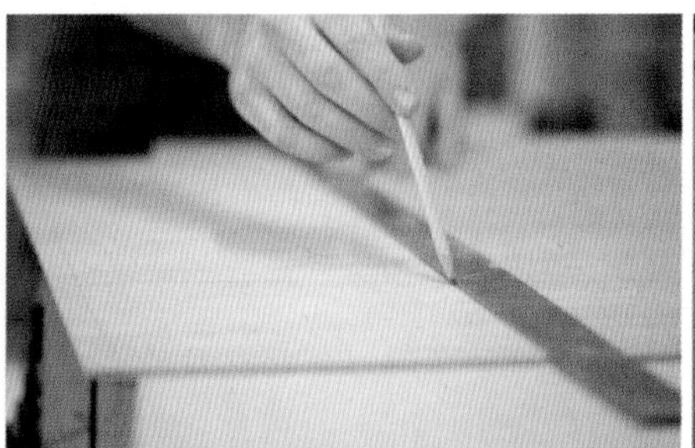

2 **Extend the marks** horizontally across the full width of the back panel, using a pencil and metal ruler.

3 **Hammer three pins** along each marked line—one at each end and one in the center—to fix the back panel to the carcass.

DETAIL OF DRAWER FRONT

DETAIL OF SHADOW GAP

FINISHES

Drawer fronts are often handled a great deal as they are opened and closed during regular use, so it is important to apply a robust finish to the timber to avoid the risk of the wood becoming permanently marked. No matter how clean your hands are, your skin emits oils that can penetrate untreated wood surfaces, leaving dull fingerprints and discoloration. On a piece of this kind it is a good idea to apply a finish, such as a clear, water-based varnish, that can be wiped clean with a damp cloth.

THE FINISHED PIECE

ALTERNATIVES

A simple way of adapting this design would be to change the shape of the false drawer-fronts, for example by incorporating a double curve on each instead of the single curve shown here. Simply make a jig of the desired shape and construct the drawers as before, but using your alternative jig. Other straightforward variations could include screwing drawer knobs or handles to the false drawer-fronts, which can be used to open the drawers instead of the finger grips. Alternatively, for a more traditional look, instead of the legs construct a plinth similar to that used in the Tool box (pp.282–87) at the base of the carcass.

Bed

The design of this bed allows it to be simply dismantled, making it easy to transport or to store it when it is not in use. The dimensions specified fit a standard single mattress, but be careful to check the exact size of the mattress you intend to use and adjust the dimensions as necessary. The design can also be adapted for a double mattress by lengthening the short rails and slats to the required size, and adding a central brace along the length to support the extra weight.

Dimensions:
80 5/8 x 40 1/8 x 35 7/16in (2050 x 1020 x 900mm)

Key techniques:
Basic mortise-and-tenon joint (pp.116–19)

CUTTING LIST

Item	Material	No.	Length	Width	Thickness
Headboard legs	Ash	2	35 7/16in (900mm)	1 15/16in (50mm)	1 15/16in (50mm)
Footboard legs	Ash	2	24 7/16in (620mm)	1 15/16in (50mm)	1 15/16in (50mm)
Side rails	Ash	2	79 3/8in (2016mm)	4 3/4in (120mm)	13/16in (20mm)
Lower head- and footboard rails	Ash	2	38 3/4in (986mm)	4 3/4in (120mm)	13/16in (20mm)
Upper headboard rail	Ash	1	38 9/16in (980mm)	4 5/16in (110mm)	13/16in (20mm)
Middle headboard rail	Ash	1	38 9/16in (980mm)	3 1/8in (80mm)	13/16in (20mm)
Slat-support battens	Ash	4	36 1/4in (925mm)	13/16in (20mm)	13/16in (20mm)
Cross-brace	Ash	1	37 3/8in (950mm)	1 3/16in (30mm)	13/16in (20mm)
Cross-brace housing	Ash	2	3 15/16in (100mm)	1 9/16in (40mm)	13/16in (20mm)
Bolt caps	Ash	4	1 15/16in (50mm)	5/8in (16mm)	1/2in (13mm)
Slats	Pine	12	37 1/2in (945mm)	2 3/8in (60mm)	3/4in (20mm)
Slat stops	Beech dowel	4	1 3/16in (30mm)	3/8in (10mm)	3/8in (10mm)

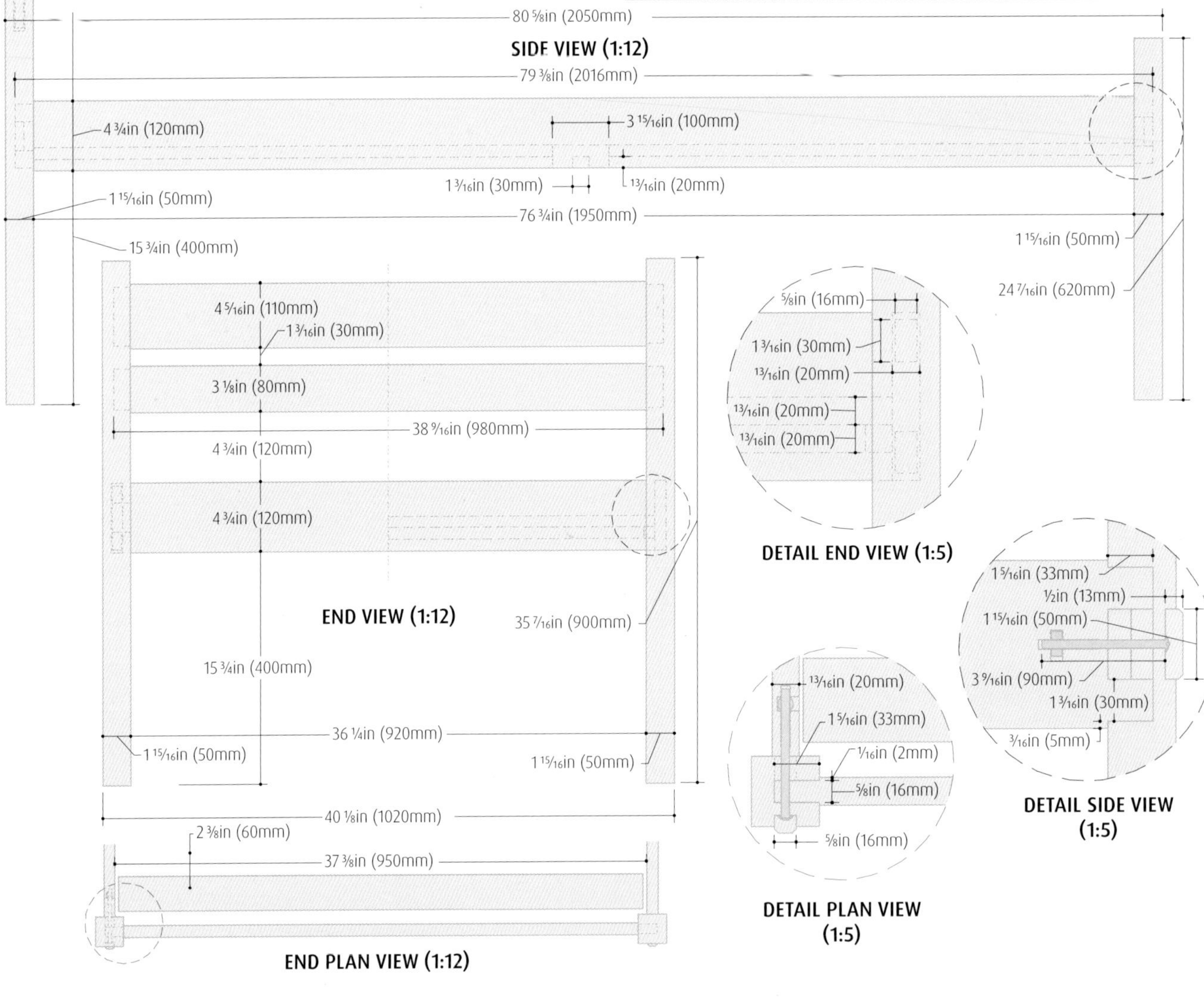

80 5/8in (2050mm)
SIDE VIEW (1:12)
79 3/8in (2016mm)
4 3/4in (120mm)
3 15/16in (100mm)
1 3/16in (30mm)
13/16in (20mm)
1 15/16in (50mm)
76 3/4in (1950mm)
15 3/4in (400mm)
1 15/16in (50mm)
24 7/16in (620mm)

4 5/16in (110mm)
1 3/16in (30mm)
3 1/8in (80mm)
38 9/16in (980mm)
4 3/4in (120mm)
4 3/4in (120mm)
END VIEW (1:12)
35 7/16in (900mm)
15 3/4in (400mm)
36 1/4in (920mm)
1 15/16in (50mm)
1 15/16in (50mm)
40 1/8in (1020mm)
2 3/8in (60mm)
37 3/8in (950mm)
END PLAN VIEW (1:12)

5/8in (16mm)
1 3/16in (30mm)
13/16in (20mm)
13/16in (20mm)
13/16in (20mm)
DETAIL END VIEW (1:5)

13/16in (20mm)
1 5/16in (33mm)
1/16in (2mm)
5/8in (16mm)
5/8in (16mm)
DETAIL PLAN VIEW (1:5)

1 5/16in (33mm)
1/2in (13mm)
1 15/16in (50mm)
3 9/16in (90mm)
1 3/16in (30mm)
3/16in (5mm)
DETAIL SIDE VIEW (1:5)

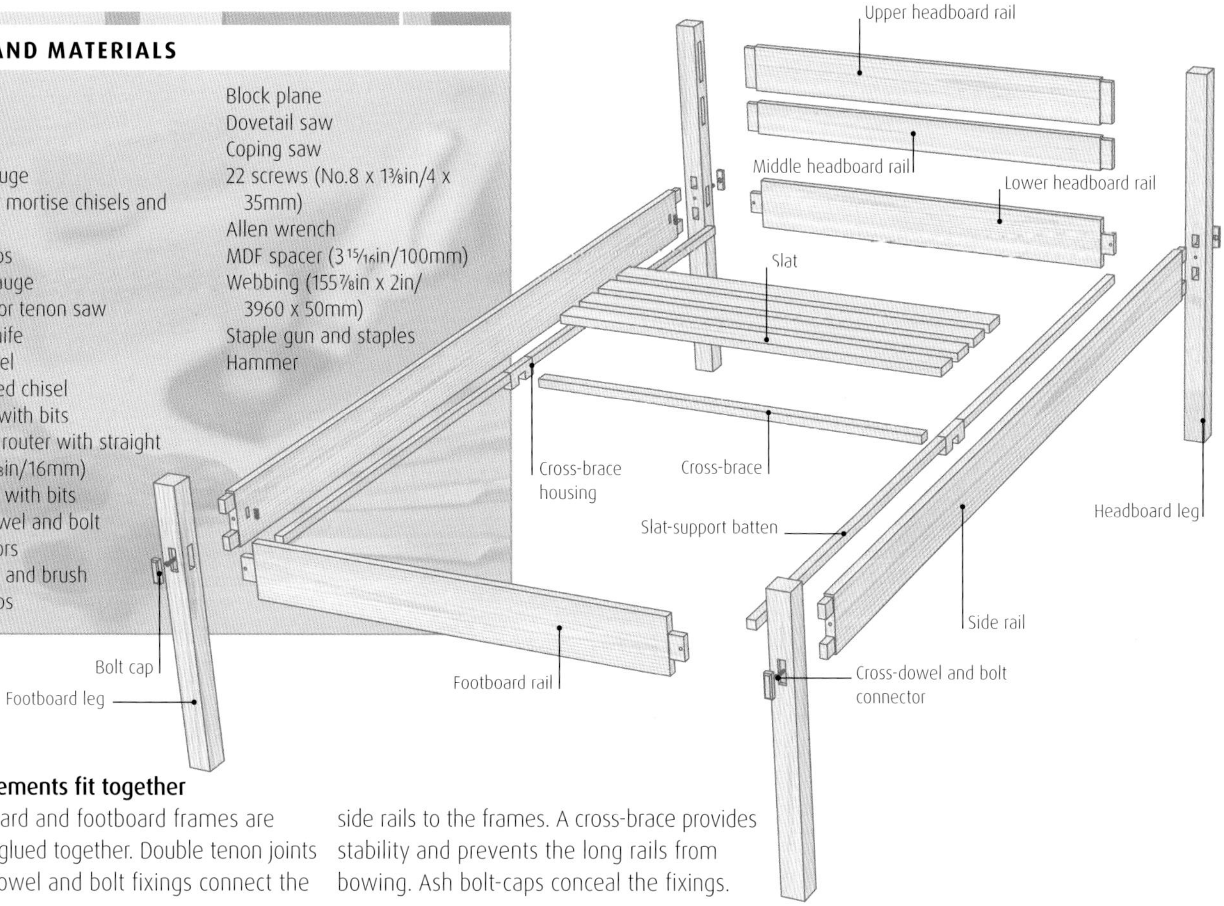

TOOLS AND MATERIALS

Ruler	Block plane
Pencil	Dovetail saw
Square	Coping saw
Mortise gauge	22 screws (No.8 x 1⅜in/4 x 35mm)
Mortiser or mortise chisels and mallet	Allen wrench
Sash clamps	MDF spacer (3 15/16in/100mm)
Marking gauge	Webbing (155⅞in x 2in/ 3960 x 50mm)
Band saw or tenon saw	Staple gun and staples
Marking knife	Hammer
Paring chisel	
Bevel-edged chisel	
Drill press with bits	
Hand-held router with straight cutter (⅝in/16mm)	
Power drill with bits	
4 Cross-dowel and bolt connectors	
Wood glue and brush	
Sash clamps	

Upper headboard rail
Middle headboard rail
Lower headboard rail
Slat
Cross-brace housing
Cross-brace
Slat-support batten
Headboard leg
Side rail
Cross-dowel and bolt connector
Footboard rail
Bolt cap
Footboard leg

How the elements fit together
The headboard and footboard frames are jointed and glued together. Double tenon joints and cross-dowel and bolt fixings connect the side rails to the frames. A cross-brace provides stability and prevents the long rails from bowing. Ash bolt-caps conceal the fixings.

MAKING THE MORTISES IN THE HEADBOARD LEGS

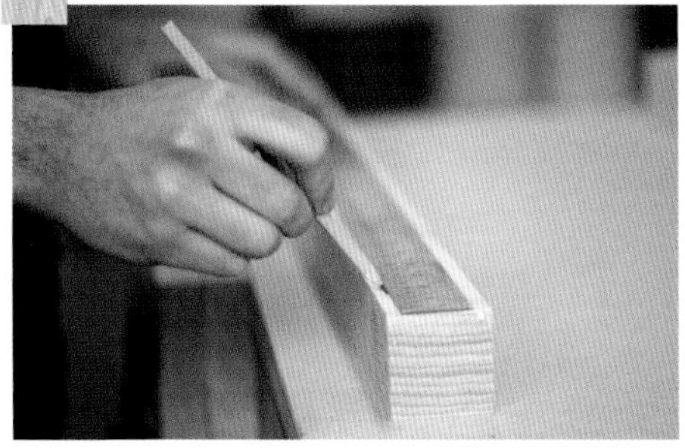

1 **Mark the start** of the first mortise on the first headboard leg 1¾in (45mm) from the end grain. Mark the other end of the mortise 3 15/16in (100mm) from the first mark.

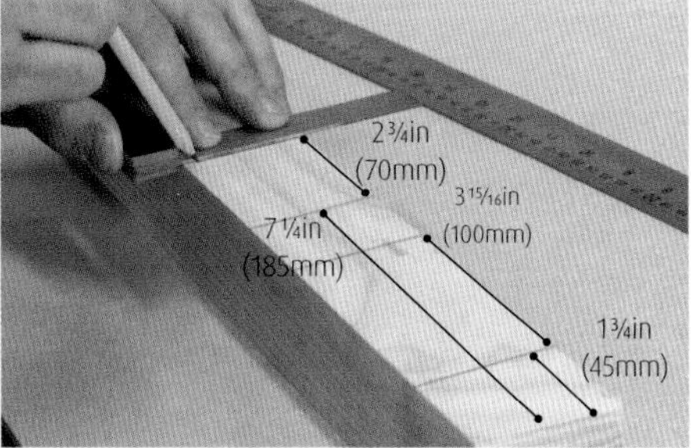

2 **Mark the start** of a second mortise 7¼in (185mm) from the end grain, then draw a second line 2¾in (70mm) from the mark just drawn.

3 **Mark a third mortise** 16⅜in (415mm) from the end grain, then mark the mortise length of 1 15/16in (50mm).

4 **Square the marks** across the face of the leg piece and extend them onto an adjacent edge (inset).

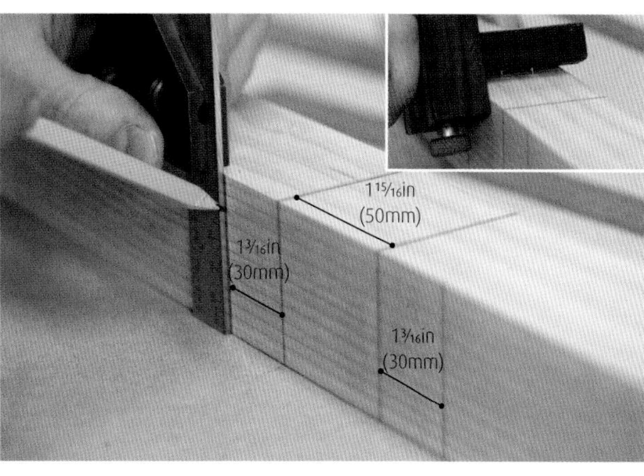

5 **Mark two lines** 1 3/16in (30mm) either side of the third mortise on both edges, to mark the position of two further mortises. Set a mortise gauge to ⅝in (16mm) and mark the width of all five mortises centrally in each of the marked positions (inset).

6 **Cut all the mortises** to a depth of 1⁵⁄₁₆in (33mm). Use a mortiser (pictured) with a bit to match the mortise width of ⅝in (16mm), or cut the mortises by hand with a mortise chisel.

7 **Repeat Steps 1–6** for the mortises in the second headboard leg, ensuring you cut the two small mortises on the opposite edge to the first leg piece.

MAKING THE MORTISES IN THE FOOTBOARD LEGS

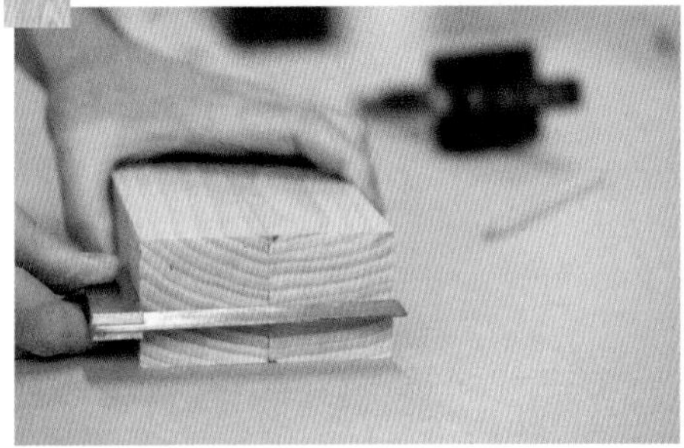

1 **Place a footboard leg** alongside one of the headboard legs, with the bottoms of both legs aligned.

2 **Clamp the legs** together, then square the position of the third mortise (1¹⁵⁄₁₆in/50mm) from the headboard leg onto the footboard leg.

3 **Turn both legs** 90 degrees, so that the small mortises on the headboard leg and the side of the footboard leg are both facing up. Square the marks across.

4 **Mark the width** of all three mortises, using the mortise gauge as previously set (⅝in/16mm). Mark the waste for removal in pencil (inset). Mark up the second footboard leg in the same way, but with the two small mortises on the opposite edge to those on the other footboard leg.

5 **Cut the three mortises** on each leg to a depth of 1⁵⁄₁₆in (33mm), using a mortiser or mortise chisel.

MAKING THE TENONS IN THE LOWER HEADBOARD RAIL AND FOOTBOARD RAIL

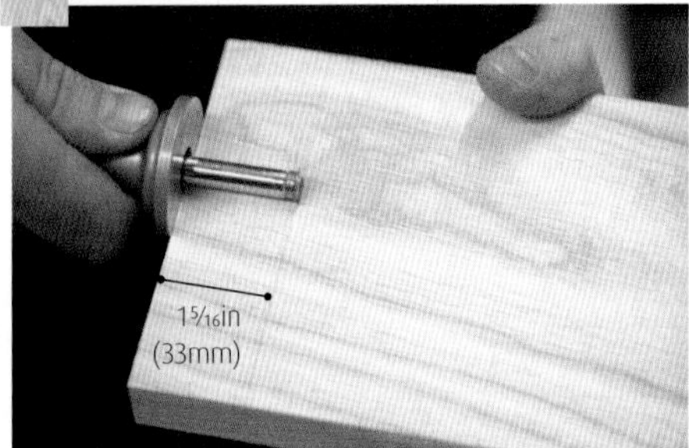

1 **With the marking gauge** set to 1⁵⁄₁₆in (33mm), scribe a shoulder on all sides of both end grains of the lower headboard and footboard rails.

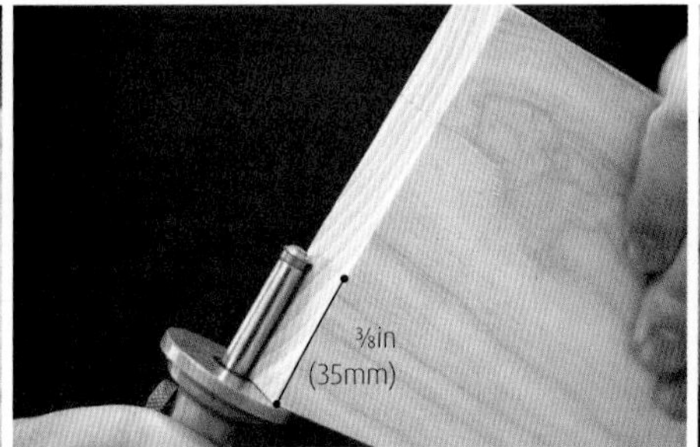

2 **Mark the tenon width** on each end grain with the marking gauge set to 1⅜in (35mm), in order to create a 1¹⁵⁄₁₆in (50mm) tenon.

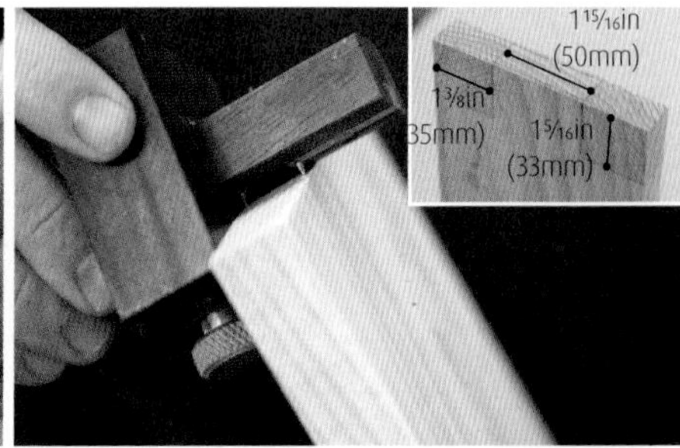

3 **Mark the tenon thickness** on each end grain with the mortise gauge as previously set (⅝in/16mm). Extend the mark around both edges and mark the waste for removal (inset).

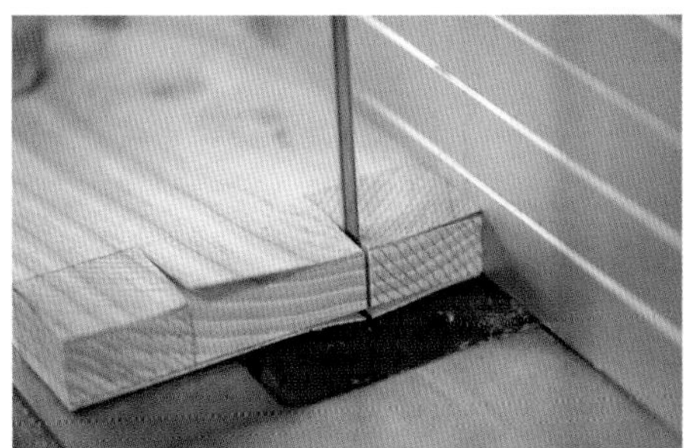

4 **Cut each rail-piece tenon** on a band saw (pictured), or by hand with a tenon saw. Cut to the waste side of the line.

5 **Use a marking knife** to score and cut the waste from the shoulders. Clean up the edges with a paring chisel.

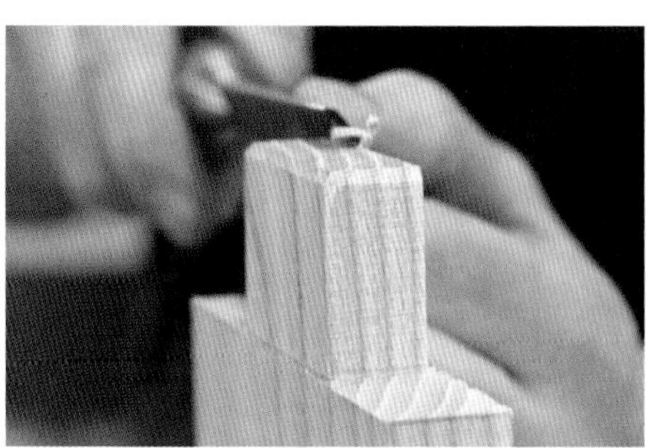

6 **Chamfer the edges** of the tenons with a bevel-edged chisel to ease the fit into the mortises.

MAKING THE TENONS IN THE UPPER HEADBOARD RAIL

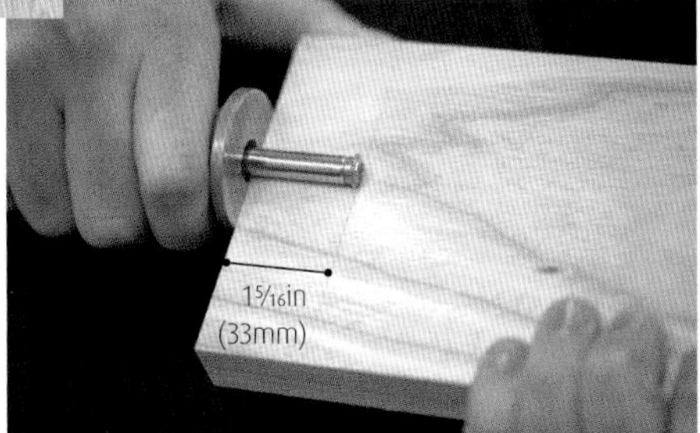

1 **With the marking gauge** set to $1\frac{5}{16}$in (33mm), mark the shoulder on all four sides and on both ends of the upper headboard rail.

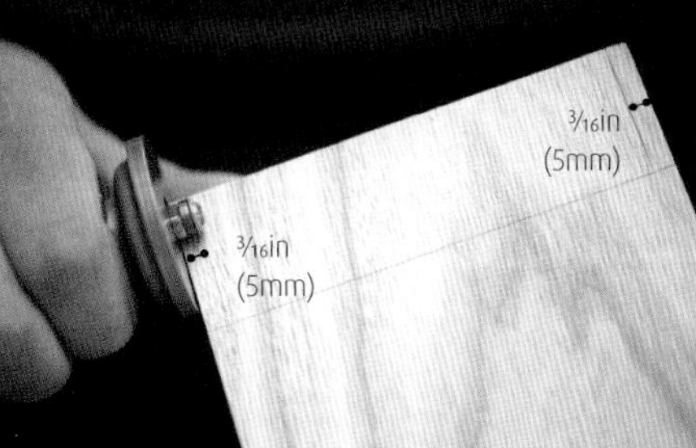

2 **Set the marking gauge** to $\frac{3}{16}$in (5mm) and scribe a line across both ends of the end grain and to the shoulder on both faces to mark the tenon width.

3 **Using the mortise gauge** as previously set ($\frac{5}{8}$in/16mm), scribe the tenon thickness onto the edges and end grain of both tenons. Mark the waste for removal (inset).

4 **Cut the tenons** with a band saw or tenon saw, then clean up the shoulders and chamfer the edges with a chisel, as described in Steps 4–6 (above).

MAKING THE TENONS IN THE MIDDLE HEADBOARD RAIL

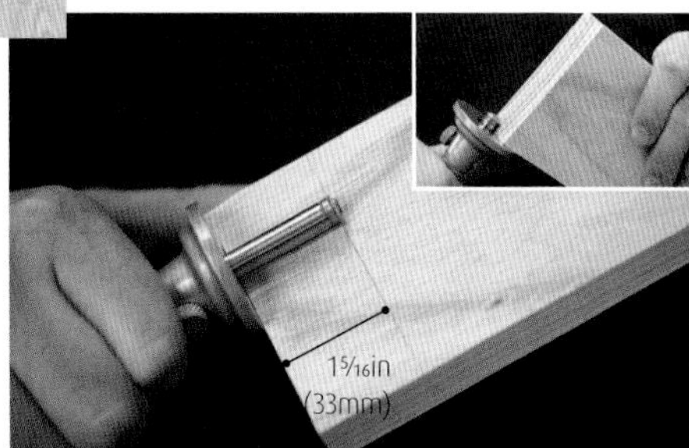

1 **With the marking gauge** set to $1\frac{5}{16}$in (33mm), scribe around both ends of the middle rail. Scribe a line $\frac{3}{16}$in (5mm) from the edges of both end grains (inset) to mark the tenon width of $2\frac{3}{4}$in (70mm).

2 **Using the mortise gauge** as previously set ($\frac{5}{8}$in/16mm), scribe the tenon thickness around the end grain and both edges of both tenons. Mark the waste for removal (inset).

3 **Cut the tenons**, clean up the shoulders, and chamfer the edges, as described in Steps 4–6 (above).

CUTTING THE DOUBLE TENONS IN THE SIDE RAILS

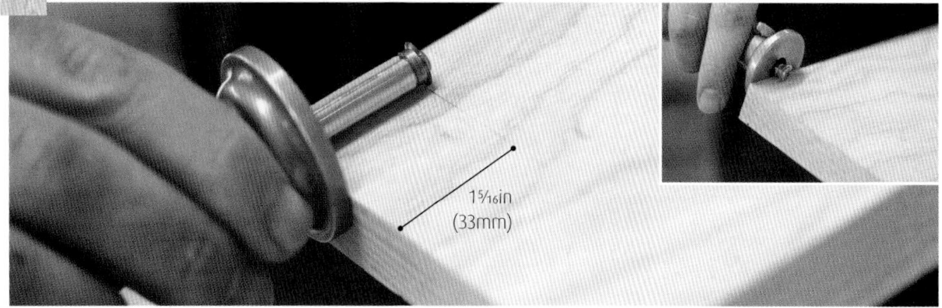

1 **Scribe a shoulder** of $1\frac{5}{16}$in (33mm) around all sides of both ends of both side rails with a marking gauge. Reset the marking gauge to $\frac{3}{16}$in (5mm), then scribe this measurement from both end grains to the shoulder at both ends of the rails (inset).

2 **Reset the marking gauge** to 1⅜in (35mm) and scribe a line from both edges of each end grain to indicate two tenons of 1³⁄₁₆in (30mm) at each end of both rails.

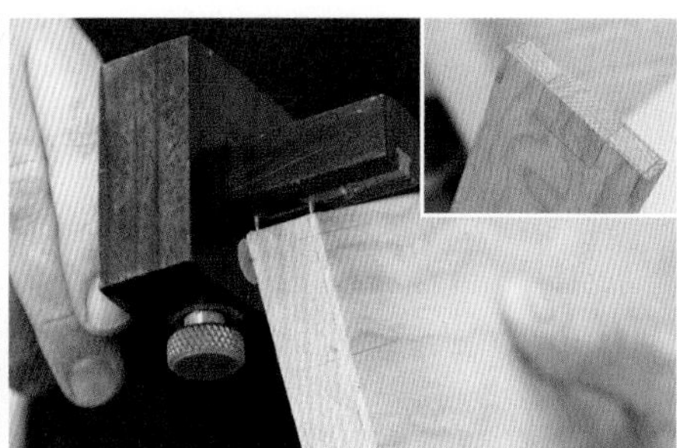

3 **Scribe a tenon width** of ⅝in (16mm) around the edges and end grain at each end of both rails and mark the waste (inset).

4 **Cut the tenons** on a band saw, then make relief cuts into the waste between the tenons. Use a marking knife to release the waste from the shoulders (inset).

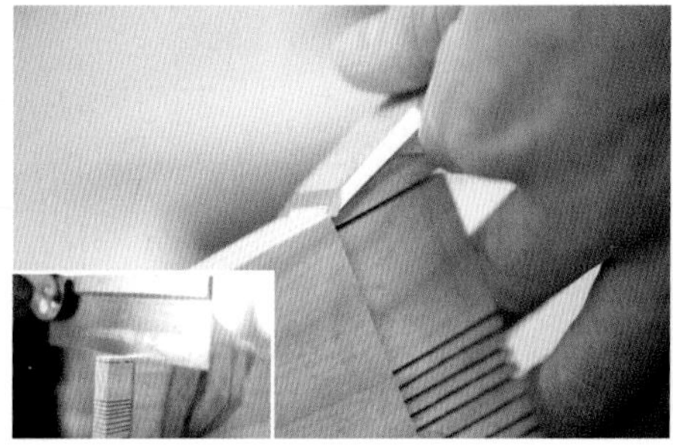

5 **Make a V-groove** along the shoulder line of the tenons on each edge of both of the end grains. Use a tenon saw to release the waste (inset).

6 **Remove the waste** from between the tenons by chopping it away with a bevel-edged chisel.

7 **Chamfer the edges** of both tenons at each end of the rails with a bevel-edged chisel, to ease the fit in the mortises.

FITTING THE CROSS-DOWEL AND BOLT CONNECTORS

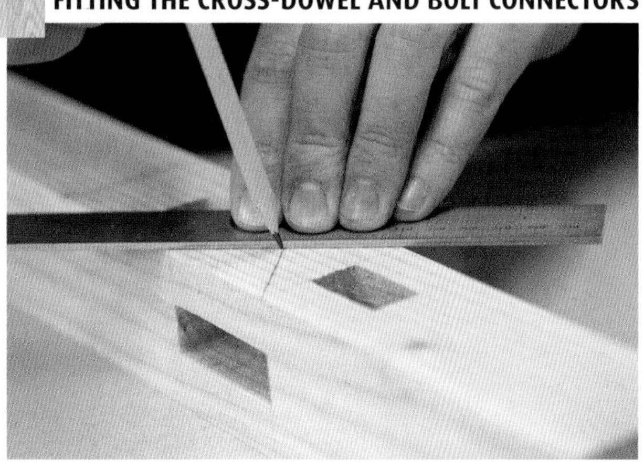

1 **The mortise-and-tenon joints** between the side rails and the legs are secured with cross-dowel and bolt connectors. Draw two diagonal lines between the edge of each pair of mortises on all four legs to mark the central point between them.

2 **Using a drill press** fitted with a ¼in (6mm) bit, drill a hole at the point marked all the way through. Repeat Steps 1–2 on the remaining three legs.

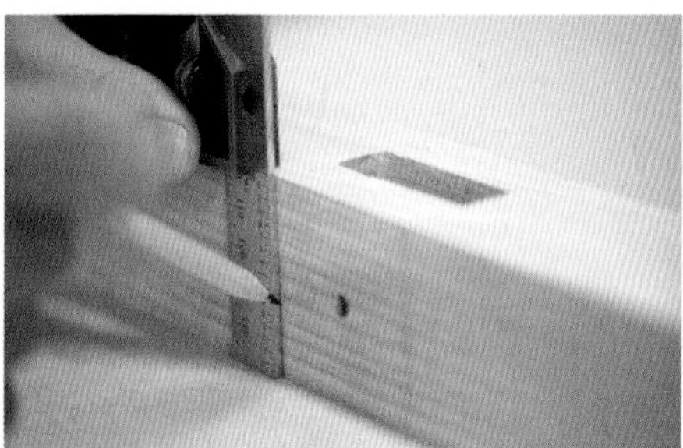

3 **Square two lines** from the ends of the mortise onto the adjacent side, across the edge where the hole emerges.

4 **Use a router** fitted with a ⅝in (16mm) cutter to cut a recess to a depth of ⅜in (10mm) centrally between the marks, through the position of the hole.

5 **Square off the ends** of the recess with a chisel. Make a similar recess in each of the remaining three legs.

6 **Use the router** to cut a recess 13⁄16in (20mm) long and 5⁄8in (15mm) deep across both ends of each side rail, 19⁄16in (40mm) from the shoulder. Square off the ends with a chisel.

7 **Insert the side-rail** tenons into the leg mortises, then drill through the existing hole (see Step 2) into the center of the recess in the side rail.

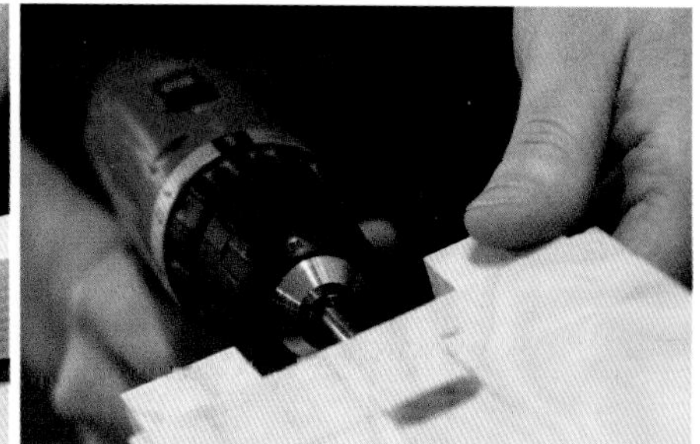

8 **If the drill bit** does not reach the recess in the side rail, remove the leg and continue to drill until you reach the recess.

9 **Insert a cross-dowel** into each recess (inset) and insert a bolt through the matching hole to test the fit, then dismantle.

GLUING AND CLAMPING THE END PIECES

1 **After test-fitting**, glue the joining parts of the headboard and footboard frames, then assemble. Clamp and allow to dry (inset).

2 **Once the glue** has dried, chamfer the top and bottom of each of the legs with a block plane.

MAKING THE CROSS-BRACE HOUSING

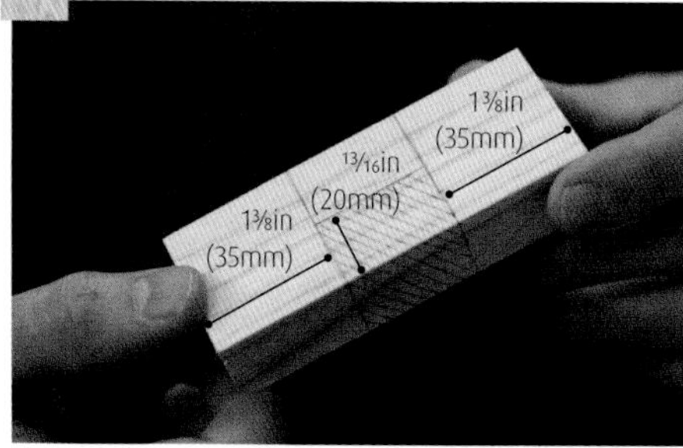

1 **Square two lines** around all four sides of the housing piece 1⅜in (35mm) from each end. Set a marking gauge to 13⁄16in (20mm) and scribe between the marks on both faces.

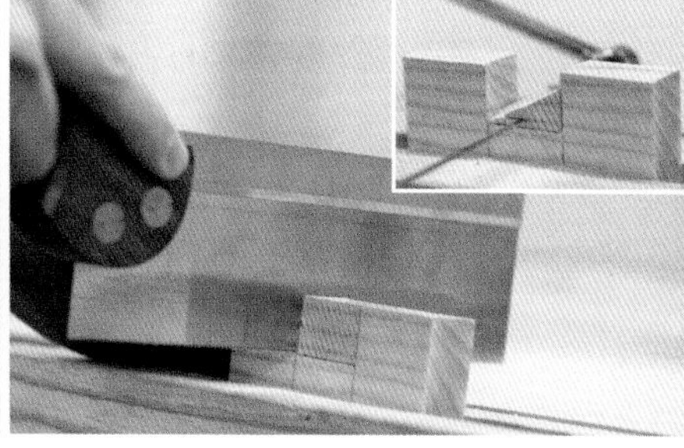

2 **Cut the housing** with a dovetail saw, then remove the bulk of the waste with a coping saw (inset).

3 **Trim the base** of the housing with a bevel-edged chisel. Cut the second housing piece in the same way, then check the fit of the cross-brace.

4 **Mark the positions** of the screw holes centrally on either side of the housing on both pieces. Drill through the marked positions with a bit to match the screws (inset), then countersink.

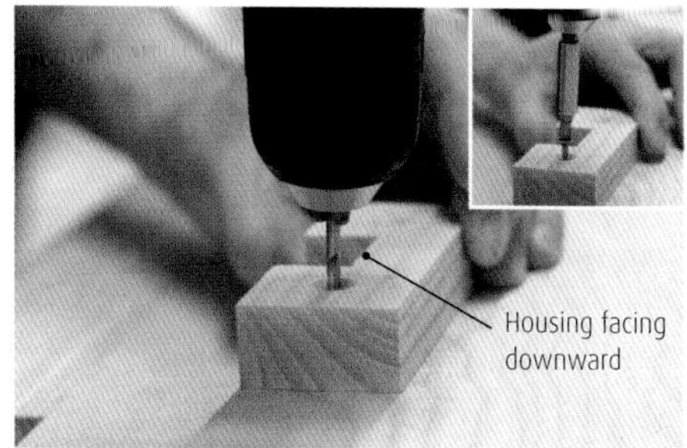

5 **Position a housing piece** in the center of each side rail aligned to the bottom edge. Drill a pilot hole into each clearance hole, then insert a screw (inset).

FITTING THE SLAT-SUPPORT BATTENS

1 **Mark the position** of four screw holes equidistantly along all four battens, using a pencil and combination square.

2 **Drill clearance holes** to match the size of the screws through each mark with a power drill, then countersink.

3 **Clamp the battens** onto the side rail aligned with the top of the housing. Drill pilot holes into the side rail through each of the clearance holes.

4 **Insert a screw** into each of the holes on both of the side rails, gripping one of the sash clamps for support if necessary.

FITTING THE SIDE RAILS TO THE FRAMES

1 **Re-drill the holes** between the mortises in the headboard and footboard through the tenon that has been glued in place.

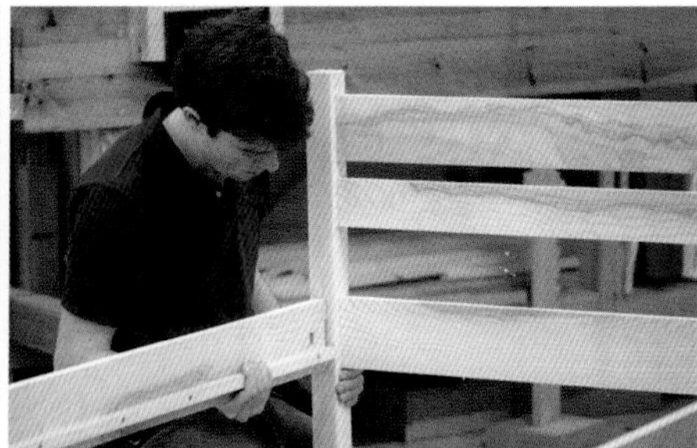

2 **Insert the side-rail tenons** into the headboard and footboard mortises to test the fit.

FIXING THE CROSS-BRACE

1 **Mark the position** of the edge of the housing on the cross-brace, then square the mark across the opposite face. Mark the center-point within this line by drawing two diagonal lines, then drill a clearance hole where the lines intersect (inset).

2 **Turn the bed** on its side, drill a pilot hole through the clearance hole into the underside of each housing, then screw the cross-brace into position.

FITTING THE CROSS-DOWEL AND BOLT CONNECTORS

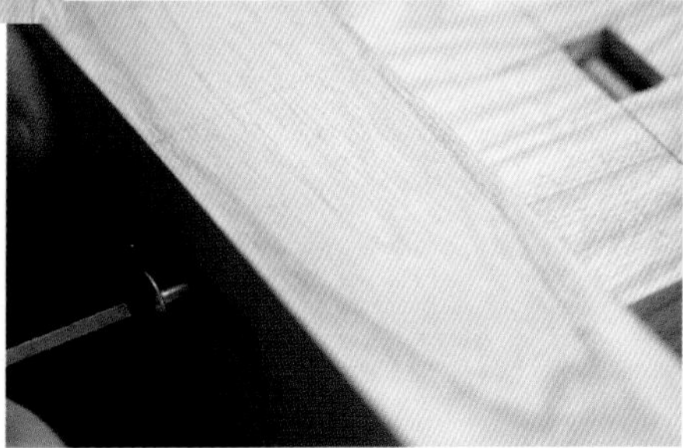

1 **Insert a bolt** into each of the recessed holes in the rear of both the headboard and footboard.

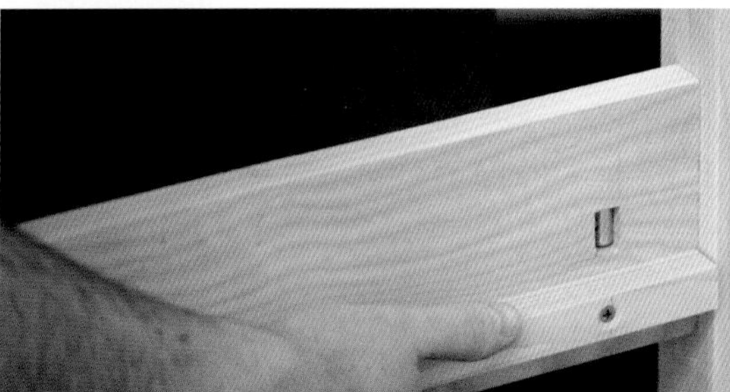

2 **Insert the cross-dowel** of the cross-dowel and bolt connector into the recess in the side rail, ensuring that the cross-dowel is oriented with the hole running from front to back. Use an Allen wrench to screw the bolt into the cross-dowel.

MAKING THE BOLT CAPS

1 **Use the bevel-edged chisel** to shape the inner side of each cap piece—which will cover the recessed holes in the headboard and footboard—to receive the head of the bolt.

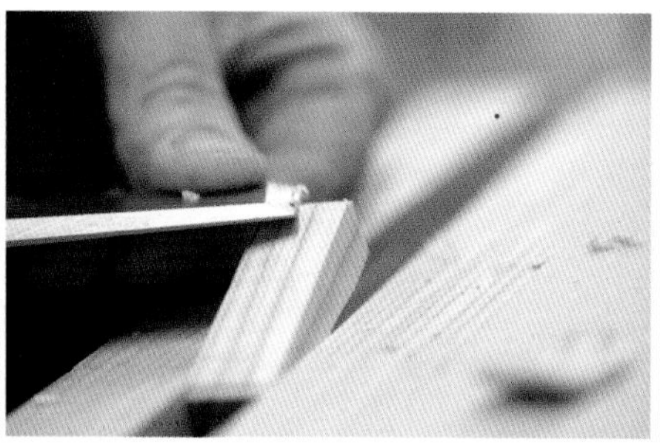

2 **Chamfer the edges** to ease the fit of the bolt cap in the holes, using the bevel-edged chisel—and a block plane if available—to finish.

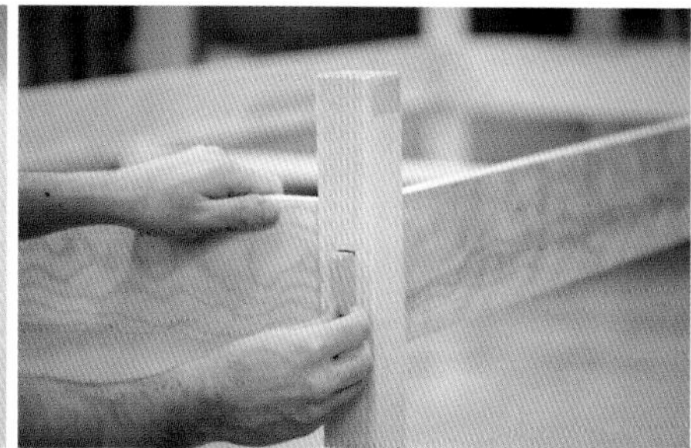

3 **Push each bolt cap** into place to cover the recessed holes. The bolt cap should be a snug fit and stand proud of the surrounding surface.

FIXING THE SLATS AND WEBBING

1 **Cut the webbing** into two equal lengths to fit the length of the bed. Using an MDF spacer (3 15/16in/100mm wide) to position the slats, fix the webbing to the slats with a staple gun.

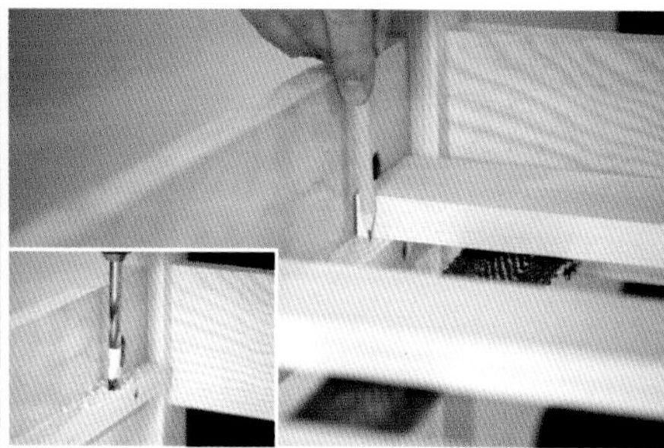

2 **Place the slats** webbing-side down into the bed frame. Mark the slat stops next to the first and last slat, centered in the width of the slat-support rail. Drill a 3/8in (10mm) hole to 5/8in (15mm) in depth (inset).

3 **Cut four dowels** 3/8in (10mm) in diameter and 1 3/16in (30mm) in length. Insert the dowels into the holes with a hammer and test the fit of the slat (inset).

FINISHES

This piece does not need any special finishing. However, you can use a clear acrylic varnish to give a good, durable finish, which retains the pale color of the timber and any interesting natural figuring. The slats should not be varnished or treated in any way.

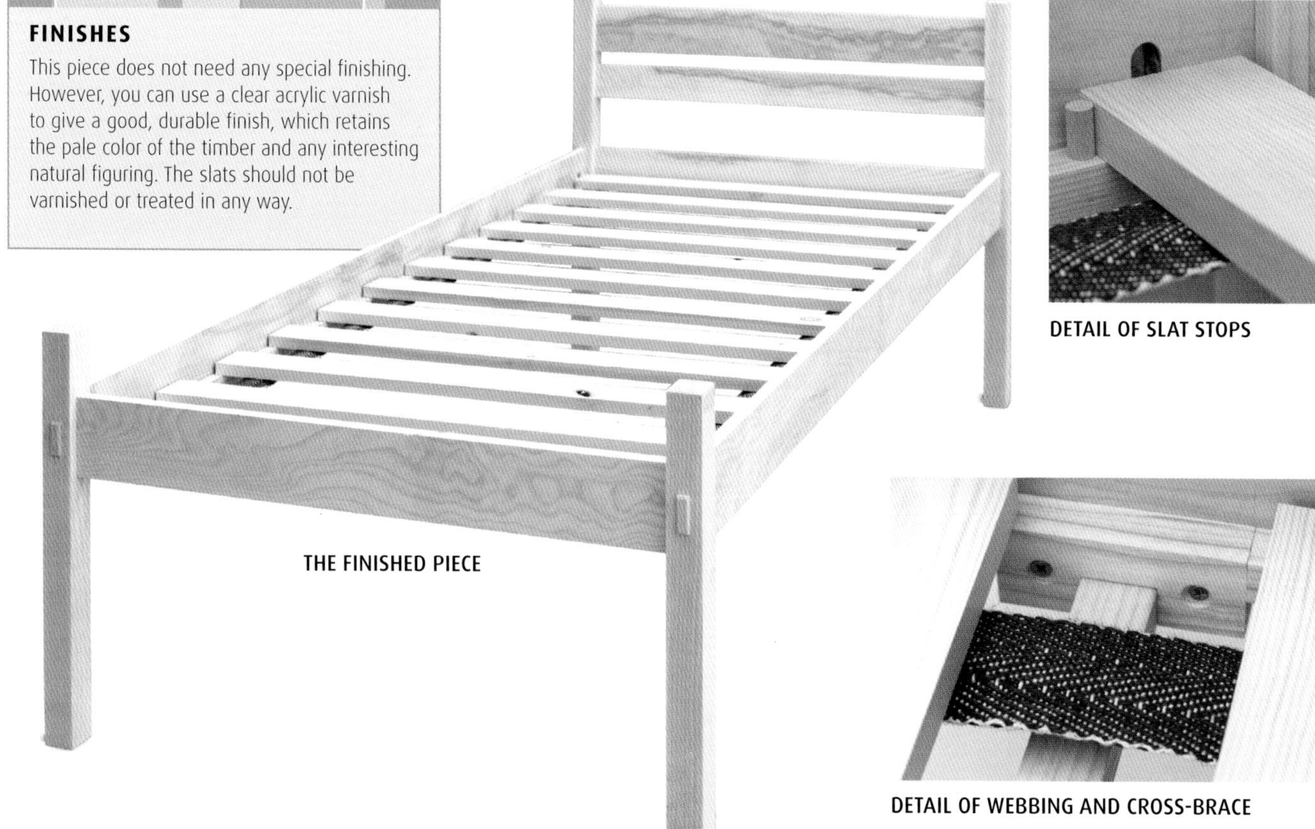

DETAIL OF SLAT STOPS

THE FINISHED PIECE

DETAIL OF WEBBING AND CROSS-BRACE

Glass-fronted cabinet

Making this wall-mounted cabinet provides the opportunity to practice a variety of carcass-construction techniques. The project employs a domino jointer (see p.65), but conventional mortise-and-tenon joints could be used instead. The doors are hinged onto the outside edges of the carcass and hang lower than the base, providing a hidden grip for opening.

Dimensions:
31 1/4 x 27 7/8 x 7 11/16in (795 x 710 x 195mm)

Key techniques:
Dovetail housing joint (pp.110–11);
Domino joints (pp.144–45)

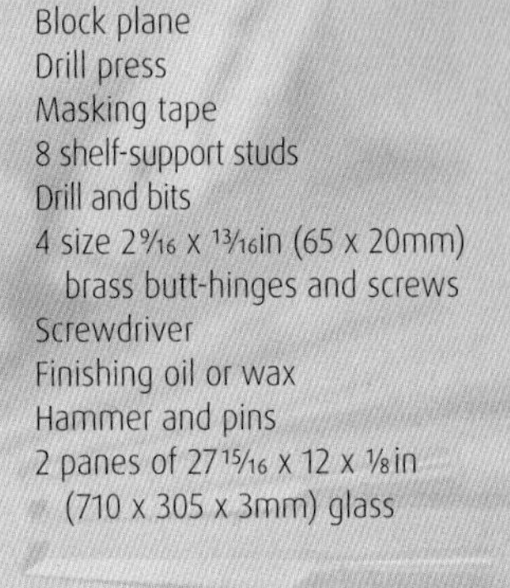

TOOLS AND MATERIALS

- Pencil
- Square
- Router, router table, dovetail cutter, straight-fluted cutter, and bearing-mounted rebate cutter
- Bevel-edged chisel
- Tenon saw
- Marking gauge
- Sandpaper
- Wood glue and brush
- Sash clamps
- Domino jointer
- 8 size 8x40 domino connectors
- MDF 29 1/2 x 7 1/16 x 11/16in (750 x 179 x18mm)
- Marking knife
- Block plane
- Drill press
- Masking tape
- 8 shelf-support studs
- Drill and bits
- 4 size 2 9/16 x 13/16in (65 x 20mm) brass butt-hinges and screws
- Screwdriver
- Finishing oil or wax
- Hammer and pins
- 2 panes of 27 15/16 x 12 x 1/8in (710 x 305 x 3mm) glass

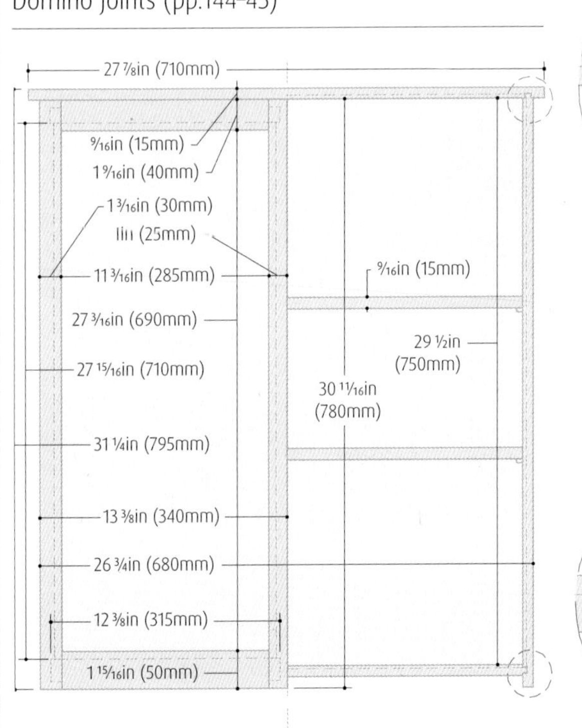

FRONT/BACK VIEW (1:10)

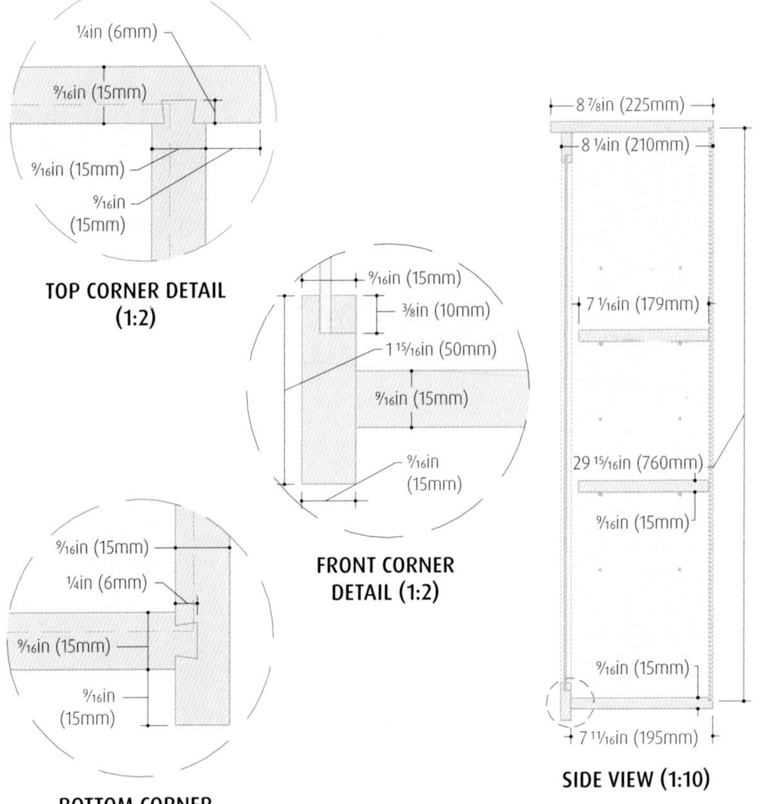

TOP CORNER DETAIL (1:2)

FRONT CORNER DETAIL (1:2)

BOTTOM CORNER DETAIL (1:2)

SIDE VIEW (1:10)

BACK

1/4in (6mm)
26in (660mm)
7 1/16in (179mm)
9/16in (15mm)
9/16in (15mm)
25 9/16in (650mm)
7 11/16in (195mm)
1 3/16in (30mm)
11 1/4in (285mm)
1in (25mm)
12in (305mm)
9/16in (15mm)

FRONT

HORIZONTAL CROSS-SECTION (1:5)

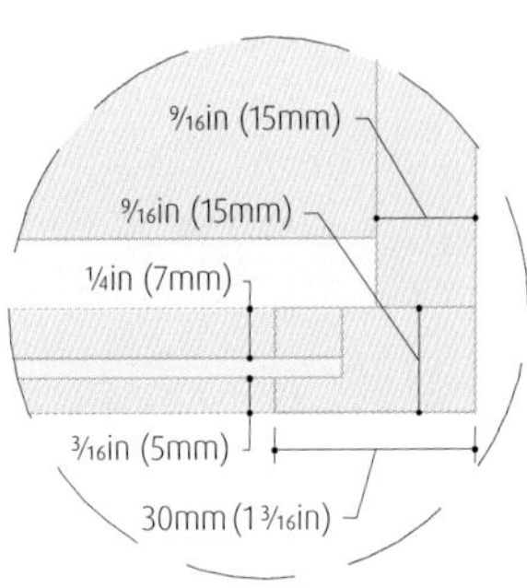

FRONT CORNER DETAIL (1:2)

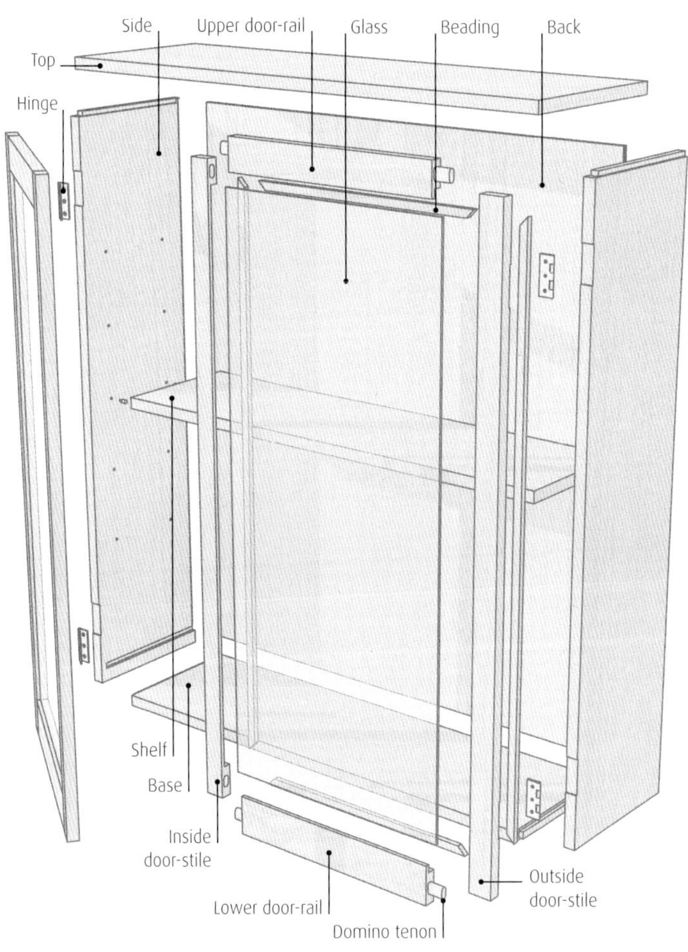

CUTTING LIST

Item	Material	No.	Length	Width	Thickness
Sides	Cherry	2	30 11/16in (780mm)	7 11/16in (195mm)	9/16in (15mm)
Base	Cherry	1	26 3/8in (670mm)	7 11/16in (195mm)	9/16in (15mm)
Top	Cherry	1	27 15/16in (710mm)	8 7/8in (225mm)	9/16in (15mm)
Shelves	Cherry	2	25 9/16in (650mm)	7 5/16in (185mm)	9/16in (15mm)
Back	Birch ply	1	30 1/4in (768mm)	26 5/16in (668mm)	1/4in (6mm)
Outside door stiles	Cherry	2	32 5/16in* (820mm)	1 3/16in (30mm)	9/16in (15mm)
Inside door stiles	Cherry	2	32 5/16in (820mm*)	1in (25mm)	9/16in (15mm)
Upper door rails	Cherry	2	11 1/4in (285mm)	1 9/16in (40mm)	9/16in (15mm)
Lower door rails	Cherry	2	11 1/4in (285mm)	1 15/16in (50mm)	9/16in (15mm)
Beading	Cherry	1	16 1/2ft* (5000mm)	3/8in (10mm)	1/4in (7mm)

*Includes excess to allow for cutting to size

How the elements fit together

The carcass is constructed with dovetail housing joints, and the birch ply-back simply drops into a rebate. The two doors consist of domino-jointed frames that hold the glass in place with beading.

MARKING OUT THE DOVETAIL HOUSING IN THE CARCASS SIDES

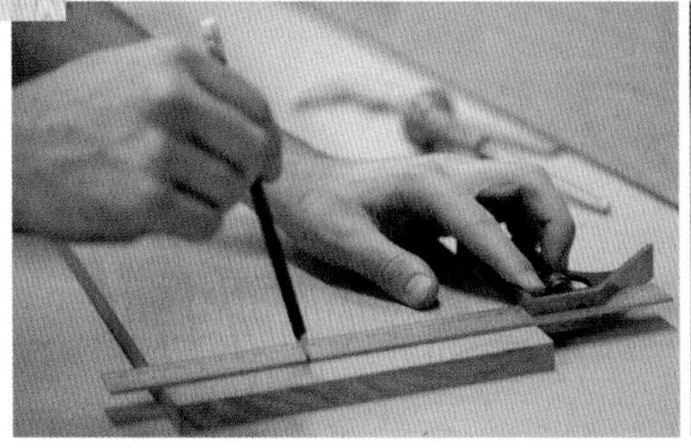

1 **Mark the position** of the center of the groove 1in (25mm) from the end grain on the inside face of each side piece.

2 **Mark the stop** 9/16in (15mm) from the front edge of each side piece with a pencil and square.

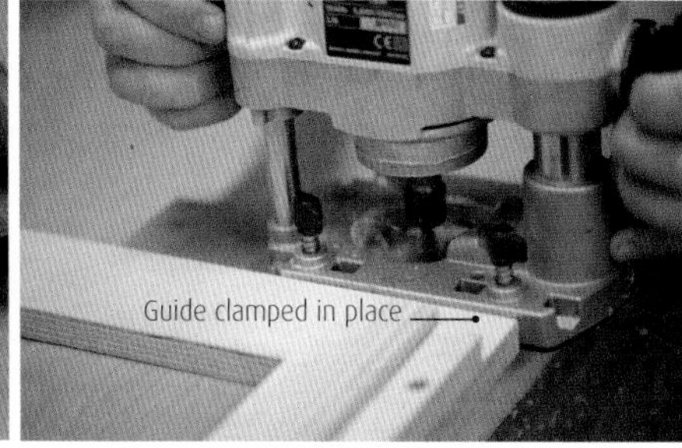

3 **Cut a groove** slightly less than 3/8in (10mm) in width from the stop to the back edge, using a router with a straight-fluted cutter, to a depth of 1/4in (6mm).

4 **Fit a 1/2in (12.7mm) dovetail bit** to the router and cut along the groove to angle the interior edges (inset) on each carcass side piece.

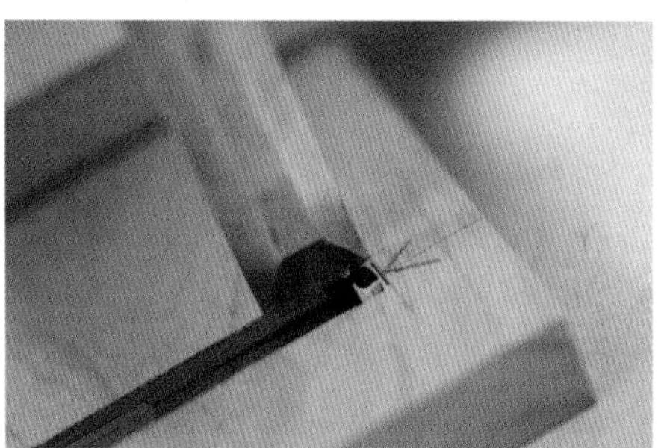

5 **Chisel the stopped end** of the groove square on each carcass side piece.

CUTTING THE REBATES AND THE DOVETAILS

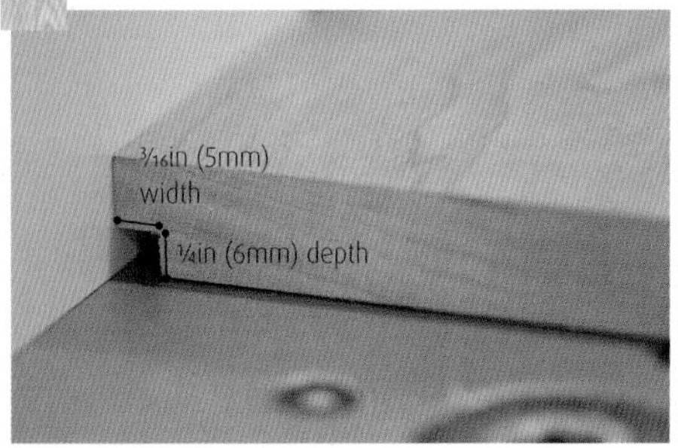

1 **Cut a rebate** along the back edges of the base and the two sides with a table-mounted router.

2 **Fit a dovetail bit** to the table-mounted router, set to a depth of 1/4in (6mm). Cut the tail into both faces of the base.

3 **Cut a stop** from the tail 9/16in (15mm) from the front edge with a tenon saw and clean up to the shoulder with a chisel (inset).

4 **Check the fit** of the dovetails in the end grains of the base by sliding them into the housings in the side pieces.

MAKING THE DOVETAIL HOUSINGS IN THE CARCASS TOP

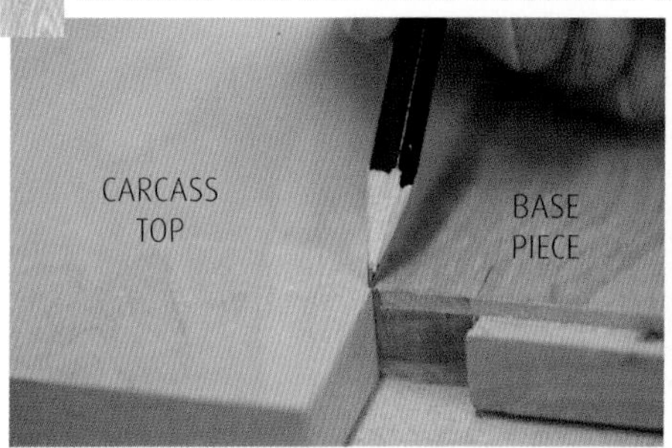

1 **Mark up the dovetail housing** on the carcass top. Determine the position by centering the base piece along its length and marking the positions of the shoulders.

2 **Mark a housing** 9/16in (15mm) wide at each end of the inside face of the carcass top. Mark a 1 9/16in (40mm) stop at the front edge (inset).

3 **Using the dovetail bit** and the hand-held router, center the cutter on the housing width (inset). Cut both housings and square off the stopped ends.

MAKING THE DOVETAILS IN THE TOP OF THE CARCASS SIDES

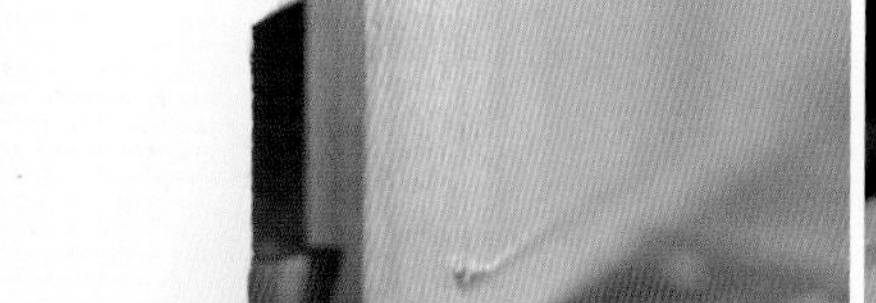

1 **Using a table-mounted router** fitted with the dovetail bit, cut along both faces of the top of both of the carcass sides to create a dovetail.

2 **Check the fit** of the dovetails in the carcass sides by sliding them into the housings in the carcass top. Adjust with a chisel if necessary.

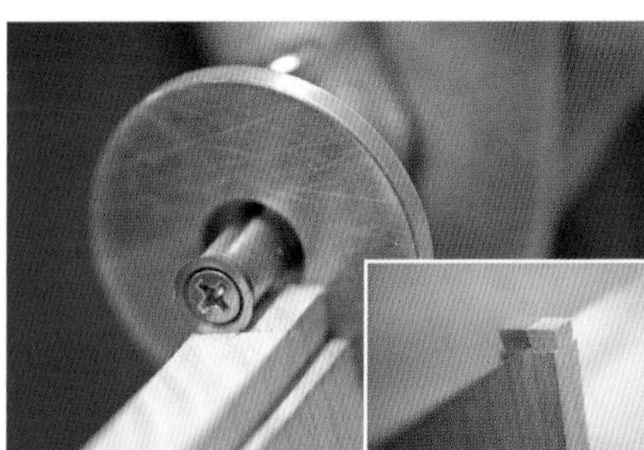

3 **Scribe a stop** in the dovetails 7/16in (11mm) from the front edge of each side. Cut with a tenon saw (inset).

CUTTING THE REBATE IN THE CARCASS TOP

1 **Using a table-mounted router**, cut a rebate to a depth of 1/4in (6mm) and a width of 3/16in (5mm) between the housings on the underside of the carcass top to house the back of the cabinet.

ASSEMBLING AND GLUING THE CARCASS

1 **Test-fit the carcass** and insert the back into the rebate. Make any adjustments that are necessary.

2 **Disassemble the carcass** and sand smooth the faces, edges, and arrises of all the carcass pieces.

3 **Glue and assemble** the carcass sides, top, and base. Insert the back piece into the rebate. Clamp and leave to dry.

MAKING THE DOORS

1 **Use a pencil** and square to mark the center of the width at each end of both door rails of the first door.

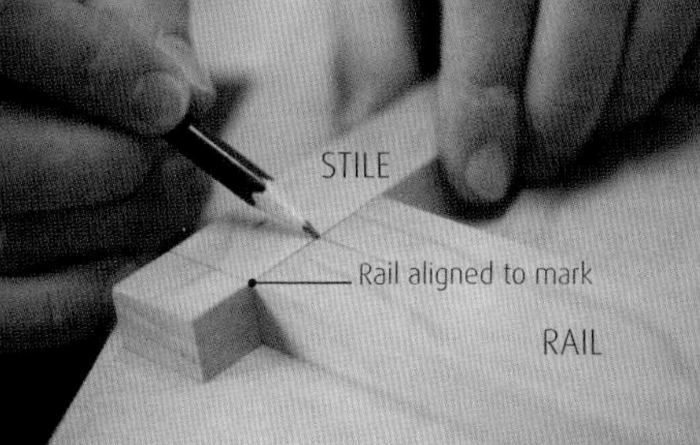

2 **Mark the door height** (30¹¹⁄₁₆in/780mm) on both door stiles, then place the rails at right-angles to these marks. Transfer the center marks from the rails to the stiles.

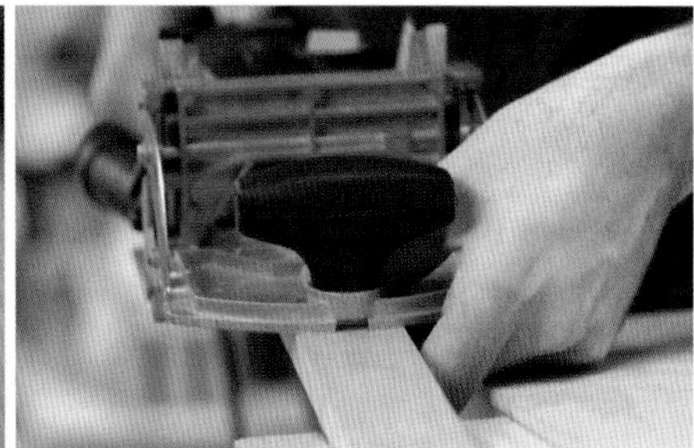

3 **Use the domino jointer** fitted with an ⁵⁄₁₆in (8mm) cutter to cut a slot to a depth of ¹³⁄₁₆in (20mm) in the center of both end grains of each rail.

4 **Cut domino mortises** to a depth of ¹³⁄₁₆in (20mm) in both marked positions in the edge of each of the stiles.

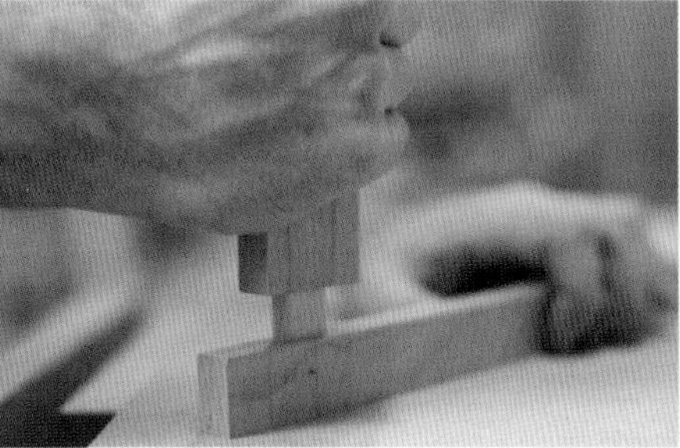

5 **Check the fit** of the dominoes in the slots in all the elements of the door frame.

6 **Glue and clamp** the door elements and allow to dry. Repeat Steps 1–5 for the second door and assemble in the same way.

FINISHING THE DOOR FRAMES

1 **Before cutting the rebate** for the glass in each door frame, make a jig from MDF to secure the frame in place and raise it from the bench surface to allow the router to run freely. Then make a wooden surround to provide a stable platform for the router (see also Routers, pp.44–49, and Jigs and templates, pp.150–51).

2 **Cut a rebate** on the inside of the inner edge of each door frame ⅜in (10mm) deep and ⅜in (10mm) wide, using a bearing-mounted rebate cutter.

3 **Mark each of the corners** on the door frames in pencil and use a chisel to pare to a right angle (inset).

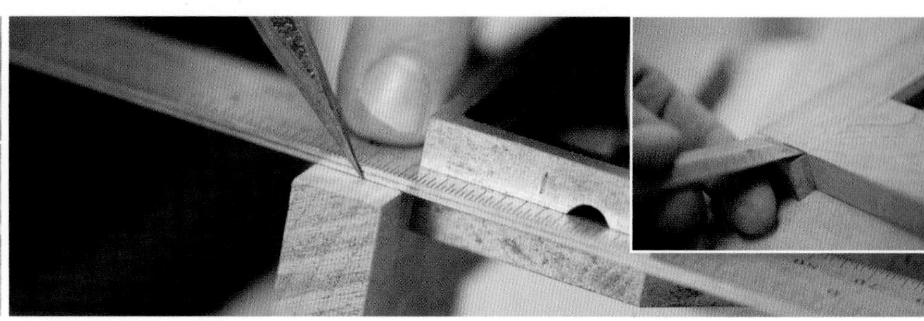

4 **Mark the excess** from the ends of the stiles with a marking knife. Chisel a V-groove to ensure a clean cut (inset).

5 **Cut across the end grain** flush with the rail using a small tenon saw. Repeat on each end of both stiles.

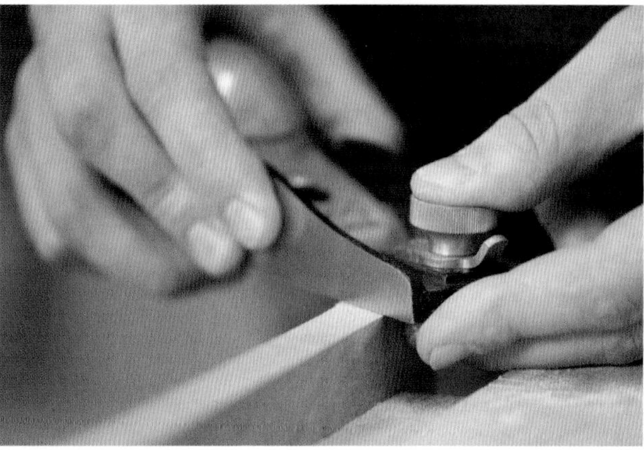

6 **Plane the edges** of the door frames flat with a block plane.

MAKING THE JIG FOR THE SHELVES

1 **Make a jig** as a guide for the holes for the movable shelf supports. Cut a piece of MDF to the same dimensions as the interior surface of the carcass sides.

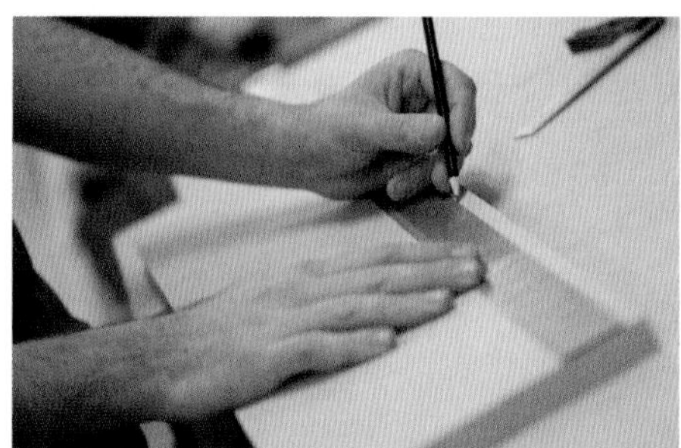

2 **Mark a range** of positions for the shelves along the length of the jig, according to your requirements.

3 **Extend the marks** square across the width of the jig using a pencil and square.

4 **Mark two positions** for the shelf supports 1³⁄₁₆in (30mm) from each edge, along the marks.

5 **Drill a hole** through each mark using a bit that matches the shelf supports. A drill press (pictured) is the best tool for the job.

FITTING THE SHELVES

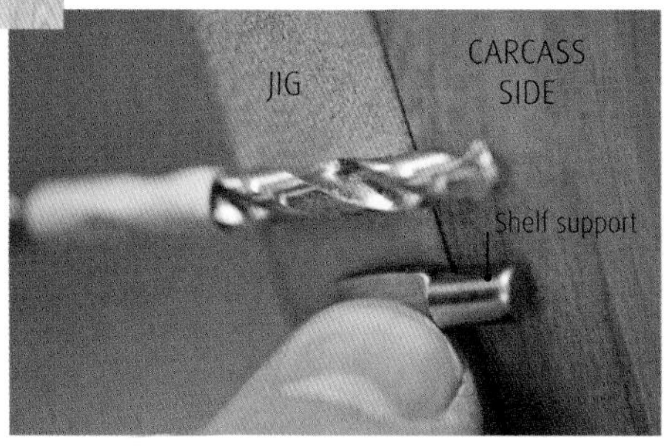

1 **Calculate the depth** of the holes to be drilled for the shelf supports by measuring the shank of a shelf support and adding the thickness of the jig. Mark the drill bit accordingly with masking tape.

2 **Set the jig** against the inside of the carcass and drill holes through each of the marks on the jig into each of the carcass sides.

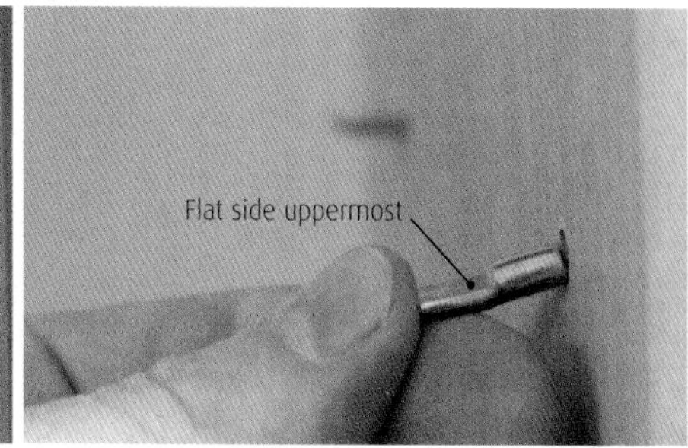

3 **Check the fit** of the shelf supports in the carcass sides. Ensure that you insert them with the flat sides sticking out and facing upward.

4 **Sand all of the surfaces** and edges of the shelf pieces and place them in position inside the carcass.

MAKING THE HINGE HOUSINGS ON THE CARCASS

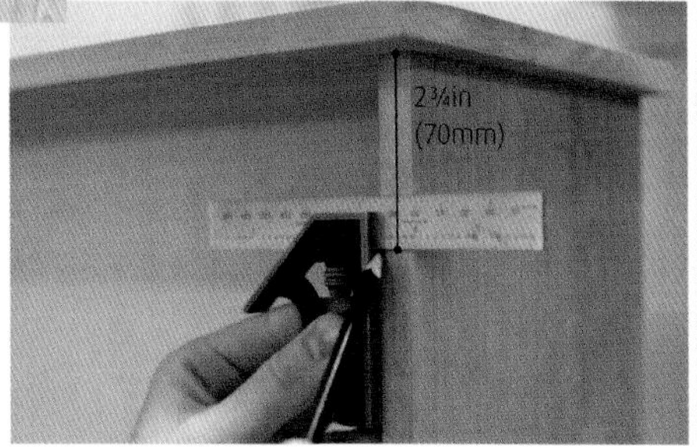

1 **Mark the position** of the top hinge on the edge of each carcass side 2¾in (70mm) from the top.

2 **Set the top edge** of the hinge against the mark on each carcass side and mark the lower edge of the hinge housing.

3 **Mark the position** of the lower hinge 2¾in (70mm) from the bottom of each carcass side and mark the size of the housing as before.

4 **Square all the marks** for the hinge housings onto both faces of the carcass sides, using a pencil and square.

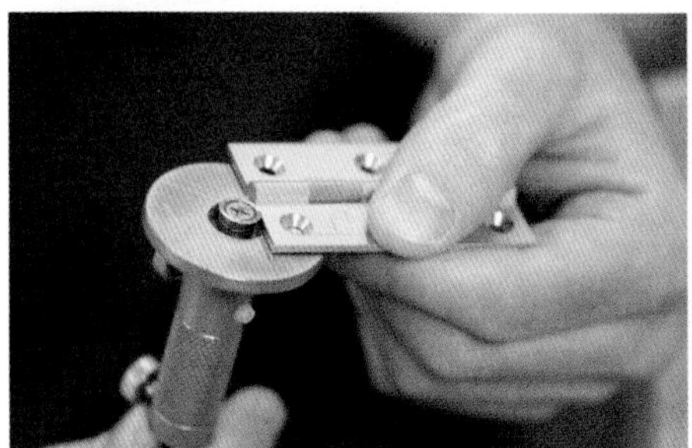

5 **Using a marking gauge**, measure the thickness of the hinge flange to determine the depth of the housing.

6 **Scribe the depth** of the housing onto both faces between the length marks. Repeat for all of the housings.

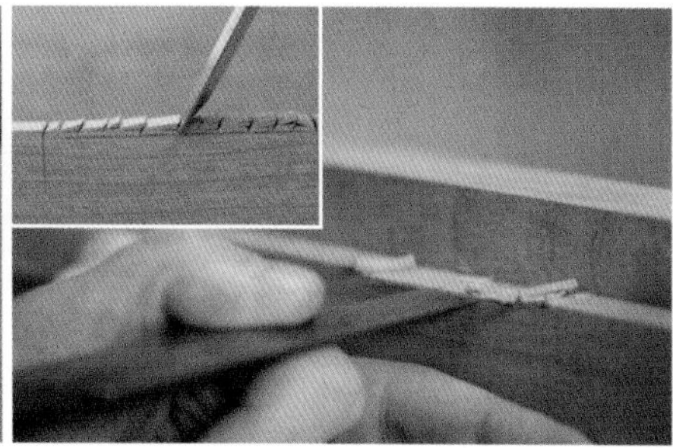

7 **Release the waste** from each of the hinge housings using a chisel (inset). Clean up the base by paring.

FITTING THE HINGES ON THE DOORS

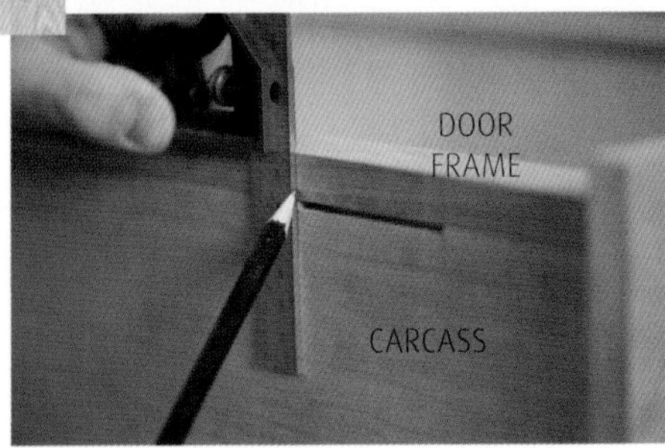

1 **Place a door frame** in position against the carcass and transfer the hinge marks from the carcass squarely onto the edge of the door frame.

2 **Square the marks** around and onto the inside face of the door frame, using a pencil and square.

3 **Use the marking gauge** as previously set to mark the thickness of the hinge between the length marks on the edge of the door frame.

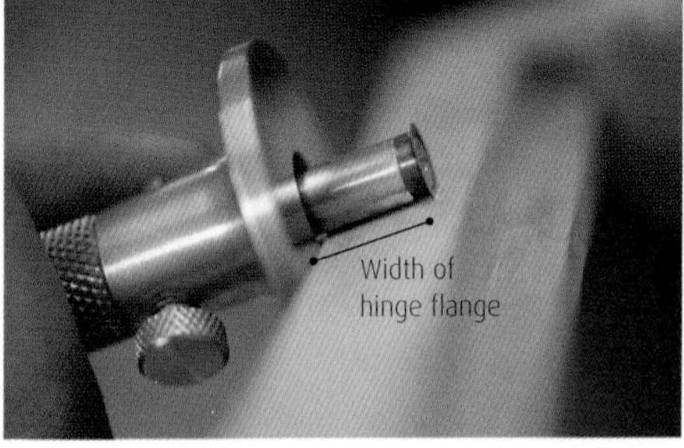

4 **Set the marking gauge** to the width of the hinge flange and scribe on the inside face of the frame between the length marks. Repeat for all other hinges on both doors.

5 **Chisel out the hinge housings** on both door frames, then test the fit of the hinges. Adjust if necessary.

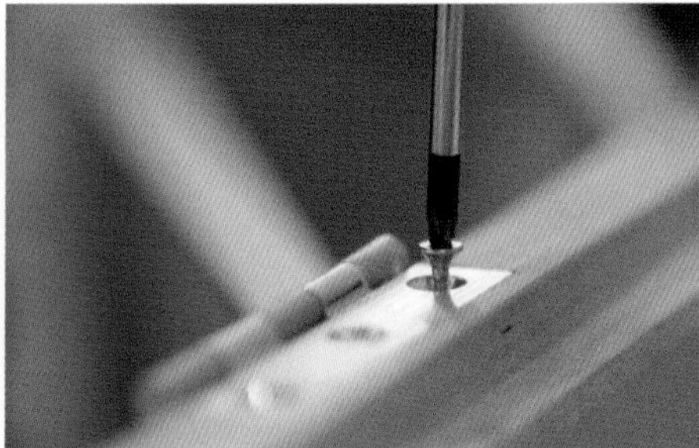

6 **With the hinge** in place, drill pilot holes through the holes in the hinge into the door frames, then insert the screws.

7 **Check the fit** of the hinges on the door frames and carcass by closing each hinge (inset), but do not screw the hinges into the carcass until the glass has been fitted.

FITTING THE GLASS

1 **Carefully place the glass** into the rebate that has been cut into the back of each door frame.

2 **Cut the stock** for the beading roughly to size: four pieces of about 31½in (800mm) and four of 15¾in (400mm). Cut a miter close to the end grain of one long piece.

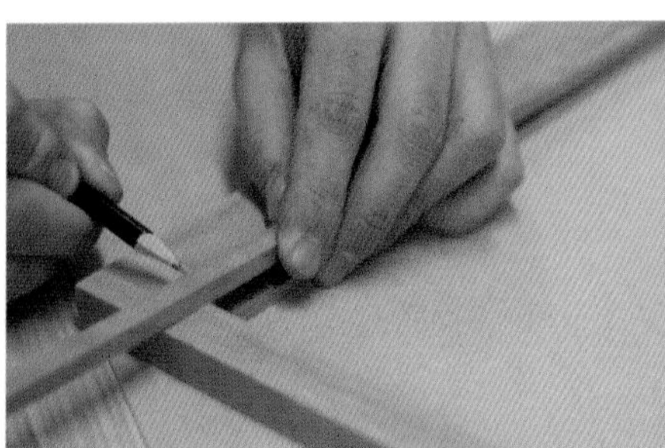

3 **Set the mitered end** into the corner of a door frame. Mark the length of the beading to fit one long inside edge. Cut a miter in that position with a tenon saw.

4 **Cut a miter** in the end of a short piece. Align it with the mitered end of the mitered long piece. Cut a miter in the other end of the short piece to fit the short side. Cut the beading for each inner edge of both door frames in the same way.

5 **Apply your chosen finish**, such as finishing oil or wax, to the door frames and beading, before affixing the beading to secure the glass in each door.

6 **Place the glass** in position in the door frames. Secure the glass with beading fitted on the inside edge of the door frame. Use a small hammer to fix the beading in position with panel pins.

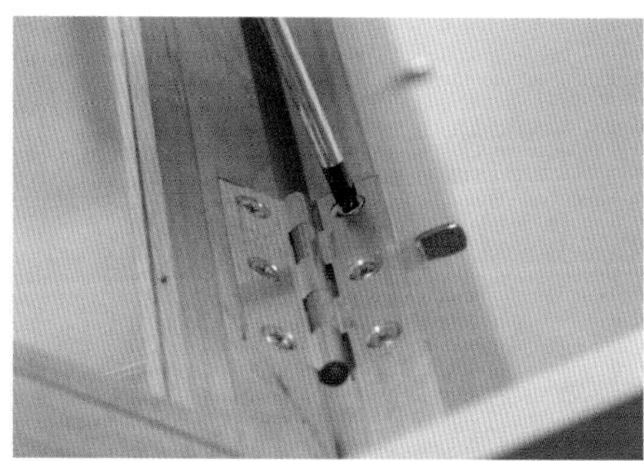

7 **Apply the selected finish** to the carcass, then fix the doors by screwing the hinges into the prepared positions.

THE FINISHED PIECE

ALTERNATIVE WITH SOLID DOORS

If you do not want to use glass in the doors, solid panels are an alternative option. A thin, veneered panel would be the best material to use for a door of this size because it would not be excessively heavy.

SHELF AND HINGE DETAIL

DOOR-FRAME DETAIL

Gateleg table

This table makes a great side table when folded and transforms into a small dining table when the gateleg is extended. The table top opens by means of a rule joint, and is supported by a gateleg that pivots on a brass rod. The table here was finished with finishing oil, but wax or varnish could be used.

Dimensions:
720 x 800 x 490mm (28⅜ x 31½ x 19⁵⁄₁₆in) with gateleg closed

Key techniques:
Basic mortise-and-tenon joint (pp.116–19)
Haunched tenon joint (p.120); Edge-to-edge joint (pp.94–95)

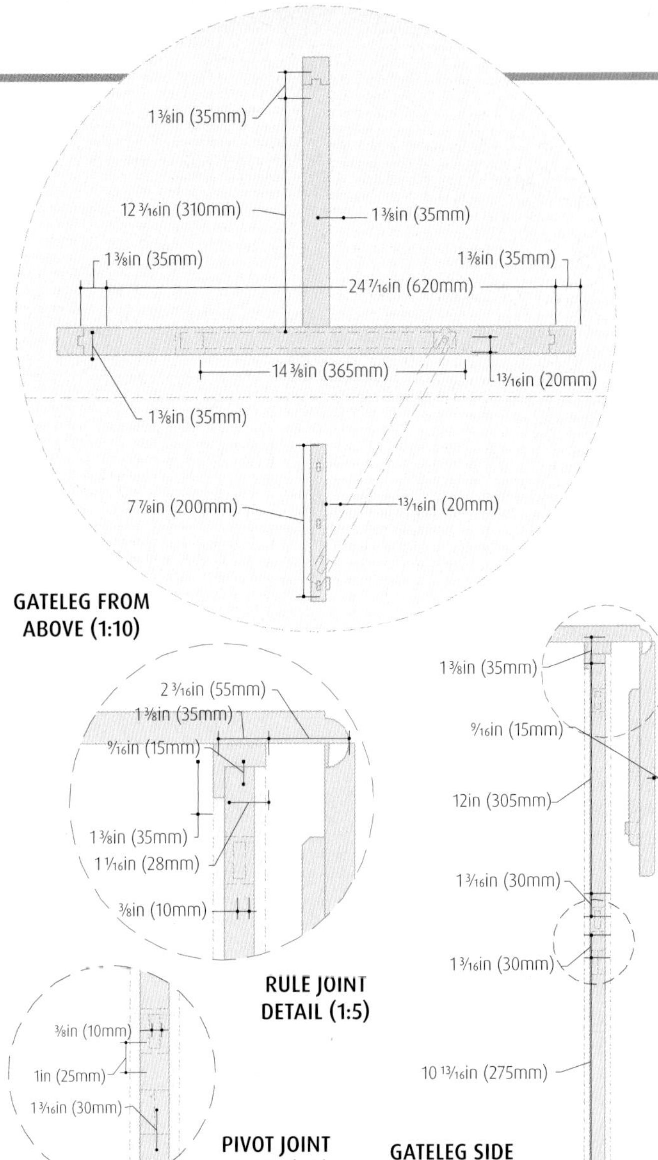

GATELEG FROM ABOVE (1:10)

RULE JOINT DETAIL (1:5)

PIVOT JOINT DETAIL (1:5)

GATELEG SIDE (1:10)

TOOLS AND MATERIALS

- Long metal ruler
- Pencil
- Wood glue and brush
- Sash clamps
- Hand-held router with straight cutters, rule-joint cutters, and bearing guide
- Cabinet scraper
- MDF (24 x 1½ x ¼in/600 x 40 x 6mm)
- Combination square
- MDF (33½ x 33½ x ¼in/850 x 850 x 6mm)
- Drill with bits
- Hammer
- Panel pins
- Band saw
- MDF (24 x 8 x ¼in/600 x 200 x 6mm)
- Table saw or panel saw
- Planer or bench plane
- Marking gauge
- Bevel-edged chisel
- 2 table hinges and screws
- Marking knife
- Screwdriver
- Sandpaper and block
- Mortise gauge
- Mortiser or mortise chisel
- Tenon saw (optional)
- Rubber mallet
- Tape measure
- Masking tape
- 2 brass rods (³⁄₁₆ x ¼in/30 x 6mm)
- Set square
- Block plane
- 2 screws (No.8 x 1in/4 x 25mm);
- 5 screws (No.8 x 1⅜in/4 x 35mm);
- 1 screw (No.4 x ¾in/3 x 20mm)
- File

CUTTING LIST

Item	Material	No.	Length	Width	Thickness
Table top	Oak	9	35½in* (900mm)	4in* (100mm)	¹³⁄₁₆in (20mm)
Legs	Oak	3	27⁹⁄₁₆in (700mm)	1⅜in (35mm)	1⅜in (35mm)
Long upper rail	Oak	1	26⅞in (680mm)	1⅜in (35mm)	1⅜in (35mm)
Short upper rail	Oak	1	14⅝in (370mm)	1⅜in (35mm)	1⅜in (35mm)
Long lower rail	Oak	1	27⁹⁄₁₆in (700mm)	1³⁄₁₆in (30mm)	¹³⁄₁₆in (20mm)
Short lower rail	Oak	1	15in (382.5mm)	1³⁄₁₆in (30mm)	¹³⁄₁₆in (20mm)
Gateleg	Oak	1	26¹⁵⁄₁₆in (685mm)	1⅜in (35mm)	¹³⁄₁₆in (20mm)
Inner stile	Oak	1	14³⁄₁₆in (360mm)	1³⁄₁₆in (30mm)	¹³⁄₁₆in (20mm)
Stretcher rails	Oak	2	13⁹⁄₁₆in (345mm)	1³⁄₁₆in (30mm)	¹³⁄₁₆in (20mm)
Leg-stop batten	Oak	1	8in (200mm)	¹³⁄₁₆in (20mm)	⁹⁄₁₆in (15mm)

*Includes excess to allow for cutting to size

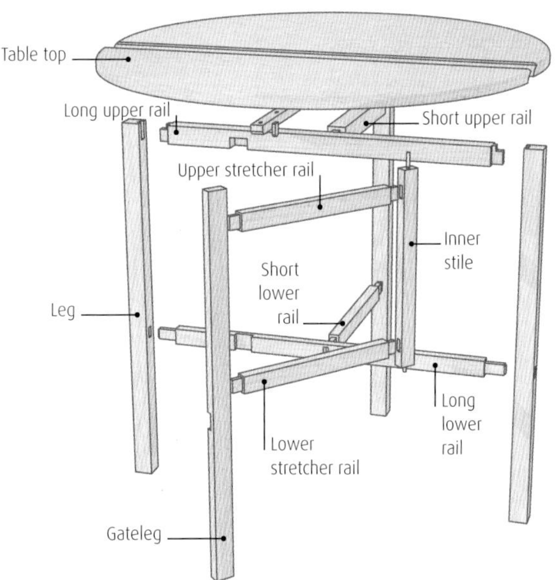

How the elements fit together
There are two frames—one fixed and one movable (the gateleg). Both are constructed with mortise-and-tenon joints. The table top is screwed in place through the upper rails.

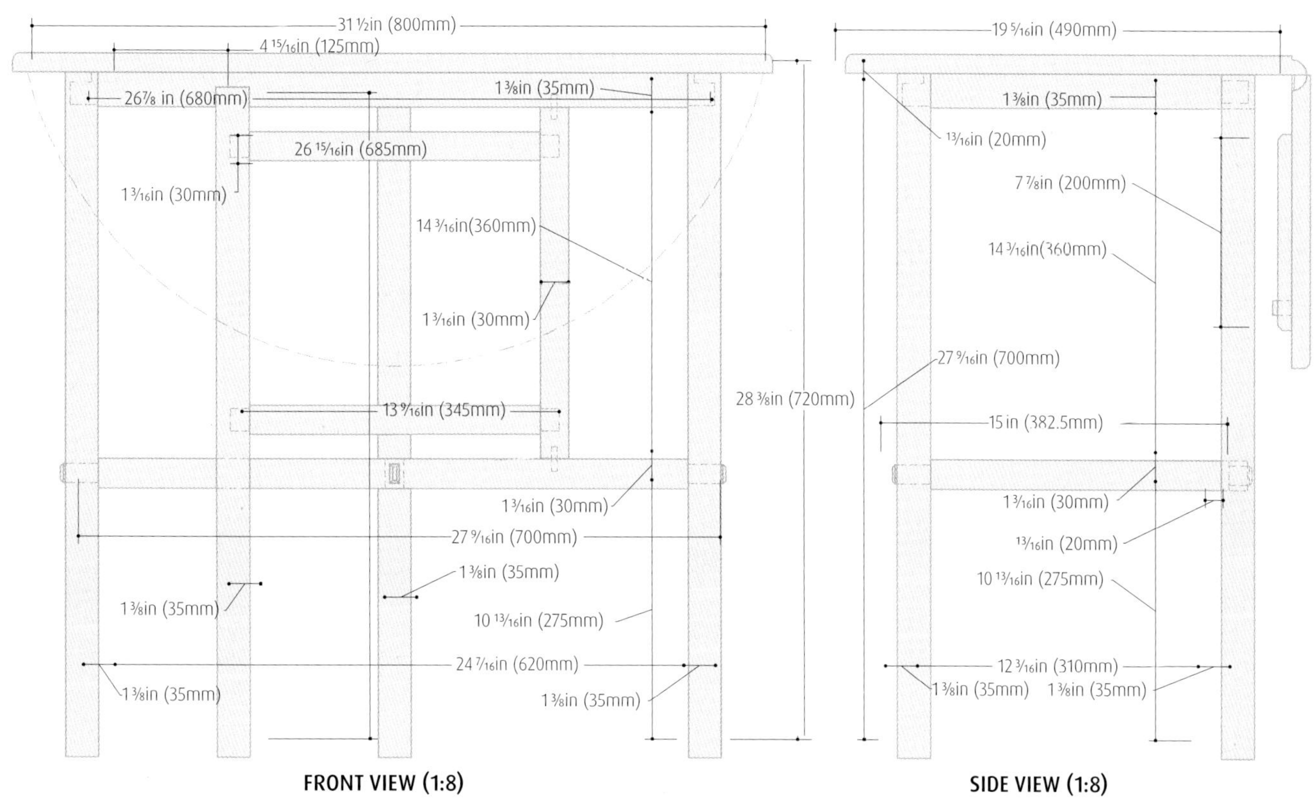

FRONT VIEW (1:8)

SIDE VIEW (1:8)

PREPARING THE TABLE TOP AND THE TABLE-TOP TEMPLATE

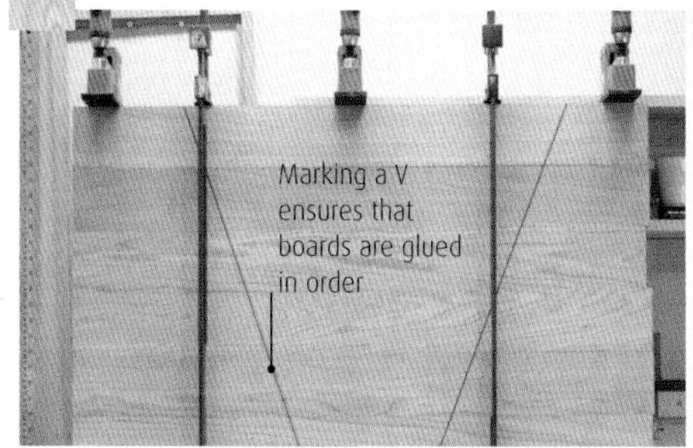

1 **Arrange the table-top pieces** to form the table top. Using a ruler, make a V-mark in pencil across the pieces in their final positions, then disassemble. Glue the pieces together (see Edge-to-edge joint, pp.94–95), arranging them with the V-mark aligned. Clamp and allow to dry.

2 **Cut the assembled table top** to form an 33 ½in (850mm) square using a table saw or panel saw. Smooth the surface with a cabinet scraper.

3 **Make a trammel** slightly longer than the radius of the table top from a strip of MDF. Mark a point a short distance from one end of the trammel and square the mark across the face.

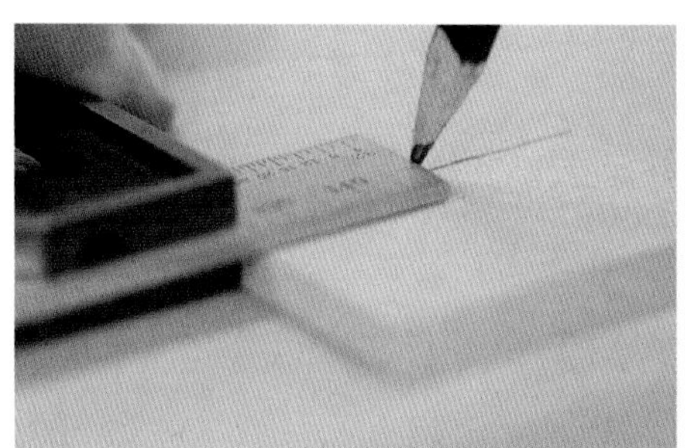

4 **Mark the radius** of the circle 15 ¾in (400mm) from that point and square off with a combination square. Make a mark at the halfway point of both lines.

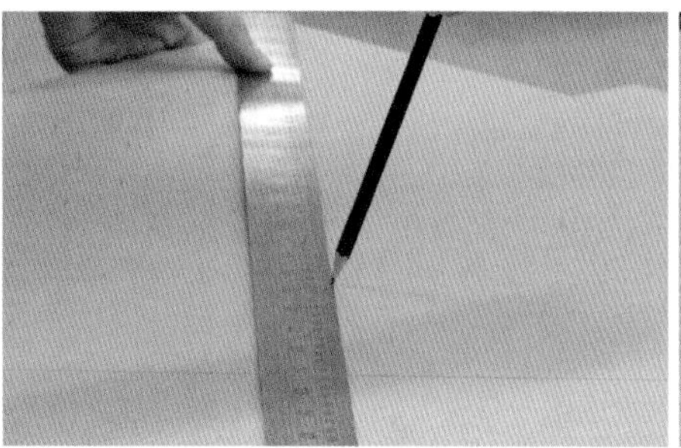

5 **Mark the centerpoint** of a square piece of MDF (33 ½ x 33 ½in/850 x 850mm), which will be used as the table-top template. Draw diagonal lines from opposite corners and mark the point at which they intersect.

6 **Drill a fine hole** for a panel pin where the lines intersect on the template and in one of the marked positions on the trammel. Drill a larger hole for a pencil in the other marked position on the trammel (inset).

7 **Use a hammer** to pin the trammel to the center of the template, then insert a pencil into the hole. As you rotate the trammel, the pencil will draw a circle with a 15¾in (400mm) radius on the template.

8 **Remove the trammel** and line up a ruler square to the edge of the template and draw a line through the center. Draw another line through the center at right-angles from the other edge.

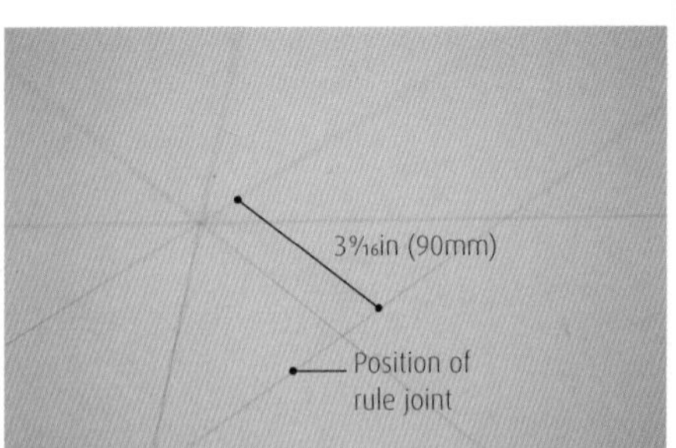

9 **Measure 3⁹⁄₁₆in (90mm)** from one of the centerlines and square the measurement across the template. This is the position of the rule joint.

CUTTING THE TEMPLATE

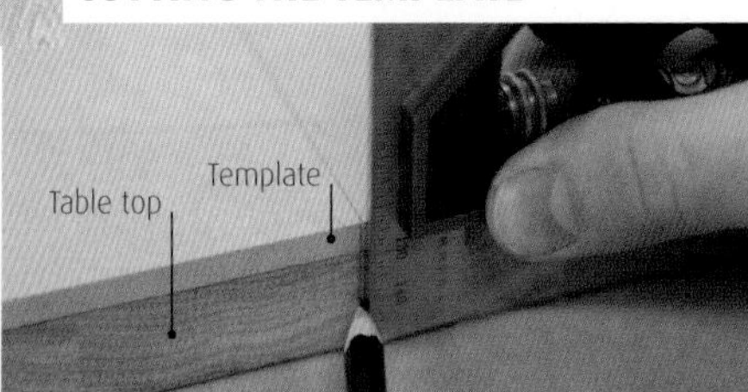

1 **Place the template** precisely over the table top and mark the position of the rule joint on the edge of the table top.

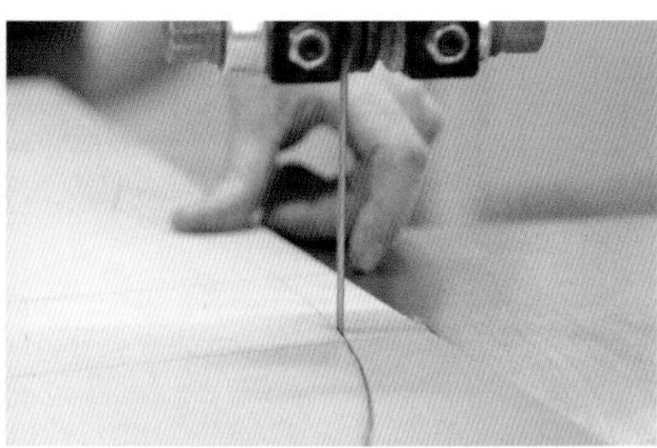

2 **Roughly cut out** the circular template on a band saw. Be careful to cut to the waste side of the marks.

3 **As you progress, use both hands** to guide the template through the blade to ensure that you do not cut through the marks.

MAKING THE ROUTER TRAMMEL

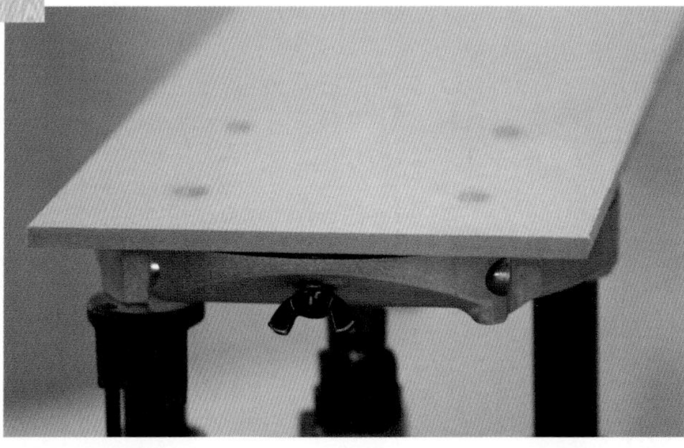

1 **Use a piece of MDF** to make a trammel for your router. Cut it to the width of the router, then mark and drill the positions of the router-locating screws at one end of the trammel. Fit a straight bit in the router and screw it to the trammel in the marked positions.

2 **With the router attached** to the trammel, drill a hole in the guide through which the router cutter can protrude.

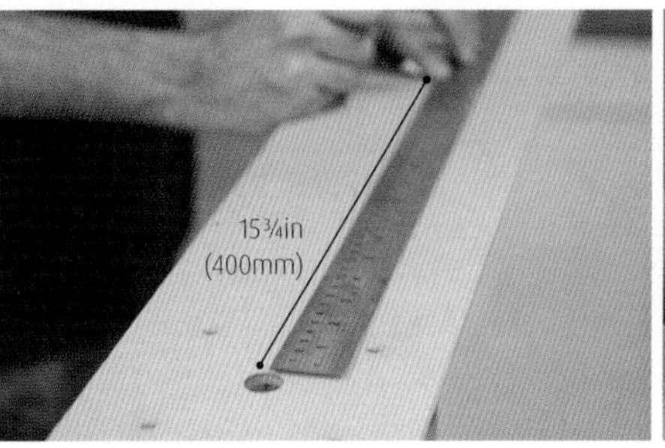

3 **Measure 15¾in (400mm)** from the inner edge of the router hole and mark that position square across the trammel.

4 **Drill a hole** for a panel pin on the router trammel at the halfway point of the marked line.

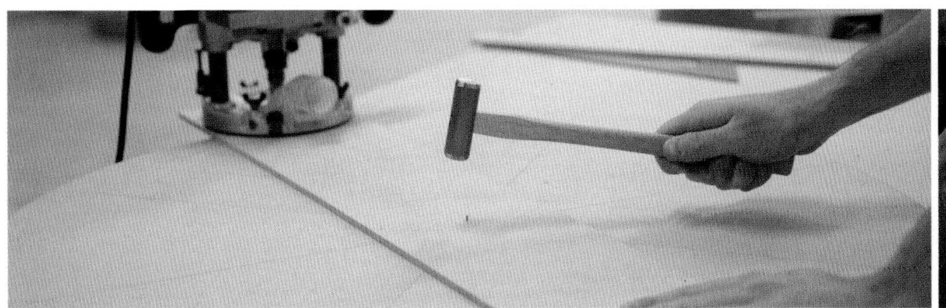

5 **Pin the router trammel**, with the router attached, through the center of the template and into the workbench. Arrange the edge of the template so it is in a position overhanging the edge of the workbench.

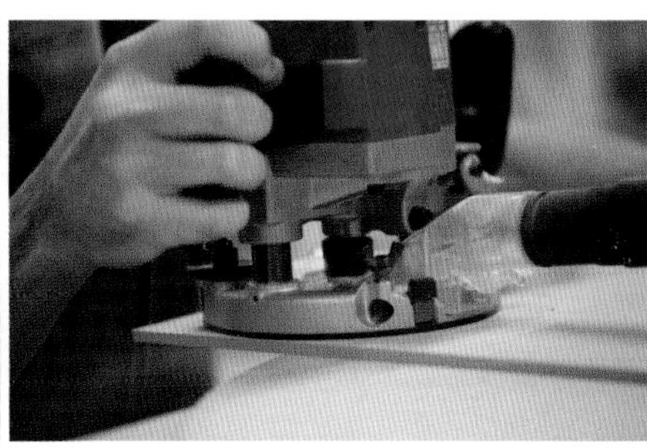

6 **Cut around the edge** of the template with the router, taking care to turn the template as you work until you have routed all the way around the circumference.

DIVIDING THE TABLE TOP

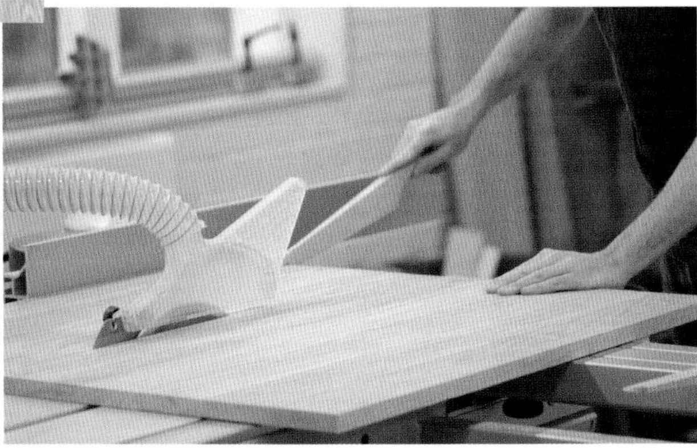

1 **Use a table saw** (or panel saw) to cut the table top in two. Align the blade with the rule-joint line.

2 **Smooth the edges** of both parts of the table top on a planer (pictured) or by hand with a bench plane.

MAKING THE RULE JOINT

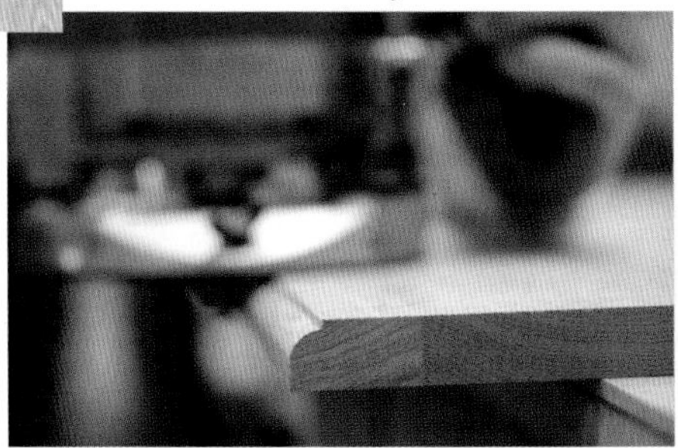

1 **Fit a router** with a round-over cutter (one of a pair of rule-joint cutters). Set the router to the full depth and cut along the newly cut edge of the larger table-top piece.

2 **Fit the matching coving cutter** to the router and cut along the newly cut edge of the smaller table-top piece. Remember to cut from the underside of the piece.

3 **Check that the covings** on both pieces of the table top fit together snugly. Make any necessary adjustments.

FITTING THE HINGES

1 **On the larger table-top piece**, use the marking gauge to scribe a line from the start of the curve on the end grain onto the underside of the table top.

2 **Mark the position** of the hinges on this line 7⅛in (180mm) from each end. Using the hinge as a guide, draw two more lines to mark the width of the hinges.

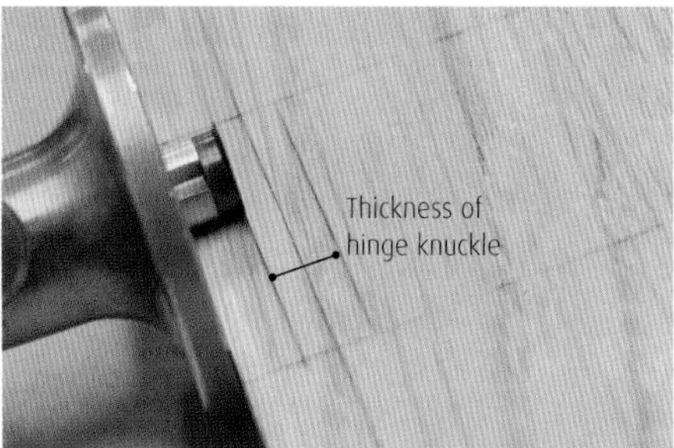

3 **Measure and mark** the thickness of the hinge knuckle by scribing that distance on either side of the line drawn in Step 1.

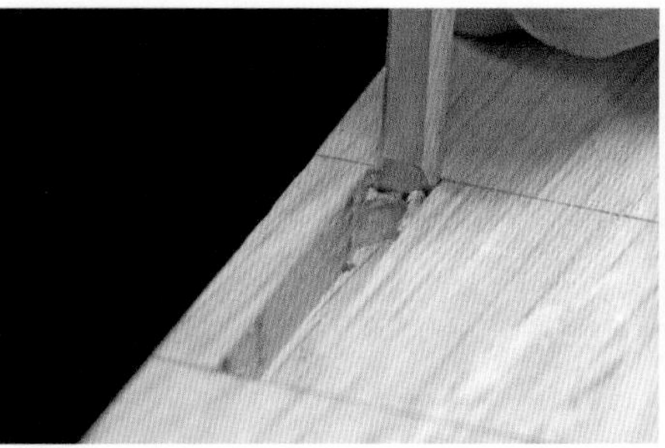

4 **Select a cutter** for your router to match the width of the knuckle, and cut a groove with the router. Square off the ends of the groove with a bevel-edged chisel.

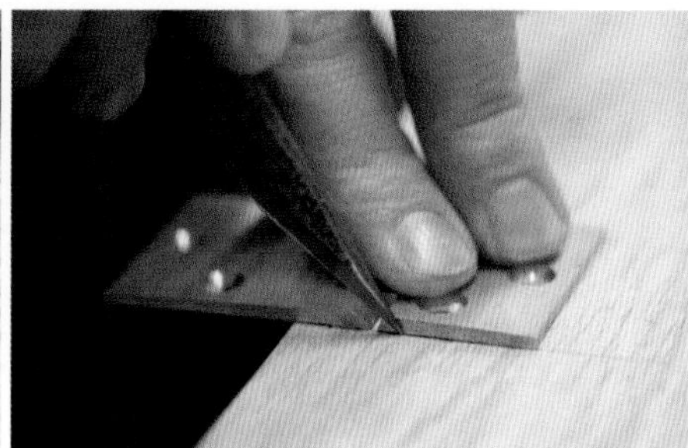

5 **Test the fit** of the hinges within the grooves and scribe around the flange to mark the dimensions of the rebates.

6 **Set the router depth** to the same as the thickness of the flange. Cut both hinge rebates with a straight cutter.

7 **Clean up the edges** of the rebate with the chisel to remove any splinters. Insert the hinge into position.

8 **Accurately position** the smaller piece of the table top alongside, and mark the position of the hinge with a marking knife.

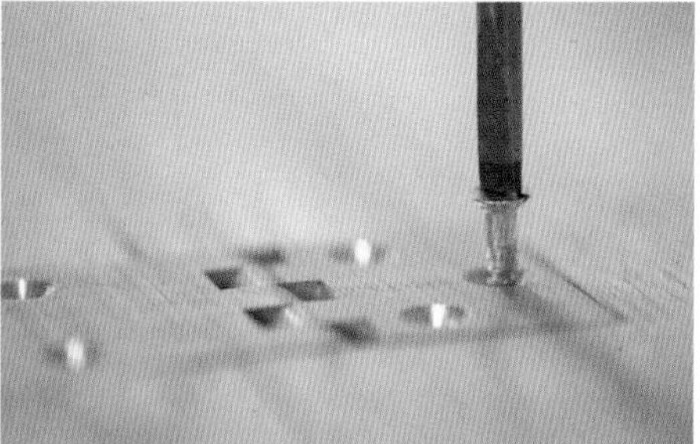

9 **Cut rebates** for the hinge on the second piece, as for the first. Drill pilot holes in all screw positions and insert the screws.

CUTTING THE CIRCULAR TABLE TOP

1 **Position the table-top template** over the underside of the assembled table top so that the rule-joint mark aligns with the actual rule joint. Draw around the template.

2 **Remove the template** and cut around the marked line with a band saw. Ensure that you cut on the waste side of the line.

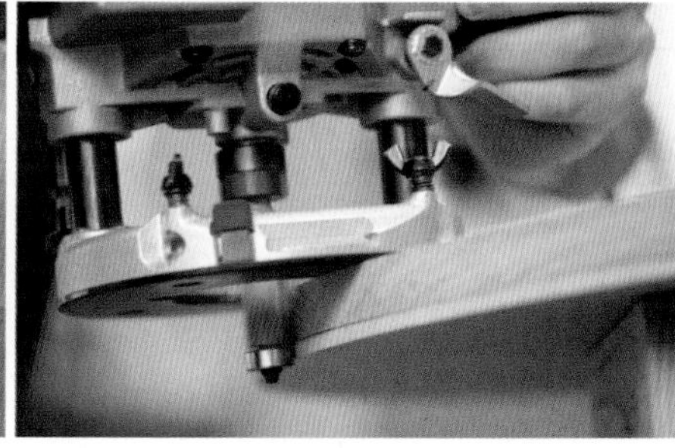

3 **Clamp the template** accurately and securely underneath the table top, then use a router with a bearing-guided straight cutter to cut accurately to the marks.

4 **Use the router** fitted with the round-over cutter that was used for the rule joint, to round off the upper edge of the table top.

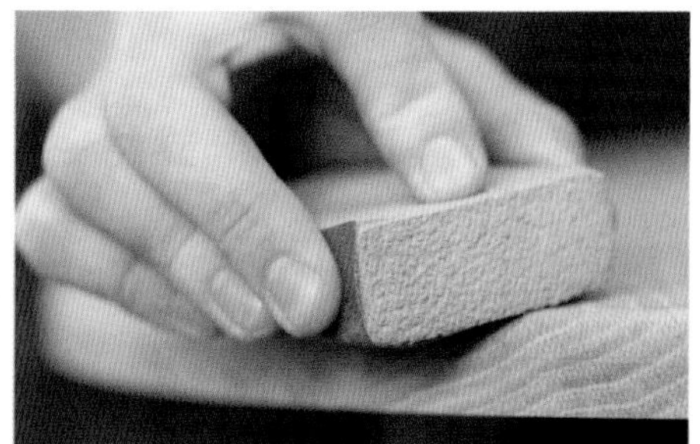

5 **Finish the table top** by smoothing the surface and edges with sandpaper wrapped around a sanding block.

MAKING THE MORTISES IN THE LEGS

1 **Each of the three fixed legs** has two mortises—a haunched one (see Haunched tenon joint, p.120) at the top of the leg for the upper rails and a second full tenon further down foı the lower rails. Prepare all three legs in the same way. Set the marking gauge to 1⅜in (35mm) and mark the length of the mortise on one edge at the top of the leg.

2 **Set the mortise gauge** to ⅜in (10mm) and scribe the width of the mortise centrally on the end grain and down the edge to the mortise-length mark.

3 **Use the marking gauge** to mark a ⅜in (10mm) haunch on the mortise edge and end grain (inset).

4 **Mark the start** of the lower mortise 15¾in (400mm) from the top of the leg. Square the mark around all four sides.

5 **Mark the bottom** of the lower mortise on all sides, 16½in (420mm) from the top end grain.

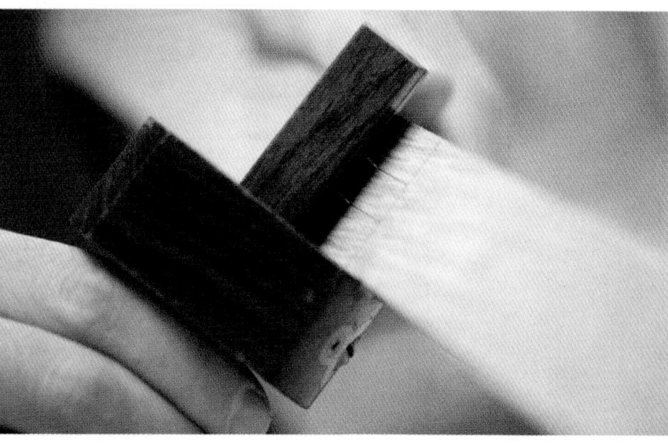

6 **Use the mortise gauge** as previously set to scribe the width of the mortise between the lines on the same side as the upper mortise.

7 **Cut the upper mortises** on all three leg pieces. Use a mortiser fitted with a ⅜in (10mm) bit (pictured) or do it by hand with a ⅜in (10mm) mortise chisel and mallet. The full depth of the upper mortise is 1³⁄₁₆in (30mm) and the depth of the haunched section of the upper mortise is ⅜in (10mm).

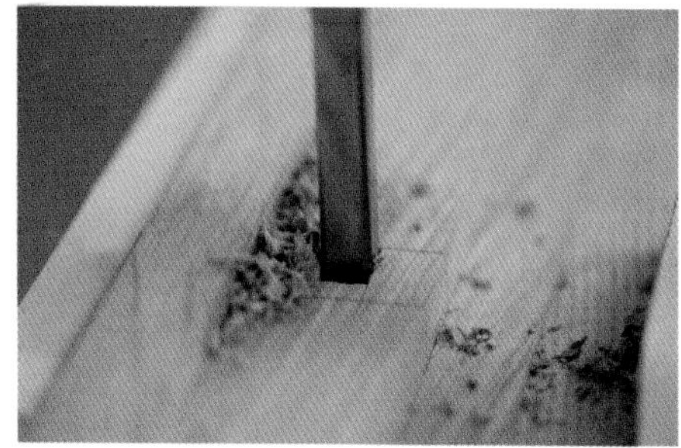

8 **Cut the lower mortise** halfway through the leg from one side and then complete it by cutting from the other side.

MAKING THE HAUNCHED TENONS IN THE UPPER RAILS

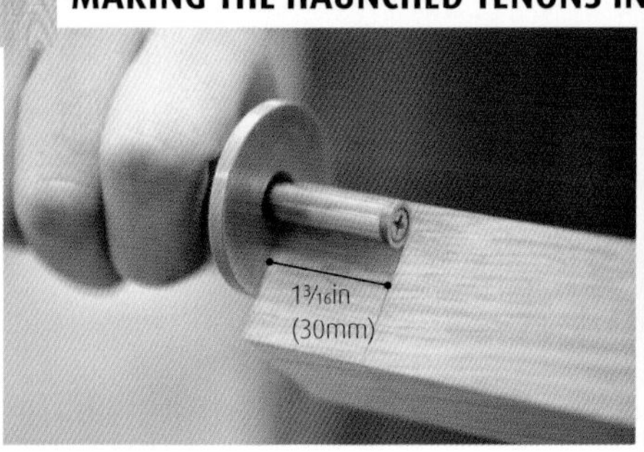

1 **On both ends** of the long upper rail and one end of the short upper rail, use a marking gauge to scribe a line on all four faces, 1³⁄₁₆in (30mm) from the end grain.

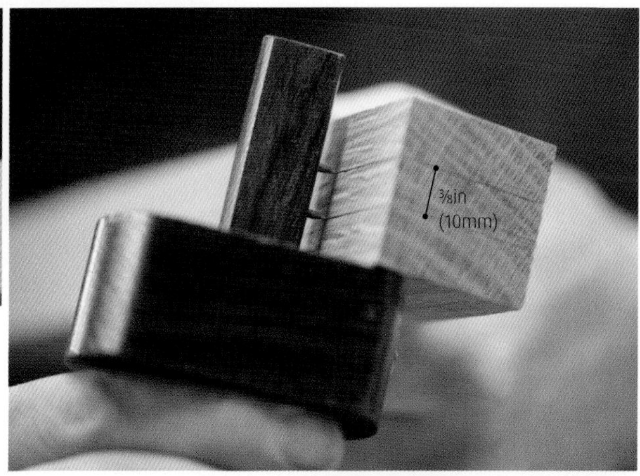

2 **Scribe the tenon thickness** of ³⁄₈in (10mm) down the edges and along the end grain of the upper rails, with the mortise gauge as previously set.

3 **Mark the haunch** at ³⁄₈in (10mm) on the end grain and ¹³⁄₁₆in (20mm) down one edge from the end grain (inset).

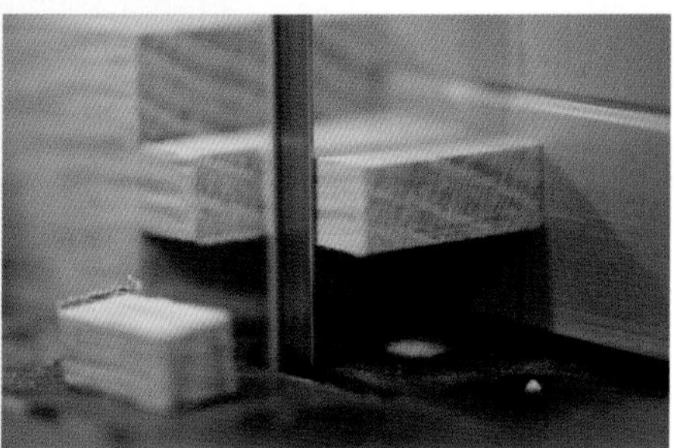

4 **Cut all three haunched tenons** either on a band saw (pictured) or by hand using a tenon saw (p.120).

MAKING THE CENTRAL MORTISE AND MATCHING TENON IN THE UPPER RAILS

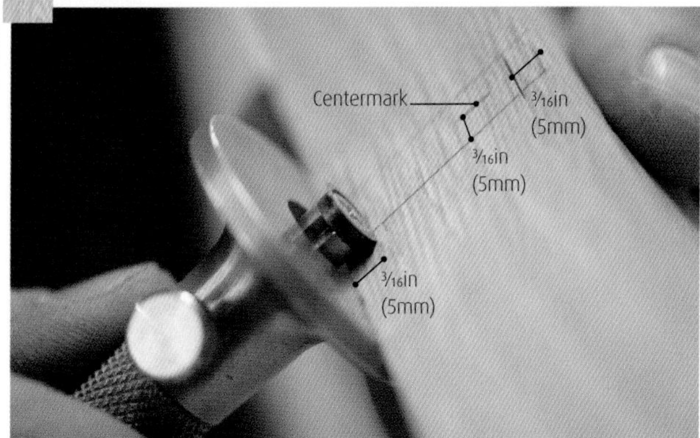

1 **Mark the central mortise** halfway down the outer side of the long upper rail. Make a centermark 12¼in (310mm) from the shoulder of one of the tenons. Mark a line ³⁄₁₆in (5mm) on either side. Scribe a line ³⁄₁₆in (5mm) from each edge to mark the length of the mortise.

2 **Use a mortiser** fitted with a ³⁄₈in (10mm) bit to cut the mortise to a depth of 1³⁄₁₆in (30mm).

3 **Make a second tenon** in the short upper rail to match this mortise. Use a marking gauge to scribe a shoulder of 1³⁄₁₆in (30mm) on all four sides of the other end of the rail.

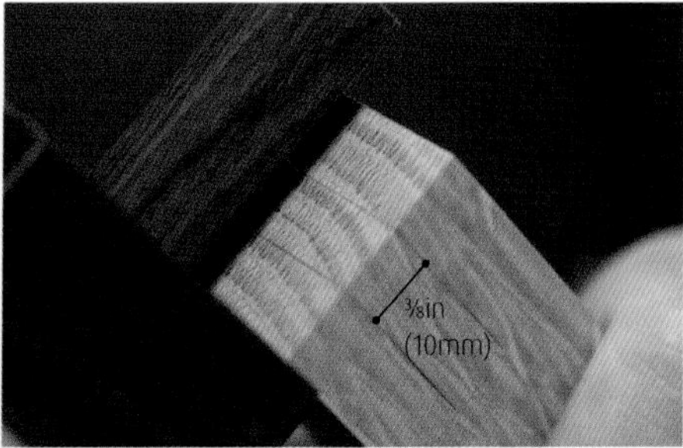

4 **Mark the tenon thickness** of ³⁄₈in (10mm) with the mortise gauge along the end grain and sides of the short upper rail. Ensure you mark the tenon on the same faces as the tenon on the other end of the rail.

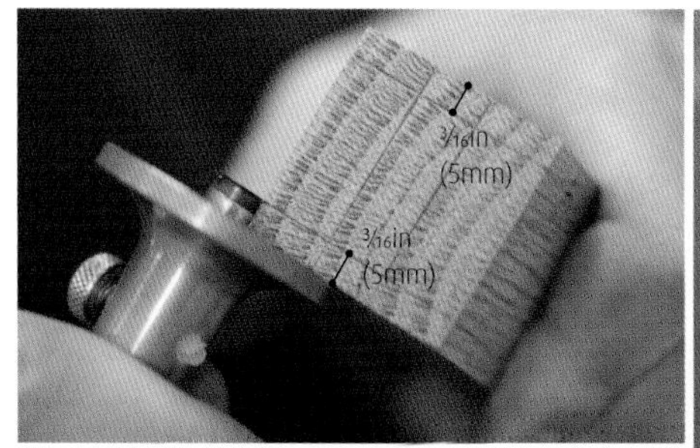

5 **Mark the width** of the tenon on the end grain with a marking gauge set to ³⁄₁₆in (5mm).

6 **Cut the tenon** on a band saw (pictured) or by hand using a tenon saw. Remove any debris.

MAKING THE TENONS IN THE LONG AND SHORT LOWER RAILS

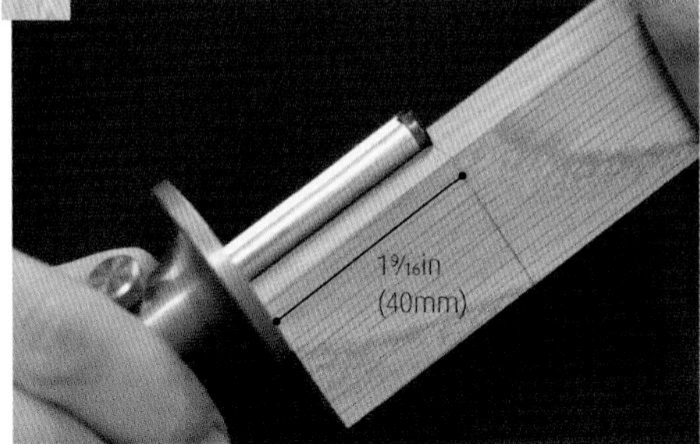

1 **Use the marking gauge** to mark a tenon 1⁹⁄₁₆in (40mm) in length on both ends of the long lower rail and one end of the short lower rail.

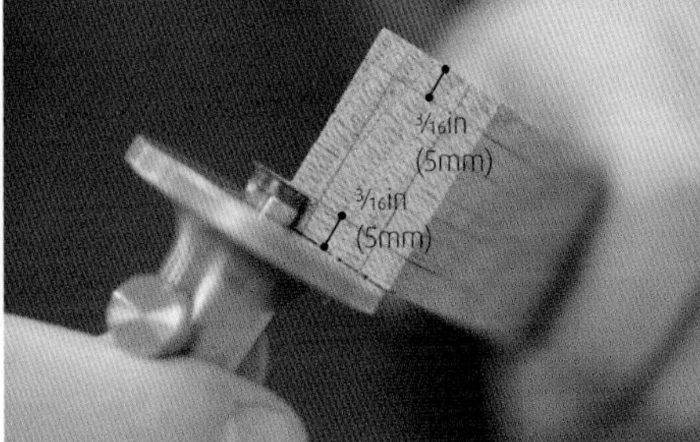

2 **Mark a 1in (25mm) tenon** on the other end of the short rail. Mark the end grains with a marking gauge set to ³⁄₁₆in (5mm).

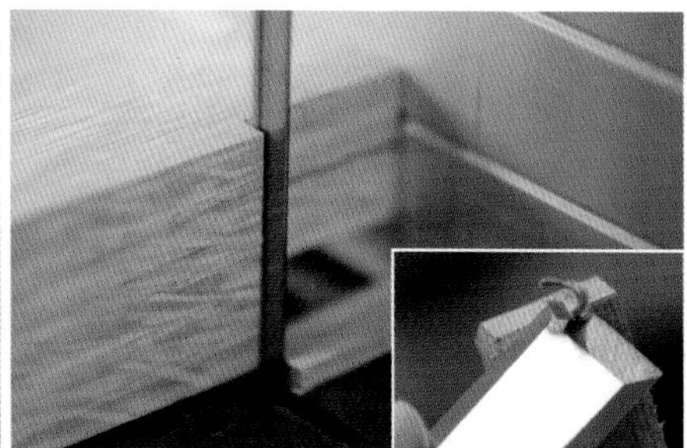

3 **Cut the tenons** on a band saw (shown) or by hand. Chamfer the ends with a bevel-edged chisel (inset) to ease the fit.

4 **Cut a through-mortise** centrally on the long lower rail, following the method shown on p.340. Make a test assembly of all the elements of the leg frame. Adjust as necessary to achieve a good fit.

MAKING THE GATELEG

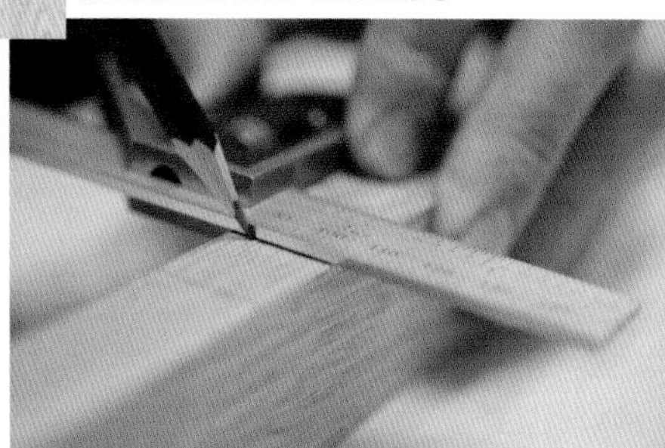

1 **Mark a mortise** on the edge of the gateleg between 13in (330mm) and 13¾in (350mm) from the end grain, giving it a length of ¹³⁄₁₆in (20mm). It should be ⅜in (10mm) wide.

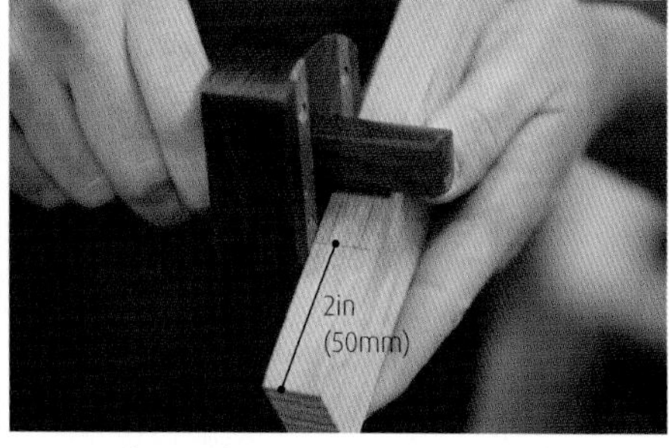

2 **Mark another mortise** with two lines 2in (50mm) and 2¾in (70mm) from the top end grain. Square all marks across the edge, then mark the mortise width of ⅜in (10mm) with a mortise gauge.

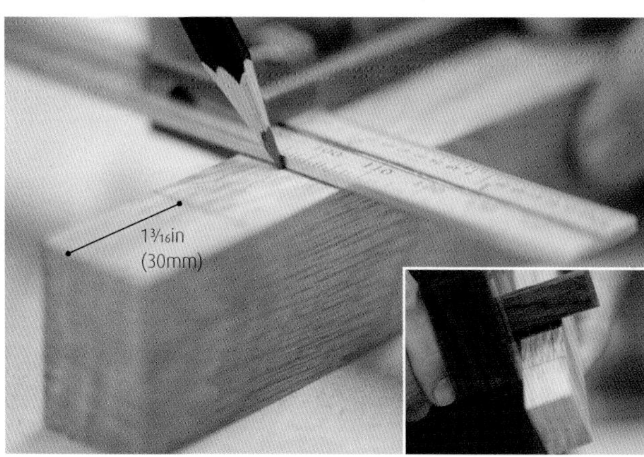

3 **Mark two mortises** of the same length ¹³⁄₁₆in (20mm) on the inner stile (the gate "pivot"), 1³⁄₁₆in (30mm) from each end grain. Mark the mortise width of ⅜in (10mm) with a mortise gauge (inset).

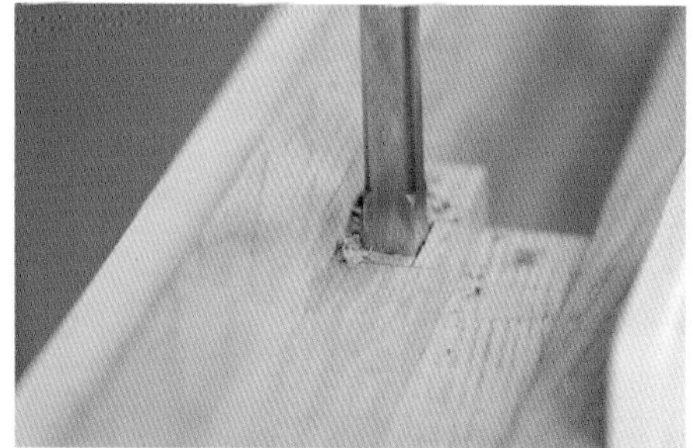

4 **Cut the mortises** to a depth of ¹³⁄₁₆in (20mm) using a mortiser fitted with a ⅜in (10mm) bit (pictured) or by hand with a ⅜in (10mm) mortise chisel and mallet.

MAKING THE TENONS ON THE STRETCHER RAILS

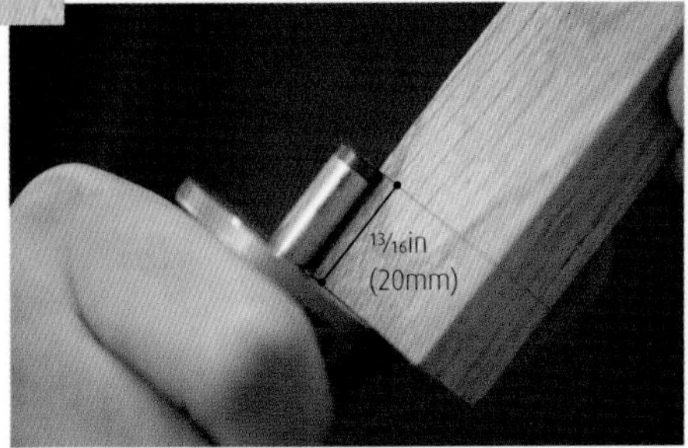

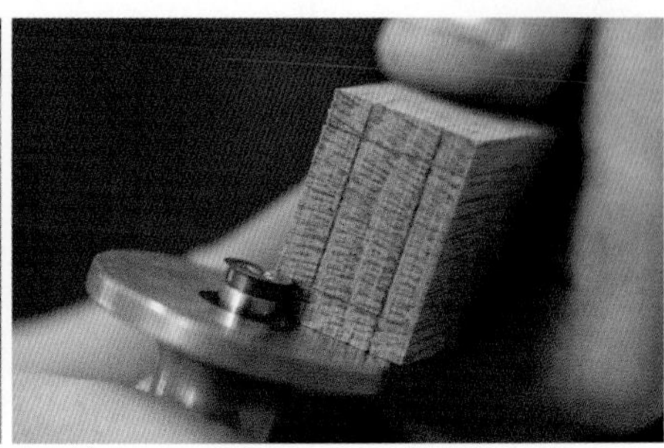

1 **Mark the tenons** on the stretcher rails to fit the mortises just made. Mark the shoulders 13⁄16in (20mm) from both end grains of both rails with a marking gauge.

2 **Mark each tenon** with a thickness of 3⁄8in (10mm) around the end grain and both edges to the shoulder with a mortise gauge.

3 **Mark the width** of the tenons across the end grain of both rails at both ends using the marking gauge set to 3⁄16in (5mm).

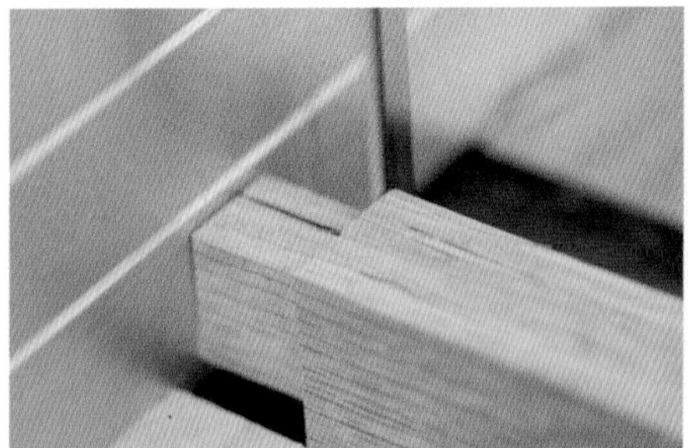

4 **Cut the tenons** and shoulders on a band saw (pictured), or by hand with a tenon saw.

5 **Test-fit the elements** of the gateleg and make any adjustments that may be necessary.

MAKING THE HOUSING IN THE LONG UPPER RAIL

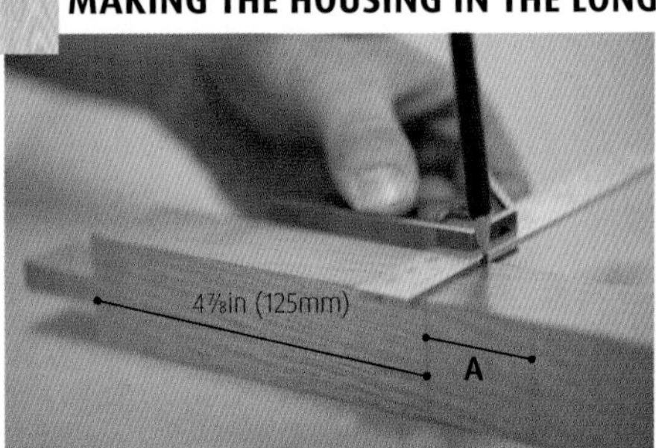

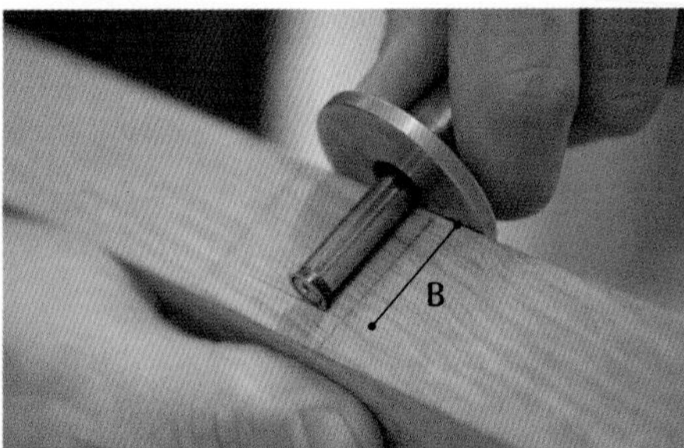

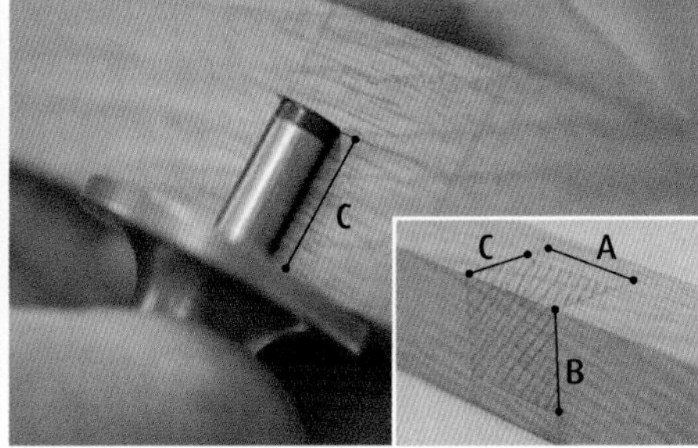

1 **Mark the housing** on the outside face and underneath edge of the long upper rail 4⅞in (125mm) from the tenon shoulder. Mark a housing width (A) of 1⅜in (35mm).

2 **Scribe a housing depth (B)** of 1 1⁄16in (28mm) between the marks on the underneath edge, with the marking gauge resting on the outside face.

3 **Scribe 13⁄16in (20mm)** on the outside face (C) with the marking gauge resting on the underneath edge. Mark the waste for removal (inset).

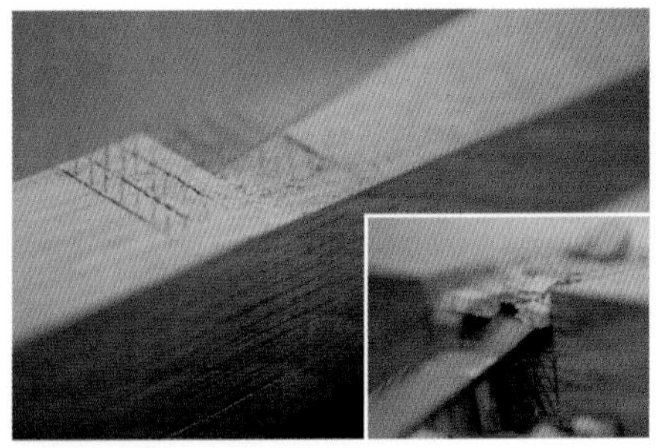

4 **Cut the housing** by making relief cuts with a tenon saw, and then use a chisel to remove the waste (inset).

MAKING THE CROSS-HALVED LAP IN THE LONG LOWER RAIL

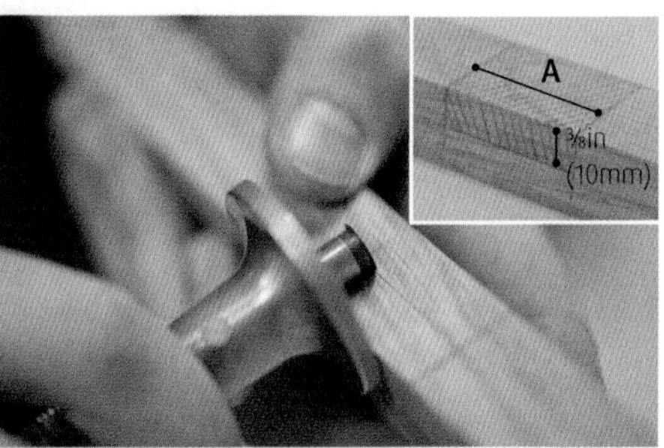

1 **Mark the lap** on the outside face of the long lower rail 5in (126mm) from the shoulder, and mark a housing width (A) of 1⅜in (35mm). Square the marks onto the edges.

2 **Set the marking gauge** to 3⁄8in (10mm) and scribe a line between the housing width lines on both edges of the rail. Mark the waste for removal (inset).

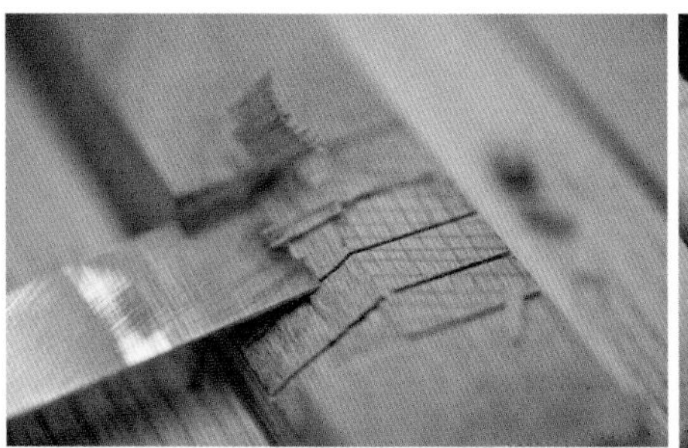

3 **Use a tenon saw** to make relief cuts, then remove the waste from the housing using a bevel-edged chisel.

4 **Mark the matching half-lap** on the gateleg 13⁄16in (30mm) down from the mortise for the lower stretcher rail of the gateleg frame. Mark the half-lap to the same dimensions as in Steps 1 and 2, and cut as in Step 3. Check the fit of both elements (inset).

EASING THE FIT AND GLUING THE GATE

1 **Assemble the frame** and gateleg in the closed position, and use a marking knife to scribe a line marking the half-lap on the edge of the leg.

2 **Chisel a slight taper** toward the half-lap and between these marks on both edges of the gateleg.

3 **Ease the fit** of the leg in the housing of the long upper rail in the same way. Avoid the chisel breaking out by first scribing the edges of the taper with a marking knife.

4 **Use a marking gauge** to scribe a line along the inner face of the top of the gateleg to indicate the size of the taper. Mark the line 1⁄16in (1mm) from each edge.

5 **Pare to the marks** using a bevel-edged chisel (inset), creating a tapered profile for the part of the end grain that fits the housing.

6 **Sand and glue all the elements** of the gateleg frame. Clamp with sash clamps and use a tape measure to check the assembly for squareness (see p.75).

FITTING THE PIVOTS

1 **Mark the midpoint** of both end grains of the inner stile of the gateleg assembly by scribing two intersecting lines halfway from the face (inset) and edge.

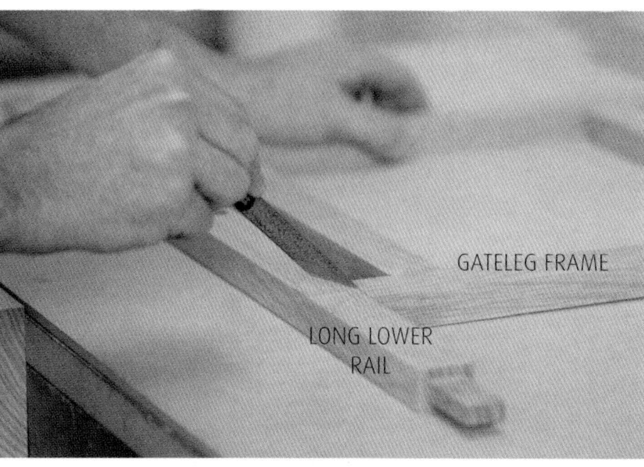

2 **Dismantle the main leg frame**. Position the gateleg assembly within the half-lap joint on the long lower rail of the leg frame. Extend the centermark from the inner stile of the gateleg frame onto the face of the long lower rail.

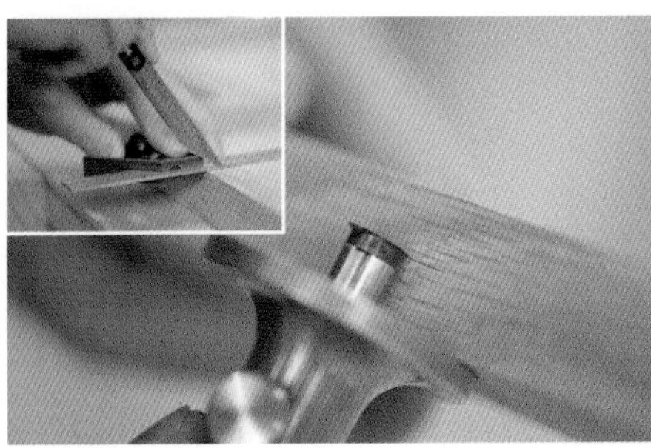

3 **Square the mark** onto the upper edge of the long lower rail (inset) and mark the midpoint of this line with a marking gauge.

4 **Place the long upper rail** of the leg frame next to the long lower rail. Align the shoulders of the two pieces.

5 **Extend the mark** from the long lower rail onto the underside of the long upper rail. Square the mark across the width (inset).

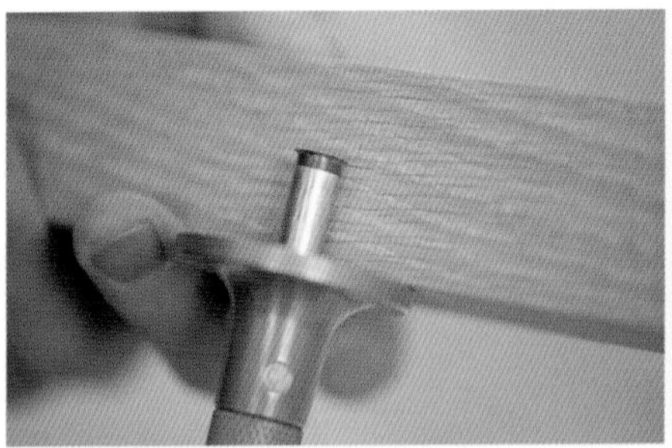

6 **Mark the midpoint** of this line with a marking gauge on the underside of the long upper rail.

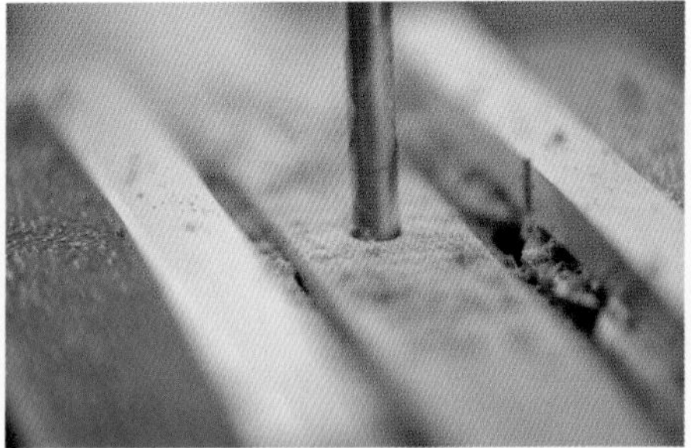

7 **Using a bit** to match the diameter of the brass rod of the pivot, drill into the marks in both rails to a depth of 13⁄16in (20mm).

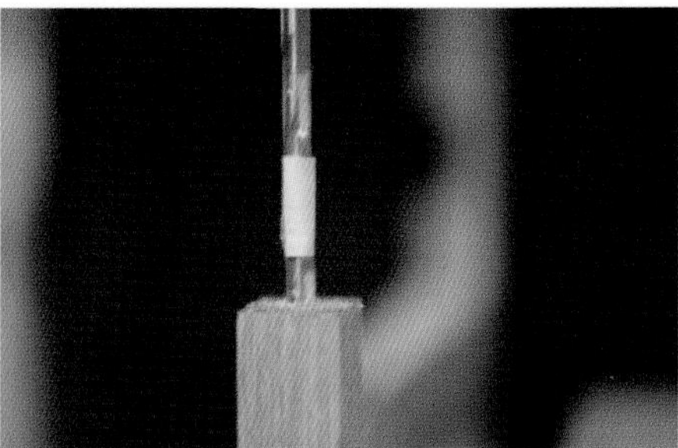

8 **Take the inner stile** of the gateleg and drill into the marked points in the center of the end grain to a depth of 3⁄8in (10mm).

GLUING THE GATELEG AND LEG FRAME

1 **Test-fit the rods** in the holes (inset) and then do a test-assembly of all the leg frame and gateleg elements.

2 **Glue the gateleg** and leg-frame elements. Glue and clamp the legs attached to the long rails first and check for squareness (inset). When dry, glue and clamp the remaining elements.

3 **When the glue** has dried, trim all the through-tenons to 3⁄16in (5mm), then chamfer the ends with a chisel.

MAKING THE LEG-STOP BATTEN

1 **On the underside** of the table top, measure the midpoint of the rule joint, then draw a line from that position at 90 degrees to the joint across the whole table top. From the midpoint of that line square another line across the diameter of the large table-top section, parallel to the rule joint.

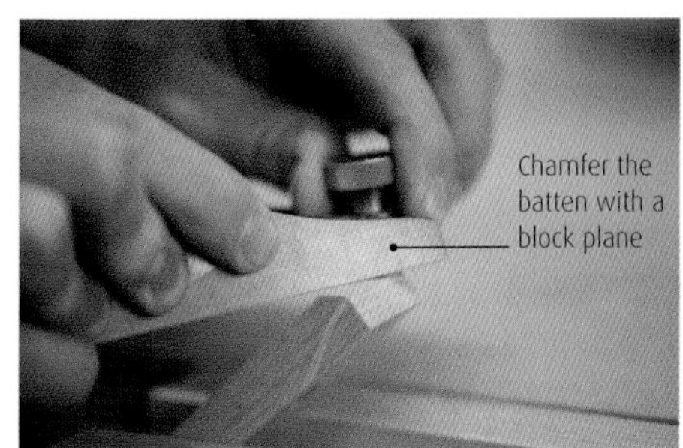

2 **Chamfer the upper edges** of the leg-stop batten. Drill and countersink two holes for size 8 x 1in (4 x 25mm) screws 13⁄16in (30mm) from each end grain.

FIXING THE TABLE TOP TO THE LEG FRAME

1 **Drill and counterbore** (p.43) four holes in the leg frame—two along the short upper rail and two along the long upper rail.

2 **Place the leg frame** on the underside of the large table-top section, with the upper rails aligned to the lines drawn in Step 1, (Making the leg-stop batten, opposite). Drill pilot holes into the table top to a depth of ⅜in (10mm) through the holes in the rails, countersink (inset), and then insert the screws.

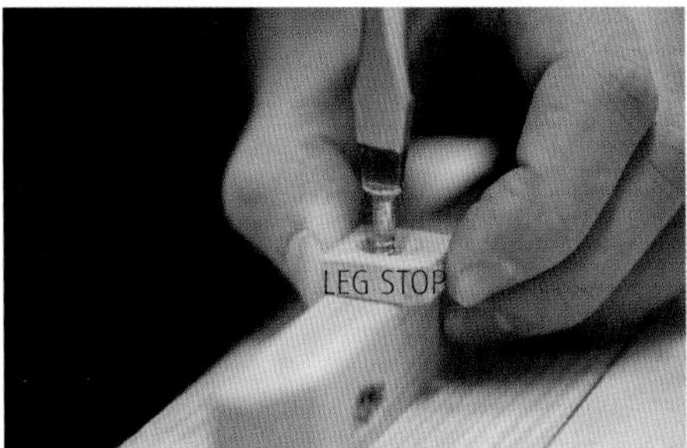

3 **Make the leg stop** from a shaped offcut approximately 13⁄16in (20mm) square and 3⁄16in (5mm) thick. Drill and countersink a hole in the center of the stop, and screw it to the side of the batten at the point where the gateleg crosses it when open.

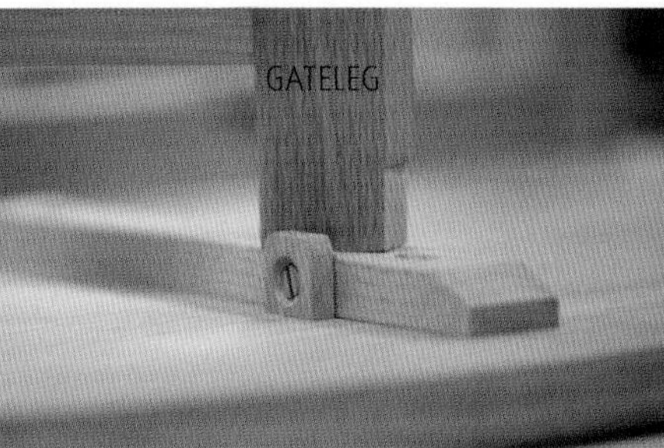

4 **Position the batten** on the underside of the small table-top section centered over the marked line, 13⁄16in (20mm) from the rule joint. Drill pilot holes into the table top to a maximum depth of 3⁄16in (10mm). Screw in place.

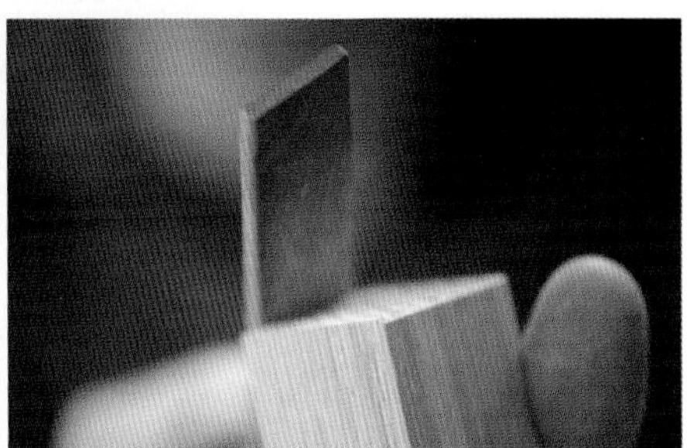

5 **File the ends** of all four legs to prevent the wood from splintering when the table is in use.

DETAIL OF RULE JOINT

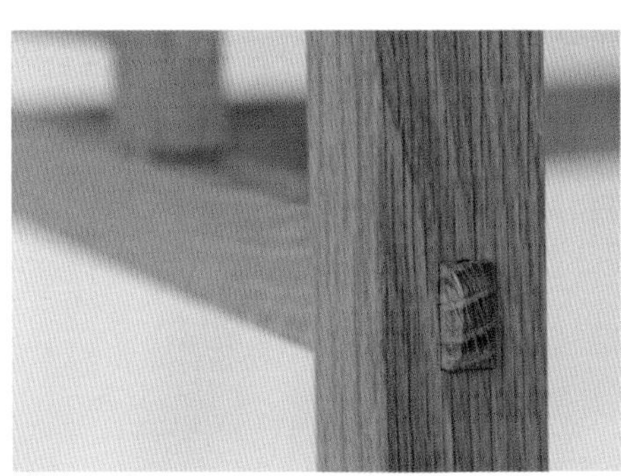

DETAIL OF TENON AND GATELEG

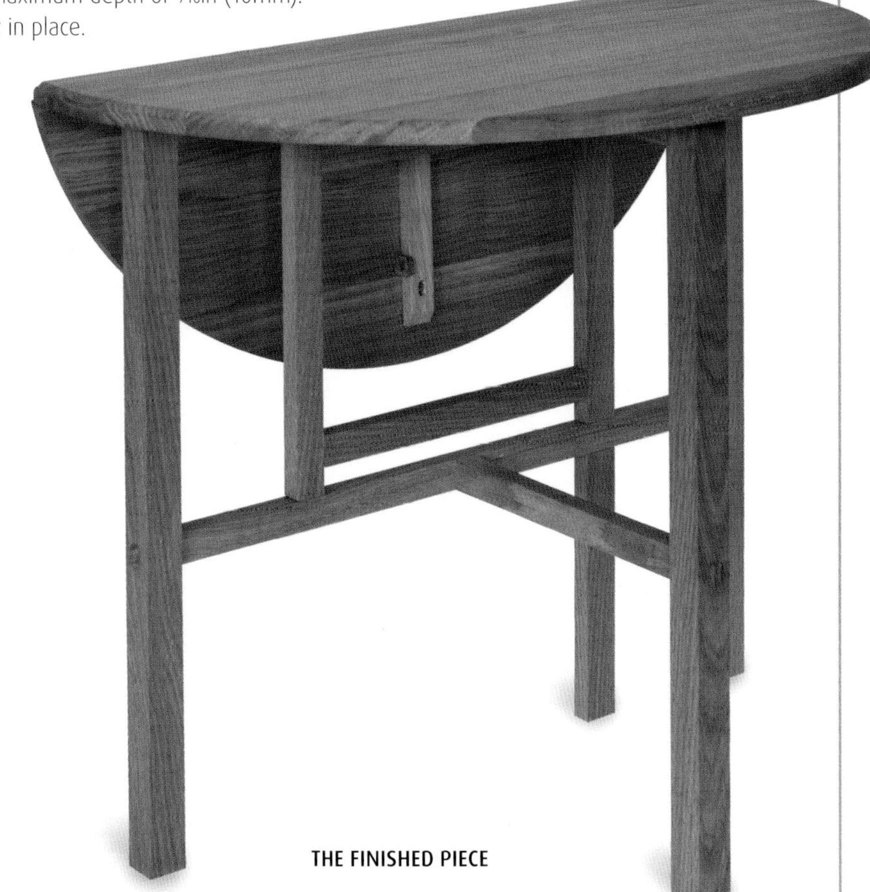

THE FINISHED PIECE

Buffet

This oak buffet and hutch is a significant undertaking for the home woodworker, but is a joy to make and will really stand out in a kitchen or dining room. The buffet is made using a wide range of construction methods—including a variety of both traditional joints and modern commercial connectors—meaning that this project is an ideal way to test and broaden your skills. It is essential to fix your completed buffet to a wall using two small brackets, screws, and wall fixings at the top to ensure that it remains steady.

TOOLS AND MATERIALS

- Square
- Pencil
- Domino jointer
- 52 size 1/4 x 1 9/16in (6 x 40mm) dominoes
- Marking knife
- Marking gauge
- Bevel-edged chisel
- Mallet
- Tenon saw
- Long metal ruler
- C-clamp
- Dovetail marker
- Drill with bits
- Biscuit jointer
- 10 No. 20 biscuit connectors
- Router with bearing-guided-beading and round-over cutters
- 3 straight cutters 3/16in (5mm), 1/4in (6mm), and 3/4in (19mm)
- Table-mounted router (optional)
- Finishing oil or Danish oil
- Flat spokeshave
- Table saw or miter saw
- Wood glue and brush
- Ratchet strap
- Tape measure
- 16 screws (No.8 x 1 1/2in/4 x 40mm)
- Mortise gauge
- Mortiser or mortise chisel
- Band saw
- Block plane and bench plane
- Sash clamps
- Rebate plane (optional)
- 18 screws (No.8 x 1 1/2in /4 x 40mm)
- 2 screws (No.8 x 3/4in 4 x 20mm)
- 6 shelf studs
- Thicknesser
- Panel saw (optional)
- Lathe (optional)
- Roughing gouge (optional)
- Parting tool (optional)
- Flush-cut saw and coping saw or jigsaw (optional)
- Sandpaper
- 4 screws (No.8 x 1 3/8in/4 x 35mm)
- 4 brass butt-hinges and screws
- Bradawl
- 4 screws (No.8 x 1in/4 x 25mm)
- Cabinet scraper
- Orbital sander
- 10 screws (No.8 x 1 3/8in/4 x 35mm)

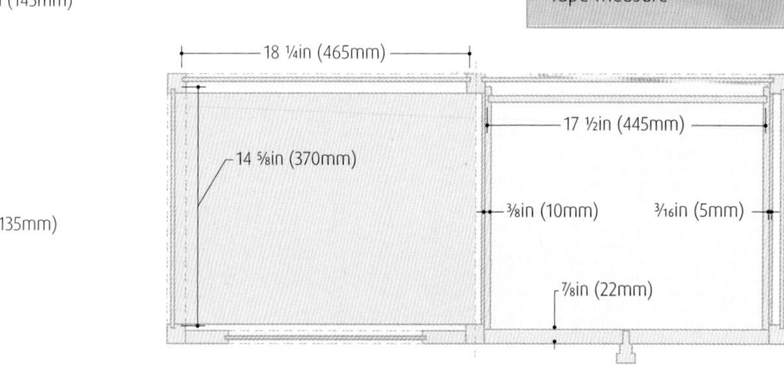

DRAWER SECTION AND PLAN VIEW (1:12)

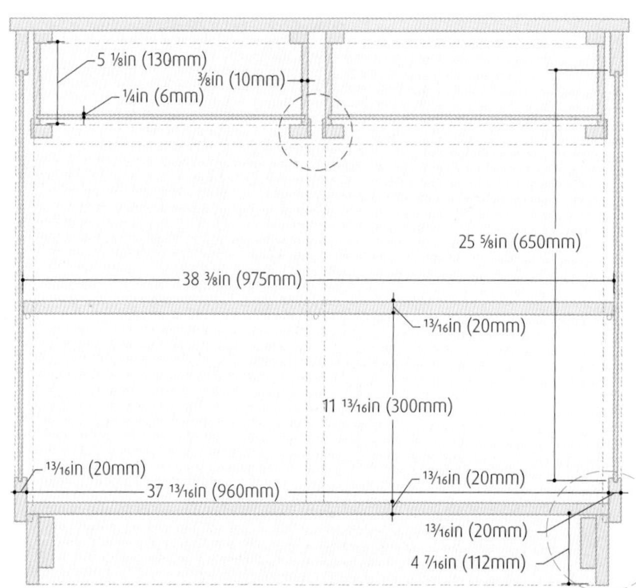

FRONT SECTION (1:12)

13/16in (20mm)
5 11/16in (145mm)
5 5/16in (135mm)
9/16in (15mm)
13/16in (20mm)
1 3/16in (30mm)
13/16in (20mm)
5 1/8in (130mm)
1 3/16in (30mm)
14 3/16in (360mm)
22 7/16in (570mm)
13/16in (20mm)
1 3/16in (30mm)

SIDE SECTION (1:12)

3/16in (5mm)
13/16in (20mm)
1 3/16in (30mm)
1 3/16in (30mm)

DETAIL, CENTRAL DRAWER RUNNERS (1:5)

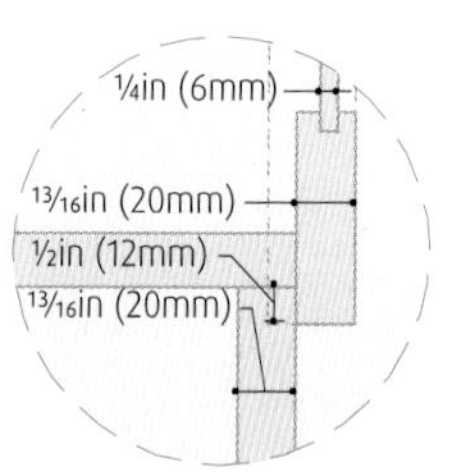

DETAIL OF BASE FITTING (1:5)

Dimensions:
73 5/16 x 40 3/16 x 17 11/16in (1860 x 1020 x 450mm)

Key techniques:
Domino joint (p.144);
Cross-halved lap joint (pp.100–101);
Loose tongue-and-groove joint (pp.96–97);
Dovetail half-lap joint (pp.102–103)

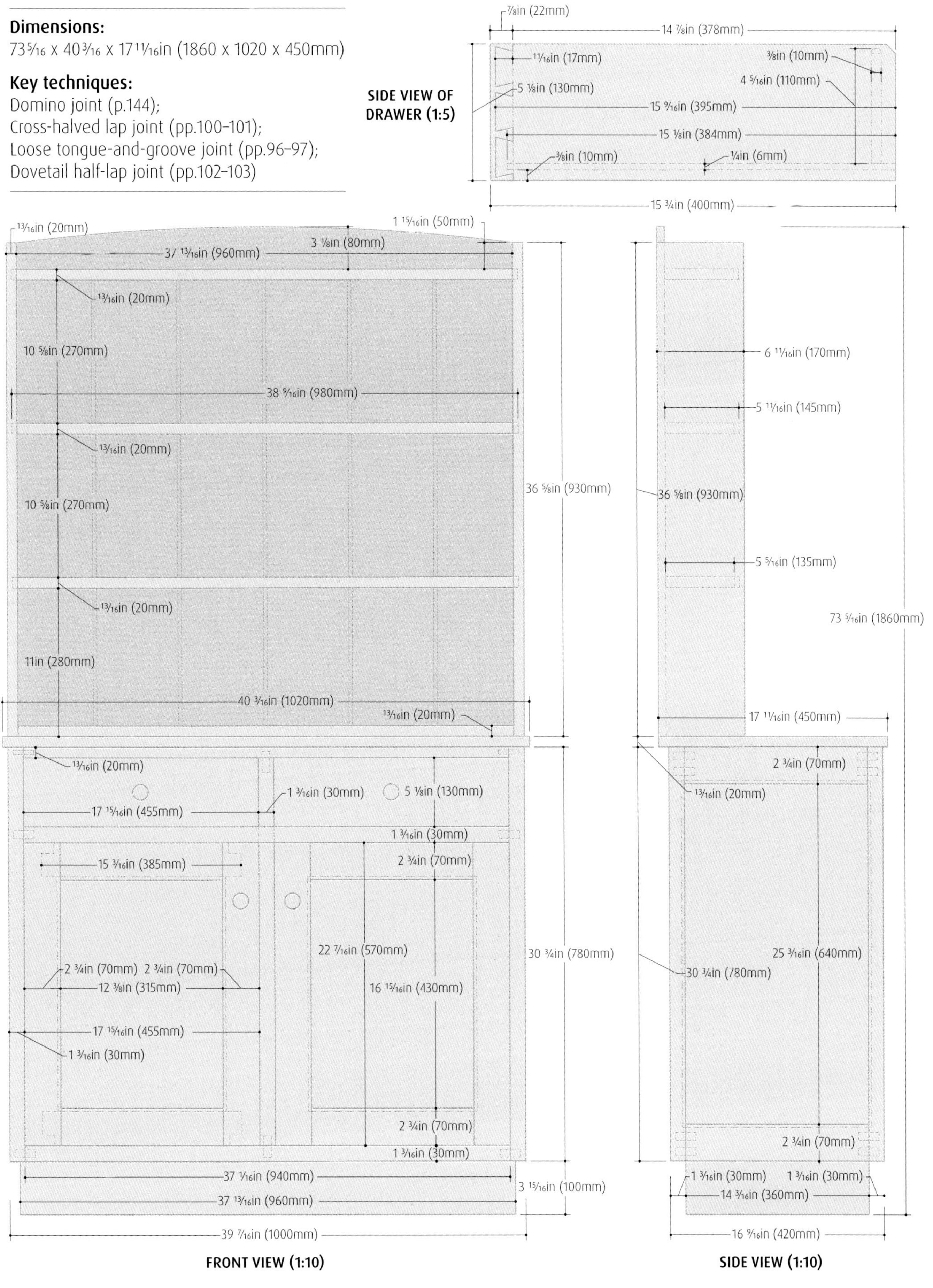

CUTTING LIST

Item	Material	No.	Length	Width	Thickness
Carcass					
Top	Oak	2	41¼in* (1050mm)	9¼in* (235mm)	13⁄16in (20mm)
Short rails (side frames)	Oak	4	14³⁄16in (360mm)	2¾in (70mm)	13⁄16in (20mm)
Stiles (side frames)	Oak	4	30¾in (780mm)	1³⁄16in (30mm)	1³⁄16in (30mm)
Long rails (front and back frames)	Oak	4	37⁷⁄16in (940mm)	1³⁄16in (30mm)	1³⁄16in (30mm)
Upper long rails (top frame)	Oak	2	38¹¹⁄16in (980mm)	1³⁄16in (30mm)	13⁄16in (20mm)
Front muntin	Oak	1	28¾in (730mm)	1³⁄16in (30mm)	1³⁄16in (30mm)
Back muntin	Oak	1	22⁷⁄16in (570mm)	1³⁄16in (30mm)	1³⁄16in (30mm)
Drawer runners and kickers	Oak	8	14³⁄16in (360mm)	1³⁄16in (30mm)	13⁄16in (20mm)
Drawer slips	Oak	4	14³⁄16in (360mm)	1³⁄16in (30mm)	³⁄16in (5mm)
Side panels	Oak-veneered MDF	2	25½in (650mm)	14⅝in (370mm)	¼in (6mm)
Lower back panels	Oak-veneered MDF	2	22¾in (578mm)	18⁵⁄16in (465mm)	¼in (6mm)
Upper back panels	Oak-veneered MDF	2	37⁵⁄16in (948mm)	5⁷⁄16in (138mm)	¼in (6mm)
Base	Oak-veneered MDF	1	37¹³⁄16in (960mm)	14³⁄16in (360mm)	13⁄16in (20mm)
Shelves	Oak	4	39in* (1000mm)	4in* (100mm)	11⁄16in* (18mm)
Doors					
Stiles	Oak	4	23⅝in* (600mm)	2¾in (70mm)	13⁄16in (20mm)
Rails	Oak	2	15³⁄16in (385mm)	2¾in (70mm)	13⁄16in (20mm)
Panels	Oak-veneered MDF	2	17⅜in (440mm)	12¾in (325mm)	¼in (6mm)
Plinth					
Long sides	Oak	2	39¼in* (1000mm)	4⁷⁄16in (112mm)	13⁄16in (20mm)
Short sides	Oak	2	15¾in* (400mm)	4⁷⁄16in (112mm)	13⁄16in (20mm)
Corner blocks	Oak	4	3¹⁵⁄16in (100mm)	1in (25mm)	1in (25mm)
Drawers					
Fronts	Oak	2	18in* (457mm)	5⅛in (130mm)	⅞in (22mm)
Sides	Oak	4	15⁹⁄16in (395mm)	5⅛in (130mm)	⅜in (10mm)
Backs	Oak	2	17½in (445mm)	4⁵⁄16in (110mm)	⅜in (10mm)
Bases	Oak-veneered MDF	2	17½in (445mm)	15⅛in (384mm)	¼in (6mm)

*Includes excess to allow for cutting to size

CUTTING LIST CONTINUED

Item	Material	No.	Length	Width	Thickness
Shelf unit					
Uprights	Oak	2	36⅝in (930mm)	6¹¹⁄16in (170mm)	13⁄16in (20mm)
Shelves	Oak	3	38⁹⁄16in (980mm)	5¹¹⁄16in (145mm)	13⁄16in (20mm)
Back board	Oak	6	34¹¹⁄16in (880mm)	6½in (165mm)	⅝in (15mm)
Tongues	Oak	5	36⅝in (930mm)	⅜in (10mm)	³⁄16in (5mm)
Top brace	Oak	1	39in (990mm)	3⅛in (80mm)	⅝in (15mm)
Batten	Oak	1	38³⁄16in* (970mm)	13⁄16in (20mm)	13⁄16in (20mm)

*Includes excess to allow for cutting to size

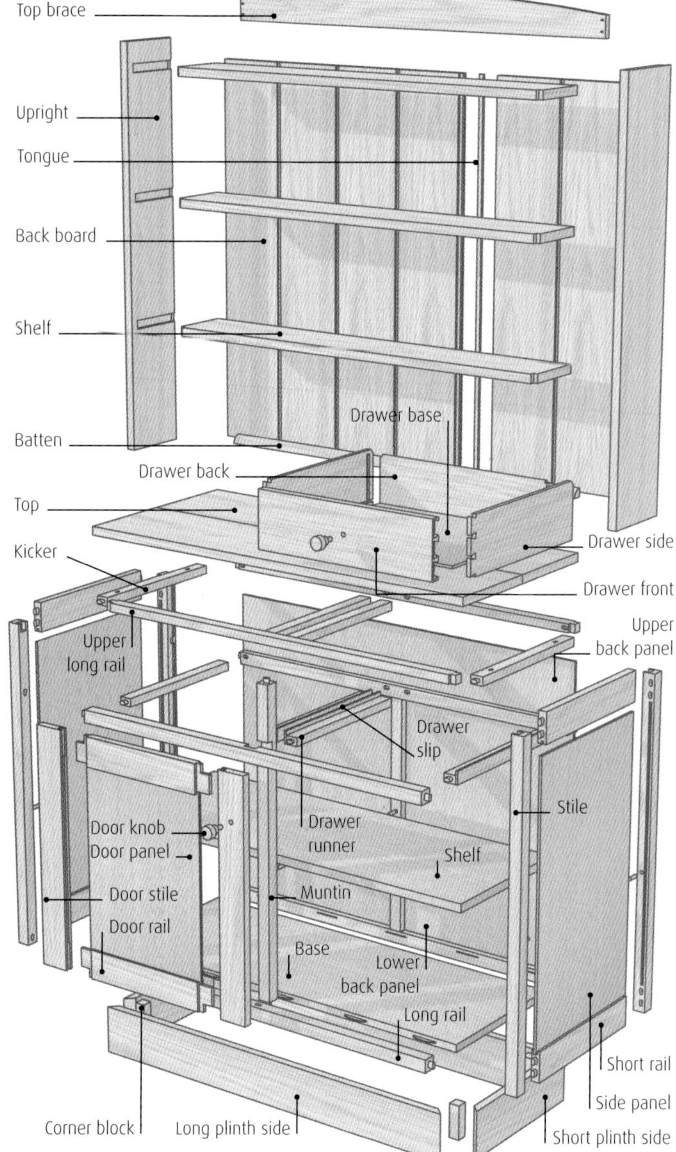

How the elements fit together

The carcass features pre-veneered oak boards and a domino-jointed frame in a frame-and-panel construction. The shelf unit locates on top of the carcass and uses loose-tongue joints for the backboard.

MAKING THE CARCASS SIDE FRAMES

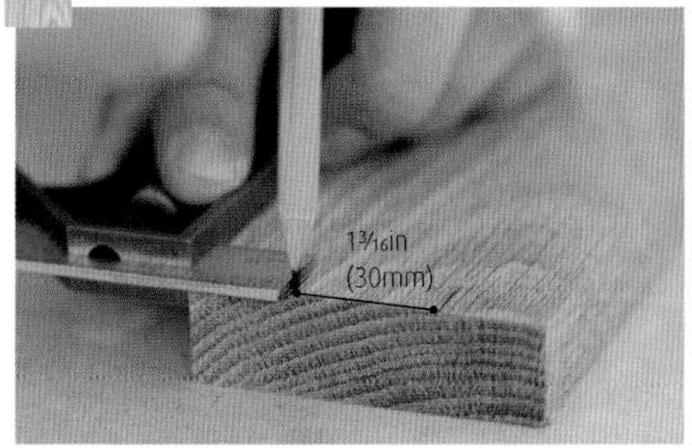

1 Mark out two mortises to take a ¼ x 1⁹⁄₁₆in (6 x 40mm) domino, centered on the thickness of each end grain of all four short rails. The center of each mortise is 1³⁄₁₆in (30mm) apart.

2 Set the domino jointer to a depth of 1⅛in (28mm) and fit a 6mm (¼in) cutter. Cut the mortises in all the marked positions in the short rails (inset).

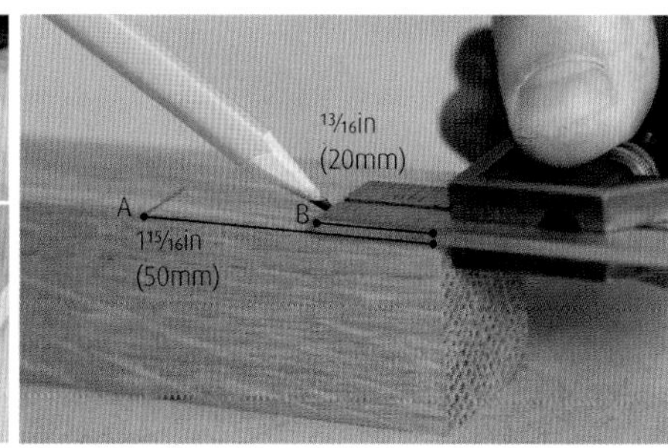

3 Mark the center-point of each mortise on both ends of all four stiles. Mark the first (A) 1¹⁵⁄₁₆in (50mm), and the second (B) ¹³⁄₁₆in (20mm), from the end grain.

4 Use the domino jointer to cut the mortises to a depth of ½in (12mm), and centered ⅜in (10mm) from the face.

5 Test the fit of the dominoes in all the mortises, dry-fitting both of the side frames (inset).

MAKING THE CARCASS BACK FRAME

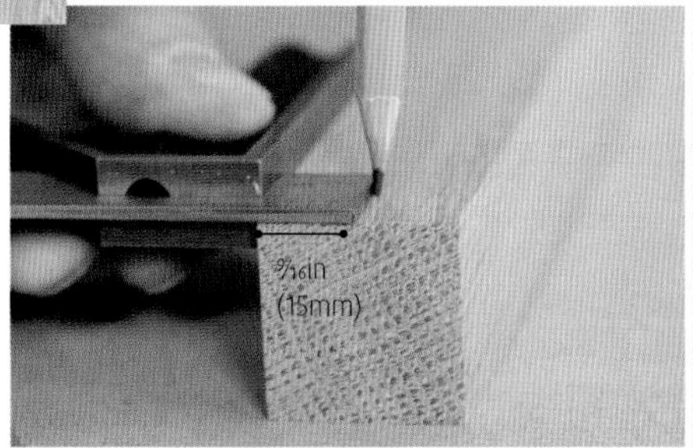

1 Mark the position of a ¼in (6mm) domino mortise in each end grain of the lower long rail, centered on the thickness and ⁹⁄₁₆in (15mm) from the top edge.

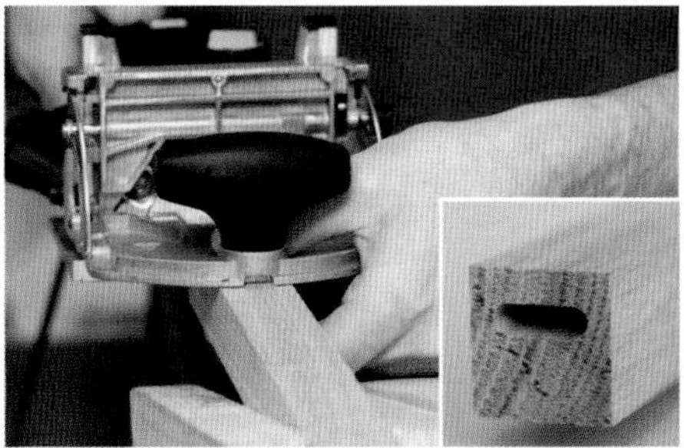

2 With the piece secured in a vise and the domino jointer set to a depth of 1⅛in (28mm) and a fence of ⅜in (10mm), cut the mortises in the end grains (inset).

3 Mark the position of a third ⁹⁄₁₆in (15mm) domino mortise in the center of the top of the rail.

4 Use the domino jointer to cut the mortise lengthwise on the rail to a depth of ½in (12mm), with the fence set to ⁹⁄₁₆in (15mm).

5 Mark and cut a ¼in (6mm) domino mortise in the center of both end grains of the back muntin to 1⅛in (28mm) in depth. Test-fit in the long-rail center mortise (inset).

6 Mark a mortise for a ¼in (6mm) domino in both end grains of the upper long rail of the back frame, centered on the width and thickness.

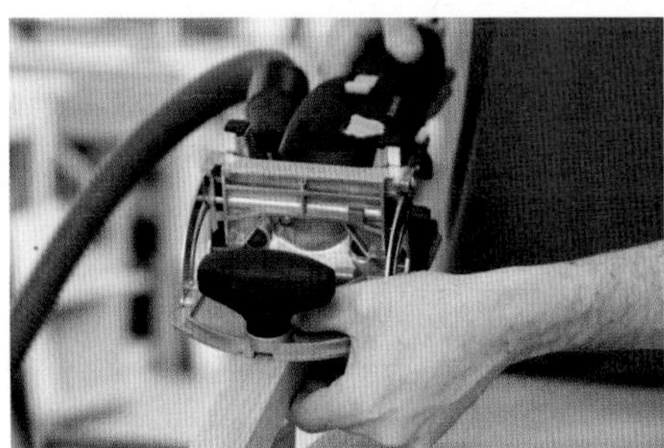

7 **Cut the mortises** to a depth of 1⅛in (28mm) using the domino jointer with the fence set to ⅜in (10mm).

8 **Mark a third mortise** for a ¼in (6mm) domino in the center of the underside of the upper long rail.

9 **Cut the mortise lengthways** to ½in (12mm) deep and a fence of 9⁄16in (15mm) (inset). Dry-fit with the muntin.

MAKING THE JOINTS FOR THE FRONT FRAME

1 **Cut three domino mortises** into the lower long rail of the front frame in the same way as the back frame (see Steps 1–4, Making the carcass back frame, p.349). The middle mortise has a fence of 9⁄16in (15mm), while the others have a fence of ⅜in (10mm).

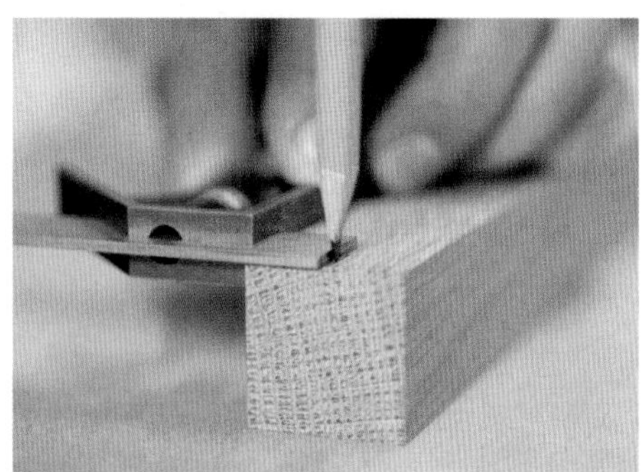

2 **Mark and cut** a ¼in (6mm) domino mortise in the center of both end grains of the front muntin.

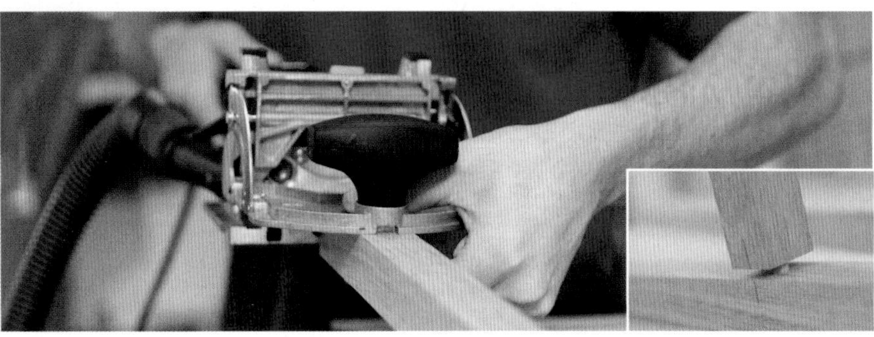

3 **Cut both mortises** to a depth of 1⅛in (28mm) with a fence setting of ⅝in (15mm). Test the fit of the dominos in the lower long rail (inset).

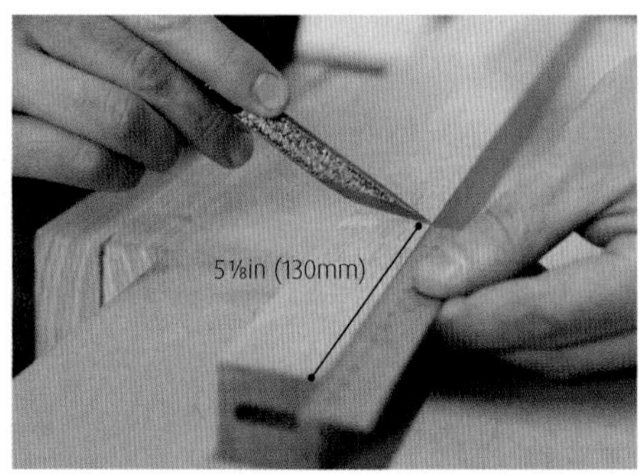

4 **Mark the cross-halved lap joint** (see pp.100–101) in the front muntin. Mark 5⅛in (130mm) from the top end grain and square the mark across with a marking knife.

5 **Mark the width of the joint** on the face of the muntin, scoring either side of the thickness of the front-frame upper long rail.

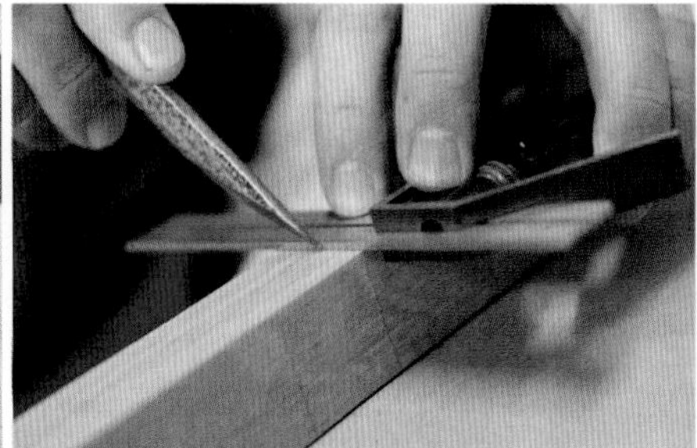

6 **Square the marks** across both edges of the muntin, using a marking knife and square.

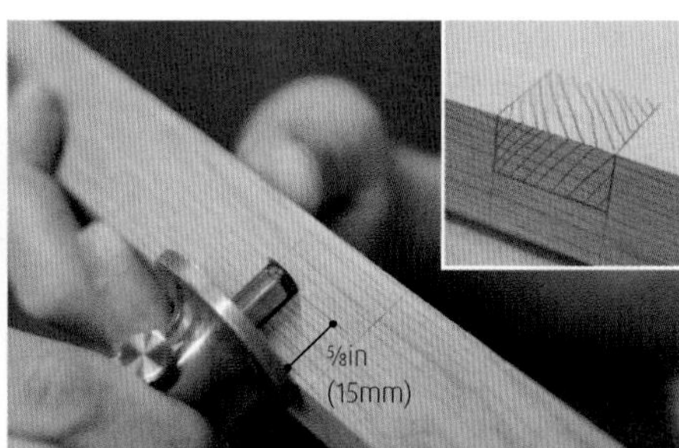

7 **Set a marking gauge** to half the thickness of the muntin—⅝in (15mm)—and scribe between the marks on both edges. Mark the waste for removal (inset).

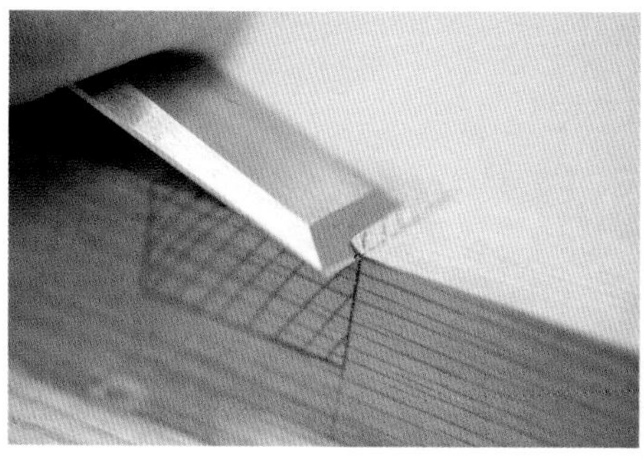

8 **Chisel a V-groove** along the edges of the waste with a bevel-edged chisel and mallet.

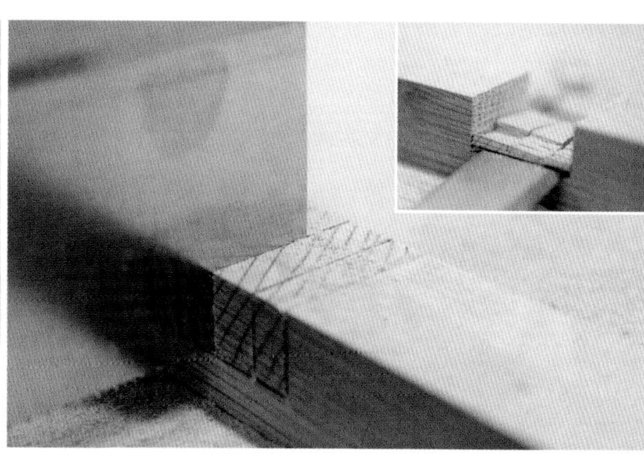

9 **Cut to the waste side** of the marks with a tenon saw, then make relief cuts through the waste. Remove the bulk of the waste with the chisel, then clean up the sides and base (inset).

MAKING THE UPPER LONG RAIL FOR THE FRONT FRAME

1 **Make the matching part** of the cross-halved lap joint in the center of the upper rail. Mark the halfway point of the rail.

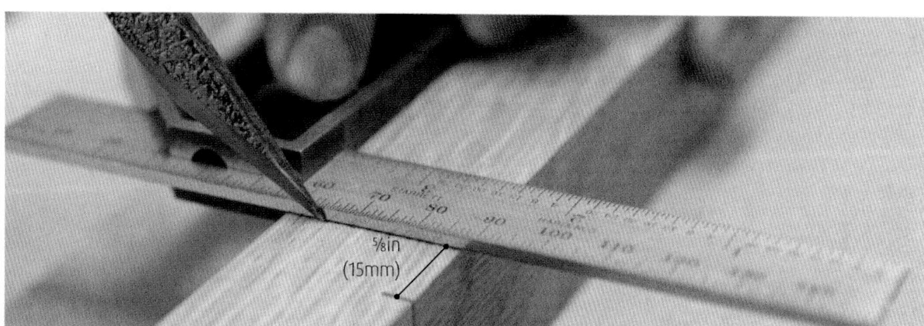

2 **Use a marking knife** to scribe a line ⅝in (15mm) to one side of the halfway point. Use this line as a guide for positioning the muntin centrally over the halfway point in Step 3 (see below).

3 **Mark the width of the joint** using the thickness of the muntin as a guide, then square the marks across both edges.

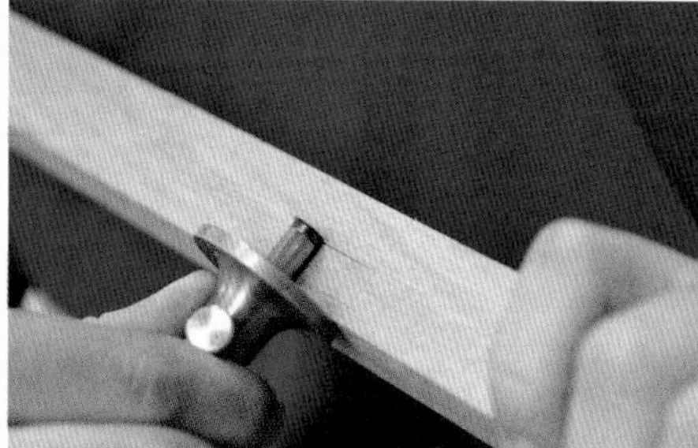

4 **Using the marking gauge** as previously set, scribe the depth of the joint between the width lines on both edges.

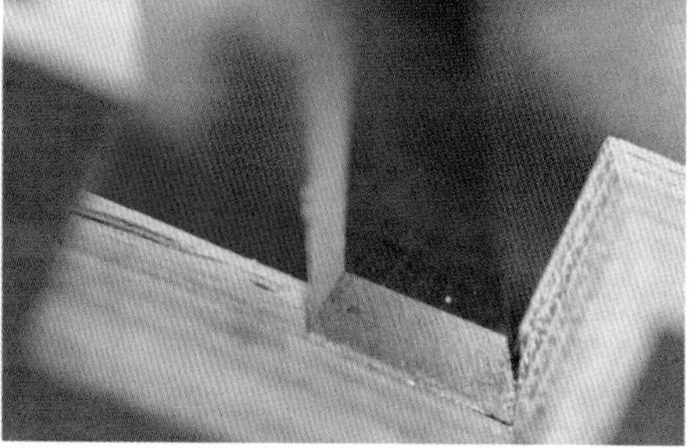

5 **Cut and clean up the joint** using a bevel-edged chisel and tenon saw, as described in Steps 8–9 (see above).

6 **Test the fit** of the joint and make any necessary adjustments.

7 **Mark and cut** a mortise for a ¼in (6mm) domino in the center of both end grains of the upper long rail to a depth of 1⅛in (28mm) and with a fence of ⅜in (10mm). Cut the mortises vertically in each end grain. Dry-fit the front frame.

JOINING THE FRAMES

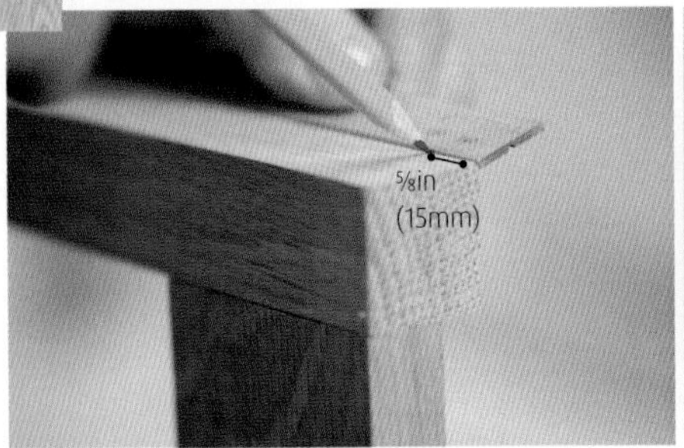

1 Mark the center of a domino mortise ⅝in (15mm) from the end grain at the bottom of each of the side-frame stiles.

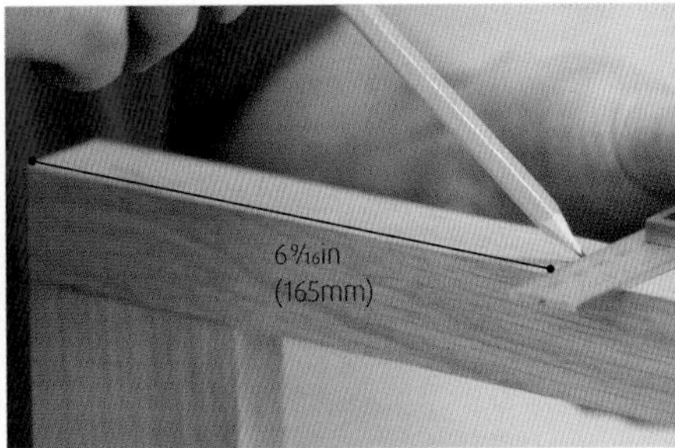

2 Mark the center of a second mortise at the top of each stile, 6 9/16in (165mm) from the end grain.

3 Cut a mortise for a ¼in (6mm) domino in each marked position to a depth of ½in (12mm) and with a fence of ⅜in (10mm).

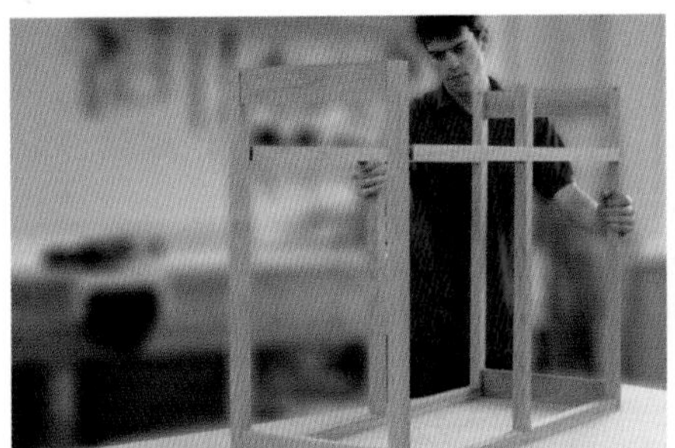

4 Check the fit of the frames by connecting the side frames with the long rails, and attaching the muntins.

MAKING AND FITTING THE DRAWER RUNNERS

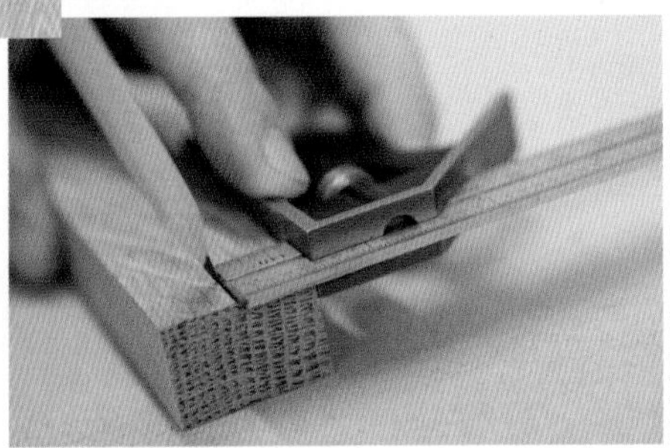

1 Mark out a mortise for a ¼in (6mm) domino in the center of both end grains of each of the four runners.

2 Cut the mortises to a depth of 1⅛in (28mm) with the fence set to ⅜in (10mm). Align the mortises to the face.

3 Cut a mortise in both end grains of all four runners, then test-fit the dominoes in each of the mortises.

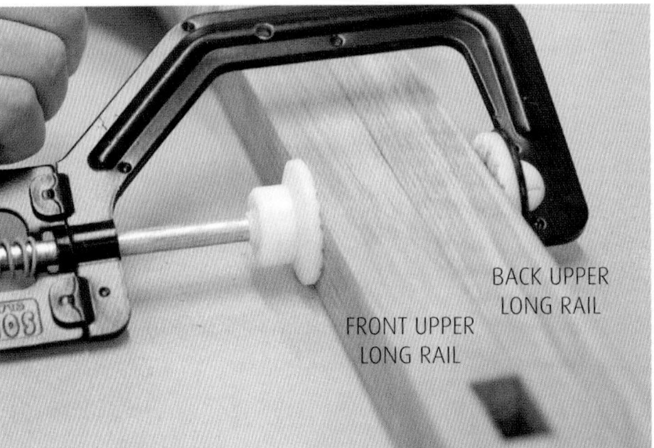
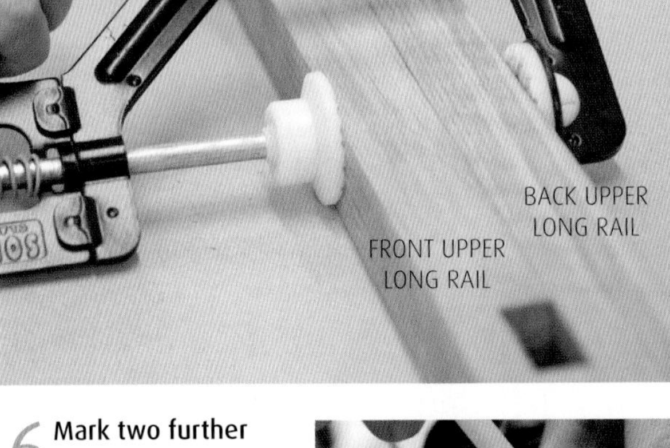

4 Use a C-clamp to fix the rails together to ensure accurate alignment. Mark the positions of the matching mortises in the upper long rails of the back and front frames.

5 Mark the position of two mortises ⅝in (15mm) from both end grains of both upper long rails.

6 Mark two further mortises ⅝in (15mm) to either side of the halving joint.

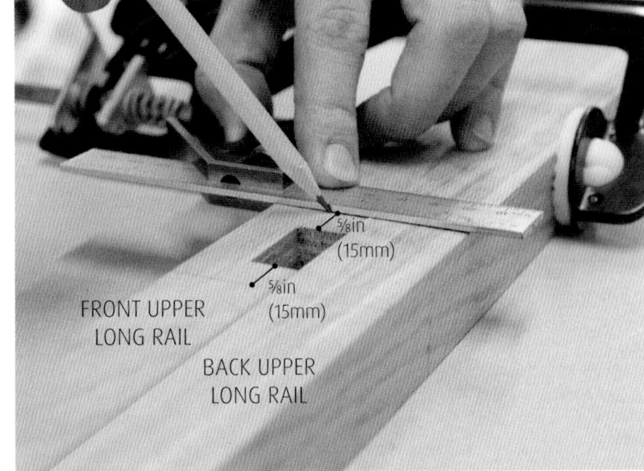

7 **Cut the mortises** on the inside face of each rail in the marked positions, working from the top edge. Set a depth of ½in (12mm) and a fence of ⅜in (10mm).

8 **Insert the dominos** into the mortises and check the fit of the frames and runners.

MAKING THE TOP FRAME

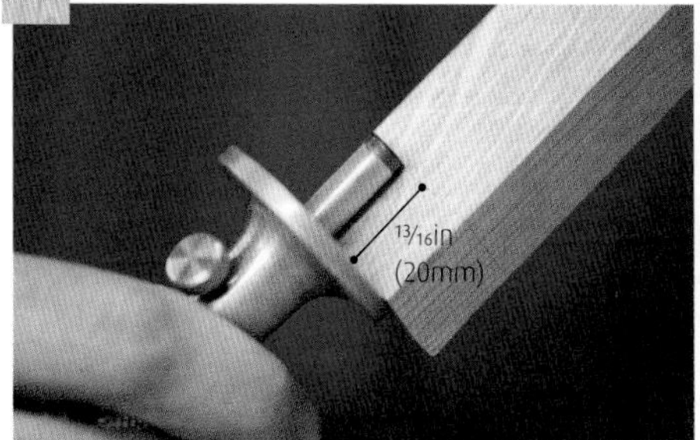

1 **Make a dovetail half-lap joint** in both ends of each of the upper long rails. Set the marking gauge to 13/16in (20mm) and scribe the shoulder around all sides.

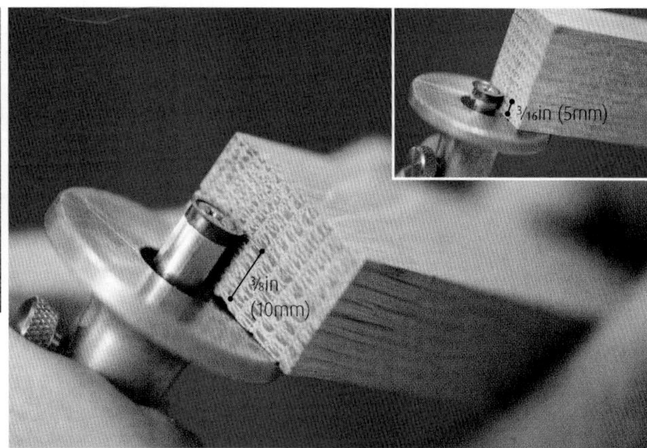

2 **Set the marking gauge** to ⅜in (10mm) and scribe along the end grain from the face. Extend the marks to the shoulder on both edges. Reset the marking gauge to 3/16in (5mm) and scribe the width of the tail from each edge (inset).

3 **Scribe the angle of the tail** from the end grain to the shoulder using a dovetail marker. Mark the waste (inset).

4 **Set the rail in a vise** so that one side of the angled tail is aligned to the vertical, to allow you to cut accurately.

5 **Use a tenon saw** to cut down to the shoulder on each side of the tail, to the waste side of the lines.

6 **Reset the piece in the vise**, then cut down to the shoulder on the waste side of the tail-thickness line.

7 **Chisel a V-groove** along the shoulder, then cut with a tenon saw to release the waste on each side of the tail (inset). Saw along the shoulder to remove the waste from the thickness of the tail.

8 **Clean up the shoulders** and edges of the tail by paring with the chisel. Cut a tail in each end of both upper long rails in the same way.

MAKING THE DOVETAIL SOCKETS

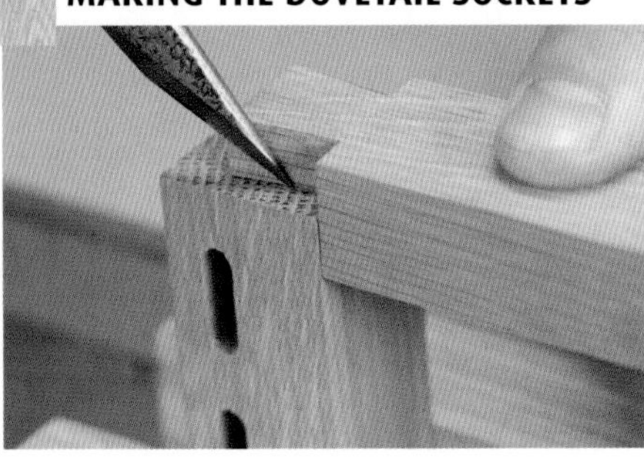

1 **Set a side-frame stile** vertically in a vise. Place the dovetail of the long rail over the top end-grain, aligned at right angles to the domino mortises in the stile. Scribe around the tail.

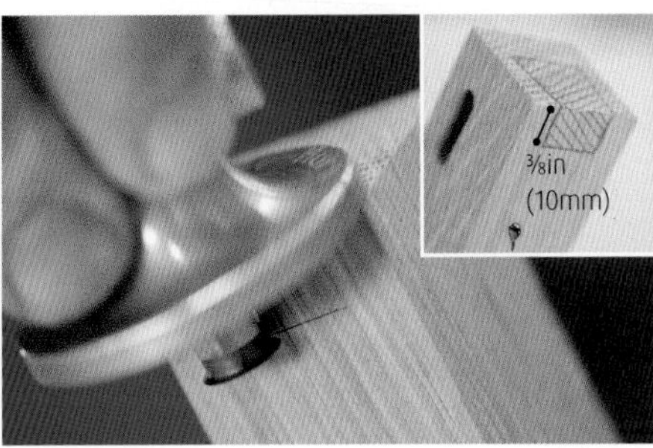

2 **Set the marking gauge** to ⅜in (10mm) and scribe the depth of the socket from the end grain. Extend the end-grain marks to the depth line, then mark the waste to be removed (inset).

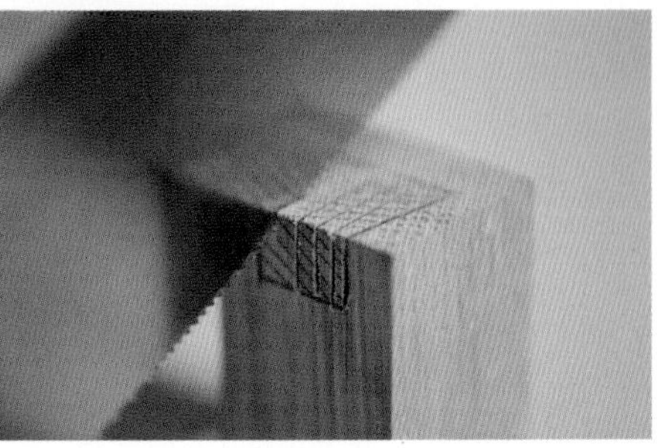

3 **Cut the waste from the socket** with the stile set in a vise, making diagonal relief cuts with a tenon saw.

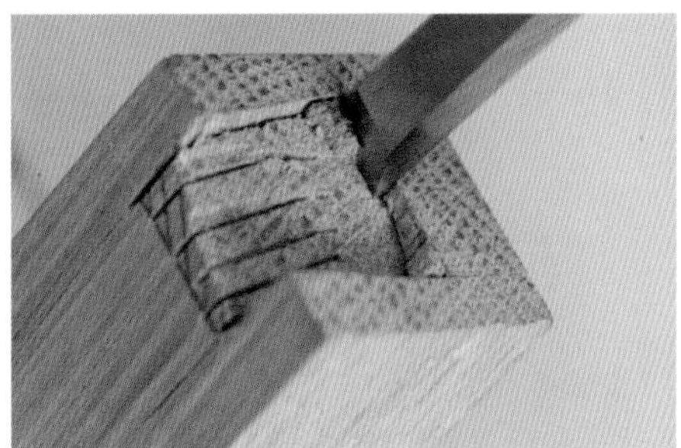

4 **Release the waste** by chopping horizontally and vertically with the chisel.

5 **Clean up the sides and edges** with the chisel. Cut sockets in the top end-grain of the other three stiles in the same way.

6 **Test the fit** of the long-rail tails in the sockets of the stiles. Adjust with the chisel to ease the fit as necessary.

MAKING THE KICKER MORTISES IN THE UPPER LONG RAILS

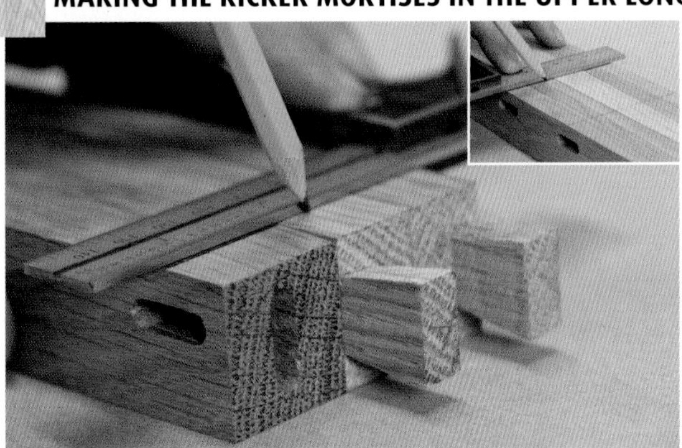

1 **Set the two upper long rails** of the top frame against the upper long rail of the back frame, ensuring the end grains are aligned precisely. Extend the position marks of the mortises from the upper long rail of the back frame to the long rails of the top frame (inset).

2 **Extend the lines** across the upper face of each of the long rails of the top frame with a pencil and square.

3 **Cut a mortise** for a ¼in (6mm) domino in each marked position to a depth of ½in (12mm), with a fence of ⅜in (10mm).

4 **The front long rail** of the top frame has an additional domino mortise in the center of the underside. Mark the halfway point between the two central mortises on the edge, then extend the line onto the face.

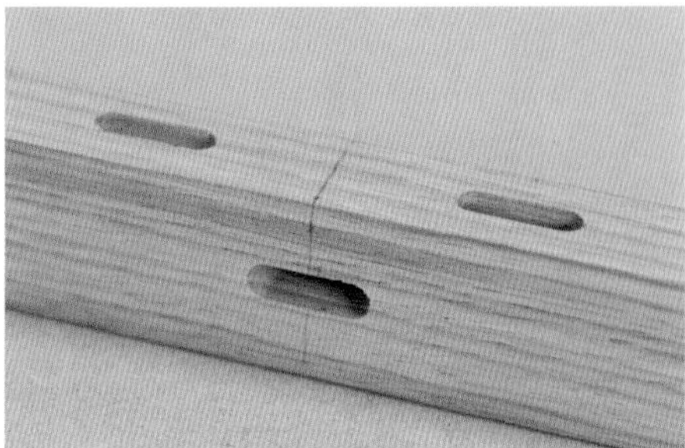

5 **Cut the domino mortise** to a depth of ½in (12mm) and with the fence set to ⅝in (15mm).

CUTTING THE MORTISES IN THE KICKERS

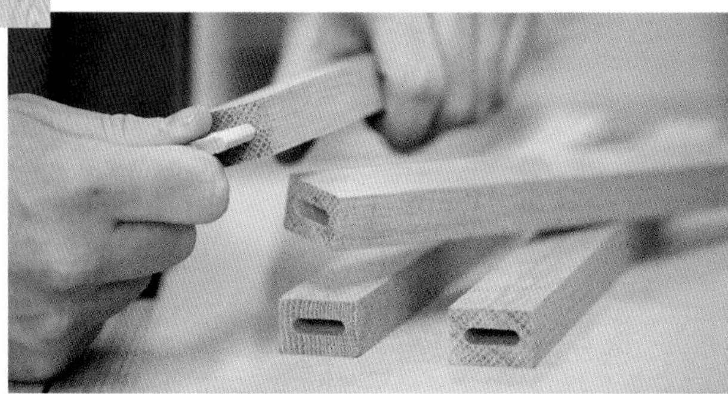

1 **Cut a mortise** for a ¼in (6mm) domino in the center of both end grains of each kicker, to a depth of 1⅛in (28mm) and with the fence set to ⅜in (10mm).

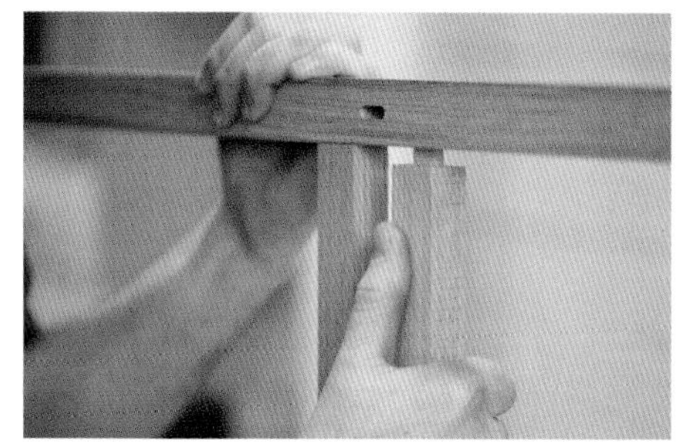

2 **Test-fit the kickers** and each of the elements of the top frame, then adjust the joints as necessary.

MAKING THE SCREW SLOTS FOR THE CARCASS TOP

1 **Mark a screw slot** on the upper face of both outside kickers 1¾in (45mm) from each end grain. Mark the length—⅝in (15mm)—of each slot.

2 **Mark the center-line** of each screw slot at half the width of the kicker, then extend the line between the length marks.

3 **Drill two holes** along the center-line, then countersink them.

4 **Use the chisel** to cut the waste between the holes to create the screw slot. Repeat Steps 1–4 for the remaining three slots.

FITTING THE BASE

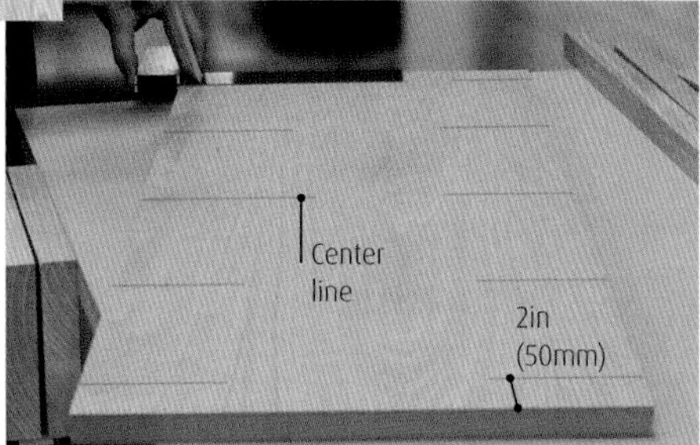

1 **Mark the position** of five biscuit grooves along both long sides of the top face of the base. Mark the first lines 2in (50mm) from each short edge, the next halfway along the length of the face, and the remaining lines centered between the two.

2 **Set the bottom long rails** of the front and back frames against the side of the base, aligned center to center, and transfer the biscuit-groove position marks.

3 **Use a biscuit jointer** to cut a groove for a No. 20 biscuit, centered in each marked position along both edges of the base (inset) and the inside edges of the rails.

4 **Insert a No. 20 biscuit connector** into each of the grooves, then check the fit of the long rails and the base.

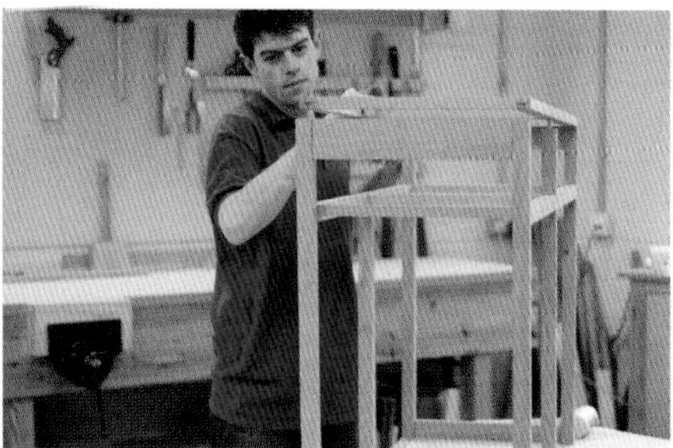

5 **Test the fit** of all the carcass elements and make adjustments to the joints as necessary.

FITTING THE CARCASS PANELS

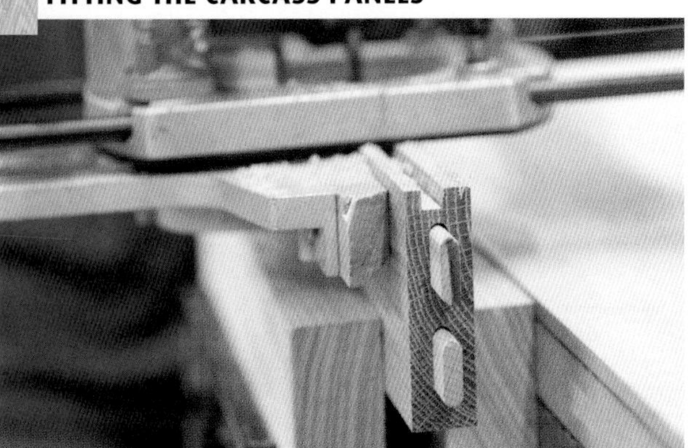

1 **Use a router** to run a groove, which will house the panels, off the front face of all elements of the side and back frames. Set the fence to 3/16in (5mm) and use a 1/4in (6mm) cutter to cut to a depth of 1/4in (6mm).

TABLE-MOUNTED ROUTER

A table-mounted router is a good choice for cutting grooves along a narrow edge. Not only does it provide greater stability than a hand-held router, but it also saves time when cutting several pieces.

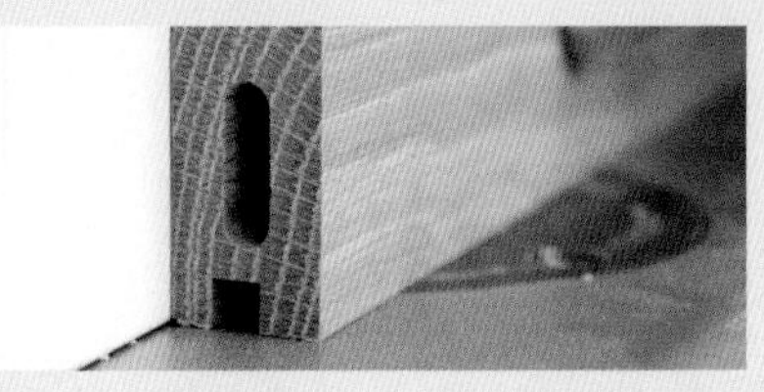

2 **Cut the groove** along the full length of each rail of the frames (pictured). For the uprights, stop the groove about 3/16in (5mm) from the mortise at each end.

3 **Mark two points** 3/8in (10mm) from the joint along the side and top inside edges of the frame elements of the side panels.

4 **Use a flat spokeshave** to cut a diminishing stopped-chamfer between the marks on the inside edge of each frame piece.

5 **Test the fit of the panels** within each of the frame elements, and adjust each piece as necessary.

6 **Use finishing or Danish oil** to protect the buffet. Apply oil to both sides of the panels, allow to dry, then glue and assemble the carcass.

MAKING THE PLINTH

1 **Cut a miter** at both ends of each plinth piece, using either a table saw (pictured) or by hand with a miter saw. Cut the pieces to make a frame with the overall dimensions of 37 13/16 x 14 3/16in (960 x 360mm).

2 **Glue each of the miters** and clamp the plinth using a ratchet strap. Use a tape measure to check the plinth for squareness.

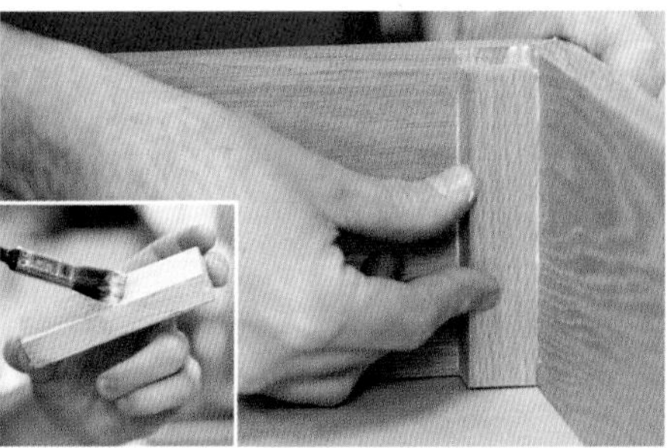

3 **Glue a block** (inset) and affix to the inside of each corner of the plinth to strengthen the joints. After the glue has dried, reinforce the joints using four screws (No.8 x 1½in/4 x 40mm) at each corner.

MAKING THE MORTISES IN THE DOOR STILES

1 Square a line 3⅜in (85mm) from the end grain, across the face of the inside edge of both ends of all four stiles of the door frames.

2 Align a rail with the line at right-angles to the stile, and mark the length of the mortise by marking the width of the rail. Extend both lines onto one adjacent edge of each stile (inset).

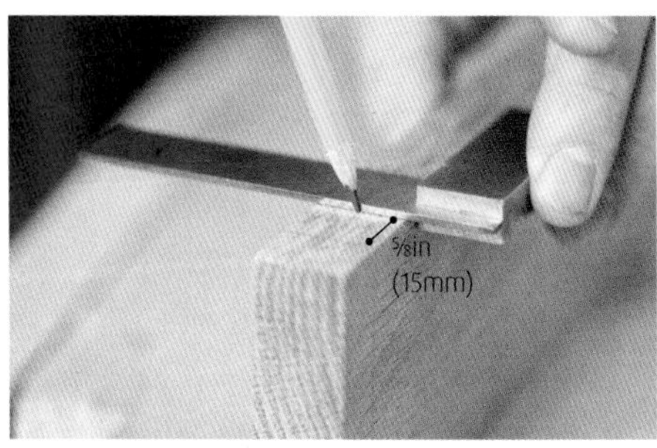

3 Square a line across the edge ⅝in (15mm) from the mark nearest to the end grain, to indicate the haunched section.

4 Use a mortise gauge set to ⅜in (10mm) to scribe the width of the mortise centrally between the marks. Mark a mortise on both ends of the stiles same way.

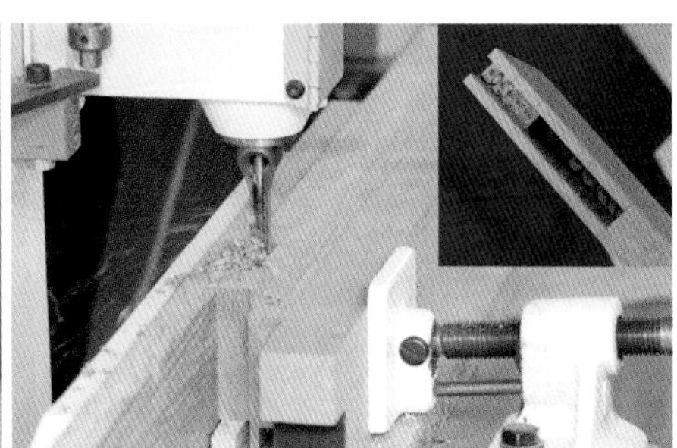

5 Use a mortiser (pictured) or a mortise chisel and mallet to cut the full depth of the mortises to 1⅜in (35mm), and the haunched part to ⅜in (10mm) in depth (inset).

MAKING THE TENONS IN THE DOOR RAILS

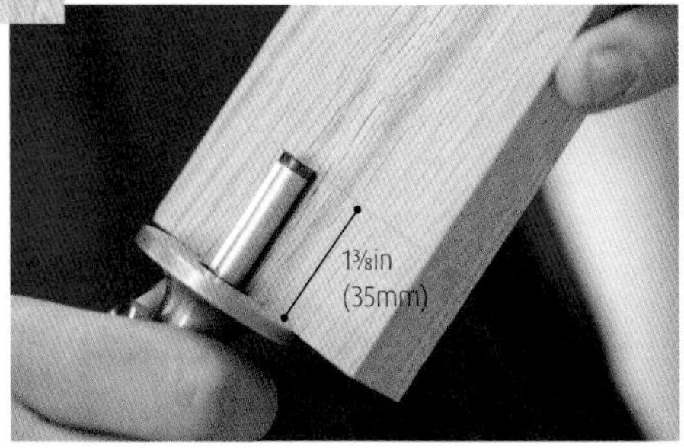

1 Mark the tenon shoulders on all the rails at 1⅜in (35mm), and square the measurement across all four sides.

2 Using the mortise gauge as previously set, mark the thickness of the tenon around the end grain and edges.

3 Mark the haunch by squaring a line across the outside edge of the tenon ⅜in (10mm) from the shoulder (inset). Square the marks onto the face.

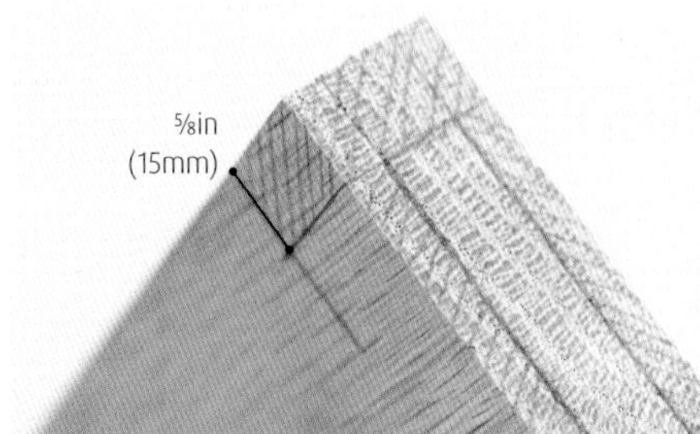

4 Measure and mark ⅝in (15mm) along the shoulder from the outside edge and square the mark onto the end grain.

5 Cut the haunch and tenons on a band saw (pictured), or by hand with a tenon saw, cutting to the waste side of the lines.

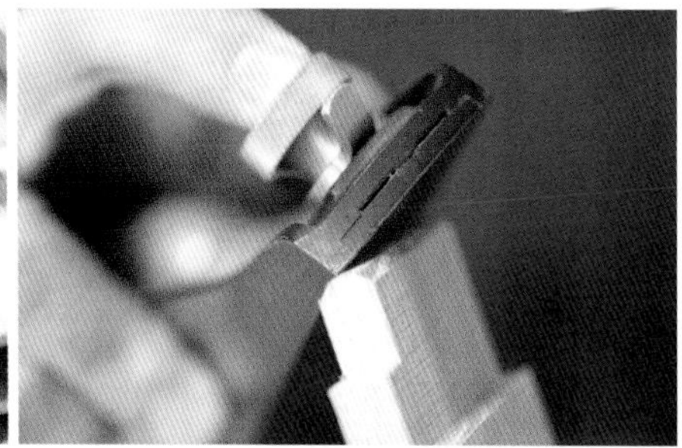

6 Use a block plane to chamfer the edges of each of the tenons to ease the fit in the mortises.

CUTTING THE GROOVES IN THE DOOR FRAMES

1 **Cut a groove** to accommodate the door panels in the inside edge of the door-frame rails and stiles with a router fitted with a ¼in (6mm) cutter. Working off the outside face, set the fence and depth to ¼in (6mm). On the rails, cut the groove at least ¼in (6mm) into the tenons.

2 **Clamp two stiles** together to provide a stable platform for the router, then continue the grooves into the mortises.

CHAMFERING THE EDGES OF THE DOOR FRAMES

1 **Mark the start** of the diminishing stopped-chamfer on the inside edge of each of the door-frame elements, ⅜in (10mm) from the inside corner.

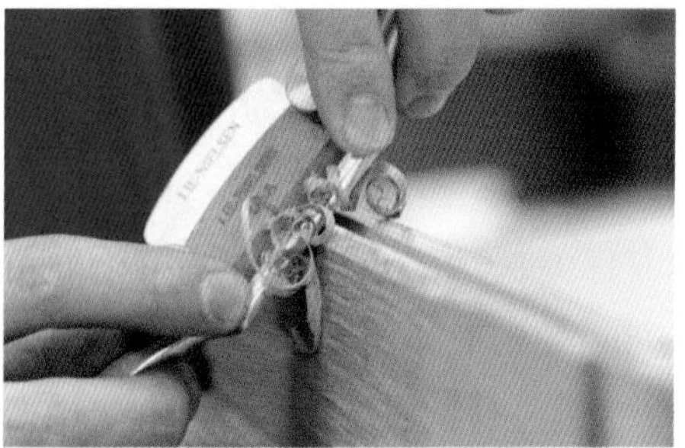

2 **Chamfer the edge** with a flat spokeshave, then test the fit of the door frames and panels.

FINISHING THE DOORS

1 **Glue the mortise-and-tenon joints** of the door frames, but insert the panels into the grooves unglued. Clamp with sash clamps and allow to dry (inset).

2 **Once the doors have dried**, square a line from the top and bottom of the frame across the excess length of the stiles—known as "horns." Cut on a band saw (inset) or by hand with a tenon saw.

3 **Plane the edges smooth** with a bench plane. Repeat Steps 1–3 for the second door.

MAKING THE SHELF UPRIGHTS

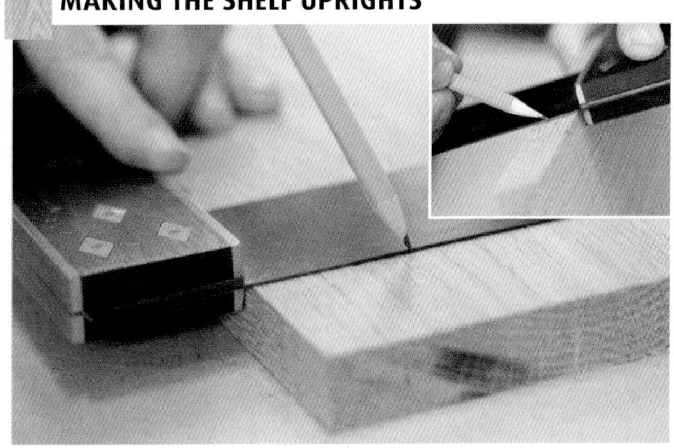

1 **Mark the position** of the stopped housings on each of the shelf uprights as shown on the diagram on pp.346–47, then square a line across the inside face. Extend the marks down the rear edge of the upright (inset).

2 **Use a marking gauge** to mark the stop in each housing 13/16in (20mm) from the front edge of the upright.

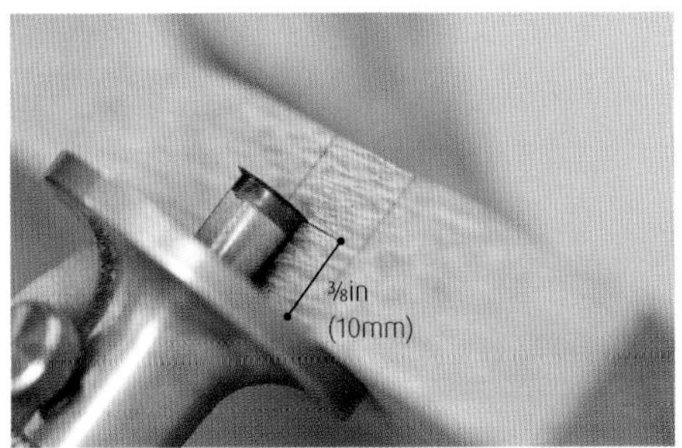

3 **Reset the marking gauge** to ⅜in (10mm), then scribe between each of the width lines to mark the housing depth.

4 **Cut the housings** either by hand, as described for the shouldered and stopped housing joint (pp.108–09), or with a router (pictured). Use a ¾in (19mm) cutter and run the router off a straight edge clamped at the necessary distance from the housing.

5 **Use a bevel-edged chisel** to square off the stopped end of each housing.

6 **Cut a rebate** along the back edge of each upright ⅝in (15mm) in depth and width. Use a router (pictured) or a rebate plane.

MAKING THE SHELVES

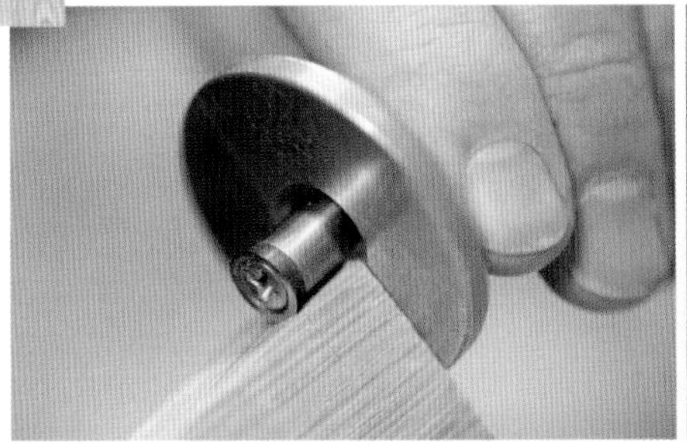

1 **Mark a stop** ⅜in (10mm) by ⅜in (10mm) in dimensions on one end grain and an adjacent edge of each shelf.

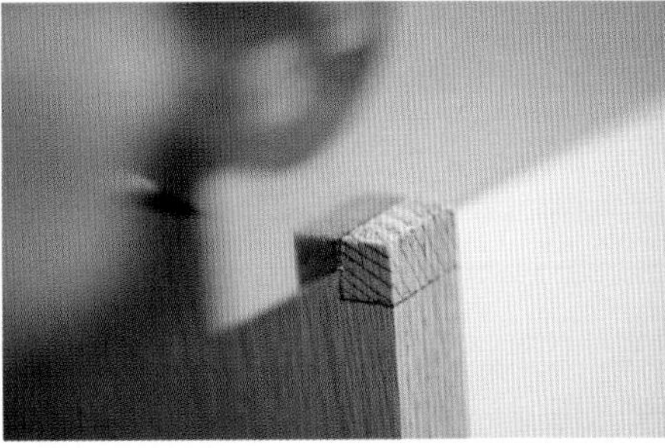

2 **Set each piece in a vise** and cut the stop using a tenon saw, being careful to cut to the waste side of the lines.

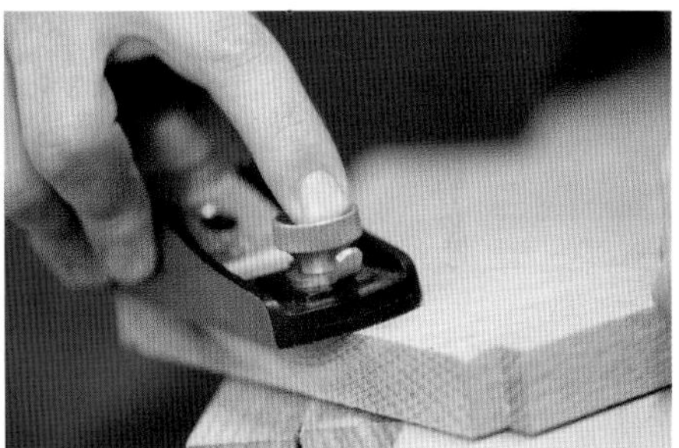

3 **Use a block plane** to create a slight taper, approximately $\frac{1}{32}$in (1mm) in size, ⅜in (10mm) from each end of the underside of each shelf.

4 **Dry-fit the shelves** and uprights, making sure that the assembly is square. This allows you to not only check the fit of the joints, but also to assess the size of the back of the shelf unit.

CUTTING THE GROOVES

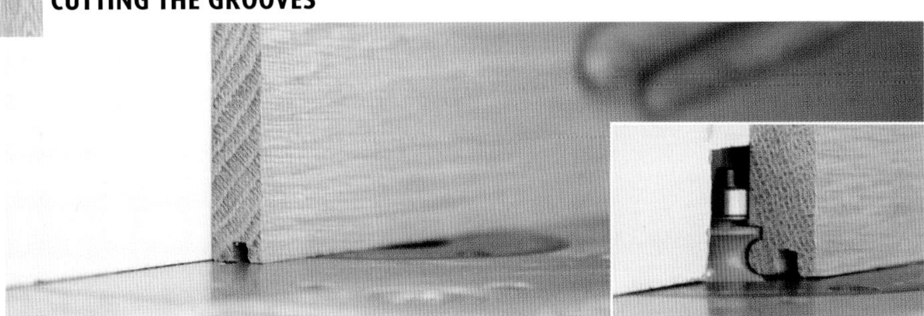

1 **Use a router** or table-mounted router (pictured) to cut a groove along a long edge of all six back boards. Use a $\frac{3}{16}$in (5mm) cutter and set a depth of $\frac{3}{16}$in (5mm) and a fence of ¼in (6mm). Cut an identical groove along the other long edge of four boards, ensuring you run the router off the same face. Then use a bearing-guided beading cutter to cut a beading in the same face on which the router has just been run (inset).

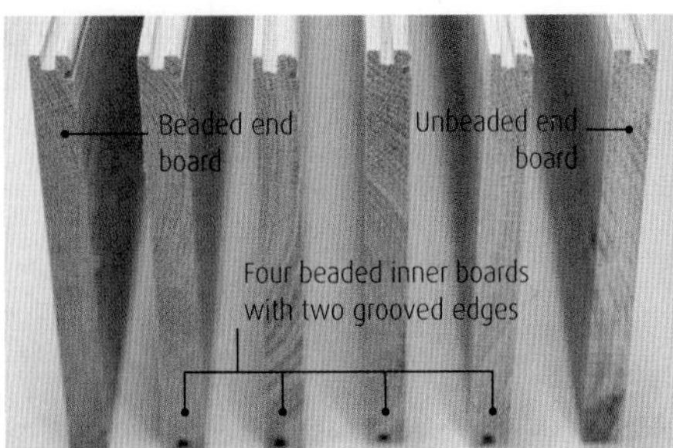

2 **Cut a beading** along the grooved edge of one of the boards with only one groove, which will both become end boards.

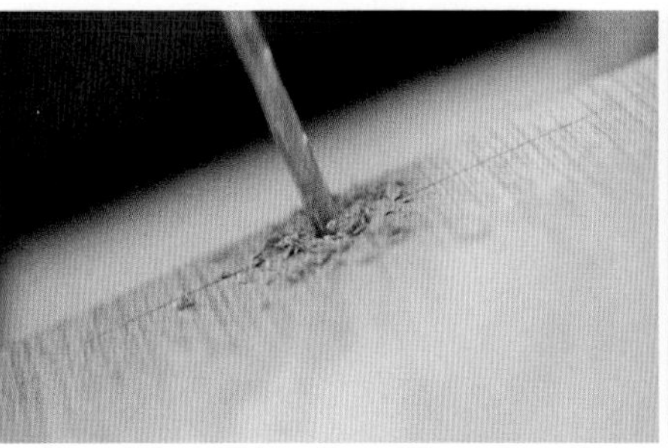

3 **Draw a line** ⅜in (10mm) from both end grains of each board. Drill a clearance hole with a ³⁄₁₆in (4mm) bit at the halfway point of the line and countersink on the back face.

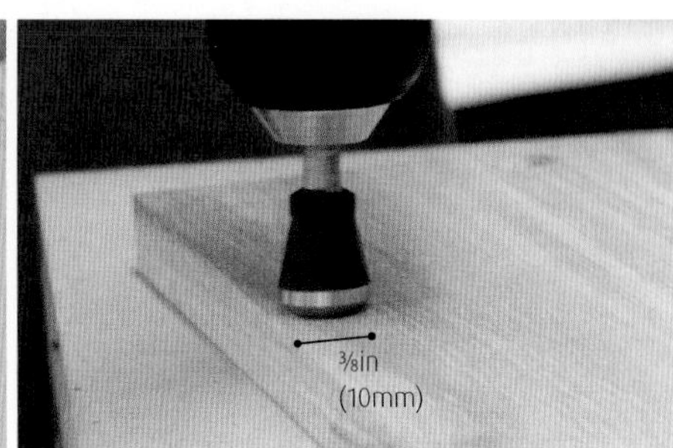

4 **Drill and countersink** three more clearance holes along the non-grooved edge of both end boards, ⅜in (10mm) from the edge, positioned equidistantly.

FITTING THE BACK BOARDS

1 **Set the beaded end board** face down in the rebate on the back of the shelf assembly. Align the board flush with the top shelf, then drill pilot holes for a No.8 x 1½in (4 x 40mm) screw into each screw position.

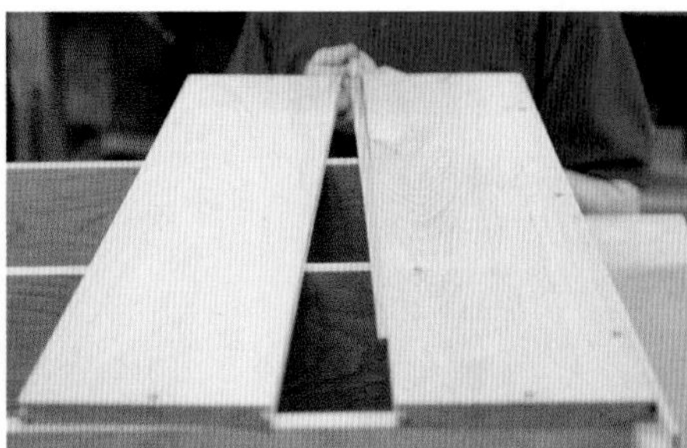

2 **Insert a tongue into the groove** of the first board, then add an inside board with the bead facedown. Affix to the top and bottom shelves with a screw at both ends of each board.

3 **Join each remaining pair** of boards with a tongue and affix to the shelves with a screw in each end.

MAKING THE DRAWERS

1 **Check the fit of the drawer fronts** in the carcass. Use a block plane to adjust the fit if necessary.

2 **Use a marking gauge** to scribe the shoulder for the lapped dovetail joint that joins the drawer sides to the drawer front. Set the marking gauge to ⅝in (15mm) and mark the shoulder at one end of each drawer side.

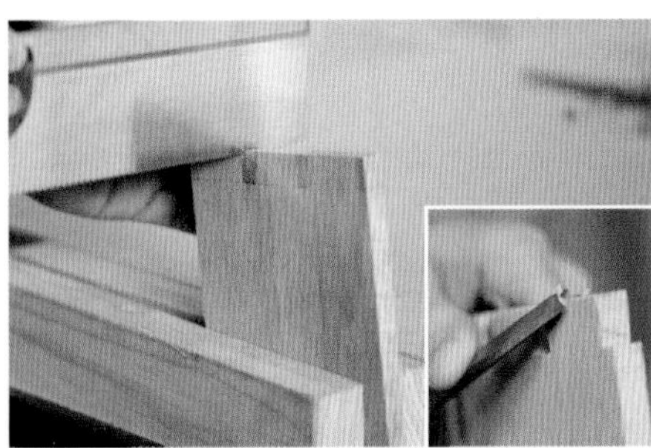

3 **Mark and cut three tails** in each drawer side (see pp.138–39), then chamfer the edges with a chisel (inset).

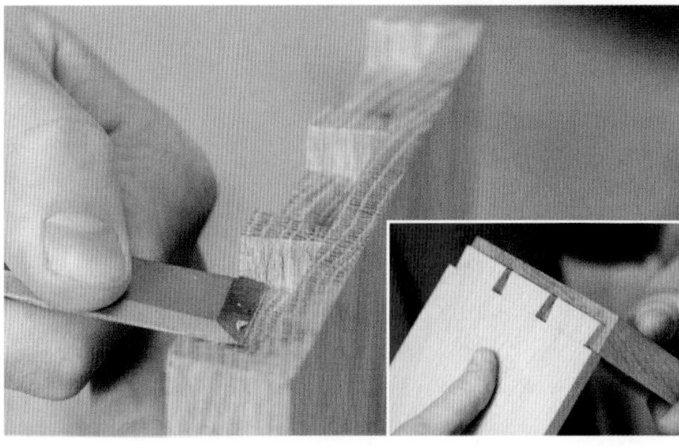

4 **Mark out and cut the sockets** in both ends of the drawer front, as described on pp.138–39. Test-fit the joints and adjust if necessary (inset).

5 **Cut a groove** ⅜in (10mm) from the inside bottom edge of the drawer front and sides (inset) to a depth of ¼in (6mm). Use a router with a ¼in (6mm) cutter or a table-mounted router (pictured).

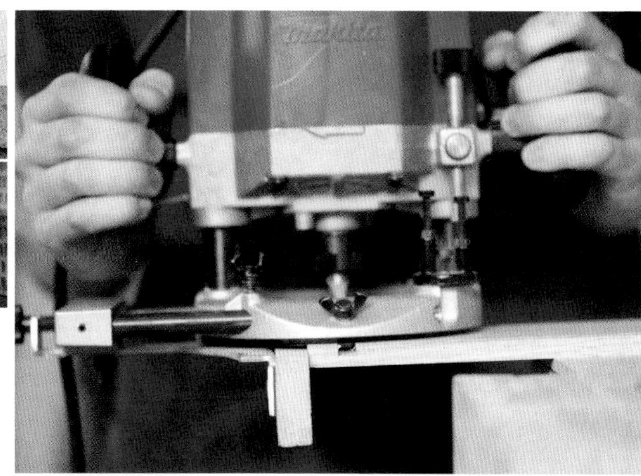

6 **Use a router** to cut a housing ⅜in (10mm) wide on the back of each drawer side, ⅝in (15mm) from the end grain and parallel to the inner edge, to house the drawer back. Stop the housing ⅜in (10mm) from the top of the drawer side.

7 **Use the chisel** to square off the end of the housing.

8 **Mark and cut a notch** ³⁄₁₆in (4mm) wide and ¼in (6mm) deep in each end of the top of the drawer back. Repeat Steps 1–8 with the second drawer.

ASSEMBLING AND FITTING THE DRAWERS

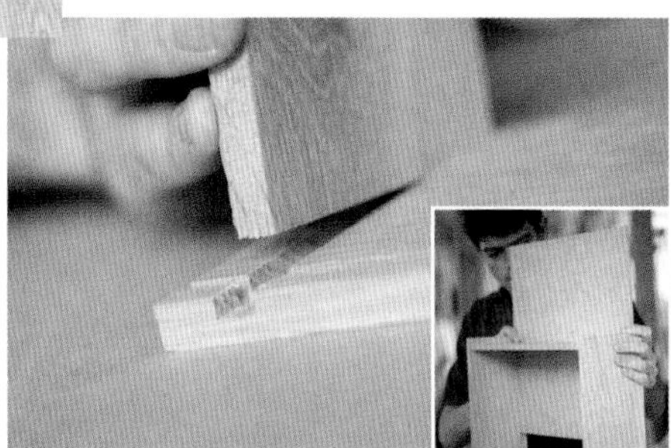

1 **Test the fit** of the drawer sides in the front and back, then insert the base into the grooves (inset).

2 **Glue all the joints** in both of the drawers, secure with sash clamps, then allow to dry.

3 **Once the glue has dried**, use a bench plane to cut the dovetail joints flush to the drawer sides.

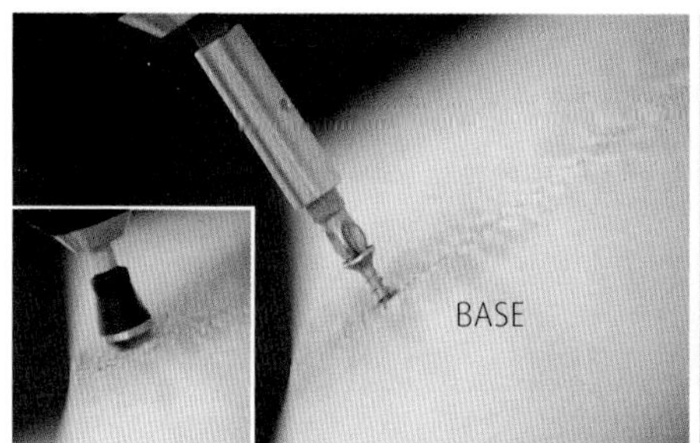

4 **Mark the center-point** of the length and width of the drawer back on the base. Drill a pilot hole in this position, countersink (inset), then insert a No.8 x ¾in/4 x 20mm screw.

5 **Fit the drawer slips** on the outside face of each runner. Glue each one in position, aligned to the bottom of the runner. Clamp the assembly and leave to dry.

6 **Once the glue has dried**, test the fit of the drawers in the carcass. Mark any sections that need adjustment and ease the fit by planing.

INSERTING THE SHELF STUDS

1 **Mark the position of the shelf studs** in the center of all six upright elements on the inside of the carcass, 11 13⁄16in (300mm) up from the base.

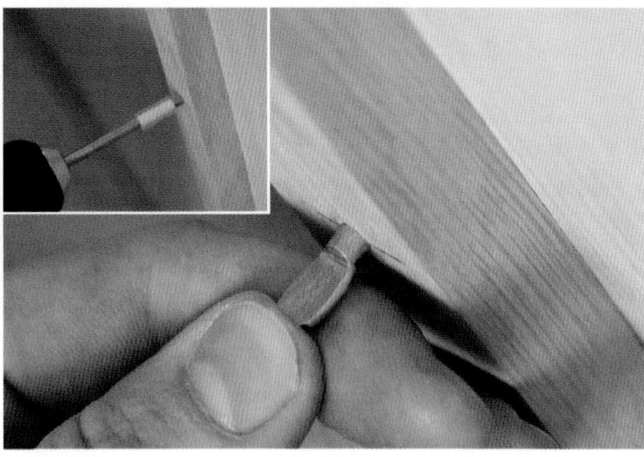

2 **Measure and mark the drill bit** with the depth of the shelf studs, then drill holes to the required depth (inset). Insert a stud in each marked position.

MAKING AND FITTING THE CUPBOARD SHELF

1 **Glue the cupboard shelf-pieces** (see Edge-to-edge joints, pp.94–95), clamp with sash clamps, then allow to dry.

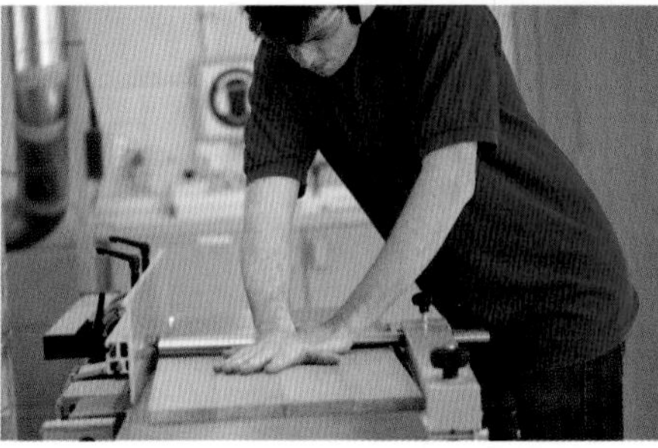

2 **Plane the glued shelf** to a thickness of approximately 5⁄8in (15mm). Do this with a thicknesser (pictured) or by hand with a bench plane (see Thicknessing, pp.58–59).

3 **Cut the shelf** to the required dimensions—38 3⁄8in (975mm) long and 14 3⁄16in (360mm) wide—on a table saw (pictured), or by hand with a panel saw.

4 **Carefully insert the shelf** in position inside the carcass, supported on the shelf studs.

MAKING THE DOOR KNOBS

1 **Use a lathe** to turn knobs for the doors and drawers. Prepare a piece of stock 12in (300mm) long, 1 3⁄8in (35mm) wide, and 1 3⁄8in (35mm) thick, by marking the center of the end grain and removing the corners with a bench plane (see also pp.152–55). Or use store-bought knobs.

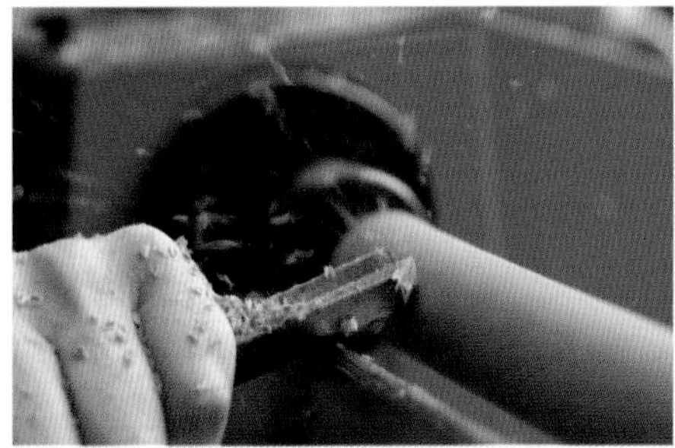

2 **Set the stock** on the lathe and use a roughing gouge to create a cylinder approximately 1 3⁄16in (30mm) in diameter.

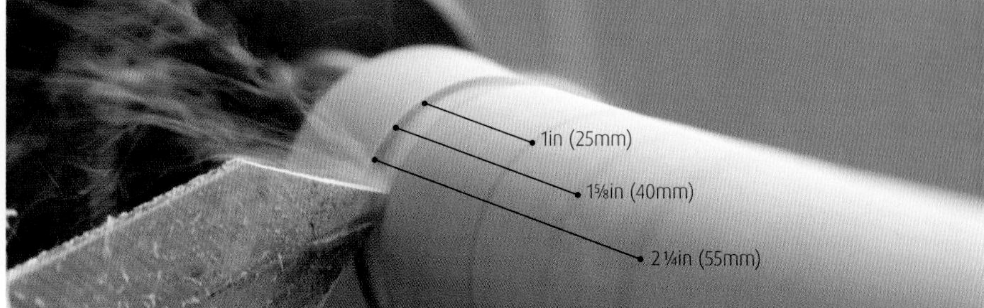

3 **Use a pencil** to mark the length (as pictured) of each cylinder of different diameter—the first cylinder is 3⁄8in (10mm) in diameter, the next is 13⁄16in (20mm), and the last is 1 3⁄16in (30mm). Then cut each section to the required diameter using the parting tool.

4 **Once the first knob is cut**, measure and mark the sections for the second knob on the stock. Continue until you have cut the profile of all four knobs.

5 **Separate the pieces** by cutting with a flush-cut saw between the stem of one knob and the thickest section of the next. Sand the knobs smooth with sandpaper.

FIXING THE KNOBS

1 **Square a line** across the stile 3 15⁄16in (100mm) from the top of the inside edge of the door. Mark the center of the line (inset).

2 **Drill a hole** through the door into the marked position, measuring 3⁄8in (10mm) in diameter.

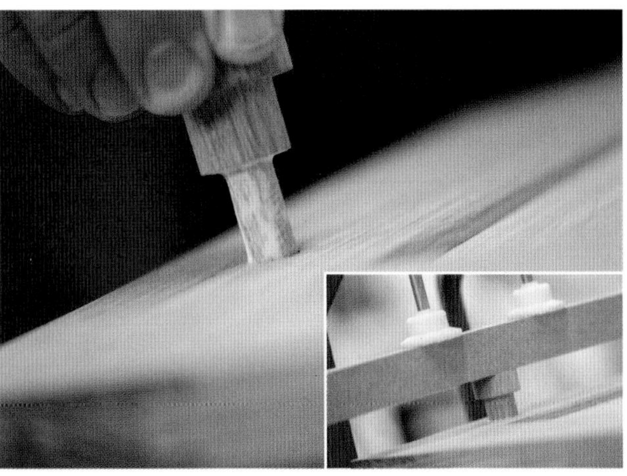

3 **After test-fitting**, glue the knobs into the doors. Clamp and allow to dry (inset). Once dry, block-plane the stem of the knob flush to the back of the door.

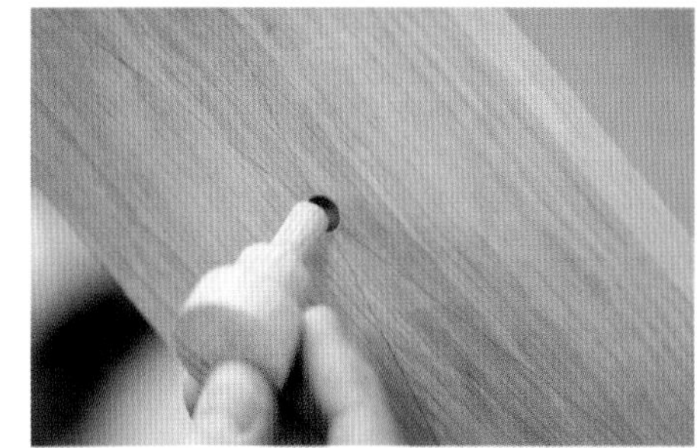

4 **Mark the center-point** of each drawer front with diagonals, then drill a hole through it 3⁄8in (10mm) in diameter. Test-fit a knob into the hole, then glue it in place. Plane the stem flush to the back of the drawer.

MAKING THE CURVED TOP BRACE

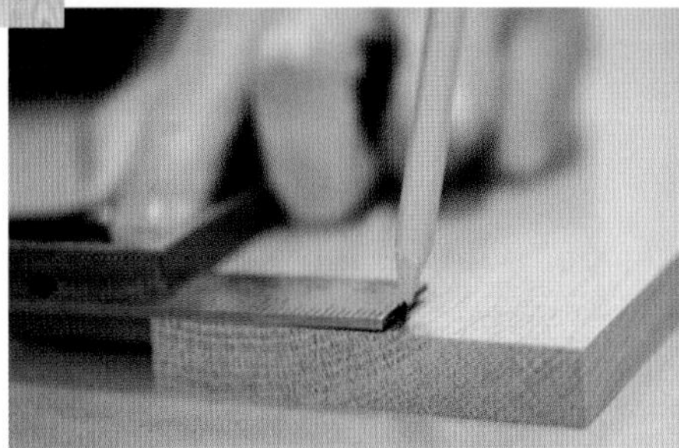

1 **Mark a point** at both ends of the top brace of the top shelf, 1 15⁄16in (50mm) from the bottom edge.

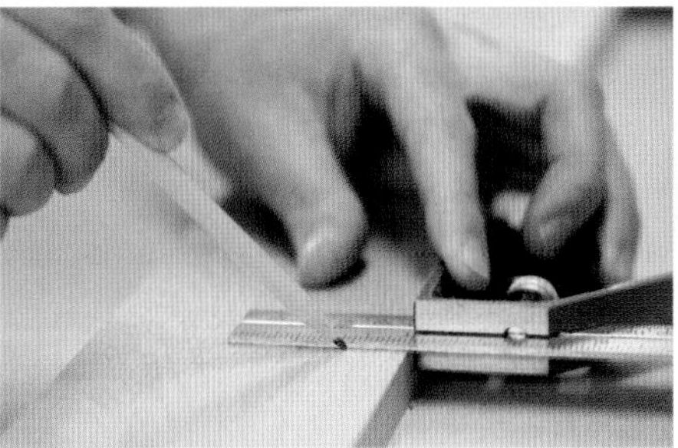

2 **Mark a line** at the halfway point of the top edge of the brace.

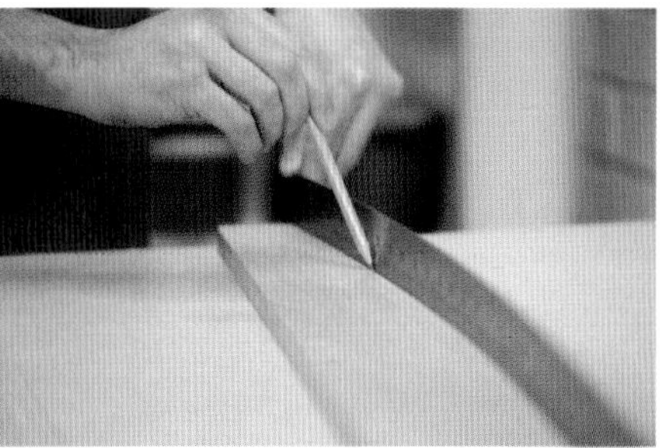

3 **Position a long metal ruler** in a curve that links the three marks (it is helpful if someone else holds the ruler in position for you). Draw the curve.

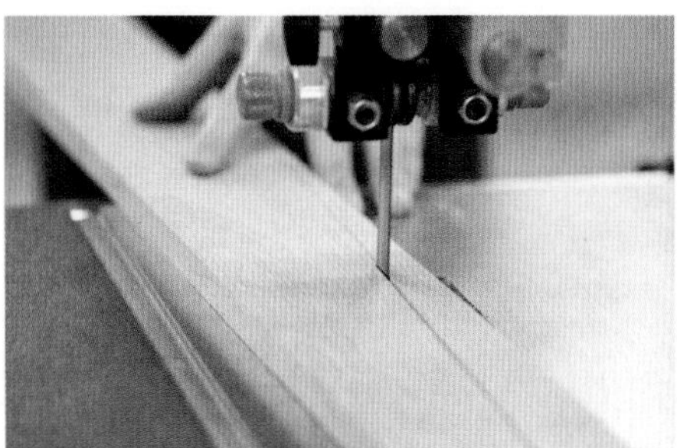

4 **Cut to the waste side** of the marked line on a band saw (pictured), coping saw, or jigsaw.

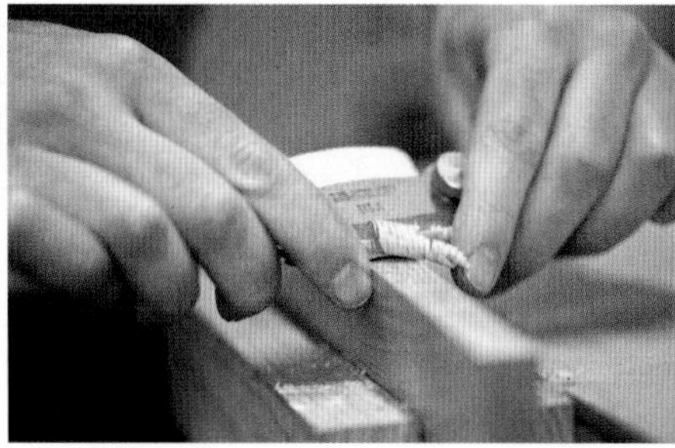

5 **Plane to the curved line** using a flat spokeshave, then remove any arrises with sandpaper.

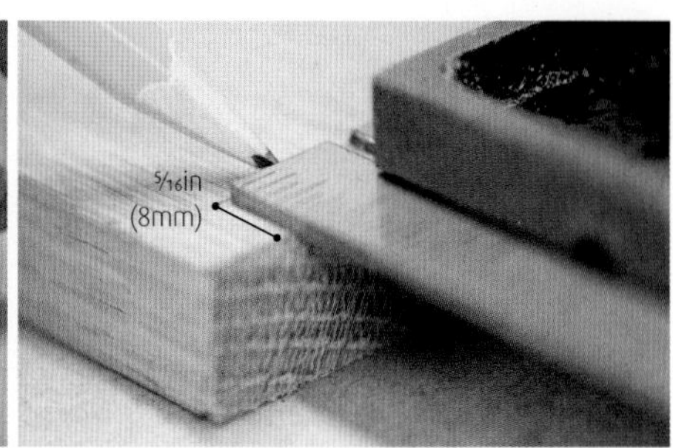

6 **Square a line** across the outside face at both ends of the brace, 5⁄16in (8mm) from the end grains.

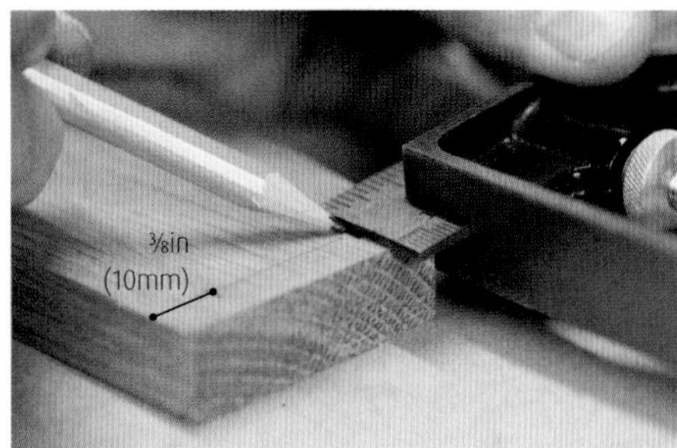

7 **Mark two points on each line** 3⁄8in (10mm) from each edge at both ends of the brace.

8 **Drill a clearance hole** in all four of the marked positions through both ends of the brace, then countersink on the outside face (inset).

9 **Position the rail** in the rebate at the back of the top shelf, then drill pilot holes to match the No.8 x 13⁄8in (4 x 35mm) screws into the side pieces through the clearance holes. Insert a screw into all four holes (inset).

FITTING THE DOOR HINGES

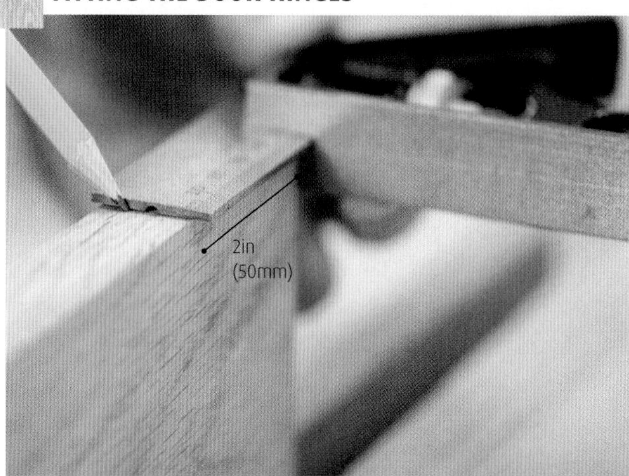

1 **Mark the position of the hinges** 2in (50mm) from the top and 2in (50mm) from the bottom on the outer edge of each door.

2 **Use a marking knife** to scribe the length and width of the butt-hinge flanges in each position.

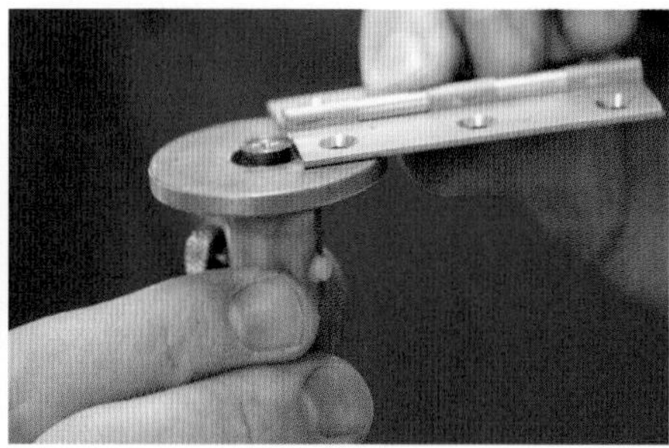

3 **Adjust the marking gauge** to the exact thickness of the hinge flange.

4 **Scribe the flange thickness** on the outside face of the door between the hinge marks. Square off the marks (inset).

5 **Chop out the waste** from each hinge housing using a mallet and chisel, being careful not to exceed the marks.

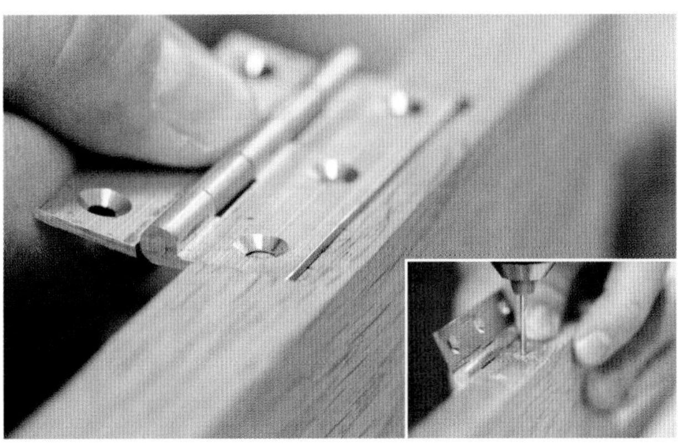

6 **Check the fit** of the hinges in the housings and adjust if necessary. Drill pilot holes (inset) and insert screws to secure the hinges.

FITTING THE DOOR TO THE CARCASS

1 **Set each door** in position in the carcass. Mark the position of the hinges on the front of the stile and the inside edge of the carcass (inset).

2 **Mark the width** of the flange in each of the marked positions on the inside edge of the carcass.

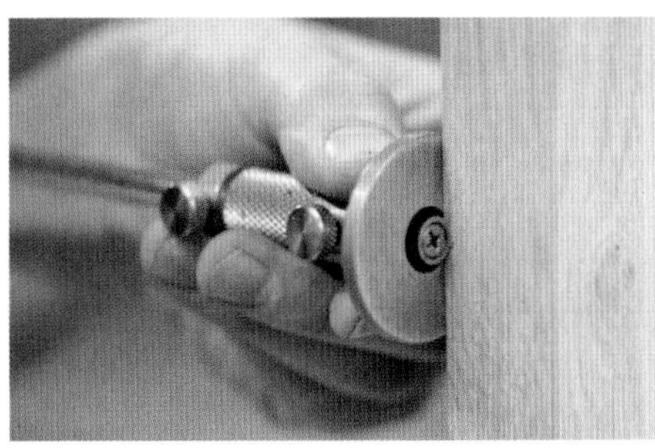

3 **Use the marking gauge** as previously set to mark the thickness of the flange on the outside face of the carcass.

4 **Set the carcass on its side** to chop out the hinge housings with a chisel. Cut the remaining three housings in the same way.

5 **Set each door** in turn in position against the frame, then mark the screw positions on the hinges with a bradawl. Screw the hinges in position on the carcass (inset).

ADJUSTING THE FIT OF THE DOORS

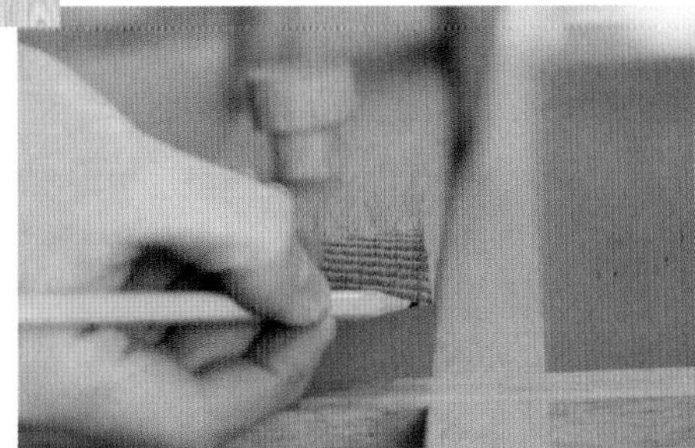

1 **Test the fit of the doors**, then mark the amount to be planed from the upper leading edge of each one.

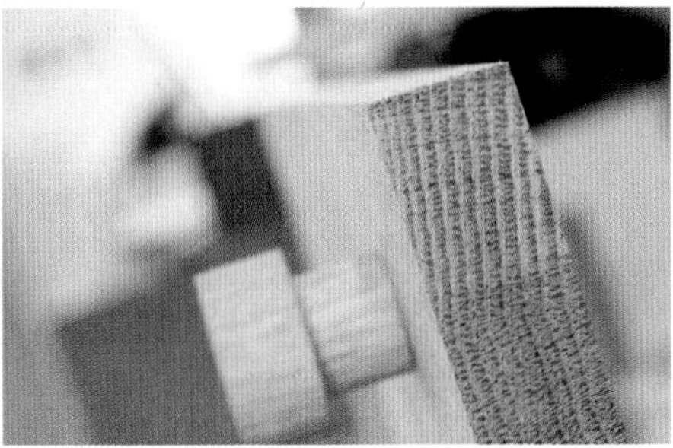

2 **Remove the doors** and set each one in a vise with the inside edge uppermost. Remove the marked amount from the leading edge using a bench plane.

3 **Cut two offcuts**, ⅜ x ⅝ x 1³⁄₁₆in (10 x 15 x 30mm) in size. Use two No.8 x 1in (4 x 25mm) screws to fix each block to the underside of the door rail butting up to the front muntin, ¹³⁄₁₆in (20mm) from the front edge.

MAKING THE BUFFET TOP

1 **Join the pieces for the carcass top** (see Edge-to-edge joints, pp.94–95). Clamp with sash clamps and leave to dry.

2 **Cut the buffet top to size**, then finish the top by scraping with a cabinet scraper and smoothing with an orbital sander.

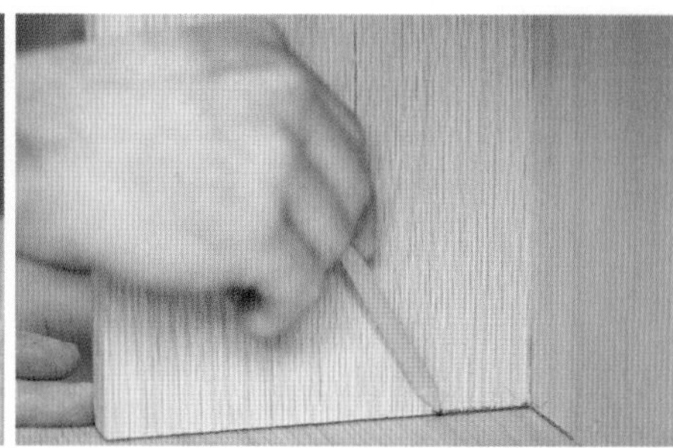

3 **Place the shelf assembly** centrally on the buffet top, flush to the back. Mark the position of the inside corner.

MAKING THE BATTEN

1 **Shape the batten** that secures the shelf assembly to the buffet top by running a round-over cutter along one edge. Use a hand-held router, a table-mounted router (pictured), or a block plane.

2 **Place the batten** on the buffet top aligned with the shelf-assembly corner marks. Mark the exact length on the batten, cut it to size, then glue and clamp it to the buffet top (inset).

FITTING THE BUFFET TOP

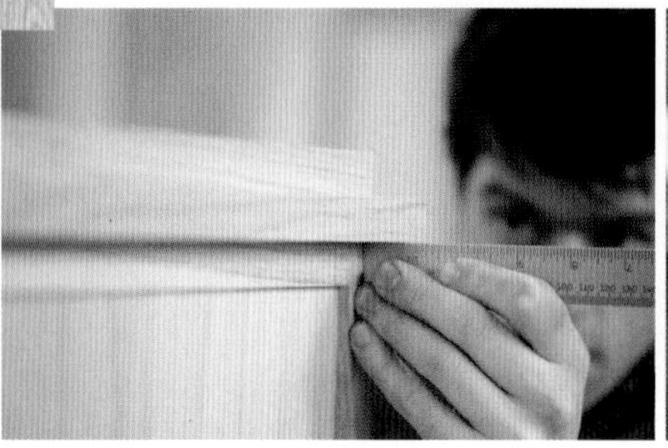

1 **Once the glue has dried**, place the buffet top on the carcass. Position it over the carcass width, overhanging the back of the carcass by 13⁄16in (20mm).

2 **Mark the position of the screw slots** in the carcass frame on the underside of the buffet top, then remove the top.

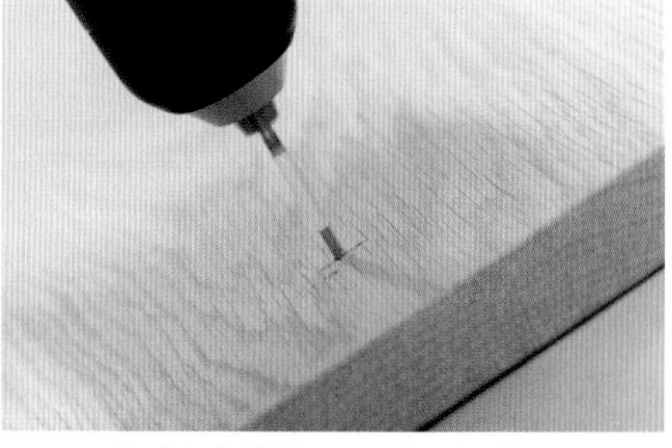

3 **Mark the drill bit** to a depth of 5⁄8in (15mm), then drill a pilot hole into the center of each of the screw-slot marks on the underside of the buffet top.

4 **Reposition the top on the carcass** and insert one No.8 x 13⁄8in (4 x 35mm) screw into each of the slots, then screw it into the pilot hole in the buffet top.

5 **Complete the assembly** by placing the carcass on the plinth and the shelf assembly on the carcass top. Affix the latter by drilling pilot holes through the clearance holes in the back of the shelf assembly part-way into the batten, then screw in place with six No.8 x 13⁄8in (4 x 35mm) screws.

FINISHES

A buffet is a piece of furniture that will be heavily used so it is essential that you add a hard coating that will prevent unwanted stains and marks. Four coats of Danish oil have been applied here, which lends a warm glow to the oak and provides a durable protective layer. A few coats of wax on top of the oil will give a nice sheen and help the wood develop a rich patina over time.

DETAIL OF DOOR HANDLE

DETAIL OF DRAWER JOINT

DETAIL OF DOOR HINGE

THE FINISHED BUFFET

Chair

A chair can be a satisfying and challenging project for every level of woodworker to undertake. The classic design shown here is simple and robust. Strength and resilience are fundamental to the design of any chair, which will usually be subject to continual and heavy use. For this reason, it is important to make the joints of the side rails as deep and as wide as possible, without compromising the integrity of the wood. Another consideration is the comfort for the person sitting in the chair, hence the gentle angle of the chair back and the subtle shaping of the back rails.

Dimensions:
34 1/16 x 18 1/8 x 17 11/16in (865 x 460 x 450mm)

Key techniques:
Basic mortise-and-tenon joint (pp.116–19);
Dowel joint (pp.145–48)

CUTTING LIST

Item	Material	No.	Length	Width	Thickness
Back leg	Oak	2	34 1/16in (865mm)	3 1/8in (80mm)	1 9/16in (40mm)
Front leg	Oak	2	17 11/16in (450mm)	1 9/16in (40mm)	1 9/16in (40mm)
Front rail	Oak	1	16 7/8in (430mm)	1 15/16in (50mm)	1in (25mm)
Side rail	Oak	2	15 7/8in (403mm)	1 15/16in (50mm)	1in (25mm)
Back rail	Oak	1	12 5/8in (320mm)	1 15/16in (50mm)	1in (25mm)
Upper back slat	Oak	1	12 5/8in (320mm)	2 3/4in (70mm)	13/16in (20mm)
Lower back slat	Oak	2	12 5/8in (320mm)	1 15/16in (50mm)	13/16in (20mm)
Seat slat	Oak	4	17 11/16in* (450mm)	3 1/2in* (89mm)	9/16in (15mm)
Arm rest	Oak	2	14 11/16in (373mm)	1 15/16in (50mm)	11/16in (18mm)
Arm-rest upright	Oak	2	8 5/8in* (220mm)	1in (25mm)	13/16in (20mm)
Dowel connector	Oak	2	24in* (600mm)	5/16in (8mm)	5/16in (8mm)

*Includes excess to allow for cutting to size

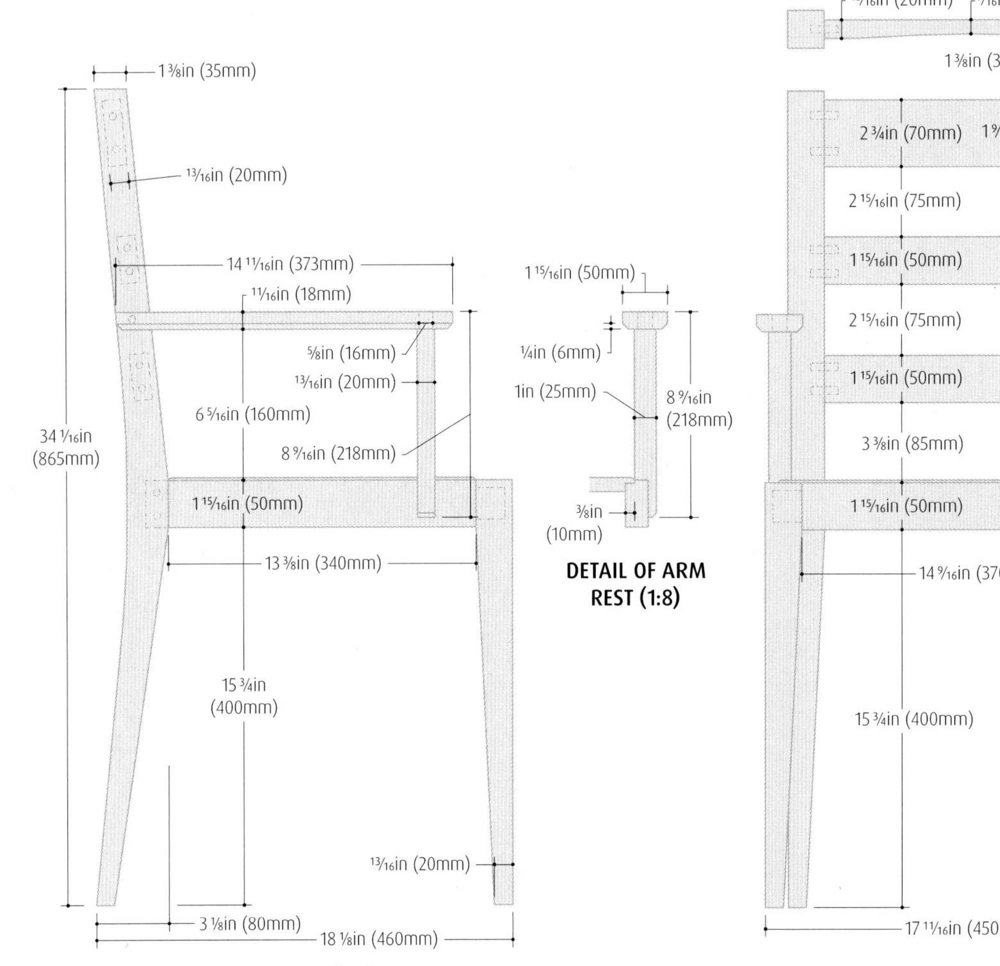

SIDE VIEW (1:8)

DETAIL OF ARM REST (1:8)

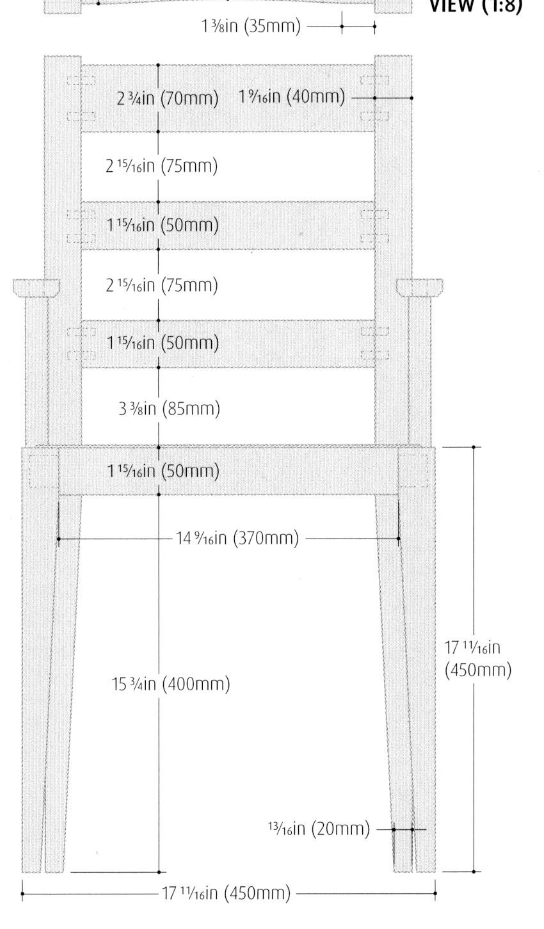

BACK TOP VIEW (1:8)

FRONT VIEW (1:8)

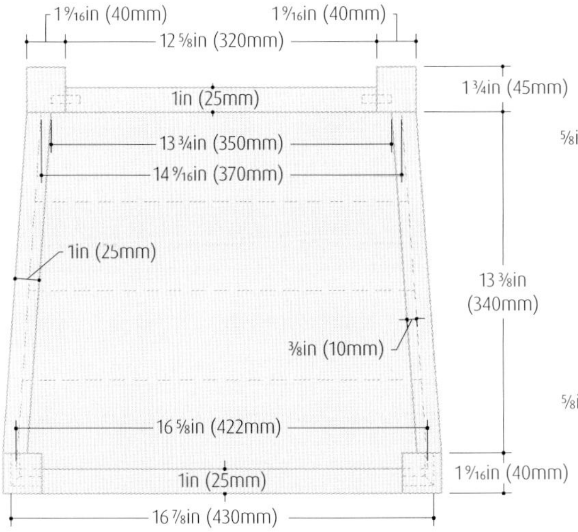

1 9/16in (40mm)
1 9/16in (40mm)
12 5/8in (320mm)
1in (25mm)
1 3/4in (45mm)
13 3/4in (350mm)
14 9/16in (370mm)
1in (25mm)
13 3/8in (340mm)
3/8in (10mm)
16 5/8in (422mm)
1in (25mm)
1 9/16in (40mm)
16 7/8in (430mm)

SEAT TOP VIEW (1:8)

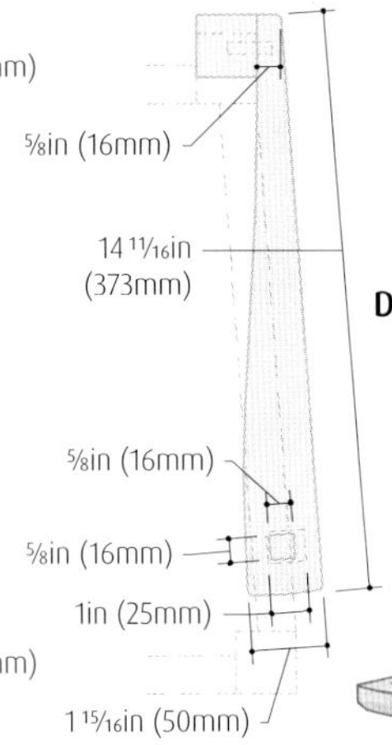

1in (25mm)
9/16in(15mm)
1/8in (3mm)
3/8in (10mm)

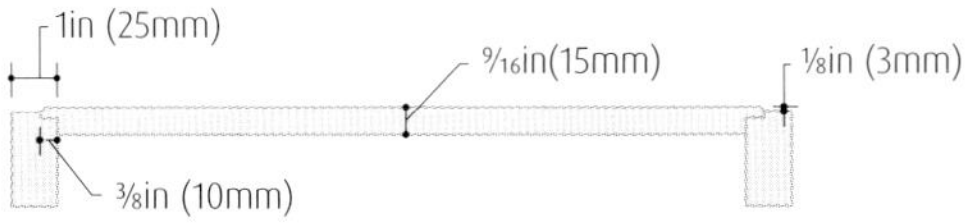

CROSS-SECTION OF SEAT (1:8)

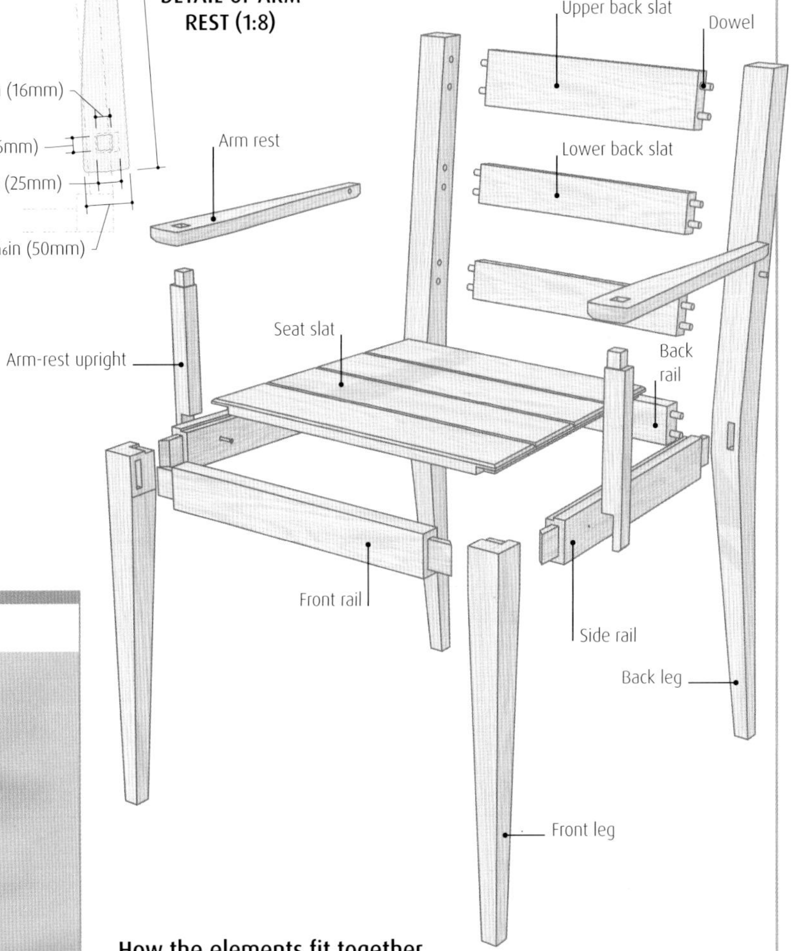

5/8in (16mm)
14 11/16in (373mm)
5/8in (16mm)
5/8in (16mm)
1in (25mm)
1 15/16in (50mm)

DETAIL OF ARM REST (1:8)

Upper back slat
Dowel
Lower back slat
Arm rest
Seat slat
Arm-rest upright
Back rail
Front rail
Side rail
Back leg
Front leg

How the elements fit together

While the back slats and rail are fixed using dowel joints, the front and side rails use mortise and tenons for greater strength, since they receive the most strain. The side rails feature angled tenons to allow the seat to splay out, making the front of the chair wider than the back.

TOOLS AND MATERIALS

- MDF (3 1/8 x 34 1/16in/80 x 865mm)
- Pencil
- Combination square
- Long metal ruler
- Band saw
- Spokeshave or sandpaper
- Bench plane
- Mortise gauge
- Mortiser or mortise chisel and mallet
- Marking gauge
- Drill with bits
- Masking tape
- Hammer
- Rubber mallet
- Tenon saw
- Protractor
- Sliding bevel
- Marking knife
- Bevel-edged chisel
- Rebate plane
- Wood glue and brush
- Sash clamps
- Tape measure
- Block plane
- Flush-cut saw
- 2 brass screws (No. 8 x 1in/4 x 25mm)
- Screwdriver
- C-clamps

MARKING UP THE TEMPLATE FOR THE BACK LEG

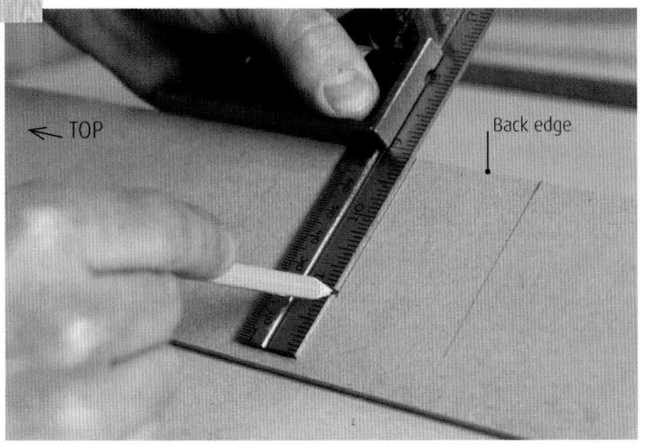

1 Make an MDF template of the back leg shape with side rail and back slat positions marked on it. Label the top and back edge of the template. Mark the location of the side rail junction 15 3/4in (400mm) and 17 11/16in (450mm) from the bottom, using a pencil and square.

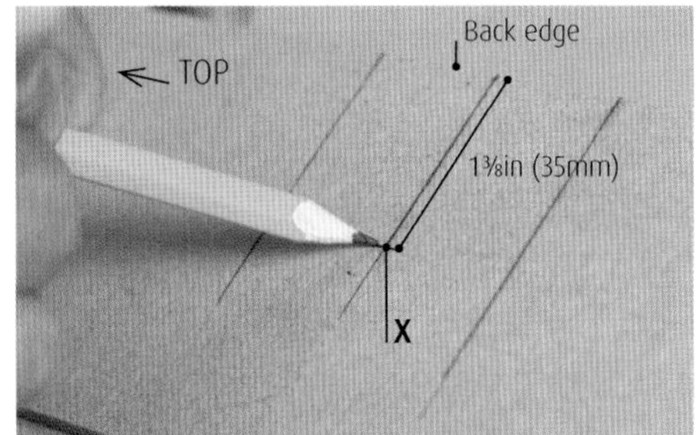

2 Mark the mid-point between the two rail width marks, then extend the line across. Mark point X on this mid-line 1 3/8in (35mm) from the back edge.

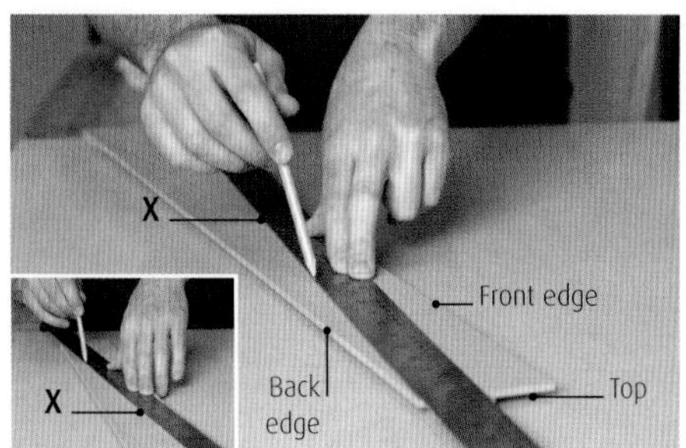

3 Draw a line between point X and a corner on the back edge. Draw a second line from X to the other corner on the back edge (inset).

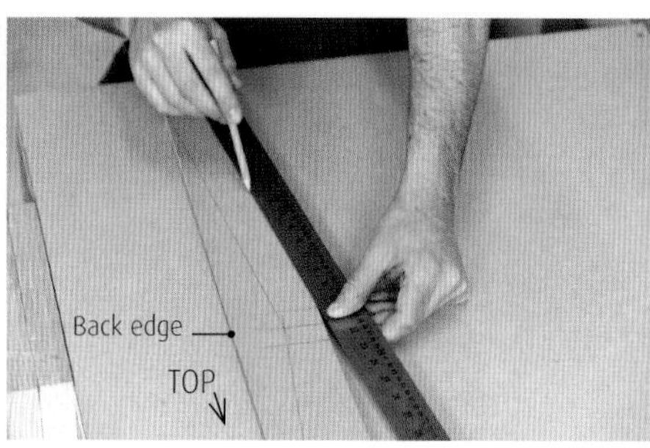

4 Mark a point on the top edge 1⅜in (35mm) from the back edge. Draw a line from here to where the upper rail mark meets the front edge. Mark a point on the bottom edge 1¹³⁄₁₆in (20mm) from the back edge. Draw to where the lower rail meets the front edge.

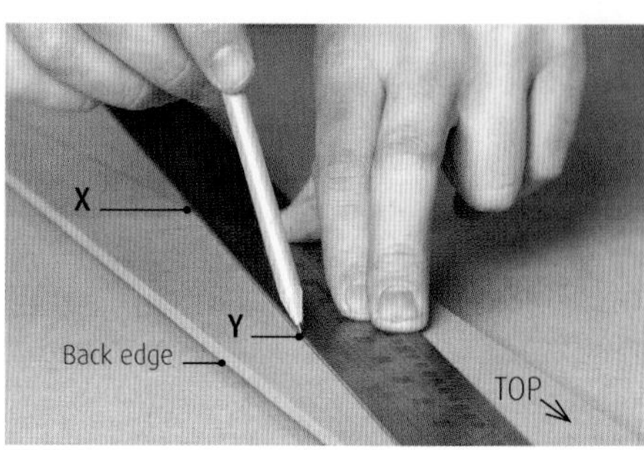

5 Mark a point (Y) 5⅞in (150mm) from point X along the line drawn in Step 3, then mark a second Y point equidistant from X along the line in the opposite direction.

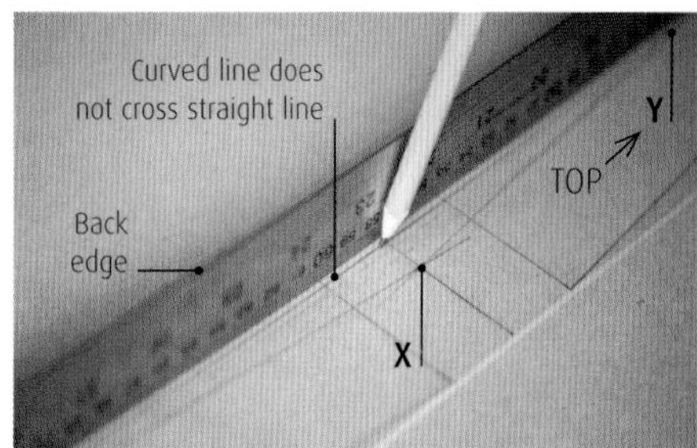

6 Bend the metal ruler between both points Y to create a curve that forms the curve of the back of the leg.

MARKING THE POSITIONS OF THE BACK SLATS

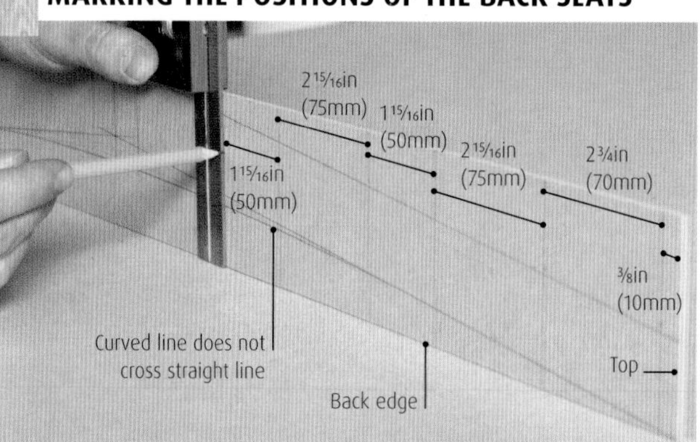

1 Mark the positions of the back slats as pictured, measured from the front edge of the template. Then square the lines across the face of the template.

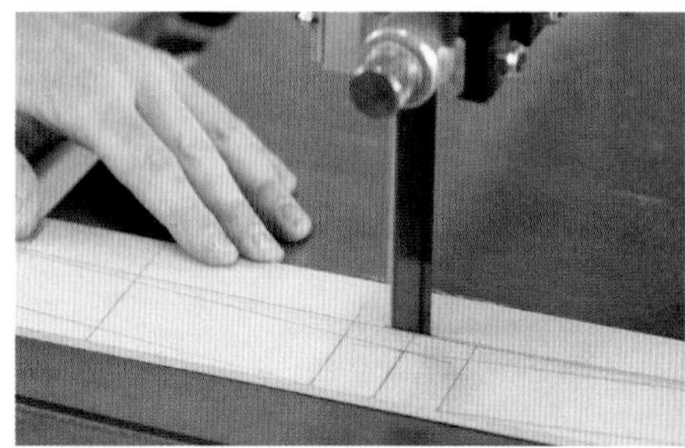

2 Cut out the template on a band saw, ensuring you cut to the waste side of the marked lines.

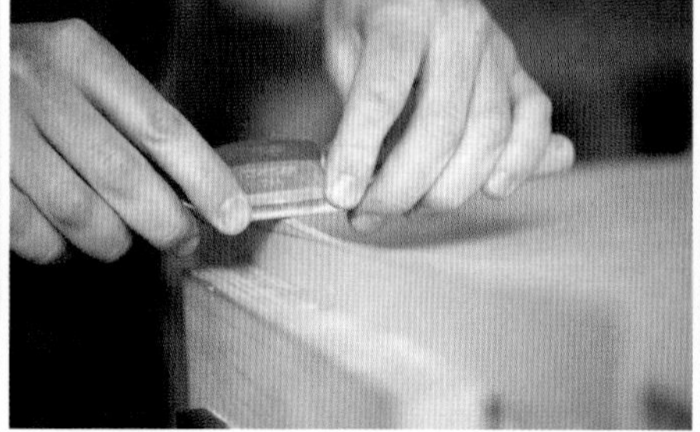

3 Use a spokeshave or sandpaper to trim to the marks on the back edge. Use a bench plane to trim the front edge.

4 Extend the marks for the back slats and rail onto the newly cut front edge of the template.

MAKING THE BACK-LEG PIECES

1 Set the template against the face of the first back-leg piece. Transfer the outline of the template and all marked positions of the slats and rails using a pencil.

2 Square the rail and slat marks across both faces and onto the front edge of the chair leg. Repeat Steps 1–2 for the second back-leg piece (inset).

3 Mark two lines ³⁄₁₆in (5mm) inward from the lines marking the rail position on the front edge of each leg piece.

4 **Use a mortise gauge** set to ½in (12mm) to mark the mortise for the side rail of the seat. Set the gauge to scribe ⅞in (23mm) from the inside face. Mark up the second back-leg piece in the same way. Cut each mortise to 1⅜in (35mm) deep with a mortiser (inset) or mortise chisels and mallet.

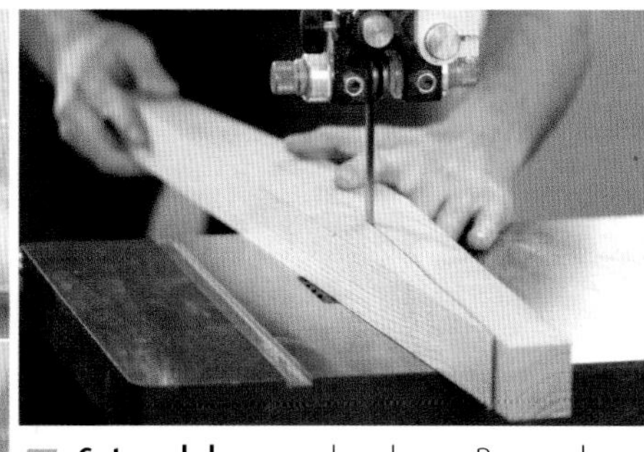

5 **Cut each leg** on a band saw. Remember to always cut to the waste side of the guide lines.

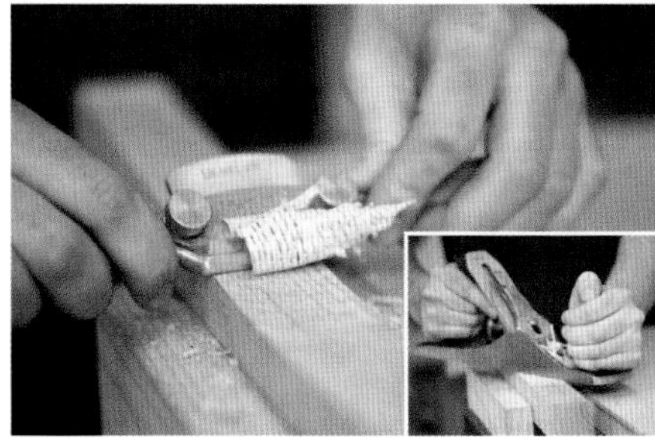

6 **Use a spokeshave** to trim to the marks and complete the shaping of the back edge of the leg. Use a bench plane to finish the shaping of the front edge (inset).

TAPERING THE BACK LEGS

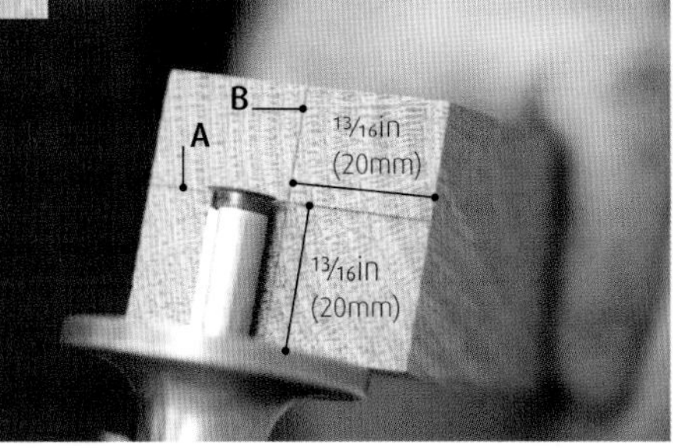

1 **Set the marking gauge** to 20mm (13/16in) and scribe two lines across the end grain of the bottom of the leg, first from the back edge (A) then from the outside edge (B).

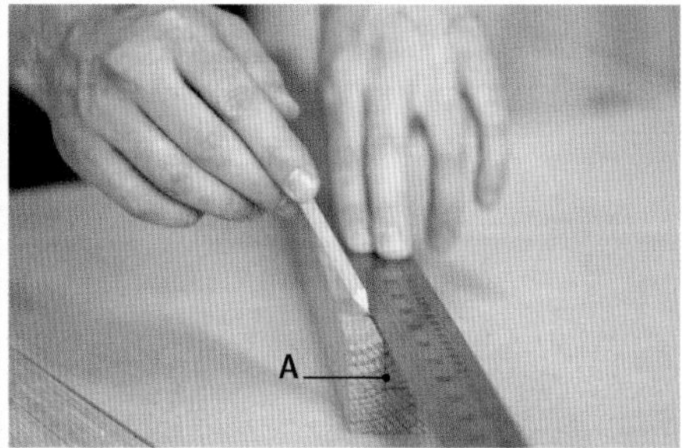

2 **Mark the taper** of the front of the leg by drawing a line between the end of line A to the position mark for the rail. Draw a second line on the other edge of the leg from the rail mark to the other end of line A.

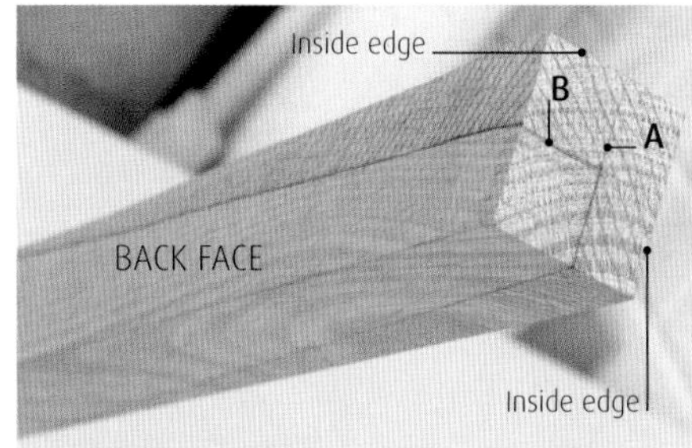

3 **Mark the taper** from the end of line B along the back face of the leg to the rail mark, then mark the waste for removal.

4 **Use a band saw** to cut the front taper, cutting to the waste side of the marked lines. Then cut the taper on the inside edge.

5 **Finish the shaping** by planing and spokeshaving to the marks. Repeat Steps 1–5 for the other back leg.

MAKING THE BACK SLATS AND BACK RAIL

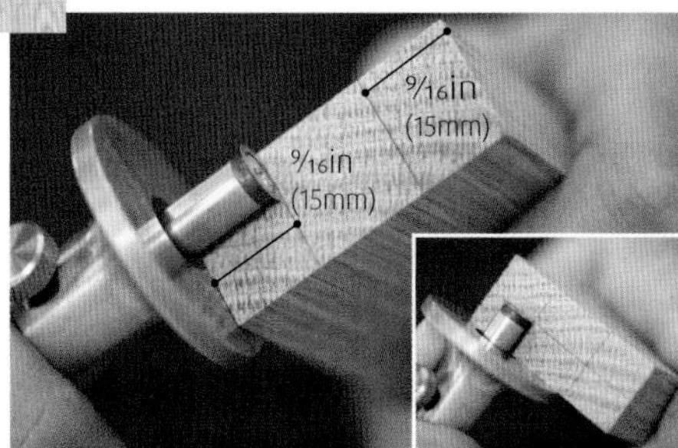

1 **Using a marking gauge**, scribe 9/16in (15mm) from each edge on both end grains of the back slats and the back rail. Scribe along the center of both end grains from the rail face and each of the slats.

2 **Drill a hole** centered on each of the intersections of these lines on both end grains of all four pieces. Use an 5/16in (8mm) bit and drill to a depth of 9/16in (15mm).

3 **Use a hammer** to insert a 1⅛in (28mm) length of 5/16in (8mm) doweling into each drilled hole.

SHAPING THE SLATS

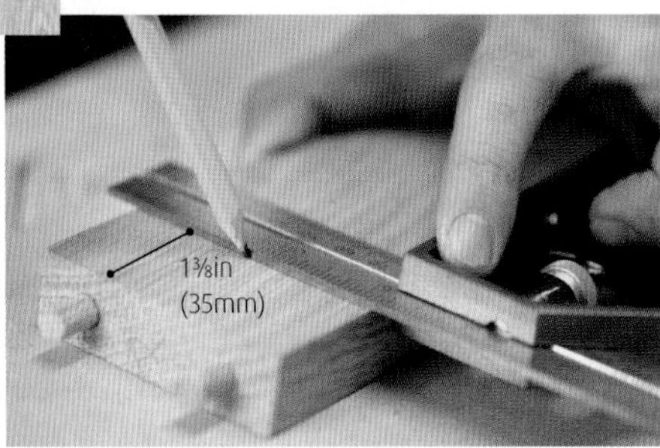

1 **Mark the start** of the curved shaping by squaring a line 1⅜in (35mm) from each end grain on the front face of all of the slats.

2 **Mark the maximum depth** of the scoop— 3⁄16in (5mm)—at the center of each slat.

3 **Shape the back slats** between the marks using a spokeshave, then smooth with sandpaper to finish.

MAKING THE DOWEL HOLES ON THE BACK LEGS

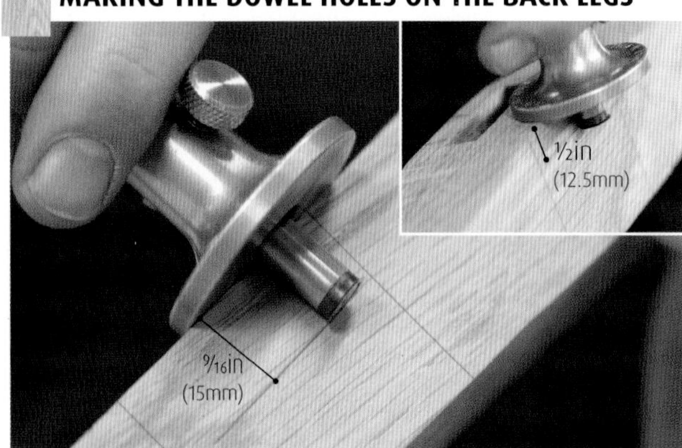

1 **Use a marking gauge** set to 9⁄16in (15mm) to scribe from the front face between each of the slat positions to indicate the position of the dowel holes. Then set the marking gauge to ½in (12.5mm) to mark the position of the dowels within the position marks of the rail on both legs (inset).

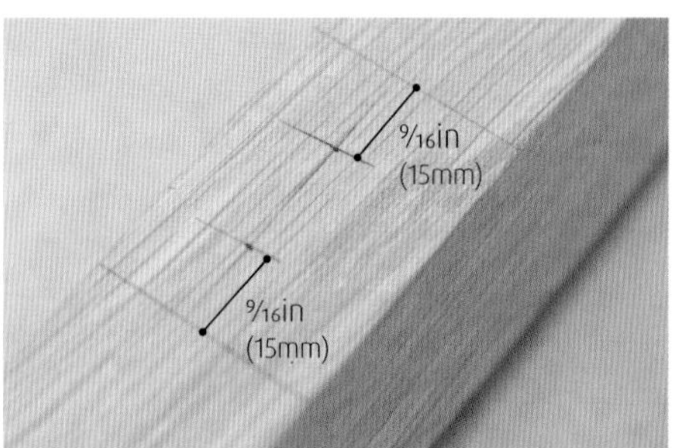

2 **Measure and mark** a point on the scribed lines 9⁄16in (15mm) inside the pencil lines marking the slats and rail.

3 **Drill an 5⁄16in (8mm) hole** to a depth of 9⁄16in (15mm) into each of the marked points. Drill a shallow countersink into each hole to ease the fit of the dowels (inset).

4 **Test the fit** of the slats (inset) and rail with the leg pieces, using a rubber mallet.

MAKING THE FRONT LEGS

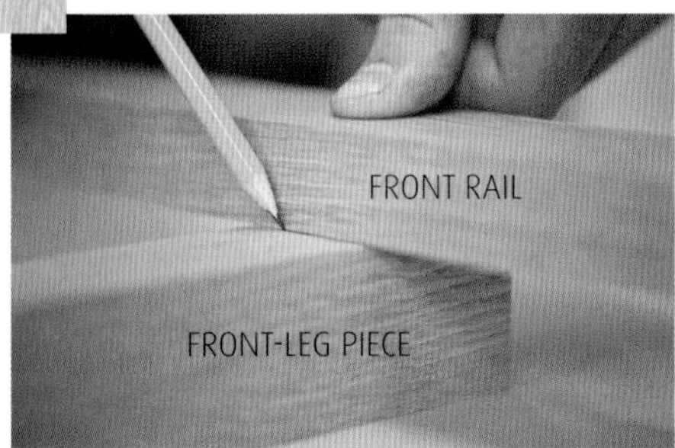

1 **Mark the position** of the two mortises at the top of each front leg. Align the long edge of the front rail with the end grain of the leg, then mark the width of the rail on the inside face of each leg.

2 **Square the mark** across the inside face and onto the edge of each leg (inset). Mark the extent of the mortises with two lines 3⁄16in (5mm) inside the rail-width line and from the end grain.

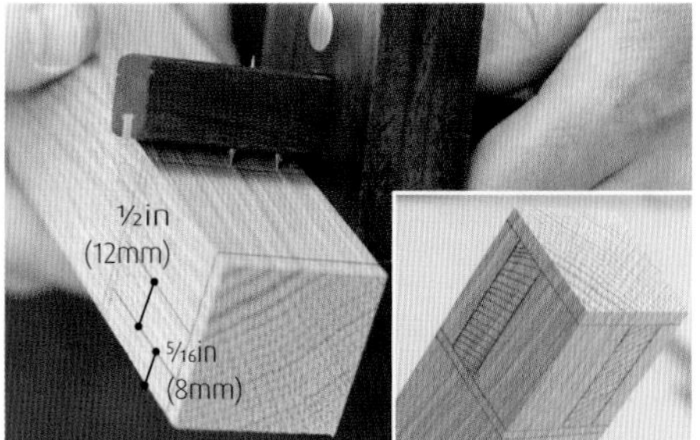

3 **Set the mortise gauge** to a width of ½in (12mm) with an 5⁄16in (8mm) fence, and scribe within the marked length of the mortise from the outside edge and outside face of each leg. Mark the waste (inset).

4 Cut all four mortises to a depth of 1 1/4in (32mm), using a mortiser (pictured) or by hand using a mallet and mortise chisel.

MAKING THE TAPER ON THE FRONT LEGS

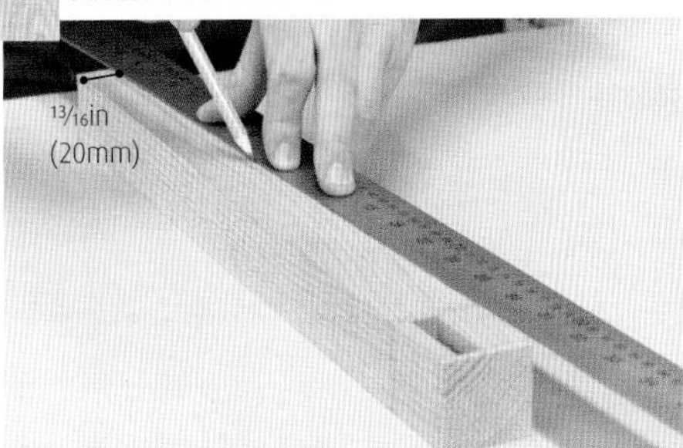

1 Scribe a mark 13/16in (20mm) along the bottom end grain from an outside edge of one leg. Join this mark to the line marking the rail width on the inside corner.

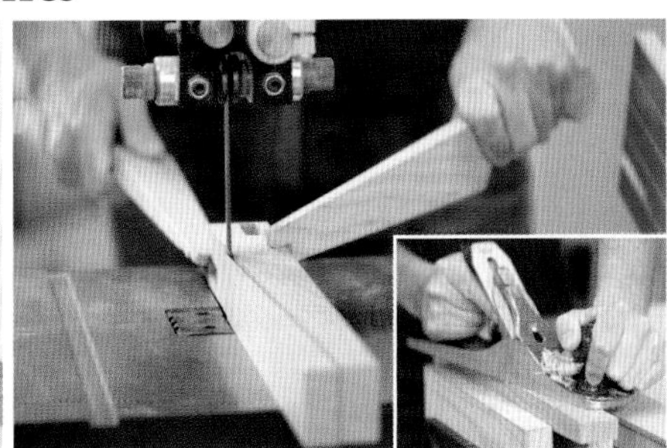

2 Use a band saw to cut along this line from the end grain. Use a bench plane to smooth the sawn edge (inset).

3 Use a marking gauge set to 13/16in (20mm) to scribe a line from the outside edge across the end grain.

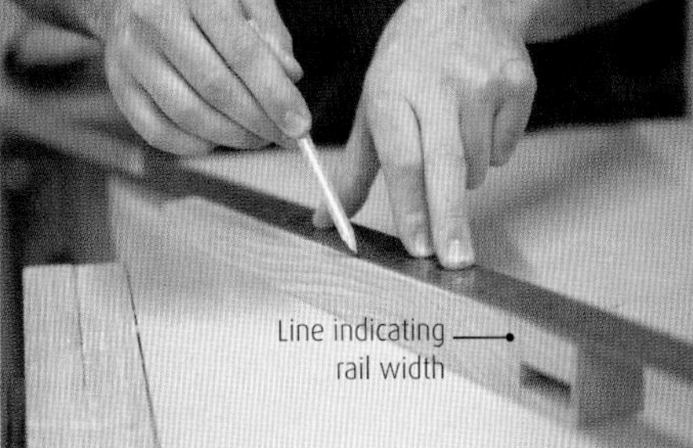

4 Draw a line from the end of this line to the inside corner at the line indicating the rail width.

5 Cut along the marked lines using a band saw, then plane the tapers to finish (inset). Repeat Steps 1–5 for other leg.

MAKING THE FRONT RAIL AND ASSEMBLING THE FRONT FRAME

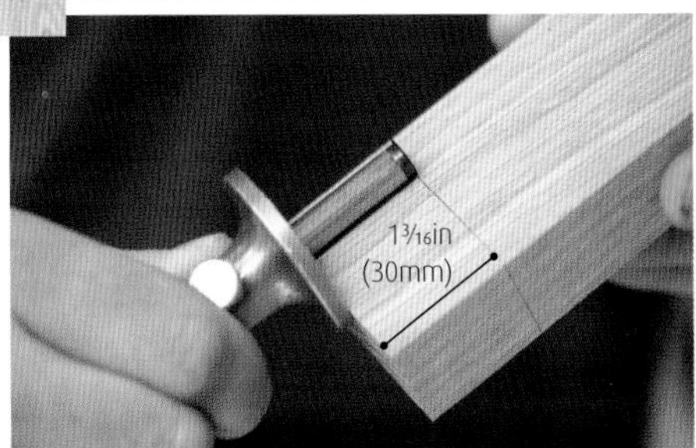

1 Mark the tenon shoulders by scribing around the face and both edges of both ends of the front rail with a marking gauge set to 1 3/16in (30mm).

2 Set the mortise gauge to a width of 1/2in (12mm) with a 5/16in (8mm) fence, then scribe the thickness of both tenons on the end grain and both edges of the front rail.

3 Reset the marking gauge to 3/16in (5mm) and mark the tenon width by scribing across the end grain from each edge and down both faces (inset) on each end of the rail. Cut the tenons on a band saw.

4 Use a combination square to mark a miter on the end of each tenon, angled toward the inside edge. Extend the mark down the inside cheek of the tenon and mark the waste (inset).

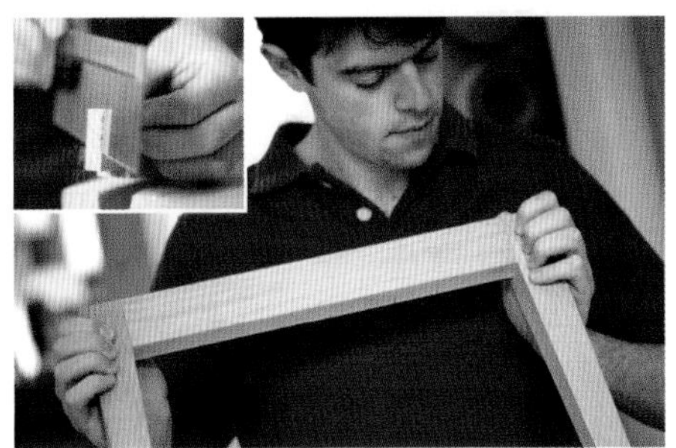

5 Cut the miters using a tenon saw (inset). Then test the fit of the front rail and front legs.

MAKING THE ANGLED TENONS IN THE SIDE RAILS

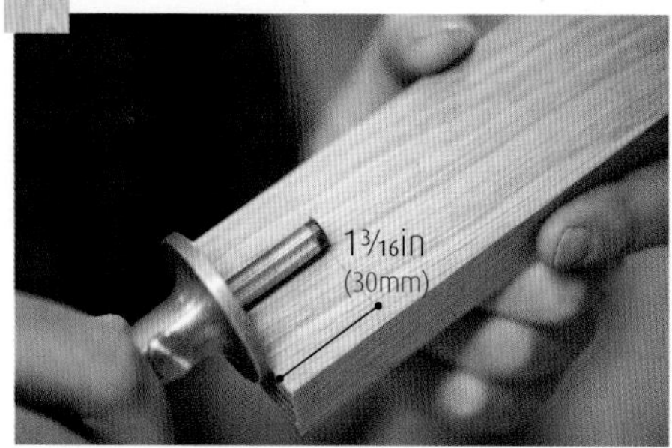

1 **Mark the tenon shoulder** on the inside face of one end of each side rail, using a marking gauge set to 1³⁄₁₆in (30mm).

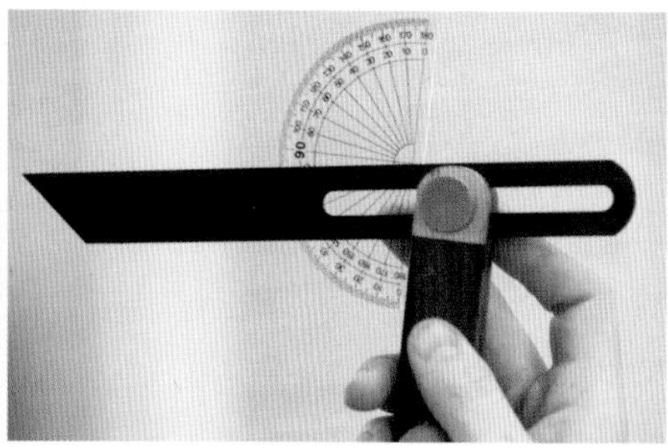

2 **Using a protractor** as a guide, set the sliding bevel—which will be used to mark the angled tenons—to 86 degrees.

3 **Set the sliding bevel** against the inside face and use a marking knife to scribe a line from the shoulder down both edges. Square the line across the outside face.

4 **Set the fence** of the mortise gauge to ⅜in (10mm) and scribe a tenon thickness of ½in (12mm) from the inside face of the rail across the end grain.

5 **With the sliding bevel** positioned against the end grain, extend the marks to the shoulder on both edges.

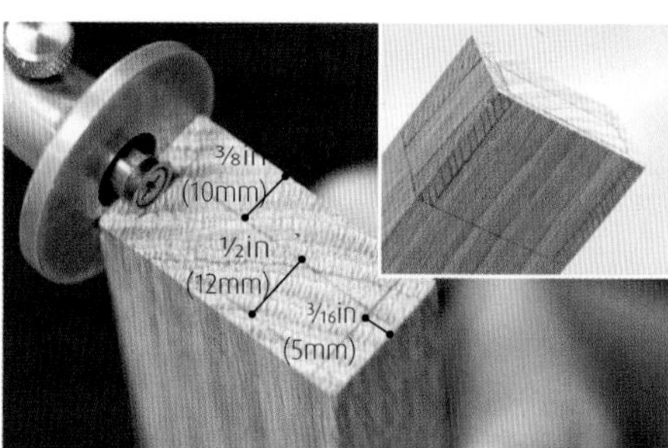

6 **Mark the tenon width** by scribing from each edge with a marking gauge set to ³⁄₁₆in (5mm). Mark the waste (inset).

7 **Cut the tenon cheeks** and ends of the tenons with a tenon saw. Reinforce the shoulder lines with a marking knife then cut a V-groove on the waste side of the shoulder lines with a bevel-edged chisel (inset).

8 **Cut through the shoulders** with a tenon saw. Repeat Steps 1–8 to mark and cut a tenon in the second side rail.

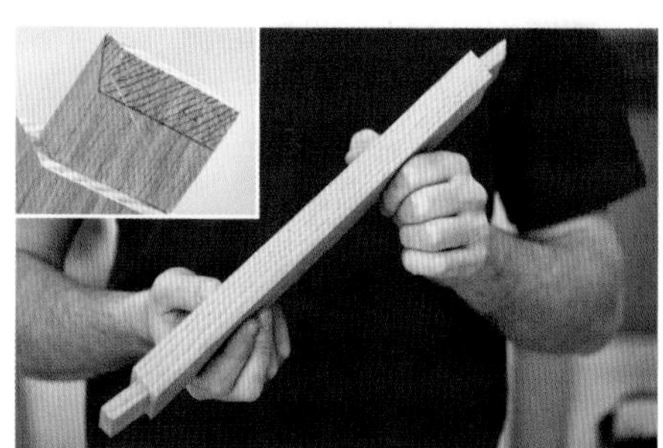

9 **Cut an angled tenon** to the same specifications in the other end of the side rails, but with the tenon angled toward the inside. Cut a miter angled toward the inside in the end of each of these tenons (inset).

CUTTING THE REBATES FOR THE SEAT

1 **Use a rebate plane** to cut a rebate ⅜in (10mm) wide along the top inside edge of each side rail, to a depth of ⅛in (3mm).

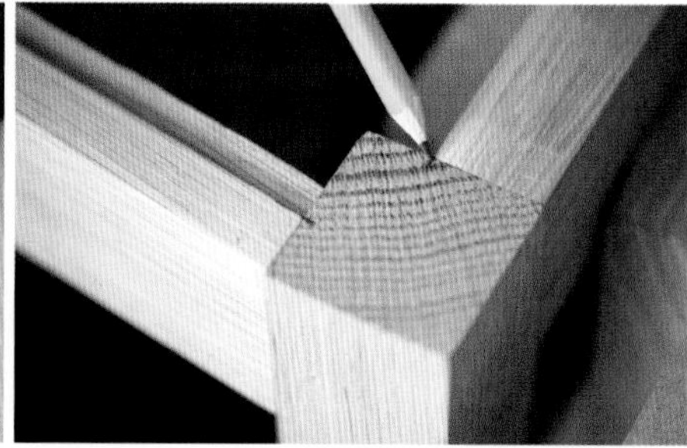

2 **Set each side rail** in position against the front-leg frame. Mark the position of both the edge of the rebate and the inside edge of the front rail onto the end grain of the leg.

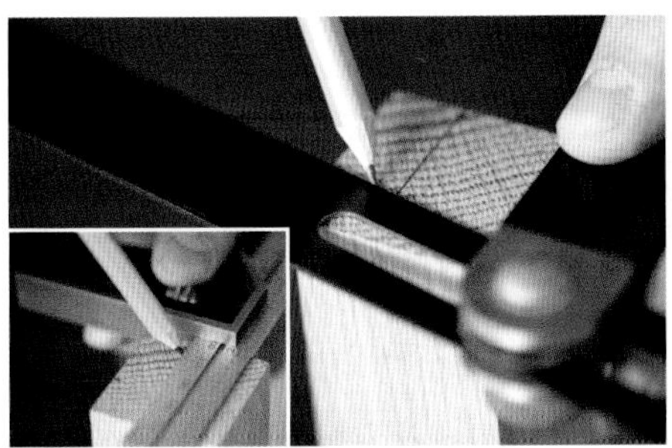

3 **Using a square**, extend the mark from the front-rail edge across the end grain (inset). With the bevel as previously set, take this line back toward the side-rail edge.

4 **Using a marking gauge** set to ⅛in (3mm), scribe the depth of the rebate from the end grain onto both inside edges. Mark the waste for removal (inset).

5 **Chop the waste** from the rebate using a chisel, being careful not to cut through the marks.

TEST-ASSEMBLING AND GLUING THE CHAIR FRAME

1 **Test the fit** of all component parts by joining the front and back frames with the side rails.

2 **Protect the wood** around the joints to be glued with masking tape, which will be removed when the glue is partly dry.

3 **When happy with the fit**, glue all the joints and dowels using a brush (inset). Clamp with sash clamps and leave to dry.

4 **Glue the side rails** in position to join the front and back frames. Clamp with blocks to spread the tension evenly, then check for squareness with a tape measure (inset).

MAKING THE SEAT

1 **Place the sliding bevel** as previously set to 86 degrees against the front edge of the first (front) slat, approximately ⅜in (10mm) from—and angled away from—the end grain. Scribe the line across the face.

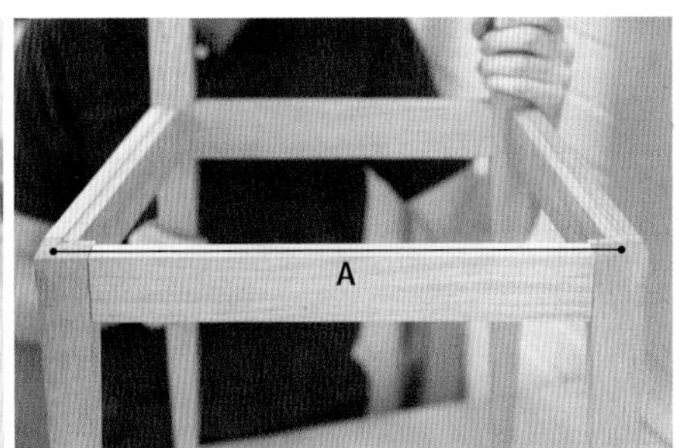

2 **Measure the distance** between the ends of the rebates in the top of each front leg (A).

3 **Angle the sliding bevel** in the opposite direction and place it measurement (A) (above) away from the mark made in Step 1. Scribe the angle across the face of the slat.

4 **Transfer the marks** from the back edge of the first slat onto the front edge of the second slat, then extend the line across the face using the sliding bevel at the appropriate angle. Square the marks onto the edges (inset). Continue the process until you have marked the length of all four slats.

5 **Cut the ends of each slat** in turn. Secure the slat to the work bench with clamps and use a tenon saw to cross-cut along the marked lines.

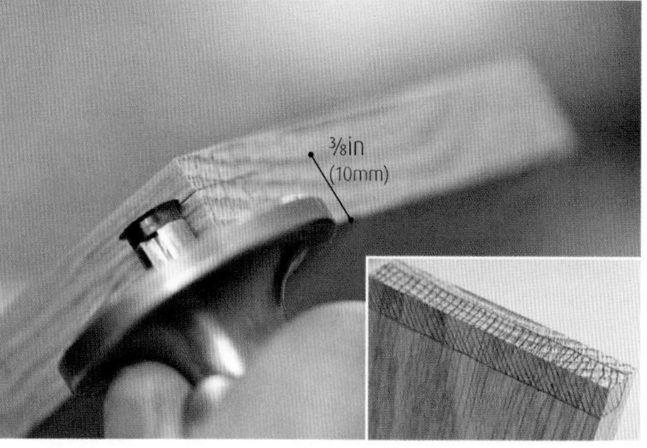

6 **Mark a rebate** along the angled end grains of each slat with a marking gauge set to ⅜in (10mm). Scribe the measurement from the underneath face along the end grain, and from the end grain along the underneath face. Extend both marks onto both edges. Mark the waste for removal (inset).

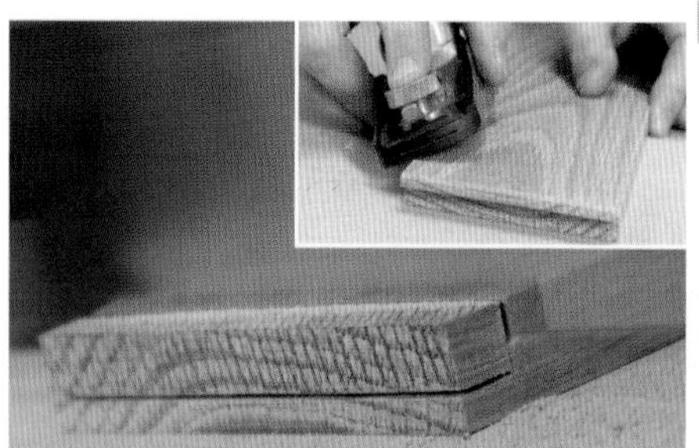

7 **Cut the rebates** with a tenon saw, then clean up the sides and edges by paring with a chisel. Chamfer the top edges of the slats with a block plane (inset).

FINISHING THE FRONT SLAT AND JOINING THE FRONT AND BACK FRAME

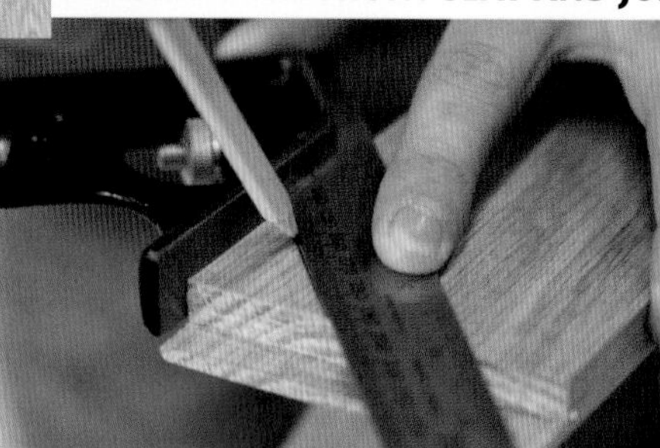

1 **Mark the front slat** 1¾in (45mm) along the underside of the front edge (including the rebate). Set a combination square to 45 degrees and draw a line to the adjacent edge.

2 **Square the marks** across the edges, then scribe the front edge to the mark with a marking gauge set to the depth of the rebate (inset). Repeat on the other front corner.

3 **Use a tenon saw** to cut through the corner to the corner marks. Cut along the marks on the face to release the waste (inset).

MAKING THE MORTISES IN THE ARM RESTS

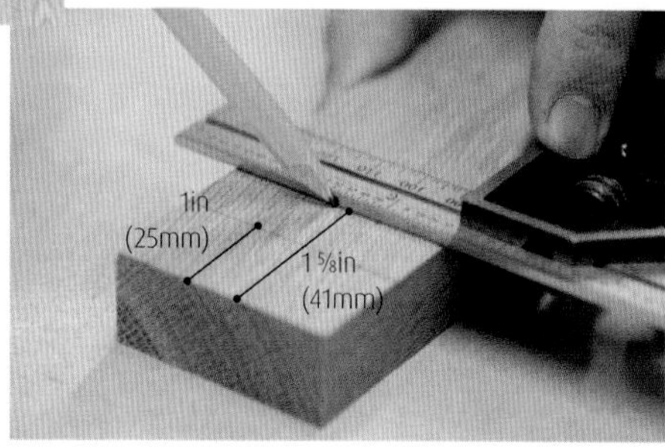

1 **Mark two points** 1⅝in (41mm) and 1in (25mm) from the end grain, then square the measurements across the face.

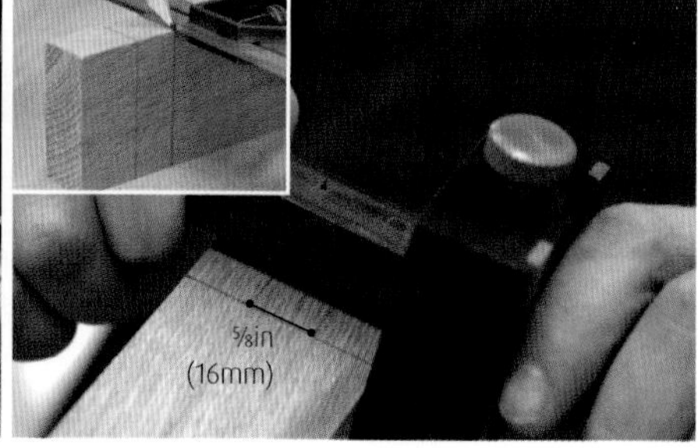

2 **Square the marks** around the edge and onto the other face (inset). Scribe a mortise ⅝in (16mm) in width centrally on both faces.

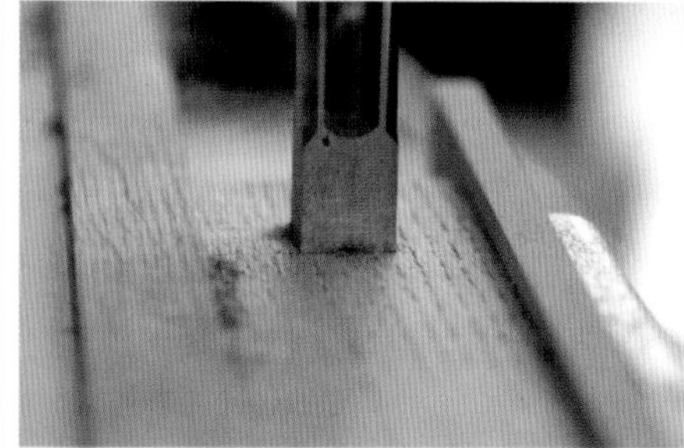

3 **Use a mortiser** fitted with a ⅝in (16mm) bit, or a mortise chisel, to cut the mortise in each arm rest. Cut halfway through the thickness from each direction.

TAPERING THE ARM RESTS

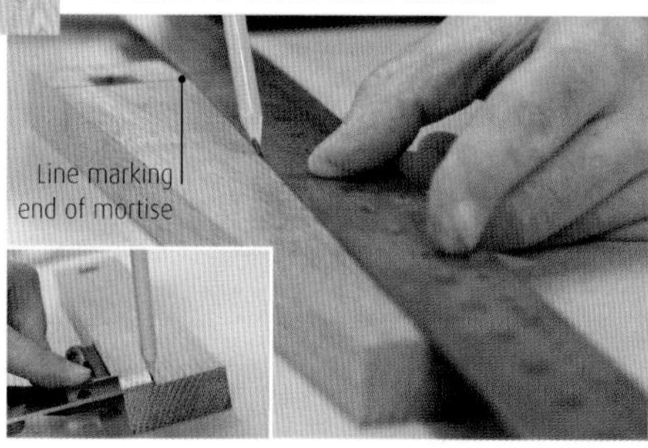

1 **Mark a point** $^{9}/_{16}$in (15mm) from the edge of the opposite end grain (inset). Draw a diagonal line from this mark to the line marking the end of the mortise.

2 **Cut the taper** on a band saw, keeping to the waste side, then plane the edges flat with a bench plane. Repeat Steps 1–2 for the second arm rest.

SHAPING THE ARM RESTS

1 **Draw a curve** with a pencil on the face of the mortised end of each arm rest (inset). Cut the shape on a band saw and smooth the edges and end grain by sanding.

2 **Use a spokeshave** to chamfer the edges on the underside of each arm rest. Stop the chamfer on the inside edge 2⅜in (60mm) from the end grain. Note that the taper is on a different side of the underneath face for each piece (inset).

MAKING THE ARM-REST UPRIGHTS

1 **Use a marking gauge** to scribe 13/16in (20mm) from the end grain around all four sides of the upright to mark the shoulder of the tenon.

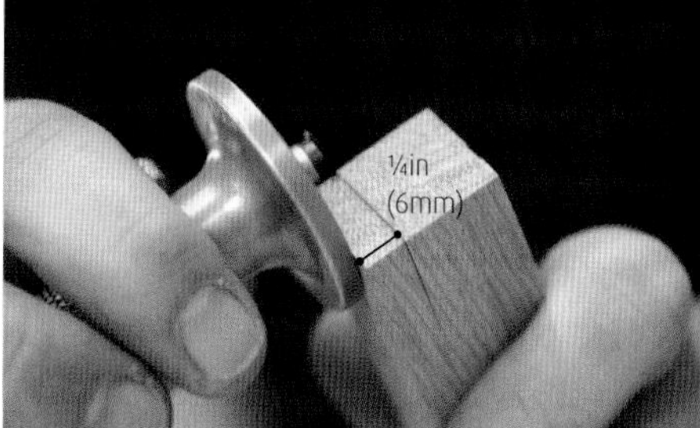

2 **Reset the gauge** to ¼in (6mm) and scribe across the end grain and both faces to the shoulder from the inside edge.

3 **Reset the marking gauge** to ⅛in (3mm) and scribe across the end grain and down to the shoulder from the other three edges.

4 **Cut the tenon** using a band saw, or by hand using a tenon saw, and then repeat Steps 1–4 for the other upright.

5 **Test the fit** of the tenons in the arm-rest mortises, and adjust as necessary with a bevel-edged chisel.

6 **Mark the length** of a notch 1 9/16in (40mm) from the end grain, then square the measurement around both faces and the inside edge.

7 **Use the marking gauge** set to 9/16in (15mm) to mark the depth of the notch. Scribe from the inside edge across the adjacent face.

8 **Cut the notch** on a band saw. Mark a chamfer on the outside edge of the end grain of the notched end, then plane the corner to the mark with a block plane (inset). Mark out and cut a notch in the other upright in the same way.

ASSEMBLING AND FITTING THE ARMS

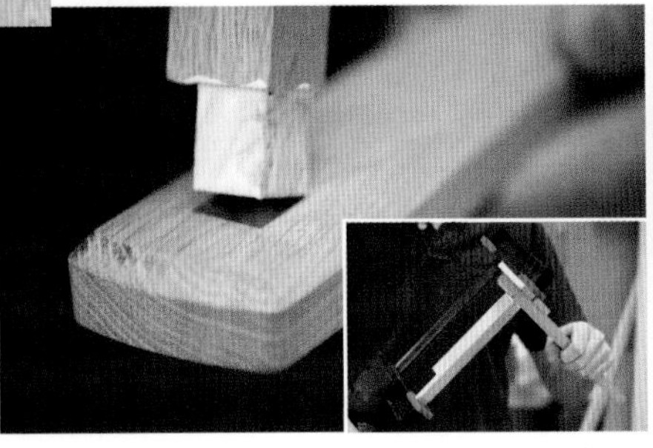

1 **Glue the tenons** of the uprights into the mortises in the arm rests. Clamp with a sash clamp and allow to dry (inset).

2 **Once the glue has dried**, use a flush-cut saw to cut the excess length from the tenons. Plane to a smooth finish with a block plane (inset).

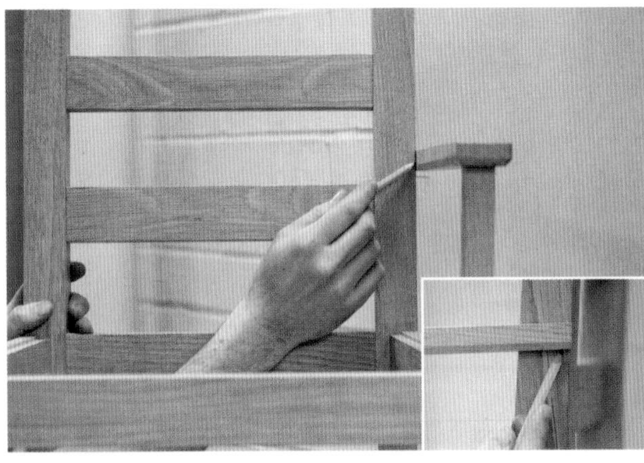

3 **Position the arm assembly** against the chair with the end of the arm rest flush to the chair back and the notch square against the seat. Mark the position of the chair back on the inside of the arm rest, and either side of the arm rest on the outside edge of the chair back (inset).

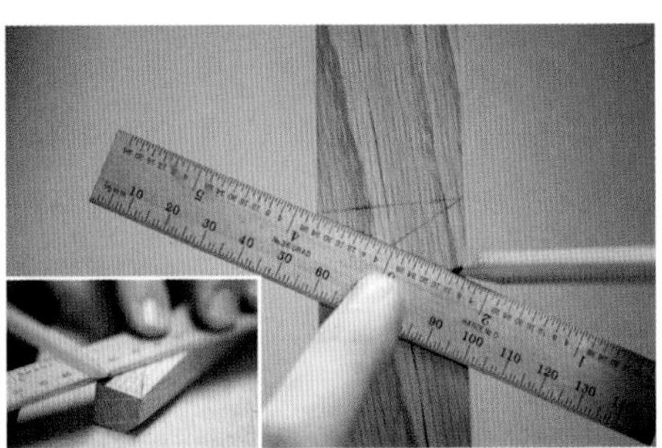

4 **Find the center point** of the arm rest on the edge of the chair back by drawing diagonals. Repeat for the center point of the chair back on the arm rest (inset).

5 **Drill a hole** 5⁄16in (8mm) wide and 13⁄16in (20mm) deep into the marked position in the chair back. Repeat on the marked position in the arm rest (inset), but drill to a depth of 3⁄8in (10mm).

6 **Cut a dowel** 13⁄16in (30mm) long and insert it into the holes to join the arm rest to the chair back.

7 **Mark the width** of the arm-rest upright on the inside of the seat frame. Mark the position of a screw hole 13⁄16in (20mm) down from the base of the seat rebate and centered between the width lines (inset).

8 **Drill a pilot hole** to a depth of 13⁄16in (30mm) from the inside of the seat frame into the upright, then countersink (inset).

9 **Attach the upright** to the seat frame with a No. 8 x 1in (4 x 25mm) brass screw. Repeat Steps 2–9 for the other arm rest.

ASSEMBLING THE FRAME AND SEAT

1 **Place the slats** in position within the frame to test the fit, and trim with a chisel or plane as necessary.

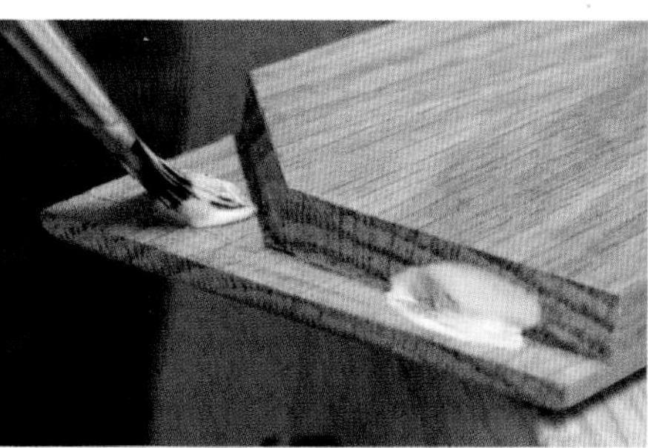

2 **Apply two small dabs of glue** on the ends of the slats, then place in position inside the chair frame.

3 **Once the slats are in position**, secure with C-clamps and leave the assembly to dry.

ALTERNATIVES

The arms are not integral to the main construction of the chair, so can be omitted if preferred. If making a set of dining chairs, it is traditional for the carver (at the head of the table) to have arm rests, but for the remaining chairs to be without. Other variations could include changing the number of back slats.

DETAIL OF ARM UPRIGHT AND RAIL

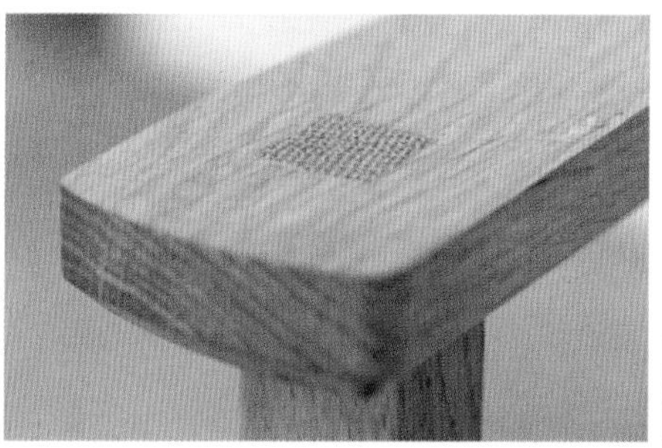

DETAIL OF ARM REST

THE FINISHED PIECE

APPE

NDIX

USA

TOOLS AND EQUIPMENT

Amana Tool
120 Carolyn Boulevard
Farmingdale, NY 11735
Tel: 800-445-0077
Email: tools@amanatool.com
www.amanatool.com
(Manufacturer of tools, router bits, and saw blades)

Bessey Tools
United States Office
PO Box 160, 1 Wright Avenue
Leroy, NY 14482
Tel: 800-828-1004
Email: info@besseytools.com
www.besseytools.com
(Manufacturer of tools and clamps)

Bosch
121 Corporate Boulevard
South Plainfield, NJ 07080
Tel: 877-267-2499, or
800-346-4103
www.boschtools.com
(Manufacturer of power tools)

Bostitch
Stanley Fastening Systems
Briggs Drive
East Greenwich, RI 02818
Tel: 800-556-6696
www.bostitch.com
(Manufacturer of air-powered tools)

Colonial Saw
122 Pembroke Street
Kingston, MA 02364
Tel: 781-585-4364
Email: info@csaw.com
www.csaw.com
(Supplier and servicer of tools and equipment, including Lamello biscuit joiners)

CMT USA Incorporated
Suite D
7609 Bentley Road
Greensboro, NC 27409
Tel: 888-268-2487
Email: info@cmtusa.com
www.cmtutensili.com
(Manufacturer of router bits and saw blades)

Delta Porter-Cable
4825 Highway 45 North
Jackson, TN 38305
Tel: 800-223-7278
www.deltaportercable.com
(Manufacturer of power tools)

DeWalt Industrial Tools
TW425, 701 East Joppa Road
Baltimore, MD 21286
Tel: 80-433-9258
www.dewalt.com
(Manufacturer of power tools)

E. C. Emmerich
7317 Chesterfield Road
Crystal Lake, IN 60012
Tel: 800-724-7758
Email: info@ecemmerich.com
(Manufacturer of cabinetmaker's tools)

FEIN Power Tools
1030 Alcon Street
Pittsburgh, PA 15220
Tel: 800-441-9878
Email: info@feinus.com
www.fein.de/corp/us/en/custom/index.html
(Manufacturer of power tools, including the Multimaster)

Festool USA
400 North Enterprise Boulevard
Lebanon, IN 46052
Tel: 888-337-8600
www.festoolusa.com
(Manufacturer of tools, including the Domino jointing system)

Freud
218 Feld Avenue
High Point, NC 27263
Tel: 800-334-4107
www.freudtools.com
(Manufacturer of cutting tools and saw blades)

Kreg Tool Company
201 Campus Drive
Huxley, IA 50124
Tel: 800-447-8638
www.kregtool.com
(Manufacturer of tools, including the Pocket Hole range)

Lee Valley Tools
PO Box 1780
Ogdensburg, NY 13669-6780
Tel: 800-871-8158
Email: customerservice@leevalley.com
www.leevalley.com
(Manufacturer and supplier of tools and steam bending equipment)

Lie Nielsen Toolworks
264 Stirling Road
Warren, ME 04864
Tel: 800-327-2520
Email: toolworks@lie-nielsen.com
www.lie-nielsen.com
(Manufacturer and supplier of hand tools)

Makita
14930 Northam Street
La Mirada, CA 90638
Tel: 800-462-5482
www.makita.com
(Manufacturer of power tools)

Milwaukee
13135 West Lisbon Road
Brookfield, WI 53005
Tel: 800-729-3878
www.milwaukeetool.com
(Manufacturer of power tools)

Senco
4270 Ivy Pointe Boulevard
Cincinnati, OH 45245
Tel: 800-543-4596
Email: actionline@senco.com
www.senco.com
(Manufacturer of air-powered tools)

Stabila
332 Industrial Drive
PO Box 402
South Elgin, IL 60177
Tel: 800-869-7460
www.stabila.com
(Manufacturer of levels)

Stanley Tools
480 Myrtle Street
New Britain
CT 06053
Tel: 800-262-2161
www.stanleytools.com
(Manufacturer of hand tools)

L. S. Starrett Company
121 Crescent Street
Athol, MA 0133
Tel: 978-249-3551
www.starrett.com
(Manufacturer of precision tools)

Woodworker's Supply
1125 Jay Lane
Graham, NC 27253
Tel: 800-321-9841
pro.woodworker.com
(Manufacturer of tools)

TIMBERS, VENEERS, AND FINISHING

Gilmer Wood Company
2211 NW St. Helens Road
Portland, OR 97210
Tel: 888-667-3979
www.gilmerwood.com
(Supplier of exotic and domestic woods)

Eisenbran Exotic Hardwoods
4100 Spencer Street
Torrance, CA 90503
Tel: 800-258-2587
Email: wood@eisenbran.com
www.eisenbran.com
(Supplier of exotic and domestic woods)

ASSOCIATIONS, COURSES, AND FURTHER INFORMATION

Architectural Woodwork Institute (AWI)
Suite 120
46179 Westlake Drive
Potomac Falls, VA 20165
Tel: 703-733-0600
www.awinet.org
(Trade association for architectural woodworkers, suppliers, design professionals, and students)

Forest Stewardship Council - US (FSC-US)
Suite 280
212 Third Avenue North
Minneapolis, MN 55401
Tel: 612-353-4511
Email: info@fscus.org
www.fscus.org
(Promotes responsible forest management worldwide)

The Windsor Institute
44 Timber Swamp Road
Hampton, NH 03842
Tel: 603-929-9801
Email: info@thewindsorinstitute.com
www.thewindsorinstitute.com
(Windsor-chair making lessons, tools, steam bending equipment, kits and materials)

Woodfinder
Tel: 877-933-4637
Email: info@woodfinder.com
www.woodfinder.com
(General woodworker's resource)

Wood Web Incorporated
RR4 Box 265A
Montrose, PA 18801
Tel: 570-278-5315
www.woodweb.com
(Woodworking industry information)

CANADA

TOOLS AND EQUIPMENT

All-In-One Wood Tools
Unit 11, 2900 Argentia Drive
Mississauga
ON L5N 7X9
Tel: 800-370-3834
Email: info@allinonewood.com
www.allinonewood.com
(Supplier of tools and equipment)

Busy Bee Tools
130 Great Gulf Drive
Concord, ON L4K 5W1
Tel: 800-461-2879
www.busybeetools.ca
(Supplier of tools and equipment)

King Canada
700 Rue Meloche
Dorval
QC H9P 2Y4
Tel: 514-636-5464
Email: info@kingcanada.com
www.kingcanada.com
(Supplier of tools and equipment)

Lee Valley Tools
PO Box 6295, Station J
Ottawa, ON K2A 1T4
Tel: 800-267-8761
Email: customerservice@leevalley.com
www.leevalley.com
(Manufacturer and supplier of tools and steam bending equipment)

MLS Machinery
Unit 4
300 Granton Drive
Richmond Hill, ON L4B 1H7
Tel: 905-731-6369
Email: sales@mlsmachinery.com
www.mlsmachinery.com
(Supplier of new and used machinery and equipment)

TIMBERS, VENEERS, AND FINISHING

A&M Wood Specialty
357 Eagle Street North
PO Box 32040
Cambridge, ON N3H 5M2
Tel: 800-265-0624
Email: mail@amwoodinc.com
www.amwoodinc.com
(Supplier of fine hardwoods and veneers)

Black Forest Wood Company
Bay 7
603-77th Avenue S.E.
Calgary, AB T2H 2B9
Tel: 877-686-6061
Email: info@blackforestwood.com
www.blackforestwood.com
(Supplier of exotic and domestic woods)

Exotic Woods
5229 Harvester Road
Burlington, ON L7L 5L4
Tel: 905-335-8066
Email: info@exotic-woods.com
www.exotic-woods.com
(Supplier of exotic and domestic woods)

Glossary

Most of the words and terms used in this book are commonplace but sometimes technical terms are used. This glossary of those terms is a useful reference, especially for those new to woodworking.

Adhesive A liquid or semi-liquid substance, such as glue or cement, which is applied to bind two or more materials together.

Aperture The gap or opening between two parts of the same structure: for example, the distance between two table legs.

Arris The sharp edge between angled surfaces (a rectangular section piece of wood has 12 arrises). It is usually rounded or beveled before finishing.

Arts and craft movement Late 19th-/ early 20th-century artistic movement, which aimed to move architecture away from the utilitarian influence of the Industrial Revolution and encourage more personal artistic expression.

Assemble Put together, in the correct formation, the various parts required to construct a particular object or section.

Auger bit A spiral-shaped drill bit that removes any wood shavings or debris that accumulate in a hole during the drilling process.

Ball catch A door fastener usually found on cabinets or wardrobes. When the door is closed, a ball presses into the claw of the catch, which is fixed to the doorframe. The claw holds the ball in place until a tug on the door handle releases it.

Bandsaw A machine that cuts via a vertical metal blade with teeth down one edge that pass through a table. Shaped like a band, the blade moves in a continuous loop. A band saw is able to cut curves.

Base The lowest supporting layer that forms the foundation of any structure.

Batten A slim strip of wood that is used to strengthen panels.

Beading A length of wood with a decorative profile (having a complex-shaped cross-section).

Bearing-guided cutter A router cutter with a bearing mounted on the shaft. The bearing rotates freely around the shaft and traces the edge of the workpiece or template, guiding the cutter without the aid of a fence or other jig. It is also called a template profile cutter.

Bench *See* Workbench.

Bench hook A wooden board with two smaller blocks of wood attached horizontally, at opposite ends and on opposite sides. Latched over a workbench, it acts as a stable barrier against which another piece of wood can be held firmly in place.

Bench plane A hand-held tool that shaves off strips of wood to smooth, flatten, or shape the surface of a workpiece.

Bevel-edged chisel The most common type of chisel. Its edges fall away at an angle on both sides while the blade itself tapers down, allowing for easy use in tight corners and joints.

Biscuit joint A joint in which circular slots are cut into two pieces of wood and a thin disc-shaped piece of wood (the biscuit) is fitted into the slots. The depth of the slots depends on the type of biscuit, which come in three standard sizes.

Biscuit jointer A machine that cuts the correct depth of circular slot into which a biscuit is fitted (*see* Biscuit joint).

Blind In the context of joints, blind is a type of joint that is less visible than alternative types.

Block plane A small, hand-held woodworking plane that is used to cut end grain.

Bore To drill a hole in a piece of wood. Also describes the hollow made by a drill bit.

Box stay A metal brace that holds a box lid open in order to stop it slamming shut or opening beyond a desired point.

Bracket An L-shaped structure that fixes an object (such as a shelf) to a wall and provides structural support. One side of the bracket attaches to the underside of the object, the other to the wall.

Bradawl A small, hand-held tool with a tip like a small, sharp screwdriver, used to make indentations in wood prior to inserting a screw or drilling a hole.

Break out The unsightly damage to a cut or hole that is sometimes made as the blade, cutter, or bit exits the wood, breaking and tearing the fibers from the surface. Using backing material to support the workpiece (an off-cut for, example) or working from both sides reduces or eliminates break out.

Butt hinge A metal hinge that connects two objects and allows a swinging motion between them. Screws are inserted through holes in each hinge panel in order to fix them in place.

Butt joint *See* Edge-to-edge joint

Butt miter joint A joint created by two pieces of wood at a 45-degree angle, used in picture frames. *See* Miter joint.

Buttons Small, step-shaped wooden fixings that are used to attach a table top to its frame.

C-clamp Named for their shape, these are the strongest clamps available, and are used for clamping (clamping) an object to a surface. An adjustable threaded bar is tightened around two or more pieces of wood, trapping the pieces in its "jaws" and securing them together.

Cabinet scraper A hand-held shaping and finishing tool used to scrape off excess wood and smooth the grain.

Carcass The basic structure of any box-shaped piece of furniture, such as a cabinet.

Caul A strong flat board (sometimes curved)—used when gluing veneer to a core—that distributes the force exerted by cross-bearers and a clamping system.

Chamfer The flattened-down (or bevelled) edge of a piece of wood, typically cut to a 45-degree angle.

Cheek (tenon) The name given to the sides of a tenon (*see* Tenon).

Circular saw A hand-held power saw with a rotating circular saw blade set in a sole plate, ideal for reducing large planks and manufactured boards in size before planing or trimming.

Comb joint Two pieces of wood joined into a corner via matching, interlocking teeth. The teeth are glued and then fit snugly into one another.

Combination square A multi-purpose measuring device that is fitted with a selection of attachments, including a ruler, protractor, set square, and 45-degree holder.

Commercial connector Joints made with commercial connectors are similar to mortise-and-tenon joints, with the difference being that instead of tenons, standard-sized connectors are used. *See* Biscuit Joint, Dowel, and Domino Joint.

Coping saw A hand saw with a thin metal blade for intricate woodworking. The blade forms the fourth side of a box-shaped metal frame, from which the handle protrudes.

Corner bridle joint In effect, this is an open mortise-and-tenon joint, where the mortise and tenon slot together in the shape of a corner, but the end of tenon remains visible.

Corner halving joint Connects two pieces of wood at a 90 degree angle—the end grains are cut into a step shape so they are mirror images of each other. The two steps slot together and are held in place with glue.

Countersink A conical hole bored into a piece of wood—when a screw is fully inserted into the hole, the top of the screw should fit neatly into the countersink and sit flush with the level of the wood.

Cross-cut A cut that is made at a right angle to the direction of the wood grain.

Cutting line A line marked with pencil or scored into the surface of the wood that forms a guide along which a saw or similar tool can cut.

De-nib Remove the nibs by raising the grain and fine sanding or after a sealing coat, just fine sanding. *See* Nibs.

Depth mark A marking on the surface of a piece of wood that indicates how deep into the wood a cut (with a saw, or similar) should penetrate.

Disassemble or dismantle Break down a structure into its component parts.

Dividers A hand-held tool shaped like a pair of tweezers, but joined by a hinge and with spikes on either end. Also known as a measuring compass, they are used to measure distances and marking equal distances.

Dividing rail A rail that is inserted into a space to create two separate cavities.

Domino joint A versatile joint that comprises a tenon with rounded, fluted sides (the domino) that fits into two mortises to connect two pieces of wood together.

Domino jointer An electrical tool that creates the domino mortise (*see above*). The cutter gouges out a section of wood (the mortise), the depth and width of which can be adjusted accordingly to match the domino size.

Double rebate Two matching grooves that are cut to leave a thin strip of wood (called a tongue) running between them.

Double/twin tenon A variation of the basic mortise-and-tenon joint that uses two identical tenons and mortises, instead of one of each.

Dovetail half-lap joint A dovetail-shaped tenon that juts out from one piece of wood to fit snugly into a slot of matching dimensions in another. It is the strongest of all lap joints, as its shape resists pull-out. *See* Pull-out.

Dovetail housing The strongest type of housing joint, it is formed by sliding a dovetailed base into a slot of matching dimensions.

Dovetail joint An interlocking joint formed by angled tails and pins, usually used in a sequence, and typically employed in traditional drawer construction.

Dovetail marker A dovetail-shaped piece of metal, which acts as a template when marking out a dovetail joint on the wood.

Dovetail saw A small type of back saw used for cutting dovetails—its thin blade allows for accurate sawing.

Dowel A round peg or pin (available in a variety of shapes and sizes), which is used to attach objects together and to reinforce a joint.

Draw-bore tenon A mortise-and-tenon joint reinforced by a dowel that passes through both parts of the joint, locking the parts together and dispensing with need for glue or clamping (although both strengthen the joint further). Importantly, the hole through the parts is deliberately misaligned so that the dowel "draws" the parts together tightly.

Drill A hand-held boring tool, with hand- or AC-powered versions, which uses a drill bit to bore holes.

Drill bit A cutting attachment inserted into a drill in order to bore a hole.

Edge The outermost side of a piece of wood.

Edge-to-edge joint Also known as a butt joint, this is the most basic joint in woodwork. It fuses the edge of one piece of wood to that of another with glue to create a smooth and seamless line.

End grain The texture and pattern of wood fibers that is exposed in the cross-section when a piece of wood is cut across the grain. In woodworking, it often refers to the top or bottom ends of a workpiece.

Excess Wood that proves surplus to requirements during woodworking and is therefore discarded.

Face The two flat sides of a piece of wood (as opposed to the edges).

Fence Usually part of a tool or machine that helps guide the tool or the workpiece. For example, the fence of a bandsaw is set a particular distance from the blade; the workpiece is passed across the machine and against the fence producing a piece of wood with parallel sides.

Figure The surface pattern of a piece of wood, including growth rings, grain patterns, color streaks, and knots.

File An abrasive surface used for filing down the rough texture of the wood to create a smooth finish—it can be either a hand-held file or sandpaper of varying textures.

Floating panel A panel fitted loosely within a frame. The panel is not glued but instead allowed to swell and shrink within grooves (or rebates and beading). Necessary in solid wood construction. *See also* Frame-and-panel construction.

Floating tenon A joint consisting of two mortises that are connected by a loose strip of wood (the tenon).

Flush A seamless connection between two surfaces, assembled so that they are exactly level.

Flush-cut saw A flexible hand-held saw with teeth that only cut on the pull stroke. It can cut protruding dowels or tenons flush to the wood's surface, without causing extraneous damage.

Frame-and-panel construction A piece of furniture is defined as "solid wood" when made solely from wood, and neither veneer nor manufactured board. A door cannot be made from a single piece of wood or wood joined edge-to-edge, as it would warp and swell and shrink: it has to be made as a frame (sometimes with divisions) with loose panels set in grooves. As such it is more flexible and able to expand and contract with fluctuating humidity and temperatures. *See also* Floating panel.

Gluing area The area of the wood that is to be glued.

Grain The orientation of a wood's fibers and the texture created as a result.

Groove A long indentation or gutter cut into a piece of wood to follow the grain.

Half-lapped dovetail joint *See* Dovetail half-lap joint.

Hardwood Hardwood timber is found in a group of broad-leaved, primarily deciduous, trees, that are classified as angiosperms (their seeds are encased in a shell). They boast a variety of colors and are more durable than softwoods. They are also usually—but not always—harder (denser) than softwoods.

Haunch (haunched tenon) Where rails meet at the top of a leg, an ordinary tenon of full width is likely to break the end grain at the top of the leg. To avoid this, the tenon is, for the most part, reduced in width (so there is a greater amount of wood at the top of the leg) but a small stub ("haunch") is left. The haunch prevents the top part of a rail warping (and adds to the strength of the joint). The same applies where a cross-rail meets a style at the corner of a frame.

Haunched tenon joint A variation on the mortise-and-tenon joint. The tenon is cut with a step (haunch) that juts out on one side of its base—the mortise itself is two-tiered to accommodate both the tenon and its haunch, thus providing additional strength.

Heartwood The hard, dark-colored, non-living wood found at the center of a tree trunk or branch. It is unaffected by water or air and as such is resistant to decay and decomposition.

Hinge A metal bearing that connects two objects and allows a swinging motion between the two.

Hinge flange The two panels that pivot on the central core of the hinge and are screwed into pieces of wood to secure the hinge.

Hinge housing Where a strip, measured to the exact dimensions of a hinge flange (*see above*) has been carved from a piece of wood and is able to fit (house) the hinge exactly, so that it sits flush with the surface of the wood.

Hinge rebate *See* Hinge housing.

Horns The excess wood on the length of the stile on a door frame, which is trimmed off.

Housing The cut-out groove in a piece of wood, into which another piece of wood is snugly fitted (housed).

Housing joint (full) One of the most basic joints. A groove is cut into a piece of wood to the exact thickness of the tenon piece, and extends across the entire width of the housing. The tenon is inserted into the housing and glued in place.

Housing piece The piece of wood into which the housing is cut.

Jig A device that positions and holds a workpiece, and works alongside a machine when drilling, cutting, planing, and so on, so that a single operation can be repeated exactly. *See also* Template.

Jigsaw A powered saw with a fine blade, used for cutting intricate designs and curves.

Joining edge The edge of a piece of wood which is joined—either by glue or another mechanism—to the edge of another.

Joint The point at which two or more pieces of wood are joined together, either by gluing, slotting, or screwing, to create a frame or structure.

Kerf The width of the groove or cut made by a cutting tool, such as saw. A dovetail saw has a narrow kerf, a bandsaw has a medium kerf, and a circular saw has a wide kerf. Also a slot for a key.

Keyed-miter joint This is constructed in the same way as a butt miter joint, but cuts are made into finished corner joint and veneer keys are inserted into the groove. These are then shaved flush to the surface of the wood. The veneer keys provide extra strength as well as an attractive finish.

Key (veneer) A miter joint can be reinforced after it is has been constructed using pieces of veneer set in kerfs that bridge the two parts of the joint. The kerfs can also be set at angles other than 90 degrees for a stronger and more decorative effect.

Knock-down tenon A mortise-and-tenon joint in which the tenon extends through the entire width of the mortise and out the other side, where a wedge-shaped peg secures it through the hole. The peg can be removed and the entire joint disassembled.

Knocked down Disassembled or taken to pieces.

Knot A defect in the surface of wood where there is variable grain direction, creating a dark knot-like mark on the wood.

Lap The strip of wood on a socket piece that encases the tails of the lapped dovetail joint (*see* Lapped dovetail joint).

Lap joint A joint that is created by the overlapping of two pieces of wood and securing them together.

Lapped dovetail joint An joint identical to the through dovetail, except that the socket is closed on one end (the lap), so the end grain of the tails is not visible.

Lip-and-spur bit A twist bit for use when drilling wood. It has the advantages of a center spur, which locates the drill more accurately than an ordinary twist bit, and a outer lip that shears a clean-sided hole. Also called a brad point or dowelling bit.

Loose-tongued miter A strong and versatile joint connecting two pieces of wood, each with a mortise cut into the end grain. A loose tongue of wood (cut to the combined depth of both mortises) is then fitted into each mortise to secure the joint.

Mark out To draw relevant guidelines or shapes on a piece of wood, in preparation for cutting.

Marking gauge A tool used for marking relative and duplicate dimensions when cutting joints, comprising a stock that slides along a beam. At the end of the beam is a point, blade, or sharp-edged wheel, which is used to mark the wood. The distance between the stock and the point is set using a ruler or a specific measurement on a workpiece. The stock acts as a fence that is slid against the workpiece.

Marking knife A type of sharp-bladed knife used to score lines in wood that will act as guides for a cutting tool, such as a saw.

Masking tape An adhesive tape set on easily tearable paper. It peels off a surface easily and leaves no residue, and is thus ideal for protecting surfaces during painting.

MDF A medium-density fiberboard made from wood fibers and resin fused together under intense heat and pressure. It is a better-quality alternative to chipboard, though it does not have the tensile strength of plywood. It is an ideal substrate for veneering and is dimensionally stable (it does not warp, swell, or shrink). Unfortunately the dust produced when it is machined is a particular health hazard and you must always wear a face mask when working with it.

Measuring compass *See* Dividers.

Miter block A cutting aid for hand-held saws, this wood block has deep grooves arranged at different angles, through which a saw can be positioned to ensure that it cuts at the required angle.

Miter joint A joint created by two pieces of wood at a 45-degree angle. *See* Butt-miter joint.

Miter saw (compound/sliding compound miter saw) Traditionally a manually-operated saw that is held in a frame that is set for specific angle cuts—usually 45 degrees—and most frequently used for making picture frames. It has been largely superseded by the motorized "compound" miter saw (with a circular saw blade that swings down onto the wood), which is more accurate and can be set at both a miter angle and a bevel angle to produce a compound angle. Sliding versions allow 1ft- (305mm-) long cross-cuts.

Mitered bridle joint A type of bridle joint that is used in the construction of frames and is neater than the cornered bridle. *See* Corner bridle joint.

Mortise The hole or recess in a piece of wood, designed to receive the matching tenon of another piece of wood, forming a joint.

Mortise chisel A type of chisel designed primarily for the cutting of mortises. It has a thick, straight blade and a strong handle that can withstand being struck by a mallet.

Mortise depth/width The depth or width to which a mortise is cut into a piece of wood.

Mortise gauge A marking gauge with a second, adjustable, pin that is used to mark out the exact dimensions of the mortise before it is cut. The distance between the pins is set to the thickness of the mortise and therefore speeds up the marking-out stage.

Mortise piece The piece of wood into which the mortise is cut.

Mortiser A machine that is specially designed to cut square or rectangular holes into a piece of wood, creating a mortise.

Muntin A framing member that separates and joins panels used in doors and wide drawer bottoms.

Nibs The raised fibers on a surface before it is truly smooth. Also the raised fibers and sealed-in dust after a sealing coat has been applied.

Off-cuts Surplus material (for example, wood) that remains after the main pieces have been cut.

Oil content Some woods, such as teak or iroko, have a very high oil content, meaning that they may require no special finish once a piece has been crafted. Oil is a natural defense against rot.

Orbital sander A power sander with an orbiting circular or rectangular pad used for fast, efficient sanding of wood.

Panel pins Slim, round nails typically used for fixing beadings and moldings in place.

Panel saw A machine for sawing large sheets into finished component sizes. Also a mid-size handsaw with small cross-cut teeth for cutting manufactured boards or fine cross-cutting of solid wood.

Pare To remove or cut away excess material in order to create a specific shape, such as using a chisel to shave wood into a right angle.

Peg A small, tapered notch of wood that is inserted into a mortise to act as a stop against tension, and hold two pieces of wood together.

Piece The completed product of your woodworking labors—an item that has been shaped and crafted through the application of various techniques.

Pilot hole A small test hole that is bored into a piece of wood: it acts as a stabilizer into which the drill can be positioned to bore a larger hole over it to the required dimensions. Pilot holes are also used for screws, to avoid shearing the screw or splitting the wood.

Pin The matching, interlocking fingers (pins) carved into the end grain of two pieces of wood. The pins of one piece fit neatly into the sockets of the other, allowing the two pieces to slot together.

Plane A tool for smoothing and shaping a piece of wood via a cutting blade, which shaves thin slices off the surface.

Planing The act of smoothing out a piece of wood by shaving off a number of strips with a plane (*see above*).

Plinth A block of wood or box-like frame that acts as the secure base for a larger structure. The plinth also raises the item of furniture off the ground, allowing cabinet doors to open and protecting the furniture from being kicked.

Plow plane A type of hand plane that takes various widths of cutter and is used for cutting grooves or housings.

Plywood A manufactured board that is molded into thin sheets and layered on top of one another, with the grains of each sheet running in opposite directions for additional strength.

Quarter-cut A means of extracting wood from its log—the log is cut into quarters and each quarter then cut into strips running perpendicular to the wood rings. This provides a consistent grain and gives the wood stability.

Racking If a structure suffers from racking it is unable to resist side-to-side movement and requires reinforcement.

Ratchet strap A strap for fastening objects together—the strap passes through a metal buckle with a ratchet handle that is cranked repeatedly to tighten the strap to its maximum capacity.

Ratio The relation in value or quantity between two different things.

Rebate A groove that is cut along one edge of a piece of wood, to give a two-tiered, or step effect.

Rebate plane A hand-held plane used for cutting a rebate into a piece of wood.

Relief cut A preliminary cut made perpendicular to the cutting line when cutting a curve. Relief cuts "relieve" the tension on the saw blades when cutting around a curve.

Ripping Sawing wood along the grain.

Router table A table with a router mounted into it. The cutter is inverted and the workpiece is passed over the table and against the fence. An advantage of a router table is that no clamping or support is required, which can speed up the cutting.

Sand To rub down a wood surface with a piece of sandpaper (*see below*).

Sandpaper Abrasive paper that can be rubbed over a rough wood surface to smooth it out.

Sapwood The young wood found on the outer edges of a tree trunk or branch. Unlike heartwood it is living wood that transfers water up from the roots toward the leaves. It is often avoided because it is a different color to the bulk of the wood, does not absorb stain in the same way as the surrounding wood, and is soft, weak, and susceptible to rot.

Sap (bleeding) A sticky substance that oozes from knots and fissures in softwood and can also sometimes bleed out after the wood has been crafted, (if this is a likelihood then a preventative knotting solution should be applied).

Sash clamp A sturdy clamp with an adjustable, screw-operated jaw that provides excellent reach and grip.

Scarf joint This acts as a lengthening device, by joining the identically shallow-beveled edges of two pieces of wood and gluing them into one long strip.

Score Mark a line along a piece of wood by cutting lightly into the surface.

Screw A metal peg with a spiral-shaped ridge running down its shaft that bores into wood and acts as a fastener.

Screw hole The hole into which a screw is inserted.

Screwdriver A hand-held tool that rotates the head of a screw, either to insert it securely into a hole, or to tighten one that is already in place.

Scribe To mark a guideline into a piece of wood with a tool, such as a marking gauge.

Seasoning Drying out wood, prior to using it for woodworking (a lengthier process for hardwoods than softwoods, as they are more dense). In theory, this ensures that the dimensions of the wood remain constant and do not fluctuate with humidity.

Shake A crack or split in the wood.

Shank The shaft or stem of a fixing or tool.

Shoot The final, accurate planing of an end or edge.

Shooting board A wooden board that attaches to a workbench and is used to assist planing.

Shoulder A protruding edge that is cut into the base of a tenon, on one or both sides.

Shoulder plane A hand-held plane that is used to shape the shoulder of tenons.

Shrinkage Occurs in timber as it dries. Seasoned wood in a finished piece is subject to shrinkage as the moisture in the air changes seasonally. All structures must permit shrinkage and expansion.

Socket piece A piece of wood that has been cut with a slot or socket, into which a tenon or tailpiece can be fitted.

Softwood The timber from a group of coniferous, primarily evergreen, trees that classified as gymnosperms (their seeds have no protective casing). They are softer than most, but not all, hardwoods and have strong growth-ring patterns.

Splay A widening of a shape or related parts. A wedged tenon is splayed at the end.

Splinters Thin, spiky shards of wood which protrude or break off from the wood's surface when it is rough.

Spokeshave A hand-held tool that is use for smoothing and shaping cylindrical objects including rods, chair legs, and wheel spokes.

Square Run a line across a piece of wood, parallel to the end grain.

Squareness When the distances between the diagonally opposite corners of a square are of equal length.

Stile The vertical part of a frame.

Stock The raw, uncrafted piece of wood from which a workpiece is created. Also part of a tool.

Stop A device in a jig or machine that restricts movement, controlling depth or size, for example. It is usually involved in performing repeat operations.

Stub tenon A short tenon which is usually square in shape and will not penetrate through a mortise.

Surface The outermost layer of a material.

Table-mounted router *See* Router table

Tailpiece The flared (tapered), "dovetail" part of a dovetail joint.

Tail *See* Tailpiece.

Taper A gradual narrowing in depth or width.

T-bridle joint A strong, T-shaped joint in which an open mortise (atop the length of the T) straddles the tenon cut into the center of another piece of wood (the T-bar) to complete the joint.

Tearing When wood is cut roughly, causing the wood fibers to rip and splinter.

Tempering The process that is applied to steel (especially tools), improving its hardness.

Template An outline drawing, shape, or pattern that provides a method for accurately transferring a design onto the final material.

Template profile cutter *See* Bearing-guided cutter.

Tenon A protrusion on the end of a piece of wood, which is designed to fit into a mortise of matching dimensions, forming a joint.

Tenon face The wide, flat sides of a tenon.

Tenon piece The piece of wood into which the tenon has been cut.

Tenon saw A type of hand-held backsaw with fine teeth that is commonly used for cutting tenons.

Tenon thickness The depth of the tenon.

Test-assemble or Test-fit Put all the pieces of a structure in position in order to check that they all fit.

Thicknesser A machine which cuts wood into boards of an even thickness—the wood is fed in at one side and emerges to a uniform size at the other end.

Through dovetail-joint One of the strongest of all woodworking joints, this consists of interlocking dovetail-shaped tails and pins.

Tolerance The scope of variation of an object's characteristics, including weight, dimensions, and density.

Tongue A protrusion of wood that is designed to fit exactly into a corresponding groove.

Tongue-and-groove joint A joint utilizing a long tongue to fit neatly into the grooves of two connecting boards.

Trammel A homemade device or beam compass which acts like a pair of compasses for drawing large circles. Also an attachment for routing circles.

Veneer A thin sheet of wood that is glued to the surface of a core material to give the impression of solid wood. Burr wood can usually only be used as a veneer in a piece of furniture. Pictures and patterns (marquetry and parquetry) are made from various veneers arranged for decorative effect.

V-groove A V-shaped groove that is cut into the surface of wood with a bevelled-edged chisel.

Vise A screw mechanism with two panels that is tightened to hold a workpiece firmly ready for cutting, planing, shaping and so on.

V-mark A V-shaped pencil mark that is made across pieces of wood when creating an edge-to-edge joint—the pieces can be accurately aligned by using the pencil marks.

Wall fixing A fixing that is inserted into a wall's surface, to allow an object to be securely attached. There are different types of fixings depending on the wall, for example if it is solid, hollow, or made of brick.

Warp A distortion within the surface of a piece of wood.

Waste The unwanted surplus material that is cut or scraped off during woodworking.

Waste side The side of a workpiece from which waste is removed. When referring to a cutting line, it is the side of the line which is considered to be waste.

Wedge A tapered piece of wood wedged securely into a slot to fix a joint in place or for another holding purpose.

Wedged-through mortise-and-tenon joint A strong, decorative joint where the tenon extends through the much longer mortise, and is held either side by two wedges (*see above*).

Winding sticks Two long, straight sticks, which are used in pairs to visually discern the flatness of a wood surface, or detect a "wind" (twist). Placed at opposite ends of a piece of wood, when you look across them, with your eyes level with the nearest stick, the sticks must be parallel, otherwise the surface is twisted.

Workbench A robust purpose-built table or work surface fitted with vices that can firmly hold a piece of wood in place, enabling it to be worked on with tools.

Workpiece A piece of wood that is being worked on or has been worked on, using either hand or machine tools.

Index

O

P

Acknowledgments

For her excellent research and legwork, thanks go to Nasim Mawji.

For help and advice during the early stages of development, thanks go to Peter Korn, Rod Wales, and Jon Binzen.

For assistance with the book and photography, special thanks go to the staff and students of the Building Crafts College: Len Conway, Dave Pearham, John Wilkie, Cornelius Lynch, Marcus Dadson, Jacob Arch, Joe Beever, John Fishwick, Keturah Hayden, Catherine James, Kelli Knight, Zuber Miah, Jason Muteham, Alfred Newall, Joseph Sivell, and Mark Tindley.

For additional photography of timbers, thanks go to David Mager Photography and Julie Renouf Photography.

For consultancy work, thanks go to Alan, Gill and Glyn Bridgewater of AG&G Books, Hamish Hill, and Marc Schmidt.

For providing tools and manufacturers' shots, special thanks go to Axminster Tool Centre (www.axminster.co.uk).

For providing additional tools and manufacturers' shots, thanks go to Bagpress; DeWalt/Black & Decker; E.C. Emmerich; Felder UK; Festool; Hegner UK; Jet; Makita; Metabo; TTS Tooltechnic Systems GB Limited; and Ulmia GmbH.

For help with the sourcing, supply and preparation of timbers and veneers, thanks go to the following merchants and individuals: Alan Curtis; Capital Crispin Veneer; Exotic Woods Incorporated; George Sykes Limited; Gilmer Wood; ITC Limited; Peter Kidman, Kidman Furniture; Mathews Timber; Ockendon Timbers; Thorogood Timber; Timbmet; Timberline; the Timber Research and Development Association (TRADA); Alan Ward; and Yandle and Sons.

For editorial and design assistance, thanks go to the team at DK India.

For indexing, thanks go to Sue Butterworth.

PICTURE CREDITS

The publisher would like to thank the following for their kind permission to reproduce their photographs:

Axminster Tool Centre (www.axminster.co.uk): 69cra, 69tl, 69tl (engineer's vice), 70cla
Dorling Kindersley: Fire Investigation Unit at Acton Police Station, London 34bc
Dreamstime.com: Lightpro 44cra
Getty Images: For endpapers: Toby Adamson
John Lloyd: 173tr, 174r, 175tl, 175tr, 175bl, 175bc, 175br
Jan Weigand/www.defcon-x.de: 2-3c,14-15c,80-81c,176-177c, 200-201c
Silverline Tools: 42bc (Forstner bit)

Barry Croucher: Jacket illustration

(Picture Key: a—above; b—below/bottom; c—centre; l—left; r—right; t—top)

About the contributors

Alan and Gill Bridgewater formed AG&G Books in 1998, and have gained an international reputation as producers of highly successful gardening and DIY books across a range of subjects including garden design, ethnic woodwork and, of course, household woodwork. They have recently moved to a smallholding and are currently writing about self-sufficiency.

Glyn Bridgewater MA(RCA) studied Furniture Design at Loughborough College of Art and Design and at the Royal College of Art, London. He now makes furniture in his workshop in Suffolk, specializing in laminated and steam-bent structures. In 1998 he formed AG&G Books with his parents (Alan and Gill Bridgewater) and helps produce their project-based books. He has written for *Woodworker*, and is co-author of *How to Make Simple Wooden Puzzles and Jigsaws* and *The Boxcart Bible*.

Colin Eden-Eadon has been involved with wood all of his working life. Having worked for the Forestry Commission in England, he trained as a furniture-maker, before moving into teaching and writing about woodworking after a period spent as a mastercraftsman with renowned furniture-maker John Makepeace. He later became a contributor to, and editor of, *Furniture and Cabinetmaking*, and is currently Senior Tutor in Fine Woodwork at the Building Crafts College, London.

Sally Francis is a post-doctoral-qualified botanist, working as a writer, journalist and consultant specialising in crops, timber and trees. Her articles and features have been published in *Furniture and Cabinetmaking*, *Woodturning*, the farming media, gardening magazines and elsewhere. Sally is also a keen woodworker and enjoys turning and furniture-making.

John Lloyd is trained in Cabinet Making and Antique Furniture Restoration and Conservation, and was awarded the City and Guilds of London Institute First Prize for Advanced Studies in Furniture for Furniture-Making and Antique Restoration. His commissions include work from Sotheby's, Christie's, St Paul's Cathedral, and numerous private clients, along with site work for the National Trust. He runs courses at his own workshops in Sussex and has lectured at West Dean College. John is a full member of The British Antique Furniture Restorers' Association.

Jonathan Tibbs studied Fine Art at Falmouth College of Arts and went on to specialize in Furniture Making at the Building Crafts College, London. Since graduating he has exhibited internationally and picked up a number of awards for his work. For the second year running, he is Furniture Maker in Residence at the Building Crafts College, from where he runs his business designing and making bespoke and batch production furniture.

J. M. Wilkie has had a lifelong interest in working with wood. A chartered civil engineer, he retrained as a furniture maker, being awarded the City and Guilds Medal for Excellence on completion of his training. He now has his own commercial workshop, is a member of the Society of Designer-Craftsmen, and holds the Master Carpenter Certificate. He teaches Fine Woodwork, part-time, at the Building Crafts College, London.

The Building Crafts College, established in 1893 by the Worshipful Company of Carpenters, has a long tradition of delivering high-quality education and training in construction crafts. Instigated at the height of the Arts and Crafts Movement, the college remains true to its original aims of promoting high-level craft skills, whilst at the same time offering training opportunities to the local community and supporting construction employers in meeting their skills requirements. Based in Stratford, East London, the Building Crafts College offers a range of construction courses from levels 1–5. Its specialist areas include timber crafts, fine woodwork, stonemasonry, multi-crafts, and conservation studies. Specialist full-cost courses are offered in Fine Woodwork/Furniture Making, and Advanced Stonemasonry, City & Guilds Diplomas and a degree in Historic Building Conservation.

The Worshipful Company of Carpenters is a City of London Livery Company that received its first Royal Charter in 1477 and was granted a coat of arms in 1466. Originally established as a medieval trade guild to safeguard the welfare and interests of carpenters in the City of London, today the cornerstones of its work are charitable activities and support for the craft of woodworking through scholarships, competitions, and the operation of its own craft training school, the Building Crafts College.